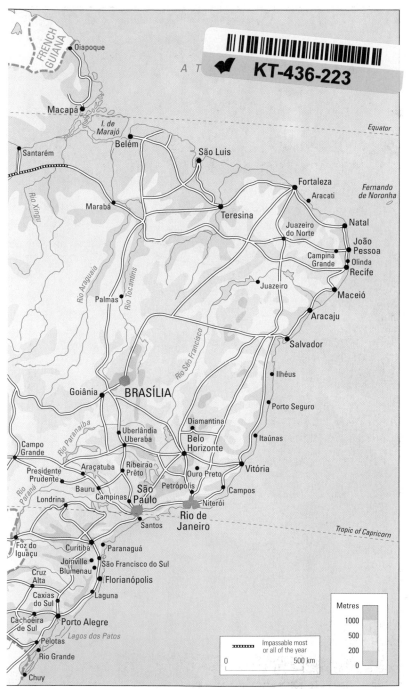

KT-436-223

Oiapoque

Macapá

Equator

I. de Marajó

Santarém

Belém

São Luis

Rio Xingu

Marabá

Teresina

Fortaleza

Aracati

Fernando de Noronha

Juazeiro do Norte

Natal

João Pessoa

Rio Araguaia

Rio Tocantins

Palmas

Campina Grande

Olinda

Recife

Juazeiro

Maceió

Rio São Francisco

Aracaju

Salvador

Goiânia

BRASÍLIA

Ilhéus

Porto Seguro

Rio Paranaiba

Uberlândia

Uberaba

Diamantina

Belo Horizonte

Itaúnas

Campo Grande

Presidente Prudente

Araçatuba

Ribeirão Prêto

Ouro Preto

Vitória

Rio Paraná

Bauru

Campinas

São Paulo

Petrópolis

Campos

Londrina

Niterói

Rio de Janeiro

Santos

Tropic of Capricorn

Foz do Iguaçu

Curitiba

Paranaguá

Joinville

Blumenau

São Francisco do Sul

Cruz Alta

Florianópolis

Caxias do Sul

Laguna

Cachoeira de Sul

Porto Alegre

Lagos dos Patos

Pelotas

Rio Grande

Chuy

Metres

1000

500

200

0

Impassable most or all of the year

0   500 km

iii

written and researched by

David Cleary, Dilwyn Jenkins and Oliver Marshall

ROUGH GUIDES

NEW YORK • LONDON • DELHI

Introduction to

Brazil

Brazilians often say they live in a continent rather than a country, and that's an excusable exaggeration. The landmass is bigger than the United States if you exclude Alaska; the journey from Recife in the east to the western border with Peru is longer than that from London to Moscow, and the distance between the northern and southern borders is about the same as that between New York and Los Angeles. Brazil has no mountains to compare with its Andean neighbours, but in every other respect it has all the scenic – and cultural – variety you would expect from so vast a country.

Despite the immense expanses of the interior, roughly two-thirds of Brazil's **population** live on or near the coast; and well over half live in cities – even in the Amazon. In Rio and São Paulo, Brazil has two of the world's great metropolises, and nine other cities have over a million inhabitants. Yet Brazil still thinks of itself as a frontier country, and certainly the deeper into the interior you go, the thinner the population becomes. Nevertheless, the frontier communities have expanded relentlessly during the last fifty years, usually hand in hand with the planned expansion of the road network into remote regions.

Other South Americans regard Brazilians as a **race** apart, and language has a lot to do with it – Brazilians understand Spanish, just about, but Spanish-speakers won't understand Portuguese. More importantly, though, Brazilians look different. They're one of the most ethnically diverse peoples in the world: in the extreme south, German and Italian immigration has left distinctive European features; São Paulo has the world's largest Japanese community outside Japan; there's a large black population con-

v

■

Fact file

- By far the largest country in South America, Brazil covers nearly half the continent and is only slightly smaller than the US, with an **area** of just over 8.5 million sq km. It shares common boundaries with every South American country except Chile and Ecuador.

- The **population** of Brazil is around 180 million, making it the fifth most populous country in the world. Of this, about 55 percent is white (Portuguese, German, Italian etc), 38 percent of mixed white and black descent and 6 percent black, with "others" (including Amerindian) accounting for a mere 1 percent.

- Almost 90 percent of Brazil's **electricity** is generated from hydropower, about 6 percent from fossil fuels and 1 percent from nuclear power.

- Paved **highways** account for a meagre 0.2 million km, while unpaved highways add up to more than 1.8 million km.

- Brazilian **exports** consist mainly of manufactured products (including automobiles, machinery and footwear), iron ore, soybeans and coffee. Brazil also produces 90 percent of the world's gems.

centrated in Rio, Salvador and São Luís; while the Indian influence is most visible in the people of Amazônia and the Northeastern interior.

Brazil is a land of profound **economic** contradictions. Rapid post-war industrialization made Brazil one of the world's ten largest economies and put it among the most developed of Third World countries. But this has not improved the lot of the vast majority of Brazilians. The cities are dotted with *favelas*, shantytowns that crowd around the skyscrapers, and the contrast between rich and poor is one of the most glaring anywhere. There are wide **regional differences**, too: Brazilians talk of a "Switzerland" in the Southeast, centred along the Rio–São Paulo axis, and an "India" above it; and although this is a simplification, it's true that

Black beans and feijoada

Brazilian food is as varied as its distinctive regions and the native Indian, African, European, Arab and Japanese origins of the country's inhabitants. While there is no clearly identifiable national cuisine, certain ingredients (and dishes) have become closely associated with Brazil. Of these, none is more important than beans, of which Brazil is the world's largest consumer and producer. The most commonly used type is feijão preto, a small black bean that features almost daily at Brazilian tables and is the main ingredient of feijoada, which is traditionally served throughout Brazil on Saturdays. Originating in Rio, feijoada is a thick, hearty stew made of beans and meat (mainly pork – including bacon, salted ear and trotter – and carne do sol, sun-dried salted beef) and served with rice, farofa (toasted manioc flour), kale and orange slices. For much more on food, see p.41.

the level of economic development tends to fall the further north you go. This throws up facts that are hard to swallow. Brazil is the industrial powerhouse of South America, but cannot feed and educate its people. In a country almost the size of a continent, the extreme inequalities in land distribution have led to land shortages but not to agrarian reform. Brazil has enormous natural resources but their exploitation so far has benefited just a few. The IMF and the greed of First World banks must bear some of the blame for this situation, but institutionalized corruption and the reluctance of the country's large middle class to do anything that might jeopardize its comfortable lifestyle are also part of the problem.

These difficulties, however, rarely seem to overshadow everyday life in Brazil. It's fair to say that nowhere in the world do people know how to enjoy themselves more – most famously in the annual orgiastic celebrations

Nowhere in the world do people know how to enjoy themselves more

of **Carnaval**, but reflected, too, in the lively year-round nightlife that you'll find in any decent-sized town. This national hedonism also manifests itself in Brazil's highly developed **beach culture**; the country's superb **music** and dancing; rich regional **cuisines**; and in the most relaxed and tolerant attitude to **sexuality** – gay and straight – that you'll find anywhere in South America. And if you needed more reason to visit, there's a strength and variety of **popular culture**, and a genuine friendliness and humour in the people that is tremendously welcoming and infectious.

Where to go

The most heavily populated and economically advanced part of the country is the Southeast, where the three largest cities – **São Paulo**, **Rio de Janeiro** and **Belo Horizonte** – form a triangle around which the economy pivots. All are worth visiting in their own right, though Rio, one of the world's most stupendously sited cities, stands head and shoulders above the lot. The **South**, encompassing the states of Paraná, Santa Catarina and Rio Grande do Sul, stretches down to the borders with Uruguay and northern Argentina, and westwards to Paraguay, and includes much of the enormous **Paraná** river system. The

River tourism

Though some might imagine it to be quite arduous, travelling by boat on the powerful Rio Amazonas (known as the Rio Solimões above Manaus) can be surprisingly relaxing. Even if you don't have your own cabin, there are few experiences as laid-back as lounging in a hammock for days on end. With a good book and a few pennies to buy the odd beer at the bar in the afternoons, the long river kilometres flow by quickly. If you've selected one of the larger boats, the top deck will probably have a massive sound system for stirring samba nights, along with satellite TV and tables for card and domino games. If you want to get a close-up view of the jungle and its wildlife, you're better off choosing the smaller boats, which travel closer to the shore going upstream and can negotiate the smaller streams; going downstream however they tend to cruise in the mid-stream currents, far from shore.

Exploring the rivers, tributaries and rainforest around Manaus by houseboat is probably the most comfortable way to see the South American jungle. The forest scenery is nothing short of breathtaking and the time easily filled with piranha fishing, forest walks and canoe rides through alligator-filled creeks. For details on planning a river trip, see pp.392 & 440.

Brazil's regions and states

For political and administrative reasons, Brazil's 25 states and one federal district are divided into five regions, referred to throughout this book and widely used in Brazil itself.

North (The Amazon)
Acre
Amapá
Amazonas
Pará
Rondônia

Centre-West
Brasília (Federal District)
Goiás
Mato Grosso
Mato Grosso do Sul
Tocantins

Northeast
Alagoas
Bahia
Ceará
Maranhão
Paraíba
Pernambuco
Piauí
Rio Grande do Norte
Sergipe

Southeast
Espírito Santo
Minas Gerais
Rio de Janeiro
São Paulo

South
Paraná
Rio Grande do Sul
Santa Catarina

spectacular **Iguaçu Falls** (at the northernmost point where Brazil and Argentina meet) are one of the great natural wonders of South America.

The vast hinterland of the South and Southeast is often called the Centre-West and includes an enormous central plateau of savanna and rock escarpments, the **Planalto Central**. In the middle stands **Brasília**, the country's space-age capital, built from nothing in the late 1950s and still developing today. The capital is the gateway to a vast interior, the **Mato Grosso**, only fully charted and settled over the last three decades; it includes the mighty **Pantanal** swampland, the richest wildlife reserve on the continent. North and west, the Mato Grosso shades into the **Amazon**, a mosaic of jungle, rivers, savanna and marshland that also contains two major cities – **Belém**, at the mouth of the Amazon itself, and **Manaus**, some 1600km upstream. The tributaries of the Amazon, rivers like the Tapajós, the Xingu, the Negro, the Araguaia or the Tocantins, are virtually unknown outside

Brazil, but each is a huge river system in its own right.

The other major sub-region of Brazil is the **Northeast**, the part of the country that curves out into the Atlantic Ocean. This was the first part of Brazil to be settled by the Portuguese and colonial remains are thicker on the ground here than anywhere else in the country – notably in the cities of **Salvador** and **São Luís** and the lovely town of **Olinda**. It's a region of dramatic contrasts: a lush, tropical coastline with the best beaches in Brazil, slipping inland into the *sertão*, a semi-arid interior plagued by drought and appallingly unequal land distribution. All the major cities of the Northeast are on the coast; the two most famous are Salvador and **Recife**, both magical blends of Africa, Portugal and the Americas, but **Fortaleza** is also impressive, bristling with skyscrapers and justly proud of its progressive culture.

When to go

Brazil splits into four distinct **climatic** regions. The coldest part – in fact the only part of Brazil that ever gets really cold – is the **South and Southeast**, the region roughly from central Minas Gerais to Rio Grande do Sul, that includes Belo Horizonte, São Paulo and Porto Alegre. Here, there's a distinct winter between June and September, with occasional cold, wind and rain. However, although Brazilians complain, it's all fairly mild. Temperatures rarely hit freezing overnight, and when they do it's featured on the TV news. The coldest part is the interior of Rio Grande do Sul, in the extreme south of the country, but even here there are many warm, bright days in winter and the summer (Dec–March) is hot. Only in Santa Catarina's central highlands does it occasionally snow.

The **coastal climate** is exceptionally good. Brazil has been called a "crab civilization" because most of its population lives on or near the coast – with good reason. Seven thousand kilometres of coastline, from Paraná to near the equator, bask under a warm tropical climate. There is a "winter", when there are cloudy days and sometimes the temperature dips below 25°C (77°F), and a rainy season, when it can really pour. In Rio and points south **the summer rains** last from October through to January, but they come much earlier in the Northeast, lasting about three months from April in Fortaleza and Salvador, and from May in Recife. Even in winter or the rainy season, the weather will be excellent much of the time.

The **Northeast** is too hot to have a winter. Nowhere is the average monthly temperature below 25°C (77°F) and the interior, semi-arid at the best of times, often soars beyond that – regularly to as much as 40°C (104°F). Rain is sparse and irregular, although violent. **Amazônia** is stereotyped as being steamy jungle with constant rainfall, but much of the region has a distinct dry season – apparently getting longer every year in the most deforested areas of east and west Amazônia. And in the large expanses of savanna in the northern and central Amazon basin, rainfall is far from constant. Belém is closest to the image of a steamy tropical city: it rains there an awful lot from January to May, and merely quite a lot for the rest of the year. Manaus and central Amazônia, in contrast, have a marked dry season from July to October.

Average temperatures (ºC) and rainfall

The first figure is the average maximum temperature; the second the average minimum; and the third the average number of rainy days per month.

To convert °C to °F, multiply by 9, then divide by 5 and add 32

	Jan	Feb	Mar	Apr	May	Jun	Jul	Aug	Sep	Oct	Nov	Dec
Belém												
max. temp.	31	30	30	31	31	32	32	32	32	32	32	32
min. temp.	23	23	23	23	23	23	22	22	22	22	22	22
rainy days	24	26	25	22	24	15	14	15	13	10	11	14
Belo Horizonte												
max. temp.	27	27	27	27	25	24	24	25	27	27	27	26
min. temp.	18	18	17	16	12	10	10	12	14	16	17	18
rainy days	15	13	9	4	4	2	2	1	2	10	12	14
Brasília												
max. temp.	27	28	28	28	27	26	26	28	30	29	27	27
min. temp.	18	18	18	17	15	13	13	14	16	18	18	18
rainy days	19	16	15	9	3	1	0	2	4	11	15	20
Manaus												
max. temp.	30	30	30	30	31	31	32	33	33	33	32	31
min. temp.	23	23	23	23	24	23	23	24	24	24	24	24
rainy days	20	18	21	20	18	12	12	5	7	4	12	16
Porto Alegre												
max. temp.	31	30	29	25	22	20	20	21	22	24	27	29
min. temp.	20	20	19	16	13	11	10	11	13	15	17	18
rainy days	9	10	10	6	6	8	8	8	11	10	8	8
Recife												
max. temp.	30	30	30	30	29	28	27	27	28	29	30	30
min. temp.	25	25	24	23	23	22	21	22	22	23	24	24
rainy days	7	8	10	11	17	16	17	14	7	3	4	4
Rio de Janeiro												
max. temp.	30	30	27	29	26	25	25	25	25	26	28	28
min. temp.	23	23	23	21	20	18	18	18	19	20	20	22
rainy days	13	11	9	9	6	5	5	4	5	11	10	12
Salvador												
max. temp.	29	29	29	28	27	26	26	26	27	28	28	29
min. temp.	23	23	24	23	22	21	21	21	21	22	23	23
rainy days	6	9	17	19	22	23	18	15	10	8	9	11
São Paulo												
max. temp.	28	28	27	25	23	22	21	23	25	25	25	26
min. temp.	18	18	17	15	13	11	10	11	13	14	15	16
rainy days	15	13	12	6	3	4	4	3	5	12	11	14

things not to miss

It's not possible to see everything that Brazil has to offer in one trip – and we don't suggest you try. What follows is a selective and subjective taste of the country's highlights: natural wonders, picturesque towns, vibrant festivals and stunning architecture. They're arranged in five colour-coded categories to help you find the very best things to see, do and experience. All entries have a page reference to take you straight into the Guide, where you can find out more.

01 Florianópolis beaches Page **679** • The island capital of Santa Catarina state has dozens of beaches to suit all tastes, from treacherous surfing beaches to those with waters safe for swimming, such as Daniela.

02 Parke Nacional da Tijuca

02 **Parque Nacional da Tijuca**
Page **112** • This impressive expanse of Mata Atlântica, close to Rio's centre, is crisscrossed by shaded trails, and features refreshing waterfalls and spectacular views across the city.

03 **Museu de Arte Contemporânea, Niterói** Page **133** • A short ferry ride from Rio, this spaceship-like museum is one of Oscar Niemeyer's architectural masterpieces.

04 **Brazilian Baroque art** Page **201** • Within this style, Aleijadinho's sculptures are remarkable, none more so than the Passion figures in Congonhas, created when the eighteenth-century sculptor was nearly blind, his hands deformed from leprosy.

06 Ilhabela Page **624** • A playground for São Paulo's rich, the island boasts some of the most beautiful beaches between Rio and São Paulo, thanks to strictly enforced environmental protection laws.

05 Parque Nacional Chapada dos Veadeiros
Page **511** • A spectacular wilderness area, dotted with interesting geological formations, caves, waterfalls and hiking trails, just a few hours north of Brasília.

07 Candomblé celebrations Page **264** • Usually identifiable by their white dress, followers of this popular Afro-Brazilian religious cult worship together in exuberant dance ceremonies as well as at fiestas.

08 Fazendas Page **619** • São Paulo's coffee-producing boom left behind some impressive rural estates (fazendas), some of which are open to visitors. The Fazenda do Pinhal near São Carlos, is among the best preserved.

09 Capoeira Page **257** • The dance-like sparring of this distinctive martial art is best seen at *capoeira* schools, where you can watch classes for free.

10 **Brasília architecture** Page **488** • Whether it looks like a futuristic dream or a nightmare, Brazil's capital is singular in its otherworldly architecture. The Aztec-inspired Teatro Nacional is just one of the monumental attractions.

12 **Colonial Rio** Page **100** • There are more colonial churches in Rio than anywhere else in Brazil, the Igreja de Nossa Senhora da Glória do Outeiro is quite simply the prettiest.

11 **Amazon wildlife** Page **440** • You can increase your chances of spotting wildlife such as alligators, monkeys and toucans by spending at least three to four days on a jungle tour, easily arranged from Manaus.

13 **Olinda** Page **312** • The cobbled streets of the city's historic centre offer up countless examples of beautiful colonial architecture.

14 **Carnaval** Page **594** • The most important of Brazil's festivals, celebrated in notably grand style in Rio, Salvador and Olinda (pictured).

15 **Avenida Paulista, São Paulo** Page **48** • Nowhere will you get a sense of the city's impressive modern face more than along this thoroughfare, though you'll also find a dozen opulent mansions worth a look as well.

16 **Iguaçu Falls** Page **662** • The power and beauty of the falls is quite simply astonishing, only rivalled by the tranquillity of the Mata Atlântica behind.

18 Rio beaches Page **107** • A major part of daily city life – on weekends, locals escape to the sands to play sports, catch up on gossip or, nowhere more than on fashionable Ipanema, to people watch.

17 Trekking in the Chapada Diamantina
Page **278** • Explore the dramatic terrain of this enormous national park, which includes mesas, forest, river beaches, waterfalls, and even a kilometre-long grotto.

19 Pedra Azul Page **236** • Located in Espírito Santo, a state rarely visited by foreign tourists, this massive stone mountain is named for the shade of blue that it appears to turn at dawn and at sunset.

20 Old world traces Page **692** • In pockets of Brazil – especially in the rural South – places like German-speaking Pomerode still show traces of old world traditions, including some lively festivals.

21 **Reggae bands** Page 372 • You'll hear appealing reggae beats throughout the Northeast, whether in atmospheric bars or on the street.

22 **River journeys**
Page **392** • Taking a slow boat on the Amazon is the most leisurely way to experience the mighty river and the spectacular jungle scenery.

23 **Parati** Page 145 • Once an important port for the export of gold, the picturesque town remains one of Brazil's best-preserved colonial towns and a great base from which to explore the surrounding Costa Verde.

25 Churrascarias
Page **42** • Sample grilled meats of all kinds at these typical *gaúcho* barbecue houses, Rio Grande do Sul's gift to Brazilian dining traditions.

24 Markets
Page **591** • For an idea of the natural abundance in Brazil, walk through any market in the country. São Paulo's Mercado Municipal is particularly impressive, crammed with produce from all over Brazil.

26 Northeast beaches
Page **363** • North of Salvador the coastline is stunning, with beaches picture-perfect and the waters good for surfing or else sailing in a traditional *jangada*.

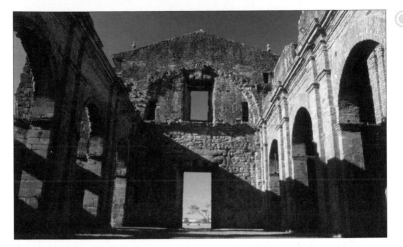

27 **The Jesuit missions** Page **729** • Admire the striking ruins of São Miguel in Brazil or combine a visit with other Jesuit missions in what is now Argentina and Paraguay.

28 **The Pantanal** Page **546** • You'll be hard-pressed not spotting wildlife, including parrots, anacondas and alligators, in the world's biggest inland swamp.

29 **Rio nightlife** Page **120** • A rather seedy inner-city *bairro* by day, Lapa at night pounds to infectious Brazilian rhythms, its nightclubs and bars teeming with locals and tourists alike.

30 **The Aquário Natural** Page **538** • Snorkel among some thirty-odd species of dourado, piripitanga and other fish in the crystalline waters of this marine sanctuary or else spy on them from above in a glass-bottomed boat.

31 **Teatro Amazonas** Page **434** • If you can't attend one of the regular concerts, be sure to take a guided tour of this remarkable opera house, painstakingly built from materials brought from Europe.

32 **Ouro Preto** Page **186** • Tucked away in the steep narrow streets of this lovely Minas Gerais town are some truly remarkable Baroque churches and, despite tourism, the place retains its small town charm.

33 **Teatro Municipal, Rio** Page **90** • If you can't catch a show inside Rio's sumptuous belle époque theatre, be sure to stop for lunch or a drink in its lavish, Assyrian-inspired café.

Contents

Using the Rough Guide

We've tried to make this Rough Guide a good read and easy to use. The book is divided into six main sections, and you should be able to find whatever you want in one of them.

Colour section

The front colour section offers a quick tour of Brazil. The **introduction** aims to give you a feel for the place, with suggestions on where to go. We also tell you what the weather is like and include a basic fact file. Next, our authors round up their favourite aspects of Brazil in the **things not to miss** section – whether it's great food, amazing sights or a special activity. Right after this comes the Rough Guide's full **contents** list.

Basics

The Basics section covers all the **pre-departure** nitty-gritty to help you plan your trip. This is where to find out which airlines fly to your destination, what paperwork you'll need, what to do about money and insurance, Internet access, food, public transport, car rental – in fact just about every piece of **general practical information** you might need.

Guide

This is the heart of the Rough Guide, divided into user-friendly chapters, each of which covers a specific region. Every chapter starts with a list of **highlights** and an **introduction** that helps you to decide where to go, depending on your time and budget. Likewise, introductions to the various towns and smaller regions within each chapter should help you plan your itinerary. We start most town accounts with information on arrival and accommodation, followed by a tour of the sights, and finally reviews of places to eat and drink, and details of nightlife. Longer accounts also have a directory of practical listings. Each chapter concludes with **public transport** details for that region.

Contexts

Read Contexts to get a deeper understanding of what makes Brazil tick. We include a brief **history**, articles on ecology, music, Indian rights and racial issues, together with a detailed section that reviews dozens of **books** relating to the country.

Language

The **language** section gives useful guidance for speaking Brazilian Portuguese and pulls together all the vocabulary you might need on your trip, including a comprehensive menu reader. Here you'll also find a glossary of words and terms peculiar to the country.

Index + small print

Apart from a **full index**, which includes maps as well as places, this section covers publishing information, credits and acknowledgements, and also has our contact details in case you want to send in updates and corrections to the book – or suggestions as to how we might improve it.

Map and chapter list

Contents

Colour section

Basics

Guide

Contexts

744–800

Language

801–811

Index and small print

813–825

Map symbols

maps are listed in the full index using coloured text

=====	Major road	⅏	Viewpoint
———	Minor road	▲	Mountain peak
▬▬▬	Railway	♟	Fort
⅏⅏⅏	Steps	●⁺⁺⁺⁺●	Funicular
—Ⓜ—	Metro station & line	●-●-●	Cable car
— —	Ferry route	ⓘ	Tourist office
———	Waterway	✉	Post office
----	Chapter division boundary	Ⓒ	Telephone office
■-■-■	International border	◉	Accommodation
■-■▬	State border	⊙	Statue/memorial
≍	Bridge/tunnel	▬	Building
✗	Airport	─┼ ↕	Church
★	Bus stop	⊤⌐	Cemetery
◓	Cave		Park, national park
⅏	Marsh		or reserve
椎	Waterfall	⦂⊛	Beach
⑰⑫	Cliffs		Swamp
⊼	Lighthouse		

8

Basics

Basics

Getting there

Unless you are entering Brazil overland from a neighbouring South American country, you'll almost certainly arrive by air. Airfares always depend on the season: the specific dates vary somewhat between airlines, but high season is generally July and August, then again mid-December to 25 December; low season is any other time. Fares don't normally rise over Carnaval (Feb–March), but getting a seat can be difficult. Airline competition is fierce, however, and special offers are often available.

You can often cut costs by going through a **specialist flight agent** – either a consolidator, who buys up blocks of tickets from the airlines and sells them at a discount, or a **discount agent**, who in addition to dealing with discounted flights may also offer special student and youth fares and a range of other travel-related services such as travel insurance, car rentals, tours and the like. If you plan on purchasing some kind of air pass or want to book a hotel room for your first few days in Brazil, it is certainly easier to go through a specialist agent. A further possibility is to see if you can arrange a **courier flight**, although you'll need a flexible schedule, and preferably be travelling alone with very little luggage. In return for shepherding a parcel through customs and possibly giving up your baggage allowance, you can expect to get a heavily discounted ticket. You'll probably also be restricted in the duration of your stay.

Apart from discounted tickets, it's worth checking fares **directly with the airlines** that fly to Brazil. Especially during low-season, airlines are increasingly offering fairly competitive fares, although they may carry certain restrictions such as having to book, and pay, 21 days before departure and having to spend at least seven days abroad (maximum stay three months).

If Brazil is only one stop on a longer journey, you might want to consider buying a **round-the-world (RTW) ticket**. Some travel agents can sell you an "off-the-shelf" RTW ticket that will have you touching down in about half a dozen cities (Rio de Janeiro and São Paulo are on some itineraries); others will have to assemble one for you, which can be tailored to your needs but is apt to be more expensive.

If you plan to do a fair amount of travelling within Brazil (or to other South American countries), think about buying an **air pass** with your main ticket. Depending on your itinerary, these passes can offer worthwhile savings, but can only be bought outside South America with your international ticket. See box on p.34 for details of the various options.

Booking flights online

Many airlines and discount travel websites offer you the opportunity to book your tickets online, cutting out the costs of agents and middlemen. Good deals can often be found through discount or auction sites, as well as through the airlines' own websites.

Online booking agents and general travel sites

Ⓦ travel.yahoo.com Incorporates a lot of Rough Guide material in its coverage of destination countries and cities across the world, with information about places to eat, sleep and etc.
Ⓦ www.cheapflights.com Bookings from the UK and Ireland only (for US, Ⓦ www.cheapflight.com; for Canada, Ⓦ www.cheapflights.ca; for Australia, Ⓦ www.cheapflights.com.au). Flight deals, travel agents, plus links to other travel sites.
Ⓦ www.cheaptickets.com Discount flight specialists (US only).
Ⓦ www.etn.nl/discount.htm A hub of consolidator and discount agent Web links, maintained by the nonprofit European Travel Network.
Ⓦ www.expedia.com (Booking from the US; for the UK Ⓦ www.expedia.co.uk). Discount airfares, all-airline search engine and daily deals for accommodation and tickets to attractions.

Ⓦ **www.flyaow.com** Online air travel info and reservations site.

Ⓦ **www.gaytravel.com** Gay online travel agent, offering accommodation, cruises, tours and more.

Ⓦ **www.geocities.com/thavery2000** Has an extensive list of airline toll-free numbers (from the US) and websites.

Ⓦ **www.hotwire.com** Bookings from the US only. Last-minute savings of up to forty percent on regular published fares. Travellers must be at least 18 and there are no refunds, transfers or changes allowed. Log-in required.

Ⓦ **www.lastminute.com** Offers good last-minute holiday package and flight-only deals (UK only; for Australia, Ⓦwww.lastminute.com.au).

Ⓦ **www.priceline.com** Name-your-own-price website that has deals at around forty percent off standard fares. You cannot specify flight times (although you do specify dates) and the tickets are non-refundable, non-transferable and non-changeable (US only; for the UK, Ⓦwww.priceline.co.uk).

Ⓦ **www.skyauction.com** Bookings from the US only. Auctions tickets and travel packages using a "second bid" scheme. The best strategy is to bid the maximum you're willing to pay, since if you win you'll pay just enough to beat the runner-up regardless of your maximum bid.

Ⓦ **www.smilinjack.com/airlines.htm** Lists an up-to-date compilation of airline website addresses.

Ⓦ **www.travelocity.com** Destination guides, hot web fares and best deals for car hire, accommodation and lodging as well as fares. Provides access to the travel agent system SABRE, the most comprehensive central reservations system in the US.

Ⓦ **www.travelshop.com.au** Australian website offering discounted flights, packages, insurance, and online bookings.

Flights from the UK and Ireland

There are plenty of choices of carriers to Brazil **from the UK**, with São Paulo and Rio being the usual points of arrival. If your ultimate destination is neither of these cities, it is almost always best to fly to connect in São Paulo, the main hub for internal flights, unless you enter the country on one of the relatively few flights into a Brazilian regional airport (see p. 000). Since direct flights can be booked up well in advance and can be more expensive, you may want to consider a flight via another country.

Two airlines operate **direct flights** to Brazil from the UK: British Airways and the Brazilian carrier Varig (Brazilian Airlines). The official fares of Varig and British Airways are usually very similar, currently starting at £499 for a thirty-day return **to Rio or São Paulo** in low season, £814 high season (July and August and 14–25 December). With these tickets return dates are in theory fixed, but once in Brazil both airlines will allow you to change the date (within the thirty days) for a fee of around £75. These fares are pretty notional and you will usually get the same tickets through travel agencies at reduced prices.

There are almost always excellent deals available from travel agencies specializing in Latin America as well as from general discount travel agencies; fares are sometimes as low as £400 in low season, rising to around £600 for high season departures. The **cheapest fares**, however, are often offered on **routes via Europe** – with Air France via Paris, TAP via Lisbon or Iberia via Madrid. Other inexpensive options include Lufthansa via Frankfurt, Alitalia via Milan, KLM via Amsterdam (to São Paulo only) and Swiss via Zurich. As prices tend to be the same whether you begin your journey in London or at one of the UK's **regional airports**, you may find it better value and more convenient to use one of these airlines rather than flying out of Heathrow with British Airways or Varig.

As Brazil is such a large country, an open-jaw ticket – flying into one city and leaving from another – may, according to your itinerary, make sense. Rio and São Paulo offer most airline possibilities, but flying with TAP broadens your options, including also Fortaleza, Recife and Salvador (see p.13).

There are currently no direct flights **from Ireland** to Brazil, although there's talk of the possibility of regular charters with the Brazilian airline TAM. There are, however, excellent connections via London or other European capitals. The best deals are available from budget or student travel agents in Ireland, but it's also worth contacting specialist agents in England for cheap fares, an unusual route or a package.

Flying out of Dublin, the cheapest discount fare is currently with Lufthansa (€850 low season, €1940 high season) via Frankfurt, though other airlines also offer competitive fares. Alternatively, it's worth checking out fares from London or Manchester, although there's unlikely to be any saving after paying for the connecting flight to the UK (see UK details above).

The Northeast and the Amazon

If you want the **Northeast** to be your point of entry into Brazil, TAP offers flights to Fortaleza, Recife and Salvador via Lisbon, though these tend to get booked up long in advance. Alternatively, Air France operates a code-shared flight with the Brazilian airline TAM (see p.16) to Recife, via Paris. **Fares** are very similar, with £415 typically offered for low season departures, rising to £640 in the high season. Competitive fares to Fortaleza are available with TACV (£520 low season, £600 high season) from Paris and Amsterdam, which allow the option of a stopover in the Cape Verde Islands, off the coast of West Africa, at no additional cost.

Flying to the **Amazon** is expensive and time-consuming. The quickest way is to catch a plane to Miami, where you can connect with the twice-weekly Lloyd Aéreo Boliviano service to Manaus (around $800 return). It is usually much easier and cheaper, however, to fly from Heathrow to Manaus with Varig, changing planes in São Paulo. An unusual, but fairly expensive and time-consuming route is with Air France via Paris to Cayenne in French Guiana (£520 low season, £680 high season), and then onwards with Surinam Airways to Macapá (£200) or Belém (£300). Similar fares are obtainable with KLM on its route from Amsterdam to Paramaribo, from where the Surinam Airways flights to Macapá and Belém originate. If you want the western Amazon to be your point of arrival, you're best off making your way to Bogotá in Colombia and taking a connecting internal flight to Leticia, just a short taxi ride from the Brazilian town of Tabatinga.

Other ticket options

Several airlines offer **stopovers** to or from Brazil at no extra cost. Apart from the airlines with European (and Cape Verdean) transit points already mentioned, stopover possibilities most commonly involve the **US**. Continental Airlines via Newark or Houston is generally the least expensive option (around £450 low season, £700 high season) with

good deals also sometimes available with American Airlines via Miami and United Airlines via New York, Chicago or Miami.

Combining Brazil with a longer trip in the southern hemisphere, or putting together a **round-the-world ticket**, is possible but expensive. The most popular ticket option is a one-way to Sydney via Brazil or Argentina (around £470 low season, £650 high season) and a separate ticket back to London via Southeast Asia or North America.

Airlines

Air France UK ☎0845/084-5111, Republic of Ireland ☎01/844 5633, ⊛www.airfrance.fr. Daily flights via Paris to São Paulo and Rio and twice weekly to Recife (code-shared with TAM).
Air Portugal Republic of Ireland ☎01/679 8844.
Alitalia UK ☎0870/544-8259, Republic of Ireland ☎01/677 5171, ⊛www.alitalia.it. Daily flights to São Paulo and Rio via Milan.
American Airlines UK ☎0345/78978, ⊛www.aa.com. A choice of daily flights via New York or Miami to São Paulo, Rio and Belo Horizonte.
British Airways UK ☎0345/78978 or 0845/773 3377, Republic of Ireland ☎1800/626747, ⊛www.britishairways.com. Direct daily flights from London Heathrow to São Paulo, continuing on to Rio.
Continental UK ☎0800/776-464, ⊛www.continental.com. Daily flights via a choice of Newark or Houston to São Paulo and onwards to Rio.
Iberia UK ☎020/7830-0011, Republic of Ireland ☎01/677 9846, ⊛www.iberia.com. Daily flights via Madrid to São Paulo and Rio.
KLM UK ☎08705/074074, Republic of Ireland ☎0870/507 4074, ⊛www.klm.com. Five flights a week to São Paulo via Amsterdam.
Lloyd Aéreo Boliviano UK ☎020/7565-9606, ⊛ww.labairlines.com. Twice weekly flights from Miami to Manaus.
Lufthansa UK ☎0845/773-7747 or 0845/773 7747, Republic of Ireland ☎01/844 5544, ⊛www.lufthansa.co.uk. Daily flights via Frankfurt to São Paulo and Rio.
Surinam Airways Netherlands Antilles ☎5999/868 4360, ⊕868 9674, ⊛www.slm.firm .sr
Swiss UK ☎0845/601-0956, ⊛www.swiss.com. Twice weekly to Rio and daily flights to São Paulo via Zurich.
TACV (Cape Verde Airlines) UK ☎01964/536599. Weekly flights from Paris to Fortaleza, touching down in Sal, one of the Cape Verde Islands.

TAP (Air Portugal) UK ☎020/7630-0900, ⓦwww.tap-airportugal.pt. Flies via Lisbon daily to São Paulo and Recife, four times a week to Rio and Salvador and three times a week to Fortaleza.
United Airlines UK ☎0845/844-4777, Republic of Ireland ☎1800/535300, ⓦwww.ual.co.uk. A choice of daily flights via New York, Washington or Miami to São Palo and Rio.
Varig (Brazilian Airlines) UK ☎0845/603 7601, ⓦwww.varig.co.uk. Direct daily flights to São Paulo, continuing on to Rio from London Heathrow.

Flight and travel agents

Bridge the World UK ☎0870/444 7474, ⓦwww.bridgetheworld.com. Specializing in round-the-world tickets, including Brazil, with good deals aimed at the backpacker market.
Flight Finders International Republic of Ireland ☎01/676 8326. Discounted flights.
Flightbookers UK ☎0870/010 7000, ⓦwww.ebookers.com. Low fares on an extensive selection of scheduled flights. Extended opening hours at their branch at Gatwick train station (☎01293/568300).
Flynow UK ☎0870/444 0045, ⓦwww.flynow.com. Large range of discounted tickets.
Joe Walsh Tours Republic of Ireland ☎01/676 0991, ⓦwww.joewalshtours.ie. General budget fares agent.
North South Travel UK ☎ & ℻ 01245/608291, ⓦwww.northsouthtravel.co.uk. Friendly, competitive travel agency offering discounted fares worldwide – profits are used to support projects in the developing world, especially the promotion of sustainable tourism.
STA Travel UK ☎0870/1600 599, ⓦwww.statravel.co.uk. Worldwide specialists in low-cost flights and tours for students and under-26s, though other customers welcome. Also over 200 offices abroad.
Trailfinders UK ☎020/7628 7628, ⓦwww.trailfinders.co.uk, Republic of Ireland ☎01/677 7888, ⓦwww.trailfinders.ie. One of the best-informed and most efficient agents for independent travellers; produce a very useful quarterly magazine worth scrutinizing for round-the-world routes. Offers competitive fares with connections out of all Irish airports.
Travel Cuts UK ☎020/725 2082 or 7255 1944, ⓦwww.travelcuts.co.uk. Canadian company specializing in budget, student and youth travel and round-the-world tickets.

Packages and tours

If your trip is short, and if your plan is simply to visit Rio for two weeks, then **package holidays**, flight and accommodation included, can be very good value. A week in a three-star hotel in Copacabana can cost less than £700, and for an extra £400 you can add on a week's tour taking in three or four key places such as Manaus, Salvador and Iguaçu. These packages can be found in brochures at any travel agent, such as Kuoni and Thomas Cook, and through some of the specialists listed here. If you want to go for Carnaval you'll need to book months in advance and pay more.

More varied **tours** are offered by many specialist operators and upmarket package companies (see list below). Journey Latin America has 22-day guided tours of Brazil (prices ranging between about £1500 and £2500), as well as larger-scale overland options which also take in Paraguay, Bolivia and Peru, or Chile and Argentina. Overland trips are offered by Exodus, Explore Worldwide and Encounter Overland, all of which visit Brazil along with one or more other South American countries on tours lasting from three weeks to three months for £1500–3000. If the ready-packaged tours don't appeal to you, Passage to South America specializes in planning itineraries to meet individual requirements, including hotels and transportation within Brazil. Last Frontiers prepares individual itineraries staying in small, comfortable hotels and also arranges occasional small groups to attend *rodeios* or to learn to play polo.

Tour and overland operators

Encounter Overland UK ☎017/2886 2222 020/7370 6845, ⓦwww.encounter.co.uk. One of the oldest overland companies going, offering activities such as hiking, climbing and rafting as well as trips off the beaten track in their own converted trucks.
Exodus UK ☎020/8675 5550, Republic of Ireland ☎01/677 1029, ⓦwww.exodus.co.uk. Adventure tour operator organizing tours for small groups, including walking, biking, overland, adventure and cultural trips.
Explore Worldwide UK ☎01252/760 000, ⓦwww.explore.co.uk. Small-group tours, treks, expeditions and safaris. Offers 17-day tours of Rio,

the Pantanal, the Amazon and Salvador, with accommodation mostly in small local hotels.

Latin American flight and tour specialists

Brazil Tours UK ☎08704/42 42 41, ⓦwww.braziltours.co.uk. Flight agents and tour operators to Brazil and elsewhere in South America.
Journey Latin America UK ☎020/8747 3108 or 8747 8315, ⓦwww.journeylatinamerica.co.uk. Flight agents and tour operators for Brazil and the rest of Latin America.
Last Frontiers UK ☎01296/653000, ⓦwww.lastfrontiers.com. Tailor-made itineraries to Brazil with a strong wildlife slant. Friendly and knowledgeable staff will point you towards small hotels in destinations throughout Brazil.
Steamond Travel UK ☎020/7730 8646, ⓦwww.easyticket.com. Flight agents and tour operators for Brazil and Latin America.
Veloso Tours UK ☎020/8762 0616, ⓦwww.veloso.com Tailor-made itineraries, especially good beach and family holidays.

By ship

It is still just about possible to get to Brazil from Europe **by ship**, though it's expensive and slow. You'll travel by cargo boat, most of which have room for around twelve passengers travelling in some luxury – most ships, for example, have a swimming pool – though the food tends to be plain. Ships take about two weeks to cross the Atlantic, depending on where they call en route.

The Strand Cruise Centre (Charing Cross Shopping Concourse, The Strand, London WC2; ☎020/7836 6363) is the agent for a range of ships departing from Tilbury and Southampton. Most ships dock in Rio and Santos (a few stop first in Recife, Salvador and Vitória), before heading south to Paranaguá, Itajaí and Buenos Aires and, less frequently, on to Rio Grande and Montevideo. The cheapest one-way berth in a shared inside cabin to any east coast port is about £950, with prices rising steeply to over £3000 for a return passage in a single outside cabin.

From the US and Canada

There are numerous gateways to Brazil in the **US and Canada**; direct flights leave from Atlanta, LA, Chicago, Dallas, Miami, New York, Orlando, Washington and Toronto. Varig and TAM are at present the only Brazilian carriers and offer the most flights from the US. The vast majority of flights go to either Rio or São Paulo, though it is possible to fly into Belo Horizonte, Recife, Salvador, Manaus and Belém. The other carriers serving Brazil are American, Air Canada, Continental, Delta, Japan Airlines and United. If your ultimate destination is somewhere other than these cities, unless you enter the country on one of the relatively few flights into a Brazilian regional airport (see p. 000), it is almost always best to fly to connect in São Paulo, the main hub for internal flights.

From the US

The greatest number of flights and destinations from the US are offered by **Varig**, the Brazilian national airline, which flies regularly to **Rio** and **São Paulo** from New York, LA and Miami (code-sharing with United and Air Canada for connections from other North American cities), as well as weekly to **Fortaleza** and **Recife** via Miami. **TAM**, a private Brazilian airline with the advantage of a newer fleet, now carries more passengers to Brazil from the United States than Varig: flights from Miami, Orlando and New York to Rio and São Paulo. Excursion-fare ticket prices vary depending on your length of stay in Brazil: count on spending at least $150 more for a ticket valid for up to three months than a ticket for up to one month. Fares to Rio and São Paulo are almost always the same. Varig offers one-month excursion fares from New York to São Paulo for $759, from Miami to São Paulo for $626, and from LA to São Paulo for $756 – all valid year-round. Unrestricted fares are much higher: a three-month ticket from New York to São Paulo, for example, costs $1345 low season, $1465 high season.

The **other airlines** serving Brazil fly chiefly out of New York, LA or Miami to Rio and São Paulo. There are also direct flights from Washington-Dulles with United, Chicago and Dallas with American, and Atlanta with Delta. In a country the size of Brazil, **open-jaw tickets** can be very good value, allowing you to fly into one city and out from another. Varig's fares from LA to Rio and São Paulo, for example, are $1244 low season and $1356 high season for an open-jaw Apex ticket valid for a minimum of 21 days.

15

If you plan to include Brazil as a stop on a **round-the-world ticket**, figure on \$1800 for a ticket including New York, Paris, overland to Madrid, São Paulo, and a return to New York. Slightly more than \$4000 will get you from London to Rio, South Africa, North Africa, Southeast Asia, Australia, Japan, the US and back to London.

Flights via other countries

If you're looking for slightly cheaper fares, and can put up with the longer flight times, or you're tempted to break your journey, it's worth checking out what the national airlines of Brazil's South American neighbours have to offer. Aerolíneas Argentinas, for instance, flies to Rio and São Paulo from Miami and New York via Buenos Aires. Others routings worth investigating include travelling via Bogotá, Lima or Panama. TACV flies from New York (Newark) to Fortaleza via Cape Verde Islands for \$1100.

If you plan on travelling in other South American countries besides Brazil, the **Mercosur Airpass** is a good-value option (see p.34).

From Canada

Direct flight choices from Canada are limited to Air Canada's service from Toronto. Expect to pay C\$1700 during high season and C\$1487 during low season, although they do post special offers throughout the year – some as low as C\$900. An alternative option is to fly to Miami, New York or LA and make your connections from there. Discount travel agents will be able to offer good prices on routes via the US. Travel Cuts is the most reliable student/youth agency, and also offers some deals for non-students; or check the travel ads in your local newspaper and consult a good travel agent. For **round-the-world tickets**, your best bet is to include a major US departure point, like New York or LA, in your itinerary.

Airlines

Aerolíneas Argentinas ☎1-800/333-0276, ⊛www.aerolineas.com. Flies daily from New York and Miami to Buenos Aires then on to Rio and São Paulo.
American Airlines ☎1-800/433-7300, ⊛www.aa.com. Flights daily from New York and Miami to Rio and São Paulo, continuing onwards to Belo Horizonte. Also direct flights from Chicago and Dallas to São Paulo.
Air Canada ☎1-888/247-2262, ⊛www.aircanada.ca. Flies out of Toronto five times a week to São Paulo, where you can pick up connecting flights to other cities in Brazil.
Continental Airlines ☎1-800/231-0856, ⊛www.flycontinental.com. Daily flights to Rio and São Paulo from Newark, NJ and Houston.
Delta Airlines ☎1-800/221-1212, ⊛www.delta-air.com. Connecting flights from all major US cities to Atlanta, then onto Rio.
Japan Airlines (JAL) ☎1-800/525-3663, ⊛www.japanair.com. Flies four times a week from New York to São Paulo, and once a week from LA.
Lloyd Aéreo Boliviano ☎1-800/337-0918, ⊛www.labairlines.com. Twice weekly flights from Miami to Manaus.
TAM Airlines ☎1-888/235-9826, ⊛www.tam-airlines.com.br. Flies twice a day from Miami to São Paulo.
United Airlines ☎1-800/538-2929, ⊛www.ual.com. Daily service from New York and Miami to São Paulo, and a daily service from Miami to Rio. Also flights from Washington to São Paulo.
Varig ☎1-800/468-2744, ⊛www.varig.com. Daily service from New York and Miami, and four flights a week from LA, to Rio and São Paulo, with connections to other cities. From Miami you can fly weekly into Recife and Fortaleza.

Discount agents and travel clubs

Council Travel ☎1-800/226 8624, ⊛www.counciltravel.com. Student/budget travel agency, with branches in many US cities. Flights from the US only. Owned by STA Travel.
Skylink ☎212/599-0430 or 1-800/633-4488, ⊛www.skylinkus.com. Consolidator with branches in Chicago, LA, Montréal, Toronto and Washington DC.
STA Travel ☎212/627-3111 or 1-800/781-4040, ⊛www.sta.com. Branches in all major US cities. Worldwide specialists in independent travel, specializing in student/youth fares; also student IDs, travel insurance and car rental.
Travel Avenue ☎312/876-6866 or 1-800/333-3335, ⊛www.travelavenue.com. Full-service travel agent that offers discounts in the form of rebates.
Travel Cuts Canada ☎1-800/667-2887, US ☎1-866/246-9762, ⊛www.travelcuts.com. Canadian student-travel organization with branches all over Canada, specializing in student fares, IDs and other travel services.
Worldtek Travel ☎1-800/243-1723 or 203/772-0470. Discount travel agency

Package deals

Package-deal vacations may not suit everyone, but don't dismiss the idea entirely. Many agents can put together surprisingly flexible deals and they can be great for your peace of mind, if only to ensure a worry-free first week while you're finding your feet on a longer tour. If you've only a week or two, you could end up getting the best value and making the most of your time, particularly if you have special interests, by using one of the specialists listed under tour operators below. For example, a simple airfare-plus-accommodation package for five nights in Copacabana in a four-star hotel can cost as little as $599. For slightly more, Festival Tours offers a five-night package to a four-star beach hotel in Rio including Brazilian breakfast every morning, day excursions and transfers for $750.

Many operators can arrange add-on trips to a Rio-based package vacation, as well as tours centred on two or three locations – Portuguese Tours offers the "Tale of Three Cities Tour" to Rio, Iguaçu and Buenos Aires for ten days for $1599. **Carnaval** tours are big business, so expect to pay up to $1000 more at this time of year – from $1650 for a five-night stay – Portuguese Tours, Solar Tours and the Brazilian Vacation Center are all specialists. The Brazilian Vacation Center is one of the largest tour operators to Brazil, offering comprehensive deals on Rio and the Amazon in particular.

Tour operators and project organisers

Abercrombie & Kent ☏1-800/323-7308 or 630/954-2944, ☮www.abercrombiekent.com. Tours to the Amazon, multi-country tours, and individually customized tours.
Adventure Center ☏1-800/228-8747 or 510/654-1879, ☮www.adventurecenter.com. Group tours of South America that include Brazil.
Brazil Nuts ☏1-800/553-9959, ☮www.brazilnuts.com. Tours that promise to take you off the beaten track to experience Brazil's cities, the Amazon basin and the Pantanal.
City Tours ☏1-800/238-2489, ☮www.citytours.com/obt. Individual and group travel throughout South America specializing in city tours and day excursions.
Conservation International ☏1-800/429-5660, ☮www.conservation.org. Offers the opportunity to work on environmental volunteer projects in Brazil.
Earthwatch Institute ☏978/461-0081 or 1-800/776-0188, ☮www.earthwatch.org. Organizes trips for volunteers to work overseas on scientific and cultural projects, with a strong emphasis on protection and preservation of the ecology and environment.
EcoAdventures ☏1-800/326-5025, ☮www.ecoadven.com. Individually tailored packages and river cruises.
Festival Tours ☏1-800/225-0117, ☮www.festivaltours.com. An all-encompassing tour operator to Central and South America focusing on main tourist sights.
Focus Tours ☏01/505 466 4688 ☮www.focustours.com. Ecology-oriented tours, custom-designed to take groups or individuals to destinations such as the Amazon, the Pantanal and the Atlantic forest regions
Lost World Adventures ☏1-800/999-0558, ☮www.lostworldadventures.com. Customized individual and group tours in Brazil, including Amazon River excursions, and multi-country tours.
Nature Expeditions International ☏1-800 /869-0639, ☮www.naturexp.com. Customized individual and group tours offering ecological adventures and Amazon River cruises.
Solar Tours ☏202/861-5864, ☮www.solartours.com. A big operator throughout Latin America, offering cruises, city tours, jungle trips and Carnaval specials.
Victor Emanuel Nature Tours ☏1-800/328-8368, ☮www.ventbird.com. Birdwatching tours.

From Australia and New Zealand

The best deals to Brazil **from Australasia** are offered by South American airlines in conjunction with Qantas and Air New Zealand. There are fewer options flying via the US and fares are generally more expensive. Round-the-world fares that include South America tend to cost more than other RTW options, but can be worthwhile if you have the time to make the most of a few stopovers.

From **Australia**, most flights to Brazil leave from Sydney, though there are also a couple of flights a week out of Brisbane and Melbourne. The most direct route is shared between Aerolíneas Argentinas and Qantas, which fly to Rio and São Paulo via Auckland and Buenos Aires. Air New Zealand/ LanChile's route is a little more long-winded, flying via Auckland, Papeete, Easter Island

and Santiago. Travelling via the US, United Airlines can fly you to Rio via either Los Angeles or San Francisco and Miami. From **New Zealand**, you can pick up one of the United, Qantas/Aerolíneas Argentinas or Air New Zealand/LanChile flights in Auckland.

In general, fares depend on the **duration of stay**, rather than the season – cut-off points when flying via Chile and Argentina are 35 days, 45 days, 90 days, 6 months and 1 year; flying via the US they are 21 days, 45 days and 180 days – but bear in mind that prices for flights (and everything else) soar during Christmas and Carnaval (Dec–March).

On the **more direct routes** you should be able to get a return fare for A$3040/ NZ$2700 in low season, rising to A$3290/ NZ$2990 in high season. Special offers with Aerolíneas Argentinas and LanChile sometimes bring the fare to Brazil down slightly, though your plans will need to be fairly flexible to take advantage of these last-minute bargains.

An **open-jaw ticket** can work out to be a convenient option. Flying into Rio and out of São Paulo (or vice versa) on Aerolíneas Argentinas or LanChile, for example, won't cost you any more than a straight through-fare to Rio.

Airlines

Aerolíneas Argentinas Australia ☎02/9252 5150, New Zealand ☎09/379 3675, ⓦwww.aerolineas.com. Two flights a week from Sydney to Rio via Auckland and Buenos Aires.
Air New Zealand Australia ☎13 24 76, ⓦwww.airnz.com.au, New Zealand ☎0800/737 000, ⓦwww.airnz.co.nz. Several flights a week from Sydney, Brisbane and Melbourne to Papeete, where you can connect with LanChile for flights on to Rio via Easter Island and Santiago.
LanChile Australia ☎1300/361 400 or 02/9244 2333, New Zealand ☎09/309 8673, ⓦwww.lanchile.com. Flies once a week from Brisbane and Sydney to Rio via Auckland, Papeete, Easter Island and Santiago – you may have to stay overnight in Santiago on some flights.
Qantas Australia ☎13 13 13, ⓦwww.qantas.com.au, New Zealand ☎0800/808 767, ⓦwww.qantas.co.nz. Code-shares with Aerolíneas Argentinas to provide an additional two flights a week to Rio from Melbourne via Auckland and Buenos Aires.
United Airlines Australia ☎13 17 77, ⓦwww.unitedairlines.com.au, New Zealand

☎09/379 3800 or 0800/508 648, ⓦwww.unitedairlines.co.nz. No direct services to Brazil or South America from Australia or New Zealand with United.

Flight agents

Anywhere Travel Australia ☎02/9663 0411, ⓦwww.anywheretravel.com.au
Holiday Shoppe New Zealand ☎0800/808 480, ⓦwww.holidayshoppe.co.nz
New Zealand Destinations Unlimited New Zealand ☎09/414 1685 ⓦwww.holiday.co.nz
Flight Centres Australia ☎13 31 33 or 02/9235 3522, ⓦwww.flightcentre.com.au; New Zealand ☎0800 243 544 or 09/358 4310, ⓦwww.flightcentre.co.nz
Northern Gateway Australia ☎1800/174 800, ⓦwww.northerngateway.com.au
STA Travel Australia ☎1300/733 035, ⓦwww.statravel.com.au; New Zealand ☎0508/782 872, ⓦwww.statravel.co.nz
Student Uni Travel Australia ☎02/9232 8444, ⓦwww.sut.com.au; New Zealand ☎09/379 4224, ⓦwww.sut.co.nz
Trailfinders Australia ☎02/9247 7666, ⓦwww.trailfinders.com.au
travel.com.au and **travel.co.nz** Australia ☎1300/130 482 or 02/9249 5444, ⓦwww.travel.com.au; New Zealand ☎0800/468 332, ⓦwww.travel.co.nz

RTW and circle tickets

Given these fares and routings, **round-the-world tickets** that take in South America are worth considering, though there are far fewer itineraries than for the more common Asian, North American and European routes. The limited choice, and the fact that most fares are mileage-based, tend to make routes via South America more expensive than other RTW options. Ultimately, your choice of route will depend on where else you want to visit besides Brazil. Qantas and Air New Zealand combine with a variety of carriers to offer tailored unlimited stopover round-the-world fares from A$3059/ NZ$3199.

Package tours

Package tours from Australia and New Zealand are few and far between and may seem a little expensive, but can be well worth it, especially if your time is limited, you're unfamiliar with the country's customs and language or you just don't like travelling alone. Specialist travel agents and operators like Adventure World and Adventure Associates offer a range of Brazilian itineraries, from the full package experience to shorter **add-on tours** that give you the flexibility of combining independent travel with say, an Amazon cruise (three days from Manaus starts at A$/NZ$600 per person, including all meals). Or, if you've got your heart set on Carnaval, pre-booked accommodation costs from A$/NZ$700 per person for four nights.

Adventure tours are worth considering if you want to cover a lot of ground or get to places that could be difficult to reach independently. Encounter Overland's 25-day Argentinian and Brazilian Encounter tour takes you from Tierra del Fuego through Patagonia to Iguassu Falls and Rio (land only A$/NZ$1600–1800, plus US$275 kitty).

Specialist agents and tour operators

The following specialize in South American travel arrangements, and can help with flights, accommodation and car rental, as well as fully inclusive tours.

Abercrombie & Kent Australia ☎02/9238 2356, ⓕ9221 1987. Offers tours in Brazil mainly on the Amazon river, some going right into Peru by boat.
Adventure Associates Australia ☎02/9389 7466 or 1800/222141, ⓦwww.adventure associates.com. Offers a wide range of tours, from four-day Pantanal eco-tours and week-long Carnaval packages, to individually tailored adventure and special interest holidays.

Adventure Specialists Australia ☎02/9261 2927, ⓦsydney.citysearch.com.au/E/V/SYDNE /0015/22/75. Overland specialist. Agents for Encounter Overland's expeditions, and G.A.P.'s Amazon river cruises.
Adventure World Australia ☎02/8913 0755, ⓦwww.adventureworld.com.au; New Zealand ☎09/524 5118, ⓦwww.adventureworld.co.nz. Agents for a vast array of international adventure travel companies – including Explore Worldwide – that offer tours in Brazil.
Contours Travel Australia ☎03/9670 6900, ⓦwww.contourstravel.com.au. Specialists in tailored city packages and eco-tours, including trips to Rio, Iguassu, the Amazon and the Pantanal.
Earthwatch Institute Australia ☎03/9682 6828. ⓦwww.earthwatch.org. Organizes volunteer work overseas on scientific and cultural projects.
Journey Latin America STA Travel (see "Flight agents" on p.18) act as agents for tours with this UK-based company.
Silke's Travel Australia ☎1800 807 860, or 02/8347 2000, ⓦwww.silkes.com.au. Tailored packages for gay and lesbian travellers.
South America Travel Centre Australia ☎1800/655 051 or 03/9642 5353, ⓦwww.satc.com.au. Specialize in tailor-made trips to Brazil.
South American Adventure Travel Australia ☎07/3854 1022. Independent and group travel specialists.
The Surf Travel Co. Australia ☎02/9527 4722 or 1800/687 873; New Zealand ☎09/473 8388, ⓦwww.surftravel.com.au. Well-established company that can advise on the best surfing beaches in Brazil as well as arrange flights and accommodation.

Red tape and visas

Citizens of most European nations, including Britain and Ireland, only need a valid passport and either a return or onward ticket, or evidence of funds to pay for one, to enter Brazil. You fill in an entry form on arrival and get a tourist visa allowing you to stay for ninety days. Australian, New Zealand, US and Canadian citizens need visas in advance, available from Brazilian consulates abroad; a return or onward ticket is usually a requirement. You'll also need to submit a passport photo with your visa application and pay a processing fee in the form of a bank cheque or money order (some consulates may accept a personal cheque or bank deposit).

Try not lose the **carbon copy of the entry form** the police hand you back at passport control; you are meant to return it when you leave Brazil, but you are no longer fined if you don't. If you do lose your passport, report to the **Polícia Federal** (see p.53) and then obtain a replacement travel document from your nearest consulate. You'll then have to return to the Polícia Federal who will put an endorsement in your passport. EU citizens can extend a tourist permit for another ninety days if you apply at least fifteen days before it expires, but it will only be extended once; if you want to stay longer you'll have to leave the country and re-enter. There's nothing in the rule book to stop you re-entering immediately, but it's advisable to wait at least a day. You'll be fined if you overstay your tourist permit or visa. For anything to do with entry permits and visas you deal with the federal police, the Polícia Federal. Every state capital has a federal police station with a visa section: ask for the delagacia federal. A $10 charge, payable in local currency, is made on tourist permit and visa extensions.

Consulates

Foreign countries are represented at **embassy level** in Brasília and most also maintain **consulates** in Rio and São Paulo. Elsewhere in this vast country, consulates, vice-consulates or honorary consulates are found in many major cities, from Manaus to Porto Alegre. Levels of service will vary depending on the nature of the particular post, but at the very least you can count on some immediate advice. Addresses and telephone numbers of embassies and consulates can be found in the "Listings" section of the cities in the *Guide*. Where their country doesn't have a representative, in an emergency a Commonwealth national can seek help at a British mission, and a European Union citizen at another EU mission.

Brazilian embassies and consulates abroad

Australia Embassy: 19 Forster Crescent, Yarralumla, Canberra, ACT 2600 ☎02/6273 2372; Consulate: 31 Market St, Sydney ☎02/9267 4414.
Canada 450 Wilbroad St, Sandyhill, Ottawa, ON K1V 6M8 ☎613/237-1090; consulates also in Montréal ☎514/499-0968; and Toronto ☎416/922-2503.
Ireland Europa House, Harcourt Centre, Harcourt St, Dublin 2 ☎01/475 6000.
New Zealand No representation – apply to Canberra through your travel agent.
South Africa Block C, 1st Floor, Hatfield Office Park, 1267 Pretorius St, Hatfield, Pretoria ☎012/426-9400; also consulate in Cape Town ☎021/421-4040.
UK Embassy: 32 Green St, London W1Y 4AT ☎020/7499 0877; Consulate: 6 St Alban's St, London SW1Y 4SQ ☎020/7930 9055).
US 3006 Massachusetts Ave NW, Washington DC 20008 ☎202/238-270) consulates also in Boston ☎617/542-4000); Chicago ☎312/464-0244); Houston ☎713/961-3063); LA ☎323/651-5833); Miami ☎305/285-6200); New York ☎917/777-7777); San Francisco ☎415/981-8170); and Washington ☎202/238-2828).

Longer stays: academic visits

Academic visitors and researchers making a short trip or attending a conference are best advised to enter on a tourist visa, which cuts down on the bureaucracy. If you're staying for a longer period, or intend to do research, you need to get a special visa, known as a "**Temporario**" before you leave home. To obtain this, you'll need to present a letter from a Brazilian institution of higher education saying it knows about, and approves, your research, and where you will have a formal affiliation during the period of your stay in Brazil. Visas are issued for six months, a year or two years; if in any doubt about exactly how long you're going to stay, apply for the two-year visa. One-year visas can be extended for a further year inside Brazil, but only after months of chasing up the police, and often involving a trip to the Ministry of Justice in Brasília.

On arrival on a Temporario you must **register** within 30 days at the *seção dos estrangeiros* office in the nearest federal police station to where you are based. You'll need to fill forms, supply an authenticated photocopy of your passport, pay a registration fee and provide some passport photo-

graphs. Several weeks later you'll be issued with an identity card; you can expect registering and getting the card to take at least a day of mindless drudgery, sitting in lines and chasing around, but it has to be done. If your work involves taking samples out of Brazil, a whole new bureaucratic ball game begins; you will need to get in touch well in advance with the Brazilian embassy in your home country and with your sponsoring Brazilian institution. New rules meant to deter bio-piracy mean that exporting plant materials from Brazil is now almost impossible.

If you are moving to Brazil, to work or because you have a Brazilian spouse, take the trouble to get a Temporario visa before entering the country as it's very difficult to arrange one after you arrive: Brazilian bureaucracy is not flexible. Brazilian consulates will advise you on what documentation you need; the process, though not complicated, takes six to nine months, so you need to start well in advance. Work visas will allow you to stay up to two years as a foreign taxpayer; from then on you pay Brazilian taxes. This is not usually an issue for Europeans, but US citizens have to deal with the double taxation issue.

Information, websites and maps

You'll find tourist information fairly easy to come by once in Brazil, and there are some sources to be tapped before you leave home. The Brazilian National Tourist Board (EMBRATUR) has representatives in Brazil's embassies or larger consulates (see p.20), where you can pick up brochure information and advice.

Useful websites

ⓦ **www.alberguesp.com.br** Information and booking service for the official youth hostel association in Brazil.

ⓦ **www.braziltourism.org** The official website of the Brazilian Tourist Office in Washington, D.C., including up-to-date information on visa requirements.

ⓦ **www.brazil.org.uk** The website of the Brazilian Embassy in London with a link to its extremely efficient and knowledgable tourism department.

ⓦ **www.cade.com.br/laturag.htm** Useful directory of Brazilian travel agencies, with hundreds of links to agencies' own websites.

ⓦ **www.candomble.com** Website in English and Portuguese offering historical and cultural information on the important African-Brazilian religion *candomblé*.

ⓦ **www.cnh.com.br** Directory of hotels and *pousadas*, restaurants, travel agents, tour operators and guides throughout Brazil, geared towards the upmarket traveller. In Portuguese only.
ⓦ **www.embratur.gov.br** Official site of EMBRATUR, the Brazilian government's national tourist service. Only in Portuguese, the site is of limited use to most foreign tourists, but there are lots of nice pictures.
ⓦ **www.worldsamba.org** This English-language site is a great introduction to samba – and Carnaval in general. Lots of links to samba schools both in Brazil and the rest of the world.
ⓦ **www.stb.com.br** Site run by the Student Travel Bureau, providing information on student discounts, air tickets and cultural exchanges.
ⓦ **www.icom.org** An excellent site for links to museum websites all over the world, including over fifty museums and public art galleries in Brazil.
ⓦ **www.isfa.com/server/web/futebol** The latest Brazilian football results, plus information on players and their teams, and links to most Brazilian teams. In Portuguese only.

Tourist offices

In Brazil, facilities vary greatly. Popular destinations like Rio, Salvador, the Northeast beach resorts and towns throughout the South have efficient and helpful **tourist offices**, but anywhere off the beaten track has nothing at all – only Manaus, Belém and Porto Velho have offices in the Amazon region, for example.

Most **state capitals** have tourist information offices, which are open during office hours, announced by signs saying "**Informações Turísticas**". Many of these provide free city maps and booklets, but they are usually all in Portuguese, although you occasionally see atrociously mangled English. As a rule, only the airport tourist offices have **hotel booking services**, and none of them is very good on advising about budget accommodation. There are EMBRATUR offices in a few of the major centres, but the local tourist offices are usually more helpful; these are run by the different state and municipal governments, so you have to learn a new acronym every time you cross a state line. In Rio, for example, you'll find national (EMBRATUR), state (TurisRio) and city (Riotur) offices.

Maps

We've provided **maps** of all the major towns and cities and various other regions. More detailed maps are surprisingly hard to get hold of outside Brazil, and are rarely very good: there are plenty of maps of South America, but the only widely available one that is specifically of Brazil is the *Bartholomew Brazil & Bolivia* (1:5,000,000) which is not very easy to read. Much better are the six regional maps in the *Mapa Rodoviário Touring* series (1:2,500,000), which clearly mark all the major routes, although these, even in Brazil, are difficult to find.

A useful compendium of **city maps** and **main road networks** is published by Guias Quatro Rodas, a Brazilian motoring organization, which also has maps to Rio, São Paulo and other cities, states and regions. These are easy to find in bookstores, newsagents and magazine stalls. Very clear maps of individual states are published by Polimapas, and are usually available in Brazilian bookstores and newspaper kiosks. At 1:1,000,000 these are the largest scale of all, though they actually have less detail than some of the above-mentioned. Topographical and hiking maps are difficult to find, though very occasionally they are available from municipal tourist offices or national parks in Brazil, or from local trekking equipment shops or tour operators.

Map outlets

In Australia and New Zealand
The Map Shop 6–10 Peel St, Adelaide, SA 5000 ☎08/8231 2033, ⓦwww.mapshop.net.au
Mapland 372 Little Bourke St, Melbourne, Victoria 3000 ☎03/9670 4383, ⓦwww.mapland.com.au
MapWorld 173 Gloucester St, Christchurch ☎0800/627 967 or 03/374 5399, ⓦwww.mapworld.co.nz
Perth Map Centre 900 Hay St, Perth, WA 6000 ☎08/9322 5733, ⓦwww.perthmap.com.au
Specialty Maps 46 Albert St, Auckland 1001 ☎09/307 2217, ⓦwww.specialtymaps.co.nz
World Wide Maps and Guides 187 George St, Brisbane ☎07/3221 4330, ⓦwww.powerup.com.au/~wwmaps

In the UK and Ireland

Blackwell's Map and Travel Shop 50 Broad St, Oxford OX1 3BQ ☎01865/793 550, ⓦmaps.blackwell.co.uk

Daunt Books 83 Marylebone High St, W1M 3DE ☎020/7224 2295, ⓕ7224 6893; 193 Haverstock Hill, NW3 4QL ☎020/7794 4006.

Easons Bookshop 40 O'Connell St, Dublin 1 ☎01/858 3881, ⓦwww.eason.ie.

Fred Hanna's Bookshop 27–29 Nassau St, Dublin 2 ☎01/677 1255.

Heffers Map and Travel 20 Trinity St, Cambridge CB2 1TJ ☎01865/333 536, ⓦwww.heffers.co.uk

Hodges Figgis Bookshop 56–58 Dawson St, Dublin 2 ☎01/677 4754.

James Thin Melven's Bookshop 29 Union St, Inverness IV1 1QA ☎01463/233500, ⓦwww.jthin.co.uk

John Smith and Sons 57–61 St Vincent St, Glasgow G2 5TB ☎0141/221 7472, ⓕ248 4412, ⓦwww.johnsmith.co.uk

The Map Shop 30a Belvoir St, Leicester LE1 6QH ☎0116/247 1400, ⓦwww.mapshopleicester.co.uk

National Map Centre 22–24 Caxton St, London SW1H 0QU ☎020/7222 2466, ⓦwww.mapsnmc.co.uk

Newcastle Map Centre 55 Grey St, Newcastle-upon-Tyne, NE1 6EF ☎0191/261 5622.

Stanfords 12–14 Long Acre, WC2E 9LP ☎020/7836 1321, ⓦwww.stanfords.co.uk, ⓔsales@stanfords.co.uk

The Travel Bookshop 13–15 Blenheim Crescent, W11 2EE ☎020/7229 5260, ⓦwww.thetravelbookshop.co.uk

Waterstone's 91 Deansgate, Manchester M3 2BW ☎0161/837 3000, ⓕ835 1534, ⓦwww.waterstones-manchester-deansgate.co.uk. In Belfast at Queens Building, 8 Royal Ave ☎028/9024 7355. In Ireland at 69 Patrick St, Cork ☎021/276 522; 7 Dawson St, Dublin 2 ☎01/679 1260.

In the US and Canada

Adventurous Traveler.com US ☎1-800/282-3963, ⓦadventuroustraveler.com

The Complete Traveller Bookstore 199 Madison Ave, New York, NY 10016 ☎212/685-9007.

International Travel Maps and Books 552 Seymor St, Vancouver, BC V6B 3J5 ☎604/687-3320, ⓦwww.itmp.com

The Map Store Inc. 1636 1st St, Washington DC 20006 ☎202/628 2608.

Open Air Books and Maps 25 Toronto St, Toronto, ON M5C 2R1 ☎416/363-0719.

Phileas Fogg's Books & Maps #87 Stanford Shopping Center, Palo Alto, CA 94304 ☎1-800/533-FOGG, ⓦwww.foggs.com

Rand McNally US ☎1-800/333-0136, ⓦwww.randmcnally.com. Around thirty stores across the US; dial ext 2111 or check the website for the nearest location.

Travel Books & Language Center 4437 Wisconsin Ave NW, Washington DC 20016 ☎1-800/220-2665.

Traveler's Bookstore 22 W 52nd St, New York, NY 10019 ☎212/664-0995.

Ulysses Travel Bookshop 4176 St-Denis, Montréal ☎514/843-9447, ⓦwww.ulyssesguides.ca

Insurance

A typical travel insurance policy usually provides cover for the loss of baggage, tickets and – up to a certain limit – cash or cheques, as well as cancellation or curtailment of your journey. Most of them exclude so-called dangerous sports unless an extra premium is paid: in Brazil this can mean scuba diving and trekking, though probably not jeep trips.

Read the small print and benefits tables of prospective policies carefully; coverage can vary wildly for roughly similar premiums.

Many policies can be chopped and changed to exclude coverage you don't need – for example, sickness and accident benefits can

Insurance

Rough Guides offers its own low-cost travel insurance, especially customized for our statistically low-risk readers by a leading British broker, provided by the American International Group (AIG) and registered with the British regulatory body, GISC (the General Insurance Standards Council).

There are five main Rough Guide insurance plans: **No Frills** for the bare minimum for secure travel; **Essential**, which provides decent all-round cover; **Premier** for comprehensive cover with a wide range of benefits; **Extended Stay** for cover lasting two months to a year; and **Annual multi-trip**, a cost-effective way of getting Premier cover if you travel more than once a year. Premier, Annual Multi-Trip and Extended Stay policies can be supplemented by a "Hazardous Pursuits Extension" if you plan to indulge in sports considered dangerous, such as scuba-diving or trekking.

For a policy quote, call the Rough Guide Insurance Line: toll-free in the UK ☏0800/015 09 06 or ☏+44 1392 314 665 from elsewhere. Alternatively, get an online quote at ⓦwww.roughguides.com/insurance

often be excluded or included at will. If you do take medical coverage, ascertain whether benefits will be paid as treatment proceeds or only after you return home, and whether there is a 24-hour medical emergency number. When securing baggage cover, make sure that the per-article limit – typically under £500 equivalent – will cover your most valuable possession. If you need to make a claim, you should keep receipts for medicines and medical treatment, and in the event you have anything stolen you must obtain an official statement from the police (at special tourist police stations or with the civil police).

Bank and credit cards often have certain levels of medical or other insurance included, and you may automatically get travel insurance if you use a major credit card to pay for your trip. If you have a good all-risks **home insurance policy** it may cover your possessions against loss or theft when overseas. Many **private medical schemes** such as BUPA or PPP also offer coverage plans for abroad, including baggage loss, cancellation or curtailment and cash replacement as well as sickness or accident.

Americans and **Canadians** should also check that they're not already covered. Canadian provincial health plans usually provide partial cover for medical mishaps overseas. Holders of official student/teacher /youth cards are entitled to meagre accident coverage and hospital in-patient benefits. Students will often find that their student health coverage extends during the vacations and for one term beyond the date of last enrolment. Homeowners' or renters' insurance often covers theft or loss of documents, money and valuables while overseas, though conditions and maximum amounts vary from company to company.

Health

Although there are no compulsory vaccinations required to enter the country, certain precautions should be taken, certainly if you're staying for any length of time or visiting the more remote regions. Taking out travel insurance is vital (see p.23), and you should take all possible precautions to guard against AIDS, a major worry in Brazil.

Pharmacies and medical treatment

Most standard drugs are available in **pharmacies**, *farmácias*, which you'll find everywhere – no prescriptions are necessary. A pharmacy will also give injections (you need a tetanus jab if you get bitten by a dog) and free medical advice, and they're a good first line of defence if you fall ill.

If you are unlucky enough to need **medical treatment** in Brazil, forget about the public hospitals – as a foreigner you have virtually no chance of getting a bed unless you have an infectious disease, and the level of health care offered by most is appalling. You can get reasonably good medical and dental care privately: North Americans will think it fairly inexpensive, Europeans used to state-subsidized health care will not. A doctor's visit will cost on average $25–45; drugs are relatively cheap. Local tourist offices and smart hotels in big cities will have lists of English- French- and German-speaking **doctors**; ask for a *médico*. Outside the larger centres, you will probably have to try out your Portuguese. If a medical emergency occurs in an out-of-the-way location, there's an excellent **air ambulance** service (℡011/5506-0606, ⊜846-8689) that guarantees collection anywhere in the country within 24 hours of calling. If considering this option, be sure to contact your travel insurance company before phoning for a plane and check that you're fully covered.

> **Emergency** phone numbers vary from place to place, but you'll always find them listed in phone boxes – look for *Bombeiros* or *Polícia Civil*.

Food and water

Many diseases are directly or indirectly related to impure **water** (see "Water purification" box on p.26) and contaminated **food**, and care should be taken in choosing what to eat and drink.

With a little common sense, it's quite easy to establish whether food is fresh or not, and always ensure that it's properly cooked. You should, of course, take particular care with seafood, especially **shellfish** – don't eat anything that's at all suspicious. Fruit and salad ingredients should be washed in bottled or purified water or, preferably, peeled. Ultimately you are going to run some risks with food, so if you're going to enjoy your stay to the full, there's no sense in being too paranoid.

Even in the most remote towns and villages **mineral water** (*água mineral*), either sparkling (*com gás*) or still (*sem gás*), is easily available and cheap. To avoid dehydration be sure to drink plenty of non-alcoholic liquids, always carry a bottle of water on long trips and check that the seal on any bottled water you use is intact.

As with food, it's difficult to be on guard all the time; fruit juices are more often than not diluted, at best with only filtered water, and while it is wise to avoid ice in general this is well-nigh impossible.

Yellow fever

Vaccinating against **yellow fever** is highly recommended if you're going to **Amazonia, Goias or Mato Grosso**. This viral disease is transmitted by mosquitoes and can be fatal. Symptoms are headache, fever, abdominal pain and vomiting, and though victims may appear to recover, without medical help, they may suffer from bleeding, shock, and kidney and liver failure. The only treatment is

Water purification

Contaminated water is a major cause of sickness due to the presence of bacteria, viruses and cysts. These micro-organisms cause diseases such as diarrhoea, gastroenteritis, typhoid, cholera, dysentery, poliomyelitis, hepatitis A, giardiasis and bilharziasis and can be present even when water looks clean and safe to drink.

Bottled water is widely available in Brazil, but, if you are considering trekking in remote regions or want to take all possible precautions, there are various methods of **treating water** whilst you are travelling. **Boiling** is the time-honoured method which will be effective in sterilizing water, although it will not remove unpleasant tastes. A minimum boiling time of five minutes (longer at higher altitudes) is sufficient to kill micro-organisms.

Chemical sterilization can be carried out using either chlorine or iodine tablets or a tincture of iodine liquid. When using tablets it is essential to follow the manufacturer's dosage and contact time; with tincture of iodine, you add a couple of drops to one litre of water and leave to stand for twenty minutes. Iodine tablets are preferred to chlorine as the latter leave an especially unpalatable taste in the water and also are not effective in preventing such diseases as amoebic dysentery and giardiasis. If you are using sterilizing tablets, a water filter is useful, not least to improve the taste.

Water filters alone will remove most bacteria and cysts, but not viruses, which, due to their microscopic size, pass through into the filtered water.

Purification, a two-stage process involving both filtration and sterilization, removes or destroys all waterborne disease-causing micro-organisms. Portable water purifiers range in size from units weighing as little as 60 grams which can be slipped into a pocket, to 800 grams for carrying in a backpack, and are available from specialist outdoor equipment retailers.

to keep the fever as low as possible and prevent dehydration. Fortunately a yellow fever vaccine is available which offers good protection for ten years.

Malaria

Malaria is endemic in **northern Brazil**, and anyone intending to travel anywhere in Amazonia should take precautions very seriously. In recent years, rates have climbed as mosquitoes have become more resistant to insecticides, and a few unwary tourists die avoidably every year. With simple precautions you can minimize the chances of getting it even in highly malarial areas, and, properly treated, a dose of malaria should be no worse than a severe bout of flu. But make no mistake – unless you follow the **precautions** outlined here, and take malaria prophylaxis before, during and after you pass through Amazonia, malaria can kill.

There are two kinds of malaria in Brazil: **falciparum**, which is more serious but less common, and **vivax**. Both are transmitted by anopheles mosquitoes, which are most active at sunrise and for an hour or so before sunset. Even in very malarial areas, only around five percent of anopheles are infected with malarial parasites, so the more you minimize mosquito bites, the less likely you are to catch it. Use **insect repellent**: the most commonly used in Brazil is **Autan**, often in combination with Johnson's Baby Oil to minimize skin irritation. The most effective mosquito repellents – worth looking out for before you leave home – contain **DEET** (diethyl toluamide). DEET is strong stuff, so follow the manufacturers' instructions, particularly with use on children. If you have sensitive skin a natural alternative is citronella or in the UK, Mosi-guard Natural, made from a blend of eucalyptus oils, though still use DEET on clothes and nets. Wear long-sleeved shirts and trousers, shoes and socks during the times of day when mosquitoes are most active. Sleep under a sheet and, crucially, use a **mosquito net**. Nets for hammocks (*mosqueteiro para rede*) cost around $15 and are easily available in Amazonian cities. Mosquito coils also help keep the insects at bay.

A traveller's first-aid kit

Among items you might want to carry with you – especially if you're planning to go trekking – are:

Antiseptic cream
Insect repellent
Plasters/band aids
Water sterilization tablets or water purifier
Lint and sealed bandages
Knee supports
A course of Flagyl antibiotics

Imodium (Lomotil) for emergency diarrhoea treatment
Paracetamol/aspirin
Multi-vitamin and mineral tablets
Rehydration sachets
Hypodermic needles and sterilized skin wipes

When taking **preventive tablets** it's important to keep a routine and cover the period before and after your trip with doses. Doctors can advise on which kind to take. As resistance to chloroquin-based drugs increases, mefloquin, which goes under the brand name of Lariam, has become the recommended prophylactic for most travellers to Brazil. This has very strong side effects, and its use is controversial. The website ⓦwww.cdc.gov/travel/regionalmalaria is a useful resource, giving advice on risk areas in Brazil and the best methods of protection. Malaria has an incubation period of around two weeks. The first **signs of malaria** are remarkably similar to flu – muscle pains, weakness and pain in the joints, which will last for a day or two before the onset of malaria fever proper – and may take months to appear: if you suspect anything go to a hospital or clinic immediately. You need immediate treatment and a blood test to identify the strain. **Malaria treatment** is the one public health area where Brazil can take some credit. Dotted everywhere around Amazonia are small malaria control posts and **clinics**, run by the anti-malaria agency SUCAM – ask for the *posto da SUCAM*. They may not look like much, but the people who staff them are very experienced and know their local strains better than any city specialist. Treatment in a *posto* is free, and if you do catch malaria you should get yourself taken to one as quickly as possible; don't shiver in your hammock and wait for it to pass. It often does, but it can also kill.

Chagas' disease

Another serious disease you should guard against is **Chagas' disease**, which is endemic in parts of the **Northeast** and **Amazonia** and, although it is difficult to catch, it can be serious, leading to heart and kidney problems that appear up to twenty years after infection. The disease is carried in the faeces of beetles which live in the cracks of adobe walls, so when sleeping in an adobe hut make sure nothing can crawl into your hammock; either use a mosquito net or sling the hammock as far from walls as you can. The beetle bites and then defecates next to the spot: scratching of the bite will rub in the infected faeces, so before scratching a bite that you know wasn't caused by a mosquito, bathe it in alcohol. If you are infected, you will have a fever for a few days which will then clear up, and though the disease can be treated in its early stages it becomes incurable once established. If you travel through a Chagas area and get an undiagnosed fever, have a blood test as soon as possible afterwards.

Dengue fever

Dengue fever, a viral disease transmitted by mosquito bites, is increasingly common in all Brazilian cities save the extreme south of the country. The symptoms are debilitating rather than dangerous: light but persistent fever, tiredness, muscle and joint pains, especially in the fingers, and nausea and vomiting. It is easily treatable, but you will feel pretty grim for a week or so. It is much more widespread than any other disease in urban areas, and is currently the focus of much educational and preventive work by the Brazilian government. The same precautions against mosquito bites outlined in the section on malaria above apply here.

Medical resources for travellers

In Australia and New Zealand

Travellers' Medical and Vaccination Centre
ⓦ www.tmvc.com.au. Australia: 27–29 Gilbert
Place, Adelaide, SA 5000 ☎ 08/8212 7522; 5/247
Adelaide St, Brisbane, Qld 4000 ☎ 07/3221 9066;
5/8–10 Hobart Place, Canberra, ACT 2600
☎ 02/6257 7156;
270 Sandy Bay Rd, Sandy Bay Tas, Hobart 7005
☎ 03/6223 7577; 2/393 Little Bourke St,
Melbourne, Vic 3000 ☎ 03/9602 5788;
Level 7, Dymocks Bldg, 428 George St, Sydney,
NSW 2000 ☎ 02/9221 7133. New Zealand: 1/170
Queen St, Auckland ☎ 09/373 3531;
Moorhouse Medical Centre, 9 Washington Way,
Christchurch ☎ 03/379 4000;
Shop 15, Grand Arcade, 14–16 Willis St, Wellington
☎ 04/473 0991.

In the UK and Ireland

British Airways Travel Clinics 156 Regent St,
London W1 (Mon–Fri 9.30am–5.15pm, Sat
10am–4pm, no appointment necessary;
☎ 020/7439 9584); 101 Cheapside, London EC2
(hours as above, appointment required;
☎ 020/7606 2977);
ⓦ www.britishairways.com/travel/healthclinintro.
Vaccinations, tailored advice from an online database
and a complete range of travel healthcare products.
Hospital for Tropical Diseases Travel Clinic
2nd floor, Mortimer Market Centre, off Capper St,
London WC1E 6AU (Mon–Fri 9am–5pm by
appointment only; ☎ 020/7388 9600,
ⓦ www.masta.org; a consultation costs £15 which
is waived if you have your injections here). A
recorded Health Line (☎ 0906/133 7733; 50p per
min) gives hints on hygiene and illness prevention as
well as listing appropriate immunizations.
Malaria Helpline 24-hour recorded advice on
☎ 0891/600350 (60p/min).
**MASTA (Medical Advisory Service for
Travellers Abroad)** 40 regional clinics (call
☎ 0870/6062782 for the nearest). Also operates a
pre-recorded 24-hour Travellers' Health Line (UK
t0906/822 4100, 60p per min), giving information
tailored to your journey by return of post.
Nomad Pharmacy surgeries 40 Bernard St,
London, WC1N 1LE; and 3–4 Wellington Terrace,
Turnpike Lane, London N8 0PX (Mon–Fri
9.30am–6pm, ☎ 020/7833 4114 to book
vaccination appointment). They give advice free if
you go in person, or their telephone helpline is

☎ 0906/863 3414 (60p per minute). They can give
information tailored to your travel needs.
Trailfinders Immunization clinics (no
appointments necessary) at 194 Kensington High
St, London W8 7RG (Mon–Fri 9am–5pm except
Thurs to 6pm, Sat 9.30am–4pm; ☎ 020/7938
3999).
Travel Medicine Services PO Box 254, 16
College St, Belfast BT1 6BT ☎ 028/9031 5220.
Offers medical advice before a trip and help
afterwards in the event of a tropical disease.
Tropical Medical Bureau Grafton Buildings, 34
Grafton St, Dublin 2, ☎ 01/671 9200,
ⓦ tmb.exodus.ie. Travel medicine specialists whose
website contains useful country-specific information.

In the US and Canada

Canadian Society for International Health 1
Nicholas St, Suite 1105, Ottawa, ON K1N 7B7
☎ 613/241-5785, ⓦ www.csih.org. Distributes a
free pamphlet, "Health Information for Canadian
Travellers", containing an extensive list of travel
health centres in Canada.
Centers for Disease Control 1600 Clifton Rd
NE, Atlanta, GA 30333 ☎ 1-800/311-3435 or
404/639-3534, ⓦ www.cdc.gov. Publishes outbreak
warnings, suggested inoculations, precautions and
other background information for travellers. Useful
website plus International Travelers Hotline on ☎ 1-
877/FYI-TRIP.
**International Association for Medical
Assistance to Travellers (IAMAT)** 417 Center
St, Lewiston, NY 14092 ☎ 716/754-4883,
ⓦ www.iamat.org, and 40 Regal Rd, Guelph, ON
N1K 1B5 ☎ 519/836-0102. A non-profit
organization supported by donations, it can provide a
list of English-speaking doctors, climate charts and
leaflets on various diseases and inoculations.
Travel Medicine ☎ 1-800/TRAVMED,
ⓦ www.travmed.com. Sells first-aid kits, mosquito
netting, water filters, reference books and other
health-related travel products.
Travelers Medical Center 31 Washington
Square West, New York, NY 10011 ☎ 212/982-
1600. Consultation service on immunizations and
treatment of diseases for people travelling to
developing countries.

Hepatitis

Wherever you go, protection against **hepatitis A** is a sensible precaution. The disease is
transmitted through contaminated water and
food, resulting in fever and diarrhoea, and it
can also cause liver damage.
Gammaglobulin injections, one before you

go and boosters every six months, are the standard protection. If you plan to spend much time in Amazonia or the Northeast, or if you know that you will be travelling rough, it's well worth protecting yourself. If you have had jaundice, you may well have immunity and should have a blood test to see if you need the injections. A newer vaccine – Havrix – is very effective and lasts for up to ten years.

Diarrhoea, dysentery and giardia

Diarrhoea is something everybody gets at some stage, and there's little to be done except drink a lot (but not alcohol) and bide your time. You should also replace salts either by taking oral rehydration salts or by mixing a teaspoon of salt and eight of sugar in a litre of purified water. You can minimize the risk by being sensible about what you eat, and by not drinking tap water anywhere. This isn't difficult, given the extreme cheapness and universal availability of soft drinks and *água mineral*, while Brazilians are great believers in herbal teas, which often help alleviate cramps.

If your diarrhoea contains blood or mucus, the cause may be dysentery or giardia. With a fever, it could well be caused by **bacillic dysentery** and may clear up without treatment. If you're sure you need it, a course of antibiotics such as tetracyclin or ampicillin (travel with a supply if you are going off the beaten track for a while) should sort you out, but they also destroy "gut flora" which help protect you. Similar symptoms without fever indicate **amoebic dysentery**, which is much more serious, and can damage your gut if untreated. The usual cure is a course of metronidazole (*Flagyl*), an antibiotic which may itself make you feel ill, and should not be taken with alcohol. Similar symptoms, plus rotten-egg belches and farts, indicate **giardia**, for which the treatment is again metronidazole. If you suspect you have any of these, seek medical help, and only start on the metronidazole (750mg three times daily for a week for adults) if there is definitely blood in your diarrhoea and it is impossible to see a doctor.

Cholera

Cholera is a waterborne bacterial disease which has become endemic to many parts of Brazil. It flourishes in a combination of hot climates and unsanitary conditions, and can be found anywhere in Brazil from Rio northwards. The disease is most common in the big cities of the Northeast, especially Fortaleza, and in the western Amazon in the border region with Peru. Rarely fatal for the young and fit if acted on immediately, the illness in most cases is no more severe than a sudden and nasty bout of diarrhoea, which can be treated with standard rehydration methods, antibiotics and a saline drip. Left untreated, it can kill within 24 hours by dehydrating its victims. Provided you take sensible precautions with food (especially shellfish) and drinking water, you shouldn't get it. If you are really concerned, vaccines are available with an effectiveness rate of between sixty and seventy percent.

HIV and AIDS

Brazil has one of the world's highest number of people with **AIDS and HIV**. There are many reasons for this: a scandalous lack of screening of either blood donors or supplies in the 1980s; the level of gay sex between Brazilian men, amongst whom bisexuality is common; the popularity of anal sex, not least amongst heterosexual couples; and the sharing of needles, both amongst drug users in large cities and, in the past, when injections were given for medical purposes, even in hospitals. Although high-profile public education campaigns are visible on TV and billboards, there is still widespread ignorance of how the disease is transmitted, and fear and persecution of its victims. Things have not been helped by the Catholic Church, in Brazil usually so liberal on many issues, which has taken a firmly conservative stance on the use of condoms. Nevertheless, it is not all doom and gloom. Brazil led the world in facing down international drug companies with the threat that they would independently manufacture AIDS drugs, with the result that all HIV positive Brazilians now receive free anti-retroviral medicines in a program that has become a global model for developing countries.

A straightforward understanding of the disease and how it is transmitted is the best defence. Firstly, AIDS is not evenly distributed throughout Brazil. A large majority of sufferers and HIV carriers are concentrated in **Rio** and **São Paulo**, where you should take extra care. As anywhere else, sex with a prostitute is a high-risk activity. Wherever you are, make sure that if you have an injection it is with a needle you see being removed from its packaging. (It is now possible to buy travellers' medical packs which contain sterile needles, attachments for intravenous drips and the like: they're available from immunization centres.) **Avoid blood transfusions unless absolutely necessary**. Although the situation with blood and blood products has improved enormously, there are still occasional slip-ups.

Finally, **use a condom**. Only a tiny minority of sexually active Brazilian men carry them as a matter of course. They are widely available in pharmacies, where you should ask for a *camisinha* or a *camiseta de Vênus*. There are often local shortages, however, and Brazilian condoms are not as durable nor as reliable as condoms in the developed world. Take a good supply along with you: you can always give them away if you don't use them.

The Amazon

Given the remoteness of many parts of the Amazon and the prevalence of insects and snakes, health care takes on a special significance. Despite the heat, you should wear long trousers all the time and use repellent to guard against disease-spreading insect bites. If you are trekking through forest or savanna, it is vital to wear good boots which protect your ankles from snake bites, chiggers and scorpions, and you should never trek alone.

Snakes are timid and only attack if you step on them, unless you are unlucky. Many of the most poisonous snakes are tiny, easily able to snuggle inside a shoe or a rucksack pocket. Always shake out your hammock and clothes, keep rucksack pockets tightly closed and take special care when it rains as snakes, scorpions and other nasty beasties quite sensibly head for shelter in huts. If you do get bitten by a snake, try to catch it for identification. Use a shoelace or a torn piece of shirt wound round the limb with a stick as a tourniquet, which you should repeatedly tighten for twenty seconds and then release for a minute, to slow down the action of the poison. Contrary to popular belief, cutting yourself and sucking out blood will do you more harm than good. It goes without saying that you should get yourself to a doctor as soon as possible. If you are well off the beaten track, small pharmacies even in remote villages usually stock serum, but you must know the type of snake involved.

Due to the humidity, any **cut** or **wound** gets infected very easily. Always clean cuts or bites with alcohol or purified water before dressing. As a general rule, leave all insects alone and never handle them. Even the smallest ants, caterpillars and bees can give you nasty stings and bites, and scorpions, large soldier ants and some species of bee will give you a fever for a day or two as well.

Costs, money and banks

Up until 1994 when the famous *Plano Real* was introduced, Brazilian inflation was astronomical, and the country was a very cheap destination for anyone who had hard currency like the dollar. At a stroke, the *Plano Real* stabilized inflation, and the tightly controlled exchange made Brazil no longer cheap to foreigners. Fortunately for tourists, a devaluation in 1999 has meant that Brazil has once again become an inexpensive destination for foreigners. With the global economic outlook still uncertain, no doubt this situation will continue for the foreseeable future.

US dollars are easy enough to change in banks and exchange offices anywhere, and are also readily accepted by luxury hotels, tour companies and souvenir shops in the big cities. Given the current instability of the *real*, we quote prices in this book in **US dollars**; this should give a reliable idea of what you'll be paying on the spot.

Money and prices

The Brazilian currency is the *real* (pronounced "hey-al"), plural *reais* (pronounced "hey-ice"). Written as R$, the *real* is made up of one hundred *centavos*, the latter written ¢. Notes, all the same size but different colours, are for 1, 2, 5, 10, 20, 50 and 100 *reais*; coins are 1, 5, 10, 25, 50 *centavos* and 1 *real*. Coins look irritatingly similar, and to tell them apart you'll have to scrutinize them closely. The notes are gorgeous, themed around Brazilian wildlife – keep an eye out for the innovative plastic 10 *real* note.

The **cost of living** in Brazil is cheap. Some things are astonishingly cheap by European and North American standards, particularly hotels, foodstuffs (including eating out in most restaurants), clothing and bus travel. Plane tickets bought in Brazil work out

around the same as a US or European budget airline, in dollar terms. Other things are more expensive: film, sun cream and anything having to do with computers. All the same, Brazil is very much a viable destination for the budget traveller, especially in urban areas. The cheapness of food and budget hotels – and the fact that the best attractions, like the beaches, are free – still makes it possible to have a very enjoyable time for under $50 a day. Staying in good hotels, travelling by comfortable buses and not stinting on the extras will cost you around $100 a day.

Changing money

Thanks to technology, changing money in Brazil is simple; just take your bank or credit card with PIN (Personal Identification Number, which you must set up with your bank before your trip), and use **ATMs** – look for a sign saying *Cartão* or *Saques por Cartão*; if there aren't any, show your card to one of the managers behind a desk, and they will point you in the right direction; this works best in large cities. Only Visa cards can be used to withdraw cash advances at the ATMs of Banco do Brasil and Banco Bradesco; only MasterCard at HSBC, Itaú and Banco Mercantil. Increasing numbers of Brazilian banks are linking their cash dispensers to the Cirrus and Maestro networks: your best bets are the Banco do Brasil followed by Itaú. Do not, however, completely count on being able to find a compatible ATM. Some machines don't read foreign-issued cards, and while you'll find that your card is acceptible in some amazingly backwater locations, it may not be – carry a reserve of cash just in case. For security rea-

> ### Exchange rates
>
> You can check current exchange rates and convert figures on ⓦ www.xe.net/currency.
> At the time of writing, the Brazilian *real* was worth R$3.50 to US$1 – this was the basis for the price calculations in this edition.

sons, between 10pm and 6am ATMs only allow the withdrawal of the equivalent of $15.

The main **credit cards** are widely accepted by shops, hotels and restaurants throughout Brazil, even in rural areas. MasterCard and Visa are the most prevalent, with Diners Club and American Express also widespread. It's a good idea to inform your credit card issuer about your trip before you leave so that the card isn't stopped for uncharacteristic use.

Given the ease of using plastic, **travellers' cheques** are not recommended, unless you want a small emergency reserve. Only the head offices of major **banks** (Banco do Brasil, HSBC, Banco Itaú, Banespa) will have an exchange department (ask for *câmbio*); whether changing cash or travellers' cheques you'll need your passport. You can also change cash and travellers' cheques in smart hotels and in some large travel agencies. The best rates, however, are usually to be found in a **casa de câmbio**, but these only operate on any scale in Rio and São Paulo. Exchange departments of banks often close early, sometimes at 1pm,

although more often at 2pm or 3pm, and it can take up to two hours to complete all the necessary paperwork. Some banks will only change a minimum of $100 per transaction. Airport banks are open seven days a week, others only Monday to Friday. You'll find life much easier if you bring only **US dollar bank notes and plastic**. Euros note are slowly being recognised, but generally only in *casas de câmbio* in Rio and São Paulo will you be able to change other currencies – and then only at very poor rates of exchange.

Exchange rates

You will see two rates being quoted for cash: the *oficial*, which is what a bank will pay you, and the *turismo*, which is what you will get in a hotel or travel agency; travellers' cheques have slightly lower rates, even in banks. The *turismo* is usually only two or three points less than the *oficial* and, unless you're changing large amounts of money, it's often worth living with this lower rate to avoid the inconvenience of changing your money in a bank.

Getting around

Local travel in Brazil is always easy. Public transport outside of the Amazon is generally by bus or plane, though there are a few passenger trains, too. However you travel, services will be crowded, plentiful and, apart from planes, cheap.

Car rental is also possible, but driving in Brazil is not for the faint-hearted. Some international car rental companies have local agencies and there are quite a few reliable Brazilian ones as well. Hitchhiking, over any distance, is not recommended.

Buses

The **bus system** in Brazil is excellent, as good as anywhere in the Americas, and makes travelling around the country easy, comfortable and economical, despite the

distances involved. Intercity buses leave from a station called a **rodoviária**, usually built on city outskirts.

Buses are operated by hundreds of private companies, but **prices** are standardized, even when more than one firm plies the same route, and are very reasonable: Rio to São Paulo is around $15, Rio to Belo Horizonte $25, Rio to Foz do Iguaçu $30, São Paulo to Brasília $40, Recife to Salvador $30 and Fortaleza to Belém $45. Long-distance buses are comfortable enough to sleep in, and have on-board toilets (which

Backpacker buses

Aimed very much at young foreign backpackers who want to combine the flexibility of independent travel with the convenience of a tour are the **hop-on hop-off bus** routes of **South America Experience** (⊛www .southamericaexperience.com), an energetic Rio-based company directly modelled on concepts developed in Australia and New Zealand. Modern air-conditioned buses ply two routes in the state of Rio and two in Bahia, passing through some of the states' most beautiful areas, both on the coast and in the mountains of the interior. The minimum recommended time for the journeys is between four and six days, but you can take as long as you want, phoning ahead to confirm the time when a bus will collect you. The buses' enthusiastic and young Brazilian guides provide as little or as much help as you want – doing no more than checking where you next want to stop or phoning ahead to book accommodation. Prices are reasonable (between $40 and $80 for a pass depending on the route) and only slightly more than using a series of ordinary local and long-distance buses which, in any case, might involve doubling back to Rio or Salvador in the case of travel from the coast into the interior. Although the buses themselves are definitely not a good way of meeting young Brazilians – almost all the passengers are foreign tourists – the guides do tap into a good informal network of pousadas and hostels which will be much more mixed. You can purchase passes from branches of STA outside of Brazil or, better still, from the Rio office of South America Experience at Rua Raimundo Corrêa 36A, Copacabana (☎021/2548 8813) who will happily discuss the itinerary and suggest places to stop off at.

can get smelly on long journeys): the lower your seat number, the further away from them you'll be. Buses stop every two or three hours at well-supplied *postos*, but as prices are relatively high it's not a bad idea to bring along water and some food to last the journey. Some bus companies will supply meal vouchers for use at the *postos* on long journeys.

There are luxury buses, too, called **leitos**, which do nocturnal runs between the major cities – worth taking once for the experience, with fully reclining seats in curtained partitions, freshly ironed sheets and an attendant plying insomniacs with coffee and conversation. They cost about a third of the price of an air ticket, and between two and three times as much as a normal long-distance bus; they're also less frequent and need to be booked a few days in advance. No matter what kind of bus, it's a good idea to have a light sweater or blanket during night journeys as the air-conditioning is always uncomfortably cold.

Tickets and luggage

Going any distance, it's best to **buy your ticket** at least a day in advance, from the rodoviária or, in some cities, from travel agents. An exception is the Rio–São Paulo route, where a shuttle service means you can always turn up without a ticket and never have to wait more than fifteen minutes. Numbered seats are provided on all routes: if you want a window ask for *janela*. If you cross a state line you will get a small form with the ticket, which asks for the number of your seat (*poltrona*), the number of your ticket (*passagem*), the number of your passport (*identidade*) and your destination (*destino*). You have to fill it in and give it to the driver before you'll be let on board. Buses have **luggage** compartments, which are safe: you check pieces at the side of the bus and get a ticket for them. Keep an eye on your hand luggage, and take anything valuable with you when you get off for a halt.

Planes

It's hardly surprising that a country the size of Brazil relies on **air travel** a good deal; in some parts of Amazonia air links are more important than either the roads or rivers. Any town has at least an airstrip, and all cities have airports, usually some distance from the city but not always: Santos Dumont in Rio, Guarulhos in São Paulo and Guararapes in Recife are all pretty central.

Air passes

When buying your international ticket, you should consider the possibility of adding an **air pass**. Although travellers used to purchase them almost automatically if flying within Brazil, the progressive decline of the *real* on the foreign exchanges and the emergence of budget carriers means that they now only make sense if you plan a series of long-haul trips – from the South to the Amazon and back via the Northeast, for example. Brazil's three main airlines – Varig (along with its regional subsidiaries RioSul and RioNordeste), VASP and TAM – all offer passes. Their route options vary somewhat but their basic conditions are virtually identical: passes can only be bought **outside Brazil** in advance of your trip with a return air ticket to the country. Only Transbrasil passes are available to anyone regardless of which airline they're travelling into Brazil on.

Varig's **Brazil Airpass** is still the most easily available of the three and gives access to the largest route network, but it can only be purchased if you travel into Brazil with British Airways or Varig (or one of its Star Alliance partners such as United, Air Canada, SAS and Lufthansa). The air pass fare is $490 low season, $540 high season, for adults and children (infants are charged ten percent) and gives you five coupons for use within a period of 21 consecutive days. Coupons are not valid for the same route in the same direction more than once. Connecting flights count as only one coupon and you can buy a maximum of four additional coupons for $100 each. You can leave your route completely open, to be decided in Brazil, or you can specify it at the time of purchase, in which case changes of route are not permitted (but flight times and dates can be altered). Bear in mind though that flights on some routes can be heavily booked long in advance. Less expensive regional Varig passes providing four coupons valid during a 21-day period are also available covering south and central Brazil ($350 low season, $400 high season) or the Northeast and the Amazon ($290 low season, $340 high season).

If Brazil is only one stop on a longer trip, consider buying the **Mercosur Airpass**, which covers eight airlines of Argentina, Brazil, Chile, Paraguay and Uruguay and can only be bought outside South America. The regulations are fairly complicated but basically allow two stopovers per country (plus point of origin) up to a maximum of eight coupons, although an extra coupon is allowed to give you use of both the Argentine and Brazilian airports at Iguaçu Falls. The route must include at least two countries and the price of a pass is based on the number of miles flown, which always works out to cost far less than purchasing regular tickets. Prices may be affected by the time of year that you travel.

The main domestic carriers are **VASP**, **Varig** and **TAM**; important regional airlines include the Varig subsidiaries **RioSul** (mainly serving the South) and **RioNordeste** (covering the Amazon region), together with **Viabrasil**, which connects São Paulo with Fortaleza, Natal, João Pessoa and Recife in the Northeast. A recent phenomenon is the appearance of budget airlines, of which the biggest is **GOL** (℡0800/7012131, @www .voegol.com.br), known to have an extensive network and cheap seats, but also for very long check-in lines and flight delays.

Flying to the Northeast or Amazonia from southern Brazil can be tiresome, as many of these long-distance routes are no more than glorified bus runs, stopping everywhere before heading north. In planning your itinerary, it's a good idea to check carefully how many times a plane stops – for example, between São Paulo and Fortaleza a flight may stop as many as four times or as few as one.

A word of **warning**: in many parts of Amazonia air travel in small planes, or **aerotaxis**, is very common – the regional word for these flights is *teco-teco*. Before taking one, you should be aware that the airstrips are often dangerous, the planes routinely fly overloaded and are not reliably maintained, and no checks are made on the qualifications of pilots – some don't have any.

Tickets and fares

Flights are rarely booked up in advance outside holiday periods, but it is always a good idea to book a *passagem* as far ahead as you can. Prices are very reasonable: Rio–São Paulo costs $110, Rio–Salvador $150, Rio–Iguaçu $180, Rio–Manaus around $300; return fares are double the one-way fares. Tickets are almost always much cheaper when purchased in Brazil rather than abroad, and you can benefit from special promotions. (For tickets bought inside of Brazil there's a $10 charge if you alter the date.) The budget airline **GOL** offers excellent fares through its website, but credit cards issued outside of Brazil are not accepted; you can, however, buy a GOL ticket from any travel agent in Brazil. If you plan on flying a lot in a relatively short time, then consider buying an **air pass** before you leave for Brazil – although they only work out cheaper if you plan on travelling long distances (see box on p.34).

For all internal flights you have to pay an **airport tax**: between $7 and $9 depending on the airport, payable in local currency usually at the airline desk of the company you're travelling with (not the check-in desk); airline desks are generally in the entrance hall of the airport. Departure tax for international flights is $36, payable in local currency or dollars when you check in – tickets sold in Brazil include the tax, as increasingly do tickets sold outside the country. Note that duty-free shops do not accept *reis* – only credit cards or dollars.

It is always a good idea to **reconfirm** onward flights a day or two in advance: this can be done over the phone – airline offices always have someone who speaks English – and you can make seat reservations at the same time. You don't need to reconfirm domestic flights. If you have an air pass and change your flights, always remember to cancel the original flight. If you don't, the computer flags you as a no-show, and all your other air pass reservations will also be cancelled.

Trains, ferries and boats

You probably won't be taking many **trains** in Brazil. Although there's an extensive rail network, much of it is for cargo only, and even where there are passenger trains they're almost invariably slower and less convenient than the buses. Exceptions are a few **tourist journeys** worth making for themselves, in the South and Minas Gerais especially.

Water travel and ferries are also important forms of transport in parts of Brazil. Specific details are included in the relevant parts of the Guide, but look out for the ferry to Niterói, without which no journey to **Rio** would be complete; **Salvador**, where there are regular services to islands and towns in the huge bay on which the city is built; in the **South** between the islands of the Bay of Paranaguá; and most of all in **Amazonia**.

Amazon riverboats

In Amazonia, rivers have been the main highways for centuries, and the Amazon itself is navigable to ocean-going ships as far west as Iquitos in Peru, nearly 3000km upstream from Belém.

In all the large riverside cities of the Amazon – notably Belém, Manaus and Santarém – there are *hidroviárias*, ferry terminals for waterborne bus services. **Amazon river travel** is slow and can be tough going, but it's a fascinating experience. On longer journeys there are a number of classes; in general it's better to avoid *cabine*, where you swelter in a cabin, and choose *primeiro* (first class) instead, sleeping in a hammock on deck. *Segundo* (second class) is usually hammock space in the lower deck or engine room. Take plenty of provisions, and expect to practise your Portuguese.

The **range of boat transport** in the Amazon runs from luxury tourist boats and large three-level riverboats to smaller one- or two-level boats (the latter normally confining their routes to main tributaries and local runs) and covered launches operated by tour companies. As a rule, most local boats cost about $10 a day (including food), more for the tourist boats and tour-based launches. The most popular route is the **Belém–Manaus trip**, which costs $35–55 (hammock space) and takes four to six days.

City transport

Shoals of **local buses** clog city streets: you enter at the back – where route details are posted – and move through a turnstile as you pay your fare. **Fares** are all flat-rate, and rarely more than 50¢. Buses often get unbelievably crowded, and in large cities are favourite targets for pickpockets. It's safer to go immediately through the turnstile even when there are seats at the rear, as *assaltantes* prefer the backs of buses where they can make a quick getaway through the rear door.

There are also good modern **metrô** systems in Rio, São Paulo, Belo Horizonte, Porto Alegre and Recife. Again, they're cheap and efficient, and they're also relatively safe – but, since they weren't built with tourism in mind, their routes are not always the most useful.

Taxis

There are enormous numbers of **taxis** in Brazilian cities, and they're very cheap, especially if there are two or more passengers. City cabs are metered, and have two rates; 1 is cheaper, 2 more expensive. Which rate the taxi is using is indicated on the taximeter, after the fare. Rate 2 is automatic on trips to and from airports and bus stations in big cities, after 8 at night, and all day Sunday and public holidays. Occasionally drivers will refer to a sheet and revise the fare slightly upwards – they are not necessarily ripping you off, but referring to price updating tables which will fill the gap until taximeters can be readjusted to reflect the official annual increases.

Taxis in small towns and rural areas do not often have meters, so it's best to agree on the fare in advance – they'll be more expensive than in the cities. Most airports and some bus stations are covered by taxi co-operatives, which operate under a slightly different system: attendants give you a coupon with fares to various destinations printed on it – you pay either at a kiosk in advance, or the driver. These are more expensive than regular taxis, but they're reliable and often more comfortable. Tipping is not obligatory, but appreciated.

Driving and car rental

Driving standards in Brazil hover between the abysmal and the appalling. Brazil has one of the highest death tolls from driving-related accidents in the world, and on any

journey you can see why, with thundering trucks and drivers treating the road as if it were a Grand Prix racetrack. City driving would make even an Italian blanch, and takes a lot of getting used to. Fortunately, inter-city bus drivers are the exception to the rule: they are usually very good, and many buses have devices fitted that make it impossible for them to exceed the speed limit. Electronic speed traps are widely in place, and if you get caught by one in a rental car, the fine will simply be added to your credit card.

Road quality varies according to region: the South and Southeast have a good paved network; the Northeast has a good network on the coast but is poor in the interior; and roads in Amazonia are by far the worst, with even major highways closed for weeks or months at a time as they are washed away by the rains. Most cities are fairly well signposted, so getting out of town shouldn't be too difficult; if city traffic is daunting, try to arrange to collect your car on a Sunday when traffic is light. If at all possible, avoid driving at night because potholes (even on main roads) and *lombardas* (speed bumps) may not be obvious, and breaking down after dark in a strange place could be dangerous. Outside the big cities, Brazilian roads are death-traps at night; poorly lit, in bad condition and lightly policed. Especially worth avoiding at night are the **Via Dutra**, linking Rio and São Paulo, because of the huge numbers of trucks and the treacherous ascent and descent of the Serra do Mar, and the **Belem-Brasilia highway**, whose potholes and uneven asphalt make it difficult enough to drive even in daylight. Where possible, avoid driving after dark in the Mato Grosso and Amazon regions as well; though rare, armed roadside robberies have been known to happen there.

An **international driving licence** is useful: although foreign licences are accepted for visits of up to six months, you may have a hard time convincing a police officer of this (the old-style paper UK licenses are not accepted by road police). It's more than likely that you'll be stopped by police at some point during your travels. Occasionally they can be quite intimidating as they point to trumped up contraventions (for example, that your driving licence isn't valid, that the car's licence plates are somehow irregular). What the police are probably angling for is a bribe and an on-the-spot *multa*, or fine, may be suggested. It's a personal judgment whether to stand one's ground (which may take up a long time) or just pay up. Whatever you do, no matter how certain you are of the righteousness of your position, try and stay calm and bend over backwards to appear polite. If your passport is confiscated, demand to be permitted to phone your consulate – there should always be a duty officer available.

Around a quarter of Brazilian cars now run on *álcool* – a mixture of petroleum-based fuel and alcohol distilled from sugar cane – which is half the price of *gasolina*, but which works less efficiently. Outside of the towns and cities, service stations can be few and far between, so keep a careful eye on the fuel gauge. Service stations in rural areas do not always accept international credit cards, so make sure you always have sufficient cash on a long trip; in urban areas plastic is almost universally accepted at petrol stations.

Parking, especially in the cities, can be tricky due to security and finding a space, and it's worth paying extra for a hotel with some kind of lock-up garage – on the street you'll often be approached by someone offering to "guard" your car, and it's usually worth a few cents just in case your self-appointed guardian might otherwise do some damage. In any event, never leave anything visible inside the car if you don't want to lose it.

Renting a car

Renting a car in Brazil is relatively straight-forward. Hertz, Avis and other big-name international companies operate here, and there are plenty of Brazilian alternatives, such as Interlocadora, Nobre and Localiza. Unidas are also represented throughout the country and are highly recommended, as their cars are always in excellent condition, service is efficient and – if you take out their comprehensive insurance policy – there is no excess payable if your car is stolen or damaged. Often, though, you'll find the lowest rates are offered by smaller, local companies, but this can be a risky proposition as their cars may be old and in poor condition and there won't be such a good breakdown service. Car rental offices (*locadoras*) can be found at every airport and in most towns

regardless of size. Try to avoid renting an alcohol-powered car: they always take two or three tries before they start, they accelerate more slowly and have a maddening tendency to cut out in lower gear if you make the slightest mistake with the clutch.

Rates start from around $20 a day for a Group A car (Fiat Punto or similar) including, depending on the company, 75 or 100km per day, though this rises to around $40 for unlimited mileage; a basic air-conditioned model will start at around $50, including unlimited mileage. Four-wheel-drive vehicles, such as Toyota Land Cruisers, are sometimes available, but are extremely expensive. Only luxury vehicles are available with automatic transmission. When you're quoted a price, make sure that it includes **insurance** (which is compulsory) and that there are no other hidden "extras". Even when insurance is included, you could well be liable to pay twenty percent of the market value of the car (around $2000 for a small car) if it's stolen or damaged in an accident, though some companies, such as Unidas, offer genuinely comprehensive policies. If you have a US or Canadian credit card, you may find that it can be used to cover the additional liability – check before leaving home. In any case, a credit card is essential as a deposit when renting a car. It's not a bad idea to reserve a car before you arrive in Brazil as you can be sure to get the best available rate quoted that will include mileage and insurance.

As you would anywhere, carefully check the condition of the car before accepting it and pay special attention to the state of the tyres (including the spare), and make sure there's a jack, warning triangle and fire extinguisher. All cars have front and back seatbelts; their use is compulsory, and stiff on-the-spot fines are imposed on drivers and front-seat passengers found not to be wearing them.

Car rental agencies

In Brazil
Interlocadora ☏ 0800/138000,
ⓦ www.interlocadora.com.br
Localiza ☏ 0800/99 2000,
ⓦ www.localiza.com.br
Nobre ☏ 0800/125888,
ⓦ www.nobrerentacar.com.br
Unidas ☏ 0800/121 121, ⓦ www.unidas.com.br

In Australia and New Zealand

Avis Australia ☎13 63 33 or 02/9353 9000, ⓦwww.avis.com.au; New Zealand ☎09/526 2847 or 0800/655 111, ⓦwww.avis.co.nz
Budget Australia ☎1300/362 848, ⓦwww.budget.com.au; New Zealand ☎09/976 2222, ⓦwww.budget.co.nz
Hertz Australia ☎13 30 39 or 03/9698 2555, ⓦwww.hertz.com.au; New Zealand ☎0800/654 321, ⓦwww.hertz.co.nz

In the UK and Ireland

Avis UK ☎0870/606 0100, ⓦwww.avis.co.uk; Northern Ireland ☎028/9024 0404; Republic of Ireland ☎01/605 7500, ⓦwww.avis.ie

Budget ☎0800/181 181, ⓦwww.budget.co.uk; Republic of Ireland ☎0903/277 11, ⓦwww.budget.ie
Hertz ☎0870/844 8844, ⓦwww.hertz.co.uk; Republic of Ireland ☎01/676 7476, ⓦwww.hertz.ie

In the US and Canada

Avis US ☎1-800/331-1084, Canada ☎1-800/272-5871, ⓦwww.avis.com
Budget US ☎1-800/527-0700, Canada ☎1-800/268-8900, ⓦwww.budgetrentacar.com
Hertz US ☎1-800/654-3001, Canada ☎1-800/263-0600, ⓦwww.hertz.com

Accommodation

Accommodation in Brazil covers the full range from hostels and basic hotels clustered around bus stations to luxury resort hotels. You can sometimes succeed in finding places to sleep for as little as $5 a night, but, more realistically, a clean double room in a one-star hotel will set you back upwards of $10–15. As is so often the case, single travellers get a bad deal, usually paying almost as much as the cost of a double room. In whatever category of place you stay, in tourist spots – both large and small – over New Year and Carnaval, you'll be expected to book a room for a minimum of four or five days.

Dormitories and hostels

At the bottom end of the scale, in terms of both quality and price, are **dormitórios**, small and very basic (to put it mildly) hotels, situated close to bus stations and in the poorer parts of town. They are extremely cheap, just a few dollars a night, but usually unsavoury and sometimes positively dangerous.

You could stay for not much more, in far better conditions, in a **youth hostel**, an *albergue de juventude*, also sometimes called a *casa de estudante*, where the cost per person is between $5 and $10 a night. There's an extensive network of these hostels, with at least one in every state capital,

and they are very well maintained, often in restored buildings. It helps to have an IYHF card (available from the youth hostel associations listed below) with a recent photograph – you're not usually asked for one, but every so often you'll find an *albergue* which refuses entry unless it's produced. The Federação Brasileira dos Albergues de Juventude in Rio produces an excellent illustrated guide to Brazil's hostels.

Demand for places far outstrips supply at certain times of year – December to Carnaval, and July – but if you travel with a **hammock** you can often hook it up in a corridor or patio. A major advantage that hostels have is to throw you together with young Brazilians, the main users of the network:

Accommodation price codes

In this guide, accommodation has been categorized according to the price codes outlined below, based on US$. These categories represent the minimum you can expect to pay for a **double room in high season** – though note that many of the budget places will also have more expensive rooms. Rates for hostels and basic hotels where guests are charged **per person** are given in US$, instead of being indicated by price code.

❶ Under $10	❹ $35–50	❼ $90–125
❷ $10–20	❺ $50–70	❽ $125–175
❸ $20–35	❻ $70–90	❾ $175 and over

they are generally friendly and intensely curious about life abroad, as they don't meet many foreigners this close up.

Youth hostel associations

In Australia and New Zealand

Australia Youth Hostels Association ☎02/9261 1111, ⓦwww.yha.com.au. Adult membership rate AUS$52 (under-18s, AUS$16) for the first twelve months and then AUS$32 each year after.
Youth Hostelling Association New Zealand ☎0800/278 299 or 03/379 9970, ⓦwww.yha.co.nz. Adult membership NZ$40 for one year, NZ$60 for two and NZ$80 for three; under-18s free; lifetime NZ$300.

In Brazil

Federação Brasileira dos Albergues de Juventude Rua da Assembléia 10, Sala 1211, Centro, Rio de Janeiro (☎021/252-4829, ⓦwww.alberguesp.com.br). Annual membership US$15.

In the UK and Ireland

Northern Ireland Hostelling International Northern Ireland ☎028/9032 4733, ⓦwww.hini.org.uk. Adult membership £10; under-18s £6; family £20; lifetime £75.
Republic of Ireland ☎01/830 4555, ⓦwww.irelandyha.org. Annual membership €10.50.
Scottish Youth Hostel Association ☎0870/155 3255, ⓦwww.syha.org.uk. Annual membership £6, for under-18s £2.50.
Youth Hostel Association (YHA) ☎0870/770 8868, ⓦwww.yha.org.uk. Annual membership £13; under-18s £6.50; lifetime £190 (or five annual payments of £40).

In the US and Canada

Hostelling International-American Youth Hostels ☎202/783-6161, ⓦwww.hiayh.org. Annual membership for adults (18–55) is $25, for seniors (55 or over) is $15, and for under-18s and groups of ten or more, is free. Lifetime memberships are $250.
Hostelling International Canada ☎1-800/663 5777 or 613/237 7884, ⓦwww.hostellingintl.ca. Rather than sell the traditional 1- or 2-year memberships, the association now sells one Individual Adult membership with a 28- to 16-month term. The length of the term depends on when the membership is sold, but a member can receive up to 28 months of membership for just $35. Membership is free for under-18s and you can become a lifetime member for $175.

Pensões, postos and pousadas

In a slightly higher price range are the small, family-run hotels, called either a **pensão** (pensões in the plural) or a hotel familiar. These vary a great deal: some are no more appealing than a dormitório, while others are friendlier and better value than many hotels and can be places of considerable character and luxury. Pensões tend to be better in small towns than in large cities, but are also usefully thick on the ground in some of the main tourist towns, where conventional hotels are pretty well non-existent. In southern Brazil, many of the **postos**, highway service stations on town outskirts, have cheap rooms and showers, and are usually well kept and clean.

You will also come across the **pousada**, which can just be another name for a pensão, but can also be a small hotel, running up to luxury class but usually less expensive than a hotel proper. In some small towns – such as Ouro Preto and Paraty – pousadas form the bulk of mid- and upper-level accommodation options. In the Amazon and Mato Grosso in particular, *pousadas* tend to be purpose-built *fazenda* lodges geared towards the growing ecotourist markets and are not aimed at budget travellers.

Hotels

Hotels proper run from dives to luxury apartments. There is a Brazilian classification system, from one to five stars, but the absence of stars doesn't necessarily mean a bad hotel: they depend on bureaucratic requirements like the width of lift shafts and kitchen floor space as much as on the standard of accommodation – many perfectly good hotels don't have stars.

Hotels offer a range of different rooms, with significant price differences: a **quarto** is a room without a bathroom, an **apartamento** is a room with (actually a shower – Brazilians don't use baths); an *apartamento de luxo* is normally just an *apartamento* with a fridge full of (marked-up) drinks; a **casal** is a double room; and a **solteiro** a single. In a starred hotel, an *apartamento* upwards would normally come with telephone, air-conditioning (*ar condicionado*) and a TV; a *ventilador* is a fan.

Rates for rooms vary tremendously between different parts of Brazil, but start at around $5 in a one-star hotel, around $15 in a two-star hotel, and around $25 in a three-star place. Generally speaking, for $25–30 a night you could expect to stay in a reasonable mid-range hotel, with bathroom and air-conditioning. Many hotels in this range in Brazil are excellent value for the standard of accommodation they offer. During the off-season most hotels in tourist areas offer hefty **discounts**, usually around 25–35 percent, but when discounts are offered credit cards are not accepted.

Most hotels – although not all – will add a ten percent **service charge** to your bill, the *taxa de serviço*: those that don't will have a sign at the desk saying "*Nos não cobramos taxa de serviço*", and it's very bad form to leave the hotel without tipping the receptionist. The price will almost invariably include breakfast – gargantuan helpings of fruit, cheese, bread and coffee – but no other meals, although there will often be a restaurant on-site. Hotels usually have a **safe deposit box**, a *caixa*, which is worth asking about when you check in; they are free for you to use and, although they're not invulnerable, anything left in a *caixa* is safer than on your person or unguarded in your room. Many hotels also offer a safe deposit box in your room, which is the safest option of all.

Finally, a **motel**, as you'll gather from the various names and decor, is strictly for couples. This is not to say that it's not possible to stay in one if you can't find anything else – since they're used by locals they're rarely too expensive – but you should be aware that most of the other rooms will be rented by the hour.

Camping

There are a fair number of **campsites** in Brazil and almost all of them are on the coast near the bigger beaches – mostly they're near cities rather than in out-of-the-way places. They will usually have basic facilities – running water and toilets, perhaps a simple restaurant – and are popular with young Argentines and Brazilians. A few fancier sites are designed for people with camper vans or big tents in the back of their cars. Having your own tent, or hiring one, is also particularly useful in ecotourist regions such as the Amazon and the Pantanal, where it can really open up the wilderness to you. In all cases, however, the problem is **security**, partly of your person, but more significantly of your possessions, which can never really be made safe. Great caution should be exercised before camping off-site – only do so if you're part of a group and you've received assurances locally as to safety.

Eating and drinking

It's hard to generalize about Brazilian food, largely because there is no single national cuisine but numerous very distinct regional ones. Nature dealt Brazil a full hand for these varying cuisines: there's an abundant variety of fruit, vegetables and spices, as you can see for yourself walking through any food market.

There are four main **regional cuisines**: *comida mineira* from Minas Gerais, based on pork, vegetables (especially *couve*, a relative of spinach) and *tutu*, a kind of refried bean cooked with manioc flour and used as a thick sauce; *comida baiana* from the Salvador coast, the most exotic to gringo palates, using superb fresh fish and shellfish, hot peppers, palm oil, coconut milk and fresh coriander; *comida do sertão* from the interior of the Northeast, which relies on rehydrated dried or salted meat and the fruit, beans and tubers of the region; and *comida gaúcha* from Rio Grande do Sul, the most carnivorous diet in the world, revolving around every imaginable kind of meat grilled over charcoal. *Comida do sertão* is rarely served outside its homeland, but you'll find restaurants serving the others throughout Brazil, although – naturally – they're at their best in their region of origin.

Alongside the regional restaurants, there is a **standard fare** available everywhere that can soon get dull unless you cast around: steak (*bife*) or chicken (*frango*), served with *arroz e feijão*, rice and beans, and often with salad, fries and *farinha*, dried *manioc* (cassava) flour that you sprinkle over everything. *Farofa* is toasted *farinha*, and usually comes with onions and bits of bacon mixed in. In cheaper restaurants all this would come on a single large plate: look for the words *prato feito*, *prato comercial* or *refeição completa* if you want to fill up without spending too much.

Feijoada is the closest Brazil comes to a national dish: a stew of pork, sausage and smoked meat cooked with black beans and garlic, garnished with slices of orange. Eating it is a national ritual at weekends, when restaurants serve *feijoada* all day.

Some of the **fruit** is familiar – *manga*, mango, *maracujá*, passion fruit, *limão*, lime – but most of it has only Brazilian names: *jaboticaba*, *fruta do conde*, *sapoti* and *jaca*.

The most exotic fruits are Amazonian (see p.403): try *bacuri*, *açaí* and the extraordinary *cupuaçu*, the most delicious of all. These all serve as the basis for juices and **ice cream**, *sorvete*, which can be excellent; keep an eye out for *sorvetarias*, ice cream parlours. For a list of common **menu** terms, see p.808.

Snacks and street food

On every street corner in Brazil you will find a **lanchonete**, a mixture of café and bar that sells beer and rum, snacks, cigarettes, soft drinks, coffee and sometimes small meals. **Bakeries** – *padarias* – often have a *lanchonete* attached, and they're good places for cheap snacks: an *empada* or *empadinha* is a small pie, which has various fillings (*carne*, meat, *palmito*, palm heart and *camarão*, shrimp, the best); a *pastel* is a fried, filled pasty; an *esfiha* is a savoury pastry stuffed with spiced meat; and a *coxinha* is spiced chicken rolled in manioc dough and then fried. In central Brazil try *pão de queijo*, a savoury cheese snack that goes perfectly with coffee. All these savoury snacks fall under the generic heading *salgados*.

If you haven't had **breakfast** (*café da manha*) at your hotel, then a bakery/*lanchonete* is a good place to head for; and for a more substantial meal *lanchonetes* will generally serve a *prato comercial*, too. In both *lanchonetes* and *padarias* you usually pay first at the till, and then take your ticket to the counter to get what you want.

You'll find a growing number of **fast food** outlets in cities that look garishly American but take the hamburger or hot dog and "Brazilianize" it, adding all sorts of things and much improving it in the process. Menus are also easy to understand because they are in mangled but recognizable English, albeit with Brazilian pronunciation. A hamburger is a *X-*

burger (pronounced "*sheezboorga*"), a hot dog a *cachorro quente*; a *bauru* is a club sandwich with steak and egg; a *mixto quente* a toasted cheese and ham sandwich.

Food sold by **street vendors** in Brazil should be treated with caution, but not dismissed out of hand. You can practically see the hepatitis bugs and amoebas crawling over some of the food you see on sale in the streets, but plenty of vendors have proper stalls and can be very professional, with a loyal clientele of office workers and locals. Some of the food they sell has the advantage of being cooked a long time, which reduces the chance of picking anything up, and in some places – Salvador and Belém especially – you can get good food cheaply in the street; just choose your vendor sensibly. In Salvador try *acarajé*, only available from street vendors – a delicious fried bean mix with shrimp and hot pepper; and in Belém go for *maniçoba*, spiced sausage with chicory leaves, or *pato no tucupi*, duck stewed in manioc sauce.

Restaurants

Restaurants – *restaurantes* – are ubiquitous, portions are very large and prices are extremely reasonable. A *prato comercial* is around $3, while a good full meal can usually be had for about $10, even in expensive-looking restaurants. Cheaper restaurants, though, tend only to be open for lunch. One of the best options offered by many restaurants, typically at lunchtime only, is self-service *comida por kilo*, where a wide choice of food is priced according to the weight of the food on your plate. Specialist restaurants to look out for include a *rodízio*, where you pay a fixed charge and eat as much as you want; most *churrascarias* – restaurants specializing in charcoal-grilled meat of all kinds, especially beef – operate this system, too, bringing a constant supply of meat on huge spits to the tables.

Many restaurants will present unsolicited food the moment you sit down – the **couvert**, which can consist of anything from a couple of bits of raw carrot and an olive to quite an elaborate and substantial plate. Although the price is generally modest, it still has to be paid for. If you don't want it, ask the waiter to take it away.

Brazil also has a large variety of **ethnic restaurants**, thanks to the generations of Portuguese, Arabs, Italians, Japanese and other immigrants who have made the country their home. The widest selection is in São Paulo, with the best Italian, Lebanese and Japanese food in Brazil, but anywhere of any size will have good ethnic restaurants, often in surprising places: Belém, for example, has several excellent Japanese restaurants, thanks to a Japanese colony founded fifty years ago in the interior. Ethnic food may be marginally more expensive than Brazilian, but it's never exorbitant.

While the bill normally comes with a ten percent service charge, you should still tip, as waiters rely more on tips than on their very low wages.

Vegetarian foods

Being a **vegetarian** – or at least a strict one – is no easy matter in Brazil. Many Brazilians are unwilling vegetarians, of course, surviving on the staple diet of rice, beans and *farinha* – and there's wonderful fruit everywhere – but this is not food that you'll find in restaurants, except as side dishes.

If you eat fish there's no problem, especially in the Northeast and Amazonia where seafood forms the basis of many meals. You can usually get a fair choice of vegetarian food at a *comida por kilo* restaurant, which offers a range of salads and vegetables, as well as rice, manioc and potatoes. However, they are often only open during the day, as are the occasional vegetarian restaurants (usually described as *Restaurante Natural*) that can be found in the larger cities. But otherwise you're up against one of the world's most carnivorous cultures. In the South and Centre-West, *churrasco* rules – served at restaurants where you eat as many different cuts of meat as you can manage, and where requests for meals without meat are greeted with astonishment. At most restaurants – even *churrascarias* – huge salads are available but, if you're a vegan, always enquire whether eggs or cheese are included. If you get fed up with rice, beans and salad, there are always pizzerias around.

Hot drinks and soft drinks

Coffee is the great national drink, served strong, hot and sweet in small cups and drunk quickly. However, coffee is often a great disappointment in Brazil: most of the good stuff is exported, and what's available often comes so stiff with sugar that it's almost undrinkable. By far the best coffee is found in São Paulo and points south. You are never far from a *cafézinho* (as these small cups of coffee are known; *café* refers to coffee in its raw state). Coffee is sold from flasks in the street, in *lanchonetes* and bars, and in restaurants, where it comes free after the meal. The best way to start your day is with *café com leite*, hot milk with coffee added to taste. Decaffeinated coffee is almost impossible to find in restaurants, and difficult even in delicatessens.

Tea (*chá*) is surprisingly good. Try **chá mate**, a strong green tea with a noticeable caffeine hit, or one of the wide variety of herbal teas, most notably that made from *guaraná* (see below). One highly recommended way to take tea is using the *chimarrão*, very common in Rio Grande do Sul: a gourd filled with *chá mate* and boiling water, sucked through a silver straw. You will need some practice to avoid burning your lips, but once you get used to it, is a wonderfully refreshing way to take tea.

The great variety of fruit in Brazil is put to excellent use in **sucos**: fruit is popped into a liquidizer with sugar and crushed ice to make a deliciously refreshing drink. Made with milk rather than water it becomes a *vitamina*. Most *lanchonetes* and bars sell *sucos* and *vitaminas*, but for the full variety you should visit a specialist *casa de sucos*, which are found in most town centres. Widely available, and the best option to quench a thirst, are *suco de maracujá*, passion fruit, and *suco de limão*, lime. In the North and Northeast, try *graviola*, *bacuri* and *cupuaçu*. Sugar will always be added to a *suco* unless you ask for it *sem açúca*; some, notably *maracujá* and *limão*, are undrinkable without it.

Soft drinks are the regular products of corporate capitalism and all the usual brands are available. Outshining them all, though, is a local variety, *guaraná*, a fizzy and very sweet drink made out of Amazonian berries. An energy-loaded powder is made from the same berries and sold in health stores in the developed world – basically, the effect is like a smooth release of caffeine without the jitters.

Alcoholic drinks

Beer is mainly of the lager type. Brazilians drink it ice-cold and it comes mostly in 600ml bottles: ask for a *cerveja*. Many places only serve beer on draught – called *chopp*. Generally acknowledged as the best brands are the regional beers of Pará and Maranhão, Cerma and Cerpa, but the best nationally available beers are Skol and Brahma. Antártica is similar and more widely available, Kaiser is a little watery. However, all Brazilian beer is stuffed with anti-oxidants and preservatives, which contributes to thumping hangovers the next day even after only a few.

Wine, *vinho*, is mostly mediocre and sweet, though some of the wines produced in the South are pretty good. In the Italian areas of Rio Grande do Sul, try the small farmers' own wines – very different from European and US wines but excellent in their own right. Among the better commercial ones are Almaden, Château Chandon, Baron de Lantier and Côtes de Blancs (white – *branco*) and Forestier, Conde de Foucaud, Château Duvalier and Baron de Lantier (red – *tinto*). The most reliable widely available Brazilian label is Miolo, a smallish producer whose wines are found in good supermarkets throughout Brazil. Best of all, though, are the wines of the Casa Valduga, sometimes available in Rio's and São Paulo's best hotels and restaurants and gourmet food stores or, better still, but rarely available even in Rio Grande do Sul, Don Laurindo. Just about drinkable wine is also produced in Santa Catarina and in Paraná, while the wine from Espirito Santo and São Paulo is pretty dreadful, produced purely for regional consumption. Commercial wine production has recently started in Bahia's São Francisco valley, with some surprisingly good results: the Miolo shiraz can be found in many supermarkets. Despite the undoubted improvement in the quality of Brazilian wines in recent years, imported wines from Chile and Argentina (or Europe) remain more reliable and can be cheaper than the best that Brazil produces.

As for **spirits**, you can buy **Scotch** (*uisque*), either *nacional*, made up from imported whisky essence and not worth drinking, or *internacional*, imported and extremely expensive. Far better to stick to what Brazilians drink, *cachaça* (also called *pinga* or in Rio, *paraty*), which is sugar-cane rum. The best *cachaça* is produced in stills on country farms; it is called *cachaça da terra* and, when produced with care, has a smoothness and taste the larger commercially produced brands lack. Apart from in the area where it's produced, you won't find it in stores. Alternatively, there are scores of brands of commercially produced rum: some of the better ones are Velho Barreiro, Pitu and 51. The best *cachaças* are produced in Minas Gerais, but those from elsewhere, particularly São Paulo, can also be good. Note that while *cachaça* produced and sold in Paraty comes in the most attractive bottles, generally it's pretty rough stuff.

Brazilians drink *cachaça* either neat or mixed with fruit juice. Taken neat, it's very fiery, but in a cocktail it can be delicious. By far the best way to drink it is in a **caipirinha**,

along with football and music one of Brazil's great gifts to world civilization – rum mixed with fresh lime, sugar and crushed ice: it may not sound like much, but it is the best cocktail you're ever likely to drink. Be sure to stir it regularly while drinking, and treat it with healthy respect – it is much more powerful than it tastes. Variants are the *caipirosca* or *caipiríssima*, the same made with vodka. Waiters will often assume foreigners want vodka, so make sure you say *caipirinha de cachaça*. You can also get *batidas*, rum mixed with fruit juice and ice, which flow like water during Carnaval: they also pack quite a punch, despite tasting like a soft drink. For a rum and Coke, ask for a *cuba libre*.

There are no **licensing laws** in Brazil, so you can get a drink at any time of day or night.

Communications

Brazil's phone network is impressive, especially considering the size of the country: public phones are everywhere, most places can be dialled direct and rates are low. Postal services within the country, too, are cheap, though sending airmail abroad is quite expensive. Brazil is fast hooking up to the Internet, and you'll come across cybercafés and Internet cabins in the most unlikely of small towns.

Phones

Public telephones are called *orelhões*, "big ears", after their distinctive conch-shaped covers. These days, phones are operated mostly by **phonecards** (*carta telefônico*) which have replaced tokens (*fichas*) and are on sale everywhere – from newspaper stands, street sellers' trays and most cafés. For local calls a 5 *reis* card will last for several conversations; for long-distance or international calls, higher-value phonecards come in 10, 20, 50 or 100 *reis* denominations. Calls to the US or Europe cost about $1.50 per minute. Before dialling direct, lift the phone from the hook, insert the phonecard and listen for a dialling tone. Note that long-distance calls are cheaper after 8pm.

The **dialling tone** is a single continuous note, **engaged** is rapid pips, and the **ringing tone** is regular peals, as in the US. The phone system in Brazil is continually overloaded. If you get an engaged tone, keep trying – nine times out of ten, the phone is not actually engaged and you get through after seven or eight attempts. The smaller the place, the more often you need to try: be patient.

Long-distance and international calls can also be made from a *posto telefônico*, which all operate in the same way: you ask at the counter for a *chave* and are given a numbered key. You go to the booth, insert the key and turn it to the right, and can then make up to three completed calls. You are billed when you return the key – around $1.50 a minute to the US or Europe. To

Long-distance telephone access codes

The privatization of Brazil's telephone system has led to a proliferation of new telephone companies and increased competition. Before making a national or international call you must now select the telephone company you wish to use by inserting a **two-digit code** between the zero and the area code or country code of the number you are calling. To call Rio, for example, from anywhere else in the country, you would dial 0xx21 (zero + phone company code + city code) followed by the seven-digit number. For local calls you simply dial the seven- or eight-digit number.

As different phone companies are responsible for different areas of the country, pay phones will display which company code should be used from that particular phone, or the hotel receptionist will let you know the correct code to be used if calling from your hotel. Only two companies (Embratel – code 21; and Intelig – code 23) allow you to make **international calls** from Brazil – one of these numbers will be an option from most phones.

make a call between cities, you need to dial the trunk code, the *código* DDD (pronounced "daydayday"), listed at the front of phone directories. For international calls, ask for *chamada internacional*; a reverse-charge call is a *chamada a cobrar*. Reversing the charges costs about twice as much as paying locally, and it is much cheaper to use a telephone charge card from home. Except in the most remote parts of Amazonia and the Northeast, everything from a small town upwards has a *posto*, though note that outside large cities they shut at 10pm.

Post offices and letters

A **post office** is called a *correio*, identifiable by their bright yellow postboxes and signs. An imposing *Correios e Telégrafos* building will always be found in the centre of a city of any size, and from here you can send telegrams as well; but there are also small offices and kiosks scattered around which only deal with mail. Because post offices in Brazil deal with other things besides post, queues are often a problem. Save time by using one of their franking machines for

Dialling codes and useful numbers

If you're dialling from abroad, the international code for Brazil is ☏55.
To call direct out of Brazil, dial ☏00 followed by the company access code (see box above) followed by the relevant country code, followed by the number.

Country codes:

Argentina ☏54	Canada ☏1	Paraguay ☏595
Australia ☏61	Ireland ☏353	US ☏1
Britain ☏44	New Zealand ☏64	

You can dial direct to operators in the following countries using these numbers:
Australia ☏0008061
Britain: use BT charge card number below
Canada ☏0008014 US: use charge card numbers below
For unlisted countries contact the international operator number.
International operator ☏000333
International operator from a public phone ☏000107
Reverse-charge international calls ☏00080 plus country code

Telephone charge cards:

AT&T ☏0008010	MCI ☏0008012
BT ☏0008044	Sprint ☏0008016

stamps; the lines move much more quickly. **Stamps** (*selos*) are most commonly available in two varieties – either for mailing within Brazil or abroad. A foreign postage stamp costs around 40¢ for either a postcard or a letter up to 10 grammes. It is expensive to send parcels abroad, however.

Mail within Brazil takes three or four days, longer in the North and Northeast, while **airmail** letters to Europe and North America usually take about a week or sometimes even less. **Surface mail** takes about a month to North America, and three to Europe. Although the postal system is generally very reliable, it is not advisable to send valuables through the mail.

Email and the Internet

Like most rapidly developing nations, Brazil has latched on to the Internet, with most hotels and businesses now online. Public access has exploded, with cybercafés (listed in the "Listings" sections throughout the Guide) in all regions of the country and hotels offering Internet access too. The general **hourly rate** for Internet access in Brazil is between $1.50 and $3.

The media

As in the US, Brazil has a regional press rather than a national one. The best of Rio and São Paulo compares well with anywhere in the world; elsewhere newspapers are at best mediocre but are always valuable for listings of local events. Brazil also boasts a lurid but enjoyable yellow press, specializing in gruesome murders, political scandals and football.

The top **newspapers** are the slightly left-of-centre *Folha de São Paulo* and the Rio-based right-of-centre *Jornal do Brasil*, usually available, a day late, in large cities throughout the country. Both are independent and have extensive international news, cultural coverage and entertainment listings. Stodgier but reasonable is the right-wing *Estado de São Paulo*, while the *Gazeta Mercantil* is a high-quality equivalent of the *Financial Times* or *Wall Street Journal*. Also widely available is *O Globo*, the mouthpiece of Roberto Marinho's Globo empire (see p.47), right of centre, but with the advantage of Caruso, the best of Brazil's political cartoonists. In Brazil, as in Argentina and Chile, the political cartoon is a widely respected art form and often screamingly funny. The most enjoyable of the yellow press is *Última Hora*, especially good for beginners in Portuguese, with a limited vocabulary and lots of pictures.

There are also two very good weekly current affairs **magazines**, *Veja* and *Isto É*. For most Brazilians, however, they are expensive, around $2, since their readership is exclusively middle class. You will find Brazilian editions of most major fashion and women's magazines. The weekly *Placar* is essential for anyone wanting to get to serious grips with Brazilian football. *Vogue Brasil*, edited in São Paulo and published by Condé Nast, is a quality magazine offering great insight into the style of the Brazilian elite, while *Plástica* is a glossy monthly magazine that offers insights into Brazil's apparent obsession with plastic surgery.

Apart from in airports, five-star hotels, Rio and São Paulo, where you can find the *International Herald Tribune* and the *Economist*, **English-language newspapers** and magazines are very difficult to find in Brazil.

TV and radio

Brazilian **TV** is ghastly, the worst you are ever likely to see, and therefore compulsive viewing even if you don't understand a word of Portuguese. There are several national channels, of which the most dominant is TV Globo, the centrepiece of the Globo empire, Latin America's largest media conglomerate. The empire was built up by Brazil's answer to Rupert Murdoch, Roberto Marinho, now over 80, one of the most powerful men in Brazil, very cosy with the military regime and prone to use his papers and TV channels as platforms for his ultra-conservative views. The other major national channels are Manchete, TV Bandeirantes, SBT and Record.

The channels are dominated by **telenovelas**, glossy soap operas which have massive audiences in the evenings; the most popular is *Terra Nostra*, a story about Italian immigrants in São Paulo at the beginning of the twentieth century. **Football coverage** is also worth listening to, a gabbling and incomprehensible stream of commentary, punctuated by remarkably elongated shouts of "Gooooool" whenever anyone scores – which is often, Brazilian defences being what they are. However, there are a few genuine highlights, notably **Jô Soares**, the funniest and cleverest of Brazilian comedians, who hosts a very civilized late-night chat show on SBT every weekday.

Radio is always worth listening to if only for the music, so a cheap transistor radio is a good thing to take with you. FM stations abound everywhere and you should always be able to find a station that plays local music. Shortwave reception for the BBC World Service is good in Brazil.

 # Opening hours, holidays and festivals

Basic hours for most stores and businesses are from 9am to 6pm, with an extended lunch hour from around noon to 2pm. Banks don't open until 10am, and stay open all day, but usually stop changing money at either 2pm or 3pm; except for those at major airports, they're closed at weekends and on public holidays. Museums and monuments more or less follow office hours but many are closed on Monday.

Although plane and bus **timetables** are kept to whenever possible, in the less developed parts of the country – most notably Amazonia but also the interior of the Northeast – delays often happen. Brazilians are very Latin in their attitude to time, and if ever there was a country where patience will stand you in good stead it's Brazil. Turn up at the arranged time, but don't be surprised at all if you're kept waiting. Waiting times are especially long if you have to deal with any part of the state bureaucracy, like extending a visa. There is no way out of this; just take a good book.

Brazilian public holidays

There are plenty of local and state holidays, but on the following **national holidays** just about everything in the country will be closed:

January 1 New Year's Day
Carnaval The five days leading up to Ash Wednesday
Good Friday
April 21 Remembrance of Tiradentes
May 1 Labour Day
Corpus Christi
September 7 Independence Day
October 12 Nossa Senhora Aparecida
November 2 Dia dos Finados (the Day of the Dead)
November 15 Proclamation of the Republic
December 25 Christmas Day

Festivals

Carnaval is the most important festival in Brazil, but there are other holidays, too, from saints' days to celebrations based around elections or the World Cup.

Carnaval

When **Carnaval** comes, the country gets down to some of the most serious partying in the world. A Caribbean carnival might prepare you a little, but what happens in Brazil goes on longer, is more spectacular and on a far larger scale. Every place in Brazil, large or small, has some form of Carnaval, and in three places especially – Rio, Salvador and Olinda – Carnaval has become a mass event, involving seemingly the entire populations of the cities and drawing visitors from all over the world.

When exactly Carnaval begins depends on the ecclesiastical calendar: it starts at midnight of the Friday before Ash Wednesday and ends on the Wednesday night, though effectively people start partying on Friday afternoon – over five days of continuous, determined celebration. It usually happens in the middle of February, although very occasionally it can be early March. But in effect the entire period from Christmas is a kind of run-up to Carnaval. People start working on costumes, songs are composed and rehearsals staged in school playgrounds and back yards, so that Carnaval comes as a culmination rather than a sudden burst of excitement and colour.

During the couple of weekends immediately before Carnaval proper there are carnival balls, *bailes carnavalescos*, which get pretty wild. Don't expect to find many things open or to get much done in the week before Carnaval, or the week after it, when the country takes a few days off to shake off its enormous collective hangover. During Carnaval itself, stores open briefly on Monday and Tuesday mornings, but banks and offices stay closed. Domestic airlines, local and inter-city buses run a Sunday service during the period.

Three Brazilian carnivals in particular have become famous, each with a very distinctive

Carnaval dates

2004 Feb 21–25
2005 Feb 4–9
2006 Feb 25–March 2
2007 Feb 16–21
2008 Feb 1–6

feel. The most familiar and most spectacular is in **Rio**, dominated by samba and the parade of samba schools down the enormous concrete expanse of the gloriously named Sambódromo. One of the world's great sights, and televised live to the whole country, Rio's carnival has its critics. It is certainly less participatory than Olinda or Salvador, with people crammed into grandstands watching, rather than down following the schools.

Salvador is, in many ways, the antithesis of Rio, with several focuses around the old city centre: the parade is only one of a number of things going on, and people follow parading schools and the *trio elétrico*, groups playing on top of trucks wired for sound. Samba is only one of several types of music being played, and, if it's music you're interested in, Salvador is the best place to hear and see it.

Olinda, in a magical colonial setting just outside Recife, has a character all its own, less frantic than Rio and Salvador; musically it's dominated by *frevo*, the fast, whirling beat of Pernambuco.

Some places you would think are large enough to have an impressive Carnaval are in fact notoriously bad at it: cities in this category are São Paulo, Brasília and Belo Horizonte. On the other hand, there are also places which have much better Carnavals than you would expect: the one in **Belém** is very distinctive, with the Amazonian food and rhythms of the *carimbó*, and **Fortaleza** also has a good reputation. The South, usually written off by most people as far as Carnaval is concerned, has major events in Florianópolis primarily aimed at attracting Argentine and São Paulo tourists, and the smaller but more distinctive Carnaval in Laguna. For full details of the events, music and happenings at each of the main Carnavals, see under the relevant sections of the Guide.

A Carnaval warning

Wherever you go at Carnaval, take care of your possessions: it is high season for **pickpockets and thefts**. Warnings about specific places are given in the text, but the basic advice is – if you don't need it, don't take it with you.

Other festivals

The third week in June sees the **festas juninas**, geared mainly for children, who dress up in straw hats and checked shirts and release paper balloons with candles attached (to provide the hot air), causing anything from a fright to a major conflagration when they land.

Elections and the World Cup are usually excuses for impromptu celebrations, too, while official celebrations, with military parades and patriotic speeches, take place on September 7 (Independence Day) and November 15, the anniversary of the declaration of the Republic.

In towns and rural areas you may well stumble across a **dia de festa**, the day of the local patron saint, a very simple event in which the image of the saint is paraded through the town, with a band and firecrackers, a thanksgiving mass is celebrated, and then everyone turns to the secular pleasures of the fair, the market and the bottle. In **Belém** this tradition reaches its fullest expression in the annual Cirio on the second Sunday of October (see p.401), when crowds of over a million follow the procession of the image of Nossa Senhora de Nazaré, but most *festas* are small-scale, small-town events.

In recent years many towns have created new festivals, usually glorified **industrial fairs** or **agricultural shows**. Often these events are named after the local area's most important product such as the Festa Nacional do Frango e do Peru (chickens and turkeys) in Chapecó (see p.702). Occasionally these local government creations can be worth attending as some promote local popular culture as well as industry. One of the best is Pomerode's annual **Festa Pomerana** (see p.692), which takes place in the first half of January and has done much to encourage the promotion of local German traditions.

Football

Brazilian football (*futebol*) is revered the world over and it is a privilege to experience it at first hand. Games are usually enthralling: the mixture of intoxicating attack and clumsy defence which has traditionally marked Brazilian international sides is to be found at all levels of the game in Brazil, which makes for plenty of goals and entertainment. The stadiums are often spectacular sights in their own right, and Brazilian crowds are fantastic: wildly enthusiastic, and bringing along their own excellent live music – a packed Maracanã has more drummers than the largest samba schools. The only downside is a recent upsurge of crowd violence, provoked by small but highly organized hooligan groups. It is not a good idea to wear a local team shirt to a match, although foreign team shirts will guarantee you a friendly conversation with curious fans.

Football was introduced into Brazil by Scottish railway engineers in the 1890s, and Brazilians took to it like a duck to water. By the 1920s the Rio and São Paulo leagues which dominate Brazilian football had been founded, and Brazil became the first South American country to compete in the World Cup (*Copas*) in Europe, sending a squad to France in 1938.

Brazil is the only country in the world to have participated in every *Copa*. Getúlio Vargas was the first in a long line of Brazilian presidents to make political capital out of the game, building the beautiful Pacaembú Stadium in São Paulo and then the world's largest stadium, the Maracanã in Rio, for the **1950 World Cup**, which Brazil hosted.

In that competition they had what many older Brazilians still think was the greatest Brazilian side ever, which hammered everybody, and then in the final, with the whole country already celebrating, came up against Uruguay. Unfortunately the Uruguayans hadn't read the script and won 2–1, a national trauma that still haunts popular memory nearly fifty years on.

Yet success was not long in coming. A series of great teams, all with **Pelé** as playmaker, won the World Cup in Stockholm in 1958 (the only World Cup won by a South American team in Europe), Chile in 1962 and, most memorably of all, **1970 in Mexico**. Mexico saw the side that is now widely regarded as the greatest in football history, with Pelé playing alongside such great names as Jairzinho, Rivelino, Carlos Alberto, Gerson and Tostão. As three-time winners, Brazil also got to keep the Jules Rimet Trophy, the original World Cup. Most also agree that the 1982 Brazilian team built around Socrates, Falcão, Eder and Cerezo was extraordinary, although they lost 3–2 to the eventual winners, Italy, in one of the greatest matches in football history.

It took Brazil until **1994** to reclaim the World Cup, deservedly beating Italy on penalties in a dramatic climax to what had been an occasionally dull final. It touched off enormous popular rejoicing, as Brazil became the first country to win the World Cup for the fourth time. This was a triumph built on such un-Brazilian virtues as a combative rather than a creative midfield, and a solid defence. Only in attack, where the genius of **Romário** found the perfect foil in Bebeto, was the 1994 side truly Brazilian.

Four years later, Brazil looked well placed to defend their crown in France, but despite the galaxy of stars they had lined up – including the prodigy **Ronaldo** – they had an unconvincing campaign, were slightly lucky to get to the final, and then lost to a good but not great French side to whom they were clearly superior on paper. This loss crystallized a feeling of unease at home about the direction of the national side, which was widely felt to have sold out to commercial interests, with stars making their living in Europe and forgetting their roots.

There is something to this: the 1990s did see an unprecedented amount of money pouring into Brazilian football, and the fact that the national side did not manage to score a single goal in open play in two World Cup finals would have been unthinkable to the 1970 and 1982 sides. It was an unease that deepened in the late 1990s, as a series of financial scandals demoralised clubs and brought the game into increasing disrepute. The malaise deepened in the qualifying campaign to the 2002 World Cup, as a series of managers chopped and changed, the great Ronaldo was sidelined by career-threatening injuries, and Brazil came close to the unprecedented indignity of having to play off against Australia to get to Japan at all.

Brazil's **winning of the 2002 World Cup** was thus a heartening surprise. There were several factors behind it, most importantly the recovery of Ronaldo and the no-nonsense approach of shrewd manager Felipe Scolari, universally revered in Brazil as Felipao, "Big Phil", who put together a settled, balanced side at just the right time. It has to be said that Brazil were lucky with the draw, with the early elimination of dangerous rivals like France and Argentina, and the fact that neither England nor Germany were good enough to put a suspect defense under pressure when it mattered. But Brazil played some fantastic football, with Ronaldo fittingly crowning his comeback with two goals in a fairytale final against Germany, and his namesake **Ronaldinho Gaucho** emerging as a great player. The only negative note was that victory took the pressure off the sleazy figures in the boardrooms, but in the final analysis, especially against the Germans – who cares?

The *favelas* and small towns, to whom football offers a glittering exit route, are a permanent conveyor belt of talent, ensuring that Brazil will always be a contender at the highest level. Brazil's domination of global football over the last decade looks set to continue, as they consolidate their position as the most charismatic and enjoyable side to watch in the world.

Going to a match

Going to a football match is something which even those bored by the game will enjoy purely as spectacle: a big match is watched behind a screen of ticker-tape and waving flags to the accompaniment of massed drums and thousands of roaring voices. The best grounds are the temples of Brazilian football, Maracanã in Rio and the

Art Deco Pacaembú in São Paulo, one of the most beautiful football stadiums in the world. Even the small cities have international-class stadiums – in essence, symbols of municipal virility.

Tickets are cheap – less than a couple of dollars to stand on the terraces (*geral*), around $5 for stand seats (*arquibancada*); championship and international matches cost a little more. Grounds are large, and stadiums usually well below their enormous capacities except for important matches, which means that you can almost always turn up and pay at the turnstile rather than having to get a ticket in advance. Most stadiums are two-tier, with terracing at the bottom surrounding the pitch, and seats on the upper deck.

The number of regional championships and national play-offs means there is football virtually all the year round in Brazil – the **national championship** is a complicated mix of state leagues and national sudden-death play-offs. Even though many major Brazilian stars play in Europe these days, there is still enough domestic talent to support very high-quality football.

Teams and shirts

Good teams are thickest on the ground in Rio and São Paulo. In Rio, **Flamengo** and **Fluminense** have historically had the most intense rivalry in Brazilian club football, though the latter are currently in steep decline and their place has been taken by **Vasco**; together with **Botafogo** they dominate *carioca* football. In São Paulo there is similar rivalry between **São Paulo** and **Coríntians**, whose pre-eminence is challenged by **Guaraní**, **Palmeiras**, **Portuguesa** and **Santos**, the last of these now a shadow of the team that Pelé led to glory in the 1960s. The only clubs elsewhere that come up to the standards of the best of Rio and São Paulo are **Internacional** and **Grêmio** in Porto Alegre, **Atlético Mineiro** in Belo Horizonte, **Vitória** and **Bahia** in Bahia, and **Sport** in Recife.

Brazilian football **shirts**, true to national character, are stylish and much more colourful than their European equivalents, making them great souvenirs. Costs range from over $30 for an official repro shirt bought at a sports shop, to around $10 for unauthorized cotton copies available in any clothes shop. The most common ones you will see are the red and black hoops of Flamengo, the green and maroon stripes of Fluminense, the white and black diagonal stripe of Vasco, the white with red and black hoop of São Paulo, and the blue, white and black stripes of Grêmio. The instantly recognizable national shirt, canary yellow and nicknamed *canarinho*, is also ubiquitous.

Crime and personal safety

Brazil has a reputation as a rather dangerous place, for both people and their possessions. It's not entirely undeserved, but it is often overblown, and many visitors arrive with a wildly exaggerated idea of the perils lying in wait for them. While you would be foolish to ignore them, don't allow worries about safety to interfere with your enjoyment of the country. Certainly, if you take the precautions outlined below, you are extremely unlikely to come to any harm – although you might still have something stolen somewhere along the way.

Robberies, hold-ups and thefts

Remember that while being a gringo can attract unwelcome attention, it can also provide an important measure of protection. The Brazilian police can be extremely violent, and law enforcement tends to take the form of periodic crackdowns. Therefore, criminals know that any injury to a foreign tourist is going to mean a heavy clampdown, which in turn means no pickings for a while. So unless you resist, nothing is likely to happen to you. That said, having a knife or a gun held on you, as anyone who's had the experience will know, is something of a shock: it's very difficult to think rationally. But if you are unlucky enough to be the victim of an **assalto**, a hold-up, try to remember that it's your possessions rather than you that's the target. Your money and anything you're carrying will be snatched, your watch will get pulled off your wrist, but within a couple of seconds it will be over. On no account resist: it isn't worth the risk.

Taking precautions

As a rule, **assalto**s are most common in the larger cities, and are rare in the countryside and towns. Most *assaltos* take place at night, in back streets with few people around, so stick to busy, well-lit streets; in a city, it's always a lot safer to take a taxi than walk. Also, prepare for the worst by locking your money and passport in the hotel safe – if you must carry them, make sure they're in a **moneybelt** or a **concealed internal pocket**. Do not carry your valuables in a pouch hanging from your neck. Only take along as much money as you'll need for the

day, but do take at least some money, as the average *assaltante* won't believe a gringo could be out of money, and might get rough. Don't wear an expensive watch or jewellery: if you need a watch you can always buy a cheap plastic digital one on a street corner for a couple of dollars. And keep wallets and purses out of sight – pockets with buttons or zips are best.

More common than an *assalto* is a simple theft, a **furto**. Bags that look like they come from the First World are an obvious target, so go for the downmarket look. You're at your most vulnerable when travelling and though the luggage compartments of buses are pretty safe – remember to get a baggage check from the person putting them in and don't throw it away – the overhead racks inside are less safe; keep an eye on things you stash there, especially on night journeys. On a city beach, never leave things unattended while you take a dip: any beachside bar will stow things for you. Most hotels (even the cheaper ones) will have a safe, a *caixa*, and unless you have serious doubts about the place you should lock away your most valuable things: the better the hotel, the more secure it's likely to be. In cheaper hotels, where rooms are shared, the risks are obviously greater – some people take along a small padlock for extra security and many wardrobes in cheaper hotels have latches fitted for this very purpose. Finally, take care at Carnaval as it's a notorious time for pickpockets and thieves.

At international **airports**, particularly Rio and São Paulo, certain scams operate; for instance, well-dressed and official-looking men target tourists arriving off international flights in the arrivals lounge, identify themselves as policemen, often flashing a card, and tell the tourists to go with them. The tourists are then pushed into a car outside and robbed. If anyone, no matter how polite or well dressed they are, or how good their English is, identifies themselves as a policeman to you, be instantly on your guard – real policemen generally leave foreigners well alone. They won't try anything actually inside a terminal building, so go to any airline desk or grab one of the security guards, and on no account leave the terminal building with them or leave any luggage in their hands.

The police

If you are robbed or held up, it's not necessarily a good idea to go to the **police**. Except with something like a theft from a hotel room, they're very unlikely to be able to do anything, and reporting something can take hours even without the language barrier. You may have to do it for insurance purposes, when you'll need a local police report: this could take an entire, and very frustrating, day to get, so think first about how badly you want to be reimbursed. If your passport is stolen, go to your consulate first and they'll smooth the path (see p.20). Stolen travellers' cheques are the least hassle if they're American Express: in Rio and São Paulo they take your word they've been stolen, and don't make you go to the police. If you have to deal with the police, there are various kinds. The best are usually the **Polícia de Turismo**, or tourist police, who are used to tourists and their problems and often speak some English or French, but they're thin on the ground outside Rio. In a city, their number should be displayed on or near the desk of reasonable hotels. The most efficient police by far are the **Polícia Federal**, the Brazilian equivalent of the American FBI, who deal with visas and their extension; they have offices at frontier posts, airports and ports and in state capitals. The ones you see on every street corner are the **Polícia Militar**, with green uniforms and caps. They look mean – and very often are –

but, apart from at highway road blocks, they generally leave gringos alone. There is also a plain-clothes **Polícia Civil**, to whom thefts are reported if there is no tourist police post around – they are overworked, underpaid and extremely slow. If you decide to go to the police in a city where there is a consulate, get in touch with the consulate first and do as they tell you.

Drugs

You should be very, very careful about **drugs**. **Marijuana** – *maconha* – is common, but you are in serious trouble if the police find any on you. You'll probably be able to bribe your way out of it, but it will be an expensive business. Foreigners sometimes get targeted for a shakedown and have drugs planted on them – the area around the Bolivian border has a bad reputation for this. The idea isn't to lock you up but to get a bribe out of you, so play it by ear. If the bite isn't too outrageous it might be worth paying to save the hassle, but the best way to put a stop to it would be to deny everything, refuse to pay and insist on seeing a superior officer and telephoning the nearest consulate – this approach is only for the patient. **Cocaine** is not as common as you might think as most of it passes through Brazil from Bolivia or Colombia for export. Nevertheless, the home market has grown in recent years, most worryingly for crack cocaine, which is generally controlled by young and vicious gang leaders from the *favelas* of the major cities.

Be careful about taking anything illegal on buses: they are sometimes stopped and searched at state lines. The most stupid thing you could do would be to take anything illegal anywhere near Bolivia as buses heading to or from that direction get taken apart by the *federais*. Much the same can be said of smuggling along the rivers into Peru and Colombia: don't even think about it!

Travellers with disabilities

Travelling in Brazil for people with disabilities is likely to be difficult if special facilities are required. For example, access even to recently constructed buildings may be impossible, as lifts are often too narrow to accept wheelchairs or there may be no lift at all. In general, though, you'll find that hotel and restaurant staff are helpful and will bend over backwards to be of assistance to try to make up for the deficiencies in access and facilities.

Buses in cities are really only suitable for the agile and for those who don't mind being thrown about. **Taxis**, however, are plentiful. Long-distance buses are generally quite comfortable, with the special *leito* services offering fully reclining seats. Internal **airlines** are helpful, and wheelchairs are available at all the main airports.

Contacts for travellers with disabilities

In Australia and New Zealand

Disabled Persons Assembly 4/173–175 Victoria St, Wellington, New Zealand ☎04/801 9100 (also TTY), ⓦwww.dpa.org.nz. Provides lists of travel agencies and tour operators for people with disabilities.

In Brazil

Centro de Vida Independente Rua Marques de São Vicente 225, Gavea, Est. da PUC, Rio de Janeiro ☎021/257-0019. Campaigning organization for disabled rights and advice on travel in Brazil.

In the UK and Ireland

Access Travel 6 The Hillock, Astley, Lancashire M29 7GW ☎01942/888844, ⓕ891811, ⓦwww.access-travel.co.uk. Tour operator that can arrange flights, transfers and accommodation.
Holiday Care 2nd floor, Imperial Building, Victoria Rd, Horley, Surrey RH6 7PZ ☎0845/124 9971, minicom ☎0845/124 9976, ⓦwww.holidaycare.org.uk. Provides free lists of accessible accommodation. Information on financial help for holidays available.

Irish Wheelchair Association Blackheath Drive, Clontarf, Dublin 3 ☎01/818 6400, ⓦwww.iwa.ie. Information provided about access for disabled travellers abroad.
RADAR (Royal Association for Disability and Rehabilitation) 12 City Forum, 250 City Rd, London EC1V 8AF ☎020/7250 3222, minicom ☎020/7250 4119, ⓦwww.radar.org.uk. A good source of advice on holidays and travel abroad.
Tripscope Alexandra House, Albany Rd, Brentford, Middlesex TW8 0NE ☎0845/7585 641, ⓦwww.tripscope.org.uk. This registered charity provides a national telephone information service offering free advice on UK and international transport for those with a mobility problem.

In the US and Canada

Directions Unlimited 123 Green Lane, Bedford Hills, NY 10507 ☎1-800/533-5343 or 914/241-1700. Travel agency specializing in custom tours for people with disabilities.
Mobility International USA 451 Broadway, Eugene, OR 97401 ☎541/343-1284, ⓦwww.miusa.org. Information and referral services, access guides, tours and exchange programs. Annual membership $35 (includes quarterly newsletter).
Society for the Advancement of Travel for the Handicapped (SATH) 347 5th Ave, New York, NY 10016 ☎212/447-7284, ⓦwww.sath.org. Non-profit travel-industry referral service that passes queries on to its members as appropriate; allow plenty of time for a response.
Wheels Up! ☎1-888/38-WHEELS, ⓦwww.wheelsup.com. Provides discounted airfare, tour and cruise prices for disabled travelers, also publishes a free monthly newsletter and has a comprehensive website.

Travelling with kids

Travelling with kids is relatively easy in Brazil as they're made to feel welcome in hotels and restaurants in a way that's not always so in Europe or North America. South Americans hold the family unit in high regard, and kids not only act as a cultural ice-breaker between foreigners and nationals, but are also much appreciated in their own right by Brazilians.

Travelling around Brazil takes time, so try not to be too ambitious in terms of how much you aim to cover. Because of frequent scheduled stops and unscheduled delays it can take all day to fly from one part of the country to another. Long bus journeys are scheduled overnight and can be exhausting. Children pay full **fare** on buses if they take up a seat, ten percent on planes if under two years old, half-fare between two and twelve, and full fare thereafter. Newer **airports** have a **nursery** (*berçário*) where you can change or nurse your baby and where an attendant will run your baby a bath, great on a hot day or if your plane's delayed. If you plan on renting a car, bring your own child or **baby seat** as rental companies never supply them and they are very expensive in Brazil. Cars are fitted with three-point shoulder seatbelts in the front, but many only have lap seatbelts in the back.

In **hotels**, kids are generally free up to the age of five and rooms often include both a double and a single bed; a baby's cot may be available, but don't count on it. It's rare that a room will sleep more than three, but larger hotels sometimes have rooms with an interlinking door. Hotels will sometimes offer discounts, especially if children share rooms and even beds with siblings or parents; the lower- to mid-range hotels are probably the most flexible in this regard. If you're planning on staying more than a few days in a city you may find it cheaper and more convenient to stay in an **apartment-hotel**, which will sleep several people and comes with basic cooking facilities. Baths are rare in Brazil, so get your kids used to **showers** before leaving home. Occasionally a hotel will provide a plastic baby bath, but bring along a travel plug as shower pans are often just about deep enough to create a bath.

Many of the mid- and upper-range hotels have TV lounges, TVs in rooms, swimming pools, gardens and even games rooms, which are often useful in **entertaining** kids. Most large towns also have cinemas, the best often being the new multiplexes found in shopping centres.

Food shouldn't be a problem as, even if your kids aren't adventurous eaters, familiar dishes are always available and there's always the ubiquitous *comida por kilo* option. Portions tend to be huge, often sufficient for two large appetites, and it's perfectly acceptable to request additional plates and cutlery. Most hotels and restaurants provide high chairs (*cadeira alta*) as well. Commercial **baby food** is sold in Brazilian supermarkets but is limited to a very small and expensive range of Nestlé products, so it's best to bring your own. If your baby is on formula, bring enough with you as the Portuguese instructions on locally produced powdered varieties may be difficult to understand and, in any case, your baby may find a change unsettling. Pay special attention to **water** and either bring a water purifier (see p.26) or a travel kettle and boil mineral water rather than tap water. Washing out bottles can be awkward, so it makes sense to bring with you an ample supply of pre-sterilized disposable bottles (not available in Brazil). Medium-category hotels usually have a **minibar** (*frigobar*) in the rooms where you can store bottles and baby food, but where there isn't one you will be able to store things in the hotel's refrigerator. A small cooler box or insulated bag is a good idea and, while ice compartments of *frigobars* are useless, you can always place your freezer blocks in the hotel's freezer (*congelador*).

In general, Brazilian infants don't use disposable **nappies/diapers** (*fraldas*), due to the cost, around $5 for twenty – very expensive for most Brazilians. As brands such as Pampers are sold in pharmacies and supermarkets, it's worth only bringing a minimum with you until you can make it to a shop.

Health shouldn't be a problem, but before planning your itinerary, make enquiries as to whether the **vaccines** recommended or required in some parts of Brazil (in particular the Amazon) are likely to have any unpleasant side effects for babies or young children.

For most of Brazil, the only likely problem will be the strength of the tropical sun and the viciousness of the mosquitoes: bring plenty of **sunscreen** (at least factor 20 for babies and factor 15 for young children) and an easy-to-apply **non-toxic insect repellent**.

Women travellers

Despite the nation's ingrained *machismo*, sexual harassment is not the problem you might expect in Brazil. Wolf-whistles and horn-tooting are less common than they would be in Spain or Italy, and, while you do see a lot of men cruising, more than you might think aren't looking for women, which spreads what hassle there is more evenly between the sexes for a change. The further north you go, blondes (men as well as women) bring out the stares, but attention which can seem threatening is often no more than curiosity combined with a language barrier.

Chances of trouble depend, to an extent, on where you are: the stereotype of free-and-easy cities and of small towns and rural areas that are formal to the point of prudishness often holds good – but not always. Many interior Amazon towns have a frontier feel and a bad, *machista* atmosphere. Also bear in mind that in any town of any size the area around the *rodoviária* or train station is likely to be a red-light district at night – not somewhere to hang around. The transport terminals themselves, though, are usually policed and fairly safe at all hours.

Women travelling alone will arouse curiosity, especially outside the cities, but the fact that you're a crazy foreigner explains why you do it in most Brazilian eyes; it shouldn't make you a target.

There is no national **women's movement** in Brazil, but there are loosely linked organizations in big cities and some university campuses, and a growing awareness of the issues. *Mulherio* is a national feminist paper.

Gay and lesbian Brazil

Gay life in Brazil still thrives in the large cities, despite the long shadow cast by AIDS (see p.29). In general, the scene has benefited from relatively relaxed attitudes towards sexuality – certainly when compared to the rest of Latin America – and the divide between gay and straight nightlife is very blurred.

Attitudes, however, vary from region to region. Rural areas and small towns, especially in Minas Gerais, the Northeast and the South, are deeply conservative; the medium-sized and larger cities less so, The two most popular gay destinations are Rio and Salvador, though even here the scene is remarkably discreet when compared to many northern European, North American and Australian cities.

And even in Brazil's big cities, there's an ugly undercurrent of homophobia present and gay visitors are advised to be cautious. Each year scores of gay men and lesbians are murdered in Brazil as a direct consequence of their sexuality, and there have been widely publicized murders in gay cruising areas.

A useful resource to consult before you trip is ⓦ www.guiagaybrasil.com.br; although the text is in Portuguese, there are enough English indicators to allow non-Portuguese speakers to navigate easily through it and benefit from the listings and tips.

Directory

ADDRESSES Trying to find an address can be confusing: streets often have two names, numbers don't always follow a logical sequence, and parts of the address are often abbreviated (Brasília is a special case – see pp.482–483). The street name and number will often have a floor, apartment or room number tacked on: thus R. Afonso Pena 111-3° s.234 means third floor, room 234. "R" is short for Rua, "s" for *sala*, and you may also come across *andar* (floor), *Ed.* (*edifício*, or building) or *s/n* (*sem número*, no number), very common in rural areas and small towns. All addresses in Brazil also have an eight-digit postcode, or *CEP*, often followed by two capital letters for the state; leaving it out causes delay in delivery. So a full address might read:

Rua do Sol 132-3° andar, s.12
65000-100 São Luís – MA

BARBERS For men, a visit to a barber is one of the cheaper luxuries Brazil affords. Wherever it says "*Cabeleireiro*" you can treat yourself to an old-fashioned haircut and shave, invariably with hot towel and cut-throat razor, and Brylcreem and facial massage as optional extras, for no more than a dollar or two. Many barbers and unisex hairdressers also offer manicures and, occasionally, pedicures, for similarly low prices.

CINEMA Most films shown in Brazilian cinemas are American with subtitles. These all reach Brazil very soon after they're released in the US (and often before the UK) and entrance is very cheap. Both Rio and São Paulo have a good art-house cinema network; in Rio the Estação chain, with branches in Botafogo, Catete, Flamengo and Copacabana, is especially good. If you understand Portuguese, look out for movies by two great Brazilian directors, the modernist Glauber Rocha, and the more conservative Nelson Pereira dos Santos. *Central do Brasil* (or *Central Station*; 1997), directed by Walter Salles, is a superb chronicle of a woman's journey with an orphaned child from Rio to the remote interior of the Northeast, while Fernando Meirelles' *Cidade de Deus* (*City of God*; 2002) is a riveting account of the growth of the drug trade in a Rio *favela* from the 1960s to the 1980s, featuring amongst its cast some of the eponymous *favela*'s inhabitants.

ELECTRICITY Electricity supplies vary – sometimes 110V and sometimes 220V – so check before plugging anything in. It's a fair bet that you'll blow the fuses anyway. Plugs have two round pins.

LAUNDRY Even the humblest hotel has a *lavadeira*, who will wash and iron your clothes. Agree on a price beforehand, but don't be too hard – livelihoods are at stake. Larger hotels have set prices for laundry services – usually surprisingly expensive. Laundries outside of hotels are not generally geared to the needs of travellers.

LEFT LUGGAGE Most bus stations will have a *guarda volume* where you can leave bags. In cities it's usually a locker system, open 24 hours – there's a booth where you buy a key, and a token for every day that you want to leave things; you leave the tokens inside the locker. In smaller places it will usually be a lock-up room operated by a bus company, so check the opening hours before you leave anything. They're safe enough to leave your bags for short periods while you look for a hotel, but don't check money or anything really valuable, especially if you are leaving it for longer periods.

MUSEUMS Many museums in Brazil do not charge for admission; when they do, entrance is almost always modest, $1 or so being typical. Brazil's few museums that have the international connections, financial means and security occasionally host special touring exhibitions from abroad, and in these cases entrance charges are somewhat higher than normal. Admission prices are given in the Guide only when they are above $1.

PHOTOGRAPHY Only regular 35mm 100 ASA Kodacolor or Fujicolour and AFS film is easily available in Brazil and even this is likely to be poorly kept, expensive and past its "use by" date. If you use anything else, bring it with you, or stock up in the first main city centre you get to. Good slide film is generally available, but only from specialist shops in major cities. In the Amazon and other forests, 400 ASA film and possibly a flash and tripod will be necessary as it can be surprisingly dark. Small batteries can also be hard to get hold of and will be very expensive if you find them. A polarizing filter is essential if you have an SLR camera. If possible try to keep the film at a constant temperature before and after use, and process it as soon as possible.

STUDENT CARDS An international student card, or an FIYTO youth card is well worth carrying. It will get you occasional reductions at museums and the like, but more importantly it serves as an extremely useful ID for bus drivers and hotels, saving you from having to keep your passport available at all times. Any official-looking card with a picture and number on it will serve almost as well.

TIME ZONES Brazil is large enough to have different time zones. Most of the country is three hours behind GMT, but the states of Amazonas, Acre, Rondônia, Mato Grosso and Mato Grosso do Sul are four hours behind – that includes the cities of Manaus, Corumbá, Rio Branco, Porto Velho, Cuiabá and Campo Grande.

TIPPING Bills usually come with ten percent *taxa de serviço* included, in which case you don't have to tip – ten percent is about right if it is not included. Waiters and some hotel employees depend on tips, so don't be too mean. You don't have to tip taxi drivers (though they won't say no),

Things to take

A universal electric plug adaptor and a universal sink plug.
A sheet or two (if staying in youth hostels).
A small flashlight.
Earplugs (for street noise in hotel rooms).
High-factor sunscreen.
A pocket alarm clock (for those early morning departures).
An inflatable neck-rest, to help you sleep on long journeys.
A multi-purpose penknife.
A needle and some thread.
Plastic bags (to sort your baggage, make it easier to pack and unpack, and keep out damp and dust).

Items for a basic first-aid kit are listed on p.27.

but you are expected to tip barbers, hairdressers, shoeshine kids, self-appointed guides and porters. It's useful to keep change handy for them and for beggars.

TOILETS Public toilets are not very common and often disgusting. The words to look for are *Banheiro* or *Sanitário*: where they're marked (less often than you might hope) *Cavalheiros* means men, *Senhoras* or *Damas* women. It's always a good idea to carry some toilet paper with you.

Guide

Guide

Rio

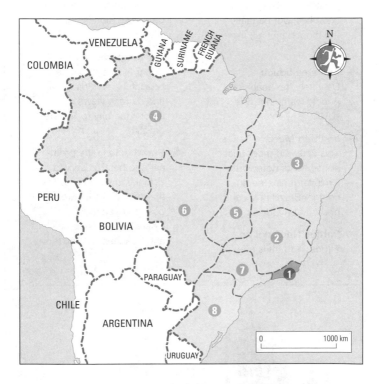

CHAPTER 1 # Highlights

✳ **Teatro Municipal** Soak up the belle époque atmosphere here and in the surrounding Praça Floriano. See p.90

✳ **Igreja de Nossa Senhora da Glória do Outeiro** One of the smallest of Rio's colonial churches, but certainly the most beautiful. See p.100

✳ **Ipanema beach** Definitely the beach for people watching. See p.107

✳ **Instituto Moreira Salles** This splendid modernist house hosts noteworthy exhibits of nineteenth-century Brazilian art and photography. See p.108

✳ **Parque Nacional de Tijuca** With trails and a wealth of flora and fauna, this fine city park offers spectacular views across Rio. See p.112

✳ **Lapa nightlife** Samba, forró and other Brazilian rhythms pound out of the bars and nightclubs of this Bohemian district of central Rio. See p.122

✳ **Museu de Arte Contemporânea** One of Oscar Niemeyer's most beautiful creations; on a fine day the views across the bay to Rio are dazzling. See p.133

✳ **Parati** Among the prettiest and best-preserved colonial towns in Brazil, the town is also a great base to explore the Costa Verde's islands and beaches. See p.145

Rio and around

The citizens of the ten-million-strong city of **Rio de Janeiro** call it the Cidade Marvilhosa – and there can't be much argument about that. Rio sits on the southern shore of a landlocked harbour within the magnificent natural setting of Guanabara Bay. Extending for twenty kilometres along an alluvial strip, between an azure sea and jungle-clad mountains, the city's streets and buildings have been moulded around the foothills of the mountain range that provides its backdrop, while out in the bay there are innumerable rocky islands fringed with white sand. The aerial views over Rio are breathtaking, and even the concrete skyscrapers that dominate the city's skyline add to the attraction.

Although riven by inequality, Rio de Janeiro has great style. Its international renown is bolstered by a series of symbols that rank as some of the greatest landmarks in the world: the **Corcovado** ("hunchback") mountain supporting the great statue of Christ the Redeemer; the rounded incline of the **Sugar Loaf** mountain, standing at the entrance to the bay; and the famous sweep of **Copacabana beach**, probably the most notable length of sand on the planet. It's a setting enhanced by the annual, frenetic sensuality of **Carnaval**, an explosive celebration which – for many people – sums up Rio and her citizens, the **cariocas**. The major downside in a city given over to conspicuous consumption is the rapacious development that is engulfing Rio de Janeiro. As the rural poor, escaping drought and poverty in other regions of Brazil, flock to swell Rio's population, the city is being squeezed like a toothpaste tube between mountains and sea, pushing its human contents out along the coast in either direction. The city's rich architectural heritage is being whittled away and, if the present form of economic development is sustained, the natural environment will eventually be destroyed, too. It's a process unwittingly hastened by Rio's citizens who look forward optimistically to the future, most with the hope of relief from poverty, some with an eye to the main chance and greater wealth.

The **state of Rio de Janeiro**, surrounding the city, is a fairly recent phenomenon, established in 1975 as a result of the amalgamation of Guanabara state and Rio city. Fairly small by Brazilian standards, the state is both beautiful and accessible, with easy trips either east along the **Costa do Sol** or west along the **Costa Verde**, taking in unspoilt beaches, washed by a relatively unpolluted ocean. **Inland** routes make a welcome change from the sands, especially the trip to **Petrópolis**, the nineteenth-century mountain retreat of Rio's rich.

The **best time to visit** both city and state, as least as far as the **climate** goes, is between May and August, when the region is cooled by trade winds and the

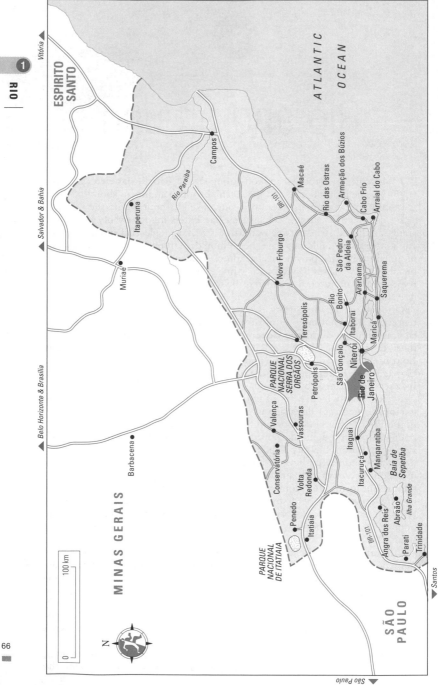

temperature remains at around 22–32°C. Between December and March, the rainy season, it's more humid, the temperature more like 40°C; but even then it's rarely as oppressive as it is in northern Brazil.

Rio de Janeiro city

Nearly five hundred years have seen **RIO DE JANEIRO** transformed from a fortified outpost on the rim of an unknown continent into one of the world's great cities. Its recorded past is tied exclusively to the legacy of the colonialism on which it was founded. No lasting vestige survives of the civilization of the **Tamoios** people, who inhabited the land before the Portuguese arrived, and the city's history effectively begins on January 1, 1502, when a **Portuguese** captain, André Gonçalves, steered his craft into Guanabara Bay, thinking he was heading into the mouth of a great river. The city takes its name from this event – Rio de Janeiro means the "River of January". In 1555, the French, keen to stake a claim on the New World, established a garrison near the Sugar Loaf mountain, and the Governor General of Brazil, Mem de Sá, made an unsuccessful attempt to oust them. It was left to his son, Estácio de Sá, finally to defeat them in 1567, though he fell – mortally wounded – during the battle. The city then acquired its official name, São Sebastião de Rio de Janeiro, after

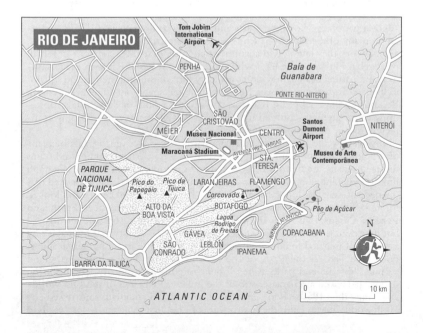

the infant king of Portugal, and Rio began to develop on and around the Morro do Castelo – in front of where Santos Dumont airport now stands.

With Bahia the centre of the new Portuguese colony, initial progress in Rio was slow, and only in the 1690s, when **gold** was discovered in the neighbouring state of Minas Gerais, did the city's fortunes look up, as it became the control and taxation centre for the gold trade. During the seventeenth century the **sugar cane** economy brought new wealth to Rio, but despite being a prosperous entrepôt, the city remained poorly developed. For the most part it comprised a collection of narrow streets and alleys, cramped and dirty, bordered by habitations built from lath and mud. However, Rio's strategic importance grew as a result of the struggle with the Spanish over territories to the south (which would become Uruguay), and in 1763 the city replaced Bahia (Salvador) as Brazil's capital city. By the eighteenth century, the majority of Rio's inhabitants were **African** slaves. Unlike other foreign colonies, in Brazil miscegenation became the rule rather than the exception: even the Catholic Church tolerated procreation between the races, on the grounds that it supplied more souls to be saved. As a result, virtually nothing in Rio remained untouched by African customs, beliefs and behaviour – a state of affairs that clearly influences today's city, too, with its mixture of Afro-Brazilian music, spiritualist cults and cuisine.

In March 1808, having fled before the advance of Napoleon Bonaparte's forces during the Peninsular War, **Dom João VI** of Portugal arrived in Rio, bringing with him some 1500 nobles of the Portuguese royal court. So enamoured of Brazil was he that after Napoleon's defeat in 1815 he declined to return to Portugal and instead proclaimed "The United Kingdom of Portugal, Brazil and the Algarves, of this side and the far side of the sea, and the Guinea Coast of Africa" – the greatest **colonial empire** of the age, with Rio de Janeiro as its capital. During Dom João's reign the Enlightenment came to Rio, the city's streets were paved and lit, and Rio acquired a new prosperity based on **coffee**.

Royal patronage allowed the arts and sciences to flourish, and Rio was visited by many of the illustrious European names of the day. In their literary and artistic work they left a vivid account of contemporary Rio society – colonial, patriarchal and slave-based. Yet while conveying images of Rio's street life, fashions and natural beauty, they don't give any hint of the heat, stench and squalor of life in a tropical city of over 100,000 inhabitants, without a sewerage system. Behind the imperial gloss, Rio was still mostly a slum of dark, airless habitations, intermittently scourged by outbreaks of yellow fever, its economy completely reliant upon human **slavery**.

However, by the late nineteenth century, Rio had lost much of its mercantilist colonial flavour and started to develop as a modern city: trams and trains replaced sedans, the first sewerage system was inaugurated in 1864, a telegraph link was established between Rio and London, and a tunnel was excavated that opened the way to Copacabana, as people left the crowded centre and looked for new living space. Under the administration of the engineer **Francisco Pereira Passos**, Rio went through a period of urban reconstruction that all but destroyed the last vestiges of its colonial design. The city was torn apart by a period of frenzied building between 1900 and 1910, its monumental splendour modelled on the Paris of the Second Empire. Public buildings, grand avenues, libraries and parks were all built to embellish the city, lending it the dignity perceived as characteristic of the great capital cities of the Old World. During the **1930s** Rio enjoyed international renown, buttressed by Hollywood images and the patronage of the first-generation jet set. Rio became the nation's commercial centre, too, and a new wave of modernization swept the city, leaving little more than the Catholic churches as monuments to the past. Even the removal of the country's political administration to the new federal capital of Brasília in 1960 did nothing to discourage the developers. Today, with the centre rebuilt many times since colonial days, most interest lies not in Rio's buildings and monuments but firmly in the **beaches** to the south of the city. For more than sixty years these have been Rio's heart and soul, providing a constant source of recreation and income for *cariocas*. In stark contrast, Rio's **favelas** (see box, p.111), clinging precariously to the hillsides, show another side to the city, saying much about the divisions within it. Although not exclusive to the capital, these slums seem all the more harsh in Rio because of the plenty and beauty that surround them.

Orientation

Arriving in a big city can be a daunting experience, and many people come to Rio de Janeiro, scramble their way to Copacabana and go no further, except on an occasional foray by guided tour. The beaches, though, are only one facet of Rio. The city is divided into three parts – centre, north and south – and the various *bairros* (neighbourhoods) have retained their individuality and charac-

Trouble – a warning

Although it sometimes seems that one half of Rio is constantly being robbed by the other, don't let paranoia ruin your stay. It's true that there is a lot of petty theft in Rio: pockets are picked and bags and cameras swiped. But use a little common sense and you'll encounter few problems. Most of the real violence affecting Rio is drug related and concentrated in the *favelas*. In addition, there are certain areas that should be avoided.

In **Centro**, contrary to popular belief, Sunday is not the best time to stroll around – the streets are empty, which means you can be more easily identified, stalked and robbed. And with nobody about, there is little hope of immediate assistance. The area around **Praça Mauá**, just to the north of Centro, should be avoided after nightfall and care should be taken at weekends. **Lapa**, one of Rio's key nightlife areas, is another place that requires caution. Along the Avenida Atlântica in **Copacabana**, the areas in front of the *Help Discoteque* and the *Rio Othon Palace Hotel* are also likely places to encounter trouble. Although Copacabana's record has improved since the authorities started to floodlight the beach at night, it's not a good idea to remain on the beach after sunset. Around the **Praça do Lido** in Leme, a red-light district, gringos are fair game; nor is it advisable to wander unaccompanied around the darker corners of the **Parque do Flamengo** after nightfall. Similarly, tourists who choose to walk between **Cosme Velho** and the **Corcovado** have sometimes been subject to robbery and assault – something that can be best avoided by taking the train, which is more comfortable anyway.

Apart from these clearly identifiable pockets of Rio, caution should generally be exercised. Drugs lords have effectively been able to shut down huge swathes of the city as a demonstration of their power, ordering shops and businesses to close under threat of violence; hijackings, burning of buses and even some bomb blasts have been known to occur in the wake of these closings. If such an event should occur during your stay – you'll notice shops' shutters being pulled down and the streets emptying in a hurry – you should immediately return to your hotel and wait until the threat passes.

teristic atmosphere. So, while you'll certainly want to get a good dose of the beaches, you may prefer to put up in a quieter quarter and explore the rich history of the centre as well. Rio's layout is straightforward and the transport system makes it easy to get around – but given the city's vast size, it's worth carrying a good map; they're available from any city kiosk.

Centro

Centro is the commercial and historic centre of Rio, and, though the elegance of its colonial and Neoclassical architecture has become overshadowed by the towering office buildings, it has by no means yet been swamped. The area is laid out in an effective grid, cut by two main arteries at right angles to each other, **Avenida Presidente Vargas** and **Avenida Rio Branco**. Presidente Vargas runs west from the waterfront and the Candelária church to Dom Pedro II **train station** and on to the **Sambódromo**, where the Carnaval procession takes place. Rio Branco crosses it in front of the Candelária church, running from **Praça Mauá** in the dockland area, south through **Praça Mahatma Gandhi** to the **Avenida Beira Mar**. On the west side of Avenida Rio Branco is **Largo da Carioca**, which provides access to the hilly suburb of **Santa Teresa**, whose leafy streets wind their way upwards and westwards towards the Corcovado. At the foot of the slope on which Santa Teresa is built lies **Lapa**, just south of Centro, an inner-city residential and red-light district, its past grandeur reflected in the faded elegance of the **Passeio Público** park.

On the east side of Rio Branco, **Rua da Assembléia** contains the TurisRio **tourist office**, and runs into **Praça XV de Novembro** – the square near the water where you'll find the **ferry station** for boats and hydrofoils to Niterói (across the bay) and the Ilha de Paquetá (to the north).

Both Avenida Rio Branco and Praça XV de Novembro are good places to catch a **bus to the southern beaches**, an area known as the Zona Sul – any bus with the name of a distant beach, like Leblon, passes along the coastline, or parallel to it.

Zona Norte

The northernmost part of Rio, the **Zona Norte**, contains the city's industrial areas and the major working-class residential *bairros* with little in the way of historic interest or natural beauty. However, the **Museu Nacional** in the Quinta da Boa Vista park is a splendid collection well worth making time for. This apart, you're not likely to go much further north than Praça Mauá, exceptions being trips to and from the international airport, inter-city bus terminal and the **Maracanã Stadium**, Brazil's football Mecca.

Zona Sul

The **Zona Sul**, the name used to cover everything south of the city centre, though generally taken to mean just the *bairros* shouldering the coastline, has much more to attract you than the Zona Norte.

Following the Avenida Beira Mar south from Centro, the zone is heralded by the **Parque do Flamengo**, an extensive area of reclaimed land transformed into a public recreation area and beach. First up is the *bairro* of **Glória**, where the whitewashed church of Nossa Senhora da Glória do Outeiro, high on a wooded hill, makes an unmistakeable landmark. Beyond, Beira Mar becomes Avenida Praia do Flamengo, which leads into the *bairros* of **Catete** and **Flamengo** – together with Glória, areas where you'll find innumerable cheap hotels. On the other side of Flamengo is the **Largo do Machado**, whose central position, between the centre and the beach areas, makes it a useful place to base yourself. From the square you can reach the *bairros* of **Laranjeiras** and **Cosme Velho**, to the west. The latter is the site of the **Corcovado** and the famous hilltop statue of Christ the Redeemer.

Further south, the bay of **Botafogo** is overshadowed by the **Sugar Loaf** mountain, looming above the *bairro* of **Urca**. From Botafogo, the **Pasmado Tunnel** leads to **Leme**, a small *bairro* whose three kilometres of beach, bordered by **Avenida Atlântica**, sweep around to **Copacabana**. Now one of the world's most densely populated areas, Copacabana is less classy than it once was, losing ground to its western neighbours, **Ipanema** and **Leblon**, which provide another four kilometres of sand and surf. These areas are the most chic of the residential *bairros*, with clubs and restaurants sitting amidst the stylish homes of Rio's more prosperous citizens.

Ipanema and Leblon are situated on a thin strip of land, only a few hundred metres wide, between the Atlantic Ocean and the **Lagoa Rodrigo de Freitas**, a lake tucked beneath the green hills of the **Tijuca National Park**. On the north side of the lake are the **Jardim Botânico** and **Jockey Club** racecourse and, just to the west, the *bairro* of **Gávea**. Further south, through Gávea, the Auto-Estrada Lagoa-Barra leads into **São Conrado** and its southern neighbour, **Barra de Tijuca**, the preserve of Rio's middle classes. São Conrado, in particular, shows up the great contradictions in Brazilian society: overlooking the elegant Gávea Golf Club and the prosperous residences that surround it is the **Favela Roçinha**, a shantytown clinging to the mountainside and reputedly home to over 160,000 people.

Arrival and information

You're most likely to fly in to Rio or arrive by bus; the city's train station is now only used for commuter services. Be warned that opportunistic thieves are active at all points of arrival, so don't leave baggage unattended or valuables exposed; be especially careful of dangling cameras and wallets stuffed into back pockets.

By air

Rio de Janeiro is served by two airports. The one at **Santos Dumont** (☎21/3814-7070) deals mainly with the shuttle services to and from São Paulo, Brasília and Belo Horizonte, and is at the north end of the Parque do Flamengo, immediately east of Centro. From here, every 40 minutes an air-conditioned **executivo bus** ($2) will take you through the Zona Sul, stopping wherever passengers want to get off along the beaches of Copacabana, Ipanema, Leblon and São Conrado. Ordinary **taxis** (yellow with a blue stripe) are readily available from outside the terminal but you're likely to be overcharged by drivers not willing to activate the meter if you're obviously new to town – the fare should amount to around $9 to Copacabana. If it's your first visit to Rio or if your Portuguese is poor, a less stressful option is to purchase a voucher from one of the many radio-taxi stands within the terminal. You'll be directed to your cab and will be charged a flat rate of around $14 to Copacabana. Alternatively, cross the road and catch an ordinary bus from Avenida Marechal Câmara, which you can reach by taking the pedestrian walkway in front of the airport terminal: #438 to Ipanema and Leblon via Botafogo; #442 to Urca; #472 to Leme. For Copacabana, #484 goes from Avenida General Justo, over which the walkway also crosses.

The Tom Jobim **international airport** (☎21/3398-4526) – usually referred to by its old name, **Galeão** – which also serves most Brazilian destinations, lies on the Ilha do Governador in Guanabara Bay, 20km north of the city. On arrival, make sure that your passport is stamped and that you retain your immigration form, as failure to do so can cause problems come departure. In the arrivals hall, consult one of the official **tourist information** desks – Riotur, TurisRio or EMBRATUR. Avoid those that represent private concerns, trying to pass themselves off as official agencies. The official desks will check hotels for vacancies for you, but not at the very cheapest places. **Changing money** is not a problem as there's a branch of the Banco do Brasil as well as several ATMs on the third floor of the airport. After 10pm you can only withdraw up to $30 from the machines but, at a pinch, you can change cash (dollars) with men hanging out in the arrivals lobby but at a poor rate of exchange.

To reach your hotel, catch one of the air-conditioned **executivo buses** ($2), which run every half-hour between 5.20am and 11pm, either via Centro to Santos Dumont, or along the coast, via Centro, to Copacabana and on to São Conrado. Outside these hours, a **taxi** ride is the only alternative. Buy a ticket at either the Cootramo, Coopertramo or Transcoopass desks, near the arrivals gate, and give it to the driver at the taxi rank; a ticket to Flamengo costs about $15, Copacabana $17 and Ipanema $20. It's best not to take the ordinary taxis – you're likely to end up being overcharged – and don't risk accepting a lift from one of the unofficial drivers hanging about in the airport. The drive takes about fifteen minutes into the centre or around half an hour to Zona Sul, unless you hit rush hour.

Heading out to the international airport, ask your hotel to arrange for a fixed-fare taxi to pick you up, or take the air-conditioned bus that follows the Zona Sul coastline and can be picked up on Avenida Delfim Moreira (Leblon), Avenida Vieira Souto (Ipanema), Avenida Atlântica (Copacabana), Avenida Beira Mar (Flamengo), or on the Avenida Rio Branco in Centro – allow at least an hour from the beaches. Inside Galeão, departure desks are split into three sections: internal Brazilian flights from Sector A; Sectors B and C for international flights. And check whether your ticket includes Brazilian **departure tax** – if it doesn't you'll have to pay $4 for internal flights or $28 for international flights, payable in either US or Brazilian currency (but not a mix of the two). Duty-free shops only accept US currency or credit cards – not Brazilian *reaís*. There's a pretty good range of shops in the departure lounge where you can buy T-shirts, fine (and expensive) jewellery and *cachaça*.

By bus

All major inter-city bus services arrive at the **Novo Rio Rodoviária** (☎21/2291-5151), 3km north of Centro in the São Cristovão *bairro*, close to the city's dockside at the corner of Avenida Rodrigues Alves and Avenida Francisco Bicalho. International buses from Santiago, Buenos Aires, Montevideo and Asunción, among others, use this terminus, too. The *rodoviária* has two sides, one for departures, the other for arrivals: once through the gate at arrivals, either grab a taxi ($4 to Centro, $8–15 to the Zona Sul), catch an *executivo* air-conditioned bus along the coast towards Copacabana and Leblon ($1.50; every half-hour from directly outside the arrivals side of the station), or cross the road to the ordinary bus terminal in Praça Hermes. Alternatively, head first for the **tourist office** desk (daily 8am–8pm) at the bottom of the stairs, in front of the main exit – they'll help with hotels, and advise which buses to catch. There are spotlessly clean showers at the *rodoviária* that you can use for around $2 (with towel included).

A more central terminal, the **Menezes Cortes Rodoviária** in Rua São José (☎21/2533-8819), handles services from some in-state towns such as Petrópolis and Teresópolis, but mainly operates buses to and from the suburbs and Zona Sul.

Leaving Rio by bus and travelling out of the state, it's best to book two days in advance. The same goes for services to popular in-state destinations, like Búzios or Paratí, which fill up at weekends; or for travelling anywhere immediately before or after Carnaval. Most **tickets** can be bought from travel agents all over the city, while inside the main *rodoviária*, on both sides, upstairs and down, you'll find the ticket offices of the various bus companies. You can reach the *rodoviária* on bus #104 from Centro, #127 or #128 from Copacabana, and #456, #171 or #172 from Flamengo.

Information

There are three official **tourist agencies** in the city, none of them particularly efficient. Information about Rio itself is from **Riotur**, which distributes maps and brochures and has a helpful English-speaking telephone information service, Alô Rio (daily 8am–8pm; ☎0800-707-1808). Riotur's main office is in Centro at Rua da Assembléia 10 (Mon–Fri 9am–6pm; ☎21/3217-7575), and it also has a branch in Copacabana at Av. Princesa Isabel 183 (daily 8am–8pm; ☎21/2541-7522). Most of Riotur's information can also be picked up at their booths at Novo Rio Rodoviária (6am–midnight) and Galeão and Santos Dumont airports (6am–midnight). Information about the state of Rio is available from **TurisRio**, at Rua da Assembléia 10 in Centro (☎21/3215-0011); and the most basic information about the rest of Brazil from **EMBRATUR**, also in Centro at Rua Uruguaiana 174 (Mon–Fri 9am–6pm; ☎21/2509-6017).

Note that if you're going to stay in Brazil for over six months, you are obliged to **register** at the Registro de Estrangeiros, Polícia Federal, Av. Venezuela 2 (Mon–Fri 11am–4pm; ☎21/3263-3747).

Getting around

Rio's **public transport** system is cheap and effective: most places can be reached by metrô, bus or taxi, or a combination of these, while for getting about the state you might want to rent a car – though driving in the city itself is not recommended unless you have nerves of steel.

The metrô

The safest and most comfortable way to travel is by using Rio's **metrô** system, in operation since 1979. It's limited to just two lines, which run from Monday to Saturday, 6am to 11pm: **Linha 1** runs from central Copacabana (Siqueira Campos station), north through Centro and then out to the Sãens Pena station in the *bairro* of Maracanã; **Linha 2** comes in from Maria de Graça, to the north of the city, via the Maracanã stadium, and meets Linha 1 at Estação Central, by Dom Pedro II train station. The system is well designed and efficient, the stations bright, cool, clean and secure, and the trains gently air-conditioned, a relief if you've just descended from the scorching world above.

Tickets are bought as singles (*ida*; 50¢) or returns (*duplo*; $1), or are valid for ten journeys (*dez*; $5). Ten-journey tickets can save time, but cost the same and can't be shared, as the electronic turnstiles only allow entrance at eight-minute

Organized tours

Well worth considering are the **organized tours** of different aspects of Rio. Carlos Roquette (℡21/3322-4872, ℻9911-3829, ℮culturalrio@uol.com.br; around $30 per person), has been leading historical and cultural tours of the city for years and while his mainstays are "colonial Rio", "Imperial Rio", "Belle Époque Rio" and "Art Deco Rio", he also designs tours to meet the particular interests of individuals or groups, not the least of which are explorations of homosexual life, past and present, in the city's varied *bairros*. Also highly recommended are Marcel Armstrong's Favela Tour ($25 per person; see p.111), and trips led by Denise Werneck and her son Gabriel of Rio Hiking (see p.113), who concentrate on Rio's green spaces ($35–50 per person) but also take visitors to Lapas bars ($35 per person).

intervals. You can also buy integrated bus/*metrô* tickets (*integrades*; 60¢), useful for making the link between the *metrô* station at Botafogo and Ipanema or Leblon. You catch the buses directly outside the *metrô* station: they run circular routes between Botafogo and Leblon, the #M21 going via the "Jóquei Clube", the #M22 via Copacabana.

Currently, Linha 1 is being extended to Ipanema but completion is still some years off. In the meantime special air-conditioned buses connect Copacabana's Cardeal Arcoverde station, the line's terminus, with Praça General Osório in Ipanema. To use this route you need a special ticket for Ipanema (*bilhete especial para Ipanema*), which costs the same as normal tickets and is valid for both the bus and metrô portion of the journey.

Buses

It's sometimes suggested that it's irresponsible to encourage tourists to use the **city buses** because they're badly driven, likely to get you lost and prone to much petty theft. But, while it's true that some of Rio's bus drivers have a somewhat erratic driving style – to say the least – it's well worth mastering the system: with over three hundred routes and six thousand buses, you never have to wait more than a few moments for a bus, they run till midnight and it's not that easy to get lost.

Numbers and **destinations** are clearly marked on the front of buses, and there are also plaques at the front and by the entrance detailing the route. You get on at the back, pay the seated conductor (the price is on a card behind his head) and then push through the turnstile and find yourself a seat. Buses are jam-packed at rush hour, so if your journey is short, start working your way to the front of the bus as soon as you're through the turnstile; you alight at the front. If the bus reaches the stop before you reach the front, haul on the bell and the driver will wait. This kind of confusion really only occurs during **rush hour**, which is 5pm to 7pm in the evening. In the beach areas of the Zona Sul, especially along the coast, **bus stops** are not always marked. Stick your arm out to flag the bus down, or look for groups of people by the roadside facing the oncoming traffic, as this indicates a bus stop.

To avoid **being robbed** on the bus, don't leave wallets or money in easily accessible pockets, or flash cameras around. If there's a crush, carry any bags close to your chest. Have your fare ready so that you can pass through the turnstile immediately, as pickpockets operate at the rear of the bus, by the entrance, so that they can make a quick escape, and don't let the turnstile come between you and anything you don't want to lose. Special care should be taken on buses known to carry mostly tourists (such as those to the Sugar Loaf) and that are consequently considered rich pickings by thieves.

Rio: some useful bus routes

From Avenida Rio Branco: #119, #121, #123, #127, #173 and #177 to Copacabana; #128 (via Copacabana), #132 (via Flamengo) and #172 (via "Jóquei Clube") to Leblon.

From Praça XV do Novembro: #119, #154, #413, #415 to Copacabana; #154 and #474 to Ipanema.

From Avenida Beira Mar, in Lapa, near the Praça Deodoro: #158 (via "Jóquei Clube"), #170, #172 (via Jardim Botânico), #174 (via Praia do Botafogo), #438, #464, #571 and #572 to Leblon; #472 to Leme; #104 to Jardim Botânico.

From Copacabana: #455 to Centro; #464 to Maracanã.

From Urca: #511 (via "Jóquei Clube") and #512 (via Copacabana) to Leblon.

From the Menezes Cortes terminal, adjacent to Praça XV de Novembro: air-conditioned buses along the coast to Barra de Guaratiba, south of Rio; on the return journey, these buses are marked "Castelo", the name of the area near Praça XV.

From Novo Rio Rodoviária: #104 from Centro, #127 or #128 to Copacabana, and #456, #171 or #172 to Flamengo.

To the train station: any bus marked "E. Ferro".

Parque do Flamengo: any bus marked "via Aterro" passes along the length of the Parque do Flamengo without stopping.

Between Centro and the Zona Sul, most buses run along the coast as far as Botafogo; those for Copacabana continue around the bay, past the RioSul shopping centre, and through the Pasmado Tunnel; those for Leblon, via the "Jóquei Clube", turn right at Botafogo and travel along Avenida São Clemente.

Taxis

Taxis in Rio come in two varieties: **yellow** ones with a blue stripe that cruise the streets; or the larger and newer, always air-conditioned **radio cabs**, white and with a red and yellow stripe, ordered by phone. Both have meters and, unless you have pre-paid at the airport, you should insist that it is activated, and check too that it has been cleared after the last fare. The flag, or *bandeira*, over the meter denotes the tariff. Normally this will read "1", but after 10pm, and on Sundays, holidays and throughout December, you have to pay twenty percent more; then the *bandeira* will read "2".

Generally speaking, Rio's taxi service is reasonably priced (Centro to Ipanema costs around $7, Botafogo to Copacabana around $3) and it is not in the cabbies' interest to alienate tourists by ripping them off; the only time to avoid ordinary (yellow and blue) taxis is when you're coming into town from an airport. However, late at night, drivers often quote a fixed price that can be up to three times the normal fare. Radio cabs are thirty percent more expensive than the regular taxis, but they are reliable; companies include Centraltáxi (☎21/2593-2598), Coopertramo (☎21/3288-4343) and Transcoopass (☎21/2560-4888).

Ferries and hydrofoils

From Praça XV de Novembro **ferries** transport passengers across Guanabara Bay to the city of Niterói (see p.132) and to Paquetá Island (see p.131), a popular day-trip destination to the north of Guanabara Bay. The ferries are extremely cheap and the view of Rio they afford, especially at sunset, is well worth the effort. The thirty-minute crossings to Niterói are very frequent and cost 50¢; just turn up and buy a ticket. The CONERJ company ferries (Companhia de Navegação do Estado de Rio de Janeiro; ☎21/2533-6661) run Monday to Saturday, every fifteen minutes from 6am to 11pm; Sunday and public holidays, every thirty minutes from 7am to 11pm. To the island of Paquetá, there are eight departures a day from 5.30am to 10.30pm and tickets cost about $1; crossings take eighty minutes. Also from Praça XV de Novembro, Transtur (☎21/2533-4343) operates **hydrofoils** to Paquetá (departures every other hour Mon–Fri from 10am to 4pm and hourly Sat, Sun & holidays 8am to 4.30pm; 30min); tickets cost around $3 on weekdays and $5 at weekends. Transtur also operates to Niterói every fifteen minutes from 6.35am to 9pm; the journey takes ten minutes and costs $2.

Trams

Rio's last remaining electric **trams**, the *bondes* (pronounced "bonjis"), climb from near Largo Carioca, across the eighteenth-century Aqueduto da Carioca, to the inner suburb of Santa Teresa and on to Dois Irmãos. Two lines run every fifteen minutes between 5am and midnight: the one for Dois Irmãos permits you to see more of Santa Teresa; the other line terminates at Largo do Guimarães. The trams still serve their original purpose of transporting locals, and haven't yet become a tourist service. The views of Rio from them are excellent, but beware of the young men who jump aboard and attempt to relieve you of your possessions. The best times of day to ride the tram are mid-morning and mid-afternoon when it's less crowded and, consequently, less chaotic. For added safety, hop on a tram that's carrying a police officer assigned to watch over tourists. The tram station is downtown behind the monumentally ugly Petrobrás building and adjacent to the Nova Catedral. Waiting passengers stand in eight lines, one for every row of seats on the tram; the fare is about 20¢, which you pay at the station turnstile going up to Santa Teresa and on board going down.

On Saturdays at 10am, a special tram service is laid on for tourists ($1.50). This goes way beyond the normal Dois Irmãos terminal, leaving the built-up area of Santa Teresa and entering the edge of the Tijuca forest, a good starting point for a stroll.

Driving in Rio

If you're renting a **car** then you must understand what you're letting yourself in for. Rio's road system is characterized by a confusion of one-way streets, tunnels, access roads and flyovers, and **parking** is not easy – all but impossible downtown. **Lane markings**, apart from lending a little colouring to the asphalt, serve no apparent practical purpose, **overtaking** on the right appears to be mandatory and, after nightfall, obeying **traffic lights** is optional. Car rental agencies are listed on p.37.

Accommodation

There's no shortage of choice of **accommodation** in Rio, but it pays to bear in mind two things. From December to February is **high season**, so if you arrive then without an advance booking, either make one through a tourist office or leave your luggage in the *guarda volumes* (baggage offices) at the *rodoviária* or at Santos Dumont airport while you look; there's no point lugging heavy bags around Rio's hot thoroughfares, and it makes you vulnerable to theft as well. The period when prices tend to soar is at **Carnaval**, when accommodation becomes that much harder to find and when most hotels accept bookings for a minimum of four nights' stay. During the low season, hotels usually lower their prices by between thirty and fifty percent but, when a discount is given, you may not be allowed to pay with a credit card – indeed most of the cheapest hotels never accept cards and require advance payment.

There is usually keen competition for tourists and you should be able to find a reasonable double room for $20–40, usually with air-conditioning. The highest concentration of budget places is in Glória, Catete and Flamengo, but reasonably priced accommodation can be found just about anywhere. Disappointingly, with a few exceptions only luxury-class hotels have pools, especially frustrating during periods when the beaches are unsafe due to pollution or strong waves.

There are no **campsites** within easy reach of Rio, but there are several very good **hostels** in Urca, Botafogo, Copacabana and Ipanema; remember, however, that Brazilian universities are on holiday between December and March, during which these places can be packed out. For **apartments**, try Rio Star Imóveis Ltda in Copacabana (☎21/3275-8393) or Rio Flat Service (☎21/3512-9922), which has apartment buildings in Copacabana, Leblon and Lagoa – from $50 a day for a studio or one-bedroom apartment, with swimming pool. If you want to be in Ipanema, call Ipanema Sweet (☎21/3239-1819), who have one- and two-bedroom apartments near the beach from $60 per day. Top Apart Service (☎21/2511-2442, ⓦwww.accorhotels.com.br) has an excellent property in Leblon with one and two-bedroom apartments and a rooftop pool from around $70 per day.

If you're stopping in Rio for a while, check out the classified ads in the *Jornal do Brasil* for **rented rooms** – "*vaga*" (vacancy) and "*quarto*" (room) signify space in someone's home; "*conjugado*", abbreviated to "*conj*", means a bedsitter.

The city centre: Centro and Lapa

Most of the cheap *pensões* are in the north of the city, or near Dom Pedro II train station, but they're mostly inhabited by full-time residents, usually single men, who are working in Rio. It's hard to find a vacancy, and you will be looking in areas that are not particularly safe. Lapa, in the southern corner of the city centre, is a far better bet. There are countless small hotels in this down-at-heel red-light area, and – surprisingly – most of them are clean and respectable enough. Though somewhat noisy at times, Cinelândia is also worth considering – an easy walk from the heart of the city centre, well connected by bus and metrô to the Zona Sul, and with some good bars.

Ambassador Rua Senador Dantas 25, Centro ☎21/2215-2910, Ⓔ ambassador@uol.com.br. Popular with Brazilian business executives, although this hotel has seen better days. Offers high standards of comfort in the heart of Cinelândia, near the Biblioteca Nacional. ④

Bragança Av. Mem de Sá 117, Lapa ☎21/2242-8116, Ⓔ hotelbraganca@rj.sol.com.br. Busy, well-equipped place where rooms come with *frigobar*, telephones and TV. Ideally situated near Lapa's nightlife. ③

Guanabara Palace Av. Presidente Vargas 392, Centro ☎21/2518-0333, ⓦ www.windsorhoteis.com.br. The only luxury hotel in the centre and the haunt of expense-account visitors. Recently renovated and although utterly soulless, it's good value and has the added bonus of a pool. ⑥

Ipiranga Rua São Joaquim da Silva 87. Cheap and friendly – well placed for walking to Centro and for buses to the Zona Sul. ②

Marajó Rua São Joaquim da Silva 99 ☎21/2224-4134. Comfy beds and efficient showers make this probably the best choice in the area. Also has some singles for around $7. ②

Nelba Rua Senador Dantas 46 ☎21/2210-3235. Simple but clean, but the street noise from surrounding Cinelândia can be considerable. ③

Glória and Santa Teresa

Glória, too, is not entirely without its share of prostitution, but the *bairro* has a slightly faded grandeur that's worth getting to know. It's not a dangerous area and is usefully located between Centro and the beaches and restaurants of Zona Sul. Behind Glória is Santa Teresa, which despite its leafy aspect and lively nightlife, has only one hotel. Santa Teresa is best reached from Centro; it is possible to walk between Glória and Santa Teresa, but keep an eye open for trouble.

Glória Rua do Russel 632, Glória ℡21/2555-7272, ⓦwww.hotelgloriario.com.br. Built in the 1920s and set amidst the cobbled roads of the Morro da Glória, this is one of Rio's most traditional hotels, strong on style and atmosphere. Most rooms are spacious and offer tremendous views, and there are two excellent pools and a fine restaurant. By far the best hotel within easy reach of downtown and it takes just 15min to reach Ipanema by taxi. Room rates vary enormously, with heavy discounts often available. ❻

Golden Park Hotel Rua do Russel 374, Glória ℡21/2556-8150, ⓔgparkrio@pontocom.com.br. A medium-sized hotel with modern facilities, including a small rooftop pool. Rooms are basic but comfortable and all are air-conditioned – be sure to request one of the front rooms, which get more light and have park views. Good value. ❹

Rio Hostel Rua Joaquim Murtinho 361, Santa Teresa ℡21/3852-0827, ⓦwww.riohostel.com. Small and friendly hostel with attractive communal areas, including a small pool. A bit isolated, but near Lapa and an easy stroll to Santa Teresa's many bars and restaurants. $10 per person.

Santa Teresa Rua Almirante Alexandrino 660, Santa Teresa ℡21/2242-0007. This no-frills, slightly shabby, *pousada* in a late nineteenth-century house is one of the few places to stay in the leafy, Bohemian *bairro* of Santa Teresa. ❸

Turístico Ladeira da Glória 30, Glória ℡21/2557-7698, ⓕ2558-9388. From the Glória metrô station, climb up round to the right of the Igreja da Glória and through the Largo da Glória to reach this hotel. Friendly, clean and cheap, with spacious, air-conditioned rooms that come with bath and balconies. Though a bit overpriced, it's a firm favourite with backpackers and usually busy, so try and book ahead. Highly recommended. ❸

Catete, Flamengo, Botafogo and Urca

Catete and Flamengo, centred around the Largo do Machado and once the chic residential *bairros* of the middle classes, are well served by hotels – all a good bit cheaper than the ones at Copacabana. These places are also convenient places to stay, handily placed between the centre and the beach zone, with buses, taxis and the *metrô* providing easy access. For some reason, Botafogo offers few hotel possibilities, but if you want to stay in what is one of Rio's best eating-out districts there are a couple of options. Finally, the only option in Urca is a youth hostel, but this upscale area is an appealing and peaceful neighbourhood.

Carioca Easy Hostel Rua Marechal Cantuaria 168, Urca ℡21/2295-7805, ⓦwww.cariocahostel.com.br. A privately owned hostel located in one of Rio's quietest neighbourhoods near the Sugar Loaf, just a ten-minute bus ride from Copacabana. The excellent facilities include a small pool, Internet access and bike rental. $12 per person in a dorm, $28 for a double room.

Chave do Rio Hostel Rua General Dionísio 63, Botafogo ℡21/2286-0303, www.riohostel.com.br. Comfortable and friendly Hostelling International-associated hostel in a beautiful renovated house just off Voluntarios da Patria in Botafogo. Beds, in dorms sleeping 4 to 8 people, go for $10 per head

(including breakfast), and not all rooms are air-conditioned. There are cooking and laundry facilities available as well. Book ahead at peak periods.

Flórida Rua Ferreira Viana 81, Flamengo ℡21/2555-6000, ⓦwww.windsorhoteis.com.br. Highly recommended for its spacious, modern rooms and excellent facilities, including a pool and free Internet usage. Popular with Brazilian business travellers, the hotels offers reduced rates at weekends. ❺

Hispánico Brasileira Rua Silveira Martins 135, Catete ℡21/225-7537. Pleasant, airy and clean hotel with comfortable beds and helpful service. ❷

Imperial Rua do Catete 186, Catete ℡21/2556-

5212, ⓦ www.imperialhotel.com.br. Spacious and comfy rooms in an attractive, renovated 1880s building, well located near to both the metrô station and park. There's also parking and a decent pool, unusual for a hotel in this price category. ❸

Inglês, Rua Silveira Martins 20, Catete ⓣ 21/2558-3052, ⓦ www.hotelingles.com.br. A recent refurbishment has made this long-established small hotel one of the best places to stay in Catete. The spacious rooms, all wth bathrooms, have good facilities including air-conditioning, TV and *frigobar*. ❸

Monte Blanco Rua do Catete 160, Catete ⓣ 21/2225-0121. Spotless and welcoming place, though with no air-conditioning and a fair amount of street noise. ❷

Monterrey Rua Artur Bernardes 39, Catete ⓣ 21/2265-9899. Safe and quiet budget option, with air-conditioning from 8pm–8am and breakfast brought to your room in the morning. ❷

Payssandú Rua Paissandu 23, Catete ⓣ & ⓕ 21/2558-7270. Clean rooms have large bathrooms and TVs, and there's a decent restaurant on the ground floor, too. ❸

Real Rua Real Grandeza 122, Botafogo ⓣ 21/2579-3863. No-frills but good value hotel in an area that's a bit of a trek from the *metrô* (convenient for buses), though close to good restaurants. Rooms are clean if rather dilapidated, and all have air-conditioning. ❸

Regina Rua Ferreira Viana 29, Flamengo ⓣ 21/2556-1647, ⓔ hotelregina@hotelregina .com.br. Good-quality rooms, plus pleasant public areas and friendly staff. Highly recommended. ❸

Copacabana and Leme

Copacabana's street life and general raucousness help to make it the kind of place you either love or hate, and while the area has certainly seen better days, it has by far the greatest concentration of places to stay, ranging from hostels to luxury hotels. Leme – really a continuation of Copacabana – is less frenetic due to being at the far end of the stretch of beach in the opposite direction of Ipanema.

Acapulco Copacabana Rua Gustavo Sampaio 854, Leme ⓣ 21/2275-0022, ⓦ www .acapulcopacabanahotel.com.br. Very comfortable hotel in a quiet location in Leme behind *Le Meridien*. Rooms are spacious and well decorated and some of the balconies even manage a beach view. Highly recommended. ❹

Apa Hotel Rua República do Peru 305, Copacabana ⓣ 21/2548-8112, ⓦ www.apahotel.com.br. A dreary-looking but perfectly respectable hotel with helpful staff and simple, clean rooms (though all have air-conditioning and balconies) in a central area of Copacabana. Some rooms sleep four people and all are excellent value. ❹

Biarritz Rua Aires Saldanha 54, Copacabana ⓣ 21/2522-0542, ⓕ 2287-7640. Just down from Av. Atlântica, this basic, but clean and friendly place is located in a quiet back street. ❸

Canadá Av. N.S. de Copacabana 687, Copacabana ⓣ 21/2257-1864, ⓔ hotel.canada@uol.com.br. A popular choice for foreign tourists, though it's difficult to understand why, with its dark rooms in need of major refurbishment. At least the noisy air-conditioners and fridges drown out the street noise. ❹

Copa Linda Av. N.S. de Copacabana 956, Copacabana ⓣ 21/2267-3399. This hotel, on the second floor, provides good, no-frills accommodation, although many rooms are small. ❸

Copacabana Chalet Hostel Rua Pompeu Loureiro 99, Copacabana ⓣ 21/2236-0047, ⓦ www .geocities.com/thetropics/cabana/7617. Just a short walk from the beach, this is a long-established, small and extremely welcoming hostel. Always popular, so advance booking at peak holiday periods is essential. $8 per head in 6-bed dorms.

Copacabana Palace Av. Atlântica 1702, Copacabana ⓣ 21/2548-7070, ⓦ www .copacabanapalace.com.br. A glorious Art Deco landmark (see p.105) where anyone who is anyone has stayed and, despite Copacabana's general decline, remains a firm favourite. Although every possible facility is on offer, there's a curious lack of communal areas, apart from the large pool in a central courtyard. All in all, this is a great place to end a trip to Brazil if you can possibly afford it. ❾

Copacabana Praia Hostel Rua Tenente Marones de Gusmão 85, Copacabana ⓣ 21/2547-5422, ⓦ www.wcenter.com.br/copapraia. Set several blocks back from the beach, off Rua Figueiredo Magalhães. This efficiently run but rather institutional hostel, by far the largest in Rio, charges $8 per head in a six-bed dorm. Rooms sleeping two to four people (including a private bathroom and basic cooking facilities) are also available. ❸

Debret Av. Atlântica 3564, Copacabana ☎21/2522-0132, ⓦwww.debret.com.br. A firm favourite among European independent travellers, though the overpriced rooms are small and long due for refurbishing, and few have ocean views, despite the address. ❺

Excelsior Copacabana Av. Atlântica 1800, Copacabana ☎21/3259-5323, ⓦwww .windsorhoteis.com.br. Reasonable upper-end choice in the middle of Copacabana's beachfront. Rooms are all well equipped, while the rooftop pool has spectacular views. One of the oldest hotels on the *avenida* (opened in 1950), it tries to maintain the atmosphere of a bygone age. ❽

Grandeville Ouro Verde Av. Atlântica 1456, Copacabana ☎21/2543-4123, ⓦwww.grandville.com.br. Viewed from the outside, this 1950s hotel looks nothing special, but it's considered by its regular guests as the only place to stay in Rio. Discreetly elegant, with spacious and well-kept rooms (go for ones looking onto the beach) and excellent service. ❻

Le Meridien Av. Atlântica 1020, Leme ☎21/3873-8888, ⓦwww.lemeridien.com. Huge hotel with all the conveniences you'd expect for the price. There's a good pool and the beach in front of the hotel is carefully watched by security patrols. With its cafés, restaurants and boutiques, this hotel is for many guests their only experience of Rio. ❽

Martinique Rua Sá Ferreira 30, Copacabana ☎21/2522-1652, Ⓕ 2287-7640. Popular hotel located near the quiet, western end of Copacabana, towards the fort. Good rooms (including some singles). ❸

Praia Leme Av. Atlântica 866, Leme ☎21/2275-3322. This cosy two-storey hotel offers the best value for a beachfront location. Due to its popularity an advance reservation is highly recommended. ❹

Santa Clara Rua Décio Vilares 316, Copacabana ☎21/2256-2650, ⓦwww.hotelsantaclara.com.br. This cosy, well-maintained hotel is excellent value and very friendly. Situated in a tranquil location five blocks from the beach, and close to the Túnel Velho leading to Botafogo's restaurants and museums. ❸

Toledo Rua Domingos Ferreira 71, Copacabana ☎21/2257-1990, ⓦwww.hoteisgandara.com.br. Small but adequate rooms (including singles and some that sleep three people) halfway down Copacabana, just one block from the beach. Good value. ❸

Ipanema and Leblon

Ipanema's safe streets and fashionable beach, along with its good shopping and dining options, make the *bairro* an attractive place to stay and, despite being one of Rio's most upscale areas, it has a pretty good range of accommodation. Just beyond Ipanema lies Leblon, an exclusive residential neighbourhood with fewer places to stay, but some good nightlife possibilities.

Arpoador Inn Rua Francisco Otaviano 177, Arpoador ☎21/2523-0060, ⓔarpoador@unisys.com.br. In a peaceful location on the edge of Ipanema (bordering Copacabana), this popular hotel is reasonable for the area, and room rates don't fluctuate much during the year and in low season the basic rooms (some sleeping three people) may seem overpriced. You'll pay double for a beachfront room. ❺

Caesar Park Av. Vieira Souto 460, Ipanema ☎21/2525-2525, ⓦwww.caesarpark.com.br. Thought of by some as Rio's finest hotel – certainly it's the city's most expensive hotel – and it features every modern luxury that its celebrity guests would expect. The rooftop restaurant and pool has superb views, and the hotel provides security and lifeguards on the beach fronting the hotel. ❾

Carlton Rua João Lira 68, Leblon ☎21/2259-1932. Small, tatty hotel in one of Rio's most classy areas, with friendly staff but somewhat gloomy rooms. ❸

Che Lagarto Youth Hostel Rua Barão de Jaguaripe 208, Ipanema ☎21/2247-4582, ⓦwww.chelagarto.com. In a great location just a block from the Lagoa and fifteen minutes' walk from Ipanema beach, with helpful staff, its own bar and occasional live music. Excellent facilities include laundry, a kitchen and Internet access. $13 per person (including breakfast) in a dorm that sleeps four.

Hostel Harmonia Rua Barão da Torre 175, Casa 18, Ipanema ☎21/2523-4904, ⓦwww .hostelharmonia.com. Nice, quiet location but near excellent bars, restaurants and the beach. Welcoming and relaxed atmosphere, plus laundry and kitchen facilities, Internet access and dorms sleeping two, four or six people. $13 per person.

Hostel Ipanema Rua Barão da Torre 175, Casa 14, Ipanema ☎21/2268-0565, ⓔjustfly@justfly.com.br. The most basic of Rio's hostels, located three blocks from the beach in a quiet area (next to the *Hostel Harmonia*), but with laundry and bike rental facilities. The hostel's owner also runs Rio's most reliable hang-gliding operation (see p.110) and offers discounts to hostel guests. $10 per person in dorms sleeping two to six people. Airport pick-up can be arranged.

Ipanema Inn Rua Maria Quitéria 29, Ipanema ☏ 21/2523-6092, ℱ 2511-5094. Excellent-value and very popular hotel with comfortable rooms that, while small, can squeeze in an extra (fold-out) bed. Just a block from the beach and in one of the best parts of Ipanema. ❹

Ipanema Plaza Rua Farme de Amoedo 34, Ipanema ☏ 21/3687-2000, ☜ www .ipanemaplazahotel.com. Excellent location in the middle of Ipanema. This discreetly luxurious hotel (part of the Dutch-owned Golden Tulip chain), is small enough that it provides individual attention. Rooms and suites are well appointed and there's a small rooftop pool with breathtaking views towards the beach. ❽

Marina Palace Rua Delfim Moreira 630, Leblon ☏ 21/2540-5218, ☜ www.hotelmarina.com.br. Excellent amenities (including a rooftop pool) and beachside location. The rooms are a bit small, but suites are also available. Hardly budget accommodation but overall good value. ❼

São Marco Rua Visconde de Pirajá 524, Ipanema ☏ 21/2540-5032, ℱ 2239-2654. A good deal for its location, on the main shopping street just a few minutes from the beach. Although air-conditioned, rooms are small and basic and there's quite a lot of street noise. ❹

Vermont Rua Visconde de Pirajá 254, Ipanema ☏ 21/2522-0057, ℱ 2267-7046. Simple, though perfectly adequate, rooms (including some that sleep three people), in a central location. Rooms are air-conditioned but not likely to suit those bothered by street noise. Excellent value. ❹

The city centre

Much of historical Rio is concentrated in **Centro**, with pockets of interest, too, in the neighbouring **Saúde** and **Lapa** quarters of the city. You'll find you can tour the centre fairly easily on foot, but bear in mind that the real interest of Rio lies elsewhere – at the beaches of the Zona Sul, and the heights of Urca and Corcovado – and it's not the most exciting city in Brazil to explore. Lots of the old historical squares, streets and buildings disappeared in the twentieth century under a torrent of redevelopment, and fighting your way through the traffic – the reason many of the streets were widened in the first place – can be quite a daunting prospect.

However, although much of what remains is decidedly low-key, there are enough churches and interesting museums to keep anybody happy for a day or two. The cultural influences that shaped the city through its five centuries of existence – the austere Catholicism of the city's European founders, the squalor of colonialism and the grandiose design of the Enlightenment – are all reflected in the surviving churches, streets and squares.

Praça XV de Novembro and around

Praça XV de Novembro is the obvious place to start. Once the hub of Rio's social and political life, it takes its name from the day (Nov 15) in 1899 when Marechal Deodoro de Fonseca, the first president, proclaimed the Republic of Brazil. One of Rio's oldest **markets** is held here on Thursday and Friday (8am–6pm). The stalls are packed with typical foods, handicrafts and ceramics, and there are paintings and prints, as well as a brisk trade in stamps and coins.

The Paço Imperial

The Praça XV de Novembro was originally called the Largo do Paço, a name that survives in the imposing **Paço Imperial** (Tues–Sun noon–6.30pm). Built in 1743, though tinkered with over the years, the building has served variously as the Governor's Palace, the headquarters of the Portuguese government in

Brazil until 1791 and, later, of the Department of Post and Telegraph. It was here, in 1808, that the Portuguese monarch, Dom João VI, established his court in Brazil (later shifting to the Palácio da Quinta da Boa Vista, now the Museu Nacional), and the building continued to be used for royal receptions and special occasions: on May 13, 1888, Princess Isabel proclaimed the end of slavery

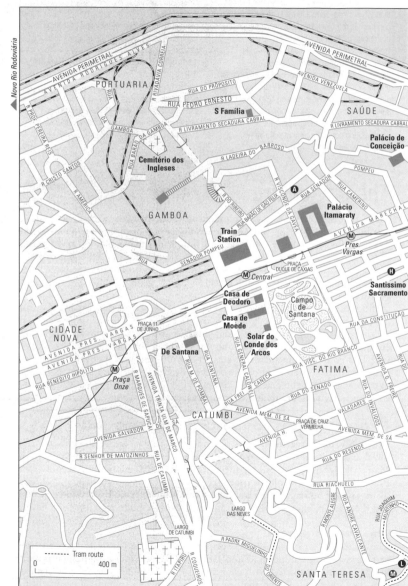

in Brazil from here. Today, the building is a popular literary meeting point, and its first floor houses the Biblioteca Paulo Santos, which specializes in books and journals on Portuguese and Brazilian architecture. Right on the square, too, is the early seventeenth-century **Convento do Carmo** (Mon–Fri 10am–5pm), the first Carmelite convent to be built in Rio. Later used as a royal residence

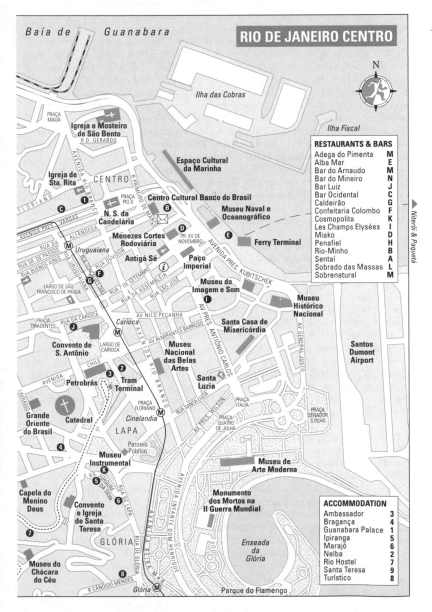

RIO DE JANEIRO CENTRO

Baía de Guanabara

Ilha das Cobras

Ilha Fiscal

RESTAURANTS & BARS

Adega do Pimenta	M
Alba Mar	E
Bar do Arnaudo	M
Bar do Mineiro	N
Bar Luiz	J
Bar Ocidental	C
Caldeirão	G
Confeitaria Colombo	F
Cosmopolita	K
Les Champs Elysées	I
Miako	D
Penafiel	H
Rio-Minho	B
Sentaí	A
Sobrado das Massas	L
Sobrenatural	M

▶ Niterói & Paquetá

PRAÇA MAUÁ

Igreja e Mosteiro de São Bento
R D. GERARDO

Espaço Cultural da Marinha

Igreja de Sta. Rita

CENTRO

Centro Cultural Banco do Brasil

N. S. da Candelária

PRAÇA PIO X

Museu Naval e Oceanográfico

Menezes Cortes Rodoviária

Uruguaiana

Antigá Sé

Paço Imperial

Ferry Terminal

Museu do Imagem e Som

Santa Casa de Misericórdia

Museu Histórico Nacional

Carioca

AV NILO PEÇANHA

Convento de S. Antônio

LARGO DA CARIOCA

Museu Nacional das Belas Artes

Santa Luzia

Santos Dumont Airport

Petrobrás

Tram Terminal

Grande Oriente do Brasil

Catedral

Cinelandia

LAPA

Passeio Público

Museu Instrumental

Museu de Arte Moderna

Capela do Menino Deus

Convento e Igreja de Santa Teresa

GLÓRIA

Monumento dos Mortos na II Guerra Mundial

Enseada da Glória

Museu do Chácara do Céu

Gloria

Parque do Flamengo

ACCOMMODATION

Ambassador	3
Bragança	4
Guanabara Palace	1
Ipiranga	5
Marajó	6
Nelba	2
Rio Hostel	7
Santa Teresa	9
Turístico	8

(after 1808 the Dowager Queen, Dona Maria I, lived here), the building has since been altered several times, and now houses the Universidade Cândido Mendes.

The Arco de Teles

The **Arco de Teles**, on the northern side of the square, was named after the judge and landowner Francisco Teles de Meneza, who ordered its construction upon the site of the old *pelourinho* (pillory) in around 1755. It's really an arcade rather an arch, linking the Travessa do Comércio to the Rua Ouvidor. The *arco* originally contained three houses; one of these was home to the Menezes family, but all were severely damaged by fire in 1790. More engaging than the building itself is the social history of the Arco de Teles and its immediate vicinity. In the luxurious apartments above street level lived families belonging to Rio's wealthy classes, while the street below was traditionally a refuge for "beggars and rogues of the worst type; lepers, thieves, murderers, prostitutes and hoodlums" – according to Brasil Gerson in his 1954 book *História das ruas do Rio de Janeiro*. In the late eighteenth and early nineteenth centuries, one of the leprous local inhabitants – **Bárbara dos Prazeres** – achieved notoriety as a folk devil: it was a common belief that the blood of a dead dog or cat applied to the body provided a cure for leprosy, and Bárbara is supposed to have earned her reputation around the Arco de Teles by attempting to enhance the efficacy of this cure by stealing newborn babies and sucking their blood. Behind the Arco de Teles is the Beco de Teles, a narrow cobblestone alley with some charming nineteenth-century buildings.

Igreja de Nossa Senhora do Carmo da Antigá Sé

At the back of Praça XV de Novembro, on the corner where Rua VII de Setembro meets Rua I de Março, stands the **Igreja de Nossa Senhora do Carmo da Antigá Sé** (Mon–Fri 9am–5pm), which served, until 1980, as Rio's cathedral. Building started in 1749 and, to all intents and purposes, continued right into the twentieth century as structural collapse and financial difficulties necessitated several restorations and delays: the present tower, for example, was built as late as 1905 by the Italian architect Rebecchi. Inside, the high altar is detailed in silver and boasts a beautiful work by the painter Antônio Parreires, representing Nossa Senhora do Carmo seated amongst the clouds and surrounded by the sainted founders of the Carmelite Order. Below, in the **crypt**, are the supposed mortal remains of Pedro Alvares Cabral, Portuguese discoverer of Brazil. In actual fact, he was almost certainly laid to rest in Santarem in Portugal.

Museu Naval e Oceanográfico and around

Close to Praça XV de Novembro, at Rua Dom Manuel 15, is the **Museu Naval e Oceanográfico** (daily noon–4.45pm). Housed in what was originally the naval headquarters, the museum's excellent collection shows the chronology of Brazil's naval history – from sixteenth-century nautical charts and scale replicas of European galleons, to paintings depicting scenes from the Brazil–Paraguay War and exhibits of twentieth-century naval hardware. Above all, the collections provide an insight into the colonial nature of Brazilian history: the exhibits show that Brazilian naval engagements were determined by the interests of the Portuguese Empire until the nineteenth century; as a primarily slave-based plantation economy until 1888, Brazil's military hardware came from the foundries of industrialized Europe. The most impressive items are the handcrafted replicas of sixteenth-century galleons – the *São Felipe* complete with its 98 cannons – and the first map of the New World, drawn by Pedro Alvares Cabral between 1492 and 1500.

If you have a serious interest in naval history, follow the bayside Avenida Alfredo Agache north a couple blocks to the **Espaço Cultural da Marinha** (daily noon–4.45pm). This long dockside building was once used as the port's main customs point, but today houses exhibition halls aimed purely at the naval enthusiast.

From the docks by the Espaço Cultural da Marinha you can reach the small **Ilha Fiscal** (Thurs–Sun noon–5.30pm) where, in the 1880s, a customs collection centre was built. It was here also that the last grand Imperial ball was held, just days before the collapse of the monarchy in November 1889. Connected by a series of lengthy causeways that lead from the mainland and the Ilha das Cobras, the Ilha Fiscal is most easily – and most enjoyably – reached by boat. Crossings ($2; 15min) are on Thursdays through Sundays at 1pm, 2.30pm and 4pm; to ensure a place, arrive at the departure point at least an hour in advance. Standing alone on the tiny island and surrounded by swaying palm trees is a wonderful fort-like structure, built in a hybrid Gothic-Moorish style, which is now an unremarkable naval museum.

Along Rua I de Março to Praça Pio X

Heading up **Rua I de Março** from the *praça* you'll pass the late eighteenth-century **Igreja da Ordem Terceira do Monte do Carmo** (Mon–Fri 8am–3.30pm, Sat 8am–noon), whose seven altars each bear an image symbolizing a moment from the Passion of Christ, from Calvary to the Crucifixion, sculpted by Pedro Luiz da Cunha. The high altar itself is beautifully worked in silver. The church and adjacent convent are linked by a small public chapel, dedicated to Our Lady of the Cape of Good Hope, and decorated in *azulejos* tiling.

A little further along Rua I de Março is the museum and church of **Santa Cruz dos Militares** (Mon–Fri 9am–3pm), its name giving a hint of its curious history. In 1628, a number of army officers organized the construction of the first church here, on the site of an early fort. It was used for the funerals of serving officers until, in 1703, the Catholic Church attempted to take over control of the building. The proposal met stiff resistance, and it was only in 1716 that the Fathers of the Church of São Sebastião, which had become severely dilapidated, succeeded in installing themselves in Santa Cruz. Sadly, they were no more successful in the maintenance of this church either, and by 1760 it had been reduced to a state of ruin – only reversed when army officers again took control of the reconstruction work in 1780, completing the granite and marble building that survives today. Inside, the nave, with its stuccoed ceiling, has been skilfully decorated with plaster relief images from Portugal's imperial past. The two owners long since reconciled, there's a **museum** on the ground floor with a collection of military and religious relics.

Across Rua I de Março from these churches is the **Centro Cultural Banco do Brasil** (Tues–Sun noon–10pm), a former bank headquarters now housing one of the Rio's foremost arts centres (see p.124).

The Igreja de Nossa Senhora da Candelária

At the end of Rua I de Março you emerge onto **Praça Pio X**, dominated by the **Igreja de Nossa Senhora da Candelária** (Mon–Fri 8am–4pm, Sat & Sun 8am–1pm), an interesting combination of Baroque and Renaissance features resulting from the financial difficulties that delayed the completion of the building for more than a century after its foundation in 1775. Inside, the altars, walls and supporting columns are sculpted from variously coloured marble, while high above, the eight pictures in the dome represent the three theological virtues (Faith, Hope and Charity), the cardinal virtues (Prudence, Justice, Strength and Temperance) and the Virgin Mary – all of them late nineteenth century work of the Brazilian artist João Zeferino da Costa. There's more grand decoration in the two pulpits, luxuriously worked in bronze and supported by large white angels sculpted in marble.

The Avenida Presidente Vargas

Until 1943 the church was hemmed in by other buildings, but it was appointed its own space when the **Avenida Presidente Vargas** was constructed, opening up new vistas. Rio's widest avenue, it runs west for almost three kilometres and has fourteen lanes of traffic, and when work started on it in 1941 there was considerable opposition from the owners of houses and businesses that were demolished in its path – not to mention clerical dissent at the destruction of a number of churches. The avenue was inaugurated with a military parade in 1944, watched by Vargas himself in the year before he was deposed by a quiet coup.

Back towards the waterfront, turn into Rua Visconde de Itaborai and you will pass the **Alfândega Antiga**, the old Customs House, which was constructed in 1820 by the French architect Grandjean de Montigny, in Neoclassical style. Although now empty apart from a small, rather ordinary restaurant occupying part of the rear of the building, it's been home to a bizarre array of organizations in its time, from the English merchants who arrived after the opening of the port to free trade in 1808, through the Mauá Gas Company and the Brazilian Society for the Protection of Animals, to the Socialist organizers of Rio's 1918 general strike.

From São Bento to the Largo da Carioca

Heading north, on the continuation of Rua I de Março, the Ladeira de São Bento leads to the **Igreja e Mosteiro de São Bento** (Mon–Fri 8–11am & 2.30–5.30pm; Sat from 7.15am; Sun from 8.15am, open also for Mass with Gregorian chant Sun 10am), in the *bairro* of **Saúde** overlooking the Ilha das Cobras. The monastery was founded by Benedictine monks who arrived in Rio in 1586 by way of Bahia; building started in 1633, finishing nine years later. The facade displays a pleasing architectural simplicity, its twin towers culminating in pyramid-shaped spires, while the interior is richly adorned. The altars and walls are covered by images of saints, and there are statues representing various popes and bishops, work executed by the deft hand of Mestre Valentim. The panels and paintings particularly, late seventeenth-century work, represent valuable examples of colonial art. There is not much else to grab your attention in the area. The monastery is next to **Praça Mauá** and the docklands, a seedy and run-down part of the city that you'd best to avoid, especially at night. There are plans for major redevelopment of this huge area as a cultural centre with a controversial **Guggenheim** museum having been committed as the centre-piece. For the time being some of the huge dockside warehouses are used as spaces for theatre productions and exhibitions.

Largo Santa Rita

Heading along Rua Dom Gerardo from the monastery leads you to the north end of Avenida Rio Branco, on the west side of which (off Visconde de

Inhaúma) is **Largo Santa Rita** and its church, the **Igreja da Santa Rita** (Mon–Sun 8am–11.30am & 2.30–5pm). Built on land previously used as a slaves' burial ground, the building dates from 1721, its bell tower tucked to one side giving it a lopsided look. It's not one of Rio's more attractive churches, but the interior stonework is a fine example of Rococo style, and it's magnificently decorated with a series of panels, three on the high altar and eight on the ceiling, painted by Ananias Correia do Amaral and depicting scenes from the life of Santa Rita.

Rua Uruguaiana: Saara and Largo de São Francisco de Paula

To return south, to the Largo da Carioca in Centro, cross Avenida Presidente Vargas and continue down **Rua Uruguaiana**. In the streets to your left (between Uruguaiana and I de Março) lies the most interesting concentration of shops in Rio, in the area known as **Saara**. Traditionally the cheapest place to shop, it was originally peopled by Jewish and Arab merchants, who moved into the area after a ban prohibiting their residence within the city limits was lifted in the eighteenth century. In recent years, a new wave of Jewish and Arab merchants – along with, most recently, Chinese and Koreans – have moved back into the area. In the maze of narrow streets you'll find everything from basic items of beachware and handicrafts to expensive jewellery. The streets are lined with stalls selling trinkets and are thronged with street traders and folk musicians, so it's always a lively place to visit: particularly good buys here include sports equipment, musical instruments, CDs and tapes.

Halfway down Rua Uruguaiana is **Largo de São Francisco de Paula**, whose church, the **Igreja de São Francisco de Paula** (Mon–Fri 9am–1pm), has hosted some significant moments in Brazil's history. Behind the monumental carved wooden entrance door the Te Deum was sung in 1816 to celebrate Brazil's promotion from colony to kingdom; in 1831, the Mass celebrating the "Swearing-in" of the Brazilian Constitution was performed here. More tangibly, the chapel of Nossa Senhora da Vitória, on the right as you enter, was dedicated by Pope Pius X to the victory of the Christian forces over the Turkish in the naval battle of Lepanto in 1571. The meticulous decoration is attributed to Mestre Valentim, who spent thirty years working on the chapel, while the paintings on the walls were created by a slave who called himself Manoel da Cunha. With the consent of his owner, Manoel travelled to Europe as the assistant of the artist João de Souza, and on his return bought his own freedom with money earned from the sale of his artwork.

Across from the church is the **Real Gabinete Português de Leitura** (Mon–Fri 9am–6pm), a library dedicated to Portugal and Portuguese literature. The building was completed in 1887 and is immediately identifiable by its magnificently ornate facade, styled after fifteenth-century Portuguese architecture. The reading room is lit by a red, white and blue stained-glass skylight and contains many of the library's 350,000 volumes. Amongst the rarest is the 1572 first edition of *Os Lusíados*, the Portuguese national epic poem by Luis de Camões, based on Vasco da Gama's voyage of exploration, occasionally on view.

The Largo da Carioca

From Largo de São Francisco de Paula, Rua Ramalho Ortigão leads the short distance to **Rua Carioca**. On the way, you can stop for a well-earned **beer** in Rio's oldest *cervejaria*, the *Bar Luiz* at no. 39. It's been here since 1887, changing its original name – the *Bar Adolfo* – following World War II, for obvious reasons. The place was once a favourite watering hole for Rio's Bohemian and intellectual groups and, though it's a little faded these days, it's still a bustling, enjoyable place. The wonderful Art Nouveau *Confeitaria Colombo* is just one block from here at Rua Gonçalves Dias 32 (see p.114).

The **Largo da Carioca** itself has undergone considerable transformation since the turn of the nineteenth century, many of its buildings demolished to allow widening of the square and the improving of nearby streets. Today street traders selling leather goods dominate the centre of the square, while a couple of things of interest remain, most notably the **Igreja e Convento de Santo Antônio** (Mon–Fri 8am–7pm, Sat 8–10.30am & 2–5pm, Sun 8.30–11am), standing above the *largo*, and known as St Anthony of the Rich (to differentiate it from St Anthony of the Poor, which is located elsewhere in the city). A tranquil, cloistered refuge, built between 1608 and 1620, this is the oldest church in Rio and was founded by Franciscan monks who arrived in Brazil in 1592. A popular saint in Brazil, St Anthony's help was sought during the French invasion of 1710: he was made a captain in the Brazilian army and in a startling lack of progress through the ranks it was 1814 before he was promoted to lieutenant-colonel, retiring from service in 1914. More improbably still, the tomb of **Wild Jock of Skelater** lies in the crypt. A Scottish mercenary who entered the service of the Portuguese Crown during the Napoleonic Wars, he was later appointed commander-in-chief of the Portuguese army in Brazil.

This aside, the interior of the church boasts a beautiful sacristy, constructed from Portuguese marble and decorated in *azulejos* depicting the miracles performed by St Anthony. There is rich wooden ornamentation throughout, carved from *jacaranda*, including the great chest in the sacristy. The image of Christ, adorned with a crown of thorns, came from Portugal in 1678 – a remarkable work of great skill.

West from Praça Tiradentes

Leave Largo da Carioca by turning left along Rua Carioca, and you're soon in **Praça Tiradentes**, named after the leader of the so-called Minas Conspiracy of 1789, a plot hatched in the state of Minas Gerais to overthrow the Portuguese regime (see p.191). In the square stands the **Teatro João Caetano**, after João Caetano dos Santos, who based his drama company in the theatre from 1840. He also notches up a bust that stands in the square, a reward for producing shows starring such theatrical luminaries as Sarah Bernhardt. In the second-floor hall of the theatre hang two large panels painted in 1930 by Emiliano di Cavalcanti, one of Brazil's great modernist artists, which, with his usual use of strong tropical colours, explore the themes of Carnaval and popular religion. The original theatre on this site, the Teatro Real, erected in 1813, had a much more political history: it was here in 1821 that Dom João VI swore obedience to the Constitution promulgated in Lisbon after the Porto Revolution. Three years later, at the end of the ceremony proclaiming Dom Pedro I Emperor of Brazil, a fire razed the old theatre to the ground.

Campo de Santana and around

Three blocks west of Praça Tiradentes, along Rua Visconde do Rio Branco, is the **Praça da República** in the **Campo de Santana**. Until the beginning of the seventeenth century this area was outside the city limits, which extended only as far as Rua Uruguaiana. Its sandy soils made it unsuitable for cultivation and the only building here was the chapel of St Domingo, sited in the area now covered by the asphalt of Avenida Presidente Vargas, and used by the Fraternity of St Anne to celebrate the festivals of their patron saint – hence the name,

Campo de Santana (field of St Anne).

By the end of the eighteenth century the city had spread to surround the Campo de Santana, and in 1811 a barracks was built to house the Second Regiment of the Line, who used the square as a parade ground. From here, Dom Pedro I proclaimed Brazil's independence from the Portuguese Crown in 1822, and after 1889 the lower half of the square became known as Praça da República. The first president of the new republic, Deodoro de Fonseca, lived at no. 197 Praça da República. At the start of the twentieth century, the square was landscaped, and today it's a pleasant place for a walk, with lots of trees and small lakes ruled by swans. In the centre lies the **Parque João Furtado**, worth visiting in the evening, when small, furry shapes can be seen scuttling about in the gloom – agoutis, happily, not rats.

Directly across Avenida Presidente Vargas is the Praça Duque de Caxias and the **Panteão Nacional**, on top of which stands the equestrian statue of the Duque de Caxias, military patron and general in the Paraguayan War – his remains lie below in the Pantheon. Nearby, the **Dom Pedro II train station** – known more commonly as the Central do Brasil and made famous by Walter Salles' 1997 film *Central Station* – is an unmistakeable landmark, its tower rising 110m into the sky and supporting clock faces measuring 7.5 by 5.5m, all linked to a central winding mechanism. Just beyond the station, at Av. Marechal Floriano 196, the **Palácio do Itamaraty** is one of Rio's best examples of Neoclassical architecture. Completed in 1853 as the pied-à-terre of the great landowner Baron of Itamaraty, it was bought by the government and was home to a number of the republic's presidents. The *palácio* now houses the **Museu Histórico e Diplomático do Itamaraty** (Mon, Wed & Fri 2–3pm), a repository of documents, books and maps relating to Brazil's diplomatic history, its collections primarily of interest to serious researchers (archives open for consultation Mon–Fri 1–5pm). Of perhaps wider interest is the part of the building that has been painstakingly restored to show how the upper classes lived in the nineteenth century.

North of Itamaraty is Gamboa, an extremely seedy port area and home to Rio's oldest *favelas*. The only reason to visit Gamboa is to go to the **Cemitério dos Ingleses** or English Cemetery, the oldest Protestant burial site in Brazil. In 1809 the British community was given permission to establish a cemetery and Anglican church in Rio, essential if English merchants were to be attracted to newly independent Brazil. Still in use today, the cemetery is set in a beautiful hillside location looking down to Guanabara Bay. The inscriptions on many of the stones make poignant reading, recalling the days when early death was almost expected. The cemetery (Mon–Fri 8am–4pm, Sat & Sun 8am–12.30pm) is at Rua da Gamboa 181 in an area with a reputation for being dangerous; you'd be wise to go by taxi and ask the driver to wait for you – under no circumstances walk alone along the approach road passing through the tunnel from the nearby central train station.

From the Nova Catedral to Cinelândia and Praça Floriano

South of the Largo da Carioca, the unmistakeable shape of the **Nova Catedral Metropolitana** (daily 7am–5.30pm) rises up like some futuristic teepee. Built between 1964 and 1976, it's an impressive piece of modern architecture and a considerable engineering feat, whatever you think of the style: the Morro de Santo Antônio was levelled to make way for the cathedral's construction, and the thousands of tons of resulting soil were used for the land reclamation project that gave rise to the Parque de Flamengo (see p.103). Similar in style to the blunt-topped Mayan pyramids found in the Yucatán region of Mexico, the cathedral is 83m high with a diameter of 104m and has a capacity of 25,000 people. Inside, it feels vast, a remarkable sense of space enhanced by the absence of supporting columns. Four huge stained-glass windows dominate, each measuring 20m by 60m and corresponding to a symbolic colour scheme – ecclesiastical green, saintly red, Catholic blue and apostolic yellow. From outside, you'll be able to see the mid-eighteenth century **Aqueduto da Carioca** (often called the Arcos da Lapa), which since 1896 has carried trams up to Santa Teresa, the beautiful *bairro* on the hill opposite (see p.93); the tram terminal is between the cathedral and the Largo da Carioca, behind what is certainly the ugliest building in Rio, the glass, steel and concrete hulk that is the headquarters of Petrobrás, the state oil company.

Along Avenida República de Chile, and right down **Avenida Rio Branco**, you'll come to Praça Marechal Floriano and the area known as **Cinelândia**, named after long-gone movie houses built in the 1930s. Rio Branco, originally named Avenida Central, must once have been Latin America's most impressive urban thoroughfare. Old photos of Avenida Rio Branco show its entire length bordered by Neoclassical-style buildings of no more than three storeys high, its pavements lined with trees, and with a promenade that ran right down the centre. Nowadays, however, the once graceful avenue has been swamped by ugly office buildings and traffic pollution.

Praça Floriano

The **Praça Floriano** is the one section of Avenida Rio Branco that still impresses. There are several sidewalk cafés on the western side of the *praça* that are popular central meeting points in the evening, when the surrounding buildings are illuminated and at their most elegant. In the centre of the square is a bust of **Getúlio Vargas**, still anonymously decorated with flowers on the anniversary of the ex-dictator's birthday, March 19. At the north end of the square the **Teatro Municipal**, opened in 1909 and a dramatic example of Neoclassical architecture, was modelled on the Paris Opéra – all granite, marble and bronze, with a foyer decorated in the white and gold characteristic of Louis XV style. Since opening, the theatre has been Brazil's most prestigious artistic venue, hosting visiting Brazilian and foreign orchestras, opera and theatre companies and singers. Tours are available round the building – enquire at the box office at the back of the building. The theatre has a decent restaurant and bar, the *Café do Teatro* (Mon–Fri 11am–4pm), which is richly adorned with elaborate Assyrian-inspired mosaics.

On the opposite side of the road, the **Museu Nacional das Belas Artes** (Tues–Fri 10am–6pm, Sat & Sun 2–6pm; $2.50 – Sun free) is a grandiose construction built in 1908 to imitate the Louvre in Paris. The European collection includes Boudin, Tournay and Franz Post amongst many others, but it's the **Brazilian collection** that is of most interest. Organized in chronological order, each room shows the various stages in the development of Brazilian painting as a result of the influences imported from Europe: the years of diversification (1919–28); the movement into modernism (1921–49); and the consolidation of modern forms between 1928 and 1967, especially in the works of Cândido Portinari, Djanira and Francisco Rebolo.

The last building of note on the Praça Floriano is the **Biblioteca Nacional** (Mon–Fri 9am–8pm, Sat 9am–3pm), whose stairway was decoratively painted by some of the most important artistic names of the nineteenth century, including Modesto Brocas, Eliseu Visconti, Rodolfo Amoedo and Henrique

Bernadelli. If you speak Portuguese and want to use the library, the staff are very obliging.

Lapa

Continuing south from Cinelândia, Avenida Rio Branco passes Praça Mahatma Gandhi, which borders the **Passeio Público** park (daily 7.30am–9pm), well into Lapa *bairro*. A little past its best, and neglected by the authorities these days, the park is, nevertheless, a green oasis away from the hustle and bustle of the city. Opened in 1783, it was designed in part by Mestre Valentim, Brazil's most important late eighteenth-century sculptor, its trees providing shade for busts commemorating famous figures from the city's history, including Mestre Valentim de Fonseca e Silva himself. One of the most recent busts to be placed in the park is that of Chiquinho Gonzaga, who wrote the first recorded samba for Carnaval – *Pelo Telefone*. Sunday morning is a good time to wander through the Passeio Público, when a stamp and coin **market** is held inside the park.

Those with an interest in musicology will appreciate the **Museu Instrumental Delgado de Carvalho** (Mon–Fri 8am–5pm), at Rua do Passeio 98, just inside the entrance to the Federal University's School of Music. The collection, initially organized by the composer Delgado de Carvalho in 1901, contains musical instruments from various parts of the world, combined with a more interesting selection of indigenous exhibits.

The rest of **Lapa** has much the same faded charm as the park, attractive enough to merit exploring – though it would be wise not to wander the streets unaccompanied at night. It's an old *bairro*; Brasil Gerson, writing in his *História das ruas do Rio de Janeiro*, noted that it was traditionally known as an "area of 'cabarets' and bawdy houses, the haunt of scoundrels, of gamblers, swashbucklers and inverteds and the 'trottoir' of poor, fallen women" – evidently a place to rush to, or avoid, depending upon your taste in entertainment. Until the mid-seventeenth century, Lapa was a beach, known as the "Spanish Sands", but development and land reclamation have assisted its slide into shabby grandeur. More recently, things have been looking up for Lapa, and the area has blossomed into one of Rio's liveliest spots for nightlife (see p.122).

From Lapa you can walk down to the Avenida Beira Mar, where the **Monumento Nacional aos Mortos na Segunda Guerra Mundial** (Monument to the Dead of World War II; Tues–Sun 10am–4pm) is a clearly visible landmark. Next to the monument, at the north end of the Parque do Flamengo (see p.103), is the glass and concrete **Museu de Arte Moderna** (Tues–Fri noon–5.30pm, Sat & Sun noon–6.30pm; $2.50; ☎21/2240-4944, ⓦwww.mamrio.com.br), designed by the Brazilian architect and urbanist Afonso Reidy, and inaugurated in 1958. The museum's collection was devastated by a fire in 1978 and only reopened in 1990 following the building's restoration. The permanent collection is still small and of little artistic significance, but the museum hosts visiting exhibitions that are occasionally worth checking out.

Northeast to the Museu Histórico Nacional

Heading northeast from the Passeio Público, along Rua Santa Luzia, you pass the **Igreja de Santa Luzia** in the Praça da Academia, an attractive eighteenth-century church whose predecessor stood on the seashore – hard to believe today, as it's overwhelmed by the surrounding office buildings. On December

13 each year, devotees enter the "room of miracles" at the back of the church and bathe their eyes in water from the white marble font – reputedly a miraculous cure for eye defects.

Rua Santa Luzia intersects with the busy Avenida Presidente Antônio Carlos, on which you'll find the imposing **Fazenda Federal**, the Federal Treasury. Directly across the road from here, the **Santa Casa de Misericórdia**, a large colonial structure dating from 1582, was built by the Sisterhood of Misericordia, a nursing order dedicated to caring for the sick and providing asylum to orphans and invalids. It was here in 1849 that, for the first time in Rio, a case of yellow fever was diagnosed, and from 1856 to 1916 the building was used as the University's Faculty of Medicine. The Santa Casa is not open to the public, but you can visit the attached church, the **Igreja de Nossa Senhora de Bonsucesso** (Mon–Fri 9am–5pm), which contains finely detailed altars, a collection of Bohemian crystal and an eighteenth-century organ.

Close by, in Praça Rui Barbosa, is the **Museu do Imagem e Som** (Mon–Fri 1–6pm), which explains Rio's social history using records, tape recordings, books and film. There's also a fascinating photographic collection (numbering some 10,000 prints, though inevitably only a fraction are displayed), documenting the city's life from the turn of the nineteenth century until the 1940s.

Museu Histórico Nacional

The nearby **Museu Histórico Nacional** (Tues–Fri 10am–5.30pm, Sat & Sun 2–6pm; $1.50 – free Sun; ℡21/2550-9255, ⓦ www.museuhistoriconacional .com.br) is uncomfortably located in the shadow of the Presidente Kubitschek flyover that runs into the Parque do Flamengo. Built in 1762 as an arsenal, it later served as a military prison where escaped slaves were detained. In 1922 the building was converted into an exhibition centre for the centenary celebrations of Brazil's independence from Portugal, and it has remained a museum ever since.

The large **collection** contains some pieces of great value – from furniture to nineteenth-century firearms and locomotives – but it's not very well organized. Nevertheless, the displays on the second floor, a documentation of Brazilian history since 1500, make this museum a must. Artefacts, charts and written explanations trace the country's development from the moment of discovery to the proclamation of the Republic in 1889 – a fascinating insight into the nature of imperial conquest and subsequent colonial society. Clearly demonstrated, for example, is the social structure of sixteenth-century Brazilian society, including the system of *sesmarias*, or royal land grants of enormous dimensions, which provided the basis for the highly unequal system of land tenure that endures today. Through the use of scale models and imaginatively arranged displays, the agrarian and cyclical nature of Brazil's economic history is explained, too, organized around a slave-labour plantation system that produced – at different times – sugar cane, cattle and cotton, rubber and coffee. The story continues into the eighteenth and nineteenth centuries, following the impact of the English industrial revolution, the spread of new ideas following the French Revolution and the transition from slavery to free labour. More recent twentieth-century developments are taken up by the Museu da República (see p.101).

Santa Teresa and the Corcovado

Before you hit the beaches of the Zona Sul, two of the most pleasant city excursions are to *bairros* to the southwest of Centro. **Santa Teresa** offers an excellent respite from the steamy hubbub of Rio's main thoroughfares, while visiting Rio without making the tourist pilgrimage up the **Corcovado** is unthinkable.

Santa Teresa

Santa Teresa, a leafy *bairro* of labyrinthine, cobbled streets and steps (*ladeiras*), and with stupendous vistas of the city and bay below, makes a refreshing contrast to the city centre. Although it clings to the side of a hill, Santa Teresa is no *favela*: it's a slightly dishevelled residential area dominated by the early nineteenth-century mansions and walled gardens of a prosperous community that still enjoys something of a Bohemian reputation. The attractions are enhanced by an absence of the kind of development that is turning the rest of Rio into a cracked, concrete nightmare. There is not a great deal of traffic on the roads up here, which are dominated instead by ageing trams (*bondes*) hauling their human load up and down the hill – a bone-rattling trip that's highly recommended.

In recent years, the *bairro* has developed into an important artistic centre, with many artists choosing to live and work here. Twice a year (the last weekend in May and November), about a hundred artists open their studios, offering the public an opportunity to buy or simply to look. For details of the participating artists, consult the organizer's Web site: Ⓦ www.vivasanta.com.br. At other times, the best place to see the work of local artists is at La Vereda, an excellent arts and crafts shop in the centre of Santa Teresa at Largo dos Guimarães.

Trams run up to Santa Teresa from Centro, from the terminal behind the massive Petrobrás building, instantly recognisable for being one of the most hideous buildings in Rio. The trams take you across the mid-eighteenth-century **Arcos da Lapa**, a monumental Roman-style aqueduct, high over Lapa, and past the **Carmelite Convento de Santa Teresa**, which marks the spot where a French force was defeated by the city's inhabitants in 1710. As you climb, the panoramic view of Guanabara Bay drifts in and out of view between the trees that line the streets. On your right, you'll pass the **Bar do Arnaudo**, a traditional meeting place of artists and intellectuals (see p.116); when the tram reaches the terminus at the top, you can stay on (and pay again) to descend the bar for something to eat. Moments from here, at Largo dos Guimarães, is the **Museu do Bonde** (daily 9am–4pm), interesting even if you're not especially interested in transport. The small and attractively displayed collection includes an old tram, photo displays and memorabilia documenting the history of trams in Rio from their nineteenth-century introduction, a means of public transport that enabled the city to expand so rapidly along the coast.

From the museum, it's an easy and enjoyable, ten-minute walk downhill to the **Museu Chácara do Céu** (daily, except Tues, noon–5pm) at Rua Murtinho Nobre 93, in a modernist stone building set in its own grounds. One of Rio's better museums, it holds a good eclectic collection including Picasso, Matisse and Dalí, as well as Cândido Portinari and Emiliano Di Cavalcanti. In the upper hall, two screens depict the life of Krishna and there are twin seventh-century iron-sculptured horses from the Imperial Palace in Beijing as well; on the second floor look for artwork by Brazilian painters Heitor dos Prazeres and Djanira.

A pathway links the museum to the **Parque das Ruínas** (Wed–Fri & Sat 10am–10pm, Sun 10am–5pm), an attractive public garden containing the ruins of a mansion that was once home to Laurinda Santos Lobo, a Brazilian heiress around whom artists and intellectuals gathered in the first half of the twentieth century. After her death in 1946, the mansion was allowed to fall into disrepair, but in the 1990s it was partially renovated as a cultural centre, and today houses art exhibitions. There's also a pleasant café and a small stage where jazz concerts are held most Thursday evenings.

The Corcovado

The most famous of all images of Rio de Janeiro is that of the vast statue of Christ the Redeemer (Cristo Redentor) gazing across the bay from the **Corcovado** (hunchback) hill, arms outstretched in welcome, or as if preparing for a dive into the waters below. The **statue** (daily 9am–7pm), 30m high and weighing over 1000 metric tons, was scheduled to be completed in 1922 as part of Brazil's centenary independence celebrations. In fact, this Art Deco symbol of Rio wasn't finished until 1931. The French sculptor Paul Landowski was responsible for the head and hands, with the rest erected by the engineers Heitor Silva Costa and Pedro Viana.

In clear weather, fear no anticlimax: climbing to the statue is a stunning experience by day, and nothing short of miraculous at night. In daylight the whole of Rio and Guanabara Bay is laid out before you; after dark the floodlit statue can be seen from everywhere in the Zona Sul, seemingly suspended in the darkness that surrounds it, and often shrouded in eerie cloud. Up on the platform at the base of the statue the effect of the clouds, driven by warm air currents, and the thousands of tiny winged insects clustering round the spotlights, help give the impression that the statue is careering through space out into the blackness that lies beyond the arc of the lights – dramatic, and not a little hypnotic.

The **view** from the statue of Christ the Redeemer can be very helpful for **orientation** if you've just arrived in Rio. On a clear day, you can see as far as the outlying districts of the Zona Norte, while on the south side of the viewing platform you're directly over the Lagoa Rodrigo de Freitas, with Ipanema on the left, Leblon on the right; on the near side of the lake, Rua São Clemente is clearly visible, curving its way through Botafogo, towards the Jardim Botânico and the racecourse; and on your left, the small *bairro* of Lagoa can be seen tucked in beneath the Morro dos Cabritos, on the other side of which is Copacabana.

It is, of course, a thoroughly exploited tourist experience. There are the usual facilities for eating, drinking and buying souvenirs. On the walk up to the statue, someone will probably take your photograph clandestinely and, when you descend, a saucer, complete with your photograph superimposed on it, will be thrust before you – if you don't want the saucer, no one is going to twist your arm though.

Back down at the bottom, if you have the time and inclination, a five-minute walk uphill from the cog-train station on Rua Cosme Velho will take you to the **Museu Internacional de Arte Naïf** (Tues–Fri 10am–6pm, Sat & Sun, public holidays noon–6pm; $2.50; ☎21/2205-8612, ⓦwww.museunaif .com.br), which boasts the world's largest naive art collection. Although most of the work displayed is by Brazilian artists, the museum features paintings from throughout the world, with work from Haiti, the former Yugoslavia, France and Italy especially well presented. Across the road, a short distance further uphill, you'll reach the much-photographed **Largo do Boticário**, named after the nineteenth-century apothecary to the royal family, Joaquim Luiz da Silva

Santo, who lived here. With its pebbled streets and fountain set in the small courtyard, this is a particularly picturesque little corner of Rio. However, as old as the Largo might appear to be, the original mid-nineteenth-century houses were demolished in the 1920s and replaced by neocolonial style homes, some with fronts decorated with *azulejos*.

Getting to the Corcovado

All major hotels organize **excursions** to the Corcovado. Alternatively, the easiest way to get there by yourself is to take a **taxi** – about $7 from the Zona Sul, a little more from Centro. **Buses** run to the *bairro* of Cosme Velho – take the #422 or #497 from Largo do Machado, the #583 from Leblon or the #584 from Copacabana – and stop at the **Estação Cosme Velho**, at Rua Cosme Velho 513. From there you take a cog-train (every 30min between 9am & 6pm; $8 return), a twenty-minute ride to the top, where only 220 steps remain between you and the viewing platform. You can also **drive** up to a car park near the top if you wish, but if you want to **walk** go in a group, as reports of assaults and robberies are becoming ever more frequent. However you choose to get there, keep an eye on the weather before setting out: what ought to be one of Rio's highlights can turn into a great disappointment if the Corcovado is shrouded in cloud.

Zona Norte

The parts of the **Zona Norte** you'll have seen on the way in from the transport terminals aren't very enticing, and they're a fair reflection of the general tenor of northern Rio. But there are a couple of places well worth making the effort to come back out of the centre for – especially the **Museu Nacional** in the Quinta da Boa Vista, west of the city centre, which you reach by metrô (get off at Estação São Cristovão) or by bus #472, #474 or #475 from Copacabana or Flamengo, or #262 from Praça Mauá.

The Quinta da Boa Vista

The area covered by the **Quinta da Boa Vista** (daily 7am–6pm) was once incorporated in a *sesmaria* held by the Society of Jesus in the sixteenth and seventeenth centuries. The Jesuits used the area as a sugar plantation, though it later became the *chácara* (country seat) of the royal family when the Portuguese merchant Elias Antônio Lopes presented the Palácio de São Cristovão (today the Museu Nacional) and surrounding lands to Dom João VI in 1808. The park, with its wide open expanses of greenery, tree-lined avenues, lakes, sports areas and games tables, is an excellent place for a stroll, best during the week as weekends can get very crowded. You may as well make a day of it and see all the sights once you're here.

The Museu Nacional

In the centre of the park, on a small hill, stands the imposing Neoclassical structure of the **Museu Nacional** (Tues–Sun 10am–4pm; ☎21/2568-8262, @acd.ufrj.br/museu), the oldest scientific institution in Brazil and certainly one of the most important, containing extensive archeological, zoological and botanic collections, an excellent ethnological section and a good display of artefacts dating from classical antiquity – altogether, an estimated one million pieces exhibited in 22 rooms.

The **archeological** section deals with the human history of Latin America, displaying Peruvian ceramics, the craftsmanship of the ancient Aztec, Mayan and Toltec civilizations of Mexico, and mummies excavated in the Chiu–Chiu region of Chile. In the Brazilian room, exhibits of Tupi–Guarani and Marajó ceramics lead on to the indigenous **ethnographical** section, uniting pieces collected from the numerous tribes that once populated Brazil. The genocidal policies of Brazil's European settlers, together with the ravages of disease, reduced the indigenous population from an estimated six million in 1500 to the present-day total of less than two hundred thousand. The **ethnology** section has a room dedicated to Brazilian folklore, centred around an exhibition of the ancient Afro- and Indo-Brazilian cults that still play an important role in modern Brazilian society – *macumba, candomblé* and *umbanda*.

On a different tack, the mineral collection's star exhibit is the **Bendigo Meteorite**, which fell to earth in 1888 (for sign-seekers, the year slavery was abolished) in the state of Bahia. Its original weight of 5360kg makes it the heaviest metallic mass known to have fallen through the Earth's atmosphere. And beyond the rich native finds you'll also come across Etruscan pottery, Greco-Roman ceramics, Egyptian sarcophagi and prehistoric remains – all in all, a good half-day's worth of exploring.

Museu da Fauna, Jardim Zoólogico and the Feira do Nordeste

Also in the Quinta da Boa Vista is the **Museu da Fauna** (Tues–Sun 9am–4.30pm), which has organized a collection of stuffed birds, mammals and reptiles from throughout Brazil, worth a look on the way to the **Jardim Zoólogico** (Tues–Sun 9am–4.30pm; $2; ℡21/2569-2024, Ⓦwww.rio .rj.gov.br/riozoo), close by. What was once a run-down and dirty zoo has been transformed in recent years – the animals look happier and the grounds are now kept scrupulously clean by zealous functionaries – but it's still basically an old-fashioned place where animals are kept in small cages.

The **Feira do Nordeste**, held every Sunday (6am–1pm) in the Campo de São Cristovão, close to the Quinta da Boa Vista, is probably the best of Rio's regular **outdoor markets**. A replica of the great Northeastern markets, with stalls run by people in traditional costume, there are typical handicrafts, food, caged birds and tropical fish – while music from the parched Northeastern backlands fills the air. Best buys are beautifully worked hammocks, leather bags and hats, folk medicines and spices. For the best selection go as early as you can, on any bus marked "São Cristovão" – #469 from Leblon, #461 from Ipanema, #462 or #463 from Copacabana.

Maracanã Stadium

To the west of Quinta da Boa Vista, a short walk across the rail line, over the Viaduto São Cristovão, stands the **Maracanã Stadium**, more formally known as the Mario Filho Stadium. Built in 1950 for the World Cup, it's the biggest stadium of its kind in the world, holding nearly 200,000 people – in the final match of the 1950 tournament, 199,854 spectators turned up here to watch Brazil lose to Uruguay (see p.49). Well over 100,000 fans attend local derbies, like the Flamengo v Fluminense fixture, and during November and December games are played here three times a week, as many of Rio's teams have followings that exceed the capacity of their own stadiums; kick-off is at 5pm.

Attending a **game** is one of the most extraordinary experiences Rio has to offer, even if you don't like football, and it's worth going for the theatrical spectacle. The stadium looks like a futuristic colosseum, its upper stand (the *arquibancadas*) rising almost vertically from the playing surface. Great silken banners wave across the stand, shrouded by the smoke from fireworks, while support for each team is proclaimed by the insistent rhythm of massed samba drums that drive the game along. *Carioca* supporters are animated to say the least, often near-hysterical, but their love of the game is infectious.

The Maracanã is open for **guided tours**, too (Mon–Fri 9am–5pm; reservations advised; ☎21/242-8806). You'll be shown through an interesting **sports museum** and get to see the view from the presidential box (reached by lift), wander through the changing rooms and have a chance to tread on the hallowed turf itself.

Getting there and seeing a game

The Maracanã is an easy and inexpensive destination to reach by **taxi**, but if you come by **metrô** (line 2) get off at the Maracanã station and walk southeast, along Avenida Osvaldo Aranha. By **bus**, catch the #464 from Leblon (Ataúlfo Paiva) via Ipanema (on Visconde de Pirajá), Copacabana (Av. N.S. de Copacabana) and Flamengo (Praia do Flamengo).

The stadium's **entrance** is on Rua Prof Eurico Rabelo, Gate 18. Arrive in plenty of time (at least a couple of hours before kick-off for big games) and buy your entrance card at any of the **ticket offices** set in the perimeter wall – a ticket for the *gerais* (lower terracing) costs about $4, the *arquibancadas* (all-seated upper terracing) about $6. Then go round to the entrance and pass your card through a machine at the turnstile. Things get frantic around the ticket offices before big games and if you're not there early enough you may get stranded outside, as the kiosk attendants leave their positions as soon as the starting whistle blows so as not to miss an early goal. After the game, it's a bit tedious getting back into town as transport is packed. Be sure to watch your belongings in the thick crowds.

Zona Sul

From Rio's Bay of Guanabara to the Bay of Sepetiba, to the west, there are approximately 90km of sandy **beaches**, including one of the world's most famous – Copacabana. Uniquely, Rio's identity is closely linked to its beaches, which shape the social life of all the city's inhabitants, who use them as a source of recreation and inspiration. For many, the beach provides a source of livelihood, and a sizeable service industry has developed around it, providing for the needs of those who regard the beach as a social environment – as significant, say, as the pub is in England.

Rio de Janeiro's sophisticated **beach culture** is entirely a product of the twentieth century. The 1930s saw Rio's international reputation emerge, as Hollywood started to incorporate images of the city in its productions, and film stars began to grace the Copacabana. Rio was one of the first destinations for the newly established jet set: "flying down to Rio" became an enduring cliché, celebrated in music, film and literature for the last seventy-odd years.

The most renowned of the beaches, **Copacabana**, was originally an isolated area, cut off from the city by mountains until 1892 when the Túnel Velho link with Botafogo was inaugurated. The open sea and strong waves soon attracted beachgoers, though Copacabana remained a quiet, sparsely populated *bairro* until the splendid Neoclassically styled *Copacabana Palace Hotel* opened its doors in 1923, its famous guests publicizing the beach and alerting enterpris-

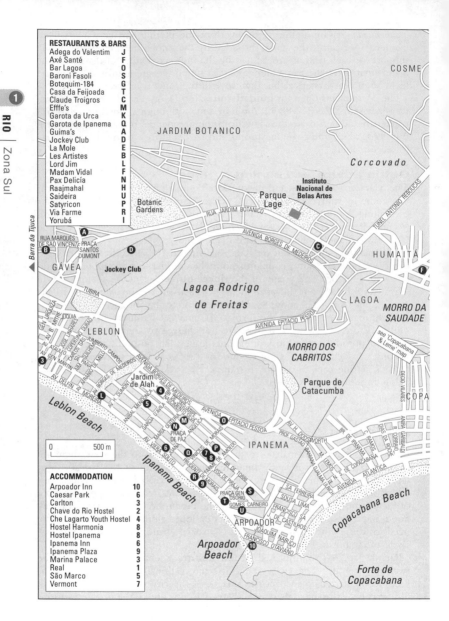

RESTAURANTS & BARS
Adega do Valentim	J
Axé Santé	F
Bar Lagoa	O
Baroni Fasoli	S
Botequim-184	G
Casa da Feijoada	T
Claude Troigros	C
Efffe's	M
Garota da Urca	K
Garota de Ipanema	Q
Guima's	A
Jockey Club	D
La Mole	D
Les Artistes	E
Lord Jim	B
Madam Vidal	L
Pax Delicía	F
Raajmahal	N
Saideira	H
Satyricon	U
Via Farme	P
Yorubá	I

ACCOMMODATION
Arpoador Inn	10
Caesar Park	6
Carlton	3
Chave do Rio Hostel	2
Che Lagarto Youth Hostel	4
Hostel Harmonia	8
Hostel Ipanema	8
Ipanema Inn	6
Ipanema Plaza	9
Marina Palace	3
Real	1
São Marco	5
Vermont	7

ing souls to the commercial potential of the area. Rapid growth followed and a landfill project was undertaken, along which the two-lane **Avenida Atlântica** now runs.

Prior to Copacabana's rise, it was the beaches of **Guanabara Bay** –

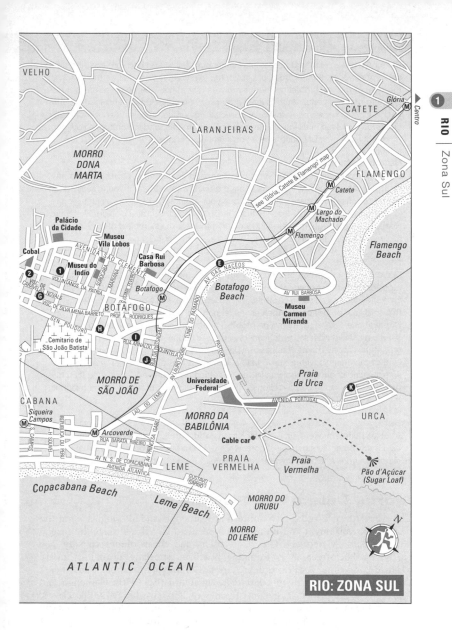

RIO: ZONA SUL

Flamengo, Botafogo, Urca and Vermelha – that were the most sought after. Today, the most fashionable beaches are those of **Ipanema** and **Leblon**, residential areas where the young, wealthy and beautiful have only to cross the road to flaunt their tans.

On the beach

Rio's beaches may attract hordes of tourists but they're first and foremost the preserve of *cariocas*. Rich or poor, old or young, everybody descends on the beaches throughout the week, treating them simply as city parks. The beaches are divided into informal segments, each identified by *postos* (marker posts) assigned a number. In Copacabana and Ipanema in particular, gay men, families, beach sport aficionados and even intellectuals claim specific segments, and it won't take you long to identify a stretch of beach where you'll feel comfortable.

Beach fashion

Looking good is important on Rio's beaches, and you'll come across some pretty snappy seaside threads. Fashions change regularly, though, so if you're really desperate to make your mark you should buy your **swimsuits** in Rio – besides, you're likely to pay considerably less for them in Brazil than in Europe or North America. Keep in mind, though, that although women may wear the skimpiest of bikinis, going topless is completely unacceptable.

Beach sports

Maintaining an even tan and tight musculature is still the principal occupation for most of Rio's beachgoers. Joggers swarm up and down the pavements, bronzed types flex their muscles on parallel bars located at intervals along the beaches, while the tradition of **beach football** is as strong as legend would have it on the Copacabana – certainly, there's no problem getting a game, though playing on loose sand amidst highly skilled practitioners of Brazil's national sport has the potential for great humiliation. There's lots of volleyball, too, as well as the ubiquitous **batball**, a kind of table tennis with a heavy ball, and without the table. It's extremely popular with the kind of people who wait till you've settled down on your towel, and then run past spraying sand in all directions – taking an electric cattle-prod to the beach is the only way to keep them off.

Eating

A lot of people make their living by plying **food** – fruit, sweets, ice cream – and beach equipment along the seashore, while dotted along the beaches are makeshift canopies, from which you can buy cold drinks. Like bars, most of these have a reg-

Glória, Catete and Flamengo

The nearest beach to the city centre is at Flamengo, and although it's not the best in Rio you might end up using it more than you think, since the neighbouring *bairros*, Catete and Glória, are useful and cheap **places to stay** (see pp.78–79). The streets away from the beach – especially around Largo do Machado and along Rua do Catete – are full of inexpensive hotels, and there's a pleasant atmosphere to this part of town. Until the 1950s, Flamengo and Catete were the principal residential zones of Rio's wealthier middle classes, and although the mantle has now passed to Ipanema and Leblon the *bairros* still have a relaxed appeal. Busy during the day, the tree-lined streets come alive at night with residents eating in the local restaurants; and though the nightlife is nothing special, it's tranquil enough to encourage sitting out on the pavement at the bars, beneath the palm trees and apartment buildings.

Glória

Across from the **Glória** *metrô* station, on top of the Morro da Glória, stands the eighteenth-century **Igreja de Nossa Senhora da Glória do Outeiro**

ular clientele and deliver a very efficient service – remember to return your bottle when you've finished. Coconut milk, *côco verde*, is sold everywhere, and is a brilliant hangover cure. You don't need to be wary of the edibles either: if the traders were to start poisoning their customers, they'd soon lose their hard-won trading space on the beach and their livelihood.

Staying safe

Many of the beaches are **dangerous**. The seabed falls sharply away, the waves are strong, and currents can pull you down the beach. Mark your spot well before entering the water, or you'll find youself emerging from a paddle twenty or thirty metres from where you started – which, when the beaches are packed at weekends, can cause considerable problems when it comes to relocating your towel and coconut oil. Copacabana is particularly dangerous, even for strong swimmers. However, the beaches are well served by **lifeguards**, whose posts are marked by a white flag with a red cross; a **red flag** indicates that bathing is prohibited. Constant surveillance of the beachfronts from helicopters and support boats means that, if you do get into trouble, help should arrive quickly.

Pollution is another problem to bear in mind. Although much has been done in recent years to clean up Guanabara Bay, it is still not safe to swim in the water from Flamengo or Botafogo beaches. While usually the water beyond the bay at Copacabana and Ipanema is clean, there are times when it and the beaches themselves aren't, especially following a prolonged period of heavy summer rain when the city's strained drainage system over-flows and deposits raw sewage on the city streets, which often later ends up on the beaches. Unfortunately, these periods are increasingly common – if you've chosen Rio essentially as a beach vacation, you may well be in for a major disappointment.

Natural dangers aside, the beaches hold other unwelcome surprises. Giving your passport, money and **valuables** the chance of a sun tan, rather than leaving them in the hotel safe, is madness. Take only the clothes and money that you'll need; it's quite acceptable to use public transport while dressed for the beach. Don't be caught out either by the young lad who approaches you from one side, distracting your attention with some request, while his mate approaches from the other side and whips your bag: it's the most common and efficient method of relieving you of things you shouldn't have brought with you in the first place.

(Tues–Fri 9am–noon & 1–5pm, Sat & Sun 9am–noon), notable for its innovative octagonal ground plan and domed roof, the latter decked with excellent seventeenth-century blue-and-white *azulejos* tiles and nineteenth-century marble masonry. Painstakingly renovated, the church, quite simply the prettiest in Rio, is an absolute gem, easily worth a quick detour, and behind it you'll find the **Museu da Imperial Irmandade de Nossa Senhora da Glória** (Mon–Fri 8am–noon & 1–4pm, Sat & Sun 8am–noon), which has a small collection of religious relics, *ex votos* and the personal possessions of Empress Tereza Cristina.

Catete

On the Rua do Catete, adjacent to the **Catete** *metrô* station, stands the Palácio do Catete, home to the **Museu da República** (Tues–Fri noon–5pm, Sat & Sun 2–6pm; ☎21/2558-6350 ⓦwww.museudarepublica.org.br; $1.50 – free Wed). The palace was used as the presidential residence from 1897 until 1960, and it was here, in 1954, that Getúlio Vargas turned his gun on himself and took his own life, believing he had been betrayed. The building was built in the mid-

1800s as the Rio home of the Barão de Nova Friburgo, a wealthy coffee *fazenda* owner. As a historical museum, the *palácio* continues where the Museu Histórico Nacional (see p.92) leaves off, with the establishment of the first Republic in 1888. The collection features both period furnishings and presidential memorabilia, though it's the opulent marble and stained glass of the building itself that make a visit so worthwhile. The grounds include a new

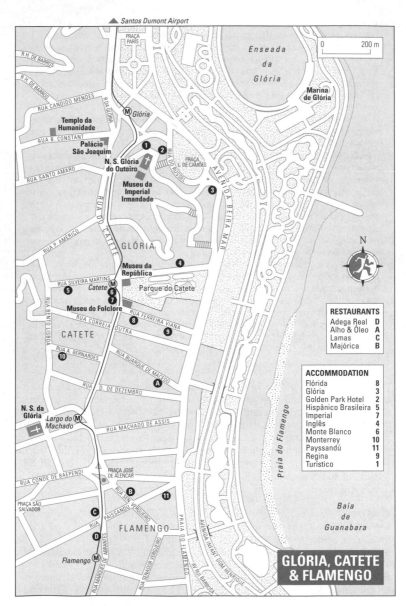

RESTAURANTS

Adega Real D
Alho & Óleo A
Lamas C
Majórica B

ACCOMMODATION

Flórida 8
Glória 3
Golden Park Hotel 2
Hispânico Brasileira 5
Imperial 7
Inglês 4
Monte Blanco 6
Monterrey 10
Payssandú 11
Regina 9
Turístico 1

GLÓRIA, CATETE & FLAMENGO

exhibition space, theatre and art gallery, which means there is often something happening here at night – the floodlit gardens make it a magical venue. The restaurant, in a glassed-in turn-of-the-century terrace overlooking the gardens, is only open at lunchtime and boasts one of the best salad buffets in Rio.

Divided between two buildings, one inside the palace grounds and the other in an adjacent house, is the **Museu de Folclore Edison Cruz** (Tues–Fri 11am–6pm, Sat & Sun 3–6pm), a fascinating folkloric collection that unites pieces from all over Brazil – leatherwork, musical instruments, ceramics, toys, Afro-Brazilian cult paraphernalia, photographs and *ex votos*. Behind the palace lies the **Parque do Catete** (daily 9am–6pm), whose birdlife, towering palms and calm walks are good for a quick break. It's a nice place to take small children as it has a pond with ducks and other waterfowl, a playground and tricycles and other toys.

Flamengo

If you follow Avenida Beira Mar away from Centro you enter the **Parque do Flamengo**, the biggest land reclamation project in Brazil, designed by the great Brazilian landscape architect and gardener, Roberto Burle Marx, and completed in 1960. Sweeping round as far as Botafogo Bay, it comprises 1.2 square kilometres of prime seafront. You'll pass through the park many times by bus as you travel between Centro and the beach zone, and it's popular with local residents who use it mostly for sports – there are countless tennis courts (open 9am–11pm) and football pitches.

The **beach** at Flamengo runs along the park for about a kilometre and offers excellent views across the bay to Niterói. Unfortunately, it's not a place for swimming as the water here is polluted. Instead, you might want to take a look at the quirky **Museu Carmen Miranda** (Tues–Fri 11am–5pm; $1.50), located in front of Av. Rui Barbosa 560, at the southern end of the park. Born in Portugal, the star made it big in Hollywood in the 1940s and became the patron saint of Rio's Carnaval transvestites. The museum contains a wonderful collection of kitsch memorabilia, as well as some of the star's costumes and personal possessions, including fruit-laden hats and posters.

Botafogo

Botafogo curves around the 800m between Flamengo and Rio's yacht club. The name derives, reputedly, from the first white Portuguese settler who lived in the area, one João Pereira de Souza Botafogo. The bay is dominated by the yachts and boats moored near the club, and again the beach doesn't have much to recommend it to bathers due to the pollution of the bay. However, there's plenty to see in the *bairro* itself.

Museu Casa de Rui Barbosa

From the Botafogo *metrô* station, walk away from the ocean along Avenida São Clemente, to reach the **Museu Casa de Rui Barbosa** at no. 134 (Tues–Fri 9am–4pm, Sat & Sun 2–5pm; ☎21/3537-0036, ⓦwww.casaruibarbosa.gov .br), set amidst the lush bowers of a garden with well-kept paths and borders. Built in 1849, it became the home of Rui Barbosa, jurist, statesman and author, in 1893, for whom the federal government established a museum here after his death. Born in Bahia state, Barbosa (1849–1923) graduated as a lawyer in São Paulo and, later, working as a journalist and critic of the monarchy, founded the newspaper *A Imprensa*. He became senator of Bahia and in 1905, and again in 1909, made unsuccessful attempts to be elected as the country's president. A liberal, he made an excellent opposition politician, earning himself exile between 1893 and 1895, years he spent in Argentina and England.

The museum is basically a collection of his possessions – beautiful Dutch and English furniture, Chinese and Japanese porcelain (including the first plumbed bathroom in Rio), and a library of 35,000 volumes, amongst which are two hundred works penned by Barbosa himself. Barbosa conferred a title on each room in the house – the Sala Bahia, Sala Questão Religiosa, Sala Habeas Corpus, Sala Código Civil – all of them identified with some part of his life.

Museu Villa-Lobos and Museu do Índio

On Rua Sorocaba, a turning off Avenida São Clemente, is the **Museu Villa-Lobos** at no. 200 (Mon–Fri 10am–5.30pm; ☎21/2266-3894, ⓦwww .museuvillalobos.org.br). Established in 1960 to celebrate the work of the Brazilian composer, Heitor Villa-Lobos (1887–1959), it's again largely a display of his personal possessions and original music scores, but you can also buy tapes and records of his music here.

Botafogo's other museum, the **Museu do Índio** (Tues–Fri 10am–5pm, Sat & Sun 1–5pm; ☎21/2286-8899, ⓦwww.museudoindio.org.br), lies in the next street along, at Rua das Palmeiras 55. Housed in a nineteenth-century mansion, the museum was inaugurated on April 19, 1953, the commemoration of Brazil's "Day of the Indian" – not that there were many around by then to celebrate. It's a broad and interesting collection, including utensils, musical instruments, tribal costumes and ritual devices from many of Brazil's dwindling indigenous peoples. Perhaps most interesting of all are the full-size shelters of the Guaraní (from Angra dos Reis), Wajãpi (from Amapá) and Kuikuro (from Mato Grosso's Xingú) peoples that have been erected in the museum's grounds. There's a good photographic exhibition, too, and an accessible anthropological explanation of the rituals and institutions of some of the tribes. The attached shop is excellent, selling a quality range of carefully sourced original artefacts at reasonable prices. The ethnographical section of the Museu HistóricoNacional (see p.92) probably provides you with more information, but this museum offers much of interest.

Urca and the Sugar Loaf

The best bet for swimming this close to the centre is around **Urca**. There are small beaches on each side of the promontory on which this wealthy *bairro* stands, its name an acronym of the company that undertook its construction – Urbanizador Construção. Facing Botafogo, the **Praia da Urca**, only 100m long, is frequented almost exclusively by the small *bairro*'s inhabitants, while in front of the cable car station (see below), beneath the Sugar Loaf mountain, **Praia Vermelha** is a cove sheltered from the South Atlantic, whose relatively gentle waters are popular with swimmers.

You should come to Urca at least once during your stay, anyway, to go to the **Pão de Açúcar**, which rises where Guanabara Bay meets the Atlantic Ocean. In Portuguese the name means "**Sugar Loaf**", referring to the ceramic or metal mould used during the refining of sugar cane. Liquid sugar cane juice was poured into the mould and removed when the sugar had set, producing a shape reminiscent of the mountain. The name may also come from the native Tamoyan Indian word *Pau-nh-Açuquá*, meaning "high, pointed or isolated hill" – a more apt description. The first recorded non-indigenous ascent to the summit was made in 1817 by an English nanny, Henrietta Carstairs. Today, mountaineers are a common sight scaling the smooth, precipitous slopes, but there is a cable car ride to the summit for the less adventurous.

The **cable car** system has been in place since 1912; sixty years later the present Italian system, which can carry 1360 passengers every hour, was installed (daily 8am–10pm, every 30min; $8). The base station is in Praça General Tibúrcio, which can be reached by buses marked "Urca" or "Praia Vermelha" from Centro, #107 from Centro, Catete and Flamengo, or #511 and #512 from Zona Sul (returning to Copacabana takes 1hr 30min as the bus first passes through Botafogo, Leblon and Ipanema). The 1400-metre journey is made in two stages, first to the summit of **Morro da Urca** (215m), where there is a theatre, restaurant and shops, and then on to the top of Pão de Açúcar itself (394m). The cable cars have glass walls and the view from the top is as glorious as you could wish. Facing inland, you can see right over the city, from Centro and the Santos Dumont airport all the way through Flamengo and Botafogo; face Praia Vermelha and the cable car terminal, and to the left you'll see the sweep of Copacabana and on into Ipanema, while back from the coast the mountains around which Rio was built rise to the Tijuca National Park. Try and avoid the busy times between 10am and 3pm: it's best of all at sunset on a clear day, when the lights of the city are starting to twinkle. Leading down from the summit are a series of wooded trails along which you'll encounter curious small marmosets, and it's easy – and safe – to get away from the crowds.

On the Morro da Urca, the Beija Flor **samba school** performs every Monday at 10pm (see p.128). This hill is also the location of the expensive Carnaval ball (see p.120).

Leme and Copacabana

Leme and **Copacabana** are different stretches of the same four-kilometre beach. Avoid walking through the Túnel Novo that links Botafogo with Leme as it's a favourite place for tourists to be relieved of their wallets. The **Praia do Leme** extends for a kilometre, between the Morro do Leme and Avenida Princesa Isabel, by the *Meridien Hotel*. From there, the **Praia de Copacabana** runs for a further 3km to the Forte de Copacabana. The fort (Tues–Sun 10am–4pm), built to protect the entrance to Guanabará Bay, is open to the public and well worth visiting for the impressive views towards Copacabana, rather than for the military hardware on display in the **Museu Histórico do Exército**; there's an outdoor café here, too, popular with tourists and elderly officers' wives, which serves light meals, cakes and cold drinks.

Leme beach is slightly less packed than Copacabana and tends to attract families. Bear in mind that the *Meridien* maintains a hawkish security watch on the part of the beach nearest the hotel, so it's a good place to park your towel.

Copacabana is amazing, the over-the-top atmosphere apparent even in the mosaic pavements, designed by Burle Marx to represent images of rolling waves. The seafront is backed by a line of prestigious, high-rise hotels and luxury apartments that have sprung up since the 1940s, while a steady stream of noisy traffic patrols the two-lane **Avenida Atlântica**. Scattered around the *bairro* are some fine examples of Art Deco architecture, none more impressive than the *Copacabana Palace Hotel* on Avenida Atlântica, built in 1923 and considered one of Rio's best hotels. Families, friends and couples cover the palm-fringed sand – at weekends it's no easy matter to find space – the bars and restaurants along the avenue pulsate, while the busy **Avenida Nossa Senhora de Copacabana** is lined with assorted stores, which – like the *bairro* in general – are in a gradual state of decline, being pushed aside by the boutiques of trendy Ipanema and the shopping malls of the Zona Sul.

Copacabana is dominated to the east by the Pão de Açúcar and circled by a line of hills that stretch out into the bay. A popular residential area, the *bairro*'s

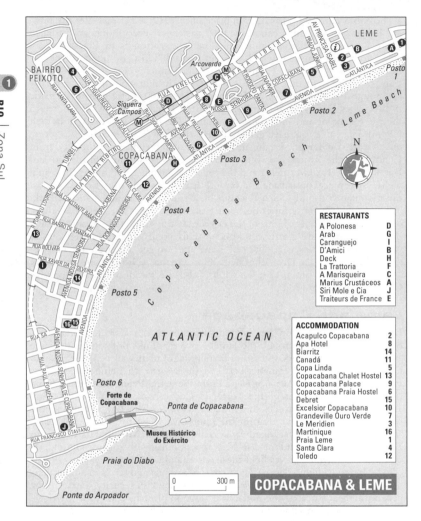

RESTAURANTS

A Polonesa	D
Arab	G
Caranguejo	I
D'Amici	B
Deck	H
La Trattoria	F
A Marisqueira	C
Marius Crustáceos	A
Siri Mole e Cia	J
Traiteurs de France	E

ACCOMMODATION

Acapulco Copacabana	2
Apa Hotel	8
Biarritz	14
Canadá	11
Copa Linda	5
Copacabana Chalet Hostel	13
Copacabana Palace	9
Copacabana Praia Hostel	6
Debret	15
Excelsior Copacabana	10
Grandeville Ouro Verde	7
Le Meridien	3
Martinique	16
Praia Leme	1
Santa Clara	4
Toledo	12

COPACABANA & LEME

expansion has been restricted by the Morro de São João, which separates it from Botafogo, and the Morro dos Cabritos, which forms a natural barrier to the west. Consequently, it's one of the world's most densely populated areas, and a frenzy of sensual activity, most of which takes place in a thoroughly impressive setting. Some say that Copacabana is past its best and certainly it's not as exclusive as it once was. You'll be frequently accosted by a stream of the dispossessed young and old – who want money, or the scraps off your plate, while the street traders work into the night, selling T-shirts, lace tablecloths and plastic Rio car numberplates. It's still an enjoyable place to sit and watch the world go by, though, and at night on the floodlit beach football is played into the early hours.

Of course Copacabana hasn't always been as it is today. Traces remain of the former fishing community that dominated the area until the first decades of the twentieth century. Each morning before dawn the boats of the *colônia de pescadores* (the descendents of the fishermen) set sail from the Forte de Copacabana, returning to the beach by 8am to sell their fish across from the *Sofitel* hotel.

Arpoador, Ipanema and Leblon

On the other side of the point from Forte de Copacabana, the lively waters off the **Praia do Arpoador** are popular with families and the elderly as the ocean here is slightly calmer than at Ipanema. From here, as far as the unkempt and balding greenery of the Jardim de Allah, a couple of kilometres away, you're in **Ipanema**; thereafter lies **Leblon**. There are few apartment buildings in either *bairro* that don't have their own pistol-toting guard, eyes alert to anyone who looks out of place in this rich person's hangout. Much calmer than Copacabana, the beaches here are stupendous, though there's not much in the way of bars and restaurants near the beach: in fact, the only bar/restaurant on the front is *Caneco*, at the far end of Leblon, a good spot to aim for anyway as you'll enjoy a fine view towards Ipanema from here. As with Copacabana, Ipanema's beach is unofficially divided according to the supposed interest of the beach users. Thus the stretch of sand east from Rua Farme de Amoedo to Rua Teixeira de Melo is where gay men are concentrated, while *posto 9* is where artists and intellectuals ponder life. On Sunday, the seafront roads – Avenida Vieira Souto in Ipanema, Avenida Delfim Moreira in Leblon – are closed to traffic, and given over to strollers, skateboarders and rollerbladers.

Since the 1960s, Ipanema has developed a reputation as a fashion centre second to none in Latin America. Although this would be disputed by many in São Paulo and Buenos Aires, certainly the *bairro* is packed with *bijou*, little boutiques flogging the very best Brazilian names in fine threads. If you do go shopping here, go on Friday and take in the large **food and flower market** on the Praça de Paz. Prices compare very well to their European or North American equivalents, but visitors are more likely to be able to afford something at the so-called **Feira Hippie**, held between 9am and 6pm on Sunday in Praça General Osório. The variety and quality of the goods – leather, jewellery, cushion covers, hammocks and crocheted tablecloths – here is very poor, and you're more likely to find something interesting that's worth buying at the Babilônia Feira Hype in Gávea (see overleaf).

Lagoa

Back from Ipanema's plush beaches is the Lagoa Rodrigo de Freitas, always referred to simply as Lagoa. A lagoon linked to the ocean by a narrow canal that passes through Ipanema's Jardim de Allah, Lagoa is fringed by apartment buildings where Rio's most seriously rich and status-conscious live. Until recently, the lagoon's water was badly polluted, but a programme to clean it up has been remarkably successful and the lagoon's mangrove swamps are now recovering. The shore surrounding the lagoon forms the Parque Tom Jobim (named in memory of Rio's famed bossa nova composer who died in 1994), and the area comes alive each Sunday as people walk, rollerblade, jog or cycle along the 7.5km perimeter pathway, play or watch baseball, or just watch the passers-by. Summer evenings are especially popular when, on the west side of the lagoon in the area known as the Parque dos Patins (Skaters' Park), there are food stalls, live music and *forró* dancing.

The steep hill slopes behind the apartment buildings are still well forested, and in 1979 a *favela* was cleared away and the **Parque da Catacumba** (daily

7am–6pm) developed in its place on one of the more accessible hills, by the southeast corner of the lagoon on Avenida Epitácio Pessoa. It's a wonderful, shaded place to relax, and the dense tropical vegetation forms an excellent backdrop for one of Brazil's few **sculpture parks**.

Jardim Botânico and Gávea

To the northwest of the Lagoa lies the *bairro* of **Jardim Botânico**, whose **Parque Lage** (daily 9am–5pm), designed by the English landscape gardener John Tyndale, in the early 1840s, consists of half a million square metres of forest, with labyrinthine path network and seven small lakes – just the spot for a little shady relaxation. A little further along the Rua Jardim Botânico at no. 1008 is the **Jardim Botânico** itself (Tues–Sun 8am–5pm; $1.50), half of it natural jungle, half laid out in impressive avenues lined with immense imperial palms that date from the garden's inauguration in 1808. Dom João used the gardens to introduce foreign plants into Brazil – tea, cloves, cinnamon and pineapples among them – and there are now five thousand plant species, amongst which live monkeys, parrots and other assorted wildlife. There are also a number of sculptures to be seen throughout the garden, notably the *Ninfa do Eco* and *Caçador Narciso* (1783) by Mestre Valentim, the first two metal sculptures cast in Brazil.

Gávea and the Jockey Club

On the **Gávea** side of Lagoa lies the **Jockey Club**, also known as the Hipódromo da Gávea, which can be reached on any bus marked "via Jóquei" – get off at Praça Santos Dumont at the end of Rua Jardim Botânico. Racing in Rio dates back to 1825 though the Hipódromo wasn't built until 1926. Today, **races** take place four times a week, every week of the year (Mon 6.30–11.30pm, Fri 4–9.30pm, Sat & Sun 2–8pm), with the international Grande Prêmio Brazil taking place on the first Sunday of August. A night at the races is great fun and foreigners can get into the palatial members' stand for just a few *reais*, but remember, no one in shorts is admitted. It's an entertaining place, especially during the floodlit evening races, when the air is balmy and you can eat or sip a drink as you watch the action. You don't have to bet to enjoy the experience – it's not very easy to understand the betting system they use anyway. On alternate weekends throughout the year, part of the club is taken over by the **Babilônia Feira Hype** (2–11pm; $1.50). You'll find a good selection of clothes, jewellery and handicrafts here, along with plenty of food stalls and live entertainment, and if you stay into the evening you can watch the horses race.

About 3km northwest of the Jockey Club, at Rua Marquês de São Vicente 476, is the **Instituto Moreira Salles** (Tues–Fri 1–8pm, Sat & Sun 1–6pm; ☎21/2512-6448, ⓦwww.ims.com.br), Rio's latest cultural centre and one of its most beautiful. Housed in the former home of the Moreira Salles family (the owners of Unibanco, one of the country's most important banks), the centre is worth a visit just to get a glimpse into the lives of the wealthy. Designed by the Brazilian architect Olavo Redig de Campos and completed in 1951, the house is stunningly beautiful – one of the most refined examples of modernist residential architecture in Brazil – with gardens landscaped by Roberto Burle Marx, who also contributed a tile mural alongside the terrace. Unibanco is a major collector of Brazilian art, and since the cultural centre opened to the public in 1999 it has hosted important exhibitions of nineteenth- and twentieth-century painting and photography. In the house a tearoom serves superb

△ Ipanema Beach, Rio de Janeiro

cakes, unusual ice creams and, at $12, an expensive high tea. It's a good half-hour walk to the Instituto Moreira Salles from the Jockey Club; you can also take bus #170 from Centro (Av. Rio Branco), Botafogo, Humaitá or Jardim Botânico, or #174 from Copacabana, Ipanema or Leblon.

Also in Gávea is the **Parque da Cidade** (daily 8am–5.30pm) and **Museu Histórico da Cidade** (Tues–Fri 1–5pm), at the end of Estrada de Santa Marinha: bus #591, #593 or #594 from Copacabana; #179 or #178 from Centro. The museum is housed within a two-storey nineteenth-century mansion once owned by the Marquês de São Vicente, and the entire collection is related to the history of Rio from its founding until the end of the Old Republic in 1930. The exhibits – paintings, weapons, porcelain, medals and the like – are arranged in chronological order; the first salon deals with the city's foundation, the rest with the colonial period.

The coast west of Leblon

Back on the coast, to the west of Leblon, lies kilometre after kilometre of white sand. **Praia do Vidigal**, tucked under the Morro Dois Irmãos, is only about 500m long, and used to be the preserve of the inhabitants of the **Favela do Vidigal** – one of the biggest shantytowns in Rio – until they lost their beach with the construction of the *Rio Sheraton Hotel*.

West again, the beautiful beach at **São Conrado**, dominated by apartment buildings and high-rise hotels, is becoming ever trendier: frequented by the famous and packed with hang-gliders and surfers at weekends, it's an area where the upper classes flaunt their wealth without shame, though some are uncomfortable with the encroachment of nearby *favelas*. Above São Conrado, on the slopes between the Tijuca mountains and the peak of Pedra dos Dois Irmãos, sits **Favela Roçinha** (see box, p.111) – spuriously picturesque and glistening in the tropical sun. Here, over 160,000 Brazilians live, for whom a salary of around $40 a month is about as much as an entire family can expect. **Bus** #500 from Urca will take you to São Conrado via Avenida Atlântica (Copacabana), Avenida Vieira Souto (Ipanema) and Avenida Delfim Moreira (Leblon).

Hang-gliding above Rio

For a bird's-eye view of Rio's beaches and forest, take off with an experienced pilot on a tandem **hang-glider** flight from the Pedra Bonita ramp on the western edge of the Parque Nacional de Tijuca (see p.112), 520m above the beach at São Conrado. Depending on conditions, flights last between ten and thirty minutes, flying alongside the mountains and over the forest and ocean before landing on the beach at São Conrado.

The most experienced and reliable operator, **Just Fly** (ⓦ www.justfly.com.br), offer flights daily (usually 10am–3pm) when weather permits, and the cost is $80 per person, which includes pick-up and drop-off from your hotel. Flights are cancelled if the chief pilot, Paulo Celani, has the slightest doubt about conditions, whether on safety grounds or because poor conditions generally make for a short, uncomfortable flight.

It's best to make your reservation directly with Just Fly on ☏21/2268-0565 or on mobile ☏21/9985-7540, as your hotel may otherwise make arrangements through another, less reliable, operator. If you're an experienced pilot and want to fly alone, you'll have to bring your own equipment to Rio as hang-gliders are not available to rent locally.

In a low-wage economy, and without even half-decent social services, life is extremely difficult for the majority of Brazilians. During the last thirty years the rural poor have descended on urban centres in search of a livelihood. Unable to find accommodation, or pay rent, they have established shantytowns, or **favelas**, on any available empty space, which in Rio usually means the slopes of the hills around which the city has grown.

They start off as huddles of cardboard boxes and plastic sheeting, and slowly expand and transform as metal sheeting and bricks provide more solid shelters. Clinging to the sides of Rio's hills, and glistening in the sun, they can from a distance appear not unlike a medieval Spanish hamlet, perched secure atop a mountain. It is, however, a spurious beauty. The *favelas* are creations of need, and their inhabitants are engaged in an immense daily struggle for survival, worsened by the prospect of landslides caused by heavy rains, which could tear their dwellings from their tenuous hold on precipitous inclines.

However, life for Rio's *favela* dwellers is beginning to change for the better. Bound together by their shared poverty and exclusion from effective citizenship, the *favelados* display a great resourcefulness and co-operative strength. Self-help initiatives – some of which are based around the *escolas de samba* (see p.126–127) that are mainly *favela*-based – have emerged, and the authorities are finally recognizing the legitimacy of *favelas* by promoting "*favela-bairro*" projects aimed at fully integrating them into city life. Private enterprise, too, is beginning to take an interest as it becomes alert to the fact that the 22 percent of the city's population living in *favelas* represent a vast, untapped market.

Favela tours

Wandering into a *favela* does not, as many middle-class *cariocas* would have you believe, guarantee being robbed or murdered. Law and order is essentially in the hands of highly organized drugs gangs, but it's simply not in their interest to create trouble for visitors as this would only attract the attention of the police who normally stay clear of *favelas*. Alone, you're liable to get lost and, as in any isolated spot, may run into opportunistic thieves, but if accompanied by a *favela* resident you'll be perfectly safe and be received with friendly curiosity. For most people, however, the best option is to take a **tour**, with the most insightful and longest-established run by Marcelo Armstrong. Marcelo, who speaks excellent English, is widely known and respected in the *favelas* that are visited and has made a point of getting community approval. It is strongly advised to make your own arrangements with Marcelo rather than through a travel agent or hotel front desk, where you may end up with an inferior tour and be charged too much. If you're worried about voyeurism, you shouldn't be: residents want outsiders to understand that *favelas* are not in fact terrifying and lawless ghettos, but inhabited by people as decent as anywhere else, eager to improve the local quality of life.

Marcelo's tours usually take in two *favelas*, **Roçinha**, Rio's largest, with over 160,000 inhabitants, and **Vila Canoas**, much smaller, with around 2500 residents. Twice a day (8.30am and 2pm; $25), tourists are picked up from their hotels or pre-arranged spots in the Zona Sul for the two-hour tour, which stops at look-out points, a day-care centre, a bar and other places of interest. Marcelo offers a fascinating commentary, pointing out the achievements of *favelas* and their inhabitants, without seeking to romanticize their lives. To reserve a place on a tour, call Marcelo on ⊤21/3322-2727, mobile 9989-0074 or 9772-1133, or for more information check out the Ⓦ www.favelatour.com.br.

The last area within the city limits is **Barra de Tijuca** where property developers have been building massive apartment buildings and shopping malls at breakneck speed. But the clean waters and white sands that run for over 16km remain popular at weekends with the beach party and barbecue set. You can reach Barra de Tijuca by **bus** from Copacabana (#553), or from Botafogo metrô station (#524).

Sítio Burle Marx

Some 25km along the coast from Barra de Tijuca is the quiet and unremarkable village of Guaratiba. The countryside around the village is popular amongst *cariocas* seeking a discreet retreat, and it was here in 1949 that the influential landscape gardener **Roberto Burle Marx** bought a forty-hectare former coffee plantation, the Sítio, and converted it into a nursery for the plants that he collected on his travels around the country. In 1973 Burle Marx moved permanently to the Sítio, living there until his death in 1994.

Today the Sítio is used as a botany research and teaching centre, and **tours** (daily 9am and 2pm; $1.50; ℡21/410-1412 or 410-1171) of the property and grounds are given to the public, though only in Portuguese. Tours last around ninety minutes and it's essential to book in advance. Burle Marx was not only a collector of plants, but also of Brazilian folk art and Peruvian ceramics – his vast collection is on display along with his own paintings and textiles inside the house. Just across the road from the Sítio's front gates, the *Restaurante do Cezar* (11.30am–6pm; weekend reservations essential; ℡21/410-1202) serves excellent local seafood and is run by Burle Marx's former cook; a full meal for two will cost around $12.

To get to the Sítio, take **bus** #387 ("Marambaia–Passeio") from the Passeio Público in Centro, which passes through Copacabana, Ipanema and Barra de Tijuca, and will leave you right outside the Sítio's entrance gate – allow ninety minutes from Centro. Alternatively, the air-conditioned "Santa Cruz–Via Barra" or "Campo Grande–Via Barra" buses follow the same route, but will leave you at the Ipiranga petrol station in Guaratiba from where you should ask for directions; the Sítio is a fifteen-minute walk away.

Parque Nacional da Tijuca and Alta da Boa Vista

When the Portuguese arrived, the area that is now the city of Rio was covered by dense green tropical forest. As the city grew the trees were felled and the timber used in construction or for charcoal. However, if you look up from the streets of Zona Sul today, the mountains running southwest from the Corcovado are still covered with exuberant forest, the periphery of the **Parque Nacional da Tijuca** (daily 7am–9pm; free), which covers an area of approximately 120 square kilometres, and is maintained by Brazil's State Institute of Forestry (IBDF).

In the seventeenth century the forests of Tijuca were cut down for their valuable hardwood and the trees replaced by sugar cane and, later, coffee plantations and small-scale agriculture. In the early nineteenth century the city authorities became alarmed by a shortage of pure water and by landslides from the Tijuca slopes. Eventually it was decided that a concerted effort was needed to restore Rio's watershed and, in 1857, a **reafforestation project** was initiated: by 1870 over 100,000 trees had been planted and the forest was reborn. Most of the seeds and cuttings that were planted were native to the region, and today the park serves as a remarkable example of the potential for the regeneration of the Mata Atlântica.

Following on from the success of the forest, the IBDF has gradually been reintroducing fauna to the extent that the forest is once again the home of insects and reptiles, ocelots, howler monkeys, agoutis, three-toed sloths and other animals. Most successful of all has been the return of **birdlife**, making Tijuca a paradise for bird-watchers. At the same time, overstretched park rangers have been struggling in recent years to keep residents of the eight neighbouring *favelas* from hunting wildlife for food or for trade.

Routes into the park

The park offers lots of walks and some excellent views of Rio, and though areas of it have been burnt by forest fires it remains an appealing place to get away from the city for a few hours. Buses don't enter the park, so a **car** is useful if you plan to do an extensive tour: you can go in via Cosme Velho *bairro*, near the **Entrada dos Caboclos**, and follow Estrada Heitor da Silva Costa. (Areas of the park are used as *terrenos*, places where *candomblé* and *umbanda* ritual ceremonies are performed: *caboclos* is the collective name for the spirits involved in these cults.) An alternative entrance is at Rua Leão Pacheco, which runs up the side of the Jardim Botânico (off Rua Jardim Botânico) and leads to the **Entrada dos Macacos** and on to the **Vista Chinesa**, above the Museu Histórico da Cidade in Gávea. From here there's a marvellous view of Guanabara Bay and the Zona Sul. Both of these entrances lead to different roads that run through the park, but they converge eventually in the *bairro* of **Alta da Boa Vista**. If you're intent upon **walking**, you should be warned that even the shorter trip from the Entrada dos Macacos will mean a hot, dehydrating climb for more than 20km.

If you don't have your own transport, it's much easier to aim for the area to the north of the park known as the **Floresta de Tijuca**. Take a bus to Alto da Boa Vista (#221 from Praça XV de Novembro; #233 or #234 from the *rodoviária*; #133 from Rua Jardim Botânico) and get off at Praça Alfonso Viseu near the **Entrada da Floresta**, with its distinctive stone columns. A few hundred metres after the entrance (where you can buy a **map**, though the main paths are well signposted) is a 35-metre-high waterfall and, further on, the **Capela do Mairynk**, built in 1860, but virtually entirely rebuilt in the 1940s. The chapel's most interesting feature is the three altar panels painted by Cândido Portinari, one of Brazil's greatest twentieth-century artists. In fact, the originals now form part of the much-depleted collection of the Museu de Arte Moderna (see p.91) and those in the chapel are reproductions. If you have the energy for an all-day climb, you can go all the way to the **Pico do Papagaio** (975m) or **Pico da Tijuca** (1021m) – peaks in the far north of the forest, above the popular picnic spot known as **Bom Retiro**. The whole park is a good place for a picnic; come well supplied with drinks and snacks as vendors are few and far between.

Alternatively, you can join an **organized tour** of the park. Most of those offered by hotels and travel agents involve nothing more strenuous than a short walk along a paved road, but more personal – and infinitely more rewarding – are the tours run by Rio Hiking (☏21/2552-9420 or mobile 9721-0594, ⓦwww.riohiking.com.br), which take small groups of people on half- or full-day hikes along the park's many trails. Operating at weekends and on some weekdays too, the tours are led by Denise Werneck and her son Gabriel, both of whom speak excellent English and are extremely knowledgeable about the park's biodiversity. Rio Hiking also run occasional three-day walking trips to Ilha Grande (see p.143) and Itatiaia National Park (see p.151), and Denise or Gabriel also take groups to sample the nightlife of Bohemian Lapa (see p.91).

Eating and drinking

As one of the world's most exotic tourist resorts and with (for Brazil) a relatively large middle-class population, Rio is well served by restaurants offering a wide variety of cuisines – from traditional Brazilian to French and Japanese. In general, eating out in Rio is not cheap – and it can be very expensive – but there's no shortage of low-priced places to grab a lunchtime meal, or just a snack and a drink: at a *galeto*, where you eat, diner-style, at the counter; or at a *lanchonete*, the ubiquitous Brazilian café, which serves very cheap combined plates of meat, beans and rice, as well as other snacks. *Cariocas* dine late, and restaurants don't start to fill up until after 9pm. Generally, last orders will be taken around midnight in most places, but there are others where you can get a meal well after 2am.

Fast food, snacks, cakes and ice cream

There's no shortage of **hamburger** joints in Rio, though it's worth bearing in mind that there's a good chance that the ground beef used comes from the Amazon, where immense ranches are displacing Indians, peasants and trees at a criminal rate. You'll get better, more authentic and cheaper food at any *galeto* or *lanchonete* – there are plenty in Centro or at Copacabana, though most are closed at night. You won't really need any guidance to find these; the places given below deal in more specialized fare.

If you're just peckish, then it's nice to take **tea and cakes** at *Confeitaria Colombo* at Rua Gonçalves Dias 32, Centro (closed Sat at 1pm and all day Sun). Founded in 1894, the *Colombo* recalls Rio's *belle époque*, with its ornate interior and air of tradition; there's also a rather plain-looking branch in Copacabana at Av. N.S. de Copacabana 890. In Leblon, *Garcia & Rodrigues*, at Av. Ataulfo de Paiva 1251, is a superb bakery serving excellent cakes (see p.119), while you'll get a fresh, crisp **salad** at *Gulla Gulla* in the *Hotel Marina Palace*, Av. Delfim Moreira 630 – a bit pricier than usual, but recommended. There are more cakes at the *Bonbon d'Or* in Ipanema at Rua Visconde de Pirajá 351, or at any branch of *Kopenhagen*. For **ice cream**, there are plenty of choices: in the *bairro* of Humaitá, try *Sanduka* at Rua Humaitá 92 or *Chaika* at Rua Visconde de Pirajá 32; in the Shopping RioSul (see p.129), the *Gelateria Parmalat*; and in Ipanema, the excellent *Felice Caffé* at Rua Gomes Carneiro 30. Best of all is *Sorvete Mil Frutas*, at Rua Garcia D'Ávila 134, which boasts dozens of flavours, varying according to the season, including exotic Brazilian fruit such as *pitanga* and *jabuticaba*; there's also a branch near the Jardim Botânico on Rua Seabra.

A note on drinking

The lists given below are for both eating and drinking. Pretty well all bars serve *pestiscos* (snacks) or even full meals while lots of restaurants allow a night's drinking, too, so you should be able to find somewhere that suits you. In most regions of Brazil, **beer** comes to your table in a bottle, but in Rio draught beer – or *chopp*, pronounced "shopee" – predominates. A good place to sample Brazil's national drink, **cachaça**, is at the *Academia da Cachaça*, Rua Cde. Bernadotte 26, Leblon, a small and always crowded bar where there are three hundred available brands to sample – treat it with respect at all times. Also well worth considering are the bars in **Lapa** (see p.91), a Bohemian neighbourhood known for some prime drinking spots; you can also eat, listen to music and dance here, too.

Check the **fruit markets** for something exotic and healthy: at Botafogo on Wednesday by Praça Canoinhas; Flamengo on Sunday in Largo do Machado; Copacabana on Thursday near Praça do Lido.

Centro and Lapa

The restaurants in the city centre cater largely for people working in the area, and at lunchtime the service is rushed. Around the Praça Tiradentes, particularly, there are lots of cheap eating places, bakeries and bars. After work, downtown office workers flock to the Arco de Teles area (see p.84), the pedestrian zone centred on Travessa do Comércio and Rua Ouvidor, for early evening drinks and *petiscos* in the many unassuming bars. Later on, the action shifts to burgeoning Lapa, one of the most important nightlife spots in Rio (see p.91).

Alba Mar Praça Marechal Âncora 186, a short walk from Praça XV de Novembro. Founded in 1933 and housed in the remaining tower of the old municipal market, this cool, green, octagonal building provides a superb view of Guanabara Bay. Stick with the moderately priced seafood, served by stern waiters in white uniforms. Lunch only, closed Sun.

Bar Luiz Rua Carioca 39. Near Largo da Carioca, this manic, but essentially run-of-the-mill restaurant and bar, serving German-style food and ice-cold *chopp*, is considered quite an institution and still a popular meeting place for journalists and intellectuals (see p.87). Closed Sun.

Bar Ocidental Rua Miguel Couto 124. One of several bars on a small pedestrianized road near the Largo de São Francisco de Paulo. Sit at a table outside and enjoy an early evening *chopp* and a plate of fresh sardines.

Caldeirão Rua do Ouvidor 26. Open at lunchtime for good, cheap seafood, with a pleasant atmosphere – try *badejo* (a type of fish) or *capixaba* (seafood stew).

Cosmopolita Travessa da Mosqueira 4, Lapa. An excellent Portuguese restaurant established in 1926 with a loyal, rather Bohemian, clientele. Fish dishes are the firm favourites here. Closed Sun.

Les Champs Elysées Av. Presidente Antônio Carlos 58, 12th floor ☏21/2220-4713. Located above the French consulate, this expensive restaurant serves creative French dishes. Popular for elegant business lunches in a part of the city with few such options available. Mon–Fri lunch only.

Miako Rua do Ouvidor 45, north side of Praça XV de Novembro. One of the first Japanese restaurants in Rio, serving reliable sushi, sashimi, *teppan-yaki* and *filé na chapa*, as well as a few Chinese dishes for good measure. Mon–Sat lunch only.

Vegetarian food

Vegetarians won't have any serious problems in Rio. While beans and rice are always available for basic sustenance, don't be shy of asking the waiter in any restaurant to have the kitchen prepare something a little more tasty: if nothing else, you'll get a plate of fresh vegetables.

Celeiro Rua Dias Ferreira 199, Leblon. Rio's best *por kilo* salad bars with a vegetable spread rarely seen at other restaurants, excellent bread and delicious desserts. Well worth the long wait for a table. Mon–Sat 10am–5.30pm.

Empório Natural Rua Barrão da Torre 167, Ipanema A great vegetarian *por kilo* restaurant with a wide range of hot and cold choices, and a decent health food store next door.

Macro Nature Travessa Cristiano Lacorte, Copacabana. An excellent health-food shop and restaurant (though the menu is limited to a narrow range of salads and bean stews). Closed Sat & Sun evening.

Natural Rua 19 de Fevereiro 118 (Botafogo) and Rua Barão de Torre 171 (Ipanema). Not strictly a vegetarian restaurant as fish can be had, too, but the food is tasty and cheap. Lunch only.

Sabor Saúde Rua da Quitanda 21, Centro. An above-average restaurant and health-food store claiming to serve only organically grown produce, slipping in the occasional fish-based dish as well. Mon–Fri 11.30am–4pm. Inexpensive.

Penafiel Rua Senhor dos Passos 121. Superb – and amazingly inexpensive – Portuguese dishes have been served here since 1912. Fish dishes and stews (such as bean, tongue and tripe) are a speciality. Lunch only, closed Sat & Sun.

Rio–Minho Rua do Ouvidor 10. Tasty Brazilian food at fair prices in a restaurant that's been going for a hundred years. The kitchen concentrates on seafood – try *badejo* fish, lobster in butter, prawn in coconut milk or the fried fish with red peppers, rice and broccoli. Lunch only, closed Sat & Sun.

Sentaí (O Rei da Lagosta) Rua Barão de São Felix 75. A wonderful daytime-only Portuguese seafood restaurant full of local colour. Take care in this rather rough part of the centre, but it's a strangely chic restaurant, well worth taking a slight risk to get to. Lunch only, Mon–Fri.

Santa Teresa

No visit to Rio is complete without going up into the airy hills of Santa Teresa. There are several good restaurants here and it's an enjoyable ten-minute tram ride from Centro. On Friday and Saturday evenings, young people congregate in the bars and restaurants around Largo dos Guimarães.

Adega do Pimenta Rua Almirante Alexandrino 296. Moderately priced German cooking – most people go for the sausage and sauerkraut, but the duck with red cabbage is excellent. The Santa Teresa tram passes the restaurant.

Aprazível Rua Aprazível 62 ☏ 21/2508-9174. Excellent and fairly expensive Franco-Mineira dishes, plus an attractive terrace with wonderful views across Rio. The quail served with a *jabuticaba* chutney is something really special, while the goat is roasted to perfection. Advance booking is advised. Thurs–Fri 8pm–midnight, Sat noon–midnight, Sun and holidays 1–6pm.

Bar do Arnaudo Rua Almirante Alexandrino 316. Just up from the *Adega do Pimenta*, an excellent mid-priced place to sample traditional food from Brazil's Northeast, such as *carne do sol* (sun-dried meat), *macaxeira* (sweet cassava) and *pirão de bode* (goat meat soup). Sat–Sun closed from 8pm & closed all Mon.

Bar do Mineiro Rua Paschoal Carlos Magno 99. Authentic country-style food in an old bar that could be in any small town in Minas Gerais. Good beers and an excellent range of *cachaças*.

Sobrado das Massas Largo dos Guimarães. Most of the week this restaurant serves up heavy pasta dishes, but on Saturday it lays out the best *feijoada* in Santa Teresa – a portion for two to three people costs just $5.

Sobrenatural Rua Almirante Alexandrino 432. Basically a fish restaurant, where the highlights are the *moquecas* and the catch of the day. Deliberately rustic looking, this is an inviting place for a leisurely meal. Closed Mon.

Flamengo

As well as the places listed below, there are numerous restaurants, *galetos* and *lanchonetes* around the Largo do Machado.

Adega Real Rua Marquês de Abrantes. No haughty *nouvelle cuisine* here, just piles of good basics – if you like decent-quality food in large quantities, this place is recommended as the friendly waiters serve up portions sufficient for at least two people. The restaurant opens onto the street, and on Fridays you can hang on to the bar and swallow draught beer until 4am; the *bolinhas de bacalhau* (cod balls) are worth trying.

Alho & Óleo Rua Barque de Macedo 13, down at the foot near Praia do Flamengo. Tasty home-made pasta and other good Italian food (try the salami flavoured with pepper and lemon) in an upmarket atmosphere, but reasonably priced.

Lamas Rua Marquês de Abrantes 18. This 130-year-old restaurant serves well-prepared Brazilian food (the Oswaldo Aranha steak – pan fried with lots of garlic – is a popular choice) to artist and journalist types. Always busy, with a vibrant atmosphere, *Lamas* is a good example of *carioca* middle-class tradition, and highly recommended. Open until 4am.

Majórica Rua Senador Vergueiro 11–15, Flamengo. A long-established, better-than-average place to tuck into some meat – the *picanha especial* (special rump steak) is the favourite. If you're not in the mood for beef, try the excellent grilled trout from near Petrópolis.

Botafogo, Humaitá and Urca

Botafogo and Humaitá undoubtedly host some of Rio's most interesting restaurants, often overlooked by tourists because they lie a bit off the beaten track, hidden away in back streets. At the Humaitá's impressive indoor market, **Cobal**, Rua Voluntários da Pátria 446, you can take your pick of the moderately priced but excellent *lanchonetes* serving Brazilian Northeastern, Italian and Japanese food. This is a very popular lunch and evening meeting point for local residents. Although there are few places to eat in Urca, one of Rio's quietest *bairros*, it's a pleasant place for a relaxing meal.

Adega do Valentim Rua da Passagem 178, Botafogo ☎21/295-2748. A comfortable restaurant (especially the front salon) serving up good Portuguese food. Expect to pay around $11 per person for a satisfying munch through cod, onions, potatoes and suckling pig. The smoked meats are especially good (though expensive) and there's a good wine list, too.

A Mineira Rua Duque de Caxias, Humaitá. A perfect introduction to the food of Minas Gerais, with all the standard dishes on offer as part of the excellent value ($6 per person) all-you-can-eat buffet.

Axé Santé Rua Capitão Solomão 55, Botafogo. A nicely decorated French-Bahian restaurant with live music. The food is well-presented and tasty – try the salad with mango and nuts, or the *carne do sol* with banana purée.

Botequim-184 Rua Visconde de Caravelas 184, Humaitá. Good, varied and inexpensive food in a lively establishment; next door, the *Overnight Bar* is a friendly place for a few drinks afterwards.

Garota da Urca Av. João Luiz Alves, Urca. Hardly stylish, but the place boasts the best views of any Rio restaurant, looking back towards Botafogo and the Corcovado. The food – Brazilian with Italian twists – is good enough, but you can also stop by

for just a drink; the *peixe a garota* is a delicious fish risotto that serves two for around $8.

La Mole Praia de Botafogo 228, Botafogo. Inexpensive, decent Italian food, long a popular venue for a family meal out. Nearby and similar are *Bella Blu*, Rua da Passagem 44, and *Bella Roma*, Rua General Gois Monteiro 18.

Madam Vidal Rua Capitão Solomão 69, Botafogo. This gay-friendly music club and restaurant serves tasty dishes that incorporate Brazilian, European and Japanese influences. The jazz nights with acclaimed singer Leila Maria are a treat. Mon–Sat until 3am; closed Sun.

Raajmahal Rua General Polidoro 29, Botafogo. An Indian restaurant that is English-owned, and extends itself well beyond the basic curry. Let the waiter know how well seasoned you want your dish, as the restaurant tends to cater for the local preference for mild curries. Closed Sun.

Yorubá Rua Arnaldo Quintela 94, Botafogo ☎21/2541-9387. Friendly restaurant serving up moderately priced Bahian cooking with its strong African influences. The beautifully presented meals always take a long time to appear, but the *bobó* (a dish based on mandioca purée), *moquecas* and other Bahian specialities are well worth the wait. Closed Mon & Tues; lunch only Sun.

Copacabana and Leme

It comes as no surprise that Copacabana is riddled with restaurants, but that doesn't mean that the choice is particularly good – unless you enjoy sitting in a restaurant swamped with holiday-makers being shuttled about by tour companies.

Arab Av. Atlântica 1936. A reasonably priced Lebanese restaurant where you can opt for a cold beer and snack on the terrace or a full meal inside (the *por kilo* lunch is excellent value). Though the menus is rather heavy on meat choices, vegetarians certainly won't go hungry. One of the very few good restaurants on Avenida Atlântica.

Caranguejo Rua Barata Ribeiro 771, corner of Rua Xavier da Silveira. Excellent, inexpensive seafood – especially the *caranguejos* (crabs) – served in an utterly unpretentious environment

packed with locals and tourists alike. Closed Mon.

D'Amici Rua Antonio Vieira 18, Leme ☎21/2541-4477. One of Rio's best – and most expensive – Italian restaurants where people go to see and be seen as much for the food. The meals, though, are excellent; besides the pastas and risottos, the roast lamb is particularly good.

Deck Av. Atlântica 2316, corner of Rua Siqueira Campos. Until 5pm, this always-busy restaurant serves an all-you-can-eat Brazilian buffet for just $5 per person, after which the offerings include *rodizio de galeto* (mouthwatering thyme-and-garlic chicken with polenta fried in palm oil) and all-you-can-eat pasta for $4.

La Trattoria Rua Fernando Mendes 7. Cheap and cheerful place serving the best Italian food in Copacabana. Amongst the excellent range of pasta dishes, the fettuccine doused in a mixed seafood sauce is especially recommended.

A Marisqueira Rua Barata Ribeiro 232. A good spot for seafood. This restaurant has been around for over forty years serving well-prepared Portuguese-style food, though it's perhaps a little unimaginative and a touch on the pricey side.

Marius Crustáceos Av. Atlântica 290, Leme ☎21/2543-6363. Definitely the place to come for oysters, crabs, crayfish, prawns and other seafood choices. The menu is varied, though Italian–Brazilian styles dominate. Expensive, but quite a treat.

A Polonesa Rua Hilário de Gouveia 116 ☎21/2547-7378. A tiny restaurant where the menu is dominated by reasonably priced, tradition-al (and rather heavy) Polish dishes, such as beet-root soup and fish in a horseradish sauce. For dessert, the soufflés and apple cake are a treat. Closed Tues–Fri lunchtime & Mon.

Siri Mole e Cia Rua Francisco Otaviano 50 ☎21/2267-0894. A rarity in Rio – an excellent Bahian restaurant, serving beautifully presented dishes (many of them spicy) in an upmarket, yet comfortable, setting. Inside, the restaurant is quite formal, but there are also a few tables outside where you can munch on *acarajé* and other Bahian snacks. There's a branch located in Centro at Av. Rio Branco 1 (☎21/2233-0107).

Traiteurs de France Av. Nossa Senhora de Copacabana 386 ☎21/2548-6440. Simple cook-ing from one of the very few affordable and good French restaurants in Rio. Mon–Thurs lunch only; Fri–Sat lunch and dinner; closed Sun.

Lagoa

Most of the restaurants in Lagoa are on the Avenida Epitácio Pessoa, which runs along the east side of the lake: generally serving uninspiring "internation-al" food, they're plush, pricey, air-conditioned and boastful of their views over the lake – which are usually obscured by trees.

Bar Lagoa Av. Epitácio Pessoa 1674, tucked into the southern shores of the lake by Ipanema. The cheapest and oldest of the lakeside restaurants, usually full of families from the adjacent neigh-bourhoods, attended to by white-coated waiters delivering beer, German sausage and smoked pork chops the size of football boots to their tables. Arrive by 9pm and grab a seat on the patio, from where there's a good view of the lake. Inexpensive and definitely recommended.

The Queen's Legs Av. Epitácio Pessoa 5030. A facsimile of a Victorian pub, good for a beer and a game of darts downstairs – but don't bother with the upstairs restaurant, which is overpriced and over-regarded.

Ipanema

There's a fair selection of good (and expensive) restaurants in Ipanema. For budget eating, however, you'll generally do rather better in Copacabana while more interesting restaurants tend to be in Leblon.

Baroni Fasoli Rua Jangadeiras 14, near Praça General Osório. Reasonably priced Italian spot in an area otherwise brimming with expensive choic-es. The pasta dishes are especially good.

Casa da Feijoada Rua Prudente de Morais 10. Usually served only on Saturdays, *feijoada* is served seven days a week here, along with other traditional, moderately priced and extremely filling Brazilian dishes.

Efffe's Rua Barão da Torre 422 ☎21/2286-2176. Modern Brazilian cooking with strong French and Italian undertones (such as chicken in a tarragon sauce, *carpaccios* and pastas). Downstairs, the restaurant serves excellent-value lunch specials, while its more formal upstairs dining room offers beautiful views of Ipanema. Expensive.

Garota de Ipanema Rua Vinícius de Morais 49. Always busy, this bar entered the folk annals of Rio de Janeiro when the song *The Girl from Ipanema* was written here one night when the muse came to Tom Jobim, the song's composer. There are few better places in Rio for a beer, but the food is unexceptional and overpriced.

Livraria da Travessa Rua Visconde de Pirajá 572. An informal restaurant in Rio's best bookshop serving breakfast, sandwiches and cakes as well as full meals. The food is excellent – modern Brazilian with Italian and other foreign touches –

and the atmosphere unhurried. Mon–Sat 9am–11pm, Sun noon–9pm.

Lord Jim Rua Paul Redfern 63. An English pub serving steak and kidney pie, fish and chips and high tea. Downstairs, there's a dart board amongst the horse brasses and fake half-timbering.

Pax Delícia Rua Quitéria 99, at Praça de Nossa Senhora da Paz. Equally suitable for a light lunch or drawn-out evening meal, this comfortable restaurant specialises in modern Brazilian cooking with dishes such as duck in a *jabuticaba* sauce, as well as excellent salads and pastas. Do save space for the desserts: the guava cheesecake is delicious! Moderate.

Saideira Rua Gomes Carneiro, near Praça General Osório. Eating and drinking through the night, until 8am. The term *saideira* means "one for the road"

and it's a place that the night-people stop off at after strenuous entertainment in the clubs round about. Worth considering for a late – or early – snack.

Satyricon Rua Barão de Torre 192 ☎21/2521-0955. Excessively formal, but many people rate the Italian food served here as the best in Rio. Seafood is the restaurant's speciality, with a sushi bar giving the place something of a cosmopolitan atmosphere. There are also plenty of meat dishes, and there's an excellent range of pasta choices, too. Very expensive.

Via Farme Rua Farme de Amoedo 47. Good Italian food – especially the pizzas and seafood. Choose from air-conditioned dining upstairs or open-air downstairs. Not cheap, but reasonable for the area.

Leblon

Many of Leblon's restaurants are situated along the Avenida Ataúlfo de Paiva, where you'll also find many of the late-opening bars. Another popular destination for food and drink is Baixo Leblon, the area around Rua Dias Ferreira three or four blocks back from the beach, which boasts some of Rio's most chic restaurants and turns very lively on weekends. Locals of all ages also flock to the Leblon's excellent **Cobal** market, at Rua Gilberto Cardoso, where the abundant and affordable *lanchonetes* serve everything from pizza and sushi to regional fare until late at night.

Alt München Rua Dias Ferreira 410. A varied menu of German and Swiss dishes; on a hot evening the veranda is a pleasant place to eat and drink. Reasonably priced.

Antiquarius Rua Aristides Espínola 19 ☎21/2294-1049. Widely rated as the best Portuguese restaurant in Rio (and possibly Brazil). Especially good for seafood (and not just cod), but goat and wild boar are other good choices here, as are the rich Portuguese and Brazilian desserts. Definitely no shorts allowed. Very expensive.

Carlota Rua Dias Ferreira 64 ☎21/2540-6821. Imaginative pan-Asian cooking with a few North African influences thrown in for good measure. The seven kinds of spring rolls are especially noteworthy. Very pleasant atmosphere. Mon–Thurs dinner only, Fri–Sat lunch & dinner, Sun lunch only. Expensive.

Garcia & Rodrigues Av. Ataulfo de Paiva 1251. A foodie's paradise: although the French restaurant is unimaginative and stuffy, there's an excellent bistro, wine shop, ice cream parlour, bakery and deli. This is one of the few places in Rio where you can buy genuinely good bread (and croissants) and there's an excellent choice of take-out salads and

other prepared meals. Open Sun–Fri 8am–midnight; Sat 8am–1am.

Nam Thai Rua Rainha Guilhermina 95 ☎21/2259-2962. Rio's top pan-Asian restaurant, although the menu is predominantly Thai-influenced. The cauliflower-coriander soup is not to be missed. Tues–Fri dinner only, Sat & Sun lunch and dinner, closed Mon.

Plataforma Rua Adalberto Ferreira 32. Upstairs, tourists are entertained by a samba show, while *cariocas* mingle at the steak house restaurant downstairs. Afterwards you can always stagger to the *Academia de Cachaça* round the corner (see p.114) and sample a few with the benefit of a good lining in the stomach.

Sushi Leblon Rua Dias Ferreira 256. Superb sushi (but expensive), along with other Japanese-inspired dishes such as grilled squid stuffed with shiitake. Mon–Sat evenings only; Sun 1.30pm–midnight.

Zuka Rua Dias Ferreira 233 ☎21/3205-7154. Food is grilled in front of your eyes, then doused in amazing sauces by a chef capable of creating unforgettable fusion cuisine: one of his specialities is seared tuna in a cashew crust, served with a potato-horseradish sauce. Around $25 per person.

Jardim Botânico and Gávea

Not an obvious choice for restaurants but a night at the races and a dip into the food available here in Jardim Botânico or neighbouring Gávea can be fun.

Claude Troigros Rua Custódio Serrão 62, Jardim Botânico ☎21/2537-8582. An early creator of Franco-Brazilian fusion food, the chef/owner Claude Troigros makes regular expeditions to the Amazon and other remote regions in search of new ingredients. Expect unusual combinations, such as quails stuffed with *farofa* and coriander and served with an *aça* sauce, and sole cooked with banana.

Guima's Rua José Roberto Macedo Soares 5, on the opposite side of Praça Santos Dumont from the Jockey Club. A small, intimate restaurant with a happy atmosphere, catering for an arty and intel-

lectual crowd. The food is delicious, and, unusually, the *couvert* (wholemeal bread and pâté) is worth the price. Try steak in a mustard and pear sauce and one of the delectable desserts. One of Rio's best restaurants but not too expensive.

Jockey Club Praça Santos Dumont. Palatial surroundings and good, reasonably priced food in this restaurant overlooking the racetrack.

Les Artistes Rua de São Vicente 75 (☎21/239-4242). An unexpected combination for Brazil: a decent, reasonably priced French restaurant. On Wednesday and Saturday, good *cassoulet* is served.

Nightlife and entertainment

The best way to find out what's on and where in Rio is to consult *Caderno B*, a separate section of the *Jornal do Brasil*, which lists cinema, arts events and concerts; *O Globo*, too, details sporting and cultural events in the city. *Veja*, Brazil's answer to *Newsweek*, includes an excellent weekly Rio supplement with news of concerts, exhibitions and other events; the magazine reaches the news stands on Sunday. Alternatively, ⓦ www.guiarj.com.br has up-to-date listings of entertainment possibilities. You shouldn't be stuck: there's no end of things to do come nightfall in the city whose name is synonymous with Carnaval (see p.125), samba and jazz.

Samba

Samba shows are inevitably tourist affairs, where members of Rio's more successful samba schools perform glitzy music and dance routines. Still, some are worth catching. Every Monday night at 10pm, the Beija Flor (☎21/791-1353) school performs at the Morro da Urca, halfway up Pão d'Açúcar; the $30 entrance fee includes dinner from 8pm, a well-executed show and spectacular city views, though the event is a tad snooty. On Thursday and Friday live music shows start at 10pm, and you can eat and drink till 2am. For a less touristy experience of a samba school, you can easily arrange to watch rehearsals held from August to February (see p.127), mainly at various points in the Zona Norte. For cheap early evening entertainment, there are the *Seis e Meia* samba shows (at 6.30pm, as the name suggests): in Centro try the Teatro João Caetano on Praça Tiradentes, or the Paço Imperial on Praça XV de Novembro.

Of the **clubs**, it's worth making the trek out to Barra de Tijuca as the *Clube do Samba*, Estrada de Barra 65 in Barra de Tijuca, is great for dancing and has a nice open-air bar. Dedicated just to samba, Saturday here often sees shows by big names like Beth Carvalho, Alcione, João and Giza Nogeuiral (check in the *Jornal do Brasil*); entrance costs about $10, which is typical for this type of set-up. Otherwise, make for the bars and clubs of Lapa (see p.91), where samba and other local rhythms play to an enthusiastic and overwhelmingly local crowd. Especially recommended there is *Carioca da Gama* (Mon–Sat from 6pm) at Av. Mem de Sá 79: look out for Teresa Cristina who brings the house down with

Gay Rio

If you're expecting **gay nightlife** to rival San Francisco's or Sydney's, you may well be disappointed. In general nightlife is pretty integrated, with gay men, lesbians and heterosexuals tending to share the same venues, and there are few areas of concentration: apart from transvestites who hang out on street corners and are visible during Carnaval, the scene is unexpectedly discreet.

A good starting point for an evening out is Rua Visconde Silva in Botafogo, which is lined with numerous gay and lesbian cafés, bars and restaurants that are liveliest on Friday and Saturday nights. The classic introduction to Rio's more traditional male gay society is *Le Ball*, a bar in the Travessa Cristiano Lacorte, just off Rua Miguel Lemos, at the Ipanema end of Copacabana. Opposite this, the *Teatro Brigitte Blair* hosts a gay transvestite show from around 10pm. Also in Copacabana, the bar and nightclub *Inc* (formerly called *Encontros*), at Praça Serzedelo Correia 15, next to Rua Siquera Campos, is open nightly and very popular, although mainly with tourists.

In Lapa, at Rua Mem de Sá 25, behind a pink facade under the Aqueduto da Carioca, is the *Casanova*, Rio's oldest and most interesting gay bar. In business since 1929, the *Casanova* features drag shows, lambada and samba music, with large ceiling fans to cool down the frenetic dancers. Very different, but also wild, are the gay nights on Saturdays at the *Cine Ideal* at Rua da Carioca 62, Centro, an informal club that always draws huge crowds. The most popular gay nightclub at the moment is undoubtedly *Le Boy* (℡21/2513-4993) at Rua Raul Pompéia 102 (in Copacabana, towards Ipanema). Based in a former cinema, this huge club is open nightly apart from Mondays and features dance floors, drag shows and much more besides.

In the daytime, the beach area in front of the *Copacabana Palace Hotel* is frequented by gay bathers, and the café next door, *Maxims*, is a fun gay place to hang out. Nearby on Avenida Atlântica at the junction with Rua Siqueira Campos, is the Gay Kiosk Rainbow, a summer-time **information point** for gay visitors – ask about circuit parties, usually held in Centro. The strip of beach between Rua Farme de Amoedo and Rua Teixeira do Melo in Ipanema is another well-known gay meeting point. For the post-beach gay crowd, there's *Boofetada*, a bar and café at Rua Farme de Amoedo 87.

See the Carnaval section, p.128, for information about Rio's gay balls. If it's tours of Rio's gay history you're after, Carlos Roquette, a rather dapper former federal judge turned tour guide, can help you to explore (see p.74).

---

her steamy samba. Excellent samba artists also perform on Friday and Saturday at *Bar Semente* at Rua Joaquim Silva 138.

Discos

Although Rio's discos attempt sophistication, the end result is generally bland and unpalatable. Too often they pump out a steady stream of British and American hits, interspersed with examples from Brazil's own dreadful pop industry. Most of the big **discos** (*boates*) are private clubs, but if you're staying in one of the five-star hotels, and are willing to spend a minimum of $7–10 per person, you can usually arrange temporary membership. Soft options for the wealthy and unadventurous are *Hippopotamus*, Rua Barão de Torre 354, Ipanema, and *Studio C*, Rua Xavier da Silveira 7, under the *Hotel Rio Othon Palace* in Copacabana. If you want to avoid fellow tourists, a good first stop is the Arco de Teles area in Centro, while fashionable nightclubs that attract both *cariocas* and tourists are all found in the Zona Sul.

00 Av. Padre Leonel Franca 240, Gávea ☎21/2540-8041. The nightclub of the moment, frequented by a rich and trendy crowd, where some of Brazil's top DJs play an eclectic mix of music; like most places it doesn't really get going until after 11pm, though on Sunday the best time to go is 7pm, immediately after returning from the beach.

Arco Imperial Travessa do Comércio 13, Lapa ☎21/2242-2695. A dance club that is always packed from the comparatively early hour of 10pm. The music is a mix of European and Brazilian disco sounds.

Biblos Av. Epitácio Pessoa 1484, Lagoa. A laid-back atmosphere, with good popular home-grown music and jazz on Tuesdays.

Casa da Matriz Rua Henrique Novaes 107, Botafogo ☎21/2266-1014. An extremely stylish, aggressively modern club that features more Brazilian music than is typical of discos – though this varies throughout the week.

Dito e Feito Rua do Mercado 21, Centro. The action starts early – from 8pm – with mainstream disco sounds. Open Monday through Saturday, but Friday is the busiest night when local office workers stream into the club.

Help Av. Atlântica 3432, Copacabana. A massive disco that gets mobbed – overwhelmingly by tourists and a fair number of prostitutes – at weekends; entrance is about $5.

Melt Rua Rita Ludolf 47, Leblon (☎21/2249-9309). A stylish, hipster haven, with a pretty good range of music, such as samba-rock on Wednesday, drum 'n' bass on Fridays.

Mess Club Rua Francisco Otaviano 20, Copacabana ☎21/2227-0419, ⊛ www.messclub .com.br. Very hip, but without a trace of snobbishness. Mainly popular with twenty-somethings, though pretty mixed. Music changes nightly, with Tuesday's "Afro Rio" especially recommended, when DJs play hip-hop, soul, reggae and other black music styles accompanied by live percussion.

Peoples Av. Bartolomeu Mitre 370, Leblon ☎21/512-8824. Long one of the trendiest spots in Rio, though with a $15 cover charge it's not the cheapest night out. Eclectic music most nights, ranging from 1970s disco beats to techno-house.

Six Electro Rua das Marrecas 38, Lapa ☎21/25103230. An old house renovated to give the place a rustic-chic air. With three dance floors featuring hip-hop and soul, trance and drum 'n' bass, this is a good place to end up after some Lapa bar-hopping.

Jazz

Rio de Janeiro has a tradition of **jazz music** that extends well beyond *The Girl from Ipanema* and which is celebrated in the **Free Jazz Festival**, a major event on the international jazz circuit. The festival usually takes place in late August or early September, and is based in the theatre inside the *Hotel Nacional* in São Conrado. In past years, Brazilian musicians like Egberto Gismonti, Hermeto Pascoal, Airto Moreira and Flora Purim have joined the likes of Art Blakey, Sarah Vaughan, Ray Charles and Stan Jordan on stage, but the future of the festival is uncertain due to the faltering state of the Brazilian *real*, which put foreign stars out of reach in 2002.

Amongst the clubs that specialize in **live jazz** and tend to have consistently good programmes are *Jazzmania*, Rua Rainha Elizabeth 769 (☎21/2287-0085) in Ipanema, near Copacabana; *Mistura Fina*, Av. Borges de Madeiros 3207, Lagoa (☎21/2537-2844); and *Peoples*, Av. Bartolomeu Mitre 370, Leblon (see above); all have cover charges of around $8–12. In each case, it's a good idea to call to find out who's playing; be prepared to be turned away if it's especially crowded and you're not dressed stylishly enough. Also worth checking out is *Cais do Oriente* in a sprawling late nineteenth-century mansion in Centro, at Rua Visconde de Itaboraí 8 (☎21/2203-0178; Tues–Sat noon to midnight), which is both a spectacularly stylish (though not very good) restaurant and a jazz club with a beautiful open patio.

Other live music

Live music options abound in **Lapa** (see p.91), an atmospheric district that in the early decades of the twentieth century was synonymous with music, and which in recent years has made a comeback as one of the city's best spots for *forró*, samba, *axé* and other kinds of Brazilian music. A good first place to make for is Rua Joaquim da Silva, where the packed bars attract a mix of *bairro* residents and college students – if walking, take care not veer onto the badly lit side streets. Visitors should take particular care around Lapa at night when it's advisable to take a taxi even from one block to the next. If you feel uncomfortable going alone – or simply want company – contact Rio Hiking (see p.113), which regularly takes small groups bar-hopping in Lapa ($35 per person, excluding drinks).

In addition to places mentioned under "Samba" (see p.120), the following bars and clubs in Lapa are well worth checking out.

(see p.113)

Arcos de Velha Av. Mem de Sá 21, Lapa. Bands play *fundo do quintal* style – around a table rather than on the stage.

Bar Semente at Rua Joaquim Silva 138, Lapa. Friday and Saturday nights are basically reserved for samba, but from Monday through Thursday other traditional styles of Brazilian music, in particular *chorô*, are performed at this easy-going bar. From 8.30pm.

Café Cultural Sacrilégio Av. Mem de Sá 81, Lapa A small old townhouse with a great atmosphere and killer *batidas* (rum drinks). The place attracts some great performers such as Nilze Carvalho, a talented young *choro* singer who performs the great classical works of this musical genre on Thursdays. Mon–Sat from 6pm until early morning.

Rio Scenarium Rua do Lavradio 20, Lapa ☎21/2233-3239. One of the liveliest places in Lapa, more to listen to music than to dance, in old baronial townhouse filled with antiques and specialising in *choro*. Visitors can sit on one of the several landings and watch the daily shows on the stage below. Reservations recommended on weekends.

Brazilian dancing

Brazilians can dance, no question about that. The various regionally rooted traditions in folk music remain alive and popular, and, if you'd like to get into a bit of Brazilian swing, go in search of the more traditional dance halls.

Gafieiras

Gafieiras originally sprang up in the 1920s as ballrooms for the poorer classes, and today they remain popular because they are places where *cariocas* can be assured of traditional dance music. The most famous of them – all highly recommended – are *Estudantina*, Praça Tiradentes 79 (Thurs 10.30pm–3.30am, Fri & Sat 11pm–4am), and *Elite*, Rua Frei Caneca 4 (Fri & Sat 11pm–4am, Sun 9pm–3am), both in Centro and, in Lapa, *Asa Branca*, at Avenida Mem da Sá (Tues–Sat from 10pm). *Estudantina's* decor recalls its 1930s roots, and with live bands on the stage busying the generally young dancers along, and a small veranda to cool off on, it's a good place to go; *Elite* is smaller, more traditional and has a famous ball during Carnaval. Both charge around $3 entrance. *Asa Branca* is a very informal dance hall that's been immensely popular for decades, always attracting big-name samba, *choro* and, especially, *forró* bands. For the most beautiful of surroundings and lively Brazilian music, try *Botanic Dancing Brazil* from Thursdays to Sundays after 10pm in the Jardim Botânico.

Forró

For some accordion-driven swing from Brazil's Northeast, look for a **forró** club. The term *forró* (pronounced "fawhaw") originates from the English "for all", a reference to the dances financed by English engineering companies for their manual labour forces, as opposed to the balls organized for the elite. As drought and poverty have forced *nordestinos* to migrate south in search of employment in Brazil's large urban centres, so the culture has followed. In recent years *forró* has gained a following across the class divide and can often be heard in *gafieras* and even in the glitzy Zona Sul discos. Nevertheless, there are still some venues dedicated to *forró*. At Rua Catete 235, in the *bairro* of Catete *Forró Forrado* (Fri–Sun 10pm–late), has an excellent band and a mixed clientele that spans Rio's social scale. On Saturday nights, there's also the *Forró da Praia*, on Avenida Nações Unidas near the Botafogo recreation ground. Also on Saturday nights in Zona Sul, *Forró do Leblon* at Rua Bartolomeu Mitre 630 in Leblon, and *Forró do Copacabana* at Av. Nossa Senhora de Copacabana 435, in Copacabana, are convenient places to check out.

Film, classical music and exhibitions

Rio is the home of the **Brazilian Symphony Orchestra**, and the orchestra of the Teatro Municipal (see p.90) – the theatre that is home to the city's **ballet** troupe and **opera** company. This is the venue for almost everything that happens in terms of "high culture", with four or five major productions a year. All kinds of events attract famous names, and prices are reasonable; check the *Jornal do Brasil*.

For musical, photographic and fine art **exhibitions**, it's worth checking at the headquarters of Funarte, around the corner from the Museu das Belas Artes in Rua Araújo de Porto Alegre; either pick up a programme from Funarte, or keep an eye on the newspapers. Particularly good are the photographic exhibitions under the direction of Walter Firmo, and the musical **recitals** that take place in the Sidney Millar room on the first floor of Funarte.

The **Centro Cultural Banco do Brasil**, Rua Primeiro de Março 66, Centro (Tues–Sun 10am–10pm; ☎21/3808-2020, ⑩ www.bb.com.br), puts on an excellent programme of films, music and plays, often free. Situated in a lovely, grand and cool building, it has several exhibition halls, a cinema, two theatres, a tearoom and a restaurant.

Film

Brazil is one of the world's largest film markets. Most European and American films are quickly released in Brazil and play to large audiences on big screens with their original soundtracks. **Cinemas** are cheap ($4) and among the best are the Largo do Machado I & II and the São Luiz I & II, both in Largo do Machado; the Ricamar and the Roxy, along Avenida N.S. de Copacabana; and Condor Copacabana in Rua Figueiredo Magalhães. *Jornal do Brasil* lists what's on and where. There's an excellent chain of art-house cinemas, called Estação, showing the latest films on the international circuit. Check out the Estação Paissandu, near the corner of Rua Senador Vergueiro and Rua Paissandu, Centro; the Estação Cinema 1 in Leme; the Estação Botafogo, Rua Voluntarios da Patria 88; and the Estação in the Museu da República, Palácio do Catete.

Since 1984 Rio de Janeiro has hosted **Rio-Cine**, an international festival of film that includes some TV and video productions as well, and ranks alongside those of Cannes, Montreal and Moscow – though it lacks the snobbery that has marred its French counterpart. The festival, which takes place over ten days in November, is based in the Convention Centre of the *Hotel Nacional* and screens over three hundred films in cinemas all over Rio. For more information, contact the organizers at Rua Paissandu 362 (☎21/285-7649), in Flamengo.

Carnaval

Carnaval is celebrated in all of Brazil's cities, but Rio's is the biggest and most flash. From the Friday before Ash Wednesday to the following Thursday, the city shuts up shop and throws itself into the world's most famous manifestation of unbridled hedonism. Its greatest quality is that Rio's Carnaval has never become stale, something to do with its status as the most important celebration on the Brazilian calendar, easily outstripping either Christmas or Easter. In a city riven by poverty, Carnaval represents a moment of freedom and release, when the aspirations of *cariocas* can be expressed in music and song.

The background

The origins of Carnaval in Rio can be traced back in a direct line to a fifteenth-century tradition of Easter revelry in the Azores that caught on in Portugal and was exported to Brazil. Anarchy reigned in the streets for four days and nights, the festivities often so riotous that they were formally abolished in 1843 – although the street celebrations have remained the most accessible and widely enjoyed feature of Carnaval ever since. In the mid-nineteenth century, **masquerade balls** – *bailes* – were first held by members of the social elite, while processions, with carriages decorated in allegorical themes, also made an appearance, thus marking the ascendancy of the procession over the general street melee. Rio's masses, who were denied admission to the balls, had their own music – *jongo* – and they reinforced the tradition of street celebration by organizing in *Zé Pereira* bands, named after the Portuguese tambor that provided the basic musical beat. The organizational structure behind today's samba schools (*escolas da samba*) was partly a legacy of those bands sponsored by migrant Bahian port workers in the 1870s. Theirs was a more disciplined approach to the Carnaval procession: marching to stringed and wind instruments, using costumes and appointing people to co-ordinate different aspects of the parade.

Music written specifically for Carnaval emerged in the early twentieth century, by composers like Chiquinho Gonzaga, who wrote the first recorded samba piece in 1917 (*Pelo Telefone*), and Mauro de Almeida e Donga. In the 1930s, radio and records began to spread the music of Rio's Carnaval, and competition between different samba schools became institutionalized: in 1932 the Estação Primeira Mangueira school won the first prize for its performance in the Carnaval parade. The format has remained virtually unchanged since then, except for the emergence – in the mid-1960s – of the **blocos** or **bandas**: street processions by the residents of various *bairros*, who eschew style, discipline and prizes and give themselves up to the most traditional element of Carnaval – street revelry, of which even the principal Carnaval procession in the Sambódromo is technically a part.

The excellent website ⓦwww.love-rio.com/samba (in English and Portuguese) gives a thorough history of Rio's Carnaval as well as links (in Portuguese) to most of Rio's samba schools and many in other parts of Brazil.

The action

Rio's street celebrations centre on the **evening processions** that fill **Avenida Rio Branco** (metrô to Largo do Carioca or Cinelândia). Be prepared for the crowds and beware of pickpockets: even though the revellers are generally high-spirited and good-hearted, it's as well to keep the little cash you take in inaccessible places (like your shoes), wear only light clothes and leave your valuables locked up at the hotel.

Most of what's good takes place down the Avenida Rio Branco. The processions include samba schools (though not the best), *Clubes de Frevo*, whose loudspeaker-laden floats blast out the frenetic dance music typical of the Recife Carnaval, and the *Blocos de Empolgação*, including the Bafo da Onça and Cacique de Ramos clubs, between which exists a tremendous rivalry. There are also *rancho* bands playing a traditional *carioca* carnival music that predates samba.

Samba schools

The **samba schools**, each representing a different neighbourhood or social club, are divided into three leagues that vie for top ranking following the annual Carnaval parades. Division 1 (the top league) schools play in the Sambódromo, Division 2 on Avenida Rio Branco and Division 3 on Avenida 28 de Setembro, up in Aldeia Campista, near the Maracanã Stadium.

Preparations starts in the year preceding Carnaval, as each samba school mobilizes thousands of supporters to create the various parts of the school's display. A theme is chosen, music written and costumes created, while the dances are choreographed by the **carnavelesco**, the school's director. By December, rehearsals have begun and, in time for Christmas, the sambas are recorded and released to record stores.

The main procession of Division 1 schools – the **Desfile** – takes place on the Sunday and Monday nights of Carnaval week in the purpose-built **Sambódromo**, further along the avenue beyond the train station, a concrete structure 1700m long that can accommodate 90,000 spectators. The various samba schools – involving some 50,000 people – take part in a spectacular piece of theatre: no simple parade, but a competition between schools attempting to gain points from their presentation, a mix of song, story, dress, dance and rhythm. The schools pass through the Passarela da Samba, the Sambódromo's parade ground, and the judges allocate points according to a number of criteria. Each school must parade for between 85 and 95 minutes, no more and no less. The **bateria**, the percussion section, has to sustain the cadence that drives the school's song and dance; the *samba enredo* is the music, the *enredo* the accompanying story or lyric. The **harmonia** refers to the degree of synchronicity between the *bateria* and the dance by the thousands of **passistas** (samba dancers); the dancers are conducted by the **pastoras**, who lead by example. The **evolução** refers to the quality of the dance, and the choreography is judged on its spontaneity, the skill of the *pastoras* and the excitement that the display generates. The costumes, too, are judged on their originality; their colours are always the traditional ones adopted by each school. The **carros alegóricos** (no more than ten metres high and eight wide) are the gigantic, richly decorated floats, which carry some of the **Figuras de Destaque** ("prominent figures"), amongst them the **Porta-Bandeira** ("flag bearer") – a woman who carries the school's symbol, a potentially big point scorer. The **Mestre-Sala** is the dance master, also an important symbolic figure, whose ability to sustain the rhythm of his dancers is of paramount importance. The **Comissão da Frente**, traditionally a school's "board of directors", marches at the head of the procession, a role often filled these days by invited TV stars or sports teams. The bulk of the procession behind is formed by the **alas**, the wings or blocks consisting of hundreds of costumed individuals each linked to a part of the school's theme.

Traditionally, every school has in addition to parade an **Ala das Baianas** – hundreds of women dressed in the flowing white costumes typical of Salvador – in remembrance of the debt owed to the Bahian emigrants, who introduced many of the traditions of the Rio Carnaval procession.

Samba schools

If you can't make Carnaval, give the fake shows in the Zona Sul a miss and get a taste of the samba schools at the *ensaios* (rehearsals) below. They take place at weekends from August to February: phone to confirm times and days. After New Year, Saturday nights are packed solid with tourists and prices triple. Instead, go to one on a mid-week evening or, better still, on Sunday afternoon when there's no entrance fee and locals predominate.

Most of the schools are in distant *bairros*, often in, or on the edge of, a *favela*, but there's no need to go accompanied by a guide. It's easy, safe and not too expensive to take a taxi there and back; there are always plenty waiting to take people home. Of the schools, Mangueira is certainly the most famous; it has a devoted following, a great atmosphere and includes children and old people amongst its dancers. The gay-friendly Salgueiro has a more white middle-class following.

Beija-Flor Rua Pracinha Wallace Paes Leme 1652, Nilopolis ☏21/2253-2860, ⓦwww.beija-flor.com.br. Founded 1948; blue and white.

Mangueira Rua Visconde de Niterói 1072, Mangueira ☏21/2567-4637, ⓦwww.mangueira.com.br. Founded 1928; green and pink.

Moçidade Independente de Padre Miguel Rua Cel. Tamarindo 38, Padre Miguel ☏21/3332-5823. Founded 1952; green and white.

Portela Rua Clara Nunes 81, Madureira ☏21/3390-0471. Founded 1923; blue and white.

Salgueiro Rua Silva Telles 104, Tijuca ☏21/2238-5564, ⓦwww.salgueiro.com.br. Founded 1953; red and white.

The **parade** of schools starts at 7.30pm, with eight schools parading on each of the two nights, and goes on till noon the following day. Two stands (7 & 9) in the Sambódromo are reserved for foreign visitors and **seats** cost over $60 per night. Though much more expensive than other areas, the seats here are more comfortable and have good catering facilities. Other sections of the Sambódromo cost from $3 to $25 and there are three seating options: the high stands (*arquibancadas*), lower stands (*geral*) and the ringside seats (*cadeiras de pista*) – the last being the best, consisting of a table, four chairs and full bar service.

Unless you have a very tough backside you will find sitting through a ten-hour show to be an intolerable test of endurance. Most people don't turn up until 11pm, by which time the show is well under way and hotting up considerably. **Tickets** are available principally from Riotur (see p.73), or through the Banco do Brasil, which has offices in most major capital cities. Book well in advance if you can, or try local travel agents who often have tickets available for a modest commission.

Blocos

In whatever *bairro* you're staying there will probably be a **bloco** or **bandas** – a small samba school that doesn't enter an official parade – organized by the local residents; ask about them in your hotel. These schools offer a hint of what Carnaval was like before it became regulated and commercialized. Starting in mid-afternoon, they'll continue well into the small hours, the popular ones accumulating thousands of followers as they wend their way through the neighbourhood. They all have a regular starting point, some have set routes, others wander freely; but they're easy to follow – there's always time to have a beer and catch up later.

Carnaval dates

The four days of Carnaval for the next few years are as follows:
21–24 Feb 2004
5–8 Feb 2005
25–28 Feb 2006
17–20 Feb 2007

Some of the best *blocos* are: the Banda da Glória, which sets off from near the Estação Glória metrô station; the Banda da Ipanema (the first to be formed, in 1965), which gathers behind Praça General Osório in Ipanema; the Banda da Vergonha do Posto 6, starting in Rua Francisco Sá in Copacabana; and the Carmelitas de Santa Teresa which gathers in the *bairro* of the same name. There are dozens of others, including several in each *bairro* of the Zona Sul, each providing a mix of music, movement and none-too-serious cross-dressing – a tradition during Carnaval that even the most macho of men indulge in.

Carnaval balls

It's the **Carnaval balls** that really signal the start of the celebrations, warm-up sessions in clubs and hotels for rusty revellers, which are quite likely to get out of hand as inhibitions give way to a rampant eroticism. They all start late, normally after 10pm, and the continual samba beat supplied by live bands drives the festivities into the new day. At most of the balls, *fantasia* (fancy dress) is the order of the day, elaborate costumes brightening the already hectic proceedings – but don't worry if you haven't got one; just dress reasonably smartly.

You'll often have to pay an awful lot to get into these affairs, as some of the more fashionable balls attract the rich and famous. If you've got the money and the silly costume, then those worth checking out include the Pão de Açúcar, on the Friday before Carnaval, halfway up the famous landmark – spectacular views, exotic company, but well over $70 a head and very snobby (☏21/3541-3737 for details). The Hawaiian Ball, hosted by the Rio Yacht Club, opens the season on the Friday of the week before Carnaval: it takes place around the club's swimming pool, amid lavish decorations, and is popular and expensive (about $50); tickets are available from the Yacht Club, on Avenida Pasteur, a few hundred metres before the Sugar Loaf cable car terminus. The Friday immediately before Carnaval (which doesn't officially start until Monday) is a big occasion, too, with the Baile de Champagne and the Baile Vermelho e Preto taking place. The latter (the "Red and Black Ball") has developed a particular reputation as a no-holds-barred affair. Named after the colours of Rio's favourite football team, Flamengo, it's a media event with TV cameras scanning the crowds for famous faces – exhibitionism is an inadequate term for the immodest goings-on at the Red and Black celebrations. In Leblon the Monte Libano (☏21/3239-0032 for details) hosts a number of "last days of Rome" festivities – the Baile das Gatas, Baile Fio Dental, even Bum Bum Night – sexually charged exercises all, though safe to attend and reasonable at around $20 a ticket.

There are a number of **gay balls**, too, which attract an international attendance. The Grande Gala G is an institution, usually held in the *Help* disco on Copacabana's Avenida Atlântica. Another is the Baile dos Enxutos, hosted by the *Hotel Itália* on Praça Tiradentes, Centro.

In recent years, the *Scala* club in Leblon has become an important centre for balls, and has hosted the Baile Vermelho e Preto amongst others. You can confirm venues by phoning the *Scala* (☏21/3274-9148), or by asking at the box office, Av. Afrânio de Melo Franco 292, Leblon.

Shopping

It's not hard to find things to buy in Rio, but it's surprisingly difficult to find much that's distinctively Brazilian. Throughout the city are shops geared to tourists, most of which sell a similar line in semi-precious stones, mounted piranha fish and T-shirts, but the best shopping area is, undoubtedly, Ipanema with a wealth of boutiques lining Rua Visconde de Pirajá and its side streets. Books and CDs, however, make good purchases – sales assistants in music stores are usually delighted to make recommendations and you'll be able to listen before you buy. Of Rio's **markets**, the Hippie Market (see p.107) at Ipanema has nowadays become rather touristy; much better is the Babilônia Feira Hype (see p.108) in Gávea, or the Feira de Antigüidades at Praça Santos (Sun 9am–5pm), good for antiques (or more accurately, bric-a-brac).

Shopping centres

Purpose-built, air-conditioned, **shopping centres** – *shoppings* – have mush-roomed in Rio during the last couple of decades. The largest, best known and most central is RioSul (Mon–Sat 10am–10pm, Sun 3–9pm), before the Pasmado Tunnel at the end of Botafogo. Inside there are department stores, a supermarket, and hundreds of fashion boutiques, record stores and places to grab a snack or meal. Other *shoppings* include Shopping Center da Gávea, Rua Marquês de São Vicente (Mon–Sat 10am–10pm), and the small, upmarket São Conrado Fashion Mall, Estrada da Gávea 899 (Mon–Thurs 10am–9pm, Fri & Sat 10am–11pm, Sun 3–9pm). Definitely worth seeking out is Originallis, which has branches at all of Rio's *shoppings*. Brazil's answer to the Body Shop or Lush, the chain sells natural soaps infused with essential oils – the colours and smells are fantastic.

Crafts

Handicraft shops are scattered all over the city but are largely a disappoint-ment. One of the best, with a varied collection from all over Brazil (including work by local artists), is La Vereda, in the centre of Santa Teresa at Rua Almirante Alexandrino 428, Largo dos Guimarães. An attractive range is also found at Andanças in the Shopping Center da Gávea. O Sol, Rua Corcovado 213, in Jardim Botânico, is a non-profit outlet selling folk art including basket-ware, ceramics and wood carvings. For Amerindian basketry and feather items, the best place to shop is the Loja Artíndia in the Museu do Índio in Botafogo (see p.104).

Music and books

CDs are much cheaper in Rio than in either Europe or North America and make great souvenirs. Many stores still have old recordings available on vinyl at bargain prices. The largest music stores in Rio include Modern Sound at Rua Barata Ribeiro 502 (near the corner of Rua Santa Clara), Copacabana, and the Saraiva Megastore, Rua do Ouvidor 98, Centro (with a branch in the RioSul shopping centre). For secondhand records, go to Top Discos, located at Rua Uruguaiana 18 and Rua 7 Setembro 139, with both branches in Centro.

Ipanema's Rua Visconde de Pirajá is the location of several of Rio's better bookshops, with the largest and best being, at no. 572, the Livraria da Travessa. The English-language section is small, but the shop has an excellent stock of art and other coffee-table books on Brazilian subjects. The shop also has a small, but very good, selection of CDs, mainly by Brazilian artists and an excel-lent restaurant as well (see p.118). A smaller branch is located at no. 462 on the same street. The Saraiva Megastore (see above) also happens to be the largest bookshop in Centro, though its English-language section is limited. A great place to browse is the Café com Letras at Av. Bartolomeu Mitre 297, Leblon, where apart from a good selection of titles there's a café with excellent light meals and cakes, and regular live music and Internet access.

Listings

Airlines Aerolíneas Argentinas ☎21/3398-3520; Air Canada ☎21/2220-5343; Air France ☎21/2532-3642; Alitalia ☎21/2292-4424 or 3398-3663; American Airlines ☎21/2210-3126 or 3398-4093; British Airways ☎21/2259-6144 or 3398-3888; Continental Airlines ☎21/2531-1142; Delta Airlines ☎21/2507-7227 or 3398-3492; Gol ☎21/3398-5131; Iberia ☎21/2282-1336 or 398-3168; Japan Airlines ☎21/2220-6414; KLM ☎21/2544-7744; Lan Chile ☎0800-55-4900; Lloyd Aéreo Boliviano ☎21/2220-9548; Lufthansa ☎21/2217-6111 or 3398-3855; Pluna ☎21/2240-8217 or 3398-2000; TAP ☎212/210-1278 or 3393-1411; United Airlines ☎21/2532-1212 or 3398-4050; Varig ☎21/2220-3821 or 3398-3522; VASP ☎0800-998-277.

Airports Galeão airport ☎21/3398-4526 or 3398-4527; Santos Dumont ☎21/3814-7070.

Banks and exchange Main bank branches are concentrated in Av. Rio Branco in Centro and Av. N.S. de Copacabana in Copacabana. It's worth remembering that although most banks remain open until 4.30pm you can usually exchange money only until 3pm or 3.30pm. There are ATMs located throughout the city.

Car rental Avis, Av. Princesa Isabel 150, Copacabana ☎21/2542-3392; Hertz, Av. Princesa Isabel 334, Copacabana ☎21/2275-3245 & 0800-701-7300; Interlocadora, Av. Princesa Isabel 186, Copacabana ☎21/2275-7440; Localiza-National, Av. Princesa Isabel 214, Copacabana ☎0800-99-2000; Unidas, Av. Princesa Isabel 350, Copacabana ☎21/2275-8496. Prices start at about $40 per day and you'll need a credit card to rent the car. It's often cheaper to reserve in advance from abroad.

Consulates Argentina, Praia de Botafogo 228, Botafogo ☎21/2553-1646; Australia, Rua Rio Branco 1, Centro ☎21/2518-3351; Canada, Rua Lauro Müller 116, Botafogo ☎21/2542-9297; Peru, Av. Rui Barbosa 314, Flamengo ☎21/2551-6296; UK, Praia do Flamengo 284, 2nd Floor, Flamengo ☎21/2553-9600; US, Av. Presidente Wilson 147, Centro ☎21/2292-7117; Uruguay, Praia de Botafogo 242, Botafogo ☎21/2552-6699; Venezuela, Praia de Botafogo 242, Botafogo ☎21/2551-5398.

Dentists Assistência Dentária, Av. das Américas 2300, Barra de Tijuca ☎21/3399-1603; Dentário Rollin, Rua Cupertinho Durão 81, Leblon ☎21/2259-2647; Clínica de Urgência, Rua Marquês de Abrantes 27, Botafogo ☎21/2226-0083.

Health matters For medical emergencies, English-speakers should try a private clinic such as Sorocaba Clinic, Rua Sorocaba 464, Botafogo (☎21/2286-0022) or Centro Médico Ipanema, Rua Anibal Mendonça 135, Ipanema (☎21/2239-4647). Your best bet for any non-emergency problems is the Rio Health Collective, Banco Nacional building (room 303), Av. das Américas 4430, Barra de Tijuca; a non-profit organization, its phone-in service (☎21/3325-9300, ext 44) is free, and provides names of qualified professionals who speak foreign languages. Alternatively, your consulate should have a list of professionals who speak your language.

Internet Rates are usually $2–3 an hour. Places to try are Comprio, Rua da Assembléia 10, basement loja 114, Centro (Mon–Fri 9am–6.30pm); Internet Café, Rua da Assembléia 10, basement loja 112, Centro (Mon–Fri 9am–7pm, Sat 9am–1pm); Internethouse, Av. N.S. de Copacabana 195, loja 106, Copacabana (Mon–Sat 9am–10pm); Conexão Copacabana Internet Access, Av. N.S. de Copacabana 374, loja 202. Internet facilities, and a very useful travellers' notice board, can be found at the office of South America Experience, a tour operator at Rua Raimundo Correa 36 in Copacabana.

Laundry All hotels have a laundry service, but these are always very expensive, while most hostels have laundry facilities. Good prices for service washes and dry cleaning are offered by Laundry Express at Rua Figueiredo Magalhães 885 and at Rua Teixeira de Melo 31.

Newspapers and magazines There are several kiosks where foreign-language newspapers are available, including ones on Rua Lauro Müller, Botafogo, at junctions along Avenida N.S. de Copacabana, Copacabana, on Rua Visconde de Pirajá, by Praça General Osório in Ipanema, and along Avenida Rio Branco in Centro. The *Herald*

Tribune, *Miami Herald* and the *Financial Times* are the most commonly available English-language newspapers in Rio, and *Time*, *Newsweek* and the *Economist* are also easy to find. The *Jornal do Brasil* and *O Globo* are Rio's two main newspapers, while the weekly news magazine *Veja* features a useful insert (*Veja Rio*) that lists and reviews cultural events in the city.

Pharmacy 24-hour service from Farmácia do Leme, Av. Prado Junior 237, Leme (℡212/2275-3847); and Farmácia Piauí, Av. Ataúlfo de Paiva 1283, Ipanema (℡21/2274-7322).

Police Emergency number ℡190. The beach areas have police posts located at regular intervals. The special Tourist Police are located at Avenida Afrânio de Melo Franco (opposite the Teatro Casa Grande), Leblon (℡21/2511-5112); they are very helpful, speak English and efficiently process reports of theft or other incidents. Open 24 hours a day, 7 days a week.

Post offices *Correios* are open Mon–Fri 8am–6pm, Sat 8am–noon. Main post offices are at Rua Primeiro do Março (corner of Rosario) in Centro; Av. N.S. de Copacabana 540 in Copacabana; Rua Visconde de Pirajá 452, Ipanema; Av. Ataúlfo de Paiva 822, Leblon.

Public holidays In addition to the normal Brazilian public holidays (see p.47), most things close in Rio on January 20 (Dia de São Sebastião) and March 1 (Founding of the City).

Rio de Janeiro state

It's easy to get out of Rio city, something you'll probably want to do at some stage during your stay. There are good **bus** services to all the places mentioned below, while the easiest trips are by ferry just over the bay to the **Ilha de Paquetá** – a car-free zone popular with locals – or to **Niterói**, whose Museu de Arte Contemporânea has become an essential sight for visitors to Rio. After that, the choice is a simple one: either head east along the **Costa do Sol** to Cabo Frio and Búzios, or west along the **Costa Verde** to Ilha Grande and Parati; both coasts offer endless good beaches and little holiday towns, developed to varying degrees. Or strike off **inland** to Petrópolis and Teresópolis, where the mountainous interior provides a welcome, cool relief from the frenetic goings-on back in Rio.

Getting out of the city is easy with inter-urban buses fanning out to all points in the state. If you planning on **renting a car** (see opposite for addresses in Rio), this is as good a state as any to brave the traffic: the coasts are an easy drive from the city and stopping off at more remote beaches is easy, while your own wheels would let you get to grips with the extraordinary scenery up in the mountains. If you've never driven in Brazil before, it's a good idea to collect your car on a Sunday when traffic in Rio is fairly light and when there are few trucks on the highways outside of the city. If you're young, seeking the companionship of other travellers, and want some flexibility with your travel plans, an excellent way to explore the coast to the north and south of Rio is with the hop-on, hop-off routes of South America Experience (see p.33).

Ilha de Paquetá

The **ILHA DE PAQUETÁ** is an island of one square kilometre in the north of Guanabara Bay, an easy day-trip that is very popular with *cariocas* at weekends. It was first occupied by the Portuguese in 1565 and later was a favourite resort of Dom João VI, who had the São Roque chapel built here in 1810.

During the naval revolt of 1893 against the government of Floriano Peixoto, the island was the insurgents' principal base: their HQ, the Chácara dos Coqueiros, still stands, though it's not open to the public. Nowadays, however, the island is almost entirely given over to tourism. About 2000 people live here, but at weekends that number is multiplied several times by visitors from the city. They come for the tranquillity – the only motor vehicle is an ambulance – and for the beaches, which sadly are now heavily polluted. Still, it makes a pleasant day's excursion – with colonial-style buildings that retain a certain shabby charm – and the trip is an attraction in itself: if possible, time your return to catch the sunset over the city as you sail back. Weekdays are best if you want to avoid the crowds, or in August come for the wildly celebrated **Festival de São Roque**.

The best way to get around is by **bike**, thousands of which are available to rent very cheaply from alongside the ferry terminal; you can also take a ride in a small horse-drawn cart (*charrete*) or rent one by the hour if you want to take your time and stop off along the way. Not that there's a great deal to see. When you disembark, head along the road past the Yacht Club and you'll soon reach the first **beaches** – Praia da Ribeira and Praia dos Frades. **Praia da Guarda**, a few hundred metres on, has the added attraction of the *Lido* restaurant and the **Parque Duque de Mattos**, with its exuberant vegetation and panoramic views from the top of the Morro da Cruz, a hill riddled with tunnels dug to extract china clay.

Practicalities

Ferries (see p.75) for Paquetá leave from near Rio's Praça XV de Novembro, Centro; the eighty-minute ride costs $1. The hydrofoil takes just half an hour and costs around $3 on weekdays and $5 at weekends.

If you want to stay over, there are a few pleasant small **hotels**, the cheapest being the *Paquetá* at Praça Bom Jesus 15 (℡21/3397-0052; ❷). More expensive, but with air-conditioning, are the *Lido*, Praia José Bonifácio 59 (℡21/3397-0377; ❸), and the *Flamboyant* at Praia Grossa 58 (℡21/397-0028; ❸), the largest hotel on the island. There's a **tourist office** on Praia José Bonifácio, near the intersection with Rua Manuel de Macedo, on the opposite side of the island from the ferry landing.

East: Niterói and the Costa do Sol

Across the strait at the mouth of Guanabara Bay lies **Niterói**, founded in 1573 and until 1975 the capital of the old state of Guanabara. Though lacking the splendour of the city of Rio, Niterói, with a population of half a million, has a busy commercial centre, an important museum and lively nightlife – well worth a visit, certainly, as it's also the gateway to the **Costa do Sol** to the east.

Buses out of Niterói head east along the Costa do Sol, which is dominated by three large **lakes** – Maricá, Saquerema and Araruama, separated from the ocean by long, narrow stretches of white sandy beach – and flecked with small towns bearing the same names as the lakes. Approximately 10km directly south of Niterói are a number of smaller lakes, too, collectively known as the **Lagos Fluminenses**, though these aren't really worth the effort to get to as the water is polluted. However, the evil-smelling sludge that surrounds them is purported to have medicinal properties. The main lakes are also muddy, but at least the water here is clean and much used for water sports of all kinds. The brush around the lakes is full of wildlife (none of it particularly ferocious), while the fresh, salty air makes a pleasing change from the city streets.

Niterói

Cariocas have a tendency to sneer at **NITERÓI**, typically commenting that the only good thing about the city are the views back across Guanabara Bay to Rio. While it's certainly true that the views are absolutely gorgeous on a clear day, Niterói has plenty more to offer, not least of which is the stunning Oscar Niemeyer–designed **Museu de Arte Contemporânea** (Tues–Fri 11am–6pm, Sat 1–9pm & Sun 11am–6pm), or MAC as it is more commonly called. Opened in 1996, and located just south of the centre on a promontory by the Praia da Boa Viagem, the flying saucer–shaped building offers 360-degree views of Niterói and across the bay to Rio. The museum boasts a worthy, though hardly exciting, permanent display of Brazilian art from the 1950s to the 1990s and also hosts temporary exhibitions, but the real work of art is the building itself, which even hardened critics of Niemeyer find difficult to dismiss out of hand. The curved lines of the building are simply beautiful, and the views of the headland, nearby beaches and Guanabara Bay as you walk around inside it breathtaking.

The Museu de Arte Contemporânea aside, Niterói has several other sights worth seeing, but they are in isolated spots throughout the city. A short distance southwest of the ferry terminal, the **Ilha da Boa Viagem** (April–Dec, 4th Sun of each month, 1–5pm), connected to the mainland by a causeway leading from Vermelha and Boa Viagem beaches, offers excellent views across the bay to Rio. On the island, guarding the entrance to the bay, are the ruins of a fort, built in 1663, and opposite there's a small chapel dating from the seventeenth century.

Praia de Jurujuba, long and often crowded, is reached from the centre along the beautiful bayside road by bus #33 ("via Fróes"). On the way, it's worth taking a look at the church of **São Francisco Xavier**, a pretty colonial church said to have been built in 1572. The church is open rather irregularly, but the priest lives next door and will open it up on request.

A short distance southeast along the coast, through Jurujuba, is the **Fortaleza de Santa Cruz** dating from the sixteenth century. The largest fort guarding the bay, it's still in use as a military establishment, but you can visit daily between 9am and 4pm (except Mon). As the nearest point across the bay to Rio's Sugar Loaf mountain, the views are particularly good from here. If you have time, also check out the **Museu de Arqueologia de Itaipu** (Wed–Sun 1–5pm), in the ruined eighteenth-century Santa Teresa convent near Itaipu beach, for its collection of ceramics and other artefacts excavated from ancient burial mounds. Around here, to the east of Niterói, beyond the bay, there are loads of **restaurants, bars and hotels**, all of which fill up with *cariocas* at weekends.

Practicalities

You can reach Niterói either by car or **bus** across the 14km of the Ponte Costa e Silva, the Rio–Niterói bridge (bus #999 from the Menezes Cortes bus terminal), or, much more fun, by catching the **ferry**, every fifteen to thirty minutes from the CONERJ docks, close to Praça XV de Novembro; ferries take about half an hour and the fare is 50¢. **Hydrofoils** ($2) leave from the same dock at similar intervals and take just ten minutes.

Tourist information is available from an office in São Francisco at Estrada Leopoldo Fróes 773 (9am–6pm), some distance from both the ferry and MAC. Although there are some good **places to eat** in Niterói, none is outstanding.

Worth considering, however, are *Coelho á Caçarola* at Av. Central 20, in Itaipu (closed Mon–Wed), which has on its menu some 25 different rabbit dishes; *Churrascaria Vacaria do Sul* at Rua do Rosário 147, the best place in town to satisfy a meat craving; *Dona Henriqueta* at Rua Francisco Dutra 147, which is a fine Portuguese restaurant; and *Marius Crustáceos* at Av. Prefeito Sílvio Picanço 479, which specialises in crab dishes.

Finally, a word of warning: although MAC is located just 1.5km from the ferry terminal, do not attempt to walk there as tourists have been robbed along the route. A taxi won't cost much, and it's also possible to take a bus to Praia de Icaraí and walk from there.

Maricá and Saquerema

MARICÁ, 40km from Niterói, is the first stop on the Costa do Sol. A sprawling fishing centre standing on the north bank of the lagoon, its peaceful waters are only narrowly separated from the ocean surf by the **Barra de Maricá** and **Ponta Negra** beaches, more laid-back than Rio's Zona Sul. From Ponta Negra the view of the coast is breathtaking. Nearby, in **UBATIBA**, the colonial farm of Rio Fundo has been turned into a museum exhibiting relics from the centuries of slavery.

SAQUEREMA, 100km east of Rio, is a smaller town in a beautiful natural setting, squeezed between the sea and its sixteen-kilometre-long lagoon, retaining vestiges of its origins as a fishing village. Local anti-pollution legislation means that the environment still sustains much wildlife, including the *microleão* monkey, which you may be able to glimpse on a walk into the nearby forests. Saquerema has a healthy agricultural sector, too, based on fruit cultivation, and orchards surround the town. The main business nowadays, though, is holiday-making: you'll find holiday homes, art and craft shops and young surfers here in abundance. Saquerema is widely rated as second only to Florianópolis (see p.673) as Brazil's surfing capital, and the **Praia de Itaúna**, 3km from town, is a favourite with the surfers, who gather every year for the National Championship in mid-May. A strong undertow makes its waters potentially dangerous for the casual swimmer, so if you want to swim without struggling against the currents head instead for the **Praia da Vila**, where the seventeenth-century church, Nossa Senhora de Nazaré (daily 8am–5pm), stands on the rocky promontory. For fishing, the **Praia de Jaconé** is a popular haunt, stretching 4km west of Saquerema.

All in all, if you're looking for a place to stop awhile, there's a lot to recommend Saquerema: a relaxed atmosphere, plenty of bars and restaurants, and lots of action at the weekend. **Places to stay** near the centre of town include the *Costa do Sol*, Av. Salgado Filho 5720 (℡22/2651-1233; ❷) an inexpensive but tidy option, and the *Lagoa Azul*, Av. Saquerema 1580 (℡22/2651-1142; ❸), which has a pool and more comfortable rooms. Further out, on the Praia de Itaúna, is the small and attractive *Pousada do Suiço*, Rua das Pitangas 580 (℡ & ℱ022/2651-2203; ❸), also with a pool.

Araruama and around

Fourteen kilometres further along the coast, **ARARUAMA** stands on the edge of one of the largest lakes in Brazil. The lake – of the same name as the town – covers an area of 192 square kilometres, its saline water fringed with sand that is said to be effective in treating rheumatic and dermatological conditions.

The town itself has sprawled considerably over recent years as holiday homes, campsites and hotels have sprung up to accommodate the growing numbers of *cariocas* who come here at the weekend. There's no shortage of unpolluted **beaches** within walking distance, though the most popular ones are located some distance away – **Praia Seca**, the nearest of these, with its impressive dunes, is some 16km away, part of the much larger **Maçambaba** beach, which continues all the way to Arraial do Cabo (see p.136). The road between Araruama and Cabo Frio passes alongside these beaches; there's an occasional bus, or you can take a taxi, though either way it can be hard to get transport back.

There are several moderately priced **places to stay** on the road out towards Praia Seca. Two good *pousadas*, both with pools, are the *Suba Pra Ver* at Km 11 (✆ & ✆ 22/2661-2171; ❸), with pleasant rooms on attractive grounds, and the *Praia dos Amores* at Km 3.5 (✆ 22/2665-6005, ⓦ www.praiadosamores .hpg.com.br), where the simple but well-decorated rooms are slightly more comfortable and afford wonderful views across the lake.

São Pedro da Aldeia

The countryside around Araruama is one of Brazil's most important salt-producing regions, and the windmills that pull the saline solution up to the surface dominate the skyline. The saltpans into which the solution emerges are of various sizes but are always square and arranged juxtaposed like a great patchwork quilt, speckled with small piles of salt brushed into heaps from the surface of the pans. At the north end of Araruama lake, the small town of **SÃO PEDRO DA ALDEIA**, a 22-kilometre bus ride east of Araruama on the way to Cabo Frio, is built around a Jesuit church and mission house (Mon–Fri 8am–noon & 2–5pm, Sat & Sun 8am–noon) which date back to 1617. Perched on a hill above the shores of the lake, the town provides a marvellous view over the saltpans and surrounding area.

The cheapest **pousada** in town, located beside an attractive lagoon, is the *Aldeia dos Ventos*, Rua João Martins 160 (✆ 22/2621-2919; ❷), with very basic rooms. It's worth paying more, however, for the colonial-style *Pousada Ponta da Peça* (✆ 22/2621-1181; ❹), 5km from town on the Praia do Sudoeste, for its well-appointed rooms, delightful grounds and excellent views across the lagoon and surrounding countryside. Excellent fish dishes can be had at the *Restaurante Vovó Chica* at Av. Getúlio Vargas 32.

Cabo Frio

During the summer months, and especially at weekends, **CABO FRIO** is at a pitch of holiday excitement, generated by the out-of-towners who come here to relax in the fresh sea breezes. The town was founded in the late sixteenth century, but it was only really in the twentieth century that it developed, thanks to the salt and tourist industries. Cabo Frio is built around sand dunes and there are **beaches** everywhere: indeed, this is the only attraction, since the town is both extremely ugly and poorly planned, but it's a relaxed place and the bars are full of happy holiday-makers at night.

The closest beaches to town are the small **Praia do Forte**, near the centre, with its fort of **São Mateus** (daily 8am–6pm) built by the French in 1616 for protection against pirates, and the larger, more popular **Praia da Barra**. The best beaches, though, all lie outside Cabo Frio, a taxi ride or decent walk away on the route to Arraial do Cabo, another small town a few kilometres to the south (see p.136). Six kilometres north in the direction of Búzios, near Ogivas, lies **Praia do Peró**, a good surfing spot, peaceful and deserted on weekdays, and further on is the small **Praia das Conchas**, with its sand dunes and clear, calm, blue waters.

On arrival, it's a three-kilometre walk in from the **bus station** to the centre, along Avenida Júlia Kubitschek. There are excellent bus connections to and from Rio, São Paulo, Belo Horizonte and Petrópolis as well as up and down the coast. Praça Porto Rocha, the location of the telephone office and a branch of Banco do Brasil, marks the centre of town. Alongside the square is one of the town's very few buildings of note, the church of **Nossa Senhora da Assunção**, built in 1615 by the Jesuits, which has been perfectly preserved. One block west of here, at Largo de Santo Antônio 55, is the post office.

Practicalities

There are plenty of **hotels** and **pousadas** in and around Cabo Frio, though during summer weekends it can be impossible to find a room. The **tourist office** (Mon–Fri 8am–6pm, Sat & Sun 9am–6pm; ☎22/2647-1684) at Praça Cristóvão Colombo near to the Praia do Forte can help find you a room. The lowest-priced *pousadas*, all offering pretty basic accommodation, are in the town centre on Rua Jorge Lóssio and Rua José Bonifácio; the best ones include *Porto Fino* on the former at no. 160 (☎22/2643-6230; ❸), and *Cochicho do Xandico* at no. 224 (☎22/2643-2525; ❸), and on the latter, *Atlântico* at no. 302 (☎22/2643-0096; ❷). Most hotels and *pousadas*, and those with better facilities, however, are concentrated along the beaches. Praia do Peró boasts Cabo Frio's most expensive hotel, the well-appointed *La Plage* (☎22/2643-1746, ⓦwwwredebela.com.br; ❻), along with the more attractive *Quintais das Dunas* (☎22/643-3894; ❹), which also has a pool. The *Porto Peró* (☎22/2644-5568, ⓦwww.pousadaportopero.com.br; ❸), a new, rather characterless pousada has the advantage of being on a particularly attractive stretch of beach. There's also a very popular **youth hostel** at Rua Goiás 266 (☎22/2645-3037; ❷), with rooms each sleeping two people.

Cabo Frio has no shortage of **restaurants** either in the town centre or on the beaches. In the centre, the *Picolino* at Rua Marechal Floriano 319, is noted for serving the town's best fish dishes, while at Praia do Forte, *La Carreta*, Av. Nilo Peçanha 443, is an excellent *churrascaria*.

Arraial do Cabo

Six kilometres south of Cabo Frio, **ARRAIAL DO CABO** nestles amongst more sand dunes, surrounded by hills. It's home to the Institute of Marine Research, based on Cabo Frio island 4km east of the town, whose object is to increase the level of marine life in the region. The aim is a laudable one, though it's uncertain whether the real purpose has more to do with replenishing stocks for next season's marine sports than preserving the area's ecology. The **beaches** around Arraial do Cabo are some of the most beautiful in the state and are usually packed in high season. Praia dos Anjos is perfectly fine considering the area behind is so built up, though you'd do much better by walking (15mins) along a path over a steep promiontory to the the unspoilt Praia do Forno. You'll have to take a boat to the absolutely stunning Praia do Pontal and the **Ilha de Cabo Frio**, a small, pristine island with powdery white beaches, sand dunes and superb views from its 390-metre peak. Boats leave from Praia dos Anjo and charge around $7 per person for a four-hour excursion. Another attractive beach is Prainha, which has the advantage of shade but can get crowded as it's easily reached by car. Even so, the water is beautiful and it's easy to ignore the people around you. At all beaches – even the most isolated – you can get drinks and snacks.

Arraial do Cabo is a much more attractive place to stay than overdeveloped Cabo Frio, but has little in the way of budget **accommodation**. Your best bet is to make for the Praia dos Anjos: the *Estalagem do Porto* (☎22/2622-2892, Ⓦwww.estalagemdoporto.com; ❸), a comfy place with rooms sleeping up to six people; a similar but rather prettier *pousada*, with the added attraction of a pool, is the *Capitão n'Areia* (☎22/2622-2720, Ⓦwww.capitaopousada.com.br; ❹). Also at Praia dos Anjos, there's an excellent IYHF **youth hostel** at Rua Bernardo Lems 145 (☎22/2622-4060; $8 per person), with dorms as well as private rooms that sleep two people (members ❷, non-members ❸). Guests can rent canoes, diving equipment and bicycles, and the staff are extremely knowledgeable about the local area.

Búzios

Keep time free for **ARMAÇÃO DOS BÚZIOS**, or Búzios as it's more commonly known; direct buses run to this peninsula from Rio at least ten times a day, or every fifteen minutes from Cabo Frio, a bumpy fifty-minute ride along a cobbled road. A place of great natural beauty and with less than 35 days of rain a year, mostly falling in September and October, it's a bit like taking a step out of Brazil and into some high-spending Mediterranean resort: Armação, the main settlement, is built in a vaguely Portuguese colonial style, its narrow cobbled streets are lined with restaurants, bars and chic boutiques, and even the surrounding landscape appears more Mediterranean than Brazilian. Búzios has been nicknamed "Brazil's St Tropez", and it comes as little surprise to find that it was "discovered" by none other than Brigitte Bardot, who stumbled upon it by accident while touring the area in 1964. Despite being transformed overnight from humble fishing village to playground of the rich, Búzios didn't change much until some serious property development took hold in the 1980s. Now, during the high season (Dec to Feb), the population swells from 20,000 to well over 150,000, the fishing boats that once ferried the catch back to shore take pleasure-seekers beach-hopping and scuba diving, and the roads connecting the town with the outlying beaches have been paved. This is the kind of place one either loves or hates: if a crowded resort full of high-spending beautiful people is your thing then you're sure to fall for Búzios, but if not give it a miss. Outside of the peak summer high season, it's hard not to be taken in by the peninsula's sheer beauty, with March and April the perfect time to visit as tourists are relatively few, prices low and the weather generally perfect.

Accommodation

Accommodation in Búzios is expensive and in the high season reservations are essential, although the tourist offices will do their best to help you find a room in one of the resort's more than 150 hotels and *pousadas*. If you can't find a room in Búzios, you could consider staying in Cabo Frio where rooms are always cheaper and easier to come by. The lower-priced *pousadas* can be found in or near Armação or Ossos; they are generally the nicest too, very friendly and mainly owned and run by Argentines, who have been an important presence in Búzios since the 1960s, even today making up two-thirds of the tourists. The price codes below are based on high-season prices; at other times you can expect discounts of up to 50 percent.

Brigitta's Guest House Rua das Pedras 131, Armação ☎22/2623-6157. Swiss-owned and -run, with four simple rooms, the best of which open directly onto the beach. Rather expensive, but very friendly. ❻

Hibiscus Beach Rua 1, Praia de João Fernandes ☎22/2623-6221, Ⓦwww.hibiscusbeach.com.br. Spacious bungalows, each with a small terrace and wonderful sea views, make up this welcoming British-owned and -run *pousada*. There's a good-sized pool and the area's best snorkelling beach is just seconds away, while Armaçao's nightlife is a five-minute taxi ride (or half-hour walk). ⑥

Meu Sonho Av. José Bento Ribeiro Dantas 1289, Ossos ☎22/2623-0902; ⓦwww .meusonho-buzios.8k.com. Located one block from the beach, this *pousada* has clean, basic rooms and a plunge pool, with the only Internet café in Búzios next door. ❸

Morombo Av. José Bento Ribeiro Dantas 1242, Armação ☎22/2623-1532. An extremely hospitable Argentine owner, good rooms and an attractive terrace all combine to make this an appealing place to stay. Located on the waterfront road leading to Ossos. ❹

Recanto do Mar Praça Santos Dumont 304, Armação ☎22/2623-4413. Simple, small rooms, an attractive lounge and rather unfriendly staff but right in the centre of Armação. ❹.

Santa Fe Praça Santos Dumont 300, Armação ☎22/2623-6404. Similar in just about every

respect to the *Recanto do Mar*, including the staff's distant attitude. Even so, it's good value and very popular thanks to its proximity to Búzios' nightlife. ❸

Seria Dourada Praia dos Ossos ☎22/2623-1131. One of the cheapest places to stay in Búzios – basic but comfortable, with a quiet beach-side location. ❸

Solar do Peixe Vivo Rua José Bento Ribeiro Dantas 999, Armação ☎22/2623-1850, ⓦwww.solardopeixevivo.com.br. The main reception building is notable for being one of the oldest structures in Búzios. The guest rooms, in cabins in the garden, are simple but spacious; the atmosphere friendly and relaxed. The beach is directly across the road, and there's a pool in the garden. ❺

Vila do Mar Travessa dos Pescadores 88, Armação ☎22/2623-1466. Very attractive rustic-chic *pousada*, with comfortable rooms, some with sea views, and a small pool. ⑥

The Town and its beaches

Búzios consists of three main settlements, each with its own distinct character. **Manguinos**, on the isthmus, is the main service centre with a tourist office (24hr; ☎0800-249-999), a medical centre, banks and petrol stations. Midway along the peninsula, linked to Manguinos by a road lined with brash hotels, is **Armação**, an attractive village where cars are usually banned from the cobbled roads. Most of Búzio's best restaurants and boutiques are concentrated here, along with some of the resort's nicest *pousadas*, and there's also a helpful tourist office on the main square, Praça Santos Dumont (daily 9am–8pm; ☎22/2623-2099). A fifteen-minute walk along the coast from Armação, passing the lovely seventeenth-century Igreja Nossa Senhora de Sant'Ana on the way, you reach **Ossos**, the oldest settlement, comprised of a pretty harbour, a quiet beach and a few bars, restaurants and *pousadas*.

Within walking distance of all the settlements are beautiful white-sand **beaches**, 27 in total, cradled between rocky cliffs and promontories, and bathed by crystal blue waters. A good way to get oriented is to hop on the **Búzio Trolley** (9am, noon, 3pm; 3 hrs; $8) at Praça Santos Dumont, which goes to twelve beaches and two look-out points, and offers an English-language commentary on the peninsula's vegetation, micro-climate and history. The beaches are varied, with the north-facing ones having the calmest and warmest seas, while those facing the south and east have the most surf. Though the beaches at Búzios' urban centre of Armação – the **Praia do Canto** and **Praia da Armação** and, to a lesser extent, the **Praia dos Ossos** – look good, the water is polluted and swimming should be avoided. A short distance to the northeast of Armação, however are the very clean waters of the small, rather isolated and extremely picturesque beaches of **Azeda** and **Azedinha** and of the rather larger **João Fernandes**, the best place around here for snorkelling. Further east is **Praia Brava**, which is rarely over-crowded as there are few hotels close by. On the north of the peninsula, to the west of Armação, is the **Praia da Tartaruga**, where the water is pristine and, apart from some bars, there are few buildings. South of Armação **is Praia da Ferradura**, a lovely bay and quite built up (and consequently crowded), but not nearly as bad as **Praia**

de Geribá, which is solidly backed by condominium developments. Further out is the appealing **Praia de Tucuns**, a long stretch of sand that attracts surprisingly few people.

Apart from walking, you can get from beach to beach by minivan (50¢), taxi (rarely more than $5) or by hitching lifts, a fairly common way of getting around though, as usual, caution should be taken. Once at the beaches, you can rent kayaks or *pedalos*, or indulge in a little windsurfing. Several dive operators, based in Armação, lead scuba trips to the Ilha Âncoa ($40 for two dives) and rent snorkelling equipment ($5 a day) for use at Praia João Fernandes.

Eating

Restaurants are, predictably, either fairly expensive or very expensive. The best places to eat, including those listed below, are concentrated in Armação, especially along Rua das Pedras and its extension, Avenida José Bento Ribeiro Dantas. Cheaper options include the *barracas* selling grilled fish on the beaches or the numerous pizza places in the town's outlying areas.

Bananaland Rua Manoel Turíbio de Farias 50. On a parallel street to Rua das Pedras, this is the best *por kilo* restaurant in Búzios and one of the cheapest for a solid meal; the choice amongst the buffet of salads and hot dishes is outstanding.

Chez Michou Crêperie Rua das Pedras 90. Belgian-owned, this has long been Armação's most popular hangout thanks to its open-air bar, cheap drinks and authentic crêpes. Open until dawn, when it serves breakfast to the patrons pouring out of the *Fashion Café* (see below).

Cigalon Rua das Pedras 265. Excellent, authentic French cooking, with the occasional uniquely Brazilian ingredient thrown in. Formal and expensive, but nevertheless remarkable value for a top restaurant.

Esotância Don Juan Rua das Pedras 178. An airy Argentine restaurant serving first-rate meat to a demanding (mainly Argentine) clientele. If cuts of beef mean little to you, opt for the *bife de chorizo*, the Argentine standard cut. Moderate.

Pizzaria Capricciosa Av. José Bento Ribeiro Dantas 500. The place for pizza in Búzios, with wood-burning ovens and dozens of varieties of pizza to choose from. Moderate.

Samsara Rua Santana Maia 684. Located just off Rua das Pedras, this vegetarian restaurant offers an excellent lunch buffet of hot and cold dishes and à la carte dining in the evening, including interesting pasta offerings. Inexpensive.

Satyricon Rua das Pedras 500. This extremely expensive Italian restaurant (with a branch in Rio) specialises in seafood. Overly formal for laid-back Búzios, but those with money to burn are in for a treat.

Sawasdee Av. José Bento Ribeiro Dantas 422. Excellent, spicy Thai food based around vegetables and seafood. Next door is *Shiitake*, a good attempt at pan-Asian cooking, drawing on Thai, Chinese, Japanese, Vietnamese and Indian cuisine. Moderate.

Sovetes Mil Frutas Rua das Pedras 24. Of the numerous ice-cream places, this is by far the best, offering flavours both familiar and exotic, from *jabuticaba* to "Romeu e Julieta" (guava and cream).

Nightlife

Nightlife – which gets going at around 10pm and continues until dawn – is largely limited to eating, drinking and people watching along Rua das Pedras. It's impossible to exaggerate how crowded Armação gets in January and February, but even in the off-season Rua das Pedras is quite lively at night. The *Pátio Havana*, a rather upscale restaurant and bar at Rua das Pedras 101, is well worth checking out for the first-rate **jazz** artists from Rio, São Paulo and abroad who are hosted there. Strangely, nightclubs haven't taken off here as they have at other similar resorts, but if you want to **dance** (or just watch with a drink), *the* place to head for is the *Fashion Café*, on Rua das Pedras, across the road from the *Chez Michou Crêperie*. Always packed with a mainly youthful crowd, the club has DJs playing a safe mix of Europop and other disco sounds, and there's usually live music by Brazilian or Argentine performers.

Northeast to Campos

If you're not yet tired of **beaches**, you'll find more beautiful examples around the pretty colonial village of Barra de São João and Rio das Ostras, an hour or so up the coast. Near the latter, the iodized waters of the **Lagoa da Coca Cola** (yes, really) boast more medicinal qualities – everyone must be very healthy in this neck of the woods. If you want to stay round here, you'll find *pousadas* in both these places, though there's been much uncontrolled development along this stretch of coast, leading to pretty hideous results.

The next town of any size is **MACAÉ**, on the edge of a large sugar-cane-producing region. The beaches here are utterly unremarkable, the city is extremely ugly and much more industrial than what has gone before, and the arrival of offshore oil drilling has not increased its attractions. From here the main road heads northeast, inland through very attractive rolling countryside to **CAMPOS**, on the River Paraíba some 50km before it flows into the sea. Again it's predominantly a sugar-cane-processing town, and its primarily agro-industrial nature makes it a less than attractive target, given the local alternatives. If you're travelling from Cabo Frio or Búzios north to Espírito Santos or Bahia, your best best is to take a bus to Campos where you'll be able to pick up a connection without much delay.

West: the Costa Verde

The mountainous littoral and calm green waters of the aptly named **Costa Verde** ("Green Coast") provide a marked contrast to the sand and surf of the coastline east of Rio. One of Brazil's truly beautiful landscapes, the Costa Verde has been made much more accessible by the **Rio–Santos BR-101 Highway** – something, however, that has led to an increase in commercial penetration of this region. The fate of this 280-kilometre stretch of lush vegetation, rolling hills and tropical beaches hangs in the balance between rational development and ecological destruction, and so far the signs augur badly. Ecologists warn that fish stocks in the Bay of Sepetiba, which covers almost half the length of the Costa Verde, are in constant danger of destruction because of pollution. Enjoy your trip; you may be amongst the last to have the privilege.

There are two ways to reach the Costa Verde from Rio. By **car**, drive through the Zona Sul by way of Barra de Tijuca, to Barra de Guaratiba. The road runs past kilometre after kilometre of white sand, but you'll need to be mobile to reach any of it. Alternatively, take one of the **buses** from Rio's *rodoviária* that leave the city by way of the Zona Norte and follow the BR-101 to Itacuruçá and beyond.

Itacuruçá and Mangaratiba

ITACURUÇÁ, around 90km from Rio, is a tranquil hamlet that draws wealthy yachting types. The attraction here is obvious: the village nestles between rolling hills and a malachite-coloured sea, its offshore **islands** – Jaguanum and Itacuruçú, with their pleasant walks and beaches – easily reached by boat. Tours of the islands can be arranged with the **tourist office** at Praça da Igreja 130, in Itacuruçá, or are operated direct from Rio (ask at Passamar Turismo, Rua Siqueira Campos 7; ☏21/3233-8835). Both islands have luxury **hotels**: on Itacuruçú the best is *Hotel Pierre* (☏21/3688-1560, ⓦwww .hotelpierre.com.br; ❻), set against a glorious Mata Atlântica backdrop, with

Time bombs in paradise

There's no doubt that the Costa Verde is one of Brazil's most beautiful stretches of coast, so it's not surprising that so many hotel and holiday home complexes are appearing on the hillsides and in the picturesque coves. What is incredible, however, is that the coast was chosen as the location of two complexes with the potential to cause the most environmental destruction – an oil terminal and a nuclear power plant.

The Petrobrás **oil terminal** is, at least, out of sight, located 25km east of Angra, so you only need contemplate the damage that an oil spill could wreak on this ecologically fragile stretch of coast when you pass the barrack-like housing complexes for the Petrobrás workers on the BR-101, the main coastal road towards Angra.

Perhaps more worrying are the **nuclear power plants**, Angra-1 and Angra-2, some 40km west of Angra. The project was directly managed by the Brazilian military, and it's difficult to imagine a more insane place to put a nuclear reactor. Not only would there be enormous difficulties should an emergency evacuation be necessary, as the mountains here plunge directly into the sea, but in addition the plant is in an earthquake fault zone, in a cove that local Indians call *Itaorna*, the moving rock.

The Angra-1's safety record is already in doubt, and since 1985 the plant has been shut down for unspecified repairs over twenty times. Officials insist that there has been no leak of radiation beyond the plant, but environmentalists, who say there may be cracks in the reactor's primary container system, want the plant shut down for good. Its future, however, looks secure: it would be humiliating for the military to abandon the project – it's claimed Angra-1 can supply twenty percent of Brazil's electricity needs while Angra-2, in operation since 1999, has similar potential – and there would be huge problems in decommissioning the plant.

Should you want to visit the plant, the **visitors' centre** offers a predictably professional public relations show (Mon–Fri 8.30am–4.30pm, Sat & Sun 8.30am–3pm).

comfortable rooms, private beaches, a good restaurant and a pool. Almost as good, but slightly cheaper and less exclusive, is *Hotel Elias C* (☎21/3680-7089; ❺). On the neighbouring island of Jaguanum, *Hotel Jaguanum* (☎21/3235-2893; ❻) offers similar accommodation but costs slightly more.

Muddy beaches and the incongruous industrial presence of the Terminal de Sepetiba put off many people stopping at **MANGARATIBA**, which lies 25km west of Itacuruçá along the BR-101. The town setting is attractive, with a mountain backdrop, a beautiful bay in front with fishing boats at anchor and a late eighteenth-century church dominating the main square. On the whole, however, the initial impression is the correct one; there are better spots to stay further along the coast. Five **buses** a day run from Rio to Mangaratiba – currently at 5.30am, 9am, 12.30pm, 3pm and 6.45pm – and if you catch the earliest bus you'll make the daily ferry that sails from Mangaratiba to Ilha Grande (see p.143). Nevertheless, if you do need to stay, Mangaratiba is by no means an unpleasant place to spend a night. There are a couple of **hotels** in town, the very basic *Rio Branco* (❷) on the main square and the air-conditioned *Pensão do Almir* (❸) on the road leading to the hospital. If you head from the main square along the seashore, you'll find several good fish restaurants.

Angra dos Reis

From Mangaratiba, the road continues to hug the coast as it wends its way westwards, rising and falling between towering green-clad mountains and the ocean. Roughly 60km west of Mangaratiba lies the shabby and rather unprepossessing little town of **ANGRA DOS REIS**. The lands around here were "discovered" by the navigator André Gonçalves in 1502, though it wasn't until 1556 that a colonial settlement was established. The port first developed as an entrepôt for the exportation of agricultural produce from São Paulo and Minas Gerais in the seventeeth century. Fifteen slave-worked sugar refineries dominated the local economy, which, with the abolition of slavery at the end of the nineteenth century, suffered a dramatic collapse. The 1930s saw the economy regenerated, with the construction of a new port, and shipbuilding remains an important local trade – although the latest venture is Brazil's first nuclear power station, located nearby.

The main reason to come here is to get out to the thirty or so local islands in the bay. Numerous leisurely **boat and fishing trips** are on offer, and most yachts have a bar at which you can fill the time between stops for swimming at beaches penned in between clear waters and tropical forest. Visiting **Gipóia** by boat, for instance, allows you a couple of hours to splash about and get something to eat in the *Luiz Rosa* bar – all very relaxing. Various companies run trips, so it's best to ask at the **tourist information office** (daily 8am–6pm; ☏24/365-1280) in Largo do Lapa, right across from the bus station and next to the **Cais de Santa Luzia**, from where the boats depart. Trips can also be arranged on the quay with independent operators, but check on the noticeboard for those boat owners who have been authorized to carry tourists. Most trips leave around 10am and return in the late afternoon; on average you'll pay around $10 a head.

Beaches in the town are nothing special. Better ones are found by following the Estrada do Contorno (by car), or catching a **bus** from the bus station (hourly) to the beaches of Bonfim, Gordas, Grande, Tanguá, Tanguazinho, Ribeira or Retiro. There are other beaches within reach, too: along the main BR-101 highway, in the direction of Rio, good spots for bathing and free camping are Garatucaia and Monsuaba.

Practicalities

The bus station, tourist information office and the passenger ferry for Ilha Grande (see p.143) are all located within a few steps of each other in Angra dos Reis. There's no shortage of **hotels** if you're planning to stay around for the beaches and islands, but most are on the pricey side. Try the modest but comfortable *Hotel Londres*, Av. Raul Pompéia 75 (☏24/3365-0044; ❷), or for only slightly more you'll get a pool at the *Acrópolis Marina* on Av. das Caravelas 89 (☏24/3365-2225; ❸).

You'll have no trouble eating and drinking either, with lots of restaurants and bars to choose from: try *Cheiro Verde*, Rua Pereira Peixoto 53, which serves satisfying Arab cuisine, or *Taberna 33* at Av. Raul Pompéia 110, for decent pizzas.

Inland from Angra

If you want to take a break from beaches, the forested **Serra do Mar** lies inland immediately behind Angra. By far the easiest and most enjoyable way to penetrate the forest is by **train**, on the line constructed a hundred years ago to export coffee from the once rich coffee region of Rio Claro. Today the line is mainly used to take coal to the Volta Redonda steel mills, but on weekends and holidays a train takes tourists 40km inland as far as Lídice. The train stops from time to time, allowing passengers to take pictures of the coast below, several waterfalls and forest. The train leaves Angra at 10.30am, arriving back at 4.30pm; tickets ($10 including lunch on the train) should be purchased at least a day in advance from Montmar Turismo, Rua do Comércio 11, Angra (☏24/3365-1705).

Some 22km beyond Angra, there's an excellent **youth hostel**, the *Hospedagem Rio Bracuí* (☎21/3531-2234; $8 per person), a little way inland on the bank of the Rio Bracuí. This is an excellent spot from which to take walks into the Serra do Mar following any of the numerous forest trails. To get here, take any bus going along the coast and get off just after the bridge that crosses the Rio Bracuí. Turn right and head inland along the Estrada do Surubim, and the hostel is located 200m on your left.

Ilha Grande

ILHA GRANDE comprises 193 square kilometres of mountainous jungle, historic ruins and beautiful beaches, excellent for some scenic tropical rambling. The entire island is a state park and the authorities have been successful at limiting development and in maintaining a ban on motor vehicles, whether owned by visitors or locals. The main drawback is the ferocity of the insects, especially during the summer, so come equipped with repellent.

Islands like this deserve a good pirate story, and Ilha Grande is no exception. According to legend, the pirate **Jorge Grego** was heading for the Straits of Magellan when his ship was sunk by a British fleet. He managed to escape with his two daughters to Ilha Grande, where he became a successful farmer and merchant. In a fit of jealousy he murdered the lover of one of his daughters and, shortly afterwards, a terrible storm destroyed all his farms and houses. From then on, Jorge Grego passed his time roaming the island, distraught, pausing only long enough to bury his treasure before his final demise. If there is any treasure today, though, it's in the island's **wildlife**: parrots, exotic hummingbirds, butterflies and monkeys abound in the thick vegetation.

Ilha Grande offers lots of beautiful **walks** along well-maintained and fairly well-signposted trails, but it's sensible to take some basic precautions. Be sure to set out as early as possible and always inform people at your *pousada* where you are going, if possible in writing. Carry plenty of water with you and remember to apply sunscreen and insect repellent at regular intervals. Darkness comes suddenly, and even on a night with a full moon the trails are likely to be pitch-black due to the canopy formed by the overhanging foliage; if possible, carry a flashlight with you – most *pousadas* will be happy to lend you one. Whatever you do, avoid straying from the trail: not only could you easily get hopelessly lost, but there are also rumours of booby traps primed to fire bullets, left over from the days when the island hosted a high-security prison.

Around the island

As you approach the low-lying, whitewashed colonial port of **VILA DO ABRAÃO**, the mountains rise dramatically from the sea, and in the distance there's the curiously shaped summit of Bico do Papagaio ("Parrot's Beak"), which rises to a height of 980m and can be reached in about three hours. There's really very little to see in Abraão itself, but it's a pleasant enough base from which to explore the rest of the island. A half-hour walk along the coast west from Abraão are the ruins of the **Antigo Presídio**. Originally built as a hospital, it was converted to a prison for political prisoners in 1910 and was finally dynamited in the early 1960s. Among the ruins, you'll find the *cafofo*, the containment centre where prisoners who had failed in escape attempts were immersed in freezing water. Just fifteen minutes inland from Abraão, and overgrown with vegetation, stands the **Antigo Aqueduto** that used to channel the island's water supply. There's a fine view of the aqueduct from the **Pedra Mirante**, a hill near the centre of the island, and, close by, a waterfall provides the opportunity for a cool bathe on a hot day.

For the most part the **beaches** – Aventureiro, Lopes Mendes, Canto, Júlia and Morcegoare to name a few – are still wild and unspoilt. They can be most easily reached by **boat**; a typical day-long excursion costs $7–12 per person, and departs from Abraão's jetty at 10.30am, stopping for snorkelling (equipment provided) before continuing on to a beach where you'll be picked up later in the day to arrive back in Abraão at around 4.30pm. Most beaches can also be reached on **foot**, and there are some lovely quiet beaches within an hour's walk of Abraão. The hike from Abraão across the island to **Praia da Parnaioca** will take about five hours, so it's no jaunt. By the coconut-fringed *praia* is an old fishing village that was abandoned by its inhabitants because of their fear of escaped prisoners from a second prison that was built on the island. This prison only closed in April 1994, not before earning the island something of a dangerous reputation as escapes were not infrequent. Today the only dangers come from *borachudos*, almost invisible but vicious gnats that bite without your feeling or hearing them. A tiny fishing community has slowly been established here, and if you need to stay over you should have little trouble finding a room to rent and something to eat. Many of the other beaches have a *barraca* or two selling snacks and cold drinks, but you should bring supplies with you.

Practicalities

There are **boats** from both Mangaratiba and Angra dos Reis to Vila do Abraão on Ilha Grande, each taking an hour or so. From **Mangaratiba** to Abraão, the boat leaves daily at 8am (with an extra boat on Friday at 10pm) and returns at 5.15pm. From **Angra dos Reis**, boats leave at 3.30pm on Monday through Friday and 1.30pm Saturday and Sunday, returning at 10am daily. Tickets cost $3 from both Mangaratiba and Angra; if you miss the ferry you can usually count on finding a small launch to do the crossing, charging around $5 per person and taking around ninety minutes. During the summer there's a constant flow of these launches from both mainland towns, but at other times Angra is the best bet. If you have a car, you'll have to leave it behind on the mainland, but you can get advice at the ferry terminals on where to find a secure, lock-up parking spot. Be sure to come with plenty of **cash**: changing dollars or travellers' cheques is impossible on the island, there's no ATM and few *pousadas* and restaurants accept credit cards.

Accommodation is mostly around Vila do Abraão, and when you arrive you'll probably be approached by youths intent on taking you to a room in a private house (around $8 per person). There are quite a few *pousadas* in Abraão, most of which are quite simple but fairly expensive. Reservations in the high season, especially at weekends, are absolutely essential; try to come in the off-season when prices are halved. One of the nicest *pousadas* is the cosy and friendly *Pousada Oásis* (☎24/3361-5549; ❹), peacefully located on the far end of the beach, a ten-minute walk from the jetty. Almost next door is the similarly sized *Pousada Porto Girassol* (☎24/979-2268; ❹) and the larger, though by no means impersonal, *Pousada do Canto* (☎21/3361-5115; ❺). More hotel-like is the *Pousada Água Viva* (☎21/3361-5166; ❺), located amidst a busy strip of shops and restaurants. There's an appealing **youth hostel** – the always popular *Pousada do Holandês* (☎24/3361-5034; ❷) – behind the beach next to the Assembléia de Deus.

Outside of Abraão there are a few more *pousadas*. One of the most attractive is the *Pousada Sankay* (☎21/3365-1090; ⓦwww.pousadasankay.com.br; ❺ half-board), one hour by boat west of Abraão on the Praia de Bananal. Further west along the coast in the quiet fishing hamlet at Praia Grande de Araçatiba, there are two more charming options, the *Cantinho de Ará* (☎24/3365-1184;

❷) and the *Refúgio do Capitão* (☎19/3272-0185; ❷). If you can cope with the bugs, **camping** is a possibility as there are several good, secure sites in Abraão; you can also camp at beaches around the island, and you can arrange for fishermen to take you from beach to beach if hiking through the forests with your gear doesn't appeal.

Summertime **nightlife** in Abraão is reasonably lively, with the *Bar Verdinho da Ilha* bashing out some eminently danceable *forró* music. Restaurants, predictably, concentrate on seafood (try the *Rei dos Caldos*, which specializes in fish soups), but there are also a couple of pizzerias. **Carnaval** is well celebrated here, much more relaxed than the Rio experience, and watch, too, for the festival of São João (Jan 20) and the Pirate Regatta, which takes place in February.

Tarituba

Back on the mainland, the road west rises amidst the most exhilarating scenery that the whole coast has to offer. About 60km from Angra is **TARITUBA**, a charming little fishing village just off the coast road, still relatively untouched by tourism. Any bus going along the coast will let you off at the side road that leads to the village, or there are buses several times a day from Parati, 35km further west.

There's not much to the village – a pier along which fishing boats land their catches, a few *barracas* on the beach serving fried fish and cold drinks, and a pretty church – it's simply a place to relax in, away from the often brash commercialism of Angra and Parati. There are a couple of decent **pousadas**, but it can be difficult to get a room in high season or even to make telephone reservations. The most comfortable place is the *Tarituba* (☎24/3365-2401; ❸), where large rooms with private verandas and hammocks overlook the pool and beach beyond. Simple, but very friendly and right on the beach is the *Pousada de Carminha* (☎24/3371-1120; ❸), offering either private or shared bathrooms. Bear in mind that here, as right along the coast, the *borachudos* and mosquitoes are murder, so bring plenty of insect repellent and mosquito coils with you.

Parati

About 300km from Rio on the BR-101 is the Costa Verde's main attraction, the town of **PARATI**. Inhabited since 1650, Parati (or more correctly, Vila de Nossa Senhora dos Remédios de Paraty, often still known as "Paraty") has remained fundamentally unaltered since its heyday as a staging post for the eighteenth-century trade in Brazilian gold, passing from Minas Gerais to Portugal. Before white settlement, the land had been occupied by the **Guaianá Indians**, and the gold routes followed the old Indian trails down to Parati and its sheltered harbour. Inland raids and pirate attacks necessitated the establishment of a new route linking Minas Gerais directly with Rio de Janeiro, and, as trade was diverted to Rio, Parati's fortunes declined. Apart from a short-lived coffee-shipping boom in the nineteenth century, Parati remained hidden away off the beaten track, quietly stagnating but intact. Nowadays, though, UNESCO considers Parati to represent one of the world's most important examples of Portuguese colonial architecture, and the entire city has been elevated to the status of a national monument.

Today, Parati is very much alive, with its population of 15,000 involved in fishing, farming and tourism. The town centre was one of Brazil's first planned urban projects, and its narrow cobbled streets, out of bounds to motorized transport, are bordered by houses built around courtyards adorned with brightly coloured flowers and teeming with hummingbirds. The cobbles of the streets

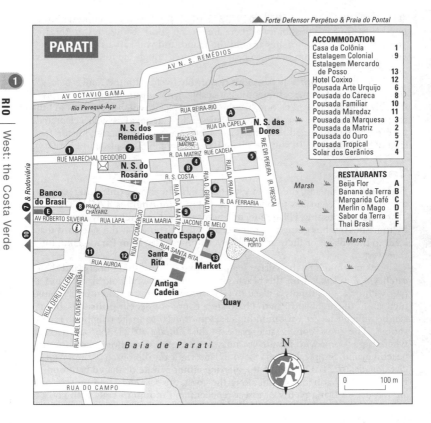

▲ Forte Defensor Perpétuo & Praia do Pontal

PARATI

AV N S REMÉDIOS

AV OCTAVIO GAMA

Rio Perequé-Açu

RUA BEIRA-RIO

N. S. dos Remédios

RUA DA CAPELA

N. S. das Dores

PRAÇA DA MATRIZ

RUE DR PEREIRA (R FRESCAL)

RUE MARECHAL DEODORO

R. DA MATRIZ   RUE CADEIA

N. S. do Rosário

R.S. COSTA

RUA D. GERALDA

RUA DA PRAIA

R. DA FERRARIA

Banco do Brasil

PRAÇA CHAYARIZ

RUA DO COMERCIO

RUA DA MATRIZ

AV ROBERTO SILVEIRA   RUA LAPA   RUA MARIA   JACONE DE MELO

Teatro Espaço

RUA SANTA RITA

PRAÇA DO PORTO

RUA AUROA

Santa Rita

Market

RUA DERIL ELENA

RUA ABEL DE OLIVEIRA (R PATIBA)

Antiga Cadeia

Quay

Baía de Parati

RUA DO CAMPO

Marsh

Marsh

Marsh

N

0   100 m

7 & Rodoviária
10

ACCOMMODATION	
Casa da Colônia	1
Estalagem Colonial	9
Estalagem Mercardo de Posso	13
Hotel Coxixo	12
Pousada Arte Urquijo	6
Pousada do Careca	8
Pousada Familiar	10
Pousada Maredaz	11
Pousada da Marquesa	3
Pousada da Matriz	2
Pousada do Ouro	5
Pousada Tropical	7
Solar dos Gerânios	4

RESTAURANTS	
Beija Flor	A
Banana da Terra	B
Margarida Café	C
Merlin o Mago	D
Sabor da Terra	E
Thai Brasil	F

are arranged in channels to drain off storm water and allow the sea to enter and wash the streets at high tides and full moon. Although businesses in Parati's historic centre are overwhelmingly geared towards tourists, the wider town also has a rather more democratic feel to it than does Búzios, and by and large provides a more satisfying experience than its chic counterpart on the Costa do Sol.

Arrival, information and accommodation

The **rodoviária** is about half a kilometre from the old town; turn right out of the bus station and walk straight ahead. The helpful **tourist office** (daily 8am–7pm; ☎24/3371-1266) is near the entrance of the historic centre, on the corner of Av. Roberto Silveira and Praça Macedo Soares, and can supply a map of the town, local bus times and a list of hotels and restaurants. There are several Internet cafés in Parati, though connections are slow, precarious and expensive ($7 an hour): try at Av. Roberto Silveira 17, or along Rua da Lapa, just after entering the historic centre.

You might well be offered **accommodation** by people waiting at the bus station, but it's usually easy to track it down yourself; the standard is high, and rooms are often amazing value for money. Most of the best **pousadas** are in the old Portuguese colonial centre, five minutes' walk from the bus station, and often young lads will guide you to the ones with vacancies. From late

December to after Carnaval, however, this entire area is packed, and hotel space becomes hard to find: if you are without a reservation try to arrive by noon, when you can hope to get a room from people leaving Parati earlier than planned. Your best hope will be to find a room outside of the historic centre, in a hotel used by tour groups – ask the tourist office for advice. At other times, expect discounts of around fifty percent from the high-season prices given below.

There's a **campsite** on the road into town from the coastal highway, and another on the Praia do Pontal, on the other side of the Rio Perequé-Açu river from the town centre.

Casa da Colônia Rua Marechal Deodoro 50 ⊕24/3371-2343. Located just outside the historic centre, this is a no-frills but attractive old *pousada*. Rooms are well equipped, and some sleep four people. ❸

Estalagem Colonial Rua da Matriz 9 ⊕24/3371-1626. All rooms at this basic but delightful small *pousada*, are attractively furnished and have lovely views, but it's worth spending a little more for the larger rooms. ❸

Estalagem Mercado de Posso Largo de Santa Rita ⊕24/3371-1114, ⓔmercadadodopouso @terra.com.br. A very comfortable *pousada* in a restored old market building. Rooms (some sleeping four) are spacious and well appointed and the courtyard garden is delightful. The rates are remarkably low because there's no pool. ❹.

Hotel Coxixo Rua do Comércio 362 ⊕24/3371-1460, ⓦwww.hotelcoxixo.com.br. Comfortable rooms, a beautiful garden and a good-size pool. One of the larger hotels in the historic centre, where you'll have a chance of securing a last-minute room. Apart from babies under 12 months, only children over the age of 10 are accepted. ❺

Pousada Arte Urquijo Rua Dona Geralda 79 ⊕24/3371-1362, ⓦwww.paraty.com.br/uruijo.htm. Somewhat pretentious six-room *pousada* with classical music in the lounge at all times and lots of artworks on the walls. Rooms are on the small side (and over-priced) and the pool is tiny. Children under 12 years not allowed. ❺

Pousada do Careca Praça Macedo Soares ⊕24/3371-1291, ⓔcareca@eco-paraty.com. Located just within the historic centre, this no-frills *pousada* has rooms that sleep two to six people. Try to get a room that looks out onto the *praça* as many of the others are somewhat airless. The owners know the area around Parati well and are happy to offer advice. ❷

Pousada Familiar Rua José Vieira Ramos 262 ⊕24/3371-1475. This no-frills *pousada* just outside the historic centre is owned by a friendly multilingual Belgian and offers clean rooms and laundry facilities. $8 per person.

Pousada Maredez Rua Derli Ellena 9 ⊕24/3371-1369. Good-value *pousada* with small rooms looking onto a courtyard, just outside the historic centre. ❷

Pousada da Marquesa Rua Dona Geralda 69 ⊕24/3371-2163. The least expensive luxury *pousada* in town, boasting wonderful views from the bedrooms, an attractive pool and all the comfort you could need. ❹

Pousada da Matriz Rua da Matriz ⊕24/3371-1610. Small, basic but clean rooms in one of the cheapest *pousadas* in the old town (❷). Very similar, and located just next door, is the *Pousada Ramiro* (⊕24/3371-1361; ❷).

Pousada do Ouro Rua Dr Pereira 145 ⊕24/3371-1378. Discreet luxury *pousada* offering a range of tastefully furnished rooms – the nicest are in the main building, while those in the annex across the road are rather dark. There's a pretty walled garden and a good-size pool, too. ❺

Pousada Tropical Rua Waldemar Mathias 38 ⊕24/3371-2020. Plain rooms in a quiet residential area next to the *rodoviária*. Ask for a room on the upper floor as they're quieter and have better ventilation. ❷

Solar dos Gerânios Praça da Matriz ⊕24/3371-1550. Beautiful Swiss-owned and -run *pousada* filled with rustic furniture and curios. The rooms are spartan but impeccably kept; most have a balcony and all have a private bathroom. Superb value (prices remain much the same throughout the year) and rightly popular, making reservations essential – request a room overlooking the beautiful *praça*. ❷

The Town

Parati is a perfect place simply to wander aimlessly, each turn of the corner bringing another picturesque view. The town's small enough that there's no danger of getting lost and, no matter what time of day or night, you can feel pretty confident that you won't be a victim of an assault. There are, however, several buildings worth seeking out if you don't happen to come across them.

As with most small colonial towns in Brazil, each of Parati's churches traditionally served a different sector of the population. Dating back to 1646, **Nossa Senhora dos Remédios** (daily 9am–5pm), on the Praça da Matriz, is Parati's main church and the town's largest building. During the late eighteenth century, the church – built for Parati's bourgeoisie – underwent major structural reforms and the exterior, at least, has remained unchanged since then. Parati's aristocracy had their own church built in 1800, the particularly graceful **Igreja das Dores** (daily 1–5pm) with its own small cemetery, three blocks from the main church by the sea. Along Rua do Comércio is the smallest church, the **Igreja do Rosário** (Mon–Fri 9am–noon), built in 1725 and used by the slaves. Finally, at the southern edge of the town is the **Igreja de Santa Rita** (Wed–Sun 10am–noon & 2–5pm), the oldest and architecturally most significant of the town's churches. Built in 1722 for the freed mulatto population, the church is notable for its elaborate facade, done in Portuguese Baroque style. Attached to the church is the small Museu de Arte Sacra, a repository of religious artefacts from Parati's churches. Next to Santa Rita you'll find the late eighteenth-century jail, the **Antiga Cadeia**, now the main tourist information office (see p.146) and a handicraft centre, while opposite to it is the lively **fish market**.

To the north of the old town, across the Rio Perequé-Açu on the Morro de Vilha Velha, is the **Forte Defensor Perpétuo**, constructed in 1703 to defend Parati from pirates seeking to plunder gold ships leaving the port. The fort underwent restoration in 1822 and today the rudimentary structure houses the Museu de Artes e Tradições Populares (Tues–Sun 10am–5pm), which has a permanent display of fishing tools and basket ware, and handicrafts for sale.

Beaches and islands

Keeping yourself amused should be no problem, even if you quickly exhaust the possibilities of the town itself. From the **Praia do Pontal** on the other side of the Perequé-Açu River from town, and from the **port quay**, *baleiras* and *saveiros* (whaling and fishing boats) leave for the beaches of Paraty-Mirim, Jurumirim, Lula and Picinguaba. In fact, there are 65 islands and about 200 beaches to choose from, and anyone can tell you which are the current favourites. Hotels and travel agents sell tickets for trips out to the islands, typically at a cost of $10 per person, leaving Parati at noon, stopping at three or four islands for a swim and returning at 6pm. Boats also leave from the quay for the **Boa Vista distillery**, or *alambique*. Home of the famous Quero Esse brand of *cachaça*, the old colonial house here was once the residence of Thomas Mann's grandfather, Johan Ludwig Brown, before he returned to Germany in around 1850. The caretaker, and master distiller, will give guided tours of the *alambique* ($10) before plying you with a liquor that has distinctly invigorating properties.

You can reach some of the mainland beaches by road – ask at the tourist office for details of bus times. If you're really feeling energetic, you can hire a **mountain bike** for $18 a day from Paraty Tours at Av. Roberto Silveira 11, who also supply maps marked with suggested itineraries covering beaches, mountains or forests. They can also arrange **car rental** for around $50 a day. To the north, the fishing village of **Tarituba** (see p.145) makes a pleasant excursion, with several delightful beaches (such as Praia Grande and Prainha) to stop off at on the way. To the southeast of Parati along an unpaved road (which should be avoided following heavy rains), is **Paraty-Mirim**, which, from a distance, looks attractive but has rather dirty beaches and shallow and utterly calm water. Best of all are the beaches near the village of **Trinidade**, 21km south of Parati and reached by a steep, but good winding road (7 buses daily; 45min). Sandwiched between the ocean and Serra do Mar, Trinidade has reached the physical limits of growth, the dozens of inexpensive *pousadas*, holiday homes, camping sites, bars and restaurants crammed with tourists in the peak summer season. The main beach is nice enough, but you're better off walking away from the village across the rocky outcrops to Praia Brava or Praia do Meio, where the only signs of development on what are some of the most perfect mainland beaches on this stretch of coast are just a few beach bars. If you plan to stay over at New Year or Carnaval, your best bet for securing a room is to arrive several days early and ask around for vacant rooms. The best place (though hardly luxurious) is the *Pousada do Pele* (☎24/3371-5125; ❹), which is situated right on the beach and has rooms that sleep two to four people. There are several modest *pousadas* slightly back from the beach, all with private bathrooms: try the *Agua do Mar* (☎24/3371-5210; ❸); the *Pouso Trinidade* (☎24/3371-5121; ❸); or the *Ponta da Trinidade* (☎24/3371/5113; ❷), which also has space to pitch a tent.

Eating

The town has a good choice of **restaurants** in all price brackets, though often the expensive-looking ones can be surprisingly reasonable, thanks to portions big enough for two people. The cheapest places to eat are outside of the historic centre – while none is remarkable, you won't have any difficulty finding a filling meal of fish, meat, beans, rice and salad for a couple of dollars. Predictably, fish is the local speciality, but there are many other options, with the restaurants listed here being the more noteworthy.

Beija Flor Rua Dr Pereira (no number). A Lebanese-Portuguese café in a quiet corner of the historic centre – a good place for a cold beer or *caipirinha* and some savoury snacks. From 4pm, closed Wed.

Banana da Terra Rua Dr Samuel Costa 198. Possibly Parati's most interesting restaurant, emphasizing local ingredients (most notably bananas) and regional cooking. The grilled fish with garlic-herb butter and served with banana is delicious, as are the wonderful banana desserts. Evenings only except Sat & Sun, when lunch is also served; closed Wed. Expensive.

Margarida Café Praça Chafariz. Well-prepared, imaginative modern Brazilian cooking. There's a nice bar, plus remarkably good live music on most nights. Expensive.

Merlin o Mago Rua do Comércio 376. Overly formal for laid-back Parati, but the French-influenced fish dishes are excellent if expensive. Evenings only, closed Wed.

Sabor da Terra Av. Roberto Silveira 180. Located outside of the historic centre, next to the Banco do Brasil, this is Parati's best *por kilo* restaurant, offering a wide variety of hot and cold dishes, including excellent seafood. Inexpensive.

Thai Brasil Rua Dona Geralda 345. Well-presented Thai dishes served in a bright and attractive setting. The food is remarkably authentic, with the fish dishes being especially good. Moderate.

Academy of Cooking and Other Pleasures

For an unusual dining experience, drop by the **Academy of Cooking and Other Pleasures** at Rua Dona Geralda 211 (☎24/3371-6468) to find out about events hosted by Yara Castro Roberts, a professional cook from Minas Gerais who lived in Massachusetts for many years doing much to encourage interest in Brazilian food through cookery classes and on television. Several evenings a week, Yara gives cooking demonstrations in her home, alternating between menus drawn from Rio, the Northeast, the Amazon and Minas Gerais, her home state. The high point of the evening comes when Yara and her guests sit around her dining room table to enjoy the meal and sample some fine *cachaças*, of which she is a connoisseur. The evening, which usually lasts from 7.30pm to 10.30pm, costs $30 per person, or $50 for a couple, with groups limited to eight or so people.

Drinking and entertainment

Parati has plenty of watering holes to keep you amused into the evening, though out of season when the town is extremely quiet you may well find yourself drinking alone. Many of the buildings in the historic centre have been converted into shops, where you can pick up clothes, artworks, *cachaça* (generally not as good as the rustic-looking bottle might suggest) and souvenirs until late at night. Otherwise, you might try the **cinema** on Av. Roberto Silveira, which usually shows English-language films, or better still, the **puppet troupe** Grupo Contadores de Estórias, internationally renowned for their wordless performances that nimbly leap between comedy and tragedy, exploring such adult themes as death, sex and betrayal (you must be 14 years or over to attend). Performances are every Wednesday and Saturday at their Teatro Espaço at Rua Dona Geralda 327 ((ⓣ24/3371-1575, ⓦwww.paraty.com.br/teatro.htm; $8), which occasionally hosts other theatre, dance or music events, too.

May, June and July see frequent **festivals** celebrating local holidays, when Parati's square comes alive with folk dances – *cerandis*, *congadas* and *xibas* – demonstrating the European and African influences on Brazilian culture.

Inland from Parati

Another good way to see a bit of the landscape is to drive, cycle or catch a bus from the *rodoviária*, following the Cunha road up into the Serra do Mar. The easiest place to head for is at Km 8, where you'll spot signs pointing to the **Cachoeira das Penhas**, a waterfall up in the mountains that offers a chance to bake on the sun-scorched rocks of the river gully and then cool off in the river. From here you can descend from rock to rock for a few hundred metres before scrambling up to a road above you. About 2km along the road, just across a small bridge, you'll enter **PONTE BRANCA** where, at the far end of the village, overlooking the river, is the *Ponte Branca restaurant*, where you can take a break and enjoy a cold beer. The walk from the waterfall takes you through the hills and valleys, and past tropical fruit plantations, all very pleasant. If you don't have your own transport, you'll probably manage to get a lift back to Parati from the restaurant when you're sufficiently refreshed.

For a more rugged experience, consider hiking along a restored segment of the **Caminho do Ouro** – the seventeenth-century mule trail that connected the port of Parati with the gold mines of Minas Gerais. If you have your own transport, you can reach the trail's access point by continuing along the Cunha road to the *Atelier Caminho do Ouro* at Km 9.5, a roadside woodworker's studio that produces and sells rustic lamps and sculptures. Here you can buy a combined map and entrance ticket ($3 per person) to the trail, which starts directly across the road from the studio. Otherwise you're better off joining a group tour organized through the Teatro Espaço in Parati (see above) – it costs $13 per person and includes transport by minibus, a bilingual guide, admission and lunch. The partially cobbled trail is very slippery after the rain, and even in dry conditions you'll need good shoes to tackle the steep uneven trail. The landscape, which appears pleasantly pastoral at first, grows increasingly impressive, and you'll have spectacular views of the forrested mountains all around, as well as Parati and the ocean. After about an hour you'll reach a gated area where display panels explain (in English and Portuguese) the region's history and ecology; there's also a waterfall to shower under and a source of fresh drinking water.

From here you can either continue along a more forested segment of the trail for a few more kilometres or follow a separate path to a **restaurant** that serves a full lunch of local dishes from Thursday to Sunday in high season (excluding

Fri in low season) and light meals the rest of the week – if no one's on duty at the gate leading to the restaurant just ring the bell and someone will eventually come out. There's also a modest **pousada** here, called the *Caminho do Ouro*, too (no phone; ❸), where the four tastefully furnished rooms have amazing views down towards the coast. Before you haul your luggage up the trail in search of a room, be sure to ask at the Teatro Espaço (☎24/3371-1575) in Parati about vacancies.

Inland: north to the mountains

Excellent bus services from Rio de Janeiro make the **interior** of the state easily accessible, and its mountainous wooded landscape and relatively cool climate are a pleasant contrast to the coastal heat. There's not a great deal in the way of historical interest, but the scenic beauty of the countryside, studded with small towns still bearing their colonial heritage, is an attraction in itself.

Volta Redonda

From Rio, the Cidade do Aço bus company runs a service along the BR-116 to **VOLTA REDONDA** and the heartland of Brazil's steel industry. Situated on the banks of the **River Paraíba**, the city is dominated by steel mills, and though it may once have been a picturesque little village it's now an expanding industrial monster.

If you feel inclined to visit the **steel mill**, you need to arrange for a guided tour about a week in advance, either with the headquarters of the Companhia Siderúrgica Nacional on Avenida XIII de Maio, Rio de Janeiro, or locally at the *Hotel Alta Bela Vista* (☎24/2348-2022; ❹). Tour buses organized by the Companhia Siderúrgica leave from Rio and travel direct to the mills; the journey takes about three hours and the price is negligible. If you want to **stay** in the town centre, apart from the *Bela Vista*, there's the *Sider Palace Hotel* at Av. Alberto Pasqualini 10 (☎24/2348-1032; ❸), and the *Embaixador* at Travessa Luís Augusto Félix 36 (☎24/3348-3665; ❷).

Volta Redonda serves as a textbook example of the (often disastrous) way in which Brazil is developing, economically and socially. To all intents and purposes, the city has been a company town since 1941, and the urban structure represents the priorities of the company – slums for the poor and nice neighbourhoods for the management sprawl sit on opposite sides of the river. The river itself is so polluted by industrial and domestic effluence that its plant and animal life have been almost completely destroyed. Apart from industrial conflict and pollution, according to a report in the *Jornal do Brazil* the citizens of Volta Redonda also have the highest incidence of hypertension and deaths caused by cardiovascular disease in the entire country. All this in what four decades ago must have been one of the healthiest climates in Brazil.

Parque Nacional do Itatiaia

Nestling in the northwest corner of the state, 165km from Rio, between the borders of São Paulo and Minas Gerais, the **Parque Nacional do Itatiaia** ($2 entrance) is the oldest national park in Brazil, founded in 1937 and covering 120 square kilometres of the Mantigueira mountain range. People come here to climb – favourites are the **Pico das Agulhas Negras** (2787m) and the **Pico de Prateleira** (2540m) – and the park is also an important nature reserve.

The park comprises waterfalls, primary forest, wildlife and orchids – but tragically a fire in 1988 ravaged some twenty percent of the park's area. In the sections affected by the fire, forest and pasture land were devastated, rare orchids and native conifers (*Podocarpus lamperti* and *Araucaria angustifolia*) destroyed; the fire reached areas of the Serra da Mantigueira, 2500m above sea level, wiping out forty kilometres of mountain pathways. In the areas most favoured by biologists, who come to study the rich fauna and flora, the once beautiful alpine scenery now resembles a lunar landscape. Also severely affected were the many natural springs and streams that combine to form the Bonito, Preto, Pirapitinga and Palmital rivers; these supply the massive hydrographic basin of the Paraíba plate, giving much needed oxygenation to the Paraíba watercourse in one of its most polluted stretches. The situation is gradually improving, but ecologists reckon that it will take more than twenty years to repair this environmental disaster. For the casual walker, however, there's still plenty of unaffected park to be seen.

Itatiaia

The town of **ITATIAIA**, situated on the BR-116, is surrounded by beautiful scenery and makes a good base: it has plenty of **hotels**, mainly found along Via Dutra, the two-kilometre-long road that links the town and park – take the minibus marked "Hotel Simon" from Praça São José. The *Hotel Simon* itself (☎24/2352-1122; ❻ full board) is extremely comfortable and in a gorgeous setting, with a wonderful orchid garden attached (daily 9–11am). Nearby is the much cheaper but pretty rustic *Pousada do Elefante* (☎24/999-2893; ❸). In town, there's a **youth hostel** at Rua João Mauricio de Macedo Costa 352 (☎24/2352-1232; $8 per person). There's **cabin accommodation** in the park, but it has to be booked about two weeks in advance at the Administração do Parque Nacional de Itatiaia (☎24/2352-1461) in Itatiaia town. You can get **information** and maps at the Visitor's Centre (daily 8am–5pm) and at the Museu Regional de Fauna and Flora (Tues–Sun 10am–4pm). Tourist information on Itatiaia and the park is also available from the Secretaría de Turismo in Itatiaia, at Rua São José 210 (☎24/2352-1660, ext 305).

Penedo

The other possible base for visting the park is the small town of **PENEDO**, 14km away and connected to Itatiaia by regular buses. Penedo was settled in 1929 by Finnish immigrants, and today much is made of this heritage, despite the fact that only a tiny minority of the population are of Finnish origin. Nevertheless, Finnish dances are performed every Saturday night at the *Clube Finlandia*, and the **Museu Finlandês da Dona Eva** at Av. das Mangueiras 2601 (Wed–Sat 10am–5pm, Sun 9am–3pm) has displays of documents, photos and furniture relating to Finnish immigration in the region. The town is popular with weekenders from São Paulo and Rio, who come for the horse riding and to buy the various jams, preserves and local liquors that are produced here. Penedo is also a good place to visit if you like saunas, since most hotels have one. It's usually easy to find a **place to stay** – there are dozens of hotels in and near the town, though few real budget places. *Pequena Suécia* at Rua Toivo Suni (☎24/2351-1275; ❸) is an excellent choice, and also features a fine Swedish restaurant; a more basic option is the *Rio das Pedras* at Rua Resende 39 (☎24/2351-1019; ❷). Most people eat at their hotels, but in town it's worth trying the delicious Finnish-style open sandwiches at the *Restaurante Skandinávia*, Av. das Mangueiras 2631.

Vassouras and Valença

Northeast of Volta Redonda, the university towns of **VASSOURAS** and **VALENÇA** make good targets if you have a car and a few spare days. Both are considered national historical monuments, key centres of Brazil's nineteenth-century coffee-based economy. Today, dairy farming has almost totally replaced coffee production, but relics from the days when the "coffee barons" reigned supreme are still visible.

Vassouras, on the main BR-393, is the smaller and more appealing of the two towns, with many late nineteenth-century buildings in the centre of town around the Campo Belo. However, it's the old **coffee fazenda houses** nearby that are the main attraction, but without your own car you won't be able to see much. The tourist information office is at Rua Barão de Capivari 20 (Mon–Fri 9am–6pm) and will give details of which of the privately owned houses are open for visits. The most impressive ones are located off the RJ-115 highway north of town, with **Santa Mônica** being the oldest, best preserved and generally the most interesting of the houses. Another beautifully preserved house that's often open to visitors is **São Fernando**, about 1km from Massambará, an outlying district in the *município* of Vassouras. If you want to **stay**, the *Gramado da Serra* at Rua Aldo Cavalli 7 (☎24/2471-2314; ❷), the *Mara Palace* at Rua Chanceler Raul Fernandes 121 (☎24/2471-2524; ❸), and the *Santa Amelia*, Av. Rui Barbosa 526 (☎24/2471-1897; ❹), are all central.

Valença is less attractive than Vassouras, but the *fazenda* houses off RJ-145 and RJ-151 to the east merit a look: ask at the tourist office at Praça XV de Novembre 676 (Mon–Fri 9am–6pm). The easiest to visit is the *Fazenda São Polycarpo* (10am–5pm) at Km 18 on the road leading to the village of Rio das Flores. Built in 1834 for the Viscount of Rio Preto, the house is decorated with period furnishings and now operates as a luxury country hotel (☎24/2458-1190; ❺ full board). The **hotels** in Valença itself are more plain and less expensive than in Vassouras, with the best being *Hotel dos Engenheiros*, Rua Teodorico Fonseca 525 (☎24/2453-4530; ❷), while, near the *rodoviária*, there's the more rudimentary *Valenciano*, Praça Paulo de Frontin 360 (☎24/2452-0890; ❷).

Petrópolis

Sixty-six kilometres directly to the north of Rio de Janeiro, high in the mountains, stands the imperial city of **PETRÓPOLIS**. The route there is a busy one, with Fácil and Única company buses leaving Rio every fifteen minutes, but even so you may have to wait a day or two for a bus with available seats. It's worth the hassle, for the journey there is glorious. On the way up, sit on the left-hand side of the bus and don't be too concerned with the driver's obsession with overtaking heavy goods vehicles on blind corners, bordered by naked rock on one side and a sheer drop on the other – it's a one-way road, and the return to Rio is made by a different route that also snakes its way through terrifying mountain passes. The scenery is dramatic, climbing among forested slopes that give way suddenly to ravines and gullies, while clouds shroud the surrounding mountains.

In 1720, Bernardo Soares de Proença opened a trade route between Rio and Minas Gerais, and in return was conceded the area around the present site of Petrópolis as a royal land grant. Surrounded by stunning scenery, and with a gentle, alpine summer climate, it had by the nineteenth century become a favourite retreat of Rio's elite. The arrival of German immigrants contributed to the development of Petrópolis as a town, and has much to do with the curious European Gothic feel to the place. Dom Pedro II took a fancy to

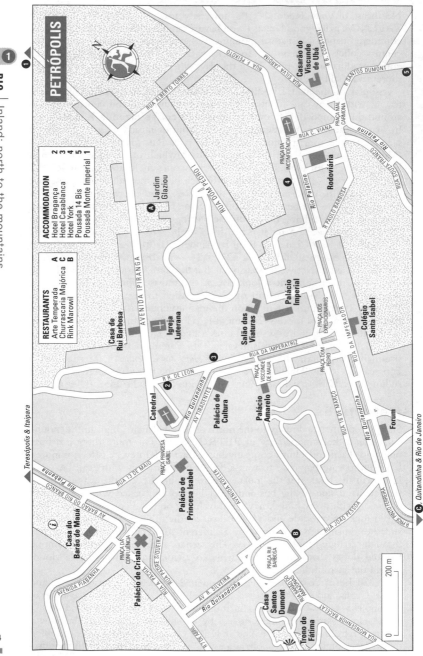

PETRÓPOLIS

Teresópolis & Itaipara

Quitandinha & Rio de Janeiro

ACCOMMODATION
Hotel Braganca 2
Hotel Casablanca 3
Hotel York 4
Pousada 14 Bis 5
Pousada Monte Imperial 1

RESTAURANTS
Arte Temperada A
Churrascaria Majórica C
Rink Marowil B

Casa do Barão de Mauá

Palácio de Cristal

Palácio de Princesa Isabel

Catedral

Casa de Rui Barbosa

Igreja Luterana

Jardim Glaziou

Palácio de Cultura

Palácio Amarelo

Salão das Viaturas

Palácio Imperial

Colégio Santa Isabel

Rodoviária

Casarão do Viscunde de Ubá

Casa Santos Dumont

Trono de Fátima

Forum

200 m

Petrópolis and in 1843 designated it the summer seat of his government. He also established an agricultural colony, which failed because of the unsuitability of the soil, and then in 1849 – with an epidemic of yellow fever sweeping through Rio – the emperor and his court took refuge in the town, thus assuring Petrópolis' prosperity.

The Town

You can easily do a tour of Petrópolis in a day, returning to Rio in the evening (or continuing inland). If you can ignore the traffic fumes, simply strolling around is as good a way to pass the time as any, taking in plenty of elegant mansions, particularly along **Avenida Koeller**, which has a tree-lined canal running up its centre, or on **Avenida Ipiranga**, where you'll also find the German **Igreja Luterana** (open only for Sunday services at 9am).

The **Museu Imperial** on Avenida VII de Setembro (Tues–Sun & holidays 11am–5.30pm; $1.50; ℡24/2237-8000, ⓦwww.museuimperial.gov.br) is a fine Neoclassical structure set in beautifully maintained formal gardens. Once the remarkably modest summer palace of Emperor Dom Pedro II, it now houses a fascinating collection of the royal family's bits and pieces. On entry, you're given felt overshoes with which to slide around the polished floors, and inside there's everything from Dom Pedro II's crown (639 diamonds, 77 pearls, all set in finely wrought gold) to the regal commode. In the former stables the royal railway carriage is displayed, while other buildings in the garden serve as space for temporary exhibitions and an excellent café and tearoom. Three nights a week (Thurs & Fri 8pm, Sat 8pm & 9.15pm; $3) the former palace is illuminated for a **sound and light show** – well worth attending for the music alone if you don't understand the Portuguese naration.

The **Catedral São Pedro de Alcântara** (Tues–Sun 8am–noon and 2–6pm) blends with the rest of the architecture around, but is much more recent than its rather overbearing neo-Gothic style suggests – it was only finished in 1939. Inside, on the walls, are ten relief sculptures depicting scenes from the Crucifixion; in the mausoleum lie the tombs of Dom Pedro himself, Princess Regent Dona Isabel and several other royal personages. If you need more direction to your strolling, then other historic buildings to track down are the **Palácio de Cristal**, Rua Alfredo Pacha (Tues–Sun 9am–5.30pm); **Casa Santos Dumont** at Rua do Encanto 22 (Tues–Sun 9am–5pm), an alpine chalet built in 1918 and the home of the Brazilian aviator of that name, containing personal memorabilia; the **Casa do Barão de Maurá** at Praça da Confluência 3 (Mon–Sat 9am–6.30pm, Sun and holidays 9am–5pm), featuring displays devoted to the baron, best known for his role in constructing Brazil's first railway; and the rather grand, half-timbered Norman-style **Quitandinha** on the Estrada de Quitandinha, just outside of town. Once the Quitandinha Casino, this last building stopped receiving the rich and famous when the Brazilian government prohibited gambling in 1946, and it was eventually converted into a luxury apartment building. Nearby, at Rua Cristóvão Colombo 1034, is the **Museu Casa do Colono** (Tues–Sun 9.30am–5pm), a simple house dating back to 1847 that has a small collection relating to the German immigrants who settled in and around Petrópolis in the early nineteenth century. German-speaking visitors may also be interested in visiting the tomb of the Austrian-born writer **Stefan Zweig**, who committed suicide with his wife in Petrópolis. You can take a look at the outside of his house at Rua Gonçalves Dias 34 in the suburb of Valparaiso, near the municipal cemetery.

Practicalities

There's an extremely helpful **tourist office** (☎0800-241516) at the entrance to town at Quitandinha (Mon–Thurs & Sun 8am–7pm; Fri & Sat 8am–8pm), with a branch at the Casa do Barão de Maurá, Praça da Confluência 3 (Mon–Sat 9am–6.30pm; Sun and holidays 9am–5pm). Town attractions aside, Petrópolis has easy access to some lovely climbing country, and if you're planning to do any **hiking** contact the Centro Alpinista, Rua Irmãos d'Angelo 28 – it's an amateur association, so go after 8pm.

There are some reasonable **hotels** in town, such as the basic *Pousada 14 Bis* at Rua Santos Dumont 162 (☎24/2231-0946, Ⓦwww.pousada14bis.com.br; ❷), and the *Hotel York* at Rua do Imperador 78 (☎24/2243-2662, Ⓦwww .hotelyork.com.br; ❸), which is handy for the *rodoviária*, but otherwise lacking atmosphere. A number of former mansions have been converted into hotels: the *Bragança*, behind the cathedral at Rua Raul de Leon 109 (☎24/2242-0434; ❹), maintains some of the residence's former style, while the *Casablanca*, next to the Palácio Imperial at Rua da Imperatriz 286 (☎24/2242-6662, Ⓦwww .casablancahotel.com.br; ❹), which has a pool, is far more institutional in character. By far the most attractive, having the air of a country inn rather than a city hotel, is the *Pousada Monte Imperial* (☎24/2237-1664; ❺), located on a hilltop at Rua José Alencar 27, which although central, is a stiff walk from the town's attractions. Rooms are quite small but appealing, and there's a nice garden with a pool, too; the English-speaking owner is extremely friendly.

Restaurants are surprisingly lacklustre in Petrópolis, most of the best being some distance from town. However, there's a good and moderately priced Portuguese restaurant in the *Hotel Bragança*, and an excellent *por kilo* choice, *Rink Marowil*, at Praça Rui Barbosa 27. Much more atmospheric is the *Arte Temperada* (Wed–Sun lunch only, Fri & Sat also dinner; ☎24/2237-2133), in a converted stable of a beautiful nineteenth-century mansion at Rua Ipiranga 716: the modern Brazilian offerings include local trout and salads. For meat, the *Churrascaria Majórica* at Rua do Imperador 754 is excellent, if formal.

If you're heading on to Teresópolis make sure you travel during the day, so as not to miss the spectacular scenery. If you're going to São Paulo or Belo Horizonte, there's no need to return to Rio as there are direct bus services from Petrópolis.

Teresópolis

While **TERESÓPOLIS** can be reached directly from Rio by bus, the best route is from Petrópolis. It's not a long journey, no more than 40km, but the road to the highest town in the state (872m) passes through the **Serra dos Órgãos**, much of which is a national park – dramatic rock formations here resemble rows of organ pipes (hence the range's name), dominated by the towering **Dedo de Deus** ("God's Finger") peak. Teresópolis, like Petrópolis, owed its initial development to the opening of a road between Minas Gerais and Rio during the eighteenth century. It, too, was a favoured summer retreat (for Empress Teresa Cristina, for whom the town was named) and though smaller than Petrópolis it also shares some of its Germanic characteristics, including a benevolent alpine climate. The town itself is extremely dull, built along one main street that changes its name every couple of blocks, and the interest lies entirely in the surrounding countryside. There are, however, magnificent views from almost anywhere in town – especially from **Soberbo**, where the Rio highway enters Teresópolis, with its panoramic view of Rio and the Baixada Fluminense.

Around Teresópolis

There's plenty to do in the surrounding countryside, within a few kilometres of town. Lakes and waterfalls – the **Cascata dos Amores** and the **Cascata do Imbuí** – make for good swimming; there's the **Mulher de Pedra** rock formation with its series of peaks rising to 2040 metres; and bird-watching opportunities amongst the lakes of the **Granja Comary** plateau (on the BR-495).

The main attraction, though, is the **Parque Nacional da Serra dos Órgãos**, where favourite peaks for those with mountain-goat tendencies are the Agulha do Diablo (2050m) and the Pedra do Sino (2263m); the latter has a path leading to the summit, a relatively easy three-hour trip (take refreshments). It costs $1.50 per person, and an additional $3 per car, to enter the park, and basic **accommodation** for climbers and hikers is available at the *Refúgio do Parque* (☎21/021/9687-4539, ✉refugiodoparque@bol.com.br; ❷; reservations essential). There are some campsites, too, but no equipment for rent, so you'll need to come prepared.

For more information about all these places, visit Teresópolis' **tourist office** (Mon–Fri 8am–5pm; ☎21/2742-3352) at Praça Olimpica. **Guidebooks and trail maps** can be purchased in front of the Igreja Matriz at the Cupelo Banco de Jornais – maps are a must because walks are not signposted. In the national park, you'll also be able to hire guides inexpensively.

Practicalities

Most of the many **hotels** in Teresópolis are located on picturesque hillsides, far from the town centre. The best of them, set in a large park with several swimming pools and an extensive network of trails, is the *Rosa dos Ventos* (☎21/2644-8833, ⓦwww.hotelrosadosventos.com.br; ❻) on the Nova Friburgo road, some 22km from town; however, the hotel does not accept children under the age of 14. Cheaper alternatives are the *Philips*, Rua Duval Fonseca 1333 (☎21/2742-1636; ❸) and the *Center*, Rua Sebastião Teixeira 245 (☎21/2742-5870; ❸), functional hotels that seem more geared for business travellers than tourists. A far better option is the *Várzea Palace*, Rua Sebastião Teixeira 41 (☎21/2742-0878; ❷), a beautiful white building that was once the most elegant place to stay. Only faint traces of its former luxury remain, but the hotel is clean, welcoming and very inexpensive. There is also a lovely **youth hostel** at Rua Luiza Pereira Soares 109 (☎21/2742-5586; $8 per person), which has private rooms as well (❷). Only a couple of **restaurants** stand out, but both are expensive: *Dona Irene*, Rua Yeda 730 (☎21/2742-2901; closed Sun evening and all Mon & Tues), serves marvellous Russian food and reservations are essential; while *Margô* at Rua Heitor de Moura Estevão 259 (closed Mon) serves up satisfying German cuisine.

In January, Teresópolis hosts the **Curso Internacional PRO–ARTE**, featuring live classical music performances (contact the tourist office for details).

Nova Friburgo

NOVA FRIBURGO, an attractive town of 90,000 people, lies in a valley surrounded by mountains to the northeast of Teresópolis. It was founded by a hundred Swiss immigrant families from the canton of Fribourg, transferred to the region by royal decree in 1818, and whose only other activity of note was that they introduced the first sauna into Brazil. The Germanic influence remains, principally in the architecture of the *bairro* of **Conego**. During the summer, Nova Friburgo's many hotels and campsites are brimming with city folk who come to enjoy the waterfalls and wooded trails or take on the local peaks – like **Caledonia**, a favourite with hang-gliders. Less of a hike, the dramatic rock formations of the **Furnos da Catete** forestry reserve on the road to Bom Jardim (23km north on the BR-492) offer an excellent walk; and for an easy view of the world a cable car (9am–5.30pm) from Praça dos Suspiros in town takes you to the summit of **Morro da Cruz**, some 1800m up.

You could easily stay awhile in this peaceful town, and there are a number of good **hotels** to choose from. Some, like the very pretty *Pousada do Riacho* (☏22/2522-2823, ⓦwww.pousadadoriacho.com.br; ⑤) at Km 60 of the Teresópolis–Nova Friburgo road lie a short distance outside of town and feature park-like grounds and every comfort; nearer the centre is the faded, though still comfortable, *Hotel São Paulo*, Rua Monsenhor Miranda 41 (☏24/2522-9135, ⓦwww.hotelsaopaulo.com.br; ❷). Other budget options include *Hotel Montanus*, Rua Fernando Bizzotto 26 (☏24/2522-1235; ❸), or the *Hotel Fabris* (☏24/2522-2852; ❷), at Av. Alberto Braune 148, the same street as the bus station.

For **food**, try the *Oberland* delicatessen on Rua Fernando Bizzotto, which doubles as a restaurant with good, cheap Swiss and German food – veal sausage, sauerkraut and the like. The *Churrascaria Majórica*, Praça Getúlio Vargas 74, is good, too, and in the same square you can buy home-made preserves and liqueurs. For a major splurge, head out to the district of Amparo, 14km east of town on the RJ-150, and try the excellent French–Swiss restaurant the *Auberge Suisse*, located in a small and rather exclusive hotel of the same name.

To reach Nova Friburgo from Rio takes about three hours by **bus** (departures from Novo Rio Rodoviária every 30min). You'll head across the Rio–Niterói bridge, and out on Highways 101, 104 and 116. It's also possible to get a bus from Teresópolis.

Travel details

Buses

International departures daily to Asunción (30hr), Buenos Aires (50hr), Montevideo (37hr) and Santiago (70hr).

Parati to: Angra dos Reis (every 30min; 2hr); Rio (9 daily; 4hr 30min); São Paulo (4 daily; 5hr); Trinidade (7 daily; 45min); Ubatuba (3 daily; 2hr).

Petrópolis to: Belo Horizonte (5 daily; 5hr); Rio (every 30min; 90min); São Paulo (3 daily; 6hr); Teresópolis (4 daily; 1hr 30min).

Rio to: Angra dos Reis (hourly; 2hr 30min); Belém (1 daily; 52hr); Belo Horizonte (20 daily; 6hr); Brasília (8 daily; 18hr); Búzios (5 daily; 4hr); Cabo Frio (5 daily; 2hr 30min); Campo Grande (1 daily; 21hr); Fortaleza (1 daily; 43hr); Foz do Iguaçu (6 daily; 22hr); Ouro Preto (1 daily; 8hr); Parati (9 daily; 4hr 30min); Petrópolis (every 30min; 90min); Recife (4 daily; 38hr); Salvador (6 daily; 27hr); São Luis (1 daily; 50hr); São Paulo (every 15min; 6hr); Teresópolis (every 30min; 2hr); Vitória (9 daily; 8hr).

Planes

Frequent **domestic** flights from Sector A of Galeão airport on Ilha do Governador to all state capitals and other internal destinations.
Rio–São Paulo shuttle from Santos Dumont, downtown, every 30min from 6.30am to 10.30pm (55min). The airport also has less frequent services to Brasília, Belo Horizonte and Curitiba.

Minas Gerais and Espírito Santo

CHAPTER 2 # Highlights

✳ **Sculptures by Aleijadinho** Amazingly, the master sculptor of Brazilian Baroque produced his best work after his hands were deformed by leprosy. See p.183

✳ **Historic Ouro Preto** Nowhere in Brazil is there a more rich concentration of Baroque art and architecture than here, in Brazil's eighteenth-century gold mining centre. See p.186

✳ **Jequitinhonha Valley** Artesanato Ceramic vessels, in human- and animal-inspired shapes of pre-colonial heritage, are still produced in remote areas of northern Minas Gerais and sold in places like the excellent Centro de Artesanato in Araçuaí. See p.213

✳ **Pedra Azul** This vast granite rock in the eponymous state park sparkles with tints of blues or greens, depending on the time of day. See p.236

Minas Gerais and Espírito Santo

The French geologist Gorceix summed up **Minas Gerais** 150 years ago, when he wrote that the state had "a breast of iron and a heart of gold". Its hills and mountains contain the richest mineral deposits in Brazil, and led to the area being christened "General Mines" when gold and diamonds were found at the end of the seventeenth century. The gold strikes sparked a wave of migration from Rio and São Paulo, which lasted a century and shifted the centre of gravity of Brazil's economy and population from the northeast decisively to the south, where it has remained ever since. In the nineteenth century new metals, especially iron, steel and manganese, replaced gold in importance, while the uplands in the west and east proved ideal for coffee production. Land too steep for coffee bushes was converted to cattle pasture, and the luxuriant forests of southern Minas were destroyed and turned into charcoal for smelting. The bare hills are a foretaste of what parts of Amazônia might look like a century from now, and only their strange beauty – sea-like, as waves of them recede into the distance – saves them from seeming desolate.

Mineral wealth still flows from Minas' hills, but iron, bauxite, manganese and steel have superseded the precious metals of colonial times. The eighteenth-century mining settlements of Minas Gerais are now quiet and beautiful colonial towns, with a fraction of the population they had two hundred years ago. They're called *as cidades históricas*, "the historic cities", and are the only colonial remnants in southern Brazil that stand comparison with the Northeast. Most importantly, they're the repository of a great flowering of Baroque **religious art** that took place here in the eighteenth century: *arte sacra mineira* was the finest work of its time in the Americas, and Minas Gerais can lay claim to undisputably the greatest figure in Brazilian cultural history – the mulatto leper sculptor, **Aleijadinho**, whose magnificent work is scattered throughout the historic cities. The most important of the *cidades históricas* are **Ouro Preto**, **Mariana** and **Sabará**, all within easy striking distance of Belo Horizonte, and **Congonhas**, **São João del Rei**, **Tiradentes** and **Diamantina**, a little further afield.

In more recent times, too, Minas Gerais has been at the centre of Brazilian history. *Mineiros* have a well-deserved reputation for political cunning, and have produced the two greatest postwar Brazilian presidents: **Juscelino Kubitschek**, the builder of Brasília, and **Tancredo Neves**, midwife to the

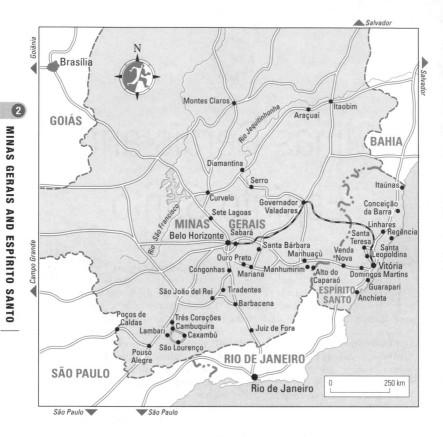

rebirth of Brazilian democracy in 1985. It was troops from Minas who put down the São Paulo revolt against Getúlio Vargas' populist regime in the brief civil war of 1932 and, less creditably, the army division in Minas which moved against Rio in 1964 and ensured the success of the military coup.

In keeping with this economic and political force, the capital of Minas, **Belo Horizonte**, is a thriving, modern metropolis – one of the largest cities in Brazil and second only to São Paulo as an industrial centre, which, with its forest of skyscrapers and miles of industrial suburbs, it rather resembles. It lies in the centre of the rich mining and agricultural hinterland that has made the state one of the economic powerhouses of Brazil, running from the coffee estates of western Minas to the mines and cattle pastures of the valley of the **Rio Doce**, in the east of the state. You can read the area's history in its landscape, the jagged horizons a direct result of decades of mining. The largest cities of the region apart from Belo Horizonte are Juiz de Fora in the south, Governador Valadares to the east, and Uberaba and Uberlândia in the west – all modern and unprepossessing; only Belo Horizonte can honestly be recommended as worth visiting.

All *mineiros* would agree that the soul of the state lies in the rural areas, in the hill and mountain villages of its vast **interior**. North of Belo Horizonte, the grassy slopes and occasional patches of forest are swiftly replaced by the stubby trees and savanna of the Planalto Central (leading to Brasília and central Brazil proper); and in northeastern Minas, by the cactus, rock and perennial drought of the *sertão* – as desperately poor and economically backward as anywhere in the Northeast proper. The northern part of the state is physically dominated by the hills and highlands of the **Serra do Espinhaço**, a range which runs north–south through the state like a massive dorsal fin, before petering out south of Belo Horizonte. To its east, the **Rio Jequitinhonha** sustains life in the parched landscapes of the *sertão mineiro*; to the west is the flat river valley of the **Rio São Francisco**, which rises here before winding through the interior of the Northeast. The extreme west of Minas Gerais state is taken over by the agricultural **Triângulo Mineiro**, a wealthy region centred on the city of Uberlândia, with far closer economic ties with São Paulo than with the rest of Minas Gerais. Many people in the Triângulo Mineiro believe that the region would benefit from being a separate state, a cause that some local politicians have adopted.

In the southwest of Minas, in fine mountainous scenery near the border with São Paulo, are a number of **spa towns** built around mineral water springs: **São Lourenço** and **Caxambu** are small and quiet, but **Poços de Caldas** is a large and very lively resort. Perhaps the most scenically attractive part of Minas Gerais – certainly the least visited – is the **eastern** border with Espírito Santo. There's some spectacular walking country in the **Caparaó** national park, where the third highest mountain in Brazil, the 2890-metre **Pico da Bandeira**, is more easily climbed than its height suggests.

Espírito Santo, the small coastal state that separates eastern Minas from the Atlantic, is the kind of place that you rarely hear about, even within Brazil. It's almost completely off the tourist map. This is hard to understand, as the interior of the state has some claim to being the most beautiful part of Brazil. Settled mostly by Italians and Germans, it has a disconcertingly European feel – cows graze in front of German-looking ranches, and, if it weren't for the heat, palm trees and the hummingbirds darting around, you might imagine yourself somewhere in Switzerland. Vast numbers of *mineiros* head for Espírito Santo for their holidays, but are only interested in the beaches, the one thing landlocked Minas lacks. This has the fortunate effect of cramming all the crowds into an easily avoidable coastal strip, leaving the interior free for you to explore.

The only place of any size is **Vitória**, a rather grimy city saved by a fine location, on an island surrounded by hills and granite outcrops. It was one of the few spots on the coast that could be easily defended, and the **Botocudo Indians** were able to restrict the Portuguese to scattered coastal settlements until the last century. This is one of the reasons the interior is relatively thinly settled; the other is the sheer difficulty of communications in the steep, thickly forested hills that rear up into mountains along the border with Minas. The semi-deciduous tropical forest that once carpeted much of the southern coast of Brazil still survives relatively unscathed here – and is what southern Minas would have looked like before the gold rushes. To a degree, the forest resembles Amazonian jungle, but if you look closely during autumn and winter (April to Sept) you'll see that many of the trees have shed their leaves. The best way to view the region is to make the round of the towns which began as German and Italian colonies: **Santa Teresa**, **Santa Leopoldina**, **Santa Maria**, **Domingos Martins** and **Venda Nova** – the last near the remarkable sheer granite face of **Pedra Azul**, one of the least-known but most spectacular sights in the country.

Belo Horizonte

The best way to approach **BELO HORIZONTE** is from the south, over the magnificent hills of the Serra do Espinhaço, on a road that winds back and forth before finally cresting a ridge where the entire city is set out before you. It's a spectacular sight: Belo Horizonte sprawls in an enormous bowl surrounded by hills, a sea of skyscrapers, *favelas* and industrial suburbs. From the centre, the jagged, rust-coloured skyline of the Serra do Espinhaço, which gave the city its name, is always visible on the horizon – still being transformed by the mines gnawing away at the "breast of iron".

Despite its size and importance, Belo Horizonte is little more than a century old, laid out in the early 1890s on the site of the poor village of Curral del Rey – of which nothing remains – and shaped by the new ideas of "progress" that emerged with the new Republic. Belo Horizonte was the first of Brazil's planned cities and is arguably the most successful. As late as 1945 it had only 100,000 inhabitants; now it has well over twenty times that number (forty times if one includes the city's metropolitan hinterland), an explosive rate of growth even by Latin American standards. It rapidly became the most important pole of economic development in the country, after São Paulo, and while it may not be as historic as the rest of the state it's difficult not to be impressed by the city's scale and energy. Moreover, Belo Horizonte's central location and proximity to some of the most important *cidades históricas* (Sabará is just outside the city, Ouro Preto and Mariana only two hours away by road) make it a good base for exploring Minas Gerais.

The **central zone** of Belo Horizonte is contained within the inner ring road, the **Avenida do Contorno**; the centre is laid out in a grid pattern, crossed by diagonal *avenidas*, that makes it easy to find your way around on foot, though difficult by car because of a complex system of one-way traffic. The spine of the city is the broad **Avenida Afonso Pena**, with the *rodoviária* at its northern end, in the heart of the downtown area. Just down from the *rodoviária* along Avenida Afonso Pena is the obelisk in the **Praça Sete**, the middle of the hotel and financial district and the city's busiest part; a few blocks further down Afonso Pena are the trees and shade of the **Parque Municipal**. A short distance south of the centre is the **Praça da Liberdade**, Belo Horizonte's main square, dominated by a double row of imperial palms and important public buildings, while beyond lies the chic residential area of **Savassi**, with its restaurants, nightlife and boutiques.

The only places **beyond the Contorno** you're likely to visit are the artificial lake and Niemeyer buildings of **Pampulha**, to the north, and the rambling nature reserve of **Mangabeiras**, on the southern boundary of the city.

Arrival, information and city transport

The nearer of Belo Horizonte's two **airports** is Pampulha (☎31/3689-2700), 9km from the centre and connected by bus #1202. All short-haul flights and an increasing number of flights from further afield arrive here. The much newer Aeroporto Internacional Tancredo Neves (☎31/3490-2001), usually refered to as Confins, the name of the nearby town, was designed to take most air traffic away from Pampulha, but its distance from the city (well over 30km, and connected by a bad road) has made it unpopular with passengers and airlines alike. Confins is linked to the centre by **airport buses** that leave you either at the *rodoviária* (the *ônibus convencional*; 75¢) or at the tourist centre, Terminal Turístico JK, west along Avenida Amazonas (the faster, air-conditioned *ônibus executivo*; $3). Both buses have rather erratic timetables (every 20min at best, every 2hr at worst) and take about an hour; if you're departing by plane, phone in advance to check departure times (*convencional* ☎31/3271-1335, *executivo* ☎31/3271-4522). **Taxis** to the city centre cost around $7 from Pampulha or $17 from Confins; there are desks in the arrivals areas from where you can purchase vouchers at rates fixed according to your destination.

The **rodoviária** is on Praça Rio Branco, an easy walk from the commercial centre of the city, and offers direct bus services to most significant destinations in the country. The information desk (☎31/3271-3000) can provide details of times and fares. Nearby is the Edwardian **train station** (☎31/3273-5976) on Praça da Estação (also called Praça Rui Barbosa), a significant sight in its own right (see p.170). Apart from the local *metrô* commuter service, only one line out of Belo Horizonte has survived the post-privatization cuts of the 1990s, namely the daily connection with Vitória on the coast, now owned by the giant industrial combine Companhia do Vale do Rio Doce (CVRD). It's an interminably slow but fascinating ride through the industrial heartland of eastern Minas (via Governador Valadares), taking about fourteen hours, much of it following the valley of the Rio Doce (see p.241 for information on departures from Belo Horizonte).

Information

The municipal Belotur organization is very knowledgeable about the city and the rest of the state, and publishes a useful, free monthly guide-booklet, the *Guia Turística*, which contains a good map. You'll find it in the city's better hotels and in the **tourist offices** at Mercado Central (Mon–Sat 8am–6pm, Sun & holidays 8am–noon); Mercado das Flores, Parque Municipal (Mon–Sat 9am–7pm); Bahia Shopping, Rua da Bahia and Avenida Afonso Pena (Mon–Fri 9am–10pm, Sat 9am–4pm, Sun & holidays 10am–4pm); Igreja São Francisco de Assis, Pampulha (daily 8am–6pm); Tancredo Neves (Confins) airport (daily 8am–10pm); Pampulha airport (daily 8am–10pm); and the *rodoviária* (Mon–Fri 8am–8pm, Sat & Sun 8am–4pm). Belotur also has a phone number ("Alô Turismo") for specific queries: ☎31/3277-9777 (daily 8am–10pm). The Minas Gerais state tourist office, Sectur, is at Praça Rio Branco 56 (Mon–Fri 9am–6pm; ☎31/3272-8585), and is well worth a visit for help planning routes in the interior.

For up-to-date **listings**, the *Estado de Minas* **newspaper** features a daily *Espetáculo* section, listing ongoing events in the city and previewing new shows. By far the most comprehensive information source, however, with detailed reviews of restaurants, films, theatre and nightlife of all sorts, is the *Roteiro Cultural* supplement of the free *Pampulha* paper, published every Saturday and generally available in the city's hotels.

City transport

The **bus system** works along the same lines as elsewhere in Brazil but is colour-coded: blue buses run up and down the main *avenidas* within the city centre, yellow buses have circular routes, white buses are "express", stopping only at selected points, and red buses are radial, connecting outlying suburbs and *favelas* with the centre. Virtually all routes include a stretch along Avenida

Useful bus routes

Yellow SCO2: from the *rodoviária* to Praça Sete and Savassi, via Praça da Liberdade.

Blue 1001: from Avenida Afonso Pena (between Rua Espírito Santo and Rua Tupis) to Praça da Savassi via Praça da Liberdade.

Blue 1202: from Avenida Afonso Pena, down the tree-lined Avenida Amazonas and out to Pampulha airport.

Blue 4001: from Avenida Afonso Pena to Praça da Liberdade.

Blue 2001: from the Parque das Mangabeiras down Avenida Afonso Pena to Praça Sete and the *rodoviária*.

Blue 6001: from the northern entrance of Parque das Mangabeiras to Savassi and the centre.

Afonso Pena, usually the most convenient place to catch a bus if you are staying in the centre. Buses are very frequent, with fares around 50¢ for all journeys in the city centre or suburbs; see the box on this page for route details.

Otherwise, with distances being short between most points of interest in the city, **taxis** (BH Táxi ☎31/3215-8081; Coopertramo ☎3454-5757) are cheap. There is a city **metrô system** but this was built with workers rather than tourists in mind and serves only to link the industrial suburbs with the centre. It runs Monday to Friday (and holidays) 5.45am–11pm, Saturday 5.45am–5pm.

Accommodation

You don't need to stray far from the centre for **accommodation**, as there are scores of hotels, most extremely reasonable, within easy reach of the *rodoviária*. There are also some good hotel options in the pleasant Savassi area, an easy taxi or bus ride (or a half-hour walk) from the centre, and a few in Funcionários, midway between the two. For those on a tight budget, the city's **youth hostel**, *Albergue de Juventude Chalé Mineiro*, Rua Santa Luzia 288 (☎31/3467-1576; $6 per person), is just a short taxi ride (or bus #2701) from the centre in the *bairro* of Santa Efigênia, 3km away, where the city's main hospitals are concentrated; the hostel has its own garden and pool and is always very popular, so phone ahead to check that they have space. Avoid the cheap *dormitórios* bunched around the *rodoviária*, which cater mainly for prostitutes and their clients.

As in most other business-oriented cities, mid- and upper-range hotels will usually offer substantial **discounts** to the official rates indicated below: you can often expect up to thirty percent off during the week and up to fifty percent at weekends, except when there's a major congress or other event taking place in the city.

Brasil Palace Rua Carijós 269, Centro ☎ & ℱ31/3273-3811. A fine 1940s building overlooking Praça Sete which still looks like the cinema it once was. The rooms are excellent value for money, with baths as well as showers, TV, *frigobar* and air-conditioning. ❷

Continental Av. Paraná 241, Centro ☎31/3201-7944, ℱ3201-7336. A respectable, inexpensive

hotel near the *rodoviária*. The rooms (both double and single) are small but clean, very quiet and newly furnished. ❷

Ibis Belo Horizonte Av. João Pinheiro, Centro ☎0800-703-7000, ⊛www.accorhotels.com.br. A renovated old house with a modern extension behind, this efficient hotel on the edge of Funcionários is typical of the French-owned chain.

The no-frills rooms are small, but each has a shower and all are air-conditioned. ③

Liberty Palace Rua Paraíba 1465, Savassi ⑦31/3282-0900, ⓦwww.libertypalace.com.br. The most expensive place to stay in Savassi, with all the facilities that you would expect of one of the city's top hotels (pool, business centre and decent restaurant). Many of the rooms on the sixth floor and above have panoramic views. ⑥

Macêdo Praça da Estação 123, Centro ⑦31/3222-9255. By far the best of the cheaper options, with good clean rooms (though some of the furniture has clearly seen better days), even cheaper *quartos*, and a basic breakfast. Some rooms have excellent views over the *praça* and the train station, but those overlooking Av. Amazonas can be noisy at night. ②

Majestic BH Centro Rua Espírito Santo 284, Centro ⑦31/3222-3390, ⑥3222-3146. Though hardly majestic, this hotel has a wide range of large, clean, basic rooms – nothing special but well priced, and *quartos* are considerably cheaper. ②

Max Savassi Suite Rua Antônio de Albuquerque 335, Savassi ⑦31/3225-6466, ⓦwww .maxsavassi.com.br. Apartment hotel located on a pleasant tree-lined street. All the apartments have a bedroom, a living room and a small kitchen, and the whole building shares a pool. Excellent value. ④

Mercure Av. do Contorno 7315, Santo Antônio ⑦31/3298-4100, ⓦwww.accor.com.br. Situated on the edge of Savassi, this is the largest, newest luxury hotel in the city. The facilities are as good as you'd expect for a hotel in this price range, with the staff efficient rather than friendly. Room rates are very competitively priced. ⑤

Metrópole Rua da Bahia 1023, Centro ⑦ & ⑥31/3273-1544. A spendid Art Deco edifice that wouldn't appear out of place in Miami's fashionable South Beach district. A very central location, but the most attractive rooms (those at the front of the hotel with balconies) are very noisy during the day. Although the rooms have seen better days, they are clean and well equipped, with air-conditioning, cable TV and *frigobar*. ③

Othon Palace Av. Afonso Pena 1050, Centro ⑦31/3247-000, ⓦwww.othon.com.br. Huge and newly refurbished 1970s skyscraper, with friendly and highly professional staff, well-equipped rooms and a fine rooftop pool. Be sure to request a room on one of the upper floors facing the front of the building: the views across the Parque Municipal and onwards to the Serra do Curral are absolutely spectacular. Good value. ⑤

Praça da Liberdade Av. Brasil 1912, Funcionários ⑦31/3261-1711, ⓦwww.pracadaliberdade.com.br. Mini high-rise hotel in a pleasant area of government offices, within easy walking distance of the city centre and Savassi. The 29 rooms, while small, are well appointed. ④

Savassi Rua Sergipe 939, Savassi ⑦31/3261-3266, ⑥3261-4328. Mid-range hotel with rather dark but perfectly comfortable rooms, and a tiny rooftop pool with fantastic views towards the Serra do Curral. Savassi's restaurants and bars are just a short walk away. ④

Sol Belo Horizonte Rua Bahia 1040, Centro ⑦31/3274-1344, ⓦwww.solmeliabh.com.br. This newish four-star downtown hotel (part of the Spanish-owned Meliá chain) has pleasant rooms, efficient though somewhat impersonal service and a pool and sauna. Popular with business executives, the place empties at weekends. ⑤

Sorrento Praça Raul Soares 354, Centro ⑦31/3272-1100, ⑥3271-2805. Clean, comfortable and efficiently run budget hotel in a pleasant downtown location on the edge of Barro Preto and its nightlife. The nicest rooms overlook the *praça*, but can be a little noisy. ②

Sun América Palace Av. Amazonas 50, Centro ⑦31/3201-1722, ⑥3212-7117. A once grand – and still quite striking at first glance – 1930s hotel that offers very basic rooms at good value. ②

Wimbledon Av. Afonso Pena 772, Centro ⑦0800-318-383, ⓦwww.wimbledon.com.br. Good mid-range hotel in the heart of downtown. The rooms are fairly small and simply furnished, but all have a rather aging *frigobar*, cable TV and air-conditioning. Ask for a room overlooking Av. Afonso Pena as these are much brighter. The hotel also has a very small pool. ④

The City

Even the most patriotic *mineiro* would make few claims for the architecture of Belo Horizonte, dominated as it is by non-descript 1960s and 1970s high-rises. Nonetheless, there are some notable exceptions, chiefly on and around **Praça da Liberdade**. And if you stand in the heart of the city, in **Praça Sete**, and look down the broad Avenida Afonso Pena towards the Parque Municipal, or

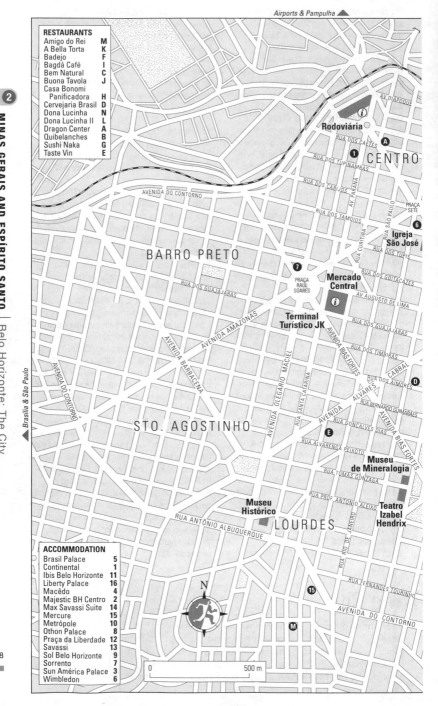

Airports & Pampulha ▲

RESTAURANTS
Amigo do Rei	M
A Bella Torta	K
Badejo	F
Bagdá Café	I
Bem Natural	C
Buona Tavola	J
Casa Bonomi Panificadora	H
Cervejaria Brasil	D
Dona Lucinha	N
Dona Lucinha II	L
Dragon Center	A
Quibelanches	B
Sushi Naka	G
Taste Vin	E

◄ Brasília & São Paulo

Rodoviária

CENTRO

Igreja São José

BARRO PRETO

PRAÇA SETE

Mercado Central

PRAÇA RAUL SOARES

Terminal Turístico JK

STO. AGOSTINHO

Museu de Mineralogia

Museu Histórico

LOURDES

Teatro Izabel Hendrix

ACCOMMODATION
Brasil Palace	5
Continental	1
Ibis Belo Horizonte	11
Liberty Palace	16
Macêdo	4
Majestic BH Centro	2
Max Savassi Suite	14
Mercure	15
Metrópole	10
Othon Palace	8
Praça da Liberdade	12
Savassi	13
Sol Belo Horizonte	9
Sorrento	7
Sun América Palace	3
Wimbledon	6

N

0   500 m

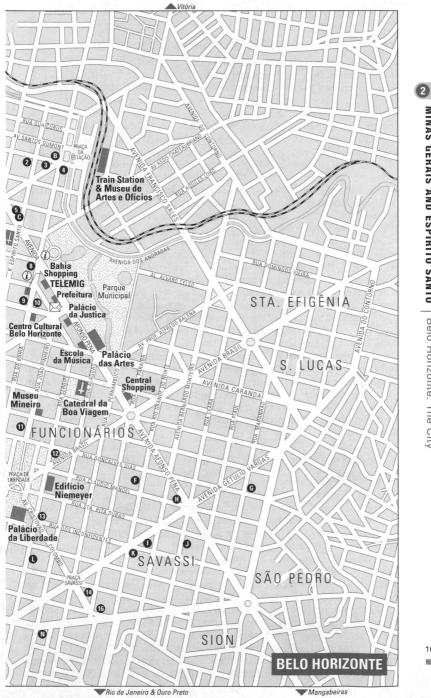

Vitória

RUA GUAICURUS

AV. SANTOS DUMONT

PRAÇA DA ESTAÇÃO

AVENIDA FRANCISCO SALES

AVENIDA DU CONTORNO

AV. ASSIS CHATEAUBRIAND

RUA AQUILES LOBO

Train Station & Museu de Artes e Ofícios

R. ESPIRITO SANTO

AVENIDA DOS ANDRADAS

RUA DOMINGOS VIEIRA

AL. ALVARO CELSO

Bahia Shopping

TELEMIG

Parque Municipal

Prefeitura

STA. EFIGÊNIA

AVENIDA DO CONTORNO

Palácio da Justiça

Centro Cultural Belo Horizonte

AFONSO PENA

AV. PROF. ALFREDO BALENA

Escola da Música

Palácio das Artes

AVENIDA BRASIL

S. LUCAS

AVENIDA CARANDA

Central Shopping

RUA GRANDE DO NORTE

AVENIDA BERNARDO MONTEIRO

RUA PIUI

RUA MARANHÃO

Museu Mineiro

RUA DA BAHIA

RUA JOÃO PINHEIRO

RUA SERGIPE

PERNAMBUCO

RUA ALAGOAS

RUA PARAÍBA

RUA TABARU

Catedral da Boa Viagem

FUNCIONÁRIOS

AVENIDA BRASIL

RUA GONÇALVES DIAS

PRAÇA DE LIBERDADE

Edifício Niemeyer

RUA CLAUDIO MANOEL

RUA STA. RITA DURÃO

AVENIDA AFONSO PENA

AVENIDA GETÚLIO VARGAS

AL. CRISTOVÃO COLOMBO

Palácio da Liberdade

RUA DOS INCONFIDENTES

SAVASSI

SÃO PEDRO

PRAÇA SAVASSI

SION

BELO HORIZONTE

Rio de Janeiro & Ouro Preto

Mangabeiras

along the graceful palm-lined Avenida Amazonas, you'll notice that the city does have attractive features.

The Praça da Estação and the Praça Sete

A good place to begin one's wanderings through downtown Belo Horizonte is the **train station** on Praça da Estação, one of the city's prettiest buildings. The Neoclassical yellow-coloured building, which replaced Belo Horizonte's original main station in 1922, is one of Brazil's finest examples of tropical Edwardiana, although these days, the station's platforms are used only by passengers on the once-daily Vitória-bound service or commuters riding the city's *metrô*. Housed inside the beautifully renovated station is the **Museu de Artes e Ofícios** (Tues–Fri 1–6pm, Sat & Sun 10am–4pm), which traces the history of work and industry in Minas Gerais. Though impressively displayed, the museum's extensive collection of handicrafts and tools provides little in the way of social or economic context, making a visit here seem somewhat pointless. You can, however, admire the craftsmanship of the hardwood staircases, stained-glass windows, and iron and plaster work inside the building, all of which are well worth a look.

Graced on both sides by imperial palms, Avenida Amazonas, one of the city's main arteries, leads up from Praça da Estação into the **Praça Sete**. Humming with activity, Praça Sete is full of office workers (the area immediately around is the city's main financial district), and is also the main venue of street draughts tournaments, when rows of hustlers set up boards on the pavement and play all comers for money. Surrounding the square are bars and *lanchonetes* which stay open until midnight, even later at weekends, and when the rest of the city has gone home to sleep the square is taken over by scores of homeless people, huddling around fires on deserted pavements.

A ten-minute stroll beyond Praça Sete, at the intersection of Rua Goitacazes and Rua Santa Catarina, is the **Mercado Central** (Mon–Sat 7am–6pm, Sun 7am–noon), a sprawling indoor market of almost four hundred stalls. There's an incredible variety of goods on offer, ranging from the usual fruit, vegetables, cheeses and meats, to *cachaças*, spices and medicinal herbs, dogs, cats and parakeets, kitchen equipment, rustic handicrafts, and *umbanda* and *candomblé* accessories.

Avenida Afonso Pena and the Parque Municipal

Running southeast from Praça Sete, the broad Avenida Afonso Pena bisects the city and is home to some of the city's showcase buildings, as well as the **Instituto Moreira Salles**, near Praça Sete, at no. 737 (Tues–Fri 1–7pm, Sat & Sun 1–6pm; ☎31/3213-7900, ⊛ www.ims.com.br), a cultural centre that hosts major exhibitions of nineteenth- and twentieth-century Brazilian art collections, often photographic, of its sponsor, Unibanco.

Further along the avenue, midway between Rua Tamoios and Rua Espírito Santo at the top of a flight of steps, is the **Igreja São José** (Mon–Sat 7–11am & 3–8pm and Sun 7am–noon & 3–8pm), which dates back to 1906 and was the first church in the new capital; its eclectic Manueline and Gothic style is characteristically Brazilian, and it is set in an attractive tree-filled garden. Further south along the avenue between Rua da Bahia and Avenida Álvares Cabral is the Art Deco–influenced **Prefeitura** (town hall), built in the 1930s as an early boast of civic pride, while just a short distance on is the imposing **Palácio da Justiça** and the **Escola da Música** with its Corinthian columns.

On the other side of the avenue is one of the very few large-scale areas of relief from the traffic and noise of downtown: the green and shade of the **Parque Municipal** (Tues–Sun 6am–6pm). Beautifully laid out by the French landscape artist Paul Villon, the park encompasses a boating lake, two thousand species of tree, shaded walks much patronized by courting couples, aviaries, a permanent fairground and exercise yards where Brazilian men make their sweaty sacrifices to the national cult of the body beautiful. It also contains the main arts complex in the city, the Palácio das Artes.

The Palácio das Artes

The **Palácio das Artes** (entrance on Avenida Afonso Pena (☎31/3237-7234, ⓦ www.palaciodasartes.com.br) is one of the finest modern buildings in the city, a complex of which the citizens of Belo Horizonte are justifiably proud. So much so that when parts of the *palácio* burned down in March 1997, reconstruction began barely a week later, and a mammoth benefit show was organized in the *mineirão* football stadium to fund the repairs. Now fully restored, the *palácio* is divided into a number of well laid-out **galleries** (daily 9am–9pm; free), with exhibitions concentrating on modern Brazilian art, a couple of small **theatres** and one big one, the **Grande Teatro**, which suffered most in the fire.

Though it's hard to believe in such a large city, the *palácio* is one of the very few places in Belo Horizonte where you'll come across a good display of the distinctive *artesanato* of the state, in the **Centro de Artesanato Mineiro** (Mon 1–6pm, Tues–Fri 9am–9pm, Sat 9am–1pm, Sun 10am–2pm). A large shop rather than a gallery proper, it's nevertheless a place you can wander around and look without being pressured to buy. Although there's a lot of dross here, there is also some excellent pottery – stubby figurines and realistic clay tableaux. Distinctive though it is, you wouldn't be wrong in thinking that the best work looks Northeastern: it comes from the valley of the Rio Jequitinhonha in the *sertão mineiro*, and contains elements of both traditions. Hammocks, clothes, wall hangings and rugs, roughly woven from the cotton that grows in northern Minas, are also of a high quality. Despite the sleek surroundings, the prices here are reasonable: not more than twice what you'd pay where the work comes from.

Feira de Arte e Artesanato

It's worth making an effort to be in Belo Horizonte on a Sunday morning for the **Feira de Arte e Artesanato**. One of the best of its kind anywhere in the country, with buyers and sellers coming from all over Brazil, this massive market takes over the Avenida Afonso Pena bordering the Parque Municipal. It's always packed, and by mid-morning, moving through the narrow avenues between rows of stalls gets difficult; by 2pm, stallholders are packing up and leaving, and by 4pm the city's efficient street cleaners will have removed all trace of the market. An excellent place for bargains, the market is split into sections, with related stalls grouped together – jewellery, leather goods, lace, ceramics, cane furniture, clothes, food, paintings and drinks, to name but a few. Prices of more expensive items and clothes are fixed, with many things on view being labelled, but otherwise there is some scope for bargaining.

As always with Brazilian markets, what's going on around you is just as interesting as what's for sale. If you can find a seat, set up camp at one of the **bars** at the corner with Rua da Bahia, and watch the stallholders hustling, buyers negotiating and people doing the same as you – just enjoying the action or listening to the buskers and serious musicians who play at the fringes of the crowds and sell tapes of their work.

Funcionários and Praça da Liberdade

Southwest of Avenida Afonso Pena, behind the grand public buildings, are the hilly tree-lined roads of **Funcionários**, a neighbourhood – as the name suggests – dominated by government offices of all sorts. The district also contains the **Catedral da Boa Viagem**, Rua Alagoas (Mon & Sat 11am–10pm, Tues–Fri & Sun 6am–10pm), inaugurated in 1922 to mark the centenary of Brazilian independence. For a cathedral of a major city, the neo-Gothic structure is surprisingly small and plain, but the grounds are beautiful.

A short walk southeast of the cathedral is the impressive, Neoclassical **Museu Mineiro**, Av. João Pinheiro 342 (Tues–Fri 11.30am–6.30pm, Sat, Sun & holidays 10am–4pm), one of the first buildings in Belo Horizonte, dating from 1897. The building served as the state Senate from 1905 to 1930, only being converted for use as a museum much later, and today houses an unremarkable sample of the tradition of religious art in Minas. One block east from Avenida João Pinheiro is the steep Rua da Bahia where at no. 1149 you'll find the **Centro de Cultura Belo Horizonte** (Mon–Fri 9am–9pm, Sat & holidays 9am–6pm, Sun 2–6pm), a curious neo-Gothic structure that was constructed in 1914 as the city's legislative assembly. The inside of the building, with its wood panelling and sweeping staircase, is worth a look, and there are often small exhibitions or concerts going on. One block down the road, the shocking-pink and blue *Hotel Metrópole* is one of the purest surviving examples of Art Deco in the city.

The park-like **Praça da Liberdade** lies to the south of Funcionários. With its beautiful trees, Edwardian bandstand and fountains, the square is a wonderful place to sit and while away the time and is especially popular on weekends when residents of neighbouring apartment buildings come out to rollerblade or sit and read in the sun. The square is dominated by the elegant French Art-Nouveau-style **Palácio da Liberdade** (Sun 9am–2pm), built between 1895 and 1898 as the residence of the president of Minas Gerais. Today, the *palácio* remains the administrative centre of the state government and the official residence of the governor, primarily used for state functions. Other buildings to look out for on the square include the flowing lines of the **Edifício Niemeyer** apartment building, designed by architect Oscar Niemeyer in the 1950s and still one of Belo Horizonte's most prestigious residential addresses. Directly across the *praça* from the apartment building, at Av. Bias Fortes 50, sits the ugly glass-and-steel **Museu de Mineralogia** (Tues–Sun & holidays 9am–5pm), whose extensive collection of minerals and local fossils is likely to be of interest only to geologists.

Museu Histórico Abílio Barreto

One of the very few museums in the city really worth a visit is the **Museu Histórico Abílio Barreto** (Tues, Wed, Fri–Sun 10am–5pm, Thurs 10am–9pm, closed Mon) at Rua Bernardo Mascarenhas in Cidade Jardim. To get there, take the #5901 bus (marked "Nova Floresta/Santa Lúcia"); the most convenient stop to catch the bus is along Avenida Amazonas between Rua Espírito Santo and Rua dos Caetés. If you ask the conductor for the Museu Histórico, you'll be dropped on Avenida do Contorno, a block away, from where there are signs to the museum on Rua Bernardo Mascarenhas. The surrounding area of Cidade Jardim is rapidly becoming one of the most fashionable, upper-class parts of the city, with new skyscrapers sprouting like weeds. It's an ironic location for the oldest building in the city, the only one that predates 1893 when construction of the new capital began.

The museum was once a *fazenda*, built in 1883, comfortable but not luxurious, and typical of the ranches of rural Minas. Though now swamped by the burgeoning city, it once stood on its own, a few kilometres away from the church and hovels of the hamlet of Curral del Rey, which straggled along what is now the stretch of Avenida Afonso Pena opposite the Parque Municipal. The *fazenda* has been perfectly preserved and now houses the usual collection of old furniture and mediocre paintings, upstairs, and in the garden an old tram and turn-of-the-century train used in the construction of Belo Horizonte. Far better is the rustic wooden veranda at the front, where you can sit with your feet up and imagine yourself back in the 1880s.

By far the most interesting part of the museum is the **galeria de fotografias**, juxtaposing images of the sleepy village before it was obliterated – mules, mud huts and ox carts – with views of the modern city through the decades; there are a couple of well-designed maps to help you get your bearings. The last remnant of Curral del Rey, the eighteenth-century Igreja Matriz, was flattened in 1932: a few photographs, and carved bits of the church piled in a shed in the garden, are all that remains of the vanished community.

Equally remarkable is the series of photographs that record the building of Belo Horizonte and its early years: a trashed building site becomes the Parque Municipal; the train station stands in glorious isolation (it's now dwarfed by the surrounding buildings); and the Praça Sete is shown as it was in the 1930s, ringed by trees and fine Art Deco buildings, of which only the Cine Brasil (now the *Brasil Palace Hotel*) is still standing. Like Rio, urban architecture in Belo Horizonte was at its peak in the 1930s and 1940s, when the city was an elegant political capital, rather than an economic centre, and it has suffered since at the hands of the developers. A classic demonstration of this is the wonderful Art Deco market building, the Feira de Amostras Permanentes, which you can now only appreciate here in the museum. It was demolished in 1970 and replaced by the *rodoviária*.

Parque das Mangabeiras

Unlikely as it may seem amid the skyscrapers of Avenida Afonso Pena, the city limits are only a short bus ride away to the south. Here, the urban sprawl is abruptly cut off by the steep hills of the **Serra do Curral**, a natural barrier that forces the city to expand in other directions. The slopes are the site of a huge nature reserve, the 600-hectare **Parque das Mangabeiras** (Tues–Sun 8am–6pm), where you can walk along forest paths that open out now and again to reveal spectacular views of the city below. To get there, catch the blue #2001-C bus, marked "Aparecida", from Avenida Afonso Pena between Avenida Amazonas and Rua Tamóios: it's a fifteen-minute steep drive to the terminus above the park entrance. When returning to the city, you can avoid having to climb back up to the main entrance by leaving the park through the small northern gate, much lower down, and catching the #6001 bus just outside.

The park is so big it has its own **internal bus service**; buses leave every thirty minutes from the left of the entrance, and end up there again twenty minutes later after making a circuit of the park. Near the entrance is a well-kept leisure area, with fountains, rows of *lanchonetes* and an open-air amphitheatre, the **Teatro de Arena**, where there's often something on on Sundays. There's an excellent view of the city from the **Mirante da Mata** viewing platform, a twenty-minute walk from the entrance; the finest walks are along the nature trails and streams of the **Parque Florestal**, a little further along. **Maps** of the park are available from the park office near the main entrance.

Mirante da Cidade

The single most spectacular view of the city is from the **Mirante da Cidade**, outside the park, largely hidden by trees behind the governor's palatial residence. Take the #2001-C bus for Mangabeiras (or the #2001-A), but get off just before at Praça do Papa, and walk east up the steep Rua Bady Salum for a short kilometre. The view is splendid: too high up for the grime and *favelas* to register (although pollution can obscure things on a bad day), it makes Belo Horizonte seem like Los Angeles, an impression reinforced if you go by night, when the carpet of lights below really is magnificent.

Pampulha

Some 10km north of the centre (an hour or so by bus) is the luxurious district of **Pampulha**, built around an artificial lake which is overlooked by some of the finest modern buildings in the city – the Museu de Arte, the modernist Igreja de São Francisco and the Casa do Baile. They are instantly recognizable as the work of architect **Oscar Niemeyer**, creator of Brasília, and landscape designer **Roberto Burle Marx** – both of whom, with their socialist ideals, were presumably horrified by the subsequent development of the area as a rich residential district.

The Igreja de São Francisco de Assis

The construction of the **Igreja de São Francisco de Assis** (Mon–Sun 8–6pm), with its striking curves, *azulejo* frontage and elegant bell tower, provides a roll call of the greatest names of Brazilian modernism: Burle Marx laid out its grounds, Niemeyer designed the church, Cândido Portinari did the tiles and murals depicting the fourteen stations of the cross and João Ceschiatti (best known for his gravity-defying angels in Brasília's cathedral) contributed the bronze baptismal font. The church's design was decades ahead of its time and it's astonishing to realize that it dates from the early 1940s. So shocked was the intensely conservative local Catholic hierarchy by the building's daring that the archbishop refused to consecrate it and almost twenty years passed before Mass could be held there. Nowadays Sunday Mass is held at 10.30am and 6pm. To get there, take bus #2004 (marked "Bandeirantes/Olhos d'Água") from Avenida Afonso Pena, between Avenida Amazonas and Rua Tupinambás.

The Museu de Arte (MAP) and Casa do Baile

The **Museu de Arte da Pampulha** (Tues–Sun & holidays 9am–7pm; ☎31/3443-4533, ⓦ www.map.art.br; $1.50) – or MAP as it is usually called – is more difficult to reach: take the #2215 bus from Rua dos Caetés and get off when you see a sign for the *museu* to the left – you then have to walk down to the lakeside Avenida Otacílio Negrão de Lima, turn right, and the museum is on a small peninsula jutting out into the lake. It's worth the trip, although the small collection of modern art it holds isn't at all compelling in itself. The building, however, is a product of two geniuses at the height of their powers: Niemeyer constructed a virtuoso building, all straight lines and right angles at the front but melting into rippling curves at the back, with a marvellous use of glass; Burle Marx set the whole thing off beautifully, with a sculpture garden out back and an exquisite garden framing the building in front. It was built as a casino in 1942, but the Brazilian government abolished gambling soon after and not until 1957 was the building inaugurated as an art museum.

Directly opposite, on the other side of the lake, the **Casa do Baile** (Tues–Sun 9am–6pm), a former dance hall, is by the same duo. After being closed for years due to renovation works, it has finally reopened as a space for temporary exhibitions of art and design, with a very nice café also on site. Get there on the #1202 bus from Rua São Paulo between Avenida Amazonas and Rua Carijós.

Football in Pampulha

Belo Horizonte's main football stadium, the **Mineirão** (☎31/3499-1100) is also situated in prestigious Pampulha. With a capacity of 90,000, the Mineirão is a world-class stadium, but it's rarely full. One of Brazil's better teams, Atlético Mineiro, play here and they're worth catching if you're in Belo Horizonte on a Sunday when they're playing at home. Local derbies, especially against Cruzeiro, are torrid and very entertaining affairs, but they often end with supporters of the rival teams destroying a large number of the city's buses. The #2004 bus passes by the stadium. Entrance costs around $4 for the *arquibancada* (stands), rising to $10 for better seats.

Eating, drinking and nightlife

You can eat well in Belo Horizonte and prices are generally quite reasonable, though outside the immediate downtown area, **restaurants** and **bars** tend to be more upmarket. Savassi has a particularly good range of options. The monthly *Guia Turístico* and the weekly paper *Pampulha* both contain up-to-date listings of Belo Horizonte's better restaurants.

The chic **nightlife** of Belo Horizonte is also concentrated in Savassi, but you'll find lively pockets of bars and clubs throughout the central area, as well as in the *bairros* of Barro Preto and Pampulha.

Snacks, street food and restaurants

The best area for moderately priced meals is **downtown**, around Praça Sete and towards the train station, where many of the *lanchonetes* serve good, simple and cheap *comida mineira*. Also downtown, there's a good range of upmarket *comida por kilo* restaurants – both *mineiro* and international – in the Bahia Shopping centre, one block west from Avenida Afonso Pena on Rua da Bahia. Rua Pernambuco in **Funcionários** is also a good place for reasonable *comida mineira por kilo* restaurants, especially popular at lunchtime with workers from nearby government offices.

Street food is worth trying, too. On Saturdays between 10am and 4pm, food stalls go up at the Feira Tom Jobim (a street market where antiques and bric-a-brac are sold) along Avenida Bernardo Monteiro on the corner with Avenida Brasil; the stands serve foreign and Brazilian regional food (including, of course, *mineiro*) which is often extremely good and is always cheap. Similar stalls crowd the busy Sunday market on Avenida Afonso Pena. Around Praça Sete you'll often find *doceiros* (sweet-sellers) in the late afternoon and early evening, hoping to tempt homebound office workers. For your own supplies, head for the modern and colourful **Mercado Central** (see p.170).

Restaurants

Oddly enough, exceptionally good **comida mineira restaurants** are not easy to find in Belo Horizonte as the state's regional specialities (see box, p.176) are more associated with small town and country life rather than city sophistication. There are, however, a good range of restaurants serving up **international cuisine**, ranging from inexpensive Lebanese, to pricey French, Italian or Japanese.

Comida mineira

Minas Gerais' delicious (if somewhat heavy) **regional food**, *comida mineira*, is one of Brazil's most distinctive – based mainly on pork, the imaginative use of vegetables, *couve*, a green vegetable somewhat like kale, and the famous *tutu*, a thick bean sauce made by grinding uncooked beans with manioc flour and cooking the mixture. Many of the dishes originate from the early mule trains and *bandeirante* expeditions of the eighteenth century, when food had to keep for long periods (hence the use of salted pork, now replaced by fresh) and be easily prepared without elaborate ingredients.

Comida mineira is not difficult to find: outside Belo Horizonte it is rare to find restaurants that serve anything else, and the capital itself has plenty of authentic establishments, provided you know where to look. There are also small stores everywhere serving Minas Gerais' *doces* (cakes and sweetmeats), local melt-in-the-mouth cheeses, made both from goats' and cows' milk and, of course, *cachaça*, usually drunk neat here before a meal "to prepare the stomach". Among the **typical dishes** are:

Brigadeiro The ultimate in chocolate snacks, so rich it should come with a health warning.

Carne picadinha A straightforward, rich stew of either beef or pork, cooked for hours until tender.

Costelinha Stewed ribs of ham.

Dobradinha Tripe stew cooked with sweet potatoes. Stews (including the two above) often include the excellent Minas sausages, smoked and peppery.

Doce de leite A rich caramel sludge.

Feijão tropeiro ("Mule driver's beans") A close relative to *tutu a mineira*, with a name that betrays its eighteenth-century origins; it features everything that is in a *tutu* but also has beans fried with *farinha* (manioc flour) and egg, often with onion, thrown into the mix.

Frango ao molho pardo Definitely one for hardened carnivores only: essentially chicken cooked in its own blood. It's better than it sounds, but rather bitter in taste.

Frango com quiabo Chicken roasted with okra and served sizzling with a side plate of *anju*, a corn porridge that *mineiros* eat with almost anything.

Tutu a mineira Most common of all dishes, found on every menu; roasted pork served with lashings of *tutu*, garnished with steamed *couve* and *torresmo* (an excellent salted pork crackling).

Amigo do Rei Rua Quintiliano 118, Santo Antônio ☎ 31/3296-3881. Simple, but very tasty Iranian food served in a casually elegant setting – the meat dishes (both stewed and grilled) are a highlight. Moderate.

A Bella Torta Rua Rio Grande do Norte 1263, Savassi ☎ 31/3281-8500. At the corner with Av. Getúlio Vargas, this is a good place to line the stomach before going clubbing; choose from a varied menu and very reasonable prices. Try the *Torta de galinha com catupiri*, a chicken-and-cheese quiche. *Comida por kilo* at lunchtimes.

Badejo Rua Rio Grande do Norte 836, Funcionários ☎ 31/3261-2023. Lots of fish and other seafood choices here at this restaurant, which specialises in the food of Espírito Santo. If you won't be visiting that state, at least try one of the distincive *mocquecas* – a tomato-based stew,

unlike the Bahian dish of the same name which uses coconut milk. Closed Mon and also Sun evening.

Bagdá Café Rua Getúlio Vargas 1621, Savassi ☎ 31/3223-7535. Inexpensive and attractive Lebanese cooking – the *cordeiro* (lamb) dishes are especially good. Evenings only.

Bem Natural Av. Afonso Pena 941, Edifício Sulacap, 2 blocks east of Praça Sete. Excellent vegetarian food, as well as some chicken and fish dishes, are served in a restaurant which is combined with a health-food shop and alternative bookstore. Inexpensive and highly recommended. Open Mon–Fri; full menu at lunchtime, soup only 5–8pm.

Buona Tavola Rua Santa Rita Durão 309, Funcionários ☎ 31/3227-6155. Near the intersection with Av. Afonso Pena, this is a relatively simple and quite authentic Italian restaurant. Expect to pay around $15 per person.

Casa Bonomi Panificadora Rua Cláudio Manoel 460, Funcionários ☎ 31/3261-3460. Located in a burgundy-coloured building without a sign near Av. Afonso Pena, this "bakery" serves excellent light meals (salads, pasta, soups and sandwiches), wonderful cakes and what is probably the best bread anywhere in Brazil. Not to be missed.

Cervejaria Brasil Rua dos Aimorés 90, Funcionários ☎ 31/3287-3299. One of the best centrally located *churrascarias* with a selection of meat likely to bewilder the most dedicated of carnivores. Pleasant surroundings and moderate prices.

Dona Derna Rua Tomee de Sousa 1380, Funcionários ☎ 3223-6954. Very good (if rather heavy) traditional northern Italian cooking with a strong emphasis on meat dishes. Moderate.

Dona Lucinha II Rua Sergipe 811, Funcionários ☎ 31/3261-5930. This and its sister restaurant (*Dona Lucinha*, Rua Padre Odorico 38, São Pedro; ☎ 31/3227-0562) offer a superb *comida mineira* buffet for just $6 per person. The vast range of meat and vegetables dishes, and the wonderful desserts, are all helpfully labelled in English, and excellent home-made liqueurs are available to sample. If you have time for just one meal in Belo Horizonte, this is the place to go. Closed Sun evening.

Dragon Center Av. Afonso Pena 549, near the *rodoviária*. This Chinese restaurant is the nearest available option for decent food if you have a couple of hours to kill while changing buses.

Emporium Av. Afonso Pena 4034, Mangabeiras ☎ 31/3281-1277. Decent *comida mineira* with lashings of *cachaça* thrown in for good measure, *Emporium* has the designer look that other *comida mineira* restaurants seem to be evolving towards. Take bus #5508 from Rua dos Caetés, or #2001 from Av. Afonso Pena in the centre.

Haus München Rua Juiz de Fora 1257, Santo Agostinho ☎ 31/3291-6900. Decent traditional German food, along the lines of pork, sauerkraut and good beer. Inexpensive. Closed Sun evening.

Mala e Cuia Av. Antônio Carlos 8305, Pampulha ☎ 31/3441-2993. Situated by the lake near Aeroporto de Pampulha and decorated in typical rustic *mineiro* style. You'll get a filling meal of regional cuisine here from around $6 a head. Live music Thursday to Sunday.

Quibelanches corner of Rua dos Caetés and Av. Amazonas. One of the cheapest Lebanese restaurants in the city, simple but with a wide range of authentic dishes, both *por kilo* (lunchtimes) and à la carte.

Sushi Naka Rua Gonçalves Dias 92, Funcionários ☎ 31/3227-2676. One of Belo Horizonte's cheapest Japanese restaurants – bear in mind that Belo Horizonte is a long way from the nearest fishing port and, although the fish served here is reliable, it's still fairly expensive. Closed Mon.

Taste Vin Rua Curitiba 2105, Lourdes ☎ 31/3292-5423. Highly rated French restaurant, with a reputation built on its excellent soufflés. Plush decor with prices to match, especially if you sample from Belo Horizonte's best wine list. Open evenings only, closed Sun.

Nightlife and entertainment

Compared to Rio and São Paulo, Belo Horizonte's nightlife is extremely measured and discreet, but there are several areas in the central part of the city where the **bars** spring to life once it gets dark. Most days of the week, the bottom end of **Rua da Bahia** between Avenida Afonso Pena and Praça da Estação is lively: the bars put out tables under the palm trees and the action goes on until the small hours. The area around the intersection of **Rua Rio de Janeiro and Avenida Augusto de Lima** is also good, but more student-like. There are a couple of small theatres and cinemas close by, and a group of bars and restaurants: a good one is *Mateus*, serving a range of light snacks and pizzas on the corner. It's also worth checking out the bars along **Rua Guajajaras** between Rua Espírito Santo and Rua da Bahia. Much further out, with outlandish performance art "happenings" at 8.30pm and the rare knack of peacefully blending in the oddest of people, is the 24-hour *Bar do Lulu*, Rua Leopoldina 415, Bairro Santo Antônio – take a taxi.

The more sophisticated bars are in **Savassi** and neighbouring **Funcionários**, both pleasant places in which to spend an evening. Drinks are only marginally more expensive here than anywhere else, and the bars get very crowded at weekends. *Chopperia Margherita Ville* and *Sausalito Point*, at the intersection of *ruas* Tomé de Souza and Pernambuco, are always busy, and most people end up drinking their beer on the street outside (both open till 4am).

Cachaça

If you want to be initiated into the wonderful world of **cachaça** (sugar-cane rum), a trip out to the *Alambique Cachaçaria*, Av. Raja Gabáglia 3200, Chalé 1, Estoril, is a must, and also offers beautiful night views of Belo Horizonte from the top of the hill. Besides the live music, the main attraction here is the *cachaça Germana*, their own brew which is available plain or infused with herbs and honey. They also serve the traditional *caipirinhas* – *cachaça* with ice, lemon and sugar – as well as straight shots. A single shot costs 35¢ and a bottle, $5. The easiest way to get here is to take a taxi from the centre: a ten- to fifteen-minute ride for about $4. While few people in Brazil would dispute a *mineiro's* claim that their *cachaça* is the best in Brazil, owing to the combination of the soil and altitude where the sugar cane is grown, bottles of *Germana* or other good quality non-industrial *cachaça* from Minas Gerais are remarkably difficult to find outside the state, even in Rio or São Paulo. If you want to take some bottles home, stock up before leaving Minas Gerais – Belo Horizonte's stalls in the Mercado Central (see p.170) have a very good selection.

Discos and live music

One of the most popular nightclubs in swish **Savassi** is *Máscaras* at Rua Santa Rita Durão 667, with its two dance floors, separate bars and video rooms, all kitted out in chic, modern style (open until 6am at weekends). It operates a system similar to many of Brazil's more upmarket nightclubs, where you pay for seats at a *mesa*, or table; if you are going in a group, it's best to book a table (☎31/3261-6050). An equally glitzy club in Savassi is *Parte Non*, popular with the scotch-drinking twenty-somethings at Rua Rio Grande do Norte 1470 (☎31/3221-9856). *Café com Letras*, Rua Antônio de Albuquerque 781 (☎31/3225-9973), is much smaller, cheaper and more laid-back, and usually features good jazz, while the small *Terra Brasilis* bar at Rua Tomé de Souza 987 has excellent live samba. Further out at Av. Bandeirantes 1299 in Mangabeiras, the downbeat *Café Concerto* hosts some interesting local bands.

For a more gritty clubbing scene, head to **Barro Preto**, where Avenida Raja Gabáglia is stuffed with good live music venues, simple *mineiro* restaurants, and small bars where you can listen to live *setaneja* (Brazilian country music) or dance to more mainstream club sounds. Quite the most outrageous is the gay club *Fashion*, Rua Tupis 1240 (11pm onwards). Strong on Bahian sounds are *Circuito*, Rua Conquista 308 (☎31/3271-3211), and the more reggae-oriented *Bar Nacional*, Av. do Contorno 10076 (Thurs–Sun; ☎31/3271-3211), while *Paco Pigalle*, Rua Ouro Preto 301 (☎31/3291-0747), plays a mix of hip-hop, reggae, salsa and disco. In **Pampulha** the nightlife caters to the wealthy students of its university. Try *Quioske Deck*, Av. Portugal 3663 (☎31/3441-3591), for samba and Bahian sounds, or *ICEX*, Campus da UFMG, which tends towards hard rock.

In the **city centre**, live music is also easy to come across, though many of the venues are well hidden and very local affairs. *Cantina do Adnan* at Rua Espírito Santo 291 (daily 5pm–sunrise; free entrance Sun–Thurs) is amongst the best of the places on that road and on Rua dos Caetés, all of them raw, energetic and distinctly dodgy (take no valuables). Another excellent place, often with live bands, is *Jequitibar*, Av. Assis Chateaubriand 573, east of the train station (☎31/3271-6522), and there's dance music at the *Café Belas Artes Liberdade*, Rua Gonçalves Dias 1581 (☎31/3222-4924), southwest of the centre in Lourdes.

Big names in music play at Minascentro, Av. Augusto de Lima 785 (☎31/3201-0122); at the Palácio das Artes (☎31/3237-7333; see p.171) and at the Teatro Izabela Hendrix, Rua da Bahia 2020 (☎31/3292-4405). Check the local papers to see who is playing: expect to pay around $7 for a ticket for a lesser-known act, or over $20 for a star performer.

Cinema and theatre

There are several **art cinemas** in Belo Horizonte with imaginative and non-dubbed programming: check out the Cine Humberto Mauro (☎31/3237-7234) in the Palácio das Artes (see p.171), and the Cineclube Unibanco Savassi (☎31/3227-6648) at Rua Levindo Lopes in Savassi. For **theatre**, there are numerous venues around town, though all productions are in Portuguese: the Palácio das Artes (☎31/3201-8900) usually has something interesting going on and there are often fine productions at the Teatro Izabela Hendrix (see above). The Palácio das Artes also occasionally shows opera and dance – try if you can to catch a performance of the Grupo Corpo, an internationally renowned dance company that emerged in Belo Horizonte in the 1970s, or watch out for the amazing puppetry of the Grupo Giramundo, also based in the city.

Listings

Airlines Aerolíneas Argentinas, Rua Tupis 204, sala 209, Centro ☎31/3224-7466; Air Canada, Av. Prudente de Moraís 135, Cidade Jardim ☎31/3344-8355; American Airlines, Av. Bernardo Monteiro 1539, Funcionários ☎31/3274-3166; British Airways, Rua São Paulo 1106, sala 305, Centro ☎31/3274-6211; Continental Airlines, Rua Espírito Santo 466, sala 1801, Centro ☎31/3274-3177; Delta Airlines, Rua Ceará 1709, sala 1202, Funcionários ☎31/3287-0001; Gol ☎31/3490-2073; Pluna, Av. Getúlio Vargas 840, Funcionários ☎31/3291-9292; TAM, Pampulha airport ☎31/3689-2233; TAP, Rua Timbiras 1200, sala 311, Funcionários ☎31/3213-1611; United Airlines, Av. Getúlio Vargas 874, 13th floor, Savassi ☎31/3269-3939; Varig/Nordeste/Rio-Sul, Av. Getúlio Vargas 840, Funcionários ☎31/3339-6000; VASP, Av. Getúlio Vargas 1492, Funcionários ☎0800-988-277.

Airports Pampulha ☎31/3490-2010; Tancredo Neves ☎31/3689-2700.

Banks and exchange Banks are concentrated downtown on Av. João Pinheiro, between Rua dos Timbiras and Avenida Afonso Pena. There are branches throughout the city and ATMs are common.

Bookshops For a city the size of Belo Horizonte, bookshops are extremely disappointing and none has more than a few books in English. The following are reasonable for Brazilian art, history and literature: Livraria da Travessa, Av. Getúlio Vargas 1427, near Praça Savassi; the *Café com Letras*,

Rua Antônio de Albuquerque 781, also near Praça Savassi; Editora Vozes, Rua Sergipe 120, Funcionários; and Livraria UFMG (the university bookshop), Av. Afonso Pena 1534, Centro.

Car rental Hertz, at the airports and Av. João Pinheiro 341 ☎31/3224-5166 or 224-1279; Interlocadora, at the airports and Rua dos Timbiras 2229 ☎31/3275-4090; Localiza, at the airports and Av. Bernardo Monteiro 1567 ☎0800-312-121; Unidas, at the airports and Av. Santa Rosa 100 ☎0800-121-121.

Consulates Argentina, Rua Ceará 1566, 3rd floor, Funcionários ☎31/3281-5288; Paraguay, Rua Guandaus 60, apto. 102, Santa Lúcia ☎31/3344-6349; UK, Rua dos Inconfidentes 1075, sala 1302, Savassi ☎31/3261-2072; Uruguay, Av. do Contorno 6777, 13th floor, salas 1301–4, Funcionários ☎31/3296-8293.

Health matters For an ambulance, phone ☎192. Hospital das Clínicas da UFMG is attached to the university, Av. Alfredo Badalena 190, Santa Efigênia ☎31/3239-7100.

Laundry Laundromat, Rua dos Timbiras 1264, beside the Igreja Boa Viagem (Mon–Sat 8am–8pm).

Police ☎190. For visa or tourist permit extension, go to the Polícia Federal at Rua Nascimento Gurgel 30, Guiterrez (☎31/3330-5200).

Post office The main post office is at Av. Afonso Pena 1270 (Mon–Fri 9am–6pm, Sat 9am–1pm). Collect poste restante round the back at Rua Goiás 77. Smaller offices are scattered around the city, including at Rua Pernambuco 1322, Savassi (Mon–Sat 9am–6pm) and at the *rodoviária* (Mon–Fri 9am–7pm, Sat 9am–1pm).

Shopping The main centres for *artesanato* in the city are the Centro de Artesanato Mineiro in the Palácio das Artes (see p.171), and the Sunday market in the Parque Municipal (see p.171). Also excellent is the range of carefully selected items at Mãos de Minas at Rua Grão Mogol 678, Sion (Mon–Fri 9am–7pm and Sat 9am–1pm). Food, medicinal plants, *umbanda* and *candomblé* (voodoo) accessories and wickerwork can be found in the Mercado Central (see p.170). Of the shopping centres, Bahia Shopping, Rua da Bahia (Mon–Fri 10am–10pm, Sat 10am–7pm and Sun & holidays 2–8pm), has a fairly good selection of shops, while similar but larger is Shopping Cidade at Rua Rio de Janeiro 910, with entrances also on *ruas* São Paulo and Tupis. In Savassi, there's a good range of elegant boutiques to be found in BHZ Fashion Mall, Rua Paraíba 1132 (daily 9am–7pm), as well as on the streets extending off Praça da Savassi.

Telephones TELEMAR offices are located at Tancredo Neves airport; the *rodoviária* (ground floor); Rua Paraíba 1441 in Savassi; and Av. Afonso Pena 1180 – all open daily until 10pm. The main branch, at Av. Afonso Pena 744, is open 24hr.

Travel and tour companies There are a number of specialist ecotourism agencies dealing with trekking, hiking, caving, canoeing, rafting and cycling trips in Minas. Contact Terra Nossa, Rua Domingos Vieira 348, sala 1309, Santa Efigênia (☏31/3241-6161); Trilhas d'Água, Rua Presidente Arthur Bernardes 409, Boa Esperança, Santa Luzia (☏31/3641-3185); or Primotur, Rua Piumí 364, loja 4, Cruzeiro (☏31/3221-3118). Trilhar, Rua Osmário Soares 310, Dom Bosco (☏31/3417-6746) organize day trips.

Around Belo Horizonte

The most popular trips out from the capital are to the *cidades históricas* (see p.182), but there are a couple of other less-frequented sites that also warrant a visit: to the north, the **Gruta Rei do Mato** is a convenient stop if you are heading for Brasília or Diamantina; to the east, lying beyond the nearest of the *cidades históricas*, Sabará, is the beautiful **Parque do Caraça**.

Gruta Rei do Mato

One of the most astonishing underground attractions of Minas Gerais lies 60km northwest of Belo Horizonte on BR-040, opposite the junction for Sete Lagoas, and makes for an excellent day-trip from the capital. Legend has it that a mysterious fugitive originally discovered this enormous cave and used it as a home. He became known as "Rei do Mato" (King of the Bush) and the name has stuck to the cave itself.

The series of caverns (guided tours daily in summer, 8am–6pm; ☏31/3773-0888; $1.50) extends for over 2000m and is 300m deep in some parts, and includes some prehistoric cave art. The third room is particularly impressive, with two parallel columns formed by interlocking stalactites and stalagmites, and is regarded as the only equal in the world to the formations in the famous caves at Altamira in Spain.

Buses from Belo Horizonte to Sete Lagoas (run by Setelagoano; every 30min from 6.30am to 1pm), Diamantina or Brasília pass the cave; the journey takes about an hour. There is a **bar** that sells refreshments at the site.

Parque do Caraça

A hundred and thirty kilometres east of Belo Horizonte lies the impressive **Parque do Caraça** (daily 7am–5pm, 9pm if you're staying in the park), named after the impression of a gigantic face in the surrounding mountains. The park is situated at 2400m above sea level; temperatures drop sharply on summer

Fazenda hotels

In recent years, with agriculture in Brazil increasingly dominated by large-scale agribusiness, small and medium-sized farms in Minas Gerais have had to look for new opportunities and many of those set in particularly attractive countryside, or retaining a grand old *fazenda* house, have turned to tourism for an alternative source of income. Within just an hour or so of Belo Horizonte there are several superb **country hotels**, full of character and with great facilities. You will generally need your own transport, though arrangements can usually be made to be picked up locally or even from Belo Horizonte – phone ahead. Reservations are essential, particularly during summer, July and holiday weekends, and rates always include full board.

Fazenda Boa Esperança Florestal ☎31/3536-2344. *Fazenda*-hotel set in a working 450-hectare dairy farm, 45km from Belo Horizonte. The buildings are colonial-style and extremely comfortable. There's a pool too, and horse riding is also available. Excellent country cooking. ❺

Fazenda das Minhocas Jaboticatubas ☎31/3681-1161, ⓦwww.fazendadasminhocas.com.br. A historic site in its own right – the *casa grande* dates from 1712 and there's an old Baroque chapel in the grounds as well as a sugar-mill and a comfortable, if rustic, *pousada*. There are pleasant walks on the property and facilities for swimming and horse riding. ❹

Fazenda Recanto dos Fonda Distrito de Ravena, Sabará ☎31/3672-3399, ⓦwww.recantodosfonda.com.br. Set amidst 200 hectares of lakes and woodland in pleasant walking country, 40km from Belo Horizonte. There's a swimming pool, and horse riding too, plus good country food. ❹

Pousada Altos de Minas Município de Nova Minas ☎31/3201-1311, ⓦwww.agendabh.com.br/altodeminas. Delightful country hotel 25km from Belo Horizonte, set in attractive gardens with a pool. The restaurant offers *mineiro* food as well as international fare. ❺

evenings and it can get very cold in winter. There are plenty of signed walks of varying difficulty on the tracks through the mountains – information is available from the hotel at the park entrance (see below). The park's imposing lake provides a good opportunity for swimming from its small beaches, and there are also several natural pools by the waterfalls within the park. **Buses** from Belo Horizonte to Santa Bárbara (about 4 daily, run by Viação Pássaro Verde) will drop you at the entrance to the park, and a trip here makes an excellent weekend break from the city.

Santuário do Caraça

Situated at the only entrance to the park is the **Santuário do Caraça**, formerly a seminary and school, and now converted into a hotel. The **school**, famous in Brazil, was founded on the site of a hermitage and seminary in 1774, and for 150 years educated the upper classes of Minas Gerais, including generations of Brazilian politicians. In 1965 a fire destroyed much of the building, the theatre was burnt to the ground and the library lost two-thirds of its thirty thousand books.

The building was restored in 1991 and transformed into a **hotel**, the *Hospedaria do Caraça* (☎31/3837-2698, reservations essential; ❸), managed by the remaining members of the order. It's a comfortable, low-key place to spend a few relaxing days. Some parts still remain from the original religious life of the building, including rooms for private prayer, a few bedrooms and the cellar. The neo-Gothic church of Nossa Senhora Mãe Dos Homens, added in 1883, was also spared by the fire, and has beautiful French stained-glass windows, marble and soapstone carvings and a seven-hundred-pipe organ built in the seminary itself.

There is a small **museum** attached to the church with exhibits rescued from the fire, including English and Chinese porcelain, furniture and a sundial. One of the greatest attractions of the place are the **wolves** (*lobo-guará*) that live in the surrounding woods. One of them comes near the church almost every day to be fed by the monks.

The cidades históricas

The **cidades históricas** of Minas Gerais – small enough really to be towns rather than cities – were founded within a couple of decades of each other in the early eighteenth century. Rough and violent mining camps in their early days, they were soon transformed by mineral wealth into treasure houses, not merely of gold, but also of Baroque art and architecture. Well preserved and carefully maintained, together the towns form one of the most impressive sets of colonial remains in the Americas, comparable only to the silver-mining towns that flourished in Mexico at roughly the same time. In Brazil, they are equalled only by the remnants of the plantation culture of the Northeast, to which they contributed much of the gold you see in the gilded churches of Olinda and Salvador.

Although some have acquired a modern urban fringe, all the historic cities have centres untouched by modern developers – and a couple, like **Tiradentes**, look very much as they did two centuries ago. All have colonial churches – **Ouro Preto** has thirteen – at least one good museum, steep cobbled streets, ornate mansions and the particular atmosphere of a place soaked in history. It was in these cities that the **Inconfidência Mineira**, Brazil's first bungling attempt to throw off the Portuguese yoke, was played out in 1789. And here the great sculptor Antônio Francisco Lisboa, **Aleijadinho** or the "little cripple", spent all his life, leaving behind him a body of work unmatched by any other figure working in the contemporary Baroque tradition.

Practicalities

The nearest *cidade histórica* to Belo Horizonte is **Sabará**, only a local bus ride away; the furthest is **Diamantina**, six hours north by bus from the capital, in the wild scenery of the Serra do Espinhaço. Two hours southeast from Belo Horizonte, **Ouro Preto** is the ex-capital of the state and the largest of the historic cities, with **Mariana** a short distance away. And two hours to the south of Belo Horizonte is **Congonhas**, where the church of Bom Jesus de Matosinhos is considered to be Aleijadinho's masterpiece. A two-hour bus ride further south are **São João del Rei** and **Tiradentes**.

Only in Sabará is **accommodation** difficult to find. All the others are well supplied with places to stay, and are worth more than a quick day-trip. If you only have a little time to spare, the best option from Belo Horizonte is probably Ouro Preto: you can easily get there and back in a day, and – though everyone has their own favourites – it is the most classically beautiful of all.

Although little is known of his life, we do know roughly what **Aleijadinho** looked like. In the Museu de Aleijadinho in Ouro Preto is a crude but vivid portrait showing an intense, aquiline man, clearly what Brazilians call *pardo* – of mixed race. His hands are under his jacket, which seems a trivial detail unless you know what makes his achievements truly astonishing: the great sculptor of the *barroco mineiro* was a leper, and produced much of his best work after he had lost the use of his hands.

Despite being recognized as a master sculptor during his lifetime, only the barest outline of the life of Antônio Francisco Lisboa is clear. He was born in Ouro Preto in 1738, the son of a Portuguese craftsman; his mother was probably a slave. For the first half of his exceptionally long life he was perfectly healthy, a womanizer and *bon viveur* despite his exclusively religious output. His prodigious talent, equally at home in wood or stone, human figures or abstract decoration, allowed him to set up a workshop with apprentices while still young, and he was much in demand. Although he always based himself in Ouro Preto, he spent long periods in all the major historic towns except Diamantina, working on commissions; but he never travelled beyond the state. Self-taught, he was an obsessive reader of the Bible and medical textbooks, the only two obvious influences in his work, one supplying its imagery, the other underlying the anatomical detail of his human figures.

In the late 1770s, his life changed utterly. He began to suffer from a progressively debilitating disease that is thought to have been leprosy, although even this is not certain. As it got worse he became a recluse, only venturing outdoors in the dark, and increasingly obsessed with his work. His physical disabilities were terrible: he lost his fingers, toes and the use of his lower legs. Sometimes the pain was so bad his apprentices had to stop him hacking away at the offending part of his body with a chisel.

Yet despite all this he actually increased his output, working with hammer and chisel strapped to his wrists by his apprentices, who moved him about on a wooden trolley. It was under these conditions that he sculpted his masterpiece, the 12 massive figures of the prophets and the 64 lifesize Passion figures for the **Basílica do Senhor Bom Jesus de Matosinhos** (see p.200) in Congonhas, between 1796 and 1805. They were his swansong: failing eyesight finally forced him to stop work and he ended his life as a hermit in a hovel on the outskirts of Ouro Preto. The death he longed for finally came on November 18, 1814: he is buried in a simple grave in the church he attended all his life, Nossa Senhora da Conceição in Ouro Preto.

Aleijadinho's prolific output would have been remarkable under any circumstances: given his condition it was nothing short of miraculous, a triumph of the creative spirit. The bulk of his work is to be found in Ouro Preto, but there are also significant items in Sabará, São João del Rei, Mariana and Congonhas. His achievement was to stay within the Baroque tradition, yet bring to its ornate conventions a raw physicality and unmatched technical skill that makes his work unique.

Sabará

SABARÁ lies strung out over a series of hills, wound around the Rio das Velhas. Many of its cobbled streets are so steep they have to be taken slowly, but ascents are rewarded with gorgeous churches, austere on the outside, choked with carving and ornamentation inside. Sabará's proximity to Belo Horizonte would make it the ideal base for seeing the metropolis, but for its lack of accommodation. Fortunately, the frequency of the **bus** link (every 15min from 4am to midnight) makes it an easy – and unmissable – day-trip from Belo Horizonte: catch the red #5509 bus on Rua dos Caetés one block up from Avenida Afonso Pena. Start early and avoid Monday when most sights are closed.

The Town

Standing in **Praça Santa Rita**, you're in the centre not just of the oldest part of Sabará, but of the oldest inhabited streets in southern Brazil. Founded in 1674, Sabará is the most venerable of the *cidades históricas*, and was the first major centre of gold mining in the state, although attention shifted southwards to Ouro Preto and Mariana by the end of the seventeenth century. It was founded by Borba Gato, a typical *paulista* cut-throat who combined Catholic fervour – the town's first name was Vila Real de Nossa Senhora da Conceição de Sabarabuçú, later thankfully shortened – with ruthlessness: his determined extermination of the local Indians made gold mining possible in Sabará.

Not until forty years after its foundation were the mud huts and stockades of the early adventurers replaced by stone buildings, and it wasn't until the second quarter of the eighteenth century, when gold production was at its peak, that serious church building began, and the village began to acquire an air of permanence. A fair proportion of the local gold ended up gilding the interiors of the town's churches, but by the turn of the nineteenth century, all the alluvial gold had been exhausted and the town entered a steep decline. Sophisticated deep mining techniques, introduced by Europeans in the nineteenth century, failed to stop the decline and Sabará became a small and grindingly poor place – today, the colonial zone is fringed by *favelas*.

Igreja de Nossa Senhora de Ó

The very early days of Sabará are represented by the tiny **Igreja de Nossa Senhora de Ó** (Mon–Fri 9am–5pm and Sat & Sun 9am–noon & 2–5pm), one of the oldest, and certainly one of the most unusual, colonial churches in Brazil. It's a couple of kilometres from Praça Santa Rita: a signposted walk, or you can take the local bus marked "Esplanada" from the square. It is extremely unusual since it doesn't look in the least Portuguese: an austere, irregularly shaped exterior is topped off by an unmistakeably Chinese tower, complete with pagoda-like upturns at the corners. The cramped interior, dominated by a gilded arch over the altar, also shows distinct oriental influences, but the church is so old – it was started in 1698 – that nobody knows who was responsible for its unique design. The most likely explanation is that the Portuguese, despairing of the local talent, imported a group of Chinese craftsmen from

Minas Baroque

There are three distinct phases of **Baroque church architecture** in Minas. The **first**, from the beginning of the eighteenth century to about 1730, was very ornate and often involved extravagant carving and gilding, but left exteriors plain; sculpture was formal, with stiff, rather crude statues. The **second phase** dominated the middle decades of the eighteenth century, with equally extravagant decorations inside, especially around the altar, and the wholesale plastering of everything with gold; the exteriors were now embellished with curlicues and panels in fine Minas soapstone, ceilings were painted and sculpture noticeably more natural, although still highly stylized. The peak was the period from 1760 to 1810, and this **third phase** of *barroco mineiro* can be stunning: the exterior decoration was more elaborate, but the interiors are less cluttered, with walls often left plain, and fine carving in both wood and stone. By now, too, the religious sculpture, with its flowing realism, had broken the stylistic bounds that confine most Baroque art.

Macau. There were certainly artisans from Macau in Diamantina, to the north, where streets are named after them, but here no other trace of them survives.

Matriz Nossa Senhora da Conceição

Sabará's main church, **Matriz Nossa Senhora da Conceição** (Mon–Fri 9am–5pm and Sat & Sun 9am–noon & 2–5pm) is on Praça Getúlio Vargas, signposted from Praça Santa Rita. Started by the Jesuits in 1720, it's a fine example of the so-called first and second phases of Minas Baroque. Succeeding generations added features to the original layout and inside it's extremely impressive, with a double row of heavily carved and gilded arches, a beautifully decorated ceiling and, once again, Chinese influence in the gildings and painted panels of the door leading to the sacristy.

Nossa Senhora do Carmo

The church of **Nossa Senhora do Carmo** (Tues–Sat 9–11.30am & 1–6pm, Sun 1–6pm) on Rua do Carmo, a vintage third-phase church, is a good contrast, while it's also a demonstration of the remarkable talents of Aleijadinho, who oversaw its construction and contributed much of the decoration between 1770 and 1783, a time when he was at the height of his powers. The interior manages to be elaborate and uncluttered at the same time, with graceful curves in the gallery, largely plain walls, comparatively little gilding and a beautifully painted ceiling. Aleijadinho left his mark everywhere: the imposing soapstone and painted wood pulpits, the banister in the nave, the flowing lines of the choir, and above all in the two statues of São João da Cruz and São Simão Stock. You can tell an Aleijadinho from the faces: the remarkably lifelike head of São Simão is complete with wrinkles and transfixed by religious ecstacy.

Nossa Senhora do Rosário dos Pretos da Barra

Despite being left half-built and open to the elements, the church of **Nossa Senhora do Rosário dos Pretos da Barra** (Tues–Sun 9–11.30am & 1–5pm), fifteen minutes' signposted walk from Praça Santa Rita on Praça Melo Viana, is just as fascinating as the more ornate buildings. It was built in typical Portuguese colonial style by slaves, who actually did the work in the gold mines: until the mines declined, a large majority of the population of all the historic cities was black. Organized into lay societies called *irmandades*, the slaves financed and built churches, but this one was begun late, in 1767, and with the decline of the mines the money ran out. Although sporadic restarts were made during the nineteenth century, it was never more than half-built, and when slavery was abolished in 1888 it was left as a memorial.

The Museu do Ouro

The **Museu do Ouro** (Tues–Sun noon–5.30pm) is a short but steep signposted walk up from Praça Santa Rita on Rua da Intendência, but well worth the effort. Built in 1732, this is the only royal foundry house remaining in Brazil. When gold was discovered in Minas Gerais, the Portuguese Crown was entitled to a fifth of the output but had to collect it first. To do so, it put a military cordon around the gold mines, and then built several royal foundries, where gold from the surrounding area was melted down, franked and the royal fifth deducted. The functional building that now houses the museum easily reveals its origins: it is built around an interior courtyard, overlooked by a balcony on three sides, from where the officials could keep an eagle eye on gold being melted into bars and weighed. Along with the other royal foundry in Ouro Preto, it was Brazil's most heavily guarded building.

Most of the museum is devoted to gold-mining history. **Downstairs** are rooms full of colonial scales, weights, pans and other mining instruments, and a strongroom where until 1986 you could see genuine eighteenth-century gold bars and jewels in the safe. Unfortunately, that year two men walked in, put a pistol to the guard's head and walked off with the safe's contents, which have never been recovered: the bars on display now are plaster casts of the real thing, although they look authentic enough. **Upstairs** you'll find the usual collection of colonial furniture and *arte sacra*, but also some interesting prints and one very fine painted ceiling, representing the four continents known at the time it was built. In a room off the courtyard, to the right of the large wooden water-driven grinding mill, is a model of the **Morro Velho** mine in nearby Nova Lima, the deepest gold mine in the world outside South Africa. There's a commemorative photograph of the 44 Welsh mining engineers and single Brazilian lawyer who began it, all working for the wonderfully named St John d'El Rey Gold Mining Company.

The rest of the town

If you tire of colonial sightseeing, just wandering around the bars and cobbled streets near the Praça Santa Rita is very pleasant, too. There are lots of impressive buildings, notably the **Prefeitura** on Rua Dom Pedro II, and the nineteenth-century **Teatro Municipal** (daily 8am–noon & 1–5pm) on the same street, which was designed as an opera house and completed just as the gold ran out. Before you leave the town, have some water from the **Chafariz do Rosário** on Praça Melo Viana, as it's believed that all those who drink from the fountain will one day come back to Sabará.

Practicalities

The nineteen-kilometre journey from Belo Horizonte takes roughly thirty minutes, though the bus station is at the far eastern end of town; ask the driver to show you the best stop for the colonial centre, from where you should easily find Praça Santa Rita. There is a rudimentary **tourist office** around the corner, but it doesn't stock maps and isn't really worth bothering with, since the colonial zone is small enough to manage without a street plan. If in doubt, any road going uphill will invariably lead you to a church, from where it's easy to get your bearings. **Buses back to Belo Horizonte** are best caught on the main road leading out of town at the bottom of the colonial zone by the river.

There are several **bars and restaurants**, which really only get busy on weekends: *Cê Qui Sabe* at Rua Mestre Caetano 56, and *Bar-Ôco* at Rua Mestre Ritinha 115, both serve a reliable *comida mineira*. Cheaper places are clustered around Praça Santa Rita, and dotted throughout the old centre, often in people's front rooms. If you want to **stay**, a very pleasant place to try is the *Solar dos Sepúlvedas*, Rua Intendência 371 (☎31/3671-2705; ❸), a restored eighteenth-century house with just seven rooms and a small pool. An equally intimate *pousada* is the *Vila Real*, Rua Serafim Mota Barro 76 (☎31/3671-2121; ❷).

Ouro Preto

The drive to **OURO PRETO**, 100km southeast of Belo Horizonte, begins unpromisingly with endless industrial complexes and *favelas* spread over the hills, but in its later stretches becomes spectacular, winding around hill country 1000m above sea level and passing several valleys where patches of forest survive: imagine the entire landscape covered with it and you have an idea of what greeted the gold-seekers in the 1690s. On arrival, the first thing that strikes you is how small the town is, considering that until 1897 it was the capital of Minas – its population is still only around 65,000. That said, you can see at a glance why the capital had to be shifted to Belo Horizonte: the steep hills the town is built around, straddling a network of creeks, severely limit space for expansion. Today, the hills and vertiginous streets (some so steep they have steps rather than pavements) of Ouro Preto's historic centre are vital ingredients in what is architecturally one of the loveliest towns in Brazil, albeit one that can no longer in all honesty lay claim to being the unspoilt eighteenth-century jewel that it was just a few years back.

Avoid coming on Monday if you want to see the sights, as all the churches and most of the museums close for the day. Also, buy your onward ticket as soon as you arrive as buses fill up quickly. Some people complain about Ouro Preto being touristy – and it is more commercialized than any other *cidade histórica* – but they miss the point: it's precisely because there really is something to savour here that the visitors come. If you have the time, aim to spend at least a night or two in Ouro Preto so that you can enjoy the city after all the day-trippers have departed.

Ouro Preto has an extremely popular street **Carnaval** that attracts visitors from far afield: be sure to reserve accommodation long in advance. Likewise, at **Easter** time, the town becomes the focus of a spectacular series of plays and processions lasting for about a month before Easter Sunday, during which the last days of the life of Christ are played out in open-air theatres throughout the town.

Some history

Less than a decade after gold was struck at Sabará, a *paulista* adventurer called **Antônio Dias** pitched camp underneath a mountain the Indians called Itacolomi, with an unmistakeable thumb-shaped rock on its summit. Panning the streams nearby, he found "black gold" – alluvial gold mixed with iron ore – and named his camp after it. It attracted a flood of people as it became clear the deposits were the richest yet found in Minas, and so many came that they outstripped the food supply. In 1700 there was a famine and legend has it that people died of hunger with gold nuggets in their hands.

The early years were hard, made worse by a war started in 1707 between the Portuguese and *paulista bandeirantes*, who resisted the Crown's attempts to take over the area. The war, the **Guerra das Emboabas**, lasted for two years and was brutal, with ambushes and massacres the preferred tactics of both sides. Ouro Preto was the Portuguese base, and troops from here drove the *paulistas* from their headquarters at Sabará and finally annihilated them near São João del Rei. From then on, Ouro Preto was the effective **capital** of the gold-producing area of Minas, although it wasn't officially named as such until 1823. Indeed, compared to places like nearby Mariana, Ouro Preto was a late developer; all but two of its churches date from the second half of the eighteenth century, and several of its finest buildings, like the school of mining and the town hall on Praça Tiradentes, were not finished until well into the nineteenth century.

The gold gave out about the time that Brazil finally became independent in 1822, but for decades the town survived as an administrative centre and university town; a school of mining was founded in 1876. After the capital moved to Belo Horizonte, steady decline set in, though the populist government of Getúlio Vargas brought back the bodies of the Inconfidêntes (see box and

▲ Mariana

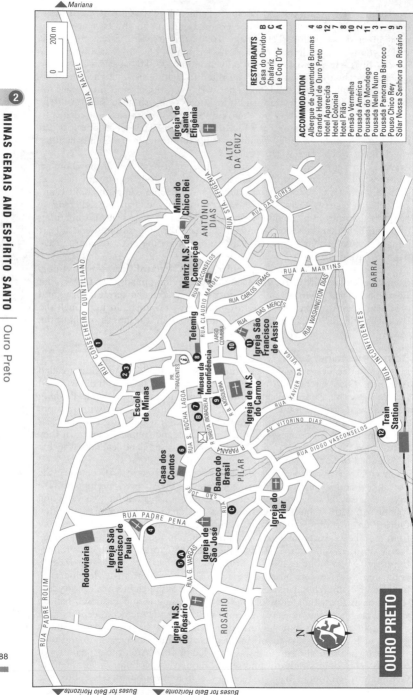

0   200 m

RESTAURANTS
Casa do Ouvidor   B
Chafariz   C
Le Coq D'Or   A

ACCOMMODATION
Albergue de Juventude Brumas   4
Grande Hotel de Ouro Preto   6
Hotel Aparecida   12
Hotel Colonial   7
Hotel Pilão   8
Pensão Vermelha   10
Pousada América   2
Pousada do Mondego   11
Pousada Nello Nuno   3
Pousada Panorama Barroco   1
Pouso Chico Rey   9
Solar Nossa Senhora do Rosário   5

Igreja de Santa Efigênia

ALTO DA CRUZ

RUA NACIEL

RUA CONSELHEIRO QUINTILIANO

Mina do Chico Rei

ANTÔNIO DIAS

Matriz N.S. da Conceição

RUA STA. EFIGÊNIA

RUA DAS DORES

RUA VASCONCELOS

RUA CLAUDIO MANUEL

RUA A. MARTINS

BARRA

RUA CARLOS TOMÁS

Telemig

RUA DAS MERCÊS

LARGO COIMBRA

Igreja São Francisco de Assis

RUA WASHINGTON DIAS

RUA INCONFIDENTES

Escola de Minas

PR. TIRADENTES

Museu da Inconfidência

RUA XAVIER DA VEIGA

Igreja de N.S. do Carmo

RUA R. B. MOSQUEIRA

RUA S. ROCHA LAGOA

R. DIREITA (BOBADELA)

AV. VITORINO DIAS

Casa dos Contos

RUA S. JOSÉ

Banco do Brasil

PILAR

RUA PARANÁ

RUA DIOGO VASCONSELOS

Train Station

Igreja do Pilar

RUA PADRE PENA

Igreja São Francisco de Paula

Rodoviária

RUA G. VARGAS

Igreja de São José

RUA PADRE ROLIM

Igreja N.S. do Rosário

ROSÁRIO

N

OURO PRETO

Museu da Inconfidência on p.191) to a proper shrine, and sensitively restored the crumbling monuments.

Since the 1980s, **tourism** has become increasingly important for the town, as has the aluminium industry, which has attracted job hungry migrants from throughout the state, many of whom end up living in the *favelas* of the surrounding hillsides. Indeed, for many locals Ouro Preto's architectural heritage and tourism are getting in the way of economic expansion; meanwhile hasty construction and heavy-vehicle traffic are threatening the city's coveted status as a UNESCO World Heritage Site, a potential embarrassment for Brazil, not least for the revenue it helps generate from tourism. There is now talk of re-routing traffic and re-housing *favela* dwellers, but tensions between various interest groups will no doubt be difficult to resolve.

Arrival, information and accommodation

Arriving from Mariana, the bus passes through the main square, Praça Tiradentes – where you should get off – before continuing to the **rodoviária**, some fifteen minutes' walk westwards on Rua Padre Rolim. Belo Horizonte buses proceed straight to the *rodoviária*, from where there are regular buses to the *praça*.

Praça Tiradentes itself is dominated by a statue of the martyr to Brazilian independence (see p.191) and lined with beautiful colonial buildings. On the east side at no. 41 is the **municipal tourist office** (Mon–Fri 8am–6pm; ☎31/3559-3269), which sells an excellent city map for $1.50; it can also provide details of some spectacular walks in the surrounding countryside. The town does get crowded at weekends and holiday periods, but there are so many establishments that you can usually find somewhere to stay; the tourist office has details and prices of even the cheapest hotels, and will phone round for you if you have problems, or keep an eye on your luggage while you search. There are ATMs at Bradesco on Praça Tiradentes, HSBC at Rua São José 105 and at the Banco do Brasil, Rua São José 189: the Banco do Brasil also changes money over the counter from Monday to Friday between 11am and 4pm.

Accommodation

The price codes below are based on weekend (Fri–Sun) and high-season prices; midweek and in low season, Ouro Preto's hotels offer discounts of around 20–30 percent.

Albergue de Juventude Brumas Ladeira de São Francisco de Paula 68 ☎31/3551-2944, ⓦwww.brumasonline.hpg.ig.com.br). Part of the Hostelling International network, this youth hostel offers fairly basic dorms, kitchen and laundry facilities. Reached by a steep 10-minute trek, with commanding views overlooking Ouro Preto's historic centre. $8 per person.

Grande Hotel de Ouro Preto Rua Senador Rocha Lagoa 164 ☎31/3551-1488, ⓦwww .hotelouropreto.com.br. Opened in 1940, this is one of Oscar Niemeyer's earliest creations, though not one of his best. If you like airport lounges you'll love this three-star hotel. Central, with good service and a small pool in the Burle Marx–designed gardens. ❹

Hotel Aparecida Praça Cesário Alvim ☎31/3551-

1091. Opposite the (freight-only) train station and requiring a steep walk up into the centre. Its *quartos* are the cheapest beds in town. ❷

Hotel Colonial Travessa Padre Camilo Veloso 26 ☎31/3551-3133, ⓕ3551-3361. An excellent place one street back from Praça Tiradentes (it's signposted), with a range of *apartamentos*, all with *frigobar*, TV, air-conditioning and telephones. The better rooms are in the wing to the right of the entrance, some of them on two levels. Much better value than the *Pousada América*. ❸

Hotel Pilão Praça Tiradentes 51, next to the tourist office ☎31/3551-3066, ⓕ3551-3275. Extremely simple rooms overlooking the square (which can be noisy at night), but not the friendliest of places; some rooms sleep up to six people. ❷

Pensão Vermelha Largo de Coimbra, at the corner with Rua Antônio Pereira ☎31/3551-1138. Quiet, family-run place, with clean if simple rooms, some overlooking the magnificent facade of the São Francisco church. ❷

Pousada América Rua Camilo de Brito 15 ☎31/3551-2525. About 100m off Praça Tiradentes along Rua Barão de Camargos (the bus from Mariana passes it). Family-run and popular with foreign tourists, with good if basic *apartamentos* and *quartos* (both same price), though slightly expensive for what it offers. ❸

Pousada do Mondego Largo de Coimbra 38 ☎31/3551-2040, ℗3551-3094. Excellent accommodation in a beautiful restored mid-eighteenth-century building beside the Igreja de São Francisco de Assis, with period furniture in all rooms – ask for one with a balcony. ❻

Pousada Nello Nuno Rua Camilo de Brito 59 ☎31/3551-3375. A very pretty small *pousada* built around a courtyard. The rooms are attractively furnished in natural woods, and the pictures are mostly by the proprietor who works in her printing atelier in the same building. Excellent value. ❷

Pousada Panorama Barroco Rua Quintiliano 722 ☎31/3551-2582. American-owned and run, this basic but friendly place is popular with young Brazilians and foreign backpackers alike. Bathrooms are shared and the proprietors offer lots of local advice. ❷

Pouso Chico Rey Rua Brigador Mosqueira 90 ☎31/3551-1274. A small eighteenth-century house converted into a beautiful *pensão*, filled with a collection of relics that would do credit to a museum, plus a wonderful view from the reading room on the first floor, excellent breakfasts and a tranquil, timeless atmosphere. There are only six rooms, so book in advance. ❸

Solar Nossa Senhora do Rosário Rua Getúlio Vargas 270 ☎31/3551-5200, ⓦwww .hotelsolardorosario.com.br. A nineteenth-century mansion (and a modern annex) transformed into the city's most luxurious hotel, with fine communal areas, including a pool. The hotel's restaurant is one of the best in the city, serving fine Franco-*mineiro* dishes. ❻

The Town

Praça Tiradentes is the best place to start a tour of the town. First stop should be the tourist office (see p.189) to pick up a map and a card that gives the latest opening hours of the churches and museums. The size of the town is deceptive. There's enough here to keep you going for days – thirteen colonial churches, seven chapels, six museums and several other sights – and if you want to explore in depth you should buy a copy of the *Guia de Ouro Preto* by Manoel Bandeira, a useful guidebook (Portuguese only) that's sold at the tourist office.

The Escola de Minas

Right on the Praça Tiradentes stands the mining school, the **Escola de Minas**, now housed in the old governor's palace. It's still the best mining school in the country, and its students, with their bars and motorbikes, lend a Bohemian air to the town. The white turrets make the building itself look rather like a fortress: the exterior, with a fine marble entrance, dates from the 1740s, but the inside was gutted during the nineteenth century and not improved by it. Attached to the school is the **Museu de Mineralogia** (daily noon–5pm), founded in 1877 from the collection of the French geologist Henri Gorceix. Although most of the exhibits are of interest only to geologists, there is one fascinating room where gold and precious stones are beautifully displayed, in contrast to the chaos in the rest of the museum.

The Paço Municipal and Museu da Inconfidência

Also in the square are the old city chambers, the **Paço Municipal** (Tues–Sun noon–5.30pm), a glorious eighteenth-century building that provides a perfect example of the classical grace of Minas colonial architecture. Its beautifully restored interior lives up to expectations: like many colonial town halls it was also a jail, and many of the huge rooms, so well suited to the display of *arte sacra*, were once dungeons.

The Inconfidência Mineira

Ouro Preto is most famous in Brazil as the birthplace of the **Inconfidência Mineira**, the first attempt to free Brazil from the Portuguese. Inspired by the French Revolution, and heartily sick of the heavy taxes levied by a bankrupt Portugal, a group of twelve prominent town citizens led by **Joaquim José da Silva Xavier** began in 1789 to discuss organizing a rebellion. Xavier was a dentist, known to everyone as Tiradentes, "teeth-puller". Another of the conspirators was **Tomas Gonzaga**, whose hopeless love poems to the beautiful **Marília Dirceu**, promised by her family to another, made the couple into the Brazilian equivalent of Romeo and Juliet: "When you appear at dawn, all rumpled/like a badly wrapped parcel, no ribbons or flowers/how Nature shines, how much lovelier you seem."

In the event the conspiracy was a fiasco and all were betrayed and arrested before any uprising was organized. The leaders were condemned to hang, but the Portuguese, realizing that they could ill afford to offend the inhabitants of a state whose taxes kept them afloat, arranged a royal reprieve, commuting the sentence to exile in Angola and Mozambique. Unfortunately the messenger arrived two days too late to save Tiradentes, marked as the first to die. He was hanged where the column now stands in the square that bears his name, his head stuck on a post and his limbs despatched to the other mining towns to serve as a warning.

The building contains the **Museu da Inconfidência** (Tues–Sun noon–5.30pm), interesting enough since the surrounding towns have been stripped of a great deal of their wealth to stock the museum; the only collection that compares with what's here is in Mariana. There are relics of eighteenth-century daily life, from sedan chairs and kitchen utensils (including the seal the bishop used to stamp his coat of arms on his cakes) to swords and pistols. A ground-floor room is dominated by a vivid life-size effigy of St George, complete with spear, which was propped up on a horse and paraded around during religious processions. And on the table opposite is the museum's highlight: four exquisite, small Aleijadinho statues that are a fitting introduction to the flowing detail of his best work.

Upstairs there's colonial furniture and more art, but the spiritual heart of the place is found at the rear of the ground floor, where the cell in which **Tiradentes** spent the last night of his life is now the **shrine to the Inconfidêntes** (see box above). An antechamber holds documents, like the execution order and birth and death registrations of Tiradentes, reverently framed, and leads into a room containing the remains of the thirteen conspirators and Tiradentes himself – all in the vaguely Fascist style the Vargas era usually chose for its public monuments. Most of the conspirators died in Africa, some in Portugal; all but Tiradentes were exiled for the rest of their lives and never returned to Brazil.

The Igreja de Nossa Senhora do Carmo

Next door to the Paço Municipal on Praça Tiradentes is one of the finest churches in Ouro Preto, the **Igreja de Nossa Senhora do Carmo** (Tues–Sat noon–4.45pm and Sun 9.30–11am & 1–4.45pm). It was designed by Manoel Francisco Lisboa, Aleijadinho's father, and construction began just before his death in 1766. **Aleijadinho** himself then took over the building of the church and finished it six years later. He contributed the carving of the exterior, and worked on the interior, on and off, for four decades. The baptismal font in the sacristy is a masterpiece, as are the carved doors leading to the pulpits. Two of the side chapels in the main church (São João and Nossa Senhora da Piedade) were among the last commissions he was able to complete, in 1809; the accounts book for the time has Aleijadinho complaining he was paid with "false gold". Much the least cluttered of the major churches in Ouro Preto, the Igreja de Nossa Senhora do Carmo is the only one to have *azulejo*-tiled panels, to make the Portuguese who patronized it feel at home.

To the side of the church is yet another **museum** of religious art (Tues–Sun noon–5pm), housed in an excellently restored mansion that was once the meeting house for the lay society attached to Nossa Senhora do Carmo. It's a high-quality collection and very well displayed, the best part being the glittering array of gold and silver religious objects downstairs in the Sala de Tesouro.

The Igreja do Pilar

It's a lovely walk from Praça Tiradentes to Ouro Preto's oldest church. **Rua Brigador Mosqueira**, which runs downhill from the square, is one of the quietest and most beautiful streets in Ouro Preto, almost every building on it worth savouring. Wander down, bear left at the bottom, and you come out onto the incredibly steep Rua do Pilar, from where you can glimpse the towers of the Igreja do Pilar well before the plunging, cobbled path deposits you in front it.

The **Igreja do Pilar** (Tues–Sun 9–10.45am & noon–4.45pm), with an exterior ornate even by Baroque standards, is the finest example anywhere of early Minas Baroque architecture. It was begun in the 1720s and the interior is the opposite of the Carmo's restraint, a wild explosion of glinting Rococo, liberally plastered with gold. The best carving was done by Francisco Xavier de Brito, who worked in Minas from 1741 until his early death ten years later – and about whom nothing is known except that he was Portuguese and influenced Aleijadinho. He was responsible for the astonishing arch over the altar, where the angels supporting the Rococo pillars seem to swarm out of the wall on either side. In the sacristy, there's a small but interesting museum featuring enormous colonial wardrobes and a collection of gold and silver relics, the latter weakened by the theft in 1973 of its most valuable items, which have never been recovered.

The Casa dos Contos

From the Igreja do Pilar, turn right up Rua Rondolfo Bretos and round into **Rua São José** (also, confusingly, called Rua Tiradentes), whose many bars and restaurants make it a good place to take a breather. Crossing the small stone bridge, you come to the perfectly proportioned **Casa dos Contos**, the old treasury building, now a museum (Tues–Sat 12.30–5.30pm, Sun 9am–3pm). Finished in 1787, it was built as a bank-cum-mansion by Ouro Preto's richest family, and in 1803 became the Fazenda Real, the place where the Crown extracted its fifth of the gold and assembled armed convoys to escort it down to Rio for shipment to Portugal. The collection is no more than moderately interesting – the usual mixture of *arte sacra* and furniture – but the building is terrific; a magnificent colonial mansion built when Ouro Preto was at its peak. The entrance hall is dominated by an imposing staircase, four storeys high, and the mansion is constructed around a beautiful courtyard, large enough for a dozen cavalry troopers. The most interesting places radiate off it: the huge furnace for melting the gold and shaping it into bars, the slave quarters, the stables (horses were definitely better accommodated than slaves) and even an eighteenth-century privy. And don't forget to go right up to the *mirante* on the top floor for one of the best views of Ouro Preto.

The Igreja de São Francisco de Assis

From Praça Tiradentes, Rua Cláudio Manoel winds downhill, lined with stores selling rather expensive precious stones and jewellery that don't in fact come from Ouro Preto but from eastern Minas. Ahead, on the right, is arguably the most beautiful church in Ouro Preto, the **Igreja de São Francisco de Assis** (Tues–Sun 8.30–11.45am & 1.30–5pm). The small square that sets it off – Largo do Coimbra – plays host to a food **market** in the morning and a mediocre arts and crafts market in the afternoon.

The church was begun in 1765, and no other in Ouro Preto contains more work by Aleijadinho. The magnificent exterior soapstone panels are his, as is virtually all of the virtuoso carving, in both wood and stone, inside; and to top it off, Aleijadinho also designed the church and supervised its construction. You would think the church commissioners would have left it at that, but in 1801 they contracted the best painter of the *barroco mineiro*, **Manoel da Costa Athayde**, to decorate the ceilings. It took him nine years, using natural dyes made from plant juices and powdered iron ore, and his work has stood the test of time far better than other church paintings of the period. The squirming mass of cherubs and saints are framed within a cunning trompe l'oeil effect, which extends the real Baroque pillars on the sides of the nave into painted ones on the ceiling, making it seem like an open-air canopy through which you can glimpse clouds. There are also painted *azulejos* that look remarkably like the real thing.

The Matriz de Nossa Senhora da Conceição and Museu do Aleijadinho

Returning to Rua Cláudio Manoel, follow the winding Rua Bernardo de Vasconcelos, to the left – this is the back way down to the last of the major churches in Ouro Preto, **Matriz de Nossa Senhora da Conceição** (Tues–Sat 8.30–11.45am & 1.30–5pm, Sun noon–5pm), and it's a steep descent. Coming this way, you're leaving the main tourist area and everything looks just as it did the day Aleijadinho died: the Matriz is famous as the church he belonged to and where he is buried. The one-time cut-throat Antônio Dias, who founded Ouro Preto and died old and rich in 1727, left his fortune to build this church on the spot of his first camp – so this is where it all began and, with the death of Aleijadinho, also where it can be said to have ended.

Despite Aleijadinho's connection with the church, he never worked on this one. All the same, it is an impressive example of mid-period Minas Baroque, and the painting and carving are very fine, especially the figures of saints in the side altars – note the pained expression and movement of St Sebastian, on the left of the nave. Aleijadinho is buried in a simple **tomb** on the right of the nave, marked "Antônio Francisco Lisboa" and covered by nothing more elaborate than a plain wooden plank.

A side door by the main altar of the church leads to the sacristy and the fascinating **Museu do Aleijadinho** (Tues–Sat 8.30–11.45am & 1.30–5pm, Sun noon–5pm), which is worth lingering over: not so much a museum of Aleijadinho's work as of his life and times. What work there is by him is in the basement, and is quite something – four magnificent lions that once served as supports for the plinth on which coffins were laid. Aleijadinho, never having seen a lion, drew from imagination and produced medieval monsters with the faces of monkeys. The ground floor is taken up by a high-quality collection of religious art, but the highlight is upstairs, in a room dedicated not just to Aleijadinho but to all the legendary figures of Ouro Preto's golden age.

There are reproductions here of the birth and death entries in the parish register for Aleijadinho, Marília Dirceu and Manoel Athayde. But even better are the eighteenth-century *ex votos* on the wall, a riveting insight into the tribulations of bygone daily life. One shows a black slave on her sickbed, with the inscription "Ana, slave of António Dias, had me made after finding herself gravely ill, without hope of life, but praying to Our Lord of the Slaves miraculously recovered". Opposite is a gruesome one from 1778 giving thanks for the successful setting of a broken leg, shown in graphic detail. Also on the wall there's a small **portrait**, crude but priceless, of Aleijadinho in middle age. It doesn't flatter so is probably a good likeness: slightly hunched, with sharp features.

Igreja de Santa Efigênia

Further out from the centre is the less important but no less fascinating **Igreja de Santa Efigênia** (Tues–Sun 8.30am–noon & 1.30–4.30pm), the church for slaves, located on the east hill some 3km from Praça Tiradentes. To get there, continue along Rua Cláudio Manoel down to the river, cross over and climb up Rua Santa Efigênia. Although plain in comparison to what you'll see in Ouro Preto's other churches, the artwork here is well worth the steep climb. The altar was carved by Javier do Briton, the mentor of Aleijadinho; the interior panels are by Manoel Rabelo de Souza; and the exterior image of Nossa Senhora do Rosário is by Aleijadinho himself. Slaves contributed to its construction by smuggling gold in their teeth cavities and under their fingernails.

Mina do Chico Rei

If you don't have time to visit the Mina da Passagem **gold mine** near Mariana (see p.197), much nearer, and cheaper too, is the **Mina do Chico Rei** (guided tours daily 8am–5pm; $1), at Rua Dom Silvério 108 in the eastern *bairro* of Antônio Dias. Founded in 1702, barely seven years after gold was first struck in Sabará, the mine had a working life of nearly two centuries. Though visually not as impressive as the Mina da Passagem, it nonetheless boasts some impressive statistics, which give some idea of just how rich Ouro Preto must once have been: the mine, constructed on five levels, contains an astonishing eighty square kilometres of tunnels, vaults and passages.

Eating and drinking

One of the nice things about Ouro Preto is the number of places where you can eat, drink or just hang out; when the students are out in force on weekend nights, it has none of the quiet atmosphere of a small interior town that you might expect. During term-time, at the weekend, the steep Rua Conde de Bobadela (also called Rua Direita), leading up to Praça Tiradentes, is packed with students spilling out of the **bars** and cafés; more congregate in the square itself, though most of the bars there have been turned into expensive restaurants. The modern wing of the mining school on the square contains a bar and a **live music** venue (see the posters in the lobby), while the *Booze Café Concerto*, a large basement area at Rua Direita 42, attracts jazz and rock bands from as far away as Belo Horizonte. If you prefer a quiet drink away from the crowds, try *Bar Sena*, a local dive on the corner outside the Igreja do Pilar.

There is no shortage of **restaurants**, either; the better-value ones (though still relatively costly) are clustered at the bottom of the hill on Rua São José, of which the best is unquestionably *Restaurante Chafariz* at no. 167, which does a superb *mineiro* buffet for about $7 and sometimes has special offers. Established in 1929, the restaurant has become something of a local institution, with pleasantly rustic décor and smooth service – altogether highly recommended.

More expensive places are clustered at the top of Rua Direita (Rua Conde de Bobadela), where you'll get good regional food in uniformly beautiful surroundings for $6–15 per person: a particularly appealing choice is the rather elegant *Restaurante Casa do Ouvidor*, Rua Direita 42. For a splurge, try *Le Coq D'Or* (℡31/3551-1032), a Franco-*mineiro* restaurant in the *Hotel Solar do Rosário*, Rua Vargas 270. Although one of the best restaurants in Minas Gerais, it's surprisingly reasonable (around $20 a head). Be sure to save room for one of the splendid desserts. If you don't want a substantial meal, the delightful *Café Geraes* at Rua Direita 122 is well worth trying for delicious sandwiches, soups, cakes and wine.

Thankfully, for those on a tight budget, there are also several **cheap places to eat**, namely the basic *lanchonetes* on Rua Senador Rocha Lagoa (also called Rua das Flôres) just off the square (the *Vide Gula* here is good, as is the *Lanchonete Ouro Grill* 20m up, which is even cheaper) and several on Rua Conde de Bobadela of which, at no. 76, the *Quinto do Ouro* has an excellent *por kilo* buffet for less than $4 for a full meal.

Mariana

MARIANA is one of the major colonial towns, and in the first half of the eighteenth century was grander by far than its younger rival 12km to the west, Ouro Preto. Despite regular riots and the war between *paulistas* and the Portuguese, Mariana was the administrative centre of the gold mines of central Minas until the 1750s. The first governors of Minas had their residence here and the first bishops their palace, and the town proudly celebrated its tercentenary in 1996. Yet today Mariana's churches are far less grand than its illustrious neighbour's, and it's really no more than a large village, albeit one that is steadily expanding. It does, however, have a fine museum and a perfectly preserved colonial centre, mercifully free of steep climbs, that is less crowded and commercialized than Ouro Preto. It's only a twenty-minute bus ride away and if you can't stand the crowds in Ouro Preto you could always stay here instead. There are also at least seven daily buses direct from Belo Horizonte, run by Viação Pássaro Verde, as well as direct services from São Paulo (3 daily; 12hr) run by Cristo Rei.

The Town

Orientation in Mariana is fairly straightforward. The colonial area begins at Praça Cláudio Manoel, in front of the large Catedral Basílica; from here, Rua

---

The Garimpeiros of Mariana

If you've got time to kill, an interesting place to stroll to is the town *garimpo*, a small **mining camp**. Stand on the last of the bridges over the Carmo creek and you can see figures digging and panning upstream. They are *garimpeiros*, gold-miners, and are using methods almost unchanged since gold was first found here in 1696 – the only difference now is that the pans are metal rather than wood. They dig channels into the stream bed, divert the flow and sift through the gravel with pans. To take a closer look, you can get there easily from Rua Rosário Velho. The *garimpeiros* are friendly, if a little bemused that gringos should find what they are doing interesting. There's another *garimpo* camp 9km out of town on the São Marco road in the *bairro* of Antônio Pereira, where topaz is mined. Again, you're free to wander as you like.

Frei Durão, lined with several of the noblest eighteenth-century public buildings, leads to the exquisite Praça Gomes Freire, with its bandstand, trees and pond, lined on all sides by colonial *sobrados*, two-storey mansions. Nearby are the two finest churches in Mariana and a lovely Prefeitura building in Praça João Pinheiro, complete with *pelourinho*, the old stone whipping post to which slaves and miscreants were tied and beaten.

The Museu Arquidiocesano

Although it has been overshadowed by its neighbour for over two centuries, you can still get a good idea of Mariana's early flourishing in one of the best museums in Minas Gerais, the **Museu Arquidiocesano** in the old bishop's palace, on Rua Frei Durão (Tues–Sun 8.30am–noon & 1.30–5pm).

The **building** itself is magnificent, with parts dating from the first decade of the eighteenth century, when it began life, bizarrely, as a prison for erring churchmen. The Franciscans were deeply involved in the *paulista* expeditions and were notorious for being the worst cut-throats of all. Between 1720 and 1756 the jail was extended into a palace: the door and window frames are massive, built in beautifully worked local soapstone. Inside, the **collection** is predictable – *arte sacra* and colonial furniture – but is distinguished by its quality and age, often predating the earliest material in Ouro Preto by two or three decades. It gives a vivid idea of how Mariana was thriving, with stone buildings and all the trappings of the early eighteenth-century good life, when Ouro Preto was still a collection of hovels.

On the ground floor there's a sobering collection of chains and manacles draped along the walls, and also the "treasure room", containing the ecclesiastical gold and silver. But the bulk of things to see are upstairs. The stairwell is dominated by a taste of things to come, a powerful painting of *Christ's Passion* by Athayde, his best-known work. The stairs lead up to a number of graceful colonial rooms, including the luxurious private quarters of the bishops, which contain an excellent collection of religious art, notably the largest number of Aleijadinho figures anywhere outside a church. They are instantly recognizable: São João Nepomuceno, the bearded São Joaquim in religious ecstasy and a marvellous São Miguel in the corner by the window.

The colonial furniture section, usually the dullest part of Minas museums, is actually worth seeing here: lovely writing desks and chests of drawers, all early eighteenth century and most made of jacaranda wood – there was a glut on the market at the time, as the forests were felled to get at the gold. The most unusual exhibit is a false bookcase, with wooden "books" painted to resemble leather. You can also wander around the bishop's audience room – the throne is also by Aleijadinho, who was nothing if not versatile – and there's a separate gallery of the bishops' portraits, incongruously included amongst which are three, rather good, local landscapes by the German artist Nobauer.

The churches

Mariana's colonial churches are smaller and less extravagant than Ouro Preto's, though most are decorated with paintings by **Athayde**, who came from here and is buried in the Igreja de São Francisco (see below).

The oldest church is the **Catedral de Nossa Senhora da Assunção** on Praça Cláudio Manoel (Tues–Sun 7am–6pm), begun in 1709 and choked with gilded Rococo detail. This is very much an Aleijadinho family venture: his father, Manoel Francisco Lisboa, designed and built it, while Aleijadinho contributed the carvings in the sacristy and a font. The interior is dominated by a massive German organ dating from 1701 and donated by the king of Portugal in 1751. Look closely and you can see Chinese-style decorations carved by slaves, who also worked the bellows. You can hear the organ in action, in recitals given at 11am on Fridays and at 12.15pm on Sundays.

The two churches on Praça João Pinheiro, around the corner, show how tastes had changed by the end of the century. Their ornate facades and comparatively restrained interiors are typical of the third phase of *barroco mineiro*. The **Igreja de São Francisco de Assis** (daily 9am–5pm), finished in 1794, has the finest paintings of any Mariana church, as befits the place where Athayde is buried. The numbers on the church floor are where members of the lay Franciscan brotherhood are buried; Athayde is no. 94. The elaborate interior contains much that is worth seeing: a fine sacristy, and an altar and pews by Aleijadinho, who also put his signature on the church in his usual way, by sculpting the sumptuous soapstone "medal" over the door. The **Igreja de Nossa Senhora do Carmo** (daily 8am–noon & 2–5pm), on the other side of the square, with its less elaborate exterior, is disappointing in comparison. But the combination of the two churches with the equally graceful **Prefeitura** makes the bare grass square an attractive place to take a break.

From here, it's a short uphill walk via the unspoilt Rua Dom Silvério to the mid-eighteenth-century **Basílica Menor de São Pedro dos Clérigos** (Tues–Sun 8am–noon & 1–4pm) that overlooks the town, framed by groves of towering palms; you pass the strange, geometric **Igreja da Arquiconfraria** on the way. The object is not so much to view the Basílica, but to enjoy the view of the town stretched out before you. If you follow the path along the top the views are even better.

Mina da Passagem

Four kilometres from Mariana, amongst steep hills bearing clear traces of centuries of mining, the ancient gold mine of **Mina da Passagem** (or Mina de Ouro) is one of the area's more unusual sights. If you don't have your own transport, take an Ouro Preto-bound bus from Mariana and get off at the bus stop opposite the mine.

Gold was first extracted here in 1719, making Mina da Passagem one of the oldest deep-shaft gold mines in Minas, although most of the seventeen kilometres of galleries date from the nineteenth century. These days the mine's eight faces are all closed and the mine survives instead as a tourist attraction, with retired miners serving as guides. Delightfully ramshackle, but engaging, **tours** operate every day from 9am until 5pm ($5).

Among the series of repair yards is probably the oldest functioning machine in Brazil – a vintage 1825 **British steam engine**, now adapted to run on compressed air. It powers a drum cable that drives railcars into and out of the mine – safer than it looks, though you do need to be careful of bumping your head once you trundle into the galleries. The guides are friendly, knowledgeable and some speak a little English and French; there are bits of nineteenth-century mining equipment knocking around, and the dripping gallery opens out into a small, crystalline floodlit lake, 120m underground. Back up on the surface, the visit is rounded off with a demonstration of gold panning, complete with real gold – not as easy as it looks.

The history of the mine is a roll call of economic imperialism. It was sold by the Portuguese to the British in 1830, and British owners happily worked it with slaves at the same time as the Royal Navy was intercepting slavers in the Atlantic. It was then offloaded onto the French in 1883, nationalized by Vargas in 1937, sold to a South African company in 1970, and finally ceased operations in 1985.

Practicalities

The local **buses from Ouro Preto** leave you right in the centre at Praça Tancredo Neves, opposite an excellent **tourist information post**, the Terminal Turístico (daily 8am–5pm; ☎31/3557-1158), which sells a good map for $1.50 and distributes free brochures and booklets. The Terminal Turístico also has up-to-date bus timetables for planning onward journeys, and supplies accredited guides for tours in the region (around $20 a day). If you're coming from further afield, you'll arrive at the new **rodoviária** (☎31/3557-1122), on the main road a couple of kilometres from the centre; if you can't be bothered to walk into the centre, catch one of the buses from Ouro Preto, which pass through the *rodoviária* every twenty minutes or so.

All the **places to stay** are within easy walking distance of Praça Tancredo Neves. One of the nicest is the *Pousada Solar dos Corrêa*, Rua Josafá Macedo 70 (☎31/3557-2080; ❸), one block up from the Terminal Turístico on the corner with Rua Direita. The hotel is full of character, with fifteen very different rooms done up with mock-colonial furniture, ranging from the rather gloomy loft conversions to a gorgeous first-floor room (no. 8) with wonderful views. It pays to come mid-week to secure the room of your choice, as at weekends you'd be lucky to get one at all. Similar in style, but slightly more expensive, is the *Pousada da Typographia* at Praça Gomes Freire 220 (☎31/3557-1577; ❸), an eighteenth-century mansion restored in period detail. The rooms are spacious and comfortable and the location especially attractive. Cheaper options include the basic *Hotel Central* (☎ & ℱ31/3557-1630; ❷), a beautiful but run-down colonial building at Rua Frei Durão 8, overlooking the Praça Gomes Freire; the modern *Hotel Faísca*, Rua Antônio Olinto 48-A (☎31/3557-1765; ❸), which you can see up the street from the tourist office and which offers both *apartamentos* or cheaper *quartos*; and excellent value is the clean and tidy *Hotel Providência*, Rua Dom Silvério 233 (☎31/3577-1444; ❷), along the road that leads up to the Basílica, which has use of the neighbouring school's pool when classes finish at noon.

Mariana has some reasonable **restaurants**, generally cheaper than those in Ouro Preto though none as good as the neighbouring city's best. Those with the nicest views look out onto Praça Gomes Freire (all open daily until midnight): the cosy *Restaurante Pizzeria Senzala* serves good food at lunchtime and turns into a lively and very friendly bar in the evenings; and *Mangiare della Mamma*, three doors up at Rua Dom Viçoso 27, does a top-notch *mineiro comida à kilo*, presented in heavy iron casseroles sizzling on a hot, wood-fired iron stove. Just up from Praça Gomes Freire at Travessa João Pinheiro 26, next to the Igreja São Francisco, is arguably the town's best *mineiro* restaurant, *Tambau* (☎31/3557-1406), while the nearby *Alvorada*, Rua Jorge Marques 101, is a good value *churrascaria*. For bargain lunches, a good place to try is the self-service *Panela de Pedra*, a restaurant attached to the Terminal Turístico.

There are simple **bars** and **sorvetaria** on most corners, and at weekends, a couple of **discos** open up on Praça Cláudio Manoel, the busiest being *Tatu's Dancing*. Lastly, the Centro de Cultura SESI-Mariana, opposite the Museu Arquidiocesano, occasionally hosts local art exhibitions, ballet and dance (☎31/3557-1041 for information).

△ Diamantina, Minas Gerais

Congonhas

CONGONHAS, a rather ugly, modern town 72km south of Belo Horizonte, sits ill as one of the historic cities. In truth, there's only one reason for coming here: to see the pilgrimage church of Bom Jesus de Matosinhos. It's a long way to come just to see one thing, but this is no ordinary church: if one place represents the flowering of *barroco mineiro*, this is it, the spiritual heart of Minas Gerais.

Getting to Congonhas is relatively easy from both Belo Horizonte (6 buses daily; 1hr) and São João del Rei (5 buses daily; 2hr). There are also two daily buses from Ouro Preto, headed for São Paulo or Barbacena; the ride takes about three hours and is a fascinating journey, much of it on country dirt roads through sleepy villages. It's possible to start out from Belo Horizonte or Ouro Preto, go to Congonhas with enough time to see Bom Jesus, and still get to São João del Rei in the evening (last bus 8.20pm, 10.20pm on Sun), but only if you set out early. To get from the main *rodoviária*, a couple of kilometres out of town, to Bom Jesus, catch the **local bus** marked "Basílica", which takes you all the way up the hill to the church; it's impossible to miss.

Most people visit Congonhas on a day-trip, and there's little reason to stay, but if you do decide to spend the night, the most comfortable option is the *Colonial Hotel* (℡31/3731-1834; ❸), overlooking the church and gardens, with its own pool. The *Max Mazza Hotel* (℡31/3731-1970; ❷) at Av. Júlia Kubitschek 410, is more modern than the *Colonial*, but lacks a pool. If you need to eat, head for the *Cova do Daniel*, a good regional **restaurant** at Praça da Basílica 76, next to Bom Jesus.

Bom Jesus de Matosinhos

Built on a hill overlooking the town, with a panoramic view of the hills around it, the **Basílica do Senhor Bom Jesus de Matosinhos** (Tues–Sun 6am–6pm) is set in a magnificent sloping **garden** studded with palms and what look like six tiny mosques with oriental domes. These are small **chapels** commemorating episodes of the Passion; each is filled with life-size statues dramatizing the scene in a tableau, 64 in all. Looking down on them from the parapets of the extraordinary terrace leading up to the church itself are twelve towering soapstone **statues** of Old Testament prophets. Everything, the figures and the statues, was sculpted by **Aleijadinho**, in what he must have known would be his last major commission. His presumed leprosy was already advanced, and he could only work with chisels strapped to his wrists. The results are astonishing, a masterpiece made all the more moving by the fact that it seems likely it was a conscious swan song on Aleijadinho's part: there is no other explanation for the way a seriously ill man pushed so hard to finish such a massive undertaking, whose theme was immediately relevant to his own suffering.

The whole complex is modelled on the shrine of Bom Jesus in Braga, in northern Portugal. The idea and money came from a Portuguese adventurer, **Feliciano Mendes**, who, towards the end of his life, planned to recreate the pilgrimage church of his native Braga, to house an image of the dead Christ he brought with him from Portugal in 1713. Mendes died in 1756, when work had only just begun, and it was forty years before the local bishop contracted Aleijadinho to produce the figures of the Passion and the prophets. Somehow, with his apprentices filling in fine detail, Aleijadinho managed to complete everything by 1805; it almost defies belief that the finished project was executed by a man who had lost the use of his hands.

The Passion

There are always **guides** hanging around, who do know their stuff and can fill in a lot of interesting detail for just a few dollars, but you're not obliged to go around with one. If you'd rather take yourself around, start at the bottom of the garden to better appreciate the deep religious mysticism that lies behind the design. The **slope** symbolizes the ascent towards the Cross and governs the sequence of tableaux, the scenes leading you up from the Garden of Gethsemane through Christ's imprisonment, trial, whipping, the crown of thorns, and the carrying of the Cross to Calvary. On top, guarded by the prophets, is the church, housing both the wooden image of Christ's body and the real body, in the Communion host: built in the shape of a cross the church represents both the Crucifixion and the Kingdom of Heaven.

Viewing of the **statues** inside the chapels isn't ideal: there are grilles to stop people getting in, and some of the figures are difficult or impossible to see. All are sculpted from cedar and were brightly painted by Athayde, using his preferred natural paints made from ox blood, egg whites, crushed flowers and vegetable dyes. They are marvellously lifelike: you can see Christ's veins and individual muscles, the bulging of a soldier's cheeks as he blows a trumpet and a leering dwarf carrying a nail for Christ's crucifixion. Too savage and realistic to be Baroque art, there is nothing with which to compare it – it's as if Aleijadinho was driven to take his genius for realism to its logical conclusion, and finally shatter the restrictions of the Baroque tradition he had worked in all his life.

Things become even more interesting on the **symbolic** front when you look closely at the figures. Christ is more than once portrayed with a vivid red mark around his neck, which make many think he also represents Tiradentes (see box p.191). Support for the theory comes from the Roman soldiers, viciously caricatured, whom Aleijadinho gives two left feet and ankle boots – which only the Portuguese wore. Although nothing is known of Aleijadinho's politics, he was a native Brazilian and lived through the *Inconfidência* in Ouro Preto. He would certainly have known Tiradentes by sight, and it is more than likely that the Congonhas Christ is meant to represent him.

The prophets and the church

If the cedar figures are outside the Baroque tradition, the statues of the **prophets** are its finest expression in all Brazil: carved from blocks of soapstone they dominate both the garden they look down on and the church they lead to. They are remarkably dramatic, larger than life-size, full of movement and expression; perched on the parapet, you look up at them against the backdrop of either hills or sky.

The **church** is inevitably something of an anti-climax, but still interesting. The effigy of the dead Christ that Mendes brought over from Portugal is in a glass case in the altar, and through the door to the right of the altar is the cross that carried the image. The lampholders are Chinese dragons, yet more of the Macau influence visible in Sabará and Diamantina.

Next to the church is a fascinating collection of **ex votos**; it keeps irregular hours but the friendly uniformed guards will open it up for you – though they're not around at lunchtime. The display will be familiar to anyone who has been to other pilgrimage centres in Brazil, and the photos, pictures and messages from grateful sufferers elicit a voyeuristic fascination. This collection is remarkable for the number of really old *ex votos*, the earliest from a slave who recovered from fever in 1722. Others record in crude but vivid paintings incidents like being gored by a bull, being seriously burnt or escaping from a bus crash.

The **bus** to take you back to the *rodoviária* leaves from the parking bay behind the church.

São João del Rei and around

SÃO JOÃO DEL REI is the only one of the historic cities to have adjusted successfully to life after the gold rush. It has all the usual trappings of the *cidades históricas* – gilded churches, well-stocked museums, colonial mansions – but it's also a thriving market town, easily the largest of the historic cities, with a population of around 80,000. This modern prosperity complements the colonial atmosphere rather than compromising it, and, with its wide central thoroughfare enclosing a small stream, its stone bridges, squares and trees, São João is quite attractive. Come evening though, it's a rather dreary place and overshadowed by **Tiradentes**, its much smaller and prettier neighbour, in terms of good places to stay. While most visitors to São João del Rei come on an easy day trip from Tiradentes, if possible, stay over in São João before a Friday, Saturday or Sunday when you can take a ride on the "Smoking Mary", a lovingly restored nineteenth-century steam train, that links the two towns (see p.206).

Founded in 1699 on the São João River, the town had the usual turbulent early years, but distinguished itself by successfully turning to ranching and trade when the gold ran out early in the nineteenth century. São João's carpets were once famous, and there is still a textile factory today. Tiradentes was born here, Aleijadinho worked here, and in more recent times the great *mineiro* politician, **Tancredo Neves**, shepherded Brazil out of military rule when he was elected president in 1985. Tragically, he died before he took office (see "History" in Contexts) and is buried in the closest thing the town has to a shrine in the cemetery of São Francisco.

Arrival, orientation and accommodation

The centre of town is fifteen minutes' walk southwest from the **rodoviária**, or you can take a local bus in: the stop isn't the obvious one immediately outside the *rodoviária's* main entrance – instead you need to turn left and take any bus from the stop on the other side of the road. Local buses enter the old part of town along **Avenida Tancredo Neves**, with its small stream and grassy verges to your left. There's a **tourist office** (daily 8am–5pm; ☎32/3379-2952), at Praça Frei Orlando, next to the Igreja São Francisco de Assis (see p.203) where you can pick up a tourist booklet with a helpful map. **Money changing** is quick at the BEMGE bank, Av. Tancredo Neves 213 (Mon–Fri 11am–4pm); should you need an ATM, the Banco do Brasil, Banespa and HSBC have branches on the same avenue.

São João is divided into two main districts, each with a colonial area, separated by a small stream – the **Córrego do Lenheiro** – which runs between the broad Avenida Tancredo Neves on the north side, and **Avenida Hermílio Alves**, which turns into **Avenida Eduardo Magalhães**, to the south. Relatively small and easy to find your way around, the districts are linked by a number of small bridges, including two eighteenth-century stone ones and a late nineteenth-century footbridge made of cast iron.

On the south side, the colonial zone is clustered around the beautiful **Igreja de São Francisco de Assis**, at the far western end of town. On the other side is the commercial centre, usually bustling with people, cars and the horse-drawn trailers of rural Minas. This commercial zone sprang up in the nineteenth century and shields the colonial area proper, several blocks of cobbled streets that jumble together Baroque churches, elegant mansions and the pastel fronts of humbler houses. For once you have the luxury of wandering around without losing your breath, as São João is largely flat.

Accommodation

Finding somewhere to stay is rarely a problem as **accommodation** in São João is plentiful and good value, though hotels and *pousadas* here are not nearly as attractive as those in neighbouring Tiradentes (see p.206). Bear in mind, however, that the town is a popular spot to spend *Carnaval* in, and Easter celebrations also attract huge numbers of visitors; at these times hotel reservations are essential. The *Hotel Brasil* (T 32/3371-2804; ❷) at Av. Tancredo Neves 395, facing the train station, is a favourite budget choice, though its high-ceilinged rooms are rather shabby. Very similar accommodation is offered by the *Pousada Portal del Rey* at Praça Severiano Resende 134 (T 32/3371-8820; ❷), above a restaurant.

Of the medium-range places, best value is the *Pousada Casarão*, Rua Ribeiro Bastos 94 (T 32/3371-7447; ❸), a wonderful converted mansion near São Francisco church, with the added attraction of a small swimming pool. At a similar price, the *Quinta do Ouro*, towards the western end of Avenida Tancredo Neves on Praça Severiano de Rezende (T 32/3371-2565; ❸), has four lovely rooms, three with salons (reservations essential). Top of the range, with a very good pool, is the very comfortable, but somewhat impersonal, three-star *Pousada do Bispo* (T 32/3371-8844, W www.becodobispo.com.br; ❸), just outside of the historic centre at Beco do Bispo 93.

The Town

São João's colonial sections are complemented by some fine buildings from more recent eras, notably the end of the nineteenth century, when the town's prosperity and self-confidence were high. The 1920s and 1930s were also good times – some of the vaguely Art Deco buildings combine surprisingly well with the colonial ones. The main public buildings line the south bank of the stream, best viewed from Avenida Tancredo Neves on the north side; there's a sumptuous French-style **theatre** (1893), and the graceful blue **Prefeitura** with an imposing Banco do Brasil building facing it. The relaxed atmosphere is reinforced by the number of bars and restaurants, and if you stumble across knots of people staring at walls take a closer look: in São João a good half-dozen traditional "**street newspapers**" still survive. Broadsheets rather than papers, they are posted on the streets for passers-by to catch up on local events, just as they were in the earliest days of the Brazilian press; their content varies from dry commentaries on agricultural issues to peppery tales with headlines like "Cobra-man speaks all!"

The Igreja de São Francisco de Assis and the Memorial Tancredo Neves

The most impressive of the town's colonial churches is the **Igreja de São Francisco de Assis** (daily 8am–noon & 1.30–5pm), one block off the western end of Avenida Eduardo Magalhães. Overlooking a square with towering palms – some more than a century old – the church, finished in 1774, is exceptionally large, with an ornately carved exterior by a pupil of Aleijadinho. The master himself contributed the intricate decorations of the side chapels, which can be seen in all their glory now that the original paint and gilding has been

stripped off. From the plaques, you'll see that the church has been visited by some illustrious guests, including President Mitterand of France. They came to pay homage at the **grave of Tancredo Neves**, in the cemetery behind the church. Sunday at 9.15am is an especially good time to visit the church, when eighteenth century music is played to accompany mass.

Tancredo was a canny and pragmatic politician in the Minas tradition, but with a touch of greatness; the transition to civilian rule in 1985 would not have happened without his skills. He was born in and spent all his life in São João, where he was loved and is still very much missed. Eerily, to some, he died on the same day of the year as Tiradentes, who was also born in São João – their statues face each other in Praça Severiano de Rezende, on the other side of the Córrego do Lenheiro. Tancredo's black marble grave has a rather fine epitaph from one of his speeches: "You shall have my bones, land that I love, the final blending of my being with these blessed hills".

Just around the corner from the Igreja de São Francisco, on Rua José Maria Xavier at the corner with Avenida Eduardo Magalhães, is the **Memorial Tancredo Neves** (Fri 1–6pm, Sat, Sun 9am–5pm). This small nineteenth-century town house shelters a collection of personal artefacts and documents relating to the president's life, and *ex votos* used to decorate his grave, thanking him "for graces granted" – only really of interest to those Brazilians for whom Tancredo was nothing less than a modern saint.

The Museu de Arte Sacra

Over on the other side of the stream, one block north from Avenida Tancredo Neves, lies the main street of the other colonial area, **Rua Getúlio Vargas**. The western end is formed by the small early eighteenth-century **Igreja da Nossa**

Senhora do Rosário (Tues–Sun noon–6pm), which looks onto a cobbled square dominated by two stunning colonial mansions. The one nearest the church is the Solar dos Neves, the family home of the Neves clan for over two centuries, the place where Tancredo was born and lived.

A couple of buildings east along from the Solar dos Neves is an excellent **Museu de Arte Sacra** (Tues–Sun noon–5pm), contained within another sensitively restored house. The collection is small but very good; highlights are a finely painted St George and a remarkable figure of Christ mourned by Mary Magdalene, with rubies representing drops of blood. As you go around, you're accompanied by Baroque church music, which matches the pieces perfectly. The museum also has a small gallery for exhibitions by São João's large artistic colony.

The Catedral Basílica de Nossa Senhora de Pilar and other churches

Almost next door to the Museu de Arte Sacra on Avenida Getúlio Vargas is a magnificent early Baroque church, the **Catedral Basílica de Nossa Senhora de Pilar** (Tues–Sun noon–6pm), completed in 1721. The interior is gorgeous: only Pilar in Ouro Preto and Santo Antônio in Tiradentes are as liberally plastered with gold. The gilding is seen to best effect over the altar, a riot of Rococo pillars, angels and curlicues. The ceiling painting is all done with vegetable dyes, and there's a beautiful tiled floor.

There are further churches to visit in this part of town, if you're enthusiastic, though none of the same standard as either São Francisco or Pilar. The **Igreja de Nossa Senhora das Mercês** (Tues–Sun noon–5pm), behind Pilar, dates from 1750 and is notable for the variety and artistry of the graffiti, some of it dating back to the nineteenth century, etched into its stone steps, while the elegant facade of **Nossa Senhora do Carmo** (daily 6.30–11.30am & 4.30–7.30pm) dominates a beautiful triangular *praça* at the eastern end of Avenida Getúlio Vargas.

The Museu Regional

More or less on a level with the cathedral, just off Avenida Tancredo Neves on Praça Severiano de Rezende, is an excellent museum, the **Museu Regional** (Tues–Sun noon–5.30pm), housed in a magnificently restored colonial mansion. Perhaps the most fascinating pieces here are the eighteenth-century *ex votos* on the ground floor, their vivid illustrations detailing the pickles that both masters and slaves got themselves into – José Alves de Carvalho was stabbed in the chest while crossing a bridge on the way home in 1765; a slave called Antônio had his leg broken and was half buried for hours in a mine cave-in. On the first floor are several figures of saints made by ordinary people in the eighteenth century: they have a simplicity and directness that makes them stand out. There's a collection of furniture and relics too, and, on the top floor, one of the oddest items – a machine used until 1928 to select the draft numbers of unfortunate army conscripts.

Eating, drinking and nightlife

On the **north side** of the Lenheiro stream, on Praça Severiano de Rezende, you'll find two of the town's best **restaurants**: the *Churrascaria Ramon*, which does a good-value *churrasco*, and the *Quinta do Ouro*, whose *mineiro* food is the best in São João. On the same *praça*, but much cheaper, is the perfectly adequate *por kilo Restaurante Rex* (11am–4pm). Alternatively, a very pleasant place for light meals and excellent afternoon teas is the *Sinhazinha* (Mon–Fri 1–6pm, Sat, Sun & holidays 8am–10pm), directly across from the Igreja de São Francisco.

The best places, however, combining good food with lively atmosphere, are on the **south side**, where tourists, young townsfolk and families flock to drink, eat and go to the cinema. Many of the **bars** have live music at weekends and get very crowded later on when people start spilling out onto the pavements. Almost all of the action is concentrated on Avenida Tiradentes, which runs parallel to Eduardo Magalhães, the avenue that runs alongside the stream. The bars are bunched both at Tiradentes' western end near São Francisco – where *Cabana do Zotti* at no. 805 (9pm onwards) is always packed and does good snacks – and halfway along Tiradentes at the junction with Rua Gabriel Passos (the road that runs in from the blue Prefeitura). Of the latter bunch, by far the best is *Miaxôu Bar*, at Rua Gabriel Passos 299 (5pm onwards), with its charming owner, excellent food (try the *bolinhos de queijo* or the pizzas) and efficient service. It gets very animated at weekends when whole families get up and shimmy to the live music (around 8pm–3am), often old sambas.

Tiradentes

TIRADENTES was founded as early as 1702, but had already been overshadowed by São João by the 1730s and is now no more than a sleepy village, with a population of only 5000. The core is much as it was in the eighteenth

The São João del Rei–Tiradentes train

If you're in São João between Friday and Sunday, don't miss the half-hour **train ride** to the colonial village of **Tiradentes**, 12km away. There are frequent buses too (8 daily from São João's *rodoviária*), but they don't compare to the trip on a nineteenth-century steam train, with rolling stock from the 1930s, immaculately maintained and run with great enthusiasm. You may think yourself immune to the romance of steam, and be bored by the collection of old steam engines and rail equipment in São João's nineteenth-century station on Avenida Hermílio Alves – the **Estação Ferroviária** (museum open Tues–Sun 9–11am & 1–5pm; ☎32/3371-8485) – but by the time you've bought your ticket you'll be hooked: the booking hall is right out of a 1930s movie, the train hisses and spits out cinders, and as you sit down in carriages filled with excited children it's all you can do not to run up and down the aisle with them.

Built in the 1880s, as the textile industry took off in São João, this was one of the earliest rail lines in Brazil and the trains were immediately christened Maria-Fumaça, "Smoking Mary". The service runs only on Friday, Saturday, Sunday and holidays, when trains leave São João at 10am and 3pm, returning from Tiradentes at 1pm and 5pm ($5 return fare). If you want to stay longer, accommodation in Tiradentes is usually easy to find, or you could get one of the many local buses back to São João. Sit on the left leaving São João for the best views, and sit as far from the engine as you can: steam trains bring tears to your eyes in more ways than one.

The half-hour ride is very scenic, following a winding valley of the Serra de São José, which by the time it gets to Tiradentes has reared up into a series of rocky bluffs. The train travels through one of the oldest areas of gold-mining in Minas Gerais, and from it you'll see clear traces of the eighteenth-century mine workings in the hills. In the foreground, the rafts on the river have pumps that suck up alluvium from the river bed, from which gold is extracted by modern *garimpeiros*, heirs to over two centuries of mining tradition.

century, straggling down the side of a hill crowned by the twin towers of the **Igreja Matriz de Santo Antônio** (Tues–Thurs, Sat & Sun 9am–noon & 1.30–5pm, Mon & Fri 9am–5pm). Begun in 1710 and completed around 1730, it's one of the earliest and largest of the major Minas Baroque churches, and in 1732 began to acquire the gilding for which it is famous, becoming in the process one of the richest churches in any of the mining towns. It was decorated with the special extravagance of the newly rich, using more gold, the locals say, than any other church in Brazil save the Capela Dourada in Recife. Whether this is true or not – and Pilar in Ouro Preto is probably as rich as either – the glinting and winking of the gold around the altar is certainly impressive. You can tell how early the altar is from the comparative crudeness of the statues and carvings: formal, stiff and with none of the movement of developed Minas Baroque. The exterior already needed restoring by 1810; the beautifully carved soapstone panels on the facade are not by Aleijadinho, as some believe, but by his pupil, Cláudio Pereira Viana, who worked with the master on his last projects.

From the steps of the church you look down an unspoilt colonial street – the old town hall with the veranda has a restored eighteenth-century jail – framed by the crests of the hills. If you had to take one photograph to summarize Minas Gerais, this would be it. Before walking down the hill, check out the **Museu Padre Toledo** (Mon, Wed–Fri, 1–4.40pm and Sat & Sun 9am–4.40pm), to the right of Santo Antônio as you're standing on the steps. Padre Toledo was one of the Inconfidêntes and built the mansion that is now the museum. He obviously didn't let being a priest stand in the way of enjoying the pleasures of life: the two-storey *sobrado* must have been very comfortable, and even though the ceiling paintings are dressed up as classical allegories, they're not the sort of thing you would expect a priest to commission, featuring so much naked flesh. The museum comprises the usual mixture of furniture and religious art, but the interesting part is the old slave quarters in the yard out back, now converted into toilets.

A more substantial reminder of the slave presence is the **Igreja da Nossa Senhora do Rosário dos Pretos** (Tues–Sun 9am–noon & 2–5pm), down the hill and along the first street to the right. There could be no more eloquent reminder of the harsh divisions between masters and slaves than this small chapel, built by slaves for their own worship. There is gilding even here – some colonial miners were freed blacks working on their own account – and two fine figures of the black St Benedict stand out, but overall the church is moving precisely because it is so simple and dignified.

Practicalities

Tiradentes might have a placid and timeless air during the week, but it gets surprisingly lively at weekends as the bars and guesthouses fill up with people attracted by its relaxed atmosphere.

Finding **accommodation** is rarely a problem, as a good proportion of the town's population have turned their homes into *pousadas* (there are well over forty), many of them exceptionally beautiful and all very good value. Nevertheless, during *Carnaval*, over Easter and in July, advanced reservations are pretty much essential, and most *pousadas* will only accept bookings of at least four nights. You'll find a selection along the road leading into the village from the train station, around the lovely Praça das Mercês it leads into, or on the main square, the Largo das Forras; the staff at the **tourist office**, Largo das Forras 71 (Mon–Fri 9am–12.30pm & 1.30–5.30pm and Sat & Sun 9am–5pm), will help you find available rooms.

The cheapest – and one of the friendliest – places to stay is the *Pousada da Bia*, Rua Frederico Ozanan 330 (⊕32/3355-1173; ❷). Rooms here are simple, but clean, there's a kitchen for the use of guests and a helpful English-speaking owner. Slightly more expensive options are the small *Pousada do Ó*, which has attractive rooms, a pleasant garden (but doesn't accept children under the age of 12) and is near the Igreja Matriz at Rua Jogo da Bola 98 (⊕32/3355-1699; ❸); the large and impersonal *Hotel Ponta do Morro*, Largo das Forras 2 (⊕32/3355-1342, ⓦwww.guiavirtual.tur.br/hponta; ❸), with a pool; and, across the square at no. 48, the very pleasant *Pousada do Largo* (⊕32/3355-11166; ❸) which also has a pool. If it's luxury you're after, the beautifully furnished colonial *Pousada Richard Rothe*, Rua Padre Toledo 124 (⊕32/3355-1333; ❺), is an excellent choice, with an attractive garden and a small pool; children under 12, however, are not accepted. The same age restriction applies to the English-owned *Solar da Ponte*, in a fine location by the Praça das Mercês (⊕32/3355-1255, ⓦwww.solardaponte.com.br; ❻) and considered to be the best hotel in town. While the converted mansion, garden and pool are undeniably appealing, a rather snooty atmosphere dominates. Much more welcoming, but offering similar top-end luxury, is the *Pousada Villa Paolucci* (⊕32/3355-1350, ⓦwww.villapaolucci.cjb.net; ❻) a mid-eighteenth-century *casa grande* located on the outskirts of town, at the end of Rua do Chafariz, and set amidst a working *fazenda* – reservations are essential.

The best **restaurant** in Tiradentes is *Viradas do Largo*, Rua do Moinho 11 (⊕32/3355-1111), which sets itself apart from other *mineiro* restaurants with the delicacy of its cooking; a full meal costs around $20 and reservations are advisable. Another fine restaurant that produces modern *mineiro* dishes is *Estalgem* at Rua Ministero Gabriel Passos 280 (⊕32/3355-1144). More orthodox (and less expensive) fare is served *Canto do Chafariz*, Largo do Chafariz 37 (closed Mon), near the São José fountain. For a break from *mineiro* food, try *Sapore d'Italia*, Rua São Francisco de Paula 13, a reasonably priced and above-average Italian restaurant; the *Mandalun*, Rua Padre Toledo 172, an attractive and very good Lebanese place; or the *Royal Dansk*, Largo das Forras 66, one of Brazil's very few Danish restaurants and especially strong on trout dishes.

Among Tiradentes' many **bars**, the *Aluarte* has the best atmosphere but is quite expensive, the *Meninasgerais* at Largo das Forras 66 is a popular dancing place, while *Xiquita Banana*, on Avenida Ministro Gabriel Passos, is the most laid-back. All have live music at weekends.

Diamantina and the Jequitinhonha Valley

DIAMANTINA, home town of Juscelino Kubitschek, the president responsible for the creation of Brasília, is the only historic city to the north of Belo Horizonte and, at six hours by bus, is by some way the furthest from it. Yet the journey itself is one of the reasons for going there, as the road heads into the different landscapes of northern Minas on its way to the *sertão mineiro*. The second half of the 288-kilometre journey is much the most spectacular, so to see it in daylight you need to catch either the 5.30am, 9am or 11.30am bus from Belo Horizonte.

Diamantina has a very different atmosphere to any of the other colonial towns. Still a functioning diamond-mining town, it is also the gateway to the

Jequitinhonha Valley, the river valley that is the heart of the Minas *sertão*. The green hills that characterise so much of the southern half of Minas are utterly absent in Diamantina, which instead is set in a rocky, windswept and often cold highland zone – be sure to bring a sweater or jacket.

The road to Diamantina

Diamantina itself, scattered down the steep side of a rocky valley, faces escarpments the colour of rust; the setting has a lunar quality you also come across in parts of the Northeast's *sertão*. In fact, at Diamantina you're not quite in the *sertão* – that begins roughly at Araçuaí, some 300km to the north – but in the uplands of the **Serra do Espinhaço**, the highlands that form the spine of the state. Almost as soon as you leave Belo Horizonte, the look of the land changes to the stubby trees and savanna of the Planalto Central, the inland plateau that makes up much of central Brazil. Some 60km from Belo Horizonte you pass the Rei do Mato cave (see p.180), and after another 54km, roughly halfway to Diamantina, the road forks – left to Brasília and the Planalto proper, right to Diamantina and the *sertão*.

You hit the highland foothills soon after the dull modern town of Curvelo, and from then on the route is very scenic. The well-maintained road winds its way up spectacularly forbidding hills, the granite outcrops enlivened by cactus, wild flowers and the bright yellow and purple *ipê* trees, until it reaches the upland plateau, 1300m above sea level. The plateau heralds yet another change: windswept moorland with few trees and strange rock formations. Look carefully on the left and you'll see traces of an old stone road, with flagstones seemingly going nowhere. This is the old slave road, which for over a century was the only communication line between southern Minas and the *sertão*.

The Town

Even if it were not set in such a striking landscape, Diamantina has a distinctive **history** that would still mark it out from the other *cidades históricas*. The Portuguese Crown had reason to feel bitter about the gold strikes in Minas Gerais: it had been forced to expend blood and treasure in prising the gold from the hands of the *paulistas*, and when diamonds were found here in 1720 the same mistakes were not repeated. **Arraial do Tijuco**, as Diamantina was called at first, was put under strict military control. People could only come and go with royal passes and the town was isolated for almost a century. This may explain Diamantina's very distinctive atmosphere. Although it has few buildings or churches to rival the masterpieces of Ouro Preto or Congonhas, the passage of time has had little effect on the large colonial centre of the town, which is the least spoilt of any of the *cidades históricas*. The narrow stone-flagged streets, with their overhanging Chinese eaves and perfectly preserved colonial houses, are exactly as they have been for generations.

Diamantina takes the *mineiro* penchant for building on slopes to extremes. Although the **rodoviária** (☎38/3531-1471) is not far from the centre of town, it's on a steep hill, and the only way back to it once in the centre is by taxi (around $2), unless you have the legs and lungs of a mountain goat. The streets are either too narrow or too steep even for Brazil's intrepid local bus drivers. Fortunately the place is small enough for you to get your bearings very quickly. The central square in the old town is **Praça Conselheiro Mota**, which has the Catedral Metropolitana de Santo Antônio built in the middle of it – everyone calls the cathedral and the square "Sé". Most of the sights and places to stay are within a stone's throw of here.

The Museu do Diamante

The **Museu do Diamante** (Tues–Sat noon–5.30pm, Sun & holidays 9am–noon) on the cathedral square is the best place to get an idea of what *garimpagem* has meant to Diamantina. It's one of the best museums in Minas, not so much for the glories of its exhibits but for the effort it makes to give you an idea of daily life in old Diamantina.

The room behind the entrance desk is devoted to the history of mining in Diamantina and filled with old mining instruments, maps and prints. Dominating everything is an enormous cast-iron English safe, brought by ox cart all the way from Rio in the eighteenth century – it took eighteen months to get here. Inside the safe is a riveting display of genuine gold, and replicas of diamond jewellery and cut diamonds: the originals are stashed in the Banco do Brasil across the road. On the upper shelf is a (genuine) pile of uncut diamonds and emeralds, much as they would appear to *garimpeiros* panning – only the occasional dull glint distinguishes them from ordinary gravel. More disturbing is an appalling display of whips, chains and brands used on slaves right up until the late nineteenth century, though the terrifying-looking tongs, underneath the chains, are in fact colonial hair-curlers, and not torture instruments.

The rest of the museum is great to wander through, stuffed with memorabilia from mouldering top hats to photos of long-dead town bandsmen: Diamantina has strong musical traditions and still supports *serestas*, small bands of accordion, guitar and flute players who stroll through the streets and hold dances around Carnaval, or on the evening of September 12, the *Dia da Seresta*.

The Catedral and other churches

Despite the comparative ugliness of the **Catedral Metropolitana de Santo Antônio**, built in 1940 on the site of an old colonial church, the cathedral square (Praça Correia Rabelo) is worth savouring. It's lined with *sobrados*, many of them with exquisite ornamental bronze- and ironwork, often imported from Portugal – look closely and you'll see iron pineapples on the balconies. Most impressive of all are the serried windows of the massive Prefeitura, and the ornate Banco do Brasil building next to it – possibly unique in Brazil in that it spells the country name the old way, with a "z".

Diamantina's **other churches** are distinctive, simple but very striking, with stubby towers and Chinese eaves: street names, like Rua Macau de Meio and Rua Macau de Cima, recall the days when these streets were home to Chinese craftsmen imported by the Portuguese during the eighteenth century. With one exception, though, the churches' exteriors are actually more interesting than the interiors.

The church that's most worth entering is the **Igreja de Nossa Senhora do Carmo** (Tues–Sat 2–6pm, Sun 8am–noon) on Rua Bonfim. Built between 1760 and 1765, legend has it that the heir of Diamantina's richest miner made sure the tower was built at the back of the church rather than the front, as was usual, so the bells didn't disturb his wife's beauty sleep. Inside is an atypically florid interior, whose two main features are a rich, intricately carved altar screen and a gold-sheathed organ, which was actually built in Diamantina.

On the cobbled street leading down the hill from here is a local curiosity. The church at the bottom, **Igreja de Nossa Senhora do Rosário dos Pretos** (Tues–Sat 2–6pm, Sun 8am–noon), has a tree growing in front of it: look closely and you can see a large distorted wooden cross embedded in the trunk and lower branches. The story behind this reads like something from Gabriel García Márquez, but did really happen. The year the old Sé church was knocked down, in 1932, the padre of Rosário planted a wooden cross outside his church to commemorate the chapel that old Diamantina had originally been built around. A fig tree sprouted up around it so that at first the cross seemed to flower – there's a photo of it at this stage in the Museu do Diamante – and eventually, rather than knocking it down, the tree grew up around the cross and ended up absorbing it. Inside the church itself is a marvellous Baroque altar and a simple, yet stunning, painted ceiling.

The Mercado dos Tropeiros

Diamantina's other important economic role, besides diamond mining, is as the market town for the Jequitinhonha Valley. It's here that the products of the remote *sertão* towns of northeastern Minas are shipped and stockpiled before making their way to Belo Horizonte. The old **Mercado dos Tropeiros** on Praça Barão do Guaicuí, just a block downhill from the cathedral square, is the focus of Diamantina's trade, and worth seeing for the building alone – an interesting tiled wooden structure built in 1835 as a trading station by the Brazilian army. Its frontage, a rustic but very elegant series of shallow arches, played a significant role in modern Brazilian architecture. Niemeyer, who lived in Diamantina for a few months in the 1950s to build the *Hotel do Tijuco*, was fascinated by it, and later used the shape for the striking exterior of the presidential palace in Brasília, the Palácio da Alvorada.

The market itself (Sat only) has a very Northeastern feel, with its cheeses, *doces* made from sugar and fruit, blocks of salt and raw sugar, and mules and horses tied up alongside the pick-ups. The food at the stalls here is very cheap, but only for the strong-stomached: the rich *mineiro* sausages (*linguiça*) are especially worth trying. The rest of the week the market is used for exhibitions and book stalls. From the market you have a fine vantage point of a square that is,

Juscelino Kubitschek

Juscelino Kubitschek was born in Diamantina and spent the first seventeen years of his life in the town. His enduring monument is the capital city he built on the Planalto Central, Brasília, which fired Brazil's and the world's imagination and which now houses his remains (he was killed in a road accident in 1976). The house where he was born and his home, Casa de Juscelino, is preserved as a shrine to his memory (Tues–Fri 9am–5pm, Sat 9am–6pm, Sun 9am–1pm), on the steep Rua São Francisco, uphill from his statue at the bottom.

Juscelino had a meteoric political career. His energy, imagination and uncompromising liberal instincts make him one of the great postwar presidents. You can understand his lifelong concern with the poor from the small, unpretentious house where he spent the first part of his life in poverty. Restoration has rather flattered it, as the photos of how it was when he lived there make plain – no Brazilian president has yet to come from a humbler background. He was of the second generation of poor Czech immigrants: you won't find many family possessions because they didn't have any. The photos and the simplicity of the house are very moving, a refreshing contrast to the pampered corruption of many of his successors.

If you're interested, the Casa da Cultura in Praça Antônio Eulálio has a folder of photographs and clippings about Juscelino, relaxing with his *seresta* group – he was an accomplished guitarist – and being feted by the proud inhabitants of the town he clearly never left in spirit. Most of the bars still display photographs of him, many dating from before he became president in 1956. And many still don't believe his death was a genuine accident, just as few *mineiros* believe Tancredo really died of natural causes. The massive turnout for Juscelino's funeral in Brasília in 1976 was one of the first times Brazilians dared to show their detestation of the military regime.

if anything, even richer than the Praça Conselheiro Mota, a cornucopia of colonial window frames and balconies and exquisite ironwork. Most of the ground floors are still ordinary shops, open throughout the week.

The **artesanato** section of the market is small and uninspiring, which is unfortunate since the most distinctive products of the Jequitinhonha Valley are its beautiful clay and pottery figures. The Casa da Cultura, on Praça Antônio Eulálio, has a very fine collection that makes a good introduction to Jequitinhonha pottery, but buying it is difficult. The most reliable place is a friendly and very reasonably priced specialist shop, Relíquias do Vale, on the same street as the *Hotel do Tijuco*, at Rua Macau do Meio 401. Besides the pottery, they also have a good stock of the rough but very rugged cotton clothes, hammocks, rugs and wall hangings that are the other specialities of the region. You'll find numerous other carpet shops dotted around town.

Diamantina practicalities

Maps are free from the **tourist office**, tucked away behind the Largo do Rosário on Rua Farinha Seca (Mon–Fri 8am–6pm, Sat 9am–5pm, Sun 8am–noon; ☎38/3531-1636). There's also a **tourist post** in the *rodoviária* (daily 8–11am & 1–6pm), but it's often shut because of staff shortages. The receptions at the *Hotel do Tijuco* and the *Dália Hotel*, and the Museu do Diamante, also hand out maps.

Hotels are plentiful. The largest, priciest and most comfortable is the *Pousada do Garimpo*, a five-minute walk from the town centre at Av. da Saudade 265, on the western continuation of Rua Direita (☎38/3531-1044, Ⓦwww .pousadadogarimpo.com.br; ❸); the hotel is friendly and well equipped (with pool), but has a somewhat soulless feel to it. Much more interesting, and cheaper too, is the town's 1951 Niemeyer creation, the *Hotel do Tijuco*, Rua Macau do Meio 211 (☎ & Ⓕ038/3531-1022; ❸), where it's worth splashing out on one of the more expensive "luxo" rooms, which are larger and brighter and have balconies offering wonderful views across Diamantina. Just up from the cathedral, at Rua Macau de Baixo 104 is the *Pousada Relíquias do Tempo* (☎38/3531-1627, Ⓕ3531-6371; ❸), in a wonderfully converted nineteenth-century house filled with period furnishings and decorated with handicrafts from the Jequitinhonha valley. The *Dália Hotel*, Praça J Kubitschek 25 (☎38/3531-1477, Ⓕ3531-3526; ❷), just down from the cathedral, is possibly the best value in town. Housed in a lovely two-storey building, it has bags of character, good rooms and fine views over the square. Another good bet is the *Pousada dos Cristais*, Rua Jogo da Bola 53, west from Rua Direita (☎38/3531-2897; ❷), an appealing family-run place with comfortable, rustic rooms. If you want somewhere cheaper still in the old part of town, the *Pousada Gameleira*, Rua do Rosário 209 (☎38/3531-1900) is an attractive choice and charges around $7 per person; ask for a room facing the Igreja do Rosário. Other cheap options, with *quartos* upwards of $4 per person, are clustered around the *rodoviária* in the upper part of town, and are ideal if you can't face the prospect of lugging your luggage uphill when it's time to leave: *Hotel JK*, for example, immediately opposite the bus station at Praça Dom João 135 (☎38/3531-1142; ❶), is perfectly decent.

The streets around the cathedral are the heart of the town, and there's no shortage of simple bars and *mineiro* **restaurants** here, though the food on offer is rather uninspiring. Reasonable ones include the *Capistrana* on Praça Antônio Eulálio, and *Espeto de Prata* on Beco da Pena just off Rua Direita, a sophisticated *churrasco* joint with live music Thursdays to Sundays. Best of all is

Cantinha do Marinho on Rua Direita 113, in front of the cathedral: the food is good and offers the best value for money in town; try a *doce de limão* to round off your meal. There's a good **cake shop** opposite the Casa da Cultura on Praça Antônio Eulálio. The main focus of weekend **nightlife** activity is Rua Direita: the busiest bar is *Oasis Clube* at no. 132 (daily 8am–late), which has live music upstairs on Friday and Sunday evenings and a disco on Saturdays. Opposite, the tiny cellar bar *Taberna do Gilmar* (Wed–Sat 8pm onwards) has the town's loudest music system, playing a mixture of Brazilian and rock. Another place to try is the cavern-like *Bar do Japão* on Beco da Tecla, an alleyway near the *mercado*.

The Jequitinhonha Valley

If you want to get a clearer idea of where the Jequitinhonha *artesanato* comes from, you have to head out into the *sertão* proper, and Diamantina is the obvious place to start your journey. Travelling into the **Jequitinhonha Valley** is not something to be undertaken lightly: it is one of the poorest and remotest parts of Brazil, the roads are bad, there are no hotels except bare flophouse *dormitórios*, and unless you speak good Portuguese you are liable to be looked on with great suspicion. There have been problems in recent years with foreigners buying up mining concessions and kicking out *garimpeiros*, and unless you can explain yourself people will assume you have ulterior motives. The region is so poor and isolated it's difficult for people to understand why outsiders, especially foreigners, would want to go there anyway.

If you need reasons, though, you don't have to look much further than the **scenery**, which is spectacularly beautiful, albeit forbidding. The landscapes bear some resemblance to the deserts of the American Southwest: massive granite hills and escarpments, cactus, rock, occasional wiry trees and people tough as nails speaking with the lilting accent of the interior of the Northeast. Here you're a world away from the developed sophistication of southern and central Minas.

Araçuaí and beyond

It seems wrong to say somewhere as off the beaten track as **ARAÇUAÍ** is easy to get to, but it is the most accessible Jequitinhonha destination from Diamantina. Booking the day before is usually essential for one of the two daily buses (currently 2am and 1.30pm) to Araçuaí – and the journey is hard: over five hours of bouncing around on dusty dirt roads, hot as hell during the day and, in winter, cold at night. **Accommodation** is unlikely to present a problem: the cheapest option is the *dormitório* (☎33/3731-2184; ❶) by the bus station (but take a hammock to avoid having to sleep in one of their beds) or, for more comfort, head for the *Pousada das Araras* (☎33/3731-1707; ❷). Although gradually expanding, Araçuaí is still not much more than a large village, but it has the best place for buying **artesanato** in the whole region – a producers' co-operative called Centro de Artesanato, open Tuesday to Saturday, best to catch on a Wednesday, Friday or Saturday morning, when craft workers come in from the surrounding villages to market. Another attraction in town is aquamarine and, especially, **tourmaline** as the mines around Araçuaí are the sources of some of the best in Brazil. Unless, however, you really know your minerals you'd be foolish to make any purchases here, although you won't have any trouble tracking down dealers at the market.

From Araçuaí, if time were no object, you could hop local buses to **Itinga** and then on 30km to the good-quality BR-116 highway into **Bahia** state.

Once you get to Vitória da Conquista there are ready connections to all Bahian cities, but it could well take you a couple of days to get that far. It is often quicker to take the bus that leaves every other day to Belo Horizonte and make your connections there.

② South to Serro

South of Diamantina, the main point of interest is the sleepy colonial village of Serro, a two-hour bus ride away. From Diamantina, there are two ways of getting there: on the main, asphalt-covered, road or on the unpaved (but good quality) road. One daily bus runs along the latter, passing through rugged, wide-open spaces with an almost lunar appearance, stopping at **MILHO VERDE** on the way, a delightful hamlet in an oasis-like setting of palm trees and intensely green fields. Apart from a small, eighteenth-century church, a colonial-style chapel, and a few houses and bars, there's very little to the place, but Milho Verde's tranquility and its natural pools and waterfalls – good for bathing – make for an enjoyable break. If you're tempted to **stay over**, try the cosy *Pousada André Luiz* (☎038/3541-1071; ❶–❷) or the slightly larger *Rancho Velho* (☎038/3541-1062; ❶–❷), or look out for the signs up outside people's houses saying "*Aluga-se*".

Situated 90km south of Diamantina, **SERRO** is set in beautiful hill country, dominated by the eighteenth-century pilgrimage church of **Santa Rita** (Sat 3–7pm) on a rise above the centre, reached by steps cut into the slope. Little-visited, this is not so much a place to see and do things, as somewhere peaceful to unwind and appreciate the leisurely pace of life in rural Minas. There are six colonial churches, but most are closed to visitors and the rest open only for a few hours on either Saturday or Sunday: a spate of thefts has made the key-holders reluctant to let you in, even once you locate them. Founded in 1702, when gold was discovered in the stream nearby, Serro was at one time a rather aristocratic place. Across the valley, easily recognizable from the clump of palms, is the **Chácara do Barão do Serro** (Mon–Sat noon–5pm, Sun 9am–noon), which now houses the village's Centro Cultural. The old house is a fascinating example of a nineteenth-century *casa grande*, and you are free to wander through the main building and the former slaves' quarters outside.

Just along the road from here on Praça Cristiano Otoni, the **Museu Regional** (Tues–Sat noon–5.30pm, Sun 9am–noon) has a reasonable collection of period drawings and paintings, kitchen equipment and furniture. From the front of the museum you get a good view of the finest buildings in the village, namely the enormous **Casa do Barão de Diamantina**, clinging to the hillside, beautifully restored and now a school, and the twin Chinese towers of the **Igreja da Matriz de Nossa Senhora da Conceição** (Sun 8am–7.30pm). The church forms one end of a main street that is completely unspoilt; at the other end, up an extremely steep incline, at the historic centre's highest point, is the very pretty eighteenth-century Igreja de Santa Rita from where there are fine **views** across the village and towards the surrounding countryside.

The *Pousada Vila do Príncipe*, just down from the Igreja de Santa Rita on the main street, Rua Antônio Honório Pires, at no. 38 (☎38/3541-1485; ❷), is the best **place to stay**; rooms are small, but the views are fantastic. Also very central are the fairly basic *Pousada Serrano*, Travessa Magalhães 55 (☎38/3541-1949; ❷), as well as several cheap *pensões*. There are few places to eat: try simple *Restaurante Itacolomi* at Praça João Pinheiro 20, which has a good *por kilo* buffet of regional dishes at lunch and an à la carte menu in the evening. The *rodoviária* (☎ 38/3541-1366) is almost in the centre: ignore the attentions of the taxi drivers, walk uphill for some thirty metres, and you're in the heart of the village.

Southern Minas: The spa towns

The drive from Belo Horizonte **south to Rio** turns into one of the most spectacular in Brazil once you cross the state border and encounter the glorious scenery of the Serra dos Órgãos, but there is little to detain you in Minas along the way. The route passes Juiz de Fora, one of the larger interior cities, but it's an ugly industrial centre, best seen from the window of a bus.

The route **southwest towards São Paulo**, however, is altogether different. The hills, rising into mountains near the state border, make this one of the most attractive parts of Minas. Six or seven hours from Belo Horizonte, to the south of the main route, there's a cluster of **spa towns** – the Circuito das Águas, or "Circuit of the Waters", as the spa resorts of Cambuquira, São Lourenço, Caxambu and Lambari are collectively known. They are all small, quiet and popular with older people, who flock there to take the waters and baths. Each is centred on a *parque hidromineral*, a park built around the springs, incorporating bathhouses and fountains. Set in spectacular volcanic mountains to the north of the São Paulo road, the city of Poços de Caldas is also based around mineral springs, but is much livelier, a traditional place for couples to spend their honeymoons.

From Belo Horizonte to the Circuito das Águas

It's five hours from Belo Horizonte, or three from São João del Rei, before you hit the gateway to the Circuito das Águas. **TRÊS CORAÇÕES** is a good place for making onward bus connections, and although not a resort town itself it is more famous, in Brazil at least, than any of the spas. This rather anonymous modern town was the birthplace of Edson Arantes do Nascimento, **Pelé** – the greatest footballer ever – and it's a holy place for any lover of the game. Keep an eye out on the left as the bus winds its way through the centre, and you'll see a bronze statue of him, holding aloft the World Cup, which Brazil (and Pelé) won in 1958, 1962 and 1970. If you find yourself stuck here overnight while waiting for a bus, the *Cantina Calabresa* hotel, Rua Joaquim Bento de Carvalho 65 (☎ 35/3231-1183, ⊛ www.hotelcalabreza.com.br; ❸), has good rooms and a pool.

After Três Corações the hill country begins, although it's hardly got going before you run into the first and smallest of the spas, **CAMBUQUIRA**, a pleasant enough place but nothing to compare with the other resorts. If you do want to **stay**, a good cheap option, with its own pool, is *Pousada Passe Fique*, 1km out on the BR-267 Lambari road (☎35/3251-1587; ❷); more central and upmarket, with a sauna as well as a pool, is *Hotel Santos Dumont*, Av.Virgílio de Melo Franco 400 (☎35/3251-1466; ❹). The baths and massages in the Parque das Águas, the village's thermal baths, are open daily between 6am and 7pm.

Caxambu

Just beating São Lourenço for the title of nicest of the smaller spas, **CAXAMBU** was a favourite haunt of the Brazilian royal family in the nineteenth century. The **Parque das Águas** in the centre of town is delightful. Built in the last decades of the nineteenth century and the early years of the twentieth, it's dotted with eleven oriental-style pavilions sheltering the actual springs, and houses an ornate Turkish bathhouse that is very reasonably priced – $4 gets you a Turkish bath in turn-of-the-century opulence, and there are also various kinds of sauna ($3) and massage ($15) available. The bathhouse, which has separate facilities for men and women, is open Tuesday to Saturday 8.30am–noon and 3–5pm, and on Sunday 8.30am–noon.

Next to the park is a good **market**, specializing in honey and homemade syrupy sweets, which leads on to a tree-shaded square, **Praça Dom Pedro**, with yet another oriental pavilion. If you're tired of walking, there's a **chairlift**, which runs from opposite the bus station up to the Cristo Redentor that overlooks the centre. At the top there's a tremendous view, not only of the town and the park but also the lovely hill country in which it nestles. There's a restaurant, too, where the views are better than the food. The only drawback is that the chairlift closes down at 4.30pm, which means you can't appreciate what would be a very spectacular sunset.

Practicalities

The *rodoviária* (☎35/3341-3999), served by direct bus services from Belo Horizonte, Rio and São Paulo, is on the far western edge of town on Praça Castilho Moreira, but Caxambu is so small that it doesn't really matter. A **tourist information post** in the terminal building hands out free town maps, but again, you don't need them to find your way around. There's just one main street, Rua Wenceslau Braz, much of which is taken up by the Parque das Águas, and around which the town is built. Although walking is easy, it's fun to get one of the **horse-drawn cabs**, or *charretes*, that seem especially appropriate to Caxambu's turn-of-the-century surroundings.

For its size, Caxambu has a surprising range of **hotels**; their rates always include full board and drop by almost half out of season. The sumptuous *Grande Hotel*, Rua Dr Viotti 438 (☎35/3341-1099, ⓦwww.grandehotelltda .com.br; ❹), and the luxury-class *Hotel Glória*, opposite the park at Av. Camilo Soares 590 (☎35/3341-3000, ⓦwww.hotelgloriacaxambu.com.br; ❺), both have pools and saunas. The best middle-range place in town – especially out of season – is the *Palace Hotel*, Rua Dr Viotti 567 (☎35/3341-3341, ⓦwww.palacehotel.com.br; ❹). Built in 1894, it's crammed with antique furniture, and has a pool and sauna, a children's games room, a drawing room, a massive lounge and a ballroom. Cheaper options include the *Santa Cecília* on Rua Dr Enout 162 (☎35/3341-3511; ❷), which offers simple apartments with private kitchens, and the *Jardim Imperial* (☎35/3341-1163; ❷), in a quiet spot near the bus station on Rua Dr Viotti.

The only **restaurant** worth going out of your way for is the Danish *La Forelle*, 5km out of town on the BR-354 towards Itamonte (Fri 7pm–midnight, Sat noon–4pm & 8pm–midnight, Sun noon–4pm; reservations essential on ☎35/3343-1900); it's fairly expensive, but does an excellent line in Scandinavian-*mineiro* cooking (a legacy of a small wave of Danish immigrants who settled in the area in the 1920s as dairy farmers), and is especially good for trout and salmon. In town, *Sputinik* at Av. Camilo Soares 648, has a varied, but hardly exciting, *por kilo* buffet.

São Lourenço

If Caxambu is the last word in Edwardian elegance, **SÃO LOURENÇO** rivals it with its displays of Art Deco brilliance. Its Parque das Águas is studded with striking 1940s pavilions and has a stunning bathhouse – the Balneário – which looks more like a film set for a Hollywood high-society comedy. The most upmarket and modern-looking of the small spas, the town is popular with young and old alike.

São Lourenço is built along the shores of a beautiful lake, a large chunk of which has been incorporated into the **Parque das Aguas** (daily 8am–5.20pm; the pavilions with the mineral water fountains are closed 11.30am–2pm), and during the day it's where everything happens. Much larger than the one in Caxambu, and much more modern, the park is kept to the same immaculate standard: again, a lovely place for a stroll, with its brilliant white pavilions, forested hillside, clouds of butterflies and birds – though steer clear of the black swans on the lake, which have a nasty temper. There are **rowing boats** for rent, and an artificial island in the middle of the lake.

The **Balneário** itself offers baths (*duchas*; $2), saunas ($3) and massages ($9), and it's worth paying for the elegant surroundings: marbled floors, mirror walls and white-coated attendants. There are separate sections for men and women.

Practicalities

The **tourist information kiosk** is on Praça Duque de Caixas in front of the *parque* (daily 8.30–noon & 2–6pm; ☎35/3349-8459), and has free town maps. The **rodoviária** (☎35/3332-5966) served by Belo Horizonte, Rio and São Paulo buses, is just off the main street, Avenida Dom Pedro II, which is lined with bars, hotels and restaurants. There is a very large **youth hostel** at no. 468, the *Albuergue da Juventude Recanto dos Caravalhos* (☎35/3799-4000; $6 per person), and a good low-price **hotel**, the *Hotel Aliança* (☎ & ⓕ035/3332-4300; ❷, full board ❸) at no. 505. Cheaper, but very decent, is the *Pousada Normandy*, Rua Batista Luzardo 164 (☎35/3332-2944; ❷), just 200m from the Parque das Aguas, or try the *Santa Rita* at Av. Getúlio Vargas 31 (☎35/3332-2522; ❸), with basic but clean rooms. For a splurge, the *Hotel Brasil*, Alameda João Lage 87 (☎35/3332-1313, ⓦwww.hotelbrasil.com.br; ❺–❻), which dominates the Praça Duque de Caixas, is luxury-class and has the works, including four pools and water-slides. Finally, just outside town, set in lovely park-like grounds, is the *Fazenda Emboaba* on Rua Jorge Amado 350 (☎35/3332-4600, ⓦwww.emboabashotel.com.br; ❺), with spacious rooms, wonderful views, a pool, sauna and horse-riding facilities.

Buses to Lambari, next town on the circuit, take about ninety minutes. Buses to Caxambu leave at 7am, 10am, 2pm, 3.50pm and 6pm, or take a taxi from the post in front of the *parque*. There's no direct bus to Poços de Caldas; you need to get the 11.45am to Pouso Alegre and make a connection there – total journey time is around six hours. Bus timetables do change frequently, so it's best to check departure times in advance with the *rodoviária*.

Lambari

LAMBARI is the nearest you get to a downmarket spa town on the Circuito das Águas, though you wouldn't guess it from the prices of its main hotels. It has a beautiful lake and the obligatory spa park, but lacks the prosperous feel of Caxambu and São Lourenço. The **rodoviária** is on Avenida Dr José Nicolau Mileo, within easy walking distance of the main square, Praça Conselheiro João Lisboa. Housed in the square, the **Parque das Águas** is small and scruffy, but has six fountains each with different types of water, as well as a fizzy *carbogasosa* pool.

There are several budget **hotels** near the *rodoviária*, while mid-range options (all with pools and rates that include full board) can be found either on or near the main square. Of these, the *Hotel Ideal*, at Rua Afonso Vilhena Paiva 245 (☎35/3271-1143, ⓕ3271-1650; ❷), is probably the best value, basic but comfortable. The *Hotel Itaici* (☎ & ⓕ035/3271-1366; ❷) at Rua Dr José dos Santos 320 is of a similar standard. The town's best hotel, the *Hotel Parque*, Rua Américo Werneck 46 (☎35/3271-2000; ❺ full board), with its own lake, thermal pools, fishing and other sports facilities, is appealing and excellent value for money.

Poços de Caldas

POÇOS DE CALDAS is the easiest of the Minas spa resorts to get to. Rich Brazilians from the large cities of Southeast Brazil like to take breaks here, and there are daily bus services to and from Rio and São Paulo as well as Belo Horizonte. It's some distance from the smaller spa towns, and is an altogether different place; with a population of over 130,000, Poços de Caldas is definitely a city rather than a town, and is quite the most animated spot in Minas after Belo Horizonte.

If possible, you should make the journey in daylight, because the countryside is something special and shouldn't be missed. After the ugly modern town of Pouso Alegre comes one of the more spectacular climbs into mountains that Brazil has to offer, with superb views of slopes clad in a mixture of pine and eucalyptus, and plains laid out like sheets behind and beneath the road. It is easy to see why the whole region became a resort area.

The city itself, almost on the state line with São Paulo, nestles in the bowl of an extinct volcano – you can trace the rim of what must once have been an enormous crater along the broken horizons. The centre is mostly modern, laid out in a grid pattern with a few skyscrapers, but made very attractive by huge tree-studded squares, an enormous but elegant bathhouse and the closeness of the thickly forested slopes of Alto da Serra, the hill crowned with the obligatory Cristo Redentor overlooking the city.

The City

If first impressions counted on arrival, you'd probably take one look at the dirty and decrepit **rodoviária** and catch the next bus out: its sole redeeming feature is that it is very central, a short distance from the huge central square, **Praça Pedro Sanchez**, easily recognizable by the large Edwardian-style bathhouse set amid gardens and fountains. Everything goes on around the square and in the blocks to the east of it, and the grid pattern makes it easy to get your bearings.

Unlike Caxambu and São Lourenço, Poços de Caldas doesn't have a single mineral-water park that encompasses all the springs; they are scattered all over the city and somehow don't seem as impressive when not set in a garden. The nearest, within easy walking distance of the centre, is **Fonte Frayha**, on the corner of Rua Amazônas and Rua Pernambuco, but you can take the same waters in style in the opulent bathhouse, the **Termas Antônio Carlos** (Mon–Sat 8–11.30am & 4–7.30pm, Sun 8–11.30am), whose Edwardian bulk looms over the main square. It's less personal than the *balneários* in the smaller resorts, but the increase in scale makes a Turkish bath in such splendid surroundings an experience.

On one side of the *praça*, not far from the bathhouse on Avenida Francisco Salles, is a **cable car** station (July & Dec–Feb daily 8am–6pm; rest of the year Mon & Wed–Fri 2–6pm, Sat & Sun 8am–6pm; $2 return), from where you're whisked up to the **Alto da Serra** and the Christ statue overlooking the city, at 1678m above sea level. It's a must: the views at the top are tremendous, there's the usual restaurant with panoramic views, and it's the starting point for an exceptionally scenic walk back down.

Although hardly a cultural hot spot, the city has an excellent **Casa da Cultura** (Tues–Fri 1–7pm, Sat & Sun 1–6pm), really a branch of Unibanco's remarkable Instituto Moreira Salles. The wooden building (one of Poços de Caldas's first houses) itself is quite wonderful, constructed in a tropical high Victorian style in 1894, but the exhibitions of historic photographs and art from Unibanco's extensive collection are usually first rate. The Casa da Cultura is at Rua Teresópolis 90, in the suburb of Jardim dos Estados, which can easily be reached by foot from the centre or on the bus marked "Santa Rosália".

Practicalities

The **Secretaria de Turismo** is located in the Palace Casino on Parque José Afonso Junqueira (Mon–Sat 8am–noon & 1.30–6pm, Sun 8am–noon; ☏35/3722-1551); they have a good free map of the town and provide information on special events.

Accommodation will be the least of your worries. The entire city is geared to catering for visitors and even during holiday periods, when people flock from as far afield as Rio and São Paulo, capacity is rarely stretched and prices are generally very keen. Many of the pricier hotels are scattered some way out of town in their own gardens or estates: the recently opened *Monreale Hotel Resort*, Av. Leonor Furlaneto Delgado 3033, 7km out on the Belo Horizonte road (☏35/3712-7777, ⓦwww.monreale.com.br; ❺ half board), is rather typical, offering splendid views, a pool and sauna and horse riding, but little in the way of character. The most luxurious hotel in the town itself is the *Palace*, at Praça Sanches (☏35/3722-3636; ❺ half board), opened in 1922 and very much in the European "grand hotel" tradition. Slightly more modest, but similarly old-fashioned is the *Minas Gerais*, Rua Pernambuco 615 (☏35/3722-1686; ❹ half board) – superb value, with two pools, a sauna and a playground. There are plenty of modern and centrally located budget places too: *Príncipe*, Rua Dr Francisco Faria Lobato 84 (☏35/3722-1740, ⓦwww .principehotelpocos.com.br; ❸ full board), which also has a pool and, very similar in style and facilities, the *Imperador*, Av Francisco Salles 273 (☏35/3722-2166; ❸ full board). For even cheaper places, try the hotels on Rua São Paulo: the *Guaranyat* at no. 106 is reasonable (☏35/3722-2585; ❷).

As you would expect in a place so popular with young couples, the **nightlife** here is very lively, especially at weekends. Busiest of all is the stretch of **Rua São Paulo** leading down to the square. There is a very good upstairs **bar** here, *Verde Amarelo*, which has high-quality live Brazilian music for free on Friday and Saturday nights; and possibly the best **juice bar** in Minas Gerais, *Casa de Sucos*, on the corner of São Paulo and Assis Figueiredo. It has an amazing variety of freshly made *sucos* and an excellent range of sandwiches and desserts. By and large, **restaurants** are unexciting, because most visitors eat at their hotels. However, *L'Itália* at Av. Francisco Salles 86 (daily to 8.30pm), offers a good Italian-based lunch *por kilo* buffet and excellent *café colonial* (high tea), while if you're in the mood for meat try the *Pampa* (closed all Mon and Sun evening), a *churrascaria* located a couple of kilometers from the centre of town in the suburb of Santana at Av. José Remígio Prézi 683.

Eastern Minas

Eastern Minas Gerais is the least-visited part of the state and, travelling along the BR-262 highway leading to Espírito Santo state and the Atlantic, it seems very clear why. Although the *mineiro* hill country is pretty enough, the towns scattered along it are ugly industrial centres, steel mills belching fumes common even in the gaps between the towns. However, if you persevere right to the border with Espírito Santo, you enter an unrivalled part of Minas, where lush hills are covered with coffee bushes in terraced rows, like contour lines on a map. These hills gradually give way to the craggy, spectacular mountains of the **Parque Nacional do Caparaó** and the highest peak in southern Brazil, the **Pico da Bandeira**. The best time to go is from June to August as at other times of year the mists and rain make it difficult to see the marvellous scenery.

Towards Caparaó

Getting to the Parque Nacional do Caparaó can be complicated, and the fact that Caparaó is the name of both the national park and a village just outside it – which itself is next to another village called Alto do Caparaó – makes things more confusing. You need to head for Alto do Caparaó to get to the park; you can make the journey from either Belo Horizonte or Vitória, the capital of Espírito Santo – Vitória is considerably nearer – but there are no direct buses and you can bank on spending most of the day to get there, and possibly longer, wherever you start from.

Initially, you should head towards the two towns in the vicinity. **Manhuaçu** is served by three daily direct buses from both Belo Horizonte and Vitória, and a midday service from the *rodoviária* outside Ouro Preto, which calls at Mariana. The town is also a stopping point for the Belo Horizonte–Vitória express buses. From Manhuaçu, local services run the 20km to **Manhumirim**, much closer to the park and a far nicer place to spend the night if necessary. There are also two direct buses a day to Manhumirim from Belo Horizonte (at 7am and 10pm), the first going via Ouro Preto (8.45am) and Mariana (9.15am), and two from Vitória (at 9.30am and 3.30pm). Journey time from either city is about five hours; the afternoon bus from Vitória is the one to Carangola. Wherever you start from you'll need to book your **ticket** the day before if possible, as these routes fill up quickly, especially on Friday and Sunday.

Once you get to **MANHUMIRIM**, your next destination will be Alto do Caparaó, 25km further on. It's an exceptionally scenic ride, so it's worth staying the night if you arrive after dark. Manhumirim is, in any case, a pleasant place, a very typical interior town where foreigners rarely appear and the people are curious and friendly. The bars in the centre get surprisingly lively on weekend evenings, and the best (though still basic) **hotel** is the *São Luis* (☎33/3341-1178; ❷), a short taxi ride from the *rodoviária*.

The easiest way to reach Alto do Caparaó is by **taxi**, which costs about $8. There are three direct local **buses** a day, too, leaving from the *rodoviária* at around 9.30am, 2pm and 4.30pm and taking about ninety minutes – check the exact times when you arrive, as they change frequently.

Alto do Caparaó

ALTO DO CAPARAÓ is a small village that lines the sloping asphalted road: wait until the bus makes its final stop at the village's Praça da Matriz before getting off. There are only a few **hotels** in the village itself, but two are unusually good value for money, namely the basic *Pousada Vale Verde* at the Praça da Matriz (☎31/3747-2529; meal and packed lunch provided; ❶), and, on the same *praça*, the excellent *Pousada Serra Azul* (☎31/3747-2674; ❶). Two other hotels lie up the winding signposted road, Rua Vale Verde, that leads from the bus stop. The *Caparaó Parque Hotel* (☎31/3747-2559; ❹ half board) is 1km along, a beautiful place with stunning mountain views out back, good food and friendly staff. The national park entrance is only a short walk on from the hotel. On the same road, and considerably cheaper, is *Pousada da Bezerra* (☎31/3747-2628; ❸), which, like the *Caparaó Parque Hotel*, has a pool and a sauna – bliss after a long day's walk. Alternative accommodation for serious hikers is camping in the park, where there are two official campsites that you can use as a base for walking (see p.222).

Opposite the *Caparaó Parque Hotel* you can **hire horses** ($6 for a daytime ride, $8 in the evening) if you feel like exploring the park in a saddle rather than on foot. Here too you'll find a simple, but welcoming, unnamed **bar** in a rustic wooden house with fantastic views back down the valley – a wonderful place from which to watch the sunsets.

Leaving Alto do Caparaó

There are three **buses** a day from Alto do Caparaó to Manhumirim, at 5.30am, 1pm and 6pm, taking about ninety minutes. Otherwise, there are always jeeps outside the entrance of the *Caparaó Parque Hotel* that will take you to Manhumirim for $10 (you can book them in advance from Transtur Turismo on ☎31/3747-2537). Direct buses from Manhumirim to Belo Horizonte leave at 11am and 10pm – there are four others during the day, but they arrive from other starting points and you may not be able to get a seat.

Parque Nacional do Caparaó

The official **park entrance** (daily 7am–10pm; $1), 4km from Alto do Caparaó, is the only way to get into the park. Here you will be handed a useful brochure, also given out free at the reception of the *Caparaó Parque Hotel*, which has a very clear **map** on the back – you'll need it, as the park is huge, 250 square kilometres of some of the most spectacular scenery in Brazil. The park covers two **ecological zones**. The lower half is extremely beautiful: thickly forested valleys, hills and streams giving way, as the hills lead into mountains proper, to treeless alpine uplands strewn with wild flowers, heather and rock formations. The major **trails** are marked on the map and are just about passable by jeep; there is an (unmapped) maze of smaller trails off these, which you can only explore on foot or horseback.

There are two official **campsites** along the trail to the Pico da Bandeira summit, each with piped spring water, a basic shelter and toilets. You need your own equipment and you'll have to **reserve a place** at least a week in advance with the park's office (☎32/3747-2555; only Portuguese spoken). You won't be allowed to camp inside the park unless you've reserved a place in advance.

Some twenty minutes into the park, the **main trail** forks: left to the mountains (see below), and right to **Vale Verde**, an enchanting forested valley where a stream forms a series of small waterfalls and shallow pools. A picnic site here is a good base for exploring several trails leading off into the forest. If you carefully pick your way downstream, after about 100m you come to a natural viewing platform looking back down Caparaó valley, framed by forest trees – a wonderfully peaceful spot.

Pico da Bandeira

Despite being 2890m high, the **Pico da Bandeira** is not difficult to climb and the four-hour (return) hike takes you through some truly spectacular scenery. The winter dry season (June to Aug) is the best time to visit for the clarity of the sky and the views, and the trail is easily walked; in the summer months (Sept to April), you can find relief from the often intense heat by taking refreshing showers beneath the park's many waterfalls. In the winter you will need a thick sweater or jacket to guard against the wind and at all times you'll need sun block, a packed lunch, a water bottle, and a good pair of walking or training shoes – the climb isn't steep enough for boots to be necessary. Be careful, too, not to be caught out after dark. Although well marked, the path is treacherous in places, and you shouldn't attempt it once the light has gone. Let the rangers at the park entrance know you are going and roughly when you expect to return.

To Tronqueira

The first **campsite** on the route to the summit is called **Tronqueira** and is 8km from the park entrance – uphill all the way, a hike that takes about three hours, or two if you're a seasoned walker. You're rewarded by stunning views, as the road winds its way out of forest into the alpine zone, with panoramic views of the Caparaó valley below. The trail culminates at *Tronqueira* itself, where a viewing platform has been built to allow you to appreciate one of the finest views in the country, as the hills far below recede to the jagged horizon. Just before you get to *Tronqueira*, a fork to the left takes you to **Cachoeira Bonita**, where the José Pedro stream, which forms the state border between Minas Gerais and Espírito Santo, plunges eighty metres down a rockface into a thickly wooded gorge; another viewing platform allows full appreciation of the spectacle.

The lazy way to do the Pico, but the only method that allows you to get back to Caparaó the same day if you're not accustomed to long hikes, is to cover the section to *Tronqueira* **by jeep**. There are usually jeeps hanging around the entrance of the *Caparaó Parque Hotel*; if not, the reception will ring for you even if you're not a guest. You need to arrange the jeep the day before, as you have to set out by 8am at the latest to be back the same day. The jeep leaves you at *Tronqueira*, taking about thirty minutes to get there, and returns at 4pm to pick you up – return fare is around $8. If you're staying at the hotel, let them know the day before and they'll prepare a packed lunch.

The hike to the summit
The path up the mountain from *Tronqueira* starts at the opposite end of the campsite from the viewing platform. The return trip to the summit from here is almost 20km, about six hours' walking time for most people, with another couple of hours for rests and lunch along the way. The very first stretch up from *Tronqueira* is extremely steep, but don't be discouraged: it soon flattens out into a pleasant stroll along a mountain valley, with the path hugging a crystalline mountain stream that forms swimmable pools at a couple of points. There is evidence of a forgotten episode in modern Brazilian history along the way, in the shape of bits of a military transport plane that crashed here in 1965. After the 1964 coup a group of left-wing militants took to these hills hoping to foment a Cuban-style popular rebellion, but were either hunted down or driven away – the plane that crashed was supplying the army patrols combing the area.

Halfway to the summit you come to **Terreirão**, the second official **campsite** and a good spot for lunch. A path to the right leads to a point overlooking a valley dominated by two mountains, the rocky crags of **Pico do Calçado** to the left, and **Pico do Cristal** to the right, both only a hundred metres shorter than Pico da Bandeira, and with trails leading up them if you felt so inclined – though only to be attempted if you are camping at *Terreirão*, or you will find yourself still on the mountain at nightfall. Fill your water bottle at *Terreirão*, as there is no drinking water between here and the summit. The path up to Pico da Bandeira continues from the opposite end of the campsite. After the first stretch it hits rocky, treeless moorland where the exact path is sometimes difficult to see, especially when cloud closes in, but there are painted arrows to help you get your bearings.

The only really steep part of the climb is right at the end, when you need to scramble up a rocky path to get to the **summit** itself. The arrows disappear, but by now you can get a bearing on the tower that marks the peak. Once there, on a clear day you are rewarded with an absolutely superb 360-degree panorama of the mountains and hills of Espírito Santo and Minas Gerais.

Espírito Santo

Espírito Santo, a compact combination of mountains and beaches, is one of the smallest states in Brazil (with a population of only 2.6 million), but as Minas Gerais' main outlet to the sea it is strategically very important. More iron ore is exported through its capital, **Vitória**, than any other port in the world. Not surprisingly the preponderance of docks, rail yards and smelters limits the city's tourist potential, despite a fine natural location. To a *mineiro*, Espírito Santo means only one thing: **beaches**. During weekends and holiday seasons, people flock to take the waters, tending to concentrate on the stretch immediately south of Vitória, especially the large resort town of **Guarapari**. The best beaches, however, lie on the strip of coastline 50km south of Guarapari, and in the north of state, heading towards Bahia.

The hinterland of Vitória, far less visited, is exceptionally beautiful, a spectacular mix of lush forest, river valleys, mountains and granite hills. It's here that the state's real pleasures lie. The soils of this central belt are fertile, and since the latter part of the nineteenth century the area has been colonized by successive waves of Italians, Poles and Germans. Their descendants live in hillside homesteads and in a number of small, very attractive country towns that combine a European look and feel with a thoroughly tropical landscape. All are easy to get to from Vitória, not more than a couple of hours over good roads, linked by frequent buses. Around the towns, the lack of mineral deposits and the sheer logistical difficulties in penetrating such a hilly area have preserved huge chunks of **Mata Atlântica**, the lush semi-deciduous forest that once covered all the coastal parts of southern Brazil. Credit should also go to the local Indians, notably the Botocudo, whose dedicated resistance pinned the Portuguese down throughout the colonial period.

Vitória

As a city, **VITÓRIA** is vaguely reminiscent of Rio, its backdrop a combination of sea, steep hills, granite outcrops and irregularly shaped mountains on the horizon. Founded in 1551, it's one of the oldest cities in Brazil, but few traces of its past remain and nowadays most of the centre is urban sprawl. Vitória is not a tourist town, and few people visit it unless they have a very definite reason. The heart of Vitória is an island connected to the mainland by a series of bridges, but the city has long since broken its natural bounds, spreading onto the mainland north and south: the major beach areas are on these mainland zones, **Canto** and **Camburi** to the north and **Vila Velha** with its beach **Praia da Costa** to the south. Vitória is renowned as the world capital of marlin fishing. It also has the unfortunate distinction of having the highest murder rate in Brazil and, although violence is unlikely to affect the casual visitor, appropriate care should be taken.

Arrival and information

The enormous, modern *rodoviária* (☎27/3222-3366) is only a kilometre from the centre and, outside, all **local buses** from the stop across the road run into town; returning from the centre, most buses from Avenida Jerônimo Monteiro pass the *rodoviária* and will have it marked as a destination on their route cards. If you're heading straight for the **beaches** on arrival, any bus that says "Aeroporto", "UFES", "Eurico Sales" or "Via Camburi" will take you to Camburi; to the southern beaches you need "P. da Costa", "Vila Velha" or "Itapoan" – all can be caught at the stops outside the *rodoviária* or in the centre. As an alternative to the buses, **taxis** are quite cheap and a good option in this small city, where the distances are relatively short.

Trains from Belo Horizonte pull into the Estação Ferroviária Pedro Nolasco (☎27/3226-4169), 1km west of the *rodoviária*, over in the mainland district of Cariacica; it's connected to the city and *rodoviária* by yellow buses marked "Terminal Itacibá" and by most of the city's orange buses, including those marked "Jardim América" and "Campo Grande".

The **airport** (Aeroporto Eurico Sales; ☎27/3327-6300) is situated a couple of kilometres from Camburi beach, some 10km from the city centre, and is

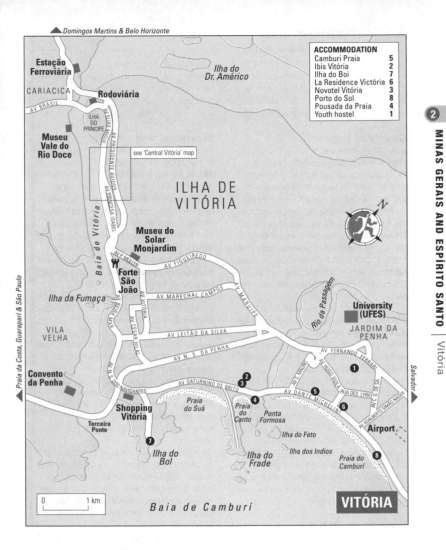

ACCOMMODATION

Camburi Praia	5
Ibis Vitória	2
Ilha do Boi	7
La Residence Victória	6
Novotel Vitória	3
Porto do Sol	8
Pousada da Praia	4
Youth hostel	1

Estação Ferroviária

CARIACICA Rodoviária

AV. BRASIL

ILHA DO PRINCIPE

Museu Vale do Rio Doce

see 'Central Vitória' map

Ilha do Dr. Américo

ILHA DE VITÓRIA

AV. PRESIDENTE AVIDOS

AV. ELIAS MIGUEL

AV. PRINCESA ISABEL

Museu do Solar Monjardim

AV. P. MÜLLER

AV. FIGUEIREDO

Baía de Vitória

Forte São João

Ilha da Fumaça

AV. BEIRA MAR

AV. VITÓRIA

AV. CESAR HILAL

AV. MARECHAL CAMPOS

AV. MARILIJE

Rio da Passagem

University (UFES)

JARDIM DA PENHA

AV. LEITÃO DA SILVA

AV. N. S. DA PENHA

AV. FERNANDO FERRARI

❶

VILA VELHA

Praia da Costa, Guarapari & São Paulo

AV. N. S. DOS NAVEGANTES

Convento da Penha

AV. SATURNINO DE BRITO

❷
❸

AV. DANTE MICHELINI

AV. S. XAVIER

AV. HUGO VILLA VERDE

RUA DES. LYRIO J.B.G.SA

AV. ADALBERTO SIMÃO NADER

❺

❻

AV. ALBERTO J.B.G.SA

Salvador

Terceira Ponte

Shopping Vitória

❼

Praia do Suá

Praia do Canto

❹

Ponta Formosa

Ilha do Fato

Airport

Ilha do Bol

Ilha do Frade

Ilha dos Indios

Praia do Camburi

❽

Baía de Camburí

0 1 km

VITÓRIA

served by frequent green buses, which can drop you on Avenida Beira Mar, its westward continuation, Avenida Getúlio Vargas, or at the *rodoviária*.

There are very helpful **tourist information** booths at the *rodoviária* (Mon–Fri 8am–9pm, Sat 9am–4pm) and at the airport (daily 8am–noon & 1–9pm; ☏27/3327-8855), both of which have lists of hotels, brochures and city maps. The central office of the state tourist company, CETUR, is at Av. Princesa Isabel 54, 4th floor (Mon–Fri 8am–6pm; ☏27/322-8888). Listings for cinema, theatre, music and art exhibitions can be found in *A Gazeta*, the main local daily newspaper.

Accommodation

The choice for **accommodation** is between the generally up-market establishments in the beach suburbs and the hotels in the centre, which are less expensive. For really **cheap** places, the row of rather grim hotels facing the main entrance of the *rodoviária* is your best bet. There's also a **youth hostel** (ⓣ27/3325-6010; $7 per person) at Av. Hugo Viola 135, Jardim da Penha, between Praia do Camburí and the campus of the federal university (UFES).

Central hotels

Alice Vitória Praça Getúlio Vargas 5 ⓣ27/3322-1144, ⓦwww.gruponeffa.com.br. This large, 1970s hotel was once considered to be the best place to stay in Vitória, but little evidence of its past elegance remains. Nevertheless, the rooms are perfectly comfortable, but the air-conditioning and *frigobars* mini-bars are noisy. There's a pool and reasonable *por kilo* restaurant, too. ❸

Avenida Av. Presidente Florentino Avidos 347 ⓣ & ⓕ027/3223-4317. A cheap central place, with a number of reasonable rooms, some with air-conditioning, TVs and *frigobar*. Single *quartos* are a particularly good deal at $7. ❷

Cannes Palace Av. Jerônimo Monteiro 111 ⓣ27/3222-1522, ⓕ222-8061. This large tower block has dowdy, but neatly kept, rooms, all equipped with aging TV and *frigobars*. Ask for a room on one of the upper floors, which at least have the benefit of views. ❷

Prata Rua Nestor Gomes 201 ⓣ27/3222-4311, ⓕ3223-0943. A reasonable budget option in the centre where the basic rooms come with high ceilings and either fans or air-conditioning. The better rooms face the pleasant Praça Climaco and the Palácio de Anchieta. ❷

Spala Av. Alexandre Buaiz 495 ⓣ27/3222-5648. The best of the budget hotels facing the *rodoviária*, with a range of spartan but tidy rooms, some with TVs. The best are at the front, while the $5 *quartos* are windowless and dingy. ❶

Beach hotels

Camburi Praia Av. Dante Michelini 1007 ⓣ27/3325-0455, ⓕ3225-7451. A reasonable medium-size hotel, with sauna and pool, and apartments facing Camburi beach. ❹

Ibis Vitória Rua João da Cruz 385, Praia do Canto ⓣ27/3345-8600, ⓦwww.accorhotels.com.br. An excellent budget hotel a couple of blocks from the local beach, as well as bars and restaurants. The

air-conditioned rooms are small but comfortable; the service efficient. The hotel is extremely popular – reservations are advised. ❸

Ilha do Boi Rua Bráulio Macedo 417, Ilha do Boi ⓣ27/3345-0111, ⓕ3345-0115. Certainly the most unexpected place to stay in Vitória, a relatively small hotel set amidst the secluded, very upscale, residential Ilha do Boi. The rooms have seen better days, but they're very comfortable and offer excellent sea or coastal views, while good facilities include a pool and a sauna. Popular with small conferences and parties, the place is often either totally full or nearly empty. ❹

La Residence Victória Av. Dante Michelini 1777, Praia de Camburí ⓣ27/3397-1300, ⓕ3397-1302. Well equipped one-bedroom beachside apartments (with kitchen) in a smart building with pool. ❹

Novotel Vitória Av. Saturnino de Brito 1327, Praia do Canto ⓣ27/3334-5300, ⓦwww.accor.com.br. Vitória's newest hotel and the one with the most extensive range of business and leisure facilities, including an excellent pool. The spacious and comfortable rooms are keenly priced and reservations highly advised. ❹

Porto do Sol Av. Dante Michelini 3957, Praia de Camburi ⓣ27/3337-2244, ⓔportodosol@vitoria.com.br. At the farthest end of the beach and convenient for the airport, this Best Western–linked property is Vitória's largest and one of its most expensive hotels. Rooms are large and well appointed, and facilities include two pools, tennis courts and a choice of restaurants. ❺

Pousada da Praia Av. Saturnino de Brito 1500 ⓣ & ⓕ027/3225-0233. A secluded, slightly dowdy *pousada* with a pool, attractive gardens and just eighteen rooms that sleep from one to five people. Offering personalised attention, the place is an ideal alternative to the large hotels that dominate the beach areas. Situated by the Ponta Formosa, overlooking the Praia do Canto. ❸

The City

Vitória is built into a steep hillside overlooking the **docks** alongside the narrow Baía de Vitória, but the main streets are all at shore level. The name of the street that hugs the shore changes as you go eastwards from the *rodoviária*; initially called Avenida Elias Miguel, then Avenida Getúlio Vargas, Avenida Mal. de Moraes and finally Avenida Beira Mar, the whole stretch is generally known to locals as **Avenida Beira Mar**. From along here, you can catch buses to the beach districts; the yellow TRANSCOL bus #500 goes over the massive **Terceira Ponte** (third bridge) to the southern district of town, **Vila Velha**, handy for the **Praia da Costa** and site of the **Convento da Penha**, with its spectacular views over the city. From the bridge itself you can also get a good idea of Vitória's layout.

From **Avenida Jerônimo Monteiro**, the main downtown shopping street, a number of stairways (*escadarias*) lead to the Cidade Alta (the upper city), the location of the colonial Palácio de Anchieta, now the state governor's palace. Just down from here the pleasant, tree-shaded **Praça Costa Pereira** is the heart of the downtown area.

At the western end of Avenida Beira Mar is the city's oldest inhabited quarter, the **Ilha do Príncipe**, a labyrinth of narrow paths and blind alleys. It occupies a small but very steep hill behind the *rodoviária*, and although no trace remains of the original dwellings the atmosphere is of a bygone age, with houses constructed one on top of another, many of them propped up on stilts, complete with the stench of broken sewers and mounds of garbage. Tourists seldom venture here, but it's well worth an hour's ramble for an alternative insight into daily Vitórian life, and harbours a few local bars should you wish to hang out a while longer. But do take care, avoid the area at night, and leave valuables in your hotel.

The centre

One of the few truly historic buildings in the centre of Vitória is the fine palace of the state governor, the **Palácio de Anchieta**, which dates from the 1650s but is almost entirely closed to visitors. The one part you can see – the **tomb of Padre Anchieta**, accessible by a side entrance (Mon–Sat noon–5pm) – is something of a curiosity. Anchieta was the first of a series of great Jesuit missionaries to Brazil, and is most famous for being one of the two founders of São Paulo, building the rough chapel the town formed around in the sixteenth century and giving his name to one of that city's main avenues, the Via Anchieta. He was a stout defender of the rights of Indians, doing all he could to protect them from the ravages of the Portuguese and pleading their case several times to the Portuguese Crown; he was also the first to produce a grammar and dictionary of the Tupi language. Driven out of São Paulo by enraged Portuguese settlers, he retired to Vitória, died in 1597 and was finally canonized. The tomb is simple, set off by a small exhibition devoted to his life.

From the *palácio*, it's a short walk along winding roads to the sixteenth-century **Capela de Santa Luzia** (Mon–Fri 9am–6pm) on Rua José Marcelino, the first building to be erected in Vitória. The simple whitewashed chapel, with its attractive Baroque altar, would not be out of place in a Portuguese village, a vivid reminder that the coast of Espírito Santo was one of the first parts of Brazil settled by Europeans. A block east of the chapel – and on an altogether different scale – is the large and unremarkable early twentieth-century neo-Gothic **Catedral Metropolitana** (Mon–Fri 7–11am & 5–8pm, Sat 8–11am & 5–8pm, Sun 7–9am & 5–8.30pm). From there walk along Rua Erothildes Rosendo to the shaded Praça Costa Pereira, a busy pedestrian intersection and always bustling with activity. There are a number of distinguished-looking buildings surrounding the *praça*, the most notable being the **Teatro Carlos Gomes**, a replica of La Scala in Milan, built between 1925 and 1927. Astride

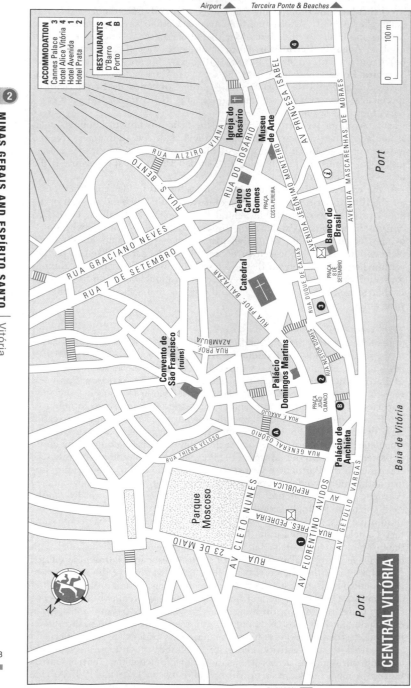

Airport ▲   Terceira Ponte & Beaches ▲

ACCOMMODATION
Cannes Palace 3
Hotel Alice Vitória 4
Hotel Avenida 1
Hotel Prata 2

RESTAURANTS
D'Barro A
Porto B

0   100 m

Igreja do Rosário

Museu de Arte

RUA ALZIRO VIANA

RUA DO ROSÁRIO

RUA S. BENTO

Teatro Carlos Gomes

PRAÇA COSTA PEREIRA

AV PRINCESA ISABEL

AVENIDA JERÔNIMO MONTEIRO

AVENIDA MASCARENHAS DE MORAES

Port

RUA GRACIANO NEVES

RUA 7 DE SETEMBRO

Banco do Brasil

RUA DUQUE DE CAXIAS

PRAÇA 8 DE SETEMBRO

Catedral

RUA PROF. BALTAZAR

RUA PROF. AZAMBUJA

RUA NESTOR GOMES

Convento de São Francisco (ruins)

Palácio Domingos Martins

PRAÇA JOÃO CLÍMACO

RUA F. ARAÚJO

RUA GENERAL OSÓRIO

Palácio de Anchieta

RUA THIERS VELOSO

AV REPÚBLICA

RUA FLORENTINO AVIDOS

AV GETÚLIO VARGAS

Baía de Vitória

Parque Moscoso

RUA PRES. PEDREIRA

RUA CLETO NUNES

23 DE MAIO

Port

N

CENTRAL VITÓRIA

◄ Rodoviária

a steep hillside just behind the *praça* on Rua do Rosário, and fronted by an impressive pair of towering imperial palms, is the whitewashed **Igreja do Rosário** (Sat 5–8pm, Sun 7–9am), which was built in 1765 by and for local slaves. Like the Capela de Santa Luzia, the church is now protected as a national monument, its plain interior housing a similarly impressive Baroque altar. Continuing along Rua do Rosário to the intersection with Avenida Jerônimo Monteiro, turn right, and at no. 631 you'll find the **Museu de Arte do Espírito Santo** (Tues–Fri 11.30am–5.30pm, Sat & Sun 1.30–5.30pm), home to a sad collection of poorly displayed, mediocre modern art (a remarkable feat considering Vitória is the capital of one of four states that make up Brazil's wealthiest region).

There is, however, one museum in the city that is really worth a look – the **Museu do Solar Monjardim** (Tues–Fri 12.30–5.30pm, Sat & Sun 1–5pm), on Avenida Paulino Müller, in the *bairro* of Jucutuquara to the southeast of the centre; take the bus marked "Circular Maruipe" or "Joana d'Arc" from Avenida Beira Mar. The museum is a restored nineteenth-century mansion filled with period furniture and household utensils, and it gives a good idea of the layout and domestic routines of a colonial estate. But if you're used to the fine displays of colonial artwork in the museums of Minas Gerais you're likely to find it disappointing.

Vitória's beach suburbs

Come evening and at weekends, downtown Vitória is pretty well deserted, and the action shifts to the middle-class **beach suburbs**, where all of Vitória's best shops, hotels and restaurants are located. Both the main city beaches here look attractive, with palm trees and promenades in the best Brazilian tradition. **Praia de Camburi** however is overlooked by the port of Tubarão in the distance, where iron ore and bauxite from Minas are either smelted or loaded onto supertankers, benefiting the economy but ruining the water. More exclusive, but still not recommended for swimming, is the **Praia do Canto,** where the rich flaunt themselves on the sands. To see where the City's truly wealthy live, walk across the bridge linking the Praia do Canto to the **Ilha do Frade**, an elite enclave of large, modern houses with spectacular views up and down the coast; there's also a small park in the centre of the island with the ruins of a Benedictine monastery. A short distance south of here, and joined to the mainland by a short causeway, is the **Ilha do Boi**, once used as a cattle quarantine station, but now visited for its two small beaches, popular with families and good for snorkelling. If you want to take a dip, you're better off crossing the *baía* to Vila Velha (see below) or travelling further afield for a perfect coast.

Vila Velha

Three bridges span the narrow Baía de Vitória, linking Espírito Santo's capital with **Vila Velha**, the state's largest city. For practical purposes, the two cities are a single metropolitan area, with people commuting in both directions. Whereas Vitória is the state's administrative centre, commercially Vila Velha is of greater significance. The city is also an important transport hub, as a railway terminus and a modern port, both featured prominently in the **Museu Vale do Rio Doce**, one of Vila Velha's few tourist attractions. Vila Vilha is no more attractive than Vitória but its **beaches**, in particularly the **Praia da Costa**, located just south of the **Convento da Penha** (one of state's oldest buildings), at least allow for safe swimming.

Museu Vale do Rio Doce

Directly across the *baía* from downtown Vitória is the fascinating **Museu Vale do Rio Doce** (Tues–Sun 10am–6pm). The museum was created by the Companhia do Vale do Rio Doce (CVRD) – a giant mining and industrial combine that's hugely important to the economy of Espírito Santo – and is housed in a former train station that was built in 1927. Focusing on the history of the **Vitória to Minas railway**, which was constructed in the early twentieth century to carry iron ore to the coast from the interior, the exhibits include a steam engine and carriages, a model railway and maps, documents, photographs and company memorabilia relating to the 664km line. The museum is also the only public venue in either Vila Velha or Vitória for the showing of important works of **modern and contemporary art**, noted for excellent exhibitions curated on themes loosely linked with the Brazilian mining industry, metallurgy or railways. There's also a pleasant **café** (Tues–Thurs & Sun 10am–6pm, Fri & Sat 10am–1am in a converted railway carriage positioned alongside the *baía*) where both snacks and full meals are served. The easiest way to get to the museum from downtown Vitória is by taxi, crossing the Ponte Florentino Avidos to the Antiga Estação Pedro Nolasco on Rua Vila Isabel. Alternatively, catch a bus marked "Vila Velha – Argolas".

The Convento da Penha

The most memorable reminder of Vitória's colonial past is on the southern mainland in Vila Velha: the chapel and one-time **Convento da Penha**, founded in 1558 (Tues–Fri 5.30am–4.45pm, Sun & religious holidays 4.30am–4.45pm, closed Mon & Sat). Perched on a granite outcrop towering over the city, it's worth visiting not so much for the convent itself, interesting though it is, as for the marvellous panoramic views over the entire city. It is a major pilgrimage centre and, in the week after Easter, thousands come to pay homage to the image of Nossa Senhora da Penha, the most devout making the climb up to the convent on their knees. It also marks the southernmost point that the Dutch managed to reach in the sugar wars of the seventeenth century; an expedition arrived here in 1649 and sacked the embryonic city, but were held off until a relief force sent from Rio drove them out – you can see how the 154-metre hill must have been almost impregnable.

You have a choice of **walks** up to the top. The steepest and most direct is the fork off the main road to the left, shortly after the main entrance, where a steep cobbled (and extremely treacherous) path leads up to the convent. Less direct, but considerably safer and with better views, is to follow the winding Rua Luísa Grinalda – a very pleasant thirty-minute walk. Once at the top, the city is stretched out below you, the centre to the north framed by the silhouettes of the mountains inland and, to the south, by the golden arcs of Vila Velha's beaches. The builders of the **chapel** thoughtfully included a viewing platform, which you reach through a door to the left of the altar. More interesting than the chapel itself is the **Sala das Milagres**, next door to the café: a collection of photos, *ex votos*, artificial limbs and artefacts from grateful pilgrims.

To **get to the convent** from the centre, take the #500 bus and ask the driver to let you off at the third stop after the Terceira Ponte, which will leave you within easy walking distance of the convent. From here there are also plenty of buses to the Praia da Costa.

Praia da Costa

Fringed by apartment buildings and a boardwalk built of granite, the **Praia da Costa** is the most popular beach hereabouts, not because of any great beauty but owing to the beach being cleaner and less polluted than its counterparts on the north side of the Baía de Vitória, a couple of kilometers to the north. For a city beach it's not bad, though you'll have to make do with people-watching if you're there on a summer weekend when it's packed solid. The Praia da Costa is easily reached from Vitória or any part of Vila Velha by buses marked "Praia da Costa".

Eating, drinking and nightlife

Local cuisine is based around seafood and is pretty good: crab is a key ingredient for many dishes, and lobster is plentiful, cheap and tastiest *na brasa* (charcoal-grilled). No stay in Vitória is complete without trying the *moqueca capixaba*, the distinctive local seafood stew in which the sauce is less spicy and uses more tomatoes than the better-known Bahian variety. For a taste of local sweets and other delicacies, try the stalls in the Sunday market (8am–noon) on Praça Costa Pereira.

Restaurants in the **centre of Vitória** are generally lacklustre, though there are a number of cheap *por kilo* places near the Palácio de Anchieta along the Escadaria Maria Ortiz stairway; the best, with a great selection of both *mineiro* and local dishes, is *D'Barro Restaurante* at no. 29. The only classy restaurant in the centre is the *Vinho do Porto* at Rua Nestor Gomes 152, near the Palácio Anchieta. Specialising in Portuguese dishes, and strong on seafood, this cosy restaurant provides a welcome contrast from the hustle and heat outside. Otherwise, even the most humble *lanchonete* will tend to have one or two local seafood dishes on offer beside the usual *salgados* and hot dogs.

For better eating, however, Vitória's beach suburbs are the places to head for. The **Praia do Canto** is especially good with numerous restaurants concentrated in the streets around the intersection of Rua Joaquim Lírio and Rua João da Cruz. But while most are good, few stand out as being exceptional. Many specialise in regional dishes, such as *mocqueca capixaba* and *torta capixaba*, a kind of seafood cake and an Easter speciality, though it's served at restaurants throughout the year. Of these, undoubtedly the best is *Pirão* at Rua Joaquim Lírio 753 (closed Mon), but there are many other similar places to choose from. Apart from regional cooking, there are many other good restaurants in this area: *Quinzinho* at Rua Aleixo Neto 1370 serves very authentic Portuguese dishes; *Mr Picuí* at Rua Joaquim Lírio 813 specialises in Northeastern food; *Canto da Roça* at Rua João da Cruz 280 offers a typical *mineiro* buffet in an attractively rustic, open-air setting; and *Kotobuki* at Rua Afonso Cláudio 60 (evenings only, closed Mon) a good, and reasonably priced, Japanese restaurant that takes full advantage of excellent seafood available here.

Praia de Camburi also has a fair number of restaurants (the green buses to the airport will take you past several), though they're spread out across a wide area. Authentic regional fare is available at many places, with *Pirata's* at Av. Dante Michelini 747, being a good moderately priced choice.

Vitória's **nightlife** is concentrated in a couple of areas. The **Praia do Canto** (particularly the streets around Rua Joaquim Lírio and Rua João da Cruz) has loads of bars, and the area attracts people from all backgrounds. There are a couple of good **live music** venues here too: *Boca da Noite*, Rua João da Cruz, and *Academeia* on the same street at no. 535, or stop by the *Oil Pub* at Rua Rômulo Samorini 33. The **Jardim da Penha** district, with the Universidade Federal do Espírito Santo (UFES) nearby, is also lively, with bars open into the small hours of the morning. The well-established *Loft Jump Bar*, Avenida Fernando Ferrari (Thurs–Sat from 11pm), opposite the university, is the city's trendiest nightclub – to get there take the airport bus or taxi. Also in Jardim da Penha, there's *forró* music every Friday (from 10pm) and samba and *pagodé* on Sunday (after 9pm) at *Chalana*, Rua Regina Vervloet 30.

Listings

Airlines Gol, at the airport ☎ 27/3327-5364; Rio Sul/Nordeste, Rua Eugênio Neto 68, Praia do Canto ☎ 27/3327-1588; TAM, at the airport ☎ 27/3324-1044; Varig, Av. Jerônimo Monteiro 1000, ground floor, Centro ☎ 27/3327-0304; Vasp, Rua Sampião 40, Praia do Canto ☎ 27/3327-0296.

Banks and exchange There's a Banco do Brasil on Av. Princesa Isabel, right in the middle of the banking district, but you can also change dollars (cash) at the Agência Esplanada, Av. Princesa Isabel 250, or the Agência Vila Velha at Av. Champagnat 1077. ATMs are found throughout the city.

Bookshops Books in English are virtually unavailable here. The best bookshops are Livraria da Ilha, Shopping Vitória (2nd floor) and the university bookshop on the UFES campus, which has a remarkable stock of books published by lesser-known Brazilian university presses.

Car rental All are based at the airport: Avis ☎ 27/3327-2348; Localiza ☎ 0800-99-2000; Unidas ☎ 27/3327-0180.

Health matters 24-hour health care at Pronto Socorro do Coração, Av. Leitão da Silva 2351, Santa Lúcia (☎ 27/3327-4833).

Police The tourist police station (open 24hr) is at Rua João Carlos de Souza 730, Barro Vermelho.

Post office There are several post offices throughout the city, including at Praça 8 de Setembre and Rua Presidente Pedreira in the centre, Rua Sampaio 204 at Praia do Canto and in the Shopping Vitória (see below for address).

Shopping Handicrafts are available at Artesanato Brasil at Praça Costa Pereira 226, Centro (Mon–Fri 8am–6pm), and at Mercado Capixaba de Artesanato at Av. Princesa Isabel 251, Centro (Mon–Fri 8.30am–6.30pm & Sat 8.30am–1pm); there's little distinctive on sale apart from rustic baskets and ceramics items, in particular *panelas de barro* (black cooking pots used for making the *moqueca capixaba*). Shopping Vitória, at Av. Nossa Senhora dos Navegantes 1440, Enseada do Suá, is the largest shopping centre in the state.

Taxis Coopertaxi ☎ 27/3200-2021; Radiotaxi ☎ 27/3336-7111; Teletáxi ☎ 27/3325-4343.

Trains The Estação Ferroviária Pedro Nolasco is just over the bridge from the *rodoviária* in Cariacica (enquiries on ☎ 27/3226-4169). There are daily services to Belo Horizonte at 6.30am, taking just over 14hr. Tickets are daily sold 5am–7pm.

The coast

Espírito Santo's **coastline** is basically one long beach, some 400km in length. With the state sandwiched between Rio and Bahia, by rights the beaches should be stunning, but the reality is rather different. There's a wide coastal plain along most of the state and with few exceptions the beaches' backdrops are hardly dramatic. Even so, if you're travelling between Rio and Bahia there are a few places where you could easily spend a few days enjoying little-visited beaches, such as **Anchieta** to the south of Vitória and **Itaunas** to its north.

South of Vitória

The most beautiful beaches near to Vitória lie around the town of **GUARA-PARI**, 54km to the south of the state capital and easily accessible from the *rodoviária* – Viação Alvorada buses run every half hour from 5am to 9pm. There are dozens of hotels here, mostly white skyscrapers catering for holiday-makers from Minas Gerais (prices are generally in the ❹ bracket), as well as a very useful eighty-bed **youth hostel**, *Guaracamping*, 800m out of the centre on Avenida F, Quadra 40, Itapebussu (☎ & ☎ 27/3261-0475; $6 per person). If you fancy raucous nightlife and holiday-making Brazilian-style, then Guarapari is the place. On the other hand, if you need some tranquillity to escape to, a mere 7km to the south of Guarapari along the ES-060 is the **Praia dos Padres**, a protected area lapped by a wonderfully green sea. Just south of here is **Meaípe**, a fishing village with some excellent restaurants: the *Cantinho do Curuca* is especially recommended for its *bolinhos de aipim* and *moqueca capixaba*. Meaípe is also a good place to stay overnight – set on a hillside with views along the coast, the *Pousada Enseada Verde* (☎27/3272-1376; ❸) is particularly comfortable and has a pool. The beaches around here are amongst the finest in Espírito Santo, with a pleasant backdrop of hills covered in tropical vegetation, and as such they're extremely popular in the summer.

Twenty kilometers south of Guarapari is the town of **ANCHIETA**, one of the oldest settlements in Espírito Santo. Of particular interest here is the imposing **Santuário Nacional Padre Anchieta** (Mon–Fri 9am–noon & 2–5pm, Sat & Sun 9am–5pm), which dominates the town from a hilltop position. Built sometime around the late sixteenth century as a Jesuit mission, the complex includes a well-kept museum commemorating the evangelical work amongst Indians of the sixteenth century Jesuit priest José de Anchieta. An important fishing port, Anchieta is one of the few places along this stretch of coast where life isn't focused on tourism, and the hotels here are mainly grim. One exception is the *Hotel Anchieta* (☎27/3536-1258; ❷), a sprawling building dating from 1911 that still offers hints of its days as a grand hotel. Heading south along the coast you pass a string of small beaches – some of which, like Praia dos Coqueiros, are quite pretty and not overly developed – before reaching **IRIRI**, some 10km from Anchieta, a busy holiday resort with a mix of low-budget *pousadas* and holiday homes.

North of Vitória

Considering what there is to look forward to in Bahia and elsewhere in the Northeast, most visitors heading northward from Vitória choose not to linger on Espírito Santo's **northern coast**. Indeed, the BR-101 remains far from the shore, never offering a glimpse of the ocean, and apart from the Serra do Mar far off to the west, this entire area is low-lying with a mix of cattle pasture and immense eucalyptus plantations and, nearer to the shore, mangrove swamps, patches of Mata Atlântica and beaches fringed with shrubs or wind-stunted coconut palms. The area does hold a few attractions, however. Coastal villages such as tiny **Regência** and **Itaúnas**, remain fundamentally fishing communities, preserving traditions that have been gradually lost elsewhere, while a visit to the **Reserva Natural da Vale do Rio Doce** is a must for amateur naturalists.

Getting around the area is usually easy as **buses** link Vitória with Espírito Santo's northern towns along the BR-101 and beyond to southern Bahia. Onward connections to the beaches however can be few and far between, so don't expect to reach them in a hurry.

Regência

Some 35km north of Aracruz on the BR-101 is the turn-off to the village of **Regência**, 40km of unpaved road leading to the fishing community of barely 1200 inhabitants. Outside the rainy season between October and December, the road is always passable, but it's slow going, with buses stopping frequently at entrances to local cattle farms. As the road reaches the ocean, look out on your right for the Projeto Tamar **turtle research station** (daily 8am–5pm, ⓦwww.projetotamar.org.br), which monitors a 35km beach nearby where, between September and March, sea turtles of all kinds come to nest. If you're lucky, you'll be invited to join the scientists in the early evening as they monitor the nests of giant leatherback turtles and watch the hatchlings crawl into the sea. At the visitors' centre, interns guide you through exhibits (in English and Portuguese) explaining the turtles' lifecycle and to tanks where you can view mature turtles.

The village of Regência itself holds little of interest, apart from the small **Museu Histórico de Regência** (Tues–Sun 10am–5pm), which charts local history through old photographs and artefacts. In summer, the village comes alive with young people from Belo Horizonte and Vitória. If you find the need **to stay**, there are several simple **pousadas**, such as, right on the beach, the *Pousada Careba* (☎27/3274-1089; ❷) and a couple of restaurants serving simple fish-based meals. When it's time to move on, you can catch a bus to Linhares (3 daily; 1hr 30min), from where you can connect with buses heading north and south.

Reserva Natural da Vale do Rio Doce

Some 30km north of the industrial town of Linhares is the **Reserva Natural da Vale do Rio Doce** (Tues–Sun 7.30am–4.30pm; ☎27/3371-9797, ✉rnvvisitas@cvrd.com.br), home to forty percent of Espírito Santo's remaining portion of Mata Atlântica. All but a tiny fraction of the 22,000-hectare reserve is open to the public, but you'll need at least a couple of days to begin to appreciate the area, which encompasses five different eco-systems ranging from tablelands forest to mangrove swamps. Although there's a wealth of flora and fauna, it's the four hundred-odd species of birds that are the biggest draw; the best time for **bird-watching** is between September and November, when the forests are most abundant with fruit. Parrots and parakeets are easily spotted, while you may see a rare cherry-throated tanager if you're very lucky.

The reserve is easily accessible: any bus heading north from Linhares will drop you at the reserve's entrance, from where you can walk 500m to the **visitors' centre** and get an excellent overview (in English and Portuguese) of the region's history and ecology; there's also a *lanchonete*, souvenir shop and playground here as well. It's best to contact the reserve in advance to arrange for a guide to lead you along the forest trails, but someone's usually available and there's no charge. Without a guide, you're only allowed to wander the lightly forested, rather park-like, trails that skirt the visitors' centre and hotel complex.

The reserve has its own **hotel** (☎27/3371-9797, ✉rnvhotel@cvrd.com.br; ❹ full board), with accommodation ranging from fairly simple rooms to chalets so luxurious that they feel at odds with the forest surroundings. There's also a large pool and a good restaurant, both reserved for hotel guests.

Conceição da Barra and Itaúnas

Some 95km further north, near the border with Bahia, is the resort town of **CONCEIÇÃO DA BARRA**. Its beaches are popular with Mineiros in the summer and there are many reasonable **pousadas** on the attractive Praia da Guaxindiba, including the *Pousada do Sol*, Av. Atlântica 226 (☎27/3762-1412; ❸), which also has a pool or, at no. 399, the simpler, but very pleasant, *Companhia do Mar* (☎27/3762-2020, ⓦwww.ciamar.tur.br; ❷). A much more pleasant place to stay, however, is the village of **ITAÚNAS**, some 20km further north on the edge of the Parque Estadual Itaúnas, best known for its thirty-metre-high sand dunes. Beneath these lies a small town that was engulfed and evacuated in the 1970s after the vegetation surrounding it had been cleared for farmland. It is said that occasionally the **dunes** shift in the wind to uncover the spire of the old church. The beaches are long and, with only low-lying vegetation, exposed, but at the height of the summer are extremely popular with college students, drawn by the party feel to the place, where *axé* music pounds from the bars until the small hours of the morning. Very different in atmosphere to coastal settlements further south, Itaúnas is said to be where northeastern Brazil begins. Keep your ears open for **forró** music – which may owe its recent popularity in Rio and São Paulo to tourists returning from Itaúnas – dances here typically getting going at around midnight and continue until 10am. There are only a few *pousadas* in Itaúnas and it's always worth calling ahead in the summer: try *Pousada das Araras* (☎27/3762-5273; ❷), *Arco Iris* (☎27/9988-8282; ❷) or *Pousada das Tartarugas* (☎27/9988-8155, ⓦwww.pousadatartarugas .com.br; ❸), all of which offer no-frills, but perfectly adequate, facilities, or for greater comfort (and a pool) the *Pousada dos Corais* (☎27/3762-5200; ❹). As for **places to eat**, there are plenty of inexpensive seafood restaurants around, of which *Cipó Cravo* is famous for its desserts. When it's time to move on, catch a bus to the road leading to Conceição from where you'll be able to pick up a bus to Vitória or to Porto Seguro in Bahia.

Inland from Vitória

In the hills and mountains inland from Vitória are several small towns surrounded by superb walking country, great for a day-trip or as a base for a relaxing few days. You can easily spot where the first immigrants came from: the houses and churches of **Santa Teresa** look as Italian as those of **Domingos Martins**, **Santa Leopoldina** or **Santa Maria** look German. The smallest of these towns, **Venda Nova**, is home to the remarkable sight of **Pedra Azul**, a grey granite finger almost 1000m high, one of the unsung natural wonders of Brazil. If you're heading for Minas Gerais, Venda Nova lies on the main Vitória–Belo Horizonte highway, Domingos Martins just off it. The area is a popular destination for residents of Vitória, so if you plan to stay over a weekend – in particular in the winter dry season, when the trails can be approached most comfortably, the sky is blue and there's a chill in the air – pre-booking accommodation is advisable.

Domingos Martins

The closest of the inland towns to Vitória is **DOMINGOS MARTINS**, 42km away on the north side of the Belo Horizonte highway. Confusingly, it has two names: Domingos Martins is the most common, but Campinho is also used. The drive there from Vitória manages to pack a remarkable amount of scenery into a very short distance – sit on the right-hand side of the bus for the best views. Almost as soon as the bus leaves the city limits the road starts to climb into the highlands, and very quickly presents wonderful views of hills and forest. Almost completely surrounded by steep hills, Domingos Martins is high enough to be bracingly fresh by day and distinctly cold at night; it looks like a run-down German mountain village, with its triangular wooden houses modelled after alpine chalets.

Get off the bus at the first stop in the town, rather than continuing to the *rodoviária*. The cheapest **accommodation** is the *Hotel Campinho* near the bus stop (❷), but if you continue the few metres to the immaculately manicured main square there's a wonderful hotel, the imposing *Imperador*, Rua Duque de Caxias 275 (☎27/3268-1115; ❸), built in German style. It's superb value for the quality of accommodation, with very comfortable rooms and a small pool.

There's not much to Domingos Martins, just a small museum, the **Casa da Cultura** (daily 8am–5pm), almost opposite the bus stop at Av. Presidente Vargas 520, which has some old documents and artefacts dating from the colony's early days after it was founded by Pomeranians in 1847. If you're into flora, it's well worth the hassle getting to the **Reserva Kautsky** (Mon–Fri 7–10am & 2–5pm, phone in advance of visit ☎27/3268-1209), some way out of town and accessible only by four-wheel-drive. which has an extensive collection of orchids and camellias – ask at any hotel for details. The main pastime in Domingos Martins in decent weather is **walking** in the surrounding forest and hills; ask at the Casa da Cultura for details and maps of possible itineraries.

In the centre of town, near the Casa da Cultura, is a very good and inexpensive *por kilo* **restaurant**, *Tia Ria*, with a buffet featuring a large variety of German- and Italian-influenced dishes, as well as more familiar Brazilian ones. For the authentic German-Brazilian culinary experience, the *Restaurante Bigosch* (open Wed–Sun), at Ladeira Francisco dos Santos Silva 50 near the Casa da Cultura, is good and reasonably priced, while for enormous and excellent high teas, try the *Café Expresso Koeler* along Rua João Batista Wernersbach. There's a good selection of jams, preserves and biscuits on offer at the town's Prefeitura-run Casa do Artesanato, all produced by local *colonos*, or smallholders.

When it's time to **move on**, you can either return to Vitória or take any Belo Horizonte-bound bus and get off in Venda Nova.

Venda Nova and Pedra Azul

VENDA NOVA DO IMIGRANTE, to give it its full name, is an Italian village some 67km further west of Domingo Martins on the Vitória–Belo Horizonte highway (the BR-262). Even by the standards of the state, the landscape in which it is set is extraordinary, a delightful mix of rich Mata Atlântica, valleys and escarpments.

Venda Nova itself is nothing more than a small village strung along the highway, with the centre, such as it is, based on Avenida Domingos Perim, the ES-166. The **Loja do Agroturismo** (Mon–Fri 7.30am–5.30pm, Sat, Sun & holidays 8am–5pm), an association of *colonos* that encourages rural tourism, is near the *Alpes Hotel* at the intersection of ES-166 and BR-262; you can pick up a very good local map there that gives the locations of the various small **farms** in the vicinity that are set up to receive visitors. There are several within a kilometre of the centre, one of the most attractive being that of the Sossai-Altoé family, south of the centre along Avenida Domingos Perim; the farm is clearly signposted and visitors are free to drop by. The Sossai-Altoé property is typical of the smallholdings (*roças*) hereabouts: the family, which emigrated to Brazil from the northern Italian province of Veneto in 1880, cultivate just five hectares of land, producing corn, beans, sugar cane and, most important of all commercially, coffee. Tourism has become vitally important for what are typically large families, and the Sossai-Altoés are happy to show their produce to visitors and demonstrate how they make their fruit wines and *cachaça*. All the farms have a small shop selling jams, wines and liquors, and it's only polite to make a purchase before leaving. An especially distinctive fruit is *jabuticaba*, a purplish-black-skinned berry that grows on the trunks of trees and has a flavour rather like that of lychees; it can be eaten fresh or as jam or wine.

Ten kilometres outside the village is the most remarkable sight in Espírito Santo, a towering bare granite mountain, shaped like a thumb, almost 1000m high – the **Pedra Azul**, or "blue stone". Its peak is actually 2000m above sea level, the other thousand accounted for by the hill country from which it sprouts, an area popular with mountaineers. It's like an enormous version of the Sugar Loaf in Rio, except that no vegetation grows on its bare surface, which rears up from thick forest and looks so smooth that from a distance it appears more like glass than stone. During the day sunlight does strange things to it – it really does look blue in shadow – but the time to see it is at either dawn or sunset, when it turns all kinds of colours in a spectacular natural show. The Pedra Azul forms the centrepiece of a state park, the **Parque Estadual da Pedra Azul** (8am–5.30pm; $2.50); there's a small visitors' centre at the foot of Pedra Azul with exhibits on local fauna and flora, and the park rangers will point you towards the trail leading up the stone – a tiring, but not very difficult, three-hour walk, though the area is closed when there's been heavy rain. Bring food and drink for the trek, and swimwear too if you want to enjoy a refreshing dip on the way up in one of the natural pools. An excellent, very detailed map ($2.50) of the Pedra Azul area is available at most local hotels.

Practicalities

There's a good range of **accommodation** in Venda Nova. The *Alpes Hotel*, on the BR-262 near the centre of Venda Nova is rather sterile but comfortable nonetheless, with its own pool and sauna (☎27/3546-1367; ❸). Cheaper, on the other side of the highway, is the simple *Hotel Canal* (☎27/3546-1322; ❷). Far more distinctive than either of these places is the *Pousada Nono Beppi* (☎27/3546-1965; ❷), 2km from the centre of Venda Nova on the BR-262 in the direction of Domingo Martins. Owned by a family of Italian descent who've farmed here since 1912, the *pousada*'s main building is a typical farmhouse. The best (though still not very good) place to eat in town is the *Ristorante Dalla Ninna*, attached to the *Alpes Hotel,* which serves reasonably priced, Italian-inspired food.

There are also several good places to stay **nearer the park**. The *Pousada dos Pinhos* (☎27/3248-1115; ❹ full board), just off Km90 on the BR-262, is an outstanding complex that would not look out of place in any European Alpine resort. A little cheaper, near the access road for the park at Km88 of the BR-262 (where it meets ES-164), is the charming *Pousasa Peterle* (☎27/3248-1243; ❹ full board), consisting of several pleasant chalets, all with superb views. On the continuation of the same access road, ES-164, some 6km beyond Pedra Azul, the basic, clean and friendly *Pousada Aargau* (☎27/3248-2175; ❷) is located in some of the most beautiful countryside in the area. Owned and run by the son of Swiss immigrants, the *pousada* also offers an enormous *café colonial* (high tea; $4), available every day.

There are three direct **buses** a day from Vitória to Pedra Azul, but any bus that goes to Minas Gerais also passes by the peak as it's on the highway to Belo Horizonte. A constant flow of local buses links Venda Nova with the access road to the Parque Estadual da Pedra Azul, from where it's an easy three-kilometre hike to the park entrance.

Santa Teresa

SANTA TERESA is only 90km northwest from Vitória but the hills between them are steep, reducing buses to a crawl for significant stretches and padding the journey out to a good two hours. The initial run up the main highway towards Bahia to the hill town of Fundão is attractive enough, but the winding road that takes you the 13km from here to Santa Teresa is something special, with great views on either side of the bus. The soils are rich, and dense forest is interspersed with coffee bushes and intensively cultivated hill farms, framed by dramatic granite cliffs and escarpments.

The closer you get to Santa Teresa, the more insistent the echoes of Europe become. The tiled hill farms look more Italian and less Brazilian, you see vines, and signs advertising local wines, and when you finally pull into the sturdy village you could be arriving somewhere in the foothills of the Italian Alps. The first colonists, mainly Italians but also several families of Polish and Russian Jews, arrived here in 1875; the last shipload of Italian immigrants docked in Vitória in 1925. Today, only the very oldest of inhabitants living in isolated smallholdings continue to speak the Italian dialects of Lombardy and Trento, although interest in the Italian heritage remains, in the form of musical bands and choirs and with young people taking Italian evening classes.

The town has grown very little in more recent times, and is still laid out along two streets in the shape of a cross. You go right down the main artery to arrive at the **rodoviária** (T27/3259-1300) at the far end of the village. There is a beautifully tended square, Praça Domingos Martins, full of flowers, trees and hummingbirds darting around. Along the adjacent street and at the far end, next to the school, is Santa Teresa's main attraction, the Museu de Mello Leitão, a natural history museum and nature reserve covering eighty square kilometres (see below).

From the square, steps cut into the hillside lead to a ridge, and five minutes' walk brings you to an unmistakeably Italian **Igreja Matriz**, complete with roundels and cupola; the names of the first colonists are engraved on a plaque on its outside wall. Rua São Lourenço, the street leading uphill from here is the oldest in the village, now lined with solidly built houses erected in the early twentieth century by the first wave of settlers. Five hundred metres along it, you come to the surviving two-storey wattle-and-daub houses put up by the first Italian and Polish immigrants; oldest of all is the Casa de Virgílio Lambert, a farmhouse opposite the tiny chapel that was built around 1876. Also around here are numerous **cantinas** where the local wines are made and sold; the limited production from grapes is, to say the least, an acquired taste, but in any case most is made from *jabuticaba*, a berry-like fruit that grows locally on tree trunks. To taste something even stronger, carry on a further 4km along the road to Cachaça da Mata, the producer of the best **cachaça** in Espírito Santo. The best time to visit the area is during the September to December harvest, during which you can see every stage of the distilling process, but visitors are welcome to tastings throughout the year.

The Museu de Biologia Professor Mello Leitão

Santa Teresa is full of flowers, and of hummingbirds feeding off them, and early this century they aroused the interest of one of the first generation of Italians to be born here, **Augusto Ruschi**. He turned a childhood fascination into a lifetime of study, and became a pioneering natural scientist and ecologist decades before it was fashionable. Specializing in the study of **hummingbirds**, he became the world's leading expert in the field and, in the later years of his life, was almost single-handedly responsible for galvanizing the state government into action to protect the exceptional beauty of the interior of Espírito Santo; that so much forest remains is due in no small measure to him. He died in 1986, at the age of 71, after being poisoned by the secretions of a tree frog he collected on one of his many expeditions into the forest.

The **Museu de Biologia Professor Mello Leitão**, Av. José Ruschi 4 (Tues–Sun 8am–5pm) was named by Ruschi as a tribute to a former teacher. It represents Ruschi's life's work, designed and laid out by him from the early

1930s. The museum contains his library and all his collections of animals, birds and insects, as well as a small zoo, a snake farm, a butterfly garden and the richest park in the state, home to thousands of species of trees, orchids, flowers and cacti – a beautiful place to wander around and a fine memorial to an extraordinary man.

Practicalities
Tourist information is available at the museum or from the Prefeitura at Av. Jerônimo Verloet 145 (Mon–Fri 8am–6pm; ☎27/3259-2268); opposite the Prefeitura is a branch of the Banco do Brasil with an ATM. The best **hotel** is the *Solar dos Colibris*, 3km from the town centre at Av. dos Manacás 400, Jardim da Montanha (☎27/3259-2200, ⊛www.hotelsolardoscolibris.com.br; ❸), which has a heated pool and sauna and park-like gardens. Slightly nearer to town, along the very pretty Estrada Lombardia, is the simple but appealing *Pousada Paradiso* (☎27/9984-9284; ❷). In town itself, the dreary-looking, but extremely welcoming *Pierazzo Hotel*, Av. Getúlio Vargas 115 (☎27/3259-1233; ❷) offers excellent value. Booking ahead is essential during the Festa do Imigrante Italiano de Santa Teresa, an annual celebration of Italian culture and traditions that takes place over a four day period coinciding with the last weekend of June. Among **restaurants**, *Mazzolin di Fiori* on Praça Domingos Martins serves local specialties (lunchtimes only), as does *Zitu's* on Avenida Getúlio Vargas, near the *Pierazzo Hotel*.

Santa Leopoldina
The drive to **SANTA LEOPOLDINA** (most people shorten it to Leopoldina) from Santa Teresa is fabulous, along a country road winding through thickly forested hills and gorges. There are a few hair-raising drops, which the bus drivers – who know every stone and curve – negotiate with aplomb, grinding gears and holding shouted conversations with the passengers, mostly blonde peasants clutching string bags and chickens. Despite the temporary look of the road and the tiny settlements you pass through – clearings in the forest uncannily like Amazon highway settlements – these are long-established communities dating from 1919, when the road was finished.

Ironically, the completion of the road to Santa Teresa meant the end of the line for Santa Leopoldina. Founded in 1857 by 160 Swiss colonists, who were followed over the next forty years by over a thousand Saxons, Pomeranians and Austrians, Santa Leopoldina was one of the earliest European colonies in Espírito Santo and also the most successful: coffee grew well on the hills and found a ready market on the coast. Built on the last navigable stretch of the Rio Santa Maria, inland from Vitória, Leopoldina was the main point of entry for the whole region. Once the road was finished, however, Santa Teresa swiftly outgrew it, leaving only a few streets of rather ugly houses and trading posts as a reminder of earlier prosperity. The town's German character has faded almost entirely, but the outlying parts of the *município* are still mainly inhabited by descendants of Germans, many of whom have retained the language or dialect of earlier generations.

The bus drops you at one end of the main street, **Rua do Comércio**. Nearby, on the same road, is the Prefeitura (Mon–Fri 8am–5pm), where you can pick up an excellent map of the *município*. Back along the street is the interesting **Museu do Colono** (Wed–Sun 9–11am & 1–5pm), housed in the mansion of what used to be the leading German family in town. The museum documents the early decades of German settlement with photographs – including some fascinating ones of the construction of the road to Santa Teresa in 1919 – along with relics and documents.

Unfortunately, there is nowhere to **stay** in town, but there are a couple of options nearby: the basic *Gasthof Tirol* (T27/3330-1042; ❷) in the hamlet of Tirol, about 15km south of Santa Leopoldina; and the charming *Pousada Parque Bosque da Prata* (T27/266-1137; ❸), 6km north of town on the unpaved road leading to Santa Teresa. There are two **buses** a day to Santa Maria and three buses covering the 28km to Santa Teresa. At a pinch, it's possible to walk to either town, but allow plenty of time, carry lots to drink and remember that the route is extremely hilly.

Santa Maria

The road leading to **SANTA MARIA DE JETIBÁ** passes through hilly terrain, densely cultivated with coffee bushes, interspersed with pine plantations and, on the steepest of hillsides, patches of Mata Atlântica. As you enter Santa Maria – essentially one long street, the Avenida Frederico Grulke – you are greeted by a "Willkommen" sign. This is an outward expression of Santa Maria's intense pride in its German (or, to be more accurate, Pomeranian) heritage, an ancestry that the village is keen to promote as a tourist attraction. Virtually the entire population is descended from late nineteenth-century immigrants from Pomerania (what is now northeast Germany and northern Poland) and today remain bound together by a common heritage based on the continued use of the Pomeranian dialect and membership in the Lutheran Church.

Santa Maria is a pleasant enough place, most of the time just a sleepy village, but there's intense activity every Monday morning as blonde-haired *colonos* arrive from their smallholdings to purchase supplies and to carry out banking and other business. Santa Maria also comes to life during the periodic **festivals** (most notably the Festa do Colono, held annually over the weekend closest to July 25), organized by the local authorities as a means of celebrating Pomeranian culture and boosting the local economy. The history of the area's settlement is well covered by the **Museu da Imigração Pomerana** (Tues–Sun 9–11am & 2.30–5.30pm) in the centre of the village at Rua Dalmácio Espíndula 260.

The very helpful **Centro de Informações Turísticas** (Mon–Fri 7.30–11am & 12.30–5pm) is housed in a German-style building on the main street. If you want to **stay** over, the excellent-value *Pommer Haus Hotel* (T27/3263-1718; ❶), in the centre at Av. Frederico Grulke 455 (above the Banco do Brasil), is comfortable and surprisingly large for a village of Santa Maria's size. If the *Pommer Haus* is full, or you'd like something even cheaper, try the extremely rudimentary *Dormitório Boa Vista* (T27/3263-1345; $4 per person). **Food** is a huge disappointment in the village, with the only places to eat being a couple of *lanchonetes* on Av. Frederico Grulke and nothing even remotely German on offer.

Travel details

Buses

Belo Horizonte to: Belém (2 daily; 50hr); Brasília (8 daily; 14hr); Campo Grande (3 daily; 23hr); Congonhas (6 daily; 2hr); Cuiabá (4 daily; 33hr); Curitiba (2 daily; 18hr); Diamantina (6 daily; 6hr); Fortaleza (1 daily; 36hr); Goiânia (5 daily; 16hr); Mariana (8 daily; 2hr); Ouro Preto (10 daily; 2hr); Poços de Caldas (4 daily; 8hr); Recife (2 daily; 40hr); Rio (20 daily; 8hr); Sabará (every 15min;

30min); Salvador (2 daily; 28hr); São João del Rei (7 daily; 4hr); São Lourenço (2 daily; 6hr); São Paulo (15 daily; 12hr); Vitória (6 daily; 8hr).

Diamantina to: Araçuaí (2 daily; 5hr); Belo Horizonte (6 daily; 6hr); São Paulo (1 daily; 16hr); Serro (1 daily; 2hr).

Ouro Preto to: Belo Horizonte (10 daily; 2hr); Brasília (Fri & Sat; 15hr); Mariana (every 20min; 30min); Rio (1 daily; 8hr); São João del Rei (2 daily; 5hr); São Paulo (2 daily; 12hr); Vitória (1 daily, except Sat; 8hr).

São João del Rei to: Belo Horizonte (7 daily; 4hr); Caxambu (4 weekly; 3hr); Ouro Preto (2 daily; 5hr); São Paulo (2 daily; 8hr); Três Corações (4 daily; 4hr); Vitória (1 daily; 13hr).

Vitória to: Belo Horizonte (6 daily; 8hr); Brasília (1 daily; 22hr); Domingos Martins (13 daily; 1hr); Fortaleza (5 weekly; 36hr); Guarapari (every 30min; 1hr); Linhares (4 daily; 3hr); Manhuaçu (2 daily; 4hr); Manhumirim (2 daily; 4hr); Ouro Preto (1 daily; 7hr); Rio (9 daily; 7hr); Salvador (2 daily; 17hr); Santa Teresa (6 Mon–Sat, 3 on Sun; 2hr); São João del Rei (1 daily; 13hr); São Paulo (5 daily; 14hr); Venda Nova (hourly; 3hr).

Trains

Calling at all stations, including Governador Valadares and Itabira:

Belo Horizonte to: Vitória (daily at 7am; 14hr).

Vitória to: Belo Horizonte (daily at 7am; 14hr).

The Northeast

CHAPTER 3

Highlights

✳ **Capoeira** Watch nimble displays of this Afro-Brazilian martial art at one of the organized capoeira schools. See p.257

✳ **Salvador's nightlife** The vibrant backstreets of Pelourinho offer the city's best live music, including samba. See p.263

✳ **Candomblé celebrations** The dance rituals of this religious cult can be memorable, if you're lucky enough to catch one. See p.264

✳ **Parque Nacional da Chapada Diamantina** There's plenty of diverse terrain to keep hikers happy in this huge national park. See p.278

✳ **Olinda** Best visited during Carnaval, when colourful parades snake through the beautifully preserved colonial streets. See p.312

✳ **Fernando De Noronha** A gorgeous archipelago visited by thousands of dolphins early each morning. See p.329

✳ **Northeast beaches** Quintessential tropical beaches line much of the region's coast, including stretches around Fortaleza. See p.363

✳ **Reggae bands** You'll hear excellent reggae throughout the region, but especially in São Luís, the reggae capital of Brazil. See p.377

The Northeast

T
he **Northeast** (*nordeste*) of Brazil covers an immense area and features a variety of climates and scenery, from the dense equatorial forests of western Maranhão, only 200km from the mouth of the Amazon, to the parched interior of Bahia, some 2000km to the south. It takes in all or part of the nine **states** of Maranhão, Piauí, Ceará, Rio Grande do Norte, Paraíba, Pernambuco, Alagoas, Sergipe and Bahia, which together form roughly a fifth of Brazil's land area and have a combined population of 36 million. When *nordestinos* living outside the region are included, they make up about a third of Brazil's total population. Within Brazil, the Northeast is notorious for its poverty, and it has been described as the largest concentration of poor people in the Americas. Yet it's also one of the most rewarding regions of Brazil to visit, with a special identity and culture nurtured by fierce regional loyalties, shared by rich and poor alike. You'll come across echoes of Northeastern culture all over Brazil – in the Amazon highway towns or the *favelas* of Rio and São Paulo – engendered by the millions of Northeasterners who migrate out of the region.

The Northeast possesses an identity forged by **geographical** contrasts, as most of the Northeastern states have three distinct areas. First is the flat coastal strip, the **zona da mata**, which literally means "forest zone". Little, apart from the name, is now left of the coastal jungle that greeted the first European settlers in the sixteenth century: at the same time as they marvelled at its beauty they cut it down and planted sugar cane, taking advantage of the heavy tropical rains and rich soils. It was on the coast that the first towns and cities of the Northeast grew up – not for nothing are all the region's state capitals, save one, coastal cities – and to this day the coastal strip is by far the most thickly populated part of the Northeast. Unfortunately, this fertile coastal belt is rather narrow, and nowhere does it extend inland for more than a hundred kilometres. This zone gives way to an intermediate area, the **agreste**, where hills rear up into rocky mountain ranges, and the lush, tropical vegetation of the coast is gradually replaced by highland scrub and cactus. Finally comes the **sertão**, the vast semi-arid interior that covers more than three-quarters of the Northeast but houses a relatively small proportion of its population. The soils here are poor, the rainfall is irregular, and only the hardy can scrabble a living out of the harsh landscape.

The contrast between the coast and the interior is the most striking thing about the region. You could have a fascinating time in the Northeast without ever leaving the *zona da mata*, but unless you make at least one foray into the interior you'll only get a partial view of what is the most varied region in Brazil. It is not just a difference in the way the country looks. Much of it also

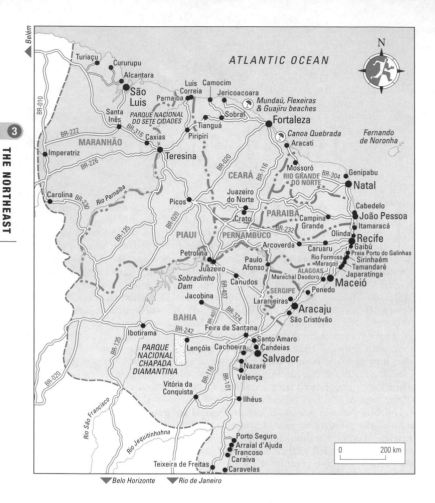

has to do with the **racial** mix, a product of the region's economic history. Blacks were imported to work on the coastal sugar plantations, and relatively few of them made it into the interior. The Northeast now has the largest concentration of black people in Brazil, but most of them still live either on or near the coast, concentrated around **Salvador**, **Recife** and **São Luís**, where African influences are very obvious – in the cuisine, music and religion. In the *sertão*, though, Portuguese and Indian influences predominate in both popular culture and racial ancestry.

As far as specific attractions go, the region has much to offer. The **coastline** is over two thousand kilometres of practically unbroken beach, much of it just as you imagine tropical beaches to be: white sands, blue sea, palm trees – the stuff advertising campaigns are made of. Brazil's **colonial heritage** survives in the Baroque churches and cobbled streets of Salvador, Olinda and São Luís, often side by side with the modern Brazilian mix of skyscrapers and shantytowns. And in Salvador and Recife, with populations of around two million each, the Northeast has two of Brazil's great **cities**. Head **inland**, and the bustling market towns of the *agreste* and the enormous jagged landscapes of the *sertão* more than repay the journeys. But above all, in both city and countryside, there's the force of a richly diverse **popular culture** that you will find reflected not only in arts and crafts, but in the texture of everyday life, most conspicuously in the Brazilian caricature of frenzied partying and football worship, which fits this region better than most.

Some history

The Northeast was the first part of Brazil to be settled by Europeans on any scale. The Portuguese were quick to recognize the potential of the coast, and by the end of the sixteenth century sugar plantations were already importing African slaves. **Salvador** and **Olinda** developed into large towns while Rio de Janeiro was no more than a swampy village. Indeed, Salvador became the first capital of Brazil, and by the end of the sixteenth century the Northeast had become Europe's main supplier of **sugar**. The merchants and plantation owners grew rich and built mansions and churches, but their very success led to their downfall. It drew the attention of the **Dutch**, who were so impressed that they destroyed the Portuguese fleet in Salvador in 1624, burnt down Olinda six years later and occupied much of the coast, paying particular attention to sugar-growing areas. It took more than two decades of vicious guerrilla warfare before the Dutch were expelled, and even then they had the last laugh: they took their new experience of sugar growing to the West Indies, which soon began to edge Brazilian sugar out of the world market.

The Dutch invasion, and the subsequent decline of the sugar trade, proved quite a fillip to the development of the interior. With much of the coast in the hands of the invaders, the **colonization** of the *agreste* and *sertão* was stepped up. The Indians and escaped slaves already there were joined by cattlemen (*vaqueiros*), as trails were opened up into the highlands and huge ranches carved out of the interior. Nevertheless, it took over two centuries, roughly from 1600 to 1800, before these regions were fully absorbed into the rest of Brazil. In the *agreste*, where some fruit and vegetables could be grown and cotton did well, market villages developed into towns. However, the *sertão* became, and still remains, cattle country, with an economy and society very different from the coast.

Life in the **interior** has always been hard. The landscape is dominated by cactus and dense scrub – *caatinga* – the heat is fierce, and for most of the year the countryside is parched brown. But it only takes a few drops of rain to fall for an astonishing transformation to take place. Within the space of a few hours the *sertão* blooms. Its plant life, adapted to semi-arid conditions, rushes to take advantage of the moisture: trees bud, cacti burst into flower, shoots sprout up from the earth, and, literally overnight, the brown is replaced by a carpet of green. Too often, however, the rain never comes, or arrives too late, or too early, or in the wrong place, and the cattle begin to die. The first recorded **drought** was as early as 1710, and since then droughts have struck the *sertão* at ten- or fifteen-year intervals, sometimes lasting for years. The worst was in the early 1870s, when as many as two million people died of starvation; 1999 was also a particularly bad year. The problems caused by drought were, and still are, aggravated by the inequalities in land ownership. The fertile areas around rivers were taken over in early times by powerful cattle barons, whose descendants still dominate much of the interior. The rest of the people of the interior, pushed into less favoured areas, are regularly forced by drought to seek refuge in the coastal cities until the rains return. For centuries, periodic waves of refugees, known as *os flagelados* (the scourged ones), have poured out of the *sertão* flee-ing droughts: modern Brazilian governments have been no more successful in dealing with the special problems of the interior than the Portuguese coloniz-ers before them.

Transport

You can reach the Northeast from almost any direction. Direct, there are **flights** to Recife and Salvador from Europe and North America, and frequent **buses** to the main Northeastern cities from all parts of Brazil. From **southern and central Brazil**, buses converge upon Salvador. From the **Amazon**, buses from Belém run to São Luís, Teresina, Fortaleza and points east, or further south to Salvador.

Getting around the Northeast is straightforward thanks to the region's extensive bus network. However, even the main highways can be a little bumpy at times, and minor roads are often precarious. This is especially true in the rainy season: in Maranhão the rains come in February, in Piauí and Ceará in March, and points east in April, lasting for around three months. These are only general rules, though: Maranhão can be wet even in the dry season, and Salvador's skies are liable to give you a soaking at any time of year.

Bahia

The oldest and most historic city in Brazil, **Salvador**, the largest city in Bahia state, possesses the largest collection of colonial architecture in Latin America and was the national capital for over two centuries, before relinquishing the title to Rio in 1763. The bay on which the city was built afforded a superb nat-ural anchorage, while the surrounding lands of **Bahia state** were ideal coun-try for sugar-cane and tobacco plantations. In the seventeeth century, Salvador became the centre of the **Recôncavo**, the richest plantation zone in Brazil before the coming of coffee the following century. Within striking distance of the city are a string of colonial towns, including **Santo Amaro** and **Cachoeira**.

The countryside changes to the south of Salvador, with mangrove swamps and fast-developing island resorts around the town of **Valença**, before revert-ing to a spectacular coastline typical of the Northeast. **Ilhéus** is a thriving beach resort, as is **Porto Seguro**, the oldest town in Brazil, site of the first Portuguese landings in 1500. **Inland**, the Bahian **sertão** is massive, a desert-like land that supports some fascinating frontier towns – the mining bases of **Jacobina** and **Lençóis** and the river terminus of **Ibotirama** are just three.

Salvador

Second only to Rio in the magnificence of its natural setting, on the mouth of the enormous bay of Todos os Santos, **SALVADOR** is one of that select band of cities that has an electricity you feel from the moment you arrive. Its founding in 1549 marked the beginning of the permanent occupation of the country by the **Portuguese**, though it wasn't easy for them. The Caeté Indians killed and ate both the first governor and the first bishop before succumbing, and Salvador was later the scene of a great battle in 1624, when the Dutch destroyed the Portuguese fleet in the bay and took the town by storm, only to be forced out again within a year by a joint Spanish and Portuguese fleet.

Much of the plantation wealth of the Recôncavo was used to adorn the city with imposing public buildings, ornate squares and, above all, churches. Today, Salvador is a large, modern city, but significant chunks of it are still recognizably colonial. Taken as a whole it doesn't have the unsullied calm of, say, Olinda

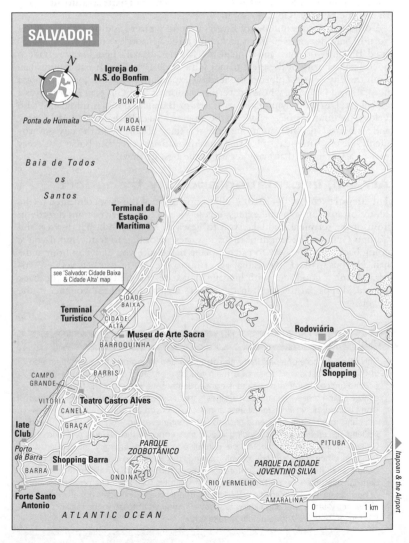

SALVADOR

N

Igreja do
N.S. do Bonfim

BONFIM

Ponta de Humaita

BOA
VIAGEM

Baia de Todos

os

Santos

Terminal da
Estação
Marítima

see 'Salvador: Cidade Baixa
& Cidade Alta' map

CIDADE
BAIXA

Terminal
Turístico

CIDADE
ALTA

Museu de Arte Sacra

BARROQUINHA

Rodoviária

CAMPO
GRANDE

BARRIS

Iquatemi
Shopping

VITÓRIA

Teatro Castro Alves

CANELA

Iate
Club

GRAÇA

*Porto
da Barra*

Shopping Barra

*PARQUE
ZOOBOTÂNICO*

PITUBA

*PARQUE DA CIDADE
JOVENTINO SILVA*

BARRA

ONDINA

RIO VERMELHO

Forte Santo
Antonio

AMARALINA

ATLANTIC OCEAN

0   1 km

but many of its individual churches, monasteries and convents are magnificent, the finest colonial buildings anywhere in Brazil.

The other factor that marks Salvador out is immediately obvious – most of the population is black. Salvador was Brazil's main slave port, and the survivors of the brutal journey from the Portuguese Gold Coast and Angola were immediately packed off to city construction gangs or the plantations of the Recôncavo; today, their descendants make up the bulk of the population. **African influences** are everywhere. Salvador is the cradle of *candomblé* and *umbanda*, Afro-Brazilian religious cults that have millions of devotees across Brazil. The city has a marvellous local **cuisine**, much imitated in other parts of the country, based on traditional African ingredients like palm oil, peanuts and coconut milk. And Salvador has possibly the richest **artistic tradition** of any Brazilian city; only Rio can rival it.

A disproportionate number of Brazil's leading **writers** and **poets** were either born in Salvador or lived there, including Jorge Amado, the most widely translated Brazilian novelist, and Vinícius de Morães, Brazil's best-known modern poet. The majority of the great names who made Brazilian **music** famous hail from the city – João Gilberto, the leading exponent, with Tom Jobim, of bossa nova; Astrud Gilberto, whose quavering version of *The Girl from Ipanema* was a global hit; Dorival Caymmi, the patriarch of Brazilian popular music; Caetano Veloso, the founder of *tropicalismo*; the singers Maria Bethânia and Gal Costa; and Gilberto Gil, who was at one time secretary of culture in the city government. The city's music is still as rich and innovative as ever, and bursts out every year in a **Carnaval** that many regard as the best in Brazil.

Arrival, information and city transport

The **airport** (☎71/204-1010) is 20km northeast of the city, connected to the centre by an hourly shuttle express bus service ($2) that leaves from directly in front of the terminal, and takes you to Praça da Sé via the beach districts and Campo Grande. The length of the ride varies according to traffic, but if you're going back the other way to catch a plane make sure you allow an hour and a half. The bus marked "Politeama" also runs to the centre, but gets very crowded and isn't a good idea with luggage. A taxi to the centre will set you back around $15; pay at the kiosk in the arrivals area and hand the voucher to the driver.

Personal safety: a warning

Salvador has more of a problem with **robberies** and **muggings** than anywhere else in the Northeast save Recife. The main tourist area around Pelourinho is heavily policed until quite late at night and is consequently safe. However, the fact that such a large police presence is needed suggests that some **precautions** are still in order. Don't wander down ill-lit side streets at night unless you are within sight of a policeman and don't use the Lacerda elevator after early evening. You should also avoid walking up and down the winding roads that connect the Cidade Alta and the Cidade Baixa, and you should be careful about using ordinary city buses on Sundays when there are few people around; the *executivo* bus is always a safe option. Give the Avenida do Contorno – the seafront road that runs north from the harbour past the *Solar do Unhão* restaurant – a miss too. It's a shame to put it out of bounds as it's a very scenic walk, but it's dangerous even in daylight as gangs lie in wait for tourists who don't know any better; if you want to go to the restaurant, or the Museu de Arte Moderna near it, take a taxi.

Salvador's superb **rodoviária** (☎71/358-4970) – well organized and packed with almost every conceivable facility – is 8km east of the centre. To get to the Cidade Alta and its hotels from here, it's best to either take a taxi (about $10) or catch the comfortable *executivo* bus from the Iguatemi shopping centre across the busy road from the *rodoviária* – there's a footbridge to stop you getting mowed down by traffic. The bus costs $2 and makes stately progress through the beach districts of Pituba and Rio Vermelho before dropping you in the Praça da Sé.

Information

Salvador's **tourist information** is better than anywhere else in the Northeast. The state tourist agency, **Bahiatursa**, is used to foreigners; most of its offices have English-speakers; and it provides a variety of maps and handouts on the city: the best two are the *Mapa Turístico de Salvador da Bahia* ($1.50) and the free *Guia do Pelourinho*. If you're travelling on to other parts of Bahia, you should also ask for whatever material they have on the rest of the state, as elsewhere the service is nowhere near as good.

There are **information posts** on arrival at the airport (daily 7.30am–11pm; ☎71/204-1244) and the *rodoviária* (daily 8am–11pm; ☎71/450-3871). Bahiatursa's **main office** is in Cidade Alta at Rua das Laranjeiras 12 (also sometimes called Rua Francisco Muniz Barreto; daily 8.30am–9pm or until 10pm at weekends; ☎71/321-2133 or 321-2463), and there are other offices at the Mercado Modelo (Mon–Sat 9am–6pm, Sun 9am–2pm; ☎71/241-0242); in Barra Shopping, Av. Centenario 2992 (Mon–Sat 10am–10pm; ☎71/264-0242); and in Iguatemi Shopping, Av. Tancredo Neves 148 (Mon–Fri 9am–11pm, Sat 9am–2pm; ☎71/480-5511). An additional source of information is the **tourist hotline**, "Disque Turismo" – just ring ☎0800/71-6622 from any telephone and you should find an English-speaker on the other end. Finally, the city of Salvador has its own tourist authority, **EMTURSA**, which has an office on Largo do Pelourinho (daily 1–7pm; ☎71/243-6555), but pales in comparison to Bahiatursa.

One thing you should bear in mind when finding your way around the city is that many **roads** have two **names**: the main seafront road, for example, is sometimes called Avenida Presidente Vargas, but more usually Avenida Oceânica. In general we've gone for the name that actually appears on the street signs.

City transport

Conveniently, many of the museums, churches and historic buildings are concentrated within **walking** distance of each other in Cidade Alta. Failing that, **taxis** are plentiful, although all the beach areas except Barra are a long ride from the centre.

There are three **local bus terminals**, and the bus system is efficient and easy to use. From **Praça da Sé**, there are local services to Barra and to **Campo Grande**, another central terminus with connections to the airport, *rodoviária* and Itapoan (also spelt Itapoã). The Praça da Sé is also the place to catch the *executivo* ($2), a comfortable express bus service, well worth using instead of the crowded city buses. There are only two routes on this service: buses marked "Iguatemi" run through the city to Barra, head down the coast to Rio Vermelho, and stop at the glossy shopping centre at Iguatemi, from where a short walkway leads to the *rodoviária* – the fastest way to reach it by public transport, though still count on at least 45 minutes in transit; the "Aeroporto" service, meanwhile, follows the same route until Rio Vermelho, before continuing along past Pituba to Itapoan, and on to the airport – cutting journey times to any of the beach areas to at least half that of a regular city bus. The third city bus terminal is **Estação da Lapa**, in Barris, which has connections to everywhere in the city; it's remarkably well laid out, with destinations clearly labelled. To reach the centre, any bus with "Sé", "C. Grande" or "Lapa" on the route card will do.

Salvador also has **ferry** services to islands in the bay and points on the mainland. There are two ferry terminals: the **Terminal Turístico**, behind the Mercado Modelo, clearly visible from Cidade Alta, is for launch services – *lanchas* – and excursion boats to the island of Itaparica, across the bay; the **Terminal da Estação Marítima** (or Terminal São Joaquim), to the north, past the the docks and Polícia Federal offices, handles the full-size car ferries to Itaparica (every 30min during the day; 1hr).

The quickest way to get to the ferry terminals – and Cidade Baixa in general – is to take the **Lacerda elevator** or the **funicular railway**, both of which connect Cidade Alta with the heart of Cidade Baixa. They run every few minutes from early morning to late at night (though see the box on "Personal Safety" on p.250), and cost only a few cents a ride.

Accommodation

Salvador is the second most popular tourist destination in Brazil and correspondingly full of **hotels**. Unless you want to stay on a beach, the best area to head for is **Cidade Alta**, not least because of the spectacular view across the island-studded bay. The wealthy suburb of **Barra** has by far the closest of the beaches to the centre; the small but lovely Praia do Porto is especially pleasant and the best for swimming. Barra is also one of the more reasonably priced beach areas and has some good medium-priced hotels. The official campsite, *Camping Ecológica Stella Maris,* at Alameda da Praia (near the *farol*) in Itapoá (☎71/374-3506), has shower and restaurant facilities, and enough space for motorhomes too.

City centre

Albergue da Juventude Solar Rua Ribeiro dos Santos 45, Pelourinho ☎71/241-0055. A good youth hostel in a relatively quiet part of the Pelourinho district. $17 a night, with breakfast.

Albergue das Laranjeiras Rua Inácio Acciole 13 ☎ & ⓕ71/321-1366, ⓦwww.alaranj.com.br. Excellent and lively youth hostel in the heart of the historic centre, with Internet access, inexpensive laundry facilities, and a trendy café. $22 per person.

Albergue do Passo Rua do Passo 3 ☎71/326-1951 or 243-1820, ⓕ351-3285, ⓦwww.passoyouthhostelH.P.G.com.br. Pleasant Pelourinho hostel in an attractive building featuring rooms with showers, good breakfasts and a communal room with cable TV. Staff speak English, French and Spanish. Prices go up twenty-fold for Carnaval, but beds come from $12 per person.

Arthemis Hotel Praca da Se 398, Edf. Themis, 7th floor ☎71/322-0724, ⓦwww.artemishotel.com.br. Located at the top of an office block in the heart of the city, with tremendous views, a patio bar and

café. Rooms are comfortable enough for the price. ❸

Chile Hotel Rua Chile 7 ☎71/321-0245. Very popular with backpackers, this is a clean and spacious hotel, though some rooms are dark. Located on the road leading away from the Praça da Sé towards Praça Castro Alves. ❸

Hotel Castro Alves Rua Aristides Milton 2 ☎71/243-6810. Located in Barroquinha in an old but charming building behind the decaying Igreja da Barroquinha, this hotel is amazingly cheap for central Salvador, but it's very basic and also rents rooms by the hour. ❶

Hotel Granada Av. Sete de Setembro 512 ☎71/243-2301. Good medium-priced option surrounded by the hustle and bustle of Cidade Alta's shopping district. ❹

Hotel Maridina Av. Sete de Setembro 6 ☎71/242-7176, ⓕ452-5269. This family-run hotel just off Praça Castro Alves is mainly frequented by Brazilians and has a friendly, laid-back atmosphere. ❸

Hotel Nogueira Rua da Ajuda 12 ☎71/241-4788,

ⓟ 322-4395. A small, anonymous-looking hotel squeezed into a tall building behind the *Hotel Palace*; all rooms are small, some dark, but most have TV and private shower. ②

Hotel Palace Rua Chile 20 ☎ 71/322-1155, ⓟ 243-1109, ⓔ palace@e-net.com.br. If you want a bit more comfort than a no-frills room for a bit more money, this is a good bet; all rooms are cosy but the ones with air-conditioning are easily the best. ④

Hotel Pelourinho Rua Alfredo de Brito 20 ☎ 71/243-2324 or 321-4653. Probably the best-known hotel in Cidade Alta, this has long been an atmospheric and popular place, but it's no longer cheap. ③

Hotel Redfish Rua Direita do Santo Antonio 454, Santo Antonio ☎ 71/243-8473, ⓔ hotelredfish @e-net.com.br. Spacious and well-appointed *pousada* run by an English artist and his Brazilian wife; the top two floors have terraces with hammock-swinging space. Located on a large residential street that runs between Pelourinho and Largo do San Antonio. Sound advice given on trips and tours. ⑤

Hotel Solara Largo Pelourinho 25 ☎ 71/326-4583. Cheap, no-frills hotel in an excellent location at the bottom end of Largo do Pelourinho; it can be wild around here at weekends, though. ②

Ibiza Hotel Rua do Bispo 6 ☎ 71/322-4503. Excellent budget hotel on the corner of Rua do Bispo and Praça da Sé. Clean, well run and good value. ③

Pousada da Praça Hotel Rua Rui Barbosa 5 ☎ 71/321-0642, ⓔ gifc@zaz.com.br. A highly recommended budget hotel offering great service, more than adequate bedrooms and a magnificent breakfast, just off Praça Castro Alves. ③

The beaches

Amaralina Praia Av. Otávio Mangabeira 197, Pituba ☎ 71/240-7377, ⓟ 248-9500, ⓦ www.amaralinapraia.com.br. Comfortable hotel set in one of the cheapest of all the beach areas, Pituba, and handily close to the airport, although a little far from the centre. Facilities include a pool, bar and decent restaurant. ③

Âmbar Pousada Rua Afonso Celso 485, Barra ☎ 71/264-6956, ⓟ 264-3791, ⓦ www .ambarpousada.com.br. A very friendly *pousada*

close to Praia do Porto da Barra. Simple but neat and cosy rooms on two storeys, set around an attractive courtyard. Excellent value. ③

Bahia Othon Palace Hotel Av. Presidente Vargas 2456, Ondina ☎ 71/203-2000, ⓦ www.othon.com.br. Superb luxury hotel standing on the seafront at the Praia Ondina. The 280 apartments, many with great views, all come with minibar and TV, and there's also a pool, sauna and an excellent restaurant. ⑦

Bahia Park Hotel Praça Augusto Severo, Rio Vermelho ☎ 71/334-6722 or 334-6724, ⓟ 330-1554. Characterless upper middle-range hotel offering most services, including pool and convention rooms, close to Rio Vermelho's fishermen's wharf and beaches. ④

Barra Turismo Hotel Av. Sete de Setembro 3691, Praia do Porto da Barra ☎ 71/264-7433, ⓟ 264-0038. Smartish hotel overlooking the beach at Barra; pretty good service and reasonable rooms for the price. ③

Hotel Barra Mar Av. Sete de Setembro 3793, Praia do Porto da Barra ☎ 71/264-9722, ⓟ 264-9954. Basic but well-kept hotel overlooking the best of Barra's beaches; great value if you can get a room with a sea view. ②

Hotel Caramuru Av. Sete de Setembro 2125, Vitória ☎ 71/336-9951. Excellent value and unpretentious, this small hotel has a nice veranda, comfortable rooms and can help organize *candomblé* visits and tours locally and to Itaparica. ④

Hotel Catharina Paraguaçu Rua João Gomes 128, Rio Vermelho ☎ 71/334-0089. One of Brazil's most elegant hotels – beautifully restored, full of character and excellent value. For some reason, taxi drivers have difficulty finding it even though it's on a main road. ⑤

Hotel Porto da Barra Av. Sete de Setembro 3783, Praia do Porto da Barra ☎ 71/264-7711, ⓟ 264-2619, ⓦ www.hotelportodabarra.com.br. Good-value, no-frills and no-nonsense hotel right by the beach; all rooms have either air-conditioning or fan. ③

Pousada Malu Av. Sete de Setembro 3801, Porto da Barra ☎ 71/264-4461. A small, exceptionally clean *pousada* on the seafront opposite the Forte de Santa Maria; a friendly place in a safe location. ②

The City

Salvador is built around the craggy, fifty-metre-high bluff that dominates the eastern side of the bay, and splits the central area into upper and lower sections. The heart of the old city, **Cidade Alta** (or simply Centro), is strung along its top, linked to the **Cidade Baixa**, below, by precipitous streets, a funicular rail-

Museu da Arte Sacra

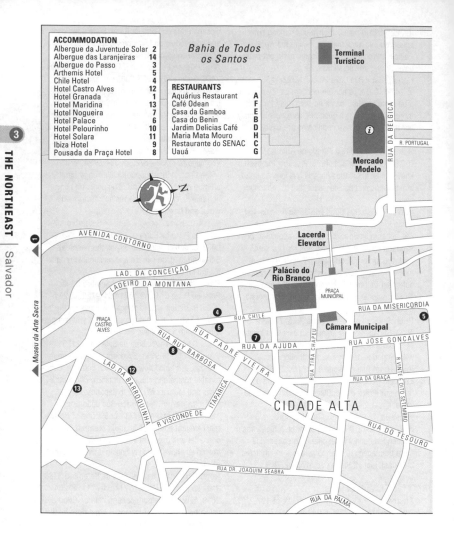

ACCOMMODATION
Albergue da Juventude Solar	2
Albergue das Laranjeiras	14
Albergue do Passo	3
Arthemis Hotel	5
Chile Hotel	4
Hotel Castro Alves	12
Hotel Granada	1
Hotel Maridina	13
Hotel Nogueira	7
Hotel Palace	6
Hotel Pelourinho	10
Hotel Solara	11
Ibiza Hotel	9
Pousada da Praça Hotel	8

Bahia de Todos os Santos

Terminal Turístico

RESTAURANTS
Aquárius Restaurant	A
Café Odean	F
Casa da Gamboa	E
Casa do Benin	B
Jardim Delicias Café	D
Maria Mata Mouro	H
Restaurante do SENAC	C
Uauá	G

R. PORTUGAL

RUA DA BELGICA

Mercado Modelo

AVENIDA CONTORNO

LAD. DA CONCEIÇAO

LADEIRO DA MONTANA

Lacerda Elevator

Palácio do Rio Branco

PRAÇA MUNICIPAL

RUA DA MISERICORDIA

PRAÇA CASTRO ALVES

RUA CHILE

RUA RUY BARBOSA

RUA PADRE VIEIRA

RUA DA AJUDA

RUA TIRA CHAPEU

Câmara Municipal

RUA JOSE GONCALVES

RUA DA GRAÇA

R.VINTE E OITO SETEMBRO

LAD. DA BARROQUINHA

R. VISCONDE DE ITAPARICA

CIDADE ALTA

RUA DO TESOURO

RUA DR. JOAQUIM SEABRA

RUA DA PALMA

way and the towering Art Deco lift shaft of the Carlos Lacerda elevator, the city's largest landmark. Cidade Alta is the administrative and cultural centre of the city, Cidade Baixa the financial and commercial district.

In the last century the city expanded into the still elegant areas of **Barris** and **Canela**, to the south of Cidade Alta, and up to the exclusive residential suburb of **Barra**, the headland at the mouth of the bay around which the city is built. From Barra, a broken coastline of coves and beaches, large and small, is linked by the twisting **Avenida Oceânica** (also known as the Avenida Presidente Vargas), which runs along the shore through **Ondina**, **Rio Vermelho** and **Pituba**, the main beach areas. Further on is the one-time fishing village of **Itapoan**, after which the city peters out.

Most of Salvador's 26 **museums** and 34 **colonial churches** are concentrat-

ed within a short distance of each other in Cidade Alta, which makes sightseeing fairly straightforward. A single meandering walk from the Praça da Sé, taking in all the highlights, but not stopping at any of them, would take no more than an hour; more realistically, you'll need at least two days, and possibly three, if you want to explore the city in depth.

From Praça Municipal to Terreiro de Jesus

The best spot to begin a walking tour is at the **Praça Municipal**, the square dominated by the impressive **Palácio do Rio Branco**, the old governor's palace. Burnt down and rebuilt during the Dutch wars, the building features regal plaster eagles added by nineteenth-century restorers, who turned a plain colonial mansion into an imposing palace. The interior is fine, a blend of

Rococo plasterwork, polished wooden floors, and painted walls and ceilings. Of lesser interest is the museum inside, the **Memorial dos Governadores** (Mon 2–6pm, Tues–Fri 10am–noon & 2–6pm; free), which houses period pieces from the colonial era. Also facing the square is the **Câmara Municipal**, the seventeenth-century city hall, graced by a series of elegant but solid arches.

To the east, Rua Chile becomes Rua da Misericórdia and leads into **Praça da Sé**, the heart of Cidade Alta, where the *executivo* buses terminate. The **Terreiro de Jesus** lies to the south in front of the plain **Catedral Basílica** (Mon–Sat 8–11.30am & 2–5.30pm, Sun 10.30am–12.30pm), once the chapel of the largest Jesuit seminary outside Rome. Its interior is one of the most beautiful in the city, particularly the stunning panelled ceiling of carved and gilded wood, which gives the church a light, airy feel that's an effective antidote to the overwrought Rococo altar and side chapels. To the left of the altar is the tomb of **Mem de Sá**, third viceroy of Brazil from 1556 to 1570, and the most energetic and effective of all Brazil's colonial governors. It was he who supervised the first phase of building in Salvador, in the process destroying the Caeté Indians. Look in on the restored sacristy, too, while you're here – portraits of Jesuit luminaries, set into the walls and ceiling, gaze down intimidatingly on intruders.

The Museu Afro-Brasileiro

Next to the cathedral stands one of the best museums in the city, the **Museu Afro-Brasileiro** (Mon–Fri 9am–5pm; $2), contained within a large nineteenth-century building that used to be the university medical faculty; in the shady yard behind is the recently restored circular lecture theatre. The main building houses three different collections, one on each of the storeys.

Largest and best is on the **ground floor**, recording and celebrating the black contribution to Brazilian culture. Four rooms are dedicated to different aspects of black culture – popular religion, *capoeira*, weaving, music and Carnaval – and everything, for once, is very well laid out. The section on *capoeira*, the balletic martial art the slaves developed (see box opposite), is fascinating, supported by photos and old newspaper clippings. But there are other highlights, too, like the gallery of large photographs of *candomblé* leaders, some dating from the nineteenth century, most in full regalia and exuding pride and authority; and the famous carved panels by Carybé, in the exhibition room past the photo gallery. Carybé, Bahia's most famous artist, was Argentinian by birth but came to Salvador 35 years ago to find inspiration in the city and its culture. The carved panels in the museum, imaginatively decorated with scrap metal, represent the gods and goddesses of *candomblé*.

The **first floor** houses a rather dull museum of the faculty of medicine, dominated by busts and dusty bookcases. A better idea is to look in the **basement**, at the **Museu Arqueológico e Etnológico**. Largely given over to fossils and artefacts from ancient burial sites, it also incorporates the only surviving part of the old Jesuit college, a section of the cellars, in the arched brickwork at the far end. A diagram at the entrance to the museum shows how enormous the college was, extending all the way from what is now the Praça da Sé to Largo do Pelourinho. It was from here that the conversion of the Brazilian Indians was organized, and one of the many Jesuit priests who passed through its gates was Antônio Vieira, whose impassioned sermons defending Indian rights against the demands of the Portuguese slavers are generally regarded as the finest early prose in the Portuguese language. After the Jesuits were expelled in 1759, most of the college was demolished by the rich for

Capoeira, which began in Angola as a ritual fight to gain the nuptial rights of women when they reached puberty, and has evolved into a graceful semi-balletic art form somewhere between fighting and dancing, is easy to find in Salvador. It's usually accompanied by the characteristic rhythmic twang of the *berimbau*, and takes the form of a pair of dancers/fighters leaping and whirling in stylized "combat" – which, with younger *capoeiristas*, occasionally slips into a genuine fight when blows land by accident and the participants lose their temper. There are regular displays, largely for the benefit of tourists but interesting nevertheless, on Terreiro de Jesus and near the entrances to the Mercado Modelo in Cidade Baixa, where contributions from onlookers are expected. The best *capoeira*, however, can be found in the **academias de capoeira**, organized schools that have classes that anyone can watch free of charge. All ages take part, many of the children astonishingly nimble: although most *capoeiristas* are male, some girls and women take it up as well. The first and most famous *academia*, the Associação de Capoeira Mestre Bimba, named after the man who popularized *capoeira* in the city from the 1920s, is still the best; it's on the first floor of Rua das Laranjeiras 1, Terreiro de Jesus, and may have classes open to tourists. Other schools are at the other end of Cidade Alta, at the Forte de Santo Antônio Além do Carmo: the Grupo de Capoeira Pelourinho, has classes on Tuesday, Thursday and Saturday from 7pm to 10pm; and the Centro Esportivo de Capoeira Angola is open all day to 10.30pm on weekdays, though you have to turn up to find out when the next class is – late afternoon is a good time, as afternoon and evening sessions are generally better attended.

building material for their mansions, part of the site used to found a university, and the rest parcelled out and sold for redevelopment.

The churches of São Francisco

Terreiro de Jesus has more than its fair share of churches; there are two more fine sixteenth-century examples on the square itself. But outshining them both, on nearby **Largo do Cruzeiro de São Francisco** (an extension of Terreiro de Jesus sometimes known as Praça Anchieta), are the superb carved stone facades of two ornate Baroque buildings, set in a single, large complex dedicated to St Francis: the **Igreja de São Francisco** (Mon–Sat 8am–5.30pm, Sun 7am–noon) and the **Igreja da Ordem Terceira de São Francisco** (Mon–Fri 8am–5pm). Of the two the latter has the edge: it's covered with a wild profusion of saints, virgins, angels and abstract patterns. Remarkably, the facade was hidden for 150 years, until in 1936 a painter knocked off a chunk of plaster by mistake and revealed the original frontage, Brazil's only example of high-relief facade carved in ashlar (square cut stones). It took nine years of careful chipping before the facade was returned to its original glory, and today the whole church is a strong contender for the most beautiful single building in the city. Its **reliquary**, or *ossuário*, is extraordinary, the entire room redecorated in the 1940s in Art Deco style, one of the most unusual examples you're ever likely to come across. From here, there's a door into a pleasant garden at the back.

To get into the complex, you have to go via the Igreja de São Francisco (the entrance is by a door to the right of the main doors). The small cloister in this church is decorated with one of the finest single pieces of *azulejo* work in Brazil. Running the entire length of the cloister, this **tiled wall** tells the story of the marriage of the son of the king of Portugal to an Austrian princess; beginning with the panel to the right of the church entrance, which shows the princess being ferried ashore to the reception committee, it continues with the procession of the happy couple in carriages through Lisbon, passing under a series of commemorative arches set up by the city guilds, whose names you can still just read – "The Royal Company of Bakers", "The Worshipful Company of Sweetmakers". The vigour and realism of the incidental detail in the street scenes is remarkable: beggars and cripples display their wounds, dogs skulk, children play in the gutter; and the panoramic view of Lisbon it displays is an important historical record of how Lisbon looked before the calamitous earthquake of 1755.

Around Largo do Pelourinho

Heading down the narrow Rua Alfredo de Brito, next to the Museu Afro-Brasileiro, brings you to the beautiful, cobbled **Largo do Pelourinho**, still much as it was during the eighteenth century. Lined with solid colonial mansions, it's topped by the oriental-looking towers of the **Igreja da Nossa Senhora dos Pretos** (Mon–Fri 9.30am–6pm, Sat 9.30am–5pm, Sun 10am–noon), built by and for slaves and still with a largely black congregation. Across from here is the **Casa de Jorge Amado** (Mon noon–6pm, Tues–Sat 9am–6pm), a museum given over to the life and work of the hugely popular novelist, who doesn't number modesty among his virtues; you can have fun spotting his rich and famous friends in the collection of photographs.

Next door, on the corner of Rua Gregório de Mattos, is the **Museu da Cidade** (Mon & Wed–Fri 9.30am–6.30pm, Sat 1–5pm, Sun 9.30am–1pm; free), housed in an attractive Pelourinho mansion. The lower levels are given over to paintings and sculpture by young city artists, some startlingly good and some pretty dire, while luxuriously dressed dummies show off Carnaval costumes from years gone by. There are models of *candomblé* deities and, on the first floor, a room containing the personal belongings of the greatest Bahian poet, Castro Alves, with some fascinating photographs from the beginning of the twentieth century. Completing the constellation of museums around Pelourinho is the **Museu Abelardo Rodrigues** (daily noon–6pm, closed Mon) at Rua Gregório de Mattos 45, which has a good collection of Catholic art from the sixteenth century onwards, well displayed in a restored seventeenth-century mansion.

From Largo do Pelourinho, a steep climb up Ladeira do Carmo rewards you with two more exceptional examples of colonial architecture: on the left is the **Convento da Ordem Primeira do Carmo** (Mon–Sat 9am–noon & 2–6pm), and on the right the **Igreja da Ordem Terceira de Nossa Senhora do Carmo** (Mon–Sat 9am–1pm & 2–6pm; 50¢). Both are built around large and beautiful cloisters, with a fine view across the old city at the back, and have chaotic but interesting museums attached. The convent museum is very eclectic, mostly religious but including collections of coins and furniture, with hundreds of unlabelled exhibits jumbled together in gloomy rooms. The highlight is a superbly expressive statue of Christ at the whipping post by Salvador's greatest colonial artist, the half-Indian slave **Francisco Manuel das Chagas**, whose powerful religious sculpture broke the formalistic bonds of the period – most of Chagas' work was completed in the 1720s. Unfortunately, Chagas died young of tuberculosis, leaving only a small body of work; this statue is appallingly displayed, jumbled together with much inferior work in a glass case in a corner of the rear gallery. In the church museum next door is another Chagas statue, a life-size body of Christ, this time sensibly displayed alone and, if anything, even more powerful. If you look closely at both statues, you'll find that the drops of blood are small rubies inlaid in the wood.

ACM and the restoration of Pelourinho

The Pelourinho district is now an attractive and much visited area, but it wasn't always this way. As recently as 1991 the area was virtually derelict, with many of the colonial buildings falling to pieces and tourism in decline. The fact that this has changed owes much to Bahia's most famous and most controversial politician, **Antônio Carlos Magalhães**. Widely disliked elsewhere in Brazil as an unreconstructed representative of the country's landed elite, the silver-haired **ACM** (as he's known) is popular in Bahia because of his tireless campaigns on behalf of his home state, and you'll see his picture hanging up in many of the city's bars. The revival of Pelourinho, which he undertook as state governor, was certainly impressive. Although there's a lot still to be done, much of the stunning colonial architecture has been restored to its original glory, the pastel pinks and blues creating a wonderfully gaudy effect. But the restoration has its critics too, who point to the fact that many local residents have had to be moved out in order for the work to take place, and complain that the area has become dominated by tourism. There is some truth to this, but you can still see plenty of locals out enjoying themselves alongside the tourists, and the economy of the area is clearly thriving; on the whole, it's hard to argue that Pelourinho was better off as a decaying shadow of its former self.

The rest of Cidade Alta is still largely colonial, and fascinating to wander around – although do it in daylight if you want to get off the main streets, and try to stick to where there are people around. Good streets to try are **Rua Gregório de Mattos** and the road on from the Carmo museums, **Rua Joaquim Távora**, which leads away from the heavier concentrations of tourists to the quiet Largo Cruz Pascoa and eventually ends up at the fort of **Santo Antônio Além do Carmo**, with a spectacular view across the bay. The simple bars on Largo Santo Antônio in front of the fort are a good place to rest your legs, have a drink and watch the stunning sunsets. Other good sundowner viewpoints on the edge of the bluff are the Praça da Sé itself, the bar of the *Hotel Pelourinho* (open to non-residents), and an unnamed bar on the left just after Largo Cruz Pascoa.

The Museu da Arte Sacra

Despite the concentration of riches in Cidade Alta, you have to leave the old city to find one of the finest museums of Catholic art in Brazil: the **Museu da Arte Sacra** at Rua Sodré 276 (Mon–Fri 11.30am–5.30pm; $1.80). It's slightly difficult to find: if you're coming into Praça Castro Alves from Rua Chile, go straight ahead and up Rua Carlos Gomes. Then take the first turning on your right down the steep Ladeira de Santa Teresa and you'll see the museum in front of you. It's housed in the seventeenth-century Santa Teresa convent, a magnificent building with much of its original furniture and fittings still intact, and with galleries on three floors surrounding a cloister. The chapel on the ground floor is lavishly decorated with elaborate, gilded carvings, and it leads into a maze of small galleries stuffed with a remarkably rich collection of colonial art, dating from the sixteenth century. The hundreds of statues, icons, paintings and religious artefacts are enough to occupy you for hours, the only real flaw in the collection being the absence of anything by Chagas or Aleijadinho (see p.183). There's still some high-quality work, though: small soapstone carvings on the top floor, marvellous tiling in the sacristy behind the chapel and a display of ornately carved religious accessories in solid gold and silver.

Cidade Baixa, the part of the city at the foot of the bluff, takes in the docks, the old harbour dominated by the circular sixteenth-century **Forte do Mar**, the ferry terminals and the main city markets. For the most part it's ugly modern urban sprawl, but for once the developers can't be blamed: the area was always the most neglected part of the city because its low-lying situation deprived it of the sea breezes and cooler air of the higher ground above. Since the sixteenth century, the city's inhabitants have only ventured down into the Cidade Baixa to work, choosing to live in the much pleasanter areas above and around.

All the same, it's not completely without interest. You are likely at least to pass through to get to the **ferry terminals** (see p.252). And there is one essential stop: the **Mercado Modelo** (daily 10am–6pm; free), an old covered market set on its own by the old harbour, across the road from the foot of the Lacerda elevator. It houses a huge and very enjoyable arts and crafts market, always crowded with Bahians as well as tourists, with the best selection of *artesanato* in the city. Not everything is cheap, so it helps to have the confidence to haggle. Some of the nicest souvenirs are the painted statues of *candomblé* deities – look for signs saying *artigos religiosos*. Even if you don't buy anything the building is a joy, a spacious nineteenth-century cathedral to commerce. There is always something going on in and around the market, with displays of *capoeira* common (and donations expected). There is an **information office** to the left of the front entrance (see p.251), and upstairs you will find a couple of good **restaurants** (see p.262).

The Igreja do Bonfim

The Igreja do Bonfim, as everyone calls the **Igreja do Nosso Senhor do Bonfim** (Tues–Sun 6.30am–noon & 2–6pm; free), sits on a hill overlooking the bay in the northwestern suburbs. The church is the focal point of colourful religious festivals that attract thousands of devotees from all over Brazil. To get there, take the buses marked "Bonfim" or "Ribeira" from the Estação da Lapa, or the bottom of the Lacerda elevator.

The church is not, by any means, the oldest or most beautiful in the city – completed in 1745 with a plain white exterior and simple interior – but it's easily the most interesting. The force of popular devotion is obvious from the moment you leave the bus. The large square in front of the church is lined with stalls catering for the hundreds of pilgrims who arrive every day, and you'll be besieged by small children selling *fitas*, ribbons in white and blue, the church colours, to tie around your wrist for luck and to hang in the church when you make your requests; it's ungracious to enter the church without a few. It's always at least half-full of people worshipping, often with almost hypnotic fervour: middle-class matrons and uniformed military officers rub shoulders with peasants from the *sertão* and women from the *favelas*.

For a clearer idea of what this place means to the people of Bahia, go to the right of the nave where a wide corridor leads to the **Museu dos Ex-Votos do Senhor do Bonfim** (Tues–Sat 8.30–11.30am & 2.30–7pm, Sun 8.30–11.30am; free). An incredibly crowded antechamber gives you an idea of what to expect: lined to the roof with thousands of small photographs of supplicants, with notes pinned to the wall requesting intervention or giving thanks for benefits received. Every spare inch is covered with a forest of ribbons, one for each request, some almost rotted away with age, and many of the written pleas are heart-rending: for the life of a dying child, for news from a husband who emigrated south, for the safe return of sailors and fishermen, for success in an exam, for money to pay for a college education, for a favourite football team to win a championship – in short, a snapshot of everyday worries and hopes. Hanging from the roof are dozens of body parts – limbs, heads, even organs like hearts and lungs – made of wood or plastic for anxious patients asking for protection before an operation, silver for relieved patients giving thanks after successful surgery. Some people blessed by a particularly spectacular escape pay tribute by leaving a pictorial record of the miracle: photos of smashed cars that the driver walked away from, or crude but vivid paintings of fires, sinkings and electrocutions.

Upstairs in the museum proper is the oldest material and recent offerings judged worthy of special display. It's not only the poor who come asking for help: there are several university classbooks deposited here, and military insignia commemorating promotion up to the rank of general. The more valuable *ex votos* are displayed here in ranks of cases, classified according to the part of the body: silver heads and limbs you might expect, even silver hearts, lungs, ears, eyes and noses, but the serried ranks of silver kidneys, spleens, livers and intestines are striking. There are also football shirts – the city's two big teams always make a visit at the start of the season – models of the church, and dozens of paintings, especially of fires and shipwrecks.

Museu Nautico da Bahia

Located on the Avenida Oceânica in the wealthy suburb of Barra, the **Museu Nautico** (closed for restoration in 2003) sits underneath the lighthouse in the picturesque white Forte de Santo Antônio on the windy Barra point – the spot where the Atlantic Ocean becomes the Bay of Todos os Santos. The museum houses an interesting collection of seafaring instruments and maps. Local buses and the *executivo* service to Barra leave from the Praca da Sé.

Eating, drinking and nightlife

Eating out is one of the major pleasures Salvador has to offer, and the local cuisine (*comida baiana*) is deservedly famous. There's a huge range of restaurants and, although Cidade Alta has an increasing number of stylish, expensive places, it's still quite possible to eat well for significantly less than $10, though

Comida Baiana: dishes and ingredients

The secret of Bahian cooking is twofold: a rich seafood base, and the abundance of traditional West African **ingredients** like palm oil, nuts, coconut and ferociously strong peppers. Many ingredients and dishes have African names: most famous of all is *vatapá*, a bright yellow porridge of palm oil, coconut, shrimp and garlic, which looks vaguely unappetizing but is delicious. Other dishes to look out for are *moqueca*, seafood cooked in the inevitable palm-oil based sauce; *caruru*, with many of the same ingredients as *vatapá* but with the vital addition of loads of okra; and *acarajé*, deep-fried bean cake stuffed with *vatapá*, salad and (optional) hot pepper. Bahian cuisine also has good **desserts**, less stickily sweet than elsewhere: *quindim* is a delicious small cake of coconut flavoured with vanilla, which often comes with a prune in the middle.

Some of the best food is also the cheapest, and even gourmets could do a lot worse than start with the street-corner *baianas*, women in traditional white dress. Be careful of the *pimenta*, the very hot pepper sauce, which newcomers should treat with respect, taking only a few drops. The *baianas* serve *quindim*, *vatapá*, slabs of maize pudding wrapped in banana leaves, fried bananas dusted with icing sugar, and fried sticks of sweet batter covered with sugar and cinnamon – all absolutely wonderful.

easier to spend $20. You should certainly treat yourself to at least one slap-up feed before leaving the city.

Restaurants

The cheapest places for a sit-down meal are around **Praça Castro Alves** and in **Cidade Baixa**. Restaurants in the **Pelourinho** area and the **beach districts** are classier and tend to be more expensive. Especially at Barra and Rio Vermelho, the seafront promenade is lined with bars, cafés and restaurants, and the best option is to take a bus and hop off wherever you fancy. The non-Brazilian cuisines tend to be concentrated in **Barra**, where Salvador's upper middle class lives.

Aquarela Av. Oceânica, Barra 141 ℡71/261-3222. Popular restaurant serving up Greek food and fish dishes. Moderate.

Aquárius Restaurant Rua Ribeiro dos Santos 37, Pelourinho. Inexpensive restaurant serving local cuisine that does good *carne do sol* and has a lovely view over the old city.

Casa da Gamboa Rua João de Deus 32, Pelourinho ℡71/321-3393. One of the district's top restaurants and worth a splurge, serving mainly Bahian dishes. Expect to pay at least $20 per head. Closed Sun.

Café Odean Rua Joao de Deus 01, 1st floor, Pelourinho ℡71/321-5725. Trendy, very modern café, with loads of weird organic material and objects woven into the fabric of the furniture. Right in the middle of the action, the place gets especially busy on Friday and Saturday nights when there's a $3 minimum consumption charge.

Casa do Benin Padre Agustinho Gomes 17, Pelourinho. Excellent, reasonably priced African food at the southern edge of Largo do Pelourinho.

Don Vitellone's Trattoria Rua Dom Marcos Teixeira 25, Barra ℡71/267-4996. Good Italian food accompanied by slightly fussy service. Notable for its great antipasto self-service plus a wide range of tasty menu choices and some fine wines.

Jardim Delicias Café Rua João de Deus 12, Pelourinho. Fantastic Bahian and international cuisine served both inside and out (in the lovely garden); the salads are especially good.

Maria de São Pedro first floor of the Mercado Modelo, Cidade Baixa. A good Bahian restaurant with great views across the bay – if you can get a table on the terrace. Next door, the *Camafeu de Oxóssi* offers much the same fare at moderate prices.

Maria Mata Mouro Rua Inacio Acioly 08, Pelourinho ℡71/326-7330. One of the finest Bahian restaurants in the district, with prices to match; whatever you choose will be divine and lovingly presented. Very busy at weekends, so it's best to book a table in advance.

Mustafa Rua Alexandre Maia 6, Clube de Bridge da Bahia, Graça ℡71/247-9884. Arabic restaurant, popular with locals and serving excellent food, though it's not cheap. Getting a taxi from the Barra seafront is the easiest way to get there, as the road is a little obscure.

Restaurante Aroma Gostoso Rua Afonso Celso 294, Barra ℡71/264-5282. A quality self-service lunchtime restaurant, quite close to the beach, offering a wide selection of dishes from the region that will appeal to vegetarians and meat-eaters alike.

Restaurante Contos dos Réis Rua do Carmo 66, Pilar. If you want maximum indulgence for both your eyes and your tastebuds, try this restaurant, beyond Pelourinho and on the way to the fort of Santo Antônio Além do Carmo. It's by no means cheap but the setting – with the whole of the bay spread out beneath you – is breathtaking.

Restaurante do SENAC Largo do Pelourinho, opposite the Casa Jorge Amado, Pelourinho ℡71/321-5502. Municipal restaurant school in a finely restored colonial mansion. It looks very expensive from the outside, but it's good value for what you get. You pay a set charge – about $15 – and take as much as you want from a quality buffet of around fifty dishes, all helpfully labelled so that you know what you're eating. If you go for dinner, try to finish before 10pm, when there's a rather touristy folklore show.

Restaurante Extudo Rua Lídio Mesquita 4, Rio Vermelho. Inexpensive, popular little bar and restaurant serving a wide range of food, including some Bahian dishes.

Sukiyaki Av. Oceânica 3562, Barra ℡71/247-5063. Excellent Japanese place, near to the Ondina seafront. There's a branch at the Aeroclube Plaza Show in Boca do Rio (℡71/461-0365). Very trendy place to eat; food's very fresh and tasty.

Uauá Rua Gregório de Mattos 36, Pelourinho. A very popular restaurant specializing in Northeastern food from both the coast and the interior, with prices on the moderate to expensive side.

Yemanjá Av. Otávio Mangabeira 45655, Pituba ℡71/461-9010. Highly recommended Bahian restaurant– a far better bet than the large, over-priced restaurants at the far end of the district.

Nightlife

Salvador's most distinctive **nightlife** is to be found in **Pelourinho**. The whole area is always very lively, and there are any number of bars where you can sit and while the evening away. The Rua das Laranjeiras, Cruzeiro de São Francisco and Rua Castro Rabelo are all good places to head for, and it's local custom to start off the evening at the *O Gravinho* bar, Largo Terreiro de Jesus 03, for a glass of specially flavoured *cachaça*; the most traditional being made from essence of clove or ginger.

Bars aside, undoubtedly the biggest attraction of the area is the chance to hear **live music**. Musically, Salvador marches to a different beat from the rest of Brazil. Instead of being connected to a single style, as Rio is to samba and Recife is to *frevo*, Salvador has spawned several, and in recent years it has overtaken Rio to become the most creative centre of Brazilian music. Some of the best music in the city comes from organized cultural groups, who work in the communities that spawned them, and have their own clubhouses and an *afoxé* or two – Salvador's Africanized version of a *bloco* – for Carnaval. They are overwhelmingly black and a lot of their music is political. In the weeks leading up to Carnaval, their *afoxés* have public rehearsals around the clubhouses, and the music is superb (see "Carnaval" p.265). For the rest of the year, the clubhouses are used as bars and meeting places, often with music at weekends.

Many find it a bit claustrophobic in Cidade Alta and head for the **beaches** instead. For **dancing** into the small hours, Amaralina and Pituba are probably the liveliest areas to head for, and Friday and Saturday nights are best. Bars, too, often have **live music**, and listings appear in the local papers at weekends; try the Sunday edition of *A Tarde*. As far as specific places go, *Travessia* at Av. Otávio Mangabeira 168 in Pituba (open 24hr Fri–Sun only) gets very busy, playing mostly samba, reggae or *forró*, and there's often good music, too, at *Canteiros*, Rua Minas Gerais in Pituba, starting after 9pm on Friday and Saturday.

There's more live music (mainly popular Brazilian and rock) and the chance to kick up your heels at the *Cachaçaria Alambique* **shows** in Rio Vermelho and at the *Rock in Rio Cafe*, Av. Otávio Mangabeira 6000, Boca do Rio (☎71/461-0300). You can sample regional cuisine and folk dancing at *Solar de União* (noon–midnight), a popular restaurant and club in the former slave market, north along the seafront from the Mercado Modelo and the new marina.

Big names in Brazilian music play the Teatro Castro Alves on Campo Grande. The SENAC building on Largo do Pelourinho has an outdoor arena and basement theatre, used for plays, concerts and displays. Also scan posters and local papers (under *Lazer*), or ask at the tourist office.

Salvador also has a lively **gay scene**. *Holmes 24th* on Rua Gamboa de Cima, opposite the Rua Banco dos Ingleses, is especially hopping on Fridays (take a taxi). *Caverna*, Rua Carlos Goma 616, Centro (☎71/358-2410), is a popular underground close to Salvador's best nightlife, while *New Look Bar Holme*, Rua Gamboa de Cima 24, in Gamboa (☎71/336-4949), is a bit more laid-back. *Beco dos Artistas* is a predominantly gay bar by the side of the Teatro Castro Alves, on Rua Leovigildo Filgueiiras (entrance beside the pizzeria).

Salvador's festivals

The two main **popular festivals** of the year, besides Carnaval, take place either in or near the Igreja do Bonfim. On New Year's Day the **Procissão no Mar**, the "Sea Procession", sees statues of the seafarers' protectors, Nosso Senhor dos Navegantes and Nossa Senhora da Conceição, carried in a decorated nineteenth-century boat across the bay from the old harbour to the church of Boa

Candomblé

Candomblé, a popular Afro-Brazilian religious cult, permeates the city. Its followers often dress in white and worship together in ecstatic dance rituals accompanied by lots of drumming and singing, or otherwise communicate with and make offerings to the Orixás spirits, personal protectors, guides and go-betweens for people and their creator-god Olorum.

A *candomblé* cult house, or *terreiro*, is headed by a *mãe do santo* (woman) or *pai do santo* (man), who directs the operations of dozens of novices and initiates. The usual object is to persuade the spirits to descend into the bodies of worshippers, which is achieved by sacrifices (animals are killed outside public view and usually during the day), offerings of food and drink, and above all by drumming, dancing and the invocations of the *mãe* or *pai do santo*. In a central dance area, which may be decorated, devotees dance for hours to induce the trance that allows the spirits to enter them. Witnessing a possession can be quite frightening: sometimes people whoop and shudder, their eyes roll up, and they whirl around the floor, bouncing off the walls while other cult members try to make sure they come to no harm. The *mãe* or *pai do santo* then calms them, blows tobacco smoke over them, identifies the spirit, gives them the insignia of the deity – a pipe or a candle, for example – and lets them dance on. Each deity has its own songs, animals, colours, qualities, powers and holy day; and there are different types of *candomblé*, as well as other related Afro-Brazilian religions like *umbanda*.

Many travel agencies offer tours of the city that include a visit to a *terreiro*, but no self-respecting cult house would allow itself to be used in this way – those which do are to be avoided. The best alternative is to go to the main Bahiatursa office (see p.251), which has a list of less commercialized *terreiros*, all fairly far out in the suburbs and best reached by taxi. Make sure that the *terreiro* is open first: they only have ceremonies on certain days sacred to one of the pantheon of gods and goddesses, and you just have to hope you strike lucky – though fortunately there's no shortage of deities.

If you go to a *terreiro*, there are certain **rules** you must observe. A *terreiro* should be respected and treated for the church it is. Clothes should be smart and modest: long trousers and a clean shirt for men, non-revealing blouse and trousers or long skirt for women. The dancing area is a sacred space and no matter how infectious you find the rhythms you should do no more than stand or sit around its edges. And don't take photographs without asking permission from the *mãe* or *pai do santo* first, or you will give offence. You may find people coming round offering drinks from jars, or items of food: it's impolite to refuse, but watch what everyone else does first – sometimes food is not for eating but for throwing over dancers, and the story of the gringos who ate the popcorn intended as a sacred offering to the spirits is guaranteed to bring a smile to any Brazilian face.

To read more on *candomblé* as practiced in Cachoeira, see box on p.270.

Viagem, on the shore down from Bonfim. The boat leaves at around 9am from Praça Cairú, next to the Mercado Modelo in Cidade Baixa, and hundreds of schooners and fishing boats wait to join the procession as the statues' boat passes: you can buy a place on the phalanx of boats that leaves with the statues, but the crowds are thick and if you want to go by sea you should get there early. On the shores of Boa Viagem, thousands wait to greet the holy images, after which there's a packed Mass in the church, and then Nossa Senhora da Conçeicão is taken back by land in another procession to her church near the foot of the Lacerda elevator. The celebrations around both churches go on for hours, with thousands drinking and dancing the night away. The spectacle, with the bay as an enormous backdrop, is impressive enough: participating in it is exhilarating.

Soon afterwards, on the second Thursday of January, comes the **Lavagem do Bonfim**, "the washing of Bonfim", second only to Carnaval in scale. Hundreds of *baianas*, women in the traditional all-white costume of turban, lace blouse and billowing long skirts, gather in front of the Igreja de Nossa Senhora da Conceição, and a procession follows them the 12km along the seafront to the Igreja do Bonfim, with tens of thousands more lining the route: the pace is slow, and there is no shortage of beer and music while you wait. At the church, everyone sets to scrubbing the square spotless, cleaning the church and decorating the exterior with flowers and strings of coloured lights, and that evening, and every evening until Sunday, raucous celebrations go on into the small hours, the square crowded with people. If you have the stamina, the focus switches on Monday to Ribeira, the headland beyond Bonfim, for a completely secular preview of Carnaval. Here you can freshen up after dancing in the hot sun by swimming at the excellent beaches.

Carnaval

Having steadfastly resisted commercialization, Carnaval in Salvador has remained a street event of mass participation. The main hubs of activity are **Cidade Alta**, especially the area around Praça Castro Alves – which turns into a seething mass of people that, once joined, is almost impossible to get out of – and, in recent years, **Porto da Barra**, equally crowded and just as enjoyable. The other focal point of Carnaval is the **northern beaches**, especially around the hotels in Rio Vermelho and Ondina, but here it's more touristy and lacks the energy of the centre.

From December onwards Carnaval groups hold **public rehearsals** and dances all over the city. The most famous are Grupo Cultural Oludum: they rehearse on Sunday nights from 6.30pm onwards in the Largo do Pelourinho itself and on Tuesdays from 7.30pm in the Teatro Miguel Santana on Rua Gregório de Mattos. On Friday night, it's the turn of Ara Ketu, who start their show at 7pm in Rua Chile, and Ilê Aiyê rehearse on Saturdays from 8pm near the fort of Santo Antônio Além do Carmo. These rehearsals get very crowded, so be careful with your belongings. One of the oldest and best loved of the *afoxés* is Filhos de Gandhi ("Sons of Gandhi"), founded in the 1940s, who have a clubhouse in Rua Gregório de Mattos, near Largo do Pelourinho, easily recognized by the large papier-mâché white elephant in the hall.

Information about Carnaval is published in special supplements in the local papers on Thursday and Saturday. Bahiatursa and EMTURSA offices also have schedules, route maps, and sometimes sell tickets for the Campo Grande grandstands. One point worth bearing in mind is that all-black *blocos* may be black culture groups who won't appreciate being joined by non-black Brazilians, let alone gringos, so look to see who's dancing before leaping in amongst them.

Listings

Airlines Air France, Rua Portugal 17, Ed. Regente Feijó, Cidade Baixa ☎71/351-6631; Lufthansa, Av. Tancredo Neves 805, Sala 601, Iguatemi ☎71341-5100; TAP Air Portugal, Av. Estados Unidos 137, Ed. Cidade de Ilhéus, Cidade Baixa ☎71/243-6122; Transbrasil, Rua Portugal 3, Cidade Baixa ☎71/326-1044; Varig, Rua Carlos Gomes 6, Cidade Alta ☎71/343-3100 or 204-1050, or Rua Miguel Calmon 19, Cidade Baixa ☎71/243-9311; VASP, Rua Chile 27, Edifício Chile, Cidade Alta ☎71/204-1304, Rua Miguel Calmon 27, Cidade Baixa, or Rua Marquês de Leão 455, Barra.

Banks and exchange There are several places where you can change money in the Pelourinho area, including Olímpio Turismo on Largo do Cruzeiro de São Francisco and Vert-Tour on Rua das Laranjeiras. You'll get lower, but still reasonable, rates for dollars (cash and travellers' cheques) at the smarter beach hotels in Ondina and Pituba. On no account change on the street, especially around the Lacerda elevator. Banco do Brasil has branches, all with Visa ATMs, at Av. Sete de Setembro 254 in Cidade Alta; Av. Estados Unidos 561 in Cidade Baixa; and in Shopping Barra, among many others around the city. Bahia Dourada shop at Praça da Sé 04/24, in the historic centre, offers reasonable money exhange rates in a relatively safe environment.

Car rental Avis Rentacar, Av. Sete de Setembro 1796 ☎71/377-2276; Localiza, based at airport ☎71/332-1999; Nobre Rent a Car, Av. Oceânica 409 ☎71/245-8022.

Consulates Canada, Av. Presidente Vargas 2400, Sala 311, Ondina Apart Hotel, Ondina ☎71/331-0064; UK, Av. Estados Unidos 4, 18-B 8th floor, Cidade Baixa; US, Rua Pernambuco 51, Pituba.

Football Salvador has a couple of good teams. The most popular, Bahia, have a tradition of playing open, attacking football in the best Brazilian tradition. The biggest matches take place on Sunday afternoons in the Estádio Otávio Mangabeira, close to the centre; take the bus marked "Nazaré" from Campo Grande, or it's a short taxi ride.

Internet CafeBrasil.com at Praça da Sé 24, in the heart of the historic centre; Groovy Dig's Cybercafe, Av. Sete de Setembro 3713, Barra (daily 8am–midnight); Internet Café at Rua João de Deus 2, Pelourinho; and *Ondina Apart Hotel*, Av. Presidente Vargas 2400, Loja 37.

Laundry Lavanderia Lavalimpo, Rua do Pilar 31, Cidade Baixa; Lav–Lev, Av. Manoel Dias da Silva 2364, Pituba.

Post office At the airport; Marquês de Caravelas 101, Barra; Shopping Barra, 3rd floor; Av. Amaralina 908, Amaralina; Rua J. Seabra 234; the *rodoviária*; Rua Rui Barbosa 19, Cidade Alta; at the Praça da Inglaterra, Cidade Baixa. Opening hours are Mon–Fri 8am–6pm.

Shopping The main place for *artesanato* is the Mercado Modelo in Cidade Baixa (see p.260). Good, cheap leatherwork is available from the street stalls of Barroquinha, the steep street lead-ing downhill just before Praça Castro Alves; and clothes and shoes can be found in the commercial area further down. For luxury items, clothes, books, CDs and food, head for either Shopping Barra or Iguatemi Shopping. Projecto Axé, Rua das Laranjeiras 22, sells great, colourful clothing – the money from which goes to support street kids. For films and camera equipment, try Fotografa, Rua Chile 10; Fotosystem, Rua Chile 4; or Minilab, on the corner of Rua Chile and Rua do Tiro Chapén. For gem stones, try Agua Marina, Terreiro de Jesus 15, Pelourinho, or Kaufmann Gems at Rua Alfredo de Brito 09, Pelourinho.

Taxis Chame Táxi ☎71/241-2266; Teletáxi ☎71/341-9988.

Telephones You can make international collect calls from a booth on Terreiro de Jesus; other *postos telefônicos* are in the airport, the *rodoviária*, in Campo da Pólvora in Cidade Alta, and in Iguatemi Shopping. International calls can be made direct with phone cards from almost any phone kiosk in Salvador.

Travel and tour companies Ceu e Mar Turismo, Rua Fonte do Boi 12, Rio Vermelho (☎71/334-7566, ⓕ335-1351 ⓔceuemar@e-net.com.br), is a good travel agent and also represents the Student Travel Bureau. LR Turismo, Rua Marques de Leao 172, Barra (☎71/264-0999, ⓔlrturismo@e-net.com.br) runs several exciting tours, from historic Bahia to boat trips to the tropical islands in the Bahia de Todos os Santos. Tours Bahia, Cruzeiro de Sao Francisco 4, Centro Historic (☎71/322-3676, ⓔtbi@compos.com.br) offer a range of services, covering city tours, airline tickets, transfers and money exchange. Privé Tur, Av. Sete de Setembro 2068, Vitória (☎71/336-7522, ⓕ337-3773) organize city tours, beach trips and schooner cruises. Dive Bahia, Av. Sete de Setembro 3809, Barra (☎71/264-3820) run scuba diving courses, while Brazil Yacht Charter, Av. Do Contorno 1010, Bahia Marina (☎71/321-1872, ⓦwww.byc.com.br) run boat trips, mainly by sail.

Around Salvador

Salvador looks onto the **Baía de Todos os Santos**, a bay ringed with beaches and dotted with tropical **islands**. To the **northeast** of the city a string of fishing villages lies along a beautiful coastline – in short, there's no lack of places to explore.

The bay: Ilha de Itaparica

Itaparica is always visible from Salvador, looking as if it forms the other side of the bay, but in reality it's a narrow island, 35km long, that acts as a natural breakwater. After the local Indians were driven out, it was taken over by the Jesuits in 1560, making it one of the earliest places to be settled by the Portuguese. Its main town, also called **ITAPARICA**, was briefly the capital of Bahia before the Portuguese were expelled from Salvador, though little evidence remains here of these times, apart from a couple of small seventeenth-century chapels. The lovely island is now very much seen as an appendage of the city, whose inhabitants flock to its beaches at weekends, building villas by the score as they go. It's quiet enough during the week, though, and big enough to find calmer spots even at the busiest times. Apart from the beaches, Itaparica is famous for its fruit trees, especially its mangoes, which are prized throughout Bahia.

Most **ferries** (see p.252) leave you at the **Bom Despacho** terminal in Itaparica town, although some boats also go to the anchorage at **Mar Grande**, a couple of kilometres away. For **getting around** once you're there, use the Kombis (minibuses) and buses that ply the coastline, or rent **bicycles** (rental places are easily spotted by the bikes piled up on the pavement). If you want to stay on the island, there are some reasonable hotels, but most are on the expensive side thanks to Itaparica's popularity as a resort for Salvador's middle classes, and cheaper ones are often full from December to Carnaval. Good options include *Club Méditerranée*, Estr. Praia da Conceição (℡71/880-7141, ℗880-7380; ❸), a luxurious hotel set directly on the beachfront; *Pousada Jardim Tropical*, Estr. da Rodagem, Praia Ponta de Areia 3.5km (℡71/831-1409; ❹), with a pool and a reasonable restaurant; and *Recanto do Guiga*, Praia da Barra do Pote (℡71/880-7268; ❸), a small *pousada* on the seafront near a fishing village.

To see anything of the **other islands** scattered across the bay – 31 of them, most either uninhabited or home to a few simple fishing villages – travel agents in Salvador offer day-long cruises in private schooners; the kiosks in the city's Terminal Turístico are the easiest places to buy tickets. It's less busy during the week, but crowded schooners have their advantages. If you manage to get on one full of Brazilian tourists you're likely to have a very lively time indeed, and drinks are often included in the price.

Northeast to Arembepe, Itacimirim and Praia do Forte

Buses from Salvador's *rodoviária* run along the coastal road (Estrada do Coco) to **AREMBEPE**, 50km away, a former hippy hangout now gone up in the world, though still peaceful and very pretty, with a pleasant little beach sheltered by a coral reef. The journey there takes you past some fine beaches and small, friendly villages, and you can get off wherever takes your fancy. Finding accommodation is easy everywhere along this route, as you're heading along a well-beaten tourist track. Don't be put off, though – it's a beautiful coastline and the beaches are long enough to swallow the crowds. There are plenty of **places to stay** in Arembepe itself: basic options on the seafront include the *Praia de Arembepe Hotel*, Largo São Francisco (℡71/824-1415; ❶), and the *Pousada Enseada do Cabral* (℡71/824-1231; ❷), the latter with a restaurant. More upmarket are the beachfront *Pousada Ondas do Mar* (℡71/824-1052; ❹), a comfortable place overlooking the harbour, and the good-value *O Turbarão Hotel*, Rua Manoel Coelho (℡71/824-1055; ❸), which has a pool, and rooms and apartments facing the beach. For **food**, the main *praça* has some options, but for cold beer and the best seafood in town head for the *Restaurant Coló*, which has a shaded terrace on the beach; try the *peixes moqueca* or the *lagosta salada* (lobster salad). Close to the harbour, the small seafood **market**, Mercado do Frutas Mar (Mon–Sat mornings), sells delicious-looking *lagosta* and *carangueijo* (crab).

Fifteen kilometres further northeast, the beach resort of **ITACIMIRIM** is not as developed as many, though there are a few hotels and lots of smart weekend residences. Out of high season and during the week, you can have this palm-fringed paradise more or less to yourself. If you want **to stay** over, the *Hotel Itacimirim* (☎71/826-1304, ⓕ826-1503; ❸) is right on the beach, while nearby, set back from the sands, there's the modern and less characterful *Hotel Beira Mar* (☎71/826-1217; ❸), which has a small pool, a bar and plain but nice rooms, some with ocean views.

A little further up the road, the hip little resort of **PRAIA DO FORTE**, 85km north of Salvador, has a couple of exceptionally nice, if small, beaches, lots of arty craft shops and some good restaurants, but is best known for the Projecto Tamar **turtle reserve** (daily 8am–7pm; $1.50). Of the seven species of sea turtle in the world, four nest off the coast of Bahia, but over-fishing and the destruction of nesting sites by human activity and urban development have seriously threatened their survival. The work of the Projecto Tamar (☎71/676-1045, ⓦwww.projetotamar.org.br) has included identifying the turtles' main nesting areas along a 1000km stretch of coastline and ensuring their protection. The local community at Praia do Forte was mainly a fishing village until eco-tourism and the turtle project arrived in the mid-1990s; today most of the 2000 residents make their income from tourism. The beaches and turtle reserve are at the end of the main drag, beyond all the craft shops and stalls. Inside the reserve, you can see many turtles in large aquariums, most of them injured and unlikely to survive in the wild. The nesting season is from September to March.

There are several good options if you want **to stay** in Praia do Forte: the *Pousada do Forte*, Almeda do Sol 4 (☎71/676-1043; ❸), offers great-value rooms and a small pool, and is located on the main sandy drag, while the *Pousada Ogum Marinho* (☎71/676-1062; ❸) is very close to the beach at the end of the main street, with cosy rooms and a nice hammock veranda. The *Do Souza*, on the first corner of the main street as you come into town, is understandably the most popular seafood **restaurant**, its terrace shaded by a massive angelin tree. There's a small sushi bar on one of the side streets, too, and an ice-cream parlour, the *Tutti Frutti*, nearby.

At the entrance to the town itself, standing alone on a small grassy mound there's a **tourist information** kiosk. **Buses** leave regularly (4 daily) from the main street for Salvador. For general tourist information and photos of the area, check out ⓦwww.praiadoforte.org.br.

The Recôncavo and Valença

The **Recôncavo**, the early Portuguese plantation zone named after the concave shape of the bay, arcs out from Salvador along 150km of coastline, before petering out in the mangrove swamps around the town of **Valença**. It's one of the most lush tropical coastlines in Brazil, with palm-covered hills breaking up the green and fertile coastal plains. And it's still one of the most important agricultural areas in Bahia, supplying the state with much of its fruit and spices. Only the sugar plantations around Recife could match the wealth of the Recôncavo, but, unlike that region, the Recôncavo survived the decline of the sugar trade by diversifying into tobacco and spices – especially peppers and cloves. It was the agricultural wealth of the Recôncavo that paid for most of the fine buildings of Salvador and, until the cocoa boom in southern Bahia in the 1920s, **Cachoeira** was by some way the second city of the state. The beau-

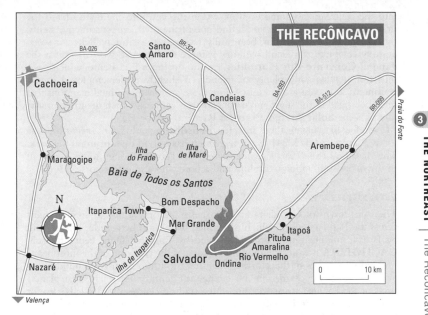

ty of the area and the richness of its colonial heritage make it one of the more rewarding parts of the Northeast to explore.

Access is good, with the main highway, the BR-324, approximately following the curve of the bay, and good local roads branching off to the towns in the heart of the Recôncavo. Thirty kilometres out of Salvador, a turn-off leads to Candéias, continuing on to Santo Amaro and the twin towns of Cachoeira and São Félix. Regular buses go to all these places from the *rodoviária* in Salvador.

Candéias and Santo Amaro

CANDÉIAS is nowhere special, a modern market town 30km from Salvador, but 7km outside there's a good introduction to the history of the area in the **Museu do Recôncavo** (Tues, Thurs & Sun 9am–5pm), situated in a restored plantation called the Engenho da Freguesia, where pictures and artefacts from three centuries illustrate the economic and social dimensions of plantation life. The owners' mansion and the slave quarters have been impressively restored, juxtaposing the horrors of slave life – there's a fearsome array of manacles, whips and iron collars – with the elegant period furniture and fittings of the mansion. The only problem is that no bus service passes the museum: if you don't go by car you have to take a taxi from Candéias, around $15.

SANTO AMARO, a further 20km from Salvador, is a lovely colonial town straddling the banks of a small river. It was the birthplace and is still the home of Caetano Veloso, one of Bahia's most famous singers and poets, who sings Santo Amaro's praises on many of his records. There's no tourist office, and the best thing to do is simply to wander around the quiet streets and squares, absorbing the atmosphere.

If you're arriving on the bus from Salvador, wait till it stops at the *rodoviária* before getting off, then turn left as you come out of the station in order to get into the centre. A few minutes' walk will bring you into the main square, the Praça da Purificação, where you'll find one of the town's most attractive sights, the **Igreja da Purificação**: beautifully restored, the church shelters a wonderfully elaborate eighteenth-century painted ceiling. Also worth a visit is the tranquil **Convento dos Humildes**, nearby on Praça Frei Bento, which has a museum attached, and plenty of friendly if slightly under-employed guides waiting to show you around. Elsewhere there are various ruined mansions that once belonged to the sugar and tobacco barons, among which the most atmospheric is the **Solar Araújo Pinto**, at Rua Imperador 1.

If you feel like staying, there are a few **pensões**, including the *Amarós*, on Rua Cons. Saraiva 27 (☎75/241-1202; ①), which has a good **restaurant** at the back. The *Agua Viva Praia*, Praia Fazenda ☎75/699-1176; ④), though some 34km out of town, has well-appointed cabins and a pool, and also offers horse riding.

Cachoeira

The twin towns of Cachoeira and São Félix are only a few kilometres apart across the Rio Paraguaçu, which is spanned by an iron box-girder bridge built by British engineers in 1885 and opened by Emperor Dom Pedro himself. **CACHOEIRA** is easily the more impressive of the two, one of the most beautiful colonial towns of the Northeast, with a profusion of fine old buildings as evidence of its importance in the eighteenth century. The rich sugar plantations of the Paraguaçu valley supported a trading centre that rivalled Salvador in size and wealth until the beginning of the nineteenth century. The town was the site of a short but vicious war in 1822 to expel the Portuguese from Bahia, when a docked Portuguese warship was stormed by the inhabitants, the city becoming the first in Brazil to declare allegiance to Dom Pedro I. The Portuguese general, Madeira de Melo, bombarded the town in retaliation, but this only provoked the countryside into general revolt, and troops from Cachoeira led a victorious assault on Salvador. After that began the long decline that turned it into the splendidly preserved small town it is today.

The Town

Get off the bus in Rua Lauro de Freitas at the bus company office; don't wait until it crosses the river into São Félix or you'll have to walk back across the bridge. A couple of blocks back along Rua Lauro de Freitas past the market

---

Candomblé in Cachoeira

Cachoeira is known for its **candomblé**, with some *terreiros* still conducting rituals in African dialects that nobody now speaks, recognizable as variants of West African and Angolan languages. One of the best-known *candomblé* events is Cachoeira's fiesta of **Nossa Senhora da Boa Morte**, which always begins on the first Friday before August 15. It's staged by a sisterhood, the Irmandade da Boa Morte, founded by freed women slaves in the mid-nineteenth century, partly as a religious group and partly to work for the emancipation of slaves by acting as an early co-operative bank to buy people their liberty. All the local *candomblé* groups turn out with drummers and singers, and although the name of the fiesta is Catholic it's a celebration of *candomblé*, with centre stage held by the dignified matriarchs of the sisterhood. The other great day in the *candomblé* year is the **Festa de Santa Barbara**, on December 4 in São Félix, dedicated to the goddess Iansã. There are several other fiestas worth catching, like the **São João** celebrations, from June 22 to 24, while five saints' days are crammed into the last three months of the year; check with Bahiatursa for exact dates (see p.251).

you'll come to the fine Praça Doutor Milton, with its Baroque public fountain and the early eighteenth-century bulk of the **Santa Casa da Misericórdia**, which has a beautiful small garden. Leaving Praça Doutor Milton in the direction of the river, go up the narrow, cobbled Rua da Ajuda, and after a short climb you'll come to a peaceful little square that contains the **Capela de Nossa Senhora da Ajuda**, the city's oldest church. Begun in 1595 and completed eleven years later, it just about qualifies as sixteenth century, which makes it a rarity. Sadly, the simple but well-proportioned interior is often closed to visitors for fear of thieves, but if you knock on the door there might be someone around to let you in.

If you go straight on down the hill as you come out of the Capela de Nossa Senhora da Ajuda, you'll find yourself in Rua 13 de Maio. On your right is the **Museu da Irmandade da Boa Morte**, which is connected with the August festival known as Nossa Senhora da Boa Morte (see box opposite). Just a few steps in the other direction is a renovated building that houses the small **Museu Hansen Bahia**, dedicated to the work of a German engraver who settled in the town. There's a lively tradition of **woodcarving** in Cachoeira and several sculptors have studios open to the public. One of the best is **Louco Junior**, who displays his wonderful elongated carvings in his studio on Rua 13 de Maio. The first turning on your left out of Rua 13 de Maio takes you up to Rua Ana Néri and the impressive **Igreja Matriz de Nossa Senhora do Rosário**. Again, the church has been robbed all too frequently and is sometimes shut, but if you can get in you'll see two huge five-metre-high *azulejo* panels dating from the 1750s.

At the end of Rua Ana Néri, in the opposite direction from Praça Doutor Milton, is the finest and most spacious square in the town, **Praça da Aclamação**. On one side it's lined with civil buildings from the golden age of Cachoeira in the eighteenth century, including the Prefeitura and the old city chambers. The other side of the square is dominated by the huge bulk of the **Conjunto do Carmo**, built in the eighteenth century and now beautifully restored, in four parts: a church, a museum, a *pousada* and a conference centre. The museum contains rare seventeenth-century furniture and some fine sacred art, including carvings and statues from Macau that bring an unexpectedly Chinese flavour to the collection. The cloister leads to the church, decorated with seventeenth-century tiles and an extravagant Rococo gold-leaf interior.

On the stretch of waterfront nearest the old centre is Praça Teixeira de Freitas, from where you can take a launch out to the Ilha do Farol in the river, and over to **SÃO FÉLIX**. The main reason for going is the great view back across the river, with the colonial facades reflected in the water.

Practicalities

Cachoeira has no **rodoviária**, just an office by the bus stop in Rua Lauro de Freitas. There's a **Bahiatursa** office in Praça da Aclamação, where you can get a map and some basic information. The nicest **place to stay** is the *Pousada do Convento de Cachoeira* (☎75/215-1716; ❸), which is part of the Conjunto do Carmo on Praça da Aclamação and has a pool, an attractive patio and a bar. Other options include the simple *Hotel Colombo*, at Rua Sete de Setembro 19 (no phone; ❶), the *Hotel Santo Antônio* on Praça Maciel (☎75/251-1402; ❶), which is handy for the bus station but noisy at times, and the friendly, no-frills *Pousada do Guerreiro*, at Rua 13 de Maio 14 (☎75/215-1104; ❷). There's also the excellent-value *Pousada do Pai Thomaz*, at Rua 25 de Junho 12 (☎75/215-1288; ❸), with spotless rooms. For fantastic regional dishes head for the *Restaurant Gruta Azul*, Praça Manuel Vitorino 2 (daily 11am–6pm).

Valença and around

After Cachoeira, the coast becomes swampy and by the time you get to **VALENÇA** you're in mangrove country. Fortunately, though, instead of alligators, the swamps are dominated by shellfish of all kinds, most of them edible. Valença lies on the banks of the Rio Una, about 10km from the sea, at the point where the river widens into a delta made up of dozens of small islands, most of which support at least a couple of fishing villages. At one time the town was an industrial centre – the first cotton factory in Brazil was built here – but it has long since reverted to fishing and boat building. Today, it's also an increasingly popular destination for tourists from Salvador, mainly as a stop-off point for the nearby island resort of Morro de São Paulo (see p.273), but the town is not yet over-commercialized.

The Town

Valença's **rodoviária** is close to the centre of town, which is just a few blocks' walk away along the riverside towards the market. There are a couple of colonial churches – the most interesting is the Igreja de Nossa Senhora do Amparo, built in 1757 on a hill affording beautiful views over the city and accessed from near the market. Valença is mostly the connection point for **Morro de São Paulo** and **Boipeba** islands (see below) or a place for walks, boat trips and lazing on beaches rather than sightseeing. By far the most absorbing thing the town has to offer is its **boatyards**, the *estaleiros*; follow the river 500m downstream from the central Praça Admar Braga Guimarães. They produce a whole series of wooden boats here, largely by hand, ranging from small fishing smacks to large schooners, and local boat builders are renowned throughout the Northeast for their skill. Provided you don't get in the way – try going around midday, when work stops for a couple of hours – and ask permission, people are pleased to let you take a closer look and often take pride in showing off their work.

Practicalities

Accommodation is easy to find. There are several hotels and *pensões*: the *Hotel Tourist* at Rua Marechal Floriano 167 (❷), and the *Guaibim* on Praça da Independência (☎75/641-1110 ❸), are welcoming and good value, the *Hotel do Porto* at Av. Maconica 50 (☎75/641-5226; ❸) offers attractive rooms and spectacular views, while the *Portal Rio Una* on Rua Maestro Barrinha (☎75/641-2383; ❺) is a more luxurious option. If you're on a tight budget, the rented hammock space at Prainha on the island of Tinharé (see p.274) costs next to nothing.

Many visitors choose to stay out of town at the beach resort of **Guaibim**, just 20 minutes' drive from Valença near the international airport. Of these, the *Aguas do Guaibim*, on Avenida Taquary (☎75/482-1047, ⓦwww .aguasdoguaibim.tur.br;❸) is hard to better, with its attractive apartments, pool and beach access; there's also the *Royal Praia Hotel* on the same road (☎75/482-1131; ❸), with stylish if slightly down-at-heel rooms and a beachside pool. Slightly cheaper is the *Taquay Hotel*, a pleasant, relatively isolated complex, with a small pool and recreation room, at the very end of Avenida Taquay, block 22 (☎75/482-1144, ⓦwww.taquary.com.br; ❸).

The **restaurants** in the town are simple and reasonably priced, and the food is excellent; the combination of fresh seafood and palm oil – Valença is famous for its *dendê* – is definitely special. Try the seafood *rodízio* (where you pay a flat fee and have all you can eat) at the *Akuarius*, on Praça da Independência, or a plate of *moqueca* at the *Bar Kardy*, on Rua Governador Gonçalves, which has the added attraction of live music. On the relaxed Praça da República, the *Skinas Bar* is a good option for drinking or munching and, opposite, there's the very cheap *Casa do Bolo*, fine for set lunch menus. You'll find other good options on the north side of the river, along a well-lit promenade with plenty of *barracas*, bars and restaurants, and a laid-back atmosphere on most evenings.

Tourist information is available from the EMVATUR office in the old Prefeitura building, Rua Comendador Madureira 10 (☎75/641-3311), facing the river by the Praça Admar Braga Guimarães. The best place to **change money** is the Banco do Brasil on Calle Calçado, the main pedestrianized street in the old centre. A good way of getting around the town is by **bicycle**. They can be rented cheaply all over the place: look out for signs saying *Aluga-se bicicleta*.

From Valença there are five daily **buses** back to Salvador, which take around five hours. Alternatively, you can travel back to Salvador via Nazaré and Itaparica, thereby reducing the journey by 150km; Excursões e Turismo, on the Praça da República (☎75/741-5305), sell combined ferry-Kombi tickets that cut the journey time by a couple of hours.

Morro de São Paulo

The obvious place to head for around Valença is the island of **Tinharé** and its famous beaches at **MORRO DE SÃO PAULO**, where there's always a great atmosphere, with reggae bars, hippy dives and great seafood restaurants. With no roads on the island, it's still relatively peaceful and undeveloped, though at the weekends, especially between December and March, Morro de São Paulo can get unbearably crowded.

There are several **boats** a day from Valença to Tinharé (more than one an hour generally) that cost about $3 and take ninety minutes to get there, plus a quicker and more expensive *lancha rapida*, which takes thirty to forty minutes and costs around $8. In high season there is also a direct boat from Salvador that you can catch from the Terminal Turístico (it's also worth enquiring about it in low season, as the boat may operate on certain days then, too). It costs about $30 for a one-way trip and takes about three hours, but the sea can be rough. There's also the occasional catamaran ($50; 1hr).

The small settlement of Morro de São Paulo sits on a hill between the port and the first of the beaches, Primeira Praia. If you don't mind being a few minutes' walk from the beach, it's a pleasant place to stay, close to the shops and restaurants. There's little in town of interest, apart from an atmospheric old fort overlooking the harbour, with a rusting canon and a Moorish-looking gun turret still standing on its crumbling battlements. To get here, follow the coastal path (clockwise round the island).

For **accommodation**, the *Pousada Natureza*, at the top of the steps leading to the pier (☎75/483-1361, ℱ483-1044, ⓦwww.hotelnatureza.com; ❹), has lovely rooms with hammock verandas, some apartments with Jacuzzis, a patio bar set in attractive gardens and a pool. Other good options are the *O Casarão* (☎75/483-1049, ℱ483-1022, ⓦwww.ocasarao.net; ❹) at Praça Aureliano Lima 190, which offers apartments and chalets plus a little pool, and the more modest but excellent-value *Porto da Cima* (❸).

The *Pizzaria Forno a Lenha* on Praça Aureliano is a good **restaurant** and one of the best places to meet people in the evenings and find out where the parties are happening. More restaurants and ice-cream parlours line the track from the square down to Primeira Praia, where *Restaurante Da Dona Elda* (☎75/483-1041) serves excellent seafood dishes, such as delicious *moqueca de* *peixe* and *bobó de camarão*, on their airy upstairs patio; there are also several shops and **tour agents** offering **money exchange** and **Internet access** along this stretch; one of the best is Marlins Viagens e Turismo (T75/483-1242). The **tourist information office** is on Praça Aureliano Lima (T75/483-1083, Wwww.morrosp.com.br), a short walk from the dock.

The beaches

There are four main beaches on the populated corner of the island, all linked by paths. The **Primeira Praia** has the best range of accommodation, but isn't the nicest of the beaches and you'd be better off heading five minutes further south round the island to **Segunda Praia**. Segunda Praia is most popular with the in-crowd tourists from São Paulo and Salvador and has the best swimming and snorkelling; the *Villa das Pedras Pousada* (T75/783-1075, F783-1122, Wwww.villadaspedras.com.br; ❺) is a good option here, with its own beach-side pool. **Terceira Praia** is narrow but pleasant, more laid-back than Segunda Praia, where wooden shack bars crowd along the lapping edge of the ocean when the tide is in. Here you'll find the plush *Villegaignon Resort* (T75/483-1010, F483-1012, Wwww.mozart.com.br/provence; ❻), the reasonable *Pousada Tia Lita* (T75/483-1532, Wwww.pousadatialita.com.br; ❷), where views come with some rooms, and the cheapest option, *Camping Natureza*, where you can put up a tent and stay for less than $3 per person. **Quarta Praia** is the least developed of the beaches, long and quite glorious, and has some of the island's best restaurants. Right on the beach here, the *Pousada Catavento Praia* (T75/483-1052, Wwww.pousadacatavento.com.br;❸), with twelve apartments, a bar and restaurant, is a good-value place to stay.

On the opposite side of the small island, 15km away, is the hamlet of **PRAINHA**. Here you'll find the **Casa da Sogra**, home of a local poet and sculptor who has papered the walls with his poems and decorative painted maps of the region. There are no hotels here but, if you want **to stay** for a few days of idyllic tranquillity, the locals – mainly fishing families – rent out hammock space: there is little except grilled fish and shellfish to eat, but it's a lifestyle you could easily get used to. At least one boat from Morro calls every day.

There's good **diving** to be had in the clear waters surrounding the island; Companhia do Mergulho, Primeira Praia (T75/483-1200, Wwww .ciamergulho@terra.com.br) offer scuba trips for certified divers both day and night ($30 per day) and also offer a six-day scuba course for beginners ($200).

Ilha de Boipeba

The beaches on the island of **Boipeba**, separated from the Ilha de Tinharé by the Rio do Inferno, are even more beautiful than those at Morro de São Paulo, but much less developed, still possessing the tranquillity that Morro hasn't seen for over fifteen years. The settlement here is small and scattered across the island, with few facilities – just a couple of restaurants and a handful of *pousadas*. The beaches are simply gorgeous, and there's good scuba diving at the coral reefs near the Ponta da Castelhauos at the southernmost point of the island.

For **accommodation**, the excellent *Pousada Luar das Aguas* on the beach (T75/653-6015, mobile T9981-1012, F641-3373, Eluardasaguas@neth .com.br) has attractive bungalow-style accommodation with hammock verandas and a palm-thatched circular beach restaurant that serves some of the best seafood cooking south of Fortaleza. The *Pousada do Outeiro*, Praia Tassimirim (T & F75/972-1535), is another good place to stay, with ten beachfront apartments. There's also a **campsite** at the Kioska Ponto do Almendeira, between the port and the beach restaurants.

Boats run to Boipeba from Valença (3hr 30min; $15), and from Segunda Praia on the Ilha de Tinharé (2hr; $10). You can save some time by renting a speed-boat (for 4–5 people) to take you between Boipeba and Morro de São Paulo for around $80–100. On the island it's possible to arrange **outdoor activities** through your *pousada*, including canoeing in the mangrove swamps, spotting wildlife in the coastal woodlands, horse riding on the beach, as well as surfing and diving.

Inland: the Bahian sertão

The **Bahian sertão** is immense: an area considerably larger than any European country and comprising about a third of the total land area of the Northeast. Much of it is semi-desert, endless expanses of rock and cactus broiling in the sun. But it can be spectacular, with ranges of hills to the north and broken highlands to the west, rearing up into the tableland of the great **Planalto Central**, the plateau that extends over most of the state of Goiás and parts of Minas Gerais. No part of the Bahian *sertão* is thickly populated, and most of it is positively hostile to human habitation: in places, no rain falls for years at a stretch. Its inhabitants suffer more from drought than anywhere else in the Northeast, and in parts of the *sertão* there's still desperate poverty.

Despite its reputation, not all the *sertão* is desert. Winding through it, like an enormous snake, is the **Rio São Francisco**, sprawling out into the huge hydroelectric reservoir of **Sobradinho**. River and lake support a string of towns, notably Paulo Afonso (see p.294) and Juazeiro (see p.328). Other possible destinations to the north are **Jacobina**, in the midst of spectacular hill country, where gold and emeralds have been mined for nearly three centuries, and **Canudos**, site of a mini civil war a hundred years ago, and a good place to get a feel for *sertão* life. By far the most popular route into the *sertão*, though, is westwards along the BR-242, which eventually hits the Belém–Brasília highway in Goiás: en route you'll pass the old mining town of **Lençóis**, gateway to the breathtaking natural wonders of the Chapada Diamantina – one of Brazil's best and most accessible trekking areas.

Travelling in the sertão requires some preparation, as the interior is not geared to tourism. Hotels are fewer and dirtier; buses are less frequent, and you often have to rely on country services that leave very early in the morning and seem to stop every few hundred yards. A **hammock** is essential, as it's the coolest and most comfortable way to sleep, much better than the grimy beds in inland hotels, all of which have hammock hooks set into the walls as a standard fitting. The towns are much smaller here than on the coast, and in most places there's little to do in the evening, as the population turns in early to be up for work at dawn. Far more people carry arms than on the coast, but in fact the *sertão* is one of the safest areas of Brazil for travellers – the guns are mainly used on animals, especially small birds, which are massacred on an enormous scale. Avoid tap **water**, by sticking to bottled water: dysentery is common, and although not dangerous these days it's extremely unpleasant.

Don't let these considerations put you off, however. People in the *sertão* are intrigued by gringos and are invariably very friendly. And while few *sertão* towns may have much to offer in terms of excitement or entertainment, the landscape in which they are set is spectacular.

Feira de Santana

Whether you choose the route north or west, you're likely to pass through **FEIRA DE SANTANA**, 112km from Salvador, known primarily for its enormous **Feira do Couro**, literally "leather market" – the best place to buy leatherwork in the Northeast. Leatherwork is the main form of *artesanato* in the *sertão*, as you'd expect from cattle country. The market happens every Monday, taking over the centre of town with tens of thousands of customers, and thousands of stalls selling cheap and very high-quality wallets, handbags, satchels, cases and bags of every shape and size, many of them beautifully tooled. You should get there early, as the market starts to wind down after lunchtime, although it does go on all day. **Buses** leave every fifteen minutes from Salvador on market day, every half-hour the rest of the week; the journey takes about two hours.

If you can't make it there on a Monday, the permanent **Mercado de Artesanato** in the centre has a wide range of leather goods every day of the week. Apart from the market, though, there's little reason to come, or to stay. The town itself is rather ugly and the countryside around is nothing special; it's best to make a day-trip from Salvador.

Jacobina

After Feira de Santana, the BR-324 strikes into the interior proper. The scenery is dull for the first couple of hours, but then the road climbs into the highlands of the **Chapada Diamantina**, with rock massifs rising out of the scrub, vaguely reminiscent of the American Southwest. At the small town of Capim Grosso the BR-407 branches off on a 300-kilometre journey north to Juazeiro, but sticking with the BR-324 for another hour brings you to the old mining town of **JACOBINA**. It nestles on the slopes of several hills with panoramic views over the **Serra da Jacobina**, one of the first parts of the *sertão* to be settled in strength by the Portuguese. The clue to what attracted them is the name of one of the two fast-flowing rivers that bisect the town, the Rio de Ouro, "Gold River". **Gold** was first found here in the early seventeenth century, and several *bandeirante* expeditions made the trip north from São Paulo to settle here. Although cattle and farming are now more important, mining still continues: there are emerald mines at nearby Pindobaçu, two large gold mines, and the diamonds that gave the Chapada Diamantina its name. The last big rush was in 1948, but miners still come down from the hills every now and then to sell gold and precious stones to traders in the town – you'll notice that many of them have precision scales on their counters.

The **town** itself is notably friendly – they don't see many tourists and people are curious – while the altitude takes the edge off the temperature most days, which makes it a good place to walk. It's a typical example of an interior town, quiet at night save for the squares and the riverbanks, where the young congregate, especially around the *Zululândia* bar in the centre, while their parents pull chairs into the streets and gossip until the TV soaps start. In all directions, **paths** lead out of the town into the surrounding hills, with spectacular views, but it still gets hot during the day and some of the slopes are steep, so it's best to take water along. The *Hotel Serra do Ouro* runs trips (around $20 per person) out to the **emerald mines** of Pindobaçu, around 60km to the north, and to the **gold mines** of Canavieiras and Itapicuru, though these are a bit disappointing in some respects: to the untrained eye uncut emeralds look like bits of gravel.

Practicalities

It's about a six-hour ride to Jacobina on the two daily **buses** from Salvador. There's no tourist office, although you might be able to get hold of a pamphlet with a street map from Bahiatursa in Salvador (see p.251). Still, it's small enough to get by without one. The bus leaves you near the centre, where there are several cheap **hotels** and *pensões*. The best, the *Hotel Serra do Ouro* (℡75/621-3324, Ⓦwww.newnet.com.br/serradoouro; ❸), is on the outskirts, built on a hillside with a magnificent view of the town. A cheaper, though less attractive, option is the *Jacobina Palace Hotel*, Rua Manoel Navares 210 (℡75/621-2600; ❷).

Jacobina is a good place for getting acquainted with the **food** of the interior: *carne do sol com pirão de leite* is rehydrated dried meat with a delicious milk-based sauce; *bode assado* is roast goat, surprisingly tender when done well; and *buchada*, a spicy kind of haggis made from intestines, is much nicer than it sounds but not for delicate stomachs. Good **restaurants** are *Carlito's*, on the banks of the Rio Ouro, and the *Cheguei Primeiro*, which only serves *caça* (game): the best dish is *tatu*, armadillo, which has a tender white flesh that tastes vaguely like pork. You should also try *doce de buriti*, a tangy, acidic-tasting paste made from the fruit of the buriti palm; it's sold in neat boxes made from the wood of the palm, which keep it fresh almost indefinitely. The favoured restaurant with locals is the *Rancho Catarinense*, at Av. N.S. da Conceição 1188, which specializes in meat. For **nightlife**, check out *Status*, a *dancetaria* on the slopes of the Serra da Caixa above the town, only accessible by taxi and worth checking out on Friday and Saturday nights.

Canudos

A different route north from Feira de Santana along the bumpy BR-116 takes you to **CANUDOS**, site of Antônio Conselheiro's rebellion in the 1890s (see box, p.278). The main reason for coming here is to get a taste of these remarkable events, but it's also a chance to sample the atmosphere of a typical small town in the *sertão*, where life is still dominated by the all-important question of rain or the lack of it. Despite the obvious poverty, it's a rewarding place to visit: everything centres on the main square, with weather-beaten *sertanejos* trudging around during the day, and the local youngsters taking over at night. If you've come from a big city, you'll certainly notice the sense of isolation provided by the *caatinga* all around.

You have to leave the town if you want to visit the **site of the Canudos war**. The valley where it all happened was flooded by a dam in the 1960s and the new Canudos is the result of a shift a few miles down the road. There is a bus that will drop you at the battlefield (ask for "Velho Canudos"), but you'll have to wait a long time to be picked up again so it may be better to arrange your own transport if you can find someone to take you. Alternatively, you could walk it in a couple of hours, but it's very hot and you should take plenty of sun protection. When you get to the edge of the valley you'll see a few houses, a statue of Antônio Conselheiro and a small museum, which is usually closed. More interesting is the valley itself, where the water has sunk to such a low level that you can now see the tops of trees and houses that may have formed part of the original Canudos. It's incredible to think that this valley was once a place that was thought to threaten the future of the Brazilian Republic.

Back in the new Canudos, there are two or three **places to stay**: *Grapiuna* on Praça Monsenhor Berenguer (℡75/275-1157; ❸) is a good bet. **Transport** there and away is also not a problem: there's a daily bus to Salvador and

Antônio Conselheiro's rebellion

The Bahian *sertão* provided the backdrop to one of the most remarkable events in Brazilian history, the **rebellion** of the messianic religious leader **Antônio Conselheiro**, who gathered thousands of followers, built a city called Canudos, and declared war on the young republic in 1895 for imposing new taxes on an already starving population. The rebels held out for two years. The forces sent confidently north from Salvador were terribly mauled by the *sertanistas*, who proved to be great guerrilla fighters, with an intimate knowledge of the harsh country and which the city troops found as intimidating as their human enemies. Twice military columns were beaten, and then a third force of over a thousand troops commanded by a national hero, a general in the Paraguayan war, was sent against the rebels. In the worst shock the young republic had suffered up to that point, the force was completely annihilated: the next expedition discovered the bleached skulls of the general and his staff laid out in a neat row in front of a thorn tree. Not until 1897, when a fourth expedition was sent, did Canudos fall, and almost all of its defenders were killed; Antônio Conselheiro himself had died of fever a few weeks before the end. One member of the force, **Euclides da Cunha**, immortalized the war in his book *Os Sertões*, generally recognized as the greatest Portuguese prose ever written by a Brazilian – it was translated into English as "Rebellion in the Backlands". It's a good introduction to the Bahian *sertão*, but a more entertaining read is *The War of the End of the World* by the Peruvian novelist Mario Vargas Llosa (see "Books", p.800), which gives a haunting fictionalized account of the incredible events in Canudos.

another daily service to Juazeiro, on the border with Pernambuco. The **food** isn't great: the local speciality is *bode assado*, roast goat, which is not particularly popular with outsiders, and there's a distinct lack of fresh fruit and vegetables. But there are plenty of biscuits in the shops, so you won't starve.

The Chapada Diamantina

The route **west** into the *sertão* is along the BR-242, which skirts Feira de Santana and swings south, where a turn-off signposted to Brasília heads inland, into the heart of the *sertão*. The scenery is remarkably similar to that along the Jacobina road 200km to the north: you're still in the tablelands of the Chapada Diamantina, with its rock spurs and mesas forming an enormous chain of foothills to the Planalto Central.

Lençóis

Five hours' ride down the BR-242, **LENÇÓIS** is another mining town and the main tourist centre in the Chapada Diamantina. The name of the town, meaning "sheets", derives from the camp that grew up around a diamond strike in 1844. The miners, too poor to afford tents, made do with sheets draped over branches. Lençóis is a pretty little town, set in the midst of the spectacular Parque Nacional da Chapada Diamantina (see p.280). Most of its fine old buildings date back to the second half of the nineteenth century, when the town was a prosperous mining community, attracting diamond buyers from as far afield as Europe. The **Mercado Municipal**, next to the bridge over the Rio Lençóis that runs through the centre, is where most of the diamonds were sold – it has Italian- and French-style trimmings tacked on to make the buyers feel at home. The centre of the town, between two lovely squares, Praça Otaviano Alves and Praça Horácio de Matos, is made up of cobbled streets, lined with well-proportioned two-storey nineteenth-century houses with high, arched windows. On Praça Horácio, the **Subconsulado Francês**, once the French

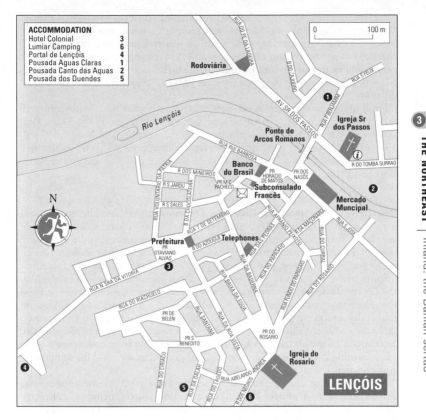

LENÇÓIS

consulate, was built with the money of the European diamond buyers, who wanted an office to take care of export certificates. **Tourist information** is available from an office on Avenida Senhor dos Passos, just below the church, on the other side of the river. You'll also find several people offering themselves as guides to the town: at a dollar or two for an extensive tour they're not expensive, and as life is not easy around here it might help someone out.

There are three **buses** a day for the six-hour journey from Salvador to Lençóis, all leaving from the main *rodoviária*. The best, and most expensive, **place to stay** in town is the *Portal de Lençóis*, Rua Altina Alves (T & F75/334-1233; ⑥). Cheaper, but still good, are the beautiful riverside *Pousada Canto das Aguas* (T & F75/334-1154; ④), with its own pool; the *Colonial*, at Praça Otaviano Alves 750 (T75/334-1114; ③), and the *Tradição*, Rua José Florêncio (T75/334-1120; ②). One of the friendliest of the basic places, the *Pousada dos Duendes*, Rua do Pires (T & F75/334-1229; ②), has kitchen access, and the owners are a mine of information on local destinations; it's a little hard to find in the back streets above the heart of town, but the effort is well rewarded. The very basic *Pousada Aguas Claras*, Rua P. Benjamin (T75/334-1236; ③), is central and good, and there's also a **campsite**, *Lumiar Camping*, in the centre on Praça do Rosário (T75/334-1241).

La Pergola, a new French-influenced **restaurant** set in the grounds of *Lumiar Camping*, has a reputation for the best cuisine in town. For *comida por kilo* lunches it's hard to beat the wide menu choice and large airy atmosphere of the *Taberna por Sol* on the corner of *ruas* 7 de Setembro and Baderna. In the evenings, the restaurant-bars on the Praça Horácio de Matos tend to be the focus of **nightlife**, with *Amigo da Onça* on Rua Jose Florencio one of the liveliest spots.

Local **artesanato** is very good, particularly the bottles filled with coloured sand arranged into intricate patterns; get a guide to take you to the **Salão das Areias** on the outskirts of town, where you can see the sand being gathered and put into bottles by local artisans – even children do it. You can buy the finished product at Gilmar Nunes on Rua Almirante Barroso, or at Manoel Reis, Rua São Félix.

Parque Nacional da Chapada Diamantina

The **Parque Nacional da Chapada Diamantina** was established in 1985 after much local campaigning, and covers over 38,000 square kilometres – an area larger than the Netherlands – in the mountainous regions to the south and west of Lençóis. Its dramatic landscape incorporates swampy valleys, barren peaks and scrubby forest, punctuated by beautiful waterfalls, rivers and streams.

Some places in the park you could just about manage without a guide, like the **Gruta do Lapão**, a remarkable grotto over a kilometre long, with a cathedral-like entrance of layered rock and stalactites. It's a short drive or a long walk (a full-day round trip) from the centre, but it's probably better to have someone take you there. The only other place within easy reach is the **Cascatas do Serrano**, a fifteen-minute walk from town, where the river flows over a rock plate forming a series of small waterfalls and pools that are good for swimming – very popular with the town's children.

Anywhere more distant and you'll need a proper guide, as the countryside can be difficult to negotiate. Reliable operators in Lençóis include Cirtur, Rua da Baderba 41 (℡75/334-1133, ⓔcirtur@neth.com.br and Lentur, on Av. 7 de Setembro (℡75/334-1271). Alternatively, if you'd rather opt for an **independent guide**, contact Roy Funch (through the Fundacao Chapada Diamantina at Rua Pé de Ladeira 212; ℡75/334-1305), a resident American and author of an excellent guidebook to the region; he may not be able to guide you himself, but can certainly recommend someone and suggest places to head for. Standard rates for independent guides are between $15 and $30 a day. Sunglasses, a hat and sun cream are all essential, as well as taking along water: it can get very hot and several of the walks are strenuous.

Amongst the most popular destinations is **Morro do Pai Inácio**, a 300-metre-high mesa formation 27km from Lençóis (don't be deceived by how near it looks). It is, though, much more easily climbed than seems possible from a distance, and you're rewarded with quite stunning views across the tablelands and the town once you get to the top, which is covered in highland cacti, trees and shrubs. Thirty kilometres away, but with much easier road access, is **Rio Mucugezinho**, another series of small waterfalls and pools that are fun to swim in; a closer river beach is the **Praia do Rio São José**, also called Zaidã. Finally, and most spectacular of all, is the highest waterfall in Brazil, the **Cachoeira Glass**, a small stream that tumbles 400m down over a mesa, becoming little more than a fine mist by the time it reaches the bottom. It's closer to town than most of the other places, and if you only feel up to one day's walking it's the best choice.

South from Salvador

The BR-101 highway is the main route to the **southern Bahian coast**, a region immortalized in the much translated and filmed novels of Jorge Amado. From the bus window you'll see the familiar fields of sugar replaced by huge plantations of *cacau*, cocoa. Southern Bahia produces two-thirds of Brazil's cocoa, almost all of which goes for export, making this part of Bahia the richest agricultural area of the state. The *zona de cacau* seems quiet and respectable enough today, with its pleasant towns and prosperous countryside, but in the last decades of the nineteenth century and the first decades of the twentieth, it was one of the most turbulent parts of Brazil. Entrepreneurs and adventurers from all over the country carved out estates here, often violently – a process chronicled by Amado in his novel *The Violent Lands* (see "Books", p.799).

Ilhéus and around

In literary terms **ILHÉUS**, Amado's birthplace, is the best-known town in Brazil, the setting for his most famous novel, *Gabriela, Cravo e Canela*, translated into English as "Gabriela, Clove and Cinnamon" – by far the most renowned Brazilian novel internationally. If you haven't heard of it before visiting Ilhéus, you soon will; it seems that every other bar, hotel and restaurant is either named after the novel or one of its characters.

The town is on the coast 400km south of Salvador, where the local coastline is broken up by five rivers and a series of lagoons, bays and waterways. Much of it is modern but it's still an attractive place, with the heart of Ilhéus perched on a small hill that overlooks one of the largest and finest-looking beaches in Bahia. Before you head for the sands, however, take time to look around the town. The modern cathedral, built in the 1930s with extravagant Gothic towers and pinnacles, is a useful landmark. Nearby, the oldest church in the city, the **Igreja Matriz de São Jorge**, on Praça Rui Barbosa, finished in 1556, has a religious art museum, while the domed roof and towers of the **Igreja de Nossa Senhora de Lourdes** dominate the shoreline nearest to the centre. Domes are rare in church architecture in Brazil, and this combination of dome and towers is unique. The **Casa da Cultura**, at Rua Jorge Amado 21, is well worth half an hour for a whistle-stop tour of the city's history, including interesting exhibits on the region's chocolate industry and Ilhéus's remarkable literary tradition. The house itself was once the home of Amado himself.

The main leisure options in Ilhéus have changed little from Amado's time: hanging around in the **bars** and squares, and heading for the beaches. The *Vezúvio* on Praça Dom Eduardo, the cathedral square, is the most famous bar in Brazil; in Amado's book it's owned by the hero Nacib, and is a watering hole of the cocoa planters. You pay a little extra for drinks, but it's a good bar, with renowned Arab food. Apart from the centre, the main concentration of bars is along the fine beach promenade of the Avenida Atlântica, the beach itself called simply **Avenida**, though much of it is now polluted and not recommended for bathing. There are other **beaches to the north**, past the port: the first is **Isidro Ramos** (bus from the centre or Avenida), followed by **Praia do Marciano** and **Praia do Norte**.

Most locals prefer the coastline to the south, particularly around the village of **OLIVENÇA**, served by local buses from the centre. Half an hour out of town is the beautiful beach at **Cururupe**, where Governor Mem de Sá trapped the Tupiniquim Indians in 1567 between his troops and the sea. It was called the "Battle of the Swimmers", after the Indians' desperate attempts to escape by water, but it was more of a massacre than a battle, and the tribe was almost wiped out. Today there are a series of bars and some holiday homes, peaceful groves of palm trees and no hint of the place's dark past. In Olivença itself the main attraction is the **Balneário**, public swimming baths built around supposedly healthy mineral water from the Rio Tororomba, which flows through the place. The healing powers of the water are exaggerated, but the baths complex is very pleasant, with an artificial waterfall, and bar and restaurant attached. The coast between Ilhéus and Olivença is very beautiful: you can **camp** virtually anywhere along the way.

Alternatively, you could head for the unspoiled beaches north of Ilhéus, arguably among the best that Bahia has to offer. Frequent buses run to the busiest beach town along this stretch, **ITACARÉ**, 70km from Ilhéus, and a fishing port in its own right. The town is a haven for **water-based adventure sports**, including rafting and canoeing, which you can arrange through Papaterra (T73/251-2252, Wwww.papaterra.com.br) and Hawaii Aqui, at Rua Pedro Longo 169 (T73/251-3050, Wwww.hawaiiaqui@bol.com.br), which is also a *pousada* and Internet café. There's no shortage of cafés, restaurants and bars in town, especially at the southern end of the beach, when you're done hanging out on the beach.

Practicalities

The **rodoviária** (T73/634-4121) is on Praça Cairu, a little way from the centre of Ilhéus, but buses outside marked "Centro" or "Olivença" take you into town. The **airport** is 4km away (T73/231-7629), connected to town by taxi ($8) and hourly buses. There's a **tourist information** post at the *rodoviária*, with good town maps, and an Ilhéustur office near the port at Av. Soares Lopes 1741 (Mon–Sat 9am–6pm; T73/634-3510, Wwww.ilheus.com.br).

Your best bet for **accommodation** in Ilhéus is probably on one of the beaches, although there's no shortage of places in town if you prefer. *Pousada Vitória* (●) is a budget option on Praça Cairu, next to the *rodoviária*. In the centre, *Ilhéus*, Rua Estáquio Bastos 144 (T73/634-4242; ●), is good value, and the *Britânia*, close to the cathedral at Rua 28 de Junho 16 (T73/634-1722; ●), is one of the cheapest central hotels. For beachside accommodation, there's the *Pousada Sol e Mar*, 14km from town on the Ilhéus–Olivença road (T & F73/269-1148; ●); frequent buses run into town. If you can afford it, one of the best places to stay is the *Pousada Aldea da Mata* (T73/9981-8692, Wwww.aldeiadamata.com.br; ●), on the edge of the Mata Atlântica roughly half way between Ilheus and Itacaré; look out for the partially hidden entrance at km 31.5 on the Ilheus–Serra Grande road. Rooms are in bungalow-style accommodation, and amenities include a terraced bar, natural hot spring shower and even massages; needless to say the beach here is empty and fabulous. If you want to stay in Itacaré, try the family-run *Pousada Sol e Mar*, Rua Nova Conquista (T73/251-2795; ●), which is away from the beach but has well-kept rooms, some with balconies and TV. There's also the lovely *Pousada Sitio Ilha Verde*, Rua A. Setubal 234 (T73/251-2056, Wwww.itacare.com.br; ●), set in beautiful grounds amid mango trees, with individually decorated rooms and a pool.

Buses to Ilhéus from Salvador take around six hours: the only one you can catch if you want to see the pleasant countryside en route is in the morning, for which you have to book at least a day in advance; otherwise take one of the three night departures. There are direct buses from Ilhéus, once a week, to Rio and São Paulo, but book at least two days ahead for these. For a **taxi**, call T73/632-6750. Messias Viagens (T73/634-1949) can arrange **city tours**; other reliable tour operators are Agua Branca Receptivo, Rua do Bonfim, Pontal 255 (☎73/231-1424) and Costa do Sol, Av. Bahia 294, Cidade Nova (☎73/231-2788). **Money exchange** is available at Emcamtur, Rua Dom Pedro II 116, in downtown Ilheus (☎73/634-6535, ✉emcamtur@maxnet.com.br). For **Internet access** try Cybercafe.com, Rua Cel. Camara 38, Centro, or Café Oclus.com.br on Rua Brigadeiro Eduardo Gomes (☎73/634-6668).

Porto Seguro

The most popular destination in southern Bahia is the resort area around the town of **PORTO SEGURO**, where Cabral "discovered" Brazil in 1500. Founded in 1526, it has some claim to being the oldest town in Brazil, and buildings still survive from that period.

The story goes that in 1500 **Pedro Alvares Cabral** and his men, alerted to the presence of land by the changing colour of the sea and the appearance of land birds, finally saw a mountain on the horizon, which must have been Monte Páscoal, to the south of today's Porto Seguro. First landfall was made on Good Friday, on a beach to the north of Porto Seguro, and the anchorage Cabral used was probably the cove where the village of Santa Cruz de Cabrália now stands. The Indians were friendly at first, though they might have been better advised otherwise, since Cabral claimed the land for the king of Portugal, and thus began over three centuries of Portuguese rule.

These days Porto Seguro is about as far as you can get from pre-colonial tranquillity. It's become one of the biggest holiday resorts in Brazil, and heaves with Brazilian tourists throughout the year, reaching saturation point at New Year and Carnaval. You may actually enjoy yourself here if your main interest is nightlife, but you've got to like crowds, and don't expect much peace and quiet. All the same, Porto Seguro has somehow managed to retain its reputation as a fairly classy destination.

The Town

The colonial area, **Cidade Alta**, is built on a bluff overlooking the town, with fine views out to sea and across the Rio Buranhém. The **Igreja da Misericórdia** here, begun in 1526, is one of the two oldest churches in Brazil. The **Igreja de Nossa Senhora da Pena**, nearby, dates from 1535 and has the oldest religious icon in Brazil, a St Francis of Assisi, brought over in the first serious expedition to Brazil, in 1503. There are the ruins of a Jesuit church and chapel (dating from the 1540s) and a small, early fort; the squat and thick-walled style of the churches shows their early function as fortified strongpoints, in the days when Indian attacks were common. Near the ruins of the Jesuit college is the **Marca do Descobrimento**, the two-metre-high column sunk to mark Portuguese sovereignty in 1503; on one side is a crude face of Christ, almost unrecognizable now, and on the other the arms of the Portuguese Crown.

Cidade Baixa, below, is where the modern action is. The riverside Avenida 22 de Abril and its continuation, Avenida Portugal, are a mass of bars, restaurants and hotels – so much so in fact that Avenida Portugal changes its name at night to become the Passarela do Álcool, or "Alcohol Street". One stretch of road – where competing stallholders urge you to try their fiendishly strong cocktails – particularly merits this name.

North of town, a string of superb beaches stretches along the Beira Mar coast road. The nearest, **Praia Curuípe**, is 3km away and has some natural pools and reefs, as well as the usual beachside restaurants. More popular, and just a few kilometres further away, is **Praia Itacimirim**. These beaches, and others further north (notably Mundaí and Taperapuã, both good for scuba diving), are connected to Porto Seguro by regular seafront buses.

Practicalities

The **rodoviária** is a little way out of town, but taxis are cheap and plentiful. Three **buses** a day make the eleven-hour journey from Salvador, but one of these is an extremely expensive *leito* service, and you should book well ahead. There are also direct **flights** from Rio and Salvador. There are **tourist information** offices at the *rodoviária*, the airport, and in the centre of town at the Secretaria de Turismo, Praça Visconde de Porto Seguro, in the Casa da Lenha (☎73/288-4124). The tour agencies Pataxó Turismo, Av. dos Navegantes 333 (☎73/288-1256), and Taípe Viagens e Turismo, Av. 22 de Abril 1077 (☎73/288-3127), are also helpful. **Internet access** is available from an office on the second floor of the Avenida Shopping Mall in the town centre ($5 per hour).

Finding **accommodation** should be the least of your worries as Porto Seguro is jammed with hotels. However, prices vary astonishingly between high and low season: a budget hotel in, say, November, could triple in price by Christmas. You need to bear this in mind when considering the high-season prices we've quoted. If you want to be right in the thick of the nightlife, you could try the *Pousada da Orla*, at Av. Portugal 404 (☎73/288-2434; ❸). A couple of roads back from the riverfront, in a wooden colonial-style building is the *Hotel Terra Á Vista*, Av. Getúlio Vargas 124 (☎73/288-2035; ❹), which is actually a relatively peaceful place to stay. A hotel with some genuine colonial character is the *Pousada Oásis do Pacatá*, at Rua Marechal Deodoro 286 (☎73/288-2221; ❹), which is run by a Frenchwoman, and has a swimming pool and a friendly atmosphere. Chalet-style accommodation is provided at the *Pousada São Luiz*, Av. 22 de Abril 329 (☎73/288-2238; ❹), and greater luxury can be found at the *Park Palace Hotel*, Av. 22 de Abril 400 (☎73/288-3777; ❻). The clean but rather noisy **youth hostel** is at Rua Cova da Moça 729 (☎73/288-1742; from $8 per person), while the best-equipped **campsite** is *Camping da Gringa* (☎73/288-2076) at the edge of town; there's another on Mundaí beach (☎73/679-2287), which starts in front of Cidade Alta.

There are a huge number of **places to eat** in Porto Seguro, though the more sophisticated ones, like the *Cruz de Malta*, Av. Getúlio Vargas 358 (11am–midnight), specializing in Bahian seafood, tend to be quite expensive. You can dine more cheaply at *Tché*, on Travessa Augusto Borges, just off the Passarela do Álcool, where a half-portion of *carne do sol* will satisfy even the most ravenous carnivore. Avenida Portugal is generally the liveliest area of town for **nightlife**. The *Sotton Bar* on Praça de Baudeira and the *Porto Prego* club on Rua Pedro Alvares Cabral are both good for live music and dancing.

South of Porto Seguro

South of Porto Seguro are three less developed, more relaxed beach resorts generally preferred by backpacking foreigners, though there are plenty of Brazilian tourists as well. You'll definitely enjoy yourself here if you're looking for beaches and nightlife, and the resorts get quieter the further south you go.

Arraial d'Ajuda

ARRAIAL D'AJUDA is the closest of the three to Porto Seguro and the easiest to get to: catch the ferry from the centre of Porto Seguro for the ten-minute journey across the Rio Buranhém. From the other side there are buses that climb the hill and drop you in the centre of town: don't stay on the bus after this or you'll find yourself making a very boring round trip. In the centre itself and on the roads running down the steep hill to the beach are an incredible number of **places to stay**. The nicest of these is the *Hotel Pousada Marambaia*, at Alameda dos Flamboyants 116 (☎73/875-1275; ❹), which has clean, chalet-style rooms around a peaceful courtyard, complete with swimming pool and gently jangling cowbells. The *Hotel Pousada Buganville*, at Alameda dos Flamboyants 170 (☎73/875-1007; ❹), also has a friendly atmosphere, while the *Pousada Vento Sul*, on the Caminho da Praia, the hill that runs down to the beach (☎73/875-1294; ❸), is for those with a taste for loud techno music, thumping out from the bar below.

The **beach** is lively and can get very crowded in places, though the further you get from the bars and the restaurants, the easier it is to find somewhere peaceful to sit in the sun. The main problem with Arraial d'Ajuda is that it's become too popular too quickly – whatever rubbish collection there is simply can't cope with the huge amounts of litter left by tourists.

Trancoso and Caraíva

Further south down the coast – more peaceful, but next in the developers' sights – is **TRANCOSO**. You can get there either **by bus** (about five a day from Arraial d'Ajuda, taking fifty minutes) or **on foot**. It's a beautiful walk – 12km down the beach from Arraial – but you have to ford a couple of rivers so be prepared to get wet. Once again, there's no shortage of **accommodation**: *Gulab Mahal* (❸), on the main square, the Quadrado, is highly recommended for its hospitality.

If you really want to get away from civilization in this part of Bahia, you have to go even further south, to **CARAÍVA**, which has no electricity apart from that provided by generators, and no cars. It's time-consuming to get to: there are **boats** from Porto Seguro (consult a travel agent) and Trancoso that take four and two hours respectively, and two **buses** a day from Trancoso – a bumpy ride, ending with a boat journey across a river. Once there, you'll find superb beaches, a few rustic places to stay, some good food and plenty of peace and quiet.

Caravelas and around

On the banks of the Rio Caravelas, in the extreme south of Bahia, lies **CARAVELAS**, an attractive, unpretentious colonial town that makes an ideal farewell or introduction to the Northeast. Founded in 1503, it became an important trading centre in the seventeenth and eighteenth centuries. Today both the town and its nearby beach are – despite the growth of tourism – extremely relaxing places to hang out. Caravelas is also the jumping-off point for the **Parque Nacional Marinho dos Abrolhos**, one of the best places in Brazil to see exotic marine life, including – at certain times of year – humpback whales.

Apart from organizing your trip to Abrolhos, there aren't a huge number of specific things to do in Caravelas, but it's an extremely agreeable place to wander round. Most of the interest lies in the streets between the river and the *rodoviária*, which is located on Praça Teófilo Otoni in the centre of town. One block to your left as you come out of the *rodoviária* is Praça Quinze, the liveliest square in this sleepy town. Another block further on and running parallel to the river is Rua Marcílio Diaz, which becomes Rua Sete de Setembro and eventually leads to the beautiful **Praça de Santo Antônio**. This is definitely the architectural highlight of Caravelas and contains the eponymous **Igreja de Santo Antônio**, which you may – if you're lucky – find open.

Practicalities

In order to get to Caravelas, you have to go first to **Teixeira de Freitas**, further inland. Águia Branca run five **buses** a day on the four-hour journey between Porto Seguro and Teixeira de Freitas. From Teixeira de Freitas, Expresso Brasileiro run five buses a day to Caravelas, an agreeable two-hour meander through lush tropical fields. From the south, you can get there from Minas Gerais or Espírito Santo or, if you want to miss out those two states altogether, São Geraldo run a daily *executivo* service from Rio that leaves in mid-afternoon and takes fifteen hours ($50).

There's an excellent **place to stay** near the *rodoviária* on Praça Teófilo Otoni, the cosy *Pousada Caravelense* (☎73/297-1182; ②), which offers friendly service and has a pool table. There are several other hotels, most of them to your left as you come out of the *rodoviária*. The *Pousada da Ponte*, on Rua Anibal Benevolo (②), is a simple, charming place built right on the riverbank. The *Pousada Caravelas* (②), on Rua Sete de Setembro, just next to the Banco do Brasil, is friendly, modern and clean, while for a real budget option you could try the *Hotel Shangri-La* (①) further down the same road. There's also accommodation **on the beach**, called Praia do Grauçá or Barra de Caravelas – a half-hour journey from the *rodoviária* in Caravelas and well worth a visit even if you don't stay there. The *Pousada das Sereias* (☎73/874-1033; ③) is the obvious choice if you don't want to spend too much money, while the *Hotel Marina Porto Abrolhos* (☎73/674-1082, ⓦwww.marinaportoabrolhos.com.br; ⑥) is for beachside luxury.

There are number of good **restaurants** in town. *Carenagem*, just by the petrol station on Praça Quinze, is very good value, as is the *Muroroa Reggae Night*, which is on the riverbank at the other end of town, near the Praça de Santo Antônio – the *carne do sol* here is amazingly good. There's another good place to eat down on the beach at Barra de Caravelas, the *Museu da Baleia*, a seafood restaurant that owes its name to the enormous whale skeleton partially assembled outside – but rest assured that whale meat is not on the menu.

Parque Nacional Marinho dos Abrolhos

For all Caravelas' attractions, there's no doubt that the main reason people come here is to see the extraordinary profusion of marine and bird life in the **Parque Nacional Marinho dos Abrolhos**. The park consists of an archipelago of five islands lying 52km offshore. Among the clear waters and coral reefs you can see all kinds of rare fish, sea turtles and birds, and between July and early November the waters are home to **whales** taking refuge from the Antarctic winter.

There are two main **tour companies** in Caravelas that offer trips to Abrolhos: the well-established Abrolhos Turismo, on Praça Dr Imbassay (☎73/297-1149), and the slightly cheaper Abrolhos Embarcações, at Av. das Palmeiras 2, more or less on Praça Quinze (☎73/297-1172). Abrolhos Turismo offers a basic day-trip to the national park in a launch, leaving at 7am and returning at 5pm, for about $120. The same sort of trip costs about $100 at Abrolhos Embarcações, though the day is shorter, starting at 8am and returning at 4pm. In either case, you can pay extra to rent snorkels, masks and more sophisticated diving equipment. Both companies also offer longer yacht trips to Abrolhos of up to three nights, for which you pay just over $100 a day at Abrolhos Turismo and about $75 at Abrolhos Embarcações. Again, hiring diving equipment costs extra.

Alagoas and Sergipe

Alagoas and **Sergipe** are the smallest Brazilian states. Sandwiched between Bahia to the south and Pernambuco to the north, they have traditionally been overshadowed by their neighbours and, to this day, still have a reputation for being something of a backwater. This isn't entirely fair. While it's true that there's nowhere comparable to the cosmopolitan cities of Recife or Salvador, there are the two state capitals of **Maceió** and **Aracaju**, together with some well-preserved colonial towns, and exceptional **beaches** in Alagoas, which many rate as the best in the Northeast. Also, the harshness of the *sertão* here is much alleviated by the São Francisco river valley, which forms the border between the two states.

Alagoas is very poor, as you immediately discover from the potholes in the roads and its rickety local buses. Thousands of Alagoanos leave every year to look for work as far afield as Rio, São Paulo and Amazonia, giving Alagoas the highest emigration rate of any state in Brazil. Don't let this put you off, however; the coast is beautiful, and Maceió is a lively city, probably the best base from which to explore the state and its neighbour, Sergipe. Sergipe was, for most of its history, in a similar position to Alagoas, but since the 1960s a minor offshore oil boom has brought affluence to parts of the coast. Brazil being what it is, this doesn't mean there's less poverty: it's simply that the rich in Aracaju tend to be richer than the rich elsewhere in the Northeast.

Maceió

Photos of **MACEIÓ**, the state capital of Alagoas, from the 1930s and 1940s show an elegant city of squares and houses nestling under palm trees. Today, while the city is still attractive in places, you can't help wishing the clock could be turned back. Some of the graceful squares and buildings remain, faded yet full of character, but the city as a whole has suffered in recent years from the attentions of planners. Their worst crime was the wrecking of a once famous waterfront parade, facing the harbour around which the city grew. An early nineteenth-century customs house once stood here, framed by offices and the fine houses of traders – all now gone and replaced by grimy concrete boxes.

The city's modern claim to fame – or infamy – is as the place where **Fernando Collor de Melo** cut his political teeth, becoming mayor and then state governor during the 1980s, before being elected Brazil's president in 1990. His term ended in disgrace after he was found to be at the centre of a huge corruption network, and further scandal was to come for Maceió with the violent death of Collor's adviser and chief accomplice in crime, **P.C. Farias**. In 1996 he and his girlfriend were found shot dead in a beachside hotel in Maceió – conspiracy theories abounded and the latest evidence suggests the deaths were an act of political revenge.

Arrival, information and accommodation

By Brazilian standards the **rodoviária** (☎82/221-4615) is relatively close to the centre, though it's still well beyond walking distance for either the old town or the beach area. Buses marked "Ouro Preto" or "Serraria Mercado" connect it

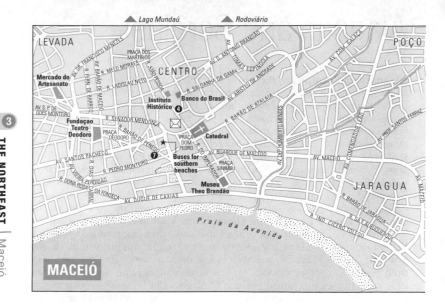

with the old town, from where, to go on to the beaches you should take the "Ponta Verde", "Jardim Vaticano" or "Jatiúca" bus. Alternatively, a taxi direct to either the old town or the beaches will cost around $5. The **airport** is 20km from the city, and is served by a bus marked "Estação Ferroviária", which takes you to the train station. A taxi will set you back around $10–12. Shoals of local buses make **getting around** very simple. All routes pass through the main squares in the centre, notably Praça Deodoro and Praça Dom Pedro II, names you'll often see on route cards propped in the front windows. The Estação Ferroviária is the place to get buses for local routes south of the city, and you may use it to go to nearby Marechal Deodoro or the glorious beach of Praia do Francês.

There's a **tourist information** booth at Avenida Dr Antônio Gouveia (Mon–Fri 8am–2pm; ☎82/315-1603), close to the small tourist market on the promenade of the Praia de Pajuçara, easily recognizable by the *jangada* sailboats offering trips a mile out to the reef. There are other tourist information offices at the *rodoviária* (daily 8am–11pm), the airport (daily 8am–11.30pm; ☎82/322-2288), in the centre at Av. 7 de Setembro 1546 (☎82/633-2850 or 652-1120) and at Rua Saldanha da Gama 71, Farol (Mon–Fri 8am–noon & 2–6pm; ☎82/223-4016). The staff are friendly, and can usually provide details of Maceió's lively **out-of-season Carnaval** (mid-December) as well as maps of the city and its nearby beaches, and information on hotels and tours. You can also check Ⓦwww.coisasalagoas.com.br and Ⓦwww.visitealagoas.com.br for general information on Maceió, and, if you're into diving, Ⓦwww.bahiascuba.com.br.

Accommodation

The area around the **rodoviária** is a good bet for budget but downmarket hotels. Otherwise, it's a largely one-sided choice between **Centro** and the beach districts of **Pajuçara** and **Ponta Verde**: the latter are only a short bus ride away, and accommodation is more plentiful and of better quality than in the centre. Buses there are marked "Ponta Verde", "Pajuçara" or "Ponta da

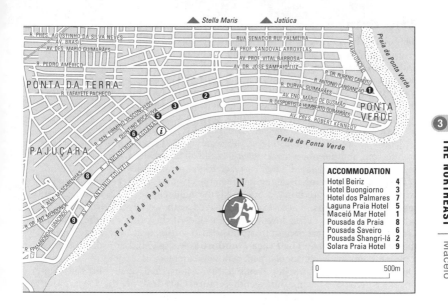

▲ Stella Maris ▲ Jatiúca

ACCOMMODATION

Hotel Beiriz	4
Hotel Buongiorno	3
Hotel dos Palmares	7
Laguna Praia Hotel	5
Maceió Mar Hotel	1
Pousada da Praia	8
Pousada Saveiro	6
Pousada Shangri-lá	2
Solara Praia Hotel	9

0 _____ 500m

Terra" and run one block in from the beach, along Avenida dos Jangadeiros Alagoanos. Conveniently, this road is strung with a series of small hotels and *pousadas*, with more down the side streets. The beach promenade is where the luxury hotels are, and there are several good medium-priced hotels on Avenida Dr Antônio Gouveia, the first stretch of promenade after the centre.

Hotel Beiriz Rua do Sol 290, Centro ☎ 82/336-6200, ℱ 336-6282. Clean mid-priced hotel, but difficult to spot from the road because there's no sign; it's next to a church. ➌

Hotel Buongiorno Av. dos Jangadeiros Alagoanos 1437, Pajuçara ☎ 82/327-4447, ℱ 327-5168. Modest but attractive little hotel, one block from the heart of the beach and close to most of the best restaurants. ➌

Hotel dos Palmares Praça dos Palmares 253, Centro ☎ 82/223-7024. A good budget option in the city centre with rooms built around a courtyard, though rooms are a bit stuffy when it gets warm. ➋

Laguna Praia Hotel Av. dos Jangadeiros Alagoanas 1231, Praia da Pajuçara ☎ 82/231-6180, ℱ 231-9737. Pleasanter than its ugly modern exterior would suggest, with friendly staff, air-conditioning, parking, an outstanding breakfast, and good discounts out of high season. ➌

Maceió Mar Hotel Av. Álavaro Octacílio 2991, Praia de Ponta Verde ☎ 82/231-8000, ℱ 327-5085, ⌨ www.maceomarhotel.com.br. Quality hotel located close to the southern end of Praia de Ponta Verde beach, with bar and sauna. A reasonably good location anytime, with fine views over

the ocean and very spacious and comfortable rooms, but especially good views for the December Carnaval. ➎

Pousada da Praia Av. dos Jangadeiros Alagoanos 545, Praia de Pajuçara ☎ 82/231-6843. A good option in the beach area, with reasonably cosy chalet-style rooms. You can arrange price reductions if you're staying for longer than a couple of nights. ➋

Pousada Saveiro Av. dos Jangadeiros Alagoanos 805, Pajuçara ☎ 82/231-9831, ⌨ www.pousadasaveiro.com.br). Very clean and friendly, this small *pousada* is one of the nicest in its range; rooms with ventilators are cheaper than those with air-conditioning. ➌

Pousada Shangri-lá Av. dos Jangadeiros Alagoanos 1089, Pajuçara ☎ 82/231-3773, ℱ 327-5229. Comfortable if fairly basic *pousada* just a block from the beach; good value with air-conditioning, TV and breakfast included. ➋

Solara Praia Hotel Av. Dr Antônio Gouveia 113, Praia de Pajuçara ☎ 82/231-4371, ⌨ www.hotelsolara.com.br. Reasonable hotel close to the beach, with clean, comfortable rooms and adequate service. ➌

The City

The small **city centre** is just inland from the modest harbour, and here what remains of Maceió's past is to be found cheek by jowl with the cheap hotels and a central shopping area. Quite distinct from this somewhat down-at-heel colonial heart is the modern, much larger and livelier area that starts at **Pajuçara**, a few minutes away by bus to the east, built along a spectacular beach. To the northwest, an undistinguished urban sprawl conceals the enormous lagoon of **Mundaú**. It's here that the city ends, an ideal place to watch a sunset and eat cheaply at the simple bars and restaurants that dot its banks.

Maceió is not exactly bursting at the seams with museums and spectacular architecture, and the places worth seeing could all be rushed around in a morning if you were so inclined. The best place to get some sense of the old Maceió is **Praça dos Martírios**, the finest square in the city, and an object lesson to those who destroyed the waterfront. At one end is the eighteenth-century **Igreja Bom Jesus dos Martírios**, whose exterior, covered with well-preserved blue-and-white *azulejo* tiling, overshadows anything inside. At the other end the colonial **Governor's Palace** faces onto the palm-shaded square, brilliantly white during the day, floodlit at night. The **Praça Deodoro** is less splendid; at its heart there's a pleasant and shady rectangular park whose centrepiece is a statue of Marechal Deodoro da Fonseca himself, gallantly astride a horse and waving his hat at an imaginary crowd. The mid-nineteenth-century **Catedral**, on the Praça Dom Pedro II, is nothing special, but it's a useful landmark in a confusing city centre.

The **commercial heart** of the old centre runs along a couple of largely pedestrianized streets, the Rua do Livramento and Avenida Moreira Lima. At the bottom end of the latter, you'll find a massive and grubby weekend **street market**, where you can buy virtually anything, from recycled car parts to fighting cocks.

There are several museums, but the one in nearby Marechal Deodoro (see p.293) outclasses them all. The **Museu Theo Brandão**, at Praça Visconde Sinimbu 206, 1st floor (also called the Museu do Folclore; Mon–Thurs 8am–noon & 2–5pm, Fri 8am–noon), has the usual bundles of Indian arrows and moth-eaten feather ornaments. Judged strictly on exhibits, the **Instituto Histórico e Geográfico** at Rua do Sol 382 (Mon–Fri 8am–1.30pm & 2–5pm) has the edge, and is worth seeing for the various relics and photographs of the bandit leader Lampião, including the famous "team photo" of his severed head, together with those of his wife, Maria Bonita, and his closest lieutenants. All were preserved in alcohol by the police detachment that shot them in 1938, so that they could be shown in market towns in the interior, the only way to convince people he really had been killed. Even now, the Brazilian media occasionally publish pictures of an old man who died in 1996, who bears a striking resemblance to Lampião. Two other museums worth a visit if you've time on your hands are the **Fundação Teatro Deodoro** on Praça Deodoro (guided tours Mon & Tues 4–7pm; ☎82/326-5252), which contains nineteenth-century furniture and fittings, and the **Museu de Arte Sacra Pierre Chalita**, Rua Loriano Peixoto 517 (Mon–Fri 8am–noon & 2–5pm), which displays a number of religious paintings and statues.

The beaches

The main city beach is at **Pajuçara**, whose curving road and wide mosaic promenade are studded with palm trees. The water is not always the cleanest here and many people hire *jangadas* (around $6 an hour) and head 2km out to sea to swim in the natural pools that form at low tide.

The bay then curves past the yacht club into the less crowded beach of **Ponta Verde**, an easy walk from Pajuçara, with some good spots to eat – try the *Sol Maior*, which has a large palm-shaded patio and serves excellent fresh fish and crab – and has wind-surfing and canoeing equipment for rent. **Diving** lessons or tours can be arranged in Ponta Verde with the Bali Hai Diving School, Av. Robert Kennedy 1473, Loja 5, Galeria 7 Coqueiros (T 82/327-3535).

Ponta Verde and the neighbouring beach of Jatiúca are the beginning of a series of fine sands to the north of Maceió. The best way to get to them is to take buses marked "Mirante" or "Fátima" from the centre, which take you along the coast as far as **Pratagi** (also called Mirante da Sereia), 13km north, where there are coral pools in the reef at low tide. You can get off the bus anywhere that takes your fancy; the main beaches, in order of appearance, are **Cruz das Almas, Jacarecica, Guaxuma, Garça Torta** and **Riacho Doce**, all of them less crowded than the city beaches during the week, but very popular at weekends.

Further afield, the large fishing village of **BARRA DE SANTO ANTÔNIO** is a popular day-trip 40km north of Maceió. Quiet during the week but crowded at the weekend, Barra has a fine beach on a narrow neck of land jutting out from the coast a short canoe ride away, and good, fresh seafood is served in the cluster of small beachside hotels. The village is a stop for some Recife–Maceió interstate buses. North again, just 15km from the border with Pernambuco state, the dozy village of **MARAGOGI** has a couple of upmarket places to stay: the superb *Hotel Salinas*, Rodoviária AL101 km 124 (T 81/296-1122; ❽), a luxury hotel with every conceivable facility set on Maragogi beach, and the *Praia dos Sonhos*, Rodoviária AL101 km 124 (T 81/222-4598; ❻), on Peroba beach.

Most visitors to Maceió flood north to the beaches, which leaves the coast **to the south** in relative calm, though the crowds are now beginning to make their way here too. Hourly buses marked "Deodoro" leave from the bus stop in front of the old train station in Maceió, near the harbour, passing out of the city over the Trapiche bridge into a flat, swampy coastline. Sixteen kilometres south, the road swings left to a beach called **Praia do Francês**, which even by Alagoan standards is something special. An enormous expanse of white sand, surf and thick palm forest, it even boasts a couple of small hotels; the *Hotel Cumarú* (❸) is the best value.

Eating, drinking and nightlife

Some of the best places to eat and drink in the city are out of the centre, at Mundaú lagoon and Pajuçara beach. From Praça dos Martírios you can take a taxi, or a local bus marked "Mundaú" or "Ponta da Barra", for the short ride to **Lagoa Mundaú**, where you can have a *caipirinha* at a **waterfront bar** to accompany the routinely spectacular sunset. There are simple but excellent **eating places** here, too, selling fish and shrimp, and the early evening is a good time to watch prawn fishermen at work on punts in the lagoon, their silhouetted figures throwing out nets against the sunset.

At **Pajuçara**, you'll find a series of **bars** built around thatched emplacements – *barracas* – at intervals along the beach. They mix excellent *caipirinhas* and serve cheaper food than you're likely to find in the seafront restaurants on the other side of the road, all much of a muchness. Seafood is, naturally, best: the *sopa de ostra* manages to get more oysters into a single dish than most gringos see in a lifetime; they're so common, you can even get an oyster omelette. Of the **restaurants**, *Spettus* (11.30am until late, daily; T 82/304-3100) at Av. Alvaro

Otacilio 3115, Ponta Verde, is probably the best place in town for steaks, but it's not cheap. Slightly more expensive again, the sophisticated French restaurant *Gstaad*, on the same street at no. 2167, is well known for its salmon dishes. Good budget options are the Chinese restaurant *Nova China* and *Restaurante Japones*, Rua Senador Rui Palmeira 46 (T82/337-0253). If you can afford to spend a bundle, there's the stylish *Sushi Bar New Hakata*, Rua Eng. Paulo Brandao Nogueira 95, in Stella Maris (T82/325-6160). More reasonable is the *Creperia Flor das Aguas*, Av. Alvaro Otacilio 3309, Ponta Verde (Mon–Fri noon–11pm, Sat & Sun 4–11pm; T82/231-2335), which serves good waffles, and of course, crèpes. For simple but tasty Italian dishes, it's hard to beat *Restaurante Carlito* (T82/231-4029) at Barraca 32, on the beach at Ponta Verde; they also deliver.

For **nightlife**, try the area around Rua Sá de Albuquerque (in the Jaragua sector), is a newly fashionable part of the city that's especially lively from Thursday through Saturday each week when the main street is closed off to traffic and the bars and restaurants put their tables outside. The liveliest of Maceió's two main clubs is here at Rua Sá e Albuquerque 588, the cavernous *Aeroporco's* (Thurs–Sat; T82/326-5145), with lots of samba, Brazilian DJs and a sushi bar. The other club, *Aquarela*, at Antônio Gomes de Barros 66, in Jatiúca, also has a large dance floor, as well as reasonably good live bands playing *pagode* and *forró*, and some tourist dance shows. The Fundação Teatro Deodoro on Praça Deodoro sometimes presents spectacular dance performances; check the cultural listings in the *Tribuna de Alagoas* newspaper or call T82/327-2727 for information.

There are a number of **gay and lesbian clubs** in Maceio, notably *Blackout* and *Heaven*, both in the Rio Uruguay sector, while *Bar Sensensura* on Rua Sá de Albuquerque has great *pagode* nights on Sundays. Stella Maris is another trendy area of town for nightlife, gay or straight.

Listings

Airlines TAM, Rua Epaminodas Gracindo 92, Pajucara T82/327-6400 or at airport T82/214-4114 or 214-4112; Varig T82/214-4100; Vasp T82/322-1414; and Transbrasil T82/221-8286. For information on flights, call the airport on T82/214-4000.

Banks and exchange Banco do Brasil and HSBC are both on the first block of Rua do Livramento, close to the corner with Rua Boa Vista. You can change money and travellers' cheques at Aero Turismo, Av. Santos Pacheco 65.

Car rental Flojos, Rua João Paulo Pelegrini 103 T82/325-5441; Comercial Locadora, Rua Zeferino Rodrigues 100, Pajuçara T82/982-5361 or 327-9145; Tropical, Rua Dr Gerson Wanderley de Oliveira 95, Mangabeiras T82/3033-5946.

Internet Emporio Jaragua Cybercafe, Rua Sá de Albuquereque 378, in Jaragua, has good food and coffee; also at Loja 7a Rua Jangadeiros Alagoanos 1292 (T82/337-4718), in a complex by the *Othon Hotel*. Also try Cafeconet, Rua Emp. Carlos da Silva Nogueira 192, Loja C, Jatiuca (T82/235-5334).

Post office The post office is at Rua João Pessoa 57 in the center near the *Asamblea* building, with

a branch in Shopping Centro de Artesabato Jaraguá, Rua Sá da Albuquerque 417.

Taxis Tele Taxi T82/320-3232; Liga Taxi T82/326-2121.

Travel and tour companies Marcão Turismo, Rua B-24, Pajuçara (T82/231-0843, W www .turismomaceio.com.br) offer city tours, trips to the Lagoa Mundaú and the southern and northern beaches, and excursions as far afield as Recife and Olinda. Jaragua Turismo, Rua Jangadeiros Alagoanos 844, Pajucara (T82/337-2780 or 9983-6129 run tours to the Praia do Frances, around the city, to nearby islands as well as the São Francisco delta. A range of local beach, city and entertainment tours are available through Status Turismo, Av. Robert Kennedy 1785, Ponta Verde (T82/327-7771, W www.statusturismo.com.br). Transamerica Turismo, Av. Dr Antonio Gouveia 487 (T82/231-7334) operate daily trips to Lagoa Mundaú and other beauty spots. For diving, contact ScuBrasil at Rua Mexihão 12, Corais do Frances, Marechal Deodoro (T82/260-1417, W www.scubrasil.com .br).

Marechal Deodoro

The beautifully preserved colonial town of **MARECHAL DEODORO** lies 22km south of Maceió. Basically it's no more than a small market town, built on rising ground on the banks of a lagoon, with streets that are either dirt or cobbled. But it's immaculately kept, with not a single building that looks as if it were constructed this century. Nor is it simply preserved for tourists to gawp at: the locals spit in the streets, gossip and hang about in bars as they would anywhere else, and there's a real air of small-town tranquillity.

The bus from Maccíó drives right to the end of town before reaching its terminus. You should get off a little earlier, in the manicured **Praça Pedro Paulinho**, which is dominated by the imposing facade of the Igreja de Santa Maria Magdalena, with the older **Convento de São Francisco**, finished in 1684, attached. The convent's plain exterior conceals an austere, yet strikingly beautiful interior, which is now turned over to the excellent **Museu de Arte Sagrada** (Mon & Wed–Sat 9am–5pm); entrance to the museum is from the road running down towards the lake from Praça Pedro Paulinho. The convent is built around a cool courtyard, with the main galleries on the first storey. Everything on display is high Catholic religious art, with little concession made to the tropical setting save for the large number of portrayals of São Benedito, the black patron saint of the slaves who manned the *engenhos* all around and built most of Marechal Deodoro itself. The highlight of the collection, extracted from churches all over the state, is the group of seventeenth- to nineteenth-century statues of saints and virgins, in the first gallery to the right. Most are no more than a foot high, made of wood or plaster, and intricately painted. Look, too, for the couple of life-size (and frighteningly lifelike) carved wooden bodies of Christ, with gruesome wounds. In comparison, the **Igreja de Santa Maria Magdalena** is not as impressive, a typical mid-eighteenth-century building, though less cloyingly Rococo than most. In front of a small side chapel, opposite the entrance from the museum, is a concealed entrance to a secret tunnel, a relic from the original chapel that stood on the site during the Dutch wars.

Down the road curving to the right past the museum is the modest house that was the birthplace of **Marechal Deodoro**, proclaimer and first president of the Republic in 1889; it's now preserved as a **museum**, Rua Mal. Deodoro 92 (daily 8am–5pm; free). Deodoro was the son of an army officer who served with distinction in the Paraguayan war, and rose to become head of the armed forces with the sonorous title "Generalissimo of the Forces of Land and Sea". He was the first Brazilian to mount a military coup, unceremoniously dumping the harmless old emperor Dom Pedro II, but he proved an arrogant and inept president, the earliest in a depressingly long line of incompetent military authoritarians. Dissolving Congress and declaring a state of siege in 1891, he did everyone a favour by resigning when he couldn't make it stick. There's no hint, of course, of his disastrous political career in the museum, which is basically a mildly interesting collection of personal effects and period furniture.

In the streets around you'll find several **lacemakers**, with goods displayed in the windows. Marechal Deodoro is famous for its lace, which you see in any sizeable market in the Northeast. It's high-quality stuff, and costs less than half the price you pay elsewhere when bought at source in the town. The Cooperative Artesanal in Rua Dr Ladislam Netto is a good place to look.

If you want to stay, there's a **pensão**, *Deodoré* (**❶**), on Praça Pedro Paulinho, but there's no sign so you'll have to ask. There's also a **campsite** (**☎**82/263-1378), clean and with good facilities, half an hour's walk beyond the square; the road is marked by a sign near the small bus company office. For **tourist information** call the municipal tourist line on ☎82/221-4615 or check out Ⓦ www.marechaldeodoro.net.com.br.

Paulo Afonso and around

Inland from Maceió, 300km to the west, the most popular destination of all in Alagoas is the **Cachoeira de Paulo Afonso**, once the largest waterfall on the Rio São Francisco and the third largest in Brazil, but now largely emasculated by a hydroelectric scheme that diverted most of the flow – a spectacular piece of ecological vandalism surpassed only by the destruction of the even more impressive Sete Quedas waterfall in Paraná by similar means in the early 1990s. These days the only time a considerable amount of water passes over the falls is during the rains of January and February, but the whole surrounding area – a spectacular deep rocky gorge choked with tropical forest and declared a national park – is very scenic all year round.

You can get there by bus from Salvador, but the journey from Maceió is shorter, with two **buses** daily from the *rodoviária* there. They leave you in the small river town of **PAULO AFONSO**, on the Bahian riverbank, where there is a cluster of reasonable **hotels** near the bus station; the *Belvedere*, Av. Apolônio Sales 457 (☎75/281-1814; ❺), is more upmarket than the others, but good value.

The **waterfall** is some way out of town and you can only get there by taxi, which will cost you about $5 an hour, but the drivers do know the best spots. Alternatively, you may be able to organize something with the tourist office in the centre of town on Rua Apolônio Sales (Mon–Sat 9am–6pm; ☎75/281-2757), which doubles up as the best place to find local guides.

Penedo

A couple of hours, and some 168km south of Maceió is the lively colonial town of **PENEDO**. Originally developed to control the illegal exportation of lumber by French merchant ships in the sixteenth century, it was occupied by the Dutch between 1637 and 1645, who built the original fort here. There are several colonial churches in town that are all marked on a useful map, obtainable at the **tourist office** (Mon–Fri 8–11am & 2–5pm) in the main central square, the Praça Barão de Penedo. The most attractive is the early eighteenth-century *azulejo*-decorated **Igreja de Nossa Senhora da Corrente**, which has a stunning gold-leaf altar inside. The **museum** in the Casa do Penedo, Rua João Pessoa 126 (Mon–Sat 9am–noon & 2–4pm; $1), is also worth a visit for its displays of period furniture and historical photographs and documents.

Penedo is strategically placed at the mouth of the Rio São Francisco, and, while the trading prosperity it might have expected as a result never quite materialized, it's still a busy little place, much of whose life revolves around the river and the waterfront. The waterfront park, with its shaded paths and kiosks selling drinks, is a good place to watch the toing and froing of the boats. You can negotiate with boat owners to go on **cruises**: the main destinations are **Piassabussu**, a sleepy and little-visited fishing village right on the mouth of the river, and the village of **Neópolis**, opposite Penedo, where there's nothing to do except have a drink and catch the boat back – but it's a nice trip.

Penedo is served by four **buses** daily from Maceió's *rodoviária* and for once they leave you in the centre of the town, which is well supplied with good **places to stay**: try *Pousada Colonial*, Praça 12 de Abril (☎82/551-2355, ℱ551-3737; ❷), which has adequate rooms plus excellent views over Penedo, or the more comfortable *São Francisco*, on Avenida Floriano Peixoto (☎82/551-2273, ℱ551-2274, ⓦwww.hotelsaofrancisco-penedo.com.br; ❹), both in the heart of town; nearer the **rodoviária** (☎82/551-2602) on Rua Siqueira Campos, are a number of budget hotels with prices starting at around $12. One of the town's better **restaurants** is *Forte da Rocheira* on Rua da Rocheira, specializing in fish dishes. Out of town, 30km east of Penedo near the town of Piaçabuço, the *Pousada Piaçabuçu* (☎82/557-1112, Ⓔroeland@sidtecnet.com.br) offers ecological tours of the surrounding countryside.

Aracaju

From Maceió seven buses a day run to **ARACAJU**, capital of the neighbouring state of **Sergipe** (population 430,000), a little-visited and rather anonymous place. Although the Portuguese founded a colony here in 1592, the capital of the infant state was moved to nearby São Cristóvão. Then, in the mid-nineteenth century, there was a sudden vogue for purpose-built administrative centres (similar to the urge that led to the construction of Brasília a century later), and the core of modern Aracaju was thrown up overnight, becoming the state capital again in 1855. Like the other state capitals planned and built in the nineteenth century, Aracaju is – to put it mildly – something of an architectural desert, built on an American-style grid layout. Oil wealth has stimulated a lot of recent building and given the city council enough money to keep everything clean and tidy, but there is a very un-Brazilian dullness about the place. However, the people are friendly, some of the beaches are good, and the small colonial towns of Laranjeiras and São Cristóvão are only a short bus ride away.

The **rodoviária** (☎79/241-2587) is miles out of town, linked to the centre by frequent local buses. The **airport** (☎79/212-8500) is also out of town (12km) but not far from the beach of Atalaia Velha; buses marked "Aeroporto" will get you into the centre. Sergipe's **tourist office**, EMSETUR, has its headquarters at Tr. Baltazar Gois 86, in the centre (☎79/3179-1940), while the SEBRAE office is at the Centro de Turismo (daily 8am–8pm; ☎79/3179-1947), in the shopping centre known as Rua 24 Horas, just next to Praça Olímpio Campos. Rua 24 Horas is actually a very pleasant place, set in a restored nineteenth-century building, with cafés, restaurants and a stage where shows are sometimes put on.

The cheaper **hotels** are as usual in the city centre, several of them near the municipal bus station, the Rodoviária Velha. For a real budget option you could stay at the *Sergipe Hotel*, Rua Geru 205 (☎79/222-7898; ❶), which is perfectly adequate for the price. Two comfortable mid-range hotels in the same area are the *Oásis*, at Rua São Cristóvão 466 (☎79/224-1181; ❸), and the *Amado*, at Rua Laranjeiras 532 (☎79/211-9937; ❸). Right next to the Rodoviária Velha is the plusher and pricier *Grande Hotel*, at Rua Itabaianinha 371 (☎79/211-1383; ❹), while down at the southern end of the city centre the *Hotel Jangadeiro*, at Rua Santa Luiza 269 (☎79/211-1350, ⓦwww .jangadeiro.com.br; ❸), has a pool and decent rooms with TV and telephone.

The two main **beaches** are Atalaia Velha and Atalaia Nova. **ATALAIA VELHA** lies about 5km south down the road from the city centre and is the more developed of the two. It's easy to get to by bus but the whole area is rather soulless and uninspiring. There are, however, a huge number of restaurants and **hotels**, including the *Pousada do Sol*, Rua Atalaia 43 (☎79/226-5500; ❸), the *Nascimento Praia*, Av. Santos Dumont 1813 (☎79/255-2090; ❹), which has a small pool, and, for total luxury, the *Del Mar Hotel*, Av. Santos Dumont 1500 (☎79/226-9000, ⓦwww.delmarhotel.com.br; ❺). **ATALAIA NOVA** lies on an island in the Rio Sergipe, accessible by boat from the *hidroviária* in the city centre. The ferry leaves every ten minutes and costs just 40¢; you can then get a bus to Atalaia Nova from the ferry terminal. Although the beach itself isn't great, the island is quite a pleasant place to stay – hotels are expensive, but there are plenty of rooms for rent.

Laranjeiras and São Cristóvão

Sergipe's main attractions are two attractive colonial towns that come as a welcome relief from Aracaju's anonymity, reminders of the time when sugar made the *sergipano* coast one of the most strategically valuable parts of Brazil. Innumerable skirmishes were fought around them during the Dutch wars, but no trace of their turbulent past survives into their tranquil present, as they slide from important market centres into rural backwaters.

The pleasantly decrepit village of **LARANJEIRAS** is forty minutes by half-hourly bus from Aracaju's Rodoviária Velha. Dominated by a hill crowned with the ruins of an old *engenho* chapel, Laranjeiras boasts a couple of small museums as well as the inevitable churches. The interesting **Museu Afro-Brasileiro**, Rua José do Prado Franco 70 (Tues–Sun 8am–noon & 2–5.30pm), concentrates on slave life and popular religion, while the **Centro de Cultura João Ribeiro**, Rua João Ribeiro (Mon–Fri 8am–10pm, Sat 8am–1pm, Sun 2–5pm), is mostly given over to *artesanato* and relics of plantation life. But the main attraction is simply wandering around the winding streets, taking in the quiet squares, pastel-painted houses and small bars where locals sit around and watch the world go by. There are a couple of **pensões**, but no hotels as yet, and with any luck it will stay that way.

The other colonial town worth visiting is the old state capital of **SÃO CRISTÓVÃO**, also reached by local bus (hourly) from Aracaju's Rodoviária Velha, a thirty-minute journey. The town was founded in 1590 and much of it hasn't changed since, as the shifting of the capital to Aracaju preserved it from the developers. Packed into its small area is the full panoply of a colonial administrative centre, including an old governor's palace, a parliament building and half a dozen period churches, together with the small **Museu de Arte Sacra e Histórico** in the Convento de São Francisco (Tues–Sun 9am–noon & 2–5.30pm). The convent contains a chapel decorated with paintings by José Teófilo de Jesus, one of the most important sacred painters from the Northeast.

Pernambuco

Recife, capital of the state of **Pernambuco**, shares with São Luis the distinction of not having been founded by the Portuguese: when they arrived in the 1530s, they settled just to the north, building the beautiful colonial town of **Olinda** and turning most of the surrounding land over to sugar. A century later, the Dutch, under Maurice of Nassau, took Olinda and burned it down, choosing to build a new capital, Recife, on swampy land to the south, where there was the fine natural harbour that Olinda had lacked. The Dutch, playing to their strengths, drained and reclaimed the low-lying land, and the main evidence of the Dutch presence today is not so much their few surviving churches and forts dotted up and down the coast, as the reclaimed land on which the core of Recife is built.

Out of Recife, there are good beaches in both directions. The Portuguese first developed the coastline as far **north** as the island of **Itamaracá**, growing sugar cane on every available inch. This erstwhile fishing village still retains its Dutch fort, built to protect the new colonial power's acquisitions, but these days it's a fairly blighted weekenders' resort. Best is the **coastal route south**, where a succession of small towns and villages interrupts a glorious stretch of palm-fringed beach.

Head **inland** and the scenery changes quickly to the hot, dry and rocky landscape of the *sertão*. **Caruaru** is the obvious target, home of the largest market in the Northeast, and close by is **Alto do Moura**, centre of the highly rated Pernambucan pottery industry. If you plan to go any further inland than this you'll need to prepare well for any kind of extended *sertão* journey, though it's straightforward enough to reach the twin river towns of **Petrolina** and **Juazeiro**.

Recife

RECIFE, the Northeast's second-largest city, appears rather dull on first impressions, but it's lent a colonial grace and elegance by Olinda, 6km to the north and considered part of the same conurbation. Recife itself has long since burst its original colonial boundaries and much of the centre is now given over to uninspired modern skyscrapers and office buildings. But there are still a few quiet squares, where an inordinate number of impressive churches lie cheek by jowl with the uglier urban sprawl of the past thirty years. North of the centre are some pleasant leafy suburbs, dotted with museums and parks, and to the south there is the modern beachside district of **Boa Viagem**. Other beaches lie within easy reach, both north and south of the city, and there's also all the **nightlife** one would expect from a city of nearly two million Brazilians.

Tourists wandering around Recife should be particularly careful with their possessions and it's best, too, to use taxis to get home after an evening out. Recife is one of Brazil's most violent cities, an unsurprising statistic given the immediately obvious disparity of wealth and stark poverty, and the large number of homeless people on the streets. On Sundays in the old centre of Recife, the streets often seem deserted except for beggars; everyone else seems to be on the beach at Boa Viagem. Tourists tend to hang out in the much pleasanter environment of laid-back Olinda.

Arrival, information and city transport

The **airport** is fairly close to the city centre, at the far end of Boa Viagem. A taxi to Boa Viagem itself shouldn't be more than $6–7, to the neighbouring island of Santo Antônio about $10–12; or take the Aeroporto bus ($2.50) from right outside, which will drive through Boa Viagem and drop you in the centre. The **rodoviária** is miles out, though this is not really a problem since the **metrô** (℡81/3424-1662 for information), an overground rail link, whisks you very cheaply and efficiently into the centre, giving you a good introduction to city life as it glides through various *favelas*. It will deposit you at the old train station, called **Estação Central** (or simply "Recife"). To get to your hotel from there, whether in the central hotel district, Boa Viagem or even Olinda, you're best off taking a **taxi** – Recife is a confusing city even when you've been there a few days, and the extra money will be well spent.

Information

Tourist information is not Recife's strong point, and what there is is directed mainly at the upper end of the market. The state tourist office, EMPETUR, runs a 24-hour information post at the **airport** (℡81/3462-4533), where you may find English-speaking staff and a few maps and calendars of events. They'll also ring hotels for you, but are no good for the cheapest places. EMPETUR has its headquarters inconveniently located at the **Centro de Convenções** (Mon–Fri 9am–6pm; ℡81/3427-8183), an ugly concrete building more or less en route between Recife and Olinda. In **Boa Viagem**, there is a Delegacia do Turista at Praca do Boa Viagem (℡81/3463-3621; 8am-8pm) that can help with accommodation at the beach. Alternatively, there's the **tourist hotline**: call ℡81/3425-8409 (Mon–Fri 8am–6pm) and you should be able to find someone who speaks English.

For up-to-date **listings** of events in and around Recife, try the *Roteiro* section of the daily *Jornal do Comércio*, or the *Viver* section of the *Diário de Pernambuco*, also daily. Alternatively, the *Agenda Cultural do Recife* is a useful guide to museums and theatre, dance, music and photography events, and is available from the Casa da Cultura (see p.305) or online at Ⓦwww.recife.pe.gov.br.

City transport

Recife's **bus network** (℡81/3452-1999) is an appalling mess. Routes change frequently, the destinations marked on the front of the buses are places you've never heard of, and unlike in Rio or Salvador there are no helpful signs on the side of the vehicle showing where it stops along the way. To make things worse, the complex layout of the city means that it's hard to get your bearings. What follows is a basic guide to getting around, but you'll probably still have to ask.

Most city buses originate and terminate on the central island of **Santo Antônio**, on Avenida Dantas Barreto, either side of the **Pracinha do Diário** (also known as Praça da Independência). There are more stops nearby on Avenida Guararapes outside the main post office. To get from the city centre **to Boa Viagem**, take buses marked "Aeroporto", "Iguatemi" or "Boa Viagem", or catch the more comfortable *frescão* (an air-conditioned bus) marked "Aeroporto", just outside the offices of the newspaper *Diário de Pernambuco*, on the Pracinha do Diário; it leaves every twenty minutes and costs about $2.50. To get to **Olinda** from central Recife, walk south down Avenida Dantas Barreto from the Pracinha do Diário to the last of the series of bus stops, and catch the bus marked "Casa Caiada" – you'll think you're heading in the wrong direction at first, but you will get there eventually. Alternatively, a taxi from central Recife to Olinda should cost around $8–10 and will take about fifteen minutes.

From Boa Viagem, most buses in either direction can be caught on Avenida Engenheiro Domingos Ferreira, three blocks in from the sea. Buses marked "Dantas Barreto" will get you **to the city centre**, and so should most of those marked "Conde de Boa Vista", though it's probably best to ask. You can get directly from Boa Viagem **to Olinda** on buses marked "Rio Doce".

If you're completely fed up with the buses, there are always **shared taxis**. These small vans tear around the city towards the end of the afternoon, offering lifts to various destinations for between 80¢ and $2.50. They'll stop almost anywhere and are a pretty good way of getting around as long as you're not too nervous a passenger, though it's clear that many locals don't like to use them.

Accommodation

It's cheapest to stay right in the rather run-down centre, and most expensive in the beach district of Boa Viagem. The other obvious area to consider staying in is Olinda (see p.312), where prices fall somewhere between the two and, although there's not much of a beach, it has a lot more culturally to offer the visitor. Recife's **youth hostel**, the *Albergue da Juventude Maracatus do Recife*, is in Boa Viagem at Rua Maria Carolina 185 (℡81/3326-1964), and is superb. Complete with swimming pool and free breakfast, it's excellent value at $15 a night.

The centre: Boa Vista and Santo Antônio

Most central hotels are concentrated around Rua do Hospício, near the bridges linking Santo Antônio with the neighbouring island of Boa Vista.

Hotel America Praça Maciel Pinheiro 48, Boa Vista ℡81/3221-1300. Two-star hotel that's not as expensive as it looks; rooms a bit run down but adequate and safe. ❸

Hotel Central Av. Manoel Borba 209, Boa Vista ℡81/3423-6411. As its name suggests, this hotel is central and is located on what remains one of Recife's quieter and more elegant streets. Also does a superb breakfast. ❸

Hotel Nassau Rua Largo do Rosário 253, Santo Antônio ℡81/3224-3977. A comfortable hotel in a good location; the spacious rooms come with private baths. ❸

Hotel Quatro de Outubro Rua Floriano Peixoto 141, Santo Antônio ℡81/3224-4900. Close to Recife's main *metrô* station, it's run-down but reasonable value; all rooms have air-conditioning and TV. ❸

Hotel São Domingos Praça Maciel Pinheiro 66, Boa Vista ℡81/3231-1388. Clean and modern two-star hotel that makes up in comfort what it lacks in style. All rooms with private baths. ❸

Recife Plaza Rua da Aurora 225, Boa Vista ℡81/3231-1200. Nondescript place close to the central river bridge, the Ponte do Coelho. Rooms are reasonable, with air-conditioning and TV, and there's a restaurant, sauna and swimming pool. ❹

Boa Viagem

In Boa Viagem, finding a hotel is the least of your problems: it sometimes seems as if they outnumber apartment buildings. The difficulty is finding a reasonably cheap one, as the majority cater for international tourists and rich Brazilians. Even so, you should be able to find somewhere for between $15 and $25 a night, certainly if you're prepared to stay a little way back from the seafront.

Atlante Plaza Av. Boa Viagem 5426 ℡81/3302-3333, freephone/toll-free for reservations ℡81/3302-3344, ⓦ www.atlanteplaza.com.br. Large, modern and well located in the centre of

beach and night life, this upmarket hotel boasts elevators with panoramic views, plus a bar, restaurant, swimming pool, saunas and fitness suite. ❼

Hotel 54 Rua Prof. José Brandão 54 ⊤81/3465-2396. A pleasant place to stay with air-conditioning and TV, but no pool. ❸

Hotel 200 Milhas Av. Boa Viagem 864 ⊤81/3326-5921. Cheap hotel that's incredible value given its seafront location. ❷

Hotel Boa Viagem Av. Boa Viagem 5000 ⊤81/3341-4144. The least expensive of all the four-star seafront hotels, this modern hotel has stylish rooms, some with ocean views, plus good showers. ❺

Hotel Park Rua dos Navegantes 9 ⊤ & ⓕ81/3465-4666. Large, modern and upmarket place but still quite good value in the centre of the action just a block from the beach, and with its own pool. ❹

Hotel Portal do Sol Av. Cons. Aguiar 3217 ⊤81/3326-9740. Moderately priced hotel, in a good location just two blocks away from the beach and on Recife's principal bus routes. ❸

Hotel Savaroni Av. Boa Viagem 3772 ⊤81/3465-4299 ⓕ3463-7664. A mid-sized good-value place with standard rooms and apartments with all mod cons, a bar, pretty good restaurant and small pool. ❻

Park Othon Hotel Rua dos Navegantes 9 ⊤81/3465-4666. An anonymous high-rise, but just a stone's throw from the beach. ❻

Pousada Aconchego Rua Felix de Brito 382 ⊤81/3326-2989, ⓦwww.hotelaconchego.com.br. This small and comfortable hotel has a swimming pool and good restaurant open 24 hours a day. ❸

Recife Monte Hotel Rua dos Navegantes 363 ⊤81/3465-7422, ⓦwww.recifemontehotel.com.br. A glorified apartment building with all mod cons, whose claim to fame is that Chico Buarque and Charles Aznavour once stayed here. ❼

Recife Palace Av. Boa Viagem 4070 ⊤81/3464-2500, ⓕ3465-6767, ⓦwww.lucsimhoteis.com.br. Superb beach views and all comforts – the cheapest of the five-star hotels by a long way. ❼

Vila Rica Ideale Hotel Av. Boa Viagem 4308 ⊤81/3465-8111. A good deal in this price range, boasting every four-star luxury. ❺

The City

Modern Recife sprawls onto the mainland, but the heart of the city is three small **islands**, Santo Antônio, Boa Vista and Recife proper, connected with each other and the mainland by more than two dozen bridges over the rivers Beberibe and Capibaribe. This profusion of waterways has led to the inevitable description of Recife as the "Venice of Brazil" – a totally ludicrous idea.

Recife island is where the docks are and therefore marks the point where the city began. Until only a few years ago it was a dangerous, run-down area inhabited mainly by drunks and prostitutes, but the investment of millions of dollars by the local authorities and private business have brought about something of a transformation in both the look and feel of the area. The brightly painted colonial buildings make the small, easily negotiable island a pleasant place to wander during the day, even though there aren't many specific things to do. And the island now has the best nightlife anywhere in the city centre, its streets jammed with revellers right through the early hours.

Avenida Dantas Barreto splits the island of **Santo Antônio**, home to the central business district and many surviving colonial churches. Just over the river is **Boa Vista**, linked to Santo Antônio by a series of small bridges; the brightly painted criss-cross girders of the **Ponte de Boa Vista** are a convenient central landmark. Santo Antônio and Boa Vista are the dirtiest areas of Recife, and although they bustle with activity during the day they empty at night, when the enormous, largely deserted streets are a little spooky and forbidding. Residential suburbs stretch to the north, but the bulk of the middle-class population is concentrated to the south, in a long ribbon development along the beach at **Boa Viagem**.

There's no excuse for being bored in Recife. There are literally dozens of colonial **churches** in the city, at least one of which it would be criminal to miss; one excellent and several lesser **museums**; and some lovely public buildings. The churches tend not to have regular opening hours, but if the main

△ Cidade Alta, Salvador

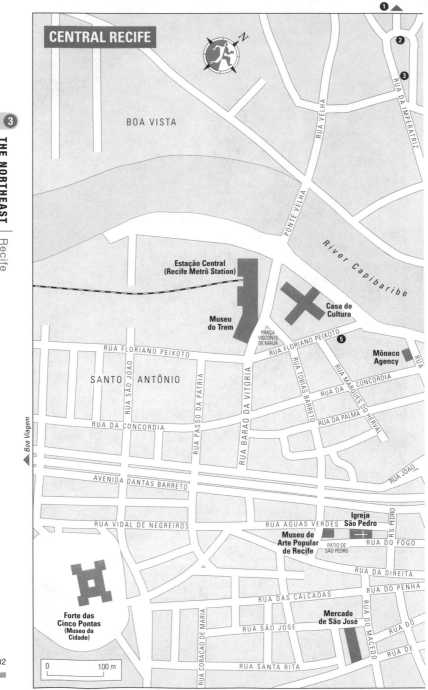

CENTRAL RECIFE

BOA VISTA

RUA VELHA

RUA DA IMPERATRIZ

PONTE VELHA

River Capibaribe

Estação Central
(Recife Metrô Station)

Museu
do Trem

PRAÇA
VISCONDE
DE MAUÁ

Casa de
Cultura

Mônaco
Agency

RUA FLORIANO PEIXOTO

SANTO ANTÔNIO

RUA SÃO JOÃO

RUA PASSO DA PATRIA

RUA BARÃO DA VITORIA

RUA TOBIAS BARRETO

RUA FLORIANO PEIXOTO

RUA MARQUES DO HERVAL

RUA DA CONCORDIA

RUA DA PALMA

RUA

RUA DA CONCORDIA

Boa Viagem

AVENIDA DANTAS BARRETO

RUA JOAO

RUA VIDAL DE NEGREIROS

RUA AGUAS VERDES

Igreja
São Pedro

R. S. PEDRO

Museu de
Arte Popular
de Recife

PÁTIO DE
SÃO PEDRO

RUA DO FOGO

RUA DA DIREITA

RUA DO PENHA

Forte das
Cinco Pontas
(Museu da
Cidade)

RUA CORAÇÃO DE MARIA

RUA DAS CALÇADAS

RUA SÃO JOSÉ

Mercado
de São José

RUA DO MACEDO

RUA DO

RUA DE

RUA SANTA RITA

0   100 m

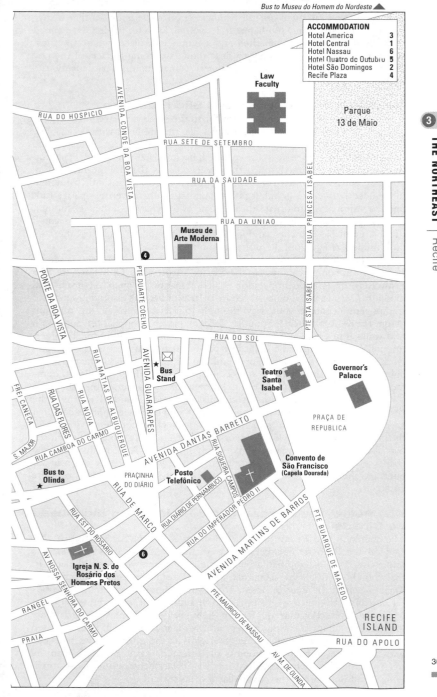

ACCOMMODATION
Hotel America 3
Hotel Central 1
Hotel Nassau 6
Hotel Quatro de Outubro 5
Hotel São Domingos 2
Recife Plaza 4

Law
Faculty

Parque
13 de Maio

RUA DO HOSPICIO

AVENIDA CONDE DA BOA VISTA

RUA SETE DE SETEMBRO

RUA DA SAUDADE

RUA PRINCESA ISABEL

RUA DA UNIAO

Museu de
Arte Moderna

❹

PONTE DA BOA VISTA

PTE DUARTE COELHO

PTE STA ISABEL

RUA DO SOL

Bus
Stand

Teatro
Santa
Isabel

Governor's
Palace

RUA MATIAS DE ALBUQUERQUE

AVENIDA GUARARAPES

FREI CANECA

RUA DAS FLORES

RUA NOVA

S. MAJOR

RUA CAMBOA DO CARMO

AVENIDA DANTAS BARRETO

RUA SIQUEIRA CAMPOS

PRAÇA DE
REPUBLICA

Convento de
São Francisco
(Capela Dourada)

Bus to
Olinda

PRAÇINHA
DO DIÁRIO

Posto
Telefônico

RUA DE MARCO

RUA DIÁRIO DE PERNAMBUCO

RUA DO IMPERADOR PEDRO II

AVENIDA MARTINS DE BARROS

PTE BUARQUE DE MACEDO

RUA EST DO ROSÁRIO

❻

Igreja N. S. do
Rosário dos
Homens Pretos

AV NOSSA SENHORA DO CARMO

RANGEL

PRAIA

PTE MAURICIO DE NASSAU

RECIFE
ISLAND

RUA DO APOLO

AV M. DE OLINDA

door is shut you can often get in by knocking on a side door – if there's anyone inside they'll be only too happy to let you in. Even for the less determined sightseer, there are parks, **beaches** and a number of places where the most interesting thing to do is simply to drift about, absorbing the feel of the city and watching people get on with their lives – something that's particularly true of the city's **markets**.

Avenida Dantas Barreto and São Francisco

The broad **Avenida Dantas Barreto** forms the spine of the central island of Santo Antônio. In southern Brazil, avenues like this are lined with skyscrapers, but, although some have sprouted in Recife's financial district, generally the centre is on a human scale, with crowded, narrow lanes lined with stalls and shops opening out directly onto the streets. Dantas Barreto, the main thoroughfare, ends in the fine **Praça da República**, lined with majestic palms and surrounded by Recife's grandest public buildings – the governor's palace (not open to visitors) and an ornate theatre. One of the charms of the city, though, is the unpredictability of the streets, and even off this main boulevard you'll stumble upon old churches sandwiched between modern buildings, the cool hush inside a refuge from the noise and bustle beyond.

Perhaps the most enticing of the central buildings is the seventeenth-century Franciscan complex known as the **Santo Antônio do Convento de São Francisco**, on Rua do Imperador – a combination of church, convent and museum. Outside, you'll be besieged by crowds of beggars displaying sores and stumps, but negotiate your way through to the entrance of the museum (Mon–Fri 8–11.30am & 2–5pm, Sat 2–5pm), pay the nominal fee, and you'll find yourself in a cool and quiet haven. Built around a beautiful small cloister, the museum contains some delicately painted statues of saints and other artwork rescued from demolished or crumbling local churches. But the real highlight here is the **Capela Dourada** (Golden Chapel), which has a lot in common with the churches in the old gold towns of Minas Gerais. Like them, it's a rather vulgar demonstration of colonial prosperity. Finished in 1697, the Baroque chapel is the usual wall-to-ceiling-to-wall ornamentation, except that everything is covered with gold-leaf. If you look closely at the carving under the gilt you'll see that the level of workmanship is actually quite crude, but the overall effect of so much gold is undeniably impressive. What really gilded the chapel, of course, was sugar cane: the sugar trade was at its peak when it was built, and the sugar elite were building monuments to their wealth all over the city.

São Pedro, the Mercado de São José and the Museu da Cicade

The church of **São Pedro** (Mon–Fri 8–11am & 2–4pm, Sat 8–10am) is situated on the Pátio de São Pedro, just off the Avenida Dantas Barreto. The impressive facade is dominated by a statue of St Peter, which was donated to the church in 1980 by a master sculptor from the ceramics centre of Tracunhaém in the interior. Inside the church there's some exquisite woodcarving and a trompe l'oeil ceiling, and on another corner of the Pátio is the **Museu de Arte Popular de Recife** (Mon–Fri 9am–7pm), which has some interesting exhibits, including pottery and wooden sculpture. If you've missed the church's opening hours, content yourself with the exterior views, best seen with a cold beer in hand from one of the several bars that set up tables in the square outside. The whole of the Pátio has in fact been beautifully restored, which lends this part of the city a charm of its own.

Recife is probably the best big Brazilian city in which to find **artesanato**, and the area around São Pedro is the best place to look for it. If you shop around, even tight budgets can stretch to some wonderful bargains. There are stalls all over the city, but they coagulate into a bustling complex of winding streets, lined with beautiful but dilapidated early nineteenth-century tenements, which begins on the Pátio de São Pedro. The streets are choked with people and goods, all of which converge on the market proper, the **Mercado de São José**, an excellent place for *artesanato*.

If you simply can't face the crowds, there's a very good **craft shop**, Penha, on the corner of the Pátio de São Pedro. It's the main city outlet for some of Recife's excellent woodcut artists. In the same shop you'll also find extremely inexpensive prints on both cloth and paper, known as **cordel**. The usual themes are stock Northeastern stories about cowboys, devils, saints and bandits, although there are also *cordel* based on political events, and educational ballads about disease and hygiene, even poems about how AIDS is transmitted and the need to use condoms. Even if you don't understand a word of Portuguese, the printed covers are often worth having in their own right, and they're extremely cheap, around $1 each. Outside the shop, you can dig out *cordel* around the *mercado* or in Praça de Sebo, where the secondhand booksellers have stalls.

Determined culture vultures could also make the hop from here to Recife's most central museum, the **Museu da Cidade** (Mon–Sat 9am–6pm, Sun 1–5pm), in the star-shaped fort, the Forte das Cinco Pontas, off the western end of Avenida Dantas Barreto; the best view of it is coming in by bus from Boa Viagem. Built in 1630 by the Dutch, the fort was the last place they surrendered when they were expelled in 1654. The building is actually far more interesting than the museum itself, which is dedicated entirely to the history of the city, shown through old engravings and photographs.

The Casa da Cultura and Estação Central

Right opposite the Estação Central, in Rua Floriano Peixoto, the forbidding **Casa da Cultura de Pernambuco** (Mon–Sat 9am–7pm, Sun 10am–5pm) was once the city's prison and is now an essential stop for visitors. It's cunningly designed, with three wings radiating out from a central point, so that a single warder could keep an eye on all nine corridors. The whole complex has been turned into an arts and crafts centre, the cells converted into little boutiques and one or two places for refreshment. The quality of the goods on offer here is good, but the prices are a lot higher than elsewhere in the city, so go to look rather than buy. The Casa da Cultura is also the best place to get **information** on cultural events in the city, providing a monthly *Agenda Cultural* listing plays, films and other entertainments; dancing displays are often laid on too, which are free and not at all bad.

Over in the Estação Central itself, on the busy little Praça Visconde de Mauá, the **Museu do Trem** (Mon–Sat 10am–6pm, Sun 2–6pm) is worth a look, too, tracing the history of the railways that played a vital role in opening up the interior of the Northeast. British visitors can wax nostalgic over the exploits of the Great Western Railway of Brazil Limited, some of whose engines and wagons decorate the forecourt between the museum and the *metrô* terminal. The fine station, lovingly restored in 1997, is a relic of the days when British companies dominated the Brazilian economy.

The Museu de Arte Moderna and the Forte do Brum

The **Museu de Arte Moderna Aloisio Magalhães**, located in Boa Vista just over the river from Santo Antônio at Rua da Aurora 256 (Tues–Sun noon–6pm), has prestigious changing exhibitions of mainly Brazilian modern artists, many amongst Pernambuco's best. Of less general interest is the **Museu Militar** on Praça Comunidade Luso-Brasileira (Tues–Fri 9am–6pm, Sat & Sun 9am–4pm). Housed in the seventeeth-century **Forte do Brum** at the northern end of Recife island, the museum displays weapons, photographs, World War II artefacts and some local ethnographic pieces – only really of interest to military enthusiasts. The fort, a prominent, white-walled four-pointed structure, also puts on occasional modern art exhibitions – check for details in the monthly *Agenda Cultural do Recife*.

The Museu do Homem do Nordeste and Museu do Estado

The **Museu do Homem do Nordeste** (Tues, Wed & Fri 11am–5pm, Thurs 8am–5pm, Sat & Sun 1–5pm) was assembled by anthropologists and is one of Brazil's great museums and the best introduction there is to the history and culture of the Northeast. It's quite a way out of central Recife in Casa Forte at Avenida 17 de Agosto 2223 (☎81/3441-5500). Take the "Dois Irmãos" bus from outside the post office or from Parque 13 de Maio, at the bottom of Rua do Hospício; there are two "Dois Irmãos" services, but the one marked "via Barbosa" is the one to get, a pleasant half-hour drive through leafy northern suburbs. The museum is not very easy to spot, on the left-hand side, so ask the driver or conductor where to get off.

The museum is split into several galleries, each devoted to one of the great themes of Northeastern economy and society: sugar, cattle, fishing, popular religion, festivals, ceramics and so on. The historical material is well displayed and interesting, but the museum's strongest point is its unrivalled collection of **popular art** – there are displays not just of handicrafts, but also of cigarette packets, tobacco pouches and, best of all, a superb collection of postwar bottles of *cachaça* (rum). A look at the designs on the labels, very Brazilian adaptations of Western 1950s and 1960s kitsch, leaves you with nothing but admiration for the imagination – and drinking capacity – of the people who put the display together.

The first floor of the museum is largely devoted to the rich regional tradition of clay sculpture and pottery that still flourishes in the *agreste* and *sertão*, especially around Caruaru. The work of **Mestre Vitalino**, a peasant farmer in the village of Alto do Moura, is a highlight. In the 1920s, he began to make small statues depicting scenes of rural life, of an astonishing vitality and power; the feeling and expression in the faces is quite remarkable, for example, in the leering devil appearing to a terrified drunk clutching a bottle of rum. As Vitalino grew older, he began to incorporate the changes happening in the countryside around him into his work. There are statues of migrants, and urban themes appear with a series of portraits of professionals: the lawyer, doctors and dentists (very gruesome), the journalist and the secretary. These themes take over in the work of the next generation of artists, the sons of Vitalino and other pioneers, like the almost equally well-known **Zé Caboclo**, whose work fills the next few cases. In the third generation the style changed, and it's interesting that the best contemporary sculptors are women, notably the granddaughters of Zé Caboclo. The statues remain true to the established themes, but they are miniaturized, and their effect comes from the extreme delicacy of detail and painting, which contrasts with the cruder vigour of their male precursors. You'll see reproductions of many of the statues here on market stalls across Brazil, but Pernambuco is the place to get the real thing: the work of many of the artists displayed in the museum can still be bought fairly cheaply, especially in Alto do Moura itself (see p.325).

The same bus, "Dois Irmãos via Barbosa", is also the one to take for the **Museu do Estado** (Tues–Fri 9am–5.30pm, Sat & Sun 2–5.30pm), a fine nine-teenth-century mansion at Av. Rui Barbosa 660, in Graças. It's on the right-hand side about twenty minutes after leaving the city centre, well before the Museu do Homem do Nordeste, but again difficult to spot, so you might need to ask. Here you'll find some fine engravings of Recife as it was in the early part of the last century, all of them English, and upstairs there are good paint-ings by Teles Júnior, which give you an idea of what tropical Turners might have looked like. On the last Sunday of the month there's also a busy little antiques fair held at the museum.

If the bus is crowded, or you can't make the driver understand where you want to get off, don't worry: after the museums it runs on to the **Horto Zoobotânico** (Tues–Sun 8am–5pm; 80¢), a combined zoo and botanical gar-dens. The gardens are the best part, with outdoor cafés and shady paths to walk along; the zoo, like most in Brazil, is shockingly bad, with the animals confined in concrete boxes far too small for them, where they're constantly taunted by children and adults who ought to know better.

The Olaria de Brennand

If you have time, try and round off your sightseeing with the bizarre **Instituto Ricardo Brennand** (Tues–Sun 10am–5pm; ☎81/3271-1544, ⓦwww .institutoricardobrennand.org.br), an industrial estate in the northern suburbs styled after a castle (complete with working drawbridge) – there can't be any-where more impressively offbeat in the whole of Brazil. One of three brothers who inherited a huge tile, ceramic and brickwork factory, Brennand became a very strange kind of tycoon. Although already rich beyond the dreams of avarice, he was driven to become an internationally famous ceramic artist. His factory estate, far from being an industrial wasteland, nestles in the middle of the only part of the old coastal forest (the Mata Atlântica) still surviving in the metropolitan area. It's a very beautiful piece of land – and it's sobering to think that without it, nothing at all would remain to show what the coast around Recife looked like before the arrival of the Europeans.

Past the rows of workers' cottages and a brickworks, you come to the *oficina*, an enormous personal gallery containing thousands of Brennand's sculptures, decorated tiles, paintings and drawings. A lot of the work is good, and has strong erotic overtones – to say that genitals are a recurring theme is putting it mildly. Nearby, you'll find the most important collection of arms in Brazil inside the **Castle Museum**, which also has beautiful tapestries, sculpture, stained-glass windows and other curiosities from the sixteenth and seventeenth centuries. The estate also has a **library** that holds some 20,000 volumes relat-ing to the Dutch period of Brazilian history.

The estate is a long way from the centre, but is definitely worth the effort. A taxi from Santo Antônio will set you back around $10 and if you don't want to walk back you'll have to arrange for it to pick you up again, because no taxis pass anywhere near. Alternatively, take the bus marked "CDU–Várzea" from outside the post office to its terminus: once there you can either take a taxi or walk – it's not far but you'll need to ask the way. Make sure you say "a oficina de Brennand" with the stress on the second syllable of "Brennand", or nobody will know what you're talking about. The staff are always pleased to see foreign visitors.

Boa Viagem: the beach

Regular buses make it easy to get down to **Boa Viagem** and the beach, an enormous skyscraper-lined arc of sand that constitutes the longest stretch of urbanized seafront in Brazil. As you'd expect of a city of islands, Recife was once studded with beaches, but they were swallowed up by industrial development, leaving only Boa Viagem within the city's limits – though there are others a short distance away to the north and south. In the seventeenth century, Boa Viagem's name was Ilha Cheiro Dinheiro, or "Smell Money Island" – as if whoever named it knew it would become the most expensive piece of real estate in the Northeast.

Much of Boa Viagem is only three or four blocks deep, so it's easy to find your way around. Take your bearings from one of the three main roads: the seafront **Avenida Boa Viagem**, with its posh hotels and a typically Brazilian promenade of palm trees and mosaic pavements; the broad Avenida Conselheiro Aguiar two blocks up; and then Avenida Engenheiro Domingos Ferreira.

The **beach** itself is longer and (claim the locals) better even than Copacabana, with warm natural rock pools to wallow in just offshore when the tide is out. It's also rather narrow, however, and more dominated by the concrete culture around it than most in the Northeast. It gets very crowded at the weekends, but weekdays are relatively relaxed. There's a constant flow of people selling fresh coconut milk, iced beers, ready-mixed *batidas* (rum cocktails), pineapples, watermelon, shrimp, crabs, oysters, ice creams, straw hats and suntan lotion.

The heart of the action emanates from Praça Boa Viagem. Close to here are some of the liveliest restaurants and *choparias*. At weekends there's a thriving and colourful food and craft fair in the Praça Boa Viagem, busiest on Sunday evenings.

The usual cautions apply about not taking valuables to the beach or leaving things unattended while you swim. There have also been a small number of shark attacks over the years, but they have almost always involved surfers far from shore.

Eating

Eating out is cheapest in Santo Antônio, more expensive in Recife island and Boa Viagem, with Olinda (see p.312) somewhere in between. *Recifense* cuisine revolves around **fish** and **shellfish**. Try *carangueijo mole*, crabs cooked in a spicy sauce until shells and legs are soft and edible, which solves the problem of digging out the meat; small crabs called *guaiamum*; and *agulhas fritas*, fried needle fish. As befits a sugar city, a favourite local drink is *caldo de cana*, the juice pressed from sugar cane by hypnotic Victorian-looking machines.

Cheapest of all, and surprisingly pleasant, are the **food sellers** and *suco* **stalls** clogging the streets of **Santo Antônio**, with the usual selection of iced fruit juices, kebabs, cakes, sandwiches and *pastel*. There's a row of reasonably priced stalls licensed by the city authorities on the pedestrianized **Rua da Palma**, across the road from the main post office, much patronized by office workers. The area also has many cheap *lanchonetes* and restaurants, although as their clientele is mainly workers they tend to close in the early evening. There's also an inexpensive lunchtime-only **vegetarian** restaurant, O *Vegetal*, which has branches on Avenida Guararapes (no. 210, 2nd floor) and Avenida Dantas Barreto (no. 507). Santo Antônio is pretty dead at night, with the exception of the cobbled square around São Pedro church, the **Pátio de São Pedro**, where there are some good regional restaurants, with tables in the square and nice views of the church. Also worth a visit is the classy *Restaurante Leite*, Praça Joaquim Nabuco 147 (☎81/3224-7977), close to the *Hotel Quatro de Outubro*, which serves tasty local dishes in a very stylish nineteenth-century interior.

Recife island has plenty of restaurants, and you may want to eat there as a prelude to going on to a bar or a nightclub. But prices are relatively high and the emphasis is on sophistication rather than good old-fashioned hearty Brazilian cooking. *Buon Gustaio*, on Rua do Bom Jesus, does superb Italian food, and *Gambrinus*, at Rua Marquês de Olinda 263, is one of the places where you can get some satisfying local dishes. There's also a branch of the vegetarian restaurant, *O Vegetal*, on Rua do Brum (lunchtime only).

Down on **the beach** there are hundreds of places to eat, with one of the biggest concentrations in the **Pina** district, between the city centre and Boa Viagem. Catch a bus in the direction of Boa Viagem and get off on Avenida Herculano Bandeira, which is just where the bus veers round to run parallel to the sea. Almost the whole of the *avenida* is taken up with restaurants, most of them concentrating on seafood; especially recommended are *Marinho's* and *Pra Vocês*.

In **Boa Viagem** itself the best value is to be found at the seafood places on the promenade near the city-centre end of the beach, and in the dining rooms of the cheaper hotels, all of which are open to non-residents. *Peixada do Lula*, at Av. Boa Viagem 244, is a reasonably priced seafood restaurant known for its shrimp and lobster dishes; *Bargaço*, on the same street at no. 670, does a mixture of traditional seafood and spicier Bahian fare; *Edmilson da Carne de Sol*, at Rua José Trajano 82, is a good for meat; and *La Pinha*, Praça Boa Viagem, is a pleasant and inexpensive little pizzeria and seafood restaurant. On either side of the main drag Avenida Domingos Ferreira, there are a number of other dining options, such as the *comida por kilo Restaurant Laçador*, or the more expensive *Shanghai Palace*, which serves tasty Chinese dishes with the added touch of fresh tropical ingredients.

Nightlife

As elsewhere in Brazil, **nightlife** in Recife starts late, after 10pm. The variety of music and dances is enormous, and Recife has its own frenetic carnival music, the **frevo**, as well as **forró**, which you hear all over the Northeast. The dancing to *forró* can be really something, couples swivelling around the dance floors with ball bearings for ankles. In the past couple of years, Recife island has become the most happening place in the city centre, but there's also plenty of action in Boa Viagem as well as in Olinda (see p.312). There are other interesting nightspots in suburbs like Graças and Casa Forte, but they're not well served by public transport, so you'll have to take a taxi.

For a taste of strongly regional music of all types it's worth trying out an **espaço cultural** or two. The Espaço Nodaloshi, at Estrada dos Remédios 1891 in Madalena (☎81/3228-3511), frequently brings together large numbers of musicians from all over Pernambuco, generally starting the shows around 10pm or later. The Espaço Cultural Alberto Cunha Melo, at Rua Leila Félix Karan 15 in Bongi (☎81/3228-6846), runs similar live music shows. These and other similar places generally promote their programmes through the *Agenda Cultural* (see p.305).

Bars

In **Santo Antônio**, virtually the only place with any zip to it is the **Pátio de São Pedro**, with its clutch of bars and restaurants. Occasionally something extra happens here, though: music and dance groups often appear at weekends, and it's one of the centres of Recife's Carnaval.

As night falls and the rest of the city centre shuts down, **Recife island** comes to life. There are all kinds of bars here, including quiet places where middle-aged professionals sit and discuss the events of the day. But the scene is mainly young and noisy: **Rua do Apolo** in particular has a string of bars with names like *Armazém da Cerveja* ("Beer Warehouse") and *Arsenal do Chopp* ("Beer Arsenal"), which gives you some idea of the spirit of the place. In the same street, the *Moritzstad* club frequently holds live concerts of the Mangue Beat bands, one of Pernambuco's modern musical movements. You should certainly sample the atmosphere here at least once just to get an idea of how seriously young *recifenses* take enjoying themselves.

In **Boa Viagem**, bars open and close with bewildering speed, which makes it difficult to keep track of them. The liveliest area, though, is around Praça de Boa Viagem (quite a long way down the beach from the city centre, near the junction of Avenida Boa Viagem and Rua Bavão de Souza Leão); the *Lapinha* bar and restaurant is a popular meeting place, as is the *Caktos* bar, Av. Conselheiro Aguiar 2328.

Quieter and classier is the northern suburb of **Casa Forte**. A good place here is *Agua de Beber*, a gem of a bar at Praça de Casa Forte 661: a large house with an expensive restaurant upstairs, it also has a leafy courtyard in which you can sit and drink magical *caipirinhas*.

Gay nightlife revolves around a handful of bars and clubs. *Banana Republica*, Rua Francisco Pesoa de Melo 260, in Candeias, and *Anjo Solto*, Rua Herculano Bandeira 513, Galeria Joanna, in D'Arc-Pina are the most popular bars, while the best-known clubs are *CATS*, Rua do Brum 85, in old Recife, *Butterfly*, Rua Raul Azedo 165 (Fri–Sun from 9pm; ☎81/465-8073) and *Cyborg 2000*, Av. real de Torre 1013, Madalena.

Dancing

If you're looking to lay down a few steps, you need to head for a **casa de forró**; the best time to go is around midnight on a Friday or Saturday. In all of them you can drink and eat fairly cheaply, too. They often have rules about only letting in couples, but these are very haphazardly enforced, especially for foreigners. There's a small entry fee, and you may be given a coupon as you go in for the waiters to mark down what you have – don't lose it or you'll have to pay a fine when you leave. Taxis back are rarely a problem, even in the small hours. Two good *casas de forró* are the *Belo Mar* on Avenida Bernardo Vieira de Melo, in Candeias, and the *Casa de Festejo* on Praça do Derby in the *bairro* of Torre. Otherwise, look in local papers or ask EMPETUR (see p.298) for details; there are dozens of others. One place that mixes *forró* with samba is the lively *Cavalo Dourado* (Fri & Sat only), at Rua Carlos Gomes 390, in the *bairro* of Prado. More westernized, but still good, is *Over Point Dancing* at Rua das Graças 261 in Graças.

Recife island has a good share of **nightclubs**, though the emphasis is on Western dance music rather than *forró*, at places like *Planeta Maluco* on Rua do Apolo. But the best nights in the docks district are Thursdays between October and March, when a large area along Avenida Marquês de Olinda is given over to hours of live music and open-air dancing, called – appropriately enough – Dançando na Rua ("Dancing in the Street"). The *Depois Dancing Bar*, at Av. Rio Branco 66 in Recife Antigo (8pm–late) is a nightclub with live Western and *forró* music from Wednesday to Saturday and a reasonable restaurant.

Carnaval in Recife

Carnaval in Recife is overshadowed by the one in Olinda, but the city affair is still worth sampling even if you decide, as many locals do, to spend most of

Carnaval in Olinda. The best place for **Carnaval information** is the tourist office, which publishes a free broadsheet with timetables and route details of all the Carnaval groups. You can also get a timetable in a free supplement to the *Diário de Pernambuco* newspaper on the Saturday of Carnaval, but be warned that it's only a very approximate guide.

The *blocos*, or **Carnaval groups**, come in all shapes and sizes: the most famous is called Galo da Madrugada; the commonest are the *frevo* groups (trucks called *freviocas*, with an electric *frevo* band aboard, circulate around the centre, whipping up already frantic crowds); but most visually arresting are *caboclinhos*, who wear Brazilian ideas of Indian costume – feathers, animal-tooth necklaces – and carry bows and arrows, which they use to beat out the rhythm as they dance. It's also worth trying to see a *maracatu* group, unique to Pernambuco: they're mainly black, and wear bright costumes, the music an interesting (and danceable) hybrid of African percussion and Latin brass.

In Recife the **main events** are concentrated in Santo Antônio and Boa Vista. There are also things going on in Boa Viagem, in the area around the *Recife Palace Lucsim Hotel* on Avenida Boa Viagem, but it's too middle-class for its own good and is far inferior to what's on offer elsewhere. Carnaval in Recife officially begins with a trumpet fanfare welcoming *Rei Momo*, the carnival king and queen, on Avenida Guararapes at midnight on Friday, the cue for wild celebrations. At night, activities centre on the grandstands on Avenida Dantas Barreto, where the *blocos* parade under the critical eyes of the judges. The other central area to head for is the Pátio de São Pedro. During the day the *blocos* follow a route of sorts: beginning in the Praça Manuel Pinheiro, and then via Rua do Hospício, Avenida Conde de Boa Vista, Avenida Guararapes, Praça da República and Avenida Dantas Barreto, to Pátio de São Pedro. Good places to hang around are near churches, especially Rosário dos Pretos, on Largo do Rosário, a special target for *maracatu* groups. The balconies of the *Hotel do Parque* are a good perch, too, if you can manage to get up there. Daylight hours is the best time to see the *blocos* – when the crowds are smaller and there are far more children around. At night it's far more intense and the usual safety warnings apply.

Listings

Airlines Aerolíneas Argentinas, Av. Mn. Borba 324 ☎81/3423-4188; Air France, Rua Sete de Setembro 42, Boa Vista ☎81/3231-7735; Air Portugal Av. Conselheiro de Aguiar 1472 ☎81/3465-8800; TAM, Praça Min. Salgado ☎81/3462-4466; Transbrasil, Av. Conde de Boa Vista 1546 ☎81/3423-2566; United Airlines, Rua Progresso 465 ☎81/3423-2444; Varig, Av. Conselheiro de Aguiar 456 ☎81/3464-4440; VASP, Rua Dr Nilo Dornelas Cámara 90, Loja 4, Boa Viagem ☎81/3421-3611.

Banks and exchange Banco do Brasil has branches at the airport (daily 10am–9pm), at Av. Dantas Barreto 541, at Av. Rio Branco 240 (4th floor), and on Rua Sete de Setembro in Boa Vista, all charging commission. You're much better off going to a *casa de câmbio* or a travel agency: the Mônaco agency at Praça Joaquim Nabuco 159 (☎81/3224-4289) in Santo Antônio will change dollars or cheques free of charge. You'll also get

reasonable rates in the seafront hotels in Boa Viagem. Exchange rates tend to drop around Carnaval time, with the influx of dollars from foreign tourists, so, if you can, delay changing large amounts until afterwards. Shopping centres have banks and money changing facilities that stay open until 9pm Monday to Saturday. The Bradesco bank on Conde de Boa Vista has an ATM that accepts most Visa cards. Don't at any time change money with people who approach you on the street.

Books New books at Livro 7, Rua Sete de Setembro 329, in the city centre, but few in English. Secondhand books (some in English) on corner of Av. Dantas Barreto and Rua Marquês do Recife.

Car rental Avis ☎81/3462-5069; Budget ☎81/3341-2505; Hertz, at airport ☎81/3800-8900 and at Av. Conselheiro Aguiar 4214, Boa Viagem ☎81/3325-2907.

Consulates UK, Av. Eng. Domingos Ferreira 4150, Boa Viagem (Mon–Fri 8–11.30am, Tues & Thurs also 2–4.30pm; ☎81/3325-0247); US, Rua Gonçalves Maia 163, Boa Vista (Mon–Fri 8am–5pm; ☎81/3421-2441).

Health matters Albert Sabin, Rua Senador José Henrique 141, Ilha do Leite ☎81/3421-5411.

Music shops Disco 7, Rua Sete de Setembro, in a small alley next to the Livro 7 bookstore (see above); small, but the best record shop for Brazilian music in the Northeast (☎81/3222-5932).

Internet Cybercafe Olind@.com at Kua Joâo Pessoalz, Carmo, by Praça Maxabomba, Olinda; and at Shopping Boavista and Shopping Center Recife.

Post office The main post office is the Correio building on Avenida Guararapes in Santo Antônio (Mon–Fri 9am–5pm). There is also a branch on Recife island at Av. Marquês de Olinda.

Taxis Disk Taxis Recife (☎81/3424-5030) and Teletaxi (☎81/3429-4242) are both safe, or you can just pick up a taxi from the ranks found on many prominent street corners all over town.

Telephones Inter-city and international telephone offices are located at the Telemar office, Praça do Carmo (next to Praça Maxambomba; daily 6am–11pm) in Olinda. International calls can also be made direct with phone cards from phone kiosks throughout the city.

Travel and tour companies Among the best tour companies in and around Recife are Soltur, Rua Matias de Albuquerque 233 (☎81/3424-1965); Káritas Turismo e Ecologia, Rua Ribeiro do Brito 1002 (☎81/3466-5447); Crystal Tour, Rua Capitão Zuzinha 22 (☎81/3462-4485); and, for flights and tickets, Flytour, Av. Rua Montevidéu 260, Graças (☎81/3221-4265, ✆www.flytour.com.br).

Olinda

OLINDA is, quite simply, one of the largest and most beautiful complexes of **colonial architecture** in Brazil: a maze of cobbled streets, hills crowned with brilliant white churches, pastel-coloured houses, Baroque fountains and graceful squares. Not surprisingly, in 1982 it was designated a cultural heritage site by UNESCO. Founded in 1535, the old city is spread across several small hills looking back towards Recife, but it belongs to a different world. In many ways Olinda is the Greenwich Village of Recife; it's here that many of the larger city's artists, musicians and liberal professionals live, and it's also the centre of Recife's gay scene. Olinda is most renowned, though, for its **Carnaval**, famous throughout Brazil, which attracts visitors from all over the country, as well as sizeable contingents from Europe.

A city in its own right, Olinda is far larger than it first appears. The old colonial centre is built on the hills, slightly back from the sea, but arching along the seafront and spreading inland behind the old town is a modern Brazilian city of over 300,000 people – known as Novo Olinda, the usual bland collection of suburbs and main commercial drags. Like Recife, Novo Olinda has a growing reputation for robberies, but the heart of colonial Olinda is safe enough. There's a calm, almost sleepy atmosphere about the place, and wandering around at night is pretty safe. Despite its size, Olinda has become effectively a neighbourhood of Recife: a high proportion of the population commutes into the city, which means that **transport links** are good, with buses leaving every few minutes.

Finally, note that the beach is awful – polluted and smelly – so you'll need to head out of town if you want to sunbathe or swim.

Arrival, information and accommodation

Buses from Recife follow the seafront road; get off in the Praça do Carmo, just by Olinda's main post office, from where it's a two-minute walk up into the old city.

A reasonable town map is available from the Secretaria de Turismo in the **Biblioteca** (daily 9am–5pm) at the foot of Rua Do Sao Francisco near Praça

ACCOMMODATION
Costeiro Olinda Hotel	1
Hostal Albergue de Olinda	3
Hotel Pousada São Francisco	4
Hotel Sete Colinas	2
Pousada Alquimia	7
Pousada d'Olinda	8
Pousada do Amparo	6
Pousada dos Quatro Cantos	9
Pousada Peter	5

OLINDA

N

Convento de São Francisco

Igreja da Sé

ATLANTIC OCEAN

Museu de Arte Sacra

ALTO DA SÉ

Igreja da Misericórdia

Igreja do Amparo

AMPARO

Biblioteca Pública

PRAÇA DO CARMO

CARMO

Buses to Recife

Museu Regional

Museu do Mamulengo

Igreja Carmo

Mercado da Ribeira

QUATRO CANTOS

Governor's Palace

AV 10 DE NOVEMBRO

RESTAURANTS
Blues Bar	B
Goya Restaurant	D
Mourisco	E
Porta D'Italia	A
Restaurante Flor do Coco	C

Museu do Arte Contemporânea

Basilica e Mosteiro de São Bento

0   500 m

Recife

3

do Carmo. The **municipal tourist office** in Rua São Bento can help with information about accommodation during Carnaval, but it's not geared up for much more than this. There's also an information kiosk on Praça do Carmo, where the buses stop, but it's not particularly useful.

There are a huge number of teenagers and young men offering themselves as **guides** to the city, and you'll probably find yourself besieged as soon as you get off the bus. Those with yellow T-shirts with the words Guia Mirim written on the back and laminated ID cards are official guides, but no longer receive support from the Municipality. They generally do their job pretty well and depend entirely on tips. They are mostly ex-street kids and a percentage of their earnings goes towards their ongoing work with street kids, so they are well worth supporting (the recommended tip for guides is $4–5 an hour per person), though few speak fluent English. Others, generally wearing white T-shirts and yellow caps with the acronym AGTIO, are from the Associação de Guias Turísticas Independentes, and should also have ID cards to prove this.

For **Internet access**, try the Olind@.com cybercafé at Rua João Pessoa 12, Carmo, and the Telemar **phone office**, where you can also make inter-city and and international calls; both places are by the Praça Maxambomba. For a reliable **taxi** driver, contact Flavio on ☎81/3429-0852 or ☎9961-9544.

Accommodation

There are dozens of **hotels** in all price ranges in Olinda. It's probably cheapest to stay in the more modern part of the city, further north down the seafront road from Recife, but you'll be seriously missing out on the old city's atmosphere if you do, and it's worth shopping around for cheaper options in the historic area. Prices vary enormously throughout the year – high-season prices are given below, but bear in mind that, if you go between March and June or between August and November, it will be cheaper. During Carnaval it's virtually impossible to get a room unless you've booked months in advance.

If you want to stay for a while and **rent a room**, look out for the signs up outside people's houses saying "*Aluga-se*". There's a **campsite**, *Camping Olinda*, just inside the old city at Rua do Bom Sucesso 262, Amparo (☎81/3429-1365), but do watch your valuables.

Costeiro Olinda Hotel Av. Ministro Marcos Freire 681, Bairro Novo ☎81/3429-4877. Three-star hotel in the modern part of the city, somewhat bland compared to the alternatives. ❻

Hostal Albergue de Olinda Rua do Sol 233, Carmo ☎81/3429-1592, ☏3439-1913, ⓦwww.alberguedeolinda.com.br. An excellent youth hostel, very comfortable and with a nice hammock area and a small swimming pool; it's also close to the seafront, though right on a busy road. $6 per person.

Hotel Pousada São Francisco Rua do Sol 127, Carmo ☎81/3429-2109, ☏429-4057, ⓦwww.pousadasaofrancisco.com.br. Located on the main road but quite close to the seafront, with a swimming pool and all mod cons. ❸

Hotel Sete Colinas Ladeira de São Francisco 307, Carmo ☎81/3439-6055, ⓦwww.hotel7colinasolinda.com.br. Fabulous hotel right in the centre of Olinda, set in beautiful gardens with modern sculpture and a fine swimming pool. There's a range of rooms, suites and luxury apartments, and a good restaurant too. It isn't cheap but it's still good value. ❼

Okakoaras Bungalow Hotel Av. Cláudio J. Gueiros 10927, Praia de Maria Farinha ☎81/3436-1754. A half-hour bus ride from Olinda, set on a palm-lined beach with a swimming pool and a peaceful

atmosphere. Cosy, bungalow-style accommodation and pleasant service. ❸

Pousada Alquimia Rua Prudente de Morais 292 ☎81/3429-1457. Cheap and cheerful, this well-located little pension has a front parlour full of paintings and nice, if basic, rooms. ❷

Pousada d'Olinda Praça João Alfredo 178 ☎81/3439-1163, ⓦwww.hoteldolinda.com.br. This centrally located *pousada* is excellent value and has everything from a fine swimming pool to a good restaurant, inexpensive bungalow-style rooms and a penthouse suite. ❹

Pousada do Amparo Rua do Amparo 199 ☎81/3439-1749. Quality place combining excellent rooms, an art gallery and a restaurant in a colonial mansion; sauna and pool, too. ❹

Pousada dos Quatro Cantos Rua Prudente de Morais 441 ☎81/3429-0220, ☏3429-1845, ⓦwww.pousada4cantos.com.br. Beautiful small mansion with a lovely leafy courtyard, right in the heart of the old city. A range of rooms and suites are available, the cheapest with shared bathrooms. ❸

Pousada Peter Rua do Amparo 215 ☎81/3439-2171, ⓦwww.pousadapeter.com.br. Located among other art galleries, this is a comfortable gallery-cum-lodging situated in a colonial-style building. Good value. ❸

The Town

Olinda's hills are steep, and you'll be best rewarded by taking a leisurely stroll around the town. A good spot to have a drink and plan your attack is the **Alto da Sé**, the highest square in the town, not least because of the stunning view of Recife's skyscrapers shimmering in the distance, framed in the foreground by the church towers, gardens and palm trees of Olinda. There's always an arts and crafts **market** going on here during the day, peaking in the late afternoon, and while much of what's on offer is pretty good, the large numbers of tourists have driven prices up, and there's little here you can't get cheaper in Recife or the interior.

The **churches** you see are not quite as old as they look. The Dutch burnt them all down, except one, in 1630, built none of their own, and left the

Portuguese to restore them during the following centuries. There are eighteen churches dating from the seventeenth and eighteenth centuries left today, seemingly tucked around every corner and up every street. Very few of them have set opening times, but they're usually open during weekday mornings, and even when they're closed you can try knocking on the door and asking for the *vigia*, the watchman.

If you have time to see only one church it should be the **Convento Franciscano** (Mon–Fri 8–11.30am & 2.30–5pm, Sat 8am–5.30pm), tucked away on Rua São Francisco. Built in 1585, the complex of convent, chapel and church has been stunningly restored to its former glory; particular highlights are the tiled cloister depicting the lives of Jesus and St Francis of Asissi, and the sacristy's beautiful Baroque furniture carved from jacaranda wood. In the north wing there's an elaborate two-tiered altarpiece in gold leaf and white, and behind the convent there's a grand patio with even grander panoramas across the ocean.

Among other churches, the **Igreja da Misericórdia**, built right at the top of an exhaustingly steep hill, has a fine altar and rear walls covered in blue *azulejo*, while the **Basilica e Mosteiro de Sâo Bento** (Mon–Fri 8am–noon & 2–6pm, Sat 8am–noon, Sun 10am–5pm) looks quite wonderful from the outside with palm trees swaying in the courtyard, though the interior is less striking. The **Igreja da Sé**, on the *praça* of the same name, is rather bland and austere inside – more of a museum than a living church – but is worth a look if only to see the eighteenth-century sedan chair and large wooden sculptures in the small room at the northeast wing. At the back of the church is a patio from where you'll have good views of the surrounding area.

By the Praça do Carmo, there's the run-down but quite splendid **Igreja do Carmo**, which sits majestically on a small hill looking down on the busy streets below, while up Rua do Amparo there's the fine eighteenth-century **Igreja do Amparo**, and within view of this the deserted ruins of the **Igreja de São João Batista dos Militares**, the one church that escaped the Dutch invaders' fires of 1630.

There's also a good sampling of religious art on display in the **Museu de Arte Sacra de Pernambuco** (Mon–Fri 8am–1pm), in the seventeenth-century bishop's palace by the Alto da Sé. The **Museu Regional** (Tues–Fri 9am–5pm, Sat & Sun 2–5pm), at Rua do Amparo 128, is well laid out, too, although the emphasis is too much on artefacts and too little on history.

There's more contemporary interest in the colourful **graffiti** in which the old city is swathed. The local council commissions artists to adorn certain streets and walls, which has the twin advantage of keeping local talent in work and ensuring Olinda has the highest-quality graffiti in Brazil. Some are political, urging people to vote for this or that candidate, some are more abstract – illustrated poems about Olinda being especially popular – but all are colourful, artistic and blend in uncannily well with the colonial architecture. One of the best places to see them is along the municipal cemetery walls on the Avenida Liberdade, but there's good graffiti all over the old city, especially during elections and Carnaval.

More serious modern art is to be found in the **Museu de Arte Contemporânea**, on Rua 13 de Maio next to the market (Tues–Fri 9am–noon & 2–5pm, Sat & Sun 2–5pm): it's a fine eighteenth-century building that was once used as a jail by the Inquisition, though the exhibits themselves are a bit disappointing. Much more interesting is the **Museu do Mamulengo** (Tues–Fri 9am–5pm, Sat & Sun 2–5pm) at Rua do Amparo 59, which houses an excellent collection of traditional puppets.

Olinda's several markets and endless *artesanato* shops make it a good place for **shopping**. The Mercado da Ribeira, built in the sixteenth century, is at Rua Bernardo Vieira de Melo 160, and offers the usual range of craft goods, while a ten-minute walk down Rua 15 de Novembro from the governor's palace brings you to another bigger *artesanato* and antique market housed in the long pink building by the main road, Largo do Varadouro.

Eating, drinking and nightlife

Olinda's relaxed atmosphere draws many *recifenses* at night, when tables and chairs are set on squares and pavements, and bars that are tucked away in court-yards amid spectacular tropical foliage make the perfect escape. There is always plenty of music around and, at weekends, a lot of young Brazilians out for a good time – all in all, a good recipe for enjoying yourself. If it's just drinks and a snack you're after, try *Bodega de Veio*, Rua do Amparo 198 (opposite *Pousada Peter*), which is occasionally the scene for live music in the evenings.

Eating and drinking

The best place to go for crowds and serious eating and drinking is the **Alto da Sé**. The good, cheap **street food** here, cooked on charcoal fires, can't be recommended too highly; try *acarajé*, which you get from women sitting next to sizzling wok-like pots – bean-curd cake, fried in palm oil, cut open and filled with green salad, dried shrimps and *vatapá*, a yellow paste made with shrimps, coconut milk and fresh coriander. If you sit in the Alto da Sé for any length of time, you're bound to be approached by one of Olinda's many **repentistas** (see p.318), who will try to improvise a song about you. The results are sometimes wonderful, sometimes embarrassing, but they will expect a small payment, so if you don't want to shell out make it clear from the start that you're not interested.

Alternatively, you can sample one of Olinda's countless **restaurants**. If you want to eat for less than $5, try the *comida por kilo* places along the seafront and in the new part of town. However, for just a little bit more, you can eat far better in the old town. The moderately priced *Blues Bar*, in the garden of an old house at Rua do Bonfim 66 (Tues–Thurs 6pm–1am, Fri & Sat 6pm–3am, Sun 11am–8pm; ☏81/9156-6415) does excellent meat dishes plays authentic blues music much of the time. More expensive – and air-conditioned – is *Mourisco*, at Praça Conselheiro João Alfredo 7, which specializes in seafood; a good meal with wine will cost $15. *Goya Restaurant*, Rua do Amparo 157, is hard to beat for imaginative Brazilian and French cuisine, the *Restaurante Flor do Coco*, Rua do Amparo 199, has excellent regional cuisine, and the *Creperia*, Praça João Alfredo 168 (☏81/3429-2935), serves great salads as well as the crepes. Other good spots at the higher end of the price range are the *Porta D'Italia*, Rua do Bonfim, which offers well-prepared Italian food and a good wine list, and the *Oficina do Sabor*, Rua do Amparo 365, excellent for local cuisine – the shrimps in mango sauce are a highlight. If it's just good coffee you're after, try the *Café Adego*, at Rua 27 de Janeiro 70.

The streets around the Alto da Sé hold a couple of good **bars** that are well worth seeking out, including the *Cantinho da Sé*, just a few steps down the Ladeira da Sé, almost always crowded and very lively indeed at night.

Nightlife

Nightlife in Olinda can be very lively, especially at the end of the week. At times the drums or bass lines carry so loudly across the town that you may think they're calling out to you. Places to check out, apart from the Alto da Sé, are the seafront restaurants and bars, many of which have *forró* groups on Friday and Saturday nights. The *Acoustico Pub*, for instance at Rua do Sol 283 has a good scene. If you get bored with *forró* – and the beat does get a bit monotonous after a while – try the more samba-like rhythms of the *Z-4 Club* or the *Clube Atlântico,* both near the Praça do Carmo. Every Friday and Saturday night (starting at 11pm) it hosts the *Noites Olindenses,* dances to an eclectic variety of music, played very loudly by energetic groups or on record – *frevo,* samba, *forró,* merengue, and even non-Brazilian styles like salsa and tango. You pay an entrance fee of about $3–5, and both the music and the dancing can be quite superb. There are sometimes extras like magicians and *capoeira* displays going on between and even during acts. To find out what's happening in the local art scene, check out ⓦ www.arte.olinda.info.

Carnaval and other festivals in Olinda

Olinda's **Carnaval** is generally considered to be one of the three greatest in Brazil, along with those of Rio and Salvador. It overshadows the celebrations in neighbouring Recife, and attracts thousands of revellers from all over the Northeast. It's easy to see why Olinda developed into such a major Carnaval: the setting is matchless, and local traditions of art and music are very strong. Like the other two great Brazilian carnivals, Olinda has a style and feel all of its own: not quite as large and potentially intimidating as in either Rio or Salvador, the fact that much of it takes place in the winding streets and small squares of the old city makes it seem more manageable. The area of town around the *Pousada dos Quatro Cantos* is one of the liveliest during Carnaval. The music, with the local beats of *frevo* and *maracatu* predominating, the costumes and the enormous *bonecos,* papier-mâché figures of folk heroes or savage caricatures of local and national personalities, make this Carnaval unique.

Carnaval in Olinda actually gets going the Sunday before the official start, when the Virgens do Bairro Novo, a traditional *bloco* several hundred strong, parades down the seafront road followed by crowds that regularly top 200,000. By now the old city is covered with decorations: ribbons, streamers and coloured lanterns are hung from every nook and cranny, banners are strung across streets and coloured lighting set up in all the squares. Olinda's Carnaval is not only famous for its *bonecos*, which are first paraded around on Friday night and then at intervals during the days, but also for the decorated umbrellas that aficionados use to dance the *frevo.* The tourist office has lists of the hundreds of groups, together with routes and approximate times, but there is something going on all the time in most places in the old city. The most famous *blocos*, with mass followings, are Pitombeira and Elefantes; also try catching the daytime performances of *travestis,* transvestite groups, which have the most imaginative costumes – ask the tourist office to mark them out on the list for you.

Inevitably, with so many visitors flocking into the city, **accommodation during Carnaval** can be a problem. It's easier to find a room in Recife, but, unless you dance the night away, transport back in the small hours can be difficult; buses start running at around 5am, and before then you have to rely on taxis. This is not always easy, as many taxi drivers stop work to enjoy Carnaval themselves. Even if you do find one, you'll have to pay an exorbitant fare, and run the risk too of **drunken taxi drivers** – dozens of people are killed on the road during Carnaval every year, and it's best to avoid travelling by road in the small hours if you can.

In Olinda itself you might as well forget about hotels, as they're booked up months in advance. Many locals, though, rent out all or part of their house for Carnaval week: the municipal tourist office has a list of places and prices. Prices start at around $250 for the week, going up to as much as $2000 – get a group together by leaving a note at the tourist office. If all the places on the tourist office lists are full – more than likely if you arrive less than a week before Carnaval starts – or if you fancy your chances of getting a cheaper and better deal on your own, wander round the side streets looking for signs saying "*Aluga-se quartos*"; knock on the door and bargain away.

The Torneio dos Repentistas

There are plenty of other festivals of one kind or another besides Carnaval in Olinda; its location and cultural traditions make it a popular venue. Definitely worth catching if you happen to be around in late January is the **Torneio dos Repentistas**. A *repentista* is a Northeastern singer-poet who improvises strictly metered verses accompanied only by a guitar. And they really do improvise, rather than repeat stock verses. Most *repentistas* make a living singing on street corners and in squares, or at markets, commenting wittily – and often obscenely – on the people going by or stopping to listen, or elaborating on themes shouted out by the audience. Even if you don't understand the lyrics, it's worth catching, especially if you can find a *cantoria*, a sing-off between two or more *repentistas*, who take alternate verses until a draw is agreed or until the audience acclaims a winner. The *Torneio dos Repentistas* in Olinda is one of the most famous events of its kind in the region, bringing in *repentistas* from all over the Northeast, who pair off and embark on singing duels while surrounded by audiences, who break into spontaneous applause at particularly good rhymes or well-turned stanzas. It's centred on and around the Praça da Preguiça, and lasts for three days.

North from Recife

North from Recife, the **BR-101 highway** runs a little way inland through low hills and sugar-cane fields, a scenic enough route but one that offers little reason to stop off anywhere, except perhaps at the small pottery centre of **Goiana**. The **coast** north of Recife is best explored along the smaller roads that branch off the highway. Nevertheless, it's as well to bear in mind that the Pernambuco coast is thickly populated by Brazilian standards. This isn't to say there aren't relatively peaceful spots, but what seems a deserted retreat during the week can fill up quickly at weekends, with *recifenses* heading for the beaches, enlivening or destroying the rural atmosphere, depending on your point of view.

Along the BR-101: Goiana and Pitimbu

At **GOIANA**, 80km north of Recife on BR-101, parts of the town are still made up of rows of nineteenth-century terraced houses, built for workers in the local cotton mill, which has been long since bankrupted. **Pottery** has taken over as the main economic activity, and Goiana is one of the most important centres of the flourishing Pernambucan ceramics industry. The town centre is dotted with workshops, their wares spilling out onto the pavements, and there are some good bargains to be had. You can watch the potters at work in many places, like Zé do Carmo in Rua Padre Batalha. Opposite here, there's a good restaurant, the *Buraco da Giá* at no. 100, where the trained crab that offers you a drink is perhaps the real highlight of any visit to the town. To get here, take one of the six daily buses from the Recife Rodoviária.

If you want to spend some time in the area, it's better to get out of Goiana and head 30km over a country road to the coastal fishing village of **PITIMBU**, just over the border in Paraíba state. There are four buses a day from Goiana, the last around 2pm; it's a crowded and bumpy ride but Pitimbu is worth it. It has friendly inhabitants and a good beach, 10km in length, although the stretch closest to town can be dirty, and there's only one **hotel**, the *Pitimbu Mar* (T83/3299-1035; ③), which has a pool and six chalets. Camping on the beach is also possible, or you can negotiate hammock space with local bar owners. It's a quiet, sleepy place, ideal for a couple of days of doing nothing at all, with excellent fresh seafood available in several beachside bars. It's also a good place to see *jangadas* – the small fishing rafts with huge curving triangular sails – in action. They go out at dawn and return in mid-afternoon, quite a sight, as they rear and plunge through the surf.

Along the coast towards Itamaracá

From Olinda, **local buses** continue 11km along the coastal road to the beautiful palm-lined beaches of **Rio Doce**, **Janga** and **Pau Amarelo**. Until recently these were pretty much deserted, and, although weekend homes are going up now, development, so far, is less obtrusive than in many places on the coast. Being close to major population centres, however, the water quality at Rio Doce and Janga is not always the best. The area gets busy at weekends, especially in Janga, when there's music and dancing in the beachside bars at night. At Pau Amarelo you can still see one of several local star-shaped forts left behind by the Dutch in 1719.

A more popular and even more scenic route north is through the pleasantly run-down colonial villages of **Igarassu** and **Itapissuma** to the island of Itamaracá. Hourly **buses** to Igarassu, with easy connections to Itamaracá, leave from Avenida Martins de Barros, on Santo Antônio island in Recife, opposite the *Grande Hotel*. Another possibility is to go there **by boat**: every travel agency in Recife runs trips, stopping at beaches on the way, for around $35–40.

Igarassu
Turning off the highway past Olinda's ugly industrial suburb of Paulista, the road wends its way through a rich green landscape of rolling hills and dense palm forest. The first town on the route is **IGARASSU**, 25km from Olinda, an old colonial settlement built on a ridge rising out of a sea of palm trees: the name means "great canoe" in the language of the Tupi Indians, the cry that went up when they first saw the Portuguese galleons. The town was founded in 1535, when during a battle with the Indians the hard-pressed Portuguese commander vowed to build a church on the spot if victorious; the **Igreja de São Cosme e Damião**, one of the oldest churches in Brazil, is still there on the ridge. Down the hill the **Convento de Santo Antônio** is almost as old, built in 1588. Both are simpler and more austere than any of the churches in Recife or Olinda.

Most of the houses in Igarassu make up the rows of tied cottages that are characteristic of the old *engenhos*, or sugar estates. You can get a good idea of what a traditional *engenho* was like at the **Engenho Monjope**, an old plantation that has been tastefully converted into a **campsite** (T81/3543-0528). The *engenho* dates from 1756; there's a decaying mansion, a chapel, water mill, cane presses and a *senzala*, the blockhouse where slaves lived. Minibuses back to

Recife from Igarassu drop you at the turn-off (ask for "*o camping*"), and the estate is an easy ten-minute walk from there. The campsite is separate from the buildings, and you can ask at the entrance to look around even if you don't want to stay. Thirteen kilometres north of Igarassu, there are a couple of more upmarket places to stay at the pleasant **Praia da Gavoa**: the *Pousada Porto Canoas*, Estr. do Ramalho 230 (☎81/3424-2845; ❸), has chalets, a pool and restaurant; and the *Hotel Gavoa Praia* (☎81/3543-7777, ⓦwww.hotelgavoa.com.br; ❻), with the full works, including pool and sauna.

Eight kilometres further on from Praia da Gavoa at **ITAPISSUMA**, a causeway connects the mainland to the island of Itamaracá.

Itamaracá

Local legend has it that Itamaracá was once the site of the Garden of Eden, and the short drive across the causeway from Itapissuma promises much, passing amongst thousands of palm trees lapped by fields of sugar cane – the rich but sickly smell just before the harvest in March is enough to make you feel distinctly queasy. So it's a shame to have to say that the town of **ITAMARACÁ** is something of a disappointment. It's very crowded and increasingly scarred by the hundreds of weekend homes springing up in ugly rashes along the beaches – alongside the humble wattle huts roofed with palm leaves where the original islanders have managed to hold on. One of the first parts of Brazil to be settled by the Portuguese, Itamaracá was so prosperous as a sugar plantation that it was also the first part of Pernambuco to be occupied by the Dutch, who built a fort here.

Itamaracá has a reputation as an idyllic rural retreat, away from the pressures of life in Recife. This might have been true fifteen years ago, but it's stretching things a little now. Nonetheless, there are a couple of places of interest. The first building you see as you arrive on the island is an enormous open prison: all the fields are cultivated by prisoners, easily recognizable in blue and grey uniforms with ID cards pinned to their chests. They run a group of cafés and shops on the road just past the prison, selling handmade jewellery and bone carvings. These shops are built near the **Engenho São João** (Mon–Sat 10am–5pm), much better preserved than Monjope (see p.319), with most of the original machinery used for pressing cane, boiling the syrup and refining sugar still intact. A turn-off just before the town (you'll probably end up walking as local buses exist but are very infrequent) leads 5km through tacky villas before rewarding you with the **Forte Oranje**, another star-shaped Dutch fort built in 1631 by Maurice of Nassau to protect the newly occupied sugar estates. There's a vicious *enfilade* at the front gate, where attackers were filtered through a zigzag corridor and exposed to musket fire from slits on all sides, and there are a few old cannons lying around on the ramparts with the makers' crests still visible. The souvenir shop inside is the most overpriced in Pernambuco, but the beachside **bars** opposite are really good value and their food excellent – a highlight is the *casquinho de carangueijo*, crab meat fried with garlic and onions, served in the shell and covered with roasted manioc flour. Downing a couple of iced beers here, looking out across the bay, should be enough to make you feel better disposed towards the island, especially if you catch somebody selling the delicious local oysters out of a bucket. You buy them by the half dozen, for around $1: the seller flicks them open with a knife and supplies a lime to squeeze over them.

There are the usual beachside bars and restaurants on Itamaracá, and a few **hotels**, including the *Hotel Do Maranjo*, Rua Padre Machado 85 (☎81/3544-1157; ❷), the *Orange Praia* (☎81/3544-1194, ⓕ3544-1176; ❹), some 8km from the town in a wonderful beachside location at the Praia do Forte Oranje and, nearby, the excellent-value *Casa da Praia* (☎81/3544-1255; ❸). **Camping** on the beach is technically illegal but possible, although not advisable with valuables. The best of the **restaurants** is the *Sargaço*, Rua Santino de Barros 270 (☎81/3544-1180), which has fine, reasonably priced seafood and a *ciranda* on Friday and Saturday nights, the latter a circular dance to lilting, rhythmic music from flutes, guitars and drums. Out at the Praia do Forte Oranje there's a superb fish restaurant, *A Peti Tosa*, but it's only open for lunch on weekdays.

The beaches

The **beaches** are very good – wide and lined with palms – and they are a popular night venue for Carnaval celebrations, which attract hundreds of visitors. Unfortunately, however, stretches around the town and along as far as the Forte Oranje have been blighted by unregulated building. There are better, deserted beaches round about, but none less than a couple of hours' walk along the shoreline in either direction.

There are *jangadas*, too, but they're a rather poignant symbol of what has happened to the town. A few years ago many families supported themselves by a combination of fishing and farming, and the *jangadas* were very much working fishing boats. A few *jangadeiros* still fish, but most of them now take weekenders and tourists out on trips; a couple of hours costs usually around $7. *Jangada* trips are not advisable unless you're a reasonable swimmer, and even then you should be careful if the sea is at all rough; there's nothing to stop you being swept overboard, and no life jackets are provided.

South from Recife

The coast south of Recife has the best **beaches** in the state and is all too quickly realizing its tourist potential – the sleepy fishing villages are unlikely to remain so for much longer. Almost all **buses** to cities south of Recife take the BR-101 highway, which runs inland through fairly dull scenery, made worse by heavy traffic. The trick is to get a bus that goes along the much more scenic **coastal road**, the PE-60, or *via litoral*; they leave from either Avenida Dantas Barreto or the Recife Rodoviária for the string of towns down the coast from Cabo, through Ipojuca, Sirinhaém, Rio Formoso, to São José da Coroa Grande. Before São José, where the road starts to run alongside the beach, you may need to catch another local bus to get to the beachside villages themselves. In theory, you could hop from village to village down the coast on local buses, but only with time to spare. Services are infrequent – early morning is the usual departure time – and you might have to sleep on a beach or find somewhere to sling a hammock, as not all the villages have places to stay. As you move south, bays and promontories disappear, and walking along the beaches to the next village is often quicker than waiting for a bus.

Gaibú and Santo Agostinho

The first stop out of Recife is the beach at **GAIBÚ**, a sizeable beach resort some 40km south of Boa Viagem – catch a bus to Cabo from Avenida Dantas Barreto, and then another local one to Gaibú. Gaibú sports the familiar set-up – palm trees, bars and surf – and is a good base for village-hopping, with a youth hostel and a couple of cheap **pensões**: the pleasant *Pousada Aguas Marinhas* (❷) is right on the beach, run by a Belgian-Brazilian couple who serve fine breakfasts in their beach garden, and have mountain bikes for rent. They can also arrange trips with local fishermen. Gaibú gets crowded at weekends, but there's a particularly beautiful stretch of coastline nearby, close enough to explore on foot. Just before Gaibú village, a turning in the dirt road heads off to the right, leading to the cape of **São Agostinho**, a pleasant walk uphill through palms and mango trees, past the odd peasant hut in the forest. Three kilometres up is a ruined Dutch chapel, so overgrown it's almost invisible, and a path to the left leads out onto a promontory where the forest suddenly disappears and leaves you with a stunning view of the idyllic, and usually deserted, beach of **Calhetas**. You can clamber down to the beach, a ring of sand in a bay fringed with palm forest, the distant oil refinery at Suape providing the only jarring note. This beach is particularly good for surfing. If you continue on from the ruined chapel, you'll come to the sleepy hamlet of **SANTO AGOSTINHO**. During the Dutch occupation there was vicious guerrilla fighting here, and an infamous massacre took place when Dutch settlers were herded into a church that was then burnt down. A small chapel still stands on the spot and there are the pulverized remains of a fort. On the cape itself are burnt-out shells of Dutch buildings from the same campaign, and there's also a plaque commemorating the Spanish conquistador, Yanez Piñon, blown south by storms on his way to the Caribbean in 1500. He put in here for shelter a couple of months before Cabral "discovered" Brazil, and sailed off without knowing where he was – thus ensuring Brazil would end up speaking Portuguese rather than Spanish. The cape is criss-crossed with several walking trails, few of which are properly signposted, and a little exploring will soon bring you to the tiny village of Nazare, where there's little to keep you apart from a ruined Dutch chapel and lighthouse keeper's bar.

If you find the need **to stay**, the Praia de Suape has two good options: the five-star *Blue Tree Park* beach resort and the delightful *Sitio Paraiso* (T81/3522-6061; ❹), a cosy *pousada* set in the middle of fruit gardens (pick your own limes for cocktails). The owner is knowledgable about local activities and will help arrange boat trips to the Suape islands through mangrove swamps.

Porto de Galinhas to Barra de Santo Antônio

A bus from Avenida Dantas Barreto in Recife (hourly 6.30am–7.30pm, last bus leaving Porto at 5.40pm) will take you direct to another glorious beach, **PORTO DE GALINHAS**, 65km from Recife, and deservedly popular – it's in danger of becoming overdeveloped, but still quiet enough during the week. *Jangadas* will take you out to the small natural coral pools just off the coast and there is some excellent surfing here, too. Good fresh fish is to be had in the beachside cafés; fried needle fish, *agulhas fritas*, is a great snack with a cold beer as you wiggle your toes in the warm sand. If you want **to stay**, there are two campsites and numerous *pousadas*, as well as an increasing number of upmarket hotels on the seafront. Right on the main beach are the luxury *Village Porto de Galinhas* (T81/3552-1038, F3552-1277; ❺), with its own pool, and the smaller *Recanto*, Avenida Beira Mar (T81/3552-1251; ❸). The *Pousada Litoral* (❷), just three blocks from the ocean at the corner of Rua da Esperança and Beijupira, has clean simple rooms. For unbelievably tasty shrimps, lobsters and local *sobremesas* visit the excellent *Beijupirá* **restaurant** (T81/3552-2354, daily from noon till 11pm) in the road of the same name.

The main drag, Rua da Esperança, is where you'll find the **tourist information** office (T81/3552-1480) and the **post office**; lines of buggies can be found at the sea end, looking for business ($20 for 2–3hrs). If you'd rather get behind the wheel, try Buggy Tour, Rua do Colegio (☎81/3461-1902 or 3552-1400).

Five kilometres away – easily reached by either a forty-minute walk along the beach or a $5 dune-buggy ride – is one of the finest beaches in the area, the **Praia de Macaripe**. The *Pousada dos Coqueiros* (☎81/3552-1294, ⓕ3552-1736, Ⓦwww.pousadadoscoqueiros.com.br; ❷) is a good place to stay, especially if you're here to surf. Another 10km further south is the beautiful **Praia da Ponta de Serrambi**, popular with windsurfers. For total luxury, *Intermares Village*, right on the beach (☎81/3527-4200, ⓕ3527-4006; ❼), has its own pool, sauna, jet skis and *jangadas*.

South again are the sleepy fishing villages of **TAMANDARÉ** and **SÃO JOSÉ DA COROA GRANDE**, where, for the time being, fishing still dominates, with *jangadas* drawn up on the beaches and men repairing nets, though even here weekend houses for city slickers are going up. In Tamandaré (served by direct bus from Recife Rodoviária), apart from the usual stunning beach, there are the ruins of the fort of Santo Inácio, destroyed in 1646, and a small hotel, *Marinas Tamandaré*, Loteamento Anaisabela, Lote 15A (☎81/3675-1388; ❺). A little way south, in São José da Coroa Grande, where the *litoral* road finally hits the coast (also served by direct bus from Recife Rodoviária), there are bars, a huge beach and the overpriced *Hotel Francês*, Rua Antonia Valdemar Acioli Belo 279 (☎81/3688-1169; ❹). Just offshore from here is the Ilha de Santo Aleixo, where there are a couple of good beaches.

Inland from Recife

In contrast to the gentle scenery of the coastal routes out of Recife, heading **inland** brings you abruptly into a completely different landscape, spectacular and forbidding. The people, too, look and speak differently; the typical *sertanejo* is short and wiry, with the high cheekbones and thin nose of an Indian ancestor. They speak a heavily accented Portuguese, much ridiculed elsewhere, but really one of the loveliest Brazilian accents.

Buses inland all leave from the Recife Rodoviária, and the best place to head for is the market town of **Caruaru**, 130km from Recife and the largest town in the *agreste*. The frequent buses there take two hours and are very comfortable; buy your ticket a day in advance. Seats on the right-hand side of the bus have the best view.

The route to Caruaru: Vitória, Gravatá and Bezerros

The **BR-232** highway heads directly away from the sea into gentle hills covered with enormous fields of sugar cane; the size of the estates gives you some idea of the inequality of land distribution in the Northeast, and explains why this part of Pernambuco has been in the forefront of the struggle for agrarian reform in Brazil. It was here in the late 1950s that the Peasant Leagues started, a social movement pressing for land reform through direct action, one of the factors that frightened the military into launching their coup in 1964. Most of the cane is destined for the first town en route, **Vitória de Santo Antão**, where, on the left-hand side of the road, is the factory that produces the most widely drunk rum in Brazil, Pitu – you can't miss the thirty-metre-high water tank cunningly camouflaged as an enormous bottle of the stuff.

After Vitória you begin to climb in earnest into the **Serra da Neblina**, threading into the hills of the *agreste* proper. Gradually the air becomes cooler, the heat drier, and highland plants replace the palms and sugar cane of the coastal strip. On a clear day the views are stunning, with rows of hills stretching into the distance on both sides and the coastal plain shimmering in the background. The fertile hills facing the sea get a lot of rain, cotton taking over from sugar as you climb, but deeper inland the hills are brown and parched, and farming becomes more difficult. You begin to see cattle and strange-looking fields filled with neat rows of cactus. This is *palma*, and it's a foretaste of the harshness of *sertão* life: in times of drought, the cactus is chopped down and fed to cattle, thorns and all. It's a feed of last resource but, remarkably, the cactus contains enough water to keep cattle alive for a few more crucial months in the wait for rain.

Gravatá

The next town, 50km down the road, is **GRAVATÁ**, one of several *agreste* towns that has optimistically tagged itself "The Switzerland of Pernambuco" on the strength of its cool hill climate – temperatures average around 21°C. There are lots of villas and a hotel built in Swiss-chalet style, rather incongruous in a landscape that is parched brown as often as not. If you want to break your journey here, the best hotels are the chalet-style *Casa Grande*, BR-232 km 83 (℡81/3533-0920, ℻3533-0812; ❺), which has a pool and sauna; the *Portal de Gravatá*, BR-232 km 83 (℡81/3533-0288, ℻3533-0610; ❻), with similar facilities; and the *Grande Hotel da Serra*, BR-232 km 83 (℡81/3533-0114; ❸), one of the cheapest hotels in the area, offering decent rooms with private showers. After Gravatá, it soon becomes obvious that you are nearing a major market from the activities at the roadside. Every few hundred yards boys and men stand as far into the road as they dare, leaping aside at the last moment, flourishing their wares at passing motorists: chickens, piglets and the delicious fruit of the interior – pomegranates, *jaboticaba* (like a cross between a plum and a sweet grape), *mangaba*, a delicious red berry that stains the mouth black, and *umbu*, which looks like a gooseberry but doesn't taste like one.

Bezerros

BEZERROS, the last town before Caruaru, is the home of a famous artist and printer, **Jota Borges**, some of whose work you may have seen in the Casa da Cultura and the Penha craft shop (see p.305) in Recife. He has a roadside workshop on the left as you leave town. Inside, you can see the carved wooden plates he makes to manufacture the prints on paper and cloth; the smaller ones are for the covers of *cordel* (see p.305), a large library of which takes up one corner of the workshop. Borges himself is often at the market in Caruaru or delivering in Recife, but a family member is usually on hand to show visitors around. The absurdly inexpensive prints are simple but powerful depictions of peasant life.

Caruaru

Home of the largest market in the Northeast, **CARUARU** is also ideally placed for excursions into the *sertão*. Saturday is the main market day, but Wednesday and Friday are busy, too.

People come from all over the Northeast for the **market**, which takes over the town, with stalls filling the squares and people clogging the streets. It's a slightly less traditional affair than it used to be, with Asian electronic goods playing an increasingly important part, but the atmosphere is still worth savouring. The market is devoted to food, arts and crafts, and famous for its songbirds and the *troca-troca*, where things are swapped rather than bought. Wandering around the **food market** introduces you to some characteristic sights and smells of the interior: the blocks of hard white *sertão* cheese, delicious when eaten with fruit; piles of leaves, roots and barks used in popular medicine; brown blocks of *rapadura*, a sweet with a rich and sickly smell made from unrefined sugar; and rows of mules having their teeth examined by prospective buyers. The **songbird market** is illegal but flourishing nonetheless, with dozens of species in small handmade cages. The so-called **troca-troca**, starting early on Saturday morning and finishing by noon, is taken over by a crowd of people wandering around with whatever they want to swap: tapes and records, an old radio, used clothes, car parts – things that it would be difficult to sell for cash, which is why you don't see livestock or food being traded. It's fascinating to watch, but keep to the sidelines as locals don't appreciate wandering tourists getting in their way. It's also used by pickpockets unloading hot goods in a hurry, so if you don't want to see your own things being bartered, keep an eye on your bag.

The **mercado de artesanato** is becoming as near to a tourist trap as the interior ever gets, and there is some dross, but there's also a large amount of interesting work at prices far lower than in Recife. It's divided into sections – straw, leather, pottery and so forth – but most popular are the small inexpensive clay statues for which this area is nationally famous, the **figurinhas de barro**. Caruaru is the main outlet for the renowned potters of Alto do Moura (see below), just up the road, and if you've seen the work of Mestre Vitalino in Recife you'll instantly recognize their vivid peasant style.

Practicalities

The **bus station** (☎81/3721-3869) is 2km out of town, but buses from Recife stop in the centre, and you can also get off there. It's perfectly possible to see the market, make a trip out to Alto do Moura and get back to Recife in a day – which is what most people do. If you want to stay over, however, or intend to move on the next day further into the interior, there is no shortage of places to sleep. The best **hotels** include the three-star *Hotel do Sol* at the crossroads between the BR-104 and BR-232, 3km from the centre (☎81/3721-3044, ℱ3721-1336; ❹); the central *Hotel Centenário*, Rua Sete de Setembro 84 (☎81/3722-4011; ❸), which has a sauna but no pool; and the excellent *Hotel Central*, Rua Vigário Freire 71 (☎81/3721-5880; ❸). Among **restaurants**, *Le Cottage* at Av. Agamemnon Magalhães 752, slightly north of the centre, serves good, low-cost meals from a varied menu; the *Bar da Perua*, Rua Aliança 175, and the *Mestre Vitalino*, to the west of town at Rua Leão Dourado 13, both offer a wide range of local dishes at lunchtime and are reasonably priced.

Alto do Moura

To explore the tradition of *figurinhas* further, it's worth making the short journey to **ALTO DO MOURA**, 6km up the road from Caruaru: take a taxi or the marked bus (departures every 2hr) from Rua 13 de Maio, one of the roads leading out of the centre towards the *rodoviária*. It's a dirt road to a small yet busy village that seems entirely unremarkable, except that every other house on the only street, **Rua Mestre Vitalino**, is a potter's workshop, with kilns resembling large beehives in the yards behind. The first house on the left was Mestre Vitalino's, and is now a small museum, with his widow and grandchildren still living in the simple hut next door. There's a plaque on the adobe wall and, inside, the hut has been kept as Vitalino left it, with his leather hat and jacket hanging on a nail. The only sign that Vitalino was somebody special is the framed photos of him being feted in Rio de Janeiro and introduced to the president. There's a visitors' book, and one of Vitalino's grandchildren is on hand to show you around. It's free, but do leave a donation: Vitalino's widow lives in penury next door without any kind of pension, a sad memorial to a man who brought fame and fortune to the town of his birth.

All the workshops are piled with pottery and *figurinhas* for sale, and are fascinating to browse around; each potter has a unique individual style. One of the most individual, and certainly the most eccentric, is **Gaudino**, on the corner opposite the solitary café. His inspiration comes to him in dreams, and much of his work consists of fantastic clay monsters, each with a poem, describing the dream that gave birth to it, stuffed into its mouth. Apart from his talents as a potter, Gaudino is a very skilled *repentista*: he can immediately improvise a stanza of welcome, rhyming your name to the last word of every line. Of the dozens of other workshops, the best are those of the children and grandchildren of Vitalino and his contemporaries: Manuel Eudócio at no. 151, who specializes in decorative pots; Luiz Antônio at no. 285; and Vitalino's son, Severino Pereira dos Santos, at no. 281. One more essential stopping point is the Casa de Arte Zé Caboclo at no. 63, one of the workshops of the large and extraordinarily talented family of **Zé Caboclo**, who along with Vitalino was the founder of the *figurinhas* tradition. His work is larger and cruder than Vitalino's, but has a vivid energy that many of the Alto do Moura potters rate more highly. Here you can also see his granddaughter Marliete's work, most of which is not for sale. She is the best of the younger generation: her delicate miniaturized figurines, superbly painted, show how the special skills of Alto do Moura are revitalized with each generation that passes, a tribute to the strength of popular culture in the interior.

Nova Jerusalém

In Easter week, Caruara's market crowds are swollen by tourists and pilgrims heading for **NOVA JERUSALÉM**, in the heart of the *agreste*, 50km from the bustling town; the turn-off is on the right just after Caruaru, on the BR-104, marked "Campina Grande". After 24km another turn-off, to the left, the PE-145, leads to the small town of **Fazenda Nova**, just outside which is the site of Nova Jerusalém.

A granite replica of the old city of Jerusalem, it was built in the early 1970s by a local entrepreneur who cashed in on the deep religious feeling of the interior by mounting a **Passion play** based on that of Oberammergau in Germany. Over the years, this Paixão do Cristo has become a tradition of the *agreste*, attracting thousands of spectators to watch five hundred costumed actors, mostly local amateurs, recreate the Passion and Crucifixion. The "replica" of Jerusalem is in fact a third of the size of the original, and is basically a setting for the twelve stages on which the action takes place, each representing a Station of the Cross. There's an enjoyable air of tackiness about the whole production, which is very free with the tomato ketchup in the whipping and crucifixion scenes. Next to the site is a **sculpture park**, where local artists have set up several impressively large granite statues of folk heroes done in the style of the interior, the largest versions you'll see of the *figurinhas de barro*.

The Passion is performed daily from the Tuesday before Easter to Easter Sunday inclusive, taking up most of the day. The most convenient way to see it is to go on one of the day tours that many travel agents in Recife – and other Northeastern cities – run there during Holy Week. It's also easy to get there under your own steam, as there are buses to Fazenda Nova from Caruaru and a **campsite** when you get there, as well as several simple *dormitórios*. Entry to the spectacle costs about $20.

Into the sertão

The **Pernambucan sertão** begins after Caruaru, though there's no sudden transition; the hills simply get browner and rockier, dense thorny scrub takes over from the hill plants, and there are cacti every few yards, from tiny flowering stumps to massive tangled plants as large as trees. And, above all, it is hot, with parched winds that feel as if someone is training a hairdryer on your face. The Pernambucan *sertão* is one of the harshest in the Northeast, a scorched landscape under relentless sun for most of the year. This is cattle country, home of the *vaqueiro*, the Northeastern cowboy, and has been since the very beginning of Portuguese penetration inland in the seventeenth century: one of the oldest frontiers in the Americas.

The main highway which runs through the hilly Pernambucan *sertão* winds through scenery unlike any you'll have seen before – an apparently endless expanse of cactus and scrub so thick in places that cowboys have to wear leather armour to protect themselves. If you travel in the rainy season here – March to June, although rain can never be relied upon in the interior – you may be lucky enough to catch it bursting with green, punctuated by the whites, reds and purples of flowering trees and cacti. Massive electrical storms are common at this time of year, and at night the horizon can flicker with sheet lightning for hours at a stretch.

Towards Petrolina

After Caruaru the highway passes through a number of anonymous farming towns. **ARCOVERDE**, 130km to the west, has a market on Saturdays and a reasonable **hotel**, the *Grande Majestic*, Av. Cel. Antônio Japiassu 326 (☎81/3821-1175; ❷), which doesn't quite live up to its name but is a cheap and handy place to break the journey. You may need to, because the best *sertão* towns to make for are buried deep in the interior, some eight or ten hours by bus from Caruaru.

The last place that could really be called a town is **SERRA TALHADA**, some 200km west of Arcoverde. Here, the *Pousada da Serra*, Rua Dr Ademar Xavier 1055, Alto da Conceição (☎81/3831-1536; ❷), is reasonable. From here on, the road passes through a succession of flyblown villages, all of which would look vaguely Mediterranean – with their whitewashed churches, café, dusty square and rows of tumbledown cottages – if it weren't for the startling landscape in which they are set. Eighty kilometres beyond Serra Talhada, a turning leads north to Juazeiro do Norte (see p.340), while one Petrolina bus turns south to follow an alternative route parallel to the São Francisco valley. The others continue for another 110km, across one of the most desolate semi-arid desert landscapes in the Northeast, before reaching **OURICURI**, quite a pleasant place to break your journey, a shady spot with a couple of hotels; from here it's another 213km south along the BR-122 to Petrolina.

Petrolina

After the villages that have gone before, **PETROLINA** seems like a city. Certainly, by the standards of the *sertão*, it's a large, thriving and relatively prosperous town, thanks to the river trade to places downstream. On the waterfront, you can occasionally see riverboats adorned with *carrancas*, carved wooden figureheads bolted onto the prow, brightly painted and with a grotesque monster's head, meant to frighten evil spirits lurking in wait for unwary mariners. Petrolina also has an interesting **Museu do Sertão** (Mon–Fri 10am–6pm, Sat 2–6pm, Sun 8am–noon), on Praça Santos Dumont on the road to the airstrip, about ten minutes' walk from the centre of town. Small but well put together, the museum documents *sertão* life and history through assorted relics and some fascinating photographs, including a couple of the bespectacled social bandit Lampião and his gang, popular heroes who roamed the *sertão* until they were shot dead in 1938. Lastly, Petrolina has a **market** on Friday and Saturday that brings people in from the *sertão* for miles around.

The **rodoviária** is quite central and there are a couple of *dormitórios* close by. Better **places to stay** are the *Hotel Central*, on Praça Dom Malan, adequate for the price (❷) and the *Hotel Reis Palace*, Rua Manuel Clementino 1157 (☎81/3861-2337; ❸), which has apartments, plus a bar and a small pool. The *Petrolina Palace*, Av. Cardoso de Sá 845 (☎81/3862-1555, ⓦwww .petrolinapalacehotel.com.br; ❹), and the *Hotel do Grande Rio*, Avenida Pe. Fraga (☎81/3862-3344; ❹) both have pools. Excellent regional **food** is served at *O Barranqueiro*, Rua Rio Beberibe 50 (☎81/3864-2356), although it's not cheap and the restaurant is some 4km from the town centre, while *Chimarrão*, Av. Mons. Angelo Sampaio, Cohab 3, is the place for hungry carnivores. There are three **buses** daily to Petrolina from Recife, which can be picked up at Caruaru.

Juazeiro

Over the bridge, or across the river by boat, and into Bahia state lies Petrolina's poorer sister town, **JUAZEIRO**, not to be confused with Juazeiro do Norte. Many of its inhabitants had their homes flooded when dams created the enormous **Sobradinho** lake just upstream in the 1960s. Since then the area around Juazeiro has become something of a showcase for **irrigation schemes**, and all kinds of fruit – including unlikely products like grapes and asparagus – are grown here. The town has several **hotels**, a good choice being the *Grande Hotel do Juazeiro*, Rua José Petitinga (☎74/611-7710; ❺), not as grand as the name would suggest, but situated on the riverfront with a pool, bar and very good restaurant. The cheaper but spotless *Rio Sol*, Rua Cel. João Evangelista 3 (☎74/611-4481; ❷), is another good bet. There is an unusual attraction in the form of a nineteenth-century paddle steamer, the *Vaporzinho*, built in 1852 to ply the São Francisco river: it's been restored, turned into a **restaurant** and is now moored on the riverfront.

Juazeiro is the northern terminus for the **river services** of the Companhia de Navegação do São Francisco, which once ran frequent boats downriver as far south as Minas Gerais but is now in decline. It still runs one monthly boat to Pirapora in Minas Gerais, from where there are bus connections to Brasília and Belo Horizonte, but its departure has become increasingly irregular: times and dates are available from tourist information offices in Recife and Salvador. The journey itself takes three or four days. There are also smaller boats to towns both upstream and downstream leaving from the waterfront in Juazeiro; most of them are river traders and are quite happy to take paying passengers – although always check during negotiations when they return, as it may not be for a couple of days. It's remarkable how appealing the idea of even a short boat trip becomes after the heat and dust of the *sertão*, whose hills crowd right down

to the Sobradinho lakeside. Tempting though it is, however, you should **avoid swimming** in the lake, as schistosomiasis – also known as bilharzia – is endemic here.

From Juazeiro you can continue south by bus along the BR-407 to Feira de Santana (see p.276) and Salvador (see p.248). Alternatively, if you're interested in the history of the *sertão*, you might want to make the five-hour journey southeast to Canudos (see p.277).

Fernando de Noronha

The beautiful archipelago of **FERNANDO DE NORONHA**, about 350km off the Brazilian coast, belongs to Pernambuco, though it's actually nearer to Rio Grande do Norte. European explorers first came here in 1503, and after a struggle between various powers the islands ended up under the control of the Portuguese. Lisbon considered the archipelago strategically important enough to build the **Forte dos Remédios**, of which only some remains can now be seen.

In recent years the archipelago has become well known as an ecotourist destination. Most of it is protected as a **marine national park**, created in order to maintain the ecological wonders that have been preserved by the islands' isolation from the rest of Brazil. The vegetation is fairly typical Northeastern *agreste*, but the wildlife is magnificent: birdwatchers will be amazed by the variety of exotic birds, including several types of pelican, while the crystal-clear sea is full of multicoloured fish, turtles, sharks, whales, sponges and coral. Perhaps most remarkable is the sight of thousands of dolphins entering the bay every day between 5am and 6am, viewed from the harbour.

The main island (Ilha de Fernando de Noronha) shelters plenty of stunning **beaches**, though the water can sometimes be turbulent and not perfectly clear; it is a fairly constant comfortable 28 degrees centigrade. The best beaches are probably Praia da Atalaia and Cacimba do Padre, and at Mirante dos Golfinhos you can watch dolphins leaping over the waves – tourists used to be able to swim with them, but this has been banned. A number of **ecological trails** allow good birdwatching, and several companies specialize in **scuba-diving** courses and trips, including Aguas Claras (☎81/3619-1225), Atlantis (☎81/3619-1371) and Noronha Divers (☎81/3619-1112). Various companies offer **boat trips** around the archipelago, leaving from the ports at the northeastern tip of the island and from the Bahia dos Golfinhos at the island's southern end. Boat trips from the latter leave most days ($15 per person including transport to the harbour; ☎81/3619-1295).

Practicalities

You can **fly** to Fernando de Noronha from either Recife or Natal with Nordeste airlines; tickets are available from a number of travel agents in both cities (see "Listings" on p.312 and p.349). A return flight from Natal will set you back at least $300, one from Recife slightly more, though there are more frequent flights from the latter. Bring plenty of local currency with you as you won't be able to change money during your stay, and also bring anything else you think you may need: prices in Fernando de Noronha are high, and you should try to avoid doing much shopping while you're there. Fernando de Noronha is best visited between August and January, when the rainfall is lowest.

The few facilities that the island's have, including the **airport**, are all found on the main island. Here you'll find the **tourist information** office (☎81/3619-1352) in the main settlement of **VILA DOS REMÉDIOS**, a small town in the northern part of the island, and, some 10km to the south near the airport, the new **Centro de Visitantes** (daily 8am–10.30pm; ☎81/3619-1171).

Tours these days are the obligatory way to get to Fernando de Noronha (an attempt to limit the impact of tourism on the fragile environment) and are generally arranged by travel agencies in Recife or Natal – such as Dolphin Travel, at Av. Eng. Domingos Ferreira 4267 (☎81/3326-3815) in Boa Viagem – and usually include a return flight, accommodation, food and tours of the island. Prices start at around $600 for two nights, $660 for three nights and $800 for five nights.

On the main island, **buggies**, **jeeps** and **motorbikes** can be rented from several operators, including Locbuggy (☎81/3619-1142) and Eduardo Galvao de Brito at the *Esmeralda do Atlântico Hotel* (☎81/3619-1335). Many hotels and *pousadas* rent out their own buggies, which can work out to be less expensive. You can arrange **diving trips** through your travel agent, but Atlantis Divers (☎81/3619-1371, ⓦwww.atlantisnoronha.com.br) are probably the best dive operator on the island.

Paraíba

Most people who are travelling north from Recife head directly for Ceará and Rio Grande do Norte's beaches, missing out **Paraíba state** and its capital of **João Pessoa** altogether. This is a big mistake, as it is the most attractive of the smaller Northeastern cities, with everything you could reasonably ask for: some of the finest town beaches in the Northeast, a beautiful setting on the mouth of the Rio Sanhauá, and colonial remains, including one of Brazil's most striking churches. In addition, not enough foreign travellers make it to the city for the *pessoenses* to have become blasé about them, and you're likely to be approached by smiling kids who are anxious to practise their hard-learned English.

Out of the city, there are even nicer beaches to the north and south, while the highway inland leads to **Campina Grande**, a market town strategically placed at the entrance to the *sertão*. The main target of the interior, though, is actually in neighbouring Ceará state (see p.340), but dealt with here since it's most easily accessible from Paraíba – the fascinating pilgrim town of **Juazeiro do Norte**.

João Pessoa

JOÃO PESSOA is one of the oldest and one of the poorest cities in Brazil. In recent years, there's been massive new development along the city's two

main beaches, but an air of dilapidated elegance remains around the old part of town. Of all the Northeast's city centres, this is the one least scarred by modern developers. Just a few kilometres away, the town beaches of **Cabo Branco** and **Tambaú** are well on the way to becoming much the same as most others in the Northeast, with towering skyscrapers stretching back towards the old town. There aren't enough of them yet, though, to detract from the stunning beauty of the vast white sandy beach, and out of season, tourists are still few and far between.

Arrival, orientation and information

The **rodoviária** (☎83/221-9611) in João Pessoa is conveniently near the city centre. Any bus from the **local bus station**, opposite the *rodoviária*'s entrance, takes you to the city's one unmistakeable, central landmark: the circular lake of the Parque Solon de Lucena, which everybody simply calls **Lagoa**, spectacularly bordered by tall palms imported from Portugal. All **bus routes** converge on the circular Anel Viário skirting the lake, some en route to the beach districts, others heading further afield – to the northern beaches, the neighbouring town of Cabedelo and the village of Penha to the south of the city. Buses for the beach can also be caught directly from the *rodoviária*; look for the ones marked "Tambaú" (#510 or 513).

The Presidente Castro Pinto **airport** (☎83/232-1200) lies just 11km west of the city centre and is connected to the *rodoviária* by regular buses; taxis into town cost around $13.

Orientation

João Pessoa's **centre** is just to the west of the Lagoa. To the east **Avenida Getúlio Vargas** leads out of town towards the skyscrapers and beachside *bairros* of Cabo Branco and Tambaú. At the city's core is **Praça João Pessoa**, which contains the state governor's palace and the local parliament; most of the central hotels are clustered around here. The oldest part of the city is just to the north of Praça João Pessoa, where **Rua Duque de Caxias** ends in the Baroque splendour of the **Igreja de São Francisco**. The steep Ladeira de São Francisco, leading down from here to the lower city and the bus and train stations, offers a marvellous tree-framed view of the rest of the city spread out on the banks of the **Rio Sanhau**.

The two sweeping bays of **Cabo Branco** and **Tambaú** are separated by the futuristic, luxury *Hotel Tambaú* – more commonly known as the *Tropical Tambaú Center Hotel* – and the nearby Centro Turístico Tambaú shopping centre. This area is also where the highest concentration of nightspots can be found. The southern boundary of the city is the lighthouse on Ponta de Seixas, the cape at the far end of Cabo Branco. Locals claim it as the most easterly point of Brazil, a title disputed with the city of Natal to the north – though the *pessoenses* have geography on their side.

Information

Official **tourist information** is available from the state tourist board, PB-Tur, at the *rodoviária* (daily 8am–6pm; ☎83/222-3537), the airport (daily 9am–4pm) and in the Centro de Turismo in Tambaú, opposite the *Tropical Tambaú Center Hotel* at Av. Almirante Tamandaré 100 (daily 8am–7pm; ☎83/247-0505). You can also find a post office and a *posto telefônico* here. An additional source of information is the English-speaking **Disque Turismo** tourist hotline (☎514).

Accommodation

The very cheapest **places to stay** are the *dormitórios* opposite the *rodoviária*. You can find good budget and medium-range hotels both in the centre and on the beaches, but five-star luxury is only available by the sea. Hotels in João Pessoa rarely seem to charge the full price displayed at the reception desk, and you can get some pretty hefty discounts if you ask.

City centre

Hotel Rio Verde Rua Duque de Caxias 263 ⊤ 83/222-4369. Right in the middle of the old centre, this is a no-frills but clean and good-value option. ❶

J.R. Hotel Rua Rodrigues Chaves 87 ⊤ & ⒻF83/241-2104. A large but good modern option, with clean rooms and friendly service. ❸

Lagoa Park Hotel Parque Solon de Lucena 19 ⊤ 83/241-1414. Not as expensive as it looks, this hotel offers adequate rooms, some with great views over the Lagoa. ❸

Paraíba Palace Praça Vidal de Negreiros ⊤ 83/221-3107. A good-value, centrally located option with simple, cosy rooms and friendly service. ❸

Pousada Raio de Luz, Praça Venancio Neiva 44 ⊤ 83/221-2169. An inexpensive hotel offering by far the best value in the city centre; rooms are tidy and some come with private showers. ❷

The beaches

Escuna Praia Hotel Av. Cabo Branco 1574 ⊤ 83/226-5611, Ⓕ 247-1442. Well located on a nice part of the beach, the *Escuna* is clean, pleasant and even better value out of season. ❸

Hotel Pouso das Aguas Av. Cabo Branco 2348 ⊤ & Ⓕ83/226-5003 ⓌWww.pousadadasaguas.com.br. Small but comfortable, with garden and a pool; right on the seafront. ❸

Hotel Praia Mar Av. Almirante Tamandaré 864 ⊤

& Ⓕ83/226-2515. Yet another inexpensive but good mid-range option right by the ocean. ❸

Mar Azul Hotel Pousada Av. João Maurício 315 ⊤ 83/226-2660. Despite not providing breakfast, this seafront budget hotel at Tambaú offers excellent value. ❷

Pousada Canta–Maré Rua Osório Paes 60 ⊤ 83/247-1047 or 226-4809. Amongst the cheapest accommodation in Tambaú, this is a small and basic but relatively comfortable lodging. ❷

Pousada Lua Cheia Mar Av. Cabo Branco 1710 ⊤ 83/247-2470. Small, clean and very friendly, this place is located at one of the best parts of the beach, between Tambaú and Cabo Branco. ❸

Tropical Tambaú Av. Almirante Tamandaré 229 ⊤ 83/226-3660, Ⓕ 247-1070, Ⓔ gegtht@tropical-hotel.com.br. One of the city's landmark modernist buildings, reminiscent of a camouflaged flying saucer, this luxury beachside hotel offers sauna, pool, the full works – though the service is not really worth the money. ❽

Victory Business Flat Av. Almirante Tamandaré 310 ⊤ 83/247-3100, Ⓕ 247-5332, Ⓦ www. victoryflat.com.br. More or less opposite the *Tropical Tambaú Center Hotel*, the *Victory* offers equally luxurious rooms at less than half the price outside high season; it also has a pool and good service. ❻

Xénius Hotel Av. Cabo Branco 1262 ⊤ 83/226-3535, Ⓕ 226-5463. Pleasant modern hotel with rooftop pool, very good restaurant and the usual mod cons. ❹

Camping

João Pessoa's beautiful **campsite**, on a promontory past the Ponta de Seixas, can be reached by taking the Cabo Branco bus to its terminal and then walking (for about 45min) past the lighthouse and along the road beyond it until the signposted fork to the left. Easier on the legs is taking the Penha bus from the Anel Viário or the local bus station: it passes near the campsite but only runs every couple of hours. Clean and well run, on a fine beach with a spectacular view of the city, the campsite is often full, especially from January to March, so it's advisable to book beforehand in the centre at Sala 18, Rua Almeida Barreto 159 (⊤83/221-4863).

The City

The centre of João Pessoa is dotted with **colonial churches, monasteries** and **convents**, some of which are extremely beautiful. Until 1992 they were all being allowed to fall into ruin but, not a moment too soon, the state government and the Ministry of Culture mounted a crash restoration programme, for once using historians and archeologists to return the buildings to their original glory, rather than gutting them. These days, modernization has certainly taken its toll on the city, but you can still see mule carts sitting alongside BMWs at the city's traffic lights.

São Francisco

João Pessoa's most spectacular church is the **Igreja de São Francisco** (Mon 2–5pm, Tues–Sun 9am–noon & 2–5pm), which sits in splendid isolation atop the hill that bears its name, at the end of Rua Duque de Caxias, and now forms part of the **Centro Cultural de São Francisco**.

The exterior alone is impressive enough. A huge courtyard is flanked by high walls beautifully decorated with *azulejo* tiling, with pastoral scenes in a series of alcoves. These walls funnel you towards a large early eighteenth-century church that would do credit to Lisbon or Coimbra: its most remarkable feature is the tower topped with an oriental dome, a form that the Portuguese encountered in Goa and appropriated for their own purposes. Older than the church by a few decades is the stone cross opposite the courtyard, at the foot of which is a group of finely carved pelicans, once believed to selflessly tear flesh from their own chests to feed their young, and so commonly used to symbolize

Christ. You reach the church through an entrance that has marvellously carved wooden panels and doors. Beyond the church are the chapels and cloister of the **Convento de Santo Antônio**, and upstairs there's an excellent **museum** of popular and sacred art.

Around São Francisco

The other places worth seeing in the centre are within a short walk of São Francisco. A little way down the steep Ladeira de São Francisco is the oldest building in town, the Casa da Pólvora, a relic of the times when the Dutch and Portuguese fought for control over this sugar-rich coastline. The squat, functional building was once the city arsenal, but is now the home of the **Museu Fotográfico Walfredo Rodriguez** (Mon–Fri 8–11.30am & 2–5pm; free), given over to a collection of enlarged photographs of the city taken in the early decades of this century.

If you go back up the Ladeira de São Francisco, turn right and right again, you'll end up on Rua General Osório. Here you'll find the cathedral, **Igreja de Nossa Senhora das Neves**, which boasts a well-proportioned interior that, for once, forgoes the Rococo excesses of many colonial cathedrals. Its large, rather plain facade fronts a small square with majestic views north to the wooded river valley and, to the west, green suburbs. Further down Rua General Osório, the seventeenth-century **Mosteiro de São Bento** (Tues–Sat 2–5pm) has a simple, beautifully restored interior with a lovely curved wooden ceiling. Other colonial churches are cheek by jowl on Rua Visconde de Pelotas, two blocks to the east: the **Igreja de Nossa Senhora do Carmo** here is well worth a look, both for its ornate Baroque exterior and the gold-leaf-covered altar inside.

The beaches

The beach areas of Tambaú and Cabo Branco are linked to the centre by frequent buses from the Anel Viário and the local bus station. The **Cabo Branco** seafront is especially stylish, with a mosaic pavement and thousands of well-tended palm trees to complement the sweep of the bay. This is best viewed from the **Ponta de Seixas lighthouse** at the southern end, where a plaque and a monument mark Brazil's easternmost point. From here, it's only 2200km to Senegal in Africa, less than half the distance to Rio Grande do Sul in the south of Brazil or the state of Roraima in the north. To get to the lighthouse, take the "Cabo Branco" bus to its terminal on the promontory at the end of the bay and walk up the hill. At the top, you'll find a park and a couple of tacky souvenir shops, but the main draw here is the view, which is glorious – Cabo Branco beach stretches out before you in an enormous arc, 6km long. Cabo Branco itself is one of the city's exclusive upper-class suburbs, where the rich stay hidden in their large detached houses, their high walls shutting out both the people and the view. The beach has the usual string of bars and several hotels, but they are sparser and less intrusive than on Tambaú, and during the week, there's not much more at the southern end of Cabo Branco than the rustle of wind in the palm trees to disturb you.

Tambaú is a lot more lively, dominated by its eponymous hotel, which forms one end of a small square. Nearby, on the corner of Avenida Nossa Senhora dos Navegantes and Avenida Rui Carneiro, is a modern building housing the **Mercado de Artesanato Paraíbano**. Although not up to the standards of Pernambuco, Paraíba has distinctive *artesanato* that's worth checking out: painted plates and bowls, and striking figurines made out of sacking and wood. North of the market you encounter busier and larger clusters of beachside bars and restaurants, and at weekends they and the beach get crowded. There are the usual simple cafés and vendors selling fruit and fish, and *jangadas* aplenty. Anywhere here is a good place for a *caipirinha* and a view of an invariably spectacular sunset.

Eating, drinking and nightlife

As usual in a coastal capital, the centre tends to get deserted after dark, as people looking for a night out head for the beaches, particularly Tambaú. However, there are several **restaurants and bars** in the centre worth trying out.

João Pessoa has a surprisingly rich but fluctuating **music scene** for a city of its size, concentrated at the beaches: the only nights it is difficult to catch something are Sunday and Monday. Venues open and close with bewildering frequency, so it's best to ask the tourist office for a current list of venues and suggestions, though they will direct you to the more expensive upmarket clubs unless you are persistent. Alternatively, look in the entertainment guide of the local paper, *O Norte*.

City centre

The *Casino da Lagoa* is a bar-restaurant in a small park looking out across the Anel Viário, on the right coming down from the centre: the food is no more than average but the view is excellent, especially at night. Some of the best **sertão food** in the city is served at the *Recanto do Picuí*, Rua Felicinano Dourado 198 (☎83/224-1400); the *carne do sol* here is excellent, best accompanied by green beans and *batata doce assado*, roast sweet potatoes. *Miralha*, on Avenida Epitácio Pessoa (☎83/226-3982), is a bar and *churrascaria* with live *forró* music on Monday evenings. For self-service lunches it's difficult to beat the quality and value offered at *Salutte*, Rua 13 de Maio 73 (open Mon–Sat). **Vegetarians** can try the reasonably priced *Natural*, Rua Rodrigues de Aquino 177, down from Praça João Pessoa – unfortunately only open for lunch.

Finally, stop by the *Bar da Pólvora*, behind the Casa da Pólvora. No more than a bar with tables set out on the patio, serving only beer, *caipirinhas* and soft drinks, it has two major advantages: one is the setting, beneath the ancient walls of the arsenal, with a stunning view out across the river; the other is the clientele – young, student-dominated and very Bohemian. The best time to go is Thursday evening, when a small fee is charged for a table and there's a show, whose basic format is a few groups/poets/singers doing spots, plus whoever else in the audience feels like doing a turn. As you might expect, some of the acts are appalling, notably the local poets reading interminable extracts from their work, but the music is sometimes excellent.

The beaches

The more expensive restaurants in the beach areas ($20–35 range) are in **Cabo Branco**. There are a couple of particularly good places on the seafront: the *Tábua do Marinheiro*, Av. Cabo Branco 1780 (☎83/247-5804), serves pasta, seafood and a range of meat; the *Olho de Lula*, Av. Cabo Branco 2300 (☎83/226-2328), is a popular, if slightly exclusive, seafood resturant. Further down, at no. 5100, is *Marina's*, one of the few seafront bars in Cabo Branco, which also does seafood: a local speciality is *polvo ao leite de coco*, octopus in coconut milk. Also in Cabo Branco, the *Restaurante Caçuá*, Rua Adolfo Loureiro 65 (☎83/247-3237), specializes in regional cuisine, and the *Sashami*

& *Grill*, Av. Beira Rio 71 (daily 6–11pm), is a reasonably good sushi restaurant. In **Tambaú**, the *Tábua de Carne*, at Av. Rui Carneiro 648, one of the roads running away from the beach, is a good place for meat and *sertão* food. *Mangai*, Av. Edson Ramalho 696, boasts a wide range of dishes, with much of the produce coming fresh from the restaurant's own ranch; this is regional cooking at its best, though it's not cheap. For a decent Italian meal, *La Boca de La Verita*, Av. Olinda 193 (☎83/247-3334; closed Tues), is easily your best option, while the *Tereré*, Av. Rui Carneiro 791 (☎83/226-1717), is an excellent *churrascaria*. For good coffee or cake, head for the *Doce Delícia*, just inside the Centro Turístico Tambaú.

The square in front of the *Tropical Tambaú Center Hotel* is a relaxed place for a drink and some **live music**. It's surrounded by restaurants and bars, and on Friday and Saturday nights tables and chairs are put out in the square, drink starts flowing and after about 9pm things start getting very lively. Every other bar has a *forró* trio, and guitarists and accordion players stroll through the crowds. There's no shortage of good, cheap food sizzling on the charcoal grills of the street vendors if your budget doesn't stretch to a restaurant. In the streets behind there are any number of small **bars and clubs**, which close down and reopen too quickly to keep track of them, so just wander around and stop by anywhere you see lights and music, though they tend not to get going until 11pm at the earliest. There are a couple of fairly lively **gay bars**, too, in the streets behind Avenida Nossa Senhora dos Navegantes in Tambaú.

Listings

Airlines TAM ☎83/232-2002; Transbrasil, Av. Presidente Pessoa 2055 ☎83/244-8544 or 244-5900; Varig, Av. Presidente Pessoa 1251 ☎83/232-1515; VASP, Parque Solon de Lucena 530, Centro ☎83/232-1757.

Banks and exchange You can change money and travellers' cheques at Câmbio Turismo, which has branches at Rua Visconde de Pelotas 54 in the city centre (Mon–Fri), and in the shopping centre on Tambaú beach (Mon–Sat).

Car rental Localiza, at Av. Epitácio Pessoa 4910 ☎83/232-1130 or at airport ☎0800/992-000; A.L.A., Av. Nego 71, Tambaú ☎83/247-5470 or 982-3583.

Post office The main office is on Praça Pedro Américo, two blocks downhill from Praça João Pessoa.

Taxis Disk taxi ☎0800/83-1310; Teletaxi ☎800-83-2056.

Telephones Domestic and international calls are easiest with a phonecard from any of the public telephones around town, though marginally cheaper from the TELPA building, off Rua Visconde de Pelotas in the centre (daily 8am–10pm).

Travel and tour companies Roger Turismo, Av. Almirante Tamandaré 229, Tambaú (☎83/247-1856 ⓕ247-1533, ⓔroger@zaitek.com.br), offer a full range of tours and travel services. Sem Fronteiras, Av. Nossa Senhora dos Navegantes 521, Loja 208, Tambaú (☎83/247-3311, ⓕ247-5352, ⓔmtulio@netwaybbs.com.br), is an innovative eco-adventure tour company offering expeditions to a number of out-of-the-way places in their four-wheel-drive vehicles. Dune-buggy trips (see p.348) can be booked through either Oswaldo (☎83/962-0962) or Evandro (☎83/984-7073).

Along the coast

Like so much of Brazil, Paraíba is blessed with many wonderful **beaches** along its 140-kilometre coastline. Unlike some other parts of the Northeast, however, many of its beaches are, for the time being, largely undeveloped and many require somewhat difficult journeys by bus and then on foot or by taxi to reach them.

South to Penha and Tambaba

Just to the **south** of João Pessoa is the fishing village of **PENHA**, served by local buses from outside the *rodoviária*. Strung out along a fine beach set in the midst of dense palm forest, Penha is distinguished from other fishing villages round about by a nineteenth-century church, the **Igreja de Nossa Senhora da Penha**, which is a pilgrimage centre and focus of much popular devotion. The beach near the church is also used by followers of *candomblé*, who identify the Virgin with Iemanjá, the goddess of the sea. According to legend, over a century ago an image of the Virgin was dredged up by fishermen in their nets, and worked so many miracles that the community adopted her as their patron saint and built the simple chapel to house her icon. Along the beach there are several rustic **bars** where you can eat and also string a hammock for a nominal fee. Discreet camping on the beach is also possible.

TAMBABA is set on a volcanic outcrop and lies some 30km to the south of João Pessoa. It's the first officially recognized nudist beach in the Northeast and is well off the beaten track. Getting here involves a bus ride from the *rodoviária* to the small seaside town of **Jacumã**, followed by an eight-kilometre walk along a rough road. If you don't want to walk, it's probably better to take a taxi than risk bringing a rented car along here as the dirt-track road is more difficult than it looks. The beach is superb and there's a small if somewhat overpriced bar here. Alternatively, and a little nearer to Jacumã, is the **Praia Coqueirinho**, which is a popular spot for the local children in the surrounding villages. Again, you'll need to take a taxi here. **Camping** is possible at the beach of Tabatinga, just to the north, otherwise there are places to stay in Jacumã.

North towards Cabedelo

Penha apart, most of the readily accessible **beaches** are to the **north**, off the road that leads to Cabedelo, 18km or 45 minutes by frequent local buses from the Anel Viário in João Pessoa – they get very crowded at weekends. The road runs a little inland and there are turn-offs leading to the beaches on the way: it seems to depend more on the drivers' whim than a timetable as to whether the bus takes you right to the beach, but hop on the Cabedelo bus anyway, and get off at the relevant turn-off if need be; it'll only be a short walk to the sea.

BESSA is the generic name for the stretch of coastline immediately north of Tambaú (see p.336). Six kilometres out of town is a turn-off that leads to the yacht club and a cluster of bars, which have a rather more upmarket clientele than the next village along, **POÇO**, where there is a chapel, some weekend homes, a fine palm-fringed beach with the obligatory bars and several good fish restaurants: *Badionaldo* serves delicious crab stew (*ensopado de carangueijo*), a local speciality, while at the *Bar e Restaurante do Marcão*, four crabs for $4 will satisfy even the greediest of appetites. From there, you could walk the 10km along the beach to Cabedelo; otherwise hourly buses to Cabedelo, or back to João Pessoa, leave during the day from the bus stop near the church.

CABEDELO itself is older than it looks. It was much fought over in the Dutch wars, and the star-shaped fort of **Santa Caterina** (Tues–Sat 8am–5pm), dating from 1585, is the major sight in the village. Unfortunately, Petrobrás have built a series of oil storage tanks right up to its ramparts, and it's difficult to get a sense of its strategic position, commanding as it does the only deep-water anchorage on this stretch of coast. Nowadays, Cabedelo's main claim to fame is as the starting point for the famous **Transamazon highway** – the Transamazônica – and there's a sign proving it over the João Pessoa road. The Transamazon was seen by its creators as the conduit along which would flow the "people without land" to the "land without people", as poor Northeasterners were funnelled towards Amazônia – a political signal to the large landowners of the Northeast that the government had no intention of tackling the region's problems by implementing agrarian reform. The only thing the poor of Paraíba got was a convenient escape route.

There's no reason to hang around in Cabedelo and plenty of reason to continue 20km to two superb and largely unspoilt beaches. For the more adventurous camper there is the **Praia do Oiteiro**, a wild and beautiful beach backed by hills covered with tropical vegetation but little in the way of modern comforts. **Campina**, just north of Oiteiro, is similarly idyllic but with the addition of a small fishing settlement. You can get to both beaches on the same bus from João Pessoa via Cabedelo, or you could try renting a boat in Cabedelo as it's only half the distance along the coast.

Inland to Campina Grande

The BR-230 highway, a good-quality asphalt road, bisects Paraíba and leads directly into the *sertão*. The green coastal strip is quickly left behind as the road climbs into the hills; two hours' driving and you arrive in the second city of Paraíba, **CAMPINA GRANDE**, linked to João Pessoa by hourly bus. It's a large town, similar in many ways to Caruaru in Pernambuco: even the slogan you see at the city limits – "Welcome to the Gateway of the *Sertão*" – is identical. Like Caruaru (see p.324), Campina Grande owes its existence to a strategic position between the *agreste* and the *sertão* proper. It's a market town and centre of light industry, where the products of the *sertão* are stockpiled and sent

Campina Grande's festivals

In June Campina Grande hosts a month-long **festival** that uses the São João holiday – the **festas juninas** – as an excuse for a general knees-up. This is the best time to visit, and the wonderfully named *forrodrómo* in the centre of town, an enormous cross between a concert hall and a *dancetaria*, is where it all happens.

Campina Grande is also famous for its out-of-season carnival, the **Micarande**, an event in late April that attracts some 300,000 people over a period of four days and is the largest of its kind in Brazil. The music, best described as frenetic electric, reaches fever pitch as the *trios elétricos* (carnival trucks), with live *frevo* bands playing on top, work their way through the crowds with their followers in train, the music lasting until dawn. Accommodation during this period is particularly scarce and expensive even for the humblest of abodes, so it's best to get in touch with one of the leading organizers, the state tourist authority, before setting out. A word of warning, however: although the event itself is very well policed, take care when making your way to it as the streets and buses are very crowded.

down to the coast, and where the people of the *sertão* come to buy what they can't make. At a large Wednesday and Saturday **market** you can see this process unfolding before your eyes.

You may also see evidence of the fierce competition between Campina Grande and João Pessoa. *Campinenses* proudly contrast their industries and commercial know-how with the decadence and stagnation of João Pessoa, and there is concerted pressure from the people of Campina Grande to make this the new capital of Paraíba. To the traveller, though, João Pessoa's elegance is something of a contrast with Campina Grande, which even locals admit is rather ugly. Still, it's a good place to sample the distinctive culture of the *sertão*, without having to suffer its discomforts, and also to experience some unforgettable **festivals**.

The **climate** in Campina Grande is always pleasant, as its height takes the edge off the coastal heat without making it cold, though you may need a sweater at night during the rainy season.

The City

Although the city sprawls out into anonymous industrial suburbs, the **central layout** is compact and easy to get the hang of. The city's heart, and most useful landmark, is the obelisk in the **Parque do Açude Novo**. The park itself straddles the **Avenida Floriano Peixoto**, which bisects Campina Grande from west to east, and the stretch of the avenue from the obelisk to the cathedral is the centre proper, where most of the things to do and see are concentrated.

The highlight of Campina Grande is its **market**, held every Wednesday and Saturday. The market takes over the area around the cathedral and the municipal market behind it, and although not quite on the scale of Caruaru or Feira da Santana in Bahia it is the largest in the northern half of the Northeast. Saturday is busiest, but to catch it at its peak you need to either arrive on the Friday or make an early start from João Pessoa, as it starts to wind down from around noon. Most entertaining are the cries, improvised verses, chants and patters of the scores of street sellers: you may be lucky enough to come across hawkers going head to head, when two vendors set up shop next to each other and try to outdo the other in extravagant claims and original turns of phrase. Sometimes sellers of *cordel* (see p.305) recite chunks of the ballads to whet the public's appetite, and clusters of people gather around to shout comments and enjoy the story. If you miss the market, but still fancy trying to get hold of **artesanato** and **cordel**, good places are the co-operative Casa do Artesão, Rua Venâncio Neiva 85, near the Rique Palace, and Kaboclinha, nearby at Rua Vidal de Negreiros 36.

There are three museums in Campina Grande. By some way the best is the **Museu de Arte Assis Chateaubriand**, part of the complex of buildings in the Parque do Açude Novo (Mon–Fri 9am–noon & 2–10pm, Sat & Sun 2–10pm). It's a source of justifiable civic pride, boasting a good gallery of modern art, devoted entirely to Brazilian artists, with a special emphasis on work from the Northeast. Some of Brazil's greatest modern painters are represented, notably Cândido Portinari, whose large canvases fuse social realism with modernist technique in their depiction of workers and workplaces. The most intriguing part of the museum is the *atelier livre*, where local painters, carvers and sculptors exhibit their works in progress. They are not very cheap, but for the quality and originality the price is often more than reasonable.

In contrast, the **Museu Histórico e Geográfico**, at Av. Floriano Peixote 825 (Mon–Fri 8am–6pm, Sat & Sun 8am–noon), is loaded with period furniture, weapons, maps and historical photos relating to the city's heritage. In a similar vein, the **Museu do Algodão** (Mon–Fri 8am–noon & 2–6pm), in the tourist centre inside the old train station, concentrates on the history of the cotton plantations of the area, including some fearsome chains, stocks, iron collars and whips used on the slaves.

Practicalities

The **rodoviária** (☎83/337-3001) is on the outskirts of town at Avenida Sen. Argemiro de Figueiredo in Catolé (☎83/341-5780); local buses marked "Centro" take you downtown. The **tourist office** is situated at Praça Clementino Procópio (Mon–Fri 8am–5pm; ☎83/3251-7717) and you can get a useful city map here.

There's a good choice of **accommodation** in Campina Grande. The cheaper *dormitórios* are clustered around the old train station and there are plenty of mid-range places close to each other around the city centre. The centrally located *Belfran*, Av. Floriano Peixoto 258 (☎83/341-1312; ❷), is one of the best budget choices in town, with cheerful, well-kept rooms. Also in the heart of the city are the comfortable *Majestic*, Rua Maciel Pinheiro 216 (☎83/341-2009, ℱ321-6748; ❷), and the *Ouro Branco*, Rua Cel. João Lourenço Porto 20 (☎83/341-2929; ❹), one of Campina Grande's luxury hotels, though hardly special. Out of the centre, the comfortable *Hotel Village*, Rua Otacílio Nepomuceno 1285 (☎83/310-8000; ❸), near the *rodoviária*, offers a pool and sauna, plus a bar and decent restaurant. Further out, in a beautiful location near a lake, the *Lago Dourado*, Açude Boqueiro, Município de Boqueirão (☎83/226-1686; ❸), is excellent value.

Two of the best **restaurants** in town, *Dona Nina*, Rua Augusto dos Anjos 183 and *Tábua de Carne* (☎83/341-1008) at Av. Manoel Tavares 1040, both specialize in regional cuisine. A meal at *Dona Nina* will run to around $10 a head, while *Tábua* is slightly cheaper.

Into the sertão

The BR-232 continues threading its way though the *sertão* to the town of **PATOS**: hot, flyblown, and looking like a spaghetti-western set with pick-ups instead of horses. If you need to stop, use the *Hotel JK*, Praça Getúlio Vargas (☎83/421-2811; ❷). Then it's on to **SOUSA**, an otherwise unremarkable *sertão* town five hours west of Campina Grande, with two hotels and one of the Northeast's more unusual sights, the **Vale dos Dinosauras**, "Dinosaur Valley", formed by the sedimentary basin of the Rio Peixe. At one time, difficult though it is to imagine in this searing semi-arid landscape, all was swamp and jungle. Various prehistoric reptiles left their footprints, preserved in stone, at several sites in the area around the town. The only way to get to them is by battered taxi over the dusty road. The nearest site is called A Ilha, about 5km out of town, which will cost you around $15 in a taxi. Here the prehistoric tracks are striking. The beast clearly lumbered along the riverbed for a while and then turned off, and you can see a regular series of footprints the size of dinner plates, some with two claws visible at the front.

Juazeiro do Norte

The main centre of the deep *sertão* is 500km west of Campina Grande – actually in the south of Ceará state – where a series of hill ranges, higher ground blessed with regular rainfall, provides a welcome respite. Food crops can be grown here, and every available inch of land is used to grow fruit and vegetables, or graze cattle. Here there are two towns within a few kilometres of each other, Crato and **JUAZEIRO DO NORTE**, and it was in this area that one of the most famous episodes in the history of the Northeast took place (see box below). It is still the site of a massive annual pilgrimage.

The pilgrim route

If you want to do what the pilgrims do, the first stop is Padre Cícero's **tomb** in the church of **Nossa Senhora do Perpétuo Socorro**, to the left of the square. A small monument sits outside, always decorated with *ex votos*, tokens brought by those praying for help. Inside the plain church you'll see a constant stream of *romeiros* praying intensely and queueing to kiss the marble slab by the altar, which you might think is the grave but isn't: that is outside to the left, an unpretentious tomb covered in flowers and ribbons. The church is surrounded by souvenir shops, which specialize in the figurines of Padre Cícero with hat and walking stick that you can find all over the Northeast.

The next destination is the **statue** of Padre Cícero on the peak of the **Serra do Horto**, the hill that looks down on the town. The soft option is to take a taxi or bus for 3km along a road that winds up the hill – a route that can be walked if you want to see the fine views of the **valley of Cariri** unfold, with the town of Crato visible to the west. The other way is to follow the **pilgrim route**, a track from the town directly up the hill: it isn't signposted but people

Miracle at Juazeiro

In 1889 Juazeiro was no more than a tiny hamlet. There was nothing unusual about its young priest, **Padre Cícero Romão Batista**, until women in Juazeiro claimed the wine he gave them at Communion had turned to blood in their mouths. At first it was only people from Crato who came, and they were convinced by the women's sanctity and the evidence of their own eyes that Padre Cícero had indeed worked a miracle. As his fame grew, the deeply religious inhabitants of the *sertão* came to hear his sermons and have him bless them. Padre Cícero came to be seen as a living saint: miraculous cures were attributed to him, things he had touched and worn were treated as relics. The Catholic Church began a formal investigation of the alleged "miracle", sent him to Rome to testify to commissions of enquiry, rejected it, sent him back to Brazil and suspended him from the priesthood – but nothing could shake the conviction of the local people that he was a saint. Juazeiro mushroomed into a large town by *sertão* standards, as people flocked to make the pilgrimage, including legendary figures like the bandit chief Lampião.

By the end of his long life, Padre Cícero had become one of the most powerful figures in the Northeast. In 1913 his heavily armed followers caught the train to the state capital, Fortaleza, and forcibly deposed the governor, replacing him with somebody more to Padre Cícero's liking. But Padre Cícero was a deeply conservative man, who restrained his followers more often than not, deferred to the Church, and remained seemingly more preoccupied with the next world than with this. When his more revolutionary followers tried to set up a religious community nearby at Caldeirão, he didn't deter the authorities from using the air force against them, in one of the first recorded uses of aerial bombs on civilians. When he finally died, in 1934, his body had to be displayed strapped to a door from the first floor of his house, before the thousands thronging the streets would believe he was dead. Ever since, pilgrims have come to Juazeiro to pay homage, especially for the anniversary of his death on July 20; an enormous white statue of the priest looks out from a hillside over the town he created.

will willingly direct you to it if you ask for *a picada dos romeiros* or *a Via Sacra*. It's a brisk hour to the top, and at several points the pilgrims have cut steps. Thousands walk the trail on July 20, "paying the promise", that is, performing penances for help received: a few hardy souls make the journey on their knees.

Once on top, the main attractions are not so much the statue – 27m high but hardly a masterpiece – as the panoramic views and the **chapel** and **museum of ex votos** next to it. Room after room is piled high with stacks of offerings from the grateful thousands for whom Padre Cícero interceded over the decades: countless artificial limbs, wooden models of body parts, photos of disasters escaped and crashes survived, even football jerseys from victorious players, including one from Brazil's winning 1970 World Cup team. As a demonstration of the hold that religion has on the daily lives of millions of *nordestinos*, only the *ex votos* at the church of Bonfim in Salvador rival it (see p.260).

The pilgrim's route finishes up at Padre Cícero's **house**, signposted from the church where he is buried, and now a cross between a museum and a shrine. It's a simple dwelling, with large rooms, a garden and glass cases displaying everything anybody could find that was even remotely connected to the great man: his glasses, underwear, hats, typewriter, bed linen, even the bed he died in.

The last act of pilgrimage is to be **photographed** to prove to the folks back home that you've made the trip. This ensures a steady flow of work for the many photographers clustered around the last church on the way to the hill, the **Igreja Matriz de Nossa Senhora das Dores**. They all have a series of props to help you pose: life-size statues of Padre Cícero, dozens of hats, toy elephants and so forth, and although the snap takes two or three hours to develop it comes ready-mounted in a mini-viewer, far more durable than a photo proper – the ideal souvenir.

Practicalities

When booking a ticket to Juazeiro make sure you specify Juazeiro do Norte, or you run the risk of ending up in Juazeiro in Bahia, several hundred kilometres south. The **rodoviária** is a couple of kilometres out of the town, which is smaller than its fame suggests. There is one central square where you'll find the best and most expensive **hotel**, the *Panorama* (☎88/512-3100, ☎512-3110; ❸), but finding somewhere to stay is the least of your worries in a town geared to putting up pilgrims: there are small hotels and *dormitórios* everywhere. Among these, the *Hotel Municipal* on Praça Padre Cícero (❷), is a good budget option.

There are two main places **to eat**: the *Restó Jardim*, in Lagoa Seca at Av. Leão Sampaio 5460 (11am–3pm & 6pm–midnight, closed Mon), serves a wide variety of regional and international dishes, while the pricier *Restaurante O Capote*, Rua José Barbosa dos Santos 83 (daily 11am–midnight), specializes in quality local cuisine.

Leaving town, seats fill up fast on the daily buses to João Pessoa, Recife and Fortaleza, so if you're staying overnight book a ticket when you arrive. Alternatively, it is usually possible to get a seat on one of the **pilgrim buses** parked around town; their drivers sell seats for the same price as on the regular bus, and busloads come from all the major cities, so just pick a bus going your way.

Rio Grande do Norte

Until the late 1980s, the small state of **Rio Grande do Norte** and its capital, **Natal**, were sleepy, conservative backwaters rarely visited by tourists. It's still true to say that there's little of historical interest among Natal's modern hotels and office buildings, and the interior is poor and thinly populated, the only place of any size being the town of **Mossoró**. But two things have transformed Rio Grande do Norte into one of the Northeast's biggest tourist centres: **beaches** and **buggies**. The beaches were always there, but the sometimes hair-raising buggy rides for which the state is famous have taken off only in the past fifteen years.

One big difference between Rio Grande do Norte and the states to the south is in its **landscape**, for this is where the Northeastern sugar belt finally peters out, drastically changing both history and landscape. The region is not without income; it supplies petroleum oil directly to several major factories and is also a major exporter of fruit. However, **north of Natal**, the *sertão* drives down practically to the coast, and the idyllic palm-fringed beaches give way to something wilder as the coastline changes character, massive sand dunes replacing the flat beaches and palm trees. The further north you go, the less fertile the land becomes and the flatter the *sertão*, given over largely to scrawny cattle scratching a living along with the people. The black Brazilian population shrinks with the sugar zone, and in Rio Grande do Norte dwindles to almost nothing.

Natal

NATAL is a medium-sized city of about 600,000 people, built on the banks of the Rio Potengi, and founded sixty years later than planned, after the Potiguar Indians stifled the first Portuguese landing on the coast in 1538. They continued to hold the invaders off until 1598, when the Portuguese built the star-shaped fort at the mouth of the river – the city's most enduring landmark. Natal is at the heart of one of the most spectacular strings of beaches in the Northeast: in fact, given that you could rent a beach buggy in Genipabu, just north of Natal, and drive along 250km of dunes uninterrupted until Areia Branca, practically on the border with Ceará, Natal is at one end of what amounts to a single enormous beach.

Stranded at the eastern tip of the Northeast, away from the main international tourist routes, and with little industry to provide employment, Natal has lately been developing tourist facilities with the desperation of a place with few other economic options. It's become a popular destination for Brazilian holiday-makers, lured by the sun and sand rather than the city itself, which is mostly modern and has a sloppily developed seafront: you will look in vain for the colonial elegance of João Pessoa or Olinda. But the glorious beaches do compensate, and amid the development and hotels there are some good nightspots and *dancetarias*.

Arrival, city transport and information

Natal's **airport**, Augusto Severo, is about 15km south of the centre on the BR-101 highway; a taxi to the centre will cost you about $10, or you can catch the bus marked "Parnamirim–Natal". Taxis from the airport to Ponta Negra (see p.350) cost around $12. The **rodoviária** is also a long way out from the centre, at Av. Capitão Mor-Gouveia 1237 in the suburb of Cidade de Esperança (☎84/205-4377), but you can get a local bus into town at the bus stop on the other side of the road, opposite the *rodoviária* entrance. Most of these buses from across the road pass through the centre: those marked "Av. Rio Branco", "Cidade Alta" and "Ribeira" are the most common. Taxis from the *rodoviária* into the centre are also plentiful and should cost around $8.

Natal's main thoroughfare is the **Avenida Rio Branco**, which runs past the oldest part of the city, **Cidade Alta**, and terminates just to the right of a scruffy square, Praça Augusto Severo, site of the useful local bus station. The main post office is on block 5 of Avenida Rio Branco, with the Banco do Brasil next door. Cutting across the *avenida* is Rua João Pessoa, graced at its western end by the city's old cathedral. East along João Pessoa, you'll come to the small **Praça Padre João Maria**, which is surrounded by some of the finest and most colourful old mansions in Natal, and which most days hosts a small but interesting *artesanato* market.

From Cidade Alta, roads descend straight to the **city beaches** of Praia do Forte, Praia do Meio and Praia dos Artistas, and the coastal road to the **southern beaches**. The most important of these is Ponta Negra, at 10km away just far enough from the city centre to have survived massive development. **Beaches to the north** of the city are generally less crowded and even more beautiful, but harder to get to. Just out of the centre are the quiet and pleasant grid-pattern suburbs of **Petrópolis** and the incongruously named **Tirol**, after the birthplace of the Austrian planner who laid them out in the 1930s.

City transport

Natal's **bus system** is easy to master, and in a hot city with hills and scattered beaches it's worth spending a little time getting used to it. At the central **bus station** on Praça Augusto Severo, and from **Avenida Rio Branco**, you can get local buses to most of the places you might want to go to: all the buses to the southern beaches, like Areia Preta and Ponta Negra, can be caught from here or the seafront; buses marked "Via Costeira" head along the southern coastal road out to Ponta Negra. Several bus routes run from the centre to the *rodoviária*, taking at least half an hour and often longer because of their circuitous routes; buses marked "Cidade de Esperança" are the most direct. **Minibuses**, acting as collective taxis, also compete with buses, stopping at all corners en route.

Information

There are **tourist information** posts at the *rodoviária* (daily 7am–11pm; ☎84/205-1000); both have good free maps of the city and can organize accommodation for you. The main tourist information facility is at the **Centro de Turismo** (Mon–Fri 7am–11pm; ☎84/211-6149) in the old prison, perched on top of a hill at Rua Aderbal de Figueiredo 980 in Petrópolis, where there are beautiful views of the beaches and city, the lovely café *Marenosso* and scores of quality arts and crafts, with an emphasis on cotton products. On the first floor there's also an interesting Galeria de Arte Antigua e Contemporanea, filled with ceramics, weavings, paintings and antiques. There is also a tourist information booth (Mon–Sat 8am–6pm; ☎84/202-5652) on Avenida Presidente Café Filho, at Praia dos Artistas, though it's not always functioning. Alternatively, you can ring the **tourist hotline** (☎84/219-4226) where you may find someone who speaks English. For information on events and films, your best bet is the *Fim de Semana* section of Friday's *Tribuna do Norte* newspaper.

If you want to take a **tour** to Fernando de Noronha (see p.329), the Reis Magos Viagens e Turismo, at Avenida Sen. Salgado Filho 1799 (☎84/206-5888, ⓕ296-6628) has information on this amazing archipelago and organizes trips there, too.

Accommodation

Hotels are plentiful in both the city centre and the beach areas. A good alternative option is to stay at one of the beaches outside the city, like Ponta Negra to the south (see p.350) or Redinha and Genipabu to the north (see p.351).

The city centre

Cidade do Sol Hotel e Albergue Av. Duque de Caxias 190 ☎84/211-3233. This youth hostel near the central bus station has decent rooms and a nice garden at the back. $10 a night per person.
Hotel Natal Av. Rio Branco 740, Cidade Alta ☎84/222-2792, ⓕ222-0232. Basic but clean, with a choice of rooms with either fan or air-conditioning. Very cheap for a central hotel. ❶
Hotel São Paulo Av. Rio Branco 697 ☎84/211-4485. Refurbished budget hotel with good breakfasts. The entrance is on Rua General Osório. ❷
Hotel Sol Rua Heitor Carilho 107 ☎84/221-1157. Good-value hotel in the older part of the upper city, with its own restaurant and smallish but pleasant rooms with private baths. ❸
Natal Center Hotel Rua Santo Antônio 665 ☎84/221-2355, ⓦwww.natalcenterhotel.com.br. One of the smartest options in the old city centre, yet surprisingly good value and welcoming. Amenities include a good restaurant, swimming pool, fitness suite and sauna. ❸

The beaches

Albergue de Juventude Ladeira do Sol Rua Valentim de Almeida 8, Praia dos Artistas ☎84/202-1699. A pleasant youth hostel offering private or shared rooms. $10 a night per person.
Bruma Hotel Av. Pres. Café Filho 1176, Praia dos Artistas ☎84/211-4947. This hotel overlooks the beach and is worth staying in mainly for the beautifully designed building. ❹
Hotel Pousada Marina Av. Pte. Café Filho 860, Praia do Meio ☎84/202-3223. Right on the seafront near the Praia das Artistas, this place

mainly attracts downmarket Brazilian business travellers, with spartan but reasonably comfortable rooms and private baths. ❷
Hotel Vila do Mar Via Costeira 4233 ☎84/211-6000. Luxury hotel close to the sea with all the facilities you'd expect, including a pool and tennis courts. ❼
Pousada Abyara Av. Pte. Café Filho 1174 ☎84/611-1042 or 880-60993. Conveniently located by Praia das Artistas, this very friendly place is clean and well run, with pleasant rooms, some of which have views and most have private baths. Rooms at front (with the views) cost more than the rest. ❷
Pousada das Dunas Rua João XXIII 601 ☎84/202-1820. A warm, family-run *pousada* just a bus ride from the Praia dos Artistas in the Mãe Luiza district; the basic rooms are spotless and comfortable. ❷
Pousada do Forte Av. Pres. Café Filho 786, Praia do Meio ☎84/211-6080. Large, well-kept rooms with all mod cons on the beachside opposite the statue of Iemanjá. ❹
Pousada Ponta do Morcego Rua Valentim de Almeida 10, Praia dos Artistas ☎84/202-2367. An extremely inexpensive, no-frills option, right next to the youth hostel. ❶
Praia Center Hotel Rua Fabrico Pedrosa 45, Petropolis ☎84/202-4407. A fairly nice concrete hotel, very close to the Praia das Artistas. Rooms are quite basic, but have TVs and private bathrooms, while the attractive breakfast patio has views over the ocean and the small hotel pool. ❺

The City

For a city that was founded nearly four centuries ago there is surprisingly little of historical interest in Natal itself, apart from the distinctive, whitewashed star of the **Forte dos Reis Magos** (daily 8am–4.45pm), dominating the river entrance. Like most of Brazil's colonial forts it looks very vulnerable, directly

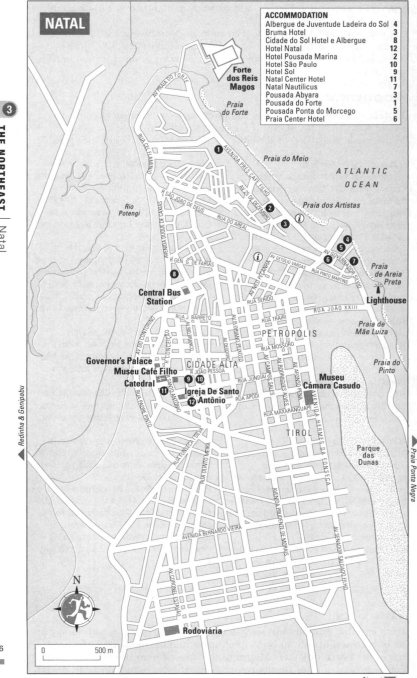

NATAL

ACCOMMODATION
Albergue de Juventude Ladeira do Sol	4
Bruma Hotel	3
Cidade do Sol Hotel e Albergue	8
Hotel Natal	12
Hotel Pousada Marina	2
Hotel São Paulo	10
Hotel Sol	9
Natal Center Hotel	11
Natal Nautilicus	7
Pousada Abyara	3
Pousada do Forte	1
Pousada Ponta do Morcego	5
Praia Center Hotel	6

Forte
dos Reis
Magos

Praia
do Forte

Praia do Meio

ATLANTIC
OCEAN

Rio
Potengi

Praia dos Artistas

Praia
de Areia
Preta

Lighthouse

Central Bus
Station

PETRÓPOLIS

Praia de
Mãe Luiza

Praia do
Pinto

Governor's Palace
Museu Café Filho
Catedral

CIDADE ALTA

Igreja De Santo
Antônio

Museu
Câmara Casudo

TIROL

Parque
das
Dunas

◄ Redinha & Genipabu

Praia Ponta Negra ►

Rodoviária

N

0   500 m

Airport ▼

overlooked by the hill behind it and with thick, surprisingly low walls. Although there is not much to see apart from a couple of token museums, the city is interesting to wander around.

The oldest part of the city is formed by the closely packed streets and small squares of Cidade Alta, but the street plan itself is one of the only things that remains from colonial times. Instead, the architecture that has survived the modern thrust for development is clustered around the administrative heart of the city, **Praça Sete de Setembro**, which is dominated by the **governor's palace**, built in tropical Victorian style in 1873. Also in the square is the **Espaço Cultural** (Mon–Fri 8am–6pm; free), with changing shows of mainly local artists, and the restored **Teatro Alberto Maranhão**, a Neoclassical structure built in 1898. In the neighbouring Praça Albuquerque, you'll find the **Instituto Histórico e Geográfico** (Mon-Fri 8am–noon & 2–5pm; free), a quaint nineteenth-century edifice housing period furniture and archives relating to the region's history, while the old **Catedral** next door (daily 4.30–6pm) was built in 1862 but is unexceptional for all that. Smaller, and rather more interesting, is the **Igreja de Santo Antônio** (Mon–Fri 8–11.30am & 2–5.30pm, Sat 8–11.30am) nearby at Rua Santo Antônio 683, a Baroque church known as the Igreja do Galo, after the eighteenth-century bronze cock crowing on top of its Moorish tower; inside you'll find a well-respected **museum of religious art** (Mon–Sat 1–6pm).

Just off Praça Sete de Setembro is the most interesting museum in a city largely bereft of them, the **Museu Café Filho** (Mon–Fri 8am–5pm, Sat 8–10am), dedicated to the only *rio grandense* to become president of Brazil – a corrupt and incompetent paternalist, despite the attempts by the museum to present him as a statesman. But he had the good taste to live in a fine two-storey mansion, at Rua da Conceição 630, which is worth seeing – more than can be said for the yellowing papers and heavy furniture of the long-dead president. Also worth a visit is the **Museu Câmara Casudo**, at Av. Hermes da Fonseca 1398, in Tirol (Tues–Fri 8–11am & 2–5pm; $1), which is dedicated to local ecology, history and geology. Sponsored heavily by Petrobrás, the museum contains a large flashy exhibit on oil drilling, but nevertheless, it's well thought out and presented, with dinosaur fossils, a *jangada* and a range of other interesting exhibits.

The beaches

What Natal lacks in attractions for the culturally minded, it makes up for in facilities for the beach bum. There are fine **beaches** right inside the city, beginning at the fort where arcs of sand sweep along the bay to the headland and **Mãe Luiza lighthouse**, a useful point to take bearings from. Buses marked "Mãe Luiza" take you from the seafront to the foot of the hill crowned by the lighthouse, which you can walk up, but you will be besieged by children offering guided tours. From the top there is a magnificent view of the **Praia do Meio**, the beach that stretches from the fort to the headland of the Ladeira do Sol, and the **Praia da Areia Preta**, curving between the headland and the lighthouse. Technically the Praia do Meio is composed of three beaches: the small Praia do Forte next to the fort, the Praia do Meio and the **Praia dos Artistas**. Here, too, you'll find dune buggies lined up looking for customers. All the beaches are lined with stalls serving the usual array of cold drinks and food, and numerous hotels and bars are strung along the inland side of the seafront, which gets lively on weekend evenings.

On the other side of the lighthouse is another enormous beach, **Praia de Mãe Luiza**, accessible along the tourist development highway known as the

Beach buggies

Going to Natal without riding a **beach buggy** is a bit like going to Ireland and not drinking Guinness – you may or may not enjoy it, but you might as well try it seeing as you're there. Buggies have become a way of life in Natal, providing employment for the young drivers or *bugeiros* who race around the city and its beaches in their noisy, low-slung vehicles. After a period of explosive, unregulated growth during which unqualified cowboy *bugeiros* risked their and their passengers' necks, the buggy industry has settled down a little bit, though you should still check that your driver has **accreditation** and **insurance** – most of them have.

There are two basic kinds of buggy rides. One possibility is to go on a **day** or **half-day trip**, which involves riding either north or south down the coast, mainly along the beaches. Many firms offer a full day's outing with the *litoral norte* in the morning and the *litoral sul* in the afternoon, or vice versa. The *bugeiro* will perform a few stunts along the way, surfing the sand dunes, but it's mainly an opportunity to explore the beautiful coastline around Natal. A day-trip costs about $100 for four people.

However, the real thrills and spills are to be found on specific beaches, especially at **Genipabu** to the north of Natal. Here you pay by the ride or by the hour for fair-ground-type stuff, with the *bugeiros* making full use of the spectacular sand dunes to push your heart through your mouth. These rides are not cheap, and you may find yourself paying over $40 for an hour's entertainment.

Conditions inside the buggies are cramped. Most *bugeiros* will try and fit three or four people in on each trip, with two people sitting outside at the back hanging on to a metal bar. You'll need plenty of **sun protection** and an extremely tight-fitting hat. However, there's no doubt that it's an exhilarating business, with the wind whipping through your hair as you bounce around the sand dunes.

Most hotels have deals with buggy companies, and you'll find yourself besieged by offers of rides wherever you are in Natal. Most rides cost between $10 and $20 per person for a day's outing. If you want to deal with the **companies** directly, try Alfatur Passeio de Buggy (⊕84/219-5542) at Av. Eng. Roberto Freire 153, Ponta Negra Buggy (⊕84/236-2521), Caninde (⊕84/982-2118) or Alto Astral (⊕84/219-2208) – all in Ponta Negra.

Via Costeira, which takes you to Ponta Negra, 10km away (see p.350). Although large, the Praia de Mãe Luiza is rarely used, much of it rocky and much of the remainder taken up by brand-new concrete developments.

Keep in mind that the beaches near the centre of town should be treated with respect: the combination of a shelving beach and rollers roaring in from the Atlantic often makes the surf dangerous, and a few tourists are drowned every year.

Eating, drinking and nightlife

Restaurants are one of Natal's strongest points, and the regional cuisine has, if anything, been strengthened by the influx of Brazilian tourists, as many see eating Northeastern food as an important part of their holiday.

Bar do Cação on the seafront near the Forte dos Reis Magos. Choose from a selection of good oyster and shellfish dishes.
Carne de Sol Benigna Lira Rua Dr José Augusto Bezerra de Menezes 9, Praia dos Artistas ⊕84/202-3914. The speciality of this moderately priced restaurant is sun-dried meat, as good as you'll find anywhere in Brazil.

Casa da Mãe Rua Pedro Afonso 230, Petrópolis. Notable for the *galinha cabidela* – chicken stewed in a sauce enriched by its own blood and giblets. The giblets are sieved out before serving, and it's delicious and inexpensive.
Chaplin Av. Presidente Café Filho 27 ⊕84/211-7457. This somewhat overpriced international restaurant and bar on the Praia dos Artistas has a

good atmosphere at weekends.

O Crustáceo Rua Apodi 414 ☎84/222-1122. Excellent, inexpensive seafood in unpretentious surroundings, right in the city centre.

Macrobiótica Rua Princesa Isabel 528 ☎84/222-6765. As the name suggests, a macrobiotic restaurant, in the centre of Natal. Mon–Sat 11am–2pm.

Restaurante Chines Rua Ulisses Caldas 144. Simple Chinese and Brazilian food at very reasonable prices and accompanied by excellent service. Close to the old city centre and Praça Sete de Setembro.

Saborosa Av. Campos Sales 609, Petrópolis ☎84/222-7338. Inexpensive restaurant serving an excellent range of regional food by the kilo.

Samó Av. Miguel de Castro 1329, Lagoa Nova ☎84/234-3666. A very appealing seafood restaurant, with delicious lobsters and some French cuisine too.

Nightlife

Most of Natal's nocturnal action takes place on or around the beaches rather than in the centre. One good spot to head for is **Praia dos Artistas**, the stretch of beach about halfway between the fort and the headland, which hosts plenty of live music at night, especially on weekends. *Chaplin Night and Shopping* presents mainly *forró* on Fridays and Saturdays while the *Balada Club* next door plays a wider variety of sounds. A few hundred yards up the beach, there's the *Casa do Pagade*, a club inside the *Bar and Restaurant Don Pedro*, and host to plenty of good *forró* and *pagode* at weekends after 9pm.

If all you want to do is sip a *caipirinha* and watch the sun set, a good place is the *Canto do Mangue* on the banks of the Rio Potengi: it's a taxi ride away near the municipal fish market in the *bairro* of **Ribeira**, where Rua Coronel Flaminio runs into Rua São João. It's also one of the best places to eat fish in the city: a speciality is fresh fish fried and served in tapioca with coconut sauce (*peixe ao molho de tapioca*). Be warned, however, that Ribeira can be a fairly rough neighbourhood, especially at night, so it's best to take a taxi there and back.

For good **live music** head for *Forró com Turista*, in the Centro de Turismo, Rua Aderbal de Figueiredo 980, Petrópolis (☎84/211-6218; Fri from 10pm). The *Kapital Eurodance*, at Praia do Meio, has a varying programme throughout the week, ending in excellent live *pagode* on Sunday nights.

Listings

Airlines Transbrasil, Av. Deodoro 429 ☎84/221-1805/6; TAM, Rua Seridó 746 ☎84/643-1624 or 202-3385; Varig, Rua Mossoró 598 ☎84644-1252 or 211-4453; VASP, Rua João Pessoa 429, Centro ☎84/644-1137 or 211-4453.

Banks and exchange There's a branch of Banco do Brasil (with ATMs) at Av. Rio Branco 510, Cidade Alta.

Car hire Avis ☎84/644-2500; Dudu ☎84/211-7000; Hertz ☎84/207-3399; Localiza (☎84/206-5296).

Post office The main branches are at Rua Princesa Isabel 711 and Av. Rio Branco 538, both in Centro.

Shopping The two best shopping centres are the Praia Shopping Centre, Av. Eng. Roberto Freire 8790, near Ponta Negra, and Natal Shopping, at Av. Sen. Salgado Filho 2234 in the Candelária district.

Taxis Radio Taxi ☎84/221-5666 and Hotel Taxi ☎84/213-6800.

Telephones TELERN is at Rua Princesa Isabel 687, Centro.

Travel and tour companies Casablanca Turismo (office at airport ☎85/466-6000) books mainly flight and bus tickets but can arrange upmarket tours in the region or elsewhere in Brazil; Manary Ecoturs, based at the *Manary Hotel* in Ponta Negra (☎84/219-2900, ⊛www.manary.com.br), operate minibus trips into the *sertão* to visit local communities, archeological sites and cave paintings; La Palma Spedizione (☎84/231-6616 or 982-9944) run tours up and down the *sertão*; and Aventura Expedições & Turismo (☎84/206-4949 or 982-1895, ⊛www .aventuraturismo.com.br) specialize in tours of the coast between Natal and Fortaleza.

South of Natal

Talking of things to do and places to go around Natal boils down to talking about **beaches**. The beach *par excellence* – and the easiest southern beach to get to from Natal – is **Ponta Negra**, 10km out of town along the Via Costeira, linked by regular buses from the local bus station that you can also catch from the seafront. **Further south**, the beaches get less crowded, but access can be difficult.

Ponta Negra

Following close on the heels of Bahia's Morro de São Paulo, **PONTA NEGRA** is one of the finest beaches in the Northeast. Running along a sweeping bay under steep sandy cliffs, the beach is magnificent, sheltered from Atlantic rollers, though still good for surfing. It's jam-packed with places to stay and often quite crowded; bars and restaurants range from trendy beach shacks to serious seafood restaurants, and there's a constant party atmosphere.

On a relatively quiet part of the beach, just a few hundred metres from the main action, there's the *Manary Praia Hotel*, Rua Francisco Gurgel 9067 (T & F 84/219-2900, W www.digi.com.br/manary; ❹), which has some **rooms** with nice hammock balconies looking over the ocean and a large beach terrace. Also right on the beach are the friendly *Blue Beach Pousada*, Av. Beira Mar 229 (T 84/641-1046, W www.bluebeach-inn.com.br; ❷), actually a hostel with its own beach café and with front rooms priced slightly more for their sea views; and the *Visual Praia Hotel*, Rua Francisco Gurgel 9184 (T 084/646-4646, F 646-4647, W www.visualpraiahotel.com.br; ❺), very comfortable and large, with a pool and a big terrace plus children's play area. The *Hotel Continental Plaza* (T 84/219-3346; ❹) is a reasonably priced and comfortable mid-range option right at the busy part of Ponta Negra beach, where the road comes down to the beach. One of the cheapest and most basic options, also very busy, is the *Hotel Costa Brasil* next door at no. 36 (T 84/236-2013; ❷). In town, the newly built *Pousada America do Sol*, Rua Erivan França 35 (T 84/219-2245, W www.pousadaamericadosol.com.br; ❸) has very comfortable rooms and great service for the price; it runs a reliable travel agency, too, organizing buggy rides, boat trips and excursions as far afield as Fernando de Noronha. If you're on a tight budget, there's the youth hostel, the appealing *Albergue da Juventude Lua Cheia* 500 (T 84/236-3696, F 236-4747, W www.luacheia.com.br; from \$10 a person), just 200m from the beach; it also has its own bar and live music Tuesday to Sunday nights from 10pm.

There are several good **places to eat**: *Don Vincenzo* serves good pasta and seafood on a pleasant veranda overlooking the beach next to the large, pink *Ingá Praia Hotel*. Close by, at Rua Erivan França 36, the *Bar Rústico* is a hectic 24-hour bar and restaurant, catering mainly to the surfing crowd. Perhaps the best of the places on the beachfront is the *Bar Pirata*, towards the southern end, just past the *jangada* boats; this bar-restaurant plays good rock and reggae music most of the time and has live *pagode* on Saturday nights. The *Churrascaria Tererê*, Estrada de Pirangi 2316, Rota do Sol (T 84/219-4081), offers excellent *gaucho*-influenced *rodízio de carne*, giving you the chance to try a wide range of beef cuts.

A ten-minute taxi ride from Ponta Negra, the *Guinza Blue*, Via Costeira 4 (T 84/219-3765), has good **live music** and dancing most weekends. For *forró*, head for the *Forró da Quartuda*, Estrada de Ponta Negra, Super Park (T 84/234-1000; Wed from 10pm).

South of Ponta Negra

The beaches **south of Ponta Negra** are more remote and consequently less crowded. The only problem is getting to them without a car, as there are usually only one or two buses a day to most of the villages from Natal's bus station. Check the times with the tourist office, but they usually leave early in the morning and you may not be able to get back to Natal the same day. The villages normally have a *pousada* or two, however, and it is easy to come to an arrangement about stringing up hammocks in bars and houses. An alternative way of reaching the beaches is to take a **bus** along the main BR-101 highway to Recife from the *rodoviária*, and get off at Nízia Floresta, from where there are pick-ups, trucks and a local bus service along the dirt road to the coastal fishing villages and beaches of **BÚZIOS** and **BARRA DE TABATINGA**, 20km and 25km from Natal.

More direct is to take the bus from the Natal Rodoviária to **PIRANGI DO NORTE**, 30km out of town. Apart from the beach, the village's other famous attraction is the biggest **caju tree** in the world, centuries old and with branches that have spread and put down new roots. Although Brazilians know *caju* as a fruit, its seeds, once roasted, become the familiar cashew nut. It's difficult to believe this enormous (over 7000 square metres) expanse of green leaves and boughs could be a single tree; it looks more like a forest. It still bears over a ton of fruit annually, so it's not surprising that Pirangi is known for its *caju*-flavoured rum.

To get away from people, you have to travel further south to the stunning **Praia da Pipa**, 80km away, and the **Praia Sagi**, which virtually lies on the border with Paraíba state some 120km from Natal. The latter is particularly inaccessible and can only be approached by four-wheel-drive vehicles or on foot, but the result is that it is virtually untouched. The **Praia da Pipa** ("Kite Beach"), on the other hand, is set in idyllic surroundings with dolphins regularly swimming near the beach, and sports a decent selection of facilities: an increasing number of *pousadas* are springing up all over the place and there are also well-established bars like *Yahoo!* where all the nightlife takes place. Once again access is only realistically possible by car or on foot, although there are some irregular local bus services.

North of Natal

Most of the recent hotel-building and development has been funnelled south of Natal by the building of the Via Costeira, which makes the **northern beaches** an attractive option. The two main places to head for are Redinha and Genipabu.

REDINHA, 16km from Natal, is a small fishing village facing the city on the northern mouth of the Rio Potengi, and marks the southern end of the enormous beach that effectively makes up the state's northern coastline. The beaches are notable for their huge shifting **sand dunes**, many metres high, which cluster especially thickly to tower over Genipabu. Redinha itself (hourly buses from the local bus station in Natal) is surprisingly undeveloped for somewhere so close to the city, retaining the air of a simple fishing village, with a small chapel and beachside stalls that fry the freshly caught fish and chill the beer.

There are regular buses to **GENIPABU** leaving from Natal's local bus station, every two hours from Monday to Saturday and hourly on Sunday.

Genipabu is still a fishing village, but these days depends more on tourism for its income. The massive dunes are spectacular and great fun to run down: the sand is so fine it often looks like it came from an egg-timer. A favourite local pastime is to roar up and down them in **beach buggies** (see box p.348). Good excursions along the dunes are to the mineral-water spring at Pitangui, and the lovely beach of Jacumã. There are plenty of *pousadas* in Genipabu, so accommodation is no problem. However, the beach stalls operate a cartel and are very expensive for what they offer; the restaurant, *O Pedro*, just to the side, compares very favourably for similar prices and serves a wide range of seafood.

West towards Ceará

The highway **west** to Fortaleza, capital of Ceará state, would be one of the most dramatic in the region if it followed the coast; sadly, though, the BR-304, a good-quality asphalt road, takes a more direct inland route and is pretty dull as a result. The **interior** of Rio Grande do Norte is flatter than the *sertão* of the states to the south, plains of scrubby *caatinga* and cacti only rarely broken up by hills or rocky escarpments. Even on a moving bus you can feel the heat, and you get some idea of why this is one of the poorest and most unforgiving areas in the Northeast. From Natal three daily **buses** make the 500-kilometre run to Fortaleza, taking around nine hours. It's a good stretch of road to do overnight: about the right length to get some sleep, and no spectacular scenery for you to regret missing.

Mossoró

The one place you might think of stopping off at before crossing into Ceará state is **MOSSORÓ**, in many ways an archetype of the *sertão* town in which so many of the inhabitants of the Northeastern interior live. Mossoró has a population of over 200,000 and is growing fast, although you wouldn't guess it from the centre, very much that of a small market town: market, square and a couple of ornate 1930s public buildings, with white plasterwork set off against walls of bright pink, looking for all the world like wedding cakes.

The Town

It's easy to get your bearings in Mossoró, despite the lack of town maps and tourist information. The main street is **Avenida Augusto Severo**, which runs down past the municipal market and local bus station to the two linked squares that are the hub of the city, **Praça Vigário Antônio Joaquim**, where the cathedral is, and **Praça da Independência**. To the left is the road leading to the old jail and town museum; straight on takes you to the Rio Apodi, where – over the bridge – is a small *artesanato* market.

The quickest way to get a flavour of Mossoró is by wandering around the **municipal market**. It gives you an instant handle on the social and economic fabric of the *sertão*, both from the goods on sale – dried meat, medicinal herbs and barks, slabs of salt – and the wiry, straw-hatted peasants and townspeople milling around. The brightly painted trucks and buses, most of which you wouldn't see outside a museum in the developed world, are the more remote villages' only link with Mossoró and, through it, to the outside world. On the fringes of the market simple stalls sell food and rum and iced *caldo de cana* (sugar-cane juice) to the shoppers, and small vendors spread their wares out on the pavement. Look for the *funilaria*, kerosene lamps and other simple household items made with great ingenuity from old tins.

However, the main places of interest in the city are connected with Mossoró's enduring claim to fame, a glorious moment in 1924 when the townspeople fought off a full-scale attack by the legendary bandit leader **Lampião** and his band. It's an event that's still celebrated every June 13 with Masses and re-enactments. To follow the Lampião trail, first stop is the **Igreja de Santo Antônio**, near the centre. In accordance with Northeastern form there was no question of a surprise assault when Lampião mounted his attack. He had announced his intention to hold the town to ransom well in advance and had taken landowners in the surrounding countryside hostage to show he meant business: an audacious thing to do, since even then Mossoró was the second city of Rio Grande do Norte. The townspeople decided to resist him, digging trenches in the main streets and fortifying public buildings. On June 13, 1924, Lampião attacked with a band of about fifty outlaws, or *cangaçeiros*, and there was fierce fighting, concentrating on the church, where the mayor, his family and retainers had barricaded themselves in. By late afternoon the bandits were driven off with several wounded, one dead, and one famous black outlaw, Jararaca, wounded and captured. Despite being a humiliating defeat for Lampião, the battle of Mossoró became one of the most famous events in his much celebrated life. On the church there's a plaque commemorating the event, and you can still see the walls and tower pockmarked with bullet holes, carefully preserved.

The next step is to make your way to the **Museu Histórico Municipal**, Praça Antônio Gomes 514 (Tues–Fri 8am–8pm, Sun 8–11am), housed in the oldest building in town, a solid late nineteenth-century structure that was once a jail: it's signposted from Praça Vigário Antônio Joaquim. It contains a remarkable collection of photographs and newspaper articles of the attack and its aftermath, together with the guns used, clothing taken from the bandits and maps of how the action developed, amongst other things. The most fascinating pieces are the powerful and eloquent photographs of the wounded **Jararaca**, kept in a cell in the very building that houses the museum. Jararaca was in jail for a day, treated by the town doctor, interviewed by the local paper, visited by town luminaries, constantly photographed by the town photographer, and then was taken out at dawn to the municipal cemetery, stabbed, thrown into a newly dug grave, and shot. Reading what he said that day, it's clear he knew his fate, but he expressed no fear or regret, only his determination to die like a man, which by all accounts he did. The final stop on the tour is a visit to his grave, in the **cemitério municipal** near the church. The grave isn't signposted, but anyone, except a priest, will point you in its direction, left of the single path as you enter. The final twist is that the outlaw got his own back in death, becoming a mythical figure and saint for the poor of the region, despite attempts by the Church and the municipal authorities to put a stop to it – hence the lack of a signpost and the fact there is no path to his grave. His grave is covered with flowers, candle stumps, *ex votos* and prayers written on scraps of paper, and regularly visited by suppliants. The best time to see this popular devotion in action is on December 13, when thousands flock to Mossoró from all over the interior of Rio Grande do Norte to celebrate the holy day of Santa Luzia, the city's patron saint.

Practicalities

Mossoró is 276km from Natal, about four hours' drive, and served by several buses a day. The *rodoviária* is on the edge of town, from where there are regular **local buses** into the centre; or it's about ten minutes by taxi. **Leaving**, you can get a bus to the *rodoviária* from the local bus station on the fringes of the municipal market.

The best **hotel**, the *Hotel Thermas*, Av. Lauro Monte 2001 (☎84/318-1200; ⑤), is a couple of kilometres out of town, built around some thermal pools. The others are simple and all in the centre of town: try the *Del Prata*, Avenida Augusto Severo, Rua Tiradentes 50 (☎84/321-3846; ❷), or the *Hotel Imperial*, Rua Santos Dumont 237 (☎& ⒻⒻ84/321-6351; ⑤). There's a pleasant **bar**, *O Sujeito*, built on the riverbank just by the *artesanato* market.

Ceará

Ceará, covering a vast area, but with less than nine million inhabitants, has long borne the brunt of the vagaries of the Northeastern climate. Droughts were recorded here as early as the seventeenth century. In the 1870s, as many as two million people may have died in a famine provoked by drought, and as recently as the early 1980s people were reduced to eating rats, while the population of Fortaleza grew by about a third as people fled drought in the interior.

Yet for all its problems Ceará has kept a strong sense of identity, making it a distinctive and rewarding state to visit. Its capital, **Fortaleza**, is the largest, most modern and cosmopolitan city in the Northeast after Recife and Salvador; the sum of its sky-scraping architecture is a futuristic cityscape. In stark contrast, the **sertão** is unforgiving to those who have to live in it, but in Ceará it rewards the traveller with some spectacular landscapes: as you travel west, the flat and rather dull plains of Rio Grande do Norte gradually give way to ranges of hills, culminating in the extreme west of the state in the highlands and lush cloud forest of the **Serra da Ibiapaba**, the only place in Brazil where you can stand in jungle and look down on desert. To the south there are the hills and fertile valleys of **Cariri**, with the pilgrim city of Juazeiro do Norte (see p.340). And the coastline boasts some of the wildest, most remote and beautiful **beaches** in Brazil.

Save for a few sheltered valleys with relatively reliable rainfall, sugar cane does not grow in Ceará and it never developed the plantation economy of other Northeastern states. Ceará was and remains **cattle** country, with the main roads and centres of population in the state following the route of the old cattle trails. As settlement by the Portuguese and serious economic development began over a century later than in the sugar-zone states, and only really got going in the last century, there are very few buildings that date back to colonial times – and, indeed, nothing colonial remains in Fortaleza.

In recent years, Ceará has developed a reputation as one of the best-governed states in Brazil. Successive governors from the **PSDB**, the Social Democratic Party of President Fernando Henrique Cardoso, have done much to reduce poverty and disease through imaginative health and education schemes. For the visitor, all this gives Ceará the feeling of an up-and-coming place where things are changing fast both economically and culturally.

Fortaleza

FORTALEZA is a sprawling city of over two million inhabitants, the centre literally bristling with offices and apartment blocks. It has, for well over a century, been the major commercial centre of the northern half of the Northeast. More recently it has poured resources into expanding its tourist trade, lining the fine city beaches with gleaming luxury hotels and developing the city centre. Taken together, this means that little trace remains of the city's eventful **early history**, the clue to which is in its name: Fortaleza means "fortress". The first Portuguese settlers arrived in 1603 and were defeated initially by the Indians, who killed and ate the first bishop (a distinction the city shares with Belém), and then by the Dutch, who drove the Portuguese out of the area in 1637 and built the Forte Schoonenborch. In fact the Portuguese were restricted to precarious coastal settlements until well into the eighteenth century, when the Indians were finally overwhelmed by the determined blazing of cattle trails into the interior. Another fort – the Fortaleza de Nossa Senhora da Assunção – was built by the Portuguese in 1816 on the site of the earlier Dutch one.

It was in Fortaleza that the independence movement in northern Brazil was organized, and it was one of the few places where the Portuguese actually made a fight of it, massacring the local patriots in 1824 before being massacred themselves a few months later. The city did well in the **nineteenth century**, as the port city of a hinterland where ranching was expanding rapidly. For decades, though, one of the city's most important exports was the people of the state: shipping lines transported *flagelados* wholesale from Fortaleza during drought years to the rubber zones of the Amazon and the cities of southern Brazil. These days, Fortaleza has something of the same atmosphere as Rio, especially when it comes to the good things in life like food, beaches and fun. It's not a beautiful city as such, though the beaches and weather make up for that. But it certainly has a safe, friendly and relaxed atmosphere; moreover, the nightlife is superb.

Arrival, city transport and information

The **rodoviária** and **airport** are some way from the centre in the southern suburb of Fátima, but getting into town is easy thanks to the comfortable *frescão* service operated by the Top Bus company ($3). The buses will stop to let you off – or can be flagged down – wherever you want along their circular route, which takes in both the airport and the *rodoviária* before winding its way through the crowded city centre to the beach areas; it's supposed to run throughout the night, but the service is less frequent then, and you should check with the tourist office if you're relying on it to catch an early-morning bus or plane. If there are more than two of you, it might be cheaper to take a taxi, which costs around $8 to the airport from most places in the city.

Fortaleza also has plenty of **local buses**. Useful routes that take you out to the main beach areas and back to the city centre are those marked "Grande Circular", "Caça e Pesca", "Mucuripe" and "P. Futuro". Two buses, the "Circular 1" and "Circular 2", run services that cover the outskirts and central part of Fortaleza respectively. The local bus station is located in the old city centre, in the square in front of the old railway station. There are loads of taxis, too, which are essential for getting around late at night. You may also choose to walk around Fortaleza quite a lot: the city is heavily policed and feels much safer than many other Brazilian cities, though the usual basic precautions are still in order.

Information and practicalities

Fortaleza is geared towards catering for visitors. The **main information office** of the state tourist office, SETUR (Mon–Sat 8am–6pm, Sun 8am–noon; ☎85/488-7411 or 212-3566), is in the Centro de Turismo in the centre, at Rua Senador Pompeu 350, and should be your first port of call; the staff know their stuff, and are especially good on the complicated bus journeys that are often necessary to get to the out-of-town beaches. The **tourist information posts** are also friendly and efficient; they give out free city maps, and if you're planning to travel in the state outside Fortaleza you should stock up on the relevant information here. There are information posts at the airport (☎85/477-1667; 24hrs) and at the *rodoviária* (daily 6am–6pm; ☎85/256-4080). The best maps of Fortaleza are usually to be obtained from the municipal tourist organization, **FORTUR**, who have an information post (daily 8am–5pm; ☎85/252-1444) on Praça do Ferreira in the centre.

You can **change money** at numerous places down on the beach, such as the blue kiosk in the shadow of the *Imperial Othon Palace Hotel*, and, in the city centre, at Tropical Viagens, Rua Barão do Rio Branco 1233 (Mon–Fri 9am–5pm, Sat 8am–noon).

Accommodation

The budget hotels, as ever, tend to be in the **centre**, which hums with activity during the day but empties at night, and the more expensive ones are generally out by the **beaches**, notably Iracema and Meireles. But this is not a hard-and-fast rule; there are literally hundreds of hotels of all shapes and sizes in the city, including luxury hotels in the centre and cheap ones in the beach areas, although very few bargains are to be had on the seafront itself. You should remember that Fortaleza can get very hot, and either air-conditioning or a fan is essential.

The city centre

Hotel Passeio Rua Dr João Moreira 221 ☎85/226-9640, ☎253-6165. Well-run hotel, located opposite the pleasant Praça dos Mártires, just a block from the Centro de Turismo. A bit musty and at the lower end of the price range, with rooms cooled by ventilator fans or air-conditioning. ❷

Hotel Sol Rua Barão do Rio Branco 829 ☎85/211-9166, ☎262-1021. A classy option with airy rooms and a swimming pool. ❹

Lidia Hotel Rua Rufino de Alencar 300 ☎85/252-4174. Friendly, very small hotel, converted from a house, with simple, clean rooms. ❷

Pousada Casa Nova Rua Pedro Ângulo 56 ☎85/252-4179. A family-run *pousada* right in the heart of the centre, with 18 spotless and air-conditioned suites. ❷

Pousada Rio Branco Rua Pedro Ângulo 46 ☎85/226-5801. Next door to the *Pousada Casa Nova*, the rooms in this converted house are small but adequate. Ring the door bell for service. ❷

Pousada Toscana Rua Rufino de Alenar 272 ☎85/231-6378, ⓦwww.pousadatoscana .hpg.com.br. Very close to the Mercado Central and

the Centro Dragão, this spick and span, well-run hostel in an attractive house has bright and airy rooms with comfortable beds. Very good value. ❷

Praia da Iracema

Albergue Praia de Iracema Av. Almirante Barroso 998, Praia de Iracema ☎85/252-3267. Fortaleza's youth hostel is in an excellent location near the best nightlife and costs $15 a night per person.

Brisa da Praia Av. Beira Mar 982, Praia de Iracema ☎85/219-4699, ☎219-1964. Modern, medium-sized hotel right on the seafront, with a small pool and rooftop terrace. ❺

Pousada Abril em Portugal Av. Almirante Barroso 1006, Praia de Iracema ☎85/231-9508. A good-value budget hotel near the youth hostel. ❷

Pousada Atalaia Av. Beira Mar 814 ☎85/219-0658, ⓦwww.pousadaatalaia.com.br. Possibly one of the best-located youth hostels in the Americas, right opposite the beach on the Praia Iracema and within shouting distance of the Fortaleza's top nightlife spots. Accommodation mostly in dormitories, with some private rooms available too. ❸

Pousada Grão de Areia Rua Dos Potiguaras 80

85/219-1704. One of the cheapest options near the busy nightlife around the Ponte dos Ingleses. Though small, the *pousada* has helpful staff, and some rooms have air-conditioning and TV. **②**
Pousada Portal de Iracema Rua dos Ararius 2, Praia de Iracema ☎85/219-0066, ⓕ219-3411, ⓔpousada@ultranet.com.br. Well-located *pousada*, very close to the sea and near the centre of the nightlife district, yet surprisingly quiet. Clean, bright rooms have TVs and *frigobars*, with good English spoken, conscientious service and lovely breakfasts. **③**
Turismo Praia Av. Beira Mar 894, Praia de Iracema ☎85/219-6133, ⓕ219-1638. Small, good-value hotel with functional rooms, a tiny pool, and modest restaurant but in a great location right opposite the beach. **③**

Praia Meireles

Hotel Beira-Mar Av. Beira Mar (Av. Presidente Kennedy) 3130, Praia de Meireles ☎85/242-5000, ⓕ242-5659, ⓦwww.hotelbeiramar.com.br. Luxury hotel with pool, right next to the Praia de Meireles. **⑤**

Hotel La Maison Av. Desembarador Moreira 201 ☎85/242-7017, ⓦwww.hotellamaison.com.br. This thirteen-room *pousada* is in a tastefully converted house just a few blocks from the beach; the rooms are pleasant and have air-conditioning, TVs, telephone. French and English spoken; parking spaces available. **③**
Hotel Marina Praia Rua Paula Barros 44 ☎85/242-7734, ⓕ242-5275, ⓦwww . hotelmarinapraia.com.br. A small, spick-and-span hotel, little bigger than a house, and less than a block from the beach in the Nautico section of Praia Meireles. It somehow fits 25 apartments into its comfortable and colourful interior, and there's also a little patio out front. Good value. **③**
Pousada do Turista Rua Dom Joaquim 351 ☎85/231-6607. Budget hotel run by French-speakers, with cool and pleasant rooms. Located in a peaceful area within ten minutes' walk from the city centre and the beach. **②**
Pousada Savoy Rua Dom Joaquim 321 ☎85/226-8426. Next door to the *Pousada do Turista*, your chance to stay at the *Savoy* at a fraction of the usual price – and comfort. **②**

The City

The only visible legacy of its crowded history in modern Fortaleza is the city's name, and a **gridded street pattern** laid out in the nineteenth century by a French architect, Adolphe Herbster. He was contracted by the ambitious city fathers to turn Fortaleza into "the Paris of the North" – you can only hope they got their money back.

The **layout of the city** is easy to grasp, despite its size. The **centre**, laid out in blocks, forms the commercial, administrative and religious heart, with markets, shops, public buildings, squares and a forbiddingly ugly concrete cathedral; it's quite possible to walk and take in most of the sights in one day, though you'd probably want to take longer. To the west of the centre, undistinguished urban sprawl finally gives way to the beaches of **Barra do Ceará**, but most of the action is to the east, where the main city beaches and the chic middle-class *bairros* of **Praia de Iracema** and **Meireles** are to be found, linked by the main seafront road, **Avenida Presidente Kennedy**, usually known as **Avenida Beira Mar**. These give way to the *favelas* and docks of the port area, **Mucuripe**, the gateway to the eastern beaches, notably **Praia do Futuro**, beyond which the city peters out.

While not the most visually attractive of Brazilian city centres, there is enough going on in the heart of Fortaleza to merit more attention than it usually gets from visitors. It certainly can't be faulted for being boring: the streets are very crowded, with shops and hawkers colonizing large areas of pavement and squares, so that much of the centre often seems like a single large market. Fortaleza is an excellent place for **shopping**, and you should stock up here if you're heading west, as you won't get comparable choice until you hit Belém, 1500km away. Clothes are plentiful and cheap, there is also good *artesanato* to be had, notably lace and leather, and Fortaleza is the largest centre for the manufacture and sale of hammocks in Brazil.

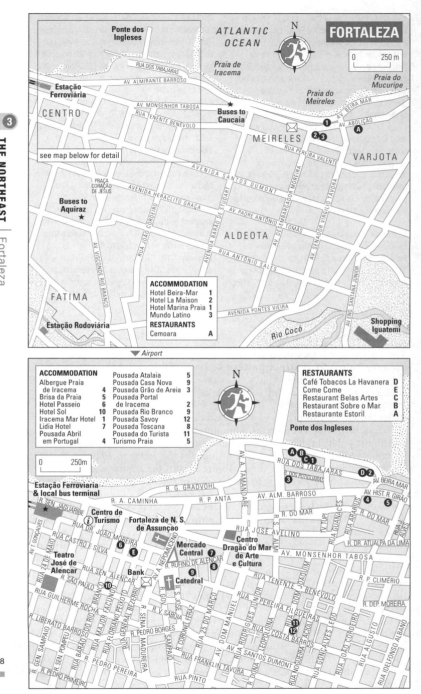

FORTALEZA

ATLANTIC OCEAN

N

0   250 m

Ponte dos Ingleses

Praia de Iracema

Praia do Mucuripe

RUA DOS TABAJARAS

AV. ALMIRANTE BARROSO

Estação Ferroviária

Praia do Meireles

AV. MONSENHOR TABOSA

RUA TENENTE BENEVOLO

Buses to Caucaia

CENTRO

AV. BEIRA MAR

AV. ABOLIÇÃO

MEIRELES

RUA PEREIRA VALENTE

VARJOTA

see map below for detail

AVENIDA SANTOS DUMONT

PRAÇA CORAÇÃO DE JESUS

AVENIDA HERACLITO GRAÇA

AV. JOÃO CORDEIRO

AVENIDA BARÃO DE STUDART

AV. PADRE ANTÔNIO TOMAS

AV. DESEMBARGADOR MOREIRA

AV. SENADOR VIRGÍLIO TÁVORA

Buses to Aquiraz

ALDEOTA

RUA ANTÔNIO SALES

AV. VISCONDE RIO BRANCO

FATIMA

AVENIDA PONTES VIEIRA

AV. ENG. SANTANA JÚNIOR

Estação Rodoviária

Rio Cocó

Shopping Iguatemi

ACCOMMODATION
Hotel Beira-Mar	1
Hotel La Maison	2
Hotel Marina Praia	1
Mundo Latino	3

RESTAURANTS
Cemoara	A

▼ Airport

ACCOMMODATION
Albergue Praia de Iracema	4
Brisa da Praia	5
Hotel Passeio	6
Hotel Sol	10
Iracema Mar Hotel	1
Lidia Hotel	7
Pousada Abril em Portugal	4
Pousada Atalaia	5
Pousada Casa Nova	9
Pousada Grão de Areia	3
Pousada Portal de Iracema	2
Pousada Rio Branco	9
Pousada Savoy	12
Pousada Toscana	8
Pousada do Turista	11
Turismo Praia	5

RESTAURANTS
Café Tobacos La Havanera	D
Come Come	E
Restaurant Belas Artes	C
Restaurant Sobre o Mar	B
Restaurante Estoril	A

Ponte dos Ingleses

N

0   250m

Estação Ferroviaria & local bus terminal

RUA DOS TABAJARAS

R. DOS POTIGUARAS

AV. BEIRA MAR

AV. A. TAMANDARÉ

R. G. GRADVOHL

R. A. CAMINHA

R. P. ANTA

AV. ALM. BARROSO

AV. HIST. R. GIRÃO

R. SEN. JAGUARIBE

Centro de Turismo

Fortaleza de N. S. de Assunção

R. DO MAR

RUA ARARIPE

RUA GUANACES

R. DO MAR

RUA DR. JOÃO MOREIRA

RUA JOSÉ AVELINO

TV. TUPI

R. DR. ATUALPA DA LIMA

RUA 24 DE MAIO

RUA CASTRO E SILVA

Teatro José de Alencar

RUA SEN. ALENCAR

Mercado Central

RUA RUFINO DE ALENCAR

Centro Dragão do Mar de Arte e Cultura

AV. MONSENHOR TABOSA

RUA SÃO PAULO

Bank

RUA TENENTE BENEVOLO

R. P. CLIMÉRIO

RUA GUILHERME ROCHA

Catedral

R. S. JOSÉ

RUA PEREIRA FILGUEIRAS

R. DEP. MOREIRA

R. LIBERATO BARROSO

RUA MAJOR FACUNDO

R. GOV. SABÓIA

AV. DOM MANUEL

RUA COSTA BARROS

R. GEN. SAMPAIO

R. SEN. POMPEU

RUA BARÃO DO RIO BRANCO

RUA FLORIANO PEIXOTO

R. GENERAL BEZERRIL

R. PEDRO BORGES

AV. 25 DO MARÇO

RUA DOM LEOPOLDINA

RUA RODRIGUES JÚNIOR

AV. DOM JOAQUIM

RUA NOGUEIRA ACCIOLI

RUA GONÇALVES LEDO

RUA JOÃO CORDEIRO

RUA IDELFONSO ALBANO

R. PEDRO PRIMEIRO

R. PEDRO PEREIRA

RUA PINTO

AV. SANTOS DUMONT

AV. DONA LEOPOLDINA

AV. SANTA FRANKLIN TÁVORA

R. CORONEL FERAZ

R. SENA MADUREIRA

The Mercado Central and around

Set right next to the grimy, neo-Gothic cathedral on Rua Conde d'Eu, the striking new **Mercado Central**, a huge complex holding hundreds of small stores, dominates the skyline. The market, along with the nearby shops on the other side of the cathedral, is the best place to buy a hammock in the city: if you're going to use one on your travels, purchase it with care. Cloth ones are the most comfortable, but are heavier, bulkier and take longer to dry out if they get wet. Less comfy in the heat, but more convenient, much lighter and more durable are nylon hammocks. Aesthetically, however, nylon hammocks are no match for cloth ones, which come in all colours and patterns. You ought to be able to get a perfectly adequate cloth hammock, which will stand up to a few weeks' travelling, for around $10 for a single and $19 for a double; for a nylon hammock, add $5 to the price. If you want a more elaborate one – and some handwoven hammocks are very fine – you will pay more. Easing the path to slinging hammocks once you get home are metal *armadores*, which many hammock and most hardware shops sell: these are hooks mounted on hinges and a plate with bolts for sinking into walls. When buying a hammock you are going to use, make sure it takes your body lying horizontally across it: sleeping along the curve is uncomfortably bad for your back.

Right opposite the Mercado Central, the nineteenth-century **Fortaleza de Nossa Senhora da Assunção** – the city's namesake – is easily identified by its thick, plain white walls and old black cannons. It belongs to the Tenth Military Regiment of the Brazilian army, but is open to visitors on request (Mon–Fri 9am–5pm; ☏85/255-1600); visits are best organized the day before.

The Centro Dragão do Mar de Arte e Cultura

The brand-new **Centro Dragão do Mar de Arte e Cultura**, a couple of blocks east of the market, makes a striking contrast to the rest of the city. Architecturally it's very modern, but its steel and glass curves blend sensitively with the attractive old terraced buildings over and around which it is built. The whole thing feels like a modern and stylish university campus and, importantly, serves as an ideal link between the beaches and the city centre, which essentially starts on the landward side of the complex on the small Praça Municipal. Within the complex, there's a small shiny-domed planetarium, cinemas, an auditorium, a couple of museums – one dedicated to contemporary art – information hall and bookshop, toilets and a good coffee bar, the *Torre do Café*, located in the tower that supports the covered walkway between the two main sections of the Centro. On the ground level there's also a shop selling quality regional *artesanato*.

The Centro de Turismo and the Museu de Arte e Cultura Popular

Overlooking the sea at the bottom of Rua Senador Pompeu is the **Centro de Turismo**, housed in the city's old prison – a perfect place to stop and have a beer in the bar in the one-time exercise yard, shaded by mango trees. The centre is also the location of the best museum in the city, the **Museu de Arte e Cultura Popular** (Mon–Fri 8am–6pm, Sat 8am–noon). Well laid out in a single huge gallery on the first floor, this is a comprehensive collection of *cearense artesanato* of all kinds, together with a sample of the painting and sculpture produced by the best of the state's modern artists. What distinguishes the museum is the imaginative juxtaposition of more traditional popular art with modernism. Both collections are of very high quality: the modern art is often startlingly original, as in the sculptures of bolts, nuts and scrap metal of Zé Pinto, but in style and subject matter you can see how profoundly it is rooted in the tradition of popular art all around it. In the same building and included in the entry price you'll find the smaller **Museu de Mineralogia** (same times), stuffed full of massive quartz crystals and a wide range of semi-precious stones.

The Passeio Público and Praça dos Mártires

Two blocks from the Centro de Turismo is another survivor of nineteenth-century Fortaleza: the old municipal boulevard, the **Passeio Público**, which sits beside the pleasant shady **Praça dos Mártires**. Both are popular with children and families – as well as prostitutes. The Passeio looks out over the waterfront, and stallholders set up chairs and tables under the trees, from where they sell cold drinks and simple food. It's a good place to go in the late afternoon or early evening, when the workers stroll around after they get out of their offices, watching the variety of street entertainers and hawkers. The municipality often lays something on: small fairs, dances – the ubiquitous *forró* pumped out by tannoy or thumped out by *trios* – or concerts. Even without entertainment, it has a relaxing feel, and is certainly the best place, away from the beaches, to watch the sunset.

Praça José de Alencar

The nerve centre of this part of the city, however, is its largest square, **Praça José de Alencar**, four blocks inland from the train station at the heart of the commercial district. In the late afternoon and early evening, the crowds here attract *capoeira* groups, street sellers of all kinds and especially *repentistas*. Fortaleza seems to specialize in these street poets, who with great skill and wit gather an audience by improvising a verse or two about those standing around watching, passing round a hat for you to show your appreciation. If you refuse, or give what they consider too little, the stream of innuendo and insults, in a variety of complicated metres, is unmistakeable, even if you don't understand a word (see p.318).

On the square you'll also find the one truly impressive building in the city, the beautiful **Teatro José de Alencar**, named after the great nineteenth-century novelist and poet, a native of the city. Built in the first decade of the twentieth century, the fine tropical Edwardian exterior is in fact only an elegant facade, which leads into an open courtyard and the main body of the theatre. It is built in ornate and beautifully worked cast-iron sections, which were brought over complete from Scotland and reassembled in 1910. Surprisingly, for a building made out of iron, it is extremely cool and pleasant to be in, even when the sun is at its height: the ironwork is open and lets in the air without trapping heat, a masterly example of Scottish design in the least Scottish setting imaginable. In 1991 it was superbly restored and is now a key venue for theatrical performances and concerts. The best time to see it is at night, when it opens for business, a favourite venue for *cearense* music of all varieties and exhibitions in the courtyard. Friday and Saturday are the likeliest nights to find something on: the staff can let you know what's happening, or try looking under the heading *Lazer* in the local papers.

The city beaches

The main city beaches are the **Praia de Iracema** and the adjacent **Praia do Meireles**, both focal points for Fortaleza's nightlife. As beaches go, the Praia do Meireles wins hands down with its greater expanse of sand, though the water is not as clean as the beaches out of town, due to the proximity of docks both east and west; the further away from the centre, the better for swimming. That said, both beaches are good for sunset watching, the seafront boulevard is well laid out, punctuated by clumps of palm trees, and there is no shortage of watering holes. By day there are surfers on the waves and beach parties at the *barracas*, and in the early evening it seems everyone in the city turns out to stroll or rollerblade down the boulevard, which has replaced the city's squares as the favoured meeting place.

If you're a beach devotee, cleaner water, higher rollers and better seafood are to be had further out past Mucuripe at **Praia do Futuro**: take buses marked "Caça e Pesca" or "P. Futuro" from Rua Castro e Silva in the centre. The beach *barracas* here are very good: the fried fish is fresh and comes in enormous portions. The ultimate surfing beaches, however, are 6km beyond the Praia do Futuro, at **Porto das Dunas** and **Prainha**, 11km in combined length. Porto das Dunas also has an aquatic theme park called **Beach Park** (daily 9am–5pm; ☎85/360-1150), the largest of its kind in Latin America.

Eating, drinking and nightlife

You'll be all right in the centre during the day if you want something to eat as there are countless places to grab a snack. However, most of what Fortaleza has to offer your palate is to be found on the beaches, especially around **Rua dos Tabajaras** on Praia de Iracema. The pier here, known as Ponte dos Ingleses, is a lovely place to have a beer and watch the sunset. Rua dos Tabajaras itself is a joy to wander around, with its brightly coloured bars and **restaurants**, and glamorous young people out enjoying themselves. The airy *Restaurant Belas Artes* (☎85/219-0330), Rua dos Tabajaras 179, has a good range of Brazilian and international dishes and an excellent bar. Nearby, the boat-like *Restaurant Sobre o Mar*, Rua dos Tremembes 2 (☎85/219-7999), serves delicious lobster and a good range of wines; there's a $1 cover charge for the frequent live music shows. *Restaurante Estoril* (☎85/219-8389) makes the best of its setting at Rua dos Tabajaras 397, serving excellent *cearense* cuisine, offering shows at weekends and comedy on Tuesday nights, but it's quite pricey. Much further south along the seafront, past Praia do Futuro at Av. Beira Mar 4566, the *Marquinhos Restaurante* (☎85/263-1204) serves excellent seafood (try the skewered lobster); it's not cheap but the service is good and the restaurant open and airy. If you happen to end up in the old city centre at lunchtime, try *Come Come*, at Rua Castro e Silva, a self-service café offering a very cheap but satisfying *comida por kilo* option near the cathedral (it's cooler and larger inside than it looks). For a filling breakfast, fresh fruit juices and excellent coffee in a relaxed café setting, you'll do no better than *Café Tobacos La Havanera* on the corner of Rua dos Ararius and Avenida Beira Mar. Arguably the best restaurant in the city is *Cemoara*, Av. Abolição 3340 (☎85/263-5001), where the service is superb and the food even better, specializing mainly in Brazilian dishes, particularly *cearense*.

Two **bars** on Avenida Beira Mar, just along from Rua dos Tabajaras, offer a wonderful combination of eating, drinking and live music: the *Pontal de Iracema* at no. 680 and the *Cais Bar* at no. 696 are extremely trendy nightspots where you have to arrive early to get a seat.

Forró: dancing and clubs

Fortaleza is justly famous for its **forró**. Nowhere is it so popular, and there is no better way to see what *cearenses* do when they want to enjoy themselves than to spend a night in a *dancetaria* in Fortaleza. And spending the night is literally what you need to do: although most *dancetarias* open at 10pm, people don't really start arriving until around midnight, and peak time is in the early hours of the morning. There always seems to be *forró* on somewhere but the venue changes every night.

Pirata at Rua dos Tabajaras 325 (☎85/219-8030), one of the most easily accessible nightclubs in Fortaleza, has live music from Tuesday through Saturday, including *forró* but with other sounds as well; it's a great night out for about $4. *Subindo ao Céu*, at Av. Zezé Diogo out on Praia do Futuro, is a popular venue on Tuesday nights. On Wednesdays the scene shifts to the *Clube do Vaqueiro* (☎85/276-2014), a taxi ride away out on the periphery of the city along the BR-116 highway leading east to Natal. As its name implies, the club has everything for the cowboy: the huge complex is sometimes used for rodeos during the day, and on Wednesday nights the cavernous interior throbs with *forró* rhythms and hundreds of dancing couples.

Other nightlife

Besides *forró*, there's plenty else in Fortaleza to keep you busy into the evenings. For **jazz**, try the *Ludvico Bar* and *Restaurante*, at Rua do Mirante 161, Mucuripe (☎85/263-1545), on most Thursday evenings. Most weekends, the *Disco Bar Desigual*, on the seafront between the pier and *Paraiso do Praia Hotel*, pulls in a young crowd with its loud live music.

One of the best venues for live **dance shows**, is *Docas Bar e Café Teatro*, beside the Centro Dragao at Rua Jose Avelino 491 (☎85/219-8209), which showcases costumed dance styles every Wednesday from 9pm, among them *Afro* (slave), *Caboclinhos* (jungle) and *Maracatu* (colonial). On Fridays the same venue usually presents local pop bands, while on weekends the music tends to be more mixed, though with heavy doses of samba.

Listings

Airlines TAM ☎85/477-1945; Varig ☎85/477-1710; Vasp ☎85/477-5001.

Banks and exchange Banco do Noreste, Rua Major Facundo 372, offers the most services, but you're likely to get faster service at Wall Street, Av. Santos Dumont 3000, Aldeota (☎85/486-3900) or Av. Beira Mar 2982, Loja 02.

Car hire RCA ☎85/219-7000; RHP ☎85/257-7533.

Internet Beira Mar Internet Café, Beira Mar 2120-A; Cachaça-Cearapontocom, Av. Beira Mar 720; Diabesso Internet Café, Av. Beira Mar 3222 (Loja 20, entrance past the restaurants up a small side street); and Interschool, Av. Abolição 3089.

Post office The main post office is at Rua Senador Alencar 38 (Mon–Fri 8am–6pm).

Taxis Cooperttur ☎85/224-6206.

Telephones There are public telephone offices for inter-urban and international calls across the city,

including one near the beach at Av. Beira Mar 730 by the *Naredomus Hotel*.

Travel and tour companies Ernahitur, Av. Barao de Studart 1165, 1st floor, Conjunto 101-107, Aldeota (☎85/244-9363, ⑤261-6782, ⑩www.ernanitur.com.br) and Wall Street, Av. Santos Dumont 3000, Aldeota (☎85/486-3900) or Av. Beira Mar 2982, Loja 02 (☎85/242-2235) arrange trips to Jericoacoara ($50), Canoa Quebrada ($12) and Lagoinha ($10), as well as city tours ($10). Praia Turismo (☎85/9989-6685), run similar tours for slightly less and will also pick up from hotels; their sales van is parked by the beach on Beira Mar (at the Praia Iracema end) on most mornings. Trip da Areia, at Av. Beira Mar 3120, sala 03 (☎85/242-3985, ⑩www.tripdaareia.com.br), run excellent one- to four-day expeditions from Fortaleza to the neighbouring beaches and resorts.

Around Fortaleza: the beaches

The **beaches** of Ceará are what attract most visitors, and both east and west of Fortaleza they stretch unbroken for hundreds of kilometres. They are invariably superb, a mixture of mountainous sand dunes, palm trees and Atlantic breakers, wilder than the sheltered reef beaches of the southern states of the Northeast. Even some of the most remote beaches have been "discovered" by tourists, but there is no need to scorn them on that account: the coastline is more than big enough to swallow large numbers of property developers and visitors without getting crowded. It's easy to bewail the passing of the simple life in the fishing villages, but talk to their inhabitants and you'll find they are still functioning communities, making money from tourists on the side. What travellers see as an idyllic, rustic existence seems more like poverty to those who live it.

Any description of the beaches becomes repetitive: they are all stunning, among the most beautiful anywhere in the world. Travelling along the coast, while often leisurely, is not difficult. To reach the beaches, as a rule, you will need to get off at a town and catch a connection to the nearby coast, and the local bus network covers most places: at the better-known beaches, shoals of pick-ups and beach buggies meet the buses from Fortaleza.

East to Aracati and Canoa Quebrada

East of Fortaleza there are two basic routes. The first heads along a coastal road that branches off the BR-116 just south of the city to Beberibe. The first coastal village along this route is **AQUIRAZ**, where there are the beaches of **Iguape** and **Prainha**. Buses to Aquiraz are run by the São Benedito company and leave from a stop on the corner of Avenida Domingos Olímpio and Avenida Aquanambi. For anywhere east of Aquiraz, buses can be caught at the *rodoviária*. Thirty kilometres beyond Aquiraz is Cascavel, 12km inland but a starting point for two more beaches: **Caponga** and, less crowded, **Aguas Belas**. Twenty kilometres further on is **BEBERIBE** itself, the drive there a lovely one on a country road through palm forests and dunes. The irregularly shaped dunes of Beberibe's beach, **Morro Branco**, are fifteen minutes away. Five kilometres from here is the small fishing village and mineral-water spring of **PRAIA DAS FONTES**, which also boasts a luxury hotel of the same name, reasonably priced and serving excellent food (☎85/338-1179; ❺).

A more direct route east takes you to **ARACATI**, two hours from Fortaleza, a once properous small textile town with half a dozen derelict, and a couple of functioning, eighteenth-century churches. It is also the jumping-off point for Ceará's best-known and most fashionable beach, **Canoa Quebrada**, half an hour along a dirt road from Aracati: pick-ups meet every bus from the city, so access is no problem. Canoa Quebrada is popular with foreigners and young Brazilians alike, the atmosphere is relaxed, and it's fairly lively at night. Certainly, if you want company and *movimento* it's the beach to head for, and there's good buggy riding here in the sand dunes of the surrounding environmental reserve. The road to Canoa Quebrada is flanked by dozens of boards advertising *pousadas* and restaurants and there's no shortage of either. The beach served directly by road from Aracati, **Majorlândia**, is less crowded and a lot quieter. It's certainly as good as Canoa Quebrada, there are *jangadas* on the beach and surf here as well, and it's just as easy to find places to stay. A good place to try is the *Pousada Fortaleza* (☎98/421-7019), 200m from the beach (☎85/242-3985, reservations at Av. Beira Mar 3120, sala 3; ❹), which has air-conditioned apartments equipped with *frigobars*, TVs and hammocks, and a pool.

West to Jericoacoara

The choice of beach strands **west of Fortaleza** is equally rich. Only 8km from Fortaleza is the town of **Caucaia**, which is served by buses from Avenida Rui Barbosa (outside the *Ideal Clube*) on Praia de Meireles. From Caucaia, local buses head out to the beaches of **Icaraí** (not to be confused with another Icaraí more than 150km to the west), **Pacheo** and **Tabuba** where, even by *cearense* standards, the coastline is really something, with dunes, lagoons, palm forests and enormous expanses of sand; the road ends up in the fishing village of Cumbuco.

Frequent buses from the Fortaleza Rodoviária (tickets from Brasileiro Transporte) go to **SÃO GONÇALO DO AMARANTE**, only an hour and 57km away. From here, you can head on to the beaches of **Pecém**, 15km away, and the glorious beach of **Taíba**, 6km on. Not all buses to São Gonçalo continue to the beaches, but if they don't there are pick-ups and local buses. The beach town of **PARACURU**, 80km from Fortaleza (frequent buses from the *rodoviária*, also with Brasileiro Transporte), is being rapidly developed and gets crowded during weekends, but is less frenetic during the week.

After Paracuru, you head out of Fortaleza's influence and the further west you go, the less crowded the beaches become. A good place to head for, reasonably remote but not impossible to get to, is **TRAIRI**, 118km from Fortaleza, served by direct buses from the *rodoviária*, which take around three hours. From here it's a few kilometres to the beautiful and usually deserted beaches of **Mundaú**, protected by a 100m reef, and **Fleixeiras**, more deserted still. When the tide is out, you can walk for an hour along the beach to the fishing hamlet of **GUA-JIRU**, named for the indigenous local fruit that still grows abundantly in the scrubby bushes scattered around the dunes. There is no electricity or running water, but the people are friendly and the scenery marvellous.

Ceará's most famous beach, **JERICOACOARA**, lies 320km west of Fortaleza, a remote hangout with huge dunes of fine white sand, and turquoise *lagoas*. Two buses a day from Fortaleza cover the seven-hour journey to the village of Gijoca, where pick-up trucks and buggies will meet you for the hour-long ride over the sands to Jericoacoara. It's still a primitive place, unconnected to the main electricity grid, but there are plenty of places to stay. *Wind Pousada*, Rua Forro 33 (☎85/9953-9596; ❸) has attractively rustic rooms just 50m from the beach, all with TVs, *frigobars*, air-conditioning and hot showers. There's also the *Pousada das Dunas*, Rua das Dunas (☎88/699-2002, or in Fortaleza at Av. Beira Mar 3120 ☎85/242-3985; ❹), which offers good service and more comfort, and the *Pousada Renata*, close to the beach, with pleasantly decorated rooms (❷). There are also tours here from Fortaleza starting at $40 per day – see p.362 for a list of tour operators.

On to Piauí: the Serra da Ibiapaba

Apart from the beaches, there is little to detain you as you head west from Fortaleza, though it's a fine drive, with rocky hills and escarpments rising out of the *sertão* and the road snaking through occasional ranges of hills. You pass through the town of **SOBRAL**, an ugly industrial centre nestling in the middle of a spectacular landscape very typical of the interior of the Northeast: fiercely hot, cobalt-blue skies, flinty hills and *caatinga*. It would be very easy to sit back, enjoy the scenery and head directly west for Piauí and Maranhão in one go, but if you did you'd miss one of the finest sights Ceará state has to offer:

the beautiful hills and cloud forest of the highlands that run down the border between Ceará and Piauí – the **Serra da Ibiapaba** – and the caves of **Ubajara**.

Serra da Ibiapaba

You reach the Serra on buses arriving from either east or west, along the BR–222 highway that links Fortaleza with Teresina, capital of the neighbouring state of Piauí. You can get off at **TIANGUÁ**, a pleasant, sleepy town on the *cearense* side of the border: from here there are frequent local connections to Ubajara, 15km away (see below), also served by direct buses from Fortaleza (Ipu Brasília line).

Whether you approach from Teresina or Fortaleza the effect is the same. The buses drive across a bakingly hot plain, which begins to break up the nearer you get to the state border, rearing up into scattered hills and mesas covered with scrub and enormous cacti. Then on the horizon, in view hours before you actually start to climb it, all the hills seem suddenly to merge into a solid wall that rears up 900m from the parched plain below, its slopes carpeted with thick forest: the **Serra da Ibiapaba**.

Ironically, the abundance of the highland forest is part of the explanation for the parched landscape below. The sheer slopes of the *serras* are well watered because they relieve any clouds of their surplus water before they drift over the plains. As the bus begins to climb, winding its way through gorges choked with forest, the broiling heat of the plain is left behind and the air gets fresher and more comfortable. When you reach the tableland on top, it seems another world. Everything is green and fertile: the temperature, warm but fresh with cool breezes, is an immense relief, and the contrast with the conditions only half an hour's drive away below couldn't be more marked. En route to Ubajara you'll see how *nordestinos* treasure those few parts of the interior blessed with fertile soil and regular rainfall: the highlands are intensively farmed by small-holders and supply fruit, vegetables, sugar and manioc for the whole region.

Ubajara

UBAJARA is a small, friendly town nestling in picturesque hills. There are a couple of simple but perfectly adequate **hotels** near the single church and quiet square, together with one or two **bars** and **restaurants**. It's a pleasant place to stay, but probably the best option is to head a couple of kilometres out of town, along the road leading away from Tianguá, to the comfortable *Pousada da Neblina*, Estrada do Teleférico (☎88/634-1270; ❸). Standing in splendid isolation at the foot of a hill covered with palm forest, it has a restaurant and swimming pool, and is remarkable value; you can also camp here. Another option is *Sítio Santana* (☎88/9961-4645), known as "Sítio do Alemão" by the locals, which provides small chalets on a coffee plantation (❷–❸). The view from the chalets is spectacular and it's only a short taxi ride away from town, or the owner will pick you up; just ask anyone in town to put you in touch with him.

Parque Nacional de Ubajara

A twenty-minute walk along the road from the *Pousada da Neblina* will bring you to the gatehouse of the **Parque Nacional de Ubajara**, which ensures that the magnificent forest remains untouched. The park, nestling attractively amidst low hills, is very small (less than six square kilometres), but tourism facilities have developed rapidly in recent years and the park now has a **visitors' centre** (daily 9am–6pm; ☎88/634-1388). There are also plenty of local guides available (starting at around $20 per day) to show you round the park's eco-trails, large caves and impressive waterfalls.

Continuing past the gatehouse brings you to the *mirante*, a viewing platform with a small café built onto the rim of an escarpment. North and south of here the *serra* breaks into ridges covered with forest and tumbles down into the plain, which stretches as far as the eye can see. The view is punctuated by jagged hills, towns and villages connected by vein-like roads, and the whole panorama is laid out as if seen from the cockpit of an aeroplane.

From here a **cable car** swoops down 400m to the cave complex of the **Gruta de Ubajara**. It's an unforgettable ride, plunging down and skimming the top of the forest before arriving at the caves. If you feel more adventurous, there is a **path** down that can be negotiated with a guide. On no account try it on your own; though it's not dangerous, it's very easy to stray off the route. The forest wardens are always on duty at the gatehouse, and can help arrange guides. Guides prefer to start early in the morning, so you do the bulk of the walk before the heat gets up: take liquids, and wear sneakers or decent walking shoes. Going down takes a couple of hours, returning twice that, but there are streams and a small waterfall to cool off in along the way. There are also caves to explore: huge caverns with grotesque formations of stalactites and stalagmites. Technically, the wardens are meant to guide you as part of their job, but as they're extremely badly paid they appreciate some recompense for spending several hours of their time making sure you come to no harm.

Piauí

Piauí is shaped like a ham, with a narrow neck of coastline 59km long that broadens out inland. It's a very distinctive state, but unfortunately most of the reasons for this are depressing. Despite its size it has fewer than two million inhabitants and by far the lowest population density in the Northeast. Subject to drought, and with virtually no natural resources except the *carnaúba* palm, it is Brazil's poorest state.

Few travellers spend much time in Piauí. The capital, **Teresina**, is strategically placed for breaking the long bus journey between Fortaleza and São Luís, but it's a modern, rather ugly city where the heat can be oppressive. The southern half of the state merges into the remoter regions of Bahia and forms the harshest part of the Northeast. Much of it is uninhabited, largely trackless, arid badlands, in the midst of which lies, ironically, the oldest inhabited prehistoric site yet found in Brazil. Cave paintings show that this desert was once jungle. Other than the capital, there are two places worth making for: the pleasant coastal town of **Parnaíba**, which has excellent beaches, and the **Parque Nacional de Sete Cidades**, good walking country with weird and striking rock formations. Strangely, this poorest of states has an excellent **highway** system and the main roads between Teresina and Parnaíba and towards Ceará are very good: as the country is largely flat, the buses really fly.

Piauí was sparsely settled by cattle drovers moving westwards from Ceará in the second half of the eighteenth century and has a violent history. The few Indians were never really conquered and were assimilated with the newcomers rather than being defeated by them, leaving their imprint in the high cheekbones and copper skin of a strikingly handsome people. Apart from cattle, the only significant industry revolves around the **carnaúba palm**, a graceful tree with fan-shaped leaves that grows in river valleys across the northern half of the state. The palm yields a wax that was an important ingredient of shellac, from which the first phonogram records were made, and for which there is still a small export market. It's also a source of cooking oil, wood, soap, charcoal and nuts, and many livelihoods depend on it.

Teresina

People from **TERESINA** tell a joke about their city: "Why do vultures fly in circles over Teresina? Because they glide with one wing and have to fan themselves with the other!" Brazil's hottest state capital, Teresina sits far inland on the east bank of the Rio Parnaíba, where it bakes year-round in an average temperature of 40°C (which means it regularly gets hotter than that). The rains, meant to arrive in February and last for three or four months, are not to be relied upon – though ironically, twice in the last fifteen years they have actually flooded Teresina. Unless you're used to such heat, you'll find it tiring to move around; rooms with at least a fan, and preferably air-conditioning, are a necessity.

There's not a great deal to do or see in Teresina, but there's enough to occupy you for a day if you feel like breaking the long bus journey from Ceará. Besides having some comfortable hotels, it's the only place between Fortaleza and São Luís where you can do things like cash travellers' cheques or have money cabled out to you.

The City

Thankfully, in such a hot place, most of the things worth seeing and doing are reasonably close to each other. The best place to start is the **market** that occupies most of the main square of the city, technically called Praça da Bandeira, but universally known by its old name, **Marechal Deodoro**. It's a smaller, more urbanized version of the typical Northeastern market, with packed stalls forming narrow streets, determined shoppers, energetic sellers, noise, loud music and plenty of *caldo de cana* kiosks, where you can slurp freshly crushed sugar cane and watch the city at work. There is *artesanato* scattered around, and the hammocks from the interior are high quality; both are cheaper here than in the craft shops run by the state tourist authority PIEMTUR.

Overlooking the market, in one of the very few fine old buildings in the city, the **Museu do Piauí** at Marechal Deodoro 900 (Tues–Fri 8am–6pm, Sat & Sun 8am–noon) is definitely worth seeing. A governor's palace, built in 1859, it has been beautifully restored, with the exhibits well displayed in simple, elegant rooms, many with high arched windows and balconies perched just above the crowded market stalls. The collection is the usual eclectic mix, and pride of place must go to a collection of early radios, televisions and stereograms, a must for lovers of 1950s and 1960s kitsch. There are also fossils as well as fine examples of the two things that distinguish *artesanato* in Piauí: sculpture in straw and beautifully tooled leather.

You might also want to investigate the crafts and culture complex run by PIEMTUR, the **Centro de Comercialização Artesanal**, also known as the Mercado Central. Located in the old military barracks at Rua Paissandu 1276, overlooking Praça Dom Pedro Segundo, it's a small but pleasant place to wander around. The *artesanato* is laid out in booths and is good quality, although a little expensive; the leatherwork is especially fine. Upstairs is a nice café with restaurant attached, where the *carne do sol* is excellent.

Practicalities

The **rodoviária** (☎86/218-1514) is on the southeast outskirts of the city and has a **tourist information post** (Mon–Fri 8am–noon & 2–6pm, Sat 8am–noon) run by PIEMTUR, where you can pick up free booklets with a city map. Frequent buses run into the centre, and there are cheap taxis, too. You will also find an information post on the corner of Magalhães Filho and Alvaro Mendes in the centre of town five blocks from the Praça da Liberdade. It's very easy to find your way around as the streets are organized in a grid pattern.

There are a number of good **hotels** opposite the *rodoviária*. Both the *Elite* (❶), and the *São Francisco* (❷), are no-frills options. Among those in the city centre overlooking the river is the luxury *Luxor do Piauí*, Praça Mal. Deodoro 310 (☎86/221-3306, ☎221-5171; ❸), with smart rooms and a pool, while cheaper places are nearby around Praça Saraiva. Mid-range hotels include the cosy *Sambaiba*, Rua Gabriel Ferreira 230 (☎86/222-4911; ❸), the *Teresina Palace*, Rua Paissandu 1219 ☎86/221-2770 ☎221-4476 (❸), and the *Royal Palace*, Rua 13 de Maio 233 ☎ & ☎86/221-7707 (❹), where you'll want to avoid the windowless basement rooms, though all have decent air-conditioning.

Restaurants in the city are not especially cheap. Good regional food is served at *Celsos*, Rua Agelica 1059 (☎86/232-2920), a short taxi ride away from the centre in the *bairro* of Fátima. You'll find excellent seafood at *Camarão de Elías*, Av. Pedro Almeida 457, in the *bairro* of São Cristóvão (☎86/232-5025; closed Sun). *Piauienses* excel at meat: a good place to try the *cabrito*, young goat, deliciously tender and served either roasted over charcoal or *ao leite de coco*, stewed in coconut milk, is *Asa Branca*, Av. Frei Serafim 2037, in the centre, with live music (Thurs–Sat). If you're after a meat feast, the *rodízio* at *Rio Poty*, Av. Mal. Castelo Branco 616, is the place to go.

The city's **nightlife** lacks the focus of the coastal capitals, but there is life here after dark. The bank of the Rio Parnaíba is the best place from which to enjoy the sunset. A kilometre or so south of the centre, along the riverfront road, is **Prainha**, a series of bars and restaurants built along the riverbank, shaded by planted trees: buses run there, but are very infrequent by late afternoon – use the taxis in Teresina, which are cheap.

Carnaúba country

Heading **west** from Ceará towards Amazônia, there are two routes you can follow. The fastest and most direct is simply to take the highway through Teresina and on to São Luís or, a day from Teresina, to Belém and Amazônia proper. But if you have the time, there is a much more interesting and scenic route **north** up the BR-343 highway, a fine drive through a plain studded with *carnaúba* palm plantations to **Parnaíba** and the coast. From Parnaíba there is a direct bus service, over country dirt roads that get seriously difficult to travel on during the rainy season, to São Luís (see p.372), capital of neighbouring Maranhão state, where the Amazon region begins.

Parnaíba

PARNAÍBA, with its attractive natural anchorage on the Rio Igaraçu, was founded over fifty years before Teresina. For the Portuguese, it was the obvious harbour from which to ship out the dried meat and *carnaúba* (a wax derived from *carnauba* palm) of the interior and, in the nineteenth century, it was a thriving little town; you can still see the chimneys of the cotton factories put up by British entrepreneurs a century ago. Then the river silted up, the port moved to Luiz Correia at the mouth of the river, and the town slipped into decline. Today, Parnaíba has a lazy feel, but is still the second largest city in the state with around 125,000 inhabitants. Located anywhere else it would be a thriving resort town; the **beaches** nearby are excellent.

There is not too much to do in Parnaíba except waste time pleasantly. The commercial area in the centre is busy, and **Praça da Graça**, with its palms and cafés, is an enjoyable place to hang about. The liveliest place in town, though, is the riverfront **Avenida Nações Unidas**, a grandiose name for a small promenade lined with cafés and restaurants. There are also boat trips to the islands at the mouth of the Rio Parnaíba, organized by the state tourist authority **PIEMTUR**, based in the Centro Cultural Porto das Barcas, beside the river at the end of Avenida Getúlio Vargas (daily 8am–1pm & 2–7pm; ☎86/321-1532).

The modern **rodoviária** is on the edge of town, and buses for the short ride to the centre leave from outside. The centre is small and contains all Parnaíba's **hotels**, best of which is the *Hotel Cívico*, Av. Chagas Rodrigues 474 (☎86/322-2470, ℱ322-2028; ❹), which has a pool, restaurant and a reasonable bar. There's also cheap, clean accommodation at the *Pousada Rio Igaraçu*, Rua Almirante Gervásio Sampaio 390 (☎86/322-3342; ❷), and the *Casa Nova Hotel*, at Praça Lima Rebelo 1094 (☎86/322-3344; ❷). For something a little different, check out the *Pousada Ecológica Ilha do Caju* (☎86/321-3044 or ℱ321-1308; ❼), located in a private eco-reserve on an island accessed by boat (4hr) from Parnaíba.

The beaches

You might as well follow the locals and head off to the **beaches** if you want to relax. Not served by bus, but only a short taxi ride away, is the **Lagoa do Portinho**, a freshwater lake with palms and chalets to stay in, and a good restaurant.

There are simple hotels and *dormitórios* if you want to stay in **LUIZ CORREIA**, a fishing village 8km north of Paranaíba, with a small modern port attached. From here you can either walk or get the bus to the huge and popular **Praia de Atalaia**. At weekends practically the entire population of Parnaíba decamps here and the crowded bars reverberate to *forró* trios. A less crowded beach, **Coqueiro**, is 12km from here, but there are only a couple of buses there a day.

Hourly **local buses** to Luiz Correia and Praia de Atalaia leave from the terminus next to Praça Santo Antônio in Parnaíba, three blocks along the pedestrianized shopping street that leads down from Praça da Graça; they take about twenty minutes to arrive in Luiz Correia, and another five to hit the beach – stay on till the end of the line to be dropped at the liveliest stretch.

Parque Nacional de Sete Cidades

The **Parque Nacional de Sete Cidades** comprises thirty square kilometres of nature reserve that could hardly be more different from the forest reserve of

Ubajara, a couple of hundred kilometres east. Here it's the spiky, semi-arid vegetation of the high *sertão* that is preserved – cacti and stubby trees. The really special feature of the reserve is its eroded **rock formations**, many streaked with prehistoric rock carvings. From the air they look like the ruins of seven towns, hence the name of the area, and their striking shapes have given rise to all sorts of theories about the area having been a Phoenician outpost in the New World. In fact the rock sculpting is the entirely natural result of erosion by wind and rain.

There are two ways of **getting to the park**, depending on whether you approach from Ceará state or elsewhere in Piauí. Coming **from Fortaleza or Ubajara**, get off the bus at the town of **Piripiri**, from where a free bus or transit van leaves at 6.45am (Tues–Fri) and takes you to the national park hostel run by the IBDF, the Brazilian forestry service. If you arrive too late, or on a day when the bus isn't running, you could take a local bus from Piripiri to the turn-off to the park 15km north, and walk (3hr) from there, or alternatively take a taxi ($18). Coming **from Teresina or Parnaíba**, get a bus to Piracuruca and take a taxi to the park – the taxi ride costs about $20. There are perfectly adequate, cheap and clean **hotels** near the bus stations in both Piripiri and Piracuruca.

Despite its good facilities and its position near the main Teresina–Fortaleza highway, not as many people visit the park as you might expect. Consequently, it's the ideal place to get off the beaten track without actually venturing far from civilization.

Into the park

There are two **places to stay** in the park. At the entrance is the *Fazenda Sete Cidades* (☎86/276-2222; ❺), with a restaurant, pool and regular pick-up shuttle into the park itself, which you can use whether you stay there or not. More convenient for walking, and just as comfortable, is the cheaper *Abrigo do Ibama* (☎86/343-1342; from $10 per person) hostel and **campsite** in the centre of the park, again with a restaurant and bathing nearby in a natural spring.

Walking in Sete Cidades is not difficult. There are a series of **trails** and several **campsites**, and the staff at both the *fazenda* and the *Abrigo do Ibama* are good at suggesting routes; there are very cursory sketch maps on sale, but don't rely on their accuracy. The walks are not especially strenuous, but take care all the same; it gets extremely hot and a stout pair of shoes, plenty of liquids and a broad-brimmed hat are essential. Start out as near sunrise as you can manage, when the park is at its most beautiful. And when you approach the rocks make some noise: rattlesnakes sometimes sun themselves on them, but they are very shy and slither away if they can hear you coming. The **rock formations** themselves make very good landmarks and their different shapes have lent them their names: the "Map of Brazil", the "Tortoise", the "Roman Soldier", the "Three Kings", the "Elephant" and so on.

Maranhaõ

Maranhão is where the separate but interlinked worlds of the Northeast and Amazônia collide. Although classed as a Northeastern state by Brazilians, its climate, landscape, history and capital of **São Luís** are all *amazônico* rather than *nordestino*. Maranhão is the only state in the Northeast to which more people migrate than emigrate from. Drought is not a problem here; the **climate** is equatorial – humid, hot and very wet indeed. The rainy season peaks from January to April, but most months it rains at least a little, and usually a lot – although only in concentrated, refreshing bouts for most of the year. Maranhão has more fertile, well-watered land than the rest of the Northeast put together. Much of it is flat, the east and north covered with palm forest, and the centre and west riddled, in typical Amazonian fashion, with large rivers and fertile riverine plains – one of the main rice-producing areas of Brazil.

Further west begins the tropical forest and savanna of Amazônia proper, as you hit the eastern boundary of the largest river basin in the world. The **coast** also changes character: the enormous beaches give way, from São Luís westwards, to a bewildering jumble of creeks, river estuaries, mangrove swamps and small islands, interspersed with some of the most remote beaches in Brazil – almost five hundred kilometres of largely roadless coastline with towns and villages accessible only from the sea.

Like most zones of geographical transition, Maranhão also marks a historical and cultural divide. The **people** are a striking contrast to the ethnic uniformity of the states immediately to the east: here blacks, Indians and Europeans form one of the richest cultural stews to be found in Brazil. Catch the great popular festival of **Bumba-meu-boi** in June and you'll get some idea of how different from the rest of the Northeast Maranhão really is.

The main population centres in the state are on and around the island of São Luís, and deep in the interior along the banks of the **Rio Tocantins**, a tributary of the Amazon but a mighty river in its own right. The contrast between the two regions could hardly be more stark. Only thirty years ago the Rio Tocantins was the boundary between Brazil and largely unknown Indian country. Today, as people flood into eastern Amazônia, **Imperatriz**, with 295,000 inhabitants, is the second city of the state, and even dozy, historic São Luís, founded in 1612, has been transformed by docks and factories linked to the huge development projects of eastern Amazônia – the subject of much international controversy.

Routes into Maranhão

There are two **routes** into Maranhão from the east: scooting along the good asphalted highway that links Teresina to São Luís, a six-hour bus ride; or lurching along country roads from Parnaíba, which is more interesting but not to be attempted in the rainy season, when the non-asphalted roads in Maranhão become quagmires. Either way, there's little to detain you before you get to São Luís, as you watch the land transforming itself into the tropics along the way. The *carnaúba* palm of Piauí gives way to the taller trunk and straight fronds of the most common tree in Maranhão, the **babaçu palm**, on which even more livelihoods depend than on *carnaúba*: it provides nuts, cooking oil, soap, charcoal, rope fibre, timber and thatch.

São Luís

Although clearly once a lovely colonial city, **SÃO LUÍS** has really been left behind by the rest of Brazil, despite President Lulas posters plastered everywhere promising change. A poor city even by Northeast standards, it's the most emphatically Third World of all the state capitals in this region. Power cuts and electricity rationing are still routine (most nights power cuts kick in around 8pm) and many things simply don't work. Some of the historic city centre is literally falling to pieces and the infant mortality rate is comparable to those of poor African countries. It has a huge black population, a legacy of plantation development during the eighteenth and nineteenth centuries. It is also far larger than it seems from the compact city centre; about 740,000 people live here, most of them in sprawling *favelas*, with the middle classes concentrated in the beach areas of Ponta da Areia, São Francisco and Olho d'Agua, linked to the rest of the city by a ring road and the bridge built out from the centre across the Rio Anil.

But, for all its problems, São Luís is still a fascinating place, and famous as Brazil's capital of reggae music. Certainly, music, street theatre, food and beaches are the city and region's main pull, along with the decrepit but impressive colonial historic centre. Built across the junction of two rivers and the sea, on an island within the larger delta formed by the **Pindaré** and **Itapicuru** rivers, it has the umbilical connection with rivers that marks an Amazon city, but is also a seaport with ocean beaches. Since 1989, two hundred buildings in the historic centre, the **Zona** (or **Praia Grande**), have benefited from a large-scale restoration programme, the **Projeto Reviver**. Meanwhile, other parts of the colonial heritage continue to crumble but have their own unique atmosphere: there are people packed cheek by jowl, workshops, stalls, brothels, *dormitórios* – in short, a living and breathing heart of a city, not something lifelessly preserved for consumption by outsiders.

The **beaches**, too, are magnificent, and for the most part have been spared intrusive urban development. Above all, try to visit in June, when you can enjoy the festival for which the city is famous, **Bumba–meu–boi** (see box p.376); here, it counts for more than Carnaval.

Arrival, information and accommodation

Both the airport and the *rodoviária* are some way from the city centre. A taxi from the **airport** to the centre will cost you about $8: pay at the kiosk on the left as you come out of the luggage collection area and hand the coupon to the driver. Alternatively you can catch the bus outside marked "São Cristóvão". From the **rodoviária** a taxi to the centre costs about $5. Buses connect the *rodoviária* with the local bus station, the **Terminal de Integração** at Praia Grande, by the waterfront in the city centre. Once there you shouldn't need to use public transport very much: the area of interest is small and most things are within walking distance.

The availability of the **tourist information** office, run by FEMTUR, at the Praca Benedito Leite (Mon–Fri 8am–7pm, Sat & Sun 9am–5pm; ☎98/231-9086) is unreliable, with opening hours being more like 10am to 5pm daily. FEMTUR's so-called 24-hour information post at the airport is not always staffed. Other offices that you may find open are at the Praça Deodoro (Mon–Fri 8am–6pm, Sat & Sun 9am–noon) and the *rodoviária* (daily 8am–11pm). You can **change money** at the Wall Street Cambio, next to the tourist office on Praca Benedito Leite, at either the HSBC bank on Rua Joao

Lisboa, by the Praça João Lisboa, or the Banco da Amazônia on Praça Dom Pedro Segundo or at the Casa 711, Av. Beira Mar 544, right next to the bridge that connects the old city with São Francisco and the other beach areas. For Internet access try the Saint Louis Internet Café at Rua da Estrela 125 or the *Antiguamente Restaurant* at Rua da Estrela 220. Radio taxis are available from Coopertaxi (ⓣ98/245-4404) and Crisbell (ⓣ244-1131); the latter also offer a minbus service.

One other thing you should bear in mind is that as in Salvador many streets have two names: Rua do Trapiche, for example, is also known as Rua Portugal.

Accommodation

Places to stay are divided between the beaches, where there are a few medium-range hotels but no cheap ones, and the centre. To get a flavour of the city's atmosphere there's no substitute for staying in the historic centre, but you should be aware that there are sometimes extremely loud reggae nights that may keep you awake.

Albergue Dois Continentes Rua 28 de Julho 129 ⓣ222-6286, ⓦwww.alberguedoiscontinentes.hpg.com.br. In the middle of Praia Grande area, this popular youth hostel is neat and comfortable, with shared or private rooms at reasonable prices. ❸.

Albergue Juventude Solar das Pedras Rua da Palma 127 ⓣ232-6694. Busy and cheerful youth hostel right in the heart of the action in Praia Grande, with tidy shared rooms and double rooms only. From $15 per person.

Athenas Palace Hotel Rua Antônio Rayol 431 ⓣ98/221-4163 or 221-4225. Quite good value as a place to stay, with some spacious quite comfortable rooms with private baths, but not ideally located for trips into the Zona. ❷

Hotel Estrêla Rua da Estrela 370 ⓣ98/232-7172. A budget option right in the heart of the old city; fairly well-kept but stuffy rooms that come with fans. ❷

Hotel Sofitel Av. Avicência ⓣ98/216-4545, ⓕ235-4921 ⓔsofitel@accor.com.br. Luxury hotel set above Calhau beach some 10km from the city centre, endowed with all possible comforts, such as a sauna, and boasting a wide range of sports facilities, including tennis, basketball, swimming and football. ❻

Hotel Vila Rica Praça Dom Pedro Segundo 299 ⓣ98/232-3535, ⓕ232-7245, ⓦwww.hotelvilarica.com.br. Comfortable but not as luxurious as it used to be, this concrete monstrosity is well located on the edge of the historic centre, close to the tourist information office. Rooms have small balconies and a pool. ❺

Lord Hotel Rua Joaquim Távora 258 ⓣ98/221-4655. Set in a colonial building with a rather grand entrance and lobby, this is a slightly faded two-star hotel that may be the ideal option if you want to stay just on the edge of the historic centre without spending too much money. Rooms come with or without both baths and air-conditioning. ❷

Pousada Colonial Rua Afonso Pena 112 ⓣ ⓣ232-2834, ⓦwww.guiasaoluis.com.br. Finely maintained mansion offering comfort and good service in pleasant surroundings. Very good value and close to the historic centre. ❸

Pousada do Francês Rua da Saavedra 160, corner of Rua Sete de Setembro ⓣ98/231-4773, ⓕ232-0879. An outstanding luxury-class *pousada*, on the edge of the Zona, in a restored eighteenth-century mansion painted in its original colours. Probably the best value accommodation in São Luís. ❸

Pousada Ilha Bella Rua da Palma 92 ⓣ98/231-3563. One of the cleanest and least expensive of the budget hotels in the Zona. ❶

Pousada Internacional Rua da Estrela 175. Friendly hostel located in one of the city's best spots for nightlife, just around the corner from the tourist information office. ❷

The City

The city's central **layout** is easily grasped. Built on a headland that slopes down to rivers on two sides, the city's largest square is **Praça Deodoro**, from where the narrow but crowded Rua da Paz and Rua do Sol, each only with room for one lane of traffic and perilously tight pavements, lead down to **Praça João Lisboa**, which marks the edge of the **Zona** – the nickname for the colonial core of the city. From here steep streets lead down to the river waterfront. It's

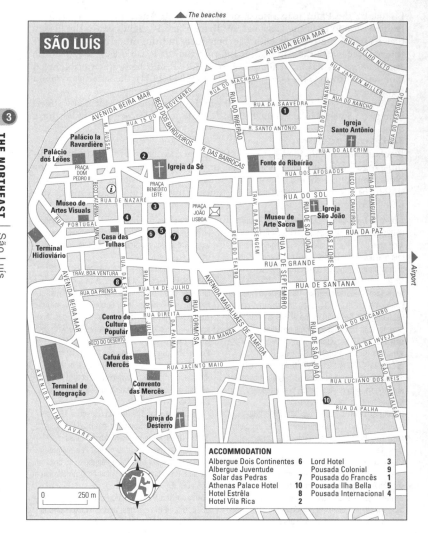

The beaches

SÃO LUÍS

ACCOMMODATION

Albergue Dois Continentes	6	Lord Hotel	3
Albergue Juventude		Pousada Colonial	9
Solar das Pedras	7	Pousada do Francês	1
Athenas Palace Hotel	10	Pousada Ilha Bella	5
Hotel Estrêla	8	Pousada Internacional	4
Hotel Vila Rica	2		

on the buildings fronting Praça João Lisboa that you will first see the lovely, glazed-tile frontages, the **azulejos**, which are the city's signature. Salvador has finer individual examples of *azulejo*, but taken as a whole the *azulejos* of colonial São Luís are unmatched for the scale of their use and their abstract beauty. Most are early nineteenth-century; some, with characteristic mustard-coloured shapes in the glazing, date back to the 1750s. Remarkably, many of the oldest tiles arrived in São Luís by accident, as ballast in cargo ships.

The Zona

The **Zona** – also called the **Reviver** after the project to restore it – covers a small headland overlooking the confluence of the Rio Anil and the Atlantic

Ocean, and though it may not look like much, a defensible harbour on this flat coastline was of some strategic importance. Now the waterfront is no more than a landing place for fishing boats and ferries, but slave ships once rode at anchor here, bringing in workers for the cotton and sugar plantations upriver. Then, the harbour was crowded with cargo boats, mostly from Liverpool, shipping out the exports of what – from about 1780 to 1840 – was a prosperous trading centre, for the first and last time in its history.

But the Zona predates even that colonial boom. São Luís shares with Rio the distinction of having been founded by the French, and is the only city in Brazil to have been ruled by three European countries. The French, decimated by a lethal combination of malaria and Indians, were soon dislodged by the Portuguese in 1615; then the Dutch sacked the city and held the area for three years from 1641, building the small fort that now lies in ruins on a headland between Calhau and Ponta da Areia. Over the next hundred years, the original shacks were replaced by some of the finest colonial buildings in northern Brazil.

The only way to explore the Zona is on foot. A good place to begin is the Praça Benedito Leite, a small leafy square where you'll find the tourist information office along with the **Igreja da Sé**, a cream and white cathedral completed in 1699 and given a Neoclassical facelift in 1922. Around the corner is the **Praça Dom Pedro II**, where the official buildings that line the square are splendidly proportioned survivors of the pre-Baroque colonial era. The oldest is the municipal hall, which dates from 1688: it still houses the Prefeitura and is called the **Palácio La Ravardiere**, after the French buccaneer who founded São Luís and is commemorated by a piratical bust on the pavement outside. In November 1985 the building was torched by an angry crowd, with the newly elected mayor inside, after an election acrimonious even by *maranhense* standards. Next door is the tropical Georgian elegance of the state governor's residence, the **Palácio dos Leões**, built between 1761 and 1776 and currently closed for restoration.

On the other side of the square from the Palácio dos Leões, steps lead down to the steep colonial street, **Beco Catarina Mina**, that takes you to the heart of the Zona, block after block of buildings, many restored whilst others are in an advanced state of decay. With its cobbled streets, *azulejos* and the vultures on the tile roofs, the Zona remains physically much as it was 150 years ago, although the colonial merchants and plantation owners who built it would have turned up their noses at its modern inhabitants. As economic decline bit deep, they sold up and moved on.

Beco Catarina Mina runs into the finest array of *azulejos* in the city, the tiled facades of the **Rua do Trapiche** (Rua Portugal), with the **Mercado da Praia Grande**'s gorgeous arches perfectly set off by the piercing-blue tiles and symmetrical windows and balconies. This area is the best-restored part of the Zona, given a magical feel by the brightly coloured *azulejos*, and has plenty of bars and restaurants and a lively street life at any time of day or night. The **Casa das Tulhas**, on Rua da Estrela, is an early nineteenth-century mansion now crammed with market stalls selling *artesanato*, including locally produced foods, quality cotton clothing, hammocks and tablecloths.

Many **churches** in the city have exteriors dating from the seventeenth century, and the most beautiful of these is the **Igreja do Desterro**, with its Byzantine domes, at the southern end of the Zona, though none of the church interiors has survived successive restorations. It was in these churches that the Jesuit **Padre Antônio Vieira** preached his sermons three hundred years ago, berating the plantation owners for enslaving Indians before the Jesuits had a chance to do so – sermons that are often taken to be the finest early Portuguese prose ever written.

Bumba-meu-boi

Bumba-meu-boi, which dominates every June in São Luís (generally starting on Sto. Antonio's day, **June 13**) is worth making some effort to catch: there's no more atmospheric popular festival in Brazil. A dance with distinctive music, performed by a costumed troupe of characters backed by drummers and brass instruments, it blends the Portuguese, African and Indian influences of both the state and Brazil. It originated on the plantations, and the troupes the *maranhenses* rate highest still come from the old plantation towns of the interior – Axixá, Pinheiro and Pindaré. To mark the day of São João on **June 24**, the interior towns send their bands to São Luís, where at night they sing and dance outside churches and in squares in the centre. Seeing the spectacular dances and costumes, and hearing the spellbindingly powerful music echoing down the colonial streets, is a magical experience.

Although the climax comes over the weekend nearest to June 24, *Bumba* takes over the city centre at night for the whole month. Dozens of stalls spring up in the areas where the troupes rehearse before setting off to the two churches in the centre around which everything revolves: the **Igreja de São João Batista**, on Rua da Paz, and the **Igreja de Santo Antônio**, four blocks north. Along the waterfront, stalls go up selling simple food and drinks, including lethal *batidas* with firewater rum – try the *genipapo*. Many choose to follow the *bois*, as the troupes are called, through the streets: if you feel less energetic, the best place to see everything is Praça de Santo Antônio, the square in front of the church where all the *bois* converge, in which you can sit and drink between troupes.

Bumba-meu-boi has a stock of characters and re-enacts the story of a plantation owner leaving a bull in the care of a slave, which dies and then magically revives. The bull, black velvet decorated with sequins and a cascade of ribbons, with someone inside whirling it around, is at the centre of a circle of musicians. The songs are belted out, with lyrics declaimed first by a lead caller, backed up only by a mandolin, and then joyously roared out by everyone when the drums and brass come in. *Bumba* drums are unique: hollow, and played by strumming a metal spring inside, they give out a deep, hypnotically powerful backbeat.

The troupe is surrounded by people singing along and doing the athletic dance that goes with the rhythm. There are certain old favourites that are the climax of every performance, especially *São Luís*, the unofficial city anthem: *São Luís, cidade de azulejos, juro que nunca te deixo longe do meu coracão* – "São Luís, city of *azulejos*, I swear I'll never keep you far from my heart", it begins, and when it comes up there is a roar of recognition and hundreds of voices join in. The sound of the people of the city shouting out their song radiates from Praça de Santo Antônio across the centre, turning the narrow streets and alleys into an echo chamber.

Bumba-meu-boi starts late, the troupes not hitting the centre until 11pm at the earliest, but people start congregating, either at the waterfront or in the square, soon after dark. *Bois* don't appear every night, except during the last few days before the 24th: ask at the place where you're staying, as everyone knows when a good *boi* is on. Bumba-meu-boi troupes are organized like samba schools; towns and city *bairros* have their own, but thankfully the festival hasn't been ruined by making them compete formally against each other. Informal rivalries are intense, all the same, and *maranhenses* love comparing their merits: most would agree that Boi de Madre de Deus is the best in the city, but they are eclipsed by the troupes from the interior, Boi de Axixá and Boi de Pinheiro. The best day of all is **June 29** (St Peter's Day), when all the *bois* congregate at the Igreja de São Pedro from 10pm until dawn.

Museums

There are two **museums** worth visiting on Rua do Trapiche. The **Salão de Bens Culturais** (daily 9am–9pm), at no. 303, houses an interesting collection of sacred and contemporary art, but the highlight is the display of brightly coloured cloth *bois*, or bulls, used in the festival of Bumba-meu-boi (see box opposite). There's also a video of the festival permanently playing in the museum. Part of this collection is also housed in the Centro de Cultura Popular Domingos Vieira Filho, Rua do Giz 221, Praia Grande (Tues–Sat 9am–7pm). Back on Rua do Trapiche at no. 273, is the **Museu de Artes Visuais** (daily 9am–7pm), a gallery that displays work by local artists.

Down at the other end of the Zona is the **Cafuá das Mercês**, the old slave market, which now houses the rather depleted collection of the **Museu do Negro**. Slaves who survived the journey across from West Africa were marched up here from the harbour and kept in the holding cells until they could be auctioned off in the small square outside. Nearby on Rua da Palma is the **Convento das Mercês**, an attractive spacious wooden building that houses a selection of presidential memorabilia belonging to one of Maranhão's most famous sons, the walrus-lookalike José Sarney. Despite having been a mediocre president, Sarney obviously benefits from having a sense of humour: many of the photographs and pictures on display mock him in one way or another.

One of São Luís's best museums lies outside the Zona. The **Museu de Arte Sacra**, Rua São João 500 (Tues–Fri 9am–6pm, Sat & Sun 2–6pm), houses some superb religious art from the seventeenth, eighteenth and nineteenth centuries. One of the outstanding pieces is a small wooden statue of St Paul embedded with incredibly lifelike glass eyes. There's also a statue of St John the Baptist with an incision in the neck: the space was used to hide jewels that were being smuggled out of the country.

The beaches

São Luís is blessed with a chain of excellent **beaches**, all of which can be reached by bus from the Terminal de Integração. The surf can be dangerous and people drown every month, so take care. It's also worth noting that swimming after sunset is not a good idea, as there are occasional attacks by sharks that are attracted by the kitchen waste dumped by ships offshore.

Ponta da Areia is the closest beach to the city centre, located by the ruins of the Forte São Marcos. Some 8km out of town, the dune beach of **Calhau** is larger and more scenic than Ponta da Areia: when the tide is out there is a lovely walk along the sands to Ponta da Areia, two hours' leisurely stroll west. After Calhau comes **Olho d'Agua**, equally fine, close to the dunes but a bit windy and well developed with houses and beach kiosks. Finally there's **Araçagi**, 19km out of town, the loveliest beach of all, an expansive stretch of sand that's also studded with bars and restaurants. It's served by hourly buses, but unless you rent a car you won't make it back the same day; there is a small hotel, though, the *Araçagi Praia* (☎98/226-3299; ❸), which offers smart rooms.

Eating, drinking and nightlife

At weekends virtually the entire city moves out to the beaches, which are large enough to swallow up the masses without getting too crowded. You will quickly discover one of the delights of this coast: the **seafood**. The seas and rivers around here teem with life, most of it edible. The beach stalls do fried fish, the prawns are the size of large fingers, and whatever they don't cook you can buy fresh from a stream of vendors – juicily tender crabs, battered open with bits of wood, or freshly gathered oysters, dirt-cheap, sold by the bagful, helpfully opened for you and sprinkled with lime juice. One thing you won't find outside Maranhão is *cuxá* – a delicious dish made of crushed dried shrimp, garlic and the stewed leaves of two native plants.

Except during Bumba-meu-boi and Carnaval, São Luís is quieter than most Brazilian cities of its size. The largest concentration of nightspots is just over the bridge, in **São Francisco**, a little on the tacky side for the most part. On Wednesday nights, when the historic centre really lets its hair down, loud reggae music blasts out till dawn.

Eating out in town is rewarding, thanks to the abundant seafood. The best in São Luís is the *caldeirada de camarão* (shrimp stew) at the *Base do SENAC*, Rua de Nazare 242 (☎98/232-6377), a piano bar located on the Praca Benedito Leite that's also a training ground for serious apprentice chefs. Good options in the Zona are *Antiguamente*, Rua da Estrela 220 (☎98/232-3964) and *La Papagaio*, more or less next door, both of which have varied menus, including local seafood dishes like *file de peixe ao molho de castanhas* (fish in a nut sauce) and pastas, too; the former also puts on decent rock music. There's also the excellent and traditional *Base do Edilson* restaurant buried deep in the *bairro* of Vila Bessa, at Rua Alencar Campos 31, but the short taxi journey from the centre is well worth the effort. Good *caldeirada* is also to be had at the *Base do Germano*, also a short taxi ride from the centre on Avenida Wenceslau Brás, in the *bairro* of Camboa. In the city centre, one of the better seafood restaurants is the *Base da Lenoca*, at Av. Dom Pedro II 181.

Along the coast

Travel in Maranhão outside São Luís is made difficult by a road system that is limited and – given the rains – often precarious. If you want to travel **along the coast** the most practical way is by boat, an option, however, that is not to be taken lightly as it's hard going: no schedules or creature comforts, and no one who speaks English. Don't do it unless you're healthy, a good sailor, not fussy about what you eat, have at least basic Portuguese and aren't too worried about time. But if you want to get completely off the beaten track, there's nothing to rival a sea journey.

The place to start is the **Estação Marítima** in São Luís, on the waterfront at the end of Praça Dom Pedro II. This is the local station for boats, which supply the nearby coastal villages and towns, take on passengers and cargo and wait for the tides. Brightly painted, these boats are built by artisans along the coast who still know how to put an ocean-going vessel together from timber.

There are sailings to the main coastal towns to the **west** about once a week. Pick a destination and ask at the booth in the Estação Marítima for the day and time: you either buy your passage there and then, or negotiate with the captain. The main coastal towns, as you head west, are Guimarães (half a day away), Turiaçu (two days) and Luis Domingues and Carutapera (three days). Take plenty of food and drink; *maranhenses* scratch limes and smell them to guard against seasickness, and it does seem to help.

If you wish to take an **organized tour** – often the simplest and fastest way to reach many of the places along this coast – it's best to go through one of the tour companies in São Luís. Simsol Turismo (☎245-9655, or ☎98/349-0260 in Barreirinhas) organize two-day trips to the Parque Nacional dos Lençóis for around $60. Rio Ave Turismo, based at Av. Dom Pedro II 221 (☎98/221-0238) in Praia Grande offer a similar tour, as well as tours of the city both day and night, trips along the coast to Ribamar and to the historic city of Alcântra, one hour away by boat from São Luís. Labotur (☎98/217-8346) run inexpensive

△ Igreja de São Francisco, Salvador

eco-tourism trips to the Ilha do Medo, usually leaving from the Ponta da Espera around 8am and returning around 5.30pm.

São José do Ribamar

Fortunately, not all the interesting places are difficult to get to. Easiest of all are the fishing towns on the island of São Luís: Raposa, a simple village on a beach, an hour away by bus from Praça Deodoro or Rua da Paz; and **SÃO JOSÉ DO RIBAMAR**, which you can reach on the bus marked "Ribamar" from the same stops, or from outside the *Athenas Palace Hotel*.

It's 32km to São José, about an hour's drive, a lovely route through thick palm forest and small hills. The bus deposits you in the small town centre, where straggling houses on a headland have sweeping views of a fine bay; it's easy to stay over, as there are several **pensões** in the centre. São José is an important fishing town, as well as being a centre of skilled boat-building by traditional methods – you can see the yards, with the half-finished ribs of surprisingly large boats, behind the houses running inland from the small landing quay and large beach. There's a very relaxing feel to the town. The people are friendly, the scenery splendid, and it's not difficult to while away a few days doing nothing in particular. There are some good **restaurants**, too: the *Ribamar*, serving mainly seafood, has a terrace looking out to the bay, and the rustic *barracas* on the waterfront are ideal spots to chat and watch the sunset from.

A lot of the **boats** that ply the coast both east and west drop in at São José, and it's a convenient place to begin a boat trip. Easiest places to head for, and with a fair degree of certainty that there'll be a boat back within a day or two, are Icatu, the mainland village on the other side of the bay, and Primeira Cruz on the east coast. From the latter, it's a short hop to the interior town of Humberto De Campos, where you can catch a bus back to São Luís.

Parque Nacional dos Lençóis

From Primeira Cruz, you can also continue to what is arguably one of the most beautiful sights in Brazil, the **Parque Nacional dos Lençóis**, a desert some 370km to the east of São Luís covering around 300 square kilometres. What makes it so special is that it is composed of hundreds of massive sand dunes that reach towering heights but are subject to prolonged rainfall. The result is that the dunes are sprinkled with literally hundreds of crystal-clear freshwater lagoons. To get there either continue from the small town of Primeira Cruz, or, direct from São Luís, catch the bus to Barreirinhas from the *rodoviária* (hours variable so check beforehand with MARATUR), which takes about eight hours to get there. If you wish to stay overnight here, there are some very modest *pousadas*, including the *Pousada Lins*, Av. Joaquim Sueiro de Carvalho 550 (☎98/349-1203; ❷), which has a good restaurant; the *Pousada do Buruti*, Rua Inácio Lins (☎98/349-1053; ❷), and the even cheaper *Pousada El Casarão*, Rua Inácio Neves 110 (☎98/349-1078; ❶). From Barreirinhas, it's a three-hour journey down the Rio Preguiças to the dunes themselves. If you don't fancy organizing the trip for yourself then there are a couple of agencies in São Luís that will: Giltur, Rua do Giz 46, in the Zona (☎98/232-6041), and Taguatur, Rua do Sol 141, inside the shopping centre (☎98/231-4197 or 232-0906), both of which organize trips by bus and boat or by plane. The overland trip takes three days and will set you back about $100; the plane trip takes a day and costs about $180. For further information on the *parque*, contact IBAMA, the national parks authority (☎98/231-3010).

Across the bay: Alcântara

Set in a wonderful tropical landscape on the other side of the **bay of São Marcos** from São Luís, **ALCÂNTARA** is now no more than a poor village built around the ruins of what was once the richest town in northern Brazil. São Luís had already eclipsed it by the end of the eighteenth century, and for the last two hundred years it has been left to moulder quietly away. The measure of its decline is that there are now no roads worthy of being called that going there; the only way is by sea from the Estação Marítima at the end of Praça Dom Pedro II in São Luís.

Alcântara is a ninety-minute chug across the bay, which can still sometimes get choppy enough to make you thankful you've arrived. The alternative is a large motorboat – the *Batevento* – which takes half the time but is twice the price ($12). The regular boat leaves at 7am, the motorboat around 9.30am. There's a fine view of ruins and the houses of the town as you arrive, strung out along a headland, the skyline dominated by imperial palms; you face a short walk uphill after you disembark. Most of the ruins you see are from the seventeenth century: Alcântara, founded in 1648, was the first capital of Maranhão and the main centre of the first stretch of coastline that the Portuguese converted to sugar plantations.

The main square, **Praça da Matriz**, gives you an idea of how grand it must have been in its heyday, surrounded on three sides by colonial mansions. In the centre of the square is a curious corroded stone post, erected in 1647, on which you can still see the carved arms of the Portuguese Crown: this is the *pelourinho*, a whipping post, set up to mark the king of Portugal's claim to the coast.

If you thought some of the buildings in the colonial zone of São Luís were in bad repair, Alcântara proves how much worse things can get, notwithstanding its more recent efforts at restoration. Very few of the oldest buildings have survived; for the most part only the facade and walls are standing, many with coats of arms still discernible. The roofs went generations ago and most have large trees growing out of them. On the main square is a small **museum**, in a restored mansion with a fine *azulejo* frontage, which has a good collection of artefacts and prints to give you an idea of what the place was once like. It doesn't keep regular opening hours, but they will open it up for you if you ask nicely; they'll know where the key is at the *Hotel Pelourinho* (see below).

The ruins, the views, the beaches and the friendliness of the people combine to make Alcântara a very atmospheric place. Short **walks** or **canoe rides** in either direction take you to deserted **beaches** where there are rustic cafés and bars serving chilled beer. Better still are boat trips through the mangroves, where you will see *guarás*, birds resembling flamingos except they are bright red instead of pink; against the green background they look extraordinary.

Practicalities

The last boat back to São Luís leaves daily at 4pm, so if you want to stay for more than eight hours you'll have to spend the night. The two **hotels** on Praça da Matriz are both good: *Pousada do Imperador* (❸), with spacious rooms and private baths, and the clean and comfortable *Hotel Pelourinho* (☎98/337-1150; ❷). There's also the more expensive *Pousada do Modomo Régio*, Rua Grande 134 (☎98/337-1197 or 337-1575; ❹), which has a decent restaurant. The cheapest option is to string your **hammock** in a house: groups of children meet incoming boats looking for tourists for exactly that purpose, so finding somewhere is easy. The deal will include an evening meal and breakfast, simple but wholesome; just don't drink the water. The best **restaurant** in town is at *Hotel*

Pelourinho, its home-brewed fruit liqueurs a speciality; try the refreshing guava (*goiaba*). Just off the main square there's a TELMA post, from where you can make **telephone calls**.

The interior

Travel in the **interior** of Maranhão is limited by the road system: there is only one highway out of São Luís, which forks east to Teresina and west to Belém (see p.394). Although asphalted, chunks of it often get washed away during the rainy season. You'll usually get through eventually – even if you have to push with the rest of the passengers – but things like timetables cease to have any meaning. The worst part of the road is the bit from São Luís to Santa Inês.

The **road to Belém** is now a lot better than it was, although the link southwest to Imperatriz can still be a bit dodgy. There's little to keep you in central Maranhão, although the journey is interesting: travel by day if you can. The area you pass through was first populated on a large scale thirty years ago and the towns, the largest en route being Bacabal and Santa Inês, are young but growing rapidly. By the time you get to Santa Inês you're in Amazônia, but don't expect to see any forest en route to Belém; most of it was cut down for cattle ranching twenty years ago.

Although there's nowhere worth getting off the bus, this final western stretch of Maranhão is fascinating. Inland, a **gold rush** has been going on since 1982. Many of the people getting on and off at the roadside villages past Santa Inês, especially at the town of Maracassumé, are *garimpeiros*, gold-miners. Just over the border with Pará you even get to see a gold camp, Cachoeira, where a village has developed around a gold strike; you can just about see the diggings from the road, but it's not advisable to get off for a closer look.

South to Imperatriz and Carolina

At Santa Inês a fork heads southwest to **IMPERATRIZ**, a mushrooming city on the Belém–Brasília highway: 280,000 people where as recently as twenty years ago there was only a small town of about 10,000. There's little reason to go to Imperatriz for its own sake. The town is teeming with people on the move, and even basic facilities have been swamped. The atmosphere here is made worse by the violent **land conflicts** in the region, and Imperatriz is where the gunmen hang out between contracts. However, it does lie en route to Brasília and, more immediately, **CAROLINA**, the only town in southern Maranhão of any conceivable interest to tourists. Situated on the banks of the Rio Tocantins, Carolina's attraction is that it lies in a region of spectacular waterfalls, the most famous being those at **Pedra Caída**, more than 30km out of town. If you're coming from São Luís, you should get the train as far as Imperatriz before changing to the bus for a four-hour ride to Carolina. There are a few **places to stay**, including the *Recanto Pedra Caída* (☎99/731-1318; ❸), an atmospheric place right by the falls, and the *Pousada do Lajes* (☎99/531-2348; ❸), which has a pool but no restaurant.

Travel details

Buses

Fortaleza to: João Pessoa (2 daily; 8hr); Natal (10 daily; 8hr); Salvador (1 daily, 21hr); São Luís (3 daily; 18hr).

João Pessoa to: Cabedelo (every 30min; 45min); Campina Grande (hourly; 2hr); Fortaleza (6 daily; 9hr); Juazeiro do Norte (2 daily; 10hr); Mossoró (several daily; 4hr); Penha (every 2hr; 45min).

Maceió to: Aracaju (6 daily; 5hr); Paulo Afonso (2 daily; 4hr); Penedo (6 daily; 2hr).

Natal to: Fortaleza (4 daily; 8hr); João Pessoa (10 daily; 3hr); Salvador (1 daily, 20hr).

Recife to: Amarelo (every 30min; 1hr); Aracaju (2 daily; 8hr); Belém (5 weekly; 35hr); Belo Horizonte (3 daily; 35hr); Brasília (3 daily; 48hr); Caruaru (at least hourly; 2hr); Fortaleza (6 daily; 12hr); Goiânia (6 daily; 2hr); João Pessoa (10 daily; 2hr); Maceió (20 daily; 4hr); Natal (20 daily; 4hr 30min); Petrolina (4 daily; 12hr); Porto de Galinhas (every 30min; 1hr); Rio (2 daily; 42hr); Salvador (6 daily; 13hr); São José da Coroa Grande (hourly; 1hr 30min); São Paulo (4 daily; 48hr).

Salvador to: Belém (4 weekly; 35hr); Brasília (6 daily; 26hr); Cachoeira (hourly; 2hr 30min); Feira de Santana (hourly; 2hr); Ilhéus (6 daily; 6hr 30min); Jacobina (2 daily; 6hr); Lençóis (2 daily; 6hr); Porto Seguro (4 daily; 11hr); Praia do Forte (4 daily; 2hr); Recife (6 daily; 13hr); Rio (2 daily; 30hr); Santo Amaro (every 30min; 2hr); São Paulo (2 daily; 35hr); Valença (6 daily; 5hr).

Teresina to: Belém (1–2 daily; 24hr); Fortaleza (2 daily; 15hr); São Luís (several daily; 10hr).

Ferries

Salvador to: Itaparicá (every 30min; 60min).

Flights

João Pessoa, Salvador, Natal, Maceió, Fortaleza and Recife are all connected by at least daily flights. Salvador also has a daily connection to Natal.

The Amazon

CHAPTER 4 # Highlights

✳ **Ver o Peso Market** Best visited in the early morning, Belém's traditional market is a great place to watch the local trade. See p.399

✳ **Teatro Amazonas** A full-blown European opera house in one of the least likely locations. See p.434

✳ **Ponta Negra clubs** Head for Manaus' Praia Ponta Negra for the best in old and modern samba music, and some lively formation dancing, too. See p.439

✳ **Amazon wildlife** Make sure to spend at least a few days in the jungle if you want to spot magnificent toucans, alligators and much more. See p.440

✳ **Jungle river trips** A great way to take in the lush forest scenery, fascinating river settlements and the beautiful sight of the river itself. See p.440

✳ **Madeira-Mamoré Museu Ferroviário** This fascinating railway museum in Porto Velho will appeal to casual visitors and railroad buffs alike. See p.459

The Amazon

④

④

THE AMAZON

The Amazon is a vast forest – the largest on the planet – and a giant river system. It covers over half of Brazil and a large portion of South America. The forest extends into Brazil's neighbouring countries, Venezuela, Colombia, Peru and Bolivia, where the river itself begins life among thousands of different headwaters. In Brazil only the stretch between Manaus and Belém is actually known as the **Rio Amazonas**: above Manaus the river is called the **Rio Solimões** up to the border with Peru, where it once again becomes the Amazonas. The daily flow of the river is said to be enough to supply a city the size of New York with water for nearly ten years, and its power is such that the muddy Amazon waters stain the Atlantic a silty brown for over 200km out to sea. This was how its existence was first identified by the Spaniard, Vicente Yanez Pinon, sailing the Atlantic in search of El Dorado. He was drawn to the mouth of the Amazon by the sweet freshness of the ocean or, as he called it, the Mar Dulce.

To many Indian tribes, the Amazon is a gigantic mythical anaconda, source of life and death. In its upper reaches, the Rio Solimões from Peru to Manaus, it is a muddy light brown, but at Manaus it meets the darker flow of the Rio Negro and the two mingle together at the famous "meeting of the waters" to form the Rio Amazonas. There are something like 80,000 square kilometres of **navigable river** in the Amazon system, and the Amazon itself can take ocean-going vessels virtually clean across South America, from the Atlantic coast to Iquitos in Peru. Even at the Óbidos narrows, the only topographical obstruction between the Andes and the Atlantic, the river is almost 2km wide and for most of its length it is far broader – by the time it reaches the ocean the river's gaping mouth stretches further apart than London and Paris.

Ecology and development

The Amazon is far more than just a river. Its catchment basin contains, at any one moment, over one-fifth of all the world's fresh water, and the **rainforest** it sustains covers an area of over six million square kilometres, stretching almost right across the continent. The Amazon forest is a vitally important cog in the planet's biosphere controls. There are over a thousand tributaries (several larger than the Mississippi), whose combined energy potential is estimated at over 100,000 megawatts daily (an endlessly renewable supply equivalent to five million barrels of oil a day). Eletronorte, the region's electricity supply company, today produces around 20,000 megawatts from Amazonian hydroelectric power.

Although in 1639 Pedro Teixeira travelled 2000 miles up the Amazon and claimed all the land east of Ecuador for Portugal, the Portuguese really gained control of the Brazilian Amazon, in a political sense, through the Treaty of

387
▬

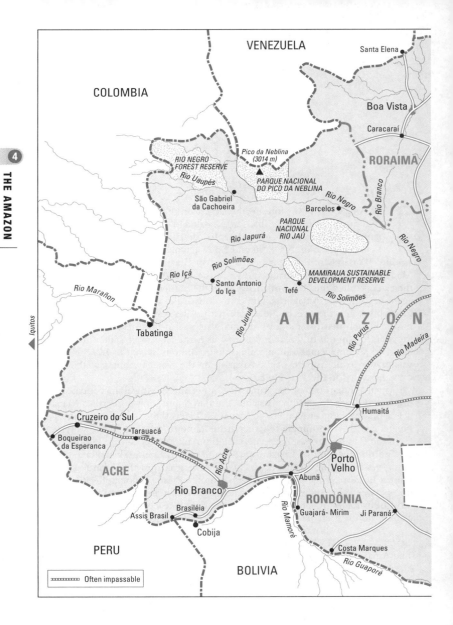

Madrid in 1750. Four years later, Governor Mendonça Furtado was appointed Boundary Commissioner and began his tour of inspection in the Amazon. He saw the prosperity of the Carmelite missions on the Rio Negro and initiated the Directorate System of controlling "official" Indian villages that were essentially labour camps. Having seen how effective the Carmelite missionaries had been in manipulating native workers, the governor was determined to do the

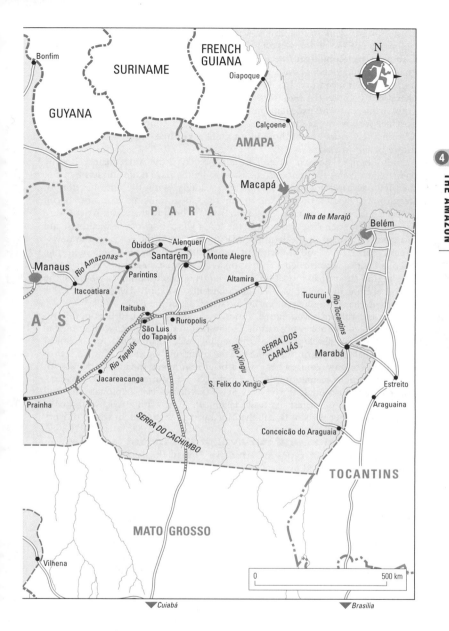

same. Some Indians, remaining free in the regions upstream on the major tributaries, tended to gather in villages at portage points like difficult rapids where they acted as guides and muscle-power for traders. Others retreated deeper into the forest.

The region was only integrated fully into the Brazilian political scene after Independence in 1822. And even then it remained safer and quicker to sail from Rio de Janeiro to Lisbon than to Manaus. Within a few years of Independence the region was almost lost to Brazil altogether when the bloody **Cabanagem Rebellion** (see p.396) overthrew white rule and attempted to establish an independent state. When things had quietened down a little, in the mid-nineteenth century, US Navy engineers were sent to the Amazon to check out its potential resources. They reported that it was wealthy in forest gums, fruits, nuts and excellent timber, and provided with a ready-made transport network in the form of rivers that gave direct contact with the Atlantic. Within a few years one of those forest gums – **rubber** – was to transform the future of the Amazon.

Until Charles Goodyear invented the rubber tyre, the Amazonian economy had run at a bare subsistence level, sustained by the slave trade and lumber. But the new demand for rubber coincided handily with the introduction of steamship navigation on the Amazon in 1858, beginning an economic boom as spectacular as any the world has seen. By 1900 both Manaus and Belém were extraordinarily rich cities, and out in the forest were some of the wealthiest and most powerful men in the world at that time, beyond the reach of the newspapers, conscience and worries of nineteenth-century Europe: men like Nicolas Suárez, who earned a reputation as an autocratic ruler of a rubber-tapping region larger than most European countries. Controlling the whole of the region around the upper Rio Madeira and into modern-day Peru, he was a legendarily harsh employer even by the standards of the day.

When the rubber boom ended, almost as suddenly as it had begun, following the success of rubber plantations established in the Far East (with smuggled Brazilian seeds), development of the region once again came to an almost complete halt, relying on the export of the traditional products of the forest to keep the economy going. There was a brief resurgence during World War II, when the rubber plantations in the Far East were controlled by the Japanese, but it is only in the last thirty years or so that large-scale exploitation – and destruction – of the forest has really taken off, along with a massive influx of people from other parts of Brazil, the Northeast in particular, in search of land.

The destruction and survival of the forest

There are three main **types of Amazon forest**: the *várzea* or flood-plain zones, regularly flooded by the rivers; the *igapós*, which are occasionally flooded; and the *terra firma*, generally unflooded land that forms the majority of the surface area. Each forest type differs in the nature of its vegetation and the potential of its land use. Much of the *terra firma* is high forest where life exists as much in the upper canopies as it does on the ground. In the extreme northern and southern limits of the Amazon Basin, and to some extent taking over where mankind has caused most devastation, there are extensive coverings of wooded and scrubby savannas. When the forest is destroyed the land generally remains productive for only a few years before turning to scrub.

The destruction of the Amazon forest obviously takes a severe toll on the area's unique **flora and fauna**. There are believed to be as many as 15,000 animal species in the Amazon – thousands of which have still to be identified – and untold numbers of so far unclassified plants. Since they remain unknown, it is impossible to say quite what damage the destruction of the rainforest is doing, but there can be no doubt that many animal and plant species will be lost before anyone has had a chance to study them. The loss of this gene pool – with its potential use for medicines, foods and other unknown purposes – is serious; perhaps only the indigenous people of the forests will really know what has been lost – if they survive.

The Brazilian riposte, of course, is that the Western nations have no right to occupy any moral high ground, or to stand in the way of what they see as the essential economic development of their country. And they generally further add that the area being lost is insignificant compared to what survives. For all the damage to the ecology and the peoples of the Amazon, it is hard to argue that Brazil should be denied the right to utilize the mineral and natural resources by people who have already exploited so much of the rest of the world.

The deforestation of the Amazon forest reached a peak in the late 1980s; large-scale ranching was mainly to blame, along with the huge number of small-scale subsistence and cash-crop farmers. In the following decade the destruction continued but at a slower pace, in part due to an increased awareness of the importance of the forest, but primarily because the world's large lumber companies were concentrating their efforts elsewhere – on the more accessible rainforests of Southeast Asia. Today, as forest cover in Southeast Asia dwindles, there is once again mounting pressure on the Amazon forest, this time from global lumber companies.

There are hopeful signs, however. People are increasingly discovering that cultivation – particularly cattle ranching – is not an efficient way to use the jungle, and that the productivity of the land decreases rapidly after the first few years. Scientists are just beginning to demonstrate (and developers to accept) that the virgin forests – with their fruits, roots, nuts, rubber trees, medicinal plants, dyes, game etc – are an endless resource that can actually be more profitable than cleared land. Another good sign is the growth of interest, among tourists and Brazilians alike, in **ecotourism**. This pursuit, properly managed, brings money into the region and provides employment for its inhabitants, through an industry that conserves rather than exploits the natural environment. For more on the Amazon environment see p.764.

Getting around the Amazon

Most people who visit Brazil will, at some time or other, have dreamt about taking a **boat up the Amazon** (see box pp.392–393). This is not hard to do, though it's not as comfortable or easy going as daydreams might have made it seem. Given the food on some boats, the trip can be tough on the stomach, and you'll need meditative patience or a botanical degree to appreciate the subtle changes in the forest scene on the often-distant riverbanks. But as many boats have a bar on their top decks, most passengers, whether Zen adepts or not, make a great time of it.

The classic journey is the five or six days from **Belém**, a friendly coastal city worth visiting in its own right, to **Manaus** in the heart of the jungle; and perhaps on from there on a wooden river boat to Iquitos in Peru via Tabatinga on the Brazilian frontier. But sticking only to the main channel of the Amazon is not the way to see the jungle or its wildlife: for that you'll want to take trips on smaller boats up smaller streams, an option that is particularly rewarding in the west where the rivers aren't quite so wide.

Thirty years ago river travel was virtually the only means of getting around the region, but in the 1960s the **Transamazônica** – Highway BR-230 – was constructed, cutting right across the south of Amazônia and linking the Atlantic coast (via the Belém–Brasília highway) with the Peruvian border at Brazil's western extremity. It remains an extraordinary piece of engineering, but is now increasingly bedraggled. Lack of money to pay for the stupendous amount of maintenance the network needs has now made much of it impassable. West of Altamira it has practically ceased to exist, apart from the Porto Velho–Rio Branco run and odd stretches where local communities find the road useful

Any journey up the Rio Amazonas is a serious affair. The river is big and powerful and the boats, in general, are relatively small, top-heavy-looking wooden vessels on two or three levels. As far as **spotting wildlife** goes, there's very little chance of seeing much more than a small range of tropical forest birds – mostly buzzards around the refuse tips of the ports en route – and the occasional river dolphin, although your chances increase the smaller the craft you're travelling on, as going upriver, the smaller boats tend to hug the riverbanks, bringing the spectacle much closer. Going downstream, however, large and small boats alike tend to cruise with the midstream currents, taking advantage of the added power they provide. Whichever boat you travel with, the river is nevertheless a beautiful sight and many of the settlements you pass or moor in are fascinating.

It's important to **prepare** properly for an Amazon river trip if you want to ensure your comfort and health. The most essential item is a **hammock**, which can be bought cheaply (from about $8) in the stores and markets of Manaus, Santarém or Belém, plus two stout pieces of rope to hang it from – hooks are not always the right interval apart for your size of hammock. Loose **clothing** is OK during daylight hours but at night you'll need some warmer garments and long sleeves against the chill and the insects. A **blanket** and some **insect repellent** are also recommended. Enough **drink** (large containers of mineral water are the best option, available in the bigger towns) and extra **food** – cookies, fruit and the odd tin – to keep you happy for the duration of the voyage may also be a good idea. Virtually all boats now provide mineral water, and the food, included in the price, has improved on most vessels, but a lot of people still get literally sick of the rice, meat and beans served on board, which is, of course, usually cooked in river water. If all else fails, you can always buy extra provisions in the small ports the boats visit. There are toilets on all boats, though even on the best they can get filthy within a few hours of leaving port. Again, there are exceptions, but it's advisable to take your own roll of **toilet paper** just in case. **Yellow fever inoculation** checks are common on boats leaving Belém to travel upriver, and for travellers unfortunate enough not to have a valid certificate of vaccination, you risk having a compulsory injection.

There are a few things to bear in mind when you're choosing **which boat** to travel with, the most important being the size and degree of comfort. The size affects the length of the journey, most small wooden boats taking up to 7 days to cover Belém to Manaus, with the larger vessels generally making the journey in 5–6 days (4–5 days downriver). The ENASA river boat company's three **catamarans** (all three-deck) are the largest boats connecting Belém with Manaus, each with at least 25 cabins ($180 upriver, $120 downriver; or up to $400 for a private bath and decent

and maintain it. The same fate has met other highways like the Santarém–Cuiabá and the Porto Velho–Manaus, on which great hopes were once pinned. With the exception of the Belém–Brasília, Cuiabá–Rio Branco and the Manaus–Boa Vista highway corridors, transport in the Amazon has sensibly reverted to rivers. Access to what remains of the Transamazônica from Belém or Brasília is via Estreito, the settlement at the junction where the BR-230 turns west off the old north–south highway, the BR-153/BR-010.

One thing to bear in mind while travelling is that there are three **time zones** in the Amazon region. Belém and eastern Pará are on the same time as the rest of the coast, except from October to February when Bahia and the states of the Southeast and the South switch to summer time, leaving Belém an hour behind. At the Rio Xingu, about halfway west across Pará, the clocks go back an hour to Manaus time. Tabatinga, Rio Branco and Acre, in the extreme west of the Amazon, are another hour behind again.

THE AMAZON

4

air-conditioning) and room for around 300 hammocks on the middle deck (around $70 upriver, $55 downriver). Like all river boats, the catamarans call at Breves, Santarém, Óbidos, Oriximiná and Parintins along the way; however, their departure times are erratic and at times there may be no service for weeks. Note also that ENASA has a poor reputation for its cuisine, and the boats tend to stick to the middle of the river, so you don't really see all that much. See also under the "Listings" for Belém, Santarém and Manaus for more on boat operators.

Better value, and usually more interesting in the degree of contact it affords among tourists, the crew and locals, is the option of taking a **wooden river boat** carrying both cargo and passengers. There are plenty of these along the waterfront in all the main ports, and it's simply a matter of going down there and establishing which ones are getting ready to go to wherever you are heading, or else enquiring at the ticket offices; like the ENASA boats, these vessels stop at most towns along the way. You'll share a deck with scores of other travellers, mostly locals or Brazilians, which will almost certainly ensure that the journey never becomes too monotonous. The most organized of the wooden river boats are the larger **three-deck vessels**, on which the Belém–Manaus trip costs $70 for hammock space ($50 downriver); this is negotiable if you're really stuck for cash, and will often come with a small discount if you buy your tickets two or more days before departure. The smaller **two-deck boats** are cosier, but often only cover shorter legs of the river. This is fine if you don't mind spending a day or two waiting for your next connection to load up. All of these wooden vessels tend to let passengers stay aboard a night or two before departure and after arrival, which saves on hotel costs.

There's room for debate about whether hammock space is a better bet than a **cabin** (camarote; currently around $110 upriver), of which there are usually only a few. Though the cabins can be unbearably hot and stuffy during the day, they do offer security for your baggage, as well as some privacy (though the cabins are shared, with either two or four bunks in each) and, in most cases, your own toilet (which can be a blessing, especially if you're not very well). The hammock areas get extremely crowded, so arrive early and establish your position: the best spots are near the front or the sides for the cooling breezes (it doesn't really matter which side, as the boat will alternate quite freely from one bank of the river to the other), though the bow of the boat can get rather chilly if the weather conditions turn a bit stormy. If it really gets unbearably crowded, you can always take your chances by slinging your hammock on the lower deck with the crew, though you'll also have to share your space with cargo and throbbing engine noise.

Eastern Amazônia

Politically divided between the states of Pará and Amapá, the eastern Amazon is essentially a vast area of forest and savanna plains centred on the final seven hundred miles or so of the giant river's course. **Belém**, an Atlantic port near the mouth of the estuary, is the elegant capital of Pará and a worthwhile place to spend some time. The city overlooks the river and the vast **Ilha de Marajó**, a marshy island in the estuary given over mainly to cattle farming, but with a couple of good beaches.

Pará has always been a relatively productive region. In the late eighteenth century it was an important source of rice (allowing Portugal to be "self-sufficient" in the commodity), and it also exported cacao and, later, rubber. Very little of the wealth, however, ever reached beyond a small elite, and falling prices of local commodities on the world markets have periodically produced severe hardship. Today, the state is booming once again, largely thanks to vast mineral extraction projects in the south. The landscape of southern Pará, below **Marabá** and the Tocantins-Araguaia rivers, is essentially a scrubby savanna known locally as *caatinga*: traditionally the home of the *Gê*-speaking Indians, it forms the major part of the central Brazilian plateau or shield. Over the last twenty years some of the most controversial developments in the Amazon have been taking place here: particularly the vast **Grande Carajás** industrial scheme, based around a huge deposit of iron and other ores, and the associated hydroelectric operation at **Tucurui**, whose dam has flooded an enormous area of forest and Indian land. Not far away are the once infamous **Serra Pelada** gold mines.

Amapá, in the northeastern corner of the Brazilian Amazon, is a fascinating place in its own right. A poor and little-visited area, it nevertheless offers the opportunity of an adventurous overland route to French Guyana and on into Surinam, Guyana and Venezuela. It's possible to do much of this journey by ocean-going boat.

Connections in the region are pretty straightforward, in that you have very few choices. The main throughway is still the Amazon, with stops at **Santarém** – a sleepy town entirely dominated by the river – and **Óbidos**, far less enticing. As far as roads go there are good highways south from Belém towards Brasília (the BR-010) and east into the state of Maranhão (the BR-316). In the north there's just one road from **Macapá**, the capital of Amapá, up towards the border with French Guyana. The BR-010 crosses the powerful Rio Tocantins near Estreito (in Maranhão) close to the start of the **Transamazônica**. If you're coming from the south, connections with westbound buses and other traffic are best made at Araguaina (in Tocantins) where there's a small *rodoviária* and several hotels. The first stop on the Transamazônica within Pará is **Marabá**, some 460km (12hr) by bus from Belém. Continuing from here, the Transamazônica reaches **Altamira**, on the navigable Rio Xingu, a small, relatively new city over 300km west of Marabá where there's another massive hydroelectric dam scheme. With a population that's grown from 15,000 in 1970 to over 130,000 today, Altamira is at the centre of an area of rapidly vanishing jungle. Beyond the city, the Transamazônica becomes impassable.

Belém

Strategically placed on the Amazon river estuary close to the mouth of the mighty Rio Tocantins, **BELÉM** was founded by the Portuguese in 1616 as the City of Our Lady of Bethlehem (Belém). Its original role was to protect the river mouth and establish the Portuguese claim to the region, but it rapidly became established as an Indian slaving port and a source of cacao and spices from the Amazon. Such was the devastation of the local population, however, that by the mid-eighteenth century a royal decree was issued in Portugal to encourage its growth: every white man who married an Indian woman would receive "one axe, two scissors, some cloth, clothes, two cows and two bushels of seed".

Despite the decree, Belém was deep in decline before the end of the century, precipitated by a shrinking labour force and, in the 1780s, the threat of

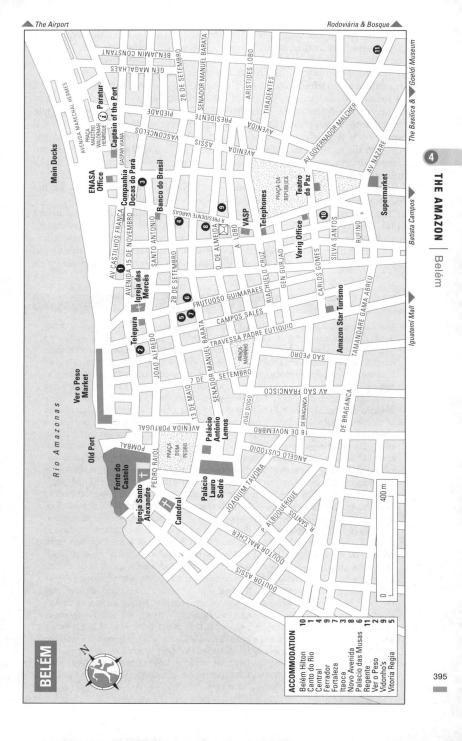

4

BELÉM

N

The Airport

Rodoviária & Bosque

Rio Amazonas

Main Docks

Ver o Peso Market

Old Port

Forte do Castelo

Igreja Santo Alexandre

Catedral

PEDRO RAIOL

Palácio Lauro Sodré

Palácio Antônio Lemos

PRAÇA DOM PEDRO

AVENIDA PORTUGAL

POMBAL

13 DE MAIO

JOÃO ALFREDO

SANTO ANTONIO

AV CASTILHOS FRANCA

AVENIDA 15 DE NOVEMBRO

Igreja das Mercés

Telepura

28 DE SETEMBRO

FRUTUOSO GUIMARAES

CAMPOS SALES

TRAVESSA PADRE EUTIQUIO

PRAÇA MARINHO

SENADOR MANUEL BARATA

7 DE SETEMBRO

JOÃO DIOGO

16 DE NOVEMBRO

ANGELO CUSTODIO

AV SÃO FRANCISCO

SÃO PEDRO

DE BRAGANCA

DE BRAGANCA

JOAQUIM TAVORA

DOUTOR MALCHER

P. A. ALBUQUERQUE

R. SANTOS

DOUTOR ASSIS

ENASA Office

Companhia Docas do Pará

Banco do Brasil

GASPAR VIANA

PRESIDENTE VARGAS

O. DE ALMEIDA

A. LOBO

RIACHUELO CRUZ

GEN GURJAO

CARLOS GOMES

SILVA SANTOS

RUFINO

VASP

Telephones

Varig Office

Amazon Star Turismo

TAMANDARE GAMA ABREU

Teatro da Paz

PRAÇA DA REPUBLICA

Supermarket

AV NAZARE

AV GOVERNADOR MALCHER

AVENIDA PRESIDENTE PIEDADE

ARISTIDES LOBO

TIRADENTES

28 DE SETEMBRO

SENADOR MANUEL BARATA

GEN MAGALHAES

BENJAMIN CONSTANT

AVENIDA MARECHAL HERMES

PRAÇA MAESTRO WALDEMAR HENRIQUE

Paratur

Captain of the Port

ASSIS

VASCONCELOS

The Basílica & Goeldi Museum

Batista Campos

Iguatemi Mall

400 m

0

ACCOMMODATION

Belém Hilton	10
Canto do Rio	1
Central	4
Ferrador	9
Fortaleza	7
Itaoca	3
Novo Avenida	8
Palacio das Musas	6
Regente	11
Ver o Peso	2
Vidonho's	9
Vitoria Regia	5

attack by a large contingent of Munduruku Indians. In the nineteenth century, it sank still further, as the centre of the nation's bloodiest rebellion (see box below), before the town experienced an extraordinary revival as the most prosperous beneficiary of the Amazon rubber boom. By the end of the nineteenth century, Belém was a very rich town, accounting for close to half of all Brazil's rubber exports. At this time rubber was being collected from every corner of the Amazon. As a result of the boom, thousands of poor people moved into Belém from the Northeast, bringing with them new cultural inputs such as music and dance, and, of course, the *candomblé* and *macumba* Afro-Brazilian religions. After the rubber crash of 1914, the city suffered another disastrous decline – but it kept afloat, just about, on the back of Brazil nuts and the lumber industry.

Belém remains the economic centre of the North, and the chief port for the Amazon. The wealth generated by the rubber boom is still evident in the shape of the modern city, whose elegant central avenues lead from the luxuriant Praça da República down to the port, past a historical sector that is replete with Portuguese colonial architecture. It's a friendly city with a Parisian feel and a surprisingly modern skyline. Always warm and often hot (and often wet, too), the **climate** is generally very pleasant, with an average temperature of 25°C.

The Cabanagem Rebellion

The **Cabanagem Rebellion** ravaged the region around Belém for sixteen months between January 1835 and May 1836, in the uncertain years following Independence and the abdication of Pedro I. What started as a power struggle among Brazil's new rulers rapidly became a revolt of the poor against racial injustice: the *cabanos* were mostly black and Indian or mixed-blood settlers who lived in relative poverty in *cabaña* huts on the flood plains and riverbanks around Belém and the lower Amazon riverbanks. Following years of unrest the pent-up hatred of generations burst into Belém in August 1835. After days of bloody fighting, the survivors of the Belém authorities fled, leaving the *cabanos* in control. In the area around the city many sugar mills and *fazendas* were destroyed, their white owners being put to death. Bands of rebels roamed throughout the region, and in most settlements their arrival was greeted by the non-white population's spontaneously joining their ranks, looting and killing. The authorities described the rebellion as "a ghastly revolution in which barbarism seemed about to devour all existing civilization in one single gulp".

The rebellion was doomed almost from the start, however. Although the leaders declared independence from Brazil and attempted to form some kind of revolutionary government, they never had any real programme, and nor did they succeed in controlling their own followers. A British ship became embroiled in the rebellion in October 1835, when it arrived unwittingly with a cargo of arms that had been ordered by the authorities before their hasty departure a couple of months previously. The crew were killed and their cargo confiscated. Five months later, the following March, a British naval force arrived demanding compensation from the rebels for the killings and the lost cargo. The leader of the *cabanos*, Eduardo Angelim, met the British captain and refused any sort of compromise; British trade was threatened, too, and the fleet commenced a blockade of the fledgling revolutionary state. Meanwhile, troops from the south prepared to fight back, and in May 1836 the rebels were driven from Belém by a force of 2500 soldiers under the command of Francisco d'Andrea. Mopping-up operations continued for years, and by the time the Cabanagem Rebellion was completely over and all isolated pockets of armed resistance had been eradicated, some 30,000 people are estimated to have died – almost a third of the region's population at that time.

Arrival, orientation and information

Belém's **rodoviária** is situated some 2km from the centre on Avenida Governador José Malcher, near the Almirante Barroso ring road: any bus from the stops opposite the entrance to the *rodoviária* will take you downtown. If you want Praça da República, catch the #316 or #904, or take one with "P.Vargas" on its route card; for the port area take the #318 bus. There are excellent facilities and services at the *rodoviária*, including a Parátur information office (not always open, even when it's meant to be). If you're coming by scheduled airline, you'll arrive at Belém **airport**, 15km out of town (☎91/210-6039). Tourist information is available here (see below) and there's the usual system of co-op taxis opposite the arrivals hall, for which you buy a ticket at the kiosk, but this is a ludicrously expensive way of getting into town ($15 for a fifteen-minute ride). Instead, you can walk to the opposite end of the terminal where you'll find the taxi stand for ordinary city cabs, which are much cheaper. Or you can take the "Marex Arsenal" bus from the airport to the *rodoviária* and continue into town from there. **Boats** dock on the river near the town centre, from where you can walk or take a local bus up Avenida Presidente Vargas (not recommended if you have luggage or late at night), or catch a taxi. For information on boat services see p.404.

Avenida Presidente Vargas is the modern town's main axis, running from the Praça da República and the landmark Teatro da Paz right down to the riverfront. Buses coming into Belém centre from the airport and *rodoviária* travel down Avenida Assis de Vasconcelos, which is more or less parallel. Most of the hotels, restaurants, shops and businesses are along Presidente Vargas, or just off it. On block 7 you'll find the FUNAI office and shop and the Varig offices, and on block 6 the VASP office and the telephone company. The central post office, one of the most impressive in South America, is on block 4, and the ENASA river boat company building at the end of the *avenida* on the riverfront.

Tourist information is available at the somewhat erratic Belémtur offices at Avenida Gov. Jose Malcher 592 (Mon–Fri 8am–6pm; ☎91/242-0033) and the airport (daily 8am–11pm; ☎91/210-6330), and also at Parátur offices downtown at the Feira de Artesanato do Estado on Praça Maestro Waldemar Henrique (previously Praça Kennedy; Mon–Fri 8am–5pm; ☎91/212-0575). There are also tourist information points operated at the Solar da Beira (daily 8am–7pm; ☎91/212-8484) in the Ver o Peso complex as well as at the *Hidroviário* on Praça Princesa Isabel (daily 8am–7pm; ☎91/249-6250). **Maps** and town guides can be bought cheaply from the newspaper stands on Avenida Presidente Vargas or in the shop inside the foyer of the *Belém Hilton*. **Yellow fever inoculations** are recommended by the Brazilian Ministry of Health at least 10 days before visiting Belém and the region (best to do this before leaving home and remember to bring your certificate with you just in case it's required for entering particular regions where there might be an outbreak).

Accommodation

There are plenty of **hotels** in Belém, many of them expensive and only some of them worth the money asked. The more expensive and mid-price hotels are located on Avenida Presidente Vargas. Other, more basic hotels tend to be found in the narrow streets behind, between Avenida Presidente Vargas and the old heart of town close to Avenida Portugal, the government palace and the fort. The nearest place to camp is at Benfica, some 15km east of town.

Belém Hilton Av. Presidente Vargas 882 ☎ 91/217-7000, ⓕ 225-2942, ⓦ www.amazon .com.br/hilton. Belém's best and most expensive hotel dominates the Praça da República, offering luxurious rooms with excellent air-conditioning, some with superb views across the cityscape and watery forests. Although usually exorbitant, the *Hilton* occasionally has radical price reductions at slack times of year. ❽

Canto do Rio Av. Castilhos Franca ☎ 91/224-7473. Situated very close to the port, this hotel has friendly staff but offers very basic (sometimes quite grubby) accommodation, in a dubious neighbourhood more or less opposite one end of the Ver o Peso market. The *Canto do Rio* also acts as an agent for boats going upstream. ❶

Central Av. Presidente Vargas 290 ☎ 91/241-4800. Probably the best value in town, this well-situated hotel is a splendid, if somewhat down-at-heel old building with a wide range of comfortable and spacious rooms and a refreshing rooftop breakfast. Most rooms have shared bathrooms, and some have windows opening onto corridors, so put valuables in the hotel safe. ❷

Equatorial Palace Av. Bras de Aguiar 621 ☎ 91/241-2000, ⓕ 223-5222. Less expensive and with a more cosy ambience than the international-flavoured *Hilton*, this hotel has pleasant enough rooms, good cheerful service, a small rooftop pool and a good restaurant, just over 500m east of Praça da República in the Nazaré sector. ❺

Ferrador Rua O. de Almeida 476 ☎ 91/242-1444. Reasonable and very central hotel, with modern rooms, catering mainly to a Brazilian business clientele. Shares the building with *Hotel Vidonho's*. ❸

Fortaleza Rua Frutuoso Guimaraes 275 ☎ 91/212-1050 or 283-0688. Undoubtedly the best value of the very cheapest places – a safe, very friendly and family-run establishment with large shared rooms in a modest and pleasant colonial house. Breakfast is quite good value at an extra $1.50. Just a few streets behind Avenida Presidente Vargas in a bustling backstreet of the commercial sector, the *Fortaleza* is pretty central and can also organize boat trips. ❶

Itaoca Av. Presidente Vargas 132 ☎ & ⓕ 91/241-3434, ⓦ www.interconect.com.br/guaras. Situated near the port, this modern hotel is comfortable and convenient, and the staff are helpful, but it's rather overpriced compared to some. ❺

Novo Avenida Av. Presidente Vargas 404 ☎ 91/223-8893, ⓕ 242-995, ⓔ avenida@hotel-novoavenida.com.br. Very central hotel with a range of rooms, some en suite with TV and air-conditioning. A little down at heel but a busy, pretty clean and friendly place. Great value. ❷–❹

Novotel Av. Bernardo Sayão 4804 ☎ 91/249-7111 ⓕ 249-7808. Located in the *bairro* of Guamá and reachable by bus (Guamá or UFA) or taxi from the centre, this international chain hotel offers great views out across the river and good service, but nothing special in the way of rooms. ❺

Palácio das Musas Rua Frutuoso Guimarães 275 ☎ 91/212-8422. Nice old hotel with some architectural merit. Basic but comfortable, with fine, if sometimes dusty, old rooms that can be shared or private. Located in a busy back street close to the heart of the city. ❶–❷

Regente Av. Gov. José Malcher 485 ☎ 91/241-1222 or 241-1333, reservations ⓕ 242-0343, ⓔ hregente@libnet.com.br. Tidy rooms in a handy location, along with helpful service, plus a good restaurant and a decent swimming pool. Excellent value. ❹

Sagres Av. Gov. José Malcher 2927 ☎ 91/266-2222, ⓔ sagres@datanetbbs.com.br. Located near the *rodoviária*, this hotel has a decent bar, sauna and reasonable pool. While the restaurant isn't worth bothering with outside of breakfast, the rooms and the views from them are fine. Worth the money if you can afford it and have to stay in this part of town. ❹–❺

Ver o Peso Av. Castilho França 308 ☎ 91/241-2022. Within a stone's throw of the old port area and the colourful Ver o Peso market, this unpretentious hotel has small basic rooms, fans, private bathrooms and a rooftop breakfast area. Good value. ❷

Vidonho's Rua O. de Almeida 476 ☎ 91/242-1444, ⓕ 224-7499. Good-value, modern hotel, with air conditioning in all rooms and good showers. Well located, if a bit noisy, just off the Avenida Presidente Vargas. ❸

Vitoria Regia Rua Frutuoso Guimarães 260 ☎ & ⓕ 091/212-2077. A modern-fronted little hotel, very reasonable and clean with a pleasant staff. Some rooms have air-conditioning but most only ventilator fans. ❷

The City

The **Praça da República**, an attractive central park with plenty of trees affording valuable shade, is a perfect place from which to get your bearings and start a walking tour of Belém's downtown and riverfront attractions. The *praça* itself is sumptuously endowed with fine statues and columns focusing on its fountain centrepiece. Overlooking it is the most obvious sign of Belém's rubber fortunes: the nineteenth-century Rococo **Teatro da Paz**, dripping with Neoclassical fixtures, the opera house where Anna Pavlova once danced. Recently restored, it's open for visits (Mon–Fri 9am–6pm; free). Beside it, modern reality is reflected in the young men cleaning other people's big cars on the pavement, using the roots of the old trees as cupboards for their buckets and sponges.

Cidade Velha

Heading down Presidente Vargas towards the river, the old part of town – the **Cidade Velha** – lies off to the left, full of crumbling Portuguese colonial mansions and churches. The oldest church of all is the **Igreja das Mercês**, Rua Frutuoso Guimarães 31. Architecturally it's nothing special, but as a living, working relic it's totally fascinating, full of quaint little touches. The holy water, for example, is dispensed from an upside-down rum bottle with the label half torn off.

This is a pleasant area to wander during business hours between 6am and 2pm daily, and it's not much further to the river docks and the hectic and anarchic market in Amazonian produce, overlooked closely by the old fort. **Ver o Peso market** is not quite the colourful spectacle it once was, but it remains the liveliest spot in town early in the morning (apart from one or two of the more energetic nightclubs). Ver o Peso ("see the weight") was originally a slave market, but these days its main commodities are fish, fruit and vegetables, manioc flour, nuts and other jungle produce. There's not much that is aimed at tourists, but Ver o Peso is one of the most interesting traditional markets in all of South America and is arguably reason enough in itself to visit Belém. There are sections devoted to aromatic oils, medicinal plants and herbs, and an expanding sector selling locally produced craft goods. It can be a dangerous place though, so leave your valuables somewhere safe, and it's not a good idea to go to the market area at any other time than the morning. Beside the Ver o Peso stands the impressive **Iron Market**, or Mercado de Ferro, built and supplied by British engineers in the nineteenth century. Nowadays the market trades in fish and you'll find an amazing selection on display.

In recent years, the riverfront promenade northeast of the market has been cleaned up and turned into an attractive pedestrian walkway lined with tourist-oriented stalls selling clothes, crafts and local gastronomic delights. As well, an old storage building by the docks on Boulevard Castilhos França has been transformed into the **Estação das Docas** (Tues–Thurs 10am–1pm, Fri–Sun 9am–3pm, closed Mon), a cultural centre where you can buy crafts and excellent local dishes or catch a performance in the theatre.

The nearby square, Praça Dom Pedro, offers views across to the **Forte do Castelo**, an old fort built by the Portuguese in 1616 that is closed to the public. Opposite the fort are two more important churches: the eighteenth-century **Igreja Santo Alexandre**, which now houses a small religious art museum, and the finer **Catedral de Nossa Senhora da Graça** (Mon 3–6pm, Tues–Fri 8–11am & 3–6pm), on Praça Frei Caetano Brandão. The cathedral was built in 1748, though it has been renovated many times since, including in the nineteenth century when the original wooden altar was replaced by one of marble and alabaster, standing over 10m high, designed by Luca Garimi; the interior of the cathedral is hung with some fine paintings.

The architectural highlights of Cidade Velha, however, dominate the square behind the old port and Ver o Peso. Together with the Opera House in Manaus, the magnificent **palaces** of Lauro Sodré and Antônio Lemos are the finest buildings left by the rubber boom. Until recently the seat of the mayor and state governor respectively, and more than a little run-down, they have been sensitively restored and thrown open to the public for under $1.50 each. No visit to Belém would be complete without seeing them.

The **Palácio Antônio Lemos** (Mon–Fri 9am–6pm, Sat 10am–6pm), completed in the 1890s at the height of the rubber boom, has an elegant blue and white Neoclassical colonnaded exterior and a series of airy arched courtyards that are occasionally used as galleries for travelling exhibitions. Upstairs is the Salão Nobre, a huge suite of reception rooms running the entire length of the frontage with crystal chandeliers, beautiful inlaid wooden floors and Art Nouveau furniture, marred only by a few grim paintings. A separate section of the palace houses the **Museu do Estado do Pará** (Mon–Fri 9am–6pm, Sat 10am–6pm, Sun & holidays 9am–1pm), which has an archive of around 6000 historical pieces plus collections of Art Nouveau and modern art.

Next door, painted a dazzling white, is the **Palácio Lauro Sodré** (Tues–Fri 9am–noon & 2–6pm, Sat 9am–1pm), built in the 1770s by Antônio Landí, a talented emigré Italian, who was also an artist and sketched the first scientifically accurate drawings of Amazonian fauna. It was from here that the joint Portuguese–Spanish border commissions set out to agree the frontiers of Brazil in colonial times. Pará's independence from Portugal in 1822 and adhesion to the Republic in 1888 were declared from here, and it was on the main staircase that President Lobo de Souza was shot down on January 7, 1835, in the early hours of the Cabanagem Rebellion (see p.396). The *palácio* later became the centre of days of street fighting at the rebellion's height, which left hundreds dead. Today it houses the Museu de Arte de Belém, containing paintings dating back to the eighteenth century, but it is the palace building itself that is the real highlight. Apart from the magnificent central staircase, carved from marble during the rubber boom, the ground floor and half of the first floor are still much as they were in the eighteenth century, uncluttered and elegant. The reception rooms overlooking the square were rebuilt at the turn of the century with no expense spared and, perhaps even more than the Manaus Opera House, give an idea of what an extraordinary period the rubber boom was.

Avenida Nazaré: the Basílica and Museu Goeldi

Two of the most important and worthwhile sights in Belém lie about fifteen minutes' walk inland from the Praça da República along Avenida Nazaré. The first is the **Basílica de Nossa Senhora de Nazaré** (daily 6.30–11.30am & 2.30–7pm) on Praça Justo Chermont. Created in 1908, and supposedly modelled on St Peter's in Rome, it rates – internally at least – with the most beautiful temples in South America. It somehow manages to be both ornate and simple at the same time, its cruciform structure bearing a fine wooden ceiling and attractive Moorish designs decorating the sixteen main arches. Most importantly, however, this is home to one of the most revered images in Brazil, **Nossa Senhora de Nazaré**. The story of the image is littered with miracles: it is said to have been originally sculpted in Nazareth in the early years of Christianity, from where it found its way to Spain by the eighth century. There it had to be hidden from the Moors, and somehow survived to end up in Portugal, where the first important miracle occurred in the twelfth century, when the mayor of Porto de Mós, Fuas Roupinho, was saved from certain death (plunging off the edge of a cliff on horseback) by the intervention of the Virgin. He built a chapel in celebration, and from there the Jesuits brought the image to Brazil in the seventeenth century. On the first attempt to bring it to

Belém, the image was lost in the jungle, and rediscovered in 1700 by a rancher, who built a rough shrine to house the Virgin. Word of its miraculous properties rapidly spread; today that shrine has grown into an impressive church, and the cult of Nossa Senhora de Nazaré is stronger than ever.

The most obvious sign of the thriving cult is the annual **Círio de Nazaré** (Festival of Candles), for which something approaching a million people flock to Belém on the second Sunday in October, many having saved all year to afford it. A copy of the image is carried in a vast parade made up of thousands of young people, who between them also carry an old 380-metre-long anchor rope that weighs well over a ton; by touching the rope, the faithful, according to traditional belief, will receive the blessing of Our Lady. The procession makes votive offerings – usually in the form of model houses, boats and trucks made out of palm trees – as it goes along its route from the cathedral to the basilica, and returns two weeks later; in between are all the usual secular festivities of a Brazilian celebration. If you hope to stay at this time of year, you'll need to book a room well in advance. To the side of the basilica is a small **museum** devoted to the cult of Círio (9am–6pm, Tues–Fri).

Two long blocks up Avenida Magalhães Barata (the continuation of Nazaré) from the basilica, you'll find the excellent **Museu Paraense Emílio Goeldi** at no. 376 (Tues–Thurs 9am–11.30am & 2–5pm, Fri 9am–11.30, Sat & Sun 9am–5pm; museum $2, botanical gardens $2; ☎91/219-3368). The gardens alone are worth a visit and, quite apart from the collections of plants, birds, animals and Indian artefacts, any money you spend here goes not only to the upkeep of the museum and its grounds but also to a wide programme of research in everything from anthropology to zoology. Founded in 1866, this is one of only two Brazilian research institutes in the Amazon, and plays a vital role in developing local expertise.

Set in the compact but beautifully laid-out botanical gardens here is a small **zoo**. Tapirs, manatees, big cats, huge alligators, terrapins, electric eels and an incredible selection of birds make this place an important site for anyone interested in the forest, and by Brazilian standards the animals are reasonably kept, too. The **museum**, particularly the geology, ecology, archeology and anthropology sections, is equally fascinating and well organized. There's an excellent description of the region from its pre-ceramic hunter-gatherer stage (10,000–1000 BC) through the period of early ceramics and incipient agriculture (3000–200 BC) until the emergence of forest agriculture as encountered by the Portuguese in the sixteenth and seventeenth centuries. Some of the early Marajó island ceramics are particularly impressive: marvellous pots and bowls that are virtually the only reminder of a culture that had already vanished when the Portuguese arrived. Finally, the museum's **souvenir shop** has probably the best selection of T-shirts and other souvenirs in Belém – it's not the cheapest place in town, but quality is high and the money goes to a good cause.

The Bosque Rodrigo Alves

About half an hour by yellow bus marked "Avenida Almirante Barroso" from Ver o Peso market, and a worthwhile outing for a breath of fresh air, the **Bosque Rodrigo Alves** botanical gardens (Tues–Sun 8am–5pm) are actually a small reserve of relatively virgin plant life – or as virgin as is possible within the confines of a large modern city. There's also a well-stocked lake and mini-zoo, and archeological exhibits from the region are on display.

Eating, drinking and nightlife

Belém is a great place to eat out and an opportunity to get acquainted with the distinctive dishes of the Amazon region (see box opposite). For quick Brazilian **snacks** and plenty of local atmosphere try the *Café Milano* on Avenida Presidente Vargas and the *Bar do Parque* (see "Nightlife" opposite) at Praça da República. The best places for **ice creams** are the *Casa dos Sucos* on Presidente Vargas, offering a wide variety of local fruit flavours, and *Tribon*, Rua Municipalidade 1643.

Avenida Av. Nazaré 1086 ☎91/223-4015. One of Belém's best restaurants, with a great setting overlooking the basilica, excellent food and air-conditioning – though it's fairly expensive and a bit short on atmosphere. Usually open until midnight but closed on Mon.

Casa dos Sucos Av. Presidente Vargas by the Praça da República. The most convenient place to sample the wide range of tropical fruit juices and ice slushes available in the city on a sultry afternoon.

Casa Portuguesa Senador Manuel Barata 897 ☎91/242-4871. Located directly behind *Restaurant Inter* with surprisingly inexpensive but superb-quality local and Portuguese food, *cabaña*-style decor and a quiet atmosphere. Usually open 11am–3pm and 6–11pm.

Cheiro Verde Av. Bras de Aguiar, near the *Equatorial Palace Hotel* and Praça de Nazaré. Excellent and cheap *comida por kilo* restaurant, with vegetarian options as well as meat and fish, and a very good salad bar. Always packed and lively; live music after 9pm on Fri and Sat nights.

Gostosão Rua Aristides Lobo 388. Just off block 4 of Av. Presidente Vargas, this inexpensive restaurant serves good evening meals from a mostly Brazilian menu – and delicious fish salads too.

Inter 28 de Setembro 304. Superb-value restaurant serving large, delicious helpings and local specialities. Frequented mostly by Belém's office workers at lunchtime who come for the self-service buffet.

Lá em Casa Av. Gov. José Malcher 247 ☎91/223-1212. Good, moderately priced food,

eaten underneath an enormous mango tree, with a retractable roof in case of rain. Regional dishes are recommended (the menu has a helpful English translation). One of the best spots in the city for local cuisine.

Miako Trav. 1 de Março 766 ☎91/242-4485. The city's large Japanese population supports this pricey restaurant, located behind the *Hilton*, which serves great Japanese food and a wide selection of *sucos* made from Amazonian fruit. Closed Mon and the third Sun of the month.

Nectar Av. Gentil Bittencourt, Travesa Padre Eutiquio 248. Superb vegetarian lunches; the choicest items are often finished before 2pm so get here early. Closed Sun.

Restó das Docas Blvd Castilhos França ☎91/212-3737. Located in the lively Estação das Docas building at the end of Av. Presidente Vargas, this air-conditioned restaurant is especially good for its lunchtime buffets. Closed Mon.

Sabor da Terra Av. Souza Franco (also called Docas) 600. The food is nothing special but the highlight is the floor show afterwards, which is touristy but very good as these things go: regional dances and music, well staged, with especially good dancers. Reasonably priced: around $15–20 a head, excluding drinks.

Trevu's 28 de Setembro 177. Perhaps the best-value budget café in town for lunch, offering a reasonable *comida por kilo* selection. The live music and dancing on Fri evenings help make up for the downmarket setting.

Drinking

Belém can be a very lively place, especially at weekends, but one of the best **bars** is also the quietest, the *Bar do Forte* on the battlements of the old Portuguese fort overlooking Ver o Peso market; the entrance is just past the *Circulo Militar* restaurant. Here you sit outside, among eighteenth-century cannons pointing out to sea, and the view is marvellous especially at sunset. The other outdoor bar in the centre is the *Bar do Parque*, a famous meeting spot right in the heart of the Praça da República in front of the Teatro da Paz. It's open all day and there's always something going on, including, very often, a *batucada* playing live music on weekend nights. There are also some bars strung along the upmarket Avenida Bras de Aguiar: the *Spazzio Verdi* and *Gío's* restaurants in block 8 of the *avenida* are popular eating and meeting places day and night.

Amazon cuisine

As you might expect from the richest freshwater ecosystem in the world, **fish** takes pride of place in Amazonian cooking. You'll come across dozens of species, the best being *peixe nobre* (the noble fish), which Amazonians prize above all others for its flavour. There are many kinds of huge, almost boneless fish, including *pirarucu*, *tambaqui* and *filhote*, which come in dense slabs sometimes more like meat, and are delicious grilled over charcoal. Smaller, bonier fish, such as *surubim*, *curimatã*, *jaraqui*, *acari* and *tucunaré* can be just as succulent, the latter similar to a large tasty mullet. Fish in the Amazon is commonly just barbecued or fried; its freshness and flavour need little help. It's also served *no escabeche* (in a tomato sauce), *a leite de coco* (cooked in coconut milk) or stewed in *tucupi* (see below).

The other staple food in Amazônia is **manioc**. *Farinha*, a manioc flour and a staple food throughout Brazil, is supplied at the table in granulated form – in texture akin to gravel – for mixing with the meat or fish juices with most meals, and is even added to coffee. Less bland and more filling, manioc is also eaten throughout Amazônia on its own or as a side dish, either boiled or fried (known as *macaxeira* in Manaus and western Amazônia or *mandioca* elsewhere). A more exciting form of manioc, **tucupi**, is produced from its fermented juices. This delicious sauce can be used to stew fish in or to make *pato no tucupi* (duck stewed in tucupi). Manioc juice is also used to make *beiju* (pancakes) and *doce de tapioca*, a tasty cinnamon-flavoured tapioca pudding. A gloopy, translucent manioc sauce also forms the basis of one of Amazônia's most distinctive dishes, *tacacá*, a shrimp soup gulped from a gourd bowl and sold everywhere from chichi restaurants to street corners. Other typical regional dishes include *maniçoba*, pieces of meat and sausage stewed with chicory leaves, and *vatapá*, a North Brazil version of the Bahian shrimp dish.

Finally, no stay in the Amazon would be complete without sampling the remarkable variety of **tropical fruits** the region has to offer, and which form the basis for a mouthwatering array of *sucos* and ice creams. Most have no English or even Portuguese translations. Palm fruits are among the most common; you are bound to come across *açaí*, a deep purple pulp mixed with water and drunk straight, with added sugar, with tapioca or thickened with *farinha* and eaten. Other palm fruits include *taperebá*, which makes a delicious *suco*, *bacuri* and *buriti*. Also good, especially as *sucos* or ice cream, are *acerola* (originally it came over with the first Japanese settlers in the 1920s, although Amazonians will swear blind it is regional), *peroba*, *graviola*, *ata* (also called *fruta de conde*) and, most exotic of all, *capuaçu*, which looks like an elongated brown coconut and floods your palate with the tropical taste to end all tropical tastes.

Nightlife

Belém's real **nightlife** rarely begins much before 10 or 11pm, when the focus switches to the western *bairro* of **Condor**, on the banks of the Rio Guamá. There are numerous clubs to choose from, particularly lively on Thursday, Friday and Saturday, and you'll need to take a taxi there and back. *Lapinha*, Trav. Padre Eutiquio 390 (☎91/249-2290; no entry charge), is the best known and most enjoyable, though it doesn't get going much before midnight. It's not too glitzy, there's usually good food and a live band at weekends, and it may be the only club in the world that has three toilet categories – "Men", "Women" and "Gay". Other places to try are the much more upmarket *Palácio dos Bares* in Condor, which often has good samba bands, and the *Bar Teatro Maracaibo*, Alcindocacela 1299 (☎91/222-4797). Other decent clubs can be found nearer the city centre in the **Reduto** urban sector, close to **Docas**; the best club here is the *Baixo Reduto*, at Rua Quintino Bocaiuva (☎9/242-6282), which usually has samba and jazz late on Friday and Saturday nights, and other themes occasionally on weekday nights. A popular area after dark is the **Avenida Souza Franco**, which everyone calls **Docas**, a short taxi ride or walk from the centre: head up Avenida Gov. José Malcher from Praça da República, turn left down Quintino Bocaiuva, take the second right and keep going for another five minutes – it's the broad street with a canal in the middle to your left. It has two nightclubs, *Spectrum* and *Back Street Bar*, which usually have DJs playing a mixture of international and Brazilian dance music to a young crowd; they occasionally host live shows by local bands, too. It's hard to call it more sedate, but at least you can sit down at the nearby *Miralha*, which has good live Brazilian music on weekend nights, and good food every night.

The other live music spot is the *African Bar* on Praça Waldemar Henrique II; it has great pseudo-African decor, complete with thatched roof, and is surprisingly cheap. Both Brazilian (mainly Samba) and international music – mostly electronic dance and some rock – is played, and at weekends only, it's lively and crowded with the city's fashionable young.

Belém is a good place for a night at the **cinema**. A couple of fine old theatres with cavernous interiors and refreshingly enormous screens make even bad films enjoyable to watch: check out the Olímpia, on Presidente Vargas almost next door to the *Hilton*, and the Nazaré, on the *praça* by the cathedral, which show mainstream releases. There's a good triple-screen arthouse, Cinema 1-2-3, behind the Iguatemi mall in Batista Campos: take any bus with an "Iguatemi" card in front, get out at the mall, and walk through it to reach the theatre. If you want to make a night of it, plenty of bars and restaurants in the same street cater for the after-show crowd.

Listings

Airlines Taba, Av. Dr. Feitas 1191, office at the airport ☎91/257-4000; TAM, Av. Assis de Vasconcelos 265 ☎91/212-2166; Tavaj ☎91/210-6257; Transbrasil, Av. Presidente Vargas 780 ☎91/212-6977; Varig, Av. Presidente Vargas 768 ☎91/210-6262; VASP, Av. Presidente Vargas 345 ☎91/257-0944.
Banks and exchange Banco da Amazônia, Av. Presidente Vargas; HSBC Bank, Av. Presidente Vargas 670; Banco do Brasil, 2nd Floor, Av. Presidente Vargas 248. Many of the larger shops, travel agents and hotels will also change both travellers' cheques and dollars cash; the *Hotel Central* generally offers reasonable rates.
Boats See also box pp.392–393. Boats leave Belém regularly for upstream Amazon river destinations, even as far as Porto Velho (at least one a day to Macapá, Santarém and Manaus) and for coastal cities such as Salvador and Rio; there are also boats every day to the port of Souré on the Ilha de Marajó (4hr). However, boats don't have set times of departure, as this depends on tides and river conditions, and there are a huge number of different companies, with no central place where you can get information. Any travel agent will book a ticket for you (just say when and where you want to go), or speak to the captains on the docks (try the waterfront by Amazém 3 and also 10). For Santarem, Manaus and Macapa, most tickets are available through the Agencia Amazonas at Av. Castilho Franca 548 (Mareques Pinto Navegaco is one of the best operators and has the most comfortable charter boats).
Car hire Avis, Rua Sen. Lemos 121 ☎91/257-2277; Dallas, Av. Bras de Aguiar 621 ☎91/212-2237; Localiza, Av. Gov. José Malcher 1365 ☎91/257-1541. The Forest Off Road Club, Av. Marquês de Herval 948, Pedreira (☎91/266-1423), hires a variety of jeeps and pick-ups with driver.
Hospital Hospital Guadalupe (private), Rua Arcipreste Manoel Teodoro 734 ☎91/241-8940.
Internet Amazon, Estação das Docas, 2nd floor, at the bottom of Av. Presidente Vargas; Cybercafé, Av. Bras de Aguiar 742; Inter-Belem, Av. Jose Malcher 189.
Laundry Lavanderia Marajo, Av. Bras de Aguiar 408; Lavanderia Tintuvana, Av. Presidente Vargas 762 (inside the arcade).
Post office The central post office (Mon–Sat 9.30am–6pm) is at Av. Presidente Vargas 498; however, as the place is frequently crowded, it's often quicker to walk to the small post office at Av. Nazaré 319, three blocks beyond the Praça da República.
Shopping Belém is one of the best places in the world to buy hammocks (essential if you are about

to go upriver) – look in the street markets between Av. Presidente Vargas and Ver o Peso, starting in Rua Santo Antônio, or try the one at Frutuoso Guimarães 273, near the *Hotel Fortaleza*. The Aplo Livros & Artes shop, at Av. Conselheiro Furtado 2956, São Braz, sells a wide range of new and secondhand books, posters and CDs. For *artesanato*, head for Casa Amazônia, Av. Presidente Vargas 512; the Loja Victoria Regia, Av. Presidente Vargas 550; or the Cantô do Virapurú, Av. Presidente Vargas 594. Orion Perumaria, Frutuoso Guimarães 270, produces and sells a wide range of rainforest oils, scents and cosmetic products. Fotoveja, Av. Presidente Vargas 526, and Fuji Image Plaza, Av. Presidente Vargas 690, both sell Kodak and Fuji film.

Taxis Aguia ☎91/276-4000; or Comista ☎91/276-0108.

Telephones Telemar operate indoor public kiosks on the corner of Av. Presidente Vargas and Rua Riachuelo; there is also a *poste telefônico* on the third block of João Alfreco (Mon–Fri 10am–7pm, Sat 10am–4pm). Alternatively, street phone booths accept phonecards for local, domestic and international calls.

Travel and tour companies Mundial Turismo, Av. Presidente Vargas 780 (☎91/223-1981) is one of the main travel agents in Belém and the best place to buy air tickets. More personal service, and a greater choice of tours around Belém, is offered by Amazon Star Turismo, Rua Henrique Gurjão 236 (☎91/212-6244, ✉amazonstar@interconect .com.br), an excellent French-run agency specializing in ecotours, including visits to Cotijuba, Icoaraçi, Mosqueiro island and Ilha de Marajó. Gran Para, Av. Presidente Vargas 676 (☎91/212-3233), operate city tours, and can also organize flights; Gaia Terra (☎91/276-3362, mobile ☎9991-9105, ✆276-1299, ⊛www.amazon.com.br/~gaia) run good boat trips to and around the *bairro* of Guamá, where they take visitors on forest trails with expert guides.

Around Belém

Although Belém is over a hundred kilometres from the ocean, there are some good **river beaches** nearby, all of them popular with city crowds at weekends and holidays. There's a reasonable beach at the village of **ICOARAÇI**, only 18km or about half an hour by bus from the bus stop next to the *Hotel Central* on Avenida Presidente Vargas, and this is also the best place to visit local **ceramic workshops** and the cheapest place to buy the very fine pottery. Still very much based on the ancient designs of the local Indians, the skill involved in shaping, engraving, painting and firing these pots is remarkable. Some of the ceramics are very large and, except to the expert eye, barely distinguishable from the relics in the Goeldi museum.

Apart from Icoaraçi, the closest and most popular of the beaches are Outeiro and Mosqueiro, both easy day-trips. **OUTEIRO**, a picturesque and often busy little town, can be reached in under an hour by bus and ferry. **MOSQUEIRO**, some 70km north of Belém, is actually an island, though it's well connected by road and bridge. The beaches here are beautiful and relatively unspoilt, but they can get very crowded at holiday times; there are all the usual beach facilities – stalls selling chilled coconut milk, bars, good restaurants and a few hotels. **Praia Murubira**, with safe swimming and sailing, is probably the best of those close to Mosqueiro town. Of the other beaches here, Praia Farol is popular and preferable to Praia Areão, which is closer to the main *praça* and bus terminal. Buses run frequently from Belém's *rodoviária*, a journey of around two hours. At Carnaval and during the July Festival de Verão, Mosqueiro is particularly lively, with *blocos* on the beach.

Just 18km east from Belém is the island haven of **Cotijuba**, replete with beautiful beaches, rainforest and access to *igarapé* creeks. It's the perfect place for bird-watching and nature walks. Trips are arranged by Amazon Star Turismo (see above), with accommodation in native-style bungalows.

Ilha do Marajó

The **Ilha do Marajó** is a vast island of some 40,000 square kilometres of largely uninhabited mangrove swamps and beaches in the Amazon river delta opposite Belém. Created by the accretion of silt and sand over millions of years, it's a wet and marshy area, the western half covered in thick jungle, the east flat savanna, swampy in the wet season (Jan–June), brown and firm in the dry season (June–Dec). Originally inhabited by the Marajoara Indians, famed for their ceramics, these days the savanna is dominated by *fazendas* where huge water buffalo are ranched; some 60,000 of them roam the island, and supplying meat and hides to the markets in Belém is Marajó's main trade. The island is also famous for its giant *pirarucu* fish which, at over 180kg, is the biggest freshwater breed in the world. Other animal life abounds, including numerous snakes, alligators and venomous insects, so be careful where you walk. There are also some beautiful sandy beaches, and the island has become a popular resort for sun-seekers and ecotourists alike.

Although it was settled by Jesuits at an early stage, the island has something of a reputation for lawlessness stemming from its violent treatment of foreign visitors during the nineteenth-century Cabanagem Rebellion. Its earliest inhabitants have left behind burial mounds, 1000 years old and more, in which many examples of the distinctive Marajó pottery were found. Mainly large pieces, decorated with geometric engravings and painted designs, these are virtually the only reminder of a vanished people – the best examples are in the Museu Goeldi in Belém. When the Jesuits arrived and established the first cattle ranches, the island was inhabited by Nhemgaiba Indians; later its vast expanses offered haven to runaway slaves and to free Indians who wanted to trade with Belém without too much direct interference from the white man's culture. Water buffalo, ideally suited to the marshy local conditions, were imported from India around the turn of the century – or, if you believe local legend, were part of a French cargo bound for Guyana and escaped when the ship sank. River navigation around Marajó is still a tricky business, the course of the channels constantly altered by the ebb and flow of the ocean tides.

Practicalities

The main port of **SOURÉ** is a growing resort offering pleasant beaches where you can relax under the shade of ancient mango trees. The *Hotel Souré*, just a few blocks from the docks in the town centre (❶), is very basic, while the *Hotel Marajó*, Praça Inhangaiba (☎91/741-1396; ❹), and the *Hotel Ilha do Marajó*, Av. Assis de Vasconcelos 199 (☎91/224-5966; ⓦwww.dadoscon.com.br/himarajo; ❺), both offer more comfort and a pool. One of the best restaurants in Souré is the *Delícias da Nalva*, Quarta Rua 1051, whose speciality *marajoara* banquet includes a *filé a marajoara* (buffalo meat covered with cheese), a *filhote* with crab sauce, fried shrimp and much more.

Other magnificent empty **beaches** can be found all around the island – the **Praia do Pesqueiro**, about 13km from Souré, is one of the more accessible and well served with places to eat, such as the *Restaurant Maloca,* excellent for fish and meat dishes. If you want to see the interior of the island – or much of the wildlife – you have to be prepared to camp or pay for a room at one of the *fazendas*: book with travel agents in Belém or take your chance on arrival. One of the best rural lodgings, the *Pousada dos Guarás* (☎ & ℻91/765-1133, ⓦwww.pousadadosguaras.com.br; ❻), is situated close to Praia Grande de Salvaterra, and has a pool, eco-trails and buffalo riding.

Organized trips can be booked at most travel agencies in the Belém (see p.405). It is also easy enough to get to Marajó yourself. By river, the trip takes four to five hours each way – boats leave weekday mornings from Belém port (Amazém 4 at the docks at the bottom end of Avenida Presidente Vargas). Be at the port before 6am (boats leave 6.30am, return 3pm) to be sure of finding an early one if you don't want to stay overnight. There are also larger **boats**, usually leaving Wednesday and Friday at 8pm and Saturday around 2pm. Tickets are best bought a day in advance.

Southern Pará

The southern half of Pará, south and west of Belém, is real frontier territory containing the notorious Serra Pelada gold mines and harbouring the Grande Carajás project (see box, pp.408–409). The region does have its fascination, but it doesn't constitute a tourist attraction, nor do locals on the whole welcome over-curious outsiders: wherever you go, take care.

Marabá

MARABÁ, on the banks of the Rio Tocantins, almost 600km south of Belém and 400km north of Araguaina on the Belém–Brasília road, is often described as the worst of all Amazon towns. It's the market centre for the region, and also the place where the ranchers, construction workers, truckers and gold-miners come for entertainment: it has a bad reputation for theft and violent crime, and it's not a place you should (or would want to) hang around any longer than you have to.

Marabá is a city of three parts, all of them easily reached by bus from Araguaina or from Belém and linked by bridges across the river. The earliest

The Serra Pelada gold mines

About 100km to the southwest of Marabá, in the **Serra Pelada**, a number of huge gold nuggets were discovered in 1980. The discovery sparked off the biggest gold rush of the century, and within a couple of years there were as many as 100,000 *garimpeiros* hacking away at the landscape. The scene here – the mountainside stripped of all vegetation, the landscape pock-marked with vast craters scraped out by the most basic of methods – is familiar from dozens of colour magazine spreads: a vision of hell unseen outside the imaginings of Hieronymus Bosch, as thousands of prospectors scraped away at the mud, barely distinguishable from it. One or two made their fortunes – above all the famous José Maria who struck a patch with over 1000 kilos of gold and became one of the richest men in Brazil overnight. But far more barely made a living, and many lost their lives. Now the mines are in terminal decline, the gold all but played out.

Serra Pelada and the surrounding Carajás region are not a tourist attraction, though they were visited by a lot of journalists in the 1980s. There have been frequent violent disturbances at the workings: in 1988, for instance, ten gold prospectors were shot dead by military police while protesting for improved safety precautions. Around 5000 miners blockaded the road and rail bridges over the Rio Tocantins until fired on indiscriminately by charging policemen. The mines are now officially closed to all visitors. The prospectors, too, have been forced out to make way for monstrous mechanical extractors, although the official line is that the area has been closed to encourage environmental recuperation.

part of town was founded on the south side of the river on ground that was prone to flooding; later settlers created the Cidade Nova on the north side, hoping to escape the waters. Then in the 1970s the completion of the Transamazônica led to the foundation of Nova Marabá, back on the south side.

Buses will drop you at the *rodoviária* at km 4 on the Transamazônica in Nova Marabá; small local buses or taxis run from here to just about every part of town. The airport (T94/324-1383) is just 3km out of town near the Cidade Nova. The choice of **accommodation** is relatively small: in Nova Marabá there's the *Hotel Itacaiúnas*, Folha 30, Quadra 14, Lote 1 (T & F94/322-1326; ❹); and the *Hotel Vale do Tocantins*, Folha 29, Quadra Especial, Lote 1 (T94/322-2321, F322-1841; ❹), both with pool, bar and restaurant; in the Cidade Nova the choice is essentially between the *Hotel Vitória*, Av. Espírito Santo 130 (T94/528-1175; ❷), and the *Hotel Keyla*, Transamazônica 2427 (T94/324-1175; ❸). Nearer the *rodoviária* there's also the basic and somewhat noisy *Pensão Nossa Senhora do Nazaré* (❶). The town's best fish **restaurant** is *Bambu*, Travessa Pedro Carneiro 111, Cidade Nova (T91/324-1290), and there's an excellent Japanese restaurant, *Kotobuki*, Av. Tocantins 746, Novo Horizonte (closed Tues).

Money can usually be changed (dollars cash only) in the larger hotels and shops, but generally at poor rates – you'd do better to change it before you arrive.

The Mineral Province of Carajás

The **Serra dos Carajás** is a range of steep hills about 160km west of Marabá. Even today, much of it is heavily forested and astonishingly beautiful, fed with moisture from the clouds and mists that are a feature of the local climate. The *serra* is also the heart of the Grand Carajás project, the most extensive, ambitious and destructive "development" project in the Amazon and one of the largest mining operations in the world today. Its story began in the 1960s, when the military authorities were making determined efforts to discover whether the Amazon's rumoured mineral deposits really existed. In 1968 a geological survey helicopter, off course, developed engine trouble and landed on one of the hills in the Carajás range. While the helicopter was being repaired the geologists on board discovered, to their astonishment, that they were standing on a hill composed almost entirely of high-grade iron ore. Further exploration established there were rich deposits of many other minerals, too.

Today **Carajás** has good roads, a modern airport and neatly planned towns where miners and technicians live, and is entirely unlike the rest of Amazônia. There are no villages strung out along the roads, no roadside vendors, no bars or cheap hotels and no bus stations. The explanation is that no one without a permit may enter: along the roads are police checkpoints, and outside them huddle the familiar shantytowns filled with people hoping for work within the officially declared **Mineral Province of Carajás**. Carajás itself is effectively a no-go zone: supplied by air, sealed off by road, with a permanent cheap labour pool to be admitted as needed and then expelled. Within the region, the massive privatized mining company CVRD (Companhia do Vale do Rio Doce) is in complete control. In the past, as a state-owned civil body, it could and did call upon military and police support whenever it needed it. Now a privately owned concern, it has even fewer controls on its activities.

The scale of it all is hard to comprehend: apart from the sophisticated open-cast mining operation itself, extracting iron, manganese, bauxite, copper and gold, a completely new network of power generation, transport and processing plants has been created, with a rail line to the coast connecting with new port facilities and aluminium factories, and an enormous hydroelectric scheme at nearby Tucurui. The original plan was for a total investment of 62 billion dollars – a substantial propor-

Tucurui

TUCURUI town, some 225km to the north of Marabá, was until 1977 no more than a pin on a surveyor's map. Today over 60,000 people live here amid air-conditioned office buildings, supermarkets, a modern hospital and even green tennis courts; it has a dusty red main street and a tendency to noise, with construction by day and rowdy construction workers by night. The entire city was built by Eletronorte to house the workers building Brazil's largest dam – over 12km long and with a flooded reservoir covering 4000 square kilometres of rainforest, the fourth largest artificial lake in the world. Now in operation, the **Barragem da Hidrelétrica de Tucurui** has a peak power output of 8000 megawatts a year, making it the largest hydroelectric project in the world.

The cost of building the dam is unknown, but it's estimated that at one stage three million dollars were being spent every day. Corruption was almost inevitable, and the **"Capemi case"** became one of the most public scandals of the years of military rule. Rather than simply drowning the vast tracts of forest in the area of the reservoir, Eletronorte invited tenders for the timber to be cleared and sold by 1983. There were plenty of companies with all too much experience in clearing rainforest, but the contract was won, in 1979, by a company called Capemi – a company that dealt mainly with investing military pen-

tion of Brazil's current foreign debt. Under military rule construction targets were met, but at an enormous environmental and political cost.

Communities living in the path of the development were moved (usually without compensation) or ignored. The rail line, for example, cuts through the Gaviões Indian reserve – a problem that was solved by simply getting dispensation from FUNAI to build there – and some 22,000 people were moved from their homes, without compensation, to allow the construction of the **Alcoa aluminium plant at São Luís**. Resentment in São Luís is fuelled by the plant's thirst for water and electricity: power to the plant comes from lines direct from Tucurui, which stop at the factory, keeping it brightly lit even when the city is suffering one of its frequent power cuts.

More recently, attention has switched to the **sem terras**, the landless rural workers who face eviction from a number of *fazendas* in the province to make way for large-scale mining and agricultural projects. Their plight hit the headlines in April 1996, when 1200 protestors blockaded the PA-150 highway near **Eldorado do Carajás**, some 100km south of Marabá, in protest against legal moves to expel them from a local *fazenda*. After two days of protest, military police responded to the stones and chants of the *sem terras* with a two-hour volley from automatic weapons, killing 19 protestors (including two infants), and wounding 69 others. The massacre brought a wave of international outcry, and bolstered the cause of the **Movimento de Trabalhadores Rurais Sem-Terra (MST)**, yet the trial of those responsible for the massacre will probably end only in the year 2010. A small memorial museum, a red road sign and 19 wooden crosses mark the site of the massacre, 9km north of Eldorado.

Meanwhile, in the *serra* itself the lands of several thousand **Indians**, and a huge chunk of **rainforest**, are being transformed into a giant industrial park. Hundreds of Indians have already died, and others are now suffering as a result of disease, pollution, deforestation and land invasions on the fringe of the project, while landless settlers moving up from Marabá are also laying claim to their lands and destroying brazil-nut groves vital to the local economy. In the Xikrin Indian reserve, which lies close to the central mines, *garimpeiros* who have managed to penetrate the cordon have polluted local rivers with mercury, used to separate out gold after panning.

sions and had no experience in the lumber industry. The decision caused outrage, millions of dollars went missing, and clearance started two years late, succeeding in removing less than a quarter of the high-quality hardwood available. The case was a textbook example of the widespread corruption that marked the final years of military rule, and has never been properly investigated: part of the deal by which the military relinquished power was that there should be no investigation of human rights or financial abuses involving military personnel. In human terms the cost was high, too. The lake flooded a section of the Parakanan Indian reserve and necessitated the re-routing of the Transamazônica through another part of it. It also destroyed the homeland of the Trocara, a group of Indians who had been "discovered" by FUNAI only in 1970.

The new city of Tucurui is served by an older settlement about 9km distant. Today this old town is the site of brothels and other entertainment for the region's workers. Many of the people working and living in the old town are refugees from the flooded area, and their number grows steadily as year after year floods strike the region, causing roads to be cut and washing away homes. There's not a great deal in Tucurui, and although it's only 350km from Belém it's not really on the way to anywhere. Nevertheless, the dam is spectacular and worth the trip. For **permission to visit the dam**, phone ☎94/787-2010 at least three days in advance for a guided tour (Tues, Thurs & Fri at 8.30am).

Practicalities

If you should need **to stay** in the city there are a number of possibilities. The *Hotel HTA*, Praça França (☎94/3787-1232; ❸–❹), the *Hotel Rio Doce*, Rua Lauro Sodré 663 (☎94/3787-1146; ❸), and the *Hotel Marajoara*, Rua Lauro Sodré 685 (☎94/3787-1489; ❸) are all reasonable value. The *CRT*, at Praça França, some 8km out of the centre (☎94/3787-1232; ❹), has the added attraction of a pool and sauna. The *Restaurante Kurika's*, on Av. Mauro Sodré 808 (☎94/3787-2061), is a good **place to eat** regional dishes; for simpler fare like soups, snacks and pasta, try the *Restaurant Hilda* on Praça Jarbas Passarinho at no. 84. The **rodoviária** is close by on Rua Lauro Sodré, and the **airport** (☎91/3787-1416) is a six-kilometre taxi ride away.

Amapá

The **state of Amapá**, north of the Amazon, is one of Brazil's poorest and least populated regions. Traditionally it was dependent primarily on rubber exports, but manganese was discovered in the 1950s and this, together with timber and other minerals, is now the main source of income. A standard-gauge rail line links the mining camps to the northwest with the Amazon port of **Porto do Santana**, near the capital Macapá, crossing the dry, semi-forested plains of the region en route. Amapá doesn't have much going for it, other than as a transit route to **French Guiana**, and it suffers the most marked dry season in the Amazon, running from June to December, when it can get extremely hot. **Macapá** fights it out with Palmas in Tocantins for the title of dullest state capital in Brazil, but at least it's cheap – also, like Manaus, it's a freeport, exempt from customs duties.

Macapá

MACAPÁ, on the north bank of the Amazon and right on the equator, is the gateway to the state of Amapá and home to three-quarters of its population.

Surrounded by uninhabited forests and hills, it dominates the northern section of the Amazon estuary. If you're coming by ferry from Belém you'll actually arrive to the southwest at **Porto do Santana**, just twenty minutes by bus or an hour by boat from Macapá, though it lies on the other side of the equator. The **airport** is 4km from town on Rua Hildemar Maia (☎96/223-2323). The **rodoviária** (☎96/242-5193) faces the Polícia Técnica, 5km outside town on the BR-156; from there, local buses run to Praça Veiga Cabral in the centre.

The countryside around Macapá is, like the Ilha do Marajó in the estuary, roamed by large herds of water buffalo. In town there is not a great deal to do. The highlight is the **Fortaleza de São José do Macapá** (daily 9am–6pm, closed Mon), one of the largest colonial forts in Brazil, built in 1782 from material brought over as ballast in Portuguese ships, in response to worries that the French had designs on the north bank of the Amazon. The fort is often closed, but nobody will mind if you slip through the enormous main gates for a stroll along the battlements. There's an interesting daily artisan market nearby on Canal da Fortaleza, and you could fill some more time checking out the eighteenth-century **Igreja São José de Macapá** on the Praça Veiga Cabral and the **Museu Histórico** at Av. Mário Cruz 17 (Tues–Sun 8am–noon & 2–6pm). The **Museu do Desinvolvimento Sustenavel**, at Av. Feliciano Coehlo 1509 (Mon–Fri 8am–noon & 2.30–5.30pm, Sat 3–5.30pm, closed Sun) has a comprehensive collection of indigenous crafts from the tribes of the region. There's also a small private museum, the **Instituto de Estudos e Pesquisas de Plantas Medicinais (IEPA)** at Av. Feliciano Coehlo 1509, holding the Valdemiro Gomes collection of minerals, Amazon woods and medicinal plants (Mon–Fri 9am–noon).

Practicalities

For **accommodation** the *Hotel Tropical*, Av. Antônio Coelho de Carvalho 1399 (☎96/231-3759; ❷), is excellent value with spacious rooms. The *Hotel São Antônio* (❶) is better placed on the main *praça*, and even cheaper, but not quite as good; or there's the clean and friendly *Hotel Mara* in Rua São José (☎96/222-0859; ❸). Out near the airport, the *Hotel San Marino*, Av. Marcílio Dias 1395 (☎96/223-1522, ℻223-5223; ❺), offers more comfort and a pool, while top of the range for creature comforts is the *Ceta Hotel* on Rua do Matadoro 640, in the Fazendinha district (☎96/227-3396, ⓦwww.ecotel.com.br; ❻). But by far the best option, if you can afford it, is the *Pousada Ekinox*, a short walk from the centre at Rua Jovino Dinoa 1693 (☎96/222-4378, ✉jef@brasnet.online.com.br; ❺). This small but lovely *pousada*, which doubles as the **French consulate**, has French and Brazilian owners, and the food is as good as that combination suggests. It's a popular place to stay, so you'll need to ring ahead and make a reservation.

As for **food**, Macapá's position as a river and sea port means that there's plenty of excellent fish to be had. The *Lennon Restaurant* downtown is a popular dining spot, but greater variety can usually be found at the *Restaurante Boscão*, Rua Hamilton Silva 997. Superb but expensive fish is served at *Martinho's Peixaria*, Av. Beira-Rio 140, and at *Cantinho Baiano*, on the same street at no. 328 (☎96/223-4153). The coast road in either direction from the fort has the most pleasant **bars** in town, always well ventilated by the sea breeze. For unrestrained night-time entertainment, try *Rithimus*, at Rua Odilardo Silva 1489, where the sounds of samba and reggae are regularly heard, or, further out at the *Marco Zero* **nightclub**, for a mix of samba and mainstream sounds; 5km on the Fazendinha road near the equatorial monument **Marco Zero**.

For information about **boats** to the north or to Belém, the Captain of the Port, Av. FAB 427 (☎96/223-9090 or 223-4755), can be contacted at his offices most weekdays between 8am and 5pm. Most boat companies sell tickets through the agency Sonave at Rua Sao Jose 2145 (☎96/223-9090). The main companies, all based at Porto do Santana, are ENAVI (☎96/242-2167), with irregular sailings via Belém as far as Santarém; and Silnave (☎96/223-4011) for car-carrying boats to Belém (Tues & Fri). Almost opposite the Banco do Brasil building, at Canal de Fortaleza 45 (☎96/223-5226), Penta offer **flights** to the eastern Amazon and Manaus, including a reasonably priced service to Santarém (from $100); Varig, at Rua Cândido Mendes 1039 (☎96/222-7724), has flights to Belém, Brasília, Rio and São Paulo; and TAM (☎96/223-2688) fly to Manaus and the south. For **car rental**, contact Localiza (☎96/223-2799).

Into French Guiana

The main reason to come to Amapá is to get to **Guyane**: the key road in the state connects Macapá with the town of **OIAPOQUE**, on the river of the same name that delineates the frontier. The road isn't asphalted all the way, but even where it's dirt road it's usually of pretty good quality: if you want to make it in one run, the regular buses to Oiapoque can take as little as twelve hours, though they can take nearer twenty in the worst periods of the rainy season. It's unfortunately a rather boring drive, largely through savanna rather than forest, with mile after mile of scrubby pine plantations blocking any view. You could break the journey in **CALÇOENE**, eight hours by bus from Macapá. A pleasant, sleepy town built around rapids on the river of the same name, Calçoene has several cheap hotels and regular bus connections on to Oiapoque. While there you may feel tempted to visit the nearby gold-mining town of Lourenço – don't, it's dangerous and very malarial.

A more leisurely option is to go **by boat** from Macapá to Oiapoque, a journey of two days (one night); boats depart once a week or so, but there's no regular schedule. If you're interested in this option, simply go to the docks and ask around: if a boat is leaving, seek out its captain and negotiate for hammock space, which should cost no more than $20 in either direction. The best hammock spaces are those with open sides, preferably on the middle deck.

If you are not a citizen of a European Union country, the US or Canada, you will need a **visa** to enter French Guiana. There is a French consulate in Macapá at the *Pousada Ekinox* (see p.411), though it's better to try to arrange the visa before you leave home. If you're going to travel overland, buy **euros** in Belém or Macapá. You can get them in Oiapoque but the rates are worse, and you can't depend on changing either Brazilian currency or US dollars for euros in the border settlement of Saint-Georges in Guyane.

Dug-out taxis (or canoes) are the usual means of transport between Oiapoque and Saint-Georges, about ten minutes downriver. Brazilian **exit stamps** can be obtained from the Polícia Federal at the southern road entrance into Oiapoque; on the other side you have to check in with the *gendarmes* in Saint-Georges. The border along the Rio Oiapoque is still a sensitive one, although the last time there were actual hostilities was in 1808–17, when a Brazilian force crossed the border and occupied Cayenne. It was during this period that Brazil obtained the lucrative cayenne pepper seeds for its own export market.

Most travellers, in fact, cross the border the easy way – by **flying** from Macapá to the capital at Cayenne (from around $200). Once you're across the border you'll probably want to fly from the border settlement of Saint-Georges to Cayenne in any case – or else catch a boat – since overland transport is atrocious.

Santarém

Around 700km west of Belém – but closer to 800 as the river flows – **SANTARÉM** is the first significant stop on the journey up the Amazon, a small city of around 130,000 people, which still makes it the fourth largest in the Brazilian Amazon. Agreeable and rather laid-back, it feels more like a large town than a city – a world away from the bustle of Belém and Manaus. But don't be deceived by its languid atmosphere, there are plenty of things to do here, and Santarém, positioned right in the centre of the area often referred to as the middle Amazon, a region still largely (and inexplicably) unvisited by tourists, is the perfect base for exploring some of the most beautiful river scenery the Amazon basin has to offer.

It is likely that this area once supported one of the highest populations in the Americas before Europeans arrived, with towns and villages stretching for miles along the riverbanks, living off the rich stocks of fish in the river, and farming corn on even richer alluvial soils, replenished annually when the Amazon flooded. On all the distinctive flat-topped hills around Santarém, there is evidence of **prehistoric Indian occupation**, easily identified by the *terra preta do Indio* (Indian black soil), a black compost deliberately built up over generations by Indian farmers. If you do any walking up and down these hills, especially around Belterra, keep your eyes open for ceramic shards. In recent years, thanks to the work of an American archeologist, Anna Roosevelt, it has become clear that Santarém and its surrounding area make up one of the most important archeological sites in the Americas.

Thirty kilometres east of Santarém, more easily accessible by river than by road, is a nineteenth-century sugar plantation called **Taperinha**. In an excavation there in 1991, Roosevelt unearthed **decorated pottery** almost 10,000 years old – twice as old as the oldest ceramics found anywhere in the Americas. This suggests that the Amazon basin was settled before the Andes, and that the Americas had been settled much earlier than previously thought. Later excavations in **Monte Alegre** confirmed that the middle Amazon played an important role in the prehistory of the Americas with cave and rock paintings dotting the surrounding hills also being dated at around 10,000 years old. About two thousand years ago, Indian culture in the region entered a particularly dynamic phase, producing some superbly decorated ceramics comparable in their sophistication with Andean crafts; there are beautiful pieces of Santarém-phase pottery in the small museum in Santarém, and even more in the Museu Goeldi in Belém (see p.401).

The very first European accounts of the middle Amazon, dating from the early sixteenth century, which talk of swarms of canoes coming out to do battle and of Indian long houses lining the riverbanks, are probably true. The river asssumed its current lightly populated look in the centuries after first contact, as disease and slavery wiped out the Indians or drove them way upriver; as late as 1960 some two hundred Indians were massacred by settlers on a sandbank just south of Itaituba.

Development and the rubber boom

Santarém in its modern form began life as a Jesuit mission in the seventeenth century. It grew only slowly during subsequent centuries, but its convenient location made it popular as a base for the several European naturalists who wrote the first travel books about the Amazon in the 1840s and 1850s. At the time, Santarém was a town of five thousand people locking themselves up after dark as jaguars prowled the streets. It was the **rubber boom** that proved the making of Santarém and the town grew into an important trading centre. The region also became a refuge for two diametrically opposed groups: escaped slaves, who founded communities along the Trombetas and Maicuru rivers on the Amazon's north bank, which were never conquered; and refugee Confederates, who made the big mistake of moving to Santarém under the misapprehension that they could grow cotton there. By the time they realized they had been misinformed, most of them had died of malaria and yellow fever; the survivors moved into sugar and prospered, although in time their descendants intermarried with locals and adopted their language and now the only trace of them is the occasional surname of Higgins or Macdonald.

Meanwhile, in 1874 an Englishman named **Henry Wickham** settled at Santarém with his wife and went on to be almost single-handedly responsible for the collapse of the Amazon rubber boom, smuggling quantities of valuable rubber seed from the heart of the Amazon (at a price of £10 for every 1000 seeds) to British-owned plantations in Asia that were already prepared and waiting. It took over twenty years for the first crop to mature to anywhere near peak production, but when it did the bottom fell out of the Brazilian rubber market. British plantations produced 4 tons of rubber in 1900, but 71,000 tons by 1914. This was not only more than Brazil was producing, but also a great deal cheaper, since the plantations were far more efficient than the labour-intensive wild rubber-tree tapping practised in the Amazon. Rubber was to feature again in local history through the development of **Fordlândia** (see p.420). More recently, Santarém underwent an explosive growth after the Santarém–Cuiabá highway was completed in the early 1970s, but, as the highway deteriorated and finally become impassable in the mid-1980s and gold-mining continued to decline in the interior, the town slumped. Tourists are therefore very welcome here and you will find prices in Santarém and the surrounding area very low. In time this may change as plans are afoot to re-open the BR-163 as a super-highway for the flow of soya bean production from the northern Panatanal and Mato Grosso to the port of Santarém.

Arrival, information and accommodation

Santarém is a busy port, serving river communities for over 300km around as well as operating long-distance services to Manaus and Belém. **Boats** to and from Manaus and Belém arrive and leave most days: the journey time is two to three days in either direction and the cost can vary, so it's worth shopping around. The appalling state of the roads in the region means that the **rodoviária** (☎93/522-3392) on the outskirts of town is largely symbolic since there are no interstate buses to anywhere. Buses to places within an hour or two of Santarém – notably Alter do Chão, Belterra and Fordlândia – leave from the Mercado Modelo or along Avenida Rui Barbosa, not from the *rodoviária*.

Santarém does have a useful little **airport** (☎93/522-4328) some 14km from the centre, with a bus connection to Avenida Rui Barbosa (travelling from the town centre, take the "aeroporto" bus, not to be confused with "aeroporto velho", which goes nowhere near the airport). There is also a Kombi (minibus) connecting the *Hotel Tropical* and the airport most mornings. The airport may not look it, but it's a regional hub, thanks to its being the headquarters of Penta, a good local airline. They run daily flights to Belém and Manaus at half Varig or Riosul rates, and have routes to Macapá and São Luís that save you at least a day by not passing through Belém.

Local buses in Santarém are sometimes useful, despite the small size of the city, to save you roasting yourself in the heat. Any bus heading left down the riverfront as you stand facing the river will take you to the Mercado Modelo, a hideous large concrete structure that houses a very useful market for stocking up on fruit and other essentials for a river journey.

For **tourist information**, try *Santarem Tur*, Rua Adriano Pimental 44 (☎93/522-4847). A useful tourist booklet, *Guia turistíco de Santarém*, is produced by the Coordenadoria Municipal de Turismo, Rua Floriano Peixoto 343 (Mon–Fri 9am–5pm; ☎93/523-2434, ⓦ www.etfa.br/santarem), and is often also available from many of the town's hotels.

Accommodation

Santarém is well supplied with **hotels** to suit every pocket. Along with Manaus, this is one of the best places to take a break from a long-distance boat trip, and you could well find yourself staying a few days.

Alvorado Rua Bittencourt 179 ☎93/522-5340. Although large and airy, this family-run hotel is very basic, and rooms come with or without air-conditioning. ❷

Amazon Park Av. Mendonca Furtado 4120 ☎93/523-2800. Located in the Liberdade district almost 5km from the heart of town, this finely refurbished hotel has an excellent restaurant and a swimming pool. The most expensive hotel in town, but the stylish rooms are good value. ❺–❻

Brasil Grande Trav. 15 de Agosto 213 ☎93/522-5660. Fine mid-range hotel right in the centre of the commercial district, with all the usual amenities, including TV, air-conditioning and a *frigo-bar*. ❸

Brisa Av. Senador Bittencourt 5 ☎93/522-1296, ⓦ www.brisahotel@tap.com.br. Basic but interesting old building that is clean and well run by a friendly family; rooms have fans. ❶–❷

Equatorial corner of Av. Rui Barbosa and Silvino Pinto ☎93/522-1135. Centrally located, no-frills hotel where you're likely to meet all sorts of travellers. Clean and airy; some rooms have air-conditioning. ❶–❷

Mirante Trav. Francisco Corréa 115 ☎93/523-3054, ⓕ523-5936. Modern hotel with small but clean rooms, all of which come with TV, *frigo-bar* and private toilets. Good value. ❸

Mistura Brasileira Av. Tapajós 23 ☎93/522-4819. Plain and basic rooms with fans, but the hotel itself is in a fantastic location and has very hospitable, if laid-back service. Good value. Up above the seafront restaurant of same name. ❶–❷

New City Trav. Francisco Corréa 200 ☎93/522-3764 or 522-4719. A clean, modern and very friendly option. The hotel also organizes river tours and airport pick-ups or boat drops. ❸

Rio Dorado Praça Rodrigues dos Santos 887 ☎93/523-2174 or 523-5782. Opposite the Mercado Modelo, this recently refurbished hotel is one of the best mid-range places around. Rooms are clean if non-descript but staff are welcoming. ❸

Santarém Palace Av. Rui Barbosa 726 ☎93/523-2820, ⓕ522-1779. A good mid-range hotel with tidy modern rooms in the centre of town. Also runs reasonably priced river tours. ❸

The city and its beaches

By far the most interesting place in Santarém, at any hour of the day or night, is the **waterfront**. There are always dozens of boats tied up here, with the accompanying bustle of people and cargoes being loaded and unloaded, and constant activity in the shops and outfitters by the water. You will probably have to wander along the front anyway to find boats to points elsewhere, but a sunset walk is reason enough to venture down this way. Many of the city's restaurants and nightspots line the waterfront, but it is especially lively during the rainy season, when the beaches are under water.

The area also boasts a surprisingly good museum, the **Centro Cultural João Foua**, a fine turn-of-the-century building constructed during the rubber

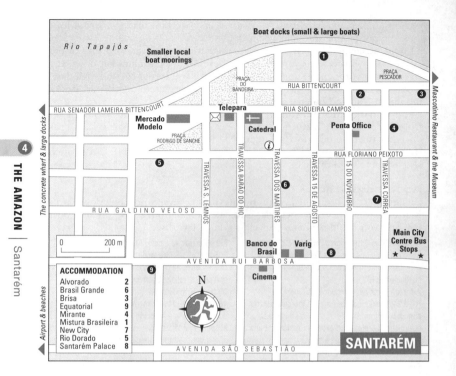

boom and standing in splendid isolation on Praça Santarém, just past the *Mascotinho* restaurant (see opposite). The highlight of the collection is some stunning Indian pottery, small but elaborately decorated and around 2000 years old. The building itself is also very pleasant and the shady internal courtyard is a good spot to hide from the sun on a hot day.

Beaches

Unlike the eastern and western reaches of the Amazon, the region around Santarém has a very distinct **dry season**, stretching from June to December. In the dry season, Santarém and its surroundings get extremely hot, even by Brazilian standards, with a particularly enervating dry heat. Fortunately this is also the time of year, especially between July and February, when the Amazon drops and the region's magnificent **river beaches** are exposed. If you are unlucky enough to be in Santarém in hot weather while the beaches are still flooded, gringos can use the swimming pools at the *Hotel Tropical* or the *Yacht Clube*, a short taxi ride from the centre.

In the city itself, the beach that forms at the waterfront in the dry season is definitely not recommended despite the number of locals you'll see swimming there: you can count the raw sewerage outlets draining directly into the water as you walk along the promenade. A much better option is to take the local bus to **Maracana** on the far side of town, which is clean. There are lots of small bars and restaurants here serving delicious, freshly caught fish. The very best beach near Santarém, however, is 15km away at Alter do Chão (see p.419).

Piranhas and stingray

One thing definitely worth bearing in mind if you are swimming anywhere in the middle Amazon is that **piranhas** and **stingrays** (*raia*) are common. Piranhas are actually much less of a problem than you would expect. Forget any films you have seen; they don't attack in shoals, and prefer still water to currents. Nevertheless, they can give you a nasty bite and are indeed attracted to blood. They frequent particular spots, which locals all know about and avoid, so ask for advice.

Stingrays are more of a problem. They love warm, shallow water and are so well camouflaged that they are practically invisible. If you tread on one, it will whip its sting into your ankle causing a deep gash and agonizing pain for at least 24 hours. However, stingrays really hate noise and crowds and so are rarely found on regularly used beaches, such as Alter do Chão, near Santarém. But off the beaten track, they are an ever-present threat. You can minimize the danger by wearing canvas boots or trainers and by splashing and throwing sand and stones into shallow water if you intend to swim there.

Eating, drinking and nightlife

You'll find many of Santarém's **restaurants** along the waterfront, but the city's side streets are also a good hunting ground, as is the beach at Maracana. As you'd expect, fish is the main cuisine, but there's also Italian, Japanese and plenty of traditional Brazilian food to be had. For delicious home-made **ice cream** using regional fruits, go to *Nido* on Mendonça Furtado between Assis Vasconcelos and 2 de Junho; try the *castanha*, the best brazil-nut ice cream you'll ever have. The ice cream at the *Panificadora Lucy*, on the Praça do Pescador, is also very good.

Amazonia Bar on the waterfront. Good bar with one of the nicest atmospheres in town; it also serves great, though not cheap, food.

Bar Mascote Praça do Pescador 10. One of the city's popular waterfront places, with regular live music at weekends. Serves a wide range of moderately priced fish and meat dishes.

Bom Paladar Av. Cuiabá. Regional fish any way you want it – the *caldeirada* (fish stew) is particularly recommended. Live music on Fri and Sat nights.

Canta-Galo Trav. Professor Antônio Carvalho. Serving very reasonably priced *carne do sol* – sundried meat grilled as you watch. This restaurant is a short taxi ride from the centre; all the taxi drivers know it.

Churrascaria Tapajós Av. Tapajós. Along the waterfront, by the gas station and just past the Mercado Modelo, this is the best option for carnivores tired of eating fish. Good range of salads as well.

Lumi Av. Cuiabá 1383. A good and moderately priced Japanese restaurant and the best option for vegetarians – the *tempura* is delicious.

Mascotinho Restaurant-Bar on the waterfront by the Praça Manoel de Jesus Moraes. The place to come for pizza and to enjoy a wonderful loca-

tion – the restaurant is built out onto the river, right in the heart of town.

Mistura Brasileira Av. Tapajós 23. A lovely place for lunch, close to the river, with tables both outside and in, and a brilliant *comida por kilo* self-service spread.

Peixaria Piracatu Av. Mendonca Furtado 174. Reputed to be the best fish restaurant in town, it's good for atmosphere as well. Generally open from 10am until after midnight.

Petit Lanche Rua Siqueira Campos. Just down from the church, this simple café is a good choice for snacks and breakfast.

Ponto Chic Restaurant Av. Rui Barbosa. Always lively at lunchtime and very good value, serving delicious river fish and a range of Brazilian dishes.

Sacy Caseiro Rua Floriano Peixoto 521. Probably the best and busiest lunchtime *comida por kilo*.

Uirapiru on the waterfront opposite *Mascotinho* (see above). The food may be adequate but the good atmosphere and great views out across the river make this a relaxing spot for a beer.

Vapt Vupt Av. Rui Barbosa, near Banco do Brasil. A *comida por kilo* buffet only open at lunchtime. Excellent quality and value, and a good option for vegetarians, too. You pay by the weight of your food and, if you guess the weight correctly, they halve the price. Otherwise a hefty lunch will set you back around $4.

Vinhoca Rua Turiano Meira 387. Just past the corner with Mendonça Furtado, this Brazilian restaurant is easily walkable from the centre. The extremely cheap and wonderful regional food includes *tacacá*, *maniçoba* and duck in *tucupi* sauce, but you have to get there by about 7pm or there won't be anything left.

Yacht Clube The restaurant here serves excellent fish and is walkable from the *Hotel Tropical*; otherwise take a taxi and arrange for it to pick you up again as no buses pass this way. Despite its name, it's not at all exclusive, nor are you likely to come across any sailing types. Good-value food, around $12 for a meal for two, and lovely views across the Tapajós.

Nightlife

There's no shortage of options when it comes to **nightlife**. On Friday and Saturday nights, the *Mascote*, *Mascotinho* and other waterfront dives have live music; people start here and then head out to the serious music places. The *Yacht Clube* usually has something going on starting at around midnight, and *Sygnus*, a nightclub at Av. Borges Leal 1227 (☎93/522-4119) gets going around the same time – most local buses from the centre pass by. One of the coolest spots these days is *La Boum*, at Av. Cuiabá 694, Liberdade (☎93/522-3632), with live Brazilian dance music until the early hours every Friday and Saturday night, or, if you want to make an all-nighter of it, *Denis Bar* on Mendonça Furtado is the place to go and, unlike the other clubs, it has no cover charge. Not far away on Mendonça is the *Babilônia*, a cavernous hangar with a stage, live music and wild crowds every weekend night. The *Bom Paladar* restaurant on Avenida Cuiabá becomes a nightclub on Friday and Saturday nights and there's good dancing here, but it's the sort of place you might expect to see Popeye and Bluto trading blows in the corner – get under the table if you hear any shots.

Listings

Airlines Penta, Trav. 15 de Novembro 183 ☎93/523-4004; Varig, Rui Barbosa 790 ☎93/522-7813; Tavaj, corner of Rua Floriano Peixoto with Travessa S. Lemnos ☎93/523-1600.
Air taxis Tapajós Taxi Aereo, Rod. Fernando Guilhon 100 ☎93/522-1467; Aquila Taxi Aereo, hangar Flavio Cesar, Santarém Airport ☎93/522-1848 or 522-4383.
Banks and exchange Changing money can be a problem in Santarém. None of the banks changes foreign currency (though cash advances on Visa cards only are available upstairs at the Banco do Brasil; bring your passport), and you have to do the rounds of the travel agents in the centre (see opposite). One possibility is to try at Fundação Esperança (see "Health matters" below), where, if they don't change the money themselves they will be able to tell you who will; dollars cash only.
Boats Head for the docks nearer the large concrete wharves for river boats to Manaus and Belém, where you can ask the various captains when they're leaving and how much they'll charge. Companies running boats to Manaus and Belém include Antônio Rocha, Rua 24 de Outubro 1047 ☎93/522-7947; ⓕ523-2328; Marquês

Pinto Navegação, Rua do Imperador 746 ☎93/523-2828, ⓕ522-2006; and Tarcisio Lopes, Rua Galdino Veloso 290-B ☎ & ⓕ93/522-2034. Wandering along the waterfront is the best way to find boats heading to the towns between Belém and Manaus; although the larger boats stop at them as well, it's better to get one of the medium-sized boats that only ply that route, since everyone on it will be local and it will probably be less crowded. These boats usually have placards hanging from their side or set out on the concrete promenade, advertising their destinations and departure times. They are very cheap, and most serve beers and soft drinks en route, but your best bet is to take your own food.
Car rental Bill Car, Av. Constantino Nery 111 ☎93/522-1705; Rede Brasil, Av. Mendonça Furtado 2449 ☎93/522-2990.
Health matters Should you have health or dental problems, contact Fundação Esperança, Rua Coracy Nunes 3344, a clinic and health centre that runs a volunteer programme for foreign health professionals, so you will be seen by an English-speaking physician or dentist, and get the best treatment in the region at minimal cost.

Santaremzinho, Starenzinho, Aeroporto Velho and Amparo/Conquista buses take you right to the door. Consultations cost less than $5.
Internet Tapajós On Line, Av. Mendosa Furtado 2454, sala A (©tapajosonline@tap.com.br).
Shopping For crafts, try the Loja Regional Muiraquita, Rua Bittencourt 131, or the Casa do Artesanato, Rua Bittencourt 69. Foto Coiety, Rua Siqueira Campos 214, sell and develop Fuji film.
Telephones Phone cards can be used in phone booths for national and international calls; alternatively, use a cabin at Telepara, beside the post office on Rua Siqueria Campos.

Travel and tour companies Amazon Turismo, Trav. Turiano Meira 1084 (T93/522-1928 or 975-1981, F522-1098), run by Steve Alexander, an expatriate American, operates trips to Belterra and Fordlândia, and reasonably priced forest and boat tours including bird-watching and dolphin-spotting. Santarém Tour, Rua Adriano Pimentel 44 (T93/522-4847, F522-3141), associated with the *Tropical Hotel*, and Santarém Viagens e Aventuras, Rua Raimundo Fona 864 (T & F091/523-2037), both offer a wide range of services and tours.

Around Santarém

The area around Santarém is richly rewarding, with a variety of day-trips possible out to **Alter do Chão**, **Belterra** or **Fordlândia** or boat journeys further afield. Due north, on the opposite bank of the Amazon, some six hours away by boat, is the town of **Alenquer**, the jumping-off point for the stunning waterfall of Véu da Noiva, on the Rio Maicuru. Similar journey times west along the Amazon will land you in **Óbidos**, east takes you to the beautiful town of **Monte Alegre**, and a slightly longer trip south up the Rio Tapajós, through gorgeous river scenery, will bring you to **Itaituba**, a classic gold-rush town, 250km from Santarém. To head into less disturbed forest and consequently have better access to wildlife, you could take a **jungle tour** from Santarém led by Amazon Turismo (see above), which run excellent trips, or else one of the tour operators looking for custom in the town's main streets.

Alter do Chão

The municipality of Santarém, which is slightly bigger than Belgium, has just 32km of asphalted road. A good two-thirds of this is accounted for by the road that leads from Santarém to its beach resort of **ALTER DO CHÃO**, and you can't fault their transport priorities. Alter do Chão is a very beautiful bay in the Rio Tapajós overlooked by two easily climbable hills, one the shape of a church altar, giving the place its name. Most of the year the bay is fringed by **white sand beaches**, which combine with the deep blue of the Tapajós to give it a Mediterranean look. In the dry season a sandbank in the middle of the bay is accessible either by wading or by canoe, and simple stalls provide the fried fish and chilled beer essential to the full enjoyment of the scene. During the week you'll almost have the place to yourself, unless you're unlucky enough to coincide with one of the periodic invasions by hundreds of elderly tourists from a cruise ship docked at Santarém. Weekends see the tranquillity shattered, as *Santarenhos* head out en masse for the beach – be careful if you're heading back to Santarém on a weekend afternoon as many drivers on the road will be drunk. If the beach is too crowded, get a canoe to drop you on the other side of the bay at the entrance to the path leading up to the higher conical hill. It's a half-hour walk through the forest and finally up above it to the top to a breathtaking view of the meeting of the Tapajós and Amazon rivers.

One essential sight is the **Centre for the Preservation of Indian Art** (daily 9am–noon & 1–5pm; $3), a spectacular collection of Indian artefacts from all over the Amazon basin put together by an American and Indian couple who settled in Alter do Chão. The centre is not difficult to find: it's by some way the largest building in the village, and its painted adobe walls might look more at home in New Mexico, were it not for the Indian masks nodding in the breeze outside. The collection is good and there is the bonus of a **gift shop** stuffed with far better Indian goods than those in any FUNAI shop, as well as a good range of books. Although prices are in dollars, and can therefore seem expensive, the reason is an honourable one: this shop is unusual in that a fair price is paid to the makers of the goods on sale.

Practicalities

At weekends there are **buses** every hour to Alter do Chão from in front of the Mercado Modelo in Santarém, with the last one returning at 7.30pm; during the week there are only three buses a day, with two daily returning to town. If you don't feel like getting the last bus back, you might as well make a night of it and stay at one of the three **pousadas** in town, all of them cheap and clean: *Pousada Alter do Chão*, on the waterfront at Rua Lauro Sodré 74 (☎93/527-1215; ❶), which has a good restaurant open to non-residents as well; *Pousada Tia Marilda* (❶–❷) on the street leading up from the square; and *Pousada Tupaiulandia*, at Rua Pedro Teixeira 300 (☎93/527-1157; ❷), a block further up, which is the best of the bunch. Away from the beach, the town square is surrounded by **restaurants**, all dependably cheap if you stick to the fish.

Fordlândia and Belterra

Fordlândia and Belterra are the fruits of an attempt by Henry Ford to revive the Amazon rubber trade in the first half of the twentieth century. Ford's intention was to establish a Brazilian plantation to challenge the growing power of the British- and Dutch-controlled rubber cartels, based in the Far East. He was sold a vast concession on the banks of the lower Rio Tapajós by a local man named Villares. What no one seemed to notice at the time was that Villares also organized the Amazon survey, which ended up visiting only his piece of land. Though it was vast – almost 25,000 square kilometres in all – the tract of land he sold had marginal potential for a plantation of any kind. It depended on seasonal rather than regular rains, it was hilly and therefore awkward to mechanize, the soil was sandy and over-leached and it was beyond the reach of ocean-going vessels for several months every year.

Nevertheless, Henry Ford went ahead with a massive investment, and the construction of **FORDLÂNDIA**, 100km south of Santarém, began in 1928. Cinemas, hospitals and shops were built to complement the processing plants, docks and neat rows of American staff homes; there was even an independent power supply, designed in Detroit. Nothing like it existed within a thousand kilometres in any direction. Unfortunately the rubber planting proceeded at a much slower rate. Difficulties were encountered in trying to clear the valuable timbers that covered the land, and even when it was cleared there was a shortage of rubber-tree seeds. After five years only about ten square kilometres a year were being cleared and planted, at which rate the process would still have been only half completed in the year 3000.

In the 1930s a new site for the plantation was established at **BELTERRA**, and high-yield rubber seeds were imported back from Asia. Belterra is a plain, around 150m above sea level and about 20km from Santarém on the east bank of the Tapajós, at a point where the river is navigable all year round. Even here, though, Ford never looked likely to recover his money, and poor labour relations combined with poor growth to ensure that he didn't. Although the plantations are still operative, they have always suffered from loss of topsoil and from South American Leaf Blight fungus, and have never made a significant contribution to the world's rubber supply. By the late 1930s Ford himself had lost interest and in 1945 he sold out to the Brazilian government for $250,000, having already invested well in excess of $20 million.

If you do visit, these are pretty bizarre places. They mimic small-town America exactly, with whitewashed wooden houses, immaculate gardens, fire hydrants, churches and spacious tree-lined streets. The only jarring note is the potholed roads. Belterra is built on a bluff overlooking the Tapajós, with spectacular views down to the river. Fordlândia, with its water towers and the ruined hulk of the rubber-processing factory, is actually on the river and more easily accessible by boat. All boats to Itaituba stop at Fordlândia, the journey taking six to twelve hours depending on the time of year. There's no accommodation but you can probably string your hammock up in the school; bring your own food as there isn't a restaurant. A daily bus runs to Belterra from the Mercado Modelo, but the road is difficult during the rains. There is one bus a day back, but in the morning – again there's no accommodation – so it's not a practical proposition unless you have a car, or can get on an excursion organized by a travel agent in Santarém.

Alenquer

Some five or six hours away from Santarém by boat, through a maze of islands and lakes on the north bank of the Amazon, is **ALENQUER**, a typical small Amazon river town rarely visited by tourists. The town is interesting enough, but wouldn't on its own detain you for more than a day. The streets are pleasant, the waterfront occasionally bustles and has a good view of the river, and there are a couple of atmospheric public buildings from the days of the rubber boom. However, the surrounding countryside is strikingly beautiful with lakes, an abundance of wildlife and the gorgeous **waterfall** of **Véu da Noiva**, all accessible by either road or boat.

Renting a boat for the day costs about the same as hiring a taxi for a day – around $30 – and, although the birdlife in the lakes surrounding Alenquer is not as rich as around Monte Alegre (see p.423), the creeks and islands you can explore are if anything more scenic. The lakes are actually quite heavily populated, by Amazonian standards, and your boatman is almost certain to take the chance to stop off and visit a relative somewhere on the way, giving you the chance to glimpse some rural life. *Botos* (river dolphins) are common and, with luck, you might even see a group of them leaping out of the water together. Unfortunately, piranhas are also common, so be careful about swimming. As for supplies, you will need to take food and water for you and the boatman.

Practicalities

There is a good **hotel** in town, the *Hotel Cirio* (☎93/526-12138; ❶), on the waterfront street to the right as you arrive at the quayside. The owner, Dona Maria José, can arrange boats for exploring the lakes and taxis for visiting the waterfall. As tourists in Alenquer are still relatively rare, things are cheap and both of these trips will set you back about $30 if you arrange them through the hotel; they're well worth it.

There are **boats** most days between Santarém and Alenquer, but you'll need to check on boats coming back before leaving Santarém if you are on a tight schedule – the crew of the departing boat will be able to tell you when the

△ Teatro Amazonas, Manaus

next boat back will be. There are also boat connections from Alenquer to Belém, Manaus and Monte Alegre, and in the dry season there are **buses** to Óbidos, Oriximiná and Monte Alegre, but the schedule is irregular and depends on the condition of the road, usually bad but passable.

Véu da Noiva

The **Véu da Noiva waterfall** is on the Rio Maicuru, a couple of hours' drive from Alenquer on a dirt road that eventually leads to Monte Alegre. A taxi will take you as far as it can and you have to walk the last 3km or so, a beautiful stroll down a forested valley with occasional glimpses of river, before the path drops down right in front of the magnificent waterfall, over 6m high and about 45m wide. The waterfall cascades into a glade in the forest with deep pools of deliciously cool water to swim in. Below the falls you can wade with care through shallow rapids, but watch your step on the sharp-edged rocks. It's an idyllic spot and well worth the effort involved in getting here. You will need to take everything for the day with you, including lunch for yourself and your taxi driver (who will wait for you at the end of the road), some water (don't drink the river water no matter how clear it looks), and, most importantly, a note from the owner of the private land on which the waterfall is located – who happens to be a relative of Dona Maria at the hotel, hence the advantage of arranging the trip through her. Without a note, the watchman on the estate won't let you in.

Monte Alegre

If you only have time to visit one river town in the middle Amazon, it should be **MONTE ALEGRE**. Most of the town is built along the brow of a steep hill with spectacular views out across marshes and freshwater lakes, with the Amazon to the south and jagged hills to the north and west, the only pieces of high ground between Belém and Manaus. With its obvious strategic advantages, this was one of the first places on the Amazon to be colonized by Europeans; a small group of English and Irish adventurers settled here in the 1570s, almost fifty years before Belém was founded. They were soon expelled by the Portuguese, and Monte Alegre was a ranching and farming settlement, then a centre of the rubber trade, before becoming the prosperous river town it is today. However, there is a much longer history of human settlement in the region. At various points the hills behind the town are covered in spectacular **Indian rock paintings**, one of the main reasons for visiting Monte Alegre. The paintings have been dated at just over 10,000 years old, making Monte Alegre one of the most important archeological sites in South America.

The paintings are only accessible by **four-wheel-drive transport** and you will need a **guide**; expect to pay around $60 for the two. Depending on how many people you can get together this can be very reasonable as it is an all-day expedition. Nelsi Sadeck, Rua do Jaquara 320 (☎93/533-1430 or 533-1215), can arrange trips. Everyone knows him and will point you in the direction of his house. Although he only speaks Portuguese, he is used to taking parties of tourists around the hills, and if he knows people want to go he can usually rustle up a few local people interested in coming along, which will bring the price of the truck rental down. The paintings themselves range from abstract geometric patterns through stylized representations of animals and human stick figures to the most compelling images of all – palm prints of the ancient painters themselves. Some of the paintings are on rockfaces large enough to be seen from the road, but others are hidden away, requiring a steep climb to see them, so wear good shoes. Whatever time of year you go, it is likely to get very hot during the day: take plenty of water, a hat and sunscreen.

Nelsi can also arrange **boat rental** for around $25 a day. The water world around Monte Alegre is one of the richest **bird** sites in Amazônia. All along the banks of the Amazon, huge freshwater lakes are separated from the river by narrow strips of land. Depending on the time of year, the lakes either flood over the surrounding land, become marshland or even, in places, sandy cattle pasture. The whole area is thick with birdlife: huge herons, waders of all kinds and a sprinkling of hawks and fish eagles. At sunset, thousands of birds fly in to roost in the trees at the foot of the town. The stunning waterscapes set against the dramatic backdrop of hills make a boat trip really worth doing, even if you can't tell an egret from your elbow. Take everything with you for the day, including lunch for you and the boat owner.

Finally, for a spot of relaxation, head for the **hot springs** at Aguas Sulforosas, 10km inland and reached by taxi or minibus; you can relax free of charge in the springs, and there's a bar, picnic area and pool close by.

Practicalities

Monte Alegre hasn't really begun to realize its tourist potential; it's only rarely visited by foreigners and still very cheap. The best **place to stay** is the *Beira Rio Hospedaria*, a very pleasant hotel situated on the riverfront opposite the fish markets; it's basic but clean, very friendly and serves excellent food (❷). There are a few other hotels, including the *Hotel das Feiras* (❷); attached to the hotel is Monte Alegre's one **restaurant**, the *Panorama*, which serves a reasonable but not exceptional range of fish dishes. The main square has a fabulous view out across the Amazon and the lakes, and there's a bar here conveniently situated for you to watch the sunset.

Transport connections are good. Monte Alegre is one of the main stops on the Belém–Santarém–Manaus **boat** route, and there are also dedicated services from both Santarém and Belém that are usually less crowded. Boats from Prainha and Macapá also stop here. Leaving, you won't wait more than two days wherever you're headed.

Itaituba

Heading south up the Rio Tapajós, between twelve and fourteen hours from Santarém depending on the time of year (the current is much stronger in the rainy season), you come to another face of the Amazon, the gold-rush town of **ITAITUBA**. The **boat journey** here is one of the main reasons for going – the broad mouth of the Tapajós, over 30km wide where it joins the Amazon just west of Santarém, soon narrows enough so you can appreciate the forest on either side. There is usually plenty of wildlife to be seen, including anteaters swimming across the river, dolphins and parrots galore.

Gold prospecting and **mining** began in the headwaters of the Tapajós in the 1950s with a few skilled prospectors from former British Guyana. Itaituba remained no more than a tiny village, living more from trade in rubber and animal pelts than gold until the early 1970s when the Transamazon highway arrived and changed everything. The highway itself was only open for a few years; it was too expensive to maintain and was soon reclaimed by forest. Nevertheless, it was long enough to channel a new wave of migrants into the area, and when the price of gold started to rise after 1974 there was capital and labour available to start exploiting the mines in a big way. The city mushroomed, and its current population of 53,000 makes it by far the biggest town on the Tapajós, even in its current depressed state (the gold has been giving out and the price has fallen since the boom years of the mid-1980s). Many mine owners are forming partnerships with big Brazilian mining companies now that the easily available gold has been mined, and Itaituba will continue to be a mining town for the foreseeable future, albeit with fewer miners and nothing like as wild a nightlife as it used to have.

The town seems unprepossessing at first, all of its buildings modern and most of them ugly, but there is a certain energy and frontier feel about the place. You'll soon start to see the gold-buying shops in the commercial area, dominating everything with their signs "*Compra-se Oura*" (we buy gold). Go inside and you can watch miners bringing in gold dust and fragments that are then burned (don't get too close, the smoke is mercury vapour), weighed and purchased with bundles of notes. Miners, despite their fearsome reputation, are quite friendly if you're polite, and are usually proud to show off their gold. Things are quieter now than they used to be but Itaituba is still the trading centre of the largest gold field in the Brazilian Amazon, supplying scores of mines (*garimpos*) scattered in the forest to the south of town and usually only accessible by air.

Practicalities

Itaituba has several **bars** and **restaurants** on the waterfront, and no shortage of **hotels**; the best is the *Juliana Park* (☎93/518-0548; ❸), with excellent breakfasts and air-conditioning – essential because it's hot here all the time. The nicest bar is the *Bar do Chico* at the far end of the waterfront, on the first corner past the church; it serves excellent *frango a caipira* (chicken in spicy gravy). It is possible to rent boats to go further upriver but you can only go about an hour or so before major rapids just past the village of São Luís do Tapajós make the river impassable. Boats back to Santarém leave every day, usually in the early evening; ask about them at the waterfront. The Banco do Brasil on Travessa 13 de Maio does cash advances on Visa cards only.

Óbidos

Around forty million years ago, when the Andes began to form themselves by pushing up from the earth, a vast inland sea burst through from what we now know as the main Amazon basin. The natural bursting point was more or less the site of modern-day **ÓBIDOS**. The huge sea squeezed itself through where the Guyanan shield to the north meets the Brazilian shield from the south, and cut an enormous channel through alluvial soils in its virgin route to the Atlantic. The river is some seven kilometres wide at Santarém, while at Óbidos, about 100km upstream, it has narrowed to less than two kilometres. Physically then, Óbidos is the gateway to the Amazon; there's an old fort to protect the passage, and most boats going upstream or down will stop here for an hour or two at least.

In the Cabanagem Rebellion (see box p.396), most of the town's leading white figures were assassinated by rebels, and Óbidos was looted and left ungoverned for years. Describing this period, the English botanist Richard Spruce remarked that anti-white feeling ran so strong in Óbidos that the mob considered the wearing of a beard as a crime punishable by death.

Óbidos is now a pretty river town with a very attractive **waterfront**, little changed since the 1920s. It makes a good stopover if you feel like breaking the journey between Manaus and Santarém or Belém. The sights won't keep you more than a morning, but it is a pleasant town to stroll around. The main thing to see is the seventeenth-century **Forte Pauxis** on the Praça Coracy Nunes, which played a crucial strategic role in Amazon history. Since that era this has been the jumping-off point for the settlement of the upper Amazon, and the cannons still in position on the ramparts command the whole width of the river. Its strategic importance meant that Óbidos was the largest town on the middle Amazon during colonial times, but the fort is the only colonial relic. Elsewhere the town has some fine buildings dating from the rubber boom and identified by metal plaques giving their history (in Portuguese only of course). Most of them are in the commercial area just off the waterfront, constructed by trading families as emporiums on the ground floor with living quarters above. Most are still shops selling simple hammocks and pots and pans.

The only really interesting **museum** in town depends on the enthusiasm of a single person, Dona Maria, who lives next door, on the road leading down from the main square. Everyone knows her so just ask for her by name. If the museum isn't open, knock on her door and she will be only too pleased to let you in. The small collection is eclectic, ranging from Indian pottery to imported British household luxuries from the rubber-boom days. There are also some intriguing old photographs: you can see that the town has hardly changed since the early years of the century. Entrance is free, but leave some money for its upkeep and sign the visitors' book; Dona Maria, who likes exotic signatures, will insist.

The town's other attractions are river-based, as you might expect. Just 25km from Óbidos along the PA-254, you can go bathing in the beautiful **Igarapé de Curuçambá**, which is served by local buses. There are also organized trips to the narrowest of Amazon river straits with impressive forested river cliffs and close-up views of river-bank homesteads and jungle vegetation. Ask about trips at the port or the *Braz Bello* hotel.

If you end up **staying** try the *Braz Bello*, Rua Marios Rodrigues de Souza 86 (☎93/547-1411;❸), which is a reasonable mid-range hotel, while along the waterfront you'll find several decent bars and restaurants. Alternatively there's the slightly cheaper *Pousada Brasil* (❷–❸) on Rua Correia Pinto, which offers a range of rooms, most with baths. **Boats** travel in and out of Óbidos every day. If you're heading to Santarém, take the smaller boats that only ply that route rather than hopping onto one of the larger Manaus–Belém boats, which tend to be slower and more expensive.

Western Amazônia

An arbitrary border, a line on paper through the forest, divides the state of Pará from the western Amazon. Encompassing the states of **Amazonas**, **Rondônia**, **Acre** and **Roraima**, the western Amazon is dominated even more than the east by the Amazon and Solimões rivers and their tributaries. In the north, the forest is centred on the Negro and Branco rivers, before phasing into the wooded savannas of Roraima. To the south, the Madeira, Purús and Juruá rivers meander through the forests from the prime rubber region of Acre and the recently colonized state of Rondônia.

The hub of this area is **Manaus**, more or less at the junction of three great rivers – the Solimões/Amazonas, the Negro and the Madeira – which between them support the world's greatest surviving forest. There are few other settlements of any real size. In the north, **Boa Vista**, capital of Roraima, lies on an overland route to Venezuela. South of the Rio Amazonas there's **Porto Velho**, capital of Rondônia, and, further west, **Rio Branco**, the main town in the relatively unexplored rubber-growing state of Acre – where the now famous Chico Mendes lived and died, fighting for a sustainable future for the forest.

Travel is never easy or particularly comfortable in the western Amazon. **From Manaus** it's possible to go by **bus** to Boa Vista and Venezuela: currently just twelve hours or so to Boa Vista on the tarmacked BR-174 through the stunning tropical forest zone of the Waimiris tribe, with over fifty rickety wooden bridges en route. You can also head east to the Amazon river settlement of Itacoatiara, but the road south to join the Transamazônica at **Humaitá** for the connection to Porto Velho is not presently open, having been repossessed by the rains and vegetation for most of its length. **From Porto Velho** the Transamazônica continues, recently paved, into Acre and **Rio Branco**, from where the route on to Peru is possible, although only in the dry season; alternatively the paved BR-364 offers quick access south to Cuiabá, Mato Grosso, Brasília and the rest of Brazil.

The rivers are the traditional and still very much dominant means of communication. Entering from the east, the first places beyond Óbidos are the small ports of **Parintins** and **Itacoatiara** – the latter has bus connections with Manaus if you're really fed up with the boat, though the roads, too, are often very hard going in the rainy season, between December and April. From Itacoatiara it's a matter of hours till Manaus appears near the confluence of the rivers Negro and Solimões. It takes another five to eight days by boat to reach the Peruvian frontier – and even here the river is several kilometres wide, and still big enough for ocean-going ships.

It rains a lot in the western Amazon – up to 375cm a year in the extreme west and about 175cm around Manaus. The heaviest rains fall in January and February most years, with a relatively dry season from June to October. The humidity rarely falls much below eighty percent, and the temperature in the month of December can reach well above 40°C. This takes a few days to get used to: until you do it's like being stuck in a sauna with only air-conditioning or cool drinks to help you escape.

Manaus and around

MANAUS is the capital of Amazonas, a tropical forest state covering around one and a half million square kilometres. The city is also the commercial and physical hub of the entire Amazon region. Most visitors are surprised to learn that Manaus isn't actually on the Amazon at all. Rather it lies on the Rio Negro, six kilometres from the point where that river meets the Solimões to form (as far as Brazilians are concerned) the Rio Amazonas. Just a few hundred metres away from the tranquil life on the rivers, the centre of Manaus perpetually buzzes with energy: always noisy, crowded and confused. Escaping from the frenzy is not easy, but there is the occasional quiet corner, and the sights of the port, markets, Opera House and some of the museums make up for the hectic pace in the downtown area. In the port and market areas, where the

Boi Bumba in Parintins

Parintins, an otherwise unremarkable small river town roughly halfway between Santarém and Manaus, has in recent years become the unlikely centre of one of the largest mass events in Brazil, the **Boi Bumba** celebrations every June (the date varies, but it generally starts the weekend before June 24 and goes on until the end of the month). Thanks to astute marketing, what began as a local custom has now become a megabucks spectacle, which attracts tens of thousands of spectators to a stadium unforgettably called the Bumbódromo, constructed in the shape of a massive stylized bull. Located in the Convention Centre of Amazonino Mendes, the stadium hosts a wild, energetic parade by something resembling an Amazonian version of Rio samba schools – and the resemblance to Rio is not coincidental, the organizers having consciously modelled themselves on Rio's Carnaval.

Boi Bumba in Parintins revolves around two schools, Caprichoso and Garantido. Each year they vie for a championship by parading through the Bumbódromo, where according to custom supporters of one school must watch the opposing parade in complete silence. You thus have the strange spectacle of 20,000 people going wild while the other half of the stadium is as quiet as a funeral, with roles reversed a few hours later. Much like the Bumba meu boi of São Luís (see p.376), Parintins' Boi Bumba has its high point with the enactment of the death of a bull, part of the legend of the slave Ma Catirina who, during her pregnancy, developed a craving for ox tongue. To satisfy her craving, her husband, Pa Francisco, slaughtered his master's bull, but the master found out and decided to arrest Pa Francisco with the help of some Indians. But, as the legend would have it, the priest and the witch doctor managed to resuscitate the animal, thus saving Pa Francisco; with the bull alive once more, the party begins again at fever pitch, to a frenetic rhythm that pounds away well into the hot and smoke-filled night.

The parade is undeniably spectacular, and the music infectious. But don't be deceived by all the references to tradition and Indian culture: the parades have only existed on this scale since the 1990s, and have about as much to do with Indian culture as the Rio samba schools that served as a model. All the same, it is enjoyable,

infamous Porto do Manaus smell is inescapable, pigs and chickens line the streets and there's an atmosphere that seems unchanged in centuries.

For the Amazon hinterland, Manaus has long symbolized "civilization". Traditionally, this meant simply that it was the **trading centre**, where the hardships of life in the forest could be escaped temporarily and where manufactured commodities to make that life easier could be purchased – metal pots, steel knives, machetes and the like. Virgin jungle seems further from the city these days – just how far really depends on what you want "virgin forest" to mean – but there are still waterways and channels within a short river journey of Manaus where you can find dolphins, alligators, kingfishers and the impression, at least, that humans have barely penetrated. Indeed, most visitors to Manaus rightly regard a **river trip** as an essential part of their stay; various **jungle tour and lodge** options are set out on pp.442–443 (see also box pp.392–393 for longer river journeys, and boat details under "Listings" on p.439). Even if you can't afford the time to disappear up the Amazon for days at a stretch, however, there are a number of sites around Manaus that make worthwhile day excursions, most notably the **meeting of the waters** of the yellow Rio Solimões and the black Rio Negro, and the lily-strewn **Parque Ecológico Januaury**.

Some history

The name Manaus came originally from the Manau tribe, which was encountered in this region by São Luís do Maranhão while he was exploring the area and is an enormous benefit to the people of the town, which has precious little else going for it economically. Thousands of people get through the rest of the year on the proceeds of catering for the huge influx of visitors during the festivities. If you're going to participate, remember that joining in with the Caprichoso group means you mustn't use yellow clothing; if you're dancing with the Carantido school, you need to avoid blue clothes as far as possible.

The number of people who descend on Parintins is considerably larger than the town's population (some 90,000 all told). During the festival, forget about **accommodation** in any of the town's few hotels: they are booked up months in advance. Your best chance in this case is simply to stay on a boat: in all the towns and cities of the region – notably Manaus and Santarém – you will find boats and travel agencies offering all-in packages for the event, with accommodation in hammocks on the boats, and this is by far the easiest way to do it. Seeing the town harbour crammed with hundreds of boats is a sight in itself. Most of the river boat companies offer three- or four-day packages, costing between $75 and $300. The trips (26hr from Manaus, 20hr from Santarém) are often booked well in advance, and are advertised from March onwards on banners tied to the boats. As you might expect, there is a lot of petty thieving and pickpocketing, so take extra care of anything you take with you. There are a couple of good places to stay during the rest of the year: *Hotel Avenida* at Av. Amazonas 2416 (⌖92/533-1158; ❷) has clean and good-value rooms, while the *Hotel Uirapuru* at Rua Herbert de Azevedo 1486 (⌖92/533-2594; ❸), though smaller, is more comfortable and has excellent service. The best **restaurant** is *Aos Amigos*, at Av. das Nacoes Unidas 2883 (⌖92/533-1446), which serves typical Amazon cuisine and is open until midnight (closed Mon).

For **tourist information**, the Secretaria de Estado da Cultura, Turismo e Desporto (SEC) has an office at Rua Jonathas Pedrosa 247-A, in Manaus Centre (daily 8am–noon & 1–6pm), which has details on accommodation in Parentins, as well as programme lists and entrance prices. The **airport** (⌖92/533-2700), on the Parananema road, is just 4km from town.

in 1616. Although he called the spot São Luís del Rio, it was Francisco do Motta Falco who really founded Manaus by building up the settlement and encouraging others to remain there with him.

The city you see today is primarily a product of the **rubber boom** and in particular the child of visionary state governor **Eduardo Ribeiro**, who from 1892 transformed Manaus into a major city. Under Ribeiro the Opera House was completed, and whole streets were wiped out in the process of laying down broad Parisian-style avenues, interspersed with Italian piazzas centred on splendid fountains. In 1899 Manaus was the first Brazilian city to have trolley buses and only the second to have electric lights in the streets.

Around the turn of the nineteenth century Manaus was an opulent metropolis run by elegant people, who dressed and housed themselves as fashionably as their counterparts in any large European city. The rich constructed palaces and grandiose mansions; time was passed at elaborate entertainments, dances and concerts. But this heyday lasted barely thirty years, and by 1914 the rubber market was collapsing fast; Ribeiro himself had committed suicide in 1900. There was a second brief boost for Brazilian rubber during World War II, but today's prosperity is largely due to the creation of a **Free Trade Zone**, the Zona Franca, in 1966. Over the following ten years the population doubled, from 250,000 to half a million, and many new industries moved in, especially electronics companies. An impressive new international airport was opened in 1976 and the floating port, supported on huge metal cylinders to cope with

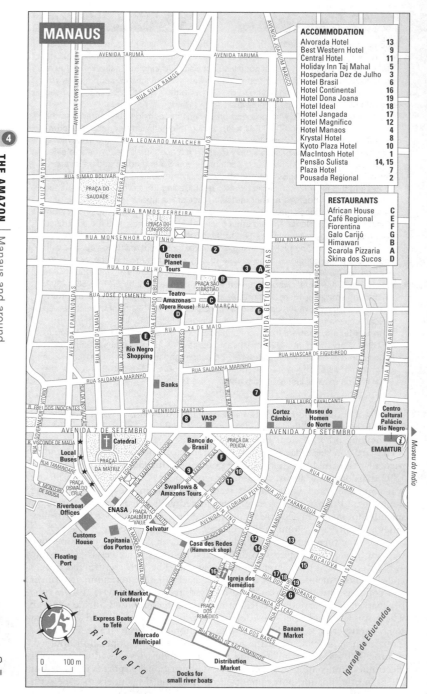

MANAUS

ACCOMMODATION

Alvorada Hotel	13
Best Western Hotel	9
Central Hotel	11
Holiday Inn Taj Mahal	5
Hospedaria Dez de Julho	3
Hotel Brasil	6
Hotel Continental	16
Hotel Dona Joana	19
Hotel Ideal	18
Hotel Jangada	17
Hotel Magnifico	12
Hotel Manaos	4
Krystal Hotel	8
Kyoto Plaza Hotel	10
MacIntosh Hotel	1
Pensão Sulista	14, 15
Plaza Hotel	7
Pousada Regional	2

RESTAURANTS

African House	C
Café Regional	E
Fiorentina	F
Galo Carijó	G
Himawari	B
Scarola Pizzaria	A
Skina dos Sucos	D

variations of as much as 14m in the level of the river, was modernized to cope with the new business.

Today, with over three million inhabitants, Manaus is an aggressive commercial and industrial centre for an enormous region – the Hong Kong of the Amazon. Over half of Brazil's televisions are made here and electronic goods are around a third cheaper here than in the south. All of this helps encourage domestic tourism – Manaus airport is crowded with Brazilians going home with their arms laden with TVs, hi-fis, computers and fax machines.

Arrival, information and accommodation

Try to avoid arriving on a Sunday, when the city is very quiet and few places are open. If you arrive in Manaus by river, your **boat** will dock right in the heart of the city, either by the Mercado Municipal or a short way along in the floating port. If you're arriving from Peru or Colombia, don't forget to have your passport stamped at the Customs House, if you haven't already done so in Tabatinga. The **rodoviária** (T92/642-6644) is some 10km north of the centre: #306 buses run every twenty minutes down Avenida Constantino Nery (two streets from the bus station), to Praça da Matriz in the heart of town, while taxis cost around $10. The **airport** (Aeroporto de Eduardo Gomes; T92/652-1212 or 654-2044) is on Avenida Santos Dumont, 17km from town in the same direction. It is also served by bus #306 (first bus 5.30am, last bus around midnight; 40min); alternatively, take a taxi for around $15. Many tour operators offer airport pickup if you're booked with them; and Geraldo Mesquita (T & F92/232-9416, mobile T9983-6273, geromesquita@hotmail.com) also offers airport pickup (approx. $11 for up to 4 passengers or $17 for 5 to 10 people).

The most central SEC **tourist office** is close to the back of the Opera House at Av. Eduardo Ribeira 666 (Mon–Fri 8am–6pm, Sat 8am–1pm; T92/231-1998), where the friendly staff can advise on the city's sights and entertainment, and provide maps and brochures. You can also check the background of any tour operator here or lodge a complaint against one if need be. The main SEC office, however, is at the side of the Palácio da Cultura at Av. Sete de Setembro 1546 (Mon–Fri 8am–6pm; T92/633-2850), and has brochures, maps and information packs about Manaus and Amazonas. There is also a SEC tourist information cabin (T92/652-1120) in the main arrivals hall at the airport (daily 24hrs).

Accommodation

Plenty of travellers end up in Manaus, so there's a wide range of places to stay, with a number of perfectly reasonable **cheap hotels**, especially in the area around Avenida Joaquim Nabuco and Rua dos Andradas. The downtown centre is just a few blocks from here, with the docks for boats up and down the Amazon and Rio Negro also nearby. Even cheaper are the hotels along Rua José Paranaguá, two blocks north of Rua dos Andradas, though this road can be unsafe at night. If you want to **camp**, the only secure option is beyond the *Tropical Hotel* at the sites around Praia Ponta Negra.

Alvorada Hotel Rua Quintino Bocaiúva 583 T92/233-5740. Among the best of the many cheap hotels on this road, though most are rented by the hour. This one is clean and friendly, and the rooms are remarkably well appointed, with TV, *frigobar* and air-conditioning. ❷

Best Western Hotel Rua Marcílio Dias 217 T92/622-7700 or 622-2844, F622-2576, www.bestwestern.com.br/manaus). Very plush, with apartments and suites; the best value hotel in central Manaus. Some rooms have views over the city centre, but there is no pool. ❺

Central Hotel Rua Dr Moreira 202 ☎ 92/622-2600, ℗ 622-2609 ✉ hcentral@terra.com.br. Wide choice of comfortable rooms, all with TV, *frigobar* and air-conditioning. There's a good restaurant on-site, too, and 24-hour room service. Excellent value for the price. ❸

Holiday Inn Taj Mahal Av. Getulio Vargas 741 ☎ 92/627-3737, ⓦ www.holidayinntajmahal .com.br. Arguably Manaus's finest hotel, with top-quality rooms, adequate service, plus a circular rotating restaurant affording the best possible views over the Opera House. The fish dishes here are especially good. Airport transfer $7. ❽

Hospedaria Dez de Julho Rua Dez de Julho 679 ☎ 92/232-6280, ✉ htdj@internext.com.br. A small family-run hotel located near the Opera House in a pleasant part of the city. Rooms are modern and clean, and the breakfasts are excellent. Also runs trips out of the city (see p.442). ❸–❹

Hotel Brasil Av. Getulio Vargas 657 ☎ 92/233-6575, ✉ hotel-brasil@internext.com.br. Modern and busy, this very adequate mid-range hotel has a bar out front by the rather noisy road, but the rooms are nice enough and the service hospitable. ❹

Hotel Continental Rua Coronel Sergio Pessoa 189 ☎ 92/233-3342. Large, clean rooms, with good showers and TVs. Some rooms overlook the Rio Negro while others face onto the Praça and Igreja dos Remédios. ❸

Hotel Dona Joana Rua dos Andradas 553 ☎ 92/233-7553. Budget hotel with large rooms that are well looked after, many offering superb views over the river, unlike most other budget places lack. ❶–❷

Hotel Ideal Rua dos Andradas 491 ☎ 92/233-9423. Opposite the *Rio Branco* and much the same, although the rooms tend to be darker. Choose between fans and air-conditioning. ❶–❷

Hotel Jangada Rua dos Andradas 473 ☎ 92/622-0264. A busy, well-kept place with a decent little restaurant. Rooms have air-conditioning and guests can use their kitchen and laundry; TVs are available. ❶–❷

Hotel Magnifico Rua Quintino Bocaiuva 450 ☎ 92/633-4690. A small dive in a handy location, with surprisingly clean rooms and hospitable staff. ❷

Hotel Manaos Av. Eduardo Ribeiro 881 ☎ 92/633-5744 ℗ 232-4443. A large modern, well air-conditioned hotel very close to the Teatro Amazonas. The service is cheerful and efficient, and the ambience unpretentious. Rooms have all mod cons. ❹–❺

Hotel Rio Branco Rua dos Andradas 484 ☎ & ℗ 92/233-4019. A secure, family-run hotel with spartan, clean rooms (shared bathrooms for some) and offering a basic breakfast. Ground-floor rooms can be damp, and some others don't have windows. ❶–❷

Krystal Hotel Rua Barroso 54 ☎ 92/233-7305, ℗ 233-7882. Near the cathedral and very good value for its modern, well-kept rooms, all equipped with TV, phone and *frigobar*. ❹

Kyoto Plaza Hotel Rua Dr Moreira 232 ☎ 92/233-7535 or 233-7305, ℗ 232-5439. Lower mid-range hotel with a friendly atmosphere in a very central location. ❸

MacIntosh Hotel Av. Eduardo Ribeiro 926 ☎ 92/234-0034 ✉ macintosh@osite.com.br. Rooms are modern but uninspired, but come with private baths. Very friendly service. Can be noisy on weekend nights due to the bar next door. ❷–❸

Pensão Sulista Av. Joaquim Nabuco 347 ☎ 92/234-5814. A pleasant old colonial-style building with clean but small rooms equipped with fans. Along with the *Rio Branco*, this is the only cheap hotel that doesn't admit prostitutes. Their annex at Rua Pedro Botelho 162, the *Hotel Sulista* (☎ 92/233-4538), has better rooms and is only marginally more expensive. ❶

Plaza Hotel Av. Getúlio Vargas 215 ☎ 92/232-7766, ℗ 234-0647 ✉ plazahotel@aol.com. Next door to the similar but twice-as-expensive *Hotel Imperial*, the towering *Plaza* has well-appointed comfy rooms and a pool – good value, though at this price the service could be better. ❹

Pousada Regional Rua Monsenhor Coutinho 768 ☎ 92/232-3505. Run by Dona Fernanda, this small, traditional family-run place is tucked away near the Teatro Amazonas. Though there are only 3–4 rooms, they're well equipped, comfortable and the service is very friendly; it's just like staying in someone's home. Downstairs there's a small street café where breakfast is served. ❸

Tropical Hotel Estrada da Ponta Negra 9015 ☎ 92/658-5000, ℗ 658-5026. This popular five-star hotel, 15km northwest of town and 8km from the airport, is right by the chic city beach, Praia Ponta Negra. Facilities include a pool, tennis courts, good nightlife, fine river beaches and even water-skiing on the Rio Negro, and the service is excellent. The *Tropical* has its own buses from the airport; from downtown, take the #120 bus from Praça da Matriz. ❼–❽

The City

It's not hard to get used to the slightly irregular **layout** of the city, and most things of interest are huddled close to the water. From the floating port where the big ships dock, river boat wharves extend round past the market, from one end of Rua dos Andradas to the other. The busiest commercial streets are immediately behind, extending up to the Avenida Sete de Setembro, with the cathedral marking one end of the downtown district, the Praça da Polícia the other. Beyond Avenida Sete de Setembro, towards the Opera House, it's a bit calmer, and the square at the entrance to the famous Teatro Amazonas is developing into an artists' quarter with bars and trendy cafes. The busy Praça da Matriz by the cathedral is the main hub of city communications, with **buses** to local points around the city and suburbs; another good connection point for city buses and taxis is the east side of Avenida Getúlio Vargas, just north of Avenida Sete de Setembro.

Around the docks

Since it's the docks that have created Manaus, it seems logical to start your exploration here – and it's certainly the most atmospheric part of town. The **port** itself is an unforgettable spectacle. A constant throng of activity stretches along the riverfront, while the ships tied up at the docks bob serenely up and down. Boats are getting ready to leave, or having just arrived are busy unloading. People cook fish at stalls to sell to the hungry sailors and their passengers, or to the workers once they've finished their shift of carrying cargo from the boats to the distribution market. Hectic and impossibly complex and anarchic as it appears to the unaccustomed eye, the port of Manaus is in fact very well organized, if organically so. During the day there's no problem wandering around, and it's easy enough to find out which boats are going where just by asking around. At night, however, this can be a dangerous area and is best avoided: many of the river men carry guns. The whole area is presently undergoing redevelopment with plans for shops, theatres and kids areas to be built largely in the old iron style of the rubber boom.

From the Praça Adalberto Valle, the impressive **Customs House** (Mon–Fri 8am–1pm), and known locally as "Alfândega" stands between you and the floating docks. Erected in 1906, the building was shipped over from Britain in prefabricated blocks, and the tower once acted as a lighthouse guiding vessels in at night. The floating docks, too, were built by a British company, at the beginning of the twentieth century. To cope with the river rising over a 14m range, the concrete pier is supported on pontoons that rise and fall to allow even the largest ships to dock here all year round (the highest recorded level of the river so far was in 1953, when it rose some 30m above sea level).

A couple of blocks east of the Customs House, on Rua dos Andradas, the **Praça Terreira Araña** has a clutch of stalls selling indigenous Amazon *artesanato*, leather sandals and jungle souvenirs, and there's a small café here too that's open only in the daytime.

Following Rua Marquês de Santa Cruz down towards the new docks will bring you to the covered **Mercado Municipal Adolfo Lisboa** (Mon–Sat 5am–6pm, Sun 5am–noon), whose elegant Art Nouveau roof was designed by Eiffel during the rubber boom and is a copy of the former Les Halles market in Paris. Inaugurated in 1882, the market features an assortment of tropical fruit and vegetables, jungle herbs, scores of different fresh fishes and Indian craft goods jumbled together on sale. Just to the east of this market is the **wholesale port distribution market**, where traders buy goods from incoming boats and sell them on wholesale to shops, market stalls and restaurants. There are also a substantial number of retail traders here where you too can buy the goods at prices only a little over wholesale. The distribution market is at its busiest first thing in the morning; by the afternoon most of the merchants have closed shop, and the place looks abandoned. In the early 1990s, this market was modernized – turning rat-infested wood and mayhem into concrete-based organized chaos. Much of the original charm has given way to the clinicality of the twentieth century, but the port and markets are still fascinating places to wander.

❹ The commercial centre and the Opera House

Things are almost as busy as the docks in Manaus's downtown commercial centre, but although it starts only a few metres inland from the water, the atmosphere is totally different. Essentially an electronics market that has evolved out of the Free Trade Zone era, this is the hub of the modern city. Everything from electronic appliances to shoes can be bought here, at prices that are very cheap by Brazilian standards.

The city's most famous symbol, the **Teatro Amazonas** or Opera House (Mon–Sat 9am–4pm; $4 including guided tour; ☎92/622-2420) seems even more extraordinary coming in the midst of this rampant commercialism. The whole incongruous, magnificent thing, designed in a pastiche of Italian Renaissance style by a Lisbon architectural firm, cost in the region of $3 million. After twelve years of building, with virtually all the materials – apart from the regional wood – brought from Europe, the Opera House was finally completed in 1896. Its main feature, the fantastic cupola, was created from 36,000 tiles imported from Alsace in France. The theatre's main curtain, painted in Paris by Brazilian artist Crispim do Amaral, represents the meeting of the waters and the local Indian water goddess Iara. The four painted pillars on the ceiling depict the Eiffel tower in Paris, giving visitors the impression, as they look upwards, that they are actually underneath the tower itself. The chandeliers are of Italian crystal and French bronze, and the theatre's seven hundred seats, its main columns and the balconies are all made of English cast iron. If you include the dome, into which the original curtain is pulled up in its entirety, the stage is a vertical 75m high.

Major restorations have taken place in 1929, 1960, 1974 and, most recently, in 1990, when the outside was returned from blue to its original pink. Looking over the upstairs balcony down onto the road in front of the Opera House, you can see the black driveway made from a special blend of rubber, clay and sand, originally to dampen the noise of horses and carriages as they arrived. Yet the building is not just a relic, and it hosts regular concerts, including in April the **Festa da Manaus**, initiated in 1997 to celebrate thirty years of the Zona Franca.

In front of the Teatro, the wavy black-and-white mosaic designs of the **Praça São Sebastião** are home to the "Monument to the Opening of the Ports", a marble and granite creation with four ships that represent four continents – America, Europe, Africa and Asia/Australasia – and children who symbolize the people of those continents. Homeless children too frequent the square, looking after cars and begging from passersby. Nevertheless, the Praça São Sebastião is getting trendier by the year, with a growing number of interesting shops, bars and arty cafés. Also on the *praça* is the beautiful little **Igreja de São Sebastião**, built in 1888, which, like many other churches in Brazil, has only one tower due to the nineteenth-century tax levied on churches with two towers. Despite being one of the more pleasant suburbs of central Manaus, the area still has its seedy side, as evident from the male and female prostitutes working the street just yards from the church. Nearby on Avenida Eduardo Ribeiro, you'll find the **Palácio da Justiça** (8am–1pm Mon-Fri), opposite the SEC tourist offices. Supposedly modelled on Versailles, the Neoclassical building functions as the main state court, and contrary to the popular image its famous statue of the Greek goddess Temis is not blindfolded,

Some three blocks further away from the river, up Rua Tapajós, you'll find the old **Central Post Office**, another imposing reminder of the glorious years of the rubber boom. On the pavement around the back there's an ornate, much-photographed antique postbox, dated 1889.

Along Avenida Sete de Setembro

Back towards the river, the **Catedral de Nossa Senhora da Conceição** (more commonly known as Igreja Matriz) on Avenida Sete de Setembro is a relatively plain building, surprisingly untouched by the orgy of adornment that struck the rest of the city – though judging by the number of people who use it, it plays a more active role in the life of the city than many more showy buildings. The original cathedral, built mainly of wood and completed in 1695 by the Carmelite missionaries, was destoyed by fire in 1850, and the present building dates from 1878, with most of the building materials brought from Europe, mainly Portugal. Around the cathedral are the **Praça Osvaldo Cruz** and the **Praça da Matriz**, shady parks popular with local courting couples, hustlers and sleeping drunks.

About 500m west of the cathedral along Avenida Sete de Setembro is the **Instituto Geográfico e Histórico do Amazonas** (Mon–Fri 2–5.30pm), Rua Bernardo Ramos 135. Founded in 1917 on one of the city's oldest streets, the building is now a heritage site and has been recently restored. The institute's small museum includes a collection of ceramics from various tribes, a range of insect displays and indigenous tools like stone axes and hunting equipment.

The **Museu do Homem do Norte** (Museum of Northern Man; Mon–Thurs 9am–noon & 1–5pm, Fri 1–5pm), in the opposite direction at Av. Sete de Setembro 1385, near Avenida Joaquim Nabuco, offers a quick overview of human life and ecology in the Amazon region. Also worth at least a quick visit is the **Centro Cultural Palácio Rio Negro** (Tues–Sun 4–9pm; free), next to the SEC tourist office, a gorgeous colonial-period mansion that houses the archives (manuscripts, drawings and plans) of the nineteenth-century Portuguese naturalist and scientist Alexandre Rodrigues Ferreira. The centre also hosts a wide range of exhibitions, drama and events, and has a good bookstore.

The excellent **Museu do Índio**, Rua Duque de Caxias 356 (Mon–Fri 8am–noon & 2–5pm, Sat 8am–noon; $2), lies about 500m further east along Avenida Sete de Setembro. The museum is run by the Salesian Sisters, who have long-established missions along the Rio Negro, especially with the Tukano tribe. There are excellent, carefully presented displays, with exhibits ranging from sacred ritual masks and inter-village communication drums to fine ceramics, superb palm-frond weavings and even replicas of Indian dwellings. Neatly complementing this collection is the **Museu Amazônico da Universidade do Amazonas**, to the north of the centre at Rua Ramos Ferreira 1036, which houses a small collection of sixteenth-century documents and engravings relating to the first explorations of the interior.

Out of the centre

The most popular and most widely touted day-trip around Manaus is to the **meeting of the waters**, some 10km downstream, where the Rio Negro and the Rio Solimões meet to form the Rio Amazonas. For several kilometres beyond the point where they join, the waters of the two rivers continue to flow separately: the muddy yellow of the Solimões contrasting sharply with the black of the Rio Negro. It's a strange sight, and one well worth seeing. If you're going under your own steam, take the "Vila Burity" **bus** (#713) from Praça da Matriz to the end of the line, from where you can take a free half-hourly government ferry over the river, passing the meeting of the waters.

Most **tours** to the meeting of the waters leave the docks at Manaus and pass by the shantytown of Educandos and the Rio Negro riverside industries before heading out into the main river course. Almost all will also stop in at the **Parque Ecológico Januaury**, an ecological park some 7km from Manaus on one of the main local tributaries of the Rio Negro. Usually you'll be transferred to smaller motorized canoes to explore its creeks (*igarapés*), flooded forest lands (*igapós*) and abundant vegetation.

One of the highlights of the area is the abundance of *Victoria Amazonica* (previously *Victoria Regia*), the extraordinary giant floating lily for which Manaus is famous. Found mostly in shallow lakes, it flourishes above all in the rainy months. The plant, named after Queen Victoria by an English naturalist in the nineteenth century, has huge leaves – some over a metre across – with a covering of thorns on their underside as protection from the teeth of plant-eating fish. The flowers are white on the first day of their life, rose-coloured on the second, and on the third they begin to wilt: at night the blooms close, imprisoning any insects that have wandered in, and releasing them again as they open with the morning sun. In the rainy season you'll explore the creeks and flood lands by boat; during the dry season – between September and January – it's possible to walk around.

The river beach at **Praia Ponta Negra**, about 13km northwest of Manaus near the *Hotel Tropical*, is another very popular local excursion, and at weekends is packed with locals. Once the home of the Manaos Indians (from whom the city name originally came), the beach is an enjoyable spot for a swim, with plenty of bars and restaurants serving freshly cooked river fish. You can also catch regular music and other events at the massive modern amphitheatre nearby. The beach is at its best between September and March, when the river is low and exposes a wide expanse of sand, but even when the rains bring higher waters and the beach almost entirely disappears, plenty of people come to eat and drink. Soltur's Ponta Negra bus (#120) leaves every half hour for the beach: catch it by the cathedral on Praça da Matriz.

The nearby military-run **CIGS Zoo** (Tues–Sun 9am–4.45pm; $1), Estrada Ponta Negra 750, also happens to be an army jungle training centre, and many of the animals in it were captured, so they say, on military exercises out in the forest. The zoo has been recently redesigned to cater better for visitors, and you can expect to see alligators, monkeys, macaws and snakes among the more than 300 animals and 73 species kept here. To get there take the #120, or the "Compensa" or "São Jorge" bus from the military college on Avenida Epaminondas.

The **Parque do Mindú**, out in the direction of the airport, is the city's largest expanse of public greenery, incorporating educational trails (on which visitors can walk along suspended walkways), an *artesanato* shop and an exhibition centre. Closer to the city centre, the **Bosque da Ciência**, Alameda

Cosme Ferreira 1756, Aleixo (Tues–Fri 9am–noon & 2–4.30pm, Sat, Sun & holidays 9am–5pm), is an ecological park created by the Instituto Nacional de Pesquisas de Amazônia (National Institute for Amazon Research; INPA), home to otters, manatees, monkeys, snakes and birds. Both sites are easiest to reach by taxi, but you can also get there on buses #508, #424, #505 or #504. INPA are based at Av. A. Araújo 1756 (daily 9am–noon & 2–5pm; ☎92/643-3377), and run free two-hour video screenings at weekends (at 10am and 2pm). A taxi ride away from here, there's more wildlife at the **Museu de Ciências Naturais da Amazônia**, Colônia Cachoeira Grande, Estrada Belém km 15 (Mon–Sat 9am–5pm; $2), including fish such as the *piraruca* – in a 37,000-gallon aquarium – butterflies, insects and a good *artesanato* shop.

The waterfalls of **Cachoeira do Tarumã**, about 20km northwest of the city, are the last of the local beauty spots within easy reach of Manaus. They don't offer unspoiled beauty any more, thanks to commercialization and weekend crowds, but the place is still fun, there's good swimming, and on busy weekends you'll often find live music in the bars. The cascades themselves, supplied by the Rio Negro, are relatively small white-water affairs that more or less disappear in the rainy season (April to Aug). Soltur buses (#11) run here approximately every twenty minutes from the Praça da Matriz, taking about half an hour.

About an hour outside the town, the **Museu do Seringal Vila Paraíso** recreates the living and working conditions of the traditional rubber tappers from one hundred years ago (Wed–Sun 8am–4pm). To get here, take the bus to Ponta Negra and then catch a dug-out taxi from the side of the *Tropical Hotel* to Igarapé São João – an affluent of the Taruma-Mirim that empties into the left bank of the Rio Negro. Tickets for the museum can be bought in advance from the SEC tourist office in the Centro Cultural Palacio Rio Negro.

Eating and drinking

There are very few places in Manaus where you can sit down and enjoy any peace, and even the cafés and bars are too full to give you much elbow room. One advantage of the crowds is that there's **street food** everywhere, especially around the docks, the Mercado Municipal and in busy downtown locations like the Praça da Matriz, where a plate of rice and beans with a skewer of freshly grilled meat or fish costs well under $2. One traditional dish you should definitely try here is **tacacá** – a soup that consists essentially of yellow manioc root juice in a hot spicy dried-shrimp sauce. It's often mixed and served in traditional gourd bowls, *cuias*, and is usually sold in the late afternoons by *tacacazeiras* (street food vendors).

For your own food, there's a **supermarket** at the corner of Avenida Joaquim Nabuco and Avenida Sete de Setembro, and another towards the market on Rua Rocha dos Santos. The following **restaurants** are closed Sundays unless otherwise stated, and be warned that prices in Manaus are roughly double what you might find in the rest of the country.

African House Praça São Sebastião. A delightful café with a vaguely Parisian feel, opening out onto the square in front of the Opera House. Choose from light meals like burgers and grilled or fried chicken, washing it down with juices mixed with vitamins or *guarana* (a health supplement made from the seeds of an Amazonian bush).
Anavilhaus Av. Joaquim Nabuco 498. One of the cheapest places in town for good cooked meals.

It's a no-frills night-time dive stacked with beer crates and playing loud music all the time, but it serves excellent fish dishes – try the *tucunaré*. Open daily.
Café Regional Rua Costa Azevedo 369 ☎92/233-1028. A small café specializing in Amazon breakfasts and vegetarian lunches, just a stone's throw from the Teatro Amazonas.
Canto da Peixada Rua Emilio Moreira 1677

92/234-3021. Considered by many to be Manaus's best regional and river-fish restaurant, and therefore not cheap, but good-value nonetheless. Closed Sun, but usually open until 11.30pm other nights.

Churrascaria Búfalo Av. Joaquim Nabuco 628A. Excellent *rodízio* and one of the best meat restaurants in downtown Manaus, but expensive at $12 a head.

Fiorentina Praça da Polícia. Upmarket Italian restaurant right in the heart of town where the menu ranges from local river fish dishes to traditional pastas and steaks; good food but quite expensive.

Galo Carijó Rua dos Andradas 536. Opposite the *Hotel Dona Joana*, this is a simple, inexpensive but excellent local fish restaurant and bar. Closed Sat evening.

Himawari Rua 10 de Julho 618 92/233-2208. A spacious Japanese restaurant with quality food and service, conveniently located on the Praça São Sebastião. Open Tues–Thurs 11.30am–2pm & 6.30–10pm, Fri & Sat 11.30–3pm & 6.30–11pm, and until 10pm Sun.

Kaktus Restaurant Av. Joaquim Nabuco, at the corner of Leonardo Marcher. This pleasant restaurant has decent self-service lunches but specializes in fish dishes in the evenings. Closed Mon.

Lanche Alternativa Rua Marquês de Santa Cruz, by the Mercado Municipal. Grilled meat and beer accompanied by the biggest and loudest PA rig in Manaus. Open daily.

Mana's Rua Dr Moreira 76. A *churrascaria* and *peixaria* that has great salads amongst its self-service *comida por kilo*–style lunches.

Mandarim Av. Eduardo Ribeiro 650, at the corner of Rua 24 de Maio. Excellent and reasonably priced Chinese restaurant, with a *comida por kilo* system for lunch and à la carte in the evening (6–10.30pm). Their *chopa* (sizzling platter) dishes are recommended.

O Naturalista Rua Sete de Setembro 752, 2nd floor. A large, clean and enjoyable vegetarian restaurant one block east from the cathedral. Open Mon–Fri lunchtime.

Scarola Pizzaria Rua Dez de Julho 739. Away from the action a little, this is a pleasant pizzeria, with a nice patio, good service and reasonable food.

Skina dos Sucos corner of Avenida Eduardo Ribeiro with the Rio Branco Shopping Centre. Superb little café specializing almost exclusively in tropical fruit juices, served iced or pure. Excellent drinks and fast service.

Sorveteria Glacial corner of Rua Henrique Martins Calvante with Avenida Getulio Vargas. Of the several tropical fruit ice-cream cafés around Manaus, this (and another across the road) are two of the busier ones.

Suzuran Rua Teresina 155 92/234-1693. Very good Japanese restaurant, worth the taxi ride to the trendy Adrianopolis suburb. The best of the city's three Japanese dining options, but without the top-tier prices. Open daily.

Nightlife

Like most large port towns, Manaus is busiest in the early mornings, and again at night, with plenty of bars, clubs and other venues that are worth exploring if you're in town for a few days; Friday editions of *Amazonas Em Tempo* carry fairly comprehensive listings.

The rowdiest **bars** are bunched around and in the Mercado Municipal, and along the entire length of Avenida Joaquim Nabuco south of Avenida Sete de Setembro. The usual starting place, for beer, snacks and a lively atmosphere, is either the Bohemian *MacIntosh Bar* on Avenida Eduardo Ribeira, just up from the Palacio da Justicia, or the *Pizzaria Scarola* on the corner of Avenida Getulio Vargas and Dez de Julho, with a patio that makes it a popular meeting place in the early evenings. Around the Mercado Municipal, the popular *Lanche Alternativa* (see above) sometimes has live music. Further around the port, to the west of Praça da Matriz on Rua M. Sousa, a couple of even louder places – *Holanda Bar* and *Recanto da Natureza* – stay open all night. There are also a number of inexpensive bars around the Praça Sebastião, including the *Bar do Amandó* in front of the Opera House, which frequently has locals playing guitars and singing inside. Also by the Opera House, under the Radio Rio Mar tower and building, is the *Jungle Disco*, usually the scene of Brazilian pop and samba dancing at weekends.

As for **clubs**, the most exciting are undoubtedly those along the Estrada Ponta Negra and around Praia Ponta Negra itself. Though their names change frequently, the music is invariably a danceable blend of old and modern sambas – it's worth coming just to see the formation dancing of the crowds. Given Manaus's prohibitive taxi fares, most of the Praia Ponta Negra clubs remain open all night, so you might as well bring a towel for a sobering early morning dip in the river. Similarly distant is *Zazoueira Disco*, located out near the airport on Estrada Torquato Tapajós at km 12, Flores. This is one of the best straight clubs in town, but drinks and entrance are expensive.

Not as chic, but more central, is the touristy *Boiart's* club, Rua Jose Clemente 500 (☎92/637-6807), near the Opera House, which puts on frequent dance presentations loosely based on Amazon tribal dances (open Wed–Sat, shows start around 11pm). The *Cheik Clube*, Av. Getúlio Vargas 773, has a solid reputation for modern dance music (house and techno as well as salsa). **Brazilian music** venues include the *Sabor Brasil Clube*, Rua Leonardo 1840, for samba (☎92/234-4520), and the *Havai Club*, Estrada da Ponta Negra (☎92/651-2797), which is great for any sort of dancing. For a more studenty feel and some live bands, try *Coração Blue*, Estrada da Ponta Negra 3701, km 6 (starts 10pm; ☎92/984-1391). The main cinemas, again very popular, include several screens at Amazonas Shopping (see "Listings", under "shopping" for address).

Listings

Airlines Lloyd Aereo Boliviano Av. 7 de Setembro 993 ☎92/6334200 or at the airport ☎92/652-1182; Penta (covering the eastern Amazon), Rua Barroso 352 ☎92/234-1046 and at the airport ☎92/652-1161; Tavaj, at the airport ☎92/652-1486; Transbrasil, Rua Guilherme Moreira 150 ☎92/621-1705; Varig, Rua Marcílio Dias 284 ☎92/652-1551; and VASP, Av. Sete de Setembro 993 ☎92/622-3470 or 652-1448.

Banks and exchange Câmbio e Turismo Cortez (Mon–Fri 9am–5pm, Sat 9am–12.30pm), at the corner of Av. Getúlio Vargas #88 and Av. Sete de Setembro, has good rates and fast service for both cash and travellers' cheques, unlike the Banco do Brasil, Rua Guilherme Moreira 315. There are several banks on Avenida Eduardo Ribeiro, just a block or two down the street from the SEC tourist offices.

Boats There are regular passenger boat services to: Belém, Santarém and all ports along the Rio Amazonas; along the Rio Solimões to Tabatinga; and up the Rio Madeira to Porto Velho. Less frequent services go up the Rio Negro to São Gabriel da Cachoeira and up the Rio Branco to Caracaraí. Tickets for the regular services can be bought from the ticket windows inside the port building off Praça da Matriz, next to where the boat departure list is posted. Before buying your ticket, ask for a paper pass (*papel do permissão*) which allows you into the docks (you'll need your passport, too) where the bigger, long-distance river boats are

moored; here you can have a look at the boats before deciding which you want to travel on. It's sensible to buy tickets in advance, which can often get you a reasonable discount, and always get on your boat a good two hours or more before it's due to depart. Standard boats from Manaus to Belém can cost anything from \$40 to \$80 and can take three to five days, often stopping off in Santarém. Smaller boats with no regular schedules, and those serving local settlements up the Rio Negro, are found to the east of the Mercado Municipal. They usually display signs marked with their destinations. The main ENASA ticket office is at Rua Marechal Deodoro 61 (☎92/633-3280 ⑤633-3093). See also the "River Journeys" box pp.392–393. For a fast boat to Tefe, it's best to take the Expreso Barcos service (13hr; \$40) from the Hidroviaria near the Mercado Municipal.

Car rental Avis ☎92/652-1579; Interlocadora ☎92/233-5288; Rede Brasil, Av. Constantino Nery 572 ☎92/233-6473; Unidas ☎92/652-1575.

Consulates Bolivia Av. Engenio Sales 2226, Quadrant B-20 ☎92/236-9988; Colombia Rua 24 de Maio ☎92/234-6777; Peru, Rua A – C/19 – Conj. Aristocratico, Chapada ☎92/656-3267 or 656-1015; UK Rua Paraque 240 ☎92/237-7869; US Rua Recife 1010 – CCI – Adrianópolis ☎92/233-4907; Venezuela, Rua Ferreira Pena 179 ☎92/233-6004.

Health matters For tropical complaints the best is the Instituto de Medicina Tropical, Avenida Pedro

Teixeira 25 ☎92/656-1441 or 656-4573. The Drogueria Nossa Senhor de Nazare, 7 de Setembro 1333 is a reasonably well-stocked pharmacy.

Internet *Amazon Cybercafé*, on the corner of Av. Getulio Vargas with 10 de Julho, has lots of terminals, serves free coffee and is inexpensive. Alternatively, try: Cybercity Internet, next to the Sorveteria Glacial in the second block of Avenida Getulio Vargas; Discover Internet, Rua Marcílio Dias 320, Loja 7; and Internext's cybercafé at Amazonas Shopping (see "Shopping", below).

Laundry Lavalux, Rua Mundurucus 77 ☎92/234-0466; Amazonas, Rua Costa Azevedo 63; Super Rápida, Rua Paraíba 1.

Police ☎190.

Post office The main one, with a reliable poste restante service (first floor), is just off the Praça da Matriz on Rua Marechal Deodoro at the corner with Rua Teodoreto Souto (Mon–Fri 9am–5pm, Sat 8am–noon). There's a smaller, quieter branch just beyond the top of Avenida Eduardo Ribeiro, on the leafy Praça do Congresso.

Shopping The best selection of *artesania* is at the lively Sunday morning street market, which appears out of nowhere in the broad Avenida Eduardo Ribeira, behind the Teatro Amazonas. The Museu do Índio (see p.435) and several shops around the square in front of the Opera House also sell *artesanato*. Indian crafts are also sold at the Mercado Municipal. Interesting *macumba* and *umbanda* items, such as incense, candles, figurines and bongos, can be found at Cabana São Jorge at Rua da Instalação 36. Duty-free electronic and all kinds of other luxury items can be bought everywhere in the centre. The modern shopping centre Amazonas Shopping, on the airport road, 4–5km from the centre by taxi or bus #306, has hundreds of shops and cafés, plus 6 cinemas. A good hammock shop is Casa des Redes on Rua dos Andradas. For photographic film and developing, try Foto Nascimento, Av. Sete de Setembro 1194.

Taxis Amazonas ☎92/232-3005; Rádio Táxi ☎92/633-3211; Tocantins ☎92/656-1330.

Telephones National and international calls can be made with phonecards in public booths around the city; alternatively, the Telmar office (Mon–Fri 8am–6pm, Sat 8am–noon) is on Av. Getúlio Vargas 950, close to the junction with Rua Ramos Ferreira.

Travel Agents Turismo Cortez, at the corner of Av. Getúlio Vargas #88 and Av. Sete de Setembro; Fontur, *Tropical Hotel*, Ponta Negra ☎92/658-3052. Both are good for flights and city tours (Fontur will arrange free hotel pick-ups in the city centre for its city tours). Tucunare Turismo, Rua Henrique Martins 116 (☎92/234-5071, Ⓦwww.tucunareturismo.com.br), offer city tours, and trips to the meeting of the waters, fishing sites and the waterfalls of Presidente Figueiredo.

Jungle trips from Manaus

Manaus is the obvious place in the Brazilian Amazon to find a **jungle river trip** to suit most people's requirements. It's not necessarily the best place if you are serious about spotting a wide range of wildlife, but it does offer a range of organized tours bringing visitors into close contact with the world's largest tropical rainforest. Unfortunately, though, since Manaus has been a big city for a long time, the forest in the immediate vicinity is far from virgin. Over the last millennia it has been explored by Indians, missionaries, rubber gatherers, colonizing extractors, settlers, urban folk from Manaus and, more recently, quite a steady flow of eco-interested tourists.

The amount and nature of the **wildlife** you get to see on a standard jungle tour depends mainly on how far away from Manaus you go and how long you can devote to the trip. Birds like macaws, jabarus and toucans can generally be spotted, and you might see alligators, snakes and a few species of monkey on a three-day-trip (though you can see many of these anyway at the Parque Janauary – see p.436). For a decent remote chance of glimpsing wild deer, tapirs, armadillos or wild cats then a week-long, more adventurous trip is the minimum, preferably more. On any trip, make sure that you'll get some time in the smaller channels in a canoe, as the sound of a motor is a sure way of scaring every living thing out of sight.

There are a few Brazilian **jungle terms** every visitor should be familiar with: a *regatão* is a travelling boat-cum-general store, which can provide a fascinating introduction to the interior if you can strike up an agreeable arrangement with one of their captains; an *igarapé* is a narrow river or creek flowing from the forest into one of the larger rivers (though by narrow around Manaus they mean less than 1km wide); an *igapó* is a patch of forest that is seasonally flooded; a *furo* is a channel joining two rivers and therefore a short cut for canoes; a *paraná*, on the other hand, is a branch of the river that leaves the main channel and returns further downstream, creating a river island.

There are scores of different **jungle tour companies** in Manaus offering very similar services and the competition is intense, which means you'll regularly get hassled by touts all over town, and the sales patter is unrelenting. While you may be able to bargain the price down a bit (groups can always get a better deal than people travelling alone), your best bet is to shop around, talk to other tourists who have already been on trips and be wary of parting with wads of cash before you know exactly what you'll be getting in return (see below). You can generally get a tour cheaper if you're prepared to hang around for the operator to find other tourists to make up a larger group. If possible, book in advance through one of the more established outfits registered with EMBRATUR.

It's always a good idea to pin your tour operator down to giving you specific details of the trip on paper, preferably in the form of a written **contract**, and you should always ask about the accommodation arrangements, what the food and drink will consist of, and exactly where you are going; ask to see photos. A circular trip may sound attractive, but the scenery won't change very much, whatever the name of the *rio*. You should also check that the guide speaks English, whether the operator has an environmental policy and what insurance cover they offer (usually nil in the case of the cheaper operators). Check, too, to see if the company is registered with EMBRATUR (if they are it is much easier to make a claim against them if something goes wrong). Ask what is not included in the price, and whether you can get your money back, or part of it, if the trip turns out to be disappointing. On a more upmarket tour, you should check that binoculars and reference books are provided on the boat, if you haven't already got your own, and, on any tour, you of course have the right to expect that any promises made – regarding maximum group size, activities and so on – are kept. If not, then a promise to complain to the SEC, Av. Eduardo Ribeira 666 (℡92/231-1998) may give you some leverage in obtaining redress. You can also check with the SEC for reports on complaints that might have been made against a particular tour operator.

The most dependable and comfortable way to visit the jungle is to take a package tour that involves a number of nights in a **jungle lodge** – though for the more adventurous traveller the experience can be a little tame. The lodges invariably offer hotel-standard accommodation, full board and a range of activities including alligator spotting, piranha fishing, trips by canoe, as well as transport to and from Manaus. You can either book a jungle lodge tour through a tour operator, or approach the lodges direct at their offices in Manaus (see box, pp.442–443). Some of the better tour companies operate their own small river boats for more leisurely exploration, sometimes with room for up to 20 people to sleep in comfortable, if small, cabins.

If you want to forgo organized tours entirely and travel independently, **milk boats** are a very inexpensive way of getting about on the rivers around Manaus. These smaller vessels, rarely more than 20m long, spend their weeks serving the local riverine communities by delivering and transporting their produce. You can spend a whole day on one of these boats for as little as $10, depending on what arrangement you make with the captain. The best place to

Jungle tour operators are not difficult to find in Manaus; but it is quite hard to identify the best and most trusted operators and guides just by meeting them at the airport or in the streets of the downtown area. If you can, it's much better to book in advance, easily done on the Web or by email. Some of the companies or agents listed below have their own lodges, river boats and houseboats, while one or two of them select and book an appropriate lodge or boat for each tour.

Tour operators

Amazonas Indian Turismo Rua dos Andradas 311 ⓣ92/633-5578. A basic but long-established operator and one of the least pushy of the budget crowd. Run by Amazon Indians, they offer good jungle trekking, wildlife (mainly birds – including toucans – dolphins and alligators), exploring *igarapés* in small canoes, piranha fishing and visits to local communities. Guides vary in quality (some speak only Portuguese) but they can be good value ($40–80 a day). Tour groups tend to be smaller than most, and more personalized itineraries are also possible. They also operate a basic but very hospitable lodge camp around 200km from Manaus.

Amazon Explorers kiosk in Praça Tenreiro Aranha, in the centre's Zona Franca shopping area (ⓣ92/613-1210), or the main office at Rua Nhamundá 21, Praça N.S. Auxiliadora (ⓣ92/232-3052, ⓕ234-6767, ⓦwww.amazonexplorers.com.br.) This reputable operator runs a reservations service for upmarket jungle lodges, luxury boat hire and fishing trips, and organizes jungle tours, with boat accommodation (from around $100 per person a day, minimum two people for two days) and a six-hour trip to the meeting of the waters and Parque Janauary ($60). As a travel agency, it offers a ticketing service for air and boat travel.

Amazon Nut Safaris Av. Beira Mar 43, São Raimundo ⓣ92/234-5860 ⓕ622-2821, ⓦwww.amazonnut.com. Upmarket ecological expeditions to the Anavilhanas archipelago. They also operate a fleet of boats and a small nine-room lodge, *Apurissawa*, on the Rio Cuieiras (Rio Negro area), 4hr by boat from Manaus. Tours include trips to the meeting of the waters, alligator and bird watching expeditions, and visits to local *caboclos* (traditional river dwellers) communities. They also have a kiosk at the airport.

Crocodile Amazon Rua Floriano Peixoto 215, Suite 807 ⓣ92/234-5907 or 9139-2620, ⓦwww.crocodileamazon.com. This company runs fishing expeditions and half-day-trips to the meeting of the waters, among other trips.

Gero's Tour ⓣ & ⓕ92/232-9416, mobile ⓣ9983-6273, ⓔamazongerostour@iamazonia.com.br, or through the *Hospedaria Dez de Julho* (see p.432). A reliable and pleasant independent guide, Geraldo (Gero) Neto Mesquita speaks English. Spanish and Portuguese. He organizes tours mainly to the Mamori and Juma areas (Rio Negro on request), and will also help book hotels, boats and arrange airport pickup. Tours include boat and canoe trips, jungle hiking and visits to native people, with accommodation in hammocks, overnight in the bush or at local family houses. Tours can be combined with luxury lodge accommodations. Prices start from $50 and depend on the size of the group.

Green Planet Tours, Rua Dez de Julho 481 ⓣ92/232-1398 mobile ⓣ989-4889, ⓦwww.planettours.com.br). A popular operator specializing in a range of trips starting around $50–60 a day, with accommodation in hammocks or tents. Most trips, which use the company's Rio Negro floating base camp, include the meeting of the waters, alligator spotting, piranha fishing and jungle walks. Travel is generally by motorised canoe but they also have a covered twin-decked river boat (though no cabin accommodation). Tours sometimes go to Mamori lake, 50km south of Manaus.

Swallows and Amazons Rua Quintino Bocaiúva 189, 1st floor, sala 13 ⓣ & ⓕ92/622-1246, ⓦwww.swallowsandamazonstours.com. A small company with an excellent reputation, specializing in private and small-group houseboat, river boat, jungle lodge and rainforest adventure tours. Most trips explore the Rio Negro river and the Anavilhanas archipelago, but custom tours are also possible. The company runs *Over Look Lodge*, 50km from Manaus on the Rio Negro. Rates $75–150 per person per day.

Lodges and camps

Jungle lodges offer travellers the opportunity to experience the rainforest while maintaining high levels of comfort, even elegance. There are scores of lodges in and around the Manaus area, most operated by tour companies.

Acajatuba Jungle Lodge Rua Lima Bacuri 345 ☎92/233-7642, ⓦwww.acajatuba .com.br. A lodge with large communal areas and spacious clean cabins, *Acajatuba* offers trips from 1 to 4 nights. It's located in the Anavilhanas archipelago and has wooden elevated footbridges joining the various parts of the site. Night-time lighting is from battery powered bulbs, so there's rarely any generator noise to drown out the sounds of the jungle at night.

Amazon Ecopark Lodge Praça Auxiliadora 4, grupo 103 ☎ & Ⓕ92/234-0027, ⓦwww.amazonecopark.com or in Rio de Janeiro, Lauro Muller 360, Suite 510 ☎21/2275-5285. Located in a nature reserve on the west bank of the Rio Tarumã, just over 20km from Manaus and an easy day-trip. Monkeys, birds, ungulates, rodents and reptiles are presented in their natural habitats at the adjacent "Amazon Monkey Jungle". From $60 per person for a day-trip, or $150 for an overnight stay, plus other options; if you can get there under your own steam (phone for transport options and opening times before setting off) you can stay overnight in a forest camp for $15.

Amazon Lodge Nature Safaris, Rua Santa Quitéria 15, Presidente Vargas ☎92/656-5464, Ⓕ656-6101, ⓦwww.natsafaris.com. Powerful motor boats take you 80km upriver to Lago Juma and the operator's comfortable floating lodge with fourteen double rooms and a restaurant. Expensive at $250 for three days and two nights.

Amazon Swiss Lodge Av. Eduardo Ribeiro 620, sala 215 ☎92/633-2322. Situated on the Rio Urubu and reached by road (182km to Lindóia), then 30min by boat. The lodge is relatively small, with sixteen wooden cabin-style rooms, collective toilets and a restaurant. Overnights in the jungle are possible. $70 per person per night, or $16 to camp.

Amazon Village Grand Amazon Turismo, Rua Ramos Ferreira 1189, sala 403 ☎92/633-1444, Ⓕ633-3217. On Lago Puraquequara, 30km from Manaus; much larger than the *Amazon Lodge* (32 rooms), with better facilities but not quite as wild in terms of the surrounding forest.

Ariau Amazon Towers Rio Amazonas Turismo, *Hotel Monaco*, Rua Silva Ramos 41 ☎92/234-7308 or 232-4160, Ⓕ233-5615, ⓦwww.ariautowers.com. (Also in the US at 905 Brickell Bay Drive, Suite 1930, Miami ☎305/371-7871). Just 65km up the Rio Negro from Manaus (3hr by boat) by Ariau lake, this is one of the largest and most developed of the jungle lodges, with a helicopter pad, swimming pool, almost 100 rooms, mostly in wooden chalets, and a 35-metre viewing tower from which you get an exceptionally close and breathtaking view of the forest canopy. It's a must if your budget isn't restricted (from $300 per person for three days and two nights).

Hotel Ecológico Terra Verde (Green Land Lodge), Rua Silva Ramos 20, Sala 305 ☎92/622-7305 Ⓕ622-4114 Ⓔterraverde@internext.com.br). Located in the Forest of Life 10,000-hectare ecological reserve, on the Fazenda São Francisco, 50km from Manaus beyond Manacapuru on the Tiririca river, this lodge has five relatively luxurious cabins, a floating swimming pool and horse-riding facilities. A comfortable and interesting place, but probably a bit tame for the adventurous traveller. $80 per person for two days and one night. Boat run daily to the lodge from the pier at the *Tropical Hotel* (8am and 2pm).

often very crowded, takes three to four days and costs upward of $45. If you want to break the journey, you can do so at **Tefé**, around halfway, and visit the beautiful **Mamiraua Sustainable Development Reserve** (see p.445), a wild but accessible area of rainforest upstream from the town or, if you really can't face the boat journey any longer, take one of the weekly flights from Tefé to Manaus and Tabatinga. There's also an *expresso* boat service connecting Tefé with Manaus (13 hr; $40).

Five large boats currently ply the river upstream from Manaus on a regular basis, all pretty similar and with good facilities (toilets with paper, showers, mineral water and enough food). Smaller boats also occasionally do the trip, but more often terminate at Tefé, from where other small boats continue. On the other side of the border, the boat trip to Iquitos from Tabatinga costs around $30–50 and takes three or four days; sometimes more, rarely less. Coming downstream from Iquitos to Tabatinga ($20-30) gives you one and a half days on the river. It's advisable to take your own food and water – all normal supplies can be bought in Tabatinga. There are also more popular superfast sixteen-seater powerboats connecting Tabatinga and Leticia with Iquitos that cost upwards of $50 and take roughly ten to twelve hours. Small planes also connect Iquitos with Santa Rosa, an insignificant Peruvian border settlement just a short boat ride over the river from Tabatinga and Leticia; there is at least one flight a week operated by the Peruvian airline TANS.

The three-way frontier

The point where Brazil meets Peru and Colombia is known as the **three-way frontier**, and it's somewhere you may end up staying for a few days sorting out red tape or waiting for a boat. Some Brazilian boats will leave you at Benjamin Constant, across the river from Tabatinga, but, if you do have to hang around, then Tabatinga, or the neighbouring Colombian town of Leticia, are the only

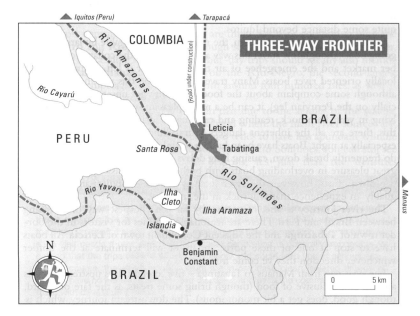

places with any real facilities. A fleet of motorboat taxis connect these places, and Islandia and Santa Rosa in Peru: Benjamin Constant to Tabatinga takes half an hour and costs around $2–3; Tabatinga to Islandia or Santa Rosa takes fifteen minutes and costs $1.80. When you're making plans, bear in mind that the three countries have differing time zones: make sure you know which you are operating on (Tabatinga is an hour behind Manaus).

For many centuries this region has been home to the Tikuna Indians, once large in numbers, but today down to a population of around 10,000. Their excellent handicrafts – mainly string bags and hammocks – can be bought in Leticia.

Tabatinga

TABATINGA is not the most exciting of towns, and many people stuck here waiting for a boat or plane to Manaus or Iquitos prefer to hop over the bor-

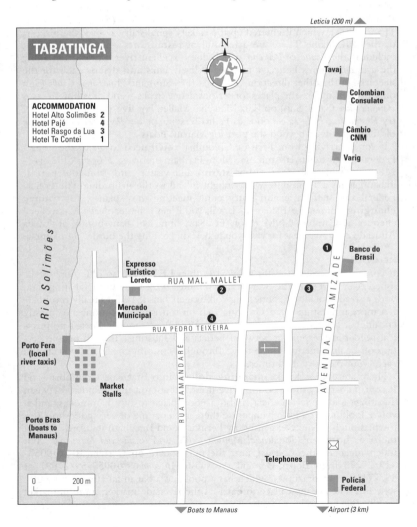

der to Leticia for the duration of their stay, even if they don't plan on going any further into Colombia. Tabatinga is the place to complete Brazilian exit (or entry) formalities with the Polícia Federal (see below for details). The town also has an airport with regular flights to Manaus. Many of the boats into Peru leave from here, and if you're coming or going the other way most downstream boats start their journeys here too (south down Rua Tamandaré, then right after the Marine base), before really filling up at Benjamin Constant.

Accommodation in Tabatinga isn't that great – a good reason to stay on the boat if you can or, if you really need a night of luxury, to try out the hotels in neighbouring Leticia (see below). In Tabatinga, your choice is limited to the friendly but very basic *Hotel Pajé*, Rua Pedro Teixeira 367 (☎92/412-2774; ❶); the fairly pleasant *Hotel Rasgo da Lua* at the start of Rua Marechal Mallet (☎92/412-2571; ❷); the *Hotel Alto Solimões*, Rua Marechal Mallet 440 (☎92/412-2827; ❷), which is something of a dump; and the nicer *Hotel Tê Contei* on the main drag Avenida da Amizade at no. 1813 (☎92/412-2377 or 413-2566; ❹), which is entered up the rickety spiral stairway over the pizzeria of the same name. There are a handful of **restaurants** on the same street, including the *Canto do Peixada*, which does excellent river fish. Further along the *avenida*, towards Leticia, a number of lively **bars and discos** cater for the sleepless. In the other direction, *Scandalo's* (Fri–Sun) and *Amazonas Clube* (Sun only, 8pm–5am) are the places for serious dance freaks – and prostitutes – as is *Banana Café* (Sat & Sun) on Rua Marechal Mallet. For **live music** (Fri & Sat), try *Restaurante Bella Epoca* on Rua Pedro Teixeira, or *Bar Porto Seguro*, a couple of kilometres west beyond the port for Manaus boats.

If you're arriving from Peru or Colombia, you'll need to go to the Polícia Federal on Avenida da Amizade (Mon–Fri 8am–noon & 2–6pm; ☎92/412-2180) for your **passport entry stamp** and visitor card; from the port at Tabatinga, it's a 15-minute walk straight inland to the main drag. The Polícia Federal also staff an airport entry point meeting most planes. For **money changing**, forget the Banco do Brasil; you'll get a better deal for travellers' cheques at Câmbio CNM (Mon–Fri 8am–5pm, Sat 8am–noon), at Av. da Amizade 2017, whereas for cash you're best off crossing the border into Leticia.

Leticia

If you are staying around for a few days then **LETICIA**, an old, more established river port – a little over twenty minutes' walk away from Tabatinga and with a steady trickle of connecting Volkswagen vans ($1) if it's really too hot – is a more interesting place. Growing rich on tourism and contraband (mostly cocaine), it has more than a touch of the Wild West about it. There's no physical border at the port or between Leticia and Tabatinga, though people getting off boats sometimes have to go through a customs check and you should carry your passport at all times.

There are endless kiosks **changing dollars** into Brazilian, Colombian and Peruvian currency, mostly on the riverfront, but also on the boundary between Tabatinga and Leticia. Leticia is also a good place to buy hammocks, and if you're looking for a little pampering there are a couple of very good hotels in town, though it's quite expensive by Peruvian (and Brazilian) standards. Best of the basic **hotels** are *Residencial Monserrate* (❸) and *Residencial Leticia* (❷), but much nicer are the *Colonial*, near the port square on Carrera 10 (☎0057-919/27273 from Brazil; ❺), and the swish *Anaconda* (☎0057-59/27891 or 59/27119 from Brazil; ❼), which has a pool and a bar in an attractive jungle-style hut. The cheapest place to **eat** is at the riverside market; more upmarket are the *Bucaneer* and *La Taguara*, both on Carrera 10.

For **tours** in the region, one of the best operators is Amaturs, at Carrera 11 7–84 (T & F0057-59/27018 from Brazil, @amaturs@impsat.net.co), who run everything from two-hour trips to see the *Victoria Regia* water lilies at Lago Yahuaracas, to day- or week-long tours to watch river dolphins and caiman and visit Witito Indian communities; they also own a jungle lodge. The Zacambu Lodge tour company, Avenida Internacional 6–25 (T0057-819/27377 from Brazil, Wwww.amazontrip.com), also offer a variety of tour packages and run a good jungle lodge. Amazons Explorers, 1st floor, Edificio Matiz, Carrera 10 785, can arrange trips out to Monkey Island or visits to local Indian communities.

Onward practicalities

If you want to go further **into Colombia**, you'll need to pick up a Colombian tourist card from the DAS (Departamento Administrativo de Seguridad) office, Calle 9, 9–62 (T0057-59/27189 or 59/24878 from Brazil; daily 24hr), just a few blocks from Leticia's port. These tourist cards are also available from the consulates at Iquitos or, coming from Brazil, Manaus. Avianca operates flights from Leticia airport to the main Colombian cities, including Bogotá, several times a week. Alternatively, an extremely adventurous option would be to cut across overland along the planned road to Tarapacá, due north of Leticia, to connect with the Rio Putumayo, where canoes to Puerto Asis connect with the Colombian road and bus system.

Heading **into Peru**, many of the boats actually leave from Tabatinga, although Peruvian authorities and passport control are in **Santa Rosa**, a military post over the river, where all Peru-bound boats have to stop for passport and customs control. The Peruvian consulate is on the main street in Leticia (Mon–Fri 9am–3pm). Powerboats (*lanchas*) to Iquitos are run by Expresso Turístico Loreto, on Rua Marechal Mallet in Tabatinga, in one of the last shacks on the left as you walk down towards the river. Other, slower boats can be found at the port in both Leticia and Tabatinga.

Up the Rio Negro

The **Rio Negro** flows into Manaus from northwestern Amazonas, one of the least explored regions of South America. There's virtually nothing in the way of tourist facilities in this direction, but it's possible to make your way up the Rio Negro by boat (see below) from Manaus to Barcelos, from Barcelos to São Gabriel, and from there on to the virtually uncharted borders with Colombia and Venezuela. Alternatively, there are reasonably fast boats from Manaus every Friday, run by Asabranc, which call in at Barcelos (two days; $40–60) on their way to São Gabriel (about five days up, three downriver; $60–90). There are also daily Tavaj **flights** to São Gabriel from Manaus, stopping off en route on alternate days at either Barcelos or Tefé on the Rio Solimões. To leave Brazil via these routes requires expedition-level planning, but it's an exciting trip nonetheless.

The first part of the journey, from Manaus to **Novo Airao**, towards the top end of the Anavilhanas archipelago, is usually reached in a day; but beyond here ice and most luxury items, including foodstuffs, are pretty well impossible to find. The best part of another day or two brings you to **Moura**, a smaller river port town with few facilities. Half a day from here the Rio Negro meets the Rio Branco and just beyond is another small town, **Carvoeiro**.

A more important settlement, **BARCELOS**, is as much as another day's boat journey up the Rio Negro from Carvoeiro. As well as the faster Asabranc boat from Manaus to Barcelos, there are ordinary boats at least twice a week ($20), taking around sixty to eighty hours; the *Irmaos Feraes* is particularly recommended, with good, fresh river food aboard. Other boats leave fairly frequently but with no predictable regularity from the docks behind the Mercado Municipal in Manaus: look for the destination signs. Alternatively, you can hire a river taxi from the floating port to help you find a boat bound for Barcelos since they also moor to the west of the main port. Fix a price with the taxi first; it should cost no more than $5–8. In Barcelos, the Nara family offer **accommodation** and good food to visitors who are going on their **jungle tours**. Run by Tatunca Nara, a local native, the tours take you deep into the forest where there's a better chance of spotting wildlife than there is closer to Manaus. Contact Tatunca's wife, who speaks English, in advance: Dr Anita Nara, c/o Unidade Mista, Barcelos, Amazonas 69700 (☎92/721-1165).

At least two days further upriver, the town of **SÃO GABRIEL DA CACHOEIRA** is the next settlement of any size. Besides the Asabranc service, boats from Barcelos leave at irregular intervals, but generally several times a week; expect to pay between $25 and $35. It's a beautiful place where the jungle is punctuated by volcanic cones, one with a Christ figure standing high on its flank. Superb views can be had across the valley from the slopes around the town, and there's a good **pensão** and several **restaurants** here as well.

A little further upriver you reach the **Rio Negro Forest Reserve**, where local guides will take you camping from around $20 a day. At present this park zone – a massive triangle between the headwaters of the Rio Negro and its important tributary the Rio Uaupés, both of which rise in Colombia – is crawling with military personnel. It's a sensitive zone, partly because of fears of narcotics smuggling, but also because it forms part of the national frontier: Venezuela, Brazil and Colombia meet here, and the Rio Negro itself serves as the border between Venezuela and Colombia for some way. There are also plans to put a highway through the park – the projected BR-210 or Perimetral Norte – which is destined to run from Macapá on the Atlantic coast to São Gabriel, passing south of Boa Vista on the way. From São Gabriel it should eventually make its way across the Amazon via Tabatinga to Cruzeiro do Sul, where it would link up with the westerly point of the Transamazônica, making it feasible to do an enormous circle by road around the Brazilian Amazon. Exactly when this will happen is anybody's guess (to date only 650km of road near Boa Vista has been built), and some of the regions that have been proposed for the road are incredibly remote.

You may also be able to get a guide to take you into the **Parque Nacional do Pico da Neblina**. The Pico da Neblina itself, Brazil's highest peak at 3014m, is on the far side of the park, hard against the Venezuelan border.

To proceed **beyond São Gabriel** by river is more difficult, particularly in the dry season from May till October. The river divides a few hours beyond São Gabriel. To the right, heading more or less north, the Rio Negro continues (another day by boat) to the community of Cucui on the Venezuelan border – there's also a very rough road from São Gabriel. It is possible to travel on from here **into Venezuela** and the Orinoco river system, through the territory of Yanomami Indians, but this involves a major expedition requiring boats, guides and considerable expense: cost aside, it is also potentially dangerous, and you should get a thorough update on the local situation before attempting this route. In recent years the region has become the focus for the *garimpeiros* who were effectively pushed out of the Yanomami territory in Roraima during the early 1990s and so moved further west into this region, which is clearly one of the last Amazonian frontiers. The left fork in the river is the **Rio Uaupés**, where the **Araripirá waterfalls** lie a day or two upstream, just before the border settlement of Iaurete. The Uaupés continues, another day's journey, along the border to the Colombian town of Mitu. Again, this is a potentially hazardous area, home to Maku Indians and, more worryingly, to coca-growing areas and members of the Colombian underworld.

Roraima

In the far north of Brazil, the **state of Roraima**, butting against Guyana and Venezuela, was only created in 1991, and came to world notice in 1998 when devastating forest fires wreaked havoc on the area. It's an active frontier zone, pushing forward the boundaries of "development", indigenous "acculturation" and, in some regions, perhaps even international borders. When the grasslands here were discovered in the mid-eighteenth century they were thought to be ideal cattle country, and it was the Portuguese who first moved in on them. But the current national borders weren't finally settled until the early part of the twentieth century. During the late 1980s, there was a massive gold rush here, with an influx of as many as 50,000 *garimpeiros* (compared to a total population of around 200,000 previously). This was centred above all in the northwest, up against the Venezuelan border in the Serra Pacaraima in the territory of the **Yanomami Indians**, Amazonian tribal peoples living on both sides of the border.

In 1989 the plight of the Yanomami, whose lands were being invaded by prospectors, brought about an international outcry that forced the Brazilian government to announce that they would evacuate all settlers from Yanomami lands. But the project was abandoned almost as soon as it began: protection of the region's valuable mineral reserves was deemed to necessitate the strengthening of the country's borders and the settlement of the area. Following the successful demarcation of Yanomami lands in 1992, and the territory's official recognition by the Federal State, things have improved, and there are now fewer *garimpeiros* prospecting in Yanomami forests. However, many vested interests were thwarted when the Yanomami's land was officially demarcated, and there remain high-level moves to take some of the land back from the Yanomami. For more on this tribe, see p.773.

Up the Rio Branco

These days it's relatively easy to get from **Manaus to Boa Vista**, the capital of Roraima, by tarmacked road, usually taking twelve hours by **bus** ($35). It is also possible to take a **boat** all the way from Manaus up the Rio Negro and Rio Branco as far as the waterfalls of **Caracaraí**, from where you can join the bus to Boa Vista (some boats also go from Caracaraí to Boa Vista, but they're few and far between). It isn't an easy trip and it has been known to take over two weeks, with lots of stopping and starting and depending on local river people for hospitality and food. If you can get a boat that is going direct, all the better. Expect to pay at least $100 for the trip, more if you're boat hopping. It's sometimes easier to travel first to Barcelos from where there are occasional boats bound up the Rio Branco, but it's all very much hit and miss once you're on the rivers.

Those who do make it up the Rio Branco are generally rewarded for their steadfastness by the sight of river dolphins, alligators and plenty of birdlife. At

Caracaraí there are very few tourist facilities, but there are two very basic **hotels**, the *Hotel Márcia*, Rua Dr Zanny (☎95/232-1208; ➊), and, marginally better, *Hotel Maroca*, Av. Pres. Kennedy 1140 (☎95/232-1292; ➋).

Boa Vista

BOA VISTA is a fast-growing city of 200,000 people, an unrelentingly hot, modern and concrete monument to its Brazilian planners who laid it out on a grand but charmless scale, with broad tree-lined boulevards divided by traffic islands and a vast Praça do Centro Cívico, swirling with traffic, from which streets radiate just unevenly enough to confuse the otherwise perpendicular grid. Clearly this is meant to be a fitting capital for the development of Roraima – and there are large stores full of ranching and mining equipment that reflect that growth. Busy as it is, though, Boa Vista has far to go to fill its ambitious designs. The huge streets seem half empty, reflecting the waning of the gold boom after the initial rush in the late 1980s and early 1990s, and many of the old hotels and gold-trading posts have closed down, or have turned into

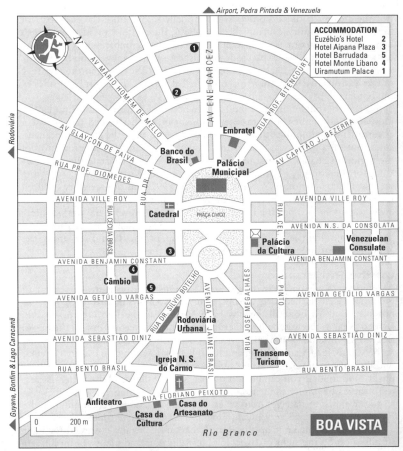

ACCOMMODATION
Euzébio's Hotel   2
Hotel Aipana Plaza   3
Hotel Barrudada   5
Hotel Monte Libano   4
Uiramutum Palace   1

Airport, Pedra Pintada & Venezuela

AV MARIO HOMEM DE MELLO

AV GLAYCON DE PAIVA

RUA PROF. DIOMEDES

AV ENE GARCEZ

RUA PROF. BITENCOURT

AV CAPITÃO J. BEZERRA

Embratel

Banco do Brasil

Palácio Municipal

AVENIDA VILLE ROY

RUA CECÍLIA BRASIL

RUA DR A

Catedral

PRAÇA CÍVICO

AVENIDA VILLE ROY

RUA CEL

AVENIDA N.S. DA CONSOLATA

Palácio da Cultura

Venezuelan Consulate

AVENIDA BENJAMIN CONSTANT

Câmbio

AVENIDA BENJAMIN CONSTANT

AVENIDA GETÚLIO VARGAS

RUA DR. SILVIO BOTELHO

AVENIDA JAIME BRASIL

RUA JOSÉ MEGALHÃES

V. PINTO

AVENIDA GETÚLIO VARGAS

Rodoviária Urbana

AVENIDA SEBASTIÃO DINIZ

AVENIDA SEBASTIÃO DINIZ

Igreja N. S. do Carmo

Transeme Turismo

RUA BENTO BRASIL

RUA BENTO BRASIL

RUA FLORIANO PEIXOTO

Anfiteatro

Casa do Artesanato

Casa da Cultura

0   200 m

BOA VISTA

Rio Branco

travel agencies, small-time banks and restaurants. The new layout obliterated many of the town's older buildings, which means that there's little of interest to see in the city itself. Most visitors to Boa Vista are on business or travellers passing through on the overland route from Venezuela to Manaus.

Arrival and information

Over 800km from Manaus, on the edge of the city, surrounded by timber yards and agricultural supply stores, stands the large, modern **rodoviária** (☎95/623-2233), housing several stores, a *lanchonete* and a local **tourist office** (Mon–Sat 10am–5pm; ☎95/623-1238). **Taxis**, which are relatively expensive here, line up outside; on the main road beyond them (from the same side as the terminal) you can catch a **local bus** towards the centre. This takes something of a detour past outlying areas before heading back to near the *rodoviária*, where it turns down past the prison and heads along the broad Avenida Benjamin Constant towards the central *praça*. Buses for the *rodoviária* from town, which bear the "Joquie Clube" sign on the route card, can be caught either at the urban bus terminal (the Rodoviária Urbana) on Rua Dr Silvio Botelho, or along the Avenida Ville Roy. Coming from the **airport** (☎95/623-0404) – where there's another tourist information office (Mon–Sat 8am–6pm, Sun 9am–1pm) – you'll have to take a taxi ($10) for the 3km ride into town.

Arrival in Boa Vista can be awkward because, thanks to the gold rush, international interest in the plight of the Yanomami Indians and the fact that the area is increasingly used by cocaine smugglers, there are lots of military personnel about who are very suspicious of foreigners: you're likely to have your luggage taken apart and to be questioned about your motives. The best bet is probably to play the dumb tourist, and say you're heading for Venezuela or Manaus.

Tourist information is available at the Roraima Tourism Office, Rua Coronel Pinto 241 (Mon–Fri 7.30am–1.30pm & 3.30–5.30pm; ☎95/623-1230). Further information and regional tours can be organized through Toca Turismo, Rua Dom Pedro 82 (☎623-8175, ⓦ www.tocaturismo.com.br).

Accommodation

Budget **accommodation** in Boa Vista, mainly along Avenida Benjamin Constant, is pretty dire, as most hotels were originally designed to meet the needs of the now ailing *garimpeiro* market, and few of them are accustomed to tourists. There are a couple of good places close to the *rodoviária*, though, while in the centre of town you'll find a handful of upmarket places, aimed at businessmen, with their own swimming pools and restaurants.

Euzébio's Hotel Rua Cecilia Brasil 1107 ☎95/623-0300, ⓕ623-9131. The most popular of the town's upmarket hotels, and often full, but not particularly central. It has a swimming pool and an expensive restaurant, yet much of its accommodation is in small, surprisingly dingy units. Make sure you get a room worth the money you're paying. ➍
Hotel Aipana Plaza Praça do Centro Cívico 53 ☎95/224-4800, ⓕ224-4116, ⓔaipana@tecbet .com.br. The best hotel in Boa Vista, with a pool, bar and a good restaurant, but it's overpriced among the hotels in its price range. ➍
Hotel Barrudada Rua Araújo Filho 228 ☎95/623-9335. Once a charming private house of a hotel, its popularity was such that it was knocked down

in 1996 and replaced by a modern six-storey edifice, but the staff remain helpful and the rooms are good value. ➋–➌
Hotel Monte Libano Av. Benjamin Constant 319 ☎95/224-7232. Probably has the edge over other budget hotels in the centre, as its staff are friendlier and the rooms are in slightly better condition. ➊
Hotel Três Nações Av. Ville Roy 1885 ☎95/224-3439. Virtually opposite the *rodoviária*, this place is spick-and-span with pleasant rooms around an open courtyard; and there aren't that many buses passing through, so it's not as noisy as many hotels near bus stations in other Brazilian cities. ➋
Itamaraty Palace Avenida N.S. da Consolata 1957 ☎95/224-9757, ⓕ623-0977,

Ⓦwww.hotelitamaraty.com.br. One of the best-value options among the mid-range hotels, the Itamaraty Palace offers a swimming pool, relatively clean and comfortable rooms, a bar, restaurant and air-conditioning. The downside is it's located a kilometre or two from the centre. ❹–❺

Pousada Beija Flor Av. Nossa Senhora da Consolata ☎95/224-8241, Ⓕ224-6536. A gem of a place run by a Brazilian–Belgian couple who are tuned in to backpackers' requirements. The accommodation is basic but clean, and Néa and

Jean offer a range of reasonably priced tours around Roraima, and a wealth of information. From the *rodoviária*, walk six blocks down Av. Ville Roy, turn right at the lights and then left onto Av. Consolata; the *pousada* is two blocks further down. ❶

Uiramutum Palace Av. Cap. Ene Garcez 427 ☎95/624-4700. Located a few blocks from the Palacio do Governo, this place is good value with nice rooms, a pool, air-conditioning and friendly service, though the restaurant is nothing special. ❹

The City

As capital city of Roraima, one of Brazil's newest states, Boa Vista makes great efforts to establish its identity. Opposite the biggest landmark in town, the huge cylindrical concrete tube pointing towards the skies from the roof of the Embratel telephone offices on the Avenida Cap. Ene Garcez, there's a semicircular **amphitheatre** with three statues – one of a *garimpeiro* holding a shovel and a gold-panning bowl; one of a *fazendeiro* wielding a lasso; and, the central one, an Indian with a bow and arrow. Just down the road, in the centre of the Praça do Centro Cívico, there's the better-known **Monument to the Garimpeiro**, which clearly speaks more to local businessmen than it does to environmentally minded foreign visitors.

On the south side of the *praça*, the modest-sized **Catedral** has an interesting curvaceous design, very airy, with a ceiling reminiscent of the hull of a huge wooden boat. On the other side of the square is the **Palácio da Cultura** (Mon–Fri 8am–7pm, Sat 8am–1pm), with its well-stocked public library and a very smart auditorium that occasionally holds theatre and music performances. Down in the old waterfront district, connected to the *praça* by the main shopping street, Avenida Jaime Brasil, you'll find a cluster of sights, including the small Portuguese-style **Igreja Nossa Senhora do Carmo**, an open-air *anfiteatro* now used as a music venue, and the **Casa da Cultura** gallery-space – an exact replica of the city's first Prefeitura that was destroyed as part of the zealous modernization of the 1960s. Facing it is an imposing concrete **Monument to the Pioneers of Roraima**. The huge bust of a Yanomami chief dominates the sculpture, his shoulder somewhat ambiguously being trampled over by a pioneer on horseback.

The **Casa do Artesanato**, on the riverbank on Rua Floriano Peixoto 192 (Mon–Sat 8am–6pm; ☎95/623-1615), is also worth a visit: its selection of handicrafts is not wide but there's some interesting stuff and it's all very cheap. There are great views from the *Restaurante Panorama Macuchik* (see below) and the riverbank near the Casa do Artesanato out across the Rio Branco, towards the large-span, modern concrete bridge and the forest stretching beyond.

Eating and drinking

Lanchonetes are everywhere in Boa Vista, though more substantial **restaurants** are surprisingly scarce as well as expensive. In the centre, the *Restaurante La Gondola*, on the corner of Avenida Benjamin Constant and the Praça do Centro Cívico, is fine for *comida por kilo* and very popular. At night, the *Hotel Euzébio*'s restaurant serves good meals and, virtually next door, the lively *Pigalle* has good pizzas and fish, but neither place is exactly on the cheap side; both also function as bars. More reasonable, and with excellent views, are a growing number of restaurants along the riverfront: the *Restaurante Panorama Macuchik*, close to the Casa do Artesanato at Rua Floriano Peixoto 114 (☏95/623-1346), is highly recommended, as is the fish restaurant *Ver o Rio* (closed Mon lunchtime; ☏95/224-6964), two buildings down on the same road. For more evening atmosphere, but without the river view, try the *Black and White Restaurant*, one road back on Rua Barreto Leite 11 (closed Mon; ☏95/224-5372).

As for **bars and clubs**, *Clube ABB* near the airport is the most popular nightspot (Fri & Sat only); also well worth trying is the *Zanzibar*, corner of Avenida Sebastião Diniz and Rua Coronel Pinto, which has a good atmosphere and hosts local bands on Friday and Saturday (9pm onwards; ☏95/224-0093). Straightforward drinking bars are surprisingly few, the best being *Meu Cantinho* opposite the *Panorama* and with equally good views (daily until midnight).

Listings

Airlines Varig have an office at Av. Getúlio Vargas 242 (☏95/224-4143). To and from Manaus, planes can be solidly booked for days if not weeks ahead, especially at holiday times, though you might get lucky with the waiting list.
Air taxis Meta (☏95/224-7677) is based at the airport.
Banks and exchange The best place to change money in Boa Vista is the private backroom office of Casa Pedro José, Rua Araújo Filho 287, which gives excellent rates and a fast, efficient service. Otherwise, the Banco do Brasil, on the *praça* near the Palácio Municipal, changes money between 8am and 12.30pm (arrive early).
Car rental Localiza ☏95/224-5222; Unidas ☏95/224-4080.
Consulates Venezuela, Av. Benjamin Constant 525 ☏95/224-2182 or 623-9285. If you hope to get a visa in a single day then arrive early: hours are officially Mon–Fri 8.30–1pm but they may open

later in the afternoon to give your completed visa back. You'll need to show your passport and have a photo and an onward ticket – though you may be able to get round the latter by having plenty of money and a good excuse. From the consulate they'll send you to a doctor for a cursory medical examination ($10 for this privilege) and from there you go to a clinic for a blood test (free), which they claim is for malaria. Having passed these you can usually go back in the afternoon, clutching the certificates, to pick up your passport and visa.
Post office Praça do Centro Cívico (Mon–Fri 9am–5pm).
Taxis ☏95/224-4223 or 224-4823.
Telephones National and international calls can be made from public booths with phonecards; alternatively the Embratel office is on Rua Cel. Pinto, close to the junction with Av. Cap. Ene Garcez.

Around Boa Vista

Situated as it is on the northern edge of the Amazon forest, where it meets the savanna of Roraima, the region around Boa Vista boasts three different forms of ecosystem: tropical rainforest, grassland savanna plains and the "Lost World"–style tepius mountain, flat plateau-like rock rising out of the savanna. Still fairly undeveloped in terms of its tourism infrastructure, the area is exceptionally beautiful, with a wealth of river beaches, and has a very pleasant climate (hot with cooling breezes). As the options for ecotourism are developed, more opportunities will no doubt emerge for visitors to explore Roraima in some depth.

Your first port of call in Boa Vista should be the tourist office (see p.453), which has details of new destinations, circuits and accommodation options in the state. At present, **independent travel** in the region can be problematic, with only sketchy bus services, so you might find it easier simply to hire a car (see "Listings" above). **Organized tours**, usually dependent on enough tourists filling spaces, are operated by Baba's Home (☏95/623-7304), Iguana tours (☏95/224-6576), Tocatur (☏95/623-2597), and ECOTUR, Rua

Barreto Leite 46 (℡95/224-6010), while the agency inside *Euzébio's Hotel* deals in six-day packages for around $450–500. Much cheaper, and virtually the only outfit in town able to arrange tours for small groups, is *Pousada Beija Flor*, who combine enthusiasm with a wealth of knowledge about the state.

Places to head for include the famous painted rock, **Pedra Pintada**, en route to Santa Elena and Venezuela; the ruined eighteenth-century **Forte São Joaquim**, two hours from Boa Vista by boat; the ecological island reserve of **Ilha do Maracá**, located on the fairly remote Rio Uraricoera; and the very pleasant **Lake Caracaranã** with its fine beaches fringed by shady cashew trees, 180km from Boa Vista in Normandia. This is currently almost the only place in the state outside Boa Vista that has adequate facilities for tourists, with fifteen chalets and ten apartments for hire, the four-bed chalets a bargain at $50; ℡95/262-1254 or contact Transeme Turismo in Boa Vista, Av. Sebastião Diniz 234 (℡95/224-9409 or 224-6271). Also of note are the **Igarape Agua Boa**, where there are islands, fine sandy beaches ($10; 2–3hr), and the **Serra Grande**, where you'll find more islands and beaches plus trails in the forest to the waterfall of the same name (1hr).

Into Venezuela and Guyana

It's now relatively straightforward to go from Boa Vista to Santa Elena in **Venezuela**, and beyond to Ciudad Guayana and Ciudad Bolívar – even right on to Puerto La Cruz on the north coast if you're that anxious to escape the interior – a daily União Cascavel bus leaves Boa Vista at 7am. Santa Elena is also served by six daily Eucatur buses (3hr, plus 2hr for border formalities). The road, the BR-174, is now fully tarmacked, which means that the União Cascavel bus arrives at the border in time for lunch; it stops at a very expensive restaurant, though, so bring your own lunch if you're running short on money. The journey from Boa Vista, across a vast flat savanna that is dusty in the dry season, boggy in the wet, offers very little in the way of scenery, but there is a great deal of wildlife, especially birds: white egrets, storks and all sorts of waders in the rainy season, flycatchers and hawks; and also the chance of some fairly large animals, including giant anteaters. As the border approaches the land begins to rise slightly: to the northeast lies **Monte Roraima**, the fourth-highest peak in Brazil at 2875m, at the point where Brazil, Guyana and Venezuela meet.

Allow a couple of hours to cross the border itself (the bus waits while everyone has passports stamped and luggage checked); **SANTA ELENA DE UAIRÉN** is barely twenty minutes further. It's not necessary to spend the night here, as the União Cascavel bus continues further up into Venezuela, but if you fancy a break Santa Elena is a tiny place with the real feel of a border town in its low, corrugated-roofed houses and dusty streets. You can see the whole place in an hour's walk, but the *Hotel Frontera* also runs tours to local waterfalls and native communities. If you're staying overnight, good **hotels** include the *Frontera* (❸), the simple *Hotel Marcia* (❷), and the *Hotel Lucas* (❹), which has a casino. There's good **food** at the *Restaurante Itália* (the spaghetti is the cheapest thing to eat in a relatively expensive town). **Money** is hard to change here: various traders will accept cash dollars or Brazilian currency – try the *Hotel Frontera* – but there's nowhere at all to change travellers' cheques. **Leaving**, there's a 5am bus to Ciudad Bolívar (12hr), as well as the União Cascavel bus late at night, and a daily flight (2hr). If you're heading for Brazil, there are at least seven buses a day. Don't forget to get your Venezuelan exit stamp from the office next to the police station on the hill behind the bus terminal. The terminal doesn't open until 8am.

Guyana is less straightforward. It's easy enough to get to **Bonfim** on the border, just over 100km away (two daily buses with Eucatur), though the road is pretty grim, but it's much less easy to continue beyond there, and strict Guyanan entry regulations on the border mean there's a fair chance you may even be refused entry. All in all, if you want to go to Guyana, it's easier to fly; there are flights from Manaus to Georgetown, but no longer any services from Boa Vista.

Rondônia and Porto Velho

A large, partially deforested region in the southwest corner of the Brazilian Amazon, the **state of Rondônia** has undergone the first phase of its environmental destruction. Roads and tracks, radiating like fine bones from the spinal highway BR-364, have dissected almost the entire state, bringing in their wake tens of thousands of settlers and many large companies who have moved in to gobble up the rainforest. Poor landless groups are a common sight, some the surviving representatives of once proud Indian tribes, living under plastic sheets at the side of the road.

The state was only created in 1981, having evolved from an unknown and almost entirely unsettled zone (then the Territory of Guaporé) over the previous thirty years. The new, fast-changing Rondônia was named after the famous explorer, Indian "pacifier" and telegraph network pioneer Marechal Cândido Rondon. It's not exactly one of Brazil's major tourist attractions, but it is an interesting area in its own right, and it also offers a few stopping-off places between more obvious destinations. **Porto Velho**, the main city of the region, is an important pit stop between Cuiabá and the frontier state of Acre. Rondônia also offers border crossings to Bolivia, river trips to Manaus and access to overland routes into Peru.

Given that it is such a recently settled region, the system of road **transport** is surprisingly good, and combines well with the major rivers – Madeira, Mamoré and Guaporé. The main focus of human movement these days is the fast BR-364, which caused a massive surge of development after its completion in the 1980s. Manaus and Porto Velho are well connected by a four-day boat journey, with usually at least three leaving weekly in either direction.

Porto Velho

The capital of Rondônia state, **PORTO VELHO**, overlooks the Amazon's longest tributary, the mighty Rio Madeira. With over 350,000 inhabitants these days, Porto Velho has evolved from a relatively small town in just twenty years. In the 1980s, settlers arrived in enormous numbers in search of land, jobs and, more specifically, the mineral wealth of the region: gold and casserite (a form of tin) are found all over Rondônia. As in most regions, the gold boom has bottomed out and the empty gold-buying stores are signs of the rapid decline. Seen from a distance across the river, Porto Velho looks rather more impressive than it does at close quarters. The two bell towers and Moorish dome of the cathedral stand out strikingly above the rooftops, while alongside the river three phallic, black water towers sit like waiting rockets beside a complex of military buildings. A little further downstream the modern port and the shiny cylindrical tanks of a petrochemical complex dominate the riverbank.

In the town itself, the main street – Avenida Sete de Setembro – has a distinct market atmosphere about it, with music stores blaring out their sounds,

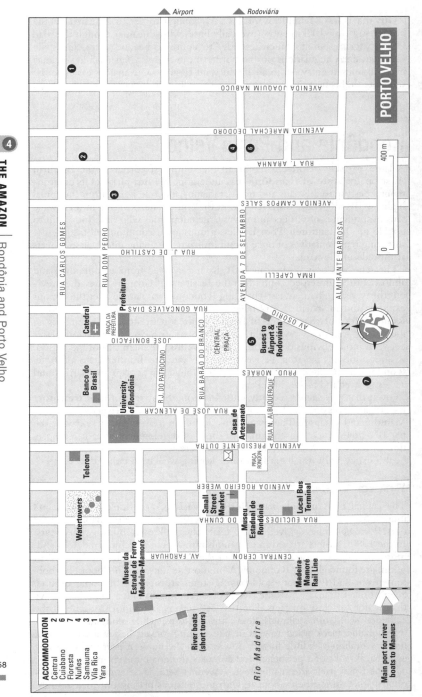

PORTO VELHO

Airport   Rodoviária

0   400 m

N

ACCOMMODATION
Central	2
Cuiabano	6
Floresta	7
Nunes	4
Samauma	3
Vila Rica	1
Yara	5

AVENIDA JOAQUIM NABUCO

AVENIDA MARECHAL DEODORO

RUA T. ARANHA

AVENIDA CAMPOS SALES

RUA CARLOS GOMES

RUA DOM PEDRO

RUA J. DE CASTILHO

AVENIDA 7 DE SETEMBRO

IRMA CAPELLI

ALMIRANTE BARROSA

AV OSÓRIO

Prefeitura

Catedral

PRAÇA DA PREFEITURA

Banco do Brasil

JOSÉ BONIFÁCIO

RUA GONÇALVES DIAS

RUA BARÃO DO BRANCO

CENTRAL PRAÇA

Buses to Airport & Rodoviária

University of Rondônia

R. J. DO PATROCINO

RUA JOSÉ DE ALENCAR

PRUD. MORAES

Teleron

Watertowers

Casa de Artesanato

RUA N. ALBUQUERQUE

AVENIDA PRESIDENTE DUTRA

PRAÇA RONDON

Small Street Market

Museu Estadual de Rondônia

AVENIDA ROGEIRO WEBER

RUA EUCLIDES DO CUNHA

Local Bus Terminal

Museu da Estrada de Ferro Madeira-Mamoré

AV. FARQUHAR

CENTRAL CERON

Madeira-Mamoré Rail Line

River boats (short tours)

Rio Madeira

Main port for river boats to Manaus

traders shouting out their wares and stallholders chattering on about their predominantly cheap plastic goods. Every other lamppost seems to have a loudspeaker attached to it. The city has a more relaxed ambience down on the far side of the old railway sheds, where you'll find outdoor bars and cafés spread along the riverfront.

Arrival and accommodation

Porto Velho's **airport** (☏69/225-1339), Belmont, is 7km out of town, served by local buses and taxis ($5). The **rodoviária** (☏69/223-2233), with daily connections to Guajará-Mirim and the Bolivian border, Cuiabá and Rio Branco, is also some way out on Avenida Kennedy; catch a local bus into town from here to Sete de Setembro. **Tourist information** is best from Funcetur on Avenida 7 de Setembro, in the same building as the Museu Estadual de Rondônia or by checking out ⊛www.rondonia.com. Regular **boats** link Manaus and Porto Velho, and the docks are located just 1km west of the main waterfront area.

There is plenty of **accommodation** to choose from in Porto Velho as it's a settlement serving a large hinterland of farmers, prospectors and businessmen, as well as a growing number of tourists.

Central Rua Tenreiro Aranha 2472 ☏69/224-2099 ⓕ224-5114, ⊛www.enter-net.com.br/central. A good mid-range place, clean but characterless, though the service aims to please, and most rooms have TVs and air-conditioning. ❸

Cuiabano Av. Sete de Setembro 1180 ☏69/221-4084. A good budget place with rooms set around a courtyard, only some of which come with a private bathroom. Can be quite noisy during the day as it's located on the main commercial drag. ❶

Floresta Rua Almirante Barroso 502 ☏69/221-5669. A popular place with a pool and a relatively quiet location, but within easy walking distance of the town centre. ❸

Nunes Av. Sete de Setembro. Opposite the *Cuiabano*, this good-value place is clean, cool and very conveniently located. Service is friendly, too. ❶

Rondon Palace Av. Gov. Jorge Teixeira 491 ☏69/224-2718, ⓕ224-6160. Close to the airport some way from the centre, this is a modern, soulless hotel with a pool and quite good restaurant. ❹

Samauma Rua Dom Pedro II 1038 ☏69/224-5300. A moderately sized and fairly modern hotel with a bar and restaurant, with very reasonable rates. Rooms are adequate and all have air-conditioning. ❷–❸

Vila Rica Rua Carlos Gomes 1616 ☏69/224-3433, ⊛www.hotelvilaricapvh.com.br. This hotel is unmissable as it is by some way the tallest building in the centre. The luxury-class rooms are tastefully redecorated, and there's a nice pool as well. Good value and hospitable. ❺–❻

Villas Gonçalves Dias. Friendly but rather basic hotel, located just off Sete de Setembro, with communal shower rooms. ❶

Yara Av. Osório 255 ☏69/221-2127. Bustling modern hotel with basic but clean rooms. The central location makes it convenient but noisy. ❶

The Town

Although it's a lively town and an enjoyable place to spend some time, Porto Velho doesn't have much in the way of a developed tourist scene beyond its main attraction, the wonderful **Madeira-Mamoré Museu Ferroviário** (daily 9am–6pm, closed Sat & Sun) and the neighbouring Museu Geologico. Run by the eloquent Sr Johnson, the railway museum is jam-packed with fascinating period exhibits, from photographs of important railway officials and operatives from the past (including Johnson's father), to station furniture, equipment and mechanical devices, including an entire and quite spectacular locomotive, built in Philadelphia in 1878. For railway buffs, there's also plenty of equipment and other locomotives to see around the old railway terminal adjacent to the museum. The Madeira-Mamoré (or Mad Maria) Railway was planned to provide a route for Bolivian rubber to the Atlantic and the markets of Europe and the eastern US, but due to a series of setbacks during its forty-year construction it was only completed in 1912 – just in time to see the price of rubber plummet and the market dry up. Some estimates say that as many as fifty thousand men died – mostly of malaria – building the rail line, though in truth the figure was probably a tenth of that. The line was closed in 1960, and in 1972 many of the tracks were ripped up to help build a road along the same difficult route. The **Museo Geologico** (daily 9am–6pm, closed Sat & Sun) is much smaller than the railway museum, but contains a few interesting exhibits of semiprecious stones and minerals.

The other museum in town, the **Museu Estadual de Rondônia** on Sete de Setembro, has an interesting collection of ethnographic artefacts gathered from indigenous tribes of the region. There's little else to see: the **University of Rondônia** is not a very inspiring building, and the **Catedral** is better appreciated from the far side of the river. One of the best things to do while you're here is to take a short trip on a **floating bar** – Fluvetur and Baretur are competing outfits that both offer much the same deal. They set out at intervals during the day – there's almost always a 5pm sundowner tour, and more frequent sailings at weekends – and for a few *reais* and the price of a beer or two you can spend a pleasant couple of hours travelling up and down the Madeira, sharing the two-storey floating bar with predominantly local groups. The atmosphere is invariably lively, and there's often impromptu music.

Eating, drinking and nightlife

There are some excellent places to **eat and drink** in Porto Velho, though beer here is more expensive than on the coast. Food, on the other hand, tends to be a little cheaper. The Mercado Central, at the bottom end of town close to the railway museum on Avendia Farqhua, is a good place to buy your own food or get a cheap meal. For decent and very good-value *comida por kilo* lunches, the best place is *Asados & Salados*, Av. Sete de Setembro 504, which also has great juices.

It may not look like it, but Porto Velho has one of the best **restaurants** in Brazil. Tucked away down an obscure side street on the riverfront, it's impossible to find without a taxi but every taxi driver knows where it is. *A Caravela do Madeira*, Rua José Camacho 104, Arigolandia (☎69/221-6641; closed Sun evening & Mon), is an amazing place, an enormous wooden construction looming out over a hillside overlooking the Rio Madeira. The restaurant would be magical even if the food was dreadful, which it most certainly isn't, with the speciality being river fish; try *costeleta de surubim*, or the equally delicious *pirarucu na brasa*. A meal with taxi to and from the centre will set you back around $20 and there's sometimes live music on Saturdays.

Otherwise, the best place for restaurants is the stretch of Avenida Joaquim Nabuco behind the *Hotel Vila Rica*, where there is a cluster of eating places including a genuine Chinese restaurant, *Oriente*, Av. Amazonas 1280 (closed Mon), catering for the Taiwanese gold buyers attracted to the region by the gold rush of the late 1980s. There are also two excellent Arabic–Brazilian restaurants, the *Habibe*, Av. Lauro Sodré 1190 (closed Mon), and the *Almanara*, Av. José de Alencar 2624.

You can find great ice cream at the *Sorveteria Mamoré*, overlooking the port side of the railway sheds, and there are reasonable drinks, snacks and fish meals available at the *barracas* (beach huts) nearby. Close to the military complex on the hill above the town, the *Restaurante Mirante II* has a good view over the river and often has live music on Friday evenings. As the night progresses, the *Wau Wau* **bar**, in the *Hotel Vila Rica*, generally offers good entertainment, and there are also a few **nightclubs,** notably *Original,* on Rua Guanabara, which plays a range of music including *forró,* samba and *pagode,* and *Bungalo,* on the same road but closer to the centre.

Listings

Airlines Tavaj, at the airport (☎69/225-2999), covers most of the western Amazon; Varig, Av. Campos Sales 2666 ☎69/224-4224, and at the airport ☎69/225-1675; VASP, A. Pena 368 ☎69/225-7356 or 224-4566; TAM, J. Castilho 530 ☎69/224-2180.

Banks and exchange Banco do Brasil at the corner of José de Alencar and Dom Pedro II (*câmbio* upstairs). Cash can also be changed at the *Hotel Floresta* and the *Vila Rica.*

Boats The main commercial port is easily located about 1km upstream from the rail yards; you'll have to go there to check out all the possibilities. For Manaus there are frequent boats offering first- and second-class passages for the four-day-trip. The boats at the port generally display their destinations; otherwise it's a matter of asking the crew of each vessel and making a deal with the captain whose itinerary suits you best.

Car hire Localiza ☎69/224-6530 and Avis ☎69/225-1011.

Post office The main post office is in Avenida Presidente Dutra, just off Sete de Setembro (Mon–Fri 9am–5pm).

Shopping The well-stocked Casa do Artesanato, Av. Sete de Setembro 488, is the best place for *artesanato.* The best places for photographic film and developing are Colortec, at Rua José de Alencar 2850, at the corner with Rua Floriano Peixoto, or the nearby Casa do Fotografo, on Avenida Presidente Dutra.

Telephones The Teleron office, where you can make international calls, is opposite the huge Caixa Economica Federal building, just up from the University on Avenida Presidente Dutra (daily 6am–11pm).

Around Porto Velho

There are several places where you can get deeper into the forest around Porto Velho. The *Pousada Rancho Grande,* c/o Haarald Schmitz, Fazenda Rancho Grande, Lote 23, Linha C20, Cacaulandia (☎69/535-4301; ❹), is a unique lodge run by a German family in the middle of rainforest and plantations. The *fazenda* is located about 260km south of Porto Velho, about 28km off BR-364, and you need to make a reservation in advance. They offer bird-watching, horse riding, jungle walks and a visit to the biggest tin mine in the world at Bom Futuro. Much nearer to Porto Velho, but around the same daily rate, the *Tapiri Selva Hotel* offers jungle lodge accommodation near Lago de Cujubim (☎69/221-4785); phone for transport arrangements.

West from Porto Velho

The backbone of modern Rondônia, the **BR-364** highway links the state more or less from north to south, connecting Porto Velho with Cuiabá, Brasília and the wealthy south coast markets. The state's main towns are strung out along the BR-364, almost all of them – including Porto Velho itself, Ji Paraná and Vilhena at the border with Mato Grosso – marking the points where the road crosses major waterways. It's a fast road, and in the final analysis there's little to stop for anywhere in this direction: you're better off heading straight through to Cuiabá.

Heading **west from Porto Velho** is a very different matter, and soon begins to feel like real pioneering. The further you go, the smaller and wilder the roads, rivers and towns become. The main attractions for the traveller are Rio Branco (see p.463) and the border crossings into Peru, in the state of Acre; and **Guajará-Mirim,** where you can cross into Bolivia or undertake an adventurous visit to the Forte Príncipe da Beira. The BR-364 in this direction is asphalted, although heavy rains still have a habit of washing great sections of it away.

Most of the land beside the road between Porto Velho and Abunã has already been bought up by big companies, and much of the forest cleared. Meanwhile, many of the smaller *fazendas* have started actively producing beef cattle and other tropical cash crops. Water birds like the *garça real* (an amazing white royal heron) can frequently be spotted from the bus, fishing in the roadside streams and ditches, but the general picture is one of an alarming rate of destruction, with columns of wood-smoke rising wherever you look and endless tracts of charred trunks sticking up into the sky like gnarled hands.

At **ABUNÃ** – some five hours out of Porto Velho – there are often long lines at the ferry that takes vehicles over the wide Rio Madeira into Acre. It's not a particularly pleasant town, caught at the end of a gold rush in which it expanded too fast for its own good, and the river itself is awash with wrecked gold-mining machinery half-sunk on large steel cylinders. Following the road towards Rio Branco, Bolivia lies across the Rio Abunã to your left, but if you want to cross the border the closest place to do so is Guajará-Mirim to the south. The road there turns off to the east of the ferry crossing at Abunã, following the Rio Mamoré via the small settlement of Taquaras.

Guajará-Mirim and beyond: Bolivia and the Rio Guaporé

GUAJARÁ-MIRIM is easy enough to reach by bus from Porto Velho (6 daily), and once you get there it's a surprisingly sophisticated place with several **hotels**, the best of which are the *Hotel Mini-Estrela*, Av. 15 de Novembro 460 (T69/541-2399; ❸), the *Hotel Lima Palace*, on the same street at no. 1613 (T69/541-3421, F541-2122; ❷), and the *Hotel Jamaica*, Av. Leopoldo de Matos 755 (T69/541-3721, F541-3722; ❷). There are good restaurants here, too, including the *Oasis*, at Av. 15 de Novembro 460, which serves a varied menu at reasonable prices. There are, however, only two reasons you might come here – to get to Bolivia or to head up the Mamoré and Guaporé rivers on a trip to the Forte Príncipe da Beira.

The valley of the **Rio Guaporé**, around 800km in length, is an obvious destination for an adventurous break from routine town-to-town travelling. Endowed with relatively accessible rainforest, a slow-flowing river and crystal-clear creeks, it is a favourite fishing region with townspeople from Porto Velho. Likely catches include the huge *dourado*, the *tambaqui*, the *pirapitanga* and *tucunaré*. Heading towards the Guaporé, there are amazing rapids on the Rio Mamoré just south of Guajará-Mirim, close to the place where the Rio Pacaás Novas flows in.

If you want a purpose to your river trip, the star-shaped **Forte Príncipe da Beira** is the place to head for. Built in 1773 by pioneering Portuguese colonists, this was an advanced border post designed to mark out Portuguese territory from the Spanish lands across the river in the Bolivian jungle. Underground tunnels and passages lead directly down to the river by the small settlement of Costa Marques. By river, it will take at least three days to reach the fort from Porto Velho: the first day by bus to Guajará-Mirim, then two or three more by boat 150km to the fort itself or 20km further to the town of Costa Marques where there is a hotel, restaurants and even a small airstrip. Another major attraction in the area is the **Reserva Biologica do Guaporé**, a swampy forest home to many birds. Contact IBAMA in Porto Velho, Av. Jorge Teixeira 3477 (T69/223-3607) for permission before setting out.

As for **Bolivia**, if all you want to do is see it, join a sightseeing tour by motor barge from Guajará-Mirim; ask at *Hotel Jamaica*, Av. Leopoldo de Matos 755 (T69/541-3721). These leave frequently, visiting the main sights, and often stopping at the islands between Guajará-Mirim and Guayaramerin, on the Bolivian side. If you actually want to cross the border it's equally easy to get a boat over the Rio Mamoré to **GUAYARAMERIN**. This is something of a contrast to the Brazilian town – far more of a border outpost, with no roads, though there is a good air taxi service to La Paz, Cochabamba and Santa Cruz with TAM and Lloyd Aéreo Boliviano. If you intend travelling into Bolivia, get your passport stamped by the Bolivian consul in Guajará-Mirim, Av. Costa Marques 495 (☎69/541-5876), and visit the Polícia Federal, Av. Presidente Dutra 70 (☎69/541-2437), for an exit stamp before crossing the river. If you want to stay in Guayaramerin, try the *Hotel Plaza* (❸), four blocks from the port. Boats to Guayaramerin leave from the port end of Av. 15 de Novembro. The tour operator Enaro, Avenida Beira Rios (☎69/541-2242), can be a helpful source of information, especially for travel arrangements.

Rio Branco

Crossing from Rondônia into the state of **Acre**, territory annexed from Bolivia during the rubber-boom days in the first years of the twentieth century, there's nowhere to stop before you reach the capital at **RIO BRANCO**. The state is a vast frontier forest zone, where it comes as a real surprise to find that Rio Branco is one of Brazil's funkiest cities. It's a small place with little of specific interest to point at, but it's exceptionally lively, with a strong student influence that means plenty of music and events to fill a stay of a few days. Arriving at night (as you usually do) after an eight-hour journey through the desolation of what's left of the jungle between here and Porto Velho, the brightly coloured lights and animated streets can make you wonder if you've really arrived at all, or simply drifted off to sleep. By the light of day Rio Branco doesn't have quite so much obvious charm, but it remains an interesting place full of interesting people.

Much of the reason for all this life is that Rio Branco is a federal **university town**, second only to Belém on the student research pecking order for social and biological studies associated with the rainforest and development. Consequently the place has more than its fair share of young people, and of Brazilian intellectuals. On top of this, the region's burgeoning development means that Rio Branco is also a thriving and very busy market town, pivotally sited on the new road and with an active, if tiny, river port.

Arrival, information and accommodation

Rio Branco is divided in two by the **Rio Acre**, whose old Indian name was Macarinarra, or "River of Arrows", because of the arrows that were cut from the flowering bamboo canes that were found here. The commercial zone, most of the hotels and much of the nightlife are situated north of the river. In the dry season, there is a good river **beach** on the curve in the river – just upstream from the bridges and on the *rodoviária* side of town.

The **rodoviária** (☎68/221-4195), 3km southwest of the river in the Cidade Nova, is just about within walking distance of the centre, or you can take a taxi; note that the area between the *rodoviária* and the river is considered unsafe at night. The **airport** (☎68/211-1000) is 25km northwest of town, but is well served by the green and white ECTA airport bus that runs more or less hourly to the centre; if you're in a hurry you'll probably want to take a taxi ($15).

The regional **tourist office**, Av. Getúlio Vargas 659 (☎68/224-3997), can supply maps of the town and information on hotels and travel in the region;

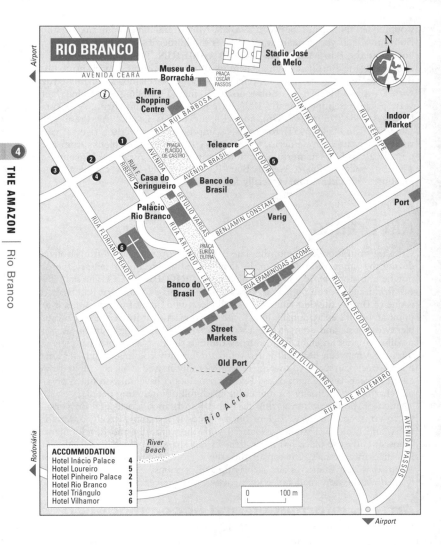

RIO BRANCO

N

Airport ◀

AVENIDA CEARÁ

Museu da
Borrachá

PRAÇA
OSCAR
PASSOS

Stadio José
de Melo

Mira
Shopping
Centre

RUA RUI BARBOSA

QUINTINO BOCAIÚVA

RUA SERGIPE

Indoor
Market

AVENIDA

PRAÇA
PLACIDO
DE CASTRO

Teleacre

RUA MAL DEODORO

AVENIDA BRASIL

Casa do
Seringueiro

Banco do
Brasil

RUA RIBEIRO

GETULIO VARGAS

BENJAMIN CONSTANT

Varig

Palácio
Rio Branco

RUA ARLINDO P. LEAL

PRAÇA
EURICO
DUTRA

RUA FLORIANO PEIXOTO

RUA EPAMINODAS JACOMÉ

Port

RUA MAL DEODORO

Banco do
Brasil

Street
Markets

AVENIDA GETULIO VARGAS

Old Port

RUA 7 DE NOVEMBRO

Rio Acre

AVENIDA PASSOS

Rodoviária ◀

River
Beach

ACCOMMODATION
Hotel Inácio Palace   4
Hotel Loureiro   5
Hotel Pinheiro Palace   2
Hotel Rio Branco   1
Hotel Triângulo   3
Hotel Vilhamor   6

0   100 m

▼ Airport

Ⓦ www.amazonlink.org is another excellent source of information. If you happen to be in Rio Branco during the third week of November, don't miss the **Feira de Productos da Floresta do Acre** (Acre's Rainforest Products Fair), usually housed in the splendid SEBRAE building on Avenida Ceará (take the Conjunto Esperança bus from the central terminal and follow the signs), and accompanied by local bands.

Accommodation

There is no shortage of **hotels** in Rio Branco, though the better ones aren't cheap. Top of the range is the *Hotel Pinheiro Palace*, Rua Rui Barbosa 450 (Ⓣ68/223-7191, Ⓕ223-6397, Ⓦ www.irmaospinheiro.com.br; ❹), with swimming pool, bar and pretty comfortable rooms with all mod cons. The *Hotel Rio*

Branco, Rua Rui Barbosa 193, on the corner of Avenida Getúlio Vargas (⊤68/224-1785, Ⓕ224-2681; ❸), is modern, with excellent service and TVs in all rooms, and is great value. The *Hotel Inácio Palace*, on the same street at no. 469 (⊤68/223-6397, Ⓕ223-7098; ❸), is of similar standard, but the atmosphere is impersonal; guests can use the *Pinheiro's* pool. Cheaper but still overpriced is *Hotel Triângulo*, Rua Marechal Peixoto 727 (⊤68/224-4117, Ⓕ224-9265; ❸), though some rooms overlook the river. The *Hotel Vilhamor*, at Rua Floriano Peixoto 394 (⊤68/223-2399; ❸), is central, modern and clean, and some rooms have views across the river valley. The *Hotel Loureiro*, Rua Marechal Deodoro 196 (⊤68/224-3110 or 224-9627, Ⓕ224-6806; ❷), also has good rooms, while the cheapest (and dirtiest) in town is *Hotel Etienne*, at Rua Jacomé 2755 (⊤68/225-7909; ❶), near the port. Very close to the *rodoviária*, the *Hotel Uirapuru* (❶) is clean, with fans in most rooms and its own pool table. There is also a decent *Albergue de Juventude* at Fronteira Verde, Travessa Natanael de Albuquerque (⊤68/225-7128; ❶–❷).

The City

If you set out to explore Rio Branco, you'll soon find that there's not a great deal to see. Of the two main tourist attractions, the more interesting is the **Museu da Borrachá**, Av. Ceará 1177 (Mon–Fri 7am–5pm; free), essentially an ethno-historical collection focusing on archeological finds, ethnographic items such as feather crafts and basketry, and a range of exhibits dealing with the rubber boom. More relevant to recent history, perhaps, though closed at the time of writing for renovations, is the **Casa do Seringueiro**, Av. Brasil 216 (Tues–Fri 7am–1pm & 2–5pm, Sun 4–7pm), near the corner with Avenida Getúlio Vargas, which houses displays about Chico Mendes and the life and times of rubber tappers in general. Nearby is the crumbling but still used **Palácio Rio Branco**.

The real attraction of Rio Branco, however, lies in the life of the bars, restaurants, streets and markets. The main square – the large **Praça Plácido de Castro** – is a lively and popular social centre for the town, with concerts, mime and all kinds of live activities happening throughout the year. Every Sunday between 5 and 10pm, the **Feira de Artesanato** takes place in the SEBRAE building on Avenida Ceará. Here you can find a good selection of rainforest crafts produced from sustainable rainforest products, including jewellery made from *tagua*, an attractive palm nut that is dense and white like ivory. The **port** is also worth seeing – small and shabby, but still an interesting spectacle in its own right. There are no regular organized **boat trips**, but it's often possible to travel on the rivers with traders and in *fazendeiros'* river boats: ask in the *Bar dos Linguarudos*, down Rua Sergipe and onto the wooden steps behind the covered market on Rua Benjamin Constant.

Acre, and in particular Rio Branco, is a strong centre for some of Brazil's fastest-growing **religious cults**. A number of similar cult groups are based in the region, connected essentially by the fact that they use forest "power plants" – like the hallucinogenic vine *banisteriopsis* – to induce visionary states. Having evolved directly out of native Indian religious practice and belief, these cults are deeply involved in a kind of green nature worship that relates easily to the concept of sustainable forest management. If you want to visit a "Santo Daime" village, contact the travel agent Acretur (see p.467) for details. The groups operate in a vaguely underground way, keeping their sanctuaries secret to non-participants. Interestingly, these cults have now spread to the fashionable coastal areas of Brazil where, behind closed doors in São Paulo and Rio de Janeiro, intellectuals participate in visionary ceremonies.

4

Acre and the rubber conflict

The relaxed air of Rio Branco masks many tensions, above all to do with population movement – people are still arriving here from the east – and the conflicting claims of small rubber tappers and multinational companies on the jungle. The tappers, who have lived here for a long time and who know how to manage the forests in a sustainable way, see the multinationals as newcomers who aim to turn the trees into pasture for beef cattle and short-term profit, destroying not only the forest but also many local livelihoods. When the leader of the rubber tappers' union, **Chico Mendes**, was shot dead by hired gunmen working for the cattle ranchers in 1988, the plight of the forest peoples of Acre came to the attention of the world. Today, the political situation in Acre remains uneasy, with the second- and third-generation tappers and gatherers joining forces with the native population in resisting the enormous economic and armed might of the advancing cattle-based companies.

Eating, drinking and nightlife

For **eating out** it is hard to beat the *Restaurante Casarão*, at Av. Brazil 110 (closed Sun lunchtime; ☎68/224-6479), by the bottom end of the Praça Plácido de Castro, near the Teleacre office (see below). The *comida por kilo* food is good and, at weekends, there's live music and an excellent atmosphere. On just about any evening it's also a good place to meet people – a hangout of students, musicians and poets. Cheaper *comida por kilo* is available at the *Restaurante El Dorado*, at the corner of Rua Deodoro and Benjamin Constant. The *Hotel Triângulo* has a good *churrasco* restaurant, and *Oscar's*, Rua Franco Ribeiro 73, is also a popular meat-house, but for a broader range of regional dishes, try the *Kaxinawá*, Rua Rui Barbosa on the corner with Avenida Ceará (closed Wed and Sun) – it's also a lively night spot. The *Pizzeria Bolota*, Rua Rui Barbosa 62, is a relatively quiet spot, next to the *Hotel Inácio Palace*, with a patio out front and occasionally live music at weekends. More or less next door is the pleasant, good-value *Inácio's*. For **street food** you'll find some good, extremely cheap stalls by the outdoor market, near the old bridge at the bottom of Avenida Getúlio Vargas. For quality local and international dishes it's hard to beat the centrally located *Restaurante Anexo*, Rua Franco Ribeiro 99 (daily 11am–2.30pm & 7–11pm; ☎69/224-1396).

There are a couple of typical wooden veranda **bars** overlooking the river and port area, down the alley leading into the main commercial market zone, by the Praça da Bandeira. A great place to meet people in the evening is in the small triangular Praça Oscar Passos, which is stuffed with chairs and tables served by a number of small bars under a giant mango tree; it's always very lively on weekend evenings. You might also try *Alek's Bar* on Rua Rio Grande do Sul near Rua Marechal Peixoto, which to all appearances is in someone's back garden. As to **clubs**, currently packing them in is *14 Bis*, right next to the airport (take a taxi), which has live salsa bands (Thurs to Sat, 7pm to very late). Also very popular is the *Maloca Club* out on Avenida Getúlio Vargas, open till late on Fridays and Saturdays.

Listings

Airlines Tavaj, at the airport (☎68/211-1008), covers most of the western Amazon including Cruzeiro do Sul, São Gabriel do Cachoeira and Tabatinga; Varig, Rua Marechal Deodoro 115 (☎68/229-2539), and at the airport (☎68/224-2719), has daily flights to Brasília, Campo Grande, Cuiabá, Manaus, Porto Velho, Rio and São Paulo; VASP, Rua Quintino Bocaiúva 105 (☎211-1133);

Andino (☎68/223-3666) organizes charter flights to Peru for between $120 and $300 (return).

Air taxis There are half a dozen air-taxi companies based at the airport, including Táxi-Aéreo Rio Branco ☎68/224-1384.

Banks and exchange The Banco do Brasil, Rua Arlindo P. Leal 85, set back from the Praça Eurico Dutra (Mon–Fri, *câmbio* between 8am and 12.30pm), will change US dollars and travellers' cheques – arrive early as it takes around two hours; you can also change dollars at the bigger hotels.

Car rental Localiza ☎69/224-7746.

Post office Rua Epaminondas Jácome (Mon–Fri 9am–5pm), by the corner with Av. Getúlio Vargas.

Shopping Aside from the Sunday-only Feira de Artesanato (see p.465), by far the best place for *artesanato* is Boutique da Floresta at Av. Getúlio Vargas 1067. The street market along Av. Getúlio Vargas sells all the usual fruit and vegetables, and there's an indoor section for everything from machetes, fishing nets and medicinal herbs to umbrellas and cassette tapes.

Telephones The Teleacre office is at Av. Brasil 378, near the bottom of Praça Plácido de Castro (daily 6am–10pm); it has external street-side booths and a telephone card sales point.

Travel and tour companies Ocitur, corner of Av. Getúlio Vargas and Rua Rui Barbosa, sells mostly plane tickets; Acretur, Rua Rui Barbosa 193 (☎68/224-2404), next to the *Hotel Rio Branco*, organizes trips to Brazil-nut forest ranges and *seringais* (rubber-tapping zones), starting at about $30 a day.

On to Peru: Brasiléia and Cruzeiro do Sul

There are really only two onward routes from Rio Branco, and both of them end up in Peru. You can either head south to Brasiléia (which is actually on the border with Bolivia) and from there continue to Assis Brasil for the border crossing, or head west to Cruzeiro do Sul and Brazil's westernmost extremity. The Peruvian jungle region of Madre de Dios, where you arrive after crossing the border between Assis Brasil and Inapari is wild territory. Cocaine smuggling does happen on this frontier and, although it's much easier to make the crossing by public transport these days, you should not undertake this route lightly.

Brasiléia and Assis Brasil

The small town of **BRASILÉIA** is six hours by bus from Rio Branco and if you're crossing the border this is where you have to visit the Polícia Federal for your exit (or entry) stamp. The office (daily 8am–5pm) is just to the right of the church as you head from the international border with Bolivia, the bus terminal just to the left. If you have to stay the night, the *Hotel Major*, Rua Salinas 326 (❶), is cheap and cheerful. Much better rooms, with air-conditioning, are at *Pousada Las Palmeras*, on Avenida G. Assis (☎68/546-3284; ❸). You can change money at the Casa Castro, over the river on the road towards Assis Brasil.

It's possible to cross to Bolivia here but there seems little point. The small town of **Cobija** on the other side, once an important rubber-collecting station, has a few expensive hotels and, at present, no onward land transport, though you can fly out, or attempt an adventurous river trip onwards to Riberalta. However, a road link between Cobija and Riberalta and the rest of Bolivia is planned.

ASSIS BRASIL is a further 90km beyond Brasiléia, and the rough road can be slow going by bus. If you can't get across the border the same day – which should be just about possible if you set off early enough from Rio Branco, and the buses connect – there's a reasonable hotel on the *praça* (❷) or you can camp near the river and leave your bags at the police station. It's then just a two-kilo-metre walk across the border to the small settlement of **Inapari** in Peru. The *Hotel Aquino* here is basic (❶); it's also possible to camp by the football pitches over the road from the hotel. From Inapari you can continue by *colectivo* (shuttle bus), bus or truck to **Puerto Maldonado** in Peru, a journey that can take a few days even in the dry season (May to Sept) and can be significantly tougher in the rainy season (Nov to March). There are also irregular flights to Puerto Maldonado from Assis: they vary in price from $40 to $80 and can be organized at the Assis airstrip. From Puerto Maldonado there are road and regular air links with Cuzco and the rest of Peru.

Cruzeiro do Sul

Totally isolated on the western edge of the Brazilian Amazon, **CRUZEIRO DO SUL** is a town of some 50,000 inhabitants, many of whom, as in Rio Branco, are social science or biology students; many others are involved in cocaine smuggling. The only dependable links with the outside world are by air either to Rio Branco (daily; 2hr) and from there the rest of Brazil, or to Pucallpa, a jungle city in the Peruvian Amazon. The road to Rio Branco is generally only passable between June and October and even then there is no bus service.

There is little obvious attraction to Cruzeiro, though it's possible to make **river trips** to extraordinarily isolated *seringais*: they can be booked through most **hotels** from around $30 a day. The *Hotel Novo Acre* (❶) is very good value, tidy and hospitable, and the *Hotel Flor de Maio* (❷), overlooking the Rio Ituí, is cheaper still. Of a better standard, *Sandra's Hotel*, Av. Celestino M. Lima 248 (☎68/322-2481; ❷), is probably the cleanest in town, and is similar to *Savone Hotel*, Trav. M. Lobão 53 (☎68/322-2349; ❷). But the only reason people come here is to cross from Brazil to Peru or vice versa – and even then this is one of the more obscure border crossings. The quickest way to Peru once you're here is to **fly** direct to Pucallpa – about one hour in a small plane that generally leaves on Tuesdays - check with TASA, Peoreira 84 (☎68/322-3086). There is no bus link between the airport and Cruzeiro's town centre some 7km away; taxis cost $6–10. The aggressively adventurous option, only possible in the rainy season between November and March, is to go by boat, which takes anything between one and two weeks and involves at least two or three days' walking between the Ucayali and Juruá watersheds. This involves travelling through a remote and relatively dangerous part of the Peruvian jungle, where terrorism and smuggling make tourism rather risky, and is not recommended.

If you've arrived from Peru, you can get up-to-date information about the road to Rio Branco from the land transport group Organização Geral Transportes, Av. Celestino M. Lima 79 (☎68/322-2093). Airlines that operate **flights within Brazil** from Cruzeiro include: VASP, Av. Celestino M. Lima 220 (☎8/322-2106); Taxi Aéreo Vale Juruá, Rua Barbosa 132 (☎68/322-2587); Tavaj, at the airport (☎68/322-2587); and Varig, Av. Celestino M. Lima 90 (☎68/322-2359).

Travel details

Buses

Belém to: Brasília (4 daily; 36hr); Marabá (3 daily; 14hr); Salvador (1 daily; 32hr).
Boa Vista to: Bonfim (2 daily; 4hr); Manaus (4 daily, 12hr); Santa Elena (6 daily; 3hr).
Manaus to: Boa Vista (4 daily; 12hr).
Marabá to: Araguaina (several weekly; 13hr); Belém (3 daily; 14hr); Tucurui (several weekly; 6hr).
Porto Velho to: Cuiabá (4 daily; 22hr); Guajará-Mirim (5 daily; 4hr); Rio Branco (4 daily; 8–9hr); São Paulo (2 daily; 36hr).
Rio Branco to: Brasiléia (3 daily; 6hr); Porto Velho (5 daily; 8hr).

Boats

Belém to: Macapá (several weekly; 1–2 days); Manaus (several weekly; 4–6 days); Santarém (several weekly; 2–3 days).
Macapá to: Belém (several weekly; 1–2 days); Oiapoque (1 weekly; 2 days); Puerto La Cruz, Venezuela (1 daily; 18hr).
Manaus to: Belém (several weekly; 3–5 days); Caracaraí (irregular; 4–8 days); Humaitá (4 weekly; 3–4 days); Porto Velho (3 weekly; 4–6 days); Santarém (daily; 2 days); São Gabriel da Cachoeira (weekly; 5–7 days); Tabatinga (several weekly; 5 days plus upstream, 3–4 downstream).

Porto Velho to: Manaus (3 weekly; 3–4 days).
Santarém to: Belém (several weekly; 2–3 days); Macapá (several weekly; 2–3 days); Manaus (1 daily; 2–3 days).
Tabatinga to: Iquitos (several weekly; 3–4 days or 12hr by speedboat); Manaus (several weekly; 4–5 days).

Planes

Belém to: Boa Vista (1 daily; 4hr); Brasília (1 daily; 2hr); Macapá (1 daily; 1hr); Manaus (2 daily; 2hr); Porto Velho (1 daily; 5hr); and at least once daily to all other major Brazilian cities.
Manaus to: Alta Floresta (1 daily; 1hr 30min); Barcelos (3 weekly; 1hr); Belém (2 daily; 2hr); Boa Vista (2 daily; 2hr 30min); Brasília (3 daily; 3hr); Cuiabá (1 daily; 3hr); Macapá (2 weekly; 2hr); Porto Velho (1 daily; 2hr); Rio Branco (several weekly; 2hr 30min); Rio de Janeiro (3 daily; 3hr 30min); São Gabriel da Cachoeira (1 daily; 3hr); São Paulo (several daily; 3hr 30min); Tabatinga (1 daily; 2hr 30min); Tefé (3 weekly; 1hr).
From **Porto Velho**, **Rio Branco** and **Marabá**, there are daily services to major Brazilian cities. Tavaj Linhas Aéreas covers most towns in the western Amazon mentioned in this chapter, including a helpful link from Rio Branco to Tabatinga (weekly; 2hr).

Brasília, Goiás and Tocantins

CHAPTER 5

Highlights

✳ **Catedral Metropolitana** Contemplate the soaring statues of St Peter and the angels from the sunken floor of this landmark cathedral. See p.487

✳ **Juscelino Kubitschek Memorial** Learn about the ambitious president who built the capital at this intriguing museum devoted to his life. See p.489

✳ **Memorial dos Povos Indígenas** Superb indigenous art is on view inside this elegant museum, itself a dazzling Niemeyer creation. See p.489

✳ **Salto de Itiquira** Best known for its 300-foot waterfall, this delightful park near Formosa makes a worthwhile daytrip from Brasília. See p.496

✳ **Goiás Velho** A picturesque colonial town, well preserved and relatively untouched by commercialism. See p.507

✳ **Parque Nacional Chapada dos Veadeiros** The varied terrain in this national park makes it an ideal spot for hiking. See p.511

Brasília, Goiás and Tocantins

The geographical heart of Brazil is the central highlands (Planalto Central), shared between the states of **Goiás**, **Tocantins** and parts of Mato Grosso. This rapidly developing and increasingly prosperous agricultural region was as recently as fifty years ago still largely Indian country, with a few colonial towns precariously linked by oxcart trails to the rest of the country. The founding of the national capital, **Brasília**, in the late 1950s changed all that, shifting Brazil's centre of gravity decisively from the coast to the interior and opening up an entire region of the country to settlement and development.

Love it or loathe it, Brazil's capital is like nowhere else on earth; the world's largest, most successful and in its own weird way most beautiful planned city, it remains the main reason for visiting the *planalto*. Brasília's chief attraction is its extraordinary **city architecture**, its late-Fifties vision of the future now charmingly retro, even sliding over into kitsch. While the capital is no metropolis, as befits a city whose main industry is politics, it is much more cosmopolitan than its relatively small size suggests, heaving with restaurants and bars where much of the city's business is transacted. Brasília is well connected by long, but good-quality, **roads** to the rest of the country – to Mato Grosso to the west, to Belém and the Northeast, to Rio, São Paulo and the South, and to the even more distant Rondônia and Acre in the western Amazon.

Although Brasília may be the region's main draw, it is by no means the only one. In recent years, the city has become the base for a significant **ecotourism** boom, still almost entirely Brazilian, and made up of middle-class punters from Brasília itself and landlocked Minas Gerais, who come for the emptiness and beauty of the landscape a few hours north of Brasília, as well as great **hiking** and more specialised outdoor pursuits like caving and rock climbing. The main centre, **Parque nacional Chapada dos Veadeiros** and environs, is an easy excursion from Brasília, and if time is limited, the spectacular waterfall of **Salto de Itiquira** is a worthwhile day trip. There is also a national park, the **Parque Nacional de Brasília**, with hiking trails on the city's periphery.

The *planalto* itself is still at that ideal stage of tourist development where there is enough infrastructure to make it accessible and enjoyable, but not so much that you ever feel things are too crowded or over-commercialised. The highlands were traversed since the earliest days by Portuguese expeditions, and

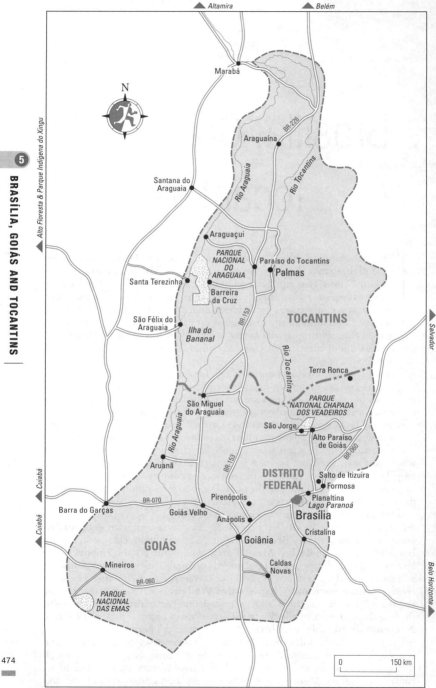

The topography and ecology of the **planalto** are unique, known within Brazil as the *cerrado*, only partly translated by the word "savanna". Much of it looks startlingly African; red earth, scrubby vegetation, dusty in the dry season, missing only giraffes and zebras for the illusion to be complete. What makes it spectacular is the topography, which begins to break up the highland plains into a series of hill ranges, cliffs, mesas, plateaus and moorlands almost as soon as you start heading north from Brasília. This irregular landscape is strategically situated between two enormous watersheds, the Paraná to the south and the Amazon to the north, both of which have the headwaters of major tributaries in the *planalto*. The hills and mountains are riddled with thousands of **rivers and streams**, forming spectacular waterfalls and swimholes within easy reach of Brasília.

As ecotourism in the region grows (see p.473), so too do the **threats** to the *planalto*. Good soils and communications, and its proximity to the markets and capital of Minas Gerais and São Paulo mean that development here is far more intense than it ever has been in the Amazon. The ranchers who spearheaded the early wave of settlement of the *planalto* are still there, but are increasingly giving way to large-scale commercial agriculture, especially soya. This has underlain the development of the two largest cities in Goiás, **Goiânia**, the state capital, and **Anápolis**, modern and prosperous by Brazilian standards, but about as interesting to visit as, say, Indianapolis. In fact, much of the *planalto* looks like the US Midwest when you fly over it, or drive through, with endless geometric fields and irrigation canals stretching to the horizon. Over 80 percent of the native vegetation has been converted to farmland or pasture, compared to 14 percent of the Amazon, and the unique flora and fauna of the *cerrado* – the giant anteater and armadillo, the maned wolf, the glorious wildflowers that speckle the *cerrado* with colour in the rainy season – are all increasingly endangered. If things continue at the present rate, within a generation the only islands of true *cerrado* left will be the national parks.

many a *planalto* town has its origins in a *paulista bandeira* looking for mines and Indian slaves. Two colonial towns in particular are worth visiting, both in Goiás; **Pirenópolis**, within easy reach of Brasília, and the old capital of Goiás state, **Goiás Velho**, a little-visited jewel that is as beautiful as any of the better known *cidades históricas* of Minas Gerais. Further north still, the **state of Tocantins** has its eastern and western frontiers defined by two of the largest tributaries of the Amazon, the **Araguaia** and **Tocantins**, but with the exception of one of the largest riverine islands in the world, the **Ilha do Bananal**, the state has little to offer the visitor and is best bypassed on the way to more interesting destinations in the North or Northeast.

Brasília

Arriving in **BRASÍLIA**, especially at its futuristic airport, is like falling into a science-fiction novel. The entire city, and especially the central area, has a startlingly space-age feel and look. Originally intended for a population of half a million by the year 2000, Brasília today has close to four million people and

Brasília's climate

Brasília's **climate** has marked seasonal differences that you should bear in mind in timing a visit. The rainy season runs from October to March, and the very best time to come is the spring, from April through June, when the trees are in bloom and the climate is pleasant and mild. July through September is the height of the dry season: during the day the sun beats down hard, everything dries out and hot winds blow fine red dust over everything. The extraordinary dryness of this time of year – humidity levels comparable with the Sahara – often cause sinus problems even among locals. If you do come during this time of year, drink as much as you can and don't stint on the sunscreen. Fortunately, night always comes as a relief; temperatures drop and freshness returns all year round.

is the only one of Brazil's major metropolitan areas that is still growing fast. Looking at the gleaming government buildings or zooming down the city's excellent roads, it really can seem that Brasília is the modern heart of a new world superpower – an illusion that is rapidly dispelled by driving ten minutes outside Brasília in any direction, when you start hitting the miles and miles of low-income housing of the millions of people who commute from the so-called *cidades satélites*, the satellite cities, serving the needs of the mainly government-employed elite who live in Brasília itself. As well as being the national capital, Brasília is also the capital of its own state, the **Distrito Federal**, the Federal District, which includes the satellite cities as well. The whole Federal District is in fact the perfect symbol of modern Brazil, though not in the way its creators intended; affluence close to but segregated from poverty, *favelas* over the horizon, and poor newcomers invading the countryside where the country's elite have their walled-off weekend retreats.

Brasília's highlights are all fairly obvious **architectural** ones. Anyone with a taste for the best of Fifties and Sixties architecture will think they have died and gone to heaven, but there are other attractions, too. Pleasant parks, popular for weekend picnics, encircle the entire city, while in the downtown zone, by the central bus station, a busy mess of people and trade generates a lively atmosphere. **Nightlife** is energetic, revolving around huge numbers of bars and restaurants that benefit from the city's marvellous nocturnal climate, fresh and pleasant all year round. **Cinema** is especially good here, patronised by a large local middle class with an appetite for foreign films, and one side-benefit of the presence of the elite is the regular appearance of top-level **performing arts**.

Brasília's design also has a **mystic** side to it. On Brazilian Republic Day – April 21 – the sun rises through the concrete "H" shape of the parallel twin towers that poke out of the National Congress building, provoking images of a futuristic Stonehenge. There is a distinct New Age feel to parts of the city and environs; it has a special attraction for the wacky religious cults and UFO enthusiasts in which Brazil abounds, who love its space-age look and feel more than anyone. Some visitors find Brasília alienating, and the central part of the city can certainly seem that way, with its jumble of undistinguished skyscrapers, malls and massive empty spaces – the absence of planned gardens and parks is the centre's major design flaw. At night the centre is deserted and dead, even at weekends, thanks to the city's rigid zoning laws, which have put all its hotels there. The popular image of Brasília as a concrete jungle comes from visitors who never leave the centre; in fact, no other Brazilian city has as many trees and parks, and the older residential areas are very pleasant to walk in, with the trees so dense it often seems the housing blocks have been built in the middle of a wood. The real life of the city, especially at night, can be found in the *asas*, the residential wings that swing north and south of the centre, where all the restaurants, clubs and barlife are to be found. At night, the outdoor bars and restaurants can make parts of it seem positively Parisian.

Some history

The idea of a **Brazilian inland capital** was first mooted in 1789, and a century later (in 1891) the concept was written into Article 3 of the Republic's Constitution, setting aside some 14,400 square kilometres for the capital's creation. Many sites were considered; indeed, in 1913 US President Theodore Roosevelt visited the western edge of the *planalto* and remarked that "any sound northern race could live here; and in such a land, with such a climate, there would be much joy of living". But fulfillment of the idea had to wait until 1956 when **Juscelino Kubitschek** became president, on the promise that he would build the city if he won the election. He had to get it finished by the end of his term of office, so work soon began in earnest.

The site was quickly selected by aerial surveys of over 50,000 square kilometres of land. In less than four years a capital city had to be planned, financed and built in the face of apparently insurmountable odds: the building site was 125km from the nearest rail line, 190km from the nearest airport, over 600km from the nearest paved road; the closest timber supply was 1200km distant, the nearest source of good steel even further. Still, in **Oscar Niemeyer**, the city's architect, Brasília had South America's most able student of Le Corbusier, founder of the modern planned city and a brilliant designer of buildings. Alongside Niemeyer, who was contracted to design the buildings, **Lúcio Costa** was hired for the awesome task of Brasília's urban planning.

Design and construction

Costa produced a **city plan** described variously as being in the shape of a bow and arrow, a bird in flight or an aeroplane. Certainly, on maps or from the air, Brasília appears to be soaring, wings outstretched, towards the eastern Atlantic coast. The main public buildings, government ministries, palace of justice and presidential palace, line the "fuselage", an eight-kilometre-long grass mall known as the **Eixo Monumental** (Monumental Axis), with the **intercity bus and train station**, the *rodoferroviária*, at one end, and the heart of government, the Praça dos Três Poderes (Square of the Three Powers) grouping the Congress building, the Supreme Court and the presidential palace at the other. The main residential districts branch out to the north and south, in the arc of the bow, while the business districts are clustered where the wings join the fuselage.

Money for the **construction** came from all over the world in the form of grants and loans, and from the printing of money, a move that increased inflation in the short term. The whole operation was incredibly expensive, not least because everything – workers, food, cement and the like – had to be flown in, as work started long before the first access roads appeared. At the time of construction, and even after inauguration, many considered the whole scheme to be a complete waste of time and money: Rio's *Correio da Manhã* newspaper famously called it "The Limit of Insanity".

Nevertheless, exactly three years, one month and five days after the master plan was unveiled, 150,000 people arrived in Brasília for the official **inauguration**, in April 1960. (The event is celebrated today as the Festa da Cidade on April 21 each year). It must have been a hectic time. There were only 150 first-class hotel rooms completed for the five thousand visiting dignitaries, but the celebrations went ahead, topped by a spectacular 38-tonne firework display. When the smoke cleared in the morning it was apparent to everyone that, despite the finished government complexes, 94 apartment buildings, around five hundred one- and two-storey houses plus their local schools and shops, there was still years of work left to do. Road junctions were not the super-slick lane mergers that had been promised, pedestrians and apartments still had to be separated from traffic, and the accommodation units had none of their intended leafy surroundings – the flats supposedly close enough to the ground for a mother to call her child. In time, the city slowly grew to fill in the spaces left for more organic expansion, most of the residential areas were landscaped and greened, and the city gradually developed some of the maladies that affect the rest of urban Brazil, like rush-hour traffic-jams.

Growth and layout

As Brasília developed it became apparent that the original **city plans**, based on Le Corbusier's notions of urban progress through geometrical order and rectilinear planning, would have to be modified if Brazilians, the least rectilinear of people, were going to feel comfortable here. Partly this was accomplished by Niemeyer's brilliant and innovative buildings, full of curves and circles. Still alive and designing away in his nineties he continues to be the city architect and all Brasília's major buildings, from the angular government ministries in the fifties to the sinuous curves of the federal prosecutors building completed in 2002, were designed by him, giving the city a unique aesthetic unity. Partly it was accomplished by time; as the city matured, its inhabitants started to subvert its rigid zoning and building codes by adding houses and expanding leisure areas, especially in the commercial sections of the Asas (see below). One essential point to bear in mind is that Brasília is dominated by its **road traffic** system like no other Brazilian city; everyone, including visitors, is obliged by its enormous spaces to move around by car and bus; **walking**, like everything else in Brasília, is zoned. There are parks and residential areas specifically designed for strolling; elsewhere you should forget about walking as the city's not made for it.

The residential wings are divided into *superquadras*, complexes of apartment buildings (see box on pp.482–483 for a complete guide to Brasília's zoning system). There are sixteen in each wing, lower numbers closer to the centre, so just by looking at the address you can tell roughly how far from the centre it is. Between every superquadra is a **commercial area**, where local shops, bars and restaurants are found; most of Brasília's nightlife is concentrated in these, and to save confusion they are referred to here as *comercials*, reflecting local usage; a *candango* (someone from Brasília) giving directions to a bar will say "*comercial 206 norte*", for example.

The costs: financial and environmental

On the face of it at least, Kubitschek lived up to his electoral campaign promise of fifty years' progress in five. What he hadn't made clear before, though, was just how much it would cost Brazil. When Kubitschek stood down in 1960, his successor, **Jânio Quadros**, broadcast a jaundiced message to the nation, saying "All this money, spent with so much publicity, we must now raise – bitterly, patiently, dollar by dollar, *cruzeiro* by *cruzeiro*". With outstanding foreign loans of two billion dollars, the city seemed an antisocial waste of resources to many, and it was certainly responsible for letting loose inflation, a problem that would take a generation to resolve.

As it turned out, however, Brasília paid for itself many times over, and very quickly. The rapid **development of the planalto** that followed transformed the entire region into one of the most developed agricultural areas in the country, and the taxes, jobs and production generated swiftly made the decision to build Brasília seem inspired; Kubitschek's reputation has steadily climbed since his death in 1976, and he is now usually thought of as Brazil's most visionary and successful president. The costs have proved to be more environmental than financial, with the rapid conversion of much of the *planalto* to farmland and the destruction of forest along the Belém-Brasília highway corridor. As ever, those with most cause to complain were the **indigenous peoples** of the *planalto*; groups like the warlike **Xavante** did what they could to halt the tide, but it was hopeless, and by the 1970s they were all confined to reservations a fraction of the size of their previous territories.

Orientation, arrival and information

Although initially quite confusing, Brasília is laid out with geometric precision. It is neatly divided into sectors: there are residential sectors – each with their own shopping and other facilities – hotel sectors, embassy sectors and banking and commercial sectors. Roads are numbered, rather than named, with digits representing their position and distance north or south of the **Eixo Monumental**, and east or west of the other main axis, the **Eixo Rodoviário**, universally known as the Eixão. The different sectors are given acronyms, most fairly easy to work out (see box pp. 482–483).

The central *rodoviária*, the urban bus station, is the main hub of movement within Brasília, with the Eixo Monumental passing around it and the Eixo Rodoviário crossing over the top of it. Up above the *rodoviária*, you can see at a glance the main areas of interest to the visitor. Looking east, towards the main government buildings that resemble great green dominoes, is the unmistakeable Aztec form of the **Teatro Nacional**, and the conical crown of the **Catedral** a little further away to the right: both are within easy walking distance. Slightly further away, but still within a half-hour's stroll, are the strange bowls and towers of the **Congresso Nacional** buildings. Immediately on either side of the *rodoviária* there are two separate, rather tacky shopping centres, the **Conjuntos de Diversões**, one to the north, another to the south. Twenty years ago these vast concrete boxes were overshadowed only by the TV Tower, but nowadays the modern towers of the nearby **Setores Hoteleiros** (hotel sectors), **Setores Comerciais** (business sectors) and **Setores das Autarquias** (government agency sectors) dominate the scene, together with the bank and government buildings on either side of the Eixo Monumental. The most distinctive is the central bank building in Setor das Autarquias Sul, black boxes hung around a central concrete framework, looking for all the world like an enormous stereo speaker.

Arrival

The **airport** (℡61/365-1941) is 12km south of the centre, and bus #102 runs every hour from there into Brasília, dropping you at the downtown *rodoviária*. A taxi will cost you about $8 to the hotel sectors. Inter-city and long-distance buses use the **rodoferroviária**, the bus and former train station at the far western end of the Eixo Monumental (℡61/233-7200). From here, the #131 bus (Platform B, stand 3) covers the 5km of the Eixo Monumental to the downtown *rodoviária*, passing the famous statue of Juscelino Kubitschek on the way. Once at the downtown *rodoviária*, go up the escalators to the second level for

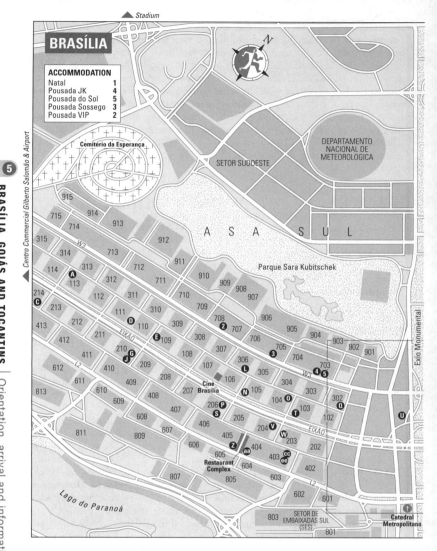

BRASÍLIA

ACCOMMODATION

Natal	1
Pousada JK	4
Pousada do Sol	5
Pousada Sossego	3
Pousada VIP	2

the shopping centres and upper roads, from where you can see most of central Brasília, and the hotel sectors are a short taxi ride. Taxis to the hotel sector from the *rodoferroviária* are about $5.

Information

The best place for **tourist information** is the kiosk at the airport (daily 8am–8pm; ☎61/365-1024), which stocks a range of leaflets, maps and brochures, and also has a surprisingly useful touch-screen computer terminal. There's also a helpful tourist office on the Praça dos Três Poderes (Mon 1.30–6pm, Tues–Sun 8am–6pm; ☎61/325-5730), and in a kiosk underneath

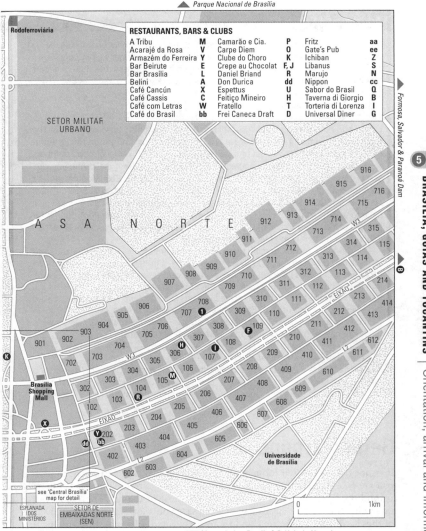

RESTAURANTS, BARS & CLUBS

A Tribu	**M**	Camarão e Cia.	**P**	Fritz	**aa**
Acarajé da Rosa	**V**	Carpe Diem	**O**	Gate's Pub	**ee**
Armazém do Ferreira	**Y**	Clube do Choro	**K**	Ichiban	**Z**
Bar Beirute	**E**	Crepe au Chocolat	**F, J**	Libanus	**S**
Bar Brasília	**L**	Daniel Briand	**R**	Marujo	**N**
Belini	**A**	Don Durica	**dd**	Nippon	**cc**
Café Cancún	**X**	Espettus	**U**	Sabor do Brasil	**Q**
Café Cassis	**C**	Feitiço Mineiro	**H**	Taverna di Giorgio	**B**
Café com Letras	**W**	Fratello	**T**	Torteria di Lorenza	**I**
Café do Brasil	**bb**	Frei Caneca Draft	**D**	Universal Diner	**G**

Museu de Arte Brasília & Palácio da Alvorada ▼

the TV tower, with the same hours. Apart from this, you can pick up leaflets from the main hotels. By far the most detailed and useful map of Brasília is to be found at the front of telephone directories and yellow pages, which you'll find in most hotel rooms. There is an excellent listings site for Brasília at Ⓦwww.candango.com.br, unfortunately with no toggle for English, but click on Mapas. The main newspaper, the *Correio Brasiliense*, publishes a daily listings supplement, the *Guia*, with comprehensive information on films, exhibitions, live music and opening hours; though in Portuguese, the details are pretty easy to work out.

Most people in Brasília live in *superquadras* – massive apartment complexes, some of which you can see coming in along the Eixão from the airport. Finding out where someone lives or works can seem impossible from the **address**, but there is a perfect internal logic to the system. For example, the address

> SQS 105
> Bloco A – 501
> 70344 Brasília - DF

means *superquadra* south no. 105, building A, apartment 501, postcode 70344. The three-digit *superquadra* number here (105) gives the location: the first digit represents the position east or west of the Eixo Rodoviário (or Eixão), with odd numbers to the west, evens to the east, increasing the further away from the centre you get. The last two digits represent the distance north or south of the Eixo Monumental, so that, for example, SQN 208 is five *superquadras* north from SQN 203, SQS 110 five south from SQS 105. Unfortunately, addresses are rarely written out in full: you'll have to watch out for "Q" (*quadra*, and often used for *superquadra*, too), "L", "lj" or "lt" (*loja* or *lote*, meaning "lot" or "shop", used for commercial addresses), "B" or "bl" (*bloco*) and "cj" (*conjunto* meaning "compound").

A similar logic applies to main roads. Even numbers apply east of the Eixão, odd to the west, prefaced for good measure by a letter that tells you which side of the Eixão it runs, L for east (*leste*), W for west (technically *oeste*, but the planners shrank from OE). The roads that run parallel to the Eixão on either side with exits to all the superquadras are the ones used by the local bus services, and are universally called the Eixinhos, the "little *eixos*", Eixinho L east of the Eixão, Eixinho W west. The main commercial street, the only one that looks anything like a normal Brazilian street in the entire city, is W3, which runs the entire length of both *asas*.

The other terms you are most likely to come across are:
Asa Norte/Asa Sul General terms for the two "wings" (*asas*) of the city, comprising the avenues Eixo Rodoviário Norte and Eixo Rodoviário Sul, and the roads running off and parallel to them (the latter lettered "W" to the west, and "L" to the east, eg W-3 Norte, L-4 Sul).

Getting around

It is not difficult to see most of Brasília's traditional sights in a day, though if you are foolish enough to walk after 10am it gets extremely tiring wandering around the open spaces of the centre in the heat of the day. There are two or three **city bus routes**, instead, which can save you a lot of shoe-leather. Details of these are given in the text, and there are also two **circular bus routes** that are very handy for a cheap overview of the city: buses #105 and #106 leave from and return to the downtown *rodoviária*, Platform A (☎61/223-0557) after a long outer city tour; just try to avoid these routes between 4pm and 6pm on weekdays when the buses are particularly crowded. Keep an eye out for pickpockets when standing in line for the buses, though once on the bus, you will be all right.

The city has a good **taxi** service. Flag a taxi down when you want one, or pick one up at the many ranks throughout the city; every *superquadra* has at least one. Most people drive their own cars, and if you want to join them see p.494 for addresses of **car rental** firms; it'll cost you from $20 a day, less if you rent over a longer period.

CLN/CLS or **SCLN/SCLS** (Setor) Comércio Local Norte/Sul. These terms describe the shopping blocks interspersed throughout the residential *superquadras* that comprise Asa Norte and Asa Sul. Their numbering follows that of the *superquadras*, so that CLN 208 is near SQN 208.

Eixinho The smaller, marginally slower main roads with exits to every quadra either side of the Eixão, the main central artery.

EQN/EQS Entrequadras Norte/Sul. Literally "between quadras", referring to the area bordering the Eixinhos.

SBN/SBS Setor Bancário Norte/Sul. The two banking sectors either side of the Eixo Monumental.

SCN/SCS Setor Comercial Norte/Sul. The two commercial office block areas, set back from the Conjuntos de Diversões shopping centres. Often confused with CLN/CLS (see above).

SDN/SDS Setor de Diversões Norte/Sul. The two shopping centres (*conjuntos*) either side of Eixo Monumental.

SEN/SES Setor de Embaixadas Norte/Sul. The embassy sectors, east of the bank sectors.

SHIN/SHIS Setor de Habitações Individuais Norte/Sul. The two peninsulas that jut into Lago Paranoá, the northern one accessible from the end of Eixo Rodoviário Norte, the southern one, also called Lago Sul, connected by bridges from Avenida das Nações.

SHN/SHS Setor Hoteleiro Norte/Sul. The hotel sectors either side of the Eixo Monumental, west of the *rodoviária*.

SQN/SQS or **SHCN/SHCS** Superquadras Norte/Sul. The individual *superquadras* in the main residential wings, Asa Norte and Asa Sul.

Although the system takes some getting used to, it's useful in pin-pointing exactly where an address is located in the city – a good defence against dishonest taxi drivers, useful when walking, and a boon if your Portuguese is too elementary for directions.

City tours

If you have limited time and want someone else to take care of things then the expensive but reliable **city tours** might be the thing for you. Most hotels in Brasília are keen to offer city tours to their guests, as they take a percentage of the fee for themselves. It's worth shopping around – the *Hotel El Pilar* can sometimes work out up to 25 percent cheaper than the *Hotel Nacional* – or you can book direct with one of the tour organizers: Power Turismo (☎61/332-6699); AeroVan Turismo (☎61/340-9251); or Monserat Turismo (☎61/326-1407, @monserrat@conectanet.com.br). Tours cost from $10 to $30 per person, and range from three-hour programmes covering commercial, banking and residential sectors as well as prominent buildings, to the night-time tour ($30–50) that ends with an evening meal. While not necessarily the best time to see most of the sights, the evening tour does give you the chance to experience the city by neon. In many ways Brasília seems easier to comprehend in the light-studded darkness when the wide-open spaces melt away. If you want to hire your own personal English-speaking guide to the city, Waldeck Costa, Caixa Postal 2983 (☎61/384-1909 or mobile 964-8673) is reliable and knows his stuff.

Accommodation

Brasília has a vast range of accommodation to suit all wallets, contrary to its reputation as being an over-expensive place to stay. The **central hotel sectors** are split into three categories of hotel, distinguishable by height, all of which post prices that are actually considerably more than they really charge if you ask for a discount. The five-star skyscrapers are the closest to the centre, offering top-range beds from around $50 a night, smaller four- and three-star hotels are to be found either side of W3 and are more than reasonable at $20–25, while $15 will get you perfectly adequate accommodation at the squat one- and two-star hotels.

If you're on a tight budget, $8–10 will get you a bed at a *pousada*; these cluster on W3 Sul, starting at *quadra* 703 to around 708. Most are squalid and none too secure; the ones recommended below are the pick of the bunch, but are still below the standards of the worst of the hotels. Staying in campsites or in the satellite cities is definitely not recommended; besides being dangerous, it costs much the same as accommodation in Brasília.

Central hotel sectors

Alvorada SHS Q.4 ℡61/222-7068. Cheap, central and good value hotel, though noisy unless you get an apartment facing away from W3. ❸

Aracoara SHN Q.5 ℡61/328-9222. Comfortable mid-range hotel, very good value, but in a marginally inconvenient location and nothing within walking distance. The surrounding area is even deader than usual for the centre at night. ❸

Aristus SHN Q.2 ℡61/328-8675, ℻326-5415. One of the cheapest options in this good location, offering a choice of basement rooms at rates slightly lower than their other rooms. ❷

Bonaparte Hotel Résidence SHN Q.2 ℡61/322-2288 or 0800-619-991, ℻322-9092, ℡www.bonapartehotel.com.br. A top-notch hotel, with a large convention facility and all mod cons. ❺

Brasília Imperial SHS Q.3 ℡61/223-7252, ℡www.brasiliaimperialhotel.com.br. Excellent value and location. ❷

Bristol SHS Q.4 ℡61/321-6162, ℻321-2690. Comfortable and with a rooftop swimming pool, this is a good-value hotel without being top of the range; highly recommended. ❸

Byblos SHN Q.3 ℡61/326-1570, ℻326-3615. Unlike most of the hotels in SHS and SHN, this one is low-rise. Clean and spartan, but its rooms aren't as nice as the *Casablanca*'s (see below) and are slightly more expensive to boot. ❷

Carlton SHS Q.5 ℡61/226-8109, ℡www.carltonhotel.com.br. Older upmarket hotel, with great 1960s decor, but slightly expensive compared to similar places. ❻

Casablanca SHN Q.3 ℡61/328-8586, ℻328-8273. Close to the Eixo Monumental and within sight of the TV Tower, a small and friendly hotel with excellent rooms and a nice restaurant. Good value at the lower end of this price bracket. ❷

El Pilar SHN Q.3 ℡61/326-5353. This cheap, low-rise hotel is a little spartan, but the location is good and the staff friendly. ❷

Eron SHN Q.5 ℡61/329-4000. Another good value mid-range hotel, with fine views from the upper floors and handy for the TV tower but little else. ❸

Hotel das Américas SHN Q.4 ℡61/321-3355 or 0800-118-844, ℻321-1972, ℡www.hoteldasamericas.com. Comfortable and modern, with an excellent restaurant, but overpriced if you don't get a discount. ❸

Kubitschek Plaza SHN Q.2 ℡61/329-3333 or 0800-613-995, ℻328-9366, ℡www.kubitschek.com.br. Among the best of the five-star hotels, built in a strange blend of Space Age and ancient Egyptian styles. Everything you'd expect at this price – pool, gymnasium, sauna, plus free medical insurance throughout your stay. ❺

Manhattan SHN Q.2 ℡61/319-3060 or 0800-612-400, ℻328-5683. Less extravagant than its stable-mate the *Kubitschek Plaza*, but still extremely smart, attracting a slightly younger clientele. ❺

Metropolitan SHN Q.2 ℡61/424-3500. Swanky but reasonably priced for all the mod cons you get – along with the excellent views. ❺

Nacional SHS Q.1, ℡61/321-7575, ℻223-9213, ℡www.hotelnacional.com.br. The oldest of the big hotels, reflected in fine retro-1960s kitsch decor. Well run with the added advantage of having all of the major airline offices out front. ❺

Planalto Bittar SHS Q.3 ℡61/322-217. Just about the best of cheaper hotels, slightly more expensive but better quality than others in this

market. Good location. ❸
St Paul SHS Q.2 ☎61/317-8400, ⓕ224-3935,
ⓔstpaul@tba.com.br). Large hotel with excellent
service, plus a sauna, pool, good restaurant and
bar. ❺

Pousadas and pensões

Natal 708 Norte, Bloco B ☎61/340-1984. Most
comfortable of the *pousadas*; breakfast included.
❷

Pousada do Sol 703 Sul, Bloco K ☎61/224-
9703. Along with neighbouring *Pousada JK*, this is
the best of a cluster of cheap places – both. ❷
Pousada Sossego 705 Sul, facing W3 ☎61/224-
5050. Aimed at the lower end of the Brazilian business market, with clean rooms. ❷
Pousada VIP 708 Sul, Bloco C ☎61/340-8544.
Doesn't quite live up to its name, but it's clean and
includes basic breakfast. ❷

The City

Brasília's overriding attraction is the unique environment produced by its stunning **architecture**. The blue sky that normally hangs over the city contrasts
well with the modern buildings and the deep red earth of the *planalto*. Visitors
normally head straight for the downtown sites, but it's best to put them in context first on one of the circular bus routes from the *rodoviária* (see p.482).

Below, the main sights in downtown Brasília are divided into three sections,
following the head, body and tail concept of the bird or aeroplane that the city
resembles; the outlying areas of the city are dealt with afterwards.

▲ *Rodoferroviária & Memorial JK*

CENTRAL BRASÍLIA

ACCOMMODATION	
Alvorada	6
Aracoara	1
Aristus	13
Bonaparte	
Hotel Résidence	11
Bristol	5
Byblos	9
Carlton	3
Casablanca	8
El Pilar	10
Eron	2
Hotel das Américas	4
Kubitschek Plaza	15
Manhattan	17
Metropolitan	16
Nacional	14
Planalto Bittar	7
St Paul	12

Praça dos Tres Poderes, ▼ *Palácio do Planalto, Palácio da Alvorada, Congress & Itamaratí*

The Esplanada dos Ministérios

Separated from the commercial centres and the downtown *rodoviária* by the Brazilian government complex known as the **Esplanada dos Ministérios**, which is focused on the unmistakable twin towers of the Congress building. All of the buildings here are within a few minutes' walk of each other, entrance is free and they can be seen in half a day, though you can easily spend more time than this exploring. All were designed by Niemeyer, and are rightly regarded as among the best, if not the best, modernist buildings in the world. The combination of white marble, water pools, reflecting glass and the airy, flying buttresses on the presidential palace and Supreme Court make these buildings remarkably elegant. At night floodlighting and internal lights make them even more impressive; a slow taxi or bus ride around the Esplanada in the early evening, when people are still working and the buildings glow like Chinese lanterns, is a must. The only blemish is the enormously ugly and vulgar flagpole at the centre of the square, which sits there like a black bluebottle on an exquisite white plate, mute testimony to the crassness and bad taste of the military regime that plonked it there over Niemeyer's protests.

At the center of the complex is the **Praça dos Três Poderes** (Square of Three Powers), representing the Congress, judiciary and the presidency. The **Congresso Nacional** is the heart of the legislative power and one of the most obvious landmarks in Brasília – in a way, everything else flows from here. If you accept the analogy of the city built as a bird, then the National Congress is its beak, something it clearly resembles with its twin 28-storey towers. The two large "bowls", one on either side of the towers, house the Senate Chamber (the smaller, inverted one) and the House of Representatives, and were designed so that the public could climb and play on them, though the only people allowed to play there now are the patrolling soldiers of the Polícia Militar. Visitors can attend debates when in session, however, something you might want to enquire about at the front entrance desk. The chambers themselves are a hoot – as Sixties as the Beatles, though they haven't aged as well. To see them, you must take one of the guided tours that leave every half hour on weekdays and hourly at weekends. Most guides speak some English and there is a strict dress code – long trousers, shirt and shoes for men, smart casual for women (Senate tours Mon–Fri 1.30–5.30pm, Sat & Sun 10am–2pm; ☎61/311-2149 for information; House of Representatives tours Mon–Fri 1–5pm, Sat & Sun 9am–2pm; ☎61/318-5092 for information).

The **Palácio da Justiça** (Mon–Fri 10am–noon and 3–5pm; same dress code as for Congress) is beside the Congress building, on the northern side of the Esplanada dos Ministerios. Created in 1960 with a concrete facade, the building was covered with fancy – and, to many, elitist – marble tiles by the military government during the dictatorship. With the return to democracy the tiles were removed, laying bare the concrete waterfalls between the pillars, but the water has been shut off for years as the pools proved to be a perfect breeding ground for the dengue mosquito. The structure is much less interesting inside than any of the other buildings, and without the waterfalls the exterior is more than a little bleak.

Much more worthwhile is the **Palácio Itamarati** (Mon–Fri. 2–4.30pm, Sat & Sun 10am–3.30pm, no guided tours but visitors are restricted to certain areas, with same dress code as for congress; ☎61/411-6159 for information), the vast Foreign Office structure. Combining modern and classical styles, it's built around elegant courtyards, sculptures and gardens, and inside its airiness and sense of space is breathtaking, well set off by a carefully chosen selection of modern art and wall-hangings. Outside, the marble *Meteor* sculpture by Bruno Giorgi is a stunning piece of work, its five parts representing the five continents.

Behind the Congresso Nacional, on the northern side, the **Palácio do Planalto** houses the president's office (Sun 9.30am–1.30pm; same dress code as for congress), which is viewable only by guided tour. Of all the Niemeyer buildings this is the most spectacular, both outside and in; the interior is dominated by sleek columns and a glorious, curving ramp, down into the reception area. On weekdays, however, visitors will have to content themselves with a changing of the guard out front at 8.30am and 5.30pm daily. Nearby in Praça dos Três Poderes, the **Museu Histórico de Brasília** (Mon–Sat 9am–1pm & 2–5pm) tells the tale of the transfer of the capital from Rio; the large-scale architectural model of the entire city, with lights for points of interest, is fun and useful to the newly arrived. The **Supremo Tribunal Federal** (Mon–Fri 1–5pm), interesting enough but not in the same class inside as the Itamaratí or the presidential palace, is open to the public; entrance is with formal dress only (jacket required). Outside there's a concrete monument to Justice, although one to Self-Importance would be more appropriate.

From here, you can take a **bus** to the downtown *rodoviária*, or it's a twenty-minute walk west through the esplanade of ministry buildings to the cathedral and downtown commercial centre. But to complete your tour of Niemeyer gems, it is worth taking the short taxi or bus ride from here to the president's official residence two miles away, the **Palácio da Alvorada** (bus #104, leaves from stand 13 of Platform A at the *rodoviária*), which some consider the most beautiful of Niemeyer's buildings. The residence is nestled behind an emerald green lawn and beautifully sculpted gardens, which perfectly set off the brilliant white of its exterior – note the architect's distinctive slender buttresses – and its blue-tinted glass. Somehow the fact that you're only allowed to see it from fifty yards away adds to its delicateness and elegance.

If you go by taxi, make sure it waits for you in the carpark to the right – taxis rarely pass by here. Guards will shout intimidatingly at you if you sit in the car in the left parking lot, the only one with the clear view, due to heightened security concerns, as everywhere else.

On your way back, look out for Niemeyer's most recent building, the circular, twin mirrored-glass towers of the attorney general's headquarters, immediately behind the Praça dos Três Poderes.

The cathedral and the commercial sectors

Between the ministries and the downtown *rodoviária*, and within walking distance of either, the **Catedral Metropolitana Nossa Senhora Aparecida** is one of Brasília's most striking edifices (daily 7am–6.30pm; no shorts allowed); it marks the spot where the city of Brasília was inaugurated in 1960 and is built in the form of an inverted chalice and crown of thorns; its sunken nave puts most of the interior floor below ground level. Some of the glass roof panels in the interior reflect rippling water from outside, adding to the sense of airiness in the cathedral, while the statues of St Peter and the angels suspended from the ceiling (the inspired gravity-defying creations of Brazilian sculptor Bruno Ceschiatti) help to highlight the feeling of elevation. Nevertheless, although some 40m in height and with a capacity of 2000, the cathedral seems surprisingly small inside.

About ten minutes' walk away, on the northern side of the Eixo Monumental, is the **Teatro Nacional**. Built in the form of an Aztec temple, it's a marvellous, largely glass-covered pyramid set at an angle to let light into the lobby, where there are often good art exhibitions with futuristic and environmental themes. Inside are three halls: the Martins Pena, the Villa-Lobos (the largest, seating 1200) and the much smaller Alberto Nepomuceno. Most theatre productions are in Portuguese, but all three venues are also used for **music concerts** – Brasília has a symphony orchestra, and popular music stars often play here as well. As the main city venue for **ballet and dance**, the theatre is always worth checking out; thanks to the presence of the government and diplomatic corps, you might luck out and catch an illustrious visitor like the Bolshoi.

The main central shopping centre, the **Conjunto Nacional**, stands on the northern side of the *rodoviária*. Contained in a huge concrete block that's covered with massive product advertisements, the flashy jewellery and furniture shops combine with restaurants and fast-food outlets, and unlike the modern shopping centres in other Latin American cities the Conjunto Nacional is not just a playground for the rich; everyone seems to shop here. The busy northern *conjunto* is much more upmarket than its neighbor across the way, the **CONIC** centre, which is increasingly rundown and now actively dangerous at night, when the only people moving are the prostitutes and clientele patronizing a basement complex of fleapit sex cinemas. Stuck underground between the two giant shopping blocks, the downtown *rodoviária* is also on three levels, and here you'll find more shops, toilets, snack bars and a bus information office.

A fifteen-minute walk west of here in the Setor Comercial Norte, on the far side of W3, is the glitzy **Brasília Shopping** Mall, a towering glass disc half sunk in the ground, and a busy meeting place packed with shops of all kinds (the Varig office is conveniently opposite). By far the most interesting place to visit within easy walking distance of the *rodoviária* can be found in the unlikely setting of the **Central Bank building**, the unmistakable concrete and black glass skyscraper in Setor das Autarquias Sul, visible from anywhere in the centre. Tucked away by the building's rear entrance is the **Museu da Moeda**, or the Museum of Money (Tue–Fri 10am–4.30pm, Sat 2–6; free, show your passport to get past reception), where you'll find a quirky but fascinating display of Brazilian currency from colonial times, very interesting as social history, but overshadowed by the second part of the display, an extraordinary exhibition behind armoured glass of the largest gold nuggets ever found in Brazil – most dating from the 1980s, when the Central Bank was buying nuggets from the Amazon gold rush. Behind the Bank building is **Centro Cultural da Caixa**, the city's main art gallery, at any one time housing at least two travelling exhibitions, dependably high quality and free as well.

The Torre de Televisão, JK Memorial and Parque Sara Kubitschek

The **Torre de Televisão** (TV Tower) on Eixo Monumental is an obvious city landmark and easily reached on foot or by bus (#131 from the *rodoviária*). The 218-metre-high tower's viewing platform (Tues–Sun 9am–9pm) is a great place from which to put Brasília into perspective, and there is no better place to watch the sunset, though frustratingly, there is no bar to watch it from. Lower down, above its weird concrete supports, is the **Museu Nacional das Gemas** (Tues–Fri 3–8.30pm, Sat & Sun 10.30am–6.30pm; $1), which is actually little more than a glorified and quite expensive gem shop. At the weekend the tower is also popular for its craft market, held around the base – a good place to pick up cheap clothes.

Further up the Eixo is the famous **Juscelino Kubitschek (JK) Memorial** (Tues–Sun 9am–5.45pm, $2 entrance charge), best reached by one of the shoals of buses heading up the Eixo as it's too far to walk. Here, a rather Soviet-like statue of Brasília's founder stands inside an enormous question mark, pointing down the Eixo towards the heart of government, while more interesting is the museum below, which reverently reproduces JK's library and study. The man himself lies in state in a black marble sarcophagus, backlit by an extraordinary combination of purple, violet and orange lights – the only thing missing is a sound system piping in "The Age of Aquarius". All around is a fascinating display of personal mementoes of JK's career and the founding and construction of the city, including photos and video clips of his funeral and dedication of the Memorial – in turning out in their hundreds of thousands in his honour, despite the desire of the military dictatorship to keep the event low key, the population of the Distrito Federal made the first important anti-military demonstration, one of the reasons for the subsequent slow relaxing of the military's grip on power.

A short walk from Setor Hoteleiro Sul, taking up one entire side of the Eixo, is the enormous **Parque Sara Kubitschek**, named after JK's wife (bus #152 from the *rodoviária* passes by) – a massive mosaic of playgrounds, jogging tracks, bars and restaurants, picnic grounds, artificial lakes, parklands and woods. If you want to walk or jog in Brasília, this is the place to do it. The southern entrance, a block away from the hotel sector, is where many of the attractions are concentrated, including an enjoyably tacky but perfectly safe (despite appearances) **funfair** that will appeal to young children, and a place to hire *pedalôs* – adult-sized tricycles that are harder work than they look, but great fun nonetheless. The best time to visit is Sunday morning, when the locals turn out en masse, jogging, working out, sunbathing, reading the paper and the like, while dozens of kiosks and streetsellers tout everything from iced green coconuts to a shiatsu massage.

The Memorial dos Povos Indígenas

Across the road from the JK Memorial is another Niemeyer building, the white and curving **Memorial dos Povos Indígenas** (Tues–Fri 10am–4pm), which houses one of the best collections of **indigenous art** in Brazil, much of it from the *planalto* itself and produced by the indigenous groups who inhabit the headwaters of the Xingú river. Highlights are the extraordinary ceramic pots of the Warao, the Xingú's ceramic specialists, beautifully adorned with figures of birds and animals, and vivid, delicate featherwork. The rotating exhibits and regular travelling shows are uniformly fascinating, but the building alone is worth the visit; the gallery is set in a long, downward curve around a circular courtyard, the smoked glass set against Niemeyer's trademark brilliant white exterior. At the lower end is a **café**, virtually never open but where Indians up from the Xingú often leave artwork for the museum staff to sell for them; bargaining for these good-quality and reasonably priced items would be churlish.

Run by the chronically hard-up state government, the museum keeps opening hours that are theoretical rather than real. If you arrive on the weekend or on Monday, and find the main entrance at the top of the ramp shut, slip down to the large metal door at ground level, to the right of the ramp, and bang hard; either a security guard or one of the museum staff will let you in. It's definitely worth making the effort.

Indigenous craft market

One of Brasília's least known but by far most interesting market of Indian *artesanato* is the impromptu **indigenous craft market** that has grown up in the patio of the headquarters of FUNAI, the federal Indian agency, in the Setor de Rádio e Televisão Sul. The market, in its own small way, is the perfect symbol of what has changed in the relationship between Brazil's Indians and the federal government in recent years. Time was when FUNAI controlled all the marketing of indigenous art, via its own chain of crafts shops, one of which you can still find inside FUNAI's entrance hall if you venture in. But too much of the revenue stayed with FUNAI rather than the producers, and they have now taken matters into their own hands; every weekday, around 9am, groups of indigenous people start setting out their wares on the patio, mainly basketware and ceramics but much more besides, most of it pretty good quality and always interesting to check out. The bulk of it comes from the Xingú, the far northeast of the Planalto, and the closest sizeable indigenous area to Brasília. But since Indians come to FUNAI from all over to sort out their many problems, and usually bring whatever they can stuff into a bag or two to sell and make a little money on the side, the anthropologically minded can find people and *artesanato* from all over Brazil, especially the Amazon. This is one of the rare places where the shopper often needs to pay more than asked; many sellers have only vague notions of market values and ask ridiculously low prices, $2 or $3 for items that are patently worth far more. The sellers are poor, not sharp middlemen; shop responsibly.

The market is a short walk from the main entrance to the Parque Sara Kubitschek, or from Setor Hoteleiro Sul along W3; go past the Pátio Brasil mall, turn right after the Assis Chateaubriand building, helpfully identified by enormous letters on its side, and the market is one block up on the other side of the road, next door to the Dom Bosco school.

Further out: the asas, Jardim Botânico and Parque Nacional de Brasília

The residential parts of Brasília are rarely thought of as a destination for visitors, but the older areas are by far the best place for a stroll during the day. The parks and gardens between the blocks are extremely well designed, and even at the hottest times of year you can walk for hundreds of yards in certain areas without leaving the shade. The oldest *superquadras* are all in Asa Sul; 108 Sul was the first to be completed in the whole city, designed as a showpiece to make the city tolerable for those bureaucrats moving here from Rio (a miserable failure that eventually improved as the trees grew). The adjacent blocks from 107 down to 104 were all built shortly after and make for a great **urban walk** – take a bus or walk up W3 Sul, get off at the 508 block, walk two blocks down, and then start strolling towards the centre. There are plenty of *comercials* along the way if you want to make a pit stop.

For a taste of the *cerrado* before heading deeper into the Planalto, or just a temporary break from the city, consider venturing to the **Jardim Botânico**, at the far end of Asa Norte, and the **Parque Nacional de Brasília**, across the striking JK Bridge over Lago Paranoá in Lago Sul. Both were created in the early 1960s to preserve large green spaces within easy reach of the city – it seemed superfluous then, but the pace of development has been so fast that there would be very little native *cerrado* anywhere near the ciy without them. The botanical garden, at Setor de Mansões Dom Bosco in Lago Sul (Tues–Sun 9am–5pm; $2

The national park is an $8 **taxi ride** from the center, but you have to arrange a rendezvous to return, since very few unoccupied taxis pass by – the **bus** is a better bet, but not easy. Astonishingly, there is no bus stop at the park entrance: the closest you can get here is by picking up the W3 Norte Circular on W3 and asking the driver to drop you off as it reaches the end of W3 and turns: look hard and you can see the park entrance on the other side of the highway.

This is the one place where it is actually easier to get a **perueiro**, one of the illegal but ubiquitous and highly organised white minibuses that shadow the bus routes. Look for *perueiro* lines #82 and #84, with an orange stripe on the side: the easiest place to catch them is the car park above the *rodoviária*, opposite the Conjunto Nacional – they wait until they fill up and then go, but you'll have to tell the driver to let you off near the park entrance.

taxi around $8 from centre; bus route #147 from *rodoviária*, stands 8 & 9 at Platform A), is a calm and well-organized retreat where you can experience the flora and fauna of the *cerrado* at first hand. There's an information centre, a large display of medicinal plants of the region, a herb garden, ecological trails and over forty square kilometres of nature reserve with an extensive network of trails. It's good hiking, but make sure you bring a hat and water.

Brasília's very own **national park** (daily 8am–4pm; admission $1), at the far end of Asa Norte, is the only area of native vegetation large enough around Brasília to support proper wildlife populations. During the week, you will have the place largely to yourself, and while the park itself is enormous, visitors are restricted to its southern corner, where the main attractions are two very large **swimming holes**, Piscina Velha and Piscina Nova, both a short, well-signposted walk from either of the two entrances, and built around a stream, preserving the natural flow of the water. When there is nobody there, this is a lovely spot – especially for a picnic. You're also likely to spot capuchin monkeys leaping acrobatically through the trees, though they have become used to scavenging picnic remains, so take care not to leave food lying around, and be sure to pack plastic bags away as the monkeys regularly choke on them.

Although the pool area gets very crowded at weekends, virtually everyone sticks to the water, so if you want space and some solitude, head up the slope to a small fenced trail through a section of gallery forest – ideal for the kids – and continue up the hill until you come up onto open *cerrado* savanna and another much longer trail, a four-mile circuit called the **Água Cristal** (crystal water trail), which lives up to its name, taking you through a number of clearwater streams before dumping you back more or less where you started. The views are beautiful, although it is frustrating that you can't hike into them.

Eating, nightlife and entertainment

One of the best things about Brasília is the wide variety of **bars and restaurants**; in fact, a combination of the government, the university and diplomats supports one of the densest concentrations of good restaurants in the country. *Candangos* eat late, hanging around in bars until at least 10pm before heading off to eat. Moreover, bars and restaurants aren't always easily distinguishable – a place that looks and feels like a bar can sometimes serve substantial meals, so the listings are somewhat arbitrary.

With some deserving exceptions, the following concentrates on the best places within easy reach of the hotel sectors. Prices are more than reasonable; unless noted, a full meal with drinks averages around $12 per head, often less. Cheaper food can be found in the street markets and stalls scattered around the *rodoviária*, Conjunto Nacional, and in the large Pátio Brasil shopping centre next to the Setor Hoteleiro Sul, dominated by *comida por kilo* places catering to lunching office workers. If you're walking, you should have no problems with safety around most places in Asa Norte and Asa Sul, but W3 and the deserted central area should be walked around with caution at night. Most restaurants close on Monday night rather than Sunday.

Restaurants

A good place to start, especially on a weekend night, is **comercial 404/405 Sul**; some *comercials* specialise and this one is known locally as *Restaurantelândia*, both sides are lined with at least a dozen different national cuisines from four continents, and are heaving with people at weekends. Although better food is to be had elsewhere, this is a good place to barhop and then have a range of eating options to choose from. Recommended places are all in the numbered *comercial*, unless otherwise indicated.

A Tribu 105 Norte. Best vegetarian food in the city, imaginative and full of flavour. Offers a lunchtime buffet, and open at night too.

Acarajé da Rosa 204 Sul. Cheap, unpretentious Bahian food, especially pleasant at night in the dry season, when you can sit outside beneath the trees.

Belini 113 Sul. Everything you need under one roof – excellent deli, good expresso bar, and classy but still reasonably priced restaurant upstairs.

Camarão e Cia. 206 Sul. Good seafood buffet at lunchtime, followed by Bahian food at night.

Carpe Diem 104 Sul. Deservedly the best-known bar/restaurant in town: great atmosphere, renowned politico hangout and very reasonably priced. Famous among locals for the best salad bar and lunch buffet in the city (you pick the salad ingredients, they whip it up for you) and the Saturday *feijoada*; food and drinks served practically 24/7, apart from a few hours in the morning.

Crepe au Chocolat 109 Norte and 210 Sul. Eat elsewhere, head here for dessert and be stretchered home – not for the faint of heart.

Don Durica 201 Norte. Serving an excellent lunch and evening buffet of traditional, quite heavy Brazilian food, such as stewed rabbit and various dishes of lamb, pork and sucking pig. If you want something lighter, try the extremely tasty soup buffet.

Espettus Setor Hoteleiro Sul. Best option if you're staying in one of the nearby hotels and don't feel like going far – good, varied *churrascaria*, infinitely preferable to any of the hotel restaurants.

Feitiço Mineiro 306 Norte. Even without the live music at weekends (see opposite), this spot is worth patronising for the food alone; a buffet of *comida mineira* (Minas Gerais food), heavy on the pork, bean sauce and sausages, prepared the traditional way on a wood-fired stove. Open for dinner only.

Fratello 103 Sul. Best pizza in town: wood-fired kiln and original ingredients. Try the eponymous Fratello, based on sweet pickled aubergine.

Fritz 404 Sul. Brazilian waiters serve very German food – stodge heaven and cheap.

Ichiban 405 Sul. Good sushi, sashimi and whatever other Japanese food you fancy; divided into western and Japanese seating sections, the latter can be hard on the knees if you're not used to it.

Kosui Academia de Tênis, Setor dos Clubes Sul – see under "Cinema", p.494, for directions). Arguably the best Japanese restaurant in the city but certainly the best location of any of them, next to the Academia's art-cinema complex, if you want to do dinner and a film. Good Italian and seafood restaurants are also part of the complex.

Nippon 403 Sul. A good, reasonably priced Japanese place, similar to Ichiban above.

Patu Anú Setor dos Mansões Lago Norte (SMLN), ML12, Conjunto 1, Casa 7l, near the Paranoá dam ℡1/369-2788 or 922-8930. The very best of Brazilian cuisine, served in a fantastic lakeside location. The menu is exclusively game – wild boar, alligator, *capivara* (the largest rodent in the world, which actually tastes great) and more, cooked with mouthwatering sauces, and regional fruits and vegetables. Dinner and drinks cost about $40 a head, plus $25 each way for the taxi. Get a taxi via your hotel and make sure you show this address to the driver before you set out. Reservations are a good idea (English spoken), and the restaurant will get you a cab for the return trip.

Porcão Pier 21 Shopping Centre, Asa Sul. A short
taxi ride from the centre, this spot ("big pig" in
Portuguese) certainly lives up to its name as the
largest and most varied *churrascaria* in Brasília,
and is strictly for carnivores. Drinks are overpriced, so concentrate on the food.

Sabor do Brasil 302 Sul. On a strict budget, this
place offers the best meal in town – for around $5
a head. A soup buffet with trimmings, very traditional Brazilian fare, good vegetarian options but
soups for carnivores too. Open for lunch and at
night. Good place to line the stomach before heading out for a night on the town, or to sober up

coming back from one.

Taverna di Giorgio 216 Norte. Tucked away
behind Bloco A but worth the trip for the very
cheap home-made pasta served with delicious
sauces by the friendly proprietor and his large collection of Brazilian friends. Impromptu live music
drifting upwards from the bar below on Saturday
nights is an occasional bonus.

Universal Diner 210 Sul. Take your pick: the lively, crowded and loud bar downstairs or the very
good restaurant upstairs, serving Brazilian and
international food.

Bars and cafés

Even discounting the hotel bars – and there are plenty of those – there's a good
selection of **places to drink**, though the scene as a whole is nothing like as
lively as Rio.

Armazém do Ferreira 202 Norte. Noted politico
hangout, best late at night when it gets very
crowded. The tables outside are very pleasant,
huddled under trees; the similar *Café do Brasil*
next door is also good.

Bar Beirute 109 Sul. Often very lively and packed
at night with a young crowd, with Lebanese food
that's no more than OK but cheap, plus a playground for kids.

Bar Brasília 506 Sul. Successful recreation of an
old-style Brazilian bar, complete with surly waiters;
as a bar very good, but the view out across a
carpark leaves something to be desired.

Café Cassis 214 Sul. Specialises in weekend
brunches for homesick Americans – they make
bagels for the American embassy – but also open
in the evening and weekday lunchtime; very
civilised, cheaper than it looks and feels.

Café com Letras 204 Sul. Pleasant café above a
good bookshop, with some English titles, open into
the small hours. The veranda is a good spot to
watch the students and young professional crowd.

Daniel Briand 104 Norte; side of Bloco A.
Essential, highly recommended spot, especially for
a late breakfast on weekends or afternoon tea any
day. French-owned patisserie and teahouse serving the best quiche and cakes in town. There's
nowhere better for coffee and reading; the only
problem is early and rigidly enforced closing at
10pm – both un-French and un-Brazilian.

Frei Caneca Entrequadra 110/111 Sul. Large beer
hall that only really gets going late at night, with
good atmosphere and live music every weekend.

Libanus 206 Sul. Perennially crowded spot serving up excellent-value, hearty Lebanese food; the
playground makes it a good place for families in
the afternoons, but turns into a young and humming scene at night.

Marujo 105 Sul. Constantly crowded bar, where
despite the terrible food, the outdoor tables under
trees make it pleasant enough as a hangout.

Torteria di Lorenza 107 Norte, 302 Sul.
Inexpensive place for gooey, tempting cakes,
expresso coffee and savouries.

Live music

Brasília is a good place to catch live music. Although not what it was – displaced by techno and house like everywhere else – the city had a lively rock
scene in the 1990s: one local band, **Legião Urbana**, achieved megastardom
and another, **Os Raimundos**, were well respected. The main place to catch
local and visiting bands is *Gate's Pub* (403 Sul), much bigger than it looks from
the outside, with a series of rooms and small stages – resembling in a weird way
a British pubrock venue. Thursday nights are particularly lively. Student hangout *Frei Caneca Draft*, in the Brasília Shopping mall, also often has local bands
on weekend nights. *Café Cancún* in the Liberty Mall, Setor Comercial Norte,
transcends its unpromising setting late on Friday and Saturday nights with live
music and great DJs, Brazilian rhythms mixed with *salsa*.

You can see more traditional first-class Brazilian music live at *Feitiço Mineiro*
(see above under "Restaurants"), and, especially, at the *Clube do Choro* (central

strip of the Eixo Monumental, next to the convention center – all the taxi drivers know it). Ask at your hotel or check the listings, but it is usually open at night from Thursday to Saturday, with live music on Thursday and Friday, turning into a *gafieira* (dance-hall), on Saturday night, with its own house band and older, intimidatingly good dancers. On Thursday and Friday, chairs and tables are set in front of the small stage, and the house specialises in *choro*, the oldest and arguably most beautiful of Brazilian musical genres, played here by masters young and old to an appreciative, knowledgeable audience. If you've never been in a crowd brought to its feet by a fast mandolin solo, you haven't lived. This is as good a club venue as you'll find anywhere in the country.

Visiting megastars, Brazilian and otherwise, will play either the Teatro Nacional or, more likely these days, the plush *Americel Hall* in the Clube de Tênis, Setor dos Clubes Sul.

Cinema

Brasília is an excellent place to go to the cinema, with a large and appreciative audience for good films. The **Clube de Tênis** hosts the annual international film festival in October and also houses the Academia, probably the best cinema complex between São Paulo and Mexico City, with twelve screens of exclusively arthouse films to choose from year-round, not to mention several restaurants and a large bar. If you want commercial films, head for the malls. Worthy of special mention is Cine Brasília, a splendid example of early 1960s kitsch at Entrequadra 106/107 Sul that has a huge screen. Run by the Ministry of Culture, the cinema is free to ignore commercial considerations completely and show the latest Iranian masterpiece, or classics of European and American cinema history.

Listings

Airlines Mostly found around the *Hotel Nacional* in various agents' shops. The main Brazilian companies are Nordeste, airport ☎61/365-1022; TAM, SHS 1, Galeria Hotel Nacional 61 ☎61/223-5168, and at the airport ☎61/365-1000; Varig/Cruzeiro, ground floor of the Conjunto Empresarial Varig building opposite Brasília Shopping mall ☎61/329-1169, and at the airport ☎61/364-9583, 24-hour reservations, English spoken on ☎0800-99-7000; and VASP, SHS 1, Galeria Hotel Nacional 53/54 ☎61/2225-5915. Cheap newcomer Gol has no agencies but has phone lines and encourages on-line bookings ☎300-789-2121, ⓦwww.voegol.com.br. Among overseas airlines are Air France, SHS 1, Galeria Hotel Nacional 39/40 ☎61/223-4152, ⓕ223-2299; Alitalia, SHS, Galeria Hotel Nacional, Loja 36/37 ☎61/321-5266, ⓕ223-2498; British Airways, SHS, Galeria Hotel Nacional, Loja 18 ☎61/226-4164, ⓕ321-9016; KLM, SHS 1, Galeria Hotel Nacional 51 ☎61/321-3636 or 225-5915; Lan Chile, SCS, Q8, Bloco B-60, Ed. Venâcio ☎61/226-0318; Lufthansa, SHS 1, Galeria Hotel Nacional, Loja 1 ☎61/223-5002 or 233-8202.

Airport enquiries ☎61/365-1941, 365-1024, 365-1224 or 365-1947.
ATMs International bankcards are accepted at Banco do Brasil and HSBC at the airport; Citibank at the Setor Bancário Sul opposite the Pátio Brasil mall, with another Citibank ATM tucked away at the Blockbuster video in 506 Norte; HSBC at 502 Sul, on W3; BankBoston next door to Citibank at Setor BancárioSul, and most central Bancos do Brasil.
Books and newspapers English-language papers, magazines and books at Sodiler, ground floor of the Conjunto Nacional, Millenium Revistas at 303 Sul, and both bookshops at the airport.
Car rental The usual suspects all line the airport road: Avis ☎61/365-2991, Localiza ☎0800-992000, Hertz ☎61/365-4747, Unidas ☎0800121 121. Avoid paying a hefty surcharge at the airport by heading into town by taxi and renting from there; highly recommended is Via Rent-A-Car ☎61/322-3181 or 9985-4717, SHS Q6 Cj. A, Bloco F, Loja 50, or, more comprehensively, the side of the *Hotel Melia*.

Consulates For the Setor de Embaixadas Sul (SES), take a bus to Av. das Nações, or just walk. Argentina, SHIS QI 01, Cj. 01, Cs. 19 ☏61/365-3000; Australia, SHIS CI 9, Cj. 16, Cs 1 ☏61/248-5569; Bolivia, SHIS QL 10, Cj. 1, Cs. 6 ☏61/364-3362; Canada, SES Av. das Nações 803, Lote 16, sala 130 ☏61/321-2171; Colombia, SES Av. das Nações 803, Lote 10 ☏61/226-8997; Ecuador, SHIS Q1 11, Cj. 09, Cs. 24 ☏61/248-5560; Paraguay, SES Av. das Nações 811, Lote 42 ☏61/242-3732; Peru, SES Av. das Nações 811, Lote 43 ☏61/242-9435; UK, SES Av. das Nações 801 ☏61/225-2710; US, SES Av. das Nações 801, Lote 3 ☏61/321-7272; Venezuela, SES Av. das Nações 803, Lote 13 ☏61/223-9325.

Driving Brasília is blanketed by radar controls. If you're caught jumping a light or speeding in a hired car, the fine will be taken off your credit card.

Emergencies Medical ☏192; police ☏197; fire brigade ☏193.

Exchange Cash and travellers' cheques are accepted at Banco do Brasil, SBS, Edifício Sede 1, Terreo (Mon–Fri 10am–5pm). Reasonable rates with no commission apply at the câmbio in the Hotel Nacional (Mon–Fri 9am–6pm).

Health matters Dr C. Menecucci, Centro Medico, Av. W3 Sul 716, Bloco D, sala 16, speaks good English. For quick blood tests, the Clínica SOS Check-Up de Brasília, SHIS 9, Bloco E, Loja 312 ☏61/248-4093, at the Centro Clínico do Lago, is efficient. Hospitals are: Da Base do Distrito Federal, SMHS 101 ☏61/325-5050; and Santa Lúcia, SHLS 716, Bloco C ☏61/245-3344.

Post office Brasília's main post office (Mon–Sat 9am–6pm) is the small, white building in the open grassy space behind the Hotel Nacional.

Shopping You can buy almost anything in the Conjuntos de Diversões or Brasília Shopping (see p.488). For artesanato and other craft goods, there's a good market underneath the TV Tower on Saturdays, Sundays and most public holidays; and see p.490. A smaller market next to the cathedral sells an incredible range of dried and dyed flowers. For regional craft specialities try the Galeria dos Estados, in the subway connecting the Setor Bancário Sul with Setor Comercial Sul. Great-value gems are available from Pedras Nativas, Conjunto Venâncio 2000, Terreo. For incense, tiger balm, tie-dye wraps and the like, try the Mercado Alternativo in the Centro Cultural Le Corbusier, at Centro Comercial Gilberto Salomão. For Kodak film go to Fujioka, and for Fuji film go to Fujifilm, both located at the front of the southern conjunto.

Taxis Cidade ☏61/321-8181, Coobras ☏61/224-1000, Radiotaxi ☏61/325-3030.

Travel and tour companies For local tours and air tickets try Buriti, CLS 402, Bloco A, Loja 27 ☏61/225-2686, ℱ226-1814; Presmic, SHS 1, Galeria Hotel Nacional 33/34 ☏61/225-5515, ℱ321-1191; and Power Turismo, SHS 1, Galeria Hotel Nacional 48 ☏61/332-6699, ℱ322-5658.

Around Brasília

Although it is sometimes difficult to imagine in the concrete heart of Brasília, the city is at the centre of some spectacular natural scenery that is easily accessible as day-trips from the capital. Here we've concentrated on straight day-trips or places where an overnight stay is possible but not really worthwhile; other destinations a little further out, like **Pirenópolis** and **Chapada dos Veadeiros**, where you can really get to grips with the cerrado rather than get a taste of it, are dealt with separately.

Lago Paranoá

Covering forty square kilometres, **Lago Paranoá** is a man-made recreation area, created by the diversion of three rivers to humidify the dry climate. Despite suffering from an algae problem, it's the scene of water sports, clubhouses and the **Ermida Dom Bosco**. This small conical hermitage, sitting alone on the edge of the lake, around 30km from the downtown rodoviária, offers fine views over the lake towards the Palácio da Alvorada, while below the nearby Paranoá dam there are amazing waterfalls during the heavy summer rains. **Buses** from the rodoviária go right around the lake in a couple of hours: #123 and #125 cover the southern half, finishing up in a shanty settlement after crossing the main dam; for the northern end of the lake, take buses #136-1 or #136-2 "Clube do Congresso".

Exploring the cerrado

If you don't have the few days necessary to go deep into the heart of *cerrado* country in the national parks (see p.509 & p.511), you can still get a sense of the wildness further north as a day trip from Brasília. It only takes a short drive from the city to drop behind a ridge to find yourself in another world of dirt roads, small villages, hills and rivers. The countryside around Brasília is dotted with walks, waterfalls, swimholes and cave systems, and has spawned a local ecotourism industry. Most of the natural attractions are difficult to get to, however: many of the best destinations, like the spectacular **Poço Azul waterfall** or the forested gorge and cave systems of **Buraco de Araras** aren't linked by roads or public transport, and part of their attraction is that they have to be hiked to over trails. Fortunately, you have the option of using local guides, and a couple of city tour operators also run specialised day trips aimed at the eco-tourism market, a wonderful option if you want to combine the comforts of staying in town with hiking the *cerrado* during the day. Expect to pay around $70 a day, which can work out to be cheap for groups, and includes everything except food and drink. Recommended English-speaking outfits and guides are Gilmar at Soul Hard Ecoturismo (☎61/944-3711), Ricardo at Be Hard Tribo Esporte (☎61/340-4816) and Leonardo at Ibiti Ecoturismo (☎61/340-6990 and 447-4523).

At all times of year the sun is hot and the altitude means you will burn quickly and imperceptibly, so a hat and lashings of sunscreen are essential. You will be able to cool off at least with regular dips in natural swimholes along the way, one of the joys of walking the cerrado. Stout sandals are the best footwear, allowing you to negotiate the rocky, uneven beds of the streams and swimholes. Be aware that flash floods are a danger in gorges during the rainy season, even when the sun is shining: rain can be falling unseen in headwaters – another reason for making sure you go with a guide.

Cristalina, Formosa and the Itiquira waterfall

From Brasília, an easy day trip involves taking one of the frequent buses from the *rodoferroviária* to the town of **CRISTALINA**, a two-hour ride south of Brasília into the Goiás plateau. Indeed, the journey itself is one of the main reasons to go, as you'll pass through the distinctive rolling hills of the Planalto along the BR-040 towards Belo Horizonte. Prospectors who came here looking for gold in the early eighteenth century came across a large quantity of rock crystal; the European market opened up over a century later, and today Cristalina is an attractive, rustic town, based around the mining, cutting, polishing and marketing of semi-precious stones. Quartz crystals and Brazilian amethyst can also be bought here at very reasonable prices, mostly from enormous warehouses on the edge of town that pull in passing motorists. If you want to stay, *Hotel Attie*, Praça José Damian 34 (☎61/612-1252; ❷), and *Hotel Goyá*, Rua da Saudade 41 (☎61/612-1301; ❷), are both good value. The town boasts an excellent *churrasco* restaurant, Churrascaria Rodeio, Rua 7 de Setembro 1237, where the Sunday lunch alone is worth the trip.

If you only have time for one day trip, though, your best bet is to take the two-hour bus ride to the town of **FORMOSA**, not so much for the place itself, pleasant though it is, as for the stunning waterfall and park of **Salto de Itiquira**, for which Formosa is the jumping-off point. The park, which is 25 miles away, is well signposted if you are in a rented car, but haggling with a local taxi driver at the bus station should get you a return trip for around $25. It's worth it: the drive is beautiful, with the spectacular 300-foot waterfall visible from miles away as a white line against the towering cliffs of the Serra Formosa. Surrounding the waterfall is a municipal park (admission $2), well laid out with a series of swimholes that make it a great place to spend the day. The most spectacular of all is at the very top of the only path, where the waterfall comes plunging down. Although there is a snack bar at the carpark, by far the best place to eat is the *Dom Fernando* restaurant, with an excellent buffet of local food, and freshly grilled meats to order. It is located in splendid isolation at km 6 on the road to the waterfall, but only open weekends and holidays – otherwise there's a restaurant to the right of the park entrance. As ever, the park is at its best during the week, when you will probably have it to yourself.

The states of Goiás and Tocantins

Beyond the city and Federal District of Brasília, the hill-studded, surprisingly green *cerrado* of **Goiás state** extends towards another planned city, **Goiânia**, and the historic old towns of **Pirenópolis** and **Goiás Velho**, the latter in particular worth going out of your way for. Although gold mining started there in a small way during the seventeenth century, the first genuine settlement didn't appear until 1725. These days agriculture is the main activity: cattle, pigs, rice and maize are important but it is soya that is booming, driving the conversion of the dwindling remnants of *cerrado* into enormous farms. The small rural towns are all increasingly prosperous as a result, the state road system is excellent by Brazilian standards, and one can imagine most of Goiás looking like the interior of São Paulo a generation from now: the main cities of **Goiânia** and **Anápolis**, with their rising affluence and acres of new high-rises, already look very like the cities of the *paulista* interior – and are about as interesting to visit, which is not very.

In the north of Goiás is the heart of the Planalto, a jumble of cliffs, spectacular valleys and mountain ranges in and around the national park of **Chapada dos Veadeiros**, excellent for hiking and a thoroughly worthwhile excursion from Brasília, although you'll need a few days to do it justice. In the south, the thermal springs of **Caldas Novas** and **Rio Quente** bubble up into giant hotel complexes, while over on the western border with Mato Grosso, the **Emas National Park** has less spectacular landscapes compared to Chapada dos Veadeiros but is wilder, a little more inaccessible (although still easily reached from Brasília), and a better place to see wildlife, in particular the large American rhea.

The mighty Rio Araguaia (which means Macaw River in Tupi Indian language), with its many beautiful sandy beaches, forms the 1200-kilometre-long western frontier of both Goiás and Tocantins states. The latter, created for political rather than geographic or economic reasons in 1989, contains the huge river island, **Ilha do Bananal**, and its **National Park of Araguaia**. The main and central section (BR-153) of the 2000-kilometre-long highway from Goiânia and Brasília to Belém also runs through Tocantins. The only town of any significance is **Araguaína**, a flyblown settlement in the middle of a largely deforested savanna.

Goiânia

The other modern, planned city in central Brazil, **GOIÂNIA** was founded in 1933, becoming the state capital four years later. Over a million strong, cheaper than Brasília, with some good hotels and only 209km from the federal capital, the city is a good stopping-off point, since it is well connected by road to most other Brazilian cities. Goiânia earns its living as a market centre for the surrounding agricultural region, which specializes in rice and soya, and while it lacks the futuristic style of Brasília it makes up for it with a more genuine heartbeat and, with its less arid climate, a lusher, greener environment.

Arrival, information and accommodation

Both the **rodoviária** (☎62/224-8466) and Santa Genoveva **airport** (☎62/207-6411 or 207-1288) lie in the northern sectors of town. The *rodoviária* is around twenty minutes by foot from Setor Central along Avenida Goiás, or a short ride by local bus. The airport is linked to the centre, 6km away, by bus (#190 or #162 "Circular Aeroporto"); a taxi to most central hotels will cost around $8. To catch local buses in town, there are main stops on Avenida Araguaia just south of Rua 4, and along Avenida Goiás opposite *Hotel Paissandu*. There's a **tourist information** booth (daily 8am–6pm; ☎62/281-2111) at the airport, which has free maps, though better maps ($1.50) can be bought from the newsagent opposite. In the centre, the regional tourist authority, SEBRAE, has an office on Rua 30 at the Centro de Convenções (☎62/217-2055, ⓦ www.goiania.net).

The wide central streets are almost handsome in their blending of pre-war Continental-style grandeur with modernist concrete and glass, skyscraping offices and homes for the rapidly growing middle-class population of the city. The main node of the concentric city plan is the Centro Cívico and Praça Dr Pedro Ludovico, at the head of the massive Avenida Goiás, whose broad and leafy pavement extends all the way down its middle between both directions of busy traffic. The city is divided into several sectors, the most important being the Setor Central, Setor Oeste and Setor Universitário, and many of the streets have numbers rather than names.

Accommodation

Goiânia has a wide range of **hotels**, wider, in fact, than Brasília. As well as giving you a greater choice of accommodation, this also means that you're more likely to be able to negotiate discounts – many of the larger hotels, as a matter of course, discount their prices out of season by 20–40 percent.

Hotel América Rua 74, #262, Centro ☎62/223-2864. Clean and family-run hotel, a little way out from the centre, but its *quartos* are probably the cheapest rooms in town. ❶

Hotel Araguaia Av. Araguaia 664, Centro ☎ & ⓕ62/224-1830. Overlooking the little Praça Antônio Lisita, this hotel has an impressive lobby, which the rooms conspicuously fail to live up to. Good value only with a discount. ❺

Augustus Hotel Av. Araguaia 702, Centro ☎62/224-1022, ⓕ224-1410. Also on the *praça* and next to the *Araguaia*, this hotel is much

Map labels:

▲ Rodoviária

► The Airport

PR SANTOS DUMONT

Estádio Pedro Ludovico

SETOR AEROPORTO

Parque Mutirama

Banco do Brasil

SETOR CENTRAL

Convention Centre

Museu de Arte Contemporanea

Pro Brazilian (Supermarket)

Teatro Goiânia

Varig

AVENIDA ANHANGUERA

Museu de Arte

Bosque dos Buritis

SETOR OESTE

SETOR UNIVERSITÁRIO

AVENIDA UNIVERSITÁRIA

CENTRO CÍVICO

Galeria Frei Confaloni

Museu Zoroastro Artiaga

PRAÇA TAMANDARÉ

AV ASSIS CHATEAUBRIAND

AVENIDA KENNEDY

Zoo

N

GOIÂNIA

0   400 m

► Museu Etnografico

▼ Setor Sul

ACCOMMODATION

Augustus Hotel	4
Castro's Park Hotel	11
Hotel América	1
Hotel Araguaia	5
Hotel Bandeirantes	7
Hotel Karajás	10
Hotel Paissandu	2
Hotel Presidente	6
Nasser's Hotel	9
Plaza Inn Suitotel	3
Pousada Ginza	12
Príncipe Hotel	8

---

flashier, with good rooms – though a little dark – plus a pool and sauna. ❻

Hotel Bandeirantes Av. Anhangüera 3278, Centro ☎ & ℱ 62/224-0066. Flashy and air-conditioned but with no pool, however; it's particularly worth bargaining over room prices here. ❻

Castro's Park Hotel Av. República do Líbano 1520, Setor Oeste ☎ 62/223-7766, ℱ 225-7070, ⓦ www.castrospark.com.br. Luxurious hotel with immaculate service, as well as swimming pools and a superb restaurant. Outside holiday times, it's a good place to try for discounted rooms. ❻

Pousada Ginza Av. Professor Alfredo de Castro 179, Setor Oeste ☎ 62/223-5118, ℱ 224-4196. A bland and fairly basic place, but it's friendly, clean and well located close to the centre, not far from Praça Tamandaré. Excellent value. ❸

Hotel Karajás Rua 3, #860, Centro ☎ 62/224-9666, ℱ 229-115. Very comfortable 20-storey block with good-sized rooms. Same price for singles, however. ❺

Nasser's Hotel Av. Araguaia 640 ☎ 62/212-2317, ℱ 212-7262. A run-down place in the busier and older part of town. Rooms are adequate, though,

with *frigobar* and air-conditioning. ❹
Hotel Paissandu Av. Goiás 1290, Centro (no phone). Situated beyond the heart of the city, though within walking distance of it, this hotel is good value, if a touch basic, with TVs in all rooms, and singles being considerably cheaper than doubles. ❸
Plaza Inn Suitotel Rua 20, #930, corner of Praça Antônio Lisita ☎62/212-8500, ⓕ212-7911. With smooth service, superb rooms (all with en-suite lounges), and a pleasant ground-floor restaurant,

by far the best value in town. The hotel offers a 30 percent discount out of season. ❻
Hotel Presidente Av. Anhangüera 5646, Centro ☎62/224-0500, ⓕ224-0551. Once a great budget option, now mid-range veering on luxury, with modern and clean rooms, and great breakfasts. ❺
Príncipe Hotel Av. Anhangüera 2936, Centro ☎62/224-0085 or 224-0962, ⓕ224-2831. Modern place with rather small rooms, where the cheaper *quartos* come with shared bathrooms. ❷–❸

The City

One of the first things visitors note when they arrive in Goiânia is the size of the place, its modern skyline dominating the horizon for some time before you reach the city's limits. The city ranks among Brazil's ten biggest, created to function as a regional agricultural and livestock market centre as gold has become less important in Goiás. Like several cities throughout South America it has a spring-like climate year-round, of which it takes good advantage through its extensive network of established green spaces – mainly large *praças*, public parks and sports grounds. Pleasant enough in its own right, Goiânia lacks any sights of outstanding interest or stunning architectural gems, though the **Complexo Memorial do Cerrado Pe Pereira** makes for an interesting out-of-town trip.

The Bosque dos Buritis and the city museums

Just two blocks due west of the Centro Cívico, the woods of the **Bosque dos Buritis** (daily 9am–6pm) spread over 140,000 square metres and contain a huge water-jet fountain as well as the free and reasonably interesting **Museu de Arte**, Rua 1, #605, Sector Oeste (Tues–Sun 8am–6pm), which has paintings of the city and stone sculptures on display. For a better selection of both Brazilian and international paintings with more frequently changing exhibits, try the **Museu de Arte Contemporânea**, lost in the concrete depths of the city's business heart in the Parthenon Centre, Rua 4, #515 (Tues–Fri 8am–6pm). Over in Praça Cívica, the **Galeria Frei Confaloni** is a small gallery displaying contemporary works by mainly local artists. Entry is free but the door is difficult to find around the back of the Centro Cultural building. Just a few yards away, the **Museu Zoroastro Artiaga**, Praça Cívica 13 (Tues–Fri 9am–5pm, Sat, Sun & holidays 9am–noon & 2–4pm), exhibits mainly artifacts, crafts and art from the region, but also houses roaming exhibitions, sometimes of ethnographic interest.

Goiânia's other museums include, in the east of the downtown area, the anthropological museum, the **Museu Antropológico**, Praça Universitária 1166 (signposted "Instituto de Artes & Escritorio Tecnico Administrativo"; Tues–Fri 9am–5pm), where enthusiasts will find a surprisingly wide range of traditional indigenous handicrafts and, nearby, the less interesting archeological museum, the **Museu Goiano de Pré-História e Arqueologia**, Praça Universitária 1440 (Mon–Fri 8–11am & 1–5pm); both museums can be reached on buses #167, #170, #164 and #162. If you're en route for some ecotourism and birdwatching in Goiás or Mato Grosso, the **Museu Ornitológia**, Av. Para 395, Setor Campinas (daily 8am–10pm), which displays around six thousand stuffed birds, may be of greater interest.

Jardim Zoológico and the Parque Mutirama

One of the town's main outdoor features, the **Jardim Zoológico** (Tues–Sun 8am–5pm; $1), located some nine long blocks west along Avenida Anhangüera from the Teatro Goiânio, is a pleasant and well-managed public park. Focused at its northern end around the muddy Lago das Rosas, the park is home to a number of semi-tame monkeys, while the southern corner houses a large and well-stocked zoo, which is a must for anyone going on to the Goiás *sertão*, Mato Grosso or the Amazon in search of wildlife. You'll see *emas* (rheas), *tuiuius* (red-throated storks) and *jacarés* (alligators) closer here than you will in the wild.

The other main public park in Goiânia, **Parque Mutirama**, in the northeast of the city at the junction of *avenidas* Araguaia and Contorno (Mon–Fri 1–6pm, Sat & Sun 9am–6pm), is very popular with local kids, who enjoy the delights of its ingenious amusement centre, skating rink and planetarium (Sun 3.30pm & 4.30pm). Opposite the park, the woods of the **Parque Botafogo** (closed Mon), with their reforested native trees, help the centre of the city to breathe; on the last Sunday of every month, there's also good live music here.

The Feira Hippie, Feira da Lua and Feira do Sol

The **Feira Hippie** is a fascinating street market open every Sunday from early in the morning until mid-afternoon, dominating the stretch of Avenida Goiás from Rua 4 up to the Praça do Trabalhador. Originally a market for local crafts people, it has evolved to incorporate a wide range of more general alternative handicrafts, plus the global variety of socks, underwear, watches, electrical goods and all kinds of imported plastics. If you're around on a Saturday between 5pm and 10pm, head for the **Feira da Lua**, which sells mainly *artesanato* in the tree-studded and lively Praça Tamandaré, a few blocks west of the Centro Cívico. Finally, the smaller **Feira do Sol**, on the Praça do Sol in the Setor Oeste, has around two hundred stalls selling crafts, antiques, foods, pets and fine arts every Sunday between 4pm and 9pm.

The Complexo Memorial do Cerrado Pe Pereira

The **Complexo Memorial do Cerrado Pe Pereira** (daily 9am–5pm; taxi to the center around $12) is an interesting museum, model village and eco-centre developed on the site of an old estate some 10km south of the city on the BR-153 towards São Paulo. The museum is dedicated to the evolution of the planet, with displays on geology, indigenous cultures, and the wildlife and flora of the region's *cerrado* ecosystem, a unique form of Brazilian savanna. There are also some botanical gardens, a plant nursery with both common and endangered *cerrado* plant species, and a fascinating model of a nineteenth-century *cerrado* village, including everything from the village shop and church to the bordello – an important public service in most *cerrado* settlements, which were after all just remote cowboy pit stops.

Eating, drinking and nightlife

Legend has it that, being a remote frontier in the eighteenth and early nineteenth centuries, the state of Goiás developed an exquisite **cuisine** in order to prolong the stay of passing travellers. Even today, in Goiânia as in Goiás Velho, the people are justly proud of their cooking. Local delicacies range from rice with *pequi* fruit through pasties (*empadões*) to roast sow with fried banana (*leitão assada com banana frita*). You may find, however, that the increasing popularity of the self-service *comida por kilo* system means that it's almost impossible to track down seriously good food at lunchtime, unless you're happy dining at the most expensive restaurants. There are, however, a number of reasonable restaurants, *lanchonetes* and pizzerias around Praça Tamandaré, plus a few more *lanchonetes* around the cheaper hotels in Setor Centro. In general, the further south you go, the more expensive the restaurant.

A Peixisqueira Praça Walter Santos 164, Setor Coimbra ☎62/233-9333. Hard to beat for moderately priced fish-based cuisine, but you will need to take a taxi to get here (it's west beyond the Jardim Zoológico).

Anhangüera Av. Anhangüera near the corner with Av. Paranaíba, Setor Central. Next to the Pro Brazilian supermarket, this is one of the cheapest and busiest lunchtime *comida por kilo* places.

Buritis at the corner of Rua 13 with Av. dos Buritis, opposite the Assembléia Legislativa building, in the Setor Central. Excellent choice of foods for self-service *comida por kilo* consumption. Open Mon–Sat lunchtimes only.

Dragão Rua Maria Cruvinel 1111 ☎62/215-1442. Just off Av. República do Líbano on the south side of Praça Tamandaré, serving good Chinese food, better in the evenings and weekends when the *comida por kilo* system makes way for old-fashioned à la carte. Offers home-delivery service as well.

Ki-sabor Rua 3, #67. This budget-priced but very pleasant *comida por kilo* restaurant is open for lunch; get there by 1.30pm to be sure of a good choice of dishes.

Piquiras Av. República do Líbano 1758, Setor Oeste ☎62/223-8168. One of the city's better all-round restaurants, with reliably good-quality food; you can eat inside or on a large terrace open to the road.

Sabor Tradição Rua 74, #194, Setor Central. Close to the corner with Rua 55, and one of a number of good lunchtime *comida por kilo* places in the centre. Closed Sun.

Tacho do Cobre Rua 72, #550, Jardim Goiás ☎62/242-1241. Located in an outer suburb to the southeast of the centre, this expensive restaurant is worth a taxi ride for its selection of the very best local dishes.

Tropeiro Chopera e Restaurante Rua 10. Located just off the western edge of Praça Tamandaré and open evenings only, this popular, moderately priced restaurant has a great atmosphere, whether you're just drinking or having a meal. This is a good place to try *mandioca frita* (fried manioc).

Vegetariano Rua 7, #475, Centro ☎62/225-7290. Simple, well-presented vegetarian dishes.

Nightlife

Goiânia has quite a lively nightlife, but most of the best **clubs** change names and venues every few months as they go in and out of fashion. Prices tend to be high, with some places charging $10 entrance as well as imposing a minimum spending limit once inside (usually also $10). Praça Tamandaré is always a good place to start your evening, with a number of bars and cafés and, later on, nightclubs. The best of these is currently the terminally designer *Draft Casual Bar & Diner*, south down Avenida República do Líbano on the corner of Rua 22 and Rua 23, Setor Oeste (Tues–Sun). Nearby, on República do Líbano almost on the Praça Tamandaré, the 24-hour *Big Paint American Bar* (open daily) is another more conventional but flashy option. A little further west, *Chocolate Chic*, Av. Portugal 719, is full of the tackiness that passes as style among Goiânia's monied youth, but it's still a fun night out. Also fairly reliable are the *Bavária*, Rua T-51, #1054, Setor Bueno, and *Boate People*, Rua 7, #1000, Setor Oeste. As for straight drinking **bars**, there aren't that many. Very busy is *O Ceará*, on the corner of Rua 2 and Rua 8. Try also *Chopp 10*, Avenida T-1, 2.215, Setor Bueno (daily 4pm until late), or the *Cervejaria Brasil* on Praça Antônio Lisita (closed Sun), which has a good range of bottled beers and cocktails.

Listings

Airlines Lufthansa, Rua 4, #1042, Setor Central ☎62/223-0036; Pantanal Linhas Aéreas, Rua Dona Gercina Borges 34, Setor Sul ☎62/224-4286; TAM, Av. 85, #944, Setor Sul ☎62/207-1800; Transbrasil, Rua 5, #813, Setor Oeste ☎62/225-1413; Varig Av. Goiás 285, Centro ☎62/207-1743 or 0800-997-000; VASP, Rua 1, #157, Centro ☎62/224-6389 or 207-1310.

Air taxis Goiás ☎62/207-1616; Anhangüera ☎62/207-2727.

Banks and exchange Good money-changing service on the first floor at the Banco do Brasil, Av. Goiás 980 (Mon–Fri 10am–6pm). The Lufthansa office (see "Airlines" above) changes cash at good rates, too.

Car rental First, Av. Araguaia 185 ☎62/212-3736; Hertz, Av. República do Líbano 1880 ☎62/223-6000; Localiza, Av. Anhangüera 3520 ☎62/261-7111; Unidas, Av. Caiapó, Quadra 85, Lote 123, Santa Genoveva ☎62/207-1297.

Health matters Hospital do Inamps, Av. Anhangüera 4379, Setor Oeste ☎62/223-5601.

Shopping The largest and flashiest shopping complex is Flambouyant Shopping, Av. Jamel Cecilio 3900, Jardim Goiás (daily 10am–10pm), followed closely by Bougainville, at Rua 9, #1855, Setor Oeste (Mon–Sat 10am–10pm). Crafts are available from the Feira Hippie along Avenida Goiás on Sunday mornings and the Feira da Lua on Saturdays (see p.501), or from the Handicraft Centre, Praça do Trabalhador, a producers' shop located in the old train station (daily 8am–6pm).

Taxis Araguaia ☎62/285-2222; Coopertaxi ☎62/229-0800; Rádio-Táxi Link ☎62/295-1513.

Travel and tour companies SINGTUR (Sindicato dos Guias de Turismo), Alameda Progresso 511 (☎62/271-6970) is the regional tour-guide syndicate, and provides accredited guides for the Parque Nacional das Emas (see p.509) and the Parque Nacional Chapada dos Veadeiros (see p.511). The staff at Castrotur, Av. República do Líbano 1520, Setor Oeste (☎62/212-7006, ⓔcastrotu@zaz.com.br), speak good English and run a range of local tours; Grupo Nativa (☎62/285-7752, ⓔnativa@nativa.tu.br) run eco-tours in canoes on the Rio Araguaia; NatureTur, Av. República do Líbano 2417, Setor Oeste (☎62/215-2000, ⓕ215-2011), are especially good for visits to Caldas Novas (see p.510); Toriua Turismo, Av. Tocantins 319, Centro (☎ & ⓕ62/223-2333), can help with flights, tickets and hotel bookings.

Pirenópolis

The picturesque town of **PIRENÓPOLIS** straddles the Rio das Almas, 112km north of Goiânia in the scrubby mountains of the Serra dos Pireneus. Founded by *bandeirantes* in 1727 as a gold-mining settlement, it's a popular weekend retreat for residents of Brasília, well supplied with accommodation to suit all wallets.

The main street, **Avenida Sizenando Jayme**, is a broad, peaceful, tree-lined avenue where the old men, with their ponies and carts, and visiting *fazendeiros* hang out chatting in the shade; on Sunday morning there's a produce market here. Just a couple of blocks down the hill is the site of the oldest church in Goiás, the **Igreja Nossa Senhora do Rosário de Meia Ponte** (1728–1732), once an attractive colonial edifice but tragically almost completely destroyed by fire in 2002 – only parts of the walls are left, a sad hulk supported by scaffolding awaiting the promised rebuilding. Opposite the church, the ruined late nineteenth-century theatre is also being rebuilt, and should, when finished, be once more the venue for plays and other distractions. The local **tourist office**, well supplied with leaflets, is just up the hill behind the Rosário ruins.

The town's only remaining colonial church is east along the very attractive Rua Bonfim da Serra dos Pireneus. **Igreja Nosso Senhor do Bonfim**, built in the 1750s, is famous for its image of Nosso Senhor do Bonfim, originally brought here by two hundred slaves. Also in the upper part of town, at Rua Direita 39 between the remains of Rosário and the *rodoviária*, you'll find the small **Museu das Cavalhadas** (Fri–Sun 9am–5pm), located in a family's front room (knock if it appears closed). The museum contains displays of incredible carnival costumes from the Festo do Divino Espírito Santo, a lively and largely horse-mounted religious festival that takes place in the town exactly six weeks after Easter Sunday. The festival combines dances with mock battles from the Crusades, and the costumes include ornate metal armour, demonic masks and animal heads. Another tiny museum, the **Museu da Família Pompeu**, in the family's home on the same road at no. 28 (Mon–Sat 9am–6pm), may in future become the *museu municipal*, with its odd collection of colonial and later bric-a-brac, including an old printing press, municipal newsletters and silver jewellery.

Below the Igreja N.S. do Rosário, the town has a different atmosphere. Swimming and sunbathing spots line the river by the old stone and wood bridge, which links the main settlement with the Carmo section of town on the north bank, and there's a vibrant **alternative scene** reflected in a handful of interesting bars, organic cafés and New Age stores: Homeostratum at Rua do Rosário 12 sells homeopathic products, natural foods, alternative magazines and *artesanato*; and Nataraja has a wide range of hippie-style clothes, crystals and alternative medicines. However, Pirenópolis is most famous in Brazil for its **silverwork**, mostly inset with semiprecious stones. The craft was introduced here just over twenty years ago by the hippies who came and stayed, and nowadays, with over two hundred artisans working in around a hundred workshops, you'll find jewellery for sale in dozens of shops, much of it inspired by Asian designs.

On the north side of the river, housed in the eighteenth-century Igreja Nossa Senhora do Carmo, the **Museu Sacro** (Mon–Sat 9am–6pm) displays an image of the town's patroness, which was originally brought here from Portugal.

One very worthwhile excursion into the surrounding countryside is the **Santuário Vagafogo** (Tues–Sun 8am–5pm; $3.50), a beautifully preserved patch of gallery forest with streams, swimholes, trails with walkways over the muddy patches and stairs up the steep sections, and a hammock-strung gazebo to relax in after your walks. Look hard and you can see the remains of colonial gold mining under the undergrowth – part of the trail is an eighteenth-century sluice bed. At weekends and on holidays, the small restaurant at the reserve entrance serves quite superb, very reasonably priced brunches, using homegrown ingredients: the jams and pickles using *cerrado* fruits are deliciously unusual. Eat first and walk it off down the trails. Access is a problem, since it is not well signposted and lies some 6km out of town. Your best bet is to catch a *moto-taxi* at the *rodoviária*, one of the motorbike taxis that hang out in groups at a pick-up point opposite the platforms (20min; around $5). It is a bumpy but enjoyable ride down a dirt track, with pleasant scenery. Once there, hiking back is easy, or arrange to be picked up again.

Practicalities

Pirenópolis is well connected by road to the other major towns of the region. There are three direct **buses** a day from Goiânia, four from the important junction town of Anápolis (which in turn has frequent connections with Goiânia). Brasília is just 172km east along the BR-070 (6 buses daily). The *rodoviária* (☎62/331-1248) is on the eastern edge of town on Avenida Neco Mendonça, five minutes' walk from the centre. **Tourist information** is available from the Secretaria de Turismo, Rua Bonfim da Serra dos Pireneus (Mon–Sat 8am–8pm; ☎62/331-1299), and the council publishes an excellent annual *Guia do Turista* (free), available in most of the hotels and establishments mentioned below.

△ Congresso Nacional, Brasília

Accommodation

As a popular local resort, Pirenópolis has dozens of **hotels** to choose from, many of them merely private homes with a few rooms for rent. The quality is generally well above average, and discounts are available mid-week or out of season. The most central hotel is the *Pousada das Cavalhadas*, Praça da Matriz (☎ & ℱ 62/331-1261; ❸), opposite the Igreja N.S. do Rosário, although its singles are overpriced. On the small square to the right of the church, the *Hotel Rex*, Praça Emmanoel Lopes 15 (☎ 62/331-1121; ❷), has several quaint rooms, some self-contained, along the edge of a traditional courtyard. Further up, *Lanchonete Pousada Central* (☎ 62/331-1625) rents out five beds in two rooms at $10 a person. One road away, at Rua Nova 25, is one of the town's nicest hotels, the *Pouso do Sô Vigário* (☎ 62/331-1206; ❺), housed in the old priest's residence, but now embellished with a pool and sauna. On the main street, at Av. Sizenando Jayme 21, is the *Pousada Imperial* (☎ 62/331-1382, ℱ 331-1340; ❸), a friendly and well-appointed place, with nice views of the Serra dos Pireneus over the river and half-price singles. On the other side of the river, the *Pousada dos Pireneus* (☎ & ℱ 62/331-1345; half board ❺) is the main upmarket place, with its own rambling gardens, a small water park with chutes that kids will love, and horse-riding facilities – including amusing half-hour jaunts by carriage through town for a mere $4.40 for four people. The *pousada* also rents bicycles for $4 an hour, but insists you stay within town, which is most unhelpful for visiting any of the surrounding attractions.

Eating and drinking

There are several good **restaurants** along Avenida Sizenando Jayme, including *As Flor* at no. 16, unprepossessing in appearance but good at lunchtime for regional cooking, though evening fare can dip in quality. *Pamonharia*, around the corner going down to the church, is also cheap. Other good, but much more expensive, restaurants can be found in the lower part of town around the river; try *Restaurante Dona Cida* (Fri–Sun only) on Rua do Carmo 22A for *galinha caipira*, small succulent chicken oven-baked with saffron, or else baked in its own blood as *galinha cabidela molho pardo*. For good basic food, the *Churrascaria Pireneus*, on the corner of Praça Matriz opposite the church, is open daily, and the *Restaurant Nena*, at Rua Aurora 4, serves good self-service *comida por kilo* lunches. There are small **supermarkets** at Av. Sizenando Jayme 30 and by the river opposite the police station. The best **bars** are down by the river, notably the communally run *Aravinda Bar* on Rua do Rosário 25, a place where beer hogs meet patchouli oil and incense in a very relaxing and friendly way (open Thurs–Sun only; live New Age music Sat night); it also serves food, including excellent *peixa na telha* (fish baked in an earthenware dish). Throughout the week, the *Pousada Central*'s bar is a popular meeting place.

Tours

A number of guides and agencies offer ecological **tours** of the surrounding region, taking in sites such as the Abade, Inferno and Corumbá waterfalls. Based at Rua Emílio de Carvalho 18 (☎ 62/331-1392), Dinis, who during the week drives a school bus, runs guided eco-tours ($20 for 3–4hr), as do Cerrado Ecoturismo, Rua Bonfim da Serra 46 (☎ 62/331-1240), who are agents for several private wildlife sanctuaries in the region. More alternative guided tours (bicycles a speciality) are offered by Calango Expedições, Bairro do Carmo (☎ 62/331-1564). Another guide worth contacting, though you'll need your own transport, is silversmith Alcides dos Santos Filho, at Rua Anduzeiro 20 (☎ 62/331-1416).

West of Goiânia

The glory of Goiás is the shiny and mighty **Rio Araguaia**. Even though most of the river now falls within the state of Tocantins (see p.514), the Goiás section has hundreds of fine **sandy beaches** suitable for camping, and some well-established resorts, very popular with the residents of Goiânia and other towns in Goiás. Rich in fish, the Araguaia is particularly busy during the dry season from May to September when the water level drops, and serious anglers come from São Paulo and Goiânia to compete. The gateway to the river is **ARUANÃ**, a small town served by only a few hotels, just over 380km northwest of Goiânia.

The **best place to stay**, and as comfortable as hotels come in this town, is the *Pousada Acuá*, Rua José Eufrasio de Lima (T & F 62/376-1294; ❹), which has a pool, bar and reasonable restaurant. The *Recanto Sonhado Hotel*, Avenida Altamiro Caio Pacheco (T62/376-1230, reservations T62/212-3955; ❹), is also very good, and has a pool, sauna and facilities for jet-skiing. At the same price but with less on offer (you should get a discount) is *Hotel Araguaia*, Praça Couto Magalhães 53 (T62/376-1251; ❹), also with a pool. Cheaper still is the *Hotel Do Sesi* (T62/376-1221; ❷). You can arrange boat trips to go fishing or rent your own boat in Aruanã, and it's also one of the main ports of access for the Ilha do Bananal (see p.515). In July, the busiest month, it can prove difficult even to get a room.

Goiás Velho

Some 144km northwest of Goiânia, and a six-hour bus ride from Brasília, is the historic town of **GOIÁS VELHO** – originally known as Vila Boa, and now often just called Goiás. Strung along and up a steep valley cut by the Rio Vermelho, it is one of the most beautiful colonial towns in Brazil, without the great churches and museums of the best of the *cidades históricas* in Minas but easily the equal of any of them in the calm elegance of its cobbled streets and squares, and much their superior in lack of commercialism. Its more remote location well to the north of the country's other eighteenth-century mining zones has made it the best-preserved colonial town in the country. With the effects of a disastrous flood in 2001 now largely repaired, the town is simply gorgeous, fully deserving its recent listing as a UNESCO World Heritage site.

Founded in 1726 as a gold-mining settlement by the *bandeirantes*, Goiás Velho remained the state capital until 1937. Nowhere else in Brazil is there a stronger sense of the colonial past, palpable in the cobbled streets and the many well-preserved eighteenth- and nineteenth-century buildings. Stone houses and quaint squares, the gaslit town centre and the occasional metallic clip-clop of mule hooves create a timeless atmosphere, one that's enhanced annually during the colourful torchlit Easter Fogareu procession.

There is more than enough here to occupy you for a few days – apart from the town itself, the surrounding countryside is worth exploring, with good hiking amid the trails, waterfalls and swimholes characteristic of the *cerrado*.

You find the usual collection of small local museums in town. The **Palácio Conde dos Arcos**, built in 1755 on the main Praça Dr Tasso de Camargo, was the old governor's palace and has the usual clunky period furniture; the best feature is an attractive Portuguese-style garden (Tues–Sat 8am–5pm, Sun 8am–noon; $2). The most interesting exhibits are actually more modern, such as a nineteenth-century photo of the great-grandfather of two-term Brazilian president Fernando Henrique Cardoso, proudly pointed out by the museum guide who accompanies you, and the original application documents for their UNESCO World Heritage listing, reverently displayed in a velvet case, though you are allowed to leaf through the supporting photos.

The **Museu das Bandeiras**, situated up the hill on the Praça Brasil Ramos Caiado (Tues–Sat 8am–noon & 1–5pm, Sun 8am–noon), recounts the story of the gold rush through artifacts like slave shackles and chains, but what's most interesting here is the building itself, which has a combined governor's office and council chamber upstairs, and jail downstairs – an arrangement typical of early eighteenth-century Brazilian towns. The room to the right of the entrance desk was once part of the jail and has changed very little since it was built.

The town's **Museu de Arte Sacra**, in the Igreja da Boa Morte on Praça Dr Tasso de Camargo (Tues–Fri noon–5pm, Sat & Sun 9am–1pm), is not very good; all of the local churches have had their interiors ruined by a combination of fires and misguided "improvements" – the worst example being the slave church of **Rosário dos Pretos** across the river, levelled on its bicentenary in 1934 and replaced by an incongruous Gothic structure. The other local museum worth checking out is the house of **Cora Coralina**, a local poet who never left the town in all of her 96 years of life but used it as raw material and became nationally famous. Located on the corner of Rua Dom Cândido, a colonial street overlooking the Rio Vermelho, the museum is a hodge-podge of old furniture, photos and manuscripts, giving you a glimpse into small-town life.

Exploring the countryside

If you need to cool off in the afternoon after walking the old city streets, there's a natural swimming pool out by the **Cachoeira Grande waterfalls** on the Rio Vermelho, just 7km east of town – the best (and cheapest) way to get there is on the back of one of the local motorbike taxis. The most beautiful sight in the area is the **Cachoeira das Andorinhas** (Swallow Waterfall), 8km out of town, which makes for a wonderful day trip. On the only road out of town, cross the Rio Vermelho, passing by the pretty church of **Igreja de Santa Bárbara**, perched on a small hill overlooking the municipal cemetery. Taking the dirt road to the left of the church, signposted *Hotel Fazenda Manduzanzan*, continue 7km through picturesque hill country until you reach a signposted trail entrance in front of the hotel. The waterfall is another kilometre from here – when in doubt, always bear left. The last few hundred yards rise steeply through a forested gorge before ending at a glorious, tree-choked swimhole with a waterfall and, true to its name, swallows darting around. A highlight is a natural rock chamber that channels part of the waterfall into a cavern – you can brace against the rock surface and have the cold water pound you into a jelly; exhilarating, especially after a hot walk.

Bear in mind that Goiás is hot year-round, and baking hot in the dry season, so the usual precautions of carrying water, sunscreen and hats apply. To save yourself some effort, consider having a motorbike taxi drop you off at the trail entrance ($2), thereby halving the distance you need to walk. Consider heading out early for the trek, stopping afterward at the hotel for its excellent lunch (open to non-guests) and a doze in its hammocks, waiting until the sun starts to set and the heat lessens before heading back.

Practicalities

The **rodoviária** (☎62/371-1510), which has connections to Goiânia and Anápolis, is down by the river, and most accommodation and eating spots are close by. The town has several good accommodation options, including the *Villa Boa Hotel*, Avenida Dr Deusdete Ferreira de Moura (℡ & ℻62/371-1000; ❻), with a decent pool and sauna; the cheaper and more central *Hotel Serrano*, on the same street, (℡62/371-1825; ❸); and the *Araguaia* at no. 8 (℡62/371-1462; ❸), which is cheaper still. Cheapest of all, but still very pleasant, is *Pousada do Sol* at Rua Americano Brasil 17 (℡62/371-1717; ❷). Highly recommended is a more upmarket pousada, *Pousada Ipê* (℡62/371-2065), on the other side of the river at Rua do Fórum 22, where $20 gets you essentials such as air-conditioning and pool access. The best-value hotel in the centre is *Hotel Casa da Ponte* (℡62/371/4467), on the Rio Vermelho right in the heart of town, with single rooms for $14 a night.

For regional **food,** the *Restaurante Caseiro*, Rua D. Cândido 31, is a cheap option for lunch. You can also try two excellent local restaurants. *Flor do Ipê*, at Rua Boa Vista 32 (across the small square from the *Pousada Ipê*, see above), serves a typical regional buffet that includes salads, pork, stewed chicken, okra and regional vegetables like *piquí*, slowly cooked on a traditional wood-fired stove; the restaurant is closed on Mondays but otherwise open for lunch and dinner. For more creative dishes based on local ingredients, the equally good *Beco do Sertão* is very central at Rua 13 de Maio 17 but open only in the evenings. On a clear night the tables in the courtyard are a great place to dine.

The best way to **get around,** other than your own two feet, are the local motorbike taxis; you'll see a stand of them in most squares, and they are usually plentiful around the bus station and its associated market.

Parque Nacional das Emas

Down in the southwestern corner of Goiás state, the **Parque Nacional das Emas** (8am–5pm) is a *cerrado* reserve that was once the domain of zoologists and botanists but is gradually opening up to regular tourism. Located in the central Brazilian highlands near the Mato Grosso do Sul border, the park consists of some 1300 square kilometres of fairly pristine *cerrado*, mostly open grasslands pocked by thousands of termite hills, but with occasional clumps of savanna forest. While it lacks the scenic grandeur of Chapada dos Veadeiros, thanks to its relative isolation the reserve is one of the last places where you can find *cerrado* wildlife in some abundance, supporting an enormous population of **emas** (South American rheas) and also large herds of **veado–campeiro** deer, often shadowed by the solitary **lobo guará** (the maned wolf); all are more easily spotted here than anywhere else in Brazil. The Emas park is also famous for its wide range of variously coloured and extremely large **anthills**, which are used by *coruja-do-campo* owls as lookout posts dotted across the flat plain, and are a good source of food for *bandeira* anteaters. Due to the activity of larvae living inside them, some of the anthills glow phosphorescently green and blue – an amazing sight on a dark night, though you can only catch it in October, when the conditions are right.

It's easy to get to the area by bus from Brasília, but a bit of a logistical challenge once you're here: without a car distances are long, local buses are almost non–existent, and you have to rely on your guide's contacts to get around. As there is no **accommodation** in the park itself, you'll have to base yourself in the small towns of **MINEIROS** or **CHAPADÃO DO CÉU**, though both are a considerable distance from the park; the former geared more to visitors but 85km away, the latter more rustic but only 27km away. You'll also need to hire a local guide, who will arrange transport, and the package will set you back around $60 a day. Within the park, as ever, you are restricted to set trails –

although here they traverse most of the park – and camping is not permitted. Beware of *mucuim*, irritating tiny ticks that jump onto legs and leave clumps of fantastically itchy reddish bites; wearing long trousers is your best defence, although this will be a drag in the dry season.

Both Mineiros and Chapadão do Céu have a highly organised association of local guides, which should be your first port of call, as they will arrange transport, quote you a price and take care of the formalities with IBAMA, the national parks authority, such as registering entry and exit and paying the $2 entrance fee (you also have to pay for your guide). Bear in mind that you will rarely be able to set out until the following day, as cars have to be rustled up and drivers found. Given the time it will take to reach the park itself, your best bet is to complete the formalities the day before and set off at dawn the next day. The association in Mineiros is located on Praça Marcelino Roque (☎62/661-7153, ✉ednaldo.marelo@bol.com.br), and although the English spoken there is rudimentary, you can get by. In Chapadão do Céu, the association is at Avenida Ema, quadra 51 (☎62/634-1228); ask for Sr Rubens or Sra Elaine on ☎62/634-1309.

Although there aren't many **accommodation** options, all are perfectly adequate and cheap. The best hotel in Mineiros is the *Pilões Palace* (☎62/661-1547), on Praça Assis; the *Dallas*, 223 Quinta Avenida (☎62/661-1534), *Líder* (☎62/661-1149) on Rua Elias Machado, and *Pinheiros* on Rua Oito are serviceable. *Chapadão do Céu* is more basic. In town, your best options are *Hotel Thesari* (☎62/634-1227), Avenida Indaia 616, *Pousada das Emas* (☎62/634-1382) on Rua Ipê, and *Hotel Rafael* on Avenida Indaia. As for **dining options**, you'll be limited to a couple of *churrascarias* in each town, plus the hotel restaurants – not *haute cuisine*, but satisfying after a day's hiking.

There are direct buses to Mineiros from both Brasília and Goiânia, to Chapadão from Goiânia only.

Caldas Novas and Rio Quente

More easily accessible than many of Goiás's attractions, the adjacent **thermal resorts** of Caldas Novas and Rio Quente, around 185km south of Goiânia, are incredibly popular with Brazilians from beyond the state. Taken together they lay claim to being the world's largest hot-spring aquifers, a massive and very hot natural subterranean reservoir. The healing reputation and the sheer joy of relaxing in the natural spa resorts lure plenty of people from the urban sprawl of the São Paulo region.

CALDAS NOVAS sometimes gets crowded in the dry season, which lasts from May to September, but there are thousands of hotel beds and over seventy hotels (which is over half the hotels in the entire state) within this relatively small town of only around 40,000 people. The therapeutic properties of the waters are said to reduce blood pressure and blood viscosity, dissolve kidney stones, improve digestion, alleviate rheumatic symptoms and even, it is claimed, stimulate endocrine glands and sexual vitality, among other things. While some people do come for long expensive courses of treatment, most visitors are simply here on holiday, relaxing, sunbathing and taking the waters for a few days or a week.

Hotel reservations are best made in advance, usually from Goiânia. Among the better **hotels**, *Thermas di Roma*, Rua São Cristóvão, Solar de Caldas, on the exit for Morrinhos (☎62/453-1718, ☎453-1945; half board ❻), has a beautiful location out of town with panoramic views, nine thermal pools and a sauna. On the whole, it's excellent value, as is *Taiyo Thermas*, in the town itself at Rua Presidente Castelo Branco 115 (T & F 62/453-1334, W www.hoteltaiyo .com.br; ⑤), with three pools and a sauna. Slightly less expensive, but with singles priced the same as doubles, is the smaller *Hotel Roma*, Praça Mestre Orlando 368 (T 62/453-1335, F 453-1340; ⑤), which has six thermal pools. Cheaper still are *Hotel Triângulo*, Av. Orozimbo Correia Neto 157 (T & F 62/453-1709, E triangulo@internetional.com.br; ④), with only one pool, although the waters are no doubt just as efficacious as elsewhere, and *Hotel Santa Clara*, Rua América 226 (T 62/453-1764; ②), which lacks a pool, but has reasonable rooms. For **camping**, *CCB-GO-2*, 4km along the road for Ipameri (T 62/223-6561), is in a beautiful location. As for **restaurants**, the better hotels have their own, but you could also try the *Restaurante Papas* at Praça Mestre Orlando 12, which serves a wide variety of Brazilian dishes. **Tourist information** is available from the SEBRAE office, on the Praça Mestre Orlando (daily 9am–6pm; T 62/453-1868), and for banking needs, head to the Banco do Brasil at Rua Santos Dumont 55.

Nearby **RIO QUENTE** consists of a huge hotel complex attached to a small service town of only 2000 inhabitants. The main feature, the *Pousada do Rio Quente* complex (T 62/452-8000, reservations T 61/224-7166, W www .rioquenteresorts.com.br; ⑦), offers superb-quality accommodation in two hotels: the four-star *Hotel Pousada* and the five-star *Hotel*. The whole complex is arranged around a natural hydrothermal spa, and in high season the minimum stay is two nights, with cheaper (but still ⑦) four-day packages offered Sunday to Wednesday.

Parque Nacional Chapada dos Veadeiros

The **Parque Nacional Chapada dos Veadeiros** in the north of Goiás is the heart of the Planalto, its stunning natural scenery among the most beautiful and distinctive in Brazil. The hundreds of square kilometers of wild and sparse vegetation, extraordinary geological formations, cave systems, waterfalls and hiking trails make this one of the best destinations for **ecotourism** in the country. A few hours north from Brasília and easily accessible by bus, the park has good local support for tourism, and apart from the occasional holidaying diplomat up from the capital, it is still remarkably unknown as a destination to foreign tourists.

Alto Paraíso

The main point of arrival for visitors to the park is **ALTO PARAÍSO DE GOIÁS**, some 240km north of Brasília and connected by regular buses; see the "Travel Details" section at the end of this chapter. The town, which lives largely on the profits of ecotourism, is also overcrowded with spiritualists, clairvoyants, astrologers and UFO-seekers – fun at first but tedious for any length of time. Alto Paraíso is a base to explore the surrounding countryside more than a place to hang out in itself. If you really want to explore the Chapadào, your best bet is to take the bus to São Jorge (see overleaf), which is much closer to the national park and the best hiking, but if you have only limited time the countryside around Alto Paraíso is also rewarding.

If you're short on time, you're better off having one of the local **ecotourism agencies** arrange everything for you; they offer a wide menu of day hikes into the countryside, and charge around $50 per head per day. Two reliably high-quality agencies are Travessia Ecoturismo at Ary Valadão 979 (☎62/446-1595, Ⓦwww.travessiatur.com.br) and Transchapada Turismo on the Praça da Rodoviária (☎62/446-1345, Ⓦwww.transchapada.com.br), but as these types of agencies are cropping up faster than mushrooms in the dark, check for more details at the tourist office, which can also advise you on **guides**.

If you want to **hike on your own**, your best best is to walk 4km up the GO-118 road north of the town, and then take the signposted dirt road right another 3km to the **Cristal waterfall**. At the head of a beautiful valley are a series of swimholes and small waterfalls created by a cool mountain stream as it plunges into the valley.

The **tourist office**, located on the main road leading into the town centre from the GO-118 (☎62/446-1159), has friendly and helpful staff. You can pick up maps of the park here, as well as the worthwhile booklet *Guia da Chapada dos Veadeiros* ($3), a comprehensive listing of all the hikes and accommodation options in and around the park, organised by town, and one of the few such publications with a good English translation. Also spend a few cents on the invaluable map *O Melhor da Chapada dos Veadeiros*, which is based on a satellite image and has all the region's roads and main sights marked.

You will be spoilt for choice for **accommodation**. Most hotels are concentrated on the central Avenida Ary Valadão, the best of which are *Hotel Central*, the *Nunes* and the *Tradição*, all very reasonably priced in the $15–25 range: the kitschiest is the *Camelot*, a Monty Pythonesque fake medieval castle on the GO-118, opposite the exit to the town centre. Slightly away from the centre is the city's best accommodation, the *Hotel Europa*, at Rua 1 Quadra 7, Setor Planalto, not far from the bus station. Dozens of *pousadas* cater to eco-tourists and weekend trippers from Brasília (all ❷–❸); recommended are the upmarket *Pousada Alfa & Ômega*, Rua Joaquim de Almeida 15 (☎62/446-1225, Ⓦwww.veadeiros.com.br) and further up on the same street the New Agey *Aquárius*, no. 326 (☎62/446-1952;); also the *Pousada Maya* (☎62/446-1200), Rua Coleto Paulino 732, even more New Age but very comfortable, and *Pousada do Sol* (☎62/446-1201), Rua Gumercindo Barbosa. Several **campgrounds** are located on the edge of town; the tourist office will have details on these. **Restaurants** are equally thick on the ground, especially on Ary Valadão; all are very similar, but the lunchtime salad bar at the *Clube da Esquina* is very good.

São Jorge

Alto Paraíso is really only an introduction to Chapada dos Veadeiros; to really come to grips with it you need to head 37km further up a good-quality dirt road to the small village of **SÃO JORGE**, which is next to the only entrance to the national park. From Alto Paraíso, there is one daily bus from the *rodoviária*, Empresa São Jorge, leaving daily at 4pm, and a more irregular Kombi run by a São Jorge tourist agency; ask at the Alto Paraíso tourist office for details.

From the village, you can either hike into the national park (see below) or explore the truly spectacular countryside around São Jorge, which is dotted with waterfalls, strange geological formations and natural swimholes. Of these, the best are the otherworldly rock formations of the **Vale da Lua**, and the swimholes and waterfalls of **Raizama** and **Morada do Sol**, both a short drive or a two-hour hike away.

Looking around São Jorge, you can see the potential that ecotourism has to protect landscapes and generate jobs and income at the same time. Before the creation of the national park in 1980, the main industry hereabouts was the mining of rock crystals. When the practice was eventually made illegal in and around the park, the parks authority, prodded and helped by the **World Wildlife Fund**, recognised the need to create jobs linked to the park and invested heavily in training local ex-miners to be guides – the perfect guides, since no-one picked over every remote nook and cranny of the landscape quite like them. So there is a good reason why IBAMA, the federal parks authority, makes it compulsory for visitors to the park to be accompanied by a guide.

Practicalities

The **tourist office** is located in a modern pavilion at the village entrance, and all restaurant and accommodation options are within five minutes of where the bus sets you down. Despite its small size, São Jorge has no shortage of accommodation. The most upmarket option, the *Pousada Casa das Flores* (reservations advisable, ☎61/9976-0603 and 234-7493, Ⓦwww.pousadadasflores.com.br; ⑤), includes very high-quality breakfast and lunch in the rates, while the pool, candlelit rooms and smoochy live music in the evenings make this a great place for a romantic weekend. More reasonably priced ($20–30) are several very pleasant pousadas, including *Trilha Violeta* (☎61/9985-6544), *Recanto da Paz* (☎61/646-1983) and *Pousada São Jorge* (☎61/9998-5384). There are also a large number of campsites and rooms from $5 upwards. For **food**, the best option is **Bar do Pelé**, which has good cheap meals, while the *Casa das Flores* restaurant is also open to non-guests, and you'll find a couple of pizzerias, *Lua de São Jorge* and *Vila de São Jorg*, as well. At all times of the year, if you're planning to stay in one of the *pousadas*, it is a good idea to ring ahead and make a reservation – most of them have a Brasília-based reservation service. At holiday periods, especially Carnaval and the New Year, São Jorge fills up and can be noisy. Bear in mind as well that at the height of the dry season (September), the village has been known to run out of water.

In the unlikely event that the villagers don't come touting for business where you're staying, let the owner you're interested and someone should be there within a few minutes. Guides charge a daily rate of around $12, not including the entrance fees to the national park, if you choose to hike there. If you want to go on a long hike outside the park, it's still a good idea to hire a guide to make sure you don't get lost.

Hiking in the park

Visitors to the park are restricted to two **trails** in its southern corner, both 10km long and each a day's worth of exploring. Although you'll only see a fraction of the park, this area is scenically the most spectacular, an unforgettable blend of hills and cliff-faces (mostly in the middle distance; fortunately you don't have to climb them), plunging waterfalls, swimholes and forests. You encounter the full range of *cerrado* vegetations as well: *veredas* (open moorlands lined by *buriti* palms), *floresta de galeria* (full-sized deciduous forest along watercourses) and *campo sujo* (the classic, shrubby savanna characteristic of Africa).

Of the two trails, one includes the park's main highlight – the marvellous **Salto do Rio Preto waterfall**, where two separate falls plunge almost 400 feet into a pool 400 yards across, the loveliest swim you are ever likely to have, after working up a sweat hiking the 5km from the park entrance. The trail's other notable sight is the **Pedreiras**, a series of natural rock pools. On the other trail, the highlight is **Cariocas falls**, a series of falls with a sand beach at the top, and you will also pass **Canion 1 e 2**, two canyons cut by the Rio Preto and lined with granite cliffs.

Your guide's first stop will be the IBAMA office to register entry and pay the fee ($2 a head); you are responsible for your guide's fee. Take plenty of water and enough food for a day, and stick to the trails, taking your rubbish home with you, and, most importantly, in the dry season **do not smoke**. Fires are the worst problem the park has, and the vegetation is tinder-dry between July and October. Bringing a change of clothes and swimwear is a good idea as you'll be cooling off in swimholes between treks.

Hikes around São Jorge

Hiking options around São Jorge are less strenuous than in the national park, but still scenically spectacular. You could easily spend a week doing a series of rewarding day hikes without even entering the national park, and for those travelling with children, for whom the long hikes in the park are not realistic, these shorter hikes are a great family outing. All destinations are reached by heading along the road that passes the village, either west or east – or, more easily, towards or away from Alto Paraíso.

The most striking hike around São Jorge leads to **Vale da Lua**, a forested valley where the river São Miguel has carved a narrow canyon through an extraordinary series of sculptured granite curves. To get there from the village, head to the main road and continue 4km east – in the direction of Alto Paraíso. On your right you come to a signposted trail into the Vale da Lua. There is a nominal entrance fee; you can either follow the trail directly to a swimhole, or else peel left to the swimhole by walking down the valley, which is the best route to see the extraordinary geology of the valley. Flash floods can be a problem here in the rainy season, given the narrowness of the gorge, so exercise caution.

Back at São Jorge, heading in the opposite direction, away from Alto Paraíso, will take you, in quick succession, to **Raizama**, a beautiful gorge with a series of swimholes and waterfalls, and **Morada do Sol**, which has less spectacular waterfalls, but more spectacular views up and down the valley. Another 5km up the main road will bring you to a private estate, **Água Quente**, where the owner has channelled a natural warm spring – tepid rather than hot – into a couple of large pools, making this a wonderful place to soak and recover from the walk. All of the above destinations charge a $1–2 entrance fee.

Tocantins

Created in 1989, the **state of Tocantins** is not an obvious geographical or cultural unit, merely a political and bureaucratic invention. Most visitors pass through the region rather than spend time around the state's hot and flyblown towns. Apart from the main north–south artery, the BR-153 highway, **transport** is difficult, and getting to the state's main attraction – the **Ilha do Bananal** – can be an expensive headache unless you're taking a guided tour (usually from Goiânia or Barra do Garças on the Mato Grosso border). As Brazilians catch on to the attractions of ecotourism, however, things are bound to change, and probably quite rapidly. The few options that do exist for the independent traveller are detailed below.

The Ilha do Bananal

Most travellers spending time in Tocantins come to explore the **Ilha do Bananal** and the **Parque Nacional do Araguaia** in the island's northern reaches, an emerging ecotourist destination. Bananal is the world's largest river island, over 300km long from head to tail, and is home to the intrepid, canoe-faring Karajá tribe, still renowned for their fine feather craftsmanship and clay dolls. You will need **permission** to enter the park from IBAMA, which is easiest to arrange through an association of local guides – for details see p.510.

Although designated a national park, the Ilha do Bananal has lost over fifty percent of its area to settlers and development. In 1958, the British explorer Robin Hanbury-Tenison, visited the island and its communities of several thousand Indians and witnessed two shamans performing ritual dances. Yet just thirteen years later, there were only eight hundred Indians left on the island, and today the few hundred survivors are far outnumbered by the many thousands of non-Indian Brazilian settlers. These days traditional Indian dances are rarely performed except on official state occasions. This apart, it's an easy place to immerse yourself in the wonders of the forest. **Wildlife** is varied and plentiful, and it's even possible to spot a maned wolf or otters if you've the time to spend searching during the rainy season. However, as there are no roads on the island, travel is only possible by boat, which means either renting one, with a boatman as guide, in one of the few settlements on the island fringes or in Aruanã (see p.507); or taking an **organized tour** from Barra do Garças on the Mato Grosso border (see p.569) or from one of the big cities. Travel agents in Goiânia (see p.503) and Brasília (see p.495) can put together tours; in São Paulo, Iate Clube, Rua Maurício Jaquei 62 (Rudge Ramos), São Bernardo do Campo (☎11/457-3277), offers fishing trips on the Rio Cristalino, a tributary of the Araguaia, including stays in their four-bed cabins in the park.

Access to the southern part of the island is usually from **SÃO MIGUEL DO ARAGUAIA**, some 480km northwest of Goiânia, where the Rio Araguaia starts to split to form the boundaries of the island. Nearby, the picturesque fishing port of **PORTO LUÍS ALVES** functions as the starting point on the river, and has a couple of good but expensive **accommodation** options: try the *Hotel Mirante do Araguaia* (☎62/702-1155, ⓕ62/271-5815; ❺), which has boats for hire, or the *Hotel Jabaru* (☎62/271-5355, ⓕ271-5815; ❺), which has a pool, and offers guided walks and information on boat trips, especially for fishing. You should also try the boat crews themselves at the docks for possible river journeys (from $200 per day for a boat carrying up to eight people). São Miguel is much cheaper for accommodation. Outstanding value, with good, clean rooms, all with TVs and fridges, is *Pousada Luz do Araguaia*, Rua 12, no. 371, Setor Oeste (☎62/772-1122; ❸); singles are especially cheap here. Another good option is the *Hotel Paraíso*, Av. José Pereira Nascimento 317 (☎62/774-1061; ❷). From here, there are daily overnight buses to São Miguel and Porto Luís Alves from Goiânia.

Further north, about halfway along the western edge of the Ilha do Bananal, is the port of **SÃO FÉLIX DO ARAGUAIA**. The only settlement of any size around the island, São Félix is one of the few places where you can buy much in the way of stores, and there's also a nice beach, the **Praia do Morro**, 2km north of town. The *Pousada Kuryala*, 20km away, is a good if expensive base (❼); you can make reservations at their Goiânia office on Avenida República do Líbano (☎62/215-1313). The *Hotel Xavante*, Av. Severiano Neves 391 (☎63/522-1305; ❷), is more central and much better value. For boat trips, ask at the port along Avenida Araguaia. Irregular **buses** link the town with Barra do Garças along the BR-158. São Félix is also served by air taxis from Brasília and Goiânia, which you can arrange at the airstrip itself.

Some 150km further north is **SANTA TEREZINHA**, the nearest point of access to the Parque Nacional do Araguaia. There are no facilities for tourists as yet, and access to the town is along a very bad dirt road or else by air. As there are no bus services, you could try hitching a lift from Santana do Araguaia (300km north), which is connected by bus to Araguaína.

Much easier to reach is the small settlement of **PARAÍSO DO TOCANTINS**, another base for visiting the northern section of Ilha do Bananal and the Parque Nacional do Araguaia. Located due west of Palmas on the BR-153, the settlement has one excellent-value hotel, *Serrano's Park*, Av. Bernardo Sayão 250 (☎63/602-1410, ℱ602-1463; ➍), with a pool and sauna. From Paraíso, a long dirt road runs to the settlement of Araguaçui, 200km northwest on the Rio Araguaia, from where it should be possible to hitch a lift on a boat south along one of the two rivers flanking the Ilha do Bananal. Alternatively, another dirt road swings off west from the BR-153 some 40km south of Paraíso to connect with the even smaller settlement of Barreira da Cruz on the eastern side of the Ilha; here there are no facilities at all for visitors and the success of your trip will depend entirely on your skills in negotiating boat rental and guides with local *fazendeiros*.

Palmas

The capital of the state, **PALMAS** lies just under 1000km north of Brasília and just over 1200km south of Belém. The town itself, with a population of some 90,000, is inconveniently set back on the banks of the Rio Tocantins, some 150km by minor roads from the main Brasília–Belém highway BR-153, and there's little reason to come here. If you do get stuck in Palmas, the best **hotel** is the *Rio do Sono*, ACSUSO 10, conjunto 1, Lote 10 (☎ & ℱ63/215-1733; ➎), with nice bright rooms and a pool. Slightly cheaper, but also with a pool, is *Casa Grande*, Av. Joaquim Teotônio Sugurado, ACSUSO 20, conj. 1, Lote 1 (☎ & ℱ63/215-1813; ➍).

Araguaína

Lying 400km north of Palmas, **ARAGUAÍNA** is many times larger, but no more attractive a place to stay. It dominates the road network in northern Tocantins, located as it is almost exactly halfway between the Araguaia and Tocantins rivers. If you do end up staying here, perhaps while changing from one bus to another, there are a few possible **places to stay**. The best, with all-important cool pools, are *Tarcisio's Palace*, Av. Perimetral 1, Qd. 3, Setor Manoel Gomes, off the BR-153 (☎63/813-1110, ℱ813-1177; ➍), and *Olyntho Estância*, BR-153 Sul, km 125, Gurupi exit (☎ & ℱ63/813-1377; ➌). For **restaurants**, *Maresia's*, Rua das Mangueiras 868, has fine fish dishes; *Gaúcha*, on the same street at no. 1246, serves good *rodízio*, and more or less opposite, at no. 1213, *Don Fabrício* has a solid reputation for traditional regional cooking.

Travel details

Buses

Brasília to: Alto Paraísɔ: (2 daily; 3hr); Anápolis (every 30min); Belém (2 daily; 36hr) Belo Horizonte (7 daily; 14hr); Cristalina (3 daily; 2hr); Cuiabá (6 daily; 20hr); Formosa: (8 daily; 2hr); Goiânia (every 30min; 2hr 30min); Pirenópolis (6 daily; 3hr); Recife (1 daily; 48hr); Rio (6 daily; 20hr); Salvador (1 daily; 26hr); São Paulo (7 daily; 16hr).

Planes

Brasilia is second only to Rio and São Paulo for number and frequency of flights, although they are exclusively domestic. There are direct flights to most state capitals, and the rest are reachable after one stop. Flights to Rio and São Paulo average at least one an hour throughout the day; several flights daily to the state capitals of southern and northeastern Brazil. If you are heading to the Amazon, there are four flights daily to Belém and Manaus, but other Amazonian state capitals have only one or two flights daily, leaving in the evening. TAM, Varig, Gol and VASP all serve Brasília, along with their regional subsidiaries like RioSul.

Mato Grosso

CHAPTER 6

Highlights

* **Piranha fishing** Fish for your supper with a simple line and hook; the peaceful town of Coxim is an excellent place to arrange fishing trips. See p.531

* **Aquário Natural** A spectacular marine sanctuary near the sleepy town of Bonito, which itself offers good opportunities for snorkelling, caving, trekking and horse-riding. See p.538

* **Bais do Chop** The perfect spot to enjoy an ice-cold beer, this waterfront restaurant/bar in Corumbá also plays excellent live music at weekends. See p.543

* **The Pantanal** Probably the best place to spot wild mammals and exotic birds in the Americas. See p.546

* **Chapada dos Guimarães** A breathtaking plateau with a pleasant small town, lots of trails, plus the true geodesic centre of South America. See p.564

Mato Grosso

V ery Brazilian, in both its vastness and its frontier culture, the **Mato Grosso** region is essentially an enormous plain rippled by a handful of small mountain ranges. Equally Brazilian, there's a firm political boundary, a line on a map, across the heart of the Pantanal swamp marking the competing ambitions of two mammoth states: **Mato Grosso** and **Mato Grosso do Sul**. The northern half of the region – the state of Mato Grosso – is sparsely populated with the only settlements of any size - Cuiabá, Rondonópolis and Cáceres – having a combined population of little over a million. Most of the state of Mato Grosso do Sul, which is marginally more populous, is either seasonal flood plain or open scrubland. To the west of Mato Grosso do Sul are Bolivian swamps and forest; the mighty rivers **Araguaia** and **Paraná** (one flowing north, the other south) form a natural rim to the east, while the **Rio Paraguai** and the country named after it complete the picture to the south. The name Mato Grosso, which means "thick wood", is more appropriate to the northernmost state, where thorny scrubland passes into tropical rainforest and the land begins its incline towards the Amazon, interrupted only by the beautiful uplifted plateau of the Chapada dos Guimarães.

The simple road network and the limited sprinkling of settlements make **getting about** within Mato Grosso fairly hard work. Distances are enormous, and although most of the buses and trunk roads are good any journey is inevitably a long one. But the variety of landscape alone makes the trip a unique one and, for the adventurous traveller, there's any one of a wide range of fascinating locations – from swamps and forests to endless cattle ranches, riverine villages or jungle Indian reservations.

The cities of Mato Grosso are particularly deceptive. Although surprisingly modern and developed, they've only recently received the full trappings of civilization. Portuguese colonists began to settle in the region fairly late, at the time of the great **Cuiabá** gold rush of the early eighteenth century, though Cuiabá town itself remained almost completely isolated from the rest of Brazil until its first telegraph link was installed in the 1890s. Masterminded and built by a local boy made good – a down-to-earth army officer named Rondon – the telegraph lines were Mato Grosso's first real attempt to join the outside world. These days, with the completion of Highway BR-364, Cuiabá has again become a staging post for pioneers; this time for thousands of Brazilian peasants in search of land or work in the freshly opened western Amazon states of Rondônia and Acre. Cuiabá can't exactly claim to be a resort town, but it is a natural stepping stone for exploring either the Pantanal, or the mountainous scenery of the Chapada dos Guimarães.

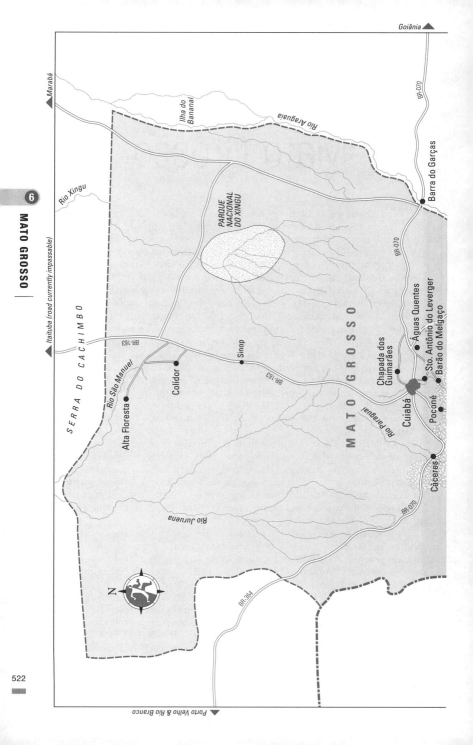

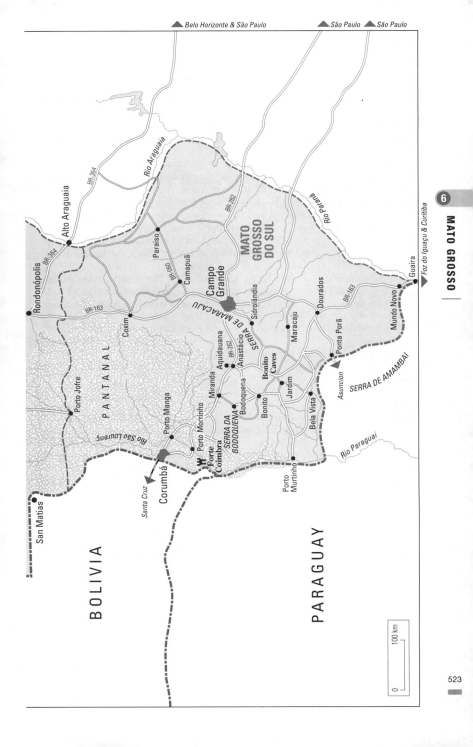

Until 1979 Cuiabá was capital of the entire Mato Grosso. **Campo Grande** in the south, however, was also growing rapidly and playing an increasingly important financial and administrative role within Brazil. The old state was sliced very roughly in half – Campo Grande becoming capital of the brand-new state of **Mato Grosso do Sul**. This tightening of political control over the various Mato Grosso regions reflects their rapid development and relative wealth – a complete contrast to the poorer, even more expansive and much more remote wilderness of the Amazon basin. These days Campo Grande is a bustling, very modern city of almost a million people, with most visitors stopping here en route to the Pantanal.

Topographically, and in terms of its tourist potential, Mato Grosso will always be dominated by the **Pantanal**, one of the world's largest swamps, which extends into both the states of Mato Grosso and Mato Grosso do Sul, and is renowned as one of the best places for spotting wildlife in the whole of South America. Between two million and five million caiman alligators are "culled" annually from the Pantanal, though it's better known for its array of birdlife and its endless supply of piranha fish – the latter used in an excellent regional soup dish. So far it's proved impossible to put a road right through the Pantanal, and travelling anywhere around here is slow.

After Cuiabá and Campo Grande, **Corumbá**, on the western edge of the swamp, is probably the next most popular urban destination and a good base for the Pantanal. Compared to Cuiabá and the northern areas, it's usually a less expensive entry point for the swamp. A relatively small city, Corumbá is only half an hour from Bolivia, but seven or eight from Campo Grande, the nearest Brazilian outpost. It is possible to travel through the Pantanal by river from Corumbá, directly to the port of Cáceres near Cuiabá, though unless you can afford a luxury tour this adventurous fluvial route takes at least a week, and often longer.

Getting around

There are three main **routes** through Mato Grosso. Two fan out around the main Pantanal swamplands in tweezer-like form and run east to west: the most heavily used road, the BR-364 through Cuiabá, and the BR-262, which runs through Campo Grande to Corumbá. The third road, the BR-163, runs from south to north, connecting Campo Grande with Cuiabá, and extending north to Santarém on the Amazon river (impassable since 1992) and south to Paraguay and Asunción. Given the distances involved, anyone in possession of a Brazilian **air pass**, or simply limited by time, might well consider the occasional plane hop.

Mato Grosso is officially one hour behind the standard **time** of Brasília and the coast. In Campo Grande, however, not everybody operates on Mato Grosso time, so it's always a good idea to synchronize with the right authority when arranging bus or plane reservations.

Mato Grosso do Sul

A fairly new state, **Mato Grosso do Sul** is nevertheless considered to be one of Brazil's better-established economic regions. It has a distinct Wild West flavour: here, close to the border with Paraguay and just a bit further from Argentinian *gaucho* territory, it's not uncommon to end up dancing Spanish polkas through the night in some of the region's bars. Until the eighteenth century the whole region was Indian territory and was considered an inhospitable corner of the New World. A hundred and fifty years and numerous bloody battles later, Mato Grosso do Sul might now be developed and "civilized" but – thankfully – it's still a place where you can forget about industrial ravages and wonder at nature's riches.

The state capital, **Campo Grande**, is a useful base from which to delve deeper into Mato Grosso. The road connection to Corumbá is well served by daily buses, and some tour companies operate from here, so reaching the Pantanal is fairly easy. But the swamp is vast, stretching into the state from north to southwest, so you can also get a bit of a feel for what it's like from a variety of road-linked places closer to Campo Grande - like **Coxim**, north of the city, or **Aquidauana**, to the west.

The south of the state is favoured by the beautiful hills of the **Serra da Bodoquena** and **Serra da Maracaju** and, deep in the Bodoquena hills, you can visit the spectacular cave systems, forests and rivers of the **Bonito** area. Further south, 319km from Campo Grande, **Ponta Porã** sits square on the Paraguayan border, from where there's a two-day overland route to Asunción. There are also several daily bus services from Campo Grande via **Dourados** and **Mundo Novo** to Guaira and the amazing falls of Foz do Iguaçu in the neighbouring state of Paraná.

Campo Grande

Nicknamed the "brunette city" because of its chestnut-coloured earth, **CAMPO GRANDE** has in less than fifty years been transformed from an insignificant settlement into a buzzing metropolis with a population of 800,000. Founded in 1889, the city was only made the capital of the new state of Mato Grosso do Sul in the late 1970s, since when it has almost doubled in size, though it retains a distinctly rural flavour: its downtown area manages to combine skyscraping banks and apartment buildings with ranchers' general stores and poky little shops selling strange forest herbs and Catholic *ex votos*. Unnervingly reminiscent of Dallas in parts, it's a relatively salubrious market centre for an enormous cattle-ranching region; it's also an important centre of South American trade routes from Paraguay, Bolivia, Argentina and the south of Brazil.

An obvious place to break a long journey between Cuiabá or Corumbá and the coast, Campo Grande tries hard to shake off the feeling that it's a city stuck in the middle of nowhere. Apart from the *gaucho* influence, the town centre is much like that of any other medium-sized city; the people are friendly and there's little manifest poverty. The generally warm evenings inspire the locals to turn out on the streets in force. People chat over a meal or sip ice-cold beers at one of the restaurants or bars around Avenida Afonso Pena and the Praça Ari

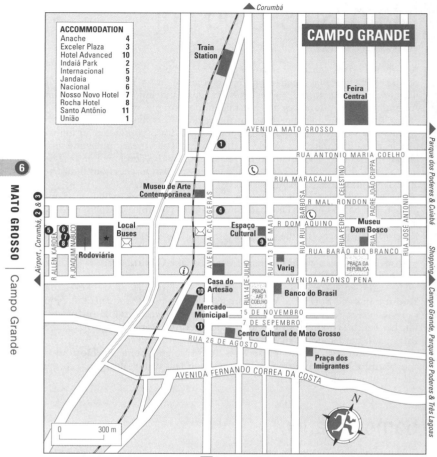

ACCOMMODATION

Anache	4
Exceler Plaza	3
Hotel Advanced	10
Indaiá Park	2
Internacional	5
Jandaia	9
Nacional	6
Nosso Novo Hotel	7
Rocha Hotel	8
Santo Antônio	11
União	1

CAMPO GRANDE

Corumbá

Train Station

Feira Central

Museu de Arte Contemporânea

AVENIDA MATO GROSSO

RUA ANTONIO MARIA COELHO

RUA MARACAJU

R MAL. RONDON

Espaço Cultural

R DOM AQUINO

Museu Dom Bosco

Local Buses

Rodoviária

RUA BARÃO RIO BRANCO

PRAÇA DA REPÚBLICA

Varig

Casa do Artesão

AVENIDA AFONSO PENA

Banco do Brasil

15 DE NOVEMBRO

Mercado Municipal

7 DE SEPTEMBRO

Centro Cultural de Mato Grosso

RUA 26 DE AGOSTO

Praça dos Imigrantes

AVENIDA FERNANDO CORREA DA COSTA

Airport, Corumbá, 2 & 3

Parque dos Poderes & Cuiabá

Shopping ▶ Campo Grande, Parque dos Poderes & Três Lagoas

N

0   300 m

Teatro Glauce Rocha, Museu José Pereira & Hipódromo

The Campo Grande railroad

Look at any map of the region, and you'll see a thin black line tracing the path of a long railroad that connects São Paulo on the Atlantic with Campo Grande, where it forks to Corumbá on the Bolivian border, and to Ponta Porã on the Paraguayan frontier. Unfortunately, the privatization of the Brazilian railways has led to the closure of all passenger lines west of Bauru, perhaps forever. This is a real shame, not least because the Corumbá line formed part of an even longer rail system, connecting with the Bolivian *Tren de los Mortes* to Santa Cruz; from there it's still possible to continue by train into Chile or via La Paz into Peru, over Lake Titicaca (by boat or around it on a bus) and on to Cuzco. There seems little chance in the immediate future of the lines being reopened (though freight trains are still running), but with ever-increasing tourist interest in the Pantanal and Mato Grosso do Sul, services may in the course of time resume.

Coelho, and guitars, maracas and congas are often brought out for an impromptu music session.

Arrival, information and accommodation

The **rodoviária** (⊕67/383-1678) is a ten-minute walk west of the central Praça Ari Coelho at Rua Joaquim Nabuco 200. A surprisingly large bus terminal, it also houses six hairdressers, a cinema, bookstores and several bars. A **word of warning**, however: the *rodoviária* is known for its unsavoury types, and though you should have no problems during the day the area is best avoided at night unless you're confident of yourself and haven't much to lose. (Similarly, the district south of Avenida Afonso Pena is also acquiring a dodgy reputation.) If in doubt, take a **taxi**: there's a rank in the bus station, or phone Rádio Táxi on ⊕67/387-1414. The other point of arrival is the **airport**, Aeroporto Internacional Antônio João (⊕67/363-2444), 7km out of town on the road towards Aquidauana. Buses from the airport to the *rodoviária* cost around 80¢, taxis $5.

Tourist information is readily available at the very helpful Morada dos Bais tourist office (Tues–Sat 8am–7pm, Sun 9am–noon; ⊕67/324-5830 or 383-1199, ✉pensao@ms-sebrae.com.br) at Av. Noroeste 5140, on the corner with Avenida Afonso Pena. Here, you'll find a notice board with details on cinema, theatre and exhibition listings. Alternatively, check out ⊛www.guiacidade .com.br or call ⊕67/351-9900, a free English-language tourist helpline operated by SEBRAE. There's also an information point at the airport (⊕67/363-3116).

Accommodation

With the demise of passenger trains, the majority of hotels around the *rodoviária* smartened up their act, and today offer quite acceptable alternatives to both the downtown and rather defunct train station options. The better budget ones are around the junction of Rua Barão do Rio Branco and Rua Allan Kardek, one street west of the *rodoviária*.

Anache Rua Cândido Mariano Rondon 1396 ⊕67/383-2841. A no-frills option but clean and safe, in a good central location, with friendly service. ❶

Exceler Plaza Av. Afonso Pena 444 ⊕67/321-0102, ⓕ321-5666. A plush hotel where you'll be coddled and swaddled in all the usual four-star treats. ❽

Hotel Advanced Av. Calógeras 1909 ⊕67/321 5000, ⓕ325 7744, ⊛www.hoteladvanced.com.br. A large modern hotel in the centre of Campo Grande, with a bar, suites and convention rooms spread over nine floors. Good service and value for money, though non-descript. ❸–❹

Indaiá Park Av. Afonso Pena 354 ⊕67/312-9400, ⓕ321-0359, ⊛www.indaia-hotel.com.br. Three-star hotel with pool, restaurant and piano bar, but rather impersonal. ❻

Internacional Rua Allan Kardek 223 ⊕67/384-4677, ⓕ321-2729, ⊛www.hotelintermetro.com.br. The largest and flashiest of the hotels around the *rodoviária*, and surprisingly well appointed, with TVs and phones

in all rooms and even a small pool for the weary to sink into. Well worth the extra few *reais*. ❸

Jandaia Rua Barão do Rio Branco 1271, on the corner with Rua 13 de Maio ⊕67/321-7000, ⓕ321-1401, ⊛www.jandaia.com.br. This excellent luxury hotel has a restaurant serving some delicious local dishes. ❻

Nacional Rua Dom Aquino 610 ⊕ & ⓕ67/383-2561. Probably the best value of the budget places around the *rodoviária*, with plenty of character. Choice of fans or air-conditioning. ❸–❹

Nosso Novo Hotel Rua Joaquim Nabuco 185 ⊕67/321-0505. Close to the *rodoviária* and linked to Youth Hostelling International, with dorms, as well as single and double rooms, solar showers, some private bathrooms, plus TVs, laundry and Internet facilities. Staff can provide information on the Pantanal, Bonito, Bolivia, Rio and Iguazu. ❶–❷

Rocha Hotel Rua Barao Rio Branco 343 ⊕67/325-6874, ✉ajcampogrande@hotmail.com. Near the bus station and offering a little more comfort than the *Nosso Novo*, with parking

facilities in front and adequate rooms. **②**
Santo Antônio Av. Calógeras 1813 ☎ 67/324-4552. Very central and excellent value with private baths and a pleasant breakfast room; basic but

stylish. **②**
União Av. Calógeras 2828 ☎ 67/382-4213. Close to the train station, simple and somewhat run-down but clean and excellent value. **②**

The City

The surprisingly modern heart of Campo Grande is based around the Praça Ari Coelho, five blocks east of the *rodoviária*. Tourism is fairly low-key in the city, but there's enough to keep you interested for a couple of days. One of the best-known attractions is the **Museu Dom Bosco** (Mon–Fri 8am–6pm, Sat 8am–5pm, Sun noon–6pm; $1), in the university building facing the Praça da República, at Rua Barão do Rio Branco 1811-43. A fascinating place, it's crammed full of exhibits, ranging from superb forest Indian artefacts to over 10,000 terrifying dead insects and some astonishingly beautiful butterflies. Most impressive of all is the vast collection of stuffed birds and animals, including giant rheas (the South American version of an ostrich), anacondas and examples of the Brazilian marsupials – the gamba and the quica.

Closer to the city centre, the **Casa do Artesão** (Mon–Fri 8am–6pm, Sat 9am–5pm), on the corner of Avenida Calógeras and Avenida Afonso Pena, is slightly disappointing considering the huge region it is supposed to represent (not least the Terena, Kadiwéu and Guato peoples). It sells mostly local craft works, the best pieces without a doubt being the woodcarvings, often depicting mythical symbols like fish-women and totemic figures. Just down the road from here, the tourist information office at Av. Noroeste 5140 (Tues–Sat 9am–8pm) also houses a small historical museum and a couple of art galleries showing changing exhibitions. Two **galleries** specializing in local contemporary art are the Museu de Arte Contemporânea de Mato Grosso do Sul (MARCO), Av. Calógeras 2499 (Tues–Fri 9am–6pm, Sat & Sun 9am–4pm), and the Centro Cultural de Mato Grosso, Rua 26 de Agosto 463.

Campo Grande also hosts several markets: the **Mercado Municipal** (daily, closed Mon morning) sells a good range of inexpensive souvenirs, including cow-horn trumpets, horn goblets and drinking gourds; the **Feira Indigena** (daily) just outside the Mercado Municipal, devotes itself almost exclusively to market-garden produce from the *mata*; and the **Feira Central**, Rua Abrão Julio Rahe, off Avenida Mato Grosso, takes place twice a week (Wed & Sat), overnight from 3pm to 6am, and attracts a large number of forest Indians selling potions and bundles of bark, beads and leatherwork, as well as a few Paraguayans selling toys. The eclectic blend of peoples is further compounded by the variety of foods on offer, ranging from *churrasquinho* to Japanese *yaki soba*.

There's good-quality *artesanato* on sale, mainly handicrafts such as cotton embroidery and leatherwork, at **Feria de Artesanato de Artistas Sul Mato Grossenses**, Praça dos Imigrantes (9am–6pm Mon–Sat), where there's also a small outdoor café. For the flip side to contemporary Mato Grosso culture, head for the **cowboy shop** at Rua Barão do Rio Branco 1296 near the *Jandaia Hotel*, which sells gun belts, holsters, saddles and boots. You can see some of this gear in action at the **horse racing**, out at the Hipódromo, run by the Jóquei Clube de Campo Grande; the Hipódromo is 5km along BR-167, beyond the exit for Dourados.

If all this is too much for you, head for the **Parque dos Poderes**, beyond the town centre at the end of Avenida Mato Grosso (Mon–Fri noon–6pm), a calm ecological reserve that's home to a variety of native plants and a small selection of the region's wild animals.

Eating, drinking and nightlife

Eating out is an important part of the local lifestyle and this is reflected in the diversity of restaurants. There are scores of **lanchonetes**, especially around the *rodoviária* and east along Rua Dom Aquino, and, during the hot afternoons, the city's many **juice bars** do brisk business: you'll find them on most street corners. This is a cattle-ranching market centre, and a lot of cows get roasted daily in Campo Grande, so if you're mad for **beef** you're in for a treat; however, there are also vegetarian options and several good Chinese restaurants.

Cantina Romana Rua da Paz 237 ℡ 67/324-9777. Wonderful Italian food, good atmosphere and very fair prices.

Casa Colonial Av. Afonso Pena 3997 ℡ 67/383-3207. Primarily a *churrascaria*, this place serves excellent traditional and rural Brazilian cooking. Expensive.

Casa do Peixe Rua João Rosa Pires 1030 ℡ 67/382-7121. Very popular spot for delicious regional dishes, with fish as the main speciality, and often with live music at weekends. Exceptional value and the service is excellent. Closed Sun evening.

China Rua Pedro Celestino 750 ℡ 67/382-4476. One of the best Chinese restaurants in town, with very reasonable prices; the fried duck (*pato frito*) is particularly recommended.

Don Leon Av. Afonso Pena 1901 ℡ 67/384-6520. A popular *churrascaria* and pizzeria, with scores of tables, fast friendly service and the added bonus of live music some evenings.

Fruta Nativa Rua Barão Rio Branco 1097. This busy lunchtime snack bar serves light and inexpensive meals, including chips and chicken, outside at the yellow tables. Next door there's an unnamed juice bar where you can sip on *sucos de guarana* and munch on *pastels* (cakes) and *tortas* (tarts).

Hong Kong Senshin-An Rua João Rosa Pires 761 ℡ 67/324-3237. An excellent Chinese restaurant specializing in local tofu and regional curry dishes. Moderately priced.

Kalil Karnes Av. Furnas 142, near Shopping Campo Grande towards the eastern end of Av. Afonso Pena ℡ 67/726-3715. Meat house with a good reputation, but somewhat out of the way, unless you're thinking of clubbing afterwards (see below).

Multiplus Vegetallis Rua 13 de Junho 756 ℡ 67/725-8109. Good vegetarian restaurant despite its vaguely homeopathic-sounding name.

Radio Clube Rua Padre João Crippa 1280 ℡ 67/321-0131. Brisk and cheap spot for basic Brazilian and international fare, popular with students and only open until midnight.

San Marino Pizzas Av. Afonso Pena 2716 ℡ 67/321-5084. One of several reasonable pizzerias on Afonso Pena, with delivery service.

Seriema Restaurante Av. Afonso Pena 1919 ℡ 67/721-2475. Near *Don Leon's* (see above), this is also a lively steak house, with cheap lunchtime *rodízio*.

Viva a Vida Rua Dom Aquino 1354, 1st floor ℡ 67/384-6524 and Av. Fernando Corréa da Costa 2177 ℡ 67/321-3208. Campo Grande's favourite vegetarian restaurant (meat also available) is self-service, and open lunchtimes only. Closed Sat.

Nightlife

Most of Campo Grande's action happens at weekends, when the *churrascarias* and other large restaurants generally serve their food to the energetic sounds of Paraguayan polkas (*Don Leon's* has them on weekdays as well). **Nightclubs** tend to change quickly, but those currently popular are *Limit* (200m off Av. Afonso Pena by Shopping Campo Grande); *Pele Vermelha* on Rua 7 de Setembro, near Rua Bahia; and *Tango*, Rua Candido Mariano 2181. All three are to the east of the city centre, and play a mix of Brazilian, European, Stateside and underground sounds. There's also *Acoustic Bar*, with mainly electronic Brazilian music on Rua 13 de Maio, close to Rua Candido Mariano, and *Club de Amistade*, with live dance music at weekends, out at Av. Tiradentes 942-B, Taveiropolis ℡ 67/331-1977.

The Glauce Rocha **theatre** is out of town, in Cidade Universitária, but often hosts interesting Brazilian works: ℡ 67/387-3311 for details, or check the local papers *Folho do Povo* or *Correio do Estado*. *Peña Eme-Ene*, on the corner of

Avenida Afonso Pena and Rua Barbosa, is a popular meeting place for artists and musicians, and has live regional music every Thursday night from 8pm – no entrance fee but you're expected to take dinner (Mon–Wed & Fri 7.30am–6pm, Thurs 7.30am–midnight, Sat noon–6pm; ☎67/383-2373).

For a more unusual night out, head for one of Campo Grande's **bingo** halls; recently introduced to Brazil, bingo has proved very popular with young and old alike. The Salas do Bingo are at Av. Mato Grosso 3566 and Rua 14 de Julho 1453.

Listings

Airlines Pantanal Linhas Aéreas, Rua Maracaju 1525 ☎67/363-1322 or 763-3859; TAM, Av. Afonso Pena 1974 ☎67/368-6161 or at airport ☎67/368-6152; Varig, Rua Barão do Rio Branco 1356 ☎67/325-4070; VASP, Av. Candido Mariano 1837 ☎67/321-8277.

Air taxis Mato Grosso do Sul, Av. Duque Caxias ☎67/363-1131; Taq-Quartin ☎67/341-4797 or 384-4127.

Banks and exchange You can change money in the Banco do Brasil, just off the main square at Av. Afonso Pena 133 (Mon–Fri 10am–5pm); at the HSBC bank, Rua 13 de Maio 2836; at the Câmbio, Rua 13 de Maio 2484; or at the airport bank.

Car rental Brascar, Rua Fernando Corréa da Costa 975 ☎67/383-1570; Lemans, Rua 7 de Setembro 334, Centro ☎0800/92-5100; Unidas, Av. Afonso Pena 829 ☎67/384-5626.

Consulates If you're heading into either Paraguay or Bolivia from Campo Grande, you should check on border procedures and visa requirements. The Paraguayan consul is at Rua 26 de Agosto 384 (☎67/324-4934), and the Bolivian consul at Rua João de Souza 798 (☎67/382-2190); both are open Mon–Fri 9am–5pm.

Health matters The Santa Casa hospital is at Rua Eduardo Santos Pereira 88 (☎67/382-5151).

Internet CH@T Room Cyber Café, Rua Pedro Celestino 992 ☎67/383-4231; and Iris Cybercafe, Av. Afonso Pena, block 20.

Laundry Planet Clean, Rua Joaquim Murtinho 135, close to the Praça dos Imigrantes.

Pharmacy Rua Barbosa, on the corner of the main square by Rua 14 de Julho and Av. Afonso Pena.

Police Emergency number ☎190.

Post offices The branch at Av. Calógeras 2309, on the corner with Rua Dom Aquino, is open Mon–Fri 8am–5pm, Sat 8–11.30am; the one on Rua Barão do Rio Branco by the *rodoviária* stays open till 6pm Mon–Fri.

Shopping Shopping Campo Grande, Av. Afonso Pena 4909, is a large and flashy shopping centre towards the eastern end of Av. Afonso Pena, replete with multiplex cinemas and over 170 shops. The busiest shopping streets in the town centre are mostly congregated in the square formed by Av. Calógeras, Av. Afonso Pena, Rua Cândido Mariano Rondon and Rua Pedro Celestino. A street market selling plastic goods and electronics sets up daily along Rua Barão do Rio Branco between the *rodoviária* and Av. Calógeras. The Barroarte shop at Av. Afonso Oena 4329, Jardim dos Estados, has a wide range of good, local ceramics, sculptures and paintings; it's some distance from the centre, but en route to Shopping Campo Grande.

Travel and tour companies Air Travel Turismo, Av. Afonso Pena 20 (☎67/382-0888), and NPQ Turismo, Av. Afonso Pena 2081, on Praça Ari Coelho (☎67/725-6789), are best for flights. If you're on a tight budget, Ecological Expeditions offer a range of affordable tours (see p.554 for more information). Impacto Turismo, Rua Padre João Crippa 1065, sala 106 (☎67/382-5197 or 724-3167), also run good Pantanal tours; Ney Gonzalves is an excellent guide. Also in Campo Grande, Lilian Borges Rodrigues is a very good English-speaking guide; contact her at Rua Octavio de Souza 464, Monte Libano (☎67/742-2204). See also the box "Upmarket Pantanal Agents and Operators" on p.550.

North to Coxim

The area of scrub forest to the east of Coxim and north of Campo Grande used to be the territory of the **Caiapó** Indian nation, who ambushed miners along the routes to Goiás and Cuiabá from São Paulo, posing a serious threat to

Portuguese expansion and development in the mid-eighteenth century. In reaction to the successful use of Bororo Indian mercenaries against their main villages in the Camapua area, the Caiapó took their revenge on the growing numbers of Portuguese settlers and their farm slaves in the area. In 1751 – the same year that the governor of Brazil declared an official military campaign against them – the Caiapó went as far as attacking the town of Goiás, beyond the northern limits of their usual territory.

Today, **COXIM** is a quiet place, easily reached by bus from Campo Grande in around three to four hours (six or seven hours from Cuiabá). Situated on the eastern edges of the Pantanal, it's a fantastic **fishing** centre: the fisherman Pirambero runs excellent trips into the swamp, down the Rio Taquari, to catch piranhas (ask for him at the port). If you're really serious about angling, contact the local fishing club, the Iate Clube Rio Verde, at Rua Ferreira, Bairro Piracema (☎67/291-1246). Besides fishing, swimming in the Rio Taquari around Campo Falls is another popular pastime, in spite of the razor-teethed fish, and, nearby on the Rio Coxim, the **Palmeiras Falls** are a good place for a picnic or to camp a while. From November through to January, the two falls are the best places to see the incredible *piracema* spectacle – thousands of fish, leaping clear of the river, on their way upstream to the river's source to lay their eggs.

Coxim offers plenty of **accommodation** possibilities, including the *Hotel Neves* one block from the *rodoviária* in an old brick farmhouse (☎67/291-1273; ❸); the very basic *Aconchega* right opposite the bus station (no ☎; ❶); and the more upmarket *Hotel Santa Ana*, Rua Miranda Reis (☎67/291-1602; ❸), with a pool and bar. There are many more hotels, mostly aimed at fishing holiday-makers, 5km away in Silviolândia. When it's time to move on, it might be worth enquiring about river boats to Corumbá. The Rio Taquari has silted up considerably in recent years – the effect of land clearance for cattle grazing and agriculture, leading to huge amounts of topsoil being shifted into the river systems – and as a result, boats along the river are now rare, though there are still a few.

South to the Paraguayan border

There's no great draw – in fact, no draw at all – in the towns south of Campo Grande en route to the Paraguayan border. The only settlement of any size is **DOURADOS**, 224km from the state capital, a violent, rapidly expanding place which recently overtook Corumbá as Mato Grosso do Sul's second-largest city. Its name is a reminder of the fact that the spot was first settled by travellers en route to the Cuiabá gold mines. These days, it's the region's most important agricultural centre, but there's little of interest to the tourist except bus connections to points further south and west (the daily bus to Bonito currently leaves at 3pm). Should you get stranded overnight, three reasonable **accommodation** options are *Dourados Park,* Avenida Guaicurus km 2 (☎67/426-1309; ⓦwww.douradosparkhotel.com.br; ❹), one of the most comfortable in town; *Hotel Alphonsus*, Av. Presidente Vargas 603 (☎67/422-5211; ❸) with pool; and, cheapest of all, *Turis Hotel*, Av. Marcelino Pires 5932 (☎67/422-1909, ⓕ421-8827; ❷).

MUNDO NOVO, about eleven hours by bus from Campo Grande, is another unattractive transport terminus. From here, buses run to the crossing point for ferries to Guaira, and to Porto Frajelli and Foz do Iguaçu. If you have to stay over, the *Hotel Marajoara*, Av. Castelo Branco 93 (☎67/474-1692; ❷), has decent rooms.

Ponta Porã

Despite the distinctly unthrilling towns that have gone before, **PONTA PORÃ** itself is an attractive little settlement, right on the Paraguayan border up in the Maracaju hills. The **Avenida Internacional** divides the settlement in two – on one side of the street you're in Brazil, on the other in the Paraguayan town of **Pedro Juan Caballero**. On the Paraguayan side you can polka the night away, gamble your money till dawn or, like most people there, just buy a load of imported goods at the duty-free shops, while the Brazilian side is a little more staid. There's a strange blend of language and character, and even a unique *mestizo* cuisine, making it an interesting place to spend a day or two. Ponta Porã also has a tradition as a distribution centre for *maté* – an herb brewed to make a tea-like drink.

There are plenty of **hotels** to choose from, though most budget travellers tend to go for the *Alvorada* (❶) or *Dos Viajantes* (❶), over the road from the train station, both of which are cheap and friendly. The *Internacional*, Av. Internacional 2604 (☎67/431-1243; ❸), is a mid-range hotel with regular hot water, while for a plusher stay it's hard to beat the *Pousada do Bosque*, just outside Ponta Porã at Av. Presidente Vargas 1151 (☎67/431-1181, ☎431-1741; ❺), with its welcoming swimming pool.

Crossing the border is a simple procedure for most non–Brazilians. An exit stamp must be obtained from the Polícia Federal at Rua Mal. Floriano 1483 (☎67/431-1428) on the Brazilian side, then it's a matter of walking four or five blocks down Rua Guia Lopes to the Paraguayan customs and control. If you need a visa for Paraguay you can get this from the consulate on Avenida Internacional on the Brazilian side. If you're pushed for time, catch a cab from the bus station to complete exit and entry formalities; the fare is about $8, including waiting time. Once in Paraguay, there's a reasonably good road direct to Concepción, a major source of imports and contraband for Brazilians; daily buses make the five- or six-hour trip in good weather. It's another five hours from there to Asunción; there's also a direct service (8–10hr) from the bus station in Pedro Juan Caballero. There's no problem **changing money** at decent rates on Avenida Internacional, but it's impossible to change traveller's cheques on Sundays and holidays.

Bela Vista and Porto Murtinho

The two other interesting destinations on the Paraguayan border are Bela Vista and Porto Murtinho, both to the west of Ponta Porã and harder to reach. While they don't serve as gateways to Paraguay (it's technically illegal to cross the frontier at these places), they are worth visiting for the splendour of their natural setting alone. Both towns are served by **bus** from Dourados (a good day's journey), and from Jardim (8hr), which in turn is connected daily with Anastácio (4hr).

In **BELA VISTA** you can explore the natural delights of the Piripacu and Caracol rivers, behind which are the unspoilt peaks of the Três Cerros and Cerro Margarida. There's also the extraordinary **Nhandejara bridge**, a water-eroded underground passage over 30m long. Most Brazilians, however, come here for the opportunity to buy imported goods: over the border is the Paraguayan town of Bela Vista, which has a road connection (a day's travel) to Concepción. If you need to stay, try the *Pousada da Fronteira*, Av. Teodoro Sativa 1485 (☎67/439-1487; ❸).

Remote and tranquil, **PORTO MURTINHO** owes its foundation to the thriving trade in the tea-type herb, *erva maté*. The town of 13,000 inhabitants sits on the banks of the Rio Paraguai, over 470km southwest of Campo Grande, near where the river finally leaves Brazilian territory. Well blessed with abundant wildlife and luxuriant vegetation, it marks the very southern limits of the Pantanal swamplands. Porto Murtinho is quite a cheap place from which to make excursions in riverboats, though you might be expected to haggle over the price a little, since there are often several boatmen to choose from at the riverfront.

For **accommodation**, *Hotel Americano*, Rua Dr Corréa 430 (☎67/287-1344, ☎287-1309, ⓦ www.donipesca.com.br); ⑤ full-board), has 38 large, air-conditioned rooms and boats for residents' use (rowing boats $15/3hr, motorboats $50/3hr); 1km out of town, in the Fazenda Saladero, is the similar *Saladero Cue* (☎67/287-1113, ☎287-1352, ⓦ www.hotelsaladerocue.com.br; ❹), which has a beautiful riverside location and also has boats for hire; slightly cheaper but not as nice is the *Pousada do Pantanal*, Rua Alfredo Pinto 141 (☎67/287-1325; ❸). Lastly, the *Americano* owns and runs *Hotel Nabileque* (⑤), 120km upriver on the Rio Nabileque, and primarily a base for anglers. The hotel is actually built on the river, supported on stilts, and has boats for hire. Daily boats (3hr) from the *Americano* will get you out there.

West towards Corumbá

Several **buses** daily connect Campo Grande with Aquidauana/Anastácio (2hr) and Corumbá (7hr), the scenery becoming increasingly swamp-like the further west you travel. It may still be worth enquiring about the axed passenger train to Corumbá (see p.526) in case someone has had the good sense to restart it.

West of Campo Grande, the savanna becomes forested as the road approaches the first real range of hills since leaving the Atlantic coast. Sticking up like a gigantic iceberg in the vast southern Mato Grosso, the **Serra de Maracaju** provided sanctuary for local Terena Indians during a period of Paraguayan military occupation in the 1860s. Under their somewhat crazy and highly ambitious dictator, Lopez, the Paraguayans invaded the southern Mato Grosso in 1864, a colonial adventure that resulted in the death of over half the invasion force, mostly composed of native (Paraguayan) Guarani Indians. This was one period in Brazilian history when whites and Indians fought for the same cause, and it was in the magnificent Serra de Maracaju hills that most of the guerrilla-style resistance took place. Beyond, interesting geological formations dominate the horizon: vast towering tors, known as *torrelones*, rise magnificently out of the scrubby savanna. Further west, around the small station of **Camisão**, is a relatively lush valley supporting tropical fruits, sugar cane and, of course, beef cattle.

Aquidauana and Anastácio

The next town, **AQUIDAUANA**, 130km from Campo Grande, is a lazy-looking place and very hot, sitting under the beating sun of the Piraputanga uplands. Since the demise of the passenger trains to Corumbá, it sweats somewhat uncomfortably some distance from the main BR-262 highway, and, though it still serves as one of several gateways into the Pantanal, it's better known for fishing and walking, with some superb views across the swamp. These days, most visitors see little more than the signpost at the crossroads where the highway bypasses town; if you stop by here, it'll most likely be to use the highway café or toilet facilities at the junction. If you do go into town or stay over here, it's worth enquiring about two nearby but seldom visited sites: the ruins of the Cidade de Xaraés, founded by the Spanish in 1580 on the banks of the Rio Aquidauana; and the **Morro do Desenho**, a series of prehistoric inscriptions on the riverbank and in the nearby hills.

The river running through the town boasts some pleasant sandy **beaches**, quite clean and safe for swimming between May and October; **fishing** championships are an integral part of the annual São João August festival here. There's a reasonable choice of **hotels**, including the quiet *Hotel Pantanal* (℡67/241-1929; ❷) at Rua Estevão Alves Correa 2611 opposite the *rodoviária*. The *Portal Pantaneiro*, Rua Pandiá Calógeras 1067 (℡67/241-4328, ℗241-4327; ❸), has a pool and very comfortable rooms; and the *Hotel Tropical*, Rua Manoel Aureliano Costa 533 (℡67/241-4113; ❸), with its smart rooms and good showers, is another one of the best in town. One of several decent restaurants is the *O Casarão*, Rua Manoel Antônio Paes de Barros 533 (℡67/241-2219), which is expensive but serves delicious, though not exclusively Brazilian, dishes.

The neighbouring town of **ANASTÁCIO** – half an hour's walk on the other side of the river – has some nice beaches of its own, but is best known for the large *jaú* fish (often weighing over 75kg) that live in its river. Anastácio is the transport hub of the region, with daily bus services to Bela Vista, Bonito, Miranda and Ponta Porã, as well as Campo Grande and Corumbá. If you're lucky enough to have your own wheels, there's an infrequently taken road that skirts the southeastern rim of the Pantanal right up to **Rio Verde do Mato Grosso**, 200km north of Campo Grande on the way to Cuiabá, which has ample opportunities for bathing in the transparent waters and cascades that feed the Rio Verde.

Fifty kilometres south of Aquidauana on the road towards Bonito, the *Cabana do Pescador* **luxury fishing lodge** on the Rio Miranda (℡67/245-2406; ❻), is another relaxing destination and a possible base from which to go horse riding or take a tour to the Bonito caves (see p.537); there are frequent buses from the *Cabana* to both Aquidauana and Bonito.

Miranda

Seventy kilometres west of Anastácio, the small town of **MIRANDA** sits straddling the BR-262 at the foot of the Serra da Bodoquena by the Rio Miranda. Once the scene of historic battles, Miranda has been somewhat ignored by visitors since the demise of the old Campo Grande to Corumbá rail service, but it's a pleasant town that is known for excellent fishing and for Terena and Kadiwéu artefacts. It's also a good base for visiting Bonito (128km) or the Pantanal swamp.

If you plan on staying, there are several reasonable **hotels**, including *Pantanal Hotel*, Av. Barão do Rio Branco 609 (℡ & ℗67/242-1608; ❹), which has a pool; and a good cheap option, the *Hotel Roma*, Praça Agenor Carrillo 356 (℡67/242-1321; ❸); *Hotel Chalé*, just up from the *rodoviária* on Rua Barão do Rio Branco (℡67/242-1216; ❸), is similarly good value, with clean, modern rooms, all with air-conditioning. The best hotel, however, is the *Pousada Águas do Pantanal*, Av. Afonso Pena 367 (℡67/242-1314, ℗242-1242; ❹), with a pool and excellent service. The management there also runs the *Fazenda San Francisco*, 36km down the road to Bonito (℡67/242-1497; ❻), which offers lots of activities, but at a cost. The *Refúgio Ecológico Caiman* (℡67/242-1450, reser-

The Terena Indians

West beyond Aquidauana lies the traditional territory of the **Terena people**, for whom there was little peace even after the Paraguayan occupation of the 1860s. The late nineteenth century saw an influx of Brazilian colonists into the Aquidauana and Miranda valleys as the authorities attempted to "populate" the regions between Campo Grande and Paraguay – the war with Paraguay had only made them aware of how fertile these valleys were. Pushed off the best of the land and forced, in the main, to work for new, white landowners, the Terena tribe remained vulnerable until the appearance of **Lieutenant Rondon** (after whom the Amazonian state of Rondônia was named). Essentially an engineer, he came across the Terena in 1903 after constructing a telegraph connection – poles, lines and all – through virtually impassable swamps and jungle between Cuiabá and Corumbá. With his help, the Terena managed to establish a legal claim to some of their traditional land. Considered by FUNAI (the federal agency for Indian affairs) to be one of the most successfully "integrated" Indian groups in modern Brazil, the Terena have earned a reputation for possessing the necessary drive and ability to compete successfully in the market system – a double-edged compliment in that it could be used by the authorities to undermine their rights to land as a tribal group. They live mostly between Aquidauana and Miranda, the actual focus of their territory being the town and train station of **Taunay** – an interesting little settlement with mule-drawn taxi wagons and a peaceful atmosphere. You'll find Terena handicrafts on sale in Campo Grande.

vations ☎11/883-6622, Ⓦwww.caiman.com.br; ➒) is one of the most luxurious of all Pantanal *fazenda*-lodges, based some 40km out of town and set in 53,000 hectares of swampland. For **camping**, ask the staff at *Perqueiro Camping Lopes* around the corner from the *rodoviária* about their site 12km away. One really good **restaurant** in town is the *Cantina del Amore*, Rua Barrão do Rio Branco 515, which serves mainly standard Brazilian dishes including fresh fish.

Bonito and around

Nestling in the Bodoquena hills, over three hours by bus from Anastácio and Miranda, four from Campo Grande and Dourados, **BONITO** is a small, somewhat sleepy sprawl of a town. But the dirt tracks that make up most of the region's roads conceal the fact that ever since Bonito starred as an "undiscovered" ecological paradise on TV Globo in 1993, it has become one of Brazil's major **ecotourist** destinations. Needless to say, tourists have been swarming to the town ever since (especially over Christmas and Easter, and in July and August), although the mood, out of season, is surprisingly relaxed and not at all pushy. Located as it is at the southern edge of the Pantanal, a visit to Bonito can happily be combined with a trip exploring the world's biggest inland swamp. Between Bonito and the Pantanal it's possible to experience a fantastic range of wildlife and ecology.

Arrival, information and accommodation

The **rodoviária** (☎67/255-1606) is located up Rua Vicente Jacques, several blocks and a ten-minute walk from the main street Rua Cel. Pilad Rebuá, where many of the town's hotels and most of its tour operators are located. Here you'll find the SETUMA **tourist information** office at no. 1780

(☎67/255-1351, ⓦ www.bonito-ms.com.br). Alternatively, the English-speaking Linha Direta con a Natureza ("Direct Line to Nature"; ☎67/255-1850) is a useful source of information and can make bookings for local tours.

Taxis are an easy way of getting about Bonito and its outlying areas, and there are several taxi points in town; Ponto Taxi, Rua Monte Castelo 824 (☎67/255-1760), charges $3–5 a ride in and around town. A cheaper alternative, particularly if you're travelling alone, is taking a **mototaxi**, or motorbike taxi (50–75¢ a ride).

Daily Cruzeiro do Sul **buses** connect Bonito with Campo Grande, Corumbá, Dourados and Ponta Porã; nevertheless, you'll need to stay two nights if you want to include even one trip to the caves or rivers (organized tours generally leave around 7.30am), though there are so many possible day- and half-day trips in the area that most people stay longer.

Accommodation

There are plenty of **places to stay** in Bonito, so finding a room should be easy even in high season. Most accommodation is budget-range – there are over a dozen cheapies on Rua Cel. Pilad Rebuá, two blocks up from the *rodoviária* – but there are also a fair number of classier options.

Outside of town, a delightful place is the *Pousada Bacuri*, 7km away beside the Aquário Natural (☎67/255-1632, or reservations in Bonito at Rua 15 de Novembro 632; ❹). It's a little paradise run by a charming family, with a number of basic but clean dormitories, and a gorgeous stretch of the Rio Formosinho for swimming, complete with four waterfalls and virgin forest inhabited by monkeys and macaws; camping is also allowed ($10 per person). A little further afield, the *Projeto Vivo* (ⓦ www.projectovivo.com.br; ❺), some 30km away, offers good-quality accommodation in a tranquil setting; there's a pool, and horse riding and river rafting are also on offer, but you need to book in advance through one of the local travel agents – try Natura Tour Vivo (see "Listings", p.539).

The town's fifty-bed youth hostel, the **Albergue de Juventude do Ecoturismo**, is ten blocks north of the *rodoviária* at Rua Lício Borralho 716 (☎67/255-1462 or 255-1022, ⓦ www.ajbonito.com.br; ❶), and besides having excellent facilities (pool, laundry, bar-café, kitchen, games area), this excellent hostel can put you in touch with local tour operators. There are also more than ten **campsites** around the Bonito area; you can get their details from the travel agents in town or, in advance, from the tourist information office in Campo Grande (see p.527). The nearest to town are *Camping Boa Vista*, Rua Ari Machado (☎67/255-1764) on the outskirts, and *Ilha do Padre* (☎67/255-1430) about 10km further out.

Hotel Alvorada Rua Luis da Costa Leite 2261 ☎67/255-1221 or 989-7393. Pretty basic and a bit run-down, with shared baths, though nicely located on the main *praça*. ❶

Hotel Gemila Palace Rua Luis da Costa Leite 2085 ☎67/255-1421, ⓕ255-1843. The best mid-range choice – a very friendly, family-run place with air-conditioned rooms and a great buffet breakfast. ❺

Hotel Pousada da Praça Rua Cel. Pilad Rebuá 2097 ☎67/255-1707. No frills but clean, with a choice between ventilators (❷) and air-conditioning (❸). Just down the street, *Hotel Florestal* at

no. 2084 (☎67/255-1409), offers much the same. **Paraíso das Aguas** Rua Cel. Pilad Rebuá 1884 ☎67/255-1296m, ⓦ www.paguas.com.br. The rooms at this tidy, welcoming and very central hotel come with air-conditioning, TV and *frigobar*. ❸

Pousada Muito Bonito Rua Cel. Pilad Rebuá 1448 ☎ & ☎067/255-1645, ⓔ muitobonito@vip2000.net. One of the best backpacker options; very friendly, and with staff who speak several languages, including English. Spotless rooms, all with private bath, and a pleasant terrace for breakfast; own tour agency. ❷

Pousada Olho d'Agua Estrada Baia das Garças, 3km from the centre ☎67/255-1430, ⓕ255-1470, ⓦwww.pousadaolhodagua.com.br. No less luxurious than the *Zagaia Resort*, but arguably more personal and affordable, this place offers delightful bungalow accommodation in intimate wooded surroundings, with excellent service food, and its own tour agency. ❺

Zagaia Eco-Resort 2km from the centre by the airfield ☎67/255-1280, ⓕ255-1710, ⓦwww.zagaia.com.br. Top of the range, an ultra-modern complex with three swimming pools, various playing fields, horse riding, numerous restaurants and even a cabaret – popular with holidaymakers from Rio. ❼

Trips from Bonito

Bonito's tour companies are unusually well tuned in to the requirements of overseas visitors, and all offer identical trips at identical – and very reasonable – prices to all the places described below, plus a wide range of other options. The municipality limits the numbers of visitors to Bonito's natural wonders and systematically enforces a whole array of regulations intended to protect this ecologically "pure" region. Many of the sites charge for entry, and for some, such as the famous Lago Azul cave, you require both authorization and a guide to visit. Such **permits** and **guides** are arranged by the tour companies or hotels. Almost all the sites require transport, which makes it virtually impossible to visit them independently. Some hotels, like *Pousada Muito Bonito*, can arrange daily **car rental** for around $30, and someone may be happy to rent you his or her bicycle for the day, but you'll still need a guide to access the main sites.

The Gruta do Lago Azul

The **Gruta do Lago Azul** (daily 8am–2pm, 7am–4pm on holidays; no children under 5; usual guide fee $5) is a cave some 20km from Bonito, out beyond the tiny municipal airstrip. It's set in forested hills that are rich in limestone, granite and marble, and full of minerals – as well as a growing number of mercury, uranium and phosphorus mines. Even before the mines, though, these hills, which reach up to about 800m above sea level, were full of massive caves, most of them inaccessible and on private *fazenda* land.

Rediscovered in 1924 by local Terena Indians, the entrance to the cave is quite spectacular. Surrounded by some 250,000 square metres of ecological reserve woodland, it looms like a monstrous mouth inviting you into the heart of the earth. At first you climb down a narrow path through vegetation, then down deeper into dripping stalactite territory some 100m below to the mists hovering above the cave's lake. The pre-Cambrian rocks of the cave walls are striated like the skin of an old elephant and there are weird rock formations such as the easily recognized natural Buddha. Light streams in from the semicircular cave opening, but only penetrates right to the lake level in the bottom of the cave for 45 minutes on 30 days each year.

Until twenty years ago the cave was used much like a local rubbish tip, but tourism revived the local council's interest in the site and since 1989 a number of expeditions have attempted to fathom the depths of the lake, but with no success (70m is the deepest exploration to date). One of these, a joint French-Brazilian expedition, discovered the bones of prehistoric animals (including a sabre-toothed tiger) and even human remains. The blue waters of the lake extend into the mountain for at least another 300m and are exceptionally clear, with only shrimps and crustacea able to survive in the calcified water.

There is another spectacular cave in the area, **Nossa Senhora Aparecida**, 30km from Bonito, which can only be visited with a guide and special permission from the Prefeitura.

The Aquário Natural

The **Aquário Natural** complex (daily 9am–6pm; all-inclusive price for a half-day excursion is around $23, covering guide, permit, and access to snorkelling equipment and boats) is justifiably Bonito's next most popular attraction. Located at the river's source, 7km from town, the Aquário itself is a small sanctuary with water so clear and full of fish that the experience is like looking into an aquarium – something you can take advantage of by a ride in one of the glass-bottomed boats. In fact, visitors are encouraged to put on a floating jacket, mask and snorkel, and to get into the water with the 35 or so species of fish, mainly *dourado* and 14-inch *piripitanga* fishes – a tickling experience with no danger from piranhas, who never swim this far upriver. The sanctuary is accessed by a path from the reception through a swamp and *mata* nature reserve, the **Parque Ecológico Bahia Bonita**, replete with wildlife, including white-collared peccaries, agouti and the majestic *caramugeiro* snail hawk. From the Aquário, the **Bahia Bonita**, a kilometre-long stretch of river, runs down to meet the Rio Formoso, where there's a death-slide (a pulley and rope system for exciting splashdowns into the river), and trampoline-based river fun.

The Aquário Natural is only one of several snorkelling locations in the area, though it has by far the most developed infrastructure. If you're on a tight budget, the nearby *Pousada Bacuri*, 500m from the Aquário Natural, has a stretch of river all of its own ($3 admission), with *dourado* fish, four small waterfalls and a small forest in which you're free to wander about. Tour companies also offer snorkelling trips to the **Rio Sucuri** ($13 half day), and the **Rio da Prata** trip ($17 full day). One of the best local scuba sites is the **Gruta do Mimosa** ($100 full day); a trip here requires both a guide and permit, best obtained through either the Pousada Olho d'Agua travel agency (see p.537) or Ygarapé Tours (see "Listings", opposite).

Ilha do Padre

Around 12km from Bonito down the Rio Formoso, there's an interesting island, the **Ilha do Padre**, which has been turned into a public nature reserve and campsite. It costs $5 to enter (no guide or authorization is required) and $8 per person to camp, or you can pay a little more ($12) to use the primitive wooden chalets. **White-water rafting** down to Ilha do Padre ($10 half day, sometimes done by moonlight) is one of the more exciting options available from tour agents in Bonito (see "Listings", opposite). The island is surrounded by 22 waterfalls of varying sizes and covers almost 50,000 square metres. Although the Formoso is an active white-water rafting river, there are also delightful natural swimming spots, lots of exotic birdlife and lush vegetation. It's not quite as beautiful as the Aquário Natural at the river's source, but still very pleasant, although come prepared for the biting flies and mosquitoes. The island is annoyingly busy at peak holiday times (such as Easter).

Fazenda da Barra Projeto Vivo

The **Fazenda da Barra Projeto Vivo**, an ecological visitors' centre 31km from Bonito at the point where the Formoso and Miranda rivers meet, provides a vivid example of how the apparently conflicting interests of ecology and business can be combined for profit, pleasure and education. The centre is one of the first of its kind in Brazil and has been very successful. Full- and half-day trips from Bonito are organized by the local travel agencies: a full day costs $35, a half-day $20 (children half-price), including transport to and from Bonito, a guided forest walk, river-rafting, horse riding and meals. There's a small eco-library for those who read Portuguese and, needless to say, it's an excellent place for children, with plenty of additional hands-on activities (painting, paper-recycling and the like) to keep them happy. If you really take a shine to the place, you can stay in one of their chalets sited 200m from the Rio Formoso: *Chalé das Artes* (❸) with eight beds, or *Chalé Eden* (❻) with only two. For more details, contact the *fazenda* direct (☎ & ℻ 067/255-1500, mobile 067/9986-4600, ⓦ www.projectovivo.com.br), or the tour companies Hapakany or Natura Tour (see "Listings" below).

Eating and drinking

Although Bonito is a small town, there are a large number of **restaurants** catering for the summer tourist trade; out of season, their quality is somewhat variable. Consistently the best are the *Pousada Olho d'Agua* (see "Accommodation" p.537) and the *Restaurante Tapera*, Rua Cel. Pilad Rebuá 1961, both serving excellent if pricey fish and other dishes in the evening. There are plenty of ice-cream parlours on Rua Cel. Pilad Rebuá, while for a quick lunch *Pousada Muito Bonito* has good home cooking in pleasant surroundings, and popular *Gula's Restaurante* at Rua Cel. Pilad Rebuá 1626, is especially good for pizzas and inexpensive *comida por kilo* lunches. The tasty and varied menu at nearby *Restaurante O Casarão*, on the same street at number 1835 (☎ 67/255-1850), is quite affordable, too, and equally popular with locals. As far as **bars** go, *Bar O Pirata*, at Rua 29 de Maio, the *Taboa Bar*, in Rua Cel. Pilad Rebuá, and *Restaurante Tapera* (see above) are all quite lively from about 9pm, but only at weekends do they stay open much beyond midnight.

Listings

Banks and exchange Bradesco, Rua Cel. Pilad Rebuá 535; Banco do Brasil, Rua Luis da Costa Leite 132; HSBC, Rua Cel. Pilad Rebuá 680.
Car rental Yes ☎ 67/255-1702; Nandai Locadora, Rua Luis da Costa Leite 1980 ☎ 67/255-1716; Translocar, Rua Cel. Pilad Rebuá 976 ☎ 67/255-1391; Unidas, Rua das Flores ☎ 67/255-1066 or 0800-121-121.
Health matters Farmácia Drogacruz, Rua Cel. Pilad Rebuá 1629.
Internet Casa do Computador, Rua Santana do Paraíso 1760 ☎ 67/255-1463 offers reasonably cheap public access ($2/hour).
Post office On the main street (Mon–Fri 8am–noon and 1–4.30pm), more or less opposite

the *Pousada Muito Bonito*.
Travel and tour companies Some of the better hotels, like *Olho d'Agua* and *Gemila Palace*, have their own tour agencies, or can help you arrange a trip with one of the tour companies. Some of the better options are: Hapakany Tours, Rua Cel. Pilad Rebuá 1837 (☎ & ℻ 67/255-1315, ⓔ hapakany @zaz.com.br); Muito Bonito Turismo, Rua Cel. Pilad Rebuá 1448 (☎ & ℻ 67/255-1645, ⓔ muitobonito @vip.2000.net), which is run by the hotel of the same name; Natura Tour, Rua Cel. Pilad Rebuá 1820 (☎ 67/255-1544, ⓦ www.naturatour.com.br); and Ygarapé Tours, Rua Cel. Pilad Rebuá 1853 (☎ & ℻ 67/255-1733), who also offer scuba diving for beginners.

Corumbá and around

Far removed from mainstream Brazil, hard by the Bolivian border and 400km west of Campo Grande, the city of **Corumbá** provides a welcome stop after the long ride from either Santa Cruz (in Bolivia) or Campo Grande. As an entrance to the Pantanal, Corumbá has the edge over Cuiabá in that it is already there, stuck in the middle of a gigantic swamp, only 119m above sea level. Its name, in Tupi, means the "place of stones" and, not surprisingly, Corumbá and the Pantanal didn't start out as a great source of attraction to travellers. As early as 1543, the swamp proved an inhospitable place to an expe-

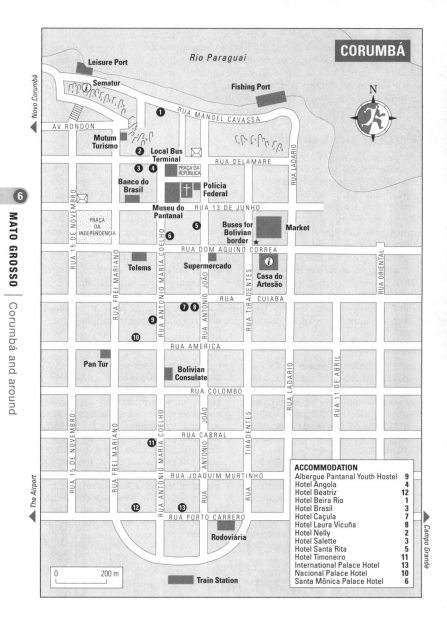

CORUMBÁ

Rio Paraguai

Leisure Port

Sematur

Fishing Port

Novo Corumbá

RUA MANOEL CAVASSA

AV RONDON

Mutum
Turismo

Local Bus
Terminal

RUA DELAMARE

RUA LADARIO

PRAÇA DA
REPÚBLICA

Banco do
Brasil

Polícia
Federal

RUA 13 DE JUNHO

Museu do
Pantanal

Buses for
Bolivian
border

Market

PRAÇA
DA
INDEPENDENCIA

RUA DOM AQUINO CORREA

Telems

Supermercado

Casa do
Artesão

RUA 15 DE NOVEMBRO

RUA FREI MARIANO

RUA ANTONIO MARIA COELHO

RUA ANTONIO JOÃO

RUA CUIABA

RUA TIRADENTES

RUA ORIENTAL

RUA AMERICA

Pan Tur

Bolivian
Consulate

RUA COLOMBO

RUA LADARIO

RUA 11 DE ABRIL

RUA CABRAL

RUA 15 DE NOVEMBRO

RUA FREI MARIANO

RUA ANTONIO MARIA COELHO

RUA JOÃO

RUA TIRADENTES

The Airport

RUA JOAQUIM MURTINHO

Campo Grande

RUA PORTO CARRERO

Rodoviária

0   200 m

Train Station

ACCOMMODATION
Albergue Pantanal Youth Hostel   **9**
Hotel Angola   **4**
Hotel Beatriz   **12**
Hotel Beira Rio   **1**
Hotel Brasil   **3**
Hotel Caçula   **7**
Hotel Laura Vicuña   **8**
Hotel Nelly   **2**
Hotel Salette   **3**
Hotel Santa Rita   **5**
Hotel Timoneiro   **11**
International Palace Hotel   **13**
Nacional Palace Hotel   **10**
Santa Mônica Palace Hotel   **6**

dition of 120 large canoes on a punitive campaign against the Guaicuru tribe. Sent by the Spanish governor of Paraguay, it encountered vampire bats, stingrays, biting ants and plagues of mosquitoes. And while it doesn't seem quite so bad today, it's easy to understand why air-conditioning is such big business here. It was Corumbá's unique location on the old rail link between the Andes and the Atlantic that originally brought most travellers to the town, but, ironically, the same swamp that deterred European invaders for so long has rapidly become an attraction, at the same time as the Brazilian part of the rail link has been closed down.

Arrival, information and accommodation

As there are now only freight trains to and from Corumbá, you're likely to arrive by either bus or plane. The **rodoviária** is close to the train station on Rua Porto Carrero (℡67/231-2033) and is served by daily buses from Campo Grande, São Paulo and even further afield. From the *rodoviária*, it's a fifteen-minute walk into town, or there are buses and taxis ($5) plying the route. The **airport** (℡67/231-3322) is a half-hour walk or a $10 taxi ride west of the city centre.

What little **tourist information** there is can be obtained from SEMATUR, Rua Manoel Cavassa 275, down at the port (Mon 1–6pm, Tues–Fri 8.30am–noon & 1.30–6pm; ℡67/231-7336 or 231-9747), or in the Casa do Artesão, Rua Dom Aquino Corréa 405 (same hours; ℡67/231-2715).

Accommodation

Hotels in Corumbá vary considerably but their sheer quantity (the following are just a selection) means you should have no trouble finding a room, even from August to October. Out of season, especially January–Easter, there are heavy discounts all round, and prices can be bargained even lower.

The most centrally located for shops and the port, and so noisiest at night, are the clutch of cheap lodgings around **Rua Delamare**, west of Praça da República; they tend to be very popular with backpackers and are good places to meet companions for trips into the Pantanal. For those travelling in a group, the tour agent Urcabar, by the river at Rua Manoel Cavassa 181 (℡67/231-3039), has a house to rent (nine beds in two rooms) for $50 plus a day.

Albergue Pantanal Youth Hostal Rua Antoni Maria Coelho 677 ℡67/231-2305, ℱ231-7740. Pleasant and well-equipped hostel with mainly dorms and shared bathrooms; tours into the Pantanal can be organized from here.

Hotel Angola Rua Antônio Maria Coelho 124 ℡67/231-7233. Safe, perfectly reasonable, and cheapest of the bunch around Rua Delamare in low season (singles from $5). ❷–❸

Hotel Beatriz Rua Porto Carrero 896 ℡67/231-7441. Facing the *rodoviária*, very cheap and pretty basic, but useful if you arrive late at night by bus and can't face the 2km hike into town. ❶

Hotel Beira Rio Rua Manoel Cavassa 109 ℡67/231-2554, ℱ231-3313. One of the more characterful hotels right by the shore, with cheerful management. Its best rooms overlook the river and the Pantanal, and there are boats for guests' use. ❷

Hotel Brasil Rua Delamare 903 ℡231-6940, ℱ231-1087. Clean and very affordable rooms, but the mood is a little impersonal and the management push their Pantanal tours a bit hard sometimes. ❷

Hotel Caçula Rua Cuiabá 795 ℡67/231-5745, ℱ231-1976. Next door and better value for money than the *Laura Vicuña*, with good clean rooms, each with TV. ❷

Hotel Laura Vicuña Rua Cuiabá 775 ℡67/231-5874, ℱ231-2663. A peaceful place, very neat and tidy in traditional fashion. All rooms have phone and TV. ❸

Hotel Nelly Rua Delamare 902 ℡67/231-6001, ℱ231-7396. Long a favourite haunt for budget travellers and kids from Rio and São Paulo, and excellent value, if a little dank. Rooms with TV cost more. ❶–❷

Hotel Salette Rua Delamare 893 ℡67/231-3768, ℱ231-4948. Similar to neighbouring *Nelly* and *Brasil* but more expensive. Cheaper rooms share bathrooms; all rooms have TV. ❶–❸

Hotel Santa Rita Rua Dom Aquino Corréa 860 ℡67/231-5453, ℱ231-4834. Rooms are clean and airy at this good-value hotel – where the more expensive ones come with air-conditioning and TV. There's also a reasonable on-site restaurant. ❷–❸

Hotel Timoneiro Rua Cabral 879 ☎ 67/231-5530. A convenient budget option near the *rodoviária*, quieter than the clutch around Rua Delamare. The ground-floor rooms are grotty, but cheaper than those on the first floor, which have fans and more light. ❷ –❸
International Palace Rua Dom Aquino Corréa 1457 ☎ 67/231-6247, ℗ 231-6852. Comfortable mid-range place with sauna, pool, restaurant and bar. ❹
Nacional Palace Hotel Rua América 936 ☎ 67/231-6868, ℗ 231-6202,

✉ hnacion@brasinet.com.br. Pretty much top of the range in Corumbá. It's convenient and has a pool (non-residents can use it for $10), but it's a bit flashy and overpriced. ❺
Santa Mônica Palace Hotel Rua Antônio Maria Coelho 345 ☎ 67/231-3001, ℗ 231-7880, ✉ stmonica@pantanalnet.com.br. Corumbá's largest hotel and best mid-range option, offering excellent value: rooms with all mod cons including air-conditioning and fridges, and the added luxury of a pool (non-residents can use it for $5), sauna and riverboats for hire. ❺

❻ The City

Commanding a fine view over the Rio Paraguai and across the swamp, the city is small (approaching 100,000 inhabitants), and is really only busy in the mornings – indeed it's one of Brazil's most laid-back towns south of the Amazon, basking in intense heat and overwhelming humidity. Even at the port nothing seems to disturb the slow-moving pool games taking place in the bars. Because of the heat, there's a very open-plan feel to the city and the people of Corumbá seem to be equally at home sitting at tables by bars and restaurants, or eating their dinners outside in front of their houses. In every street, there's at least one television blaring away on the pavement, and it's not unusual to be invited into someone's house for food, drinks or – at weekends – for a party.

Corumbá's life revolves around its **port**, while its transport connections are at the other end of town around the *rodoviária* and airport; if you're intending to stay more than one night, the port end is your best bet. Within a few blocks of the riverfront you'll find the **Praça da Independência**, a large, shaded park with ponds, a children's playground and a few unusual installations dotted around: a streamroller, imported from England around 1921, whose first job was flattening Avenida General Rondon, and an antique water wheel, also English, which served in a sugar factory until 1932. Early in the day, the *praça* is alive with tropical birds, and by evening it's crowded with couples, family groups and gangs of children relaxing as the temperature begins to drop. The large but otherwise unimpressive church on this square is useful as a prominent landmark to help you get your bearings in this very flat, grid-patterned city.

A stone's throw away on the smaller **Praça da República** stands the stark late nineteenth-century Igreja Matriz Nossa Senhora da Candelária. Next door at Rua Delamare 939, facing the local bus terminal, is the fascinating **Museu do Pantanal** (Mon–Fri noon–5pm), which encompasses a collection of stuffed animals, artefacts from various indigenous tribes of the region, some archeological specimens, and changing exhibits of modern art. If you need advice or information about the local flora or fauna, contact the museum office. The only other thing to see is the **Casa do Artesão** at Rua Dom Aquino Corréa 405 (Mon–Fri 8–11am & 2–5pm, Sat 8–11am). It's housed in Corumbá's most historic edifice – the old prison, dating from 1900 – and is a great place to track down some local craft work (especially wood and leather), as well as local liquors and *Farinha da Bocaiúva*, a flour made from palm-tree nuts and reputed to be an aphrodisiac.

Eating, drinking and nightlife

For **self-catering**, there's a branch of Supermercado Ohara on the corner of Rua Dom Aquino Corréa and Rua Antônio João, and three butchers opposite.

The covered market, one block east, should complete your provisions. There's only one place for really good coffee and great juices – *Centre Coffee*, at Rua Delamare 967. For ice cream try *Scorpius Sorvetes* at the corner of Rua Cuiabá and Rua Frei Mariano, and *Sorveteria Cristal* on the corner of Rua Delamare and Rua 7 de Setembro.

There's no shortage of **restaurants** in Corumbá. The best are to be found on Rua Frei Mariano and Rua 15 de Novembro, though there are plenty of cheap snack bars throughout town, especially on Rua Delamare west of the Praça da República, serving good set meals for less than $5. Being a swamp city, fish are the main local delicacy, with *pacu* and *pintado* among the favoured species. For upmarket local cuisine try *Peixaria do Lulu*, Rua Antônio João 410 (℡67/232-2142), or the smart *Cantina Casa Mia*, opposite the telephone office at Rua Dom Aquino Corréa 928 (closed Mon; ℡67/231-1327). *Mauro's Restaurante*, facing the Praça da Independência at Rua Frei Mariano 383, is one of the classiest and most popular eateries, particularly at lunchtimes when it has a splendid selection of surprisingly good-value self-service dishes. There's a huge choice of inexpensive meat and fish in vast portions from *Galpão*, Rua 13 de Junho 797 at the corner of Rua Antônio Maria Coelho; more modest is the calm *Restaurante Trivial* at Rua 15 de Novembro 146/188, which has self-service *comida por kilo* most lunchtimes and evenings. For pizza freaks, there's *Fiorella Pizza*, on the eastern corner of Praça da República and Rua Delamare. Lastly, for those who like to **cruise** with their food, the restaurant-boat *La Barca Tur* (℡67/231-3106) does five-hour lunch trips in high season, including the inevitable piranha soup, for $25.

As to **bars**, you'll find these all over town, though with few exceptions they're spit-and-sawdust joints, rough-looking and a little intimidating at first. Among the more relaxed are those down on the riverfront – where you can usually get a game of pool with your drink – and the friendly *Bar da China* on Rua Ladário off Rua Dom Aquino Corréa. **Nightlife** is thin on the ground. *Restaurante Estalagem Canecão*, at the corner of Rua Frei Mariano and Rua Dom Aquino Corréa, brightens up its undistinguished menu with occasional live music, and the *Bais do Chop* restaurant, a lovingly restored waterfront mansion down at the port next to the *artesanato* shops, plays good live music at weekends. Two other lively options, both on Avenida Marechal Rondon overlooking the Rio Paraguai, are the *Millennium Petisqueria*, which has live music at weekends, and *Stadium 54*.

Listings

Airlines Note that the Varig air pass is not valid for Corumbá. Aerosul flies twice daily to Santa Cruz in Bolivia (℡67/231-6091 or 231-6939, ℱ231-4477; office at the *rodoviária* open 8am–noon, office at the airport from 2pm), and Lloyd Boliviano (℡67/231-4308) fly there daily, both companies charging $58. TAM (℡67/231-7177), Pantanal Linhas Aéreas (℡67/231-1818 or 231-7095) and VASP (℡67/231-4441) fly regularly from Corumbá to Campo Grande, and from there to other destinations. Tickets for all companies can be brought from Mutum Turismo (see "Travel and tour agencies" below), or at the airport after 9.30am.
Air taxis Visa Aérotáxi (℡67/231-1745) are the best; Ocorema (℡67/231-3823) are also reliable;

check at their airport desks.
Banks and exchange You can change cash and travellers' cheques at the *casa de câmbio* at Rua 15 de Novembro 212 (Mon–Fri 8.30am–5pm). Otherwise, there's a host of banks on Rua Delamare west of Praça da República (all Mon–Fri 10am–3pm), as well as the Banco do Brasil, Rua 13 de Junho 914 (10am–5pm). Out-of-hours exchange is sometimes possible at the desk in the *Nacional Palace Hotel*, Rua América 936.
Boats There are plenty of boats waiting on the riverfront off Rua Manoel Cavassa that will take you into the Pantanal swamp or Bolivia. See box on p.550 for details of Pantanal operators, or ask around at the numerous offices on the waterfront.

Small motorboats can be hired (two to four passengers) from *Hotel Beir Rio* and Urcabar, also on Rua Manoel Cavassa, for about $60–80 a day (fuel is extra, and costs around $1 a litre – you'll need up to 50 litres in a day). The demise of the luxury liner *Sabrina* means there are no direct passenger connections to the Atlantic. Those vessels that still cover part of the route invariably now begin in Paraguay. Another option, equally hit or miss, is joining a cargo boat bound for Asunción. If you do find a Paraguayan trading boat, you should take care of the necessary paperwork with the Polícia Federal, Praça da República (℡67/231-5848 or 231-2413), and the Paraguayan consulate (see below) before leaving town, as well as with the Capitania dos Portos (℡67/231-6444) at Rua Delamare 806, next to the post office.

Car rental Localiza is at Rua Frei Mariano 51 (℡67/231-6379); Unidas, Rua América 810 (Mon–Sat 8am–6pm; ℡67/231-1239, ℱ231-6992), has reliable Volkswagens that can be taken out of Brazil, but must be returned to Corumbá. Both charge $90 a day upwards.

Consulates Bolivia, Rua Antônio Maria Coelho 852 (℡67/231-5605); Paraguay, Rua Cuiabá (℡67/231-4803).

Health matters The hospital is at Rua 15 de Novembro, between Rua América and Rua Colombo.

Laundry There's an expensive same-day laundry service at Apae, Rua 13 de Junho 1377.

Post office The main post office is at Rua Delamare 708, opposite the church on Praça da República (Mon–Fri 9am–5pm, Sat 8–11.30am). A smaller office is near Praça da Independência on Rua 15 de Novembro (same hours).

Shopping For the Casa do Artesão and for food shopping, see p.542. Two of the shops on Praça da Independência are devoted entirely to hunting, fishing and cowboy paraphernalia, like saddles and guns, and there's a shop on Rua Antônio Maria

Coelho, three blocks from the river, stuffed with garish Catholic *ex votos* and plastic icons. There are numerous photographic shops throughout town; Fotocor, Rua Delamare 871, has a good reputation.

Taxis Ponto Taxi (℡67/231-4043) – the taxi rank is at the southeast corner of Praça da Independência; Mototaxis (℡67/231-7166).

Travel and tour agencies Corumbá Tur, Rua Antônio Maria Coelho 852 (℡ & ℱ67/231-1532 or 1260), an upmarket operator dealing with *fazendas* and luxury angling cruises, also does half-day cruises to Puerto Suarez in Bolivia ($18; no passport required), a good place for silverwork and tax-free goods. Green Track, Rua Delamare 576 (℡67/231-2258, ℠www.travel.to/green-track), runs highly recommended packages of up to five days in the Pantanal; Mutum Turismo, Rua Frei Mariano 17 (℡67/231-1818, 231-1826 or 231-1768, ℱ 231-3027), deals with flights and ticketing, and has a list of approved Pantanal guides; Tucantur, Rua 13 de Junho 744 (℡67/231-5323), has staff that speak good English and will arrange most things from flights to *fazenda*-lodge bookings. Fishing-based tours are operated by Pérola do Pantanal, Rua Manoel Cavassa 255, Porto Geral (℡67/231-1460, ℠www.msinternet.com.br/perola). Down on the riverfront there are several smaller boat-tour company offices that run fishing and safari trips; the best include Pantanal Tours, Rua Manoel Cavassa 61 (℡67/231-5410), and Urcabar, Rua Manoel Cavassa 181 (℡67/231-3039). See also the list of upmarket Pantanal operators on p.550. Budget Pantanal tours are run by all of the cheap hotels around Rua Delamare, whose touts will probably find you as soon as you get off the bus. Make sure you get authorised receipts for any money or valuables you deposit with a tour company or hotel; there have been reports of problems with this kind of practice in Corumbá.

Around Corumbá

Apart from the Pantanal itself (see p.546), there isn't a great deal to visit around Corumbá. Probably the most interesting place is the **Forte de Coimbra** (daily 8.30–11.30am & 1.30–4pm), 80km to the south. Theoretically, the fort can only be visited with previous permission from the Brigada Mista in Corumbá, Av. General Rondon 1735 (℡67/231-2861 or 231-9866), although visitors unaware of this fact are sometimes allowed in. On the other hand, the Brigada Mista is as good a place as any to find out about transport to the fort. The fort is accessible only by water, and is most easily reached via Porto Esperança, an hour's bus ride from Corumbá (buses leave from outside *Hotel Beatriz* several times a day). The journey there is an interesting one along the edge of the swamp, and once in Porto Esperança you should have little difficulty renting a

Crossing into or out of Bolivia from Corumbá is a slightly disjointed procedure. **Leaving Brazil**, you should get an exit stamp from the Polícia Federal at Praça da República 51 in Corumbá (easiest before 11am or between 7pm and 9pm), before picking up a Bolivian visa (if you need one) from the consulate at Rua Antônio Maria Coelho 881 (☎67/231-5605 or 231-5606). After that, it's a matter of taking the bus (from Rua Dom Aquino Corréa) the 10km to the border, checking through Bolivian immigration and receiving your passport entry stamp. **Money** can be changed at decent rates at the border.

Train tickets for Santa Cruz should be bought at La Brasilena train station in **Quijarro**, a few minutes by *colectivo* (a type of shuttle bus; $1.50) or bus from the Bolivian immigration office. First class to Santa Cruz costs $25, second class $15. The first-class carriages are comfortable, with videos, but everything sways and the toilets are dirty. Limited food is available on board, and also from the track-side villages during the train's frequent stops. Insect repellent and clothes that cover your flesh are essential, as the lights of the carriages attract all manner of biting insects at night. Drinking water and a torch are also useful. As timetables vary considerably, check at the station in Corumbá or Quijarro at least a couple of days in advance. It's worth going to Quijarro the day before departure to actually make your booking.

Entering Brazil from Bolivia is essentially the same procedure in reverse, although US citizens should remember to pick up visas in the Brazilian consulate in Santa Cruz before leaving.

boat, or finding a guide, to take you a couple more hours downriver to the fort. It's also possible to approach the fort in traditional fashion, by following the Rio Paraguai all the way from Corumbá in a boat, but this takes around seven hours and involves going through a tour agency in town. One bonus of going by this route, however, is that you'll pass two little-visited natural caves, **Gruta do Inferno** and **Buraco Soturno**, sculpted with huge finger-like stalactites and stalagmites.

The Forte de Coimbra was built in 1775, three years before Corumbá's foundation, to defend this western corner of Brazilian territory and, more specifically, to protect the border against invasion from Paraguay. In 1864 it was attacked by the invading Paraguayan army, which had slipped upriver into the southern Mato Grosso. Coimbra provided the first resistance to the invaders, but it didn't last for long as the Brazilian soldiers escaped from the fort under cover of darkness, leaving the fort to the aggressors. Nearly 3000 Paraguayans continued upstream in a huge convoy of ships and, forging its way north beyond Corumbá, the armada crossed the swamps almost as far as the city of Cuiabá, which was saved only by the shallowness of its river. Nowadays the fort is a pretty dull ruin (except perhaps for military enthusiasts), and it's the journey there that's the real draw.

You may also be able to visit one of the planet's largest manganese deposits, currently being mined in the Urucum hills, just south of Corumbá off the BR-262. The hills rise more than 950m above the level of the swamp, and, although much of the area is technically out of bounds, organized visits to the **Minas do Morro do Urucum at Mineradora**, 24km from Corumbá, with their subterranean galleries (Grutas dos Belgas), can still be arranged through most tour agencies in Corumbá – or contact the company office at Av. General Rondon 1351 (☎67/231-1661). If you decide to chance a visit unaccompanied, buses to Urucum depart from a lot next to *Hotel Beatriz* on Rua Porto Carrero.

Finally, if you're not going to have the time to get any further into the Pantanal, you can get a taste of the swamp life, without spending a lot of money, at two settlements on the Rio Paraguai. **PORTO MORRINHO** is the easier to get to, 67km or an hour by bus from Corumbá, just west of Porto Esperança on the main road to Campo Grande, with ample birdlife and creeks to explore. The town has a few cheap hotels, as well as mid-range ones such as the *Hotel Tuiui* (❹), 200m by *balsa* (raft) from Porto Morrinho on the banks of the river. The hotel rents out motorboats for $35 a day, rowing boats for $12. About the same distance from Corumbá on the old Campo Grande road (the unsurfaced MS-184/MS-228) is **PORTO MANGA**, which is renowned as a centre for wildlife-spotting and fishing on the Rio Paraguai, particularly in September. There are a couple of hotels here, including the *Hotel Pesqueiro* (☎67/231-1987; ❸), whose clean rooms have private baths, as well as some riverboats and boatmen for hire, and various potential camping locations in and around the settlement. From Porto Manga onward it's only 70km via Passo do Lontra to rejoin the BR-262.

The Pantanal

An open swampland larger than France, extending deep into the states of Mato Grosso and Mato Grosso do Sul, **THE PANTANAL** is a slightly daunting region to visit, one of the rare places in Brazil where you're more likely to find wildlife than nightlife. In fact, you see so many birds and animals that you start to think you're in a well-stocked wildlife park – the wildlife is wild, but not at all shy. *Jacarés* (alligators), jaguars, anacondas and *tuiuiú* (giant red-necked storks) are all quite common sights in the Pantanal, and it's probably the best place for wild mammals and exotic birds in the whole of the Americas. Having said that, it's only fair to mention that you'll still see more cattle than any other creature.

Taking off into the Pantanal is what most independent travellers have in mind when they arrive in Mato Grosso, but as no road or rail track crosses the swamp it's a tricky place to travel. The easiest and one of the best ways to experience the Pantanal is by taking an **organized tour**, perhaps spending a night or two at a **fazenda-lodge** (called **pousadas** in the northern Pantanal). The *fazenda*-lodges, mostly converted ranch-houses with decent facilities, are generally reached by jeep; those that require access by boat or plane are usually deeper into the swamp, which increases your chances of spotting the more elusive wildlife. At least one night in the swamp is essential if you want to see or do anything other than sit in a bus or jeep the whole time; three- or four-day excursions will give you a couple of full days in the swamp. Without an organized trip, unless you've got bags of money or are travelling in a large group in which case you can hire boats to get you almost anywhere, you're dependent on local **cargo boats**, which inevitably take much longer than expected. Organized tours are also more likely to go out of their way to show you the wildlife than will a captain whose boat is brimming over with livestock. **Renting a car** is also a slim possibility, though without four-wheel drive you're limited to only a few tracks on the fringes of the swamp where the wildlife makes itself scarce.

THE PANTANAL

Cuiabá
Cáceres
São Antônio do Leverger
Poconé
Barão do Melgaço
Rio Jauru
Rio Cuiabá
Porto Cercado
Rio Mutum
Rondonópolis
Rio Paraguai
Rio São Lourenço
CARACARA NATIONAL PARK
Porto Joffre
Rio Itiquira
Rio Correntes
BOLIVIA
Rio São Lourenço
Rio Taquari
Coxim
Puerto Suarez
Corumbá
Porto Manga
NHECOLÂNDIA
Rio Verde de Mato Grosso
Porto Morrinho
Passo da Lontra
Rio Negro
Rio Aquidauana
Posto Florestal
Rio Paraguai
Rio Miranda
Miranda
Aquidauana
Campo Grande
Anastácio
BR-070
BR-163
BR-163
BR-267

6

MATO GROSSO | The Pantanal

ACCOMMODATION
Baia Bonita	11
Cabana do Lontra	15
Fazenda Rio Negro	13
Hotel Cabanas do Pantanal	1
Hotel Pouso da Garça	9
Hotel Recanto Barra Mansa	14
Passo do Lontra	15
Pousada Arara Azul	12
Pousada Araras	5
Pousada Beira Rio	7
Pousada Pantaneiro	8
Pousada Passargada	2
Pousada Pixaim	6
Pousada Porto Cercado	4
Pousada São Sebastião do Pantanal	3
Rancho Kue	10
Refúgio Ecológico Caiman	16

N

0   100 km

PARAGUAY

Most organized tours enter the Pantanal by road and spend a couple of days exploring in canoes, small motorboats or on horseback from a land base. The most obvious initial target is **Corumbá** in Mato Grosso do Sul. There is lots of accommodation here and no end of agencies and operators running trips into the swamp. Other routes into the swamp are from **Campo Grande** in the east or **Cuiabá**, to the north, through settlements like **Porto Jofre** and

Cáceres. The **best time** to explore the Pantanal is probably towards the end of the rainy season, around April, when your chances of spotting wildlife are high.

Some background

There are very few places on earth where it is so easy to see so much wildlife as in the Pantanal, which occupies an arguably unique ecological niche as an unparalleled bio-genetic reservoir. It's almost unnerving spending the afternoon on the edge of a remote lagoon in the swamp, surrounded by seemingly streams of flying and wading birds – toucans, parrots, red and even the endangered hyacinth macaws, blue herons, and the symbol of the Pantanal, the magnificent *jabiru*, or giant red-throated storks, known locally as *tuiuiú*. Unlike in most other areas of wilderness, the birdsong and density of wildlife in the Pantanal frequently lives up to the exotic soundtrack of Hollywood jungle movies, and in the middle of the swamp it's actually possible to forget that there are other people in the world – though it's difficult to forget the **mosquitoes**. (Malaria is supposedly absent in the Pantanal, so you'll only have the insufferable itching to worry about.) The mosquitoes should be no surprise really, given that the Pantanal is the biggest inland swamp in the world, covering some 230,000 square kilometres of the upper Rio Paraguai basin. It acts as an immense sponge, seasonally absorbing the swollen waters of three large rivers – the Paraguai, Taquari and Cuiabá.

During the **rainy season**, from November to March, river levels rise by up to 3m, producing a vast flooded plain with islands of scrubby forest amidst oceans of floating vegetation. Transport is necessarily dominated by the rivers, natural water channels and hundreds of well-hidden lagoons. The small islands of vegetation created during the rains crawl with wild animals – jaguars, tapirs, capybaras (the world's largest rodents) and wild boar living side by side with domesticated cattle.

At other times of the year, much of the Pantanal is still very boggy though interspersed with open grassy savannas studded with small wooded islands of taller vegetation, mainly palm trees. The **dry season**, from April to October, with its peak normally around September, transforms the swamp into South America's most exciting natural wildlife reserve. Its infamous piranha and alligator populations crowd into relatively small pools and streams, while the astonishing array of aquatic birds follows suit, forming very dense colonies known here as *viveiros*. Treeless bush savanna alternates with wet swamp, while along the banks of the major rivers grow belts of rainforest populated with colonies of monkeys (including spider monkeys and noisy black gibbons). Note, however, that the previously metronomic regularity of the seasons has become most unpredictable of late, with the onset of global warming.

History and development

Very little is known about the Pantanal's **history**. At the time of early Portuguese explorations, and the first unsuccessful attempts at populating the region by the Spanish in the sixteenth century, the region was dominated by three main tribes. In the south lived the horse-riding **Guaicuru**, who adopted stray or stolen horses and cattle from the advancing white settlers, making the tribe an elite group amongst Indians. Wearing only jaguar skins as they rode into battle, they were feared by the neighbouring **Terena** (Guana) tribe, who lived much of their lives as servants to Guaicuru families. In many ways, the nature and degree of their economic and social interaction suggests that the two might once have been different castes within the same tribe. Another powerful people lived to the north – the **Paiaguá**, masters of the main rivers, lagoons and canals of the central Pantanal. Much to the chagrin of both Spanish and Portuguese expeditions into the swamps, the Paiaguá were superbly skilled with both their canoes and the bow and arrow.

It wasn't until the **discovery of gold** in the northern Pantanal and around Cuiabá during the early eighteenth century that any genuine settlement schemes were undertaken. A rapid influx of colonists, miners and soldiers led to several bloody battles. In June 1730 hundreds of Paiaguá warriors in 83 canoes ambushed the annual flotilla, which was carrying some 900kg of gold south through the Pantanal from Cuiabá. They spared only some of the women and a few of the stronger black rowers from the flotilla: all of the gold and most of the white men were lost. Much of the gold eventually found its way out of Brazil and into Spanish Paraguay where Cautiguacu, the Paiaguá chief, lived a life of luxury in Asunción until his death 55 years later.

The decline of the gold mines during the nineteenth century brought development in the Pantanal to a standstill and the population began to fall. The twentieth century saw the establishment of unrestricted **cattle-grazing** ranches – *fazendas* – and today over 20 million head of cattle roam the swamp. To the east, the BR-163 between Campo Grande and Cuiabá skirts around the Pantanal, and Ministry of Transport plans for a Transpantaneira road from Cuiabá to Corumbá have been shelved for the sake of the region's ecological balance. For all that, tourism has developed greatly in the region over the last few years, which has coincided with a slump in the price for cattle. The papers are full of auction notices for *fazendas*, livestock and equipment, though some *fazendeiros* have been quick to realize the potential of converting their farms and land into ecological reserves.

The Pantanal, however, is still **under threat** from the illegal exploitation of skins, fish and rare birds, and even gold panning. The chemical fertilizers and pesticides used on the enormous *fazendas* to produce cash crops such as soya beans are also beginning to take their toll. **Ecotourism** has been heralded as a potential savior for the swamp, but this will only work if sufficient money is ploughed back into conservation. The Pantanal has its own Polícia Florestal who try to enforce the environment-friendly regulations now being strictly applied to visitors and locals alike: no disposal of non-biodegradable rubbish, no noise pollution, no fishing without a licence (it costs $100) or between November and January during the breeding season, no fishing with nets or explosives and no removal of rocks, wildlife or plant life.

Practicalities

If you talk to locals about visiting the Pantanal they will almost certainly recommend going in by road. This is usually cheaper and quicker than renting a boat or going on one of the cruises. The main problem, though, is knowing where and how to go, and which company or lodge to choose. This section gives a rough overview of the various options, together with a box listing a selection of recommended **tour operators** (see p.550). The following sections describe some possible **routes**, from Corumbá and from Cuiabá, together with

The following is a selection of the more upmarket Pantanal operators who deal with both complete packages and bookings for boats and/or lodges; for other agents and guides, see under "Listings" for Cuiabá, Campo Grande and Corumbá.

Aguas do Pantanal Av. Afonso Pena 367, Miranda ☎67/242-1242. This company owns and runs several *pousadas* around Miranda, Passo do Lontra and Porto Morrinho on the Rio Paraguai.

Anaconda Rua Marechal Deodoro, Cuiabá 2142 ☎65/624-4142. Short but well organized and comfortable tours in the Pantanal and elsewhere in the Brazilian wilderness.

Confiança Turismo Rua Cândido Mariano 434, Cuiabá ☎65/623-4141. A well-established company with a strong track record operating a variety of Pantanal tours.

Corumbá Tur Rua Antônio Maria Coelho 852, Corumbá ☎ & ⓕ067/231-1532. Corumbá's leading upmarket agency, dealing with all the main *fazendas* and luxury boat cruises, as well as organizing its own fishing and photography tours (anywhere from $120 per person per day). Prices for the fishing cruises (departing Sun on a variety of boats) range from $675 to $1300 per person per week.

Fish World Rua Lucélia 85, Vila Castelo, Campo Grande ☎67/383-3709, ⓕ 382-8152. Efficient agents for a large number of luxury boat trips, specializing in angling trips, as well as bookings for *fazenda*-lodges.

Pantanal Explorers/Expediturs Av. Gov. J.P. Arruda 670, Várzea Grande, Cuiabá ☎65/682-2800 or 682-1260. Agents and operators for tours and boats based around Cuiabá and Cáceres.

Pantanal Express Av. Afonso Pena 2081, Campo Grande ☎67/382-5333. Agents for some of the more upmarket tour operators and *fazenda* holidays.

Pan Tur Rua America 969, Corumbá ☎67/231-2000. Agents for almost everything, who also run their own Pantanal tours from around $70 a day.

Pérola do Pantanal Rua Manoel Cavassa 255, Corumbá ☎67/231-1460, ⓕ231-6585, ⓦwww.msinternet.com.br/perola. Agents for upmarket cruises from Corumbá.

SuperPesca Pantanal Rua Marechal Cândido Rondon 2300, Campo Grande ☎67/721-5713. Specialists in angling tours, and especially knowledgeable on which boats go down which rivers, potentially useful information for hitching a ride.

details of **accommodation** in *fazenda*-lodges and *pousadas*. The box on pp.552–553 describes the options for **boat trips** from Cáceres and Corumbá.

If you want to go **independently** remember that the Pantanal is a difficult and dangerous place to travel in. There are very few roads and, although hundreds of tracks sneak their way into the swamp, they are used only by *fazenda* workers who know them inside out. An inexperienced driver or hiker could easily get lost – or worse. That said, there's no better way to see the wildlife than to camp or stay on a boat deep in the swamp, away from roads, tracks or *fazenda*-lodges, but to do this you will need a local **guide**; these are generally available only at lodges or in end-of-the-track settlements like Porto Jofre. Also, it's important to take all the **equipment** you need with you if you're going it alone like this in the Pantanal – food, camping gear, a first-aid kit and lots of mosquito repellent. It's possible to take **buses** and **boats** from Cuiabá and Corumbá to places such as Cáceres, Coxim, Porto Jofre or Aquidauana, and it's then a matter of finding a boat going your way deeper into the swamp or paying a local guide or *fazendeiro* to take you on a trip. This will cost around $20–50 per person per day, including canoe or vehicle transport and a guide/boatman/driver. Local guides and *fazendeiros* usually prefer to use the

△ Storks, The Pantanal

Pantanal boat tours

At present, two basic types of **cargo boat** cross the swamp between Cáceres and Corumbá on a fairly regular basis – **soya** and **cattle barges**. Neither has fixed schedules or itineraries, so it's a matter of checking on departure dates when you arrive at either town. The trip usually takes about six to ten days upstream from Corumbá, three to six downstream, with plenty of time for relaxing and looking out for wildlife. The barges, though, do tend to keep to the main channel of the Rio Paraguai, which obviously doesn't give you a good chance of spotting anything particularly shy or rare. However, if you can find space on one of these boats, then it's a very inexpensive as well as unusual way of seeing some of the Pantanal. Apart from your hammock, take some extra food (tins, biscuits, bottled drinks and the like), insect repellent and a few good books. And a bottle of whisky or good *cachaça* wouldn't go amiss with the captain.

The only other problem is that travelling on the barges hasn't been strictly legal since 1985, when the son of a naval minister accidentally died while on board one of the cement barges that used to ply the same route. Passengers have consequently been "smuggled" aboard in dinghies, under cover of darkness. However, you might find it's still possible to buy a ride simply by asking the *comandante* of Portobras, one of the barge companies – they have offices on the waterfront in both Corumbá and Cáceres (☎65/222-1728). The cattle barge between Corumbá and Cáceres run by Serviço de Navegação da Bacia da Prata also often picks up passengers from the ports at either end, but leaves at irregular intervals. Other cattle boats leaving Corumbá are willing to take passengers on return journeys within the swamp, delivering and picking up cattle from various *fazendas*.

Luxury fishing boats are the other option, prohibitively expensive for most, but an ideal way to encounter the swamp's wildlife on the end of a line and ultimately on your plate. Essentially floating hotels designed with the Brazilian passion for angling in mind, one of these for a week costs anything from $500 to $2000 a head, though the price is full-board and usually includes ample drink, food and unlimited use of their small motorboat tenders for exploring further afield. Note that for **families with small children**, any river trip is inadvisable as none of the boats currently in use has guard-rails safe enough to keep a toddler from falling in.

Most of the boats are based in Corumbá, with some others in Cáceres, Barão do Melgaço and Cuiabá, and all can be booked through the upmarket agents on p.550. In high season, they tend to run pre-scheduled trips, departing and returning Sundays; routes are mentioned where they remain fixed from year to year. Out of season, they're up for rent, with a minimum number of passengers and days invariably demanded, though bargaining is possible. You can find them tied up at their home ports.

---

road networks to reach *fazenda*-lodges within the swamp, and explore in canoes or on horseback from there. Cheaper still, and certainly the most unusual alternative, is to buy a passage (around $10–20 a day; hammock essential) on one of the few **trading boats** still crossing the Pantanal between Corumbá and Cáceres, and occasionally Porto Jofre (both connected by road to Cuiabá).

Most people, however, go on **organized tours**, entering the swamp in jeeps or trucks and following one of the few rough roads that now connect Corumbá, Aquidauana, Coxim and Cuiabá (via Poconé or Cáceres) with some of the larger *fazenda* settlements of the interior. The short **jeep trips**, often run by freelance operators, are relatively cheap (especially from Corumbá, where a hammock and truck tour can cost as little as $25–30 a day per person; from Cuiabá, it's more like $50–60), but they offer little more than a flavour of the

Luxury boats from Cáceres

Botel Pantanal Explorer II ☎65/682-2800. Mainly covering the Rio Paraguai, this boat is very small with only three quadruple cabins. Upwards of $130 per person per day.

Cobra Grande ☎65/223-4203. A small boat with five cabins and an adequate dining room. Book well in advance.

Rei do Rio and Velho do Rio Contact Moretti Serviços Fluviais, Cuiabá ☎65/361-2082, ℱ322-6553. A couple of Louisiana-style houseboats intended primarily as bases for fishing expeditions.

Luxury boats from Corumbá

Arara Tur Rua Manoel Cavassa 47, by the port, Corumbá ☎67/231-4851, ⓦwww.araratur.com.br. This company runs a fine boat – the *Albatroz* – beautifully furnished with bars and cosy but very comfortable cabins. Choose from a wide range of short and longer boat tours in the Pantanal, specializing in photo safaris on the Rio Paraguai. $200 per person per day, 5 days minimum.

Barco Hotel Falcão Rodrigues Turismo, Rua Manoel Cavassa 331, Corumbá ☎67/231-5186, ℱ231-6746. Conceived as a floating base for sports anglers, the *Falcão* holds six to eight passengers. There's a five-day minimum rent, $180 per person per day. The boat is also available for return trips along the Rio Paraguai to Cáceres, at $2000 per person (the trip takes around eight days upriver, five days down).

Cabexy I & II Pantanal Tours, Rua Manoel Cavassa 61, Corumbá ☎67/231-4683 or 231-1559, ℱ231-2523, ⓦwww.pantanaltours.tur.br. Two two-tiered riverboats for rent, similar in style to the *Kalypso* (see below) but holding a maximum of eight passengers each, and rather more exclusive. Motorboats and fishing accessories provided. Five-day minimum period, $200 per person per day. Reservations and $3000 deposit required.

Cidade Barão do Melgaço Book direct on ☎67/231-1460 or through upmarket agent Fish World. This converted tour boat with eight double cabins is only for rent from Corumbá: five days and eight people minimum, starting at $180 per person per day.

Kalypso Book direct on ☎67/231-1460 or through agents Corumbá Tur, Mutum Turismo or Pan Tur. Brazil's answer to Nile cruisers, the *Kalypso* is a spacious three-tier affair with berths for 120 passengers, and looks for all the world like a pile of portacabins on a barge (which is what it once was). The interior is wood-panelled, the restaurant is self-service, and there's a pool on top in which to escape the mosquitoes and the heat. Originally designed as a base for fishing trips, it has a number of small motorboats and a giant fridge in which you can keep your catch. Prices start at $120 per person per day, with a minimum stay of six nights.

swamp. Details of these freelance operators are given on p.563 (Cuiabá), p.530 (Campo Grande) and p.544 (Corumbá). Instead, it's better to seek out **small boat trips** (around $40–80 a day, from Corumbá, Porto Jofre or Cáceres; there are no agencies for this sort of trip, so just ask around), or a **combination of jeep and boat**, over four or five days, which would certainly give the trip a taste of adventure, and could work out cheaper if you and your companions (there's usually a minimum number of passengers needed for boats) are happy braving the mosquitoes in hammocks. Note that if you're in Campo Grande, the trips you might be offered will invariably be luxury cruises.

Swamping it **upmarket** is much easier, at one of an increasing number of **fazenda-lodges** in the Pantanal, well away from towns and main roads. However, with few exceptions these cost upwards of $100 a night per person, and $200 is not uncommon. In their favour, though, is that the prices invariably include various activities, including trips by boat or jeep, horse riding, guided walks or fishing expeditions, as well as meals. Prices are generally more reasonable in the northern Pantanal (accessible from Cuiabá) than in the south (Corumbá, Miranda and Aquidauana). Also including nights in *fazenda*-lodges are **all-inclusive package tours**, though their prices vary wildly, sometimes undercutting the official lodge price, at other times almost doubling it – it's worth shopping around and bargaining (the tour operators listed in the box on p.550 all have a selection). As a general rule, however, you'll pay less if you deal direct with a *fazenda*-lodge owner in Porto Jofre, Cáceres, Aquidauana and even Corumbá, rather than through their agents. Most of the *fazenda*-lodges are located east and northeast of Corumbá, and also on either side of the Rio Cuiabá in the north, accessible for the most part via the aborted Transpantaneira road between Poconé and Porto Jofre. If you really have money to burn, signing up for a **luxury cruise**, or even **hiring a boat** for a week or so is the ideal option – see the box on pp.552–553. If you want to arrange tours from home before you leave for Brazil, see the Basics section of this guide for operators.

Into the swamp: routes from Corumbá and Campo Grande

Of the three main Pantanal towns, **Corumbá** is best placed for getting right into the Pantanal by bus or jeep, and has a welter of guides and agencies to choose from, as well as boats for hire. Though farther from the action, Campo Grande has better hotels and communications with the rest of Brazil, so it's as likely an entry point as Corumbá. Currently the most popular *fazenda*-lodges are those in Nhecolândia, roughly speaking the area between the *rios* Negro and Taquari east of Corumbá. These benefit from a well-established dirt access road, the MS-184/MS-228 (the old Campo Grande road), which loops off from the main BR-262 highway 300km from Campo Grande near Passo do Lontra (it's well signposted), and crosses through a large section of the swamp before rejoining the same road some 10km before Corumbá. The track also passes through Porto Manga (see p.546).

If you're coming from Campo Grande, your best bet is to hook up with Ecological Expeditions, Rua Joaquim Nabuco 185 (☏67/382-3504 or 321-0505, ⓦwww.pantanaltrekking.com), who offer the cheapest option for going deep into the swamp area by using camping facilities. They also run various tours including bush walking, horse riding, vehicle safaris, canoeing (in the wet season), piranha fishing, and wildlife spotting. Tour prices are also reasonable, with a three-day tour at around $90 (4 days $100 and 5 days $120).

Fazenda-lodges in the southern Pantanal

The following *fazenda*-lodges are accessible from Corumbá, Miranda or Aquidauana, offer full-board accommodation and swamp trips, and can be booked through the addresses given below or through the upmarket Pantanal operators listed in the box on p.550.

Baia Bonita Nhecolândia ☏ & ⓕ 67/231-9600, ⓦwww.pantanalnet.com.br/baiabonita. On reasonably dry land approximately 160km northeast of

Passo do Lontra (turn right before you reach Porto Manga), a two-storey block beside a ranch house. Homely atmosphere with safari-style tours on foot, in four-wheel-drive vehicles or on horseback. Minimum two people for two nights. ❼

Cabana do Lontra Passo do Lontra ☎67/987-3311 or 383-4532. Situated near where the MS-184 crosses the Rio Miranda, some 100km southeast of Corumbá and 7km off the main BR-262. The *Cabana*, with over twenty rooms and its own motorboats, is located in a good spot for most wildlife; excellent for fishing. ❺

Fazenda Rio Negro Rio Negro (owned by Orlando Rondon, Rua Antônio Correa 1161, Bairro Monte Libano, Campo Grande); ☎67/351-5191, ⓦwww.fazendarionegro.com.br. One of the Pantanal's oldest ranches, founded in 1895 by Cicíaco and Thomázia Rondon. Located up the Rio Negro with access from Aquidauana, this is a small, upmarket place with boats, horses and good guides. Air transfer from Campo Grande or Aquidauana is $100 return. ❽

Hotel Recanto Barra Mansa Rio Negro (owned by Guilherme Rondon) ☎67/383-5088, ⓦwwwhotelbarramansa.com.br. Further east from *Fazenda Rio Negro* (see above) on the north shore of the river, 130km from Aquidauana, with room for twelve guests. Specialises in game and fly fishing. Daily buses run here from Corumbá. ❽

Passo do Lontra Some 8km into the Pantanal from the BR-262 between Campo Grande and Corumbá (☎67/231-6136). One of the rare cheap options (with substantial reductions in low season), although a minimum of six guests may be required. They also allow camping. ❺

Pousada Arara Azul Rio Negrinho ☎67/384-6114, ⓦwww.pousadaararaazul.com.br. Close to the Rio Negro in Nhecolândia 38km up the MS-184 past Passo do Lontra, this *pousada* offers all the comforts you could want, plus guaranteed access to virtually all the bird and mammalian wildlife apart from the rarer jaguars and wolves. Excellent for piranha fishing, night-time *jacarés* viewing and horse riding. Camping allowed, too ($10 a night), though they may require a minimum stay of two days in the lodge. ❼

Refúgio Ecológico Caiman Rio Aquidauana. Reservation center in São Paulo where most bookings are taken (☎11/3079-6622, ⓦwww.caiman.com.br), with agents in Campo Grande (☎67/382-5197). The luxurious Pantanal jungle lodge experience. The *Refúgio* is located some 240km west of Campo Grande, 36km north of Miranda, and covers over 530 square kilometres. There are four *pousadas*, all with good facilities and a distinctive style to match the surroundings. Main activities include horse riding, nocturnal safaris, hikes, boat trips and cattle-drives (around 70 percent of the reserve's income still derives from cattle). The *Refúgio* has its own airstrip and offers transfer services leaving from Campo Grande four times a week. Full board, all activities and bilingual guide services are included in the daily rate of $200 per person per night in a double room.

Into the swamp: routes from Cuiabá

One of the simplest ways into the swamp is to take a **bus** (3hr) from Cuiabá south to **BARÃO DO MELGAÇO**, a small, quiet village on the banks of the Rio Cuiabá. Although not quite in the true swamp, and therefore with less in the way of wildlife, Barão is perfect if you're short on time and just want a taste of the Pantanal. There's a reasonable hotel by the river in town, the *Barão Tour Pantanal Hotel* (bookings at Rua Joaquim Murtinho 1213, Cuiabá; ☎65/713-1166, Ⓕ624-8743; ❸), which also has boats for hire; while the exclusive *Pousada do Rio Mutum* is just an hour away by boat, in a stunning location on the Baía de Siá Mariana bay near the Rio Mutum (☎65/623-7022; ❹); or book through Eldorado Exec. Centre, Av. Rubens de Mendonça 917, sala 301, Cuiabá (☎ & Ⓕ65/321-7995; ❺). Although Barão is no longer served by regular boats from Corumbá, it might still be worth asking around should a shallow-draught vessel be covering the journey – an unforgettable experience right through the centre of the swamp.

Poconé and Porto Jofre

The most exploited option from Cuiabá is to follow the route south to Poconé and Porto Jofre. There are daily **buses** from Cuiabá's *rodoviária* as far as **POCONÉ** along a paved and fairly smooth hundred-kilometre stretch of road. Like Barão do Melgaço, Poconé is not real Pantanal country, but it's a start and there are plenty of **hotels in town** if you need to stay over. On the main square, Praça Rondon, the *Hotel Skala* at no. 64 (☎65/721-1407; ❸), and a couple of restaurants take most of the trade. At the southern end of town at the start of the road to Porto Jofre, the cheaper *Hotel Santa Cruz* (☎65/721-1439; ❸) is recommended for relatively clean and comfortable lodging. Cheaper still, but slightly grubby, is *Dormitório Poconé* (❶), near the *rodoviária*.

The swamp proper begins as you leave the town going south, along the aborted Transpantaneira road. In fact it's just a bumpy track, often impassable during the rains, but you'll see plenty of wildlife from it, as well as signs marking the entrances to a number of *fazenda*-lodges and *pousadas* set back from the road around various tributaries of the Rio Cuiabá, notably the Pixaim. Although pricey, they're cheaper than their counterparts in the southern Pantanal, and all have restaurants and facilities for taking wildlife day-trips into the swamp by boat, on horseback or on foot. Another track from Poconé, in an even worse state, trails off southeast to Porto Cercado on the banks of the Rio Cuiabá itself, and also has a few *pousadas*.

After 145km, having crossed around a hundred wooden bridges in varying stages of dilapidation, the track eventually arrives at **PORTO JOFRE**. After Cuiabá, Porto Jofre appears as little more than a small fishing hamlet, literally the end of the road. This is as far as the Transpantaneira route has got, or ever looks like getting, thanks to technical problems and the sound advice of ecological pressure groups. As far as **accommodation in town** goes, the *Hotel Porto Jofre* (closed Nov–Feb; ☎65/322-6322; ❻) has the monopoly and therefore charges through the nose. If you have a hammock or a tent, it's usually all right to sleep outside somewhere, but check with someone in authority first (ask at the port) and don't leave your valuables unattended. There are no other options unless you can get someone to invite you to their house.

From Porto Jofre, there are irregular cargo **boats** to Corumbá (about twice a month), normally carrying soya or cattle from Cáceres, and the journey takes between two and five days, depending on whether the boats sail through the night. It's also possible to arrange a day or two's excursion up the Piquiri and Cuiabá rivers from Porto Jofre.

Pousadas around Poconé and Porto Jofre

All of the following can be booked through the addresses given below or through upmarket travel agents in Cuiabá (see p.563); some lodges insist on advance reservations and won't let you in unannounced, but others might relent if you just drop by. All the lodges below offer full-board accommodation, with swamp trips included in the price; they're listed in loose geographical order, from northeast to southwest.

Hotel Cabanas do Pantanal ☎65/345-1887 or Confiança Turismo, Rua Cândido Mariano 434, Cuiabá ☎65/623-4141. Situated 50km from Poconé on the Rio Pixaim, left off the Porto Cercado track. Confiança prefer you take one of their various three- to five-day packages, including trips to Aguas Quentes and Chapada dos Guimarães. ❺–❻

Hotel Pouso da Garça ☎65/322-8823 or 322-4916; bookings at Rua Miranda Reis 38, Cuiabá, or through ☎11/299-5353 or 267-9966. On the Rio São Lourenço near its confluence with the Rio Cuiabá (access by light aircraft), with a pool, motorboats and horses for guests' use. ❻

Pousada Araras office at Cuiabá airport, or Av. Ponce de Arruda 670, Várzea Grande; ☎65/682-2800, ⓦwww.araraslodge.com.br. At km 32 of the Transpantaneira, this long-established *pousada* is an old brick ranch building, more atmospheric than most of the more modern *pousadas*, with a pool, as well as boats and horses, but its fourteen rooms are likely to be full in high season. ❺

Pousada Beira Rio ☎65/721-1642, reservations ☎65/321-9445. On the opposite bank of the Rio Pixaim at km 65, with good-quality, air-conditioned apartments, as well as boats and horse riding for

guests. Mainly used by package tours. ❺
Pousada Pantaneiro (bookings through Cuiabá's travel agents). Approximately 100km south of Poconé, a small place (five rooms) and one of the more reasonably priced *pousadas* which, although not on a river itself, offers swamp trips on horseback. It should be OK to camp here, too, and they also have tents for hire. ❸–❹
Pousada Passargada (bookings through Cuiabá's travel agents, or in Rio ☎021/235-2840 or São Paulo ☎011/284-5434). Linked in the dry season by the Porto Cercado track, most of the year it's 1hr 30min by boat from Barão do Melgaço. A good place directly on the Rio Pixaim. ❻
Pousada Pixaim ☎65/721-2091; reservations ☎65/721-1172. At km 64 on the Rio Pixaim, and not always reachable by road (this and the more southerly *pousadas* are often cut off in the rains, but all have airstrips). Ten wooden three-bed rooms on stilts, with motorboats for hire and a

number of swamp tracks to follow on foot. ❺
Pousada Porto Cercado ☎65/721-1726, reservations 682-1300. Near the end of the Porto Cercado track, 79km from Poconé with direct access to the Rio Cuiabá. The *pousada* has thirty double rooms, and a restaurant specializing, not surprisingly, in fish. Pool and boats also available for messing about in. ❻
Pousada São Sebastião do Pantanal ☎65/322-0178, ⓕ 321-0710. Situated 34km from Poconé at km 27 of the aborted Transpantaneira road, and usually reachable even in bad weather. A first-class establishment (with pool) located close to the river in pleasant wooded surroundings, offering horse and boat safaris. Good for families. ❻
Rancho Kue ☎67/241-1875. This is one of the best-located *fazendas*, right in the centre of the swamp and close to the confluence of the big *rios* Paraguai and São Lourenço. Access by plane. ❼

Cáceres

Although less frequented than the Porto Jofre route, **CÁCERES** is another good target from Cuiabá, 233km west of the city. It's a very pleasant, laid-back place, and given the prices of accommodation along the Transpantaneira, definitely deserves consideration as a base for visiting the Pantanal. It's a three- to four-hour journey by bus, several of which leave daily from the *rodoviária* in Cuiabá. On the upper reaches of the Rio Paraguai, which is still quite broad even this far upstream, Cáceres is a relatively new town, made up largely of wooden shacks, bars and pool rooms. There are lots of cheap **hotels**, the best of which is the *Santa Terezinha*, Rua Tiradentes 485 (☎65/223-4621; ❷), which is clean and hospitable. The *Hotel Comodoro*, Praça Duque de Caxias 561 (☎65/223-2078, ❹), has **motorboats** for hire, as do the *Barco Hotel Santa Maria*, Rua Marechal Deodoro 73 (☎65/223-5455, ❸), and the small but well-equipped Lancha Gaiva tour boat company(☎65/223-4956) whose office is at the Praça Duque de Caxias 206. The *Hotel Turbo* at Av. São Luis 1399 (☎65/223-1984; ❹) has a pool and restaurant. The **travel agency** Natureza, at Rua Coronel José Dulce 304 (☎65/223-1997), can arrange *pousada* accommodation and a number of good-value tours.

About 60km away on the confluence of the *rios* Paraguai and Jauru is the touristy, Japanese-owned *Hotel Fazenda Barranquinho* (☎65/223-1081; ❼), which can be reached by track or boat in around three hours from Cáceres. It's a beautiful spot, but is still not far enough into the swamp for the best chance of spotting wildlife. Best bet for this is to take one of the **cargo boats** to Corumbá from Cáceres – see the box on pp.552–553, which also gives details of luxury fishing boats. For an even more adventurous option, you could rent a small motorboat for a week or two, which would certainly give you greater freedom (though a guide would be advisable). The Cáceres Iate Clube, Rua Maravilha (☎65/223-2148) may be of help. Other potentially useful contacts are on Rua Boa Vista: the Oficina Náutica São Luiz at no. 115 (☎65/223-1427), and Nautica Turismo at no. 119 (☎65/223-1565).

The only road to go further into the Pantanal is the track that leads on to the **Bolivian border** settlement of San Matias; from here you can fly to Santa Cruz.

Mato Grosso state

The state of Mato Grosso is dominated completely by **Cuiabá** in spite of the fact that this city is located in the very south of the state. Roads radiating from this commercial and administrative centre appear on a map like the tentacles of a gigantic octopus extending hungrily over the plains in every direction. The city is over 1000km from Brasília, almost 1500km from Porto Velho and more than 1700km from São Paulo: an opportune place to break a long overland haul. Beyond its strategic importance, though, Cuiabá's friendly personality and interesting city centre, combined with the breathtaking scenery of the nearby Chapada dos Guimarães, can easily lure you into staying longer than planned.

Cuiabá is a good springboard for a trip into or through the **Pantanal** (see p.546) but, as far as other long expeditions go, the state has disappointingly little to offer. No longer a true frontier zone, it's an established cattle-ranching region where cows are much bigger business than tourism. With almost no tourist development outside Cuiabá and the Pantanal, the reality for most travellers will be an intrepid journey by bus (and perhaps river) to some other distant city. The most arduous of the options used to be the awful **Highway BR-163** from Cuiabá to Santarém, which, in theory, connects at Itaituba with the BR-230 Transamazônica Highway for Altamira, Marabá and Belém. However, around 400km of road has been reclaimed by jungle along the Rio Jamanxim in southern Pará, making it impassable to anything other than four-wheel-drive vehicles for the foreseeable future: the furthest north you can drive is the Serra do Cachimbo on the fringes of Pará state. The fastest road is **Highway BR-364** through Cuiabá (known as the BR-070 in Mato Grosso), which ultimately links São Paulo with Rio Branco.

Cuiabá

The southern gateway into the Amazon, **CUIABÁ** has always been firmly on the edge of Brazil's wilderness. Following the discovery of a gold field here in 1719 (one version of the town's name means the "river of stars"), the town mushroomed as an administrative and service centre in the middle of Indian territory, thousands of very slow, overland miles from any other Portuguese settlement. To the south lay the Pantanal and the dreaded Paiaguá people who frequently ambushed convoys of boats transporting Cuiabá gold by river to São Paulo. The fierce Bororo tribe, who dominated Mato Grosso east of Cuiabá, also regularly attacked many of the mining settlements. Northwest along a high hilly ridge – the Chapada dos Parecis, which now carries BR-364 to Porto Velho – lived the peaceful Parecis people, farmers in the watershed between the Amazon and the Pantanal. By the 1780s, however, most Indians within these groups had been either eliminated or transformed into allies: the Parecis were needed as slave labour for the mines; the Bororo either retreated into the forest or joined the Portuguese as mercenaries and Indian hunters; while the Paiaguá fared worst of all, almost completely wiped out by cannon and musket during a succession of punitive expeditions from Cuiabá.

The most important development came during the 1890s, when a young Brazilian army officer, Lieutenant **Cândido Rondon**, built a telegraph system

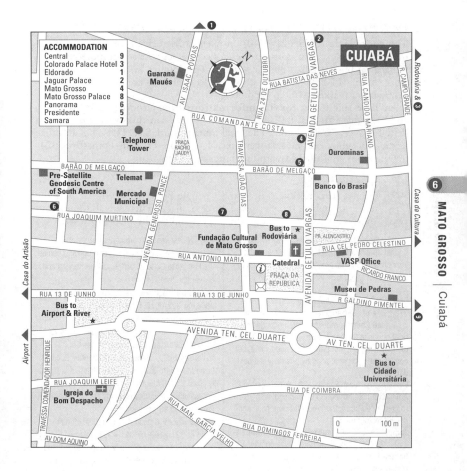

from Goiás to Cuiabá through treacherous Bororo territory – assisted no doubt by the fact that he had some Bororo blood in his veins. By 1903 he had extended the telegraph from Cuiabá south to Corumbá, and in 1907 he began work to reach the Rio Madeira, to the northwest in the Amazon basin. The latter expedition earned Rondon a reputation as an important explorer and brought him into contact with the Nambikwara Indians. Since then, Cuiabá has been pushing forward the frontier of development and the city is still a stepping stone and crossroads for pioneers, with a population approaching one million. Every year, thousands of hopeful settlers stream through Cuiabá on their way to a new life in the western Amazon.

The established farmlands around the city now produce excellent crops – maize, fruits, rice and soya. But the city itself thrives on the much larger surrounding **cattle-ranching region**, which contains almost a quarter of a million inhabitants. Future prosperity is assured, too: a large lead ore deposit is being worked close to the town, and oil has been discovered at Várzea Grande; but it is more sustainable industries, like rubber, palm nuts and, of course, tourism, that will provide income in years to come.

Arrival, information and accommodation

The **rodoviária** (☎65/621-1040) on Avenida Marechal Rondon is an ultra-modern complex, 3km north of the city centre: it's a fifteen-minute ride into Cuiabá on buses #202, #304 or #309, or ten minutes by taxi ($10). The **airport** (☎65/614-2500), 8km south in Várzea Grande, is connected to the centre by buses marked "Tuiuiu" and taxis.

You'll be able to get **tourist information** at the airport (☎65/381-2211) and *rodoviária* (☎65/321-0102); both offices are – in theory at least – open daily between 8am and 6pm. The local tourist board, SEDTUR, has an office in the city centre on Praça da República 131 (Mon–Fri 8am–6pm; ☎65/624-9060), and is well stocked with brochures and a few maps.

Accommodation

With the *rodoviária* relatively close, most people prefer to stay in or near the busy city centre, where there's a good range of places. There are also numerous two- and three-star hotels around the airport and on the way into town.

Central Rua Galdino Pimentel ☎65/321-8309. A budget option in the heart of the old town, with very basic rooms. Its neighbor *São Marcos*, on the same street (☎65/624-2300), offers much the same. **①**

Colorado Palace Av. Jules Rimet 32 ☎65/621-3763. One of a dozen three-star hotels along the main road from the *rodoviária* into town, this one's right opposite the bus station. The rooms are predictably noisy and not particularly good value, but convenient if you're leaving by bus early the next day. **④**

Eldorado Av. Isaac Póvoas 1000 ☎65/624-1480. A five-star hotel at the top of its range, with 182 rooms, arctic-strength air-conditioning, pool, and decent restaurant. **⑥**

Jaguar Palace Av. Getúlio Vargas 600 ☎65/624-4404, ℱ 623-7798, ℰjaguarph@zaz.com.br. A little run-down but still very good value, with a restaurant and pool that non-residents may be able to use for a fee. **③**

Mato Grosso Rua Comandante Costa 2522 ☎65/614-7777, ℱ 614-7053. Within three blocks of Praça da República and offering excellent-value rooms with private showers. **②**

Mato Grosso Palace Rua Joaquim Murtinho 170 ☎65/614-7000 or 0800-110-098, ℱ321-2386,

ⓦwww.bestwestern.com.br. Part of the Best Western chain. Situated in a grand building behind the Fundação Cultural, with excellent service and convention facilities. No pool. **⑥**

Panorama Praça Moreira Cabral 286 ☎65/322-0866, ℱ 322-0072. On the corner with Rua Ferreira Mendes, this basic but good value option has views over the city from its upper floors. **②**

Portal do Pantanal Av. Isaac Póvoas 655 ☎65/624-8999, ⓦwww.portaldopantanal.com.br. Linked to Youth Hostelling International, this friendly place has all the usual facilities, plus Internet access, kitchen and surprisingly comfortable beds. From around $8 per person.

Presidente Av. Getúlio Vargas 345 ☎65/624-1386 or 321-6162, ℱ 321-4323. Just two blocks from Praça da República, in a crumbling building on the corner of Rua Barão de Melgaço, this place has seen better days but is reasonable for the price (air-conditioning is extra). Can be loud, though. **②**

Samara Rua Joaquim Murtinho 270 ☎65/322-6001. Clean and hospitable hotel that's cheaper than *Hotel Presidente* and just as centrally located. **①**

The City

Perhaps because of its busy feel, Cuiabá is an exciting place to spend a few days. There's certainly a lot to see and do in the city's relatively self-contained centre, where modern skyscrapers long ago won the battle for attention with the now hidden ornate facades of crumbling, pastel-shaded colonial villas, churches and shops.

The central **Praça da República** is a hive of activity from daybreak onwards. It's the city's main meeting spot, and the cathedral, post office, the cultural foundation and university all face onto the square, while under the shade of its large trees, hippies from the Brazilian coast sell crafted jewellery and leather work. The most interesting old mansion in town, the **Palácio da Instrução**, is on the square at no. 151. Now the **Fundação Cultural de Mato Grosso**, it houses three excellent **museums** of history, natural history and anthropology, with exhibits spanning prehistoric to colonial times (Mon–Fri 8.30am–4.30pm). There are some fascinating old photos of Cuiabá, along with rooms full of stuffed creatures from the once forested region and, best of all, a superb array of Indian artefacts. The **Catedral do Bom Jesus**, next door, was built in the 1960s to replace the old cathedral, a beautiful Baroque affair that was then thought old-fashioned. Constructed of pinkish concrete with a square, vaguely Moorish facade, the new cathedral has a predictably vast, rectangular interior; its main altar is overshadowed by a mural reaching from floor to ceiling that depicts a sparkling Christ floating in the air above the city of Cuiabá and the cathedral.

The only other church of any real interest in Cuiabá is the early twentieth-century **Igreja de Nossa Senhora do Bom Despacho**, though both it and its splendid religious art collection are currently closed to visitors. Sitting on the hill to the south, across the Avenida Tenente Coronel Duarte from the cathedral side of town, Bom Despacho used to dominate the cityscape before office buildings and towering hotels sprang up to dwarf it in the latter half of the twentieth century.

Just to the northeast of Praça da República, a few narrow central lanes – Pedro Celestino, Galdino Pimentel, Ricardo Franco and Rua 7 de Setembro – form a crowded pedestrian shopping area. It's here that you'll find the city's oldest church, the simple but run-down **Igreja Nossa Serhora do Rosário e Capela de São Benedicto**, completed in 1722, and the unusual **Museu de Pedras**, Rua Galdino Pimentel 195 (Mon–Fri 7–11am & 1–4pm; $2). Packed tightly into just two rooms, the museum contains the marvellously eccentric collection of local man Ramis Bucair, comprising gemstones, crystals, fossils, Stone Age artefacts, stuffed animals, birds and snakes. The exhibits are a hotch-potch of genuinely fascinating pieces – rocks containing liquid and loose diamonds, and a dried catfish tongue, once used as a rasp for grating guaraná (a tropical berry) – mixed with some outrageous fakes, such as the inch-high carved stone purported to be a shrunken human skull from some remote Indian tribe, and a display case containing a large fossilized bone, discovered locally and boldly claimed to be that of a *Tyrannosaurus rex*. An equally dubious claim is made in Praça Moreira Cabral, along Rua Barão de Melgaço by the state assembly buildings: a small post enclosed by a tall thin pyramid marks what was considered to be, until the advent of satellite topography, the geographical centre of the South American continent. The actual place, for what it's worth, is actually 67km away in the Chapada dos Guimarães.

Having exhausted the central possibilities, there are a couple of other museums in Cuiabá, which are worth an hour or so of your time if you have any interest at all in the indigenous culture. The **ethnographic collection** belonging to the offices of FUNAI, the Foundation for Indian Affairs, is difficult to track down, as they keep moving location; it's currently on Avenida C.P.A., the easterly continuation of Avenida Tenente Coronel Duarte (☏65/644-1850), but it's worth checking first with the tourist office. Easier to find is the smaller university-run **Museu do Índio Marechal Rondon**, on Avenida Fernando Corréa da Costa (Mon–Fri 7.30–11.30am & 1.30–5.30pm, Sat & Sun 7.30–11am), which also focuses on local Indian culture. The museum is beside the university pool, 5km east of town off BR-364, in the sector known as Cidade Universitária; buses #133, #505, #513, #514 and others from Avenida Tenente Coronel Duarte will take you there. Also in the Cidade Universitária is a small **zoological garden** (daily 8am–5pm; closed Mondays) where you'll find swamp creatures including caimans, tapirs and capybaras, a small consolation if you don't have time for a Pantanal tour.

Finally, focusing mainly on work by early Republican and modern Brazilian artists, there are two **art galleries** in Cuiabá – one in the Casa da Cultura, Rua Barão de Melgaço, the other, Laila Zharan, at Av. Marechal Deodoro 504.

Eating, drinking and nightlife

Cuiabá has a surprising range of cuisine and some excellent **restaurants**, although you'll find almost everything closed on Sundays. Avenida Getúlio Vargas hosts an array of very swish and expensive modern Italian restaurants, such as *Adriano* at no. 985 and *Tavola Piena* at no. 676; *Getúlio's* at no. 1147 offers decently priced drinks and cocktails, if you want to watch the cream of Cuiabá cruise by in their dream wagons in the evenings. For **cheaper eating** and *lanches* there are plenty of places in the area around Praça Alencastro, at the north end of Travessa João Dias near Rua Comandante Costa, and in the shopping zone between Rua Pedro Celestino and Rua Galdino Pimentel. **Ice cream parlours** are an essential ingredient of any city with temperatures well over 40°C. The best in Cuiabá are *Alaska*, Rua Pedro Celestino 215, *Patotinha*, Av. Generoso Ponce 761, and *Flocky's* on Avenida Isaac Póvoas. For your own supplies, the busy **Mercado Municipal** is on Avenida Generoso Ponce (Mon–Sat 7.30am–6pm, Sun 7.30am–noon).

Restaurants

Barranco Bar Rua Pedro Celestino. Inexpensive food and drinks and live Brazilian music, in a modest but inviting place – as good as any to meet the local people. One of the few inexpensive spots open Sun.

Casa Branca Rua Comandante Costa 565. Cheap and cheerful restaurant, 500m east of *Hotel Mato Grosso*, serves mainly Brazilian meat dishes and salads. Closed Sun.

Chopp Dourado Av. Ten. Coronel Duarte. Large and very busy place on the *avenida*, serving up good, reasonably priced meals (about $10 a head). It tends to get packed at night with crowds dancing to its frequent live music shows.

Le Bam Rua Comandante Costa. Around the corner from *Hotel Presidente*, a gem of a *lanchonete*: cheap and delicious food with exceptionally friendly owners. Closed Sun.

Meridiano 56 Av. Isaac Póvoas 1039 ☎65/322-4321. Reasonably priced, fairly central and well-regarded fish restaurant. Tues–Sat evenings, Sunday mornings.

Papagaio Grill Av. Mato Grosso 764 ☎65/621-1020. Five blocks down from Avenida Getúlio Vargas, one of Cuiabá's trendiest restaurant-bars and the evening focus for brash, young Cuiabanos, with excellent but expensive food of a wide range of Brazilian and international dishes, everything form pizza to Amazon swamp fish as well as very potent cocktails. Daily 4pm–3am.

Presto Pizzas Av. Getúlio Vargas 1371 ☎65/624-4600. Good popular pizza restaurant with fast service; also operates a delivery service.

Regionalíssimo Rua 13 de Junho ☎65/623-6881. Excellent, moderately priced regional dishes. On Wednesdays they serve a speciality of beef with green bananas, and there's sometimes live music at weekends. Closed Mon.

The Best Rua Pedro Celestino 8. Refreshingly cool coffee bar with friendly service. Mon–Fri 7am–6pm, Sat 7am–4pm.

Tio Ari Natural Restaurante Rua Comandante Costa 770. Excellent, largely vegetarian food near the Caixa Economica bank, all at very low prices.

Bars and nightlife

Although beer is twice as expensive here as it is on the coast, you'll find that **nightlife** in Cuiabá revolves mainly around the bars and restaurants in the town centre, especially along Rua Isaac Póvoas. *Barranco Bar* and *Papagaio Grill* (see "Restaurants" above) have a good atmosphere, while beyond the downtown area, along the large Avenida C.P.A., there are several more bars and

Tour operators and guides in Cuiabá

All of Cuiabá's travel agents offer trips into the Pantanal (see also the list of upmarket operators on p.550) or to the closer sites, like Chapada dos Guimarães, although their primary occupation is selling flights within Brazil. For more personal service, however, you'd do better to contact one of the **tour operators**: Anaconda Pantanal Operator, Rua Comandante Costa 649 (☎65/624-4142 or 624-5128, ℗624-6242), is the biggest; Tuiu Tur, Rua 12 de Outubro 170 (☎65/622-2030), runs occasional charter flights to Bolivia, as well as being specialists in arranging Pantanal hotel bookings. If you're short of time, Ametur, Rua Joaquim Murtinho 242 (☎65/624-1000), runs day-trips by boat to Barão de Melgaço as well as offering the usual ticketing agency services. Tours within the region tend to cost upwards of $50 a day per person (though it's often worth bargaining). Note that in low season you may have to wait a few days for enough tourists to make up your group, unless you're happy paying more.

Individual **guides** to the Pantanal tend to approach arriving passengers at the airport, as well as leaving their brochures at the SEDTUR office on Praça da República. Well worth contacting for their more personal tours are Joel Souza, an excellent guide who operates from an office next door to *Hotel Presidente*, at Av. Getúlio Vargas 155-A (☎65/624-1386 or 321-6162, ℗321-4323); the ever-enthusiastic Munir of Natureco, Rua Barão de Melgaço 2015 (☎ & ℗65/624-5116); and Edivaldo Oliveira (☎65/935-3640), a local taxi driver with a huge knowledge of local history and geology. Guides charge from $25–30 per day.

clubs, continuously opening and closing at the fickle whim of Cuiabá's monied youth. Currently recommended – provided you have plenty of cash – are *Deck Avenida*, at no. 635, which has live music, a wide range of food and a lively atmosphere; *Terraço*, which offers live music at weekends; and *Tucano*, a spot with diverse dance music. The *Veneza Palace Hotel*, Av. Cel. Escolastico 738 in Bandeirantes (☎65/661-1480 or 321-4847), has occasional big-name bands from Rio playing live, while the main gay venue, though not exactly a scream, is the bar under *Hotel Presidente*. Lastly, if you're desperate for a fix of Hollywood movies, the main cinema is Cine Bandeirantes, Rua Pedro Celestino 199 (☎65/624-3550), which screens relatively new releases.

Listings

Airlines TABA, at the airport ☎65/682-1049; TAM, Av. Isaac Póvoas 586 ☎65/682-1702; Varig, Av. 15 de Novembro 230 ☎65/682-1140; VASP, Rua Pedro Celestino 32 ☎65/682-5996.

Air taxis Cheap if you're travelling in a big group, an air-taxi service is a useful way of getting to some of the more remote places, and the only way during the rains to reach most of the Pantanal *pousadas*. About ten companies are based at the airport, among them Guara (☎65/682-2288), Protaxi (☎65/321-2287) and Universal (☎65/381-2352).

Banks and exchange Cuiabá is the only place in the region where you're likely to be able to change travellers' cheques – Visa cards cash advances can be obtained and cheques and notes exchanged in the Banco do Brasil (first floor) on

Praça Alencastro (Mon–Fri 10am–3pm). Dollars cash can be exchanged at good rates at a number of *casas do câmbio* along Rua Ricardo Franco, at Ourominas at Rua Cândido Mariano 401, or in some of the larger hotels.

Car rental Localiza, Av. Dom Bosco 965 (☎65/624-7979); Trescinco, Av. Fernando Corréa da Costa 1751 (☎65/627-3500 or 682-2004), which also has a branch at the airport; Unidas, Praça do Aeroporto (☎65/682-4052).

Post office At Praça da República (Mon–Fri 9am–6pm, Sat 9am–noon).

Shopping Explore the streets between the Praça da República and the Igreja do Rosário or try the Casa do Artesão, corner of Rua 13 de Junho and Rua Senador Metello, or FUNAI's ArtIndia shop, Rua São Joaquim 1047, for local handicrafts. More curious is the magic shop on Av. Tenente Coronel Duarte, near the corner with Av. Generoso Ponce – its shelves are stacked with ceremonial swords, North American Indian ceramic figurines, incense, pots decorated in gods and demons, strings of jungle beads and seed pods. Also worth a visit is the shop Guaraná Maués, Av. Isaac Póvoas 611, which specializes in *guaraná*, grown locally in Mato Grosso state. There are two decent photographic shops on Rua Joaquim Murtinho: Cuiabá Color at no. 789, and the friendly Artcolor next door. **Telephones** International and national calls can be made easily with phone cards at any public booth. The Telemat office is at Rua Barão de Melgaço (Mon–Sat 7.30am–5.30pm).

Around Cuiabá

Although it's a major staging post for the Pantanal, there isn't a lot in terms of organized tourism in the immediate region **around Cuiabá**, and what there is, is mostly aimed at local people. Nevertheless, the scenery around **Chapada dos Guimarães** makes for a rewarding side-trip from the city – much more of a draw than either the hot springs of **Aguas Quentes** or the beach at **São Antônio do Leverger**.

Chapada dos Guimarães

A paved road winds its way up to the scenic and increasingly popular mountain village of **CHAPADA DOS GUIMARÃES**, set on the plateau of the same name just 64km from Cuiabá. Nine daily **buses** run by Expreso Rubi make the one-hour journey from Cuiabá's *rodoviária*.

It is here on this plateau that the true geodesic centre of South America was pinpointed by satellite, much to the chagrin of the Cuiabanos who stick resolutely to their old 1909 mark; the actual spot, the **Mirante da Geodésia**, is located on the southern continuation of Rua Clariano Curvo from Praça Dom Wunibaldo, 8km away. Parochial disputes aside, Chapada is an interesting settlement in its own right, containing Mato Grosso's oldest church, the **Igreja de Nossa Senhora de Santana do Sacramento**, a fairly plain colonial temple built in 1779, which dominates the top end of the town's leafy Praça Dom Wunibaldo. These days, with a population nearing 16,000, the town has something of a reputation as a centre for the Brazilian "New Age" movement, with crystal shops, health food stores and hippy communities springing up over the last years. If you're here in July, you're in for a treat, with the staging of the **Festival de Inverno** – a mix of drama, exhibitions and music, the latter ranging from traditional, sacred and Indian music to funk and rap.

Most of the year, however, it's not the town itself that brings most people out to Chapada. The stunning countryside, of which over 300 square kilometres is protected as the **Parque Nacional da Chapada dos Guimarães**, consists of a grassy plateau – at 800m, the highest land in Mato Grosso – scattered with low trees, a marvellous backdrop for photographing the local flora and birdlife. Within walking distance, there are waterfalls, fantastic rock formations and precipitous canyons, as well as some interesting, partially excavated archeological sites. The most spectacular of all the sights around the village is the **Véu de Noiva waterfall**, which drops over a sheer rock face for over 60m, pounding into the forested basin below. If you don't want to take a tour, you can get there by walking or, if you're lucky, hitching from the village of Buruti, on the road from Cuiabá, about 12km before Chapada dos Guimarães. Alternatively, the falls lie within a couple of kilometres of the road if you jump off the bus some 6km beyond Salgadeira (ask the driver to show you the track).

Other highlights in the park include, about 25km to the north of town, the impressive and weird rock formations of **Cidade da Pedra**, some of them up to 300m tall, the spectacular waterfalls of **Cachoeira da Martinha**, 30km further north, and a couple of interesting cave systems – the **Casa de Pedra**, not far from Véu da Noiva and, further afield, the **Caverna Aroe Jari**, the latter with cave paintings. Good views of the Cidade da Pedra can be had from **Porto do Inferno**, a viewing point some 16km from the village on the road into the Chapada from Cuiabá.

Practicalities

There's a good range of **places to stay**, both in the village and in the surrounding countryside. *Pousada Bom Jardim* on the Praça Dom Wunibaldo 641 (℡65/301-1244 or 301-1201; ❹), is clean and very friendly, with nice breakfasts; the *Quincó*, also on the square, is the cheapest option, and perfectly reasonable (℡65/301-1284; ❷); and the *Hotel Turismo*, Rua Fernando Corréa 1065 (℡65/301-1176; ❹), has exceptionally comfortable beds and good showers. Just three blocks from the *praça* is *Rios Hotel*, Rua Tiradentes 333 (℡65/301-1126; ❷–❸), one of the best basic places.

There are also a number of good *pousadas* dotted about the Chapada, many with superb views: *Pousada Penhasco*, on the outskirts of the village (℡65/624-1000 or 301-1555, ⓦwww.penhasco.com.br; ❺), is a large, quite plush place with apartments, pool and sports facilities; similarly upmarket is the *Pousada Estáncia*, Rod. Emanuel Pinheiro km 60, some 2–3km from the village (℡65/981-0335, 391-1269 or 972-2773; ❻), which also offers horse riding; a further 3km along the same road, the *Hotel Pousada da Chapada*, Rod. Emanuel Pinheiro km 63 (℡65/624-1515 or 301-1171; ❺), is smaller but still comfortable with a pool, sauna and decent bar. One of the best spots for **camping** is the *Vale da Boçátina Camping Ecológico* (℡65/301-1393, 301-2074 or 301-1154), 10km from the village on a beautiful site near waterfalls and streams, but they need to be contacted in advance to arrange transport.

Most of Chapada dos Guimarães best **restaurants** can be found, not surprisingly, around the Praça Dom Wunibaldo: *Felipe's*, Rua Cipriano Curvo 598, is one of the most popular restaurant-bars with *comida por kilo* at lunchtimes; next door, the *Trapiche* has an airy terrace and good self-service lunches; while the *Casa do Artesão* in Rua Quinco Caldas serves excellent local dishes at very reasonable prices. A busy spot in the evenings is the *Santos Bar* on the *praça*.

Tourist information is available from the helpful Secretaria de Turismo just off Praça Dom Wunibaldo on Rua Quinco Caldas (daily 9am–7pm; ℡65/301-1690, which usually has details of bus times, information on campsites, contact lists for local guides and maps of the Chapada. There are also a couple of good **tour agents** in town: Eco Turismo, Praça Dom Wunibaldo 464 (℡65/301-1393, ⓦwww.chapadadosguimaraes.com), organize tours of the region and have an English-speaking guide; Chapada & Pantanal, Rua Tiradentes 28 (℡65/301-1836), specialize in adventure tours, mainly trekking and canoeing, but also offer trips to the Cidade de Pedra, the Mirante da Geodésia and the other main sites in the area. Joel Souza, who operates from Cuiabá (see p.563), is also worth contacting for his guide services. For **changing money**, the Banco do Brasil is on the Praça Dom Wunibaldo.

Águas Quentes and São Antônio

The hot baths of **ÁGUAS QUENTES**, 86km east of Cuiabá in the Serra de São Vicente, just off BR-364 towards Rondonópolis, function as a weekend and honeymoon resort for locals. Apart from the baths, though, there is little of interest. The water, said to be mildly radioactive, comes in four different pools, the hottest at around 42°C, and is regarded as a cure for rheumatism, liver complaints and even conjunctivitis. There are daily **buses** to the town from the *rodoviária* in Cuiabá, but be warned that the resort has only one **hotel**, the expensive hydrotherapy centre of *Hotel Águas Quentes* (☎65/614-7500, ☏321-2386 ⓔhomat@zaz.com.br; ⓺); or you can also book in advance at the *Hotel Mato Grosso Palace* in Cuiabá (see p.560).

The closest **beach** to Cuiabá is at **SÃO ANTÔNIO DO LEVERGER**, 35km south of the city on the Rio Cuiabá. It's as much fun as most of the beaches on the coast, even if it seems a little incongruous given the jungle backdrop, but the waters are now far from clean, carrying with them much of Cuiabá's effluent. The dry and relatively cool month of July is designated a beach festival. Again, there are **buses** every day from the *rodoviária* in Cuiabá.

On from Cuiabá

Cuiabá is a central point for all sorts of long-distance trips within Brazil, and a launching pad for onward travel into neighbouring countries. The two main regional highways, the **BR-163** and the **BR-364**, are accessible from the city: the BR-364 is particularly important as a link between the Amazon and almost all other regions, although parts of its westernmost sections are impassable for much of the year. Whether you're coming from São Paulo, Rio, Brasília or the Northeast, this is the route to take if you want to travel overland into the western Amazon. See p.555 for routes from Cuiabá into the Pantanal.

West to Rondônia and Porto Velho

Heading **west from Cuiabá**, Porto Velho and Rio Branco are both possible destinations in their own right, or would serve as relaxing stops on the way to Manaus, Peru or Bolivia. Following Rondônia's telegraph link to Manaus in the early twentieth century, **Highway BR-364** to northern Mato Grosso and southwestern Amazon was the next development to open up the region. Paving the BR-364 cost around $600 million – partly financed by the World Bank – but construction was held up for a while when anthropologists realized that it was planned to cut straight through **Nambikwara** tribal lands. The road was eventually completed by making a large detour around these Indians, who still live in small, widely scattered groups that have very little contact with each other.

Leaving the industrial fringes of Cuiabá, the road soon enters the well-established pastoral farmlands to the west. At **Cáceres** (see p.557), three hours out of Cuiabá, the highway starts to leave the Pantanal watershed and climbs gradually towards the inhospitable but beautiful ridges of the **Chapada dos Parecis** and the state frontier with Rondônia. Here everyone normally has to pass through the **yellow fever checkpoint**: busloads of people spend half an hour either getting inoculated or showing their vaccination certificates. The Nambikwara and Sararé Indians live to the south of the Chapada escarpment, while to the north there are settlements of Parecis and various other groups. The process of occupation in this region is so recent and intense that the Indians have suffered greatly. Most of their demarcated lands have been invaded already and the situation is worsening all the time; local newspapers are full of reports concerning police operations aimed at removing the illegal *garimpeiros* from the reserves. The Indians don't generally come out to the highway, though sometimes you'll see a family or two selling crafted goods – bows and arrows, beads or carvings – beside the road at small pit stops.

The road from Cuiabá to Porto Velho passes through the remains of tropical rainforest. There's the occasional tall tree left standing, but more usually it's acres of burnt-out fields and small frontier settlements, crowded with people busy in mechanics' workshops or passing the time playing pool. This is **Rondônia** (see p.457), a relatively recently established jungle state, which has already, even by official reckoning, lost over fifteen percent of its original forest. **JI PARANÁ** is the only town of any real size along the BR-364, with a population that's grown from 9000 in 1970 to over 120,000. Now Rondônia's second-largest city, its main drag is dominated by a massive Ford showroom, while thousands of gigantic tree trunks sit in enormous piles by the roadside. Even from the bus you can hear the grating noise of circular saws, slicing the forest into manageable and marketable chunks. And on the outskirts of town, hundreds of small, new wooden huts are springing up every month. It's another five hours, through decimated jungle scenery, before you reach the jungle frontier town of Porto Velho (see p.457), capital of Rondônia state.

North towards the Serra do Cachimbo

Crossing the hills to the **north of Cuiabá**, the BR-163 heads up towards the Serra do Cachimbo; the 2000-kilometre continuation to the Amazon and Santarém – a bold but untenable attempt to cross what is still essentially a vast wilderness – is currently impassable. As the road climbs towards the rim of the Amazon basin, the forest becomes thicker and the climate muggier, and the road surface soon deteriorates. This transitional zone is one of the best areas south of Boa Vista for large-scale ranching, and there are plenty of open grasslands, dry enough in the dry season for ranchers to burn off the old pastures to make way for fresh shoots with the first rains. Interspersed among the grasses and tangled bamboo and creeper thickets are large expanses of cane, grown as fodder for the cows after the pasture has been burnt. It's still very much a frontier land, with small settlements of loggers and brick-firers springing up along the roads as the forest is cleared away forever.

Colonel P.H. Fawcett, the famous British explorer, vanished somewhere in this region in 1925, on what turned out to be his last attempt to locate a lost jungle city and civilization. He'd been searching for it, on and off, for twenty years, the story entertainingly told in his edited diaries and letters, *Exploration Fawcett* (see "Books", p.788). This last expedition was made in the company of his eldest son, Jack, and a schoolfriend of Jack's, and following their disappearance various theories were put forward as to their fate, including being kept as prisoners of a remote tribe or, more fancifully, adopted chiefs. Possibly, they were murdered out in the wilds, as were dozens of other explorers over the years, although Fawcett had travelled for years among the Indians without coming to any harm. More likely, they merely succumbed to one of the dozens of tropical diseases that were by far the biggest killer at the time. The fate of the colonel remains a mystery: in 1985, the same team who had identified the body of the Nazi Josef Mengele announced that they had identified bones found in a shallow grave as those of the colonel; but in 1996 another expedition, Expedição Autan, dissatisfied with the Mengele team's proofs, set off to try to make a DNA match, but found no trace of either the colonel or his companions.

Alta Floresta

Turning west off the BR-163 some 150km before the Serra do Cachimbo, a dirt road leads to **ALTA FLORESTA**, a rapidly growing frontier town of around 43,000 people. Located almost 800km north of Cuiabá, it's a remote but thriving agricultural settlement with regular bus and plane connections to Cuiabá and elsewhere. There's little of immediate interest unless end-of-road towns are your thing, but the town has in recent years opened its doors to **eco-tourism** in the form of a four-star **hotel**, the *Floresta Amazonica*, Av. Perimetral Oeste 2001 (T65/521-3601, F521-2221; ❺), a tastefully developed place with expansive jungle grounds that serves as a base for the associated *Cristalino Jungle Lodge* (❻). Deeper in the forest on a tributary of the Rio Teles Pires, which ultimately flows into the Amazon, the lodge offers a wide choice of trips and activities (around $80–150 per person per day), including visits to an *escola rural productiva* where you can buy paintings and other artefacts from local Kayaby Indians. The forest around here is particularly rich in **birdlife**, and there are several set birding trails. A similar but even more remote development, accessible only by air taxi, lies 140km northwest of Alta Floresta on the Rio São Benedito, on the Pará state border: *Pousada Thaimaçu* (T65/521-3587; ❼), offers fishing and boat trips, and pleasant chalet accommodation.

Back in town, the *Grande Hotel Coroados*, Rua F-1, 118 (T65/521-3111; ❷), is exceptionally good value, with cosy rooms, an excellent pool and even a sauna. Difficult to find (there are few street signs in Alta Floresta), the hotel is one street back from Avenida Ludovico da Riva Nato in "Bloco F" at the end of a cul-de-sac. *Lisboa Palace Hotel*, at Av. do Aeroporto 251 (T65/521-2876 or 521-2969, F531-3500; ❸), has larger rooms but no pool. A surprisingly good budget option is the *Hotel e Restaurante Luz Divina*, opposite the *rodoviária* on Avenida Ludovico da Riva Nato (T65/521-2742 or 521-4080; ❶), offering a wide choice of clean, modern rooms.

As buses no longer connect Cuiabá with Santarém, **flying** is the only way **northwards from Alta Floresta**. The **airport**, 2km northwest of Alta Floresta on the Avenida Ariosto da Riva (T65/521-3177; $8 by taxi), has daily flights (Varig air passes are valid) north to Itaituba, Santarém and Belém, and south to Cuiabá and São Paulo.

Southeast to Rondonópolis and São Paulo

For those who have arrived in Cuiabá from the Amazon, the city acts as a gateway to the rest of Brazil. From the earliest times, São Paulo was the main source of settlers arriving in Mato Grosso, though until the twentieth century the route followed the river systems. These days, the **BR-364** runs all the way (over 1700km) from Cuiabá to São Paulo, with several daily buses taking around 24 hours minimum.

On the headwaters of the Pantanal's Rio São Lourenço, two to three hours from Cuiabá, the industrial town of **RONDONÓPOLIS** serves as a base for visiting the local **Bororo Indians**. In the present political climate, visits to Indian reservations are not always permitted – and you might consider the ethics of such visits before you decide to go. In any case, permission must be obtained first from FUNAI (see below), and they'll decide if, when and where you can go. Meanwhile, if you decide to stay here, there's a range of **hotels**, including the cheap but clean *Turis Hotel* on Rua Alagoas 61 (T65/421-7487; ❷). Good mid-range hotels include the *Hotel Nacional*, right by the *rodoviária* at Av. Fernando Corrêa da Costa 978 (T65/423-3245; ❹); and the *Guatujá*, at

Av. Fernando Corréa da Costa 624 (☎65/423-2111; ❹).The more luxurious *Novotel* is at Rua Floriano Peixoto 711 (☎65/423-1050; ❼).

JATAÍ is almost halfway to São Paulo, about ten hours from Cuiabá in the state of Goiás.This is where many passengers will be getting off and on the bus, changing to one of the other routes which emanate from here – to Brasília, Goiânia, Belo Horizonte, Rio de Janeiro, the Northeast and Belém.

East towards Goiânia and Brasília: Barra do Garças

An alternative route from Cuiabá to Goiás Velho, Goiânia and Brasília runs east via the **BR-070**. Over 500km from Cuiabá, on the frontier between Mato Grosso and Goiás states, **BARRA DO GARÇAS** is a useful and interesting point at which to break a long bus journey.This small and isolated, but still fast growing town of some 70,000 people sits astride the Rio das Garças, one of the main headwaters of the Araguaia, underneath low-lying wooded hills. It's a surprisingly good base for a variety of nature-based hikes or relaxing in hot-water springs, and the nearest beach, the **Praia de Aragarças**, is barely 1km away. In the mountainous terrain that stretches from Barra do Garças up to the Serra do Cachimbo, the most impressive feature is the highly eroded red-rock cliff of the 700-metre **Serra do Roncador**, 150km due north of the town. Waterfalls and caves abound in the region; close to the limits of the town there are fourteen waterfalls in the Serra Azul alone, a range that rises to over 800m.

Much nearer, just 6km northeast of town, there are more fine river beaches and the popular natural hot baths of the **Parque Balneário das Águas Quentes** (daily 6am–9.30pm). Besides curing all the usual complaints, the waters are proudly proclaimed by the town's tourist office to have the capacity to augment one's *vitalidade sexual* – you have been warned! Nearby, too, there are the reserves of the Xavante and Bororo Indians. For information and to find out about written authorization to enter one of the reserves, contact FUNAI at Rua Muniz Mariano 3, Setor Dermat (☎65/861-2020).

Practicalities

The swishest **place to stay** is the *Serra Azul Plaza*, at Praça dos Garimpeiros 572 (☎66/401-6663; ❺); followed closely by *Toriuá Parque*, with a beautiful pool some 4km beyond Barra do Garças on Avenida Min. João Alberto (BR-158), Chácara Rio Araguaia (☎ & ⑤66/638-1811; ❹). In the centre, the *Hotel Presidente*, Av. João Alberto 55 (☎66/861-2108; ❸) has the most comfortable rooms, while similar but slightly more down at heel is *Novo Mundo*, opposite at no. 48 (☎66/861-1762; ❷).There are also two **campsites**, one at the Porto Bae on the banks of the Rio Araguaia (access from Avenida Marechal Rondon), and the other at the Parque das Águas Quentes, 6km from town.

There's not a huge choice of **restaurants** in Barra do Garças, but the food is reasonably good and not particularly expensive. The floating *Restaurante El Barco*, at the Porto dos Pioneiros, is great for fish and open from 10am to midnight every day. The *Rock Café*, Av. Rio das Garças 4 (opposite *Aquarius Pizzeria*), is a trendy place to be seen eating and drinking in the evenings, with a wide range of snacks and light Brazilian meals.

There is a municipal **tourist office**, FUNDATUR, on Praça Tiradentes (Mon–Sat 9am–6pm; ☎66/861-2227 or 861-2344), and there are also three **environmental organizations** in town who may be able to help with information on the region and eco-tours, as well as possibilities for **rock-climbing**, **pot-holing** and **canyoning**: CELVA, Centro Etno-Ecológico do Vale do

Araguaia (℡66/861-2018); União Eco-Cultura do Vale do Araguaia, Av. João Alberto 100; and the Fundação Cultura Ambiental do Centro Oeste (Caixa Postal 246). Barra do Garças also serves as a possible starting point for visits to the world's largest river island, the Ilha do Bananal, in Tocantins state (see p.515).

You can **change money** at the Banco do Brasil on Praça Tiradentes, or nearby at HSBC, Av. Min. João Alberto 528. The central **post office** is at Rua 1 de Maio 19, and **car hire** is available from Localiza (℡66/861-2140). Bus connections from the **rodoviária** on Rua Bororós (℡66/401-1766) along the BR-070 between Cuiabá and Brasília are good, and there is also an **airport**, Julio Campos, 15km out of town (℡66/401-2218), which is served by the local air taxi service BRC (℡66/861-2140) and operates flights to Brasília, Cuiabá, Goiânia and Rondonópolis.

Travel details

Buses

Except on the Campo Grande-Corumbá route, which is monopolized by Andorinha, there are scores of different bus companies competing for the same routes as well as opening up new ones. Each company advertises destinations and departure times at its ticket office windows, making it relatively easy to choose a route and buy a ticket. Note that going north from Cuiabá, buses only go as far as Alta Floresta, or to Rio Branco via Porto Velho. Manaus, Itaituba, Santarém and Belém are all advertised by the bus companies, but are reachable only by enormous detours taking several days via Goiânia. Cruzeiro do Sul has no reliable road access.

Anastácio to: Bonito (1 daily; 4hr); Campo Grande (8 daily; 2hr); Corumbá (8 daily; 5hr); Ponta Porã (2 daily; 4–6hr).

Bonito to: Anastácio (1 daily; 4hr); Campo Grande (1 daily; 5hr); Corumbá (Mon–Sat 1 daily; 8hr); Dourados (1 daily; 5hr); Miranda (Mon–Sat 1 daily; 4hr); Ponta Porã (1 daily; 7hr).

Campo Grande to almost everywhere in Brazil, including: Alta Floresta (3 daily; 22hr); Anastácio/Aquidauana (8 daily; 2hr); Belo Horizonte (1 daily; 23hr); Bonito (1 daily; 5hr); Brasília (1 daily; 24hr); Corumbá (11 daily; 7hr); Coxim (4 daily; 3–4hr); Cuiabá (5 daily; 11hr); Dourados (5 daily; 4hr); Foz do Iguaçu (10 daily; 15hr); Miranda (11 daily; 3hr); Ponta Porã (4 daily; 5–6hr); Rio de Janeiro (4 daily; 22hr); São Paulo (6 daily; 14hr).

There is also a weekly service to Asunción in Paraguay, leaving Sunday mornings (Amambay company).

Corumbá to: Campo Grande, via Anastácio/Aquidauana and Miranda (11 daily; 7hr; change in Campo Grande for most onward destinations); Rio de Janeiro (4 daily; 32hr); São Paulo (4 daily; 26hr).

Cuiabá to: Alta Floresta (4 daily; 12hr); Brasília (6 daily; 20hr); Campo Grande (6 daily; 11hr); Chapada dos Guimarães (9 daily; 1hr); Coxim (6 daily; 6–7hr); Goiânia (6 daily; 14hr); Porto Velho (4 daily; 23hr); Rio Branco (4 daily; 32hr); Rio de Janeiro (1 daily; 31hr); Rondonópolis (10 daily; 3hr); São Paulo (1 daily; 24hr-plus).

Planes

Campo Grande Several daily flights (VASP, Varig, TAM, Pantanal Linhas Aéreas) to Brazil's main cities; also to Vilhena (halfway between Cuiabá and Porto Velho).

Corumbá Daily flights (TAM, VASP and Pantanal Linhas Aéreas) to Campo Grande, Rio de Janeiro and São Paulo; and to Santa Cruz in Bolivia (Aerosul, Lloyd Aereo Boliviano or air-taxi service). Note that for Corumbá flights the Varig air pass is not valid.

Cuiabá VASP, Varig and TAM cover the main cities. Rio-Sul flies daily to Alta Floresta, Itaituba, Santarém and Belém, and Lloyd Aereo Boliviano flies Mon and Fri to Santa Cruz.

São Paulo

CHAPTER 7 # Highlights

✳ **Memorial do Imigrantes museum** Explore this fascinating museum, once a hostel through which tens of thousands of immigrants passed through at the start of their new lives in Brazil. See p.590

✳ **Mercado Municipal** Look out especially for the lovely stained-glass windows depicting scenes of Brazilian agricultural production. See p.591

✳ **Avenida Paulista** A showcase for modern São Paulo, along with some lavish mansions from bygone eras. See p.594

✳ **Paranapiacaba town** This remarkable late nineteenth-century British railway village is a popular base for walks in the surrounding Mata Atlântica. See p.614

✳ **Fazenda do Pinhal** An intriguing relic of the state's nineteenth-century coffee boom: this typical estate preserves the main house and slave quarters. See p.619

✳ **Ilhabela** The most beautiful spot on São Paulo's coast, this island remains unravaged by tourism, protected as a state park. See p.624

São Paulo

The citizens of the **São Paulo state**, *paulistas*, never tire of saying that their state is Brazil's economic powerhouse, and they produce a mountain of statistics to sustain the boast. The state's forty million inhabitants represent about a quarter of Brazil's total population, yet the state contributes forty percent of the federal tax revenues, and consumes sixty percent of the country's industrial energy to produce two-thirds of its industrial output. A highly capitalized agricultural sector produces eighty percent of Brazil's oranges, half of its sugar, forty percent of its chickens and eggs, and a fifth of its coffee. Yet while *paulistas* crow that without their muscle Brazil's economy would collapse, other Brazilians feel that São Paulo has developed at their expense. The state, it is argued, attracts capital away from the other regions, which are basically seen as sources of cheap labour and as guaranteed markets for São Paulo's products.

This economic pre-eminence is a relatively recent phenomenon. In 1507, São Vicente was founded on the coast near present-day **Santos**, the second-oldest Portuguese settlement in Brazil, but for over three hundred years the area comprising today's state of São Paulo remained a backwater. The inhabitants were a hardy people, of mixed Portuguese and Indian origin, from whom – in the seventeenth and eighteenth centuries – emerged the **bandeirantes**: frontiersmen who roamed far into the South American interior to secure the borders of the Portuguese Empire against Spanish encroachment, capturing Indian slaves and seeking out precious metals and gems as they went.

Not until the mid-nineteenth century did São Paulo become rich. Cotton production received a boost with the arrival of Confederate refugees in the late 1860s, who settled between **Americana** and **Santa Bárbara d'Oeste**, about 140km from the then small town of **São Paulo** itself. But after disappointing results with cotton, most of these plantation owners switched their attentions to coffee and, by the end of the century, the state had become firmly established as the world's foremost producer of the crop. During the same period, Brazil abolished slavery and the plantation owners recruited European and Japanese immigrants to expand production. Riding the wave of the coffee boom, British and other foreign companies took the opportunity to invest in port facilities, rail lines, power and water supplies, while textile and other new industries emerged, too. Within a few decades, the town of São Paulo became one of Latin America's greatest commercial and cultural centres, sliding from a small town into a vast metropolitan sprawl.

If the thought of staying in the city of São Paulo doesn't particularly appeal to you, the state does have other attractions. Although unpleasantly crowded in the Brazilian summer, the beaches north of Santos, especially on **Ilhabela** and

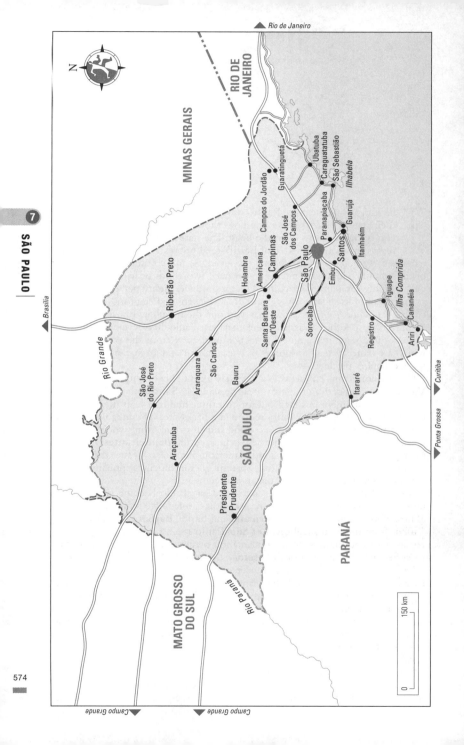

around **Ubatuba**, rival Rio's best, while those to the south – near **Iguape** and, especially, **Cananéia** – remain relatively unspoiled. **Inland**, the state is dominated by agribusiness, with seemingly endless fields of cattle pasture, sugar cane, oranges and soya interspersed with anonymous towns where the agricultural produce is processed. Even so, some impressive **fazenda houses** remain as legacies to the days when São Paulo's economy was pretty well synonymous with coffee production. To escape scorching summer temperatures – or for the novelty in tropical Brazil of a winter chill – make for **Campos do Jordão**, São Paulo's main mountain resort.

São Paulo City

Rio is a beauty. But São Paulo – São Paulo is a city.

Marlene Dietrich

In 1554, the Jesuit priests José de Anchieta and Manuel da Nóbrega established a mission station on the banks of the Rio Tietê in an attempt to bring Christianity to the Tupi-Guarani Indians. Called São Paulo dos Campos de Piratininga, it was 70km inland and 730m up, in the sheer, forest-covered inclines of the Serra do Mar, above the port of São Vicente. The gently undulating plateau and the proximity to the Paraná and Plata rivers facilitated traffic into the interior and, with São Paulo as their base, roaming gangs of *bandeirantes* set out in search of loot. Around the mission school, a few adobe huts were erected and the settlement soon developed into a trading post and a base from which to secure mineral wealth. In 1681, São Paulo – as the town became known – became a seat of regional government and, in 1711, it was made a municipality by the king of Portugal, the cool, healthy climate helping to attract settlers from the coast.

With the expansion of **coffee** plantations westwards from Rio de Janeiro, along the Paraíba Valley, in the mid-nineteenth century, São Paulo's fortunes looked up. The region's rich soil – *terra roxa* – was ideally suited to coffee cultivation, and from about 1870 plantation owners took up residence in the city, which was undergoing a rapid transformation into a bustling regional centre. British, French and German merchants and hoteliers opened local operations, British-owned rail lines radiated in all directions from São Paulo, and foreign water, gas, telephone and electricity companies moved in to service the city. In the 1890s, enterprising "coffee barons" began to place some of their profits into local industry, hedging their bets against a possible fall in the price of coffee, with textile factories being a favourite area for investment.

As the local population could not meet the ever-increasing demands of plantation owners, factories looked to **immigrants** (see box pp.590–591) to meet their labour requirements. As a result, São Paulo's **population** soared, almost tripling to 69,000 by 1890 and, by the end of the next decade, increasing to 239,000. By 1950, when it had reached 2.2 million, São Paulo had clearly established its dominant role in Brazil's urbanization: today the city's population stands at around ten million, rising to at least sixteen million when the sprawling metropolitan area is included.

As industry, trade and population developed at such a terrific pace, buildings were erected with little time to consider their aesthetics; in any case, they often became cramped as soon as they were built, or had to be demolished to make way for a new avenue. However, some grand **public buildings** were built in the late nineteenth and early twentieth centuries, and a few still remain, though none is as splendid as those found in Buenos Aires, a city that developed at

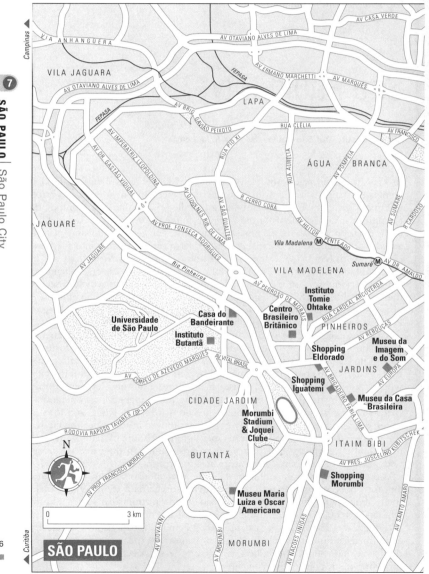

SÃO PAULO

much the same time. Even now, conservation is seen as not being profitable, and São Paulo is more concerned with rising population, rising production and rising consumption – factors that today are paralleled by rising levels of homelessness, pollution and violence.

Residents of the city, *paulistanos*, talk smugly of their work ethic, supposedly superior to what dominates the rest of Brazil, and speak contemptuously of the

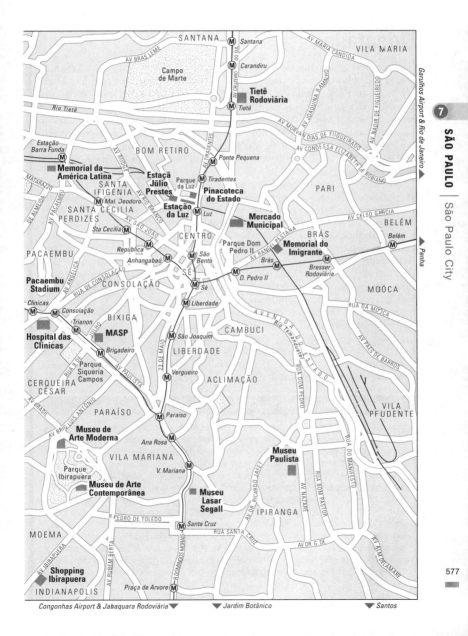

Congonhas Airport & Jabaquara Rodoviária ▼   ▼ Jardim Botânico   ▼ Santos

idleness of *cariocas* (in reply, *cariocas* joke sourly that *paulistanos* are simply incapable of enjoying anything, sex in particular). But work and profit aside, São Paulo does have its attractions: the city lays claim to having long surpassed Rio as Brazil's **cultural** centre, and is home to a lively music and arts world. The city's **food**, too, is often excellent, in part thanks to immigrants from so many parts of the world and a new wave of imaginative cooks.

Orientation

The prospect of arriving in South America's most populous city, spread over an area of 30,000 square kilometres, is likely to seem a little daunting. However, while it's true that urban development has been carried out with an almost complete lack of planning, São Paulo is far more manageable than you might imagine. Greater São Paulo is enormous, but the main shopping, entertainment and hotel districts are easy to move between, and the areas of historic interest are extremely limited. Even so, São Paulo's streets form something of a maze and even for the briefest of visits it's well worth buying a street guide, available at any newspaper kiosk.

São Paulo's traditional centre is the area around **Praça da Sé** and **Praça da República**, the two squares separated by a broad avenue, the **Vale do Anhangabaú**, which in turn is bridged by a pedestrian crossing, the **Viaduto do Chá**. The area around Praça da Sé is where you'll find both the Pátio do Colégio, which dates back to the early years of the Jesuit mission settlement, and the commercial district of banks, offices and shops, known as the **Triângulo** – originally comprising Rua Direita, Quinze de Novembro, São Bento, and Praça Antônio Prado. The area around Praça da República now forms an extension of the main commercial district, but there are many hotels and apartment buildings here, too.

The *bairros* to the **east** of the centre contained some of the city's first industrial suburbs and were home for many immigrants, but with the exception of the Museu da Hospedaria do Imigrante there's hardly anything of interest here. **North** of the centre is the red-light district of **Luz**, until recently known only as the rather seedy location of the city's railway stations, but now being developed into a major cultural hub. Due north of here, across the Rio Tietê, is the

Avoiding trouble in São Paulo

Assaults and robberies are favourite topics of conversation amongst *paulistanos*, with the city's crime statistics now consistently higher than those of Rio. Nevertheless, by using a little common sense you're unlikely to encounter any real problems. With such a mixture of people in São Paulo, you're far less likely to be assumed to be a foreigner than in most parts of Brazil, and therefore won't make such an obvious target for pickpockets and other **petty thieves**.

At night, though, pay particular attention around the central red-light district of **Luz**, location of the city's main train stations and – though not as bad – around **Praça da República**. Also take special care late at night in **Bixiga** (also known as Bela Vista), or if you venture into **Praça Roosevelt**. Always carry at least some money in an immediately accessible place so that, if you are accosted by a **mugger**, you can quickly hand something over before he starts getting angry or panicky. If in any doubt at all about visiting an area you don't know, don't hesitate to take a taxi.

Rodoviária Tietê, the city's main bus station serving points throughout Brazil and neighbouring countries.

Just **south** of the commercial district are **Bela Vista** – usually referred to as "Bixiga", São Paulo's "Little Italy", focused on Rua 13 de Maio – and **Liberdade**, with its centre around Praça da Liberdade and Rua Galvão Bueno. Traditionally a Japanese neighbourhood, Liberdade is gradually being transformed by the arrival of new immigrants from other east Asian countries.

To the southwest of the centre is **Avenida Paulista**, an avenue of high-rise office buildings that divides the city's traditional centre from the **Jardins**, one of the most prestigious of São Paulo's middle- and upper-class suburbs. Extending south and west are yet more plush suburbs, such as **Itaim Bibi** and **Vila Olímpia**, with upmarket restaurants and nightspots and a new business district that stretches along **Avenida Brigadeiro Faria Lima**. Cutting across Avenida Paulista into the Jardins is **Rua Augusta**, which begins in the centre at Praça Franklin Roosevelt; many of São Paulo's best restaurants and shopping streets are located around here. West of the Jardins is **Vila Madalena**, and beyond here **Pinheiros**, mainly residential neighbourhoods that are amongst the city's most fashionable nightspots. Just across the Rio Pinheiros is the vast campus of the **Universidade de São Paulo** and the Instituto Butantan, while to the southeast lies the **Parque Ibirapuera**, one of the city's great parks.

Greater São Paulo includes huge, sprawling, industrial suburbs where people are housed in a mixture of grim-looking high-rise tenements, small houses and, on just about every patch of wasteland, *favelas* – the slum homes for some two million of the city's inhabitants. The most important **industrial areas** are the so-called "A B C D" *municípios* of Santo André, São Bernardo, São Caetano and Diadema, the traditional centre of Brazil's motor vehicle industry and of the city's militantly left-wing political tradition. In the 1940s, Santo André elected Brazil's first Communist Party mayor, while out of the Metal Workers' Union and the auto workers' strikes of the late 1970s – which heralded the end of the country's supposed economic "miracle" – emerged Lula, the leader of the PT, the Workers' Party, who was inaugurated as Brazil's president in January 2003.

Arrival, information and tours

You'll probably **arrive** in São Paulo by plane or bus, though there are train connections with Bauru and Campinas in the interior of the state. Watch your belongings at all times, as thieves thrive in the confusion of airports and stations.

By air

São Paulo is served by two airports. Just to the south of the centre, the always congested **Congonhas** (☏11/5090-9000 or 5090-9195) handles services within the state of São Paulo, but also operates the shuttle service (the Ponte Aérea) to Rio, as well as flights to some other destinations, including Curitiba and Belo Horizonte. Most other domestic flights (including some Curitiba, Belo Horizonte and Rio flights), and all international flights use the much newer **Guarulhos** (sometimes called 'Cumbica') airport (☏11/6445-2945), 30km from the city. Note that bad weather frequently leads to the diversion of planes from Guarulhos to Congonhas.

Congonhas and Guarulhos are connected to each other by air-conditioned *executivo* **buses** leaving at roughly half-hourly intervals (5.30am–11pm; $5). At similar intervals, buses link both airports with the western side of Praça da República (7am–9pm; $5). From Guarulhos there are more options: every 35 minutes there are buses to the Rodoviária Tietê (5.40am–10.10pm); and there's also a bus service ($5) to the *Maksoud Plaza Hotel*, which stops off at the other top hotels around Avenida Paulista. If you are staying at a hotel in Itaim Bibi or elsewhere to the southwest of Jardins, your best bet is to take the airport bus to the *Hotel Renaissance* from where you can take a taxi onwards. Even cheaper, but only really practical if you have little luggage, is to take a bus to the Bresser *metrô* station (5am–11pm; 70¢) where you can catch a train into the city centre. **Taxis** are readily available at both airports: the fare from Congonhas to the centre is around $12, from Guarulhos about $20. At both airports there are taxi desks in the arrivals halls and you pay a fixed price depending on the distance of your destination.

SET (Secretaria de Esportese Turismo) maintains helpful state **tourist information** desks at the airports (daily 7.30am–10.30pm); there are banks and *casas de câmbio* at both airports where you can change cash or travellers' cheques and use the ATMs.

By bus

Inter-city bus services arrive at one of four *rodoviárias*. To the south of the centre, **Jabaquara** (☎11/5581-0856) is for buses to and from the Santos region and São Paulo's south shore as far as Peruíbe. **Barra Funda** (☎11/3666-4682), near the Memorial da América Latina, serves destinations in southern São Paulo and Paraná. **Bresser** (☎11/6692-5191) is for buses to Minas Gerais. The largest bus station, serving all state capitals as well as destinations in neighbouring countries, is the **Tietê** terminal to the north (☎11/3235-0322). All four *rodoviárias* are on the *metrô* system, and a night bus (#510M) runs between the Jabaquara and Tietê, passing through the centre at Praça da Sé. Bus tickets to most destinations can be bought at many of the city's travel agents.

By train

There are very few train services now to São Paulo's **Estação da Luz** (see p. 592) at the edge of the city centre to the north. The train still runs to Bauru in the interior of the state of São Paulo, but the connection on to Campo Grande for Corumbá has been suspended. The only other useful inter-city service is to Campinas, though buses are considerably faster. Some suburban trains leave from here, including the service to Rio Grande da Serra that has connections to Paranapiacaba (see p.614). To get to the city centre from the station, take the *metrô* (from the Luz station) or a taxi, which will cost $5–10.

An extensive suburban train network also operates from the **Estação Júlio Prestes**, located just a couple of blocks from the Estação da Luz. For practical purposes, however, you're more likely to enter the station complex to attend a concert (see p. 592) than to catch a train.

Information

Anhembi Turismo, the city's tourism department (☎11/6971-5511), maintains several **information booths** scattered about the city whose English-speaking staff are especially helpful for general directions, or for local bus and *metrô* details. Booths can be found on Praça da República (across from Rua Sete de Abril; daily 9am–6pm); at Praça da Liberdade (daily 9am–6pm); at the Teatro Municipal (Mon–Fri 9am–6pm, Sat 9am–1pm); at Avenida Paulista (across from MASP; daily 9am–6pm); and outside the Morumbi (daily 9am–6pm) and Iguatemi (daily 9am–6pm) shopping centres (see p.611). A good map, and information on the state of São Paulo, is available from the state **tourist office** at Avenida São Luís 97 (Mon–Fri 10am–5pm).

For up-to-date **listings** of what's going on in the city, the São Paulo edition of the weekly magazine *Veja* contains an excellent entertainment guide, and the daily newspaper *Folha de São Paulo* lists cultural and sporting events and, on Friday, contains a useful entertainment guide, the *Guia da Folha*. The Guia Internet São Paulo (*www.guiasp.com.br*) is a good source of up to the moment information on São Paulo's restaurants, bars, cinemas, theatres and nightclubs as well as current exhibitions in museums and galleries.

Tours

For people with little time available, there is an excellent and inexpensive **tour** run by the city authorities. An air-conditioned bus with a bilingual guide departs hourly from Barra Funda *metrô* station's Terminal Turístico (Tues–Sun from 9.30am, last departure at 4.30pm), and visits the Memorial da América Latina, Pinacoteca do Estado, Museu de Arte Sacra, Memorial do Imigrante (Sundays only), the Museu de arte de São Paulo and the Museu de Arte Moderna – before returning to Barra Funda. The tour is just $1 and the ticket entitles you to half-price admission to the museums. You can get off the bus at any of the sights and rejoin the tour on a following bus.

City transport

São Paulo's **public transport** network is extensive but traffic congestion and a seemingly perpetual rush hour can make travelling by bus or taxis frustratingly slow going. Matters are made even worse when it rains: São Paulo's drainage system cannot cope with the summer rains and, as many roads are transformed into rivers, the city seemingly grinds to a halt – just take cover in a bar or *lanchonete* and sit it out. The city's *metrô* network, by contrast, is fast, clean and efficient, though limited in extent. As a **safety precaution**, when using public transport always make sure you have some small notes at hand, so as not to attract attention to yourself by fumbling through your wallet or bag for change.

With your own car, the main difficulties of driving in São Paulo are the volume of traffic and finding a parking space – given this, it doesn't make much sense to rent a car for getting around the city. Roads are, however, well signposted and it's surprisingly easy to get out of the city. For a list of **car rental firms**, see p.613.

Buses

Traffic congestion rarely allows São Paulo's **buses** to be driven at the same terrifying speeds as in Rio, though drivers do their best to compete. Despite everything, the network is remarkably efficient and includes trolley buses as well as ordinary buses, for which there is a flat fare of 35¢.

On the downside, **bus routes** often snake confusingly through the city, and working out which bus to take can be difficult. The number of the bus is clearly marked at the front, and there are cards posted at the front and the entrance (towards the back) that indicate the route. At **bus stops** (usually wooden posts) you'll have to flag down the buses you want: be attentive or they'll speed by. Buses run between 4am and midnight, but avoid travelling during the height of the evening rush hour (around 5–7pm) when they are overflowing with passengers.

From Praça da República along Avenida Paulista (via Liberdade): #595P.
From Praça da República to Avenida Brigadeiro Faria Lima (via Rua Augusta): #702P.
From Praça da República to Butantã (via Rua Augusta and Avenida Brigadeiro Faria Lima): #7181 and #107P.
From Avenida Ipiranga to Butantã and Universidade de São Paulo: #702U.
From *metrô* Ana Rosa along Avenida Paulista: #875P.
From Rodoviária Tietê to Rodoviária Jabaquara via Largo de São Bento and Avenida Liberdade: #501M (midnight–5am only).

The metrô

Quiet, comfortable and fast, São Paulo's **metrô** would be by far the easiest way to move around the city were it not limited to just three lines. The north–south **Linha Azul** (blue line) has terminals at Tucuruvi in the far north of the city and Jabaquara (the *rodoviária* from where buses to Santos depart) and also serves the Tietê Rodoviária and Luz train station. The **Linha Vermelha** (red line) extends east–west with terminals at Corinthians–Itaquera and Barra Funda, and intersects with the Linha Azul at Praça da Sé. There's also the **Linha Verde** (green line), a shorter east–west line that runs underneath Avenida Paulista from Ana Rosa to Vila Madalena, stopping at the Museu de Arte de São Paulo (Trianon-MASP station). You can transfer between the Linha Verde and the Linha Azul at either Ana Rosa or Paraíso stations.

The *metrô* operates every day from 5am until midnight, although the ticket booths close at 10pm. **Tickets** cost 45¢ for a one-way journey and come either as singles (*ida*), doubles (*duplo*), or valid for ten journeys (*bilhete com dez unidades*). You can also buy integrated bus and *metrô* tickets; many buses stop at the *metrô* stations, with the names of their destinations well marked.

Taxis

Taxis in São Paulo are reliable and abundant but, given the volume of traffic and the often considerable distances involved in navigating the city, fares quickly mount. With irregular – or no – bus services at night, taxis are really the only means of transport after midnight. There are two main types: the yellow *comuns* and the *rádiotáxis*.

The **comuns**, generally small cars that carry three passengers, are the cheapest and are found at taxi ranks or hailed from the street. **Rádiotáxis** are larger and more expensive, and are ordered by phone: try Coopertax (☎11/6941-2555) or Ligue Táxi (☎11/3262-2633). Both types of taxi have meters with two fare rates, and a flag, or *bandeira*, is displayed on the meter to indicate which fare is in operation: fare "1" is charged from 6am to 10pm Monday to Saturday, but after 10pm and on Sunday and public holidays, fare "2" is charged, costing twenty percent more.

Accommodation

Finding somewhere to stay in São Paulo is rarely a problem and, as there are several areas where hotels are concentrated, you should get settled in quite quickly. The **prices** of hotels vary enormously throughout the year, with hefty **discounts** offered during the quieter summer months of December, January and February. Weekend discounts of fifty percent or even more are usually given, especially at the better hotels that otherwise cater largely to business executives.

Rooms at even the top hotels cost just a small fraction of what business travellers pay in European or North American cities. With some notable exceptions, most budget and medium-priced places are located in parts of the city where visitors, especially women, may feel distinctly uncomfortable walking alone at night. The dangers, however, are often more imaginary than real and, by simply being alert and taking taxis late at night, you should have no problems.

Downtown

In the traditional centre of São Paulo, there are lots of inexpensive and medium-priced hotels in the streets around Praça da República and Avenida São Luís. Cheap rooms can be found in hotels towards Estação da Luz in the Santa Ifigénia district, but most of these are aimed at either long-stay guests or couples checking in for an hour or two, and at night the area has a distinctly dangerous edge to it. The Praça da República area has a much more comfortable feel and there are a number of fine hotels here that would command far higher rates if in the Jardins. But at night, when there are a lot of suspicious-looking individuals milling around the *praça*, you're best off relying on taxis.

Cambridge Av. 9 de Julho 216 ☎11/3101-4376, ⓦ www.cambridgehotel.com.br. If it wasn't for its location on an ugly, multi-lane inner-city avenue, this hotel would command far higher rates. Rooms are well equipped, if rather tatty, and the communal areas – in particular the very popular bar – have a cosy old-fashioned feel. Located near the central banking and business district and on the edge of the city's lively "Little Italy". ❸

Copacabana Rua Aurora 26 ☎11/222-0511. A basic crash pad, offering rooms with or without bath. There are plenty of similar, cheap hotels on this street. ❷

Eldorado Boulevard Av. São Luís 234 ☎11/3214-1833, ⓦ www.hoteiseldorado.com.br. A good mid-range hotel popular among budget-oriented Brazilian and foreign executives for its comfortable rooms and huge suites. The 24-hour coffee shop attracts theatre-goers, journalists and other late-nighters. ❹

Gávea Palace Rua Conselheiro Nébias 445 ☎11/222-4655. Clean and comfortable hotel situated on a quiet street just behind Praça da República towards Avenida São João. ❸

Marian Palace Av. Cáspar Libero 65 ☎11/228-8433, ⓦ www.marian.com.br. This late Art Deco gem has been updated over the years but retains many of its original features in its guest rooms and public areas. A nice pool and garden terrace help

compensate for the location, which can be dodgy at night. ❺

Municipal Av. São João 354 ☎11/228-7833. Located in a part of the centre that, while busy, feels safe day and night, this friendly hotel is now protected as a historic monument. The hotel's simple rooms have hardly been updated since opening in the 1940s, but are perfectly adequate. ❷

Normandie Design Hotel Av. Ipiranga 1187 ☎11/3311-9855, ⓦ www.normandiedesignhotel .com.br. One of the most stylish hotels in São Paulo. You either love or hate the general look – everything white, black and chrome – but the staff are all enthusiastic, the bedrooms comfortable (if on the small side) and the price very reasonable. ❻

República Park Av. Vieira de Carvalho 32 ☎11/3361-8636, ⓦ www.republicaparkhotel .com.br. The chandeliers, velvet furnishings and marble bathrooms have clearly seen better days, but the hotel is comfortable and great value. Ask for a room on an upper floor with a balcony overlooking the Praça da República. ❸

São Sebastião Rua Sete de Abril 364 ☎11/257-4988. Quiet but dark and rather musty rooms, all with shower, just minutes from the entrance to the Praça da República *metrô* station. A popular choice with European backpackers, with safe night-time access. ❷

Liberdade

Liberdade, São Paulo's Japanese *bairro*, has a few low and medium-priced hotels that are well worth considering – not least because the area is considered one of the safest parts of central São Paulo. Although the overwhelming majority of people staying here are either Japanese-Brazilians or visiting Asian businessmen, other guests are made to feel just as welcome.

Barão Lu Rua Barão de Iguape 80 ⊤ 11/3341-4000, Ⓦ www.hotelbaraolu.com.br. Chinese owned and managed, this budget hotel features spacious rooms and a decent restaurant on-site serving Shanghai food. ❸

Nikkey Palace Rua Galvão Bueno 425 ⊤ 11/270-8511, Ⓦ www.nikkeyhotel.com.br. Comfortable hotel geared towards Japanese businessmen and particularly well known for its health club, which guests can use for free. Choose between standard or more expensive Japanese-style bedrooms and either a continental or Japanese buffet breakfast. ❺

Osaka Plaza Praça da Liberdade 149 ⊤ 11/3270-1311, Ⓦ www.hotelosaka.com.br. Neither remarkable nor recognisably Japanese, this hotel remains a good budget choice for those wanting to be in the heart of Liberdade. Rooms (including some singles) are spacious, with the brightest overlooking the *praça*. ❸

Rua Augusta and around

The area is best known for the *Cá d'Oro*, *Caesar Park* and *Maksoud Plaza* – three of São Paulo's finest hotels. However, along and just off Rua Augusta in the direction of downtown are some more affordable options worth seeking out. The hotels here are ideally located, convenient for the city centre, the international banks of Avenida Paulista and the fashionable Jardins. The area is quite safe, though walking along Rua Augusta late at night can be unpleasant as you're likely to be accosted by men touting on behalf of sleazy nightclubs.

Augusta Palace Rua Augusta 467 ⊤ 11/256-1277. This hotel is nearer to Rua da Consolação than Av. Paulista, which makes it handy for the Praça da República area. Very much a business hotel and worth calling in advance for weekend discounts. ❹

Augusta Park Residence Rua Augusta 922 ⊤ 11/3255-5722, Ⓦ www.augustapark.com.br. Medium-sized hotel with small but well equipped rooms and helpful service. ❸

Cá d'Oro, Rua Augusta 129 ⊤ 11/3256-4300, Ⓦ www.cadoro.com.br. An easy stroll from Av. Paulista, this excellent hotel offers five-star standards in a more tasteful environment than is generally the case with São Paulo's luxury hotels. The large and simply furnished rooms are extremely comfortable and also excellent value. ❻

Caesar Park Rua Augusta 1508 ⊤ 11/285-6622, Ⓦ www.caesar-park.com. Almost on the corner with Av. Paulista, this is one of the most sumptuous hotels in the city, with everything you'd expect in this price band. The most unusual rooms are those in traditional Japanese style, but otherwise the hotel is rather soulless. ❽

Maksoud Plaza Alameda Campinas 150 ⊤ 11/3145-8000, Ⓦ www.maksoud.com.br. Up against severe competition in recent years, the *Maksoud Plaza* clings nervously to its reputation as the city's most distinguished hotel. The rooms are as comfortable as you'd expect, the staff are efficient and welcoming and there's a pool and several decent on-site restaurants. Hardly cheap, but a comparative bargain. ❼

Pergamon Rua Frei Caneca 80 ⊤ 11/3120-2021, Ⓦ www.pergamon.com.br. Very modern and chic, and much more reasonably priced than the similarly trendy *Emiliano* (see opposite). Ask for a room on one of the upper floors for a great view of downtown São Paulo. ❼

Pousada dos Franceses Rua dos Franceses 100 ⊤ 11/3262-4026, Ⓦ www.pousadadosfranceses.com.br. In a quiet location, just behind the *Maksoud Plaza* and a couple of blocks from both Bixiga and Av. Paulista, this small property has been newly coverted into a simple but very friendly *pousada*. Guests have use of the kitchen, and breakfast is available at a small extra cost. Rates vary from $6 per person per night in a dorm, to $15 for a double room with private bathroom. Single and triple rooms are also available.

Jardins

The south side of Avenida Paulista marks the beginnings of Jardins, a wealthy residential neighbourhood that houses some of the city's most fashionable (and expensive) shops and restaurants. There are some excellent accommodation options here, and as an area where one feels safe both in the daytime and at night, it makes a good place to base oneself.

Emiliano Rua Oscar Freire 384 ☎ 11/3069-4369, ⓦwww.emiliano.com.br. São Paulo's most trendy – and most expensive – hotel. With just 57 rooms, the *Emiliano* is small compared with the city's other luxury hotels and prides itself on providing discreet individual attention. For an extra charge you can arrange to be transferred to and from Guarulhos airport by helicopter. If you can't afford to stay here but are curious, stop by at the bar for a drink and to people watch. ❾

Formule 1 São Paulo Paraiso Rua Vergueiro 1571 ☎ 11/5085-5699, ⓦwww.hoteis-accor .com.br. This small and extremely simple French-owned hotel offers a double bed (with a single bunk bed above), a shower and toilet, and TV (but no telephone) in all rooms. A very popular choice, thanks to a good location by the Paraiso *metrô* station and rates that are the same whether single, double or triple occupancy: reservations are always highly recommended. ❷

Metropolitan Plaza Alameda Campinas 474 ☎ 0800/553-600 and 11/3288-0369, ⓦwww.metropolitanplaza.com.br. Attractive rooms, all with fully equipped kitchenette, and a smallish pool at this hotel, where rates are very reasonable given the high quality of the place and the neighbourhood. Deluxe rooms are only $5 more but have a separate living room and a larger bathroom. ❺

Paulista Center Rua Consolação 2567 ☎ & ⓕ 11/3852-0733. Almost at the intersection with Av. Paulista at the edge of Jardins, this basic hotel

is by far the cheapest hereabouts and is just a couple of blocks from fine restaurants and bars. The lack of air-conditioning, however, makes staying here in the summer rather unpleasant. ❷

Pousada Dona Ziláh Alameda Franca 1621 ☎ 11/3062-1444, ⓦwww.zilah.com. This large house converted into a simple, but extremely pretty *pousada* – is the only one in Jardins, and the cheapest place to stay in an otherwise upmarket neighbourhood. The atmosphere is friendly but unintrusive, and there's always someone on hand to offer local advice. Discounts offered for stays of a week or more, and bikes available for rent for exploring Jardins. ❷

Regent Park Rua Oscar Freire 533 ☎ 11/3064-3666, ⓕ 3064-7507. A very good apartment-hotel, mainly with one-bedroom units, but also a couple of two- and three-bedroom ones. All units include a living room and a small, but fully equipped kitchen. There's also a rooftop pool with panoramic views across the city. ❺

Renaissance Alameda Santos 2233 ☎ 11/3069-2233, ⓦwww.renaissancehotels.com. Just a couple of blocks from the city's best dining and shopping area, this burgundy-coloured tower designed by the renowned Brazilian architect Ruy Ohtake (see p.597) boasts a high-tech business centre, a helipad, large and well-appointed guest rooms, a good pool and health club – though it offers little that isn't available at the similarly luxurious *Maksoud Plaza* for a quarter of the price. ❾

Itaim Bibi and Pinheiros

The stretch along Avenida Brigadeiro Faria Lima that links Itaim Bibi with Pinheiros is a rapidly expanding business district. There are still few hotels here but those that do exist offer good facilities. At night these areas offer plenty of street life, thanks to the many excellent restaurants and clubs, and walking feels quite secure.

Hotel de la Rose Praça dos Omáguas 106, Pinheiros ☎ 11/3812-9097, ⓦwww.hoteldelarose .com.br.This rather charming hotel offers small and simple rooms, but all have a private bathroom and air-conditioning. ❸

Meliá Confort Iguatemi Rua Iguatemi 150, Itaim Bibi ☎ 11/3065-2450, ⓦwww.solmelia.com. This new hotel offers comfortable rooms, a small business centre, a fine buffet breakfast and a small rooftop pool. Although a typically characterless

example of the Spanish Meliá chain, the hotel has pleasant staff who provide helpful and efficient service. ❻

Radisson Hotel Jardins Av. Cidade Jardim 625, Itaim Bibi ☎ 11/3093-5960, ⓦwww.radisson.com. The most luxurious hotel in the area, located in the heart of the Faria Lima business district. Besides well-equipped rooms, the hotel offers a business centre and meeting rooms, and, for winding down, a sauna, fitness centre and attractive pool. ❼

The City

For visitors and locals alike, the fact that São Paulo's history extends back for over four centuries, well beyond the late nineteenth-century coffee boom, usually goes completely unnoticed. Catapulted virtually overnight from being a sleepy, provincial market town into one of the western hemisphere's great cities, there are few places in the world that have as comprehensively turned their backs on the past as São Paulo has done. In the nineteenth century, most of colonial São Paulo was levelled and replaced by a disorganized patchwork of wide avenues and large buildings, the process repeating itself ever since; today, not only has the city's colonial architectural heritage all but vanished, but there's little physical evidence of the coffee boom decades either.

Nevertheless, a few relics have, somehow, escaped demolition and offer hints of São Paulo's bygone eras. What remains is hidden away discreetly in corners, scattered throughout the city, often difficult to find but all the more thrilling when you do. There is no shortage of **museums**, but with a few significant exceptions they are disappointing for a city of São Paulo's stature. Collections have frequently been allowed to deteriorate and exhibits are generally poorly displayed. Fortunately, museum **charges** are negligible, around $1, and are only given in the text below where they are above this figure.

There are several sights associated with the vast influx of immigrants to the city (see box pp.590–591), and it's worth visiting some of the individual *bairros*, detailed in the text, where the immigrants and their descendants have established communities: the food, as you'd expect, is just one reason to do this.

Around Praça da Sé

Praça da Sé is the most convenient starting point for the very brief hunt for **colonial São Paulo**. The square itself is a large expanse of concrete and fountains, dominated by the **Catedral Metropolitana**, a huge neo-Gothic structure with a capacity of 8000 but otherwise unremarkable. Completed in 1954, it replaced São Paulo's eighteenth-century cathedral, which was demolished in 1920. During the day the square outside bustles with activity, always crowded with hawkers and people heading towards the commercial district on its western fringes. At night it's transformed into a campsite for homeless children, who survive as best they can by shining shoes, selling chewing gum or begging.

Along Rua Boa Vista, on the opposite side of the square from the cathedral, is where the city of São Paulo originated. The whitewashed Portuguese Baroque **Pátio do Colégio** is a replica of the college and chapel that formed the centre of the Jesuit mission founded here by the priests José de Anchieta and Manoel da Nóbrega in 1554. Although built in 1896 (the other buildings forming the Pátio were constructed in the twentieth century), the chapel (Mon–Fri 8am–5pm) is an accurate reproduction, but it's in the **Museu Padre Anchieta** (Tues–Sun 9am–5pm), part of the Pátio, that the most interesting sixteenth- and early seventeenth-century relics – mostly old documents, maps and watercolours – are held.

Virtually around the corner from the Pátio do Colégio at Rua Roberto Simonsen 136 is the **Museu da Cidade** (Tues–Sun 9am–5pm). More interesting than the museum's small collection chronicling the development of São Paulo is the building that it's housed in, the **Solar da Marquesa de Santos**, an eighteenth-century manor house that represents the sole remaining residential building in the city from this period. A couple of hundred metres from here, at Av. Rangel Pestana 230, is the well-preserved **Igreja do Carmo** (Mon–Fri 7–11am & 1–5pm, Sat & Sun 7–11am), which was built in 1632 and still retains many of its seventeenth-century features, including a fine Baroque high altar.

It is in these streets, particularly around Rua 25 de Março, that São Paulo's **Lebanese and Syrian community** is concentrated. At Rua Comandante Abdo Schahin 40, the Empório Syrio sells Middle Eastern delicacies, and on the same road there are some excellent Arab restaurants, always full with local merchants. The community is fairly evenly divided between Muslims and Christians, and hidden away at Rua Cavalheiro Basilio Jafet 15 there's a beautiful **Orthodox church**.

Over the other side of the Praça da Sé, a two-minute walk down Rua Senado Feijó to the Largo de São Francisco is the **Igreja de São Francisco de Assis** (Mon–Fri 7.30am–8pm, Sat & Sun 7–10am), one of the best-preserved colonial buildings in the city. Built between 1647 and 1790, it is a typical Portuguese Baroque church of the period, featuring intricately carved ornaments and an elaborate high altar. While here, step inside the courtyard of the Faculdade de Direito de São Paulo – one of Brazil's first higher education institutions, founded in 1824 – which adjoins the church, and take a look at the huge 1930s stained-glass window depicting the Largo de São Francisco in the early nineteenth century. Before leaving this area, it's worth visiting the **Igreja de Santo Antônio**, at Praça do Patriarca, by the Viaduto do Chá (the pedestrian bridge linking the two parts of the commercial centre). Built in 1717, its yellow and white facade has been beautifully restored; the interior, meanwhile, has been stripped of most of its eighteenth-century accoutrements, though its simple painted wooden ceiling deserves a glance.

Bixiga and Liberdade

Since the early twentieth century, the Italian immigrant population of the *bairro* of **Bixiga**, lying to the southwest of Praça da Sé, has given it the name "Little Italy" (it's also known as Bela Vista). Calabrian stonemasons built their own modest homes with leftover materials from the building sites where they were employed, and the narrow streets are still lined with such houses. In an otherwise ordinary house at Rua dos Ingleses 118, the **Museu Memória do Bixiga** (Wed–Sun 2–5pm) enthusiastically documents the history of the *bairro*, and has a small collection of photographs and household items. Italian **restaurants** exist throughout the city, but the area with the greatest concentration (if not the greatest quality) is Bixiga. The central Rua 13 de Maio, and the streets running off it, are lined with *cantinas*, pizzerias and bars and small theatres. This normally quiet neighbourhood springs to life in the evening, and during the day on Sunday there's a lively flea market, Antiguidades e Artesanato do Bixiga, at Praça Dom Orione (see p.612).

Just east of Bixiga is the *bairro* of **Liberdade**, traditional home of the city's large Japanese community. Rua Galvão Bueno and intersecting streets are largely devoted to Japanese and other east Asian restaurants and shops selling semiprecious stones, Japanese food and clothes. The **Museu da Imigração Japonesa**, Rua São Joaquim 381 (7th and 8th floors; Wed–Sun 1.30–5.30pm), has a Japanese-style rooftop garden and excellent displays on the Japanese community in Brazil, from their arrival in 1908 to work on the coffee plantations to their transition to farming and their varied contributions to modern Brazil. On the same road, alongside drab-looking office and apartment buildings is the instantly recognisable **Templo Busshinji** at no. 285 (9am–7pm), a Japanese Buddhist temple built in 1995; visitors are welcome to look around the wooden

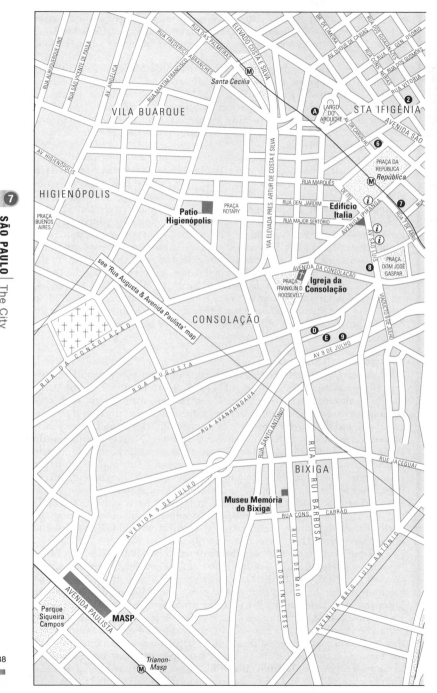

SÃO PAULO | The City

7

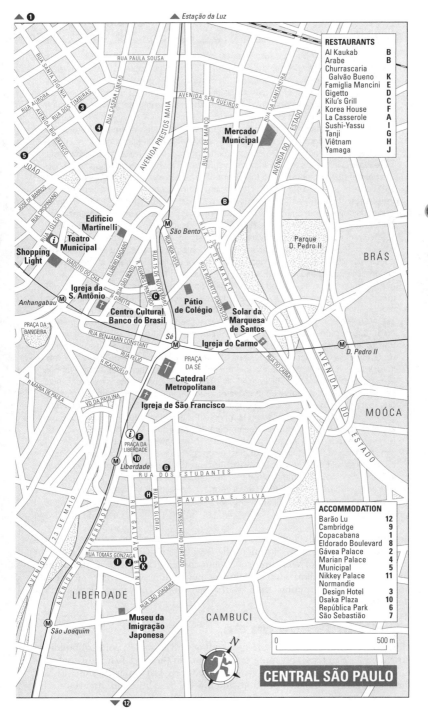

RESTAURANTS

Al Kaukab	**B**
Arabe	**B**
Churrascaria Galvão Bueno	**K**
Famiglia Mancini	**E**
Gigetto	**D**
Kilu's Grill	**C**
Korea House	**F**
La Casserole	**A**
Sushi-Yassu	**I**
Tanji	**G**
Viêtnam	**H**
Yamaga	**J**

RUA PAULA SOUSA

RUA SANTA IFIGENIA

RUA AURORA

AVENIDA RIO BRANCO

RUA DOS TIMBIRAS

RUA GASPAR LIBERO

AVENIDA SEN QUEIROS

RUA DA CANTAREIRA

③

④

⑤

JOÃO

JOSE DE BARROS

RUA CRISPINIANO

AVENIDA PRESTES MAIA

RUA 25 DE MARÇO

AVENIDA DO ESTADO

Mercado Municipal

Ⓑ

Ⓜ *São Bento*

Parque D. Pedro II

BRÁS

Edifício Martinelli

RUA TOLEDO

ⓘ **Teatro Municipal**

Shopping Light

VIADUTO DO CHA

RUA BOA VISTA

RUA LIBERO BADARÓ

RUA 15 DE NOVEMBRO

RUA ALVARES PENTEADO

RUA SÃO BENTO

R DIREITA

RUA ROBERTO SIMONSEN

RUA 25 DE MARÇO

Ⓒ

Igreja da S. Antônio ✝

Ⓜ *Anhangabaú*

Centro Cultural Banco do Brasil

Pátio de Colégio

Solar da Marquesa de Santos

PRAÇA DA BANDEIRA

RUA BENJAMIN CONSTANT

Sé

Ⓜ

Igreja do Carmo

Ⓜ *D. Pedro II*

RUA DO CARMO

AVENIDA D. PEDRO II

RUA FEIJÓ

R RACHUELO

PRAÇA DA SÉ

Catedral Metropolitana ✝

R MARIA DE PAULA

VD DA PAULINA

AVENIDA DO ESTADO

MOÓCA

ESTADO

Igreja de São Francisco ✝

ⓘⒻ

PRAÇA DA LIBERDADE

⑩

Ⓜ *Liberdade*

Ⓖ

RUA DOS ESTUDANTES

Ⓗ RUA DA GLORIA

AV COSTA E. SILVA

RUA CONSELHEIRO FURTADO

AVENIDA 23 DE MAIO

AVENIDA DA LIBERDADE

RUA GALVÃO BUENO

RUA TOMÁS GONZAGA

Ⓘ Ⓙ ⑪ Ⓚ

RUA SÃO JOAQUIM

LIBERDADE

CAMBUCI

Ⓜ *São Joaquim*

Museu da Imigração Japonesa

N

ACCOMMODATION

Barão Lu	12
Cambridge	9
Copacabana	1
Eldorado Boulevard	8
Gávea Palace	2
Marian Palace	4
Municipal	5
Nikkey Palace	11
Normandie Design Hotel	3
Osaka Plaza	10
República Park	6
São Sebastião	7

0   500 m

CENTRAL SÃO PAULO

▼ ⑫

São Paulo is a city built on **immigrants**: largely due to immigration, São Paulo's population grew a hundred-fold in 75 years to make it the country's second-largest city by 1950. Besides sheer numbers, the mass influx of people had a tremendous impact on the character of the city, breaking up the existing social stratification and removing economic and political power from the traditional elite groups at a much earlier stage than in other Brazilian cities.

Although there had been attempts at introducing Prussian share-croppers in the 1840s, mass immigration didn't begin until the late 1870s. Initially, conditions were appalling for the immigrants, many of whom succumbed to malaria or yellow fever while waiting in Santos to be transferred inland to the plantations. In response to criticisms, the government opened the Hospedaria dos Imigrantes in 1887, a hostel in the eastern suburb of Moóca. Now open to the public as the **Memorial do Imigrante**, Rua Visconde de Paraíba 1316 (☎11/6693-0917; ⓦwww .memorialdoimigrante.sp.gov.br), the hostel buildings house an immigration research centre, a basic café and one of the best museums in São Paulo (Tues–Sun 10am–5pm; research facilities available only 1–4pm). The museum has a permanent collection of period furniture, documents and photographs, and regularly hosts temporary exhibits relating to individual nationalities or particular aspects of immigration history. The main building itself is the most interesting feature of the complex, however, with vast dormitories and its own rail siding and platform for unloading immigrants and their baggage. Near the entrance, a separate building contained the rooms where new arrivals met their prospective employers, the government providing interpreters to help the immigrants make sense of work contracts. Designed to hold 4000 people, the hostel housed as many as 10,000 at times, the immigrants treated little better than cattle. In its early years, it was a virtual prison: the exit ticket was securing a contract of employment. Control was considered necessary since few immigrants actually wanted to work in the plantations, and there was a large labour leakage to the city of São Paulo itself. In 1978 the last immigrants were processed here. During most of the week the Memorial do Imigrante is little visited – perhaps due to its grim location, an unpleasant five-minute walk from Brás *metrô* station and the fact that adjoining the museum is a hostel for homeless men – but on Sundays and holidays, a wonderful nineteenth-century train connects the complex with Bresser *metrô* station (10am–5pm) and succeeds in drawing larger crowds.

Immigration to São Paulo is most closely associated with the **Italians**, who constituted 46 percent of all arrivals between 1887 and 1930. In general, soon after arrival in Brazil they would be transported to a plantation, but most slipped away within a year to seek employment in the city or to move on south to Argentina. The rapidly expanding factories in the districts of Brás, Moóca and Belém, east of the city cen-

building and attend ceremonies. In recent years, Liberdade's ethnic character has been changing and, although the area is still Japanese-dominated, an increasing number of Vietnamese, Chinese and especially Korean immigrants are settling in the area and introducing new businesses – most noticeably restaurants – and touting their wares on Sunday morning at the Praça Liberdade market.

North of Praça da Sé

The coffee boom that led to the dismantling of São Paulo's colonial buildings provided little in terms of lasting replacements. In the city's first industrial suburbs, towering brick chimneys are still to be seen, but generally the areas are now dominated by small workshops and low-income housing, and even in the tre, were desperately short of labour, and well into the twentieth century the population of these *bairros* was largely Italian. But it is **Bixiga** (or, officially, Bela Vista) where the Italian influence has been most enduring, as catalogued in the **Museu Memória do Bixiga** (see p.587). Originally home to freed slaves, Bixiga had by the early twentieth century established itself as São Paulo's "Little Italy". As immigration from Italy began to slow in the late 1890s, arrivals from other countries increased. From 1901 to 1930 **Spaniards** (especially Galicians) made up 22 percent, and **Portuguese** 23 percent, of immigrants, but their language allowed them to assimilate extremely quickly. Only Tatuapé developed into a largely Portuguese *bairro*.

The first 830 **Japanese** immigrants arrived in 1908 in Santos, from where they were sent on to the coffee plantations. By the mid-1950s a quarter of a million Japanese had emigrated to Brazil, most of them settling in the state of São Paulo, and unlike most other nationalities the rate of return migration among them has always been small: many chose to remain in agriculture, often as market gardeners, at the end of their contract. The city's large Japanese community is centred on **Liberdade**, a *bairro* just south of the Praça da Sé and home to the excellent **Museu da Imigração Japonesa** (see p.587).

São Paulo's **Arab** community is substantial. Arabs started arriving in the early twentieth century from Syria and the Lebanon and, as they were then travelling on Turkish passports, they're still usually referred to as *turcos*. Typically starting out as itinerant traders, the community soon became associated with small shops, with many Arabs becoming extremely successful in business. Family ties remain strong and, with the 1980s civil war in the Lebanon, the community was considerably enlarged. Many of the boutiques in the city's wealthy *bairros* are Arab-owned, but it's in the streets around **Rua 25 de Março**, north of Praça da Sé, that the community is concentrated (see p.587).

The **Jewish** community has also prospered in São Paulo. Mainly of East European origin, many of the city's Jews started out as itinerant pedlars before concentrating in **Bom Retiro**, a *bairro* near Luz train station (see p.593). As they became richer, they moved to the suburbs to the south of the city, but some of the businesses in the streets around Rua Correia de Melo are still Jewish-owned and there's a fine Eastern European restaurant (*Cecília*; see p.605) and a synagogue in the area. As the Jews moved out, **Greeks** started moving in during the 1960s, followed in larger numbers by **Koreans**, with many eventually prospering. The area has long been known as a centre of the rag trade and in the Korean-owned sweatshops the latest immigrant arrivals – **Bolivians** – are employed, often illegally and enduring appalling conditions.

city centre there are very few buildings of note, most of the area being given over to unremarkable shops and offices.

To the north of Praça da Sé, at Rua da Cantareira 306, you'll find the **Mercado Municipal**, an imposing, vaguely German neo-Gothic hall, completed in 1933. Apart from the phenomenal display of Brazilian and imported fruit, vegetables, cheese and other produce, the market (Mon–Sat 4am–4pm) is most noted for its enormous stained-glass windows depicting scenes of cattle raising, market gardening and coffee and banana plantations. Just across the Viaduto do Chá, in the direction of Praça da República, is the **Teatro Municipal**, São Paulo's most distinguished public building, an eclectic mixture of Art Nouveau and Italian Renaissance styles. Work began on the building in 1903, when the coffee boom was at its peak and São Paulo at its most confident. The theatre is still the city's main venue for classical music, and the auditorium, lavishly decorated and furnished with Italian marble, velvet, gold leaf and mirrors, can be viewed only if you're attending a performance.

If you need a break from pavement bashing, a good place to escape to is **Shopping Light**, an imposing mid-1920s building across from the theatre, one of São Paulo's newest shopping centres and the only upmarket collection of shops downtown.

Luz

Further north, the once affluent and still leafy *bairro* of Luz is home to São Paulo's two main train stations, around which one of the city's seediest red-light districts has sprung up – normal care should be taken in the area, especially when alone and at night. In recent years, Luz has been undergoing a remarkable renaissance, with massive city and state government investment aimed at transforming the *bairro* into a top-rank cultural centre.

At the intersection of Rua Duque de Caxias and Rua Mauá is the **Estação Júlio Prestes**, built between 1926 and 1937 and drawing on late nineteenth-century French and Italian architectural forms. The building's most beautiful features are its large stained-glass windows, which depict the role of the railway in the expansion of the Brazilian economy in the early twentieth century. Although part of the building still serves as a train station for suburban services, its Great Hall was transformed in the late 1990s into the Sala São Paulo, a 1500-seat concert hall – home of the world-class Orquestra Sinfônica do Estado de São Paulo, and centrepiece of the **Complexo Cultural Júlio Prestes** (☎11/3337-5414).

Nearby, along Rua Mauá at Largo General Osório 66, there are signs of further changes to the area, with the recent renovation of the **Edifício DOPS** (Tues–Sun 10am–5pm), a large, anonymous-looking building. During the military rule of the 1960s to 1980s (see p.756), this was the headquarters of the infamous Departamento de Ordem Política e Social, and was used as one of the two main torture centres in São Paulo. Today the building is an exhibition centre, and commemorates its ugly past with displays charting Brazil's history of repression, from the rise of Getulio Vargas in the 1930s to the more recent military dictatorship and the struggle for democracy. Temporary art exhibitions on related themes are also held here.

Further along Rua Mauá, towards Avenida Tiradentes, is the **Estação da Luz**, part of the British-owned rail network that did much to stimulate São Paulo's explosive growth in the late nineteenth century. The station was built in 1901, and everything was imported from Britain for its construction, from the design of the project to the smallest of screws. Although the refined decoration of its chambers was destroyed by fire in 1946, interior details – iron balconies, passageways and grilles – bear witness to the majestic structure's original elegance. Also worth a look is the **Vila Inglesa** at Rua Mauá 836, a group of 28 distinctively English-style houses built in 1924 to house British railway engineers and their families but which have long since been used as shops and offices.

The **Parque da Luz** (daily 10am–6pm) is one block north on Avenida Tiradentes. Dating back to 1800, the park was São Paulo's first public garden, and its intricate wrought-iron fencing, Victorian bandstands, ponds and rich foliage attest to its former glory. Until recently, the park was considered off limits, but security is now excellent and, as one of the few centrally located patches of greenery in the city, it is popular with local residents and visitors to the surrounding cultural centres. Now fully renovated, the space includes large display panels (in English and Portuguese) on the history of the Luz district and has been developed as a sculpture park.

Adjoining the park, at Av. Tiradentes 141, is the **Pinacoteca do Estado** (Tues–Sun 10am–6pm; $1.50), the gallery of São Paulo state. Housed in an imposing Neoclassical building constructed in 1905 and thoroughly renovated in 1998, this is one of the most pleasant and professionally maintained galleries in Brazil, with an excellent permanent collection of Brazilian paintings. Pride of place in the nineteenth-century galleries goes to images of rural São Paulo by Almeida Júnior, of which the Pinacoteca boasts some major pieces, but the work of other Brazilian landcape, portrait and historical artists of the period is also represented. The twentieth-century galleries include Cubist-influenced engravings, important paintings by the German expressionist turned Brazilian modernist Larsar Segall (see p. 000), plus works by other painters, such as Emiliano Di Cavalcanti, noted for his choice of Afro-Brazilian and urban themes, Cândido Portinari, whose work contained clear social and historical references, and the vibrant paintings of Tarsilla do Amaral. There is also a very pleasant café with a large terrace opening onto the Parque da Luz.

A short walk north of the Pinacoteca, by the Tiradentes *metrô* station at Av. Tiradentes 676, is one of the city's few surviving colonial churches, the **Igreja do Convento da Luz** (daily 6.30–11am & 2–5pm), a rambling structure of uncharacteristic grandeur. Built on the site of a sixteenth-century chapel, the former Franciscan monastery and church date back to 1774, though they've been much altered over the years and today house the **Museu de Arte Sacra** (Tues–Fri 11am–6pm, Sat & Sun 10am–7pm; $1.50). The museum's fine collection includes examples of Brazilian seventeenth- and eighteenth-century wooden and terracotta religious art and liturgical pieces.

To the north, the adjoining *bairro* of **Bom Retiro** is known for its shops selling cheap clothes and fabric. At the turn of the twentieth century the neighborhood was predominantly Italian, with successive waves of Jewish, Greek, Korean and Bolivian immigrants becoming the most prominent ethnic groups as the century progressed.

Around Praça da República

Praça da República is now largely an area of offices, hotels and shops but was once the site of the lavish **mansions** of the coffee-plantation owners who began to take up residence in the city from about 1870. However, no sooner had the mansions been built – constructed from British iron, Italian marble, Latvian pine, Portuguese tiles and Belgian stained glass – than they were abandoned as the city centre took on a brash and commercial character, and the coffee barons moved to new homes in the Higienópolis district, a short distance west of Praça da República. The central mansions were all knocked down, though a few remain in Higienópolis: completed in 1902, the Art Nouveau-influenced **Vila Penteado**, on Rua Maranhão, is a fine example and was one of the last to be built in the area. While extremely hectic, on weekdays the area feels perfectly safe, but in the evenings and, for the most part at weekends, the area is too quiet for comfort. On Sundays, however, Avenida Ipiranga, extending southwest of the *praça*, is closed to traffic and given over to the **República das Artes**, a huge tented street market (9am–4pm) where stalls sell tacky paintings, some interesting handicrafts and semiprecious gems.

The Triângulo

Southeast of the Praça da República lies the **Triângulo**, the traditional banking district and a zone of concentrated vertical growth. At the northern edge of the Triângulo, at Av. São João 35, stands the 35-storey **Edifício Martinelli**, the city's first skyscraper. Modelled on the Empire State Building, Martinelli was inaugurated in 1929 and remains an important downtown landmark – the rooftop observation area (Mon–Fri 10.30am-4pm) can be visited with permission of the building manager on the ground floor. A couple of blocks south of Edifício Martinelli, at Rua 15 de Novembro 275, is the **BOVESPA** building (Mon–Fri 9am–noon and 2–6pm; ☎11/3233-2178, ⓦwww.bovespa .com.br), São Paulo's stock exchange: next to New York's, it's the most active stock exchange in the Americas. A tour can easily be arranged (☎11/3233-2178, ⓔvisite@bovespa.com.br) if you have official links to a foreign or Brazilian investment institution, but otherwise you can observe the frenetic activity of the trading floor from the observation gallery.

The arts are hardly a driving force behind the Triângulo, but a distinctive Beaux Arts–style former bank building at Rua Álvares Penteado 112 has been developed as the **Centro Cultural Banco do Brasil** (Tues–Sun noon–7.30pm; ☎11/3113-3600, ⓦwww.cultura-e.com.br) and is a refreshing contrast to the surrounding mammon. Always worth at least a brief look are the temporary exhibitions on display, which are taken from the bank's own important collections of Brazilian art or those of prominent private collectors. Inside, the café and small restaurant is a convenient place for lunch.

On Avenida São Luís, the street leading south from the Praça da República, is Latin America's tallest office building, the 46-storey **Edifício Itália**, built in 1965 to dwarf the Edifício Martinelli. On cloud- and smog-free days, the *Terraço Itália* restaurant on the 41st and 42nd floors is a good vantage point from which to view the city; the food is expensive and not particularly good, so you're best off just having afternoon tea (3–5.30pm) or an early evening drink at the bar (from 6pm, when shorts may not be worn). In the 1940s and 1950s, **Avenida São Luís** itself was São Paulo's version of New York's Fifth Avenue, lined with high-class apartment buildings and offices, and, though no longer fashionable, it still retains a certain degree of elegance. Admirers of the Brazilian architect Oscar Niemeyer will immediately recognise the serpentine curves of the **Edifício Copan**. Constructed in 1950 and with over 4,000 people occupying its 1,850 apartments, this is by far the largest of the apartment and office buildings on the avenue.

The Memorial da América Latina

Northwest of Praça da República along the Avenida São João is the strikingly ugly **Memorial da América Latina** (Tues–Sun 9am–6pm; ☎11/3823-4600, ⓦwww.memorial.org.br), located close to the Barra Funda *metrô* station. Designed by Oscar Niemeyer in 1989, this is a building that even the most avid fans of the architect find it hard to say anything good about, looking as it does more like a nuclear weapons site than a showcase for Latin American culture. Unfortunately, the concrete structure is in a poor condition and apart from a permanent display of Latin American folkloric art, the Memorial hosts only occasional exhibitions, concerts and conferences.

Along Avenida Paulista

By 1900, the coffee barons had moved on from Higienópolis, to flaunt their wealth from their new mansions set in spacious gardens stretching along the three-kilometre-long **Avenida Paulista** – then a tree-lined avenue set along a ridge 3km southwest of the city centre. In the late 1960s, and throughout the 1970s, Avenida Paulista resembled a giant building site, with banks and other companies competing to build ever-taller buildings. There was little time for

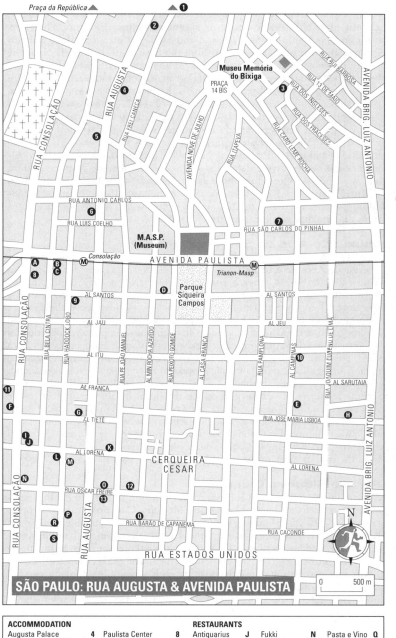

SÃO PAULO: RUA AUGUSTA & AVENIDA PAULISTA

Praça da República▲

Museu Memória do Bixiga
PRAÇA 14 BIS

RUA ANTONIO CARLOS
RUA LUIS COELHO

M.A.S.P. (Museum)

RUA SÃO CARLOS DO PINHAL

Consolação

AVENIDA PAULISTA

Trianon-Masp

Parque Siqueira Campos

AL SANTOS
AL SANTOS
AL JAU
AL JEU
AL ITU
AL FRANCA
AL SARUTAIA
AL TIETÊ
RUA JOSÉ MARIA LISBOA
AL LORENA
CERQUEIRA CESAR
AL LORENA
RUA OSCAR FREIRE
RUA BARÃO DE CAPANEMA
RUA CACONDE
RUA ESTADOS UNIDOS

RUA AUGUSTA
RUA BELA CINTRA
RUA CONSOLAÇÃO
RUA HADDOCK LOBO
RUA PE JOÃO MANUEL
AL MIN ROCHA AZEVEDO
RUA PEIXOTO GOMIDE
AL CASA BRANCA
RUA PAMPLONA
RUA CAMPINAS
RUA JOAQUIM EUGENIO DE LIMA
AVENIDA BRIG. LUIZ ANTONIO

RUA RUI BARBOSA
RUA 13 DE MAIO
RUA DOS INGLESES
RUA DOS FRANCESES
RUA CARD LEME ROCHA
RUA ITAPEVA
AVENIDA NOVE DE JULHO
RUA BELCANECA
RUA CONSOLAÇÃO

N

0   500 m

ACCOMMODATION			
Augusta Palace	4	Paulista Center	8
Augusta Park Residence	5	Pergamon	1
Cá d'Oro	2	Pousada Dona Ziláh	11
Caesar Park	6	Pousada	
Emiliano	12	dos Franceses	3
Maksoud Plaza	7	Regent Park	13
Metropolitan Plaza	10	Renaissance	9

RESTAURANTS					
Antiquarius	J	Fukki	N	Pasta e Vino	Q
Arábia	M	Jun Sakamoto	H	Sara	P
Dona Lucinha	P	L'Arnaque	O	Sativa	F
Esfiha Chic	A	Le Vin Bistro	G	Templo	
Esplanada Grill	S	Massimo	D	da Bahia	E
Fasano	R	Mr Fish Grill	K	Tucupy	B
Folha de Uva	C	Namesa	I	Z-Deli	L

creativity, and along the entire length of the avenue it would be difficult to single out more than one example of decent modern architecture. There are, however, about a dozen Art Nouveau and Art Deco mansions along Avenida Paulista, afforded official protection from the developers' bulldozers. Some lie empty, the subjects of legal wrangles over inheritance rights, while others have been turned into branches of *McDonald's* or prestigious headquarters for banks. One mansion that is well worth visiting is the French-style **Casa das Rosas**, Av. Paulista 35 (Tues–Sun 1–8pm; ☎11/251-5271, ⓦwww.casadasrosas .sp.gov.br), near Brigadeiro *métro* station at the easterly end of the *avenida*. Set in a rose garden with a beautiful Art Nouveau stained-glass window, and constructed in 1935 as a private residence, it contrasts stunningly with the mirrored-glass and steel office building behind it. The Casa das Rosas is now a cultural centre owned by the state of São Paulo, where interesting art exhibitions are often held. A block from here at Av. Paulista 149 is the **Instituto Itaú Cultural** (Tues–Fri 10am–9pm, Sat, Sun & holidays 10am–7pm; ☎11/238-1883, ⓦwww.itaucultural.org.br), an arts centre worth a look for its exhibitions of contemporary Brazilian art.

Museu de Arte de São Paulo (MASP)

One of the few interesting modern buildings along Avenida Paulista is that of the **Museu de Arte de São Paulo** at no. 1578 (Tues–Sun 11am–6pm; $2, free on Thurs; ☎11/251-5644, ⓦwww.masp.art.br). Designed in 1957 by the Italian-born naturalized-Brazilian architect Lina Bo Bardi and opened in 1968, the monumental concrete structure appears somehow to float above the ground, supported only by remarkably delicate pillars. MASP is the great pride of São Paulo's art lovers, and is considered to have the most important collection of Western art in Latin America, featuring the work of great European artists from the last five hundred years. For most North American and European visitors, notable though some of the individual works of Hieronymus Bosch, Rembrandt and Degas may be, the highlights of the collection are likely to be the seventeenth- to nineteenth-century landscapes of Brazil by European artists, none more important than the small but detailed paintings by Frans Post. MASP is one of Brazil's few museums that regularly hosts international visiting exhibitions; and the museum's excellent and very reasonably priced restaurant (Mon–Fri 11.30am–3pm, Sat, Sun & holidays noon–4pm) makes for an excellent escape from the crowds, exhaust fumes and heat of Avenida Paulista outside.

Parque Siqueira Campos

Almost directly across Avenida Paulista from MASP is one of São Paulo's smallest but most delightful parks, the **Parque Siqueira Campos** (daily 6am–6pm) created in 1912 when building in the area began. It was planned by the French landscape artist Paul Villon, based around local vegetation with some introduced trees and bushes, and in 1968 underwent a thorough renovation, directed by the great designer Roberto Burle Marx. The park consists of 45,000 square metres of almost pure Atlantic forest with a wealth of different trees, and there's a network of trails, as well as shaded benches to sit and relax on away from the intense summer heat. The park is well patrolled by wardens but a degree of alertness is still called for – don't doze off.

The Jardins, Itaim Bibi and Pinheiros

Avenida Paulista marks the southwestern boundary of downtown São Paulo, and beyond that are Jardim Paulista, Jardim America and Jardim Europa – the **Jardins** – an area laid out in 1915 and styled after the British idea of the garden suburb. These exclusive residential neighbourhoods have long since taken over from the city centre as the location of most of the city's best restaurants and shopping streets, and many residents never stray from their luxurious ghettos – protected from Third World realities by complex alarm systems, guards and fierce dogs. At the northeastern edge of the Jardins is **Jardim Paulista**, a neighbourhood within the wider district of Cerqueira César that straddles both sides of Avenida Paulista. Just a few blocks into the Jardins from Avenida Paulista one finds a mixed bag of hotels, offices and apartment buildings interspersed with shops, restaurants and bars geared towards the city's upper middle class. This is one of the few parts of the city with street life that's pleasant to walk in late into the evening – wander along Rua Oscar Freire and the intersecting *ruas* Haddock Lobo, Bela Cintra and da Consolação for some of the neighbourhood's most exclusive boutiques, lively bars and excellent restaurants.

Rua Augusta, lined with shops of all sorts, bisects Jardim Paulista and then turns into Rua Colômbia and Avenida Europa in the adjoining **Jardim America** and then **Jardim Europa**. Unfortunately, the winding tree-lined roads of these largely residential neighbourhoods afford only occasional glimpses of the Victorian or Neoclassical houses that are all but hidden behind their gardens' high walls. In Jardim Europa, it's worth stopping off at Av. Europa 158, near the intersection with Rua Groenândia in Jardins, to see what's on at the **Museu da Imagen e do Som** (Tues–Sun 2–10pm), which hosts often fascinating exhibitions of contemporary and historic Brazilian photography. Continuing along Avenida Europa one reaches Avenida Brigadeiro Faria Lima, where, at no. 2705, the **Museu da Casa Brasileira** (Tues–Sun 1–5pm, T 11/3032-3727, W www.mcb.sp.gov.br) boasts a varied collection of seventeenth- to twentieth-century Brazilian furniture and decorative items. Of interest is the building itself, which is typical of the mansions in Jardim Europa – an imposing ochre-coloured Palladian villa built in the 1940s. In the villa's kitchen, and extending into the garden, there's an excellent restaurant, the *Quinta do Museu* (see p.604).

The traffic-choked Avenida Brigadeiro Faria Lima, with the mixed residential and commercial neighourhoods of **Itaim Bibi**, towards its southern end, and **Pinheiros** to the north, is the main artery of São Paulo's newest business expanse. Although the new buildings around here have generally been constructed at a break-neck speed, leaving little time for architectural reflection, there are at least a couple of interesting creations in Pinheiros, both some distance from the main concentration of office development. At Av. Brigadeiro Faria Lima 201 is one construction that you won't fail to notice, a striking purple and blue office building designed by **Ruy Ohtake**, one of Brazil's most important contemporary architects (see also his *Hotel Renaissance*, p.585). Opened in 2002, the building is notable for its curved lines and use of colour, both characteristic of Ohtake's work and a deliberate move away from the modernist tradition that has been so dominant in Brazilian architecture.

Housed on the lower floors of the building (and with its entrance on Rua Coropés) is the **Instituto Tomie Ohtake** (Tues–Sun 11am–8pm; T 11/6844-1900), which honours the Japanese-Brazilian artist Tomie Ohtake (the architect's mother). The artist's early Brazilian work (notably landscapes) is most closely informed by her Japanese background, but this is even apparent after her shift to abstraction, in which the restrained brushstroke remains the key element. Although only a small proportion of the exhibition space features her work, in rotating displays that highlight particular periods or themes, this section is always well worth a look. Otherwise the galleries are devoted to temporary exhibits of contemporary Brazilian artists or influential twentieth-century Brazilian constructivists. There's also a good giftshop focusing on modern Brazilian art and design, as well as a restaurant (see p.601).

Four blocks west of Avenida Brigadeiro Faria Lima is the **Centro Brasileiro Britânico** (opening hours vary, call ☎11/2029-0508) at Rua Ferreira de Araújo 741, which houses the British Consulate and various British cultural and community organisations. Opened in 2000, the building is almost boastfully modern, its steel, plate-glass and concrete construction managing to appear both imposing and inviting. And while the exhibition centre has so far showcased mostly second-rate contemporary British and Brazilian art, at least the bar – *Poet's Corner* (see p.608) – and restaurant (see p.606), are both open to the public and worth lingering in.

The Parque do Ibirapuera and around

The **Parque do Ibirapuera** (daily 6am–8pm), southeast of the Jardins, is the most famous of São Paulo's parks and is the main sports centre for the city. It's a ten-minute bus ride from the bus stops on Avenida Brigadeiro Luís Antônio. The park, officially opened in 1954, was created to mark the 400th anniversary of the founding of the city of São Paulo. Most of the buildings were designed by Oscar Niemeyer and impressive designs for landscaping were produced by Roberto Burle Marx. Unfortunately, these plans remained on paper only.

The park contains the peaceful and unusual **Bosque de Leitura** (reading woods), where you can borrow books and sit amongst the trees reading them, and is also home to several of the city's museums. The **Museu de Arte Contemporânea** (Tues, Wed & Fri 10am–7pm, Sat, Sun and holidays 10am–4pm; $2; ☎11/3818-3039, ⓦ www.mac.usp.br), located in the Pavilhão da Bienal in the park – and also on a larger site at Rua da Reitoria 160 (Mon–Fri noon–8pm, Sat 9am–1pm) in the university complex – regularly alters its displays, drawing upon its huge stored collection. Although the collection includes work by important European artists, such as Picasso, Modigliani, Léger and Chagall, and Brazilians including Tarsilla do Amaral, Di Cavalcanti and Portinari, the pieces that are selected for exhibition can be disappointing.

Next door to the Pavilhão da Bienal in the Marquise do Parque do Ibirapuera, the **Museu de Arte Moderna**, or MAM (Tues, Wed & Fri noon–6pm, Sat, Sun & holidays 10am–6pm; $3, free Tues; ☎11/5549-9688, ⓦ www.mam.org.br), is a much smaller museum that mainly hosts temporary exhibits of the work of Brazilian artists. There's an excellent café here serving light meals and snacks, and a good bookshop.

If you're on the art-gallery trail, there are a couple of other museums nearby that are well worth seeking out. The *bairro* due east of the Parque do Ibirapuera, Vila Mariana, contains the wonderful **Museu Lasar Segall** at Rua Afonso Celso 388 (Tues–Sat 2–7pm, Sun 2–6pm; $2). As most of Lasar Segall's work is contained in this museum (his home and studio from 1932 until his death in 1957), the Latvian-born naturalized-Brazilian painter is relatively little known outside Brazil. Originally a part of the German Expressionist movement at the beginning of the twentieth century, he settled in Brazil in 1923 and became increasingly influenced by the exuberant colours of his adopted homeland. East of here in the *bairro* of Ipiranga, the **Museu do Ipiranga** – also known as the Museu Paulista – (Tues–Sun 9am–4.45pm; ☎11/6165-8000, ⓦ www.mp.usp.br), at the intersection of *avenidas* Nazareth and Dom Pedro in the Parque da Independência, is worthwhile if you have a passing interest in

The **São Paulo Bienal** has been held in the Parque do Ibirapuera every two years since 1951. It's widely considered to be the most important exhibition of contemporary visual art in Latin America and is only rivalled in the world by the similar event held in Venice. Each country sponsors work by its most influential contemporary artists, while a select few artists (living or dead) are also chosen by the Bienal's curators. At best, the Bienal can be an exhilarating venue to see important retrospectives and experience a wealth of innovative art, but at worst it can be little more than an embarrassing – or amusing – showing of fourth-rate global art. The Bienal was traditionally held in October and November in odd-numbered years, but the 1993 event was postponed until 1994 and it is now scheduled for even-numbered years. For advance information contact the cultural attaché of any Brazilian embassy, or write directly to São Paulo Bienal, Parque do Ibirapuera, Portal 3, 04090-900 São Paulo – SP (☎11/5574-5922, ⓕ5549-0230).

Brazilian history: the museum is especially strong on the nineteenth century, featuring many paintings, furniture and other items that belonged to the Brazilian royal family. The park is also significant as the site where, in 1822, Brazilian independence was declared; in the park is a monument celebrating the event – a replica of the **Casa do Grito**, the simple house where Dom Pedro I slept – and the chapel where he and his wife were later buried.

Butantã and Morumbi

In the southwest of the city, the two *bairros* of Butantã and Morumbi are worth the trek. No houses from the colonial era remain standing in the city centre, but out here in the suburbs a few simple, whitewashed adobe **homesteads** from the time of the *bandeirantes* have been preserved. The easiest to visit is the **Casa do Bandeirante**, by the university at Praça Monteiro Lobato, Butantã (Tues–Sun 9am–5pm): it's no more than a typical early eighteenth–century *paulista* dwelling containing period furniture and farm implements.

One of the city's more popular attractions is also situated in the *bairro* of Butantã. Founded in 1901, the **Instituto Butantan**, Av. Vital Brasil 1500 (Tues–Sun 9am–4.30pm), was one of the world's foremost research centres for the study of venomous snakes and insects and the development of anti-venom serums. Sadly, financial cuts have had a devastating effect on the institute, and what was once one of the highlights of a tour of São Paulo is now, despite its enduring reputation, a large disappointment for adults and children alike. There's a dark and dusty museum that documents the history of the institute's work, huge, mostly empty, snake pits, and rooms where spiders and scorpions are bred; the work of the institute, however, now goes on almost entirely behind closed doors.

Fundação Maria Luiza e Oscar Americano

Situated in the elegant suburb of Morumbi, the **Fundação Maria Luiza e Oscar Americano**, Av. Morumbi 3700 (Tues–Fri 11am–5pm, Sat & Sun 10am–5pm; $1.50; ☎11/3742-0077; ⓦwww.fundacaoosaramericano.org.br), is a sprawling modernist house full of eighteenth-century furniture, tapestries, religious sculptures and collections of silver, china, coins and tapestry. Amongst the most valuable works are Brazilian landscapes by the seventeenth-century Dutch artist Frans Post, and drawings and important paintings by Cândido Portinari and Emiliano di Cavalcanti. The hilltop house, designed by Oswaldo

Arthur Bratke, is clearly influenced by the work of the American architect Frank Lloyd Wright, and the beautiful wooded estate, which mainly features flora native to Brazil, helps to make this an excellent place to escape the city. There's a superb tearoom, serving English-style high teas ($6 per person) until 6pm daily as well as light lunches on weekends, and concerts at 4pm on Sundays. Courses on music, art and architecture are offered during the week.

Parque do Estado

South of the city centre, near Congonhas airport, is the largest expanse of greenery within the city – the **Parque do Estado**. The park features an extent of Mata Atlântica, trails and picnic areas, but by far the biggest draw is the **zoo** – the Zoológico de São Paulo (Tues–Sun & holidays 9am–5pm; $2.50; ☎11/5073-0811, ⓦ www.zoologico.com.br), ranked as one of the largest and best in the world and housing an estimated 3200 animals from around the world, predominantly Brazilian and African species. The reptile and monkey houses have especially important collections of the latter, while several thousand migratory birds are drawn annually to the natural habitat of the park. The easiest way to get to the park and zoo is by *metrô* to Jabaquara station, followed by a short taxi ride.

Eating

Eating out is a major pastime for middle- and upper-class *paulistanos*, who take great pride in the vast number of restaurants in the city. Certainly, the variety of eating options is one of the great joys of São Paulo although quality and taste can be disappointing, even at the more expensive end of the scale. Fortunately, though, things are changing, with chefs becoming more creative with traditional Brazilian dishes as well as adapting European and Asian ones to suit Brazilian tastes and make use of local ingredients.

Fast food, coffee, tea and ice cream

paulistanos are reputed to be always in a hurry and on just about every block there's somewhere serving **fast food**. *Lanchonetes* do snacks and cheap, light meals and – in direct competition – so too do the likes of *McDonald's* and *Pizza Hut*. Claiming to have invented the traditional *bauru* sandwich (made with roast beef, salad and melted cheese) is the *Ponto Chic* at Largo do Paissandu 27, Centro, while **sandwich bars** popular with a younger crowd include the *Frevo*, Rua Oscar Freire 603, Cerqueira César, the *Companhia Paulista de Sanduíches* at Rua Prof. Arthur Ramos 395, Jardim Europa, and *The Bagel Factory*, Rua Padre João Manoel 881, Jardim Europa. There are plenty of **pizzerias**, too: highly recommended are the *Margherita*, at Alameda Tietê 255, Cerqueira César and the *Marco Polo*, Rua Franz Schubert 35, Jardim Europa, both of which serve fairly authentic Italian, thin and crispy pizzas, while *Castelões*, Rua Jairo Góis 126, Brás (one of the most traditional pizza houses in the city), and the long-established *Camelo*, Rua Pamplona 1873, Jardins, offer heavier, thicker varieties that are more typical of Brazil.

Oddly, for a city built on immigrants and coffee, São Paulo has no **café** tradition. **Coffee**, though, is drunk endlessly in the form of *cafézinhos* (small cups of strong, black coffee). It's not usually lingered over, but if you want to take your time look out for one of the ever-increasing number of places with an

espresso machine. Among several branches of *Fran's Café* in downtown São Paulo, the most popular is on the ground floor of the Edifício Itália just round the corner from Praça da República. Open 24 hours a day, it serves delicious *canelinha* – espresso with milk and cinnamon.

There are a few good **tearooms**, among which *Jasmin* at Rua Haddock Lobo 932 and *La Baguette* at Rua Haddock Lobo 1604 (both in Jardins) are both especially inviting, serving good-quality tea and excellent varieties of cakes. For a novel experience, try *As Noviças*, Rua Gaivota 1216, Moema (closed Mon), where waitresses dressed as nuns serve teas against a background of religious music. If you have time, to escape the crowds and fumes of the hectic business districts, head out to the Fundação Maria Luiza e Oscar Americano (see p. 599), where superb English-style high teas are served.

Perhaps it's due to the Italian element in the population that you can find such good **ice cream** in São Paulo. For Italian-style ice cream and fruit sorbets at their absolute best try *Gelatería d'Arte* at Alameda Lorena 1784 or, almost as good, *Gelatería Parmalat* at Rua Oscar Freire 518, both in Jardim Paulista. *La Basque* at Alameda Lorena 1444, Cerqueira César, is always reliable, too.

Restaurants

São Paulo's restaurants are concentrated where the money is, in the city centre and especially in the middle- and upper-class suburbs of the city's southwest in neighbourhoods like **the Jardins**, **Itaim Bibi**, **Morumbi** and the newly fashionable **Pinheiros** and **Vila Madalena** area. You can get away with paying $2 or even less for a standard dish of rice, beans and meat at a small, side-street restaurant, and even at the most elegant places in the wealthiest neighbourhoods you'll be very hard-pressed to pay more than $40 per person unless you opt for expensive imported wines. There is, of course, a huge choice of good options between these price extremes, so you won't have any trouble finding places to suit your tastes and budget.

Asian

As home to the largest Japanese community outside Japan, it's no surprise that São Paulo has many excellent Japanese restaurants, though you won't find anything resembling the new wave, fusion, Japanese food found in Japan or the United States. Make for **Liberdade**, traditionally considered São Paulo's "Japanese quarter", where restaurants and sushi bars are everywhere. In recent years other Asian restaurants have opened across the city, but their quality is generally disappointing.

China Massas Caseiras Rua Mourato Coelho 140, Pinheiros. Huge quantities of extremely cheap, unsophisticated, Cantonese-style food recommended for the restaurant's lively atmosphere and super-low prices.

Churrascaria Galvão Bueno Rua Galvão Bueno 451, Liberdade. Korean barbecue cooked on a small grill at your table. The menu includes a range of spicy Korean dishes and Japanese items as well. Around $12 per person.

Fukki Rua da Consolação 3447, Jardins. This small restaurant, near the corner of Rua Oscar Freire, is notable for its lunchtime buffet, which includes a pretty good range of sushi and sashimi – amazing value at around $6 per person. Open until late.

Govinda Rua Princesa Isabel 379, Brooklin Paulista. The oldest Indian restaurant in the city, with dishes tempered to suit Brazilian tastebuds. Fairly expensive, the restaurant is worthwhile more for the lavish decoration than the food. Closed Sun evening.

Instituto Tomie Ohtake Av. Brigadeiro Faria Lima 201 (entrance on Rua Coropés), Pinheiros. Even if the art in the cultural centre (see p.597) leaves you cold, the restaurant is well worth a visit. A rare – and generally successful – attempt at fusing Brazilian dishes with pan-Asian (especially Japanese and Thai) flavours. Expect to pay around $15 per person for a full meal, or $5 for a sandwich lunch. Tues–Sun noon–6pm.

Jun Sakamoto Rua José Maria Lisboa 55, Jardim Paulista ☎ 11/3088-6019. This expensive restaurant stands out amongst São Paulo's many Japanese eateries, with its attractive steel and wood setting and a daring chef who adds modern twists to otherwise classic dishes. The sushi is creatively presented, and the tempura, in a light batter with sesame seeds, is excellent. Very popular at weekends, when a reservation is advisable. Evenings only.

Kabuki Mask Rua Girassol 384, Vila Madalena. Good Japanese food drawing a rather trendy crowd, with live Brazilian music in the evenings. Open daily for dinner and also lunch Sat & Sun.

Korea House Rua Galvão Bueno 43, Liberdade. One of the very few Korean restaurants in São Paulo, despite the city's sizeable Korean community. Many dishes are prepared at the table, and the often spicy meals are very different to Chinese or Japanese cooking. Around $5 per person.

Oriental Rua José Maria Lisboa 1000, Jardim Paulista. Flavours of the Far East feature here in this rather formal restaurant with interesting Chinese-, Thai- and Vietnamese-inspired dishes.

Expect to pay at least $20 per person at what is considered the best pan-Asian restaurant in the city. Closed Sun.

Sushi-Yassu Rua Tomás Gonzaga 110 A, Liberdade. Excellent, traditionally presented sushi, sashimi, noodle and other Japanese dishes, but not cheap (about $20 a person). Unusually for Brazil, eel (sautéed with soy sauce and sake) is regularly served, and sea urchins are often on the menu.

Tanji Rua dos Estudantes 166, Liberdade. The speciality here is sushi, although how attractively it's presented depends on the cook's general mood. The fish, however, is always extremely fresh. Evenings only; closed Wed.

Viêtnam Rua da Glória 224, Liberdade. More Chinese than Vietnamese, but still pretty good for a country where Vietnamese food is virtually unknown. Tues–Sun dinner only.

Yamaga Rua Tomás Gonzaga 66, Liberdade. Small and mainly attracting Japanese diners; an excellent meal here will cost around $12 a head with a choice from a wide-ranging Japanese menu.

Middle Eastern

In general, Middle Eastern restaurants in São Paulo are extremely reliable and excellent value, catering both to the city's substantial Arab community and to non-Arabs alike. Almost all serve Lebanese or Syrian food, typically a large variety of small dishes of stuffed vegetables, salads, pastries, pulses, minced meat, spicy sausages and chicken, with a strong emphasis on meat in individual dishes.

Agadir Rua Fradique Coutinho 950, Vila Madalena. Unique in São Paulo, this restaurant serves Moroccan food – in this case entirely based on couscous, served with a good choice of chicken, lamb, beef or vegetable stews or tagines. Quite simple but pleasant; expect to pay around $10 per person. Tues–Sat dinner, Sun lunch only.

Al Kaukab Rua Com. Abdo Schahin 130, Centro. A meeting point for the local Arab community, this lively restaurant serves excellent and cheap food, and outsiders are always made to feel welcome.

Arabe Rua Com. Abdo Schahin 102, Centro. Crowded at lunchtime with Lebanese diners, for the rest of the day this inexpensive restaurant mainly sees elderly men who live in this traditionally Arab neighbourhood spending hours dawdling

over their coffees or mint tea.

Arábia Rua Haddock Lobo 1397, Cerqueira César. Excellent Middle Eastern fare, with an emphasis on Lebanese cuisine, served in very pleasant and spacious suroundings. The fixed-price lunch menus are good value and include some unusual vegetarian choices.

Esfiha Chic Rua da Consolação, near the junction with Av. Paulista, Cerqueira César. A good Lebanese restaurant serving delicious, attractively presented food at very low prices and excellent service to match.

Folha de Uva Rua Bela Cintra 1435, Cerqueira César. A combination of fast food and a buffet of Middle Eastern snacks – popular with the lunchtime crowds.

Traditional Brazilian

Apart from *lanchonetes* and *churrascarias* (see opposite), "typical" Brazilian food is surprisingly hard to come by in São Paulo – perhaps because of the immigrant origins of so many of the city's inhabitants. If Brazilians do go out for Brazilian food, they'll often search out restaurants serving Bahian, Minero or other regional food.

Andrade Rua Artur de Azevedo 874, Pinheiros. Moderately priced restaurant (dishes easily serve two people) specializing in northeastern food, in particular *carne do sol* (sun-dried beef) served with pumpkin, sweet potato and mandioca. From 9pm and at Sunday lunch there's live *forró* music.

Bargaço Rua Oscar Freire 1189, Jardim Paulista. A branch of what is considered by many to be Salvador's best Bahian restaurant. Certainly the food here is excellent, with the varied menu concentrating on seafood dishes. Upmarket, yet reasonably priced. Closed Mon lunch.

Bolinha Av. Cidade Jardim 53, Jardim Europa. Traditionally *feijoada* is served throughout Brazil only on Wednesdays and Saturdays, but here it's the house staple every day, served as a *rodízio* along with *farofa*, rice, sliced oranges and other trimmings. Either opt for the traditional *feijoada* – complete with ear, nose, trotter and bacon – or the leaner "*feijoa* lite". Moderate.

Capim Santo Rua Arapiraca 152, Vila Madalena. Excellent and moderately priced food served in an attractive setting. The lunch buffet is a great way to sample at will the highlights of Bahian food, and in the evening the à la carte offerings provide a similarly wide choice of dishes. On fine summer evenings sit outside in the very attractive garden. Tues–Sat lunch and dinner, Sun lunch only.

Consulado Mineiro Praça Benedito Calixto 74, Pinheiros. Inexpensive (around $7 per person) restaurant serving authentically hearty *mineiro* food, extremely popular on weekends when the square hosts an antique and crafts market. Closed Sun and Mon evenings.

Deli & Cia Rua Tabapua 716, Itaim Bibi. Although this busy restaurant has a varied a la carte menu, you're best off opting for the buffet for variety and value (salads, meat, fish, pasta dishes), while the special *feijoada* buffet on Saturday is not to be missed. Outstanding value and friendly service. Mon–Sat lunch only.

Dona Lucinha Rua Bela Cintra 2325, Jardim Paulista. The best *mineiro* food that you're likely to taste in São Paulo is served at this branch of the highly regarded *Don Lucinha* in Belo Horizonte (see p.177). Begin with one of the many *cachaças* before sampling a huge range of typical, and more unusual, vegetable and meat dishes and desserts that make up the excellent value fixed-price buffet. Tues–Sat lunch and dinner, Sun lunch only.

Espírito Capixaba Rua Francisco Leitão 57, Pinheiros. Unique in the city, this restaurant specializes in food from the usually overlooked state of Espírito Santo. Lots of seafood dishes are on offer, most notably distinctive *moquecas* (fish stews) cooked in tomato sauce, rather than coconut milk as in Bahia. Around $13 per person.

O Profeta Alameda dos Aicás 40, Indianópolis. Authentic, and fairly inexpensive, food from Minas Gerais. The extensive buffet includes over thirty different dishes.

Santa Gula Rua Fidalga 340, Vila Madalena. Brazilian food with French and Italian influences. The food is generally excellent (and always expensive), but it's the exotic decor that will hold the attention. Tues–Sat lunch and dinner, Sun lunch only.

Templo da Bahia Alameda Campinas 720, Jardim Paulista. Hugely popular Bahian restaurant with beautifully presented – and extremely tasty – dishes. If you're new to Bahian food, choose one of the many *moquecas* (stews) or try the Festival do Templo, a large platter of seafood and tasty street food such as *acarajé* (fried bean cakes) and *bolinhos de bacalhau* (small cod pastries). Expect to pay around $25 for a meal for two people.

Tia Carly Alameda Ribeirão Preto 492, Bela Vista. Excellent *paulistano* home-style cooking at very cheap prices, with *feijoadas* served on Wed and Sat. Closed Sun evening.

Tucupy Rua Bela Cintra 1551, Jardins. If you don't make it to the Amazon, this is your opportunity to try the food of the state of Pará, including distinctive fish and duck dishes. Helpful waiters take you through the menu, which is extremely unusual for São Paulo. Closed Mon.

Churrasco

Beef in a bewildering variety of cuts is the centre of any **churrasco** (barbecue), but lamb, chicken, pork and even fish are also usually served, along with huge salads.

Baby Beef Rubaiyat Av. Brigadeiro Faria Lima 2954, Itaim Bibi ☎11/3849-9488. Airy, modern surroundings and meat of the highest quality has helped to make this a firm favourite of the city's more upmarket *churrascarias*. The menu is bewildering, but if in doubt choose the house speciality – the exceptionally tender baby beef, sourced from the restaurant's own ranch. An excellent *feijoada* is served on Wednesdays and Saturdays when it's advisable to reserve a table.

Costela de Ripa Rua João Cachoeira 298, Itaim Bibi. Beef ribs are the speciality of this unpretentious and reasonably priced *churrascaria*. Closed Sun evening.

Dinho's Place Alameda Santos 45, Paraíso. One of the city's oldest *churrascarias*, distinctive because of its Wednesday and Saturday *feijoada* buffets, where the ingredients are cooked and served separately; fairly expensive but consistently high quality.

Esplanada Grill Rua Haddock Lobo 1682, Jardins. This elegant and expensive place is one of the best *churrascarias* in the city – the thinly sliced *picanha* (rump) steak is outstanding.

Fogo de Chão Av. Moreira Guimarães 964, Moema. A bit of a trek, but this authentic *gaúcho*-style *churrascaria* – a branch of a Porto Alegre-based chain – is rated by some to have the best meat in São Paulo. Expect to pay $15–20 per person for a full meal.

Kilu's Grill Rua 15 de Novembro 250, Centro. Just off Praça da República, this *churrascaria* and *por*

kilo restaurant is always packed with local office workers. There's a huge selection of salads, Brazilian stews and other dishes, and, of course, lots of meat – various cuts of beef as well as pork, chicken and fish. Excellent value: expect to spend around $5 per person. Mon–Fri lunch only.

Galeto's Alameda Santos 1112, Jardins. Barbecued chicken is the only meat here, served with salad and *pollenta*. Inexpensive.

Grill da Villa Rua Inácio Pereira da Rocha 422, Vila Madalena. Quality meat and pleasant surroundings in this restaurant, located in one of São Paulo's most fashionable neighborhoods for nightlife. Moderate. Closed Mon–Thurs lunch.

Sujinho-Bisteca d'Ouro Rua da Consolação 2078, Cerqueira César. No-frills *churrascaria* popular with local residents, serving excellent meat at amazingly low prices.

Contemporary Brazilian

A welcome addition to São Paulo's restaurant scene has been the emergence of more modern, often lighter, forms of culinary craft that combine the enormous wealth of exotic Brazilian flavours with traditional Italian, French or Asian styles of cooking. These places tend to be expensive and can be as popular for seeing and being seen as for the actual food.

Cantaloup Rua Manoel Guedes, Itaim Bibi ☎11/3846-6445. Known for simply placing ingredients from the tropics alongside French and Italian ones, always with mouthwatering results. Lush foliage and efficiently friendly service create an intimate atmosphere in this converted warehouse. Fairly expensive but excellent.

Carlota Rua Sergipe 753, Higienópolis ☎11/3661-8670. One of the most successful East Asian/Italian/Brazilian fusions you'll find in São Paulo, thanks to careful selection and matching of ingredients. As reservations are not taken at this elegant restaurant, expect a long wait for a table if you arrive after 9pm. Closed Mon lunch and Sun evening.

Quinta do Museu Av. Brigadeiro Faria Lima 2705, Jardim Europa. Located in the old kitchen and gardens of a 1940s villa that now houses the Museu da Casa Brasileira (see p.597), this is a wonderful place for an al fresco lunch or afternoon tea. The

menu is a successful blend of Brazilian and Italian, much lighter than the standard Italo-Brazilian fare. Tues–Sun noon–6pm.

Santa Gula Rua Fidalga 340, Vila Madalena ☎11/3812-7815. Located in the back garden of an old house, this small restaurant must rate as one of the most beautiful in São Paulo, its style a blend of Mediterranean rustic chic and tropical touches. The menu is a mix of Italian and Brazilian and includes *carne seca* and pumpkin ravioli, creative risottos, grilled meats and delicious mousses made from unusual Brazilian fruit. Fairly expensive, reservations essential. Closed Sun evening and Mon lunch.

Tribeca Rua Jerônimo da Veiga 163, Itaim Bibi. Choose from a small but carefully thought-out menu that's strong on fish and vegetables, with Thai hints and Brazilian ingredients (for example, *madioca* rather than potato puree). The appealing dining room has a light and airy ambience.

French

French restaurants are often excellent but always expensive – expect to pay at least $30 a head, and possibly even double that amount.

La Casserole Largo do Arouche 346, Centro ☎11/3331-6283. An old favourite for a romantic evening out, with ever-reliable – though fairly expensive – classic French food. Closed Sat lunch and Mon.

L'Arnaque Rua Oscar Freire 518, Cerqueira César. Interesting, but not always successful, French-Brazilian *nouvelle cuisine*. Pleasant surroundings attract a trendy clientele; the fixed-priced menu is good value, but still not for the budget-conscious.

Le Coq Hardy Rua Jerônimo da Veiga 461, Itaim Bibi ☎ 11/3079-3344. Arguably São Paulo's best traditional French restaurant, and almost certainly its most expensive. The food is well prepared and rich in a very old fashioned way – as far removed from *nouvelle cuisine* as you can get. On weekdays there's a comparatively good-value ($15) *executivo* menu. Closed Mon.

Le Vin Bistro Alameda Tietê 184, Jardim Paulista. Simple but attractively presented food, particularly good as a light lunch.
Roanne Rua Henrique Martins 631, Jardim Paulista. *Nouvelle cuisine* of a high standard in this relaxed, yet sophisticated French restaurant. Closed Sat lunch and Sun.

Italian

With so many immigrants from Italy, it's hardly surprising that the city has a huge number of Italian restaurants, ranging from family-run *cantinas* and pizzerias to elegant, expensive establishments. For the most part, São Paulo's Italian restaurateurs are the children or grandchildren of immigrants, and have adapted their mainly northern recipes to suit Brazilian tastes and the availability of ingredients. São Paulo's "Little Italy", the Bixiga *barrio*, is good for a fun night out, with countless inexpensive cantinas, but the food there is nothing special, and you'll find better fare elsewhere in the city.

Bricola Alameda Gabriel Monteiro da Silva 1040, Cerqueira César. Pretty courtyard restaurant serving a simple, low-priced menu.
Famiglia Mancini Rua Avanhandava 81, Centro. Fun atmosphere, especially late at night when it's crowded with young people. Long queues for a table are common (reservations aren't accepted), though the food is rather mediocre apart from the fabulous *por kilo* antipasto buffet. If you want a hot meal, there's a very good choice of pasta dishes, all of which easily feed two people. Inexpensive.
Fasano Rua Taiarana 78, Cerqueira César ☎ 11/3062-4000. Often rated as the best Italian restaurant in São Paulo, this elegant (and very expensive – expect to pay over $50 per person) restaurant is a place to go to for very special occasions. Renowned for its fine ingredients and unusual vinegar marinades, interesting pastas and simple but delicious vegetable and meat dishes.
Gero Rua Haddock Lobo 1629, Cerqueira César ☎ 11/3064-0005. With the same owners as *Fasano* (see above), this relaxed restaurant has a smaller menu but it's still very good. The food is more moderately priced than other places like it (but still expect to pay at least $25 per person), the diners rather trendy.

Gigetto Rua Avanhandava 63, Centro. Just off Rua Augusta on a road lined with several other Italian restaurants, this one is always crowded with Brazilian families. The food's excellent and very inexpensive.
Jardim de Napoli Rua Dr Martinico Prado 463, Higienópolis. A simple *cantina* where some of São Paulo's best Italian food is served at very reasonable prices.
La Locandeira Rua Dr Mário Ferraz 465, Itaim Bibi. A varied menu, but it's the fine pasta dishes that stand out in this modestly priced, lunchtime-only restaurant, sited in one of the city's most exclusive shopping districts.
Massimo Alameda Santos 1826, Cerqueira César ☎ 11/3284-0311. Unusual among São Paulo's Italian restaurants for exploring the diversity of Italy's regional cooking. The pasta and polenta dishes are reliable and the main courses – such as roast lamb or suckling pig – can be excellent. Fairly expensive, but the atmosphere is relaxed.
Pasta e Vino Rua Barão de Capanema, Cerqueira César. The pasta and other Italian dishes served here are adequate, but what makes this moderately priced restaurant something of a godsend is that it's open 24 hours.

Jewish

São Paulo has by far the largest Jewish population in Brazil and while community life has traditionally been centred on downtown in Bom Retiro, today it's the *bairro* of Higienópolis that has the greatest concentration of residents. There are a few Jewish restaurants here, all very authentic.

Cecília Rua Tinhorão 122, Higienópolis. The restaurant serves authentic, moderately priced (about $12 per peron) Polish Jewish dishes and on weekends a Central European version of *feijoada* made with white beans, beef and potato. Tues–Fri

& Sun lunch only; Sat lunch and dinner; closed Mon.
Sara Rua da Graça 32, Bom Retiro. Busy café/snack bar serving Eastern European food to a largely Jewish clientele who still do business in

this once predominantly Jewish neighbourhood. Mon–Fri 11am–7pm, Sat & Sun 11am–3pm.
Shoshi Delishop Rua Correia de Melo 206, Bom Retiro. Eastern European Jewish food (such as *gefilte fish* and ox-tongue accompanied by buckwheat) and dishes incorporating contemporary Italian-Brazilian touches (such as salmon risotto) Mon–Fri 8am–5pm, Sat 9am–3pm, Sun 10am–4pm.

Z-Deli Alameda Lorena 1214, Cerqueira César. People who live or work in this trendy neighbourhood come to this small Jewish deli for gefilte fish, falafel, cheesecake and more. Two other branches operate with the same hours: Alameda Lorena 1449, Cerqueira César; Alameda Gabriel Monteiro da Silva 1350, Jardim Paulistano. Mon–Fri 9am–6.30pm, Sat 9am–4pm.

Portuguese

Considering the size and overall importance of the Portuguese community in São Paulo, there are surprisingly few Portuguese restaurants, and you get what you pay for: if it's cheap, it tends not to be very good.

Antiquarius Alameda Lorena 1884, Jardim Paulista ☎11/3064-8686. Excellent – but very expensive – Portuguese food and wine. The seafood is especially good, but the rustic nature of many Portuguese dishes sits uncomfortably with the formal, not to say gaudy, surroundings. Closed Mon lunch & Sun evening.
Presidente Rua Visconde de Parnaíba 2424, Brás.

Very good food, reasonably priced, in an area that once had a large Portuguese community. Closes daily at 9.30pm and all day Sun; open on Sat for dinner only.
O Rei do Bacalhau Av. Brigadeiro Faria Lima 2174, Pinheiros. An up-scale Portuguese restaurant specializing in cod dishes; expect to pay upwards of $20 per person. Closed Mon.

Other European

Restaurants specializing in German food are especially popular places to go for a few drinks, and while the food tends to be cheap – you'll eat heartily for around $6 per person – they are generally unimaginative in their range of dishes, with menus usually based on pork, potatoes and sauerkraut.

Acrópoles Rua da Graça 364, Bom Retiro. Long-established, popular and inexpensive restaurant serving traditional Greek food. Evenings only.
Alt Nürnberg Av. João Carlos da Silva Borges 543, Santo Amaro. São Paulo's swankiest German restaurant; though the menu is pork-based, there's a wide range of accompanying dishes. Closed Sat lunch and Sun.
Bierquelle Av. Professor Papini 169, Interlagos. A cosy place serving German and Swiss dishes – try their delicious fried, grated potato with apple sauce.
Centro Brasileiro Britânico at Rua Ferreira de Araújo 741, Pinheiros. There's no modern British cooking here to match the centre's forward-looking British design; instead you'll find an excellent value ($7 per person) buffet of mainly Brazilian and Italian dishes, and traditional British dishes a la carte, such as Irish stew and shepherd's pie.

Mon–Fri lunch; evening opening hours vary, call ☎11/2029-0508.
Don Curro Rua Alves Guimarães 230, Pinheiros. This large and longstanding Spanish restaurant serves excellent *paellas* (serving two or three people) and seafood, including octopus and squid. Expensive.
Juca Alemão Rua Min. José Galotti 134, Brooklin Paulista. Plain German food – heavy on sausages and potato salad – of the kind that's strangely popular amongst Brazilians. Cheap, with a following of mainly young people drawn more by the beer than the food.
Mediterraneo Rua Girassol 67, Vila Madalena. Attractively presented dishes influenced by cuisines from throughout the Mediterranean, catering to a trendy clientele, as befits this newly fashionable part of town. Closed Sat & Sun evening, and Mon.

Seafood

São Paulo's close proximity to the coast makes seafood an excellent option though, as is often the case, it tends to be rather expensive. The following places specialize in seafood, although Japanese, Portuguese and Bahian restaurants are generally strong on fish too.

Amadeus Rua Haddock Lobo 807, Cerqueiro César ℡ 11/3061-2859. The best and probably the most expensive seafood in the city. The oysters are especially good, but all the prawn and fish dishes can also be relied on. Expect to pay over $40 per person.

Crab Rua Wisard 193, Vila Madalena. As the name suggests, this moderately priced restaurant specialises in only one ingredient but, depending on availability, different types of crabs are served, all creatively prepared and presented. Tues–Fri dinner only, Sat lunch and dinner, Sun lunch only.

Mr Fish Grill Alameda Lorena 1430, Cerqueiro César. Simply prepared but extremely fresh fish served with a choice of sauces and accompaniments. Somewhat sterile atmosphere, but prices are reasonable – around $15 per person.

Vegetarian

There's nowhere easier in Brazil to be vegetarian than in São Paulo: barring *churrascarias*, most restaurants offer non-meat dishes. Most of the following specifically vegetarian restaurants are very inexpensive, and have an unusually varied selection of dishes that extends beyond brown rice and beans.

Apfel Rua Barão de Itapetinga 207 (1st floor), Centro. The excellent vegetarian buffet features both hot and cold dishes at around $3 per person. Mon–Fri lunch only.

Cheiro Verde Rua Peixoto Gomide 1413, Jardim Paulista. Comfortable and fairly sophisticated vegetarian restaurant serving excellent and inexpensive fare. The simple menu changes with the season.

Da Fiorella Rua Bernardino de Campos 294, Brooklin Paulista. Vegetarian Italian restaurant whose staple dish is a delicious cold tomato, herb and mozzarella sauce served over hot pasta. Closed Sun evening and Mon.

Lótus Rua Brigadeiro Tobias 420, Luz. Inexpensive vegetarian *por kilo* restaurant with a mainly Chinese menu, well located for the nearby cultural centres. Closed Sun evening.

Mel Rua Araújo 75, Centro, and also Av. Brigadeiro Faria Lima 1138, Jardim Europa. One of the best places for an inexpensive lunch downtown. The menu is only half vegetarian – fish and chicken are also served. Mon–Fri lunch only.

Namesa Rua Consolação 2967, Jardins. Well-presented health food, strong on fresh vegetables, salads and fruit. An excellent place to stop by for a light meal, snack or juice. Closed Sun evening & Sat.

Sativa Rua Consolação 3140, Jardins. Very comfortable place with reasonably priced food, and one of the few vegetarian restaurants that serves beer.

Bars, nightlife and entertainment

Whether you're after "high culture", live music, a disco or just a bar to hang out in, you won't have much of a problem in São Paulo. The city has four main centres for nightlife: **Bixiga**, with good bars and live music; **Jardins**, with some good neighbourhood bars; **Itaim Bibi** and **Vila Olímpia**, together best known for their flashy nightclubs; and **Vila Madalena** and adjoining **Pinheiros**, which have a trendier, slightly alternative scene. Some suggestions are detailed below, but for the full picture of what's on, consult the weekly *Veja*, the daily *Folha de São Paulo* (especially its Friday *Noite Ilustrada* supplement) or the *Guia Internet São Paulo* website (Ⓦwww.guiasp.com.br). Places come and go in São Paulo continually and so on-the-spot advice is vital. Bear in mind that it's often difficult to draw neat distinctions between bars, live music venues and clubs.

São Paulo has a large gay population but, with some exceptions, clubs and bars tend to be mixed rather than specifically gay, with the scene mainly in the Jardins area.

Bars

The bars that you'll find scattered throughout the city depend largely upon the neighbourhoods that they're in for their character. Some of the liveliest, often with live music, are found around Rua 13 de Maio in Bixiga (Bela Vista), and in fashionable Vila Madalena and Pinheiros.

All Black Irish Pub Rua Oscar Freire 163, Jardins. A swish and very successful Irish-theme pub serving expensive Irish and European beers (plus affordable Brazilian lagers), a range of Irish whiskeys and bar food that extends from Irish to Thai. Especially popular on Tues, Thurs and Fri when the pub hosts live modern Brazilian music.

All of Jazz Rua João Cachoeira 1366, Vila Madalena. Nice intimate place with excellent live jazz.

Astor Rua Delfina 163, Vila Madalena. This well-established bar is one of the neighbourhood's trendiest meeting points. Excellent beer and *petiscos* (snacks) make this is a good place to start or end a night out in Vila Madalena.

Balcão corner of Alameda Tietê and Rua Melo Alves, Cerqueira César. Pleasant neighbourhood bar attracting well-heeled trendies.

Bar Brahma Av. São João 677 (at the corner with Avenida Ipiranga), Centro. Opened in 1948, this is one of the city's oldest bars. Once a haunt for musicians, intellectuals and politicians, it draws a post-theatre crowd to the bar and insomniacs to its 24-hour café.

Bar do Sacha Rua Original 45, Pinheiros. Open from noon and located on a hill with a pleasant garden, this is a particularly pleasant place to come for a drink on a sunny day.

Barnaldo Lucrecia Rua Abilio Soares 207, Paraíso. An instantly recognizable yellow house, this place attracts a young crowd. Especially lively on Fridays, and live music most evenings.

Cachaçaria Paulista Rua Mourato Coelho 593, Pinheiros. A great place for sampling *cachaça*: there are over 200 kinds here and it's open from 6pm until the last customer leaves.

Café do Bixiga Rua 13 de Maio 76, Bela Vista. Excellent *chopp* and a carefully nurtured Bohemian atmosphere are the main attractions here – a good place to stop for a post-theatre drink.

Café Piu-Piu Rua 13 de Maio 134, Bela Vista. Although the bar has a nice neighbourhood feel to it, the wide range of Brazilian music – including live samba, MPB and jazz – draws a mixed crowd into the early hours of the morning.

Charles Edward Av. Pres. Juscelino Kubitschek 1426, Itaim Bibi. Renowned as something of a meat market, this bar is popular with people in their 30s and 40s; often features live music and dancing.

Fidalga Rua Fidalga 32, Jardins. Besides live jazz and Brazilian music during the week, this cosy club also has its own small bookstore.

Finnegan's Alameda Itú 1529, Jardins, and Rua Cristiano Viana 358, Pinheiros. Both branches of this Irish-theme bar are busy late into the evening (it's almost always impossible to get a table), and often feature live blues and jazz. Hugely popular with English-speaking residents.

Morro de São Paulo Rua Leopoldo Couto de Magalhães 928, Itaim Bibi. Attracts the young and beautiful who flaunt themselves under palm-thatched roofs. Live MPB and bursts of *axê* (a Bahian variant of samba) help to create a permanent festive atmosphere.

Pirajá Av. Brigadeiro Faria Lima 64, Pinheiros. Trendy and attractive "traditional"-looking bar serving tasty Spanish-style tapas.

Poets Corner Centro Brasileiro Britânico, Rua Ferreira de Araújo 741, Pinheiros. Popular amongst older Brits with nostalgia for eccentric opening hours (last orders at 11pm) and warm English and Irish beers (though ice-cold Brazilian lager is also served). Closed Sun.

Ritz Alameda Franca 1088, Cerqueira César. During the day a quiet restaurant serving hamburgers and sandwiches, at night a lively bar for young people, popular with the gay crowd.

Quinta do Mandioca Rua Oscar Freire, Jardim Paulista. This rustic bar and café opens out somewhat incongruously onto one of São Paulo's most chic shopping streets. The menu features good snacks (including fired mandioca) and light meals.

Live music and dancing

São Paulo has quite an imaginative **jazz** tradition. The *Bourbon Street Music Club*, Rua dos Chanés 127, Moema, has a consistently good, though very expensive (entrance is $17), programme including visiting international artists and frequent festivals. Fashionable Vila Madalena has several jazz venues, probably the best being *Blen Blen Brasil* (see under "Discos and clubs"), though check in advance as diverse musical styles are on offer here throughout the week – often *forró*, popular Brazilian music. In Bixiga, the *Café Piu-Piu* (closed Mon), at Rua 13 de Maio 134, is a lively venue for some very good jazz and *choro*, as well as the most appalling rock and country-and-western music.

If it's more obviously **Brazilian music** that you're seeking, check the newspaper entertainment listings for touring artists or, for something slightly adventurous, you could go to a **gafieira**, a dance hall where working-class and Bohemian chic meet. A *gafieira* that's always packed to the rafters with migrants from the Northeast dancing to *forró* is *Pedro Sertanejo*, Rua Catumbi 183, Brás (Sat 9pm–4am, Sun 8pm–midnight). Be warned that *gafieiras* tend to be out of the centre in poor neighbourhoods. Very much community gatherings, these *gafieiras* can seem rather alien and disconcerting places if you've only just arrived in Brazil, but in no time you'll be made to feel welcome. The *Avenida Club*, Av. Pedroso de Morães, Pinheiros, is the best-known place in São Paulo for **formal dancing** – everything from ballroom to samba, *forró* and *merenque*. To discover how the *lambada* should really be danced, try the *Som de Cristal* at Rua Rego Freitas 470, Centro. Regular performances of Brazilian folk, popular and New Wave music are given at the Centro Cultural de São Paulo, at Rua Vergueiro 1000 (by the Vergueiro *metrô* station), and are either free or charge only a modest admission fee. If you're around on a weekend night, one of the most enjoyable outings is to the *Clube do Choro*, held in Jardim América (at Rua João Moura, between Rua Artur Azevedo and Rua Teodoro Sampaio); the street is closed off, a stage erected and tables and chairs put out so that you can sit and listen to some excellent music. There's a small cover charge and food and drink are available, too.

Discos and clubs

A Lanterna Rua Fidalga 531, Vila Madalena. A fun place to drop by, attracting a youthful crowd. The house band plays music from the 1960s to the 1980s. Open 6pm–2am; closed Mon.

BCBG Rua Tabapuã 1410, Itaim Bibi. One of São Paulo's chicest club venues – very expensive and smart – where the city's beautiful people congregate. Techno music. Wed–Sat 10pm–5am.

Blen Blen Brasil Rua Inácio Pereira da Rocha 520, Vila Madalena. Besides being a nice place for a drink and a jazz venue, this fashionable, yet not overly trendy, club has several dance floors with a constantly changing mix of everything from techno to *forró* to MPB. Open daily 7pm–late.

Brancaleone Rua Luís Murat 298, Vila Madalena. One of the trendiest dance places in São Paulo, attracting a young and suitably stylish crowd. The music is eclectic and you can also get a remarkably good Italian meal here. Open 8.30pm till late; closed Sun.

Carioca Club Rua Cardeal Arcoverde 2899, Pinheiros. Live samba, *pagode* and MPB bands interspersed with a house DJ playing a range of Brazilian disco sounds. Attracts a good mix of the over-20s. Mon–Sat 10pm–4am.

Clube Massivo Alameda Itú 1548, Jardins. Open from midnight onwards, this is a shrine to the sounds of the 1970s.

Dado Bier Av. Juscelino Kubitschek 1203, Itaim

Bibi. Arrive for an early evening drink (the club boasts one of the city's few micro-breweries), stay for dinner (pizza or sushi), check out the art gallery, and then dance to techno, ska and rock music until dawn. Mon–Fri 6pm–late, Sat 8pm–late.

Diesel B.A.S.E. Av. Brigadeiro Luis Antonio 1137, Bela Vista. A hugely popular venue drawing a predominantly gay and lesbian crowd with house and techno music. Sat only, 11.30pm–7am.

Ipis Club Rua Padre Garcia Velho 63, Pinheiros. Large modern club with some great DJs and occasional live music – one of the most popular gay and lesbian hangouts in the city. Thurs–Sat 11pm–5am; Sun 7pm–3am.

Lov.E Club Rua Pequetita 189, Vila Olímpia. A mixed club playing techno and trance. Decent Italian food and breakfast is served here, too. Tues–Fri midnight–6am, Sat midnight–10am.

Muzik Rua da Consolação 3032, Jardim Paulista. Huge disco playing a mixed bag of '70s disco and house, overwhelmingly popular with young gay men. 11pm to dawn.

Nostro 2000 Rua da Consolação 2554, Jardins. A mainly gay venue, the most popular night being Sunday from 6pm until midnight.

Rubi Rua Bandeira Paulista 742, Itaim Bibi. Relax in the lounge area of this small club or dance to house and techno. Tues–Sat 9pm until the last client leaves.

Cinema, theatre and classical music

In general, **films** arrive in São Paulo simultaneously with their release in North America and Europe, and are subtitled rather than dubbed. Charging around $4, most cinemas are on Avenida Paulista, but there are also several downtown on Avenida São Luís. All the shopping centres (see below) have cinema complexes and show the latest blockbusters. Keep a special eye out for what's on at CineSesc, Rua Augusta 2075 (Cerqueira César); Bixiga, Rua 13 de Maio (Bixiga); Espaço Unibanco de Cinema, Rua Augusta 1475 (Cerqueira César); and the Centro Cultural de São Paulo, Rua Vergueiro 1000, by the Vergueiro *metrô* station – all of which are devoted to Brazilian and foreign art films. Arthouse films are also shown at the Belas-Artes at Rua da Consolação 2423, on the corner of Avenida Paulista.

São Paulo is Brazil's theatrical centre and boasts a busy season of classical and avant-garde productions; a visit to the **theatre** is worthwhile even without a knowledge of Portuguese. Seats are extremely cheap, available from **ticket offices** that have details of all current productions: Casa do Espectador, Rua Sete de Abril 127, Centro (Mon–Fri 10am–6pm); and Vá ao Teatro, Shopping Ibirapuera, Moema (Mon–Fri 9am–9pm, Sat 9am–3pm). The Brasileiro de Comédia, Rua Major Diorgo 311, and the Teatro Sérgio Cardoso, Rua Rui Barbosa, both in Bixiga, have particularly good reputations.

The traditional focal point for São Paulo's vibrant **opera** and **classical music** season is the Teatro Municipal (☎11/222-8698; see also p.591), in Praça Ramos de Azevado in the city centre, where, in the 1920s, Villa-Lobos himself performed. As an operatic and classical music centre, São Paulo has always been less important than Rio, but now Brazilian and foreign performers divide their time between the two cities. The beautifully renovated Estação Júlio Prestes (☎11/3337-5414; see also p.592) in the *bairro* of Luz is the home of the world-class Orquestra Sinfônica do Estado de São Paulo and has a new 1500-seat concert hall. Many of São Paulo's churches have free **recitals**, most notably the beautiful Gregorian chant at the Basílica de São Bento, Largo de São Bento, every Sunday at 10am.

Shopping

São Paulo's **shopping** possibilities are as varied as the city's restaurants and, for *paulistanos* with the means, as important an activity. In the wealthy southwestern Jardins suburb, shops are far more impressive than those in just about any other Brazilian city, and the quality way above par. Even if you're not intent on a spree, the shopping centres and stores are worth a tour to experience the opulent surroundings. And there's a fine selection of **markets**, too, where you can pick up a decently priced souvenir or two and some good food.

The widest selection of Brazilian **music** shops in the city can be found in the Galeria do Rock at Av. São João 439, Centro. A more limited, but still good, range of CDs are sold at FNAC Centro Cultural at Av. Pedroso de Moraes 858, Pinheiros. For secondhand Brazilian records try Sebo do Disco, Rua Lisboa 45, Jardim América, while for Brazilian musicians of the 1940s and 1950s, try Grandes Galerias, a down-at-heel shopping centre at Rua 24 de Maio, just behind the Teatro Municipal. Casa Amadeus at Av. Ipiranga 1129, near Praça da República, has a good selection of Brazilian sheet music, percussion and stringed instruments.

By far the best **bookshops** in São Paulo are Cultura in the Conjunto Nacional building, Av. Paulista 2073 at the intersection of Rua Augusta, Cerqueira César (Mon–Sat 10am–7pm) and FNAC Centro Cultural (see above; 10am–10pm). Both have a good selection of English-language titles and high-quality Brazilian art and other coffee-table books. Livraria Corrêa do Lago, Rua João Cachoeira 267, Itaim Bibi, has what is probably Brazil's most extensive collection of antiquarian and out-of-print books for sale.

Shopping centres

São Paulo's shopping centres – air-conditioned temples to hedonism – are hugely popular amongst the city's middle classes as places to escape to, where they can feel utterly insulated from their less fortunate fellow citizens. Each centre tries to outdo the other, with mirrored walls and ostentatious fountains – you won't feel closer to North America than this during your stay in Brazil. All the shopping centres are open Monday–Saturday 10am–10pm, and Sunday after lunch to around 7pm.

Eldorado Av. Rebouças 3970, Pinheiros (bus from Praça da República). Rather downmarket, but nevertheless vast and with one of the largest ranges of shops.

Ibirapuera Av. Ibirapuera 3103, Moema (bus from *metrô* Ana Rosa, or Praça da República). Plush shopping centre in an upmarket residential area.

Iguatemi Av. Brigadeiro Faria Lima 1191, Jardim Europa (bus from Av. Ipiranga or trolley along Rua Augusta). The oldest of the city's many shopping centres – and constantly being remodelled and relaunched.

Morumbi Av. Roque Petroni Jr 1089, Morumbi (bus from *metrô* Ana Rosa). Shopping centre serving one of the city's wealthiest neighbourhoods, with a huge recreation area and, by shopping mall standards, gourmet restaurants.

Patio Higienópolis Av. Higienópolis 615 (bus from Praça da República or Av. Paulista). A glass and wrought-iron building, considered to be the most exclusive of the city's shopping centres. Features lots of top-end boutiques and an above-average food hall.

Shopping Light corner of Rua Xavier de Toledo and the Viaduto do Chá, Centro. The newest shopping centre and, while quite small, boasts the best collection of shops downtown.

Downtown shopping

The main shopping streets in the centre of the city are near **Praça da República**, especially the roads running off Avenida Ipiranga: Rua Barão de Itapetinga, Rua 24 de Maio, Rua do Arouche and, between them, Rua Dom José de Barros. Most of the stores around here sell clothes, but you'll rarely find the latest fashions. One particularly curious shopping area can be found on Rua São Caetano, opposite the Parque da Luz, where over a hundred shops sell everything that you could possibly need for a wedding.

In recent years, the downtown area has been characterized by the huge number of street traders who have taken over the pavements. Their presence has become a major issue in the city, with regular calls to clamp down on their activities.

Cerqueira César and the Jardins

South of Avenida Paulista is where the money is, and where all the best stores are. There are lots of boutiques selling clothes and accessories of Brazilian, European and US designers, especially in the streets running parallel to and crossing Rua Augusta, most notably Rua Oscar Freire, Alameda Lorena, Rua Haddock Lobo, Rua Bela Cintra and Rua Dr Melo Alves. Although expensive, prices compare well to Europe and the US, even for imports. There are no obvious "**souvenirs**" of São Paulo, but the following places are worth checking out for unusual Brazilian items:

Arte-India (FUNAI), Rua Augusta 1371, Cerqueira César. Basketwork, pottery, necklaces and feather handicrafts made by Indians, sold at fair prices and authenticity guaranteed.

Casa Santa Luzia Alameda Lorena 1471, Jardim Paulista. An amazing gourmet supermarket – the perfect place to stock up if you're staying in an apartment hotel in the area. Otherwise, a good source of luxury Brazilian food items – preserves, wines and liquors – to take home. Open until late.

Galeria Arte Brasileira Alameda Lorena 2163, Jardim Paulista. A mix of tacky souvenirs and well-chosen handicrafts from throughout Brazil, especially the Amazon and the northeast.

Galeria Brasiliana Rua Artur de Azevedo 520, Jardim America. Popular Brazilian art – not cheap, but of excellent quality, with the pieces made by top craftspeople.

Kabuletê Rua Dr Melo Alves, Cerqueira César. An excellent choice of unique – but expensive – Brazilian crafts drawn from throughout the country.

O Bode Rua Bela Cintra 2009, Cerqueira César. Carefully selected handicrafts from throughout Brazil, including items from the state of São Paulo.

Markets

There's lots of choice here, from handicrafts to flowers, and one – the Mercado Municipal – that ranks as one of the best **markets** in Brazil. The different *bairros* also have their own markets.

Antiguidades do MASP Museu de Arte de São Paulo (MASP), Av. Paulista 1578 (Sun 10am–5pm). A fun place to browse, but don't expect to find much worth buying.

Antiguidades e Artes Praça Benedito Calixto, Pinheiros (Sat & Sun 9am–5pm). You may pick up the odd bargain here; cheaper, livelier and with a larger collection of bric-a-brac than the similar market beneath MASP (see above). There are also some good restaurants around the square and food stalls in the market itself.

Antiguidades e Artesanato do Bixiga Praça Dom Orione, Bela Vista (Sun 9am–6pm). A flea market with little worth purchasing, but lots of local atmosphere.

Feira Oriental Praça da Liberdade, Liberdade (Sun 10am–7pm). Japanese-Brazilian handicraft stalls are now few and far between, but Japanese horticulturalists still sell house plants here and the market includes some good stalls selling Japanese meals and snacks – usually prepared and sold by kimono-clad Afro-Brazilians.

Mercado de Flores Largo de Arouche, Centro. A dazzling daily display of flowers (8am–4pm).

Mercado Municipal Rua da Cantareira 306, Centro (Mon–Sat 4am–4pm; see also p.591). About the most fantastic array of fruit, vegetables, herbs, meat, fish and dairy produce that you're likely to find anywhere in Brazil. Very cheap and often excellent meals and sandwiches are also available.

República das Artes Av. Ipiranga, Centro (Sun 9am–4pm). Amongst the tack, there are some interesting handicrafts and semiprecious gems in this vast tented street market located near Praça da República, between Av. São Luís and Rua da Consolação.

Listings

Airlines Aerolíneas Argentinas ☎ 11/3214-4233 & 6445-3806; Air Canada ☎ 11/3259-9066; Air France ☎ 11/3049-0900 & 6445-2211; Alitalia ☎ 11/3218-7600 & 6445-2324; American Airlines ☎ 11/3214-4000 & 6445-3234; British Airways ☎ 11/3145-9700 & 6445-2021; Continental ☎ 0800-554-777 & 11/6445-4188; Delta ☎ 0800-221-121 and 11/6445-4153; GOL ☎ 0800-701-2131 and 11/4331-6885; Iberia ☎ 11/3218-7130 & 6445-2060; Japan Airlines (JAL) ☎ 11/3251-5222; KLM ☎ 11/3457-3230 & 6445-2887; Lan Chile ☎ 11/3259-2900 & 6445-3532; Lloyd Aéreo Boliviano ☎ 11/3258-8111 & 6445-2425; Lufthansa ☎ 11/3048-5800 & 6445-2220; Pluna ☎ 11/3231-2822 & 6445-2130; Qantas ☎ 11/3145-9700; SAS ☎ 11/3259-4300 & 6445-3934; South African Airways ☎ 11/3065-5115 & 6445-4151; Swiss ☎ 11/3251-4000 & 6445-2535; TAM ☎ 0800-123-100; TAP ☎ 11/3255-5366 & 6445-3215; United Airlines ☎ 0800-162-323 & 11/6445-3039; Varig ☎ 11/5091-7000; VASP ☎ 11/5532-3838.

Airports Flight information: Congonhas ☎ 11/5090-9000 & 5090-9191; Guarulhos ☎ 11/6445-2945.

Banks and exchange Branches are scattered throughout the city, but are concentrated along Av. Paulista, Av. Brigadeiro Faria Lima and Rua 15 de

Novembro. Remember that between 10pm and 6am only the equivalent of $20 can be withdrawn from ATMs. If you need to change cash at weekends, ask your hotel or try the souvenir shops and jewellers in Liberdade, the Japanese *bairro*.

Car rental Avis, Rua da Consolação 335, Centro ☎0800/118-066; Hertz, Rua da Consolação 439, Centro ☎0800/147-300; Localiza, Rua da Consolação 419, Centro ☎0800/312-121; Unidas, Rua da Consolação 347, Centro ☎0800/121-121.

Consulates Argentina, Av. Paulista 1106, 9th floor Cerqueira César ☎11/3284-1355; Australia, Rua Tenente Negrão 140, 12th floor, Chácara Itaim ☎11/3829-6281; Bolivia, Rua da Consolação 37, 3rd floor, Centro ☎11/881-1688; Canada, Av. Paulista 1106, 1st floor, Cerqueira César ☎11/3253-4944; Chile, Av. Paulista 1009, 10th floor, Cerqueira César ☎11/3284-2044; Colombia, Rua Peixoto Gomide 996, 10th floor, Cerqueira César ☎11/3285-6350; Ireland, Av. Paulista 2006, 5th floor, Cerqueira César ☎11/3287-6362; New Zealand, Al. Campinas, 15th floor, Cerqueira César ☎11/3148-0616; Paraguay, Rua Bandeira Paulista 600, 15th floor, Itaim Bibi ☎11/3020-1412; Peru, Rua Votuverava 350, Morumbi ☎11/3870-1793; South Africa, Av. Paulista 1754, 12th floor, Cerqueira César, ☎11/3285-0433; UK, Rua Ferreira de Araújo 741, Pinheros ☎11/3094-2700; Uruguay, Al. Santos 905, 10th floor, Cerqueira César ☎11/3284-0998; US, Rua Padre João Manoel 933, Jardim Paulista ☎11/3081-6511; Venezuela, Rua Veneza 878, Jardim Europa ☎11/3087-2318.

Cultural institutes Being Brazil's economic capital (and arguably its cultural capital), São Paulo has a vast number of privately and publically supported cultural centres and institutes, with exhibition spaces, cinemas and theatres often boasting first-rate programmes. Many of these are discussed in the Guide, but in addition the activities of the following overseas-based institutes may be of interest: Alliance Française, Rua Gen. Jardim 182, Vila Buarque ☎11/3259-8211; Cultura Inglesa, Rua Ferreira de Araújo 741, Pinheros ☎11/3222-3866; Goethe Institut, Rua Lisboa 974, Pinheiros ☎11/280-4288; Instituto Italiano de Cultura, Rua Frei Caneca 1071, Bela Vista ☎11/3285-6933; União Cultural Brasil–Estados Unidos, Rua Cel. Oscar Porto 208, Paraíso ☎11/3885-1022.

Dress Business travellers in particular will notice a very different dress code in São Paulo than in Brazilian cities to the north. For men, suits and ties are pretty much the order of the day though jackets tend to be carried rather than worn. Evenings are as informal as anywhere else in Brazil and even in top restaurants people lean firmly towards the casual. Nightlife, too, follows the Brazilian pattern of casual dress – even the trendiest clubs don't base entry on this.

Football There are three First Division teams based in São Paulo: Corinthians, who play at Parque São Jorge (Rua São Jorge 777; *metrô* Bresser and bus #278A); São Paulo, at Morumbi Stadium (*metrô* Ana Rosa and bus #775P; or bus #775P from Av. Paulista); and Palmeiras, at Palestra Itália (Parque Antártica; bus #208A or #208C from Av. São João). Matches are generally held on Wed and Sat.

Health matters The private Albert Einstein Clinic, Av. Albert Einstein 627, Morumbi (☎11/3747-1233) is considered to be the best hospital in Brazil. For dentistry, Dental Office Augusta, Rua Augusta 878, Cerqueira César (☎11/256-3104), or, open 24 hours, Consultorio Dentario, Av. 9 de Julho 3446, Jardins (☎11/3062-0904), are both expensive, but have good reputations.

Internet Almost all hotels offer Internet access to their guests. Internet cafés are surprisingly few and far between in São Paulo, but FNAC Centro Cultural (the city's best book and music store) at Av. Pedroso de Moraes 858, Pinheiros has terminals and is open 10am–10pm.

Laundry There are very few self-service laundries in São Paulo and it is expensive to have your hotel wash your clothes. Conveniently located self-service places are at Alameda Tietê 96, near the intersection with Rua Augusta, Cerqueira César and at Alameda Joaquim Eugenio Lima 1696, Cerqueira César.

Newspapers and magazines Most newspaper kiosks downtown and in Jardins sell English-language newspapers: the *Financial Times*, *Miami Herald* and *International Herald Tribune* are the most widely available. Haddock Lobo Books and Magazines, Rua Haddock Lobo 1503, Cerqueira César (open until midnight), has a particularly good selection of European magazines and newspapers, as do Jardim Europa, corner of Av. Europa and Rua Groenlândia (open 24hr) and FNAC Centro Cultural at Av. Pedroso de Moraes 858, Pinheiros, open 10am–10pm.

Police Emergencies ☎190. DEATUR, a special police unit for tourists (☎11/3214-0209), is located at Av. São Luís 91, one block from Praça da República. To extend your visa, visit the Polícia Federal, Av. Prestes Maia 700, Centro (Mon–Fri 10am–4pm; ☎11/3223-7177 ext 231).

Post office The main post office is downtown on Praça Correio, at the corner of Av. São João, and is open 8am–10pm. Yellow-coloured postal kiosks are scattered throughout the city, including several along Av. Paulista.

Public holidays In addition to the normal
Brazilian public holidays (see p.47), most things
close in São Paulo on January 25 (Founding of the
City) and on Ash Wednesday.

Telephones TELESP (the state telephone company) have a 24-hour office on Rua Sete de Abril
(just off Praça da República).

Around São Paulo

What only a few years ago were clearly identifiable small towns or villages have
since become swallowed up by Greater São Paulo. Despite the traffic, however, escaping from the city is surprisingly easy, and there are even some points
on the coast that can make good day-trips (see p.621).

Embu

Founded in 1554, **EMBU** was a mere village before São Paulo's explosive
growth in the twentieth century. Located just 27km west of the city, Embu has
now effectively merged with its massive neighbour, and yet, surprisingly, it has
managed to retain its colonial feel. Quaint buildings predominate in the town's
compact centre, which is traffic-free on weekends and makes for a pleasant and
easy day trip.

In the 1970s, Embu was a popular retreat for writers and artists from São
Paulo, many of whom eventually set up home here. Today, the **handicraft
market** (9am–6pm) in the main square, Largo 21 de Abril, every Saturday and
Sunday, makes the town a favourite with *paulistano* day-trippers, although during the week Embu is far quieter. The shops around the main square stock a
similar selection to what's on offer in the market – pseudo-antiques, rustic furniture, ceramics, leather items, jewellery and homemade jams – but they are
open daily. Nearby, on Largo dos Jesuítas, the basic structure of the eighteenth-
century **Igreja Matriz Nossa Senhora do Rosário** is typical colonial
Baroque, but its interior retains almost no original features. Attached to the
church is the **Museu de Arte Sacra dos Jesuítas** (Tues–Fri 1–5pm, Sat &
Sun 10am–5pm), with an interesting collection of eighteenth-century religious
artefacts. Otherwise, you might as well sit down and eat at one of several
restaurants on Largo 21 de Abril and along the adjoining streets: *Patacão* at
Rua Joaquim Santana 90 is a particularly good place to sample traditional
regional cooking, rare in the city of São Paulo itself, or try *Orixás* at Rua Nossa
Senhora do Rosário 60 for excellent Afro-Brazilian cooking. There's a well-
organized **tourist information** office on Largo 21 de Abril (9am–5.30pm;
☎11/4704-5333).

It takes less than an hour to get to Embu from São Paulo; catch the "Embu
Cultural" **bus** (every 30min) from outside the Tietê Rodoviária.

Paranapiacaba

For most of its history, communications from São Paulo to the outside world
were slow and difficult. In 1856 the British-owned São Paulo Railway
Company was awarded the concession to operate a rail line between Santos
and Jundaí, 70km north of São Paulo city, in what was then a developing cof-
fee-growing region. The 139-kilometre line was completed in 1867, remaining under British control until 1947. Overcoming the near-vertical incline of
the Serra do Mar that separates the interior of the state from the coast, the line
was an engineering miracle and is slowly being restored today.

PARANAPIACABA, 40km southeast of São Paulo and the last station
before the rack railway plunges down the coastal escarpment, was the admin-

istrative and engineering centre for the rail line and at one time was home to four thousand workers, many of them British. Neatly laid out in the 1890s in a grid pattern, the village has remained largely unchanged over the years. All that remains of the original train station is the clock tower, said to be a replica of London's Big Ben, but the workers' cottages, locomotive sheds (which house old British-built carriages and steam engines) and funicular cable station are in an excellent state of preservation, and some are open to the public. On a hilltop overlooking the village is the wooden Victorian-style Castelinho: once the residence of the chief engineer, today the building houses the **Centro Preservação da História de Paranapiacaba** (Tues–Sun 9am–3.30pm), which displays old maps and photographs of the rail line's early years.

You don't have to be a railway buff to appreciate Paranapiacaba, however. The village is set amidst one of the best preserved areas of Mata Atlântica in the country and most visitors use it as a starting place for fairly serious hikes into the thickly forested **Parque Estadual da Serra do Mar**, notable for its amazing orchids and bromelias. Employing a guide is strongly advised as trails are unmarked, often very narrow and generally hard going, and poisonous snakes are common. There's an office of the association of licensed guides as you enter the settlement from the station; expect to pay around $20 for a day and bring food, drink and sturdy footwear. The weather in this region is particularly unreliable but, as a general rule, if it's cloudy in São Paulo you can count on there being rain in Paranapiacaba.

Getting to Paranapiacaba is easy. Take a train from São Paulo's Luz station to Rio Grande da Serra (every 15min; 45min; 45¢), where, if you're lucky, there'll be a connecting service continuing the two stops to Paranapiacaba. If there's no train, take a bus from outside the station (35¢), or a taxi (about $3). Most visitors return to São Paulo the same day, but guides can point you towards villagers who charge around $8 per person for simple bed and breakfast accommodation.

The state of São Paulo

Away from the city, the state's main attraction is its coastline. **Santos**, Brazil's leading port, retains many links with the past, and many of the **beaches** stretching north and south from the city are stunning, particularly around **Ubatuba**. The towns and cities of the state's **interior** are not so great an attraction – the rolling countryside is largely devoted to vast orange groves and fields of soya and sugar. Good-quality roads run through this region, including major routes to the Mato Grosso and Brasília.

The interior

Although there's not much to detain you inland from São Paulo, **Americana** and **Santa Bárbara d'Oeste** do have traces of Confederate history, while more recent Dutch immigrant arrivals have had a far greater impact on nearby **Holambra**. Further into the interior is coffee country, where it's possible to visit some old *fazenda* houses. To escape the summer heat, the resort of **Campos do Jordão**, northeast of the city, offers some attractive hill scenery and plenty of walking possibilities.

Campinas

One hundred kilometres northwest of São Paulo is **CAMPINAS**, in relative decline compared to its neighbour since the nineteenth century when it was by far the more important of the two cities. It started life as a sugar plantation centre, produced coffee from 1870 and later made its money as a centre for agricultural processing and, more recently, high-tech industry and education. An attractive city, with a reasonably compact centre, it doesn't offer many reasons for visiting, though it's interesting enough to take a tour around Largo do Rosário, with its **Catedral**, inaugurated in 1883. A few blocks southwest of here – around the train station – is the **Vila Industrial**, rows of small houses built for the city's new working class in the late nineteenth century. Better known is **Unicamp**, the Universidade Estadual de São Paulo, 13km from the city centre. The university was founded in 1969 on land belonging to Colonel Zeferino Vaz and, during the worst years of military terror, became – thanks to the protection afforded by Vaz – a refuge for left-wing teachers who would otherwise have been imprisoned or forced into exile. Unicamp rapidly acquired an international reputation and today is widely considered to be Brazil's best university, though you're only likely to visit on academic business as the campus is architecturally unremarkable.

With a student population of 100,000, Campinas has a reasonably lively cultural life, centred on the **Centro de Convivência Cultural**, at Praça Imprensa Fluminense in the centre. Aside from a theatre and art galleries, the center is home to the fine Orquestra Sinfonia. To the south of the *praça*, the **museums** dedicated to folklore, history, Indian and natural history (Tues–Sat 9–10.50am & 1–5pm, Sun 9am–noon & 1–5pm) in the **Bosque dos Jequitbás** contain little of interest, though the park itself is a pleasant place to while away an hour or two.

If you have a car, one of the most interesting places to visit near Campinas is the **Fazenda Monte d'Este**, 12km from town, just off the SP-340 (the road leading to Holambra). Built during the nineteenth-century coffee boom, the beautiful *fazenda* house is open to the public and contains a small museum outlining the development of the area's former coffee-based economy. A tour of the place, which lasts 1hr 30min, costs $9, or $30 including an excellent lunch (bookings essential on ☎ 19/3257-1236).

Practicalities

Campinas is a major transport hub, and there are **buses** from the city to most places in the state and many beyond. The highway to São Paulo itself is one of Brazil's best, and the hourly buses take an hour and a quarter. The **rodoviária** in Campinas is at Rua Barão de Itapura, a twenty-minute walk from the city centre down Rua Saldanha Marinho. There are also several daily **trains** between Campinas and São Paulo's Estação da Luz, though they take around twenty minutes longer than the bus.

With São Paulo so close you won't necessarily need to stay in Campinas, but there is plenty of centrally located **accommodation**: the *Royal Palm Tower* at Praça Carlos Gomes (☎ 19/3731-5900, ⓦ www.royalpalmhoteis.com.br; ❺) is a very comfortable, newly built business hotel, while the *Ermitage* at Av.

Francisco Gilcério 641 (☎19/3234-7688, Ⓦwww.ermitage.com.br; ❹) and the *Opala Barão* at Rua Barão de Jaguara 1136 (☎19/3232-4999, Ⓦwww.hoteisopala.com.br; ❸) are cheaper but perfectly decent. There is no shortage of **places to eat** in town. The three branches of *Giovanetti* in Praça Carlos Gomes and Largo do Rosário are popular student hangouts selling drinks and excellent sandwiches. *Cenat*, at Rua Barão de Jaguara 1260, serves excellent vegetarian food; *Trattoria Tevere* (owned by a Unicamp philosophy professor), Av. Coronel Silva Teles 439, has good Italian dishes; the *Steiner Bar do Alemão* at Av. Benjamim Constant 1969 offers reasonable German food and cold beer amidst a sometimes raucous atmosphere; the *Santa Gertrudis* at Rua Olavo Bilac 54 is the city's best *churrascaria*; excellent Japanese food is served at the *Restaurante Taka* in the *Hotel Vitória* at Av. José de Souza Campos 425; and the *Éden*, Rua Barão de Jaguara 1224, is just a large hall serving huge portions of cheap, plain Brazilian food.

Americana and Santa Bárbara d'Oeste

Although there are perhaps as many as 100,000 Brazilians of Confederate descent, there are few obvious signs of this in the two towns most associated with them. **AMERICANA**, an hour beyond Campinas, is a bustling city of about 180,000 people, but there are only 25 English-speaking families. If curiosity does bring you here, the **rodoviária** is just a short walk from the centre of town; walk across the bridge in front of the station and keep straight on for about ten minutes. On the main square, Praça Comendador Muller, you'll find the simple but adequate **hotel** *Cacique* (no phone; ❶), and for a bit more comfort there's the *Nacional* at Rua Washington Luís 399 (☎19/3461-8210, Ⓦwww.hotelnacionalamericana.com.br; ❷), and the *Florença Palace*, Av. Cillos 820 (☎19/3461-6393, Ⓦwww.hotelflorenca.com.br; ❸). For **food** there are plenty of *lanchonetes*, as well as a very good *churrascaria*, the *Cristal*, at Av. Fortunato Faraoni 613. But apart from the odd Confederate emblem, don't expect much to do with the South.

Santa Bárbara d'Oeste

Thirteen kilometres west of Americana, **SANTA BÁRBARA D'OESTE** has more Confederate ties. Much the smaller of the two, it has about thirty families of Confederate origin, most of whom still speak English with more than a touch of Dixie in their voice. Near the main square, a short walk from the *rodoviária*, the excellent **Museu da Imigração** (Tues–Sat 10am–10pm, Sun 10am–10pm) has displays relating to the history of the Confederates in the area, and that of other nationalities, chiefly Italian. About 10km from town, the **Cemitério do Campo** is a cool and shaded cemetery on a hill overlooking endless fields of sugar cane. It dates back to 1910 and all the tombstones, as well as the monument commemorating the Confederate immigrants, bear English inscriptions. There's a small chapel here, too, and a picnic area where, four times a year (the second Sunday of January, April, July and October) around 250 members of the Fraternidade Descendência Americana arrive from throughout Brazil to renew old ties. The cemetery is very isolated and can only be reached by car: a taxi will charge around $15 to take you there, and will wait for you while you look around. However, as not all taxi drivers know exactly where the cemetery is, ask the museum attendant to order a taxi for you and give your driver precise directions.

As for **accommodation** in Santa Bárbara, there's only one hotel, the very simple *Municipal* (no phone; ❷), right by the *rodoviária*, and just one **restaurant**,

Confederates in Sao Paulo

In the face of humiliation, military defeat and economic devastation, thousands of former American **Confederates** resolved to "reconstruct" themselves in often distant parts of the world, forcing a wave of emigration without precedent in the history of the United States. Brazil rapidly established itself as one of the main destinations, offering cheap land, a climate suited to familiar crops, political and economic stability, religious freedom and – more sinisterly – the possibility of continued slave ownership. Just how many Confederates came is unclear: suggested numbers vary between 2000 and 20,000, and they settled all over Brazil, though it was in São Paulo that they had the greatest impact. Although Iguape, on the state's southern stretch of coast, had a large Confederate population, the most concentrated area of settlement was the Santa Bárbara colony, in the area around present-day **Americana** and **Santa Bárbara d'Oeste**.

The region's climate and soil were ideally suited to the growing of **cotton** and the Confederates' expertise soon made Santa Bárbara one of Brazil's biggest producers of the crop. As demand for Brazilian cotton gradually declined, many of the immigrants switched to **sugar cane**, which remains the area's staple crop, though others, unable to adapt, moved into São Paulo city or returned to the United States.

the *Bela Mesa*, at Rua General Osório 676, which serves both standard Brazilian food and pasta dishes.

Holambra

Some 40km northeast of Americana is the small town of **HOLAMBRA**, established in the nineteenth century by settlers from the Netherlands and retaining to this day a great deal of its Dutch character. Attracted by the rich farming opportunities of the São Paulo region, many Dutch emigrated here in the post-World War II years, spurred on by disastrous flooding in their own country. Their numbers were further boosted by Dutch departing from newly independent Indonesia. The settlement of Holambra (its name is a contraction of Holândia, América and Brasil) was created by the arriving migrants, who bought a large, fertile *fazenda* and farmed co-operatively, while the new arrivals established their own farms, specializing – predictably – in the cultivation of flowers. Today's residents like to boast that their prosperity is based on the work ethic that the immigrants brought with them. There may be something in this, but without the substantial financial investments from the Netherlands, Holambra would probably have foundered like so many foreign agricultural schemes in Brazil.

Holambra maintains a strong Dutch character, despite the arrival of non-Dutch migrants attracted by the town's growing prosperity. To boost sales of its agricultural products and flowers (Holambra is responsible for 35 percent of flowers produced commercially in Brazil), Holambra has been keen to play up its Dutch origins, and the urban centre can best be described as Dutch kitsch. Most people get around by bicycle, many of the buildings have Dutch-style facades, and gardens are neatly tended and filled with flowers, while the public telephone stands are in the ludicrous shape of a giant wooden clog. The highlight of the year here is **Expoflora**, the annual spring flower festival, which takes place on most weekends throughout September; the event attracts not only commercial buyers but also ordinary individuals drawn by the colourful displays, Dutch folk dancing, musical shows and food.

Practicalities

Holambra is located 40km north of Campinas at the km 141 turn-off of the SP-340 Campinas to Moji-Mirim road. There are hourly bus services between Holambra and Campinas and several buses day from São Paulo. One of the main reasons to visit is the **restaurants**. The best choice in town is *Warong* on Rua Campo de Pouso 607, the only restaurant in Brazil specializing in the spicy food of Indonesia. The excellent *Confeitaria Martin Holandesa*, Rua Doria Vasconcelos 15, serves up tea and cakes, while for meals that are more traditionally Dutch try the *Clube Holambra* at Alameda Mourício de Nassau 894, a *por kilo* restaurant (weekends only) or *Old Dutch* (closed all Mon and Sun evening), 1.5km from the centre of town at Fazenda Ribeirão. There are several good **hotels**, the most attractive being *Lago do Holandês* (☎ & ℻ 19/3820-1781; ❸), which also serves Dutch food, on the outskirts of town at Av. das Tulipas 245; at no. 57 on the same avenue is the simpler but more central *Hotel Sheller* (☎ 19/3820-1329; ❷).

Fazenda do Pinhal

During the late-nineteenth-century coffee boom, the interior of the state of São Paulo was synonymous with coffee, with the area around **SÃO CARLOS**, today a bustling university city 150km northwest of Americana, a particularly important producer of the commodity. Today the farms around the city are largely given over to sugar cane and oranges, and little evidence remains of the area's coffee-producing past. However, the **Fazenda do Pinhal**, one of the oldest surviving and amongst the best-preserved rural estates in the state of São Paulo, is well worth a visit. It's an easy day trip from either Americana or Campinas, but you'll need your own transport. The *fazenda* is located off the SP-310 highway: at km 227 take the exit for Riberão Bonito and then turn immediately onto the much smaller Estrada da Broa. After about 4km you'll see a sign marking the *fazenda's* entrance. It's essential to call in advance (☎ 16/272-7142); the entrance charge, including an excellent two-hour tour, is $20 – a fixed fee for either a large group or an individual.

The *casa grande*, the main house, was built in 1831 and, typical of the period, was modelled after the large, comfortable Portuguese city dwellings of the eighteenth century. Although the house was enlarged and renovated several times over the following century, its basic structure and appearance have remained much the same, and it retains its original furnishings. For its first few decades, Pinhal's main source of income was cattle raising, and it only switched to coffee in the late nineteenth century; the large *terreiro*, or terrace for drying coffee beans, is evidence of this. There are numerous outbuildings, including *senzalas* (slave quarters), warehouses and a simple, but very pretty, chapel.

It's not possible to stay at the Fazenda do Pinhal, but 47km to the northwest at SP-310 km 274, just outside Araraquara, there's another *fazenda*, which, although architecturally not nearly as important as the Fazenda do Pinhal, has been developed into a superb **hotel**, the *Fazenda Salto Grande* (☎ 16/222-4169, ⓦ www.hotelfazendasaltogrande.com.br; ❻ full board). Developed as a coffee plantation in the late nineteenth century, the main house and outbuildings of the estate now form the basis of a luxury hotel, which offers two swimming pools, horse riding, very comfortable rooms and excellent country cooking.

Campos do Jordão

When temperatures plunge to 15°C, São Paulo's citizens generally shiver and reach for their mothballed woollens. But to experience something approaching genuine cold weather they have to head into the highlands. East of the city, in the direction of Rio, is the **Serra da Mantiqueira**, which boasts the lively winter resort of **CAMPOS DO JORDÃO**, 1628m above sea level. Founded by the British in the late nineteenth century, the town lies on the floor of a valley, littered with countless hotels and private houses resembling English country houses and Swiss chalets, and divided into three sections: **Abernéssia**, the older commercial centre and location of the *rodoviária*; and, a fifteen-minute bus ride away, **Juaguaribe** and **Capivari**, where most of the boutiques, restaurants and hotels are concentrated.

The novelty of donning sweaters and legwarmers draws the crowds, who spend their days filling in the time before nightfall when they can light their fires. Nevertheless, it also makes perfect sense to come here in the winter when day-time temperatures are typically very pleasant, the sky clear and the **trails** dry. Although in the summer the altitude offers some relief from the searing heat of the coast, the often heavy rains can make walking unpleasant, if not treacherous.

In all directions from Capivari there are good walks, and the trails are well signposted. **Horse riding** is also possible with treks lasting between 30 minutes ($5) and four hours ($25) and taking in hilltop view points and pine forests; your hotel or the tourist information office will be able to provide information. Much of the land has been stripped of forest cover to make way for cattle pasture, but in the higher reaches you'll still come across remains of the graceful *araucária* (Paraná pine) trees that once dominated the natural vegetation hereabouts. For a good **view** over Campos do Jordão and the surrounding Paraíba valley, take the **ski lift** from near the small boating lake in the centre of Capivari: it whisks you up to the **Morro do Elefante**, where you can hire horses.

Practicalities

A very helpful tourist information office, located by the town gate on the main road (SP-123) leading into Campos do Jordão, has maps of the resort and outlying areas and can advise you on room availability. Despite there being dozens of **hotels**, finding a room is difficult, and finding an affordable one – at any rate during the winter months of June and especially July – can be impossible. One of the more reasonable places is the small and pleasant *Pousada Recanto do Sossego*, Praça Benedito Albino Rodrigues (☎12/262-4224; ❸), in Abernéssia. Otherwise, you're best off walking along the tree-lined Avenida Macedo Soares (Capivari), where many of the cheaper, but still comfortable, hotels are located, including the *Casa São José* at no. 827 (☎012/262-8206; ❸), and the *Nevada* at no. 27 (☎012/262-3735; ❸). Before accepting a room, check that it has an electric fire as even on warm summer days it can get quite chilly at night. Also in Capivari there's a small **youth hostel**, *Elis Regina II* (☎012/263-2732; $8 a night), at Rua Benigno Ribeiro 320, but at weekends it's often fully booked. One of Campos de Jordão's more appealing hotels, the *Duas Quedos Park*, Rua Manoel Ribeiro de Toledo 255, Vila Britânia (☎012/262-2492; ❺), is situated in a beautiful park with waterfalls nearby; the hotel also rents simple chalets that sleep six to eight people for $50–90 per chalet. Another attractive place, the *Villa Capivary*, Av. Victor Godinho 131 (☎012/263-1746, ⓦwww.capivari.com.br; ❼ full board), is a very comfortable Swiss chalet-style hotel in Capivari.

The choice of **restaurants** is comparatively limited as most people eat in their hotels, but you won't go hungry since there are several fairly expensive pseudo-Swiss restaurants: try *Só Queijo*, Av. Macedo Soares 642, or the *Matterhorn*, Rua Djalma Forjaz 10, both in Capivari. Also in Capivari, the *Bia*

Kaffee, Rua Professora Isola Orsi 33, is a very good and reasonably priced German restaurant serving full meals, teas and coffee. **Nightlife** is very much hotel-oriented, but people also congregate around the splendidly kitsch "medieval" shopping arcade in Capivari, drinking hot mulled wine at the top of the arcade's tower or – for a really big evening out – watching the electronic thermometer.

The coast

Despite its proximity to the city, most of the four hundred kilometres of São Paulo's **coast** have until recently been overlooked by sun and beach fiends in favour of more glamorous Rio. Although this situation is changing all too fast, the area becoming a victim of uncontrolled development, this part of the coast still offers great contrasts, ranging from long, wide stretches of sand at the edge of a coastal plain, to idyllic-looking coves beneath a mountainous backdrop. Having the use of a car is an advantage for exploring the more isolated, less spoilt, beaches (p.613 and p.130 for car rental addresses in São Paulo and Rio). Southwest of Santos, however, tourism has still to take hold, in part because the roads aren't as good, but also because the beaches simply aren't as beautiful.

Santos

SANTOS, one of Portugal's first New World settlements, was founded in 1535, a few kilometres east of São Vicente. The city stands on an island, its port facilities and old town facing landwards with ships approaching by a narrow, but deep, channel. In a dilapidated kind of way, the compact centre retains a certain charm that has not yet been extinguished by the development of an enormous port complex.

Arriving in Santos and getting oriented couldn't be easier. The **rodoviária**, at Praça dos Andradas, is within easy walking distance of the Centro, on the north side of the island: from it, walk across the square to Rua XV de Novembro, one of the main commercial streets. One block on, turn left at **Rua do Comércio**, along which you'll find the remains of some of Santos' most distinguished buildings. Although only the facades remain of some of the nineteenth-century former **merchants' houses** that line the street, they are gradually being restored, the elaborate tiling and wrought-iron balconies offering a hint of the old town's lost grandeur. At the end of Rua do Comércio is the **train station**, built between 1860 and 1867, and, while the city's claim that the station is an exact replica of London's Victoria is a bit difficult to swallow, it is true that the building wouldn't look too out of place in a British town. Next to the station in Largo Marquês de Monte Alegre is the **Igreja de Santo Antônio do Valongo** (Mon–Sat 8am–noon and 2–6pm, Sun 8am–7pm), built in 1641 in colonial Baroque style but with its interior greatly altered over the following centuries; few of its original features remain. Back on Rua XV de Novembro, at no. 95, is the former **Bolsa de Café** (Tues–Sat 9am–5pm, Sun 10am–5pm), where coffee prices were fixed and the quality of the beans assessed; the building retains its original fixtures, but is now an exhibition centre charting the history of the coffee trade. And at the end of the street is another Baroque building, the **Convento do Carmo** (Tues–Sat 9am–7pm and Sun 8–11am) again seventeenth-century in facade only.

Across town from Centro on the south side of the island, twenty minutes by bus from Praça Mauá by Rua do Comércio, are Santos' **beaches**. They're huge, stretching around the Atlantic-facing Baía de Santos, and are attractive in a rather brash kind of way. The problem, though, is that while the beaches themselves are kept tidy the water is of doubtful cleanliness, so it's best to stick to the sands.

Practicalities

Coming from São Paulo, be sure to remember that buses to Santos leave from the Jabaquara Rodoviária and not from Tietê. In Santos, there are **tourist offices** at the *rodoviária* in Centro, and at the corner of Avenida Ana Costa and the seafront Avenida Presidente Wilson in Gonzaga, but their opening hours are very haphazard. **Banks** in Santos, concentrated around Praça da República in Centro and on Rua XV de Novembro, all have ATMs and many change dollars.

Hotels in Santos are concentrated in **Gonzaga**, a *bairro* of apartment buildings, restaurants and bars alongside the beach, facing the Baía de Santos. Good places include the simple but very pleasant *Pousada do Marquês*, Av. Floriano Peixoto 202 (☎13/3237-1951; ❷); the comfortable *Gonzaga*, at Av. Presidente Wilson 36 (☎13/3244-1411; ❷); the once grand, but now slightly rundown, *Avenida Palace* (☎013/3289-3555, ⓦwww.avenidapalace.com.br; ❸) at Av. Presidente Wilson 10; the *Ritz*, set back at Av. Marechal Deodoro 24 (☎13/3284-1171; ❸); and the *Parque Balneário* (☎13/3289-5700, ⓦwww .parquebalneario.com.br; ❻) at Av. Ana Costa 555, a luxurious high-rise hotel with a pool. There are some reasonable seafood **restaurants** in Centro: try *Café Paulista* at Praça Rui Barbosa 8, or *Rocky* at Praça dos Andradas 5. Otherwise most restaurants are in Gonzaga: for reliable Japanese food, there's *Tike* at Rua Bahia 93 (closed Tues and Sun evening), or for good Portuguese food there's *Último Gole* at Rua Carlos Afonseca 214. For souvenir hunters, the most distinctive local items are embroideries, made by the descendants of immigrants who came to Santos in the late nineteenth century from the Portuguese island of Madeira. The best source for these is the Unidade Regional de Produção do Morro de São Bento, Largo do São Bento 120, near the Igreja do Valongo in Centro (☎013/3222-2211).

Guarujá, Boiçucanga and Maresias

GUARUJÁ is São Paulo's most popular beach resort, very commercialized and usually crowded. Getting there is easy: there are half-hourly buses from the city's Jabaquara Rodoviária that take little more than an hour to travel the 85km to the resort. From Santos, take a bus from Gonzaga east along the beach avenue to Ponta da Praia, from where a ferry makes the ten-minute crossing of the Santos channel, and then it's a fifteen-minute bus ride on to Guarujá itself. The resort features a set of large apartment buildings alongside lengthy, rather monotonous beaches. In the summer, finding space on the main beach, **Pitangueiras**, can be difficult, and the beaches within walking distance, or a short bus ride, to the northeast are little better. In fact, without a car and considerable local knowledge, Guarujá is best avoided; in any case, finding a reasonably priced **hotel** in the summer can be almost impossible. Your best bet around Praia das Pitangueiras is the small and friendly *Hotel Rio Guarujá* at Rua Rio de Janeiro 131 (☎13/3286-6081; ❷), just a block from the sea, or at the adjoining Praia Guarujá, the *Guarujá Praia*, Praça Brigadeiro Franco Faria Lima 137 (☎13/3286-190; ❸). For a local map, detailed instructions on outlying beaches and hotel information, there's a helpful **tourist office** at Rua Quintino Bocaiúva 248 (Mon–Fri 9am–6pm; ☎13/3387-7199).

From Guarujá's *rodoviária*, buses run east as far as Ubatuba (see p.627), stopping off at points along the way. For much of the first 90km the road passes inland, but approaching **BOIÇUCANGA** it again skirts the coastline, and the landscape grows increasingly mountainous as the forested Serra do Mar sweeps down towards the sea. Set on a large bay fringed by a fine beach, this once quiet resort has fallen victim to the worst excesses of uncontrolled development, and you'll find hastily built holiday homes, *pousadas* and shopping galleries occupying every square meter of land. If you need to stay overnight you won't have any problem finding a *pousada* but, as elsewhere along the coast, summer availability is limited. Two worth trying are the *Casarão* at Rua Apiacás 44 (☎12/3865-1690; ❸) and the *Marambaia* at Rua Itaberaba 534 (☎012/3865-2372, ⓦwww.pousadamarambaia.com.br; ❸); both are small and simple, but have pools. The **tourist office** at Rua Hilário de Mattos (daily 8am–7pm) should be able to point you towards *pousadas* with rooms that are available. The best beach near Boiçucanga is Praia Brava – reachable only by walking along a 2km trail, it remains fairly undeveloped but is often crowded nonetheless.

From Boiçucanga the road rises steeply inland through the Serra do Mar, from which you'll catch the occasional glimpse of the distant ocean through the trees. The road eventually descends into the neighbouring resort of **MARESIAS**, which, though over-developed, is smaller and marginally more pleasant than Boiçucanga. Accommodation here is plentiful and expensive: the *Pousada Brig a Barlavento*, set just 50 metres from the beach at Av. Francisco Loup 1158 (☎12/3865-6527, ⓦwww.brig.com.br; ❹) is a very attractive option with a nicely landscaped garden, a good pool and rooms of varying standards, while 2km from the beach, the *Pousada Pé da Mata*, at Rua Nova Iguaçu 1992 (☎12/3865-5019; ❹) has a pretty forest setting and a nice pool. Alternatively, try the youth hostel at Rua Sebastião Romão César 406 (☎12/3865-6612; $7 per person), though in the summer it's likely to be packed out. Some 10km further on from Maresias is the much quieter and more appealing **Praia Toque–Toque Pequeno**, where there are just a few shops and simple restaurants, while 6km further is **Praia Toque–Toque Grande**, also beautiful and still largely undeveloped.

São Sebastião

Twenty-seven kilometres further northeast is **SÃO SEBASTIÃO**, a bustling little town on the mainland directly opposite the island of Ilhabela (see p.624). Founded in the first years of the seventeenth century, São Sebastião relied on its sugar cane and coffee farms until the eighteenth century, when the town entered a period of decline. Emerging from this stagnation only in the last few decades with the growth of the fishing industry and the development of a large oil refinery, São Sebastião has retained many of its colonial and nineteenth-century buildings. Unlike in other similar towns, these have not been taken over by wealthy city-dwellers, since São Sebastião's beaches, in both directions from the centre, are poor and completely cut off from the open sea by the much more beautiful Ilhabela, directly opposite.

The narrow roads that make up the historic centre allow for pleasant wanderings among the pastel-coloured Portuguese colonial style facades. Praça Major João Fernandes is the heart of São Sebastião and the location of the **Igreja Matriz**, built in 1636 and almost as old as the town (although its interior is twentieth-century plaster). Along the waterfront Rua da Praia (more formally called Avenida Dr Altino Arantes), are innumerable **bars** and unpretentious seafood **restaurants**, where meals cost less than $6. Especially pleasant is the *Gyokai*, with its excellent-value *rodizio* of sushi, tempura and other Japanese standards.

The **tourist office** (daily 8am–10pm; ☎12/3452-1808), located on the waterfront in São Sebastião's visitor centre complex, has information on both the town and the surrounding villages and countryside. It also has a good selection of free maps and can provide details on trails and hotel room availability. The visitor centre itself has some fascinating displays (daily 10am–6pm), including old photographs and scale models that chart the town's development, and handicrafts by Tupí-Guaraní Indians who live in outlying parts of the *município*.

Accommodation

Due to its proximity to Ilhabela, São Sebastião has a good selection of **hotels** and **pousadas**, which have rooms just as nice and considerably cheaper than those on the island. As hotels are usually booked solid during the summer, it's worth booking ahead.

Hotel Beira Mar Rua Expedecionário Brasileiro 258 (no telephone). Very basic accommodation in the centre. The rooms – some of which have attractive sea views – all share bathrooms. ❶

Hotel Porto Grande Av. Guarda Mór Lobo Viana 1440 ☎12/3452-1101. A ten-minute walk from town, this is a pretty, whitewashed colonial-style building, with a pool in park-like gardens that stretch down to the hotel's own beach. Rooms are spacious and well equipped, but even at night there's ample road noise from the adjacent coastal highway. ❹

Hotel Roma Praça Major João Fernandes ☎12/3452-1016. A rather rundown but visually imposing and welcoming 100-year-old hotel on the city's main square. The good range of rooms (sleeping 1 to 4 people either with or without a private bathroom) are all set around an attractive garden. ❷

Pousada Beira da Prainha Av. Vereador Antônio Borges 88 ☎12/3862-6250, ⓦwww

.pousadabeiradaprainha.com.br). Extremely attractive colonial-style building, situated 3km south of town, on a promontory with wonderful views towards Ilhabela. Rooms are well equipped, and amenities include a nice pool on a terrace and a secluded beach a short walk down from the pousada. ❹

Pousada da Ana Doce Rua Expedecionário Brasileiro 196 ☎12/3452-1615, ⓦwww .litoralvirtual.com.br/anadoce). The prettiest, and one of the friendliest, places to stay in the town's historic centre. The small but perfectly adequate rooms are set around a delightful courtyard garden and there's a nice handicraft store. ❸

Pousada da Sesmaria Rua São Gonçalo 190 ☎12/3892-2347, ⓦwww.pousadadasesmaria .com.br). A charming, recently renovated *pousada* with colonial-style furnishings in the town centre. Rooms are small but comfortable and an excellent breakfast is served. ❷

Ilhabela

Without a shadow of a doubt, **Ilhabela** is one of the most beautiful spots on the coast between Santos and Rio, though it's best avoided during the crowded summer tourist season. Of volcanic origin, the island's startling mountainous scenery rises to 1370m and is covered in dense, tropical foliage. With much of the island protected within the boundaries of the **Parque Estadual de Ilhabela**, the dozens of waterfalls, beautiful beaches and azure seas have contributed to the island's popularity; old or new, most of the buildings are in simple Portuguese colonial styles, as far removed from brash Guarujá as you can get. The island is a haunt of São Paulo's rich who maintain large and discreetly located homes on the coast, many with mooring facilities for luxury yachts or with helicopter landing pads. Hotels and *pousadas* are expensive and often fully booked, so many people choose to stay in São Sebastião instead – not a bad idea, since transport connections are good. **Ferries** (24 hr; pedestrians free, cars $4) depart from São Sebastião's waterfront every half an hour and the crossing takes about twenty minutes. If you're driving, be prepared for a long

△ Catedral Metropolitana and fountains, São Paulo

queue for the ferry during the summer unless you book in advance (☎0800-55-5510). The ferry is met by a bus, which goes to **Vila Ilhabela** at the north-western end of the island.

Vila Ilhabela

Almost all of the island's 20,000 inhabitants live along the sheltered western shore, with the small village of **VILA ILHABELA** the main population centre. After about twenty minutes from the ferry landing, look out on the right-hand side of the road for the grand eighteenth-century main house of the **Fazenda Engenho d'Agua**, which is located a few kilometres outside the village. This was one of the largest sugar plantations on the island, famous for its high-quality *cachaça*. Today there's virtually no agricultural production on the island, its economy completely geared to tourism. On the outskirts of the village at Rua Bartolomeu de Gusmão 140, there's a **tourist office** (Mon–Fri 9am–6pm, Sat 10am–4pm; Sun 10am–2pm; ☎12/3896-1091) that produces a very detailed map of the island.

The village, which has a few pretty colonial buildings, is dominated by the **Igreja Matriz**, a little church completed in 1806. Apart from the church, there's little here apart from a branch of Bradesco bank (with an ATM), a few grocery stores, some snack bars and boutiques selling overpriced T-shirts and yachting gear. In the evenings, people congregate on the pier, catching swordfish with remarkable ease.

The rest of the island

Getting around the island can be a problem as the only bus route is along the island's western shore north as far as the lighthouse at Ponta das Canas and south to Porto do Frade – the limits in both directions of good-quality roads. The beaches along this mainland-facing shore are small, but pleasant enough, and the calm waters are popular with windsurfers. Far more attractive are the small beaches in the coves along the northern coast, such as the **Praia do Jabaquara**, but access is difficult, involving clambering down steep trails hidden from view from the road. It's along this stretch of coast that some of the island's most exclusive villas are located, and their owners have an interest in making sure the road remains in bad condition and that the beaches are difficult to reach. The road is also poor along the southern shore, where some of the best beaches are located: after the road ends at Borifos, it's a two-hour walk along an inland trail to the tiny fishing hamlet at **Praia do Bonete**, just beyond which lie a couple of other fine beaches. Along the way you'll pass an impressive waterfall, the **Cachoeira do Late**, beneath which a natural pool has formed.

The entire eastern half of the island falls within the **Parque Estadual da Ilhabela** and, as such, is protected from commercial tourist development. The east coast beaches of the **Baia de Castelhanos**, 25km across the island via a steep mountain road often washed out by heavy rain, have the most surf and are considered by many to be the island's most beautiful. They are linked to one another by cliff-top trails. Seven kilometres along the mountain road, stop at the *Jardim Tropical* (daily 9am–6pm; $1.50, including insect repellent) for a drink and a refreshing shower under a waterfall or a dip in a natural pool. To get any further east, a **jeep** is essential; you can hire one at Locatudo, Av. Princesa Isabel 1634, Praia do Perequê, near the ferry landing (☎12/3472-2468; $50 per day). Alternatively, most hotels and local travel agencies will reserve a place on an all-day tour to the Baia de Castelhanos at around $8 per person.

Practicalities

Throughout the year the island is the most expensive spot on São Paulo's coast, and in the summer it can be difficult to find a **place to stay** – reservations are essential. In Vila Ilhabela the cheapest place to stay is the *Hotel Costa Azul* (☎12/3472-1365; ❸), just to the north of the main commercial area and next to the yacht club at Rua Francisco Gomes da Silva Prado 71. For the price, the hotel provides very basic accommodation, though it's extremely friendly. A little more expensive, more comfortable (rooms sleep 2 to 4) and with a large, pleasant garden leading down to the beach is the *Hotel da Praia* (☎12/3896-1218, ⓦwww.hoteldapraiadeilhabela.com.br; ❹), located at Av. Pedro Paulo de Moraes 578, on the southern outskirts of the village. Nearby on the same street, at no. 151, is the *Hotel Ilhabela* (☎12/272-1083; ❹), completely devoid of character but with large rooms and a good-sized pool. Much prettier, at no. 720, is the *Pousada dos Hibiscos* (☎12/3896-1375; ⓦwww.ilhabela.com.br /pousadadoshibiscos; ❹–❺), also with a pool. For a splurge, there's the *Maison Joly* (☎12/472-2364; ⓦwww.maisonjoly.com.br; ❼–❽), on a hill above the village at Rua Antônio Lisboa Alves 278, with luxurious, but tastefully furnished rooms (all have private terraces with spectacular ocean views), a pool and the island's best restaurant, which is strong on seafood dishes in a mix of Brazilian and French styles. Further south at Saco da Capela, the *Porto Pousada* (☎12/472-2255; ❺) has beautiful rooms with verandas, lush tropical gardens and a pool, while the *Pousada d'Ajuda* (☎12/472-042; ❹) offers more basic accommodation. Near the ferry landing at Praia do Perequê there are a number of hotels, the cheapest of which is the *Hotel Rafimar* (☎12/472-1539; ❸), small but with a pool, and the simple but attractive *Hotel Perequê* (☎12/472-1813; ❸). Inland, an attractive option is the *Pousada Ecológica Recanto da Cachoeira* (☎12/3896-3098, ⓦwww.ecoilha.com.br; ❹), on the edge of the Parque Estadual just off the road leading to the Baia de Castelhanos. The rooms are basic but comfortable, there's also a pool, and the property is entirely surrounded by tropical forest – making a good supply of insect repellant essential.

Ilhabela has several **campsites**, including the *Camping Clube de Ilhabela* at Praia do Perequê and, south of the ferry landing, *Camping Porto Seguro* at Praia Grande. In general, camping on beaches is strictly forbidden, but no one cares if you camp on the virtually uninhabited eastern side of the island.

Eating, like everything else on Ilhabela, is quite expensive. Most restaurants are concentrated in and just south of Vila Ilhabela and at Praia do Perequê. Apart from the excellent and rather elegant seafood restaurant in the *Maison Joly* (see above), the other notable restaurant on the island is *Viana*, just north of the village at Av. Leonardo Reale 1560 (closed Mon–Thurs March–June & Aug–Nov), which also specialises in seafood. When it's time to **move on**, you can take the twice-daily bus to São Paulo from near the pier in the main village of Vila Ilhabela, or from São Sebastião take one of the buses that run along the mainland coast.

Ubatuba and beyond

From São Sebastião, the highway continues along the coast passing frustratingly close to deserted coves of dazzling beauty, with occasional detours through forested areas inland. Buses stop in Caraguatatuba, an extremely ugly sprawling town with a long, gently curving beach alongside the main road, but you're better off carrying on towards **UBATUBA**. The town is only slightly more attractive than Caraguatatuba, but that's of little importance when you consider the local beaches, 72 in all, on islands and curling around inlets.

Ubatuba is centred on Praça 13 de Maio, a couple of blocks from the *rodoviária* on Rua Conceição. On the square there's a very helpful **tourist office** (daily 8am–6pm; ☎12/3832-4255), which supplies maps of the coast and will make hotel reservations for you. Also worth a visit is the local branch of the environmental organisation Projeto Tamar, Rua Antônio Athanásio 273 (daily 10am–noon and 2–6pm), which has display panels (in English and Portuguese) on their work protecting **sea turtles** (mainly loggerheads) that graze offshore, and live turtles on view in pools, too. Otherwise Ubatuba's main urban area has little going for it apart from hotels, rather uninspired bars and restaurants, banks and other services.

As far as **accommodation** goes, Ubatuba makes a good base if you plan to explore the outlying beaches, but the hotels are generally expensive, especially during the summer; they are concentrated in the area around Rua Conceição, towards the beach. On Rua Conceição itself, comfortable and reasonably cheap are the *Parque Atlântico* at no. 185 (☎12/3832-1336; ❸), the *São Nicolau* at no. 213 (☎12/3832-5007; ❸), and the *Xaréu*, around the corner at Rua Jordão Homem da Costa 413 (☎12/3832-1525; ❸). There are plenty of other places to stay in outlying parts of the *município*: a short distance south of Ubatuba are the charming *Pousada da Ana Doce* (☎12/3842-0102; ❸–❹) at Praia do Lázaro and, at Praia das Toninhas, the pretentious but comfy *Pousada das Artes* (☎21/3842-0954; ❹–❺). To the north there are fewer options: try the basic *Pousada Todas as Luas* (☎12/3845-3129; ❸), near Praia Itamambuca, which is surrounded by lush forest, or the even simpler *Pousada da Praia* (☎12/3845-1196; ❸), situated on one of the prettiest beaches, the Praia do Félix. For travellers on tighter budgets, the only alternative is to head for a **campsite** – the nearest to town is the *Sítio Usina Velha* (☎12/3832-3629), some 3km north on the road to Parati, where you can pitch a tent for $5 per night or rent a small cabin (❷). Most **restaurants** are on Avenida Iperoig, which curves alongside the town's beach, the Praia de Iperoig, and you'll find a good variety of seafood, Italian and other types to choose from. For outstanding seafood at low prices, head for *Peixe com Banana* in town at Rua Guarani 255, which specializes in the local dish, *azul-marinho* – essentially fish stewed with green banana.

The beaches

Although there's nothing wrong with the town's **Praia de Iperoig**, Ubatuba is best used as a base from which to visit some of the numerous other beaches accessible by bus or private boat. The least developed – and the most attractive – are to the **northeast** of town, with the furthest, Camburi, 46km away on the border with Rio state. To get to these beaches, take the **local bus** marked "Prumirim" from the *rodoviária* and ask the driver to stop at whichever stretch takes your fancy. One possible point to make for is the Bairro do Picinguaba, a fishing village with a couple of bars and simple restaurants that's set alongside a very pretty beach, and is connected to the main road by a 3km long, narrow winding road.

To the south of town are the more popular beaches, again easily reached by bus from the town centre, although almost all of them are fringed with hastily built condominiums, and shopping and entertainment complexes. **ENSEADA**, 9km from Ubatuba, is lined with beachfront hotels, none of which has rooms for less than $35. Nestled in a bay protected from the lively surf, the beach is popular with families, and in the summer it's always uncomfortably crowded.

Across the bay from Enseada are a series of beautiful isolated beaches that draw fewer people. Walk out of town on the main road for about 2km until you reach **RIBEIRA**, a yachting centre and colourful fishing port. From here, there are trips on sailing boats to the **Ilha Anchieta**, a nearby island where only a few fisherfolk live, or further afield along the coast: these will cost between $10 and $20, depending on the itinerary. Beyond Ribeira are sandy coves that you can reach by clambering down from the trail on the cliff above the sea.

Southwest of Santos

The coastal escarpment **southwest of Santos** begins its incline 20–30km inland from the sea. Lacking the immediate mountain backdrop, and with large stretches of the coast dominated by mangrove swamp, this region was for years left more or less untouched by tourism. However, holiday development companies have been moving in recently, aiming at *paulistanos* who can't afford places further north.

Heading south from Santos, the road follows the coast as far as Peruíbe, then moves inland onto higher, firmer terrain before heading back to the coast down the Serra do Mar. The road is slow but, passing through small fishing villages, banana and sugar plantations and cattle-grazing land, you're reminded that there's more to Brazil than just beaches. Incidentally, from São Paulo, rather than travelling via Santos it's much faster to take a direct bus to Iguape and Cananéia.

Itanhaém

The coastline between Santos and **ITANHAÉM**, 61km south, is, in effect, one long beach which – were it not for the holiday complexes that line the entire stretch – would be unremarkable. Founded in the sixteenth century, the village has a few remaining facades from its early years, most notably the **Convento de Nossa Senhora da Conceição** (daily 9–11am and 1–6pm), a semi-ruined chapel and monastery.

If you do decide to stay overnight, you're likely to have problems finding a **hotel** room in the summer. Most of the people coming on holiday here are lower-middle-class *paulistanos* staying in holiday complexes owned by workers' associations, but there are a few small hotels. The most likely place to find rooms available is the *Hotel Atlântico* (☎13/292-3154; ❸) at Rua Cunha Moreira 68, or failing that, the *Hotel da Barra* (☎13/422-3222; ❸) at Praça 22 de Abril.

Iguape

IGUAPE, roughly two and a half hours further south by bus, was founded in 1538 by the Portuguese to guard against the possibility of Spanish encroachment on the southern fringes of the empire. On the southern tip of the estuarine island of Papagaio, Iguape was well placed as a base for exploring the state's southern interior, up the Rio Ribeira do Iguape. Far from possible markets, however, it was slow to develop and attempts to settle immigrants – most notably Confederate refugees – were met with abject failure. But because Iguape remained a backwater for so long, many of its colonial buildings survive today in good condition. The greatest concentration of these are found around **Largo da Basílica**, Iguape's main square, which is rimmed by white-washed and brightly coloured buildings built in colonial, nineteenth-century and even Art Deco styles.

During the summer, Iguape is popular with *paulistas* seeking a beach vacation away from the sophistication, crowds and expense of resorts further north. The nearest good beach on the mainland is **Barra do Ribeira**, popular with surfers; to get there it's a fifteen-minute boat ride from Iguape, or a twenty-kilometre car ride over rough track. Facing Iguape is another island, the **Ilha Comprida**, 86km long but just 3km wide, with an interior of light forest; an uninterrupted beach stretches the entire Atlantic-facing length of the island. In the summer it gets very crowded near the access road that crosses the island, where ugly urban development is increasing apace, but if you want to be alone just walk south for a few kilometres. A bridge links the island to the mainland, and frequent buses head inland from both the centre of Iguape and the **rodoviária**, located a good twenty minutes' walk (or short taxi ride) from the town centre.

Iguape has a good selection of **accommodation**, with by far the nicest being the *Pousada Solar Colonial* at Largo da Basílica 30 (☎13/6841-1591; ❷). The comfortable rooms in this refurbished nineteenth-century mansion are tremendous value, with the best rooms overlooking the main square. A few blocks away are the *Pousada Casa Grande* at Rua Major Rebelo 768 (☎13/6841-1920; ❸) and the *Itamiaru* at Rua Princesa Isabel 731 (☎13/6841-1428; ❷), both less characterful, but pleasant nonetheless. For **food**, you'll find very good fish dishes at the *Panela Velha* at Rua 15 de Novembro 190 and at the *Itacurumins* at Rua Porto do Rosário 2, while the *Cantina Sapore d'Italia* at Rua 7 de Setembro offers reasonable Italian dishes. The helpful **tourist information office** is located at Largo da Basílica 272 (☎13/6841-1626; 8am–5.30pm).

Elsewhere on the island, you'll find several **hotels**: budget choices include the *Alpha* (☎13/6842-1270; ❷) and the *Vila das Palmeiras* (☎13/6842-1349; ❷), both offering spartan rooms. A couple of kilometres south of the main access road crossing the island, there are several **campsites**, and numerous bars and *lanchonetes*. You'll get good inexpensive steak, fish, chicken, rice and beans at the *Nordestão* on Avenida Beira Mar, and there are numerous restaurants serving up cheap fresh fish.

Cananéia

Like Iguape, **CANANÉIA**, 50km further south, is on an island, lying between the mainland, to which it's linked by a short bridge, and the Ilha Comprida. Frequent **ferries** runs between the town centre and the Ilha Comprida, from where you can either take a bus (every hour) or follow the road for 3km straight ahead by foot or cycle to the beach (bikes are available for around $5 per day from *Silva Rent a Bike,* at Av. Independencia 840, and also from *Kurt Kaffee* – see below). Where the road hits the beach, there are a couple of very simple *pousadas* and bars. In the summer it gets quite crowded here, but for the rest of the year, both the town and beaches are extremely quiet, with Cananéia being even more of a backwater than Iguape.

In the old centre of Cananéia, in particular along *ruas* Tristão Lobo, Bandeirantes and Dom João II, there are many simple ochre-coloured and whitewashed colonial and nineteenth-century buildings. Except for a few, such as the well preserved, seventeenth-century **Igreja São João Batista** (Wed–Sun 8.30am–noon & 2–6pm) on Praça Martim Afonso de Souza, they're in very poor condition and for some only the facade remains. Worth a brief look is the **Museu Municipal** (Mon–Fri 8am–noon & 2–6pm, Sat, Sun and holidays 8am–noon & 2–8pm), with pride of place among the exhibits going to a preserved shark that weighed 3500kg. The area to the south of Cananéia is a protected **nature reserve**, with isolated beaches and fishing villages that can most easily be reached by chartering a small launch. Karl Beitler

(☎13/3851-3437 and 3851-1683, ⓦwww.lagamar.tur.br), a long-term German resident in Cananéia who runs the ecotourism agency Lagamar (Av. Independência 885), knows the area well and leads tours to offshore islands, taking in some wonderful Mata Atlântica trails, waterfalls and pristine beaches. Schooner trips to outlying islands, departing from the wharf that fronts onto Praça Martim Afonso de Souza, last five or six hours (weekends only Dec–Feb; $15 per person), allowing time to stop and swim or view marine birds.

Most of Cananéia's **hotels** and **pousadas** are located on Avenida Independência, the main road leading into town. The most comfortable place to stay, and the only property with a pool, is the *Golfinho Plaza* (☎13/6851-1655; ❸), at no. 885, while the *Pousada Bom Abrigo* at no. 374 (☎13/6851-1546; ❷) offers good-value basic accommodation. Most other hotels are along or near the waterfront in the same vicinity: good bets are the *Beira-Mar* at Av. Beira Mar 219 (☎13/851-1115; ❸), the *Recanto do Sol* at Rua Pedro Lobo 271 (☎13/851-1162; ❸), or the *Pousada Caropá* (☎13/6851-1601; ❸), in a beautifully renovated mid-nineteenth century building, at Av. Beira Mar 13 on the corner of the *praça* which, while basic, is by far the most attractive place to stay.

You can **eat** quite well in Cananéia, where apart from pizza, the mainstays are fish, mussels, octopus and, the town's speciality, oysters. Restaurants are mainly found on Av. Independência, and straightforward but good choices include the *Camaroeiro*, at no. 655 and *Bacharel*, at no. 835, both strong on seafood. Near the *praça*, the *Naguissa do Silêncio* at Av. Luís Wilson Barbosa 401 is a slightly more upmarket restaurant specialising in seafood. Even in summer, nightlife is low key, but there are several bars on the waterfront alongside the *praça* while, a block away at Av. Beira Mar 71 there's the appealing *Kurt Kaffee*, a bar, antique shop and **internet café** that stays open until late at night and attracts an eclectic mix of people.

At low tide, cars are permitted to drive along the beach between Iguape and Cananéia, a journey that can be completed in less than an hour – check and double check tidal times and drive carefully, neither too near the water's edge nor too high up the beach or you risk getting stuck in the sand. Otherwise, **buses** have to take a circuitous route inland, an 80km trip that takes about two hours, with departures several times a day between the towns.

On from Iguape and Cananéia

If travelling south to Paraná, you'll have to change buses in **REGISTRO**, a bustling and rather ugly town an hour inland from both Iguape and Cananéia in the heart of Brazil's main tea-growing region. Registro's once overwhelmingly Japanese character has been greatly diluted in recent years with the arrival of migrants from other parts of the state and with a gradual exodus of young people of Japanese descent drawn to greater opportunities in the city of São Paulo or Japan. If you're unlucky with connections and need to **stay**, the best places in town are the *Lito Palace* (☎13/6821-1055; ❷), Av. Jonas Banks Leite 615, and the *Regis* (☎13/6821-1988; ❶), at Rua São Francisco Xavier 83. You'll find numerous *lanchonetes* in the centre or, if you have time for a meal, try the *Parada Oriental*, at Rua Presidente Getúlio Vargas 401, which serves inexpensive though not very good Japanese food and is the only real restaurant in town.

It's also possible to reach Paraná by **boat**: five days a week there are launches from Cananéia (Mon 1pm; Wed, Thurs, Sat & Sun 8am; ☎13/851-1268) that travel via a tranquil, inland waterway to Ariri (see p.658), a small fishing community just within the state of Paraná. Although the journey there takes only three hours, there is a small risk of no connecting launch if you're planning to visit Guaraqueçaba or Paranaguá. If you find yourself stuck for a night, there are a couple of rustic *pousadas* (❶–❷) in the fishing village of Marujá, a couple of kilometres away, where there's also a great beach and wonderful forest trails.

Travel details

Buses

Campinas to: Curitiba (5 daily; 6hr); São Paulo (hourly; 1hr 15min).
Cananéia to: Registro (6 daily; 1hr); Santos 1 daily; 5hr); São Paulo (2 daily; 4hr 30min).
Iguape to: Registro (13 daily; 1hr); Santos 3 daily; 4hr); São Paulo (4 daily; 4hr).
Santos to: Cananéia (1 daily; 5hr); São Paulo (every 15min; 1hr).
São Paulo to: Americana (14 daily; 2hr); Bauru (7 daily; 4hr 30min); Belo Horizonte (hourly; 12hr); Campinas (hourly; 1hr 15min); Campo Grande (8 daily; 16hr); Cananéia (2 daily; 4hr 30min); Corumbá (4 daily; 26hr); Curitiba (hourly; 6hr); Embu (every 30min; 1hr); Florianópolis (8 daily; 12hr); Guarujá (every 30min; 1hr); Holambra (6 daily; 2hr); Iguape (4 daily; 4hr); Recife (4 daily; 40hr); Rio (every 30min; 6hr); Salvador (4 daily; 30hr); Santa Bárbara d'Oeste (8 daily; 2hr); Santos (every 15min; 1hr); São Sebastião (6 daily; 3hr); Ubatuba (6 daily; 3hr 30min).
Ubatuba to: Parati (3 daily; 1hr 30min); Rio (2 daily; 5hr); São Paulo (6 daily; 3hr 30min).

Trains

São Paulo to: Bauru (4 daily; 5hr 30min); Campinas (8 daily; 1hr 50min); Rio Grande da Serra (for Paranapiacaba; every 15min; 45min).

The South

CHAPTER 8

Highlights

* **Ilha do Mel** One of Brazil's most gorgeous islands, blessed by little development and no cars. See p.655

* **Iguaçu Falls** No trip to the South is complete without a visit to these breathtaking falls. See p.662

* **Florianópolis beaches** Known as one of Brazil's surfing hot spots, Florianópolis offers plenty of calm swimming beaches as well. See p.678

* **Old-world settlements** Head to the rural south for a taste of the Old World, from German Pomerode (see p.692) and Italian Flores da Cunha (see p.718) to Ukrainian Serra do Tigre (see p.661).

* **Erva maté** Porto Alegre's Mercado Público is a fun place to browse all grades of this herb, which is brewed to make chimarrão, a popular tea. See p.708

* **Churrascarias** Choose from a staggering selection of cuts at these popular barbecue houses – two good options are *Chef's Grill* and *Galpão Crioulo* in Porto Alegre. See p.710

* **Sáo Miguel** The fine Jesuit ruins of Sáo Miguel are dramatically sited in the sparsely inhabited interior of Rio Grande do Sul. See p.730

The South

T he states forming the **South** of Brazil – **Paraná**, **Santa Catarina** and **Rio Grande do Sul** – are generally considered to be the most developed part of the country. The smallest of Brazil's regions, the South maintains an economic influence completely out of proportion to its size. This is largely the result of two factors: the first is an agrarian structure that, to a great extent, is based on highly efficient small and medium-sized units; and the second is the economically over-active population that produces a per capita output considerably higher than the national average. With little of the widespread poverty found elsewhere in the country, the south tends to be dismissed by Brazilians as being a region that has more in common with Europe or the United States than with South America.

Superficially, at least, this view has much going for it. The inhabitants are largely of European origin, anyway, and live in well-ordered cities where there's little of the obvious squalor prevalent elsewhere. Beneath the tranquil setting, however, there are tensions: due to land shortages – people are constantly forced to move vast distances, as far away as Acre in the western Amazon – to avoid being turned into mere day-labourers, and *favelas* are an increasingly common sight in Curitiba, Porto Alegre and the other large cities of the South. From time to time these tensions explode as landless peasants invade the huge, under-used *latifúndios* found in the west and south of the region, and it is no coincidence that it was here that the Landless Movement (Movimento dos Sem Tera) first emerged.

For the tourist, though, the region offers much that's attractive. The **coast** has a subtropical climate that in the summer months (November to March) draws people who want to avoid the oppressive heat of northern resorts, and a vegetation and atmosphere that feel more Mediterranean than Brazilian. Much of the Paraná's coast is still unspoilt by the ravages of mass tourism, and building development is essentially forbidden on the beautiful islands of the **Bay of Paranaguá**. By way of contrast, tourists have encroached along Santa Catarina's coast, but only a few places, such as **Balneário Camburiú**, have been allowed to develop into a concrete jungle. Otherwise, resorts such as most of those on the **Ilha de Santa Catarina** around **Florianópolis** remain small and do not seriously detract from the region's natural beauty.

The **interior** is less frequently visited. Much of it is mountainous, the home of people whose way of life seems to have altered little since the arrival of the European pioneers in the nineteenth and early twentieth centuries. Cities in the interior that were founded by Germans (such as **Blumenau** in Santa Catarina), Italians (**Caxias do Sul** in Rio Grande do Sul) and Ukrainians (**Prudentópolis** in Paraná) have lost much of their former ethnic character, but

only short distances from them are villages and hamlets where time appears to have stood still. The highland areas between **Lages** and **Vacaria**, and the grasslands of southern and western Rio Grande do Sul, are largely given over to vast cattle ranches, where the modern *gaúchos* (see box p.727) keep alive many of the skills of their forebears. The region also boasts some spectacular natural features, the best known being the **Iguaçu** waterfalls on the Brazilian–Argentine frontier and the incredible canyons of the **Aparados da Serra**.

Travelling around the South is generally easy, and there's a fine **road** network. Most north–south **buses** stick to the road running near the coast, but it's easy to devise routes passing through the interior, perhaps taking in the Jesuit ruins of **São Miguel**.

Paraná

Paraná is the northernmost of Brazil's southern states and one of the wealthiest in all Brazil. Its economy is based on small land holdings, modern industries which, unlike those of neighbouring São Paulo, have been subject to at least limited planning controls, and a population comprised largely of the descendants of immigrants. All of which combine to give Paraná something of the feel of an American Midwestern state transplanted to the subtropics.

For several decades after breaking away from São Paulo in 1853, Paraná's economy remained based on pig-raising, timber extraction and *erva maté* (a South American bush, the leaves of which are used to make a tea-like beverage), and in its early years the province was linked to the rest of Brazil only by a network of trails along which cattle and mules passed between Rio Grande do Sul's grasslands and the mines and plantations of the northern provinces. Paraná was sparsely populated by Indians, Portuguese and mixed-race *caboclos*, who worked on the *latifúndios*, scratched a living as semi-nomadic subsistence farmers or, on the coast, fished.

Then, because of a labour shortage in Brazil brought about by the end of the slave trade, the provincial government turned to **immigration** as a means to expand Paraná's economy and open up land for settlement. The first immigrant colonies of British, Volga-Germans, French, Swiss and Icelanders were utter failures, but, from the 1880s onwards, others met with some success. As mixed farmers, coffee or soya producers, Germans moved northwards from Rio Grande do Sul and Santa Catarina; Poles and Italians settled near the capital, Curitiba; Ukrainians centred themselves in the south, especially on Prudentópolis (see box p.659 & p.660), Japanese spread south from São Paulo, settling around Londrina and Maringá; and a host of smaller groups, including Dutch, Mennonites, Koreans, Russian "Old Believers" and Danube-Swabians established colonies elsewhere with varying success rates. Thanks to their isolation, the immigrants' descendants have retained many of the cultural traditions of their forebears, traditions that are gradually being eroded by the influences of television and radio, the education system and economic pressures that force migration to the cities or to new land in distant parts of Brazil. Nevertheless, this multi-ethnic blend still lends Paraná its distinct character and a special fascination.

Unless you're heading straight for the **Iguaçu** waterfalls, **Curitiba** makes a good base. Transport services fan out in all directions from the state capital and there's plenty to keep you occupied in the city between excursions. The **Bay of Paranaguá** can be visited as a day-trip from Curitiba, but the bay's islands and colonial towns could also easily take up a week or more of your time. Inland, the strange geological formations of **Vila Velha** are usually visited as a day-trip from Curitiba, but – by changing buses in Ponta Grossa – you can head west to the Ukrainian-dominated region around the towns of **Prudentópolis** and **Irati**; and from there, head yet further west to Foz do Iguaçu.

Curitiba

Founded in 1693 as a gold-mining camp, **CURITIBA** was of little importance until 1853 when it was made capital of Paraná. Since then, the city's population has steadily risen from a few thousand, reaching 140,000 in 1940 and

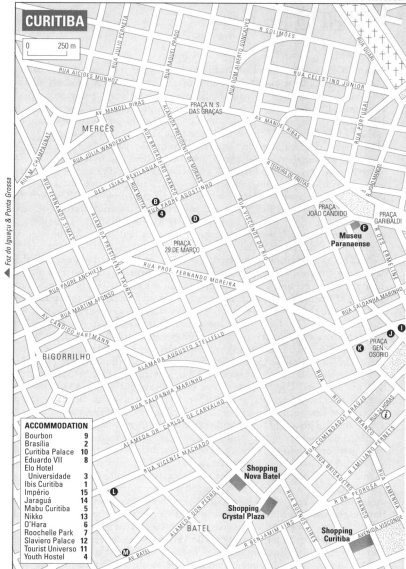

CURITIBA

0   250 m

RUA JÚLIO PERNETA

RUA AICIDES MUNHOZ

RUA ODM ALBERTO GONÇALVES

R SOLIMÕES

RUA RAQUEL PRADO

RUA GUARI

RUA CELESTINO JÚNIOR

PRAÇA N. S.
DAS GRAÇAS

AV. MANOEL RIBAS

MERCÊS

AV. MANOEL RIBAS

ALAMEDA PRESIDENTE TAUNAY

RUA JULIA WANDERLEY

RUA BRIGADEIRO FRANCO

RUA PORTUGAL

R TEIXEIRA DE FREITAS

RUA M. CHAMPAGNAT

DES. ISIAS BEVILAGUA

RUA FERNANDO SIMAS

RIO MOTTA

RUA PADRE AGOSTINHO

B
④
D

R DALMANDER

PRAÇA
JOÃO CANDIDO

PRAÇA
GARIBALDI

F

**Museu
Paranaense**

R DES. ERMELINE

PRAÇA
29 DE MARÇO

RUA VISCONDE DO RIO

RUA PROF. FERNANDO MOREIRA

RUA PADRE ANCHIETA

ALAMEDA PRESIDENTE TAUNAY

RUA MARTIM AFONSO

AV. CANDIDO HARTMANN

BIGORRILHO

RUA SALDANHA MARINHO

ALAMEDA AUGUSTO STELLFELD

PRAÇA
GEN
OSORIO

J
K

RUA SALDANHA MARINHO

RUA

RIO

RUA 24 HORAS

RUA

BRANCO

i

ALAMEDA DR CARLOS DE CARVALHO

RUA COMENDADOT ARAUJO

R EMILIANO PERNETS

R EMILIANO PERNETS

ACCOMMODATION

Bourbon	9
Brasília	2
Curitiba Palace	10
Eduardo VII	8
Elo Hotel	
Universidade	3
Ibis Curitiba	1
Império	15
Jaraguá	14
Mabu Curitiba	5
Nikko	13
O'Hara	6
Roochelle Park	7
Slaviero Palace	12
Tourist Universo	11
Youth Hostel	4

RUA VICENTE MACHADO

**Shopping
Nova Batel**

RUA BRIGADEIRO FRANCO

RUA TAMENHA

L

ALAMEDA DON PEDRO II

**Shopping
Crystal Plaza**

RUA BUENOS AIRES

R DR PEDROSA

R BENJAMIM LINS

BATEL

**Shopping
Curitiba**

AVENIDA VISCONDE

M

AV. BATEL

some 1.6 million today. It's said that Curitiba is barely a Brazilian city at all, a view that has some basis. The inhabitants are descendants of Polish, German, Italian and other immigrants who settled in Curitiba and in surrounding villages that have since been engulfed by the expanding metropolis. On average, *curitibanos* enjoy Brazil's highest standard of living: the city boasts health, education and public transport facilities that are the envy of other parts of the

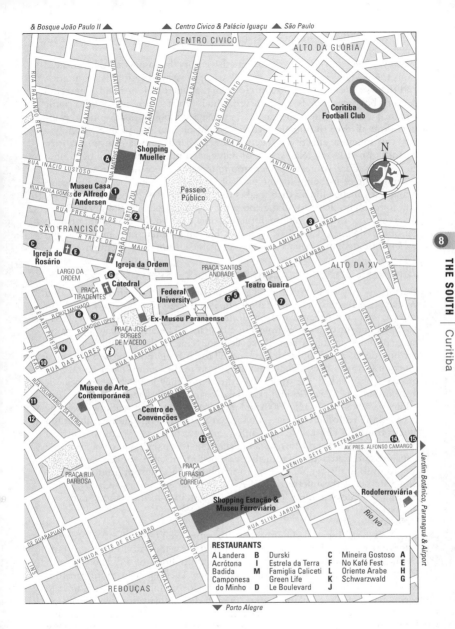

country. There are *favelas*, but they're well hidden and, because of the cool, damp winters, sturdier than those in cities to the north. The wooden houses of Curitiba's lower and middle classes often resemble those of frontier homesteads and frequently betray their inhabitants' Central or Eastern European origins, with half-hip roofs, carved window frames and elaborate trelliswork. As elsewhere in Brazil, the rich live in mansions and luxury condominiums, but even these are a little less ostentatious, and need fewer security precautions, than usual.

Many nineteenth- and early twentieth-century buildings have been saved from the developers who, since the 1960s, have ravaged most Brazilian cities, and there's a clearly defined **historic quarter** where colonial and nineteenth century buildings have been preserved. Much of the centre is closed to traffic and, in a country where the car has become a symbol of development, planners from all over Brazil and beyond descend on Curitiba to discover how a city can function effectively when pedestrians and buses are given priority. Thanks in part to the relative lack of traffic, it's a pleasure just strolling around and, what's more, you can wander around the city, day or night, in safety.

One result of its being so untypical of Brazil is that few visitors bother to remain in Curitiba longer than it takes to change buses or planes. At most, they stay for a night, prior to taking the early morning train to the coast. But it deserves more than this: although there's some truth in the image of northern European dullness, Curitiba's attractive buildings, interesting museums and variety of restaurants make a stay here pleasant – if not over-exciting.

Arrival, information and city transport

Curitiba is easy to reach from all parts of Brazil and, once here, you'll find yourself in a Brazilian city at its most efficient. Flights to most major Brazilian cities as well as to Argentina depart from the ultramodern **airport** (℡41/381-1515), about thirty minutes from the city centre. The airport features a good range of shops (including several excellent souvenir and local handicraft shops), car hire desks, a post office, banks, and ATMs, a hotel booking service and a tourist information desk. Taxis from the airport to the centre charge about $15, or take a bus marked "Aeroporto" (in the centre, they leave about every hour from outside the *Hotel Presidente* on Rua Westphalen by Praça Rui Barbosa).

The main bus (℡41/320-3000) and train (℡41/323-4008) stations – together-er called the **rodoferroviária** – are located adjacent to one another, about ten blocks from the city centre. The only remaining passenger trains to Curitiba run along the line from Morretes and Paranaguá (see p.653), which has become a major tourist attraction. From the *rodoferroviária*, it takes about twenty minutes to walk to the centre, or there's a minibus from almost in front of the station: catch it at the intersection of Avenida Presidente Afonso Camargo and Avenida Sete de Setembro, to the left of the entrance to the station's drive.

Information

The Secretaria Especial do Esporte e Turismo (SETUR), the state **tourist information** organization, has its headquarters near the Palácio Iguaçu at Rua Deputado Mário de Barros 1290, on the third floor of Edifício Caetano Munhoz da Rocha (Mon–Fri 9am–6pm). They keep up-to-date information on changes to rail and boat schedules and provide useful maps of trails in state parks; many of the employees speak English. For information specifically on Curitiba, go to the well-organized tourist office on Rua da Glória 362 (Mon–Fri 8am–noon & 2–6pm); there are other branches in an old yellow tram carriage on Praça Tiradentes (Mon–Fri 9am–1pm & 2–6pm), and in Rua 24 Horas (daily 8am–10pm), though they can keep rather eratic hours.

City transport

Curitiba is small enough to be able to **walk** to most places within the city centre. For exploring outlying areas, there's an extremely efficient municipal **bus** network that's considered the envy of all other Brazilian cities. In the city centre, the two main bus terminals are at Praça Tiradentes and Praça Rui Barbosa, from where buses head out into the suburbs as well as to neighbouring *municípios*. **Taxis** are easy to come by and, as distances are generally small, they're not too expensive.

If you have limited time in Curitiba, an excellent way to view the city's main attractions is to take a **bus tour**. Buses of the Linha Turismo depart from Praça Tiradentes every half-hour (Tues–Sun; first bus leaves 9am, last bus 5.30pm; $2.50) and stop at twenty-two attractions around the city centre and suburbs. The bus takes just over two hours to complete the itinerary, but tickets allow passengers to get off at three of the stops and rejoin the tour on a later bus.

Accommodation

If your sole reason for being in Curitiba is to catch the dawn train to the coast, there are numerous cheap **hotels** within a few minutes' walk of the *rodoferroviária*. Otherwise, places to stay in the city centre are widely scattered but within walking distance of most attractions and are generally excellent value. Many of the better hotels offer substantial discounts at weekends as they are primarily used by business executives. Curitiba's **youth hostel** is at Rua Padre Agostinho 645 (℡41/233-2746; $7 per person). It's friendly and has no curfew but is located twenty minutes' walk from the city centre in the pleasant residential suburb of Mercês, and on the opposite side of town from the *rodoferroviária*.

Bourbon Rua Cândido Lopes 102 ℡41/322-4001, ⓦwww.bourbon.com.br. Widely considered the best hotel in the city, with an atmosphere of traditional elegance combined with every modern facility, including a pool, business centre and very good restaurants. ⑥

Brasília Rua Presidente Carlos Cavalcanti 518 (℡41/221-6811). A good option if you're seeking inexpensive accommodation near the historic centre. Rooms are clean but, located by a busy intersection, there's a lot of traffic noise. ①

Curitiba Palace Rua Ermelino de Leão 45 ℡41/322-8081, ⓦwww.curitibapalace.com.br. Centrally located and comfortable mid-range choice; all the rooms have balconies. ④

Eduardo VII Rua Cândido Leão 15 ℡41/322-6767, ⓦwww.hoteleduardovii.com.br. Perfectly located near the historic centre, close to Praça Tiradentes and surprisingly quiet. Friendly service and good-sized rooms. ③

Elo Hotel Universidade Rua Amintas de Barros 383 ℡41/3028-9400, ⓦwww.hoteiselo.com.br. Modern, rather characterless hotel with a pool, situated next to the university's main administrative building. The rooms are clean and comfortable and the staff are very helpful: excellent value and highly recommended. ③

Ibis Curitiba Rua Mateus Leme 358 ℡41/324-0469, ⓦwww.ibis-brasil.com.br. An attractive, German-style house with small but well appointed guest rooms. Superb value and central location

near the historic centre and the Shopping Mueller. ③

Império Av. Presidente Afonso Camargo 367 ℡41/264-3373. Located virtually opposite the *rodoferroviária*, with good rooms and a nice atmosphere, this is a decent budget option hereabouts. ② Next door, at no. 355, is the *Hotel Maia* (℡41/264-1684) which has the edge on comfort (and a better breakfast) but is slightly more expensive. ②

Jaraguá Av. Presidente Afonso Camargo 279 ℡41/362-2022, ⒻGold264-7763. Directly opposite the *rodoferroviária*, this has the best facilities of all hotels in the vicinity. The rooms are comfortable and clean, the service efficient. ③

Mabu Curitiba Praça Santos Andrade 830 ℡41/322-1122, ⓦwww.hoteismabu.com.br. Good location and attentive service but its small rooms are overpriced – presumably for the convenience of being part of the Best Western Hotel network. ⑤

Nikko Rua Barão do Rio Branco 546 ℡41/322-1808, ⓦwww.hotelnikko.com.br. Modern Japanese-style hotel set behind a pretty nineteenth-century facade. The small rooms are simply and attractively furnished, with mineral water supplying the bath and shower, and there's a small Japanese-style garden, a tiny swimming pool and a sushi bar. ④

O'Hara Praça Santos Andrade 770 ℡41/232-6044. Well located on the continuation of Rua XV

de Novembro, just ten minutes' walk from the *rod-oferroviária*. Its central location rates mean that it's very popular, though rooms are small, dark, musty and rather overpriced. ❸
Roochelle Park Rua Tibagi 307 ☎41/322-8989, ⓦwww.roochelle.com.br. Comfortable but characterless modern hotel located between the *rodoferroviária* and the historic centre. Rooms are large, the staff courteous and there's an efficient business centre. ❸

Slaviero Palace Rua Senador Alencar Guimarães 830 ☎41/322-7271, ⓦwww.hotelslaveiro.com.br. Situated a couple of blocks from Rua das Flores, this well-established hotel is popular with business travellers. The rooms are pleasant, large and fully equipped and there's an excellent restaurant. ❺
Tourist Universo Praça Osório 63 ☎41/322-0099, Ⓕ223-5420. Attractively situated with the nicest rooms overlooking the tree-lined *praça*. Friendly atmosphere and well-equipped rooms; good value. ❸

The City

Being comparatively compact, much of Curitiba is best explored on foot and, apart from the museums – many of which are located in the central commercial district – most interest is concentrated in the historic centre, around the Largo da Ordem. The main commercial district, with Rua das Flores (part of Avenida XV de Novembro) at its heart, is only a couple of blocks south of the historic quarter.

The commercial district: Rua das Flores and around

The **Rua das Flores** – a pedestrianized precinct section of the Rua XV de Novembro lined with graceful, and carefully restored, pastel-coloured early twentieth-century buildings – is the centre's main late afternoon and early evening meeting point, its bars, tearooms and coffee shops crammed with customers. Few of the surrounding streets are especially attractive, but the former city hall, at Praça José Borges across from the flower market, is definitely worth a visit. Built in 1916, the magnificent Art Nouveau construction was later converted for use as the Museu Paranaense. In 2003, however, the museum was transferred to a new site (see opposite) and the building has since stood empty, its future undecided. Just off Praça General Osório, at the far end of Rua das Flores, there's a small shopping arcade, the **Rua 24 Horas**, an attempt by city planners to keep the centre of Curitiba alive outside of office hours. As its name suggests, businesses here are open around the clock, useful if you have a 4am urge to buy a T-shirt, have a snack or get a haircut.

There are a number of other museums within the commercial centre (the tourist office has a complete list), but only two are really worth going out of your way for. Of obvious interest to rail buffs, the **Museu Ferroviário**, in Praça Eufrásio Correia (Mon–Fri 1–8pm, Sat, Sun & holidays 11am–8pm), contains relics from Paraná's railway era. The building housing the museum was the original terminus of the Curitiba–Paranaguá line, and now forms the centrepiece of the **Estação Shopping**, which encompasses over a hundred shops, ten cinema screens and plenty of places to eat. **The Museu de Arte Contemporânea**, at Rua Westphalen 16 (Mon–Fri 10am–7pm, Sat–Sun 10am–4pm), concentrates on local artists in its permanent and temporary exhibits. A brief look round the museum's diminutive collection will be enough to recognize that Paraná has not established itself as a trendsetter in the Brazilian contemporary art scene.

A couple of blocks north from Rua das Flores is Praça Tiradentes where the **Catedral Metropolitana** is located. Inaugurated in 1893, and supposedly inspired by Barcelona's cathedral, it's a totally unremarkable neo-Gothic construction. If you feel the need for a break from the city crowds, head east for a few blocks to the **Passeio Público**, Curitiba's oldest park. Opened in 1886, it has two large boating ponds at its centre and a network of paths to wander along, shaded by tall trees. Of particular interest here are the aviaries housing local species of brightly feathered birds.

The historic quarter

Near the cathedral, a pedestrian tunnel leads to Curitiba's **historic quarter**, centred on Largo da Ordem and the adjoining Praça Garibaldi, an area of impeccably preserved eighteenth- and nineteenth-century buildings. With few exceptions, the whitewashed buildings of the old town are of a style that would not be out of place in a small village in Portugal. Today the buildings all have state preservation orders on them and do duty as bars, restaurants, art and craft galleries and cultural centres. On Sundays (9am–2pm) in the Largo da Ordem and Praça Garibaldi, the **Feira de Artesanato** has a range of local handicrafts and cuisine representing the state's diverse ethnic traditions.

Two of Curitiba's oldest churches physically dominate the historic quarter. Dating from 1737, with the bell tower added in the late nineteenth century, the **Igreja da Ordem Terceira de São Francisco das Chagas**, on Largo da Ordem, is the city's oldest surviving building and one of the best examples of Portuguese ecclesiastical architecture in southern Brazil. Plain outside, the church is also simple within, its only decoration being typically Portuguese blue and white tiling and late Baroque altars. The church contains the **Museu de Arte Sacra** (Tues–Fri 9am–noon & 1–6pm, Sat & Sun 9am–2pm), with relics gathered from Curitiba's churches. Opposite the church is the mid-eighteenth-century **Casa Romário Martins**, Curitiba's oldest surviving house, now the site of a cultural foundation and exhibition centre for artists from Paraná. A short distance uphill from here, on the same road, the church of **Nossa Senhora do Rosário** dates back to 1737, built by and for Curitiba's slave population. However, after falling into total disrepair, the church was completely reconstructed in the 1930s and remains colonial in style only.

Further up the hill is the newly opened **Museu Paranaense**, on Praça João Cândido (Tues–Fri 9am–5pm, Sat 10am–4pm, Sun 11am–3pm), in a beautifully renovated building that used to house the *Museu de Arte do Paraná*. One of Curitiba's more interesting museums, it displays an attractive collection of artefacts charting the history of Paraná from pre-colonial times into the twentieth century. Also here are some paintings, from the art museum's collections, by local artists of the nineteenth and early twentieth centuries, who were important for documenting the local landscape and population of their time. There's an excellent tea room here and a shop selling a good selection of local books and handicrafts. Although only a small number of items from the former *Museu de Arte do Paraná* is now on display here, a completely new museum – the *Novo Museu* – will house its collection, and it will also receive important temporary exhibitions from elsewhere in Latin America. Designed by Oscar Niemeyer, the *Novo Museu* is due to open soon on the outskirts of Curitiba and will be one of the stops on the Linha Turismo (see p.641).

Back down the hill, at Rua Mateus Leme 336, off the Largo da Ordem, is a much smaller art museum that's worth a visit. The well organised **Museu Casa de Alfredo Andersen** (Mon–Fri 9am–6pm, Sat 10am–4pm) is dedicated to the work of the eponymous Norwegian-born artist and is located in his former home and studio. Although a gifted painter, Andersen is hardly known in his native country, in part because the majority of his artistic output is in Brazil and because his subject matter – late nineteenth and early twentieth century landscapes – solely concerned Paraná. The museum's gift shop, selling books and souvenirs relating to Andersen, opens at 1pm.

The outskirts

North of the old town, about 3km from the centre of Curitiba, the **Bosque João Paulo II** (daily 6am–8pm) was created to commemorate the papal visit to Curitiba in 1980. In the heart of the park, the **Museu da Imigração Polonesa** (Tues–Sun 9am–6pm) celebrates Polish immigration to Paraná. It's made up of several log cabins, built by Polish immigrants in the 1880s and relocated here from the Colônia Thomaz Coelho. The cabins contain displays of typical objects used by pioneer families, and one building has been turned into a shrine to the "Black Madonna of Czestochowa". There's a **shop** attached to the museum selling Polish handicrafts and wonderful postcards marking the papal visit. On the side road as you enter the park, there's a tearoom, *Kawiarnia Krakowiak* (daily 10am–9pm), where you can get delicious homemade Polish–Brazilian cakes, light meals and superb locally produced vodkas.

To get to the park, take the yellow bus going to Abranches (a suburb with a high concentration of Poles) from Praça Tiradentes and get off at the **Portal Polaco**, a huge concrete structure extending over the road leading north out of town. Alternatively, take any bus that goes to the Palácio Iguaçu, a massive complex of state government buildings bordering the park. You can enter via a back gate and then follow the footpaths through the wood to the museum.

A short distance north of the park is the **Universidade Livre do Meio Ambiente**, hardly a university in the traditional sense but more a park and exhibition centre promoting environmental awareness. Established in 1991 as one of the centrepieces of Curitiba's self-proclaimed status as the "environmental capital of Brazil", the grounds – a former quarry – are certainly an attractive place for a stroll. The university's building (daily 8am–8pm) is visually striking – it forms an arch and aims at evoking the four elements of fire, earth, wind and water – and hosts stimulating exhibits on themes such as the regeneration of the Atlantic forest, recycling and alternative forms of energy as well as courses for adults and children relating to environmental studies. The easiest way to get there is to catch a yellow bus marked "Bosque Zaninelli" or "Jardim Kosmos" from Praça Tiradentes. Just west of here in the Parque Tingüi, the **Memorial da Imigração Ucraniana** (Tues–Sun 9am–6pm) is a newly constructed Ukrainian-style onion-domed church modelled on the much larger one in Serra do Tigre (see p.661) and small historical museum that celebrates Paraná's Ukrainian heritage, with a shop selling Ukrainian-Brazilian handicrafts; catch the yellow bus marked "Raposo Tavares" from Praça Tiradentes.

On the other side of town is the **Jardim Botânico** (daily 8am–6pm; $1.50), another high-profile project promoting the city's green image. Created in 1991, in the formal style of a French garden, the Jardim Botânico is still in its infancy, its limited attraction being its flowerbeds and the small Museu Botânico (Mon–Fri 8am–noon & 1–6pm). To get to the gardens, take a red express bus from Praça Tiradentes marked "Capáo da Imbuia/Centenário".

Eating, drinking and nightlife

Given Curitiba's prosperity and its inhabitants' diverse ethnic origins, it's not surprising that there's a huge range of **restaurants**. There are also numerous **cafés**, and a fair amount of evening **entertainment**, too, based around the usual bars, cinemas and theatres. There's an excellent selection of produce available at the Mercado Municipal at Av. Sete de Setembro 1865.

Restaurants

Acrótona Rua Cruz Machado 408. A cheap restaurant where the speciality is unusual Brazilian, Portuguese, Ukrainian and other soups. Evenings only.

A Landerna Rua Padre Agostinho 690. Just across the road from the youth hostel in Mercês, this is a very good though fairly expensive pizzeria. Mon–Sat evening and Sun lunch.

Al'Dar Rua Visconde do Rio Branco 1376. Relatively sophisticated Lebanese dishes at very reasonable prices. Closed Sun evening.

Badida Av. Batel 1486, Batel. A slightly up-market *churrascaria* with a menu extending beyond beef to include other meats and salads. Good lunch specials. Closed Sun evening.

Camponesa do Minho Rua Padre Anchieta 978, Mercês. A good Portuguese restaurant, but fairly expensive as many of the dishes are based on imported dried cod (*bacalhau*). Closed Sun evening and all Mon.

Cantinho do Eisbein Av. Dos Estados 863, Água Verde. German restaurant with excellent duck and pork dishes that easily feed two people. Good value. Closed Mon and Sun evening.

Durski Rua Jaime Reis 254. Curitiba's only Ukrainian restaurant, located in a renovated house in the heart of the historic centre looking onto Largo da Ordem. The food (including Polish, Russian and Brazilian dishes) is attractively presented and very tasty. Closed Sun evening.

Estrela da Terra Rua Kellers 95 (corner with Praça Garibaldi). An excellent and moderately priced restaurant, providing *paranense* cooking at its most varied. For lunch there's an excellent *por kilo* buffet; in the evenings the menu includes *barreado* (see p.652) and *charque* (dried salted beef), as well as dishes representing the Italian, Dutch and Polish immigrant traditions. Closed Sun evening.

Famiglia Caliceti (Bologna) Rua Carlos de Carvalho 1367. Most of Curitiba's Italian restaurants are concentrated in Santa Felicidade (see p.647); this is one of the few decent ones close to the downtown area. The moderate-to-expensive food is quite good and served in pleasant surroundings. Closed Sun evening and all Tues.

Green Life Rua Carlos de Carvalho 271. A large, varied and inexpensive all-you-can-eat buffet drawing on produce from the restaurant's own organic farm located near Curitiba. Attached is a natural food store. Lunchtimes only.

Le Boulevard Rua Voluntarios da Pátria 539 (☎41/224-8244). By far the best French restaurant in the city, with prices to match, in a somewhat vulgar atmosphere. Closed Sat lunch and all Sun.

Mineira Gostosa Rua Mateus Leme 491. An inexpensive self-service restaurant with a range of typical Minas Gerais dishes. Closed Sun evening.

No Kafé Fest Rua Duque de Caxias 4. Located along an alley next to the Igreja do Rosário in the historic centre. An excellent and reasonably priced *por kilo* buffet of hot and cold dishes is served at lunch, and a German-style high tea in the afternoon in a building shared with an art gallery.

Oriente Arabe Rua Ébano Pereira 26 (1st floor). Central and cheap, offering large helpings of simple, but fairly good, Lebanese food. Closed Sun evening.

Schwarzwald Rua Claudino dos Santos 63. Excellent German food served with cold beer – a popular evening student meeting point in the Largo da Ordem. Daily 5pm to late.

Warsóvia Av. Batel 2059. Moderately priced traditional Polish dishes – in many ways as "typical" a Curitiba meal as you're likely to find. Situated south of the centre in Batel, it's a short taxi ride or take a bus from Praça Tiradentes. Closed Sun evening & all Mon.

Cafés and tearooms

Modern Paraná was founded on coffee and European immigrants, and one result in Curitiba has been a profusion of old-world-style **cafés** and **tearooms**, most concentrated on the Rua das Flores. Virtually unchanged in style and clientele since opening in the 1920s (elderly ladies and gentlemen in ill-fitting grey suits predominate) are the *Confeitaria Schaffer* (at no. 424), the *Confeitaria das Famílias* (no. 372) and the *Confeitaria Cometa* (no. 410), at all of which the coffee's good, the tea's bad and the cakes are sticky. In the historic centre, a very good high tea is served in attractive surroundings at *No Kafe Fest* (see above). For superb cakes, it's well worth making the trek out to the Bosque João Paulo II where there's an excellent Polish tearoom, the *Kawiarnia Krakowiak* by the entrance (see p.644). For a pre-dawn coffee or snack, you can always join the crowds at Rua 24 Horas (see p.642).

Bars

During the late afternoon and early evening locals congregate in the pavement cafés at the Praça Osório end of Rua das Flores, but as the evening progresses the historic centre comes to life, its **bars** and restaurants attracting a mainly young and well-heeled crowd. On Praça Garibaldi, and the streets extending off it, there are numerous bars, many with **live music** – typically Brazilian rock music, jazz and what seem to be parodies of country and western. Also in the historic centre, several small bars popular with students dot Rua Mateus, just off the Largo da Ordem.

Cinema and theatre

Films reach Curitiba fast, and details of the latest releases are found in *Bom Programa*, a weekly events leaflet distributed by the tourist office and most hotels. There are two good arts cinemas showing non-Hollywood productions, the Cine Groff in the Galleria Schaffer, Rua das Flores 424, and the Cine Ritz on the same street.

During the winter, the Teatro Guaira at Praça Santos Andrade, across from the Federal University, has a varied schedule of **theatre**, **ballet** and **classical music**. With three excellent auditoriums, the Guaira is justified in its claim to be one of the finest theatres in Latin America and is often host to companies from the rest of Brazil, and even international tours.

Listings

Airlines Aerolíneas Argentinas ☎41/232-9012; Gol ☎41/381-1744; Rio-Sul ☎41/381-1644; TAM ☎41/323-5201; Varig 41/381-1588; VASP ☎41/381-1727.

Banks and exchange Main offices of banks are concentrated at the Praça Osório end of Rua das Flores. ATMs are found throughout the city.

Books The best bookshop in Curitiba – and probably the best anywhere south of São Paulo – is the Livraria do Chain at Rua General Carneiro 441 (near the intersection with Rua Amintas de Barros).

Car rental Avis ☎41/381-1381; Hertz ☎41/269-8000; Localiza ☎41/253-0330; Unidas ☎41/332-1080.

Consulates Argentina, Rua Benjamin Constant 67, 15th floor ☎41/222-9589; UK, Rua Presidente Faria 51, 2nd floor ☎41/322-1202.

Health matters In emergencies use the Pronto-Socorro Municipal hospital at Av. São José 738 (☎41/262-1121). Otherwise, go to Nossa Senhora das Graças hospital at Rua Alcides Munhoz 433 (☎41/222-6422).

Laundry There's a self-service laundry on the corner of Trajano Reis and Treze de Maio, near Praça João Cândido in the historic quarter.

Post office The main office is at Rua XV de Novembro 700, by Praça Santos Andrade.

Shopping On Sundays (9am–2pm) the Feira de Artesanato takes over the Largo da Ordem and Praça Garibaldi, with stalls selling handicrafts produced in Curitiba and elsewhere Paraná. For Polish and Ukrainian items, including simple embroideries and intricately painted eggs, try the shops at the Memorial da Imigração Ucraniana and in the Bosque João Paulo II (both on p.644). There's a surprisingly good selection of handicrafts, T-shirts and other souvenirs available at the airport. Shopping centres include Shopping Mueller, Av. Cândido de Abreu 127, with over 200 shops; Shopping Curitiba, Rua Brigadeiro Franco 2300; the upscale Crystal Plaza Shopping, Rua Comendador Araújo 731, Batel, which has dozens of shops as well as a cinema; the small and exclusive Shopping Novo Batel, Alameda Dom Pedro II 5259, Batel, which specializes in women's clothing and accessories; and the enormous Shopping Estação, behind the old railway station (see p.642), which has over 130 shops, numerous restaurants, ten cinema screens and a huge bowling alley.

Telephones The telephone office is next to the main post office on Praça Santos Andrade and there are small kiosks along Rua das Flores.

Around Curitiba

Apart from heading down to the coast (see "Bay of Paranaguá", p.649), there are several places easily reachable by bus that are well worth seeing on day-trips from Curitiba. On the city's outskirts, **Santa Felicidade** is near enough to visit for an evening, to eat at one of the many Italian restaurants there, while **Lapa**, a small colonial country town 80km southwest of the city is a pleasant place to go for a typical *paranaense* Sunday lunch. **Araucária** offers interesting insights into Polish pioneer life, while just under 100km west of Curitiba is **Vila Velha**, home of a strange rock formation that's the basis of a state park.

Santa Felicidade

An outer suburb of Curitiba, about 8km northwest of the city, **SANTA FELICIDADE** was founded as a farming colony in 1878 by Italians transferred from failed coastal settlements and by newly arrived immigrants from northern Italy. Only the oldest inhabitants still speak the Veneto dialect of their immigrant forebears and Santa Felicidade now has little Italian feel to it; the European legacy is essentially that of grape and wine production, culinary traditions and periodic music and folk-dancing festivals (the highlights of which are the annual grape harvest festival in February and the wine festival in late June and early July). Across the road from the church there's an interesting **cemetery**, dating from 1886, but the only real reason to visit Santa Felicidade is for the **restaurants** that line the main road, Avenida Manoel Ribas, alongside shops selling plants, wooden furniture, wicker items, wine and other produce of the local smallholders.

The restaurants compete fiercely for the custom of Curitiba's *nouveaux riches*, each vying to surpass the next in vulgarity. Many of the restaurants are enormous – with some seating over two thousand diners – and are favourites of visiting tour groups and Curitiba families alike. As far as the food goes, in theory most varieties of Italian regional cooking can be found, but it's best to avoid those claiming to specialize in Sicilian or Neapolitan dishes and instead try those with no particular regional claim. These places generally offer the northern Italian food in which the local cooking is rooted, with chicken and polenta being the centrepieces of any meal. Don't expect the same style of food (not to say wine, made from locally grown American grapes) that you may have tasted in Italy. Dishes have been adapted according to the availability of ingredients and the results are, at best, an interesting blend of local Brazilian and Italian influences – rustic dishes as eaten by the *colonos* themselves. At worst, they're simply poor imitations of Italian cooking. Whether in a restaurant decked out to look like a pseudo-Italian palazzo, a medieval castle or somewhere less pretentious, charges remain much the same: about $4 per person for the *rodízio di pasta*, a continuous round of pasta, salad and meat dishes.

Yellow **buses** to Santa Felicidade can be caught on Travessa Nestor de Castro, at the intersection of Rua do Rosário, just below Curitiba's historic quarter; the journey out along Avenida Manoel Ribas takes about 45 minutes. The Linha Turismo (see p.641) also includes Santa Felicidade on its route.

Lapa

Also worth visiting for culinary reasons, if for little else, is **LAPA**, a sleepy provincial town founded in 1731 on the trail linking Rio Grande do Sul to the once important cattle market in Sorocaba. It's only because Lapa is one of the very few towns in Paraná's interior that has made any efforts to preserve its late eighteenth- and early nineteenth-century buildings – typical rustic Portuguese-style colonial structures – that the town has become a favourite place for Sunday excursions from Curitiba.

Four blocks behind the *rodoviária*, Lapa's main church, the **Igreja Matriz de Santo Antônio** (Tues–Sun 9–11.30am & 1–5pm) dominates the principal square, Praça General Carneiro. Built between 1769 and 1784, but reformed over subsequent years, the church's interior displays – all too typically – no original features. However, there are several small museums of mild interest, most notably the **Museu de Epoca** (Tues–Sun 1.30–5pm), an early nineteenth-century house furnished in period style, on Rua XV de Novembro 67, opposite the Panteon dos Herois. The **Museu de Armas** (Sat & Sun 9–11.30am & 1–5pm), on the corner of Rua Barão do Rio Branco and Rua Henrique Dias, in a house of the same period, contains a poor collection of nineteenth-century weaponry.

It's the chance to sample **paranaense cooking**, rare in Curitiba itself, that makes Lapa really worth a visit; the inexpensive and excellent *Lipski Restaurante* (closed Sun & Mon evenings) is just a few metres uphill from the *rodoviária* at Av. Manoel Pedro 1855. There are ten **buses** a day between Curitiba and Lapa covering the 80km in less than an hour; if you want to **stay** over, modest but perfectly comfortable accommodation is available at the *Pousada da Lapa*, Av. Manoel Pedro 2069 (✆41/822-1422; ❷).

Araucária

The ethnic group most often associated with Paraná are the Poles who settled in tightly knit farming communities around Curitiba in the late nineteenth and early twentieth centuries. Poles came to Brazil in three main waves: the smallest number between 1869 and 1889, the largest during the period of so-called "Brazil fever" that swept Poland and the Ukraine between about 1890 and 1898, and the next largest contribution in the years just before World War I. Most of the Poles settling in the vicinity of Curitiba arrived in the 1880s with subsequent immigrants settling further afield in south-central Paraná.

Well into the twentieth century, the Polish community was culturally isolated, but as Curitiba expanded, absorbing many of the Polish settlements, assimilation accelerated and today the lives of most *paranaenses* of Polish origin are indistinguishable from those of their non-Polish neighbours. In recent years, however, there has been a tremendous revival of interest in people's Polish heritage, and, wherever there are large concentrations of Poles, children are encouraged to join Polish language classes, and folk dance and music groups are being established to preserve folk traditions.

One small town within easy reach of Curitiba that is making a strong effort to promote and preserve elements of the Polish immigrant heritage is **ARAUCÁRIA**, situated some 30km south of the state capital. In most respects a thoroughly unremarkable agricultural processing town, Araucária has made particular efforts to record its history. Within walking distance of the town centre is the **Parque Cachoeira**, a large recreational area with a small lake, dotted with distinctive *araucária* (Paraná pine) trees that once characterized the region's landscape. The park is the location of the **Museu da Mata e Imigração Polonesa** (Tues–Sun 10am–5pm), an outdoor museum that serves as a tribute to the area's first Polish settlers who arrived in 1886. Resembling a small village, the museum is similar to the one in Curitiba's Bosque João Paulo II, but larger. Abandoned buildings from outlying parts of this largely rural *município* have been transported to the park and renovated and, so far, the village consists of early pioneer log cabins, a granary, chapel and school, as well as a pig pen, beehive and various agricultural implements. There's an excellent book and gift store, and traditional Polish food is available.

Buses leave Curitiba's Praça Rui Barbosa hourly for the 45-minute journey to Araucária. **Tourist information** and details of special cultural events in and around Araucária are available from the Secretaria Municipal de Cultura e Turismo at Praça Dr Vicente Machado 25 (Mon–Fri 9am–noon & 2–6pm; ☎41/843-1300).

Parque Estadual de Vila Velha

At **Vila Velha** stand 23 rock pillars, carved by time and nature from glacial sandstone deposits, and looking from a distance like monumental, abstract sculptures. The sandstone formation is a result of sand deposited between 300 and 400 million years ago during the Carboniferous period, when the region was covered by a massive ice sheet. As the glaciers moved, the soil was affected by erosion and the ice brought with it tons of rock fragments. When the ice thawed, this material remained and, as natural erosion took its course and rivers rose, these deposits were gradually worked into their current formations.

The **Parque Estadual de Vila Velha** (daily 8am–6pm; ☎42/228-1138) is 97km, an hour and a half by **bus**, from Curitiba. From the city's *rodoviária*, take a *semi-direito* bus (roughly every two hours) to Ponta Grossa and ask to be let off at the park's entrance, a half-hour walk from the rock formations. If you're lucky, the driver may enter the park itself, leaving you only a few metres from the beginning of the area where you can wander between and above the fantastically shaped stones and in the partially wooded section behind. Views over the surrounding countryside from here are tremendous. There's a small entrance charge to the park, but it gets you a detailed map, an elevator ride into a crater-lake (located 4km away from the pillars) and use of the **swimming pool** – a welcome relief from the midday heat since, at an altitude of 1000m, the sun is deceptively strong.

Facilities in the park are excellent due to a complete redevelopment of infrastructure in 2002 and include a couple of modest but good **restaurants**, and a **campsite**. You can also stay in considerable comfort just outside the park at the *Fazenda Capão Grande* (☎ & ⑤42/228-1198; reservations essential; ❺ full board), which offers horse riding on trails around the *fazenda*. If you decide not to stay the night, there are good late afternoon bus services back to Curitiba, so there's no chance of being left stranded. If you're travelling on to Iguaçu, there's no need to return to Curitiba: instead, take a bus the 20km to Ponta Grossa from where you can catch an overnight bus to Foz do Iguaçu. If you don't make the connection in Ponta Grossa, the *Hotel Casimiro*, next to the *rodoviária* at Rua Fernandes Pinheiro 49 (☎42/224-0205; ❶) is a decent place to stay.

The Bay of Paranaguá

Sweeping down from the plateau upon which Curitiba lies, the **Serra do Mar** has long been a formidable barrier separating the coast of Paraná from the interior. Until 1885 only a narrow cobblestone road connected Curitiba to the coast and the **Bay of Paranaguá**, and it took two days for carriages to cover the 75km from what was, at the time, the main port, **Antonina**. In 1880, work

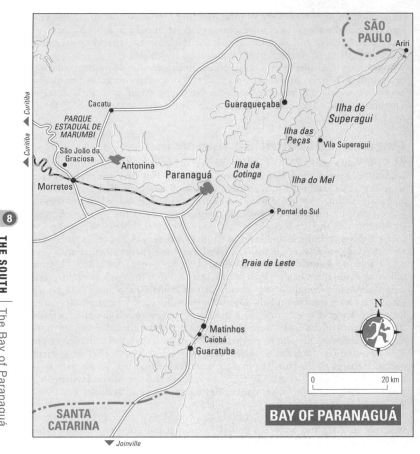

began on the construction of a **rail line** between Curitiba and **Paranaguá**. Completed in 1885, this remains a marvel of late nineteenth-century engineering and the source of much local pride, as it is one of the country's few significant rail lines developed with Brazilian finance and technology. Sufferers from vertigo be warned: the line grips narrow mountain ridges, traverses 67 bridges and viaducts and passes through 14 tunnels as the trains gradually wind their way down to sea level (see below for details of schedules). Passing through the **Parque Estadual de Marumbi**, on a clear day the views are absolutely spectacular, and the towering Paraná pines at the higher altitudes at the beginning of the journey and the subtropical foliage at lower levels are unforgettable.

If the fight to save the Amazon rainforest is now on, that for the **Mata Atlântica**, the Brazilian Atlantic forest, today covering barely three percent of its original area, has been all but lost. But the forbidding terrain of Paraná's Serra do Mar has provided limited natural protection from exploitation by farming and lumbering interests and, since 1986, legal protection for a wider area has been granted by the state government. In theory, the region's future development must serve the needs of local communities, though the regulations are being blatantly flouted, most persistently by ranchers and plantation owners in remote regions. It remains to be seen to what extent the Paraná's coastal zone will remain unspoilt.

Passenger **trains** (*trem convencional*) depart from Curitiba's *rodoferroviária* to the coast at 8am every day except Monday, arriving at Morretes at 11am and at Paranaguá at noon; the return train departs Paranaguá at 3pm and Morretes at 4pm, arriving in Curitiba at 7.20pm. It's advisable to buy tickets in advance ($4–15, single); they are sold at the *rodoferroviária*. There's also an air-conditioned tourist train, the *Litorina*, which operates at weekends (Fri–Sun) and holidays, stopping at scenic points along the way. It departs Curitiba at 9am and arrives in Morretes at 11.25am and in Paranaguá at 12.15pm; on the return leg it leaves Paranaguá at 3pm and Morretes at 4pm to arrive in Curitiba at 6.15pm. Tickets for the *Litorina* ($23 return) must be purchased several days before, either from a travel agent, or direct from the operating company, Serra Verde Express (☎41/323-4007, ⓦwww.serraverdeexpress.com.br). Note that only hand luggage can be carried. For the best views, sit on the left-hand side going down to the coast and on the right when returning. Avoid being persuaded on the train to buy the video of the route as it's really terrible!

If timing doesn't allow you to travel by train to the coast, take a **bus** from Curitiba that follows the Graciosa road (2 daily), a route almost as beautiful as the rail line's. There are also hourly buses between Curitiba and Antonina and Paranaguá by the new highway (journey time approximately 1hr 30min); many people return by bus rather than on the train. Buses between Guaraqueçaba and Curitiba take six hours (2 daily), and between Guaraqueçaba and Paranaguá four hours (2 daily), both services going via Antonina. If travelling to or from Santa Catarina, Curitiba can be avoided by taking a bus between Paranaguá and Guaratuba (15 daily, most via Pontal do Sul for access to the Ilha do Mel), and another between Guaratuba and Joinville.

Antonina

An important port until the mid-1940s, **ANTONINA** has all the atmosphere of a town that has long since become an irrelevance. As ships grew larger and access to Antonina's harbour was restricted by silt, the town abandoned its role as Paraná's main port and entered a long period of stagnation. Due to its decline, many of Antonina's eighteenth- and nineteenth-century buildings have largely been saved from the developers, leaving the town with a certain dilapidated, backwater charm. With neither masterpieces of colonial architecture, nor beaches immediately accessible, the town attracts few other than Sunday visitors from Curitiba. Nonetheless, along with its much smaller neighbour, Morretes, Antonina is the most pleasant of Paraná's coastal towns, and is a considerably better place to stay than Paranaguá, only a 45-minute bus ride away. It also has an important Carnaval.

The **rodoviária** is located right in the town centre. Turn right onto Rua XV de Novembro, the main commercial thoroughfare, and walk two blocks, past once elegant nineteenth-century merchants' houses, then one block along Rua Vale Porto to reach Antonina's main square and evening meeting point, **Praça Coronel Macedo**. The **tourist office** is in the Theatro Municipal at Rua Carlos Gomes da Costa (Mon–Tues 9am–noon & 2–5pm, Wed–Sun 8am–8pm; ☎41/432-4134).

On Praça Coronel Macedo is the town's principal church, **Nossa Senhora do Pilar**. Imposing rather than interesting, the church dates back to 1715 and is built in typical Portuguese colonial style. Its interior has sadly been completely remodelled and preserves no original features. Across from the church at no. 214 is Antonina's oldest house, which is of late seventeenth-century origin.

If you want to **stay**, the *Hotel Regency Capela* (T & F41/432-1357; ❹), built amid the ruins of an eighteenth-century Jesuit mission right on the main square, is worth a splurge, especially if you want a pool. Also on Praça Coronel Macedo is the *Pousada Atlante* (T & F41/432-1256; ❸), more basic with a smaller pool, as well as the *Hotel Monte Castelo* (❷), which offers basic and much cheaper accommodation.

As for **meals**, avoid the *Regency Capela*'s mediocre "international" restaurant and go instead to one serving seafood or the regional speciality, **barreado**, a dish typical of the Paraná's coast and most easily found in Antonina. *Barreado* used only to be eaten by the poor during Carnaval as it can provide food for several days and requires little attention while cooking. Traditionally, it's made of beef, bacon, onion, cumin and other spices, placed in successive layers in a large clay urn, covered and then "*barreada*" (sealed) with a paste of ash and *farinha* (manioc flour); and then slowly cooked in a wood-fired oven for twelve to fifteen hours. Today pressure cookers are often used (though not by the better restaurants), and gas or electric ovens almost always substitute for wood-fired ones. *Barreado* is served with *farinha,* which you spread on a plate; place some meat and gravy on top and eat with banana and orange slices. In Antonina good *barreado* (as well as fine seafood) can be found at the *Restaurante Albatroz*, Travessa Marquês do Herval 14. For lunch try the excellent food stalls in the municipal market by the *rodoviária*, serving fresh seafood at low prices, or for Dutch specialities and seafood there's the *Buganvills*, at Avenida Conde Matarzzo 721.

Morretes

MORRETES, a small colonial town founded in 1721, lies 16km inland of Antonina at the headwater where the Rio Nhundiaquara meets the tidal waters of Paranaguá Bay. Buses constantly pass Morretes on their way between Curitiba and Antonina, and Antonina and Paranaguá, but it's an unremarkable place noted mainly for its production of excellent *cachaças*, for its *balas de banana* (the *doce* typical of the region) and for *fandango*, a local dance introduced into the area during Spanish colonial times. However, Morretes is a good base for visiting the Parque Estadual de Marumbi (see below). You can get park information from the **tourist office** in the Casa Rocha Pombo, Largo José Pereira 43.

Most visitors stay closer to the Parque Estadual de Marumbi, but there are several basic **hotels** in Morretes; the best is the *Nhundiaquara Hotel*, Rua Carneiro 13 (T41/462-1228; ❷), picturesquely positioned on the river in the town centre. With less character, but more expensive and with air-conditioning, is the *Porto Real Palace*, Rua Visconde do Rio Branco 85 (T41/462-1612; ❸). The cheapest option, 500 meters from the *rodoviária* at Rua 15 de Novembro 1000, is the well-kept *Pousada Vista do Marumbi* (T41/462-1573; ❶). As well as sampling the excellent local *cachaças*, you can eat extremely well in the town's **restaurants**, mostly specializing in seafood and *barreado*. For the best *barreado*, head for the pleasant surroundings of the *Armazém Romanus*, at Rua Visconde do Rio Branco 141 (closed Sun & Mon evening), though the restaurant at the *Nhundiaquara Hotel* also serves good food.

Parque Estadual de Marumbi

The original **Graciosa trail** (Caminho Colonial da Graciosa), constructed between 1646 and 1653 to link Curitiba with the coast, passes through the

Parque Estadual de Marumbi alongside the newer road, and is slowly being reclaimed from the forest. A network of other trails provides stunning views on clear days, and there's a wealth of flora and fauna in this, one of the largest and least spoilt stretches of Mata Atlântica in the country. If you're travelling by car, the Graciosa road takes you through the park, with rest areas, picnic tables and fire grills.

From Morretes, there's a **bus** to the village of São João de Graciosa, a two-kilometre walk from the park's entrance; if you're coming directly from Curitiba, get off the train at the Marumbi stop. At the entrance there's a **park office** (☎41/432-2072), where you can pick up a trail map and information about the very basic **camping sites**; the only site hereabouts that's equipped with any kind of facilities is in São João. In any case, it's not the best spot to camp because of the heavy rainfall and mosquitoes that are characteristic of the entire region. If you don't camp, you're best off staying either in Morretes or one of the several *pousadas* located just off the road between the town and São João. Especially attractive is the *Ilha do Rio*, Estrada da Graciosa km 7.5 (☎41/462-1400, Ⓦwww.pousadailhadorio.com.br; ❹ half-board) with a rustic main building and cabins set within a beautiful garden with a pool. Slightly larger and closer to Morretes, is the *Hakuna Matata* (☎41/462-2388, Ⓦwww.hakuna.matata.com.br; ❸), similar in facilities to *Ilha*, but not nearly as pretty. In the park itself there are no places to eat, but São João sports numerous small **restaurants** and bars.

Paranaguá

Propelled into the position of Brazil's second most important port for exports within a couple of decades, **PARANAGUÁ** has now lost most of its former character. It was founded in 1585, and is one of Brazil's oldest cities, but only recently have measures been undertaken to preserve its colonial buildings. While both Antonina and Morretes boast less of interest than Paranaguá, they have at least remained largely intact and retain instantly accessible charm. Paranaguá doesn't, though what is worth seeing is conveniently concentrated in quite a small area, allowing you the possibility of spending a few interesting hours between boats, trains or buses.

The **train station** is three blocks from the waterfront on Avenida Arthur de Abreu. Inside the building is a very helpful **tourist office** (☎41/423-2155), which has useful maps of the city, hotel lists and boat, bus and train information. The **rodoviária** (☎41/420-2925) is located on the waterfront, a few hundred metres beyond the Jesuit college. Both bus and train stations are only a few blocks from Paranaguá's historic centre, and in walking from one to the other you'll pass most of what's worth seeing of the city. Left out of the train station, it's three blocks or so to Rua XV de Novembro. Here, on the corner, is the **Teatro da Ordem**, housed in the very pretty former **Igreja São Francisco das Chagras**, a small and simple church built in 1741 and still containing its eighteenth-century Baroque altars. Along Rua XV de Novembro is the **Mercado Municipal do Café**, a turn-of-the-century building that used to serve as the city's coffee market. Today the Art Nouveau structure contains handicraft stalls and simple restaurants serving excellent and very cheap seafood.

Just beyond the market, Paranaguá's most imposing building, the fortress-like **Colégio dos Jesuítas**, the old Jesuit college, overlooks the waterfront. Construction of the college began in 1698, sixteen years after the Jesuits were invited by Paranaguá's citizens to establish a school for their sons. Because it lacked a royal permit, however, the authorities promptly halted work on the college until 1738, when one was at last granted and building recommenced. In 1755 the college finally opened, only to close four years later with the Jesuits' expulsion from Brazil. The building was then used as the headquarters of the local militia, then as a customs house, and today is home to the **Museu de Arqueologia e Etnología** (Tues–Sun noon–5pm). The stone-built college has three floors and is divided into 28 rooms and a yard where the chapel stood, until it was destroyed by a fire in 1896. None of the museum's exhibits relates to the Jesuits, concentrating instead on prehistoric archeology, Indian culture and popular art. The displays of local artefacts are of greatest interest, and there are some fine examples of early agricultural implements and of the basketry, lace-making and fishing skills of the Tupi-Guarani Indians, early settlers and *caboclos*.

Away from the waterfront, in the area above the Jesuit college, the remaining colonial buildings are concentrated on Largo Monsenhor Celso and the roads running off it. The square is dominated by a cathedral that dates from 1575 but which has since suffered innumerable alterations. On nearby Rua Conselheiro Sinimbu is the charming little **Igreja São Benedito**, a church built in 1784 for the use of the town's slaves, and one that is unusual for not having been renovated. Beyond the church is the **Fonte Velha** or **Fontinha**, a mid-seventeenth-century fountain, and Paranaguá's oldest monument.

Practicalities

In the end, though, Paranaguá remains basically a place to pass through – it's worth getting details about leaving immediately you get here, and only later setting out to explore the city. If you find you have no alternative but to spend a night, there are several inexpensive and centrally located **hotels**, including the excellent-value *Pousada Itiberê*, just a few blocks back from the waterfront at Rua Princesa Isabel 24 (☎41/423-2485; ❶), and the more comfortable *Monte Líbano*, nearby at Rua Júlia da Costa 152 (☎41/422-2933; ❷). The best hotel in town is the *Camboa*, on Rua João Estevão (☎41/423-2121, ⓦwww .hotelcamboa.com.br; ❺), which has large, well-equipped rooms and a pool. There are numerous **restaurants** specialising in seafood and *barreado*, the best of which is the *Casa do Barreado* at Rua Antonio da Cruz 9 (weekend lunches only), which offers an excellent buffet of regional dishes at a remarkably low price. Alternatively, the *Danúbio Azul*, right on the waterfront at Rua XV de Novembro 95, is reliable, or for lunch only try the excellent and inexpensive seafood restaurants in the Mercado Municipal do Café.

For information about **boat departures** ask at the fish market below the Jesuit college. Every morning, fishermen from all around the bay land their catches in Paranaguá and it's usually possible to find boats returning to most points. Keep a careful eye on the weather as storms blow up quickly (especially in September and October, the months of heaviest rainfall), making crossings uncomfortable and potentially dangerous, as few boats carry life jackets. Apart from short tourist excursions from the new municipal market near the bus station, the only **scheduled boat service** from Paranaguá – and one which does pay heed to safety – is the three-hour crossing to Guaraqueçaba, stopping off at the Ilha das Peças and at the Ilha de Superagüi (departures Mon–Sat 6am & 3pm and Sun 9am; 3hrs).

The Ilha do Mel and the southeast coast

To the east of Paranaguá are Paraná's main beach resorts, principally attracting visitors from Curitiba seeking open sea and all the familiar comforts of home.

The surrounding countryside is relentlessly flat and the beaches can't really compare with those of Santa Catarina or, for that matter, most other parts of Brazil. There is, however, one notable exception, the Ilha do Mel, which, despite being Paraná's most beautiful island, has been protected from tourism's worst effects by being classified as an ecological protection zone – the number of visitors to the island is limited to 5000 per day, building is strictly regulated and the sale of land to outsiders is carefully controlled.

The Ilha do Mel

ENCANTADAS is the smaller of the two settlements but the one that attracts most of the day-trippers. Apart from fishermen's clapboard houses, all there is to Encantada is some **bars**, three or four **pousadas** offering basic but good-value accommodation (❸), a few simple restaurants, a campsite (☎41/9959-6132; $4 per person) and a police post. In a sheltered position facing the mainland, it can feel rather claustrophobic due to the mountains all around, but only minutes' walk behind the village on the east side of the island is the **Praia de Fora** where powerful waves roll in from Africa.

Livelier than Encantadas, but lacking the intimate fishing-village atmosphere, is **NOVA BRASÍLIA**, where the bulk of the island's 1200 inhabitants are con-

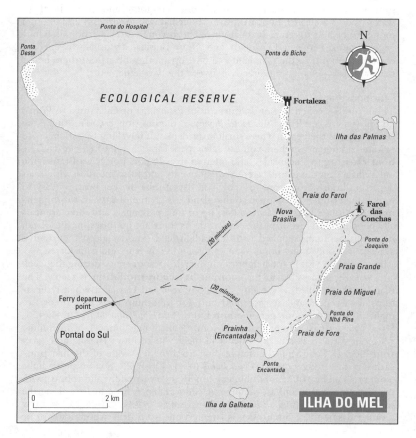

centrated. Stretched between two gently curving, sheltered bays on a narrow strip of land linking the flat western section of the island to the rugged, smaller, eastern portion, this is the area of the island where most tourist facilities (such as they are) are located. Close to the jetty where the passenger boats land, there's a **campsite**, the ecological station, a police, medical and telephone post, and beyond this an immense beach along which are several *pousadas*, as well as **restaurants** and **bars** that are crowded with young people in the evenings. These are not always immediately visible, as many are hidden along paths leading from the beach, up to a 45-minute walk from Nova Brasília's "centre". For a pleasant and undemanding fifty-minute stroll, wander along the beach towards the ruins of **Fortaleza**, the Portuguese fort (built in 1769 to guard the entrance of the Bay of Paranaguá), in the opposite direction from the lighthouse that overlooks Nova Brasília.

The most beautiful part of the island is the series of **beaches** along its mountainous southeast side, between Encantadas' Praia de Fora and the Praia do Farol, near Nova Brasília – an area of quiet coves, rocky promontories and small waterfalls. It takes about three hours to walk between the two settlements but, because of the need to clamber over rocks separating the beaches, the journey should only be undertaken at low tide. As the tide comes in, be extremely careful on the rocks: it's easy to slip or get pulled into the ocean by a wave. Let someone where you're staying know where you're going, and carry a bottle of water (there's a clean mountain stream about halfway for a refill) and enough money to be able to return by boat if need be. If you're carrying too much luggage to walk between Encantada and Nova Brasília, it's usually easier and cheaper to return to the mainland and pick up another boat from there rather than wait for a boat going directly between the two settlements.

Practicalities

The island is reached by hourly **buses** from Paranaguá or Guaratuba to Pontal do Sul (where you'll find the *Hotel Jhonny*, at the bus stop, if you're stuck); the last bus stop is the beach, where small boats depart. If travelling by car, there are private parking areas where you can safely park for a charge of $5 per day. The **boat crossing** to Encantadas (also referred to as Prainha) or Nova Brasília, the only villages on the island, takes between twenty and forty minutes, with boats departing hourly from 8am to 5pm ($2). If you miss the last boat, it's easy to find a small launch to take you to the island at a charge of $10–15 for the ten-minute crossing. These boats can take up to four passengers and there are usually people around to share the costs with. As there are no shops on the island, it is worth coming supplied with a flashlight and candles (electric current is available for only a few hours a day), mosquito coils, fruit and fruit juices.

If you plan to visit in the height of summer, it's best to arrive during the week and as early as possible in the morning as **accommodation** is scarce. The island is always filled to capacity over New Year and Carnaval when reservations are essential and are accepted only for minimum stays of four or five nights. There's only one genuine **hotel**, the *Park Hotel Ilha do Mel* ☎41/426-8075, ⓦwww.parquehotelilhadomel.com; ❹ including dinner), a 45-minute walk out towards Fortaleza – they will meet you in Nova Brasília and carry your luggage. Following the trail leading from the jetty, one of the first **pousadas** is the justly popular *Pousadinha* (☎41/426-8026 ⓦwww.pousadinha .com.br; ❷). The young, multilingual employees are friendly, and rooms (with or without a bathroom) are simple but comfortable. A little further along the trail, the more intimate *Pousada das Meninas* (☎41/426-8023, ⓦwww .pousadadasmeninas.com.br; ❷), is largely built from drift wood, local stone and recycled materials. The owner, Suzy, speaks some English and, if you gather together a small group, her husband will take you to outlying islands with his motorboat. There's also the extremely pretty *Pousada Praia do Farol* (T41/426-8014, Wwww.praiadofarol; ❸ including dinner), on a beautiful stretch of beach, with thirteen rooms (half of which have private bathrooms) and a shady garden. In Encantadas try the *Ephira Pousada* (T41/426-9056, Wwww.ephira.cjb.net; ❸ including dinner), where the well-appointed rooms (all with private bathroom) sleep up to five people.

The southern coast of Paraná

In contrast to the Ilha do Mel, it's hard to find anything positive to say about the rest of the **southern coast of Paraná**, except that it's easy to get to it from Curitiba, thus making it a popular location for second homes for the city's inhabitants. Twenty kilometres south of Pontal do Sul is the first such resort, **PRAIA DE LESTE**, attracting families and campers. **MATINHOS**, 20km further down the coast, is Paraná's surfing capital and, during the summer months, **hotels** here are fairly expensive – though, in any case, they tend to be fully booked. If you're stuck, however, the *Casarão* and the *Beira-Mar*, both on Rua Reinoldo Schaffer, and the *Praia e Sol* on Rua União (all ❸), are the cheapest hotels in town and worth a try.

Ten kilometres further south down the coastal road, and a ten-minute ferry ride from Caiobá, across the entrance of Guaratuba Bay, is **GUARATUBA** itself, Paraná's most upmarket resort. The best beaches are only accessible by car or private boat, so unless you enjoy being surrounded by luxury hotels and multistorey apartment buildings, Guaratuba offers little but the buses going to and from Santa Catarina.

Guaraqueçaba and its islands

North of Paranaguá, directly across the bay, lies Guaraqueçaba, Paraná's poorest and fifth-largest *município*. With 55 isolated settlements, a few poor roads and a widely scattered population of only 8000 (including a few surviving Tupi-Guarani Indians, sometimes seen by roadsides selling basketware), Guaraqueçaba's mountainous interior, coastal plain and low-lying islands give the authorities huge administrative headaches. The sole town, also called **GUARAQUEÇABA**, is really only visited by the most dedicated of fishing enthusiasts and people interested in the conservation zone which, in theory at least, encompasses ninety percent of the *município*. Guaraqueçaba is marked by a tremendous feeling of isolation, connected as it is to the outside world only by sea and an unpaved and severely potholed road, which winds about the interior for the convenience of the *latifúndios*. The owners – usually São Paulo-based corporations – are illegally cutting down the forest, most of which falls within the Guaraqueçaba conservation zone, for development as buffalo pasture or banana and *palmito* plantations. Isolation apart, the town's lack of beaches, and rain that seems to pause only long enough to enable mosquitoes to breed, do little to encourage visitors. The town is, however, useful as a starting point for visiting nearby islands, and you'll find two **places to stay** with rooms that sleep up to six people: the air-conditioned *Hotel Eduardo I* on the waterfront at Rua Paula Miranda 165 (T41/482-1225; ❸) and the more basic *Pousada Chauá* nearby on Rua Ferreira Lopes (T41/482-1265; ❷). There are several restaurants serving home-style dishes, usually some sort of fish option. In town try *Barbosa* (closed Sun evening) located on the waterfront and *Thaíco*, on the outskirts of town on Rua Luís Ramos Figueira 144.

None of Guaraqueçaba's buildings bear witness to the fact that, in the seventeenth century, the town was a more important port than Paranaguá. Nor, apart from the former banana producers' co-operative building at Rua Dr Ramos Figueira 3 (now the local headquarters for IBAMA, the national environmental protection body), do more than a few buildings remain from its heyday between 1880 and 1930 when ships sailed from here to Europe and the River Plate laden with bananas and timber. Today, a shadow of its former self, the port is used only by local fishermen and by boats belonging to the ecological station and municipal authorities, which are used to visit otherwise inaccessible parts of the *município*. In the IBAMA building, there's a visitors' information centre and fascinating small **museum** (Wed–Sun 9am–9pm; ☎41/482-1262) depicting the history of the *município*; reproductions of the paintings of William Michaud, a settler from Switzerland, provide vivid images of the area in the nineteenth century. Some interesting **handicrafts** are produced in Guaraqueçaba, with the best outlet being the non-profit Casa do Artesanato on Rua 15 de Novembro (7–10pm), which sells sculptures and basket work produced by Guarani Indians and ceramics, violas and other musical instruments crafted by local artisans.

Boats and islands

The only scheduled **boat services** are run by the *município*; precise times are available from the the the operators (☎41/482-1232) and you would be wise to confirm the schedule before going to Guaraqueçaba. If there are no municipal boats for your destination, ask at the waterfront whether a fishing boat's heading there. Alternatively, it's easy, but very expensive, to charter a boat. Though rare, good weather is highly desirable for exploring this, one of the more inaccessible and least spoilt parts of Brazil's coastline, but what is absolutely essential is plenty of time, patience, mosquito repellent and anti-mosquito coils for overnight stays. You may get stuck somewhere for days if there are storms.

A daily boat (Mon–Sat 6am, Sun 3pm) makes the three-hour crossing to Paranaguá, stopping off at the **Ilha das Peças**, which forms part of the Parque Nacional de Superagüi and is noted for its marine and Atlantic forest birds. You can be let off on the island and collected again later in the day on the boat's return journey (though confirm that the boat will in fact collect you).

The other regular service is a fortnightly boat to **ARIRI** (first and third Thursday of the month, returning the next day), a small fishing village just within Paraná on the border with São Paulo. On this extremely rewarding trip, the boat stops off at **VILA FATIMA**, a tiny settlement on the northwest coast of the island of Superagüi (see below), before passing through the **Canal da Varadouro**, a long, narrow mangrove-fringed channel. Ariri is only a very short boat trip from **ARARAPIRA**, a village just inside the state of São Paulo, from where another boat leaves the following day (though schedules are extremely fluid) for Cananéia and Iguape.

An occasional boat service also links Guaraqueçaba with the island of **Superagüi** and its village, **VILA SUPERAGÜI**, but as departures depend on the islanders' medical needs the village is more easily reached by fishing boat from Paranaguá; a crossing that takes between one and three hours depending on the type of boat. By asking around it's easy to find **accommodation** with a family but in a village where tourism is only just emerging don't expect much comfort. There are two basic *pousadas*, the *Sobre as Ondas* (☎41/9978-4213; www.superagui.net; $7 per person in a shared room or $17 for a double room with a private bathroom) or the *Bella Ilha* (☎41/9978-3893; www.lol.com.br/~bellailha; $7 per person in a shared room or $15 for a double room); both arrange boat trips to outlying beaches and to other islands. On the east side of the island, a short walk from the village, is **Praia Deserta**, a beach stretching 34km. In March the beach attracts thousands of migratory birds. There are many trails on the island but only researchers working with IBAMA may venture out of the immediate area of the village or Praia Deserta.

South-central Paraná

The hilly – and in places almost mountainous – region of **south-central Paraná** makes a good stopover between Curitiba and Iguaçu Falls for anyone interested in European, especially **Ukrainian**, immigration. As none of the towns in the region is especially distinctive, it's better to use them more as bases from which to visit nearby villages and hamlets where the pioneering spirit of the inhabitants' immigrant forebears remains. The houses, made of wood and sometimes featuring intricately carved details, are typically painted in bright colours and are usually surrounded by flower-filled gardens. Because of the ethnic mix, even small villages contain **churches** of several denominations; most hamlets have at least a chapel with someone on hand to open it up to the rare visitor.

Ukrainians in Paraná

In the late nineteenth and early twentieth centuries, European and North American companies were contracted to construct a rail line linking the state of São Paulo to Rio Grande do Sul. As part payment, large tracts of land were given to the companies and, as in the United States and the Canadian West, they subdivided their new properties for sale to land-hungry immigrants who, it was hoped, would generate traffic for the rail line. Some of the largest land grants were in southern central Paraná, which the companies quickly cleared of the valuable Paraná pine trees that dominated the territory. Settlers came from many parts of Europe, but the companies were especially successful in recruiting **Ukrainians**, and between 1895 and 1898, and 1908 and 1914, over 35,000 immigrants arrived in the Ukraine's "other America". Today, there are some 300,000 Brazilians of Ukrainian extraction, of whom eighty percent live in Paraná, largely concentrated in the southern centre of the state.

As most of the immigrants came from the western Ukraine, it's the Ukrainian Catholic rather than the Orthodox Church that dominates – and dominate it certainly does. Throughout the areas where Ukrainians and their descendants are gathered, onion-domed churches and chapels abound. While the Roman Catholic hierarchy, in general, is gradually becoming sensitive to the need to concentrate resources on social projects rather than in the building of more churches, new Ukrainian Catholic churches are proliferating in ever more lavish proportions. In Brazil, the **Ukrainian Catholic Church** is extremely wealthy, and its massive landholdings contrast greatly with the tiny properties from which the vast majority of the poverty-stricken local population eke out a living. Priests are often accused of attempting to block measures that will improve conditions: they are said to fear that educational attainment, modernization and increased prosperity will lessen the populace's dependence on the Church for material and spiritual comfort, so reducing their own influence.

The Ukrainians' neighbours (*caboclos*, Poles, Germans and a few Italians and Dutch) frequently accuse them and their priests of maintaining an exclusiveness that is downright racist in character. While inter-communal tensions are easy to detect, the few non-Brazilian visitors to this part of Paraná are treated with the utmost civility, and if your Portuguese (or Ukrainian) is up to it you should have no problem finding people in the region's towns and hamlets who will be happy to talk about their traditions and way of life.

8

Prudentópolis and around

The administrative centre of a *município* where 75 percent of the inhabitants are of Ukrainian origin, **PRUDENTÓPOLIS** is heralded as the capital city of Ukrainian Brazil. However, in common with the other regional urban centres, there's little in the city of Prudentópolis to indicate the ethnic background of most of its citizens. Blonde heads and pink noses do predominate but, if you're expecting plump, Tolstoyesque peasants wearing elaborately embroidered smocks and chatting to one another in Ukrainian, you'll be extremely disappointed.

At a glance, Prudentópolis is much like a thousand other nondescript small towns in the interior of southern Brazil. At the heart of the city is a large Roman (not Ukrainian) Catholic church set in a park-like square totally disproportionate in size to the town. The surrounding buildings are the usual mix of anonymous breeze-block and concrete-slab municipal buildings, houses, *lanchonetes* and small stores. Still, committed Ukrainophiles should not despair. A closer look around town will reveal some traces of the Ukraine: many of the older houses bear a resemblance to peasant cottages of Eastern Europe, in particular in the style of the window frames and roofs. As throughout the region, the Ukrainian Catholic Church displays a strong presence, most visibly in the form of the **seminary**, a large mustard-coloured building located next to the Ukrainian Catholic cathedral of São Josafat (masses held in Ukrainian Mon–Sat 6am & 7pm, Sun 6am, 8am, 10am & 5pm). Across the road from the seminary is the church's printing press where Ukrainian-language propaganda is churned out on machinery that has remained unchanged since soon after the first Ukrainians arrived in Brazil. The **Museu do Milênio** (Mon–Sat 8–11.30am & 1.30–6pm), in Praça Ucrânia, traces the history of Ukrainian settlement in Brazil. For traditional Ukrainian **handicrafts**, including intricately painted eggs and embroidery, head for the Casa do Artesanato at Avenida São João 330 (1–6pm, Sat 8.30am–noon) or to the handicraft stall on Praça Ucrânia (Mon–Fri 1–6pm).

There are two relatively modest **places to stay** in town, both a couple of blocks from the main square: *Hotel Lopes*, Av. São João 2595 (☎42/446-1476; ❷) and the *Hotel Mayná Palace*, Rua Osório Guimarães 935 (☎ & ⓕ42/446-2091; ❷). Close by is the *Churrascaria do Penteado*, at Rua Domingos Luiz de Oliveira 1378, which offers cabbage rolls, *borscht* and *pirogi* alongside its standard *churrascaria* offerings. Also serving Ukrainian fare is the *Restaurante Familiar* on Avenida São José.

It's a fairly simple matter to reach Prudentópolis, well served by **bus** from Curitiba (4 daily), Foz do Iguaçu (3 daily) and most nearby centres. However, as one of Paraná's largest and most sparsely populated *municípios*, travelling far beyond the city without a car is difficult. To see some of the rural environs, though, you could always take a **local bus** (2 daily) about 10km northwest of town to the village of **ESPERANÇA**, where there's a large domed church, and a school staffed by Ukrainian nuns; and then turn off the road and head north for 6km to **BARRA BONITA**, another extremely poor and overwhelmingly Ukrainian settlement. Jeeps with local drivers can be hired at the *Hotel Mayná Palace* for excursions to outlying villages and impressive waterfalls.

Bairro dos Binos

While descendants of Ukrainian immigrants form the great majority of Prudentópolis' population, immigrants have arrived from elsewhere as well. Perhaps the strangest, as well as earliest, arrivals were the **French** of **BAIRRO**

DOS BINOS. In 1858, 87 French families arrived in Brazil to form a farming community in what was then – and still is – an extremely isolated part of Paraná. After a few years the colony all but disintegrated, with only a few families remaining. Disappointingly, but not surprisingly, there remains barely the faintest trace of Bairro dos Binos' French origins today – the odd family carrying French surnames, and some uncharacteristic stone houses of the early settlers.

Getting to Bairro dos Binos is very time-consuming; take a **bus** from Prudentópolis to **Teresa Cristina** (140km north), and it's then a ten-kilometre walk west. Still, the journey to Teresa Cristina is fascinating, with the road passing through isolated communities and mountainous terrain, and Bairro dos Binos itself is quite pretty. Aim to return to Prudentópolis on the same day, but if you get stuck ask the priest at Teresa Cristina's church if he can help find a bed for the night.

Irati, Mallet and around

Smaller, and with a greater ethnic diversity than Prudentópolis to the north, **IRATI** and **MALLET** are not especially interesting in themselves, but both are useful jumping-off points for visiting the Ukrainian villages and hamlets nearby. The two towns are very similar in character, both straddling the rail line to which they owed their existence and growth during the first decades of the twentieth century. Mallet – smaller and generally less developed – is marginally the more attractive of the two, and its small Ukrainian Catholic church is worth a visit, as is the train station that dates back to 1903.

Regular **buses** link Irati and Mallet with each other, as well as with União da Vitória, useful if you're travelling to or from Santa Catarina; and there are three buses a day to and from Prudentópolis, and two to and from Curitiba. On weekdays, finding **accommodation** in Irati can be a problem, but if the *Hotel Colonial Palace*, across from the bus station (T42/423-1144; ❷), is full, try the *Hotel Luz*, Rua 15 de Julho 522: walk downhill to the end of the road, turn left and take the second right (T42/422-1015; ❶). In Mallet, there's always room at the *Hotel Brasil* (❶), next to the bus station. **Food** here means meat, with *churrascarias* located near the bus stations of both towns.

Gonçalves Júnior

About 12km west of Irati, the small village of **GONÇALVES JÚNIOR** is well worth a visit if you want to get an idea of local rural traditions. Of the village's four **churches** (Lutheran, Roman Catholic, Ukrainian Catholic and Ukrainian Orthodox) the only one that deserves much attention is the Orthodox, which serves 24 local families. The small church, built in 1934, has an extremely beautiful interior featuring Orthodox icons, and a ceiling and walls bearing intricately painted traditional frescoes. From Gonçalves Júnior, take the Linha "B" road, along which there's a pretty chapel cared for by Ukrainian Catholic nuns. If you're walking to the chapel (allow at least an hour), you will no doubt come across plenty of *colonos*, Ukrainian-, Polish-, German-, Italian- and Dutch-speaking peasant farmers who live in the colourful wooden houses that front the dirt road, who will be happy to chat to you about their lives and those of their parents and grandparents.

Serra do Tigre

Without any doubt, the most interesting and most beautiful Ukrainian church hereabouts is in **SERRA DO TIGRE**, a small settlement south of Mallet that still retains much of its Ukrainian character. Built in 1904, the church, spectacularly positioned high upon a mountain-top near the heart of the village, is the oldest Ukrainian Catholic church in Paraná. In traditional fashion, the church was constructed totally of wood – including, even, the roof tiles – and both the exterior and the elaborately painted interior frescoes are carefully maintained as a state monument.

Without your own transport, getting to Serra do Tigre is not terribly easy. Immediately on arrival in Mallet, go to the Prefeitura and ask for a lift to Serra do Tigre on the school bus, which departs very early in the morning and then again at about noon. Alternatively, take a bus the 10km from Mallet to **DORIZON** from where it takes about an hour to walk up the very steep hill to Serra do Tigre. The *Hotel Dorizon* is a spa resort with good food and a natural swimming pool (☎42/542-1272; ❹ full board).

⑧ The Iguaçu Falls and around

The **Iguaçu Falls** are, unquestionably, one of the world's great natural phenomena. To describe their beauty and power is a tall order, but for starters cast out any ideas that Iguaçu is some kind of Niagara Falls transplanted south of

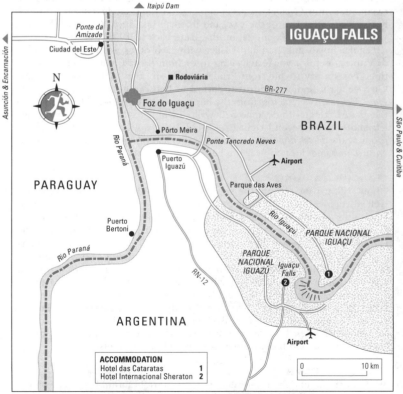

the equator – compared to Iguaçu, with its total of 275 falls that cascade over a precipice 3km wide, Niagara is a ripple. But it's not the falls alone that make Iguaçu so special: the vast surrounding subtropical **nature reserve** – in Brazil the Parque Nacional do Iguaçu, in Argentina the Parque Nacional Iguazú – is a timeless haunt that even the hordes of tourists fail to destroy.

The Iguaçu Falls are a short distance from the towns of **Foz do Iguaçu** in Brazil, **Puerto Iguazú** in Argentina and **Ciudad del Este** in Paraguay – which makes the practical details of getting in and out that bit trickier. Foz do Iguaçu and Puerto Iguazú are both about 20km northwest of the entrances to the Brazilian Parque Nacional do Iguaçu and the Argentine Parque Nacional Iguazú, while Ciudad del Este is 7km northwest of Foz do Iguaçu. Most tourists choose to stay in Foz do Iguaçu, much the largest of the three towns, though many visitors prefer the relative tranquillity and frontier atmosphere of Puerto Iguazú.

Foz do Iguaçu

The **airport** at **FOZ DO IGUAÇU** is served by flights from Curitiba, São Paulo, Rio de Janeiro, Brasília, Salvador and Belém. Regular buses (5am–midnight, Mon–Sat every 15min, Sun every 50min; 35¢) head to the **local bus terminal** in the centre of town on Avenida Juscelino Kubitschek. If you want to go straight to Argentina, get off the bus at the Hotel Bourbon and then cross the road for a bus to Puerto Iguazú (80¢). By taxi, the fixed fare into Foz is $8, or $15 to Puerto Iguazú (see p.666). Arriving by bus, Foz do Iguaçu's

rodoviária (℡45/522-3633) is located on the northern outskirts of town by the road to Curitiba and is served by buses from throughout southern Brazil, and from as far north as Rio and Mato Grosso do Sul, as well as Asunción and Buenos Aires. Buses #01, #02 and #03 link the *rodoviária* with the local bus terminal in town; taxis cost around $5.

There are **tourist offices** at the airport (daily 9am–11pm), at the *rodoviária* (daily 6am–6pm), and on the Brazilian side of the Ponte Tancredo Neves (daily 8am–6pm). In town, there are offices at the local bus terminal (daily 9am–6pm), on Rua Barão do Rio Branco (daily 7am–10pm), and at Rua Almirante Barroso 1300 (Mon–Fri 9am–5pm). For information by phone, call the Foz tourist office, Teletur on ℡800-451-516.

Accommodation

Finding **somewhere to stay** in Foz do Iguaçu is usually easy, and as occupancy rates are generally low you are likely to be offered a knock-down rate, especially outside the peak tourist months of January, February and July, and over Easter. Many of the **hotels**, including some of the best, are located some distance from town on the road leading to the falls, and most of the cheaper ones in town cater largely to shoppers bound for Paraguay. During the summer months, the town is very hot, but all mid-range hotels have air-conditioning and most have a pool.

There's an excellent **campsite** run by the *Camping Club do Brazil* (℡45/529-6034 and 0800-22-7050) situated alongside the visitors' centre of the Brazilian *parque nacional*; at $4 per person, facilities are good (including a laundry area, clean swimming pool, and praiseworthy, inexpensive meals), and the experience of sleeping surrounded by jungle is unforgettable.

Albergue da Juventude Paudimar Avenida das Cataratas km 12.5 ℡45/529-606, ⓦwww .paudimar.com.br. An excellent international hostelling establishment with superb facilities. Cabins (each with a private bathroom) sleep five to eight people and there are family rooms with private facilities and access to a swimming pool. Dinner is available for $2 or you can use the kitchen. Located near the airport, it's easy here to flag down a bus going to the Brazilian *parque nacional*, and arrangements can be made to be taken to the Argentine *parque nacional*. $7 per person.
Continental Inn Hotel Av. Paraná 1089 ℡45/523-5000, ⓦwww.continentalinn.com.br. Excellent value for a centrally located and high-quality – if somewhat anonymous – hotel. The well-equipped rooms are spacious, breakfasts are ample, the staff are efficient and there's a good pool. ❹
Dany Palace Hotel Av. Brasil 509 ℡45/523-1530. No frills, but prides itself on cleanliness. Air conditioned rooms, some sleeping three people. Centrally located. ❷
Hotel Internacional Foz Rua Almirante Barroso 2006 ℡45/521-4100, ⓦwww.internacionalfoz.com.br. The most upmarket hotel in town with luxury facilities including a large pool, gift shop and nightclub. ❻

Hotel Rafain Centro Rua Marechal Deodoro 984 ℡45/523-1213, ⓦwww.rafaincentro.com.br. The rooms are large here, with balconies, and the service friendly. Ask for a room overlooking the pool at the rear of the building. ❹
Hotel Três Fronteiras Av. Jorge Schimmelpfeng 605 ℡45/523-2202. Modern, clean and comfortable. The buses to Argentina and the Brazilian falls stop on this avenue. ❷
Pousada da Laura Rua Naipi 629 ℡45/574-3628. Friendly, small B&B-style accommodation has become a favourite for backpackers. Although the house is located in a central, pleasant residential section, care should be taken as young men from the neighbouring *favela* have been known to rob tourists. $9 per person.
Pousada Evelina Navarrete Rua Kalichewski 171 ℡ & ⒻÐ45/574-3817. An extremely friendly place with a youth hostel atmosphere that mainly attracts foreign backpackers. Rooms are simple but spotless, breakfasts are adequate, there's internet access and multilingual Evelina goes out of her way to be helpful. Well located for buses to the falls. ❷
Tropical das Cataratas Eco Resort Parque Nacional do Iguaçu ℡45/521-7000 and 0800-701-2670, ⓦwww.tropicalhotel.com.br. The only hotel within the Brazilian national park, discreetly

located just out of sight from the falls. Rooms are comfortable and pleasantly furnished. Even if you can't afford to stay here, you can wander around the hotel's grounds or eat in the restaurant (see below). Reservations are usually required; do not expect discounted rates. ❽

Eating and drinking

Foz do Iguaçu is certainly no gastronomic paradise, but it's possible to **eat** well without paying too much. On Rua Marechal Deodoro there are numerous buffet-style *por kilo* restaurants, and if you're really on a tight budget cross into Ciudad del Este for dinner (see p.667).

Antônio Maria Rua Almirante Barroso 1466 (Galeria Viela). Remarkably authentic – though expensive – Portuguese food. Sun lunch only.

As Portugalios Av. das Cataratas 569 ☎45/572-3927. Friendly and attractive establishment serving excellent Portuguese food at reasonable prices. Evenings only.

Bier Kastell Av. Jorge Schimmelpfeng (corner with Rua Marechal Deodoro). A lively beer garden where you can enjoy ice-cold *chopp* and German-style sausage and other light meals.

Búfalo Branco Rua Rebouças 530. Upmarket *churrascaria* with the all-you-can-eat *ródizio* system and an excellent salad bar.

Churrascaria Bianco Rua Quintino Bocaiúva 839. Excellent quality all-you-can-eat meals for $6 per person make this popular with visitors and locals alike.

Clube Maringá Porto Meira ☎45/527-3472; reservations advised on Sun. Justly popular among locals for its superb *rodízio de peixe* lunch and stunning views of the Iguaçu river. Apart from a selection of local freshwater fish, there's an excellent salad bar and you can pay a little extra for fresh sashimi.

Expect to pay $8–10 per person. Take the "Porto Meira" bus and ask for directions or a taxi ($3).

Recanto Gaúcho Av. Cataratas, km 15 – near the Brazilian park entrance ☎45/572-2358 or 572-1694. A favourite Sunday outing for locals: the atmosphere's lively, the meat's excellent and cheap ($5 per person for all you can eat) and the owner (who always dresses in full *gaúcho* regalia) is a real character. Turn up soon after 11am; food is served until 3pm. It's advisable to phone ahead. Closed Dec and Jan.

Trigo & Cia Rua Almirante Barroso 1750. Adjoining the *Hotel Internacional Foz*, this busy café serves tasty savoury snacks, good coffee and the best cakes in Foz. Open until 11pm.

Tropical das Cataratas Parque Nacional do Iguaçu. The only hotel restaurant worth trying. In peak season an excellent buffet lunch of typical Brazilian dishes is available for $12.

Zaragoza Rua Quintino Bocaiúva 882. Decent Spanish restaurant specialising in fish but, being so far from the coast, opt for the fresh-water options like *surubí* or, if available, *dourado*. A meal will cost around $13 per person.

Listings

Airlines TAM ☎45/523-8500; Varig/Rio-Sul ☎45/529-6601; VASP ☎45/529-7161.

Banks and exchange Dollars (cash or travellers' cheques) can be easily changed in travel agencies and banks along Avenida Brasil; the latter also have ATMs.

Car rental Avis (☎45/529-6160), Localiza (☎45/529-6300), and Yes (☎45/522-2956) are all represented at the airport and will deliver a car to your hotel. Note that, if you are just travelling between Foz do Iguaçu and Puerto Iguazú or the two national parks, then no special car documentation is required to cross the Brazilian/Argentine border. If, however, you intend taking your rental car to the Paraguayan or Argentine Jesuit missions (see p.729) or anywhere else south of Puerto Iguazú, you will need to request the correct papers from the rental agency (an extra $5 per day is charged), or you will be turned back by customs officers.

Consulates Argentina, Rua Dom Pedro II 28 ☎45/574-2969; Paraguay, Rua Bartolomeu de Gusmão 777 ☎45/523-2898.

Horse riding You can hire horses at the *Recanto Gaúcho* (see above). Reservations are essential and the cost is $10 per person for a two-hour ride accompanied by a guide through forested and open country trails.

Post office Praça Getúlio Vargas near Rua Barão do Rio Branco.

Travel and tour companies Martin Travel, Travessa Goiás 200 (☎45/523-4959; ✉fernando @martintravel.com.br), is a reliable local travel agency that specializes in ecotourism and puts together groups to go mountain-biking through forest trails, and canoeing. Many travel agents organize day-trips to the Argentine Jesuit ruins of San Ignacio Miní (see p.731) for around $45 per person.

Fishing on the Rio Paraná

The upper reaches of the Rio Paraná are the home of one of the world's greatest freshwater game fish, the **dourado**, a beautiful silver and gold fish with deep orange marking on its fins and tail. Known as the "golden salmon", these immensely powerful fish have long been popular with South American and European anglers alike. Similar in character to the better-known East African tiger fish, the migrating *dourado* is found as far north in Brazil as the Pantanal, but it's in the fast-flowing stretch of the Rio Paraná between Argentina and Paraguay around Iguaçu that the largest fish can be caught. *Dourado* are caught from boats positioned side-on and allowed to drift with the current, and they weigh between 13 and 18kg. The *dourado* season is from October to March, with the best time to fish being November, December and January.

A British-run company, Dourado Sports Fishing (☏45/523-2076), which operates out of Foz do Iguaçu's Cataratas Yacht Club, organizes well-equipped fishing trips in large, safe aluminium launches. For half a day (4 hours) on the river, including collection from your hotel and all fishing equipment and bait, the rate is $60 per person for a minimum of two people. A full day costs $100 and includes lunch.

Puerto Iguazú and around

If you want to avoid the crowds, **PUERTO IGUAZÚ** is a better **place to stay** than Foz do Iguaçu, especially if you're on a tight budget, as simple hotels are more pleasant on the Argentine side of the border. There's also a good youth hostel, *Corre Caminos* near the bus station at Rua Paulino Amarante 48 (☏3757/420-967, ⓦwww.correcaminos.com.ar; ❶ for a double room with a private bathroom or $4 for a cramped bunk). Near the bus terminal there are several basic, family-run hotels, including the recommended *Residencia Paquita*, at Av. Córdoba 731 (☏3757/420-434; ❷), and the *Hostería Los Helechos*, Calle Paulino Amarante 76 (☏3757/420-338; ❷), which is particularly good value and has a small pool. Only a little more expensive, *Residencial King*, Av. Victoria Aguirre 916 (☏3757/420-360; ❸), has an attractive garden setting and a pool. The best mid-range place, however, is the *Hotel Saint George* at Av. Córdoba 148 (☏3757/420-249 or 420-566; ❸), which has a pool. At the luxury end, the rather hideous *Sheraton Internacional Iguazú* (☏3757/421-600;ⓦwww .iguazufalls.com; ❼) offers views of the forest or the falls. If you want to **camp**, use the good site at Puerto Canoas in the national park on the Argentine side (see p.670).

If you have your own transport, a wonderful hotel that's well worth considering as a base for both the falls and the Jesuit missions (see p.729) is the *Estancia Las Mercedes* (☏3751/15660921, ⓦwww.estancialasmercedes.com.ar; reservations essential; $65 per person full board), 95km south of Puerto Iguazú (an easy 90min drive) near the bustling little town of Eldorado. The *estancia* was established as an *erva maté* plantation by immigrants from New Zealand in 1923, who built the main house and outbuildings in a style akin to that of a sheep station in their home country. Today the grandchildren of the founder run *Las Mercedes* as a cattle ranch and country hotel. There's a pool in the attractive grounds, and horse riding and canoeing are included in the rates.

Puerto Iguazú is a sleepy, safe and small town (its population is just 16,000, compared to Foz do Iguaçu's 230,000). The **Museu Mbororé**, at the intersection of Avenida Misiones and Brasil (irregular hours, usually open in the afternoon), is worth a brief look, for its small exhibition relating to the indigenous Guaraní Indians. What nightlife there is in Puerto Iguazú takes place in the "downtown" **bars** on Avenida Victoria Aguirre, where the town's two Internet cafés are also located. This being Argentina, **food** means meat accompanied by decent wine, with a couple of excellent *parrillas* (grills) including *Charo* and *La Rueda*, near the bus terminal on Avenida Córdoba.

There's a **tourist office** at Av. Victoria Aguirre 396 (daily 8am–8pm; ☏3757/420-800), but only the most basic of information concerning Puerto Iguazú and the wider area is supplied. Puerto Iguazú has daily **flights** to and from Buenos Aires and Cordoba, with connections to elsewhere in Argentina; buses to town meet arriving flights. Aerolíneas Argentinas' office is on Avenida Victoria Aguirre (☏3757/420-168). Puerto Iguazú's combined local and long-distance **bus terminal** is in the town centre, with several daily departures to Buenos Aires and Posadas, near the Jesuit ruins of San Ignacio Miní (see p.731).

Ciudad del Este and around

At first sight, **CIUDAD DEL ESTE** must rank as one of South America's more unpleasant cities. When it rains, the city is awash with mud and it can be dangerous to cross a road for fear of vanishing into one of the many potholes. In dry weather, the place is coated with a thick layer of red dust. In former years, Ciudad del Este's tax-free status made it a magnet for Brazilian shoppers, but the devaluation of the Brazilian currency, combined with the lowering of duty-free allowances, has resulted in a sharp decline in cross-border trade. In response, the city is redefining its economy, stressing the financial services sector and, curiously, higher education – its two universities attract significant numbers of Brazilian students in fields as diverse as medicine and philosophy.

The **bus terminal** is located just south of the centre, to which it is linked by local buses. If you arrive from Asunción or Encarnación (see p.734) after dark it makes sense to cross into Brazil the next morning. Buses between Ciudad del Este and Foz do Iguaçu (daily 7am–8.50pm) stop on the main street, Avenida Monseñor Rodríguez, and the parallel Avenida Adrián Jara. Depending on traffic, it can take between fifteen minutes and two hours to go from city centre to centre – heading out of Ciudad del Este, it's often faster to walk across the international bridge and pick up a bus heading into Foz do Iguaçu. Day and night there are taxis available for around $4. If you're just crossing for a day you need only wave your passport at the immigration officials, but otherwise remember to be stamped in or out of the respective countries. The Brazilian **consulate** is at Tenente Coronel Pampliega 337 (☏61/31-2309).

Ciudad del Este's **tourist office** is at the Paraguayan immigration post but don't expect any more than basic directions by way of assistance. Dollars, *pesos* and *reis* are all accepted in town, but if you're travelling further into Paraguay you'll need Paraguayan **guaranies**, available at similar rates in *casas de câmbio* in Foz do Iguaçu, Puerto Iguazú and, in Ciudad del Este, on Avenida Monseñor Rodríguez. The **post office** is opposite the bus station at Alejo García and Oscar Rivas Ortellado (the Paraguayan postal service is much cheaper than the Brazilian or the Argentine).

If you need **accommodation**, there are two good hotels located opposite one another on Avenida Adrián Jara, near the intersection with Alejo García. The *Mi Abuelo* (☏61/62373; ❷) is friendly, quiet and has an attractive courtyard, and the *Convair* (☏61/62349; ❸) is more impersonal but with air-conditioning, TVs and minibars. German-speakers may be attracted to the *Hotel Munich* (☏61/62371; ❷) or the *Hotel Vienna* (☏61/68614; ❷), both in Calle Emiliano Fernández, between Calle Miranda and Calle Morgelos; the two hotels are predictably clean and remarkably friendly, and the latter has a good Austrian restaurant. If you're staying in Foz, it's worth crossing into Ciudad del Este just for dinner: you can **eat** well and inexpensively here, and Paraguayan beer is excellent. Like the shops, most restaurants are owned by Arab and east Asian immigrants and cater mainly for the shop owners. The best choices are on Avenida Adrián Jara: the *Oriental* serves reasonable Chinese food, the *New Tokio* serves excellent Japanese food and the *Lebanon* serves somewhat over-priced Lebanese food. Also check out the side roads, such as Calle Abay, where many of the smaller Chinese, Japanese and Korean restaurants are located. For more traditional Paraguayan offerings, try *Mi Ranchito*, an outdoor *parrilla* at the corner of Calle Curupayty and Avenida Adrián Jara.

Puerto Bertoni

Definitely worth the effort is a visit to **Puerto Bertoni**, 20km south of Ciudad del Este and home of the Swiss naturalist and ethnologist Moises Bertoni, who settled in the area in 1890, remaining until his death in 1929. Surrounded by a small jungle reserve, Bertoni's house and outbuildings are now a museum, housing a small botanical collection and excellent panels (in English and Spanish) describing Bertoni's life and work. A few hundred metres from the buildings is a small village inhabited by Guaraní Indians who survive by subsistence farming and the sale of simple handicrafts to visitors. Trips to Puerto Bertoni can be arranged from most travel agents in Foz do Iguaçu; they last about three and a half hours and cost $25. From Porto Meira, the old Brazilian ferry landing, you'll be taken by launch to the Puerto Bertoni land-ing, from where it's a steep fifteen-minute walk up the river embankment along a jungle trail to the house.

The falls

The **Iguaçu Falls** are formed by the Rio Iguaçu, which has its source near Curitiba. Starting at an altitude of 1300m, the river snakes westward, picking up tributaries and increasing in size and power during its 1200-kilometre jour-ney. About 15km before joining the Rio Paraná, the Iguaçu broadens out, then plunges precipitously over an eighty-metre-high cliff, the central of the 275 interlinking cataracts that extend nearly 3km across the river. There is no "best time" to visit since the falls are impressive and spectacularly beautiful whatev-er the season. That said, the rainy season is during the winter months of April to July, and at this time the volume of water is at its greatest – but then the sky is usually overcast and the air, especially near the falls themselves, is quite chilly. By the end of the summer dry season, around March, the volume of water crashing over the cliffs is reduced by a third (only once, in 1977, did the falls dry up altogether), but even then there's no reduction in impact, with the added attraction of the rainbow effects from the splashing of falling water and the deep-blue sky. The one time to avoid at all costs is Easter, when the area attracts vast throngs of Argentine and Brazilian tourists.

Although many people arrive at Iguaçu in the morning and depart the same evening, the falls should really be viewed from both the Brazilian and the Argentine sides of the river: at least two days are needed to do them justice and you could easily spend longer. Crossing the **frontier** to see both sides is easy, and if you're of a nationality that normally requires a visa to visit either Argentina or Brazil you won't need one just for a day-trip. If, however, you're not returning to Foz do Iguaçu or Puerto Iguazú the same day, you'll have to go through normal **immigration** formalities on either side of the **Ponte**

Presidente Tancredo Neves, the bridge that crosses the Rio Iguaçu between the two towns. There are good bus services between the two cities and onwards to the falls, but consider renting a car if your time is limited; see "Listings" p.665 for car rental details.

The Brazilian side

The finest overall view of the falls is obtained from the Brazilian side, best seen in the morning when the light is much better for photography. You'll only need about half a day here (longer if you're also visiting the Parque das Aves – see p.671), since, although the view is magnificent and it's from here that you get the clearest idea as to the size of the falls, the area from which to view them is fairly limited.

From the local bus terminal in central Foz do Iguaçu, there are **buses** every half hour (daily 8am–7pm) to the "Parque Nacional", which cost around 80¢ and take about 45 minutes. Buses stop at the park entrance where, after paying the $2.50 entrance fee, you transfer onto another bus that takes you to the falls. Buses stop on the road beneath the renowned hotel the *Tropical das Cataratas* (see p.665), where you're only a couple of minutes' walk from the first views of the falls.

From the bus stop, there's a stairway that leads down to a 1.5-kilometre cliff-side **path** near the rim of the falls. From spots all along the path there are excellent views, at first across the lower river at a point where it has narrowed to channel width. At the bottom of the path, where the river widens again, there's a catwalk leading out towards the falls themselves. Depending on the force of the river, the spray can be quite heavy, so if you have a camera be sure to carry a plastic bag. From here, you can either walk back up the path or take the elevator to the top of the cliff and the road leading to the hotel.

Every fifteen minutes or so you'll hear the buzzing from a **helicopter** flying overhead. It takes off just outside the park's entrance, across from the *Parque das Aves*, and offers eight-minute flights over the falls for $60, or a 35-minute flight over the falls and Itaipu for $150. In recent years the helicopter has been the cause of a minor rift between Brazil and Argentina: the Argentines refuse to allow it to fly over their side of the falls as they claim that it disturbs the wildlife. Whether this is in fact true is a matter of fierce debate, but certainly the view from above is spectacular and the ride exhilarating.

The Argentine side

For more detailed views, and greater opportunities to experience the local flora and fauna at close range, Argentina offers by far the best vantage points. The falls on the Argentine side are much more numerous and the viewing area more extensive and this, combined with the fact that many people only visit the Brazilian side, means that you'll rarely be overpowered by fellow tourists. With a good eye, toucans and other exotic birds can be spotted, and brilliantly coloured butterflies are seen all about in the summer months. In warm weather, be sure to bring your bathing gear as there are some idyllic spots to cool off in the river.

Getting to the Argentine side of the falls from Foz do Iguaçu is straightforward enough, but if your time is very limited it makes sense to join an **excursion**, which most travel agencies and the better hotels organize (from around $28). Otherwise, from Foz do Iguaçu's local bus terminal take a **bus to Puerto Iguazú** 80¢; departures every half-hour 7am–6.45pm; 30min); if you miss the last bus in either direction a taxi will cost $10. From Puerto Iguazú's bus terminal, there are then buses every hour (6.30am–7.30pm, returning 8am–8pm;

$2) that take thirty minutes to reach the national park's new visitor's complex where you pay an entrance fee of $2.60, and you'll be given a very useful map. Bear in mind that Argentine time is one hour behind the Brazilian; Brazilian *reís*, US currency and Argentine *pesos* are all accepted for the bus fare between Puerto Iguazú and the falls, snacks and drinks, and the Argentine park entrance charges.

At the visitor's complex you'll find a large car park, souvenir shops, a café and a restaurant as well as an impressive **Centro de Interpretación de la Naturaleza** (7.30am–8pm). This makes a good first stop with its **museum** focusing on the region's natural history. It's here that you'll see the extremely shy, and mainly nocturnal, forest animals – though they're all stuffed. From the centre transfer to the grandly named **Tren de la Selva**, a miniature railway that winds its way through the forest between the park's entrance and the falls. The first stop is the *Estación Cataratas* for the Sheraton Hotel and the fall's Circuito Inferior and the second is the Estación Garganta del Diablo.

The **Circuito Inferior** involves an easy walk that, with a few interruptions to admire the scenery, is likely to take a couple of hours. Despite not being as dramatic as the falls upriver, few parts of the park are more beautiful and the path passes by gentler waterfalls and dense vegetation. At the river shore, **boats** (9am–4pm; $3 return) cross to the **Isla San Martín**, whose beaches are unfortunately marred by the streams of sand flies and mosquitoes present. One of the many enchanting spots on the island is **La Ventana**, a rock formation that's framed, as its name suggests, like a window. From here you can continue around the marked circuit, but, if you are at all agile, haul yourself instead across the rocks in front and behind La Ventana where, hidden from view, is a deep natural **pool** fed by a small waterfall, allowing some relaxing swimming.

The Argentine falls embrace a huge area, and the most spectacular spot is probably the **Garganta del Diablo** (Devil's Throat) at **PUERTO CANOAS**. The Garganta del Diablo marks a point where fourteen separate falls combine to form the world's most powerful single waterfall in terms of the volume of water flow per second. Catwalks lead into the middle of the river to a central viewing platform, from where it's easy to feel that you will be swallowed by the tumbling waters: be prepared to get drenched by the spray, mist and rain. From Puerto Canoas the train will take you back to the park's entrance complex from where there are frequent buses that link directly with Puerto Iguazú.

The forest

One of the remarkable aspects of the park is that visitors can gain access to a **tropical rainforest** without any difficulty and without posing a threat to people or nature. Even by keeping to the main paths around the falls, it's easy to get a taste of the jungle. The forest is home to over two thousand plant varieties, four hundred bird species, dozens of types of mammals and innumerable insects and reptiles. It's essentially made up of four levels of vegetation: a nearly closed canopy reaching over 35m; a layer of trees between 3 and 10m in height; a lower layer of shrubs; and a herbaceous ground level. In reality the levels are not so pronounced, as epiphytes and other plants intertwine, at times creating a mass of matted vegetation.

Within the forest lives a rich diversity of **wildlife** species, but they are spread out over a wide area, are often nocturnal and are usually extremely timid. However, if you get up early, walk quietly away from other people and look up into the trees as well as towards the ground, you have a good chance of seeing something. Jaguars and mountain lions have been seen in Iguaçu, but they keep so well hidden and so few remain that realistically your chances of observing them are minimal. Around the water's edge, you may occasionally see **tapirs**, large animals shaped rather like a pig with a long snout. Smaller, but also with a pig-like appearance is the **peccary**, dangerous when cornered, but shy of humans.

Far more common is the **coatimundi**, the size of a domestic cat but related to the racoon. Even on the main paths on the crowded Brazilian side of the falls, you often come face to face with coatimundi, begging food from tourists. The *caí*, or **capuchin monkey**, is also often seen and is recognizable by its long legs and tail, small size and black skullcap mark that gives it its name. These monkeys travel the forest canopy in large groups and emit strange bird-like cries. Far bigger and with a deep voice is the **howler monkey**. You may not see any, but you're likely to hear their powerful voices emanating from the jungle.

The forest is also home to a rich variety of **birdlife**, and with a good eye you should be able to see toucans, parakeets and hummingbirds even without straying from the main paths. Again, their most active hours are soon after dawn when it's cooler. For a more reliable view of local birdlife, a visit to the **Parque das Aves** (daily 8.30am–6.30pm; $8) is highly recommended although serious bird watchers are likely to be scornful of a place that allows such effortless viewing. Located just 100m from the entrance to the national park on the Brazilian side of the falls, the bird park maintains both small breeding aviaries and enormous walk-through aviaries, still surrounded by dense forest. There's also a large walk-through butterfly cage – butterflies are bred throughout the year and released when mature. All the butterflies and eighty percent of the birds are Brazilian, most of them endemic to the Atlantic forests, the main exception being those in the Pantanal aviary.

Trips into the forest are organized in the Argentine park, and tickets are available at the offices of Iguazú Jungle Explorer (☎3757/421-600) located at the Circuito Inferior. A typical trip lasts around two hours ($25), and involves being driven in the back of a truck along a rough road through the forest, a walk down a narrow trail to the river, and a wild boat ride down some rapids towards the Garganta del Diablo. Don't expect to see any wildlife (much of which is nocturnal), but guides may point out some of the flora. You stand a better chance of seeing some animals – or at least hearing them – at night; escorted moonlit walks take place on two or three nights a month around the time of the full moon (8–10pm; $3). Sign up at the Centro de Visitantes.

It's also possible to rent **mountain bikes** from Iguazú Jungle Explorer; you will be given a map with which you can explore some of the trails. Also on the Argentine side, at Puerto Canoas you can rent an inflatable **boat** and float smoothly downriver 4km to the Puerto Tres Marinas. Expert **guides** are also available who can lead serious birdwatchers, botanists and photographers into the forest: in Foz do Iguaçu, contact the reliable Martin Travel (see "Listings" p.665) for details of upcoming excursions.

Yacutinga

About 50km east of the Parque Nacional Iguazú in Argentina the smaller **Refugio de Vida Silvestre Yacutinga** is in many ways a more appealing experience for visitors. The reserve is located on the Yacutinga peninsula, on the south bank of the Iguaçu River, and covers 570 hectares, almost all of it Mata Atlântica. Apart from conducting environmental research projects on the property, the privately run reserve works with neighbouring farming communities to encourage environmental awareness and sustainable agriculture. Expert English-speaking **guides** take you along trails within the refuge, with walks typically lasting an hour or two, while float trips on the Iguaçu River and tributaries are also offered on most days. What you see, of course, varies enormously, but capuchin monkeys, deer, otters, caimans and other lizards are common sights, and there are ample birdwatching opportunities to satisfy both casual and serious birdwatchers alike. Although the longer trails require a guide, there is one clearly signposted trail that you can take unaccompanied, and you'll also find walkways strung between trees from where you can look out for birds or animals or just take in the serenity of the rainforest.

Visits to Yacutinga (ⓦ www.yacutinga.com) must be arranged in advance through a **travel agent**; contact the reserve by e-mail for an agent in your locality. Yacutinga's agent in Foz do Iguaçu is Martin Travel (see p.665). The cost for two nights and three days at the *Yacutinga Lodge*, with full board and the services of the local guides, is about $350 per person. The price includes transfer by truck and river to the lodge – the road is atrocious, the three-hour drive is bone shattering, but the scenery is wonderful, at first passing through the Parque Nacional before entering a zone of smallholdings, mainly farmed by families of German descent. Accommodation is in rustic but extremely comfortable cabins, all of which have a private bathroom and a wood stove (essential for the chilly winter nights). The Mexican pueblo-style main lodge has a lounge, bar and restaurant, while outside there's a swimming pool and an open-air bar. Meals are superb, with an emphasis on varieties of local squash, beans and other vegetables.

Itaipu

While there's complete agreement that Iguaçu is one of the great natural wonders of Brazil, there's bitter debate as to what **Itaipu** – the world's largest hydroelectricity scheme – represents. Work on the dam, 10km north of Foz do Iguaçu, began in the early 1970s at a cost of US$25 billion, and its eighteen 700,000 kilowatt generators became fully operational in 1991. Proponents of the project argue that the rapidly growing industries of southeastern Brazil needed nothing less than Itaipu's huge electrical capacity, and that without it Brazilian development would be greatly impeded. However, critics claim that Brazil neither needs nor can afford such a massive hydroelectric scheme and that the country would have been much better served by smaller and less prestigious schemes nearer to the centres of consumption. In addition, they point to the social and environmental upheavals that have been caused by the damming of the Rio Paraná and the creation of a 1350-square-kilometre reservoir: forty thousand families have been forced off their land; a microclimate with as yet unknown consequences has developed; and – critics say – the much publicized animal rescue operations and financial assistance for displaced farmers barely address the complex problems.

Visiting Itaipu is easy, with hourly **buses** from Foz do Iguaçu's local bus terminal. You're dropped at the **Visitors' Centre** where a film about the project, in English and other languages, is shown, and from where **free guided tours** depart (Mon–Sat 6 daily; 1hr). The film is extremely slick and, until you stand on the dam and look across the massive reservoir stretching into the horizon, it's easy to be convinced by Itaipu's PR machine that the project was, at worst, no more than a slight local inconvenience.

Santa Catarina

Santa Catarina shares a similar pattern of settlement with other parts of southern Brazil, the indigenous Indians rapidly being displaced by outsiders. In the eighteenth century the state received immigrants from the Azores who settled along the coast; cattle herders from Rio Grande do Sul spread into the higher reaches of the mountainous interior around **Lages** and **São Joaquim**; and European immigrants and their descendants made new homes for themselves in the fertile river valleys. Even today, small communities on the **island of Santa Catarina**, and elsewhere on the coast, continue a way of life that has not changed markedly over the generations. Incidentally, to prevent confusion with the name of the state (though barely succeeding at times), most people call the island of Santa Catarina **Florianópolis**, which is actually the name of the state capital – also situated on the island. Elsewhere, cities such as **Blumenau** and **Joinville**, established by German immigrants, have become totally Brazilianized, but in the surrounding villages and farms many people still speak the language of their forebears in preference to Portuguese.

On the coast, tourism has become very important and facilities are excellent, though the considerable natural beauty is in danger of being eroded by the uncontrolled development that has been taking place in recent years. Inland, though, visitors rarely venture, despite the good roads and widely available hotels. Here, with the minimum of discomfort, it's possible to get a sense of the pioneering spirit that brought immigrants into the interior in the first place – and keeps their descendants there.

The island of Santa Catarina

The **island of Santa Catarina** is noted throughout Brazil for its Mediterranean-like scenery, attractive fishing villages and the city of Florianópolis, the state's small and prosperous capital. The island has a subtropical climate, rarely cold in winter and with a summer heat tempered by refreshing South Atlantic breezes; the vegetation is much softer than that further north. Joined to the mainland by two suspension bridges (the longest, British-designed, has been closed for several decades to all but cyclists and pedestrians), the island is served by frequent **bus** services connecting it with the rest of the state, other parts of Brazil, Buenos Aires, Asunción and Santiago. During January and February the island is extremely popular with Argentine, Uruguayan and Paraguayan tourists who can usually enjoy a summer holiday here for much less than the cost of one at home.

Florianópolis

FLORIANÓPOLIS – or "Desterro" as it was originally called – was founded in 1700 and settled fifty years later by immigrants from the Portuguese mid-Atlantic islands of the Azores. Since then, it's gradually developed from being a sleepy provincial backwater into a sleepy state capital. With the construction of the bridges linking the island with the mainland, Florianópolis as a port has all but died, and today the city thrives as an administrative, commercial and tourist

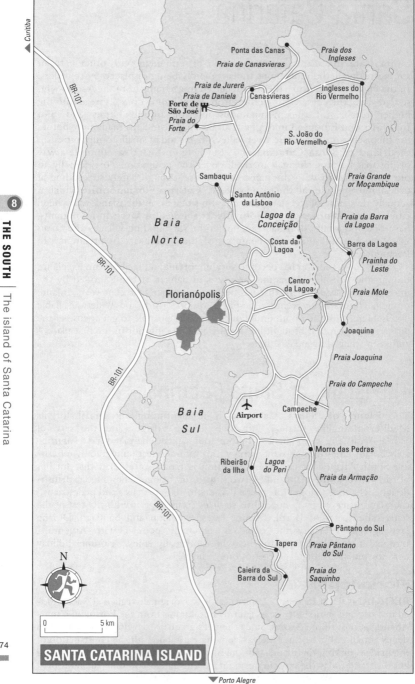

8

Curitiba ▲

BR-101

BR-101

BR-101

BR-101

Ponta das Canas
Praia de Canasvieras
Praia dos Ingleses

Praia de Jurerê
Praia de Daniela Canasvieras
Forte de São José
Praia do Forte

Ingleses do Rio Vermelho

S. João do Rio Vermelho

Sambaqui

Santo Antônio da Lisboa

Praia Grande or Moçambique

B a i a   N o r t e

Lagoa da Conceição

Praia da Barra da Lagoa

Costa da Lagoa

Barra da Lagoa

Prainha do Leste

Centro da Lagoa

Florianópolis

Praia Mole

Joaquina

Praia Joaquina

Praia do Campeche

B a i a   S u l

✈ **Airport**

Campeche

Morro das Pedras

Ribeirão da Ilha

Lagoa do Peri

Praia da Armação

Pântano do Sul

Tapera

Praia Pântano do Sul

Caieira da Barra do Sul

Praia do Saquinho

N

0   5 km

674

SANTA CATARINA ISLAND

▼ Porto Alegre

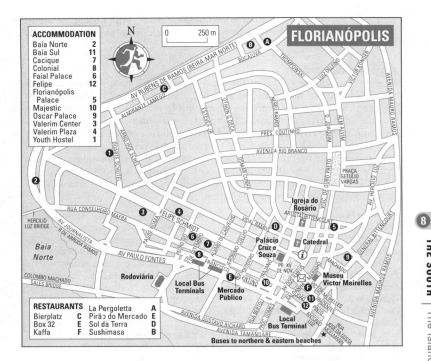

ACCOMMODATION

Baía Norte	2
Baía Sul	11
Cacique	7
Colonial	8
Faial Palace	6
Felipe	12
Florianópolis Palace	5
Majestic	10
Oscar Palace	9
Valerim Center	3
Valerim Plaza	4
Youth Hostel	1

FLORIANÓPOLIS

0   250 m

RESTAURANTS

Bierplatz	C	La Pergoletta	A
Box 32	E	Pirão do Mercado	E
Kaffa	F	Sol da Terra	D
		Sushimasa	B

Buses to northern & eastern beaches

centre. Land reclamation for a multi-laned highway and new bus terminals has totally eliminated the character of the old seafront, and with it vanished much of the city's former charm. Despite all the changes, though, the late nineteenth-century pastel-coloured, stuccoed buildings still recall faint "old world" images, while the relaxed, small-town atmosphere provides a total contrast to the excitement of São Paulo or Rio.

Arrival and information

Buses arrive at the modern **rodoviária** (☎48/224-2777) situated between the two bridges that link the island to the mainland. Outside the main entrance, beyond the car park and dual carriageway, is the former waterfront area where one of the **municipal bus terminals** is situated. From here, frequent buses (50¢) set out for most parts of the city as well as to all points in the south of the island. Otherwise, buses to the northern and eastern beach resorts depart from the corner of Rua José da Costa Moelmann and Avenida Mauro Ramos, a fifteen-minute walk around the hillside. These buses run to a surprisingly accurate timetable (check times at the information booths) and are cheap, though generally crowded. Alternatively, from both terminals there are faster, more comfortable and more expensive *executivo* minibuses ($1) to most of the beaches.

The **airport** (☎48/331-4000) is 12km south of the city and is served by taxis ($12) and "Aeroporto" buses (50¢), which take about forty minutes.

In Praça XV de Novembro, there's a **tourist information kiosk** (Dec–March Mon–Sat 7am–10pm, Sun 7am–7pm; April–Nov Mon–Sat 8am–6pm; ☎48/223-7796), where very good, free maps of the island and city are available, and a branch at the *rodoviária* (daily 8am–7pm). Listings of events in Florianópolis and elsewhere in Santa Catarina can be found in the daily newspaper *Diário Catarinense*.

Accommodation

Most tourists choose to stay at the beaches and resorts around the island (see under "The rest of the island" pp. 678–682), but staying in Florianópolis itself has the benefit of a concentration of reasonably priced hotels, and direct bus services to all parts of the island. Try to arrive early in the day as **accommodation** is snapped up quickly during the peak holiday periods, and it's especially difficult to get a bed at the well-cared-for **youth hostel** at Rua Duarte Schutel 227 (open year-round; ☏48/225-3781, ⊛www.albuerguedajuventurafpolis .com.br; $12 per person). Many of the cheapest **hotels** are located on, or just off, Rua Felipe Schmidt, only a few minutes from both Praça XV de Novembro and the bus terminals.

Baía Norte Av. Beira Mar Norte ☏48/225-3144, ℻225-3227. Pleasant rooms, but be sure to ask for one facing the ocean. Although just a short walk from good bars and restaurants, it's a longer trek into the commercial centre itself. ⑤

Baía Sul Rua Tiradentes 167 ☏48/224-0810. Small and rather outdated rooms, but good value. Favoured by Brazilian business travellers. ③

Cacique Rua Felipe Schmidt 423 ☏48/222-5359. Always popular and therefore difficult to get a room. Good for the price and location in the heart of the city centre. ②

Colonial Rua Conselheiro Mafra 399 ☏48/222-2302. Simple, good-sized rooms, often none too clean, but the service is friendly. ②

Faial Palace Rua Felipe Schmidt 603 ☏48/225-2766, ℻225-0435. Large, modern hotel with spacious, if rather bland, rooms, and helpful staff. Good value. ⑤

Felipe Rua João Pinto 26, at the intersection with Rua Antônio Luz ☏48/222-4122. The rooms here are neat and small, with ten percent discounts offered to youth hostel association card-holders. ②

Florianópolis Palace Rua Artista Bittencourt 2 ☏48/222-9633. The only luxury hotel in the city centre, with excellent facilities, the *Palace* has a minibus service to its private beach at Canasvieras. ⑥

Oscar Palace Av. Hercílio Luz 760 ☏48/222-0099, ℻222-0978. Favoured by Argentine tourists and business travellers, this hotel offers comfortable rooms and friendly service. ④

Valerim Center Rua Felipe Schmidt 554 ☏48/225-1100, ⊛www.hotelvalerim.com.br. The largest of the budget hotels with rooms (some sleeping up to six) that are air-conditioned and equipped with TV and *frigobar* (③). At no. 705 of the same road, the more upmarket *Valerim Plaza* (☏48/225-3388, ⊛www.hotelvalerim.com.br; ③) has similar, but newer facilities.

The City

With the notable exception of Carnaval – rated as the country's fourth most elaborate, and certainly the liveliest south of Rio – few tourists visit the island for the limited charm and attractions of Florianópolis itself. However, being so centrally located, the city does make a good base for exploring the rest of the island, as most points are easily reached within an hour by bus. Take time, though, for at least a stroll around Florianópolis before heading out to the beaches.

On the former waterfront, you'll find two ochre-coloured buildings, the **Mercado Público** (Mon–Fri 8am–9pm & Sat 8am–4pm), which contain some excellent bars and small restaurants, and the **Alfândega** (Mon–Fri 8am–7pm), a former customs house that has been converted for use as a crafts market. From here, there's a steep walk up to the Praia de Fora, the "new town", centred on the main, tree-filled square, **Praça XV de Novembro**. On one side of the square is the **Palácio Cruz e Souza**, an imposing pink building built between 1770 and 1780 as the seat of provincial government. It's now open to the public as the **Museu Histórico de Santa Catarina** (Tues–Fri

10am–6pm, Sat & Sun 10am–4pm) and, as there's no admission charge, it's worth taking a brisk walk around the building to admire the nineteenth-century interior decoration, rather than to examine the unexciting collection of guns, swords and official scrolls. On the other side of the *praça* is Florianópolis' main post office and, just behind it at Rua Victor Meirellas 59, the **Museu Victor Meirellas** (Tues–Fri 1–6pm, Sat & Sun 3–6pm). Meirellas was born in this building in 1832 and went on to become famous for his historically themed paintings. The museum is surprisingly interesting: sixteen of Meirellas' paintings are displayed on the first floor (most notable being the *Battle of Guararapes*, which celebrates Portugal's acquisition of Northeastern Brazil from the Dutch in 1649), and the first floor is used for visiting exhibits of other Brazilian artists.

Overlooking the square from the highest point is the utterly unremarkable **Catedral Metropolitana**; it was originally constructed between 1753 and 1773, but was enlarged and totally remodelled in 1922, so you'd be hard-pressed to identify any original features. The only church in the city centre dating back to the colonial era is the mid-eighteenth-century **Igreja de Nossa Senhora do Rosário**, higher up from the cathedral and best approached by a flight of steep steps from Rua Marechal Guilherme.

On the campus of the Federal University (UFSC), twenty minutes by bus from the city centre, the **Museu de Antropologia** (Mon–Fri 9am–noon & 1–5pm) has a small collection of artefacts belonging to Santa Catarina's decimated Kaingang and Xokleng forest Indians and objects relating to early Azorean immigrants that's worth an hour or so on a rainy day. The **Museu de Arte de Santa Catarina** (Mon–Fri 9am–noon & 3–9pm, Sat & Sun 5–10pm), in the Centro Integrado de Cultura (reached by buses marked "Agronomica"), hosts permanent and temporary exhibitions by local and national artists of often dubious talent. The centre itself also boasts an arts cinema; a detailed programme is published in the *Diário Catarinense*.

Eating, drinking and nightlife

In **the centre**, on the roads that run off the main square in all directions, are numerous cheap, but largely uninspiring **restaurants**. One of the more distinctive is *Kaffa*, on Rua Victor Meirellas behind the main post office, which offers huge portions of satisfying and very reasonably priced Lebanese food. Good vegetarian meals are available in the centre at *Vida*, Rua Visconde de Ouro Preto 62 (Mon–Sat lunch only), as well as at the *Sol da Terra*, Rua Nereu Ramos 13, and *Natural Familia Doll*, Rua Vidal Ramos 43a (both close at 5pm), and out near the federal university (UFSC) at *Soul Salada* in Trinidade Shopping, Rua Lauro Linhares (Mon–Sat to early evening). There are several excellent bars and simple restaurants in the Mercado Público, serving cold beer, light meals and tasty snacks: *Box 32* (Mon–Fri 10am–10pm, Sat 10am–3pm) is especially good and is known as a meeting point for local politicians and artists, while *Pirão do Mercado* (Mon–Sat lunch only) specializes in local dishes of Azorean origin.

Come evening, there's very little life in the commercial centre around Praça XV de Novembro. Instead, people concentrate in the **bars and restaurants** that spread out along the **Beira Mar Norte** (or Avenida Rubens de Arruda Ramos as it is officially called), a dual carriageway that skirts the north of the city along reclaimed land starting at the Hercílio Luz bridge, or head for much more fashionable Lagoa (see p. 679). Places move in and out of popularity rapidly and in summer you'll find that the bars – the first two of which are situated virtually under the bridge itself – are either packed solid with wealthy young people or, for no apparent reason, totally empty. Unfortunately the restaurants here aren't particularly good either and are generally expensive, but there is at least a fair choice, which is more than can be said for the commercial centre. Towards the far end of Beira Mar Norte (take any bus that reads "via Beira Mar Norte") there are several worth noting: at no. 1990 on the avenue itself, *Sushimasa* (closed Tues–Fri lunch & Mon) is a competent Japanese restaurant, and nearby are some pretty good Italian places, the best being *La Pergoletta* (open Tues–Sat evening and all Sun) at Travessa Carreirão 62. Nearby, *Sushimasa* at Travessa Harmonia 2 (open Mon–Sat evenings) is a very pleasant Japanese restaurant specialising in sushi and other fish dishes. Cold beer and hearty German dishes are available at the *Bierplatz* at Beira Mar Norte 210 until late into the night. Further north, in the Beira Mar Norte Shopping Center (Mon–Sat 10am–10pm), there are a dozen fast-food outlets including the usual hamburgers as well as seafood and a decent vegetarian restaurant. The best Japanese food on the island is at *Miyoshi*, located yet further north, at km 3.5 of the SC-401 highway, in the suburb of Saco Grande; a taxi there will cost around $7. The best times to go are Tuesday and Friday evenings when there's a very reasonably priced *por kilo* buffet that includes an excellent sushi and sashimi selection – on other evenings the restaurant is much more expensive.

Listings

Airlines Aerolíneas Argentinas, Rua Tenente Silveira 200, 8th floor, and at the airport (☎48/224-7835); Gol, at the airport (☎48/331-4127); TAM, at the airport (☎48/331-4085); Varig/RioSul/Pluna, Rua Felipe Schmidt 228, and at the airport (☎48/331-4154); VASP, Av. Osmar Cunha 105, and at the airport (☎48/236-3033).

Banks and exchange Banks are located on Rua Felipe Schmidt and by Praça XV de Novembro.

Books Florianópolis' bookshops are poor, but you may find something of local interest at Livros e Livros, Rua Deodoro 191, sala 2; Lunardelli, Rua Victor Meirellas 28; Insular, Rua Felipe Schmidt 51, sala 103; Livraria Catarinense, Rua Deodoro 425 and in the Beira Mar Norte Shopping Center.

Car rental Avis (☎48/236-1426), Hertz (☎48/236-9955), Localiza (☎48/236-1244), Unidas (☎48/236-0607) and Yes (☎48/284-4656)

are all represented at the airport and can arrange delivery in the city centre. During the peak summer season advance reservations are strongly recommended.

Consulates Argentina, Rua Saldanha Marinho 392, 5th floor ☎48/216-4903; Uruguay, Rua Tenente Silveira 94, 10th floor ☎48/216-8800).

Post office The main post office is on Praça XV de Novembro.

Shopping The Beira Mar Norte Shopping Center is on Avenida Rubens de Arruda Ramos heading north from the centre. Apart from numerous surf-oriented shops, it contains all the usual Brazilian fashion brand-name shops. At the former waterfront, the Alfândega building (see p.676) is now an arts and crafts market, though the quality of the merchandise is disappointing.

The rest of the island

Most people arriving in Florianópolis head straight for the **beaches**, undoubtedly the best of which are found on the **north** and **west** coasts. With 42 beaches around the island to choose from, even the most crowded are rarely unbearably so, and they're all suited to a few days' winding down. Despite the existence of a good **bus network**, this is one place where **renting a car** (see "Listings" above) should be seriously considered, especially if you have limited time and want to see as much of the island as possible: the roads are excellent, though crowded in mid-summer, and the drivers fairly civilized.

The north coast

The island's increasingly built-up **north coast** offers safe swimming in calm, warm seas and, as such, is particularly popular with families. The long, gently curving bay of **CANASVIERAS** is the most crowded of the northern resorts, largely geared towards *paulista*, Argentine and Uruguayan families who own or rent houses near to the beach. Most of the bars along the beach cater to the tourists, playing Argentine and North American pop music, and serving Argentine snacks accompanied by Brazilian beer. By walking away from the concentration of bars at the centre of the beach, towards the east and Ponta das Canas, it's usually possible to find a relatively quiet spot. Unless you're renting a house for a week or more (agencies abound), finding **accommodation** is difficult, as the unappealing hotels are usually booked solid throughout the summer months. However, if you are set on staying here, by asking in the souvenir shops and restaurants you'll eventually be directed to someone with a spare **room to rent**. The local **restaurants** mostly offer the same menu of prawn dishes, pizza and hamburgers, with only the *Restaurante Tropical* and its Bahian dishes standing out as different.

Heading westwards you'll reach **JURERÊ**, another long beach that almost exclusively attracts families, and is separated from Canasviera by a rocky promontory. Still further west, a series of coves fringed by luxuriant vegetation – reached by clambering down from the road skirting the coast, or by climbing over the rocks that separate one cove from another – link Jurerê to **DANIELA**, a smaller and less developed beach. Though it amounts to nothing special, the turquoise waters of the nearby coves are well worth the small effort needed to reach them, and **rooms** are available next to the *Lancheria Palheiro*. Roughly midway between Jurerê and Daniela, stunning views of the coast and across to the mainland can be appreciated from the ruins of the **Forte de São José** (usually referred to as Forte Jurerê), built in 1742 to guard the northern approaches to Desterro. Next to the fort there's a small eighteenth-century chapel.

The east coast

If you find the north coast too crowded and developed, head for the **east coast**, where Atlantic rollers scare away most of the families. Take extreme care yourself, though, as the undercurrents here make for dangerous swimming. There are a couple of places to avoid: **PRAIA BRAVA** (the most northerly of the east coast beaches) is dominated by huge condominium complexes that have resulted in this beautiful stretch of coast becoming the island's ugliest corner. There's been similar uncontrolled development at **INGLESES**, a little further south. Instead you're better off returning to Florianópolis and crossing the island to the Lagoa da Conceição, a large saltwater lagoon in the centre of the island.

Lagoa da Conceição

The **Lagoa da Conceição** is very popular amongst families and others who want to swim, canoe or windsurf. **CENTRO DA LAGOA** (usually simply referred to as Lagoa), a bustling little town at the southern end of the lagoon, is a very pleasant place to stay: there are good bus services from here into Florianópolis and to the east coast beaches, a post office, a branch of Banco do Brasil (with an ATM), grocery stores and numerous restaurants and bars on the main road. This is one of the most lively nightspots on the island during the summer and at weekends throughout the year, with restaurants always crowded and people overflowing into the street from the bars. **Accommodation** is scarce, however: try the rather spartan *Pousada A'guia Pequena*, a couple of minutes' walk from the bridge that crosses the lagoon, at Rua Rita Lourenço da Silveira 114 (℡48/232-2339; ❹), or the very similar *Pousada do Grego* at Rua Antônio da Silveira 58 (℡48/232-0734; ❸). If they're fully booked, try the large, rather institutional *Hotel Samuka*, Travessa Pedro Manuel Fernandes 96, at the intersection with Avenida Das Rendeiras (℡48/232-5024, Ⓦwww .hotelsamuka.cjb.net; ❹). An alternative option (only really practical if you have a car) is the *Chalés do Canto*, chalets set in pleasant park-like grounds, 4km south of town at Rua Laurindo Januário da Silveira 2212 (℡48/232-0471; ❹).

The town's beaches are close by; cross the small bridge on the road leaving Centro da Lagoa and it's a ten-minute walk. There are also some attractive beaches on the isolated northwest shore of the lagoon – one of the most beautiful parts of the island – around **COSTA DA LAGOA**, a charming fishing village barely touched by tourism. The area is impossible to reach by road and involves either a three-hour walk along a trail skirting the lagoon, or an hour's boat ride; boats leave every hour (75¢) from beneath the bridge in Centro da Lagoa, stopping off at isolated houses and tiny fishing hamlets on the way. Once at Costa da Lagoa, a ten-minute walk along a rough trail will take you to a nearby waterfall, where you can take a refreshing dip in the natural pool. Back in the village there are swimming beaches and a couple of restaurants, but you'd do better taking the trail that hugs the shore of the lagoon back south towards Centro da Lagoa; a twenty-minute walk will bring you to a much more attractive beach, which has an excellent seafood restaurant and bar. If you're tempted to stay, rooms are available above the restaurant here (❷), but otherwise you can either continue back along the trail to Centro da Lagoa, or wait at the pier for the hourly boat.

BARRA DA LAGOA, the village at the entrance to the Lagoa da Conceição, has succeeded fairly well in allowing tourism to develop alongside the inhabitants' traditional main activity – fishing. There are beautiful cliffside walks from here, the best reached by crossing the Ponte Pêncil, a rickety suspended footbridge that leads to the very pretty **PRAINHA DO LESTE**, a small cove flanked by forbidding rock formations where beach parties are often held in summer. Barra da Lagoa has several **restaurants**, a **campsite** and plenty of **rooms** and cabins to rent. There are also several **pousadas** in Prainha, including the *Gaivota* (℡48/232-3253; ❷), which offers no-frills bed and breakfast accommodation, and the rather more comfortable *Vipaz* (℡48/232-3193; ❸), across the Ponte Pêncil, with spacious rooms sleeping two to four people, and cooking facilities as well. You may, however, have better luck finding a room at the much larger *Recanto dos Pinhais* (℡48/232-3662, Ⓦwww.recantodospinhais.odi.com.br; ❸), located amidst pleasant park-like gardens just outside Barra, alongside the Reserva Florestal do Rio Vermelho (see below).

North of Lagoa da Conceição

Stretching north for kilometres, Barra da Lagoa's beach merges into **PRAIA DA MOÇAMBIQUE** (also known as Praia Grande). Praia da Moçambique is the longest beach on the island, over 12km, and also one of the least developed, due to the **Reserva Florestal do Rio Vermelho** that takes up most of its hinterland. Inland from here on the Estrada Geral do Rio Vermelho – the road that leads to the village of Rio Vermelho – is one of the most outstanding, and surprising, **restaurants** on the island, well worth going out of your way for. *Chez Altamiro* (℡48/9971-3387; reservations strongly advised) is run by an islander who, despite having never set foot in France, cooks extremely good traditional French food for around $20 a head. The restaurant is in the middle of nowhere, but is easily recognized by the tricolor that adorns the outside of the wooden building.

South of Barra da Lagoa, the road climbs steeply, passing mountain-sized sand dunes to the secluded **PRAIA GALHETA**, the only nudist beach on the island, and **PRAIA MOLE**, whose beautiful beach is slightly hidden beyond the sand dunes and beneath low-lying cliffs. Mole is extremely popular with young people but, rather surprisingly, commercial activity has remained low key, probably because there's a deep drop-off right at the water's edge.

Approached by a road passing between gigantic dunes, the next beach is at **JOAQUINA**, very popular with surfers, particularly so during the Brazilian national surf championships, held annually in the last week of January. The water's cold, however, and the sea rough, only really suitable for strong swimmers. If you have the energy, climb to the top of the dunes where you'll be rewarded with the most spectacular views in all directions. The dunes are a popular location for sandboarding and no skill is required if you sit, rather than stand, on a board as you hurtle down a dune (board rentals at the roadside for $2 an hour) and paragliding (see box below). Accommodation at Joaquina is limited to one hotel, the *Joaquina Beach* (T48/232-5059, Wwww.joaquinabeachhotel.com.br; ●), usually booked solid in the summer. The beach stretches 3.5km to the south, blending into **PRAIA DO CAMPECHE**, so by walking for fifteen minutes or so you can escape the Joaquina's crowds and be almost alone. Campeche, which itself merges into Morro das Pedras and Armação (see below), is considered by many to be the most beautiful stretch of the island's coast, but due to the strong current and often ferocious surf fewer people are attracted here than to the beaches to the north. Consequently, there's been comparatively little building work, and only slowly are houses, bars and beach houses appearing, concentrated around the southern portion of the beach.

Continuing south, you reach the fishing village of **ARMAÇÃO**, whose lovely hilly backdrop gives it a stunning location. There's an attractive beach – though, here too, the waves and currents are unforgiving – and well-marked trails leading both inland and to more protected coves. Of the **places to stay**, the *Alemdomar* (T48/237-5600, Wwww.alemdomar.com.br; ●), some 250 meters south of the village near the Lagoa do Peri, is a relaxing if rather exclusive option, while the beds at the well-equipped youth hostel, the *Albergue Armação* (T48/389-5542, Ealbergue@brturbo.com; $8 per person). fill up fast; in summer reservations are essential. Armação is also the nearest point to the **Ilha do Campeche**, where pristine white sand beaches are protected from any form of development – only four hundred visitors are permitted at any one time, along with a few people selling refreshments. Boats from Armação take about 30 minutes to complete the three-kilometre crossing ($5 return).

Beyond here, practically at the end of the road, is **PÂNTANO DO SUL**, a rather larger fishing village at the end of a well-protected bay with a moun-

---

Paragliding on Santa Catarina

The state of Santa Catarina has some good **paragliding** locations, with the Joaquina sand dunes on the island of Santa Catarina being an excellent place to learn. Parapente Sul, based at Rua João Antônio da Silveira 201, Centro da Lagoa da Conceição (T48/232-0791 or 982-6811), has an excellent reputation and offers courses for $230. Courses generally run over a four-week period, with as many lessons given as needed (usually about 15) before you graduate with a jump off the cliff and flight over Praia Mole. If you want to simply get a taste of paragliding, you can fly tandem over Praia Mole with an instructor for $18.

tainous backdrop. The village itself is not at all attractive, but the water is calmer here than elsewhere on the east coast, the views of the small, uninhabited islands offshore are pleasant, and you can eat well. There are several **restaurants** right on the beach, including the *Bar do Arante*, known for serving some of the best seafood on the island, and a couple of **pousadas**, the very pleasant *Sol de Costa* (☎48/222-5071; ❷), and the *Pescador* (☎48/237-7122; ❸). Tourism has had only a minimal impact on the inhabitants' lives and Azorean traditions have remained strong, most visibly during Carnaval when brass bands wind their way through the streets and along the beach, the rhythms very different from the familiar beat of samba drums.

The west coast

The principal places of interest on the **west coast** are **SAMBAQUI** and **SANTO ANTÔNIO DE LISBOA** to the north of Florianópolis, and **RIBEIRÃO DA ILHA** to the south. As the island's oldest, most attractive and least spoilt settlements, the houses in these places are almost all painted white and have dark blue sash windows – in typical Azorean style – and each village has a simple colonial church. As was the case with most of the island's settlements, these villages were founded by immigrants from the Azores, and their present-day inhabitants – who still refer to themselves as being Azorean – retain many traditions of the islands from which their forefathers came. Fishing, rather than catering to the needs of tourists, remains the principal activity of the three villages, and the waters offshore from Santo Antônio are used to farm mussels and oysters, considered the best anywhere in the island. Azorean immigrants brought their lace-making skills to Santa Catarina, too, and intricately fashioned lace tablecloths, mats and other items are displayed for sale outside some of the houses in Ribeirão da Ilha – or you can buy them at the Casa Açoriana, Rua Cônego Serpa, in Santo Antônio. Local handicrafts are also on display, along with exhibits on the Azorean settlement of the island, at the **Ecomuseu** (Tues–Fri 10am–6pm, Sat, Sun & holidays noon–6pm; $1.50) in Ribeirão da Ilha. Because the beaches are small and face the mainland, tourism has remained minimal, the few visitors who are about are on day-trips from resorts elsewhere on the island. They stay just long enough for a meal: especially recommended is the superb *Gugu*, in Sambaqui, with an excellent choice of local seafood and dishes, but *Restaurante Rosemar*, outside Sambaqui towards Santo Antônio, and *Pizzeria Lisboa*, in Santo Antônio itself, are also good options for seafood.

South of Ribeirão da Ilha, hugging the steep hillside as it passes tiny, deserted coves, the dreadfully potholed road leading to Barra do Sul runs through some of the most stunning scenery on the island. The rainfall here is extremely heavy, nurturing a profusion of rich foliage, most noticeably flamboyants and bougainvillaea.

If you choose **to stay** in one of the west coast villages, finding a room can be quite a problem, but if successful you'll be rewarded by complete tranquillity of a kind lost to most of the rest of the island over the course of the last couple of decades. Your best chance is in Santo Antônio: the *Pousada Caminho dos Açores* (☎48/235-1363; ❸) is set in a lovely garden and has an attractive pool, or there's the *Pousada Mar de Dentro* (☎48/235-1521; ❹), very similar, with a tiny pool, but right on the beach. In Ribeirão da Ilha try the modest *Pousada do Museu* (☎48/237-8148; ❷), which fronts onto the beach by the Ecomuseu.

Around Florianópolis: the mainland

On the mainland, 30km inland and southwest of Florianópolis, lies the small resort of **SANTO AMARO DA IMPERATRIZ**, served by four buses daily from Praça da Bandeira. In the late nineteenth century, Imperatriz (the name commemorating the visit in 1845 of Brazil's emperor, Dom Pedro II and his wife, the Empress Teresa Cristina) was quite a fashionable spa town. The *Hotel Caldas da Imperatriz* (☎48/245-7088, ⓦwww.hotelcaldas.com.br; ❹ half board) was opened to celebrate the imperial visit, and for years afterwards succeeded in mimicking the European idea of the Grand Hotel, attracting wealthy Brazilians from as far away as Rio. Today most of the hotel's visitors are elderly *catarinenses* and *gaúchos*, especially chronic sufferers of rheumatism and those with digestive or nervous disorders, though the baths are also open to non-guests on payment of a small fee.

A few kilometres up the narrow, tree-filled valley is another spa, the more recently developed **ÁGUAS MORNAS** and its luxury *Palace Hotel* (☎48/245-7015, ⓦwww.aguasmornaspalacehotel.com.br; ❺ half board), favoured by the seriously rich. The spa itself is not particularly attractive, but the approach road and general setting are delightful.

Parque Estadual da Serra do Tabuleiro

For anyone with even a vague interest in the fauna of Santa Catarina, a visit to the nature reserve of the **Serra do Tabuleiro** (daily 9am–5pm; $1.50) is a must. Animals and birds from throughout the state live in as near to natural conditions as is possible, and endangered species are bred in the hope that they will eventually be returned to the wild. You'll see alligators, tortoises, twenty species of birds (including rheas, emus and flamingos – and even the odd lost penguin from Patagonia), anteaters and deer and, best of all, get no feeling that you're in, essentially, a zoo.

To get to the reserve from Florianópolis, take a **bus** (Empresa Paulo Lopez line, or any bus heading south along the main coastal highway, the BR–101) and ask to be let off at the entrance to the "Parque da Serra". From the park's entrance, it takes about half an hour to walk to the reserve. As the journey time there is about two hours, you'd do best to take the 7am or, at the latest, the 10.30am bus from Florianópolis; count on returning on the 2pm or 4.30pm bus. It's a tiring excursion, but well worth it.

The north coast to São Francisco do Sul

If you're going to travel by bus on Santa Catarina's coastal highway (the BR–101) **north of Florianópolis** in the Brazilian summer you're best off keeping your eyes firmly closed. The bumper-to-bumper traffic moves at terrifying speeds, with cars, trucks and buses constantly leapfrogging one another for no apparent advantage; the wrecked cars that litter the highway are enough to make you get out of the bus and walk to your destination – something that, at times, might be faster anyway. But worse, if you don't have a car of your own, is that much of the BR–101 passes alongside absolutely stunning beaches, some of which have remained totally devoid of buildings and people. If you're on the bus, there's no hope of stopping for a refreshing dip, and you'll just have to make do with the idyllic images out of the window.

Porto Belo

Although the stretch immediately north of Florianópolis is probably the most beautiful part of the Santa Catarina coast, during the peak summer season it is completely overrun by Argentine and *paulista* tourists. Less than two hours from Florianópolis, the peninsula and city of **PORTO BELO** is easily reached by bus, and although the local authority's claim that there are 32 beaches around Porto Belo is highly suspect, the beaches there certainly are numerous and large enough to cope with the visitors – at least outside of the peak months of January and February.

The "city" of Porto Belo is, in reality, just an overgrown village containing a tourist office, post office, and a few bars and restaurants, but from here frequent local buses fan out around the peninsula, stopping along the road to pick up passengers. The most attractive beaches are **Bombas** and **Bombinhas**, 5km and 8km east of Porto Belo respectively and separated from one another by a rocky promontory. The bay in which they're found is very pretty, with rich vegetation behind, and the waves here are suitable for inexperienced surfers. South of Bombinhas, if you're looking for open sea and more powerful waves, the east-facing **Praia do Mariscal** is better, but should be braved by only the most expert of surfers. In complete contrast, the nearby **Praia do Canto** is ideal for anyone merely seeking a gentle swim.

Hotels in Porto Belo are generally small and fairly expensive – you're unlikely to find a room for less than $40 a night, and you may have to pay considerably more. The best hope of finding somewhere to stay is in Bombinhas: try the Spanish colonial-style *Pousada Águas* (☎47/340-5799; ❸) or, with panoramic views and a small pool, the *Pousada das Palmeiras* (☎47/369-2222; ❸). Expensive, but worth every *real* is the *Pousada do Arvoredo* (☎47/369-2355; ❺), which has attractive rooms with balconies overlooking the gardens and the ocean, and a pool. Back in Porto Belo itself, there's the *Pousada Enseada das Garoupas* (☎47/369-4383; ❹) or the more basic *Pousada das Vieras* (☎47/369-4468; ❸). The only bargain around, at $7 per head, is the **youth hostel** (☎47/369-4327; summer reservations essential), about ten minutes' walk away, on Av. Governador Celso Ramos 1442, the approach road to town.

Balneário Camboriú

Just 20km north of Porto Belo lies **BALNEÁRIO CAMBORIÚ**, Brazil's answer to the worst wall-to-wall concrete high-rise Spanish resort. It's got the lot, though you probably won't want any of it: high-rise hotels, a towel-sized patch of beach per person, and nightclubs which celebrate "Carnaval" all summer, with dance troupes imported from the tropical, more "exotic" Brazil to the north.

Stretching for 5km along the Avenida Atlântica, Camboriú is only a few streets deep. With the mountains behind the resort plunging almost straight into the sea, it's just about possible to imagine how beautiful it once was before the developers moved in, back in the 1930s. Today, there's precious little natural beauty still in evidence but, if you do want to stick around, there's rarely a problem finding a room, although many hotels are block-booked by Argentine tour operators; the cheapest **hotels** are centrally located, near the *rodoviária* (from where buses leave for just about every city in South America south of Rio; ☎47/367-2901), and on the streets set back from the beach. The **tourist office** (Dec–March daily 8am–8pm, April–Nov Mon–Fri 8am–noon & 2–6pm; ☎47/367-8122), with branches at Praça Papa João Paulo I 320 and Praça Tamandaré, provides helpful information on hotel availability, a list of the phenomenal number of **restaurants**, most of which only open between December and March, and the latest information on the constantly changing nightclub and disco scene.

Itajaí

Santa Catarina's most important port, **ITAJAÍ**, is located at the mouth of the Rio Itajaí-Açu, 10km north of Balneário Camboriú. Although it was founded in the early eighteenth century, Itajaí looks fairly new, with few buildings dating back to before 1950 – and with nothing of any tourist interest. However, it's an important transport centre, and it may not be possible to avoid the city altogether. Fortunately, most buses pass straight by it, with only a minority actually stopping to pick up and put down passengers in the city. And as there's a constant flow of buses to Blumenau, Joinville and Florianópolis, as well as further afield in all directions, there are few reasons actually to stay in Itajaí. One reason might be to catch an early morning plane from nearby Navegantes **airport** (☏47/342-1132), from where you can fly to Florianópolis, Porto Alegre and São Paulo. To get to the airport, take the ferry from Avenida Argentina, across the river, and then a taxi at around $4; for slightly more, taxis will take you direct from Itajaí, via the ferry, to the airport. Should you need a **hotel**, a couple are clearly visible from the *rodoviária*: the *Itajaí Tur* (☏47/348-4600; ❷) is convenient and has rooms of varying levels of comfort and price. A few blocks away from the *rodoviária*, on the way to the centre, is the *Hotel San Remo* (☏47/348-0968; ❶), offering basic accommodation. Downtown at Rua Felipe Schmidt 198, the *Grande Hotel* (☏47/348-2179; ❸) is a comfortable, executive-style place.

If for some reason you really can't get out of Itajaí, and have some time to spare, the city's **beaches** aren't bad. From the local bus terminal in the city centre, near the intersection of Rua Joinville and Avenida Victor Konder, buses take about twenty minutes to reach the nearest beaches, **Atalaia** and **Geremias**, or a little longer to get to the cleaner **Praia Cabecudas**.

The Ilha de São Francisco

North of Itajaí, the highway gradually turns inland towards Joinville (see p.687), but 45km east of here is the **Ilha de São Francisco** lies 45km off-shore, a low-lying island separated from the mainland by a narrow strait that is spanned by a causeway. As Joinville's port and the site of a major Petrobras oil refinery, São Francisco may seem like a place to avoid, but this isn't the case. Both the port and refinery keep a discreet distance from the main town, São Francisco do Sul, and the beaches, while the surprisingly few sailors who are around blend perfectly with the slightly dilapidated colonial setting.

São Francisco do Sul

The island was first visited by European sailors as early as 1504, though not until the middle of the following century was the town of **SÃO FRANCIS-CO DO SUL** established. It's one of the oldest settlements in the state and also one of the very few places in Santa Catarina where colonial and nine-teenth-century buildings survive concentrated together. During most of its first two hundred years, São Francisco do Sul was little more than a naval outpost, its simple local economy based on fishing and sugar-cane production. In the nineteenth century, with the opening of nearby areas to immigrants from Germany, the town grew in importance as a transhipment point for people and produce. Merchants established themselves in the town, building grand houses and dockside warehouses, many of which remain today – protected from demolition and gradually undergoing restoration. Dominating the city's skyline is the **Igreja Matriz**, the main church, originally built in 1665 by Indian slaves; completely reconstructed in 1884, the church has lost all of its original features. You might want to visit the **Museu Histórico** (Tues–Fri 9am–6pm, Sat & Sun 11am–6pm) on Rua Coronel Carvalho, housed in São Francisco's nineteenth-century prison building (which, incidentally, stayed in use until 1968). The former cells have been converted into small exhibition halls; the most interesting exhibits are nineteenth-century photographs of the town. The **Museu Nacional do Mar** on Rua Manoel Lourenço de Andrade (Tues–Fri 9am–6pm, Sat & Sun 11am–6pm) has a collection devoted to the technology of ocean travel and the people who make their living from the sea, with an emphasis on southern Brazil.

Most of the island's visitors bypass the town altogether and head straight for the beaches to the east, so, even in midsummer, there's rarely any difficulty in finding a **hotel** with room. Quite comfortable, and with sea views, is the *Hotel Kontiki* (✆47/444-2232; ❷) at Rua Camacho 33, near the market or, if you want a pool, there's the relatively luxurious *Hotel Zibamba* (✆47/444-2020; ❹) at Rua Fernandes Dias 27. Eating out holds no great excitement, with the *Hotel Zibamba*'s seafood restaurant the best of a generally poor bunch.

From the market in the town centre, there are **buses** to the *rodoviária*, beyond the town's limits, from where there are hourly connections to Joinville as well as daily services to São Paulo and Curitiba.

The island's beaches

The prettiest beaches, **Paulos** and **Ingleses**, are also the nearest to town, just a couple of kilometres to the east. Both are small, and have trees to provide shade, and surprisingly few people take advantage of the protected sea, ideal for weak swimmers. On the east coast, **Praia de Ubatuba** and the adjoining **Praia de Enseada**, about 15km from town, are the island's most popular beaches, with enough surf to have fun in but not enough to be dangerous. At Enseada there are a couple of **campsites** and an overpriced hotel, while Ubatuba caters mainly for families who rent or own houses that front the beach. By way of contrast, a ten-minute walk across the peninsula from the eastern end of Enseada leads to **Praia da Saúde** (or just Prainha), where the waves are suitable for only the most macho surfers.

Buses to Enseada and Ubatuba leave from the market in the town centre, with the last buses in both directions departing at about 9.30pm.

Northeast Santa Catarina

Although the northeast of Santa Catarina is populated by people of many ethnic origins, it's an area most associated with **Germans**, who so obviously dominate both culturally and economically. **Joinville** and **Blumenau** vie with each other to be not only the economic powerhouse of the region, but also the cultural capital. However, both cities lose out in terms of tourist interest to the small towns and villages of the interior, where old dialects continue to be spoken and survive. One such community is **Pomerode**, which is set in a picturesque area and does much to promote its German heritage.

In the nineteenth century, as it became more difficult to enter the United States, land-hungry European immigrants sought new destinations, many choosing Brazil as their alternative America. Thousands made their way into the forested wilderness of Santa Catarina, attempting to become independent farmers, and of all of them, it was the **Germans** who most successfully fended off assimilationist pressures. Concentrated in areas where few non-Germans lived, there was little reason for them to learn Portuguese, and, as merchants, teachers, Catholic priests and Protestant pastors arrived with the immigrants, complete communities evolved, with flourishing German cultural organizations and a varied German-language press. After Brazil's entry into World War II, restrictions on the use of German were introduced and many German organizations were proscribed, accused of being Nazi fronts. Certainly, "National Socialism" found some of its most enthusiastic followers among overseas Germans and, though the extent of **Nazi activity** in Santa Catarina is a matter of debate, for years after the collapse of the Third Reich ex-Nazis attracted sympathy in even the most isolated forest homesteads.

Later, due to the compulsory use of Portuguese in schools, the influence of radio and television and an influx of migrants from other parts of the state to work in the region's rapidly expanding industries, the German language appeared to be dying in Santa Catarina. As a result, in **Joinville** and **Blumenau** – the region's largest cities – German is now rarely heard. However, in outlying villages and farming communities such as **Pomerode**, near Blumenau, German remains very much alive, spoken everywhere but in government offices. Recently, too, the German language and Teuto-Brazilian culture have undergone a renaissance and the German government has provided financial support. Property developers are encouraged to heed supposedly traditional **German architectural styles**, resulting in a plethora of buildings that may be appropriate for alpine conditions, but look plain silly in the Brazilian subtropics. A more positive development has been the move to protect and restore the houses of the early settlers, especially those built in the most characteristic local building style, that of **enxaimel** ("Fachwerk" in German) – exposed bricks within an exposed timber frame. These houses are seen throughout the region, concentrated most heavily in the area around Pomerode. Keen to reap benefits from the new ethnic awareness, local authorities have also initiated pseudo-German **festivals**, such as Blumenau's Munich-inspired "Oktoberfest" and Pomerode's more authentic "Festa Pomerana", both of which have rapidly become major tourist draws.

Joinville and around

An hour from São Francisco, the land on which **JOINVILLE** was settled was originally given as a dowry by Emperor Dom Pedro to his sister, who had married the Prince of Joinville, the son of Louis-Philippe of France. A deal with Hamburg timber merchants meant that, in 1851, 191 Germans, Swiss and Norwegians arrived in Santa Catarina, to exploit the 25 miles of virgin forest, stake out homesteads and establish the "Colonia Dona Francisca" – later known as Joinville. As more Germans were dispatched from Hamburg, Joinville grew and prospered, developing from an agricultural backwater into the state's foremost industrial city. This economic success has diluted much of Joinville's once solidly German character, but evidence of its ethnic origins remains: the largely Germanic architecture and the impeccably clean streets produce the atmosphere of a rather dull small town in Germany.

The Town

Shops and services are concentrated along Rua Princesa Isabel, while Rua XV de Novembro and Rua IX de Março run parallel to each other, terminating at the river. However, the points of interest associated with Joinville's German heritage are more widely scattered. The first place to head for is the **Museu Nacional de Imigração e Colonização** at Rua Rio Branco 229, near Praça da Bandeira (Tues–Fri 9am–5pm, Sat & Sun 11am–5pm), an excellent introduction to the history of German immigrants in Santa Catarina in general and Joinville in particular. In the main building, formerly the Prince of Joinville's palace, built in 1870, there are some late nineteenth- and early twentieth-century photographs, though the museum's most interesting features are an old barn containing farm equipment used by early *colonos*, and a typical nineteenth-century *enxaimel* farmhouse with period furnishings. If you've more than a passing interest in Joinville's history, also visit the superbly organized **Arquivo Histórico** (Mon–Fri 8am–noon & 2–9pm, Sat 8am–noon), on Rua Rio de Janeiro, where temporary, mainly photographic, exhibitions are held.

As throughout the region, Joinville's municipal authorities are making efforts to preserve the surviving **enxaimel houses**. Although scattered throughout the city, they can be seen in some concentration along the former main approach road, the cobbled **Rua XV de Novembro**. On the same road, about twenty minutes' walk from the centre, is the **Cemitério do Imigrante**, the final resting place of many of Joinville's pioneer settlers. Covering a hillside from where there are fine views of the city, the cemetery has been preserved as a national monument, the tombs and headstones serving as testimony to Joinville's ethnic origins. If you have some time on the way to the cemetery, take a brief look around the **Museu de Arte**, Rua XV de Novembro 1400 (Tues–Fri 9am–9pm, Sat & Sun 11am–6pm). The museum, housed in a small German-style mansion built in 1864, has a small collection of works by mainly local artists and also hosts visiting exhibitions. There's a **cinema** featuring non-commercial, often German, films as well.

It's also worth popping into the **Mercado Municipal**, near the local bus terminal, which sells food and some handicrafts produced by local German *colonos*. On the second Saturday of each month a **handicraft market** is held in the nearby Praça Nereu Ramos.

Practicalities

The **rodoviária** (☎47/433-2991) is 2km from the city centre, reached in five minutes by bus or in half an hour on foot by walking down Rua Ministro Calógeras and then left along Avenida Kubitschek. Bus services to neighbouring cities are excellent. The terminal for **city buses** and those to Dona Francisca (see opposite) is in the centre, at the end of Rua IX de Março. There's an **airport** (☎47/467-1000), 13km north of the city, with flights to Florianópolis, Porto Alegre and São Paulo.

Opened in 1910, Joinville's **train station** – an imposing construction with a German half-hipped roof – is the oldest one still functioning in Santa Catarina. Today, the only passenger trains are laid on for tourists in the summer months, going east to São Francisco do Sul; enquire at the **tourist information** office at Rua XV de Novembro 4305 (daily 8am–8pm; ☎47/453-0177).

Finding a comfortable, spotlessly clean and reasonably priced **hotel** is usually easy, though Joinville has become a popular place for conferences, during which accommodation is scarce. In the city centre, on Rua Jerônimo Coelho near the local bus terminal, try the *Ideal* (☎47/422-3660; ❶) at no. 98, or, if you prefer a private bathroom, the *Príncipe* (☎47/422-8555; ❷) at no. 27. Nearby is Joinville's priciest place to stay, the *Tannenhof* (☎47/433-8011, ⓦ www.tannenhof.com.br; ❺) at Rua Visconde de Taunay 340, with all the features one expects of a large, luxury hotel. Smaller but with much more character is the *Anthurium Parque Hotel*, Rua São José 226 (☎47/422-6299, ⓦwww .anthurium.com.br; ❹), a curious building supposedly of "Norwegian–German" style, located in pretty grounds near the cathedral. Around the corner from here at Rua Ministro Calógeras 612 is the *Germânia* (☎47/433-9886, ⓦwww.hotelgermania.com.br; ❹), which to all appearances is just another small modern tower block, but which has extremely comfortable rooms, helpful staff and very friendly owners.

Not surprisingly, **German restaurants** abound, but most are of the sausage, pig's knuckle, potato and sauerkraut level of sophistication. The *Bie-keller*, conveniently located at Rua XV de Novembro 497 (closed Mon), is typical, or try one of the many self-service restaurants in the Shopping Müeller, a large shopping centre next to the *Hotel Tannenhof*. If you're desperate for a decent meal, you'll have to go out to the suburbs (a $3 taxi ride) to the *Sopp* (evenings only, closed Sun) at Rua Marechal Deodoro 640, the best restaurant in Joinville. The excellent menu, based on German cooking, is varied enough for most tastes and the beer is excellent. For **afternoon tea**, you'll get good cakes at the *Delicatesse Viktoria* at Rua Felipe Schmidt 400, near to the Shopping Müeller; alternatively, all the upmarket hotels serve a good high tea (*café colonial*)

There's a cultural institute in Joinville, the Instituto Cultural Brasil-Alemanha on Rua Princesa Isabel, near Rua Sergipe, and students congregate in the nearby **bars** in the evenings after classes. Since 1937, the **Festa das Flores** has been held for ten days during the second half of November, the height of the orchid season – flower shows, German folk dancing, music and food are the main attractions. Pride of place in the cultural calendar goes to the annual **Festival Internacional de Dança**, the largest event of its kind in Latin America. For twelve days around mid-July, dance companies from around the world descend on Joinville, attracting an audience from throughout Brazil. So strong is Joinville's association with dance, that in 1999 it was chosen by the Bolshoi as the location of its first ballet school outside Russia.

Around Joinville: Estrada Bonita and Estrada Dona Francisca

Although Joinville itself has developed increasingly into a rather anonymous big city, its rural, German-speaking hinterland to the west has changed little over the past few decades. There are two distinct areas to head for: the **Estrada Bonita**, with its well-organized small farms selling homemade jams, *cachaça* and biscuits, and the **Estrada Dona Francisca**, where you'll find some of the oldest and best-cared-for *enxaimel* houses in Santa Catarina. In both areas, visitors are warmly received. For Estrada Bonita's *colonos*, tourism enables them to sustain a reasonable standard of living and keep young people from moving to Joinville, while in the Dona Francisca area local awareness of the historic importance of the old buildings is high, and people are happy to show their homes to visitors. The landscape is also beautiful in this region: flat, rich farmland set against a dramatic forested mountain backdrop.

Joinville's tourist office distributes a useful free **brochure** and **map** covering the Estrada Bonita area, as well as details of the *colonos* who are members of the Turismo Rural project and therefore happy to open their farms to visitors. The homesteads are widely scattered, however, and a car is pretty essential; alternatively, the tourist office runs a weekly bus **tour** of the area, departing from the tourist office at 9.30am ($7 including lunch). In the Dona Francisca area, the most interesting houses are dispersed over a large area and often hidden in forest, and you're best off accompanied by someone who knows the area well; ask at the tourist office for the name of a taxi driver who's familiar with the area, and negotiate a price (about $15 for a couple of hours).

Blumenau

Despite Joinville's challenge, **BLUMENAU** has succeeded in promoting itself as the "capital" of German Santa Catarina. Picturesquely located on the right bank of the Rio Itajaí, Blumenau was founded in 1850 by Dr Hermann Blumenau, who served as director of the colony until his return to Germany in 1880. Blumenau always had a large Italian minority, but it was mainly settled by Germans and, as late as the 1920s, two-thirds of the population spoke German as their mother tongue. In the surrounding rural communities an even larger proportion of the population were German-speakers, many of them finding it completely unnecessary to learn Portuguese. Well into this century Blumenau was isolated, with only poor river transport connections with the Brazil beyond the Itajaí valley – circumstances that enabled its German character to be retained for longer than was the case in Joinville.

Today, Blumenau's municipal authority never misses an opportunity to remind the world of the city's German origins, the European links helping tourism and attracting outside investors. And, superficially at least, Blumenau certainly looks, if not feels, German. The streets are sparkling clean, parking tickets are issued by wardens dressed in a uniform that Heidi would have been comfortable in, most buildings are in German architectural styles and geranium-filled window boxes are the norm. But since German is almost never heard, and the buildings (such as the half-timbered Saxon-inspired department store and the Swiss chalet-like Prefeitura) are absurd caricatures of those found in German cities, the result is a sort of "Disneyland" interpretation of Germany.

It's easy to sneer, but tourists from São Paulo are impressed by Blumenau's old-world atmosphere and visit in large numbers, especially during the annual **Oktoberfest**. Held, since 1984, over three weeks in October, the festival is basically an advertising gimmick thought up by Hering, the Blumenau-based textile and agro-industrial giant. Besides vast quantities of beer and German food, the main festival attractions are the local and visiting German bands and German folk-dance troupes. Performances take place at PROEB, Blumenau's exhibition centre, located on the city's outskirts (frequent buses run during the festival period), as well as in the downtown streets and the central Biergarten. So successful has the Oktoberfest been in drawing visitors to Blumenau – a million people attended the festivities during its peak year in 1992 – that the city's authorities came to realize that the event's local flavour had been swamped by outsiders and have now successfully halved attendance.

The rest of the year, local German bands perform every evening from 5pm in the **Biergarten**, the city's main meeting point, in the tree-filled Praça Hercílio Luz. In the oldest part of Blumenau, across a small bridge on the continuation of the main street, Rua XV de Novembro, the Biergarten is only a short walk from the **Museu da Família Colonial**, one of the city's few museums, at Alameda Duque de Caxias 78 (Tues–Fri 8am–5.30pm, Sat 9am–noon & 2–4.30pm, Sun 9am–noon). The museum's buildings, constructed in 1858 and 1864 for the families of Dr Blumenau's nephew and secretary-librarian, are two of the oldest surviving *enxaimel* houses in Blumenau. Exhibits include nineteenth-century furniture and household equipment, documents relating to the foundation of the city, photographs of life in the settlement during its early years, and artefacts of the Kaingangs and Xoklengs – the indigenous population displaced by the German settlers. But it's in the beautiful forest-like garden that you'll find the most curious feature: a cemetery, the final resting place for the much loved cats of a former occupant of one of the houses.

A good half-hour walk from Praça Hercílio Luz, on the river at Rua Itajaí 2195, is the **Museu de Ecologia Fritz Müller** (daily 8–11.30am & 2–5pm), built in 1867 and the former home of the eponymous German-born naturalist. Born in 1822, Müller lived in Santa Catarina between 1852 and 1897, and was a close collaborator of British naturalist Charles Darwin; the small museum is dedicated to the work of the lesser known scientist.

Practicalities

The **rodoviária** (℡47/323-0690) is 7km from the city centre in the suburb of Itoupava Norte (the "Cidade Jardim" bus runs into the centre). There are hourly services to Florianópolis, Joinville and Itajaí, and frequent services to western Santa Catarina, Curitiba and São Paulo. Buses to Pomerode leave roughly hourly from Rua Paulo Zimmermann, located near the Prefeitura and Praça Victor Konder; if in doubt, ask for the bus stop of the Volkmann company.

Tourist information offices are found at Rua XV de Novembro 420, at the corner of Rua Nereu Ramos (daily 9am–9pm; ℡47/326-1516), at the *rodoviária* (daily 9am–6pm), and in the Prefeitura (Mon–Fri 9am–5pm) at Praça Victor Konder. There's a **German consulate** at Rua Caetano Deeke 20 on the 11th floor.

Centrally located **hotels** are plentiful, so accommodation shouldn't pose a problem, except during the Oktoberfest. At the lower end of the price range, look no further than the wonderful *Hotel Hermann* (℡47/322-4370; ❷), an early twentieth-century *enxaimel* building in the heart of the city at Rua Floriano Peixoto 213, by the intersection with Rua Sete de Setembro. Another charming small German-style hotel, on Rua Ângelo Dias, is the *Christina Blumenau* (℡47/322-1198; ❷), owned by a granddaughter of the town's founder. Blumenau's most expensive hotel is the *Plaza Blumenau*, Rua Sete de Setembro 818 (℡47/231-7000, Ⓦwww.plazahoteis.com.br; ❻), but there are several other medium-priced hotels on the same road, including the *Glória* at no. 954 (℡47/326-1988, Ⓦwww.hotelgloria.com.br; ❹). If you want to stay with a German-speaking family, contact the tourist information office.

The cheaper hotels don't serve **breakfast**, but a superb one – a $4 buffet affair – can be found at the *Café Haus* in the *Hotel Glória*. The same place also serves the best cakes in Blumenau and is an excellent spot for afternoon tea. In general, though, food in Blumenau is poor and largely takes the form of **snacks** to accompany beer.

There are several **German restaurants**, by far the most pleasant-looking being the *Frohsinn* (closed Sun). The food here is not at all special (it's fairly expensive and the service is poor), but the location – on a beautiful, cool, pine-clad hill with excellent views over the city – makes the journey worthwhile. It's a bit of an effort to get there: from Praça Hercílio Luz, walk for about fifteen minutes along Rua Itajaí and turn right on Rua Gertrud Sierich – the restaurant is at the top of this very steep road. Nearer to the centre, huge portions of passable German food are served at the *Cavalinho Branco*, Alameda Rio Branco 165, but it's accompanied by loud Teutonic music. If you're sick of pork, cross the bridge to the *Restaurante Moinho do Vale* at Rua Paraguai 66, which serves more typically Brazilian and international food. It's rather expensive but worth it for the beautiful setting overlooking the river. If you're craving something really different, there are several cheap **Chinese restaurants** – one of the best is the *Chinês* at Rua XV de Novembro 346.

You could also take a **dinner cruise** down the river. Cruises depart at noon, 4pm and 8pm (dinner served on 8pm cruise only) from Avenida Castelo Branco, near the intersection with Rua Nereu Ramos – the two-hour paddle-steamer excursion costs from $5, food extra.

Pomerode

Thirty kilometres to the north of Blumenau, **POMERODE** probably has the best claim to be the most German "city" in Brazil. Not only are ninety percent of its 22,000 widely dispersed inhabitants descended from German immigrants, but eighty percent of the *município's* population continue to speak the language. Unlike Blumenau, in Pomerode German continues to thrive and is spoken just about everywhere, although in schools it takes second place to Portuguese. There are several reasons for this: almost all the immigrants – who arrived in the 1860s – came from Pomerania, and therefore did not face the problem of mixing with other immigrants speaking often mutually unintelligible dialects; as ninety percent of the population are Lutheran, German was retained for the act of worship; and, until recently, Pomerode was isolated by poor roads and communication links. This isolation has all but ended, though. The road to Blumenau is now excellent, buses are frequent, car ownership is common and televisions are universal. However, despite the changes, German looks more entrenched than ever. The language has been reintroduced into the local school curriculum, cultural groups thrive and, where the government has exerted pressure, it has been to encourage the language's survival.

Pomerode is renowned for its **festivals**, the chief of which is the **Festa Pomerana**, a celebration of local industry and culture held annually for ten days, usually from around January 7. Most of the events take place on the outskirts of town, on Rua XV de Novembro, about 1km from the tourist office, and during the day thousands of people from neighbouring cities descend on Pomerode to sample the local food, attend the song and dance performances and visit the commercial fair. By late afternoon, though, the day-trippers leave and the Festa Pomerana comes alive as the *colonos* from the surrounding areas transform the festivities into a truly popular event. Local and visiting bands play German and Brazilian music, and dancing continues long into the night. In July, Pomerode organizes the smaller, though similar, **Festa da Tradição Alemã**.

There are more regular festivities too, as every Saturday the local hunting clubs take turns to host **dances**. Visitors are always made to feel welcome, and details of the week's venue are displayed on posters around town, or ask at the tourist office. As many of the clubs are located in the *município's* outlying reaches, a bus is laid on, leaving from outside the post office, on Rua XV de Novembro.

The main activity for visitors, other than attending the town's famous festivals and dances, is **walking**. Pomerode has Santa Catarina's greatest concentration of *enxaimel* buildings, the largest number found in the Wunderwald region: to reach them, cross the bridge near the Lutheran church, turn left and walk for about twenty minutes, then turn right just before a bridge across a small stream. If you're feeling energetic, return to the main road and cross the bridge, walk on another hundred metres or so and turn left along the Testo Alto road; about 3km up the steep valley, you'll arrive at the **Cascata Cristalina**, where you'll be able to cool off under the tiny waterfall or use the swimming pool (Oct to mid-Dec & mid-Jan to March Sat, Sun & holidays 8am–7pm, mid-Dec to mid-Jan daily 8am–7pm; $1.50). The views are marvellous and you may well be tempted to stay at the basic *pousada* here (**2**). An alternative way of getting round is by **bike**: the tourist office rents them out at about $1 for two hours, along with a useful map.

Practicalities

Buses to and from Blumenau stop outside the *Hotel Schroeder* and the Lutheran church on Rua XV de Novembro, the main street, which sprawls alongside the banks of the Rio do Testo. At no. 818 the very helpful **tourist office** (Mon–Fri 7.30am–6pm, Sat & Sun 10am–4pm; ☎47/387-2627) provides a good map and details of forthcoming events, and has a small selection of local wooden and ceramic handicrafts for sale.

Accommodation is always easy to find, even during the Festa Pomerana. The largest hotel in town is the rather soulless *Hotel Bergblick* (☎47/387-0952, Ⓦwww.bergblick.com.br; **3**), on the outskirts at Rua George Zepelin 120. Just as comfortable, much more central and cheaper is the *Hotel Schroeder*, Rua XV de Novembro 514 (☎47/387-0933; **2**). If these are full or too expensive, the tourist office will find you a **room** with a local family.

You can **eat** well in Pomerode. There's no attempt to reproduce "old world" cooking, but instead simple local dishes are prepared. Pork is, of course, ever present, but it's *marreco* (wild duck) that's considered the local speciality. The *Wunderwald* (closed Sun evening & Mon) is, without doubt, Pomerode's best restaurant, serving typical regional food at bargain prices in a perfectly preserved early twentieth-century *enxaimel* farmhouse. To get to the restaurant from the centre, cross over the bridge near the church and turn left; the *Wunderwald* is at Rua Ricardo Bahr 200, a small road to the left immediately after the hospital. For a reasonable **café colonial** try the *Torten Paradies* at Rua XV de Novembro 211.

There are almost hourly **buses** to and from Blumenau, but as the last goes to Blumenau at 6pm and returns at 10.30pm, going into the city for an evening out is only just about possible.

The south coast to Laguna and Criciúma

Unlike the northern stretch of coast, heading south from Florianópolis doesn't offer as many temptations to leap off the bus and into the sea. Most of this part of the BR-101 highway is too far inland to catch even a glimpse of the sea but, in any case, south of Laguna, the beaches are less attractive and more exposed. Many of the coastal settlements were founded by Azorean immigrants in the late seventeenth century and early eighteenth century, and they've retained the fishing and lace-making traditions of their ancestors. Inland, settlement is much more recent and the inhabitants are a blend of Germans, Italians and Poles, whose forebears were drawn in the late nineteenth century by promises of fertile land and offers of work in the region's coal mines. However, apart from a handful of farms and villages where Portuguese-influenced Italian dialects are spoken, only surnames and scattered wooden and stone houses of the early settlers remain of the immigrant heritage.

Garopaba and Imbituba

The first accessible spot worth stopping at is **GAROPABA**, a fishing village inhabited by people of Azorean origin, which, despite attracting more and more people every summer, has not yet been totally overwhelmed by tourism. In the 1970s, Garopaba was "discovered" by hippies from Porto Alegre, attracted to the area by the peaceful atmosphere and beautiful beaches. During the 1980s, surfers from throughout Brazil and beyond descended on the village, which fast developed a reputation for having some of the best surfing in the country.

The **beaches** are excellent, but are located a short distance from the village. The main village beach is fine, and large enough to take the summer crowds, but try to make it to the outlying beaches. Ten kilometres to the north is Praia Siriú, backed by huge dunes, while 6km further on, Praia da Gambora is a good beach for swimming, with a beautiful mountain backdrop. The best beaches for surfing are to the south, the most challenging being Praia do Silveira (3km from Garopaba) and Praia do Rosa (18km). Most visitors arrive in the summer, but between mid-June and mid-November, Garopaba is the most popular place on the Brazilian coast for whale watching. With luck you should be able to spot humpback whales swimming just thirty meters from the beach, but for near-certain viewing of both adult whales and their calves it's best to take a boat excursion: the *Pousada Vida, Sol e Mar* ($40; see below) is the most experienced operator, with boats especially designed for whale watching.

Facilities in Garopaba are mainly geared to campers and there are very few **restaurants**, mainly simple places serving fried fish. Of Garopaba's dozen or so **hotels**, amongst the cheapest is the very pretty *Pousada Casa Grande e Senzala* at Rua Dr Elmo Kiseki 444 (☏48/254-3177; ❷), but being small, it's often full in summer. However, by asking around you can nearly always find a room in a private house. There's a small, and in the summer usually full, **youth hostel** at Estrada Geral do Capão, Praia da Ferrugem, opposite the Paulotur bus terminal. There are also plenty of places to stay around Praia do Rosa, 18km to the south, the most picturesque and least developed beach hereabouts, with several attractive *pousadas* (all ❻ and with pools) hidden amidst the hills behind the beach: try *Quinta do Bucanero* (☏48/355-6056, ⓦwww.bucanero.com.br), *Morada dos Bougainvilles* (☏48/355-6100, ⓦwww.pousadabougainville.com.br) or the largest, the *Vida, Sol e Mar* (☏48/355-6111, ⓦwww.vidasolemar.com.br). Despite Garopaba's size, **bus** services are good, with buses to Florianópolis leaving from Rua Marquês Guimarães, and those destined for points south as far as Porto Alegre leaving from Praça Silveira.

Thirty kilometres south of Garopaba, **IMBITUBA**, once one of the most attractive points along the coast, should be approached with caution. Imbituba's main function is that of a port serving the nearby coalfields; from here coal is sent north to the steel mills of Volta Redonda for coking. The town's beaches are polluted and, so too is the air, thanks to the carbo-chemical plant.

Laguna and around

LAGUNA, 125km from Florianópolis and the closest Santa Catarina gets to having a near-complete colonial town, is an excellent place to break your journey. Located at the end of a narrow peninsula, at the entrance to the Lagoa Santo Antônio, Laguna feels like two distinct towns. Facing west onto the sheltered lagoon is the old port (long surpassed by Imbituba) and Lagoa's historic centre, protected as a national monument. Two kilometres away, on the far side of a granite outcrop of mountainous proportions that separates the city's two parts, is the new town, facing east onto the Atlantic Ocean.

The Town

As a beach resort, Laguna's attraction is limited. The city's importance lies in its **old town** which, even during the height of the summer tourist season, attracts few people – just as well, as it's quite small and could easily be overwhelmed. The one time of year that Laguna gets unbearably crowded is during Carnaval as the town is rated as having one of the best celebrations south of Rio.

Laguna was significant as early as 1494, being the southern point of the line dividing the Americas between Spain and Portugal (the northern point was at Belém), 370 leagues west of the Cape Verde Islands. A **monument**, near the *rodoviária*, a few minutes' walk from the centre, marks the exact spot. However, a permanent settlement wasn't established until 1676, but it rapidly became the pre-eminent port of the southern fringes of the Portuguese empire, and a base for the exploration and colonization of what is now Rio Grande do Sul.

Although by no means all of Laguna's old town dates from the eighteenth century, its general aspect is that of a Portuguese colonial town. The oldest streets are those extending off **Praça Vidal Ramos**, the square that holds the **Igreja Santo Antônio dos Anjos**. Built in 1694, the church retains its late eighteenth-century Baroque altars and, though rather modest, is considered the most important surviving colonial church in Santa Catarina.

On the same square as the church is the **Casa de Anita** (daily 8am–6pm), a small museum housed in a modest early eighteenth-century house and dedicated to Anita Garibaldi, the Brazilian wife of Giuseppe Garibaldi, maverick military leader of the Italian unification movement. Garibaldi was employed as a mercenary in the Guerra dos Farrapos, between republicans and monarchists, and it was in Laguna that a short-lived republic was declared in 1839. There are some fine photographs of nineteenth-century Laguna on display, but – oddly perhaps – there's little on Anita's life and republican activities; scissors and hairbrushes that once belonged to her are typical of the exhibits. In Praça República Juliana in the former town hall and jail, built in 1747, is the **Museu Anita Garibaldi** (daily 8am–6pm), housing a rather dreary collection of local Indian artefacts and items relating to the Guerra dos Farrapos. Close by, on Praça Lauro Muller, the **Fonte da Carioca** is the oldest surviving fountain in Laguna, dating back to 1863, covered in blue and white Portuguese tiles.

Practicalities

The **rodoviária** (☎48/644-2441) is at Rua Arcângelo Bianchini, a couple of minutes' walk from the waterfront and the old town. Located at the official entrance to town, 3km from central Laguna, on Av. Calistralo Muller Salles is the **tourist office** (Mon–Sat 8am–6pm, Sun 8am–1pm), which provides excellent maps of Laguna and the surrounding area.

Most of Laguna's hotels and restaurants are located in the new town, alongside and parallel to the **Praia do Mar Grosso**, the city's main beach. **Hotels** here tend to be large and fairly expensive, but moderately priced exceptions are the *Mar Grosso*, Av. Senador Galotti 644 (☎48/644-0298; ❸), the *Hammerse*, Av. João Pinho 492 (☎48/647-0598, ⓦwww.hammers.com.br; ❷), and the *Monte Líbano*, Av. João Pinho 198 (☎48/647-0671; ❷). The clutch of seafood **restaurants**, in the middle of Avenida Senador Galotti, are good, if similar.

Apart from during Carnaval, **rooms** in the old town are easy to find. The *Hotel Farol Palace* (☎48/644-0596; ❷), on the waterfront opposite the market, is a good choice. There are also a couple of extremely cheap *dormitórios* behind the hotel. **Restaurants** in this part of town are poor, the best being two pizzerias on Praça Juliana, but there's a little *confeitaria*, the *Docelândia*, at Rua Voluntário Carper 78 with a superb range of desert offerings.

Around Laguna: the Farol Santa Marta

About 19km out of town to the south is the **Farol Santa Marta**, a lighthouse that was transported piece by piece from Scotland in 1891. The third tallest lighthouse in the Americas, it's surrounded by bleak but beautiful scenery offering wild seas (suicidal for even the strongest of swimmers) and protected beaches. Between June and September this stretch of shore is a popular spot from which to watch the migrating **humpback whales**, which are clearly visible from shore with binoculars. There are no buses here, but if you have your own transport (most of the road is unpaved, so drive especially carefully after heavy rain) or are prepared to hitch a lift you'll discover a comfortable **hotel**, *Farol de Santa Marta* (T48/9986-1257; ❸), complete with a heated pool, as well as the *Jurikão* (T48/691-8000; ❸), a basic hotel, and a couple of **restaurants**.

South to Criciúma

The **coastline** between Laguna and the Rio Grande do Sul border is effectively one long beach – though it's of no great beauty and can be passed without much regret. The coastal plain, which stretches inland some 30km, provides little in the way of natural attractions, and the region's two largest towns, Tubarão and Criciúma, were founded as coal-mining centres; the area remains one of Brazil's very few producers of the mineral. Should you need to stay, **CRICIÚMA** is marginally the more pleasant and less polluted of the two.

The **rodoviária** is centrally located on Avenida Centenário, the main artery that bisects the town, and as there are frequent buses to all points in Santa Catarina it's unlikely that you'll have to stay the night. However, if you arrive late, there are two very good **hotels**, virtually alongside the *rodoviária* – the luxury *Crisul* (T48/437-4000; ❹) and the medium-priced *Turis Center* (T48/633-8722; ❸) – plus two basic *dormitórios*. Cheap and comfortable, the *Cavaller Palace* (❷) is on Rua Anita Garibaldi, near the town's central square, Praça Nereu Ramos. The square is also where you'll find the **tourist office**, a five-minute walk from the back of the *rodoviária*.

Killing time in Criciúma is fairly easy. The **Museu da Colonização**, Rua Cecília Daros Casagrande (Mon–Fri 9am–6pm; take the "Bairro Comerciario" bus), with its exhibits relating to Italian and German immigrants, is worth a look, but, if you've only got a couple of hours to spare, a visit to the **coal mine** (daily 8–11.30am & 1–6pm; $1.50), Criciúma's prime tourist attraction, is really the best idea. It's 3km from the city centre: take the "Mina Modelo" bus from the local bus terminal, which is next to the *rodoviária*. Coal seams were discovered around Criciúma in 1913, and this mine entered production in 1930, ceasing production in the late 1950s. Visitors are taken through the coal mine by retired workers from other local mines, who grind out, in exhausting detail, information about the local geological structure and mining techniques. The deepest the mine goes is just 42 meters, but the squeamish should note that it is home to huge numbers of – quite harmless – fruit bats.

Central and western Santa Catarina

Until the road-building programme of the 1970s, mountainous **central and western** Santa Catarina was pretty much isolated from the rest of the state. Largely settled by migrants from neighbouring states, this territory has inhabitants of diverse origins including Germans and Italians in the extreme west, Austrians, Italians and Ukrainians in the central Rio do Peixe Valley, and *gaú-*

chos – and even Japanese – in the highlands of the Serra Geral. In the more isolated areas, dominated by a single ethnic group, traditions and languages have been preserved but, as elsewhere in southern Brazil, they are under threat.

Any route taken to reach the **Serra Geral** is spectacular, but if you enter the region directly from the coast the contrasts of landscape, vegetation and climate unfold most dramatically. From the subtropical lowlands, roads have been cut into the steep escarpment and, as the roads slowly wind their way up into the *serra*, dense foliage emerges – protected from human destruction by its ability to cling to the most precipitous of slopes. Waterfalls can be seen in every direction until suddenly you reach the *planalto*. The graceful Paraná pine trees are fewer in number on the plateau but are much larger, their branches fanning upwards in a determined attempt to re-form the canopy that existed before the arrival of cattle and lumber interests.

For tourists, towns in the *serra* are generally places to travel towards rather than destinations in their own right. Even if it means going a considerable distance out of the way, most **bus** services to Lages, from the coast, travel via the BR-470 – Santa Catarina's main east–west highway – before turning onto the BR-116, which cuts north–south through the state. To and from Florianópolis, for example, it's usually much faster and more comfortable for buses to travel via Blumenau; however the twice-daily services from Florianópolis direct to Lages via Alfredo Wagner are far more picturesque. From the southern coast of Santa Catarina, the *serra* can be approached by bus from Criciúma on the even more spectacular road leading up via São Joaquim to Lages.

Urussanga and Orleans

The route into the Serra Geral from Criciúma at first passes through a gently undulating landscape, inhabited largely by the descendants of northern Italian immigrants who settled in the region in the 1880s, before climbing the steep escarpment into the highlands. If possible choose a clear day to make the trip as the views east towards the coast are absolutely spectacular.

Some 20km from Criciúma the road passes through **URUSSANGA**, a small agricultural processing town. Urussanga and the surrounding countryside is noted for its stone farm buildings dating from the arrival of the first Italian settlers and, with federal government support, the authorities have been making tremendous efforts to restore them. A handful are located in the town itself, but to see those in outlying areas you'll need to get detailed directions from the Prefeitura. If you need somewhere **to stay**, make for the *Pousada da Vinícola Mazon* (℡48/465-1500; ❷), some 6km from town towards the village of São Pedro. The *pousada* is set in pretty countryside, the hillsides covered in grape vine, and you can eat here too – the meals are superb examples of local Italian country cooking.

A further 20km along the road is **ORLEANS**, lying on a fairly busy crossroads, from where it's easy to pick up buses to São Joaquim, Criciúma or Laguna. If you decide to stop over, there are a couple of modest **hotels**: the *São Francisco* (℡48/666-0282; ❷), at Rua Aristiliano Ramos 120, and the *Brasil* (❶), at Rua Getúlio Vargas 9. An unremarkable little town in most ways, Orleans does boast the excellent outdoor **Museu ao Ar Livre** (daily 8.30am–6pm; $2), which records early immigrant life and industry and features a water-powered sawmill and other buildings moved here from the surrounding area.

São Joaquim

Formerly a small ranching centre, **SÃO JOAQUIM**, ninety steep kilometres beyond Orleans, has only really been on the Brazilian map since the mid-1970s when apple orchards were introduced here. Within twenty years, Brazil changed from importing nearly all the apples consumed in the country to becoming a major exporter of the fruit. At an altitude of 1360m (making this the highest town in Brazil), apple trees are in their element in São Joaquim, benefiting from the very pronounced seasonal temperature variations. Temperatures in the winter regularly dip to -15°C and, as this is one of the few parts of Brazil that sees regular snowfalls, there is a surprising amount of tourism in the winter, with camping being especially popular amongst Brazilians as a way of truly experiencing the cold. Anyone with a specific interest in apples can visit the **Estação Experimental de São Joaquim**, on the outskirts of town, which does research into fruit. On Sundays there's a handicrafts market on the town's main square, Praça João Ribeiro, with stalls selling local food produce too, including apples.

The **rodoviária** (℡49/233-0400), a couple of minutes' walk from the city centre, has good connections to Lages, Criciúma and Florianópolis. For accommodation, there's a reasonable **hotel**, the *Nevada*, on Rua Manoel Joaquim Pinto (℡49/233-0259; ❷) as well as the newer, and more comfortable, *São Joaquim Park* at Praça João Ribeiro 58 (℡49/233-1444, ⓦwww .saojoaquimparkhotel.com.br; ❹). Despite the presence of some fifty Japanese apple-growing families, the only **restaurants** are a pizzeria, the *Agua na Boca* on Rua Marcos Batista 907, and the *Casa de Pedra* on Rua Manuel Joaquim Pinto 360, which offers a buffet of varied hot and cold dishes and a *rodízio de carnes*; if you just want a snack you're best off heading to the *Confeitaria Rogéria* at Rua Manuel Joaquim Pinto 240, for delicious savoury and sweet pastries.

Lages

Although founded in 1766, nothing remains in **LAGES** from the days when it was an important resting place for cowhands herding cattle and mules on the route northwards to the market in Sorocaba. Nowadays, Lages, 76km northwest of São Joaquim, is a collection of anonymous post-1950s buildings, and only the presence in town of visiting ranchers and cowhands, dressed in the characteristic baggy pantaloons, sash and poncho, reminds you that the town is at the northern edge of *gaúcho* country. Because of the presence of so many knife-carrying men, who come into town at the weekend for supplies and a good time, Lages is reputed to be the most violent town in the state. However, the general atmosphere is dull rather than menacing, and tourists are unlikely to get caught up in any trouble.

The reason to visits Lages is for a taste of life in the *gaúcho* high country. The tourist office promotes the **Turismo Rural project**, which provides opportunities for people to visit typical cattle *fazendas* and catch a glimpse of life in outlying parts of the *serra* – otherwise extremely difficult for tourists to see. For daytrips, only groups are catered for, so ask at the tourist office whether you can join one that has already been formed. Alternatively, several *fazendas* accept guests, who are encouraged to participate in the everyday activities of the cattle stations (see p.699). Otherwise, the best way to get a feel of the region is to attend one of the periodic **rodeios**; again, the tourist office can provide information.

Practicalities

The **rodoviária** (℡49/227-0022) is a half-hour walk southeast of the centre, or you can take a bus marked "Dom Pedro". The **tourist office** (Mon–Fri

8am–noon & 2–6pm; ☎49/222-5225) is in the centre of town at Rua Hercílio Luz 573, and distributes a good map of Lages.

Reasonable, modestly priced **hotels** are easy to come by. The *Hotel Presidente*, Av. Presidente Vargas 106 (☎49/224-0014; ❷), is quite good and only minutes' walk from the cathedral and main square, Praça Waldo da Costa Avila. If you want a bit more luxury, try the *Grande Hotel Lages*, Rua João de Castro 23 (☎49/222-3522; ❸) or the newer, but otherwise similar, *Le Canard* at Av. Presidente Varga 255 (☎49/224-5566, ⓦwww.lecanard.com.br; ❸). However, to really experience *serra* life you should arrange to stay on a **cattle fazenda**, all located some distance from town. A full list and advice is available from the tourist office, but recommended are the rustic *Seriema* (☎49/9986-0051; ❸ full board), *Nossa Senhora de Lourdes* (☎49/9983-0809; ❹ full board), a nineteenth-century *fazenda* house with period furnishings and a pool (no children accepted) and the more hotel-like *Barreiro* (☎49/236-1226, ⓦwww.fazendadobarreiro.com.br; ❺ full board), which traces its origins to the late eighteenth century though its buildings are all of recent contruction – reservations are essential for all three. While the landscape of the *serra* is extremely rugged and the life of the highland *gaúcho* is often harsh, the *fazendas* provide comfortable accommodation, and excellent food and facilities.

Restaurants are, of course, largely meat-oriented, the best being the *Laghões*, at Rua João de Castro 27. There are also a number of vaguely Italian restaurants: *Cantina d'Italia*, at Rua Francisco Furtado Ramos 122, is worth a try.

Rio do Peixe valley

Immigrants were introduced to the **Peixe valley** in around 1910 by the American-owned Brazil Railway Company. For completing the São Paulo–Rio Grande rail line, the company received land from which they could extract valuable timber and which they could divide for sale to homesteaders. Due to the region's isolation, war in Europe, anti-immigration legislation and the discovery that the soil was not as fertile as had been believed, fewer people than hoped moved into the area. Of those who did come, most were from neighbouring states, mainly Slavs from Paraná, and Germans and Italians from Rio Grande do Sul.

Joaçaba

The region's most important town is **JOAÇABA**, 462km west of Florianópolis, on the Peixe's west bank, directly across the river from the smaller town of Herval d'Oeste. Perhaps due to the narrowness of the valley, whose slopes rise precipitously along one entire side of town, Joaçaba has an oppressive, almost menacing, atmosphere. Although the population is dominated by descendants of Italian immigrants, no obvious Italian influences remain, and, as Joaçaba developed into an important centre of light industry and agribusiness, it lost any frontier charm that might have once existed. However, if you're visiting the Rio do Peixe area, Joaçaba is difficult to avoid altogether. Buses serve all surrounding districts and towns to the west, and there are regular departures to Blumenau, Florianópolis, São Paulo and Foz do Iguaçu.

With the **rodoviária** located just minutes' walk from the town centre, arriving in Joaçaba couldn't be easier. On leaving the *rodoviária*, turn right onto Avenida XV de Novembro, the road that follows alongside the river through town; turn right again on Rua Sete de Setembro and you'll find an inexpensive **hotel**, the *Hotel Comércio* (☎49/522-2211; ❷). A few doors away is the modern luxury *Hotel Jaraguá* (☎49/522-4255; ❸), which has a pool and a reasonable restaurant. Also on Avenida XV de Novembro are a couple of *churras-carias* and pizzerias.

Treze Tílias

Of the region's ethnic groups, it is one of the smallest – the Austrians – who have been most stubborn in resisting cultural assimilation. The claim of the *município* of **TREZE TÍLIAS** to be the "Brazilian Tyrol" is by no means a baseless one. In 1933, 82 Tyroleans led by Andreas Thaler, a former Austrian minister of agriculture, arrived in what is now Treze Tílias. As the dense forest around the settlement was gradually cleared more settlers joined the colony, but after Germany's annexation of Austria in 1938 immigration came to an end – as did funds to help support the pioneers during the difficult first years. With the onset of war, communications with Austria ceased altogether and, with no country to return to, abandoning the colony was not an option. During the immediate post-war years, contacts with Europe were minimal, but as Austria grew more prosperous Treze Tílias began to receive assistance. The area eventually came to specialize in dairy farming and today its milk products are sold in supermarkets throughout Santa Catarina.

Treze Tílias is only an hour north of Joaçaba and west of Videira and it's perfectly practical to use it as a base for getting to know the wider region. All buses stop outside the *Hotel Áustria* (☎49/537-0132; ❷), the oldest, most basic and one of the friendliest of the town's numerous **hotels**. The *Hotel Tirol* (☎49/537-0239, ⓦ www.hoteltirol.com.br; ❹), a Tyrolean-style chalet right in the centre, complete with geraniums hanging from every balcony, has very comfortable rooms and a pool. You'll get similar floral comforts at the more intimate *Campestre Recanto da Áustria* (☎49/537-0287; ❸). Both these hotels have good restaurants serving standard Austrian dishes at lunch, and *café colonial* in the late afternoon and evening. If you want to **eat** somewhere with more local character, make for the *Berenkamp*, located right behind the Prefeitura. The food here is good, cheap and abundant, and the atmosphere is about as close as you're likely to come outside Austria to an ordinary Tyrolean pub. The best time is early evening, when elderly locals drop by to eat and chat – German-speakers will be intrigued by the local Tyrolean-Brazilian dialect that has developed in Treze Tílias over the past seventy years. Even better Austrian food, however, is served at the *Estíria Haus* (closed Mon), deep in the countryside some 30km from town along the road to Joaçaba.

But for the absence of snow-capped mountain peaks, the general appearance of Treze Tílias is not dissimilar to that of a small alpine village. Walking in any direction, you'll pass through peaceful pastoral landscapes. The seven-kilometre walk to the chapel at **Babenberg** is particularly rewarding; if you decide to visit the local **waterfalls** a few kilometres outside town, get very detailed directions before setting out.

In the village itself, try and visit some of the **woodcarvers**. The best of them learned their craft in Europe, and their work is in demand by churches throughout Brazil. On the main street, the **Museu do Imigrante** (Mon–Sat 9.30am–noon & 2–6pm, Sun 10am–noon & 2–5pm) features a small collection of photographs and paintings of the area in the 1930s and 1940s, as well as items brought with the immigrants from Austria. The **Tirolerfest** during the first two weeks of October is a lively display of Austrian folk traditions including singing and dancing.

Videira

On the eastern fringes of Treze Tílias, along the Linha Pinhal road leading to **VIDEIRA**, the population is mainly of Italian origin, descended from migrants who came from Rio Grande do Sul in the 1940s, their brightly painted wooden houses instantly distinguishable from the Austrians' chalets. Vines dominate the landscape, and if you visit a *colônia* you'll probably be invited to taste their home-produced salami, *cachaça* or the wine – it's only polite to buy a bottle before leaving. In Videira itself the small, but well-organized **Museu do Vinho** (Mon–Fri 8.30–11.30am & 1.30–5.45pm) next to the main church, is worth half an hour or so. The displays relate to the local wine-making skills in the early years of settlement.

Videira itself doesn't justify more than the briefest of pauses between buses, which are, unfortunately, far less frequent than those from Joaçaba. If you need a **hotel**, and there's no time to go to Treze Tílias, walk down the hill on Avenida Dom Pedro II from the *rodoviária* and turn right at the Shell station onto Rua Brasil (the main commercial street); the inexpensive *Savannah Hotel* (❶) and **restaurant** is the first building on the left. Alternatively, crossing the river over the bridge at the bottom of Rua Brasil, next to the local bus terminal, you'll come to Videira's luxury *Hotel Verde Vale Palace* (☎49/566-1622; ❹), whose reasonably priced restaurant serves the town's best food – a mix of standard Brazilian and Italian dishes. If you're looking for somewhere cheaper to stay, try the *Hotel das Videiras* (☎49/566-0421; ❷) at Rua Paulo Ogliari 52.

Caçador

The next town on the Rio do Peixe, 35km north of Videira, is very different in character, with a workaday atmosphere and a landscape dominated by pine plantations. The one reason to stop is to visit the small **Museu do Contestado** (Tues–Sun 8.30–11.30am & 1.30–5.30pm), housed in the old railway station. The museum commemorates the brutal war that took place in the Rio do Peixe valley from 1912 to 1916 between the Brazilian government, which was protecting the interests of the American-owned railway company that had been awarded huge land grants in the region, and the displaced native and *caboclo* population. The war eventually led to the deaths of 20,000 people, and well-presented exhibits in the museum commemorate the lives of the local Indians and *caboclos* who fought in the conflict. Outside the station is a perfectly preserved 1907 Baldwin locomotive and passenger carriage.

There are several **hotels** within minutes of the museum if you need to stay over, the best being the modern *Le Canard* (☎49/663-1000, ⓦ www.lecanard .com.br; ❸). Otherwise there are good bus services to Florianópolis, União da Vitória and Curitiba from the **rodoviária** (☎49/563-0225) across from the museum. If you are travelling north towards Paraná by car there are two possible routes: the paved SC-451 road connecting to the BR-153 is the fastest, but much more interesting is to take the road to Calmon, a village on the banks of the Rio do Peixe and continue on north to União da Vitória. The road is absolutely appalling but the landscape is bleak and beautiful, dominated by huge plantations of imported pine trees and the occasional patch of original Paraná pine.

The extreme west

Until the 1950s, most of the population of the extreme west of Santa Catarina were Kaingang Indians and semi-nomadic *caboclos* who harvested the *erva maté*. As land became increasingly unavailable in Rio Grande do Sul, peasant farmers moved north into Santa Catarina and the area has since become the state's foremost producer of pigs and chickens.

Chapecó and around

Unless you have an interest in agriculture, **CHAPECÓ** – or indeed any other town in the region – is unlikely to hold your attention for longer than the time it takes to change buses. Fortunately, Chapecó is well served with **buses** to points throughout Santa Catarina and Rio Grande do Sul, to Dionísio Cerqueira (for Argentina), Curitiba and Cascavel (for connections to Foz do Iguaçu) in Paraná. If you have to stick around for a while, frequent buses connect the *rodoviária*, on the city's outskirts, with the local bus terminal, which is located virtually on the main square. There are a couple of **places to stay** near the bus terminal – *Hotel Eston* is comfortable (T49/323-1044; ❸) – and two more on the main street, Avenida Getúlio Vargas.

Chapecó's self-proclaimed status as regional capital simply means that its slaughterhouses are larger than those in the surrounding towns. If you happen to be in town during the month of August, you'll coincide with the **Festa Nacional do Frango e do Peru**, an absurdly contrived affair celebrating chicken and turkey production – almost as ridiculous as the town's **Wurstfest**, an annual jamboree in November in celebration of the sausage. Otherwise there's not much to delay you, though if you're stuck browse around Bolicho do Gauderio, on the main square – a general outfitters aiming at fashion-conscious young *gaúchos* and a good place to pick up souvenirs. On a sadder note, souvenirs can also be purchased from forlorn-looking Kaingang Indians, who wander around town attempting to sell their brightly coloured basketwork and bows and arrows. One possible excursion, however, is to the **Museu Entomológico Fritz Plaumann** (7am–noon & 1–5pm, closed Fri & Sun; T49/452-119, Wwww.fritzplaumann.cjb.net) in **Nova Teutônia**, an overwhelmingly German district some 45km east of Chapecó near Seara (any bus between the two towns will drop you off there). Housed in a large 1940s wooden house typical of the region, the museum boasts what is quite possibly the most important collection of insects in Latin America. Plaumann arrived in Nova Teutônia in 1924 and went on to dedicate his life to entomological studies, collecting 170,000 species, including 1500 that had previously been unknown. Pride of place goes to the displays of butterflies at every stage of development, but what's truly impressive is that the entire collection is supported by detailed notebooks and other documentation representing over seventy years of Plaumann's professional and personal life.

Abelardo Luz

Ninety kilometres north of Chapecó is **ABELARDO LUZ**, a small town near Paraná's border. In the mid-1980s Abelardo Luz briefly hit the headlines in Brazil, when thousands of landless peasants from neighbouring areas moved onto the huge estates of absentee landowners in this, one of the poorest and most sparsely populated parts of Santa Catarina.

The unrest has long since subsided and the reporters from throughout Brazil who descended on this little town are now just an exciting memory for this otherwise sleepy place. However, small numbers of tourists do stop off in Abelardo Luz, on their way between eastern Santa Catarina, Rio Grande do Sul and Foz do Iguaçu, to see the beautiful waterfalls, **Quedas do Rio Chapecó**, a 45-minute walk from town. To reach the falls, walk up Abelardo Luz's main street and, at the top, turn left and walk until you reach an asphalted highway where you turn right. Walk along the road past the horseshoe-shaped entrance to the park, cross a bridge and continue until you come to signs for the "*quedas*", indicating a road to the left. You'll be charged a small entrance fee, but facilities are good; there's a **campsite**, a very basic **hotel** (☎49/445-4811; ❷), a **restaurant** and snack bar. The falls themselves extend across the river and take the form of eight steps varying in breadth and width. Walkways cross parts of the waterfalls and there are numerous small natural pools by the side of the tourist complex. But to swim properly, you need to go 3km upriver to **Prainha**, a beach where there's also a campsite.

Apart from at the falls themselves, the only **place to stay** is a very grim, but cheap, hotel on the main street in town. **Buses** leave from virtually outside the hotel and there's an hourly service to Xanxerê, an hour south of Abelardo Luz, from where there are frequent connections to points within Santa Catarina and Rio Grande do Sul. If you're travelling to or from Foz do Iguaçu, take a bus to Cascavel (Paraná) or Dionísio Cerqueira and change there.

Dionísio Cerqueira

Situated in the extreme northwest corner of Santa Catarina, **DIONÍSIO CERQUEIRA** virtually merges with the smaller town of **Barracão** in Paraná and, just across the Argentine border, **Bernardo de Irigoyen**. Dionísio Cerqueira has become quite a busy shopping centre, attracting Argentines eager to purchase cheap food, household goods and clothes in Brazil, but it's an unremarkable border town and you're unlikely to want to stay longer than is needed to catch a bus out. Fortunately each of the border towns is well served by **bus** companies. Dionísio Cerqueira's *rodoviária*, a few blocks back from the border, has frequent departures to all main towns in Santa Catarina, Rio Grande do Sul and Posadas in Argentina. The nearby Barracão Rodoviária serves Paraná, including Curitiba and Foz do Iguaçu. From Bernardo de Irigoyen's bus station, there are services throughout the Argentine province of Misiones including Posadas (for the nearby Jesuit ruins, or travel further south or west into Argentina) and Puerto Iguazú.

If you do need to stop over, it's easy to find a **hotel**. The best place to stay (and eat) is the very reliable *Motel ACA* (☎751/92218; ❸) near the bus station in Bernardo de Irigoyen. In Barracão, the *Hotel Província* (☎49/844-1261; ❷) is comfortable and has a restaurant, while in Dionísio Cerqueira there's the very basic *Hotel Iguaçu* (☎49/844-1029; ❶), at Rua Mário Cláudio Turra 260. Dionísio Cerqueira has only one real **restaurant**, the *Medieval* at Av. Santa Catarina 190, which serves standard Brazilian fare.

The **border crossing** is very relaxed and is open between 7am and 7pm. Argentine passport control is located right on the border, whereas the Brazilian Polícia Federal is two blocks back from the border on Dionísio Cerqueira's main road, at Rua República Argentina 259.

Rio Grande Do Sul

For many people the state of **Rio Grande do Sul**, bordering Argentina and Uruguay, is their first or last experience of Brazil. More than most parts of the country, it has an extremely strong regional identity – to the extent that it's the only state where the possibility of independence is discussed. Today, the Santa Cruz do Sul-based **Movimento Pro-Pampa** campaigns for the separation of Brazil's three southernmost states to create the República Federal da Pampa Gaúcha. Central government's authority over Brazil's southernmost state has often been weak: in the colonial era, the territory was virtually a no-man's land separating the Spanish and Portuguese empires. Out of this emerged a strongly independent people, mostly pioneer farmers and the descendants of European immigrants, isolated fishing communities and, best known, the *gaúchos* (see p.727), the cowboys of southern South America whose name is now used for all inhabitants of the state, whatever their origins.

The **road and bus network** is excellent and it's easy to zip through the state without stopping if need be. However, Rio Grande do Sul is as Brazilian as Bahia or Rio and it would be foolish to ignore the place. The capital, **Porto Alegre**, is southern Brazil's most important cultural and commercial centre but, like all the other cities in Rio Grande do Sul, has little to detain tourists. However, it's also the state's transportation axis and at some point you're likely to pass through the city. For a truer flavour of Rio Grande do Sul, visit the principal region of Italian and German settlement, around the towns of **Caxias do Sul**, **Bento Gonçalves** and **Nova Petrópolis**, a couple of hours north of Porto Alegre. And for the classic image, head for the cattle country of the *serra* and *campanha* where old *gaúcho* traditions still linger.

Porto Alegre

The capital of Rio Grande do Sul, **PORTO ALEGRE**, lies on the eastern bank of the Rio Guaiba, at the point where five rivers converge to form the **Lagoa dos Patos**, a giant freshwater lagoon navigable by even the largest of ships. Founded in 1755 as a Portuguese garrison, to guard against Spanish encroachment into this part of the empire, it wasn't until Porto Alegre became the port for the export of beef that it developed into Brazil's leading commercial centre south of São Paulo.

With a rather uninteresting feel to it, like a cross between a southern European and a North American city, most people will be tempted to move straight on from Porto Alegre, unless they're waiting to make a transport connection. Fortunately the city has considerable life, if not much visible history, and you'll find many ways to occupy yourself, particularly if your visit coincides with one of the main festivals: Semana Farroupilha (Sept 13–20) features traditional local folk dancing and singing, while the highlight of Festa de Nossa Senhora dos Navegantes (Feb 2) is a procession of fishing boats.

Arrival, information and accommodation

There's hardly an airport in southern Brazil that doesn't serve Porto Alegre, and there are international services to Buenos Aires, Montevideo and Santiago, too. The **airport** (℡51/3358-2000) is linked by *metrô* to the Mercado Público, in the city centre just 6km away, or take the L.05 bus, which links the airport with Praça Parobe (next to the Mercado Público). Taxis into the city cost about $6.

Buses from throughout Brazil and neighbouring countries stop at Porto Alegre's **rodoviária** (℡51/3210-0101), which is within walking distance of the centre; however, because the *rodoviária* is virtually ringed by a mesh of highways and overpasses, it's far less confusing, and safer, to use the *metrô* from here. Porto Alegre used to be a major **rail** hub but, apart from suburban routes, the only remaining services are to Santa Maria, from where the line branches out to Santana do Livramento and Uruguaiana. Trains depart from the **ferroviária**, just outside the city centre in the direction of the airport, also accessible by *metrô*.

The **metrô** (Mon–Fri 6am–11pm, Sat & Sun 5am–10pm; 40¢) has its city centre terminal at the Mercado Público, but as the system is very limited in extent it's only really of use when you arrive and leave Porto Alegre.

The city's **tourist office** (℡0800-51-7686), has very helpful branches at the airport (7am–midnight), at the *rodoviária* (7am–10pm), the Usina do Gasômetro (Tues–Sun 10am–6pm) and at the Mercado Público (Mon–Sat 9am–6pm). SETUR, the state tourist office (℡51/3228-7377, 🌐www.turismo.rs.gov.br), has kiosks at the *rodoviária* (daily 7am–7pm) and the airport (same hours), but is of more limited assistance. Both agencies hand out excellent free maps of Porto Alegre. For up-to-date **listings**, consult the monthly *Programa*, produced by the tourist office, or the events listings in the newspaper *Zero Hora*.

Accommodation

Most **hotels** are scattered around the city centre, but distances are small and it's possible to walk to most places, although great care should be taken at night when the area is usually eerily quiet. There are a couple of upscale options in the residential and business suburb of Moinhos de Vento, a good area to stay in that allows for evening walks, and offers a choice of bars and restaurants.

Blue Tree Towers Av. Coronel Lucas de Oliveira 995 ℡51/3333-0333, 🌐www.bluetree.com.br. A recent addition to the pleasant residential district of Bela Vista, with very comfortable rooms and its own sushi bar but rather pretentious. **6**

Lancaster Travessa Acelino de Carvalho 67 ℡51/3224-4630, 🌐www.hotel-lancaster-poa .com.br. Located in one of the liveliest commercial areas downtown, this modern hotel is set behind an imposing 1940s facade. Rooms are small but well equipped, and excellent value for money. **3**

Master Express Rua Sarmento Leite 865 ℡51/3211-3636, 🌐www.master-hoteis.com.br. Efficient but rather sterile hotel in a good location, with low rates and helpful staff. **3**

Metropolis Rua Andrade Neves 59 ℡ & ℻51/3226-1800. Basic but neatly kept rooms, popular with business travellers from outlying parts of the state. The best of several places to stay on this busy road in the heart of the commercial district. **3**

Palácio Rua Vigário José Inácio 644 ℡51/3225-3467. One of the city's oldest hotels, the *Palácio* is welcoming, secure and popular with budget travellers. Situated on a busy lane in the commercial district, the hotel has small rooms (sleeping 2–4) that come with or without bathrooms and are somewhat noisy. **2**

Parthenon Manhattan Rua Miguel Tostes 30 ℡51/3024-3030, 🌐www.accor.com.br. An apartment hotel with a pool in Minhos de Vento, with well-appointed apartments sleeping up to four people. **5**

Plaza São Rafael Av. Alberto Bins 514 ℡51/3221-5767, 🌐www.plazahoteis.com.br. Downtown hotel with all of the features you'd expect from the city's best (and most expensive) accommodation. Rates are usually heavily discounted, especially at weekends, and include an evening meal in the hotel's reasonable restaurant. Ask for a room overlooking the river. **5**

Porto Alegre City Rua Dr José Montaury 20 ℡51/3212-5488, 🌐www.cityhotel.com.br. This one-time luxury hotel is now rather frayed at the edges, but it still offers considerable comfort, as well as large rooms and helpful service. **4**

Praça da Matriz Largo João Amorim do Albuquerque ℡51/3225-5772. Located in an early nineteenth-century house on a large tree-lined square near the cathedral, just a few blocks back from the main commercial district. The hotel has seen better days, but the ornate building retains its original grace and there's an attractive courtyard as well. Rooms are plain ("luxo" ones are a bit larger), and come with telephone and minibar. **2**

Ritter Largo Vespasiano Júlio Veppo 55 ℡51/3221-8155, 🌐www.ritterhoteis.com.br. Across the road from the *rodoviária*, this hotel is devoid of character but is clean, efficient and serves an inexpensive buffet supper. You can use the swimming pool, sauna and other facilities of the adjoining upmarket *Porto Alegre Ritter Hotel*. **3**

Sheraton Porto Alegre Rua Olavo Barreto Viana 18 ℡51/3323-6000, 🌐www.sheraton-poa .com.br. Located in the suburb of Moinhos de Vento, above the shopping mall of the same name, this ultra-modern hotel has lured much of the expense account business away from the Plaza São Rafael. The rooms are as well appointed as you'd expect, with good fitness and business centres. **7**

Terminal-Tur Largo Vespasiano Júlio Veppo 125 ☎51/3227-1656. Small rooms but with air-conditioning, very important during Porto Alegre's summer. The cheapest secure hotel near the *rodoviária*. **2**

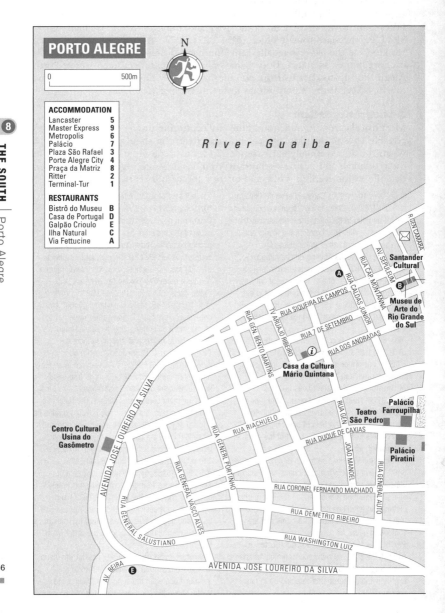

PORTO ALEGRE

N

0   500m

ACCOMMODATION
Lancaster	5
Master Express	9
Metropolis	6
Palácio	7
Plaza São Rafael	3
Porte Alegre City	4
Praça da Matriz	8
Ritter	2
Terminal-Tur	1

RESTAURANTS
Bistrô do Museu	B
Casa de Portugal	D
Galpão Crioulo	E
Ilha Natural	C
Via Fettucine	A

River Guaiba

R. BENTO CAMARA

AV. SEPÚLEIM

RUA CAP. MONTANHA

Santander Cultural

RUA CALDAS JUNIOR

RUA SIQUEIRA DE CAMPOS

TV. ARAÚJO RIBEIRO

RUA GEN. BENTO MARTINS

RUA 7 DE SETEMBRO

Museu de Arte do Rio Grande do Sul

RUA DOS ANDRADAS

i

Casa da Cultura Mário Quintana

Palácio Farroupilha

RUA GEN.

Teatro São Pedro

RUA RIACHUELO

RUA DUQUE DE CAXIAS

Palácio Piratini

Centro Cultural Usina do Gasômetro

AVENIDA JOSE LOUREIRO DA SILVA

RUA GENERAL PORTINHO

JOÃO MANOEL

RUA GENERAL AUTO

RUA GENERAL VASCO ALVES

RUA CORONEL FERNANDO MACHADO

RUA GENERAL SALUSTIANO

RUA DEMETRIO RIBEIRO

AV. BEIRA

RUA WASHINGTON LUIZ

AVENIDA JOSE LOUREIRO DA SILVA

The City

Porto Alegre sprawls out over a series of hills with the centre spread between two levels, the older residential area on the higher level and the commercial area below. In the 1960s and 1970s the city centre underwent dramatic rede-

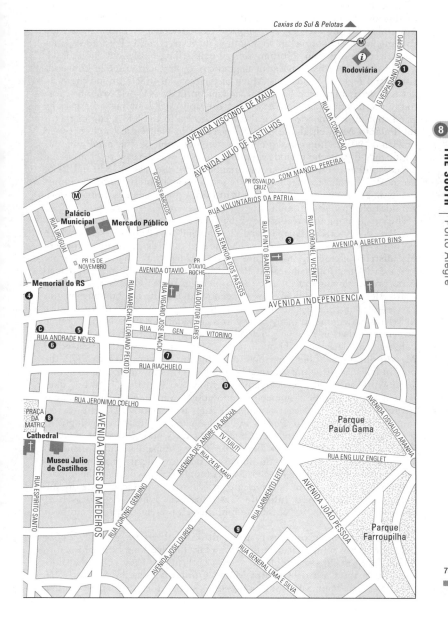

Caxias do Sul & Pelotas

velopment with new urban highways, ever larger office buildings and landfill schemes to improve the docks. Despite the destruction accompanying the construction boom, many of Porto Alegre's nineteenth- and early twentieth-century buildings escaped demolition, and the city has succeeded in retaining some of its former dignity. In the city centre itself, everything is within an easy walk, and a half-day or so is enough to visit most places of interest.

The ochre-coloured **Mercado Público** (Mon–Sat 9am–5pm) is at the heart of the lower town, located alongside Praça Rui Barbosa and Praça XV de Novembro. Dating back to 1869 and said to be a replica of Lisbon's Mercado da Figueira, this imposing building, with its intricate, typically Portuguese, stuccoed detail, contains an absorbing mix of stalls selling household goods, food, a vast variety of herbs, *erva maté* of all grades of quality, items used in Umbanda rituals and regional handicrafts. Much of the maze of streets around the market is pedestrianized; the bar and restaurant on Praça XV de Novembro, formerly the meeting place of the city's artists and intellectuals, is an especially good spot from which to watch the world go by. To the left of the market is the **Palácio Municipal**, the old *prefeitura*, built in Neoclassical style between 1898 and 1901, its impressive proportions an indication of civic pride and self-confidence during the period when Porto Alegre was developing from being a mere southern outpost into an important city. Between about 1880 and 1930, Porto Alegre attracted large numbers of southern and eastern European immigrants and in front of the palace is a **fountain**, a gift to the city from its once considerable Spanish community.

The streets along the steep slope rising from the low-lying parts of the centre (Rua dos Andradas, Rua General Vitorino and Rua Andrade Neves, which becomes Avenida Senador Salgado Filho) mark Porto Alegre's main **commercial district** of clothing stores, travel agents and banks. Further up the hill are Praça da Matriz (officially called Praça Marechal Deodoro) and Largo João Amorim do Albuquerque, where the former legislative assembly and some of Porto Alegre's oldest buildings are concentrated. Despite the buildings in this part of the city having late eighteenth- to mid-nineteenth-century origins, they have undergone so many renovations and additions over the past couple of centuries that only vaguely, if at all, do they bear any resemblance to their colonial predecessors. Though the foundations of the **Catedral Metropolitana** are built over those of a church that dates back to 1772, the present Italianate structure was only begun in 1921, and wasn't completed until 1986. Work on the former legislative assembly also started in 1772 but, likewise, it has undergone innumerable renovations over the years. The **Palácio Piratini** (the state governor's residence) dates from only 1909, while across from it the **Teatro São Pedro** was inaugurated in 1858. Surprisingly, its Portuguese Baroque appearance has remained largely unmolested, and the theatre is an important venue for local and visiting companies. The **Consulado Italiano** (Italian consulate) is an impressive mansion and its prominent position, on the east side of the Praça da Matriz (no. 134), is a symbol of the important role Italians played in Porto Alegre and elsewhere in Rio Grande do Sul. Near here is the **Museu Júlio de Castilhos**, Rua Duque de Caxias 1231 (Tues–Fri 10am–7pm, Sat & Sun 1–5pm), which presents a patchy and poor history of the state.

Porto Alegre's other **museums and cultural centres** are generally a poor bunch, which is somewhat surprising for a city that has long been prosperous and is the most important cultural centre south of São Paulo. One that does stand out is the **Casa de Cultura Mário Quintana**, Rua dos Andradas 736 (Tues–Fri 9am–9pm, Sat & Sun noon–9pm), one of the city's largest cultural

△ Iguaçu Falls

centres. Designed in Neoclassical style by the German architect Theo Wiederspahn in 1923, the extremely elegant rose-coloured building was a hotel until 1980 and as such was once a popular meeting point for local artists, intellectuals and politicians, including presidents Vargas and Goulart. The poet Mário Quintana was a long-time resident, hence the name, and pride of place is given to his room, which is maintained as it was while he lived there. Apart from numerous exhibition galleries, the Casa de Cultura houses a library, a bookshop, a cinema, a decent restaurant and a café. Nearby, on Praça da Alfândega, are three other exhibition centres housed in imposing French-style Neoclassical buildings that are always at least worth a peak. Although the **Museu de Arte do Rio Grande do Sul** (Tues–Sun 10am–7pm; Ⓦwww.ccmq.rs.gov.br), has been devastated by thefts, it still has a small collection of work by *gaúcho* artists, among which the nineteenth-century landscapes deserve particular attention; it also hosts occasional special exhibitions. Alongside, the **Santander Cultural** (Mon noon–8pm, Tues–Sat 10am–8pm, Sun 10am–6pm; Ⓦwww.santandercultural.com.br) puts on temporary exhibits of Brazilian art, often important collections first displayed in São Paulo. The building itself, a converted 1920s bank, features some remarkable stained-glass windows depicting positivist themes. Next door, the **Memorial do Rio Grande do Sul** (Tues–Sun 10am–7pm; Ⓦwww.memorial.rs.gov.br) houses the state archives, along with an oral history centre and various other collections preserving the history of Rio Grande do Sul. Pride of place goes to the large permanent exhibit explaining the origins and mission of the **World Social Forum**, the anti-globalization coalition that came together in Porto Alegre in 2001.

Eating, drinking and nightlife

As you'd expect, meat dominates menus here and *churrascarias* abound. However, the city centre has only a limited selection of **restaurants** of any sort, with the best located in the suburbs – which, fortunately, are rarely more than a $4 taxi-fare away.

Although during the daytime you can walk around most places in the city in safety, take care after dark, as Porto Alegre is developing a reputation for street crime to rival the worst of Brazilian cities. Nevertheless, it's a lively place with plenty going on until late into the evening.

Restaurants

Al Dente Rua Mata Bacelar 210 ☏51/3343-1841. The best of several very good Italian restaurants in the suburb of Auxiliadora, 3km northeast of the centre. Fairly expensive northern Italian food served in attractive surroundings. Reservations advised at weekends. Evenings only, closed Sun.

Bistô do Museu Praça da Alfândega. In the Museu de Arte do Rio Grande do Sul and with tables on the *praça* itself, this is one of the few restaurants in the area. Food is simple – pastas, steak, salads and the like – but good. Open Tues–Sun 11am–10pm.

Café do Porto Rua Padre Chagas 293. Excellent light meals, sandwiches, cakes and wine are served in this pleasant Moinhos do Vento café in an area filled with similar places.

Chef's Grill Rua Miguel Tostes 424. East of the centre in the suburb of Rio Branco, this small moderately priced place is one of the best *churrascarias* in the city.

Galpão Crioulo Parque da Harmonia. An excellent *churrascaria* in the city centre, with a bewildering selection of meats in its *rodízio* and good range of salad and vegetable offerings. In the evenings there's *gaúcho* music and dance performances.

I Puritani, Rua Hilário Ribeiro 208. A plush bistro in Moinhos de Vento serving a mix of French-, Italian- and Brazilian-influenced dishes, such as artichoke risotto, wild boar in an apricot sauce and passion-fruit mousse served with a *jabuticaba* sauce.

Ilha Natural Rua Andrade Neves 42, 1st floor. One of Porto Alegre's rare vegetarian restaurants, but the food is fairly unimaginative. Inexpensive. Mon–Fri lunch only.

Koh Pee Pee, Rua Schiller 83. A brave and rather successful attempt to introduce Thai food to Porto Alegre, offering a good assortment of dishes, appealing surroundings and reasonable prices. Mon–Sat evenings only.

O Galo Av. Aureliano Figueiredo Pinto 904. Located in Cidade Baixa and moderately priced, this is the best Portuguese restaurant in the city centre. Closed Mon.

Polska Rua João Guimarães 377. Extremely well-presented and fairly expensive Polish cooking that tastes delicious on a cold Porto Alegre winter's day. Closed Mon.

Pulperia Travessa do Carmo 76. Good, affordable regional food, a short walk from Largo João Amorim do Albuquerque. Evenings only.

Stübel Rua Quintino Bocaiúva 940. Hearty German food in the suburb of Moinhos de Vento. Moderate. Evenings only, closed Sun.

Via Fettuccine Largo Visconde de Cairú 17, 7th floor. A good-value buffet of hot and cold Brazilian and international dishes draws business diners to this anonymous downtown office block. But what's really special is the stunning view out towards the lake and beyond. Mon–Fri lunch only.

Nightlife and entertainment

Bars, some with live music and most with a predominantly young and arty clientele are spread out along, and just off, Avenida Osvaldo Aranha, alongside the Parque Farroupilha and near the Federal University. Favourites change constantly, but the *Ocidente*, on Avenida Osvaldo Aranha itself, is usually lively and good for dancing as well. Also try the upscale suburb of Moinhos do Vento, especially along Rua Padre Chagas and Rua Fernando Gomes, near the Moinhos do Vento shopping mall. On Rua Fernando Gomes, there's excellent beer at *Dado Pub* and good music at the *Jazz Café*. Be warned, though, that things don't get going until around 11pm.

Porto Alegre boasts a good popular **music scene** and a considerable **theatrical** tradition. Foreign performers of all kinds usually include Porto Alegre on any Brazilian or wider South American tour. The *Sala Jazz Tom Jobim* at Rua Santo Antônio 421 (☎51/3225-1229) features the city's best **jazz**, and there are live afternoon jazz sessions at the *Café Concerto* within the Casa de Cultura (see p.708). These days *the* place to go dancing is the huge *Dado Bier* complex in the eastern suburb of Chácara das Pedras (take a taxi). Inauspiciously located in the Bourbon Country shopping mall, the club features top bands bands from all over Rio Grande do Sul.

There's a good **art-house cinema** in the Casa de Cultura, and three more screens at Espaço Unibanco, Rua dos Andradas 736 (☎51/221-7147), another place for art-house films. The Centro Cultural Usina do Gasômetro, a converted 1920s power station on the banks of the river just west of the centre is well worth a visit; there's always something going on in its cinema, theatre and galleries, and it also has a café and a good bookshop. Finally, throughout the year, Porto Alegre's numerous Centros de Tradição Gaúcha organize traditional meals, and also music and dance performances that are hugely popular with locals; for full details, contact the Movimento Tradicionalista Gaúcho, Rua Guilherme Schell 60 (☎51/3223-5194).

Listings

Airlines Aerolíneas Argentinas, Av. Salgado Filho 267 ☎51/3221-3300; Gol, at the airport ☎51/3358-2028; TAP, Rua dos Andradas 1237 ☎51/3226-1211; Varig and Rio-Sul, Rua dos Andradas 1107 ☎51/3358-2595; VASP, Rua Uruguai 396 and Av. Farrapos 2059 ☎51/3358-2233.

Banks and exchange There are numerous banks and *casas de câmbio* (Mon–Fri 10am–4.30pm) along Rua dos Andradas and Avenida Senador Salgado Filho near Praça da Alfândega, and ATMs throughout the city. The *casa de câmbio* at the *rodoviária* changes travellers' cheques and dollars cash.

Boats Two-hour excursions on the Rio Guaiba leave from the tour-boat berth (Doca Turística) on

Avenida Mauá, near the train station. Schedules vary seasonally, so check with the tourist office. There are also boat excursions from the Centro Cultural Usina do Gasômetro (see p.711).

Consulates Argentina, Rua Coronel Bordini 1033 ℡51/3321-1360; Uruguay, Av. Cristóvão Colombo 2999 ℡51/3325-6200; UK, Rua Itapeva 110 ℡51/3341-0720; US, Rua Riachuelo 1257 ℡51/3226-3344.

Health matters Pronto-Socorro Municipal hospital is on Av. Osvaldo Aranha at the intersection with Venâncio Aires (℡51/231-5900).

Post offices At Rua Siqueira Campos 1100, Rua Sete de Setembro 1020 and Rua General Camara, near the waterfront Avenida Mauá.

Shopping Handicrafts from throughout the state are available at Artesanato Rio Grande do Sul, Av. Senador Salgado Filho 366, and the Feira do Artesanato on Praça da Alfândega (between *ruas* da Praia and Sete de Setembro) is worth a look, too. Casa do Peão, Av. Alberto Bins 39,3 has a fine stock of *bombachas*, lassoes and other *gaúcho* paraphernalia. The Sunday Redenção Bric-a-Brac in the Parque Farroupilha is well worth a visit for regional handicrafts; there's a lively atmosphere, with street performers and thronging bars and restaurants.

⑧ The Serra Gaúcha

North of Porto Alegre is the **Serra Gaúcha**, a range of hills and mountains populated mainly by the descendants of German and Italian immigrants. The Germans, who settled in Rio Grande do Sul between 1824 and 1859, spread out on fairly low-lying land, establishing small farming communities, of which **Nova Petrópolis** is just one that still retains strong elements of its ethnic origins. The Italians, who arrived between 1875 and 1915, settled on more hilly land further north and, being mainly from the hills and mountains of Veneto and Trento, they adapted well and very quickly specialized in **wine production**. Caxias do Sul has developed into the region's most important administrative and industrial centre, but it is in and around smaller towns, such as **Bento Gonçalves** and **Garibaldi**, that the region's – and, in fact, Brazil's – wine production is centred.

To the **east**, and at much higher altitudes, are the resort towns of **Gramado** and **Canela**, where unspoilt landscapes, mountain trails and refreshing temperatures, luxurious hotels and the *café colonial* – a vast selection of cakes, jams, cheeses, meats, wine and other drinks produced by the region's *colonos* – attract visitors from cities throughout Brazil.

Nova Petrópolis and around

The main road north from Porto Alegre passes **São Leopoldo** and **Nova Hamburgo** (Rio Grande do Sul's first two German settlements but now mere industrial satellites of the city) before entering more hilly terrain inhabited by peasant farmers. In most of the family farms, German-based dialects are still spoken, but in the majority of towns and villages Portuguese is the dominant language. However, in architecture and culture, the ethnic origins of the townsfolk are quite obvious, and considerable pride is taken in the German heritage.

Thoroughly unremarkable in most respects, **NOVA PETRÓPOLIS**, 100km north of Porto Alegre, makes the greatest effort in promoting its German character, and the German language is almost universally spoken here. The municipal authorities encourage new building to be in "traditional" German architectural styles (which is why there's a plethora of alpine chalet-like structures around), and **festivals** take on a distinct German flavour. Principal amongst these are the *Festa de Verão* (weekends during Jan & Feb), the *Festa do Folklore* (weekends in July) and the *Oktoberfest* (October weekends), all held in the **Parque do Imigrante**. But while clearly German-inspired, the events have little in common with the popular culture of the region's *colonos*. Indeed, of rather more interest is the Parque do Imigrante itself, where a village much like many in the region during the late nineteenth century has been created (daily 8am–6pm). The black-and-white half-timbered buildings, dating from between 1870 and 1910, were brought to the park from outlying parts of the *município* and include a Protestant chapel and cemetery, a general store with a dance hall, a credit agency (*Bauernkasse*), a school house and a smithy.

Disappointingly, Nova Petrópolis is not a place for walks as there are no trails leading out from town. Instead, take a bus to the nearby hamlet of **Linha Imperial** and walk from there into the surrounding countryside. The scenery is hilly and pastoral and it's a good area to view rural life close up. There are a couple of hotels here, the *Veraneio Schoeler* (℡54/298-1052; ❷) and the *Vila Verde* (℡54/298-1161; ❸), which are remarkably comfortable for such a backwater.

Practicalities

The **rodoviária** is centrally located just off Avenida XV de Novembro, with good connections to Porto Alegre, Gramado and Caxias do Sul. You'll find the helpful **tourist office** (daily 8am–6pm; ℡54/281-1398) at the entrance to the Parque do Imigrante.

As you might expect of somewhere so German-influenced, **hotels** here are always clean and usually relatively expensive. The most pleasant by far is the *Hotel Recanto Suiço*, Av. XV de Novembro 2195 (℡54/281-1229, ⓦwww.recantosuico.com.br; ❸), on the principal road running through town. The main building of the hotel feels like a diminutive Swiss inn, and in the extensive tree-filled gardens there's a small pool and chalets. The friendly owner speaks excellent English and, of course, German. There are several other hotels on the same road or just off it, all providing similar facilities at around the same price. Typical of the rather characterless alternatives is the *Hotel Petrópolis*, near the *rodoviária* at Rua Coronel Alfredo Steglich 81 (℡54/281-1091, ⓦwww.hotelpetropolis.com.br; ❸), in a modern chalet-style building with an attractive garden, pool and beautiful mountain views.

You can **eat** well in town, too, and the *Hotel Recanto Suiço* has an excellent and inexpensive restaurant featuring standard German dishes. If you want to have supper there, advance notice is required. At lunchtime, *Colina Verde*, 3km from Nova Petrópolis heading towards Porto Alegre (closed Mon), serves superb local German, Italian and highland *gaúcho* dishes in a pretty country setting. *Opa's Kaffeehaus* at Rua João Leão 96 (closed Mon) offers a wonderful *café colonial* in a spot with spectacular views.

Gramado

Thirty-six kilometres due east of Nova Petrópolis, along a beautiful winding road, is **GRAMADO**, Brazil's best-known mountain resort. At 825m you're unlikely to suffer from altitude sickness, but Gramado is high enough to be refreshingly cool in summer and positively chilly in winter. Architecturally, Gramado and the neighbouring resort of Canela try hard to appear Swiss, with alpine chalets and flower-filled window boxes the norm. It's a mere affectation, though, since hardly any of the inhabitants are of Swiss origin – and only a small minority are of German extraction. The most pleasant time to visit the area is during the spring (Oct & Nov) when the parks, gardens and roadsides are covered in flowers, but the hydrangeas remain in bloom well into January. During the first two weeks of August, the resort is overrun by the prestigious

Festival de Cinema, (☎54/286-9544), the most important event of its kind in Brazil. In winter the festival **Natal Luz** (mid–Nov to early Jan) stirs things up with concerts, an ersatz German Christmas market, topped by Carnaval-style parades in December that end in an (artificial) snow storm, but unless the kitchness of it all appeals to you, the entire event is something to avoid.

At other times there isn't much to do in town, but a stroll around the large and flower-filled **Parque Knorr** (daily 9am–6pm) and the secluded **Lago Negro**, surrounded by attractive woodland, can fill the hours between meals. The surrounding region is magnificent, but difficult to explore properly without a car, though tours taking in the back roads are available (see below). Just 6km from town is the beautiful **Vale do Quilombo**, where much of the original forest cover has survived intact. It's a difficult trek, though, and you'll need a local map (available from the tourist office), to identify the incredibly steep, unpaved approach road, Linha 28. For **guided tours** along the forest trails ($6), contact the *Sítio da Família Sperry*, an organic farm where an amazing diversity of primary forest remains. The English-speaking owner is extremely knowledgeable about the local flora and takes individuals or small groups through the forest. A neighbouring family-owned *cantina*, the *Quinta dos Conte*, offers tours of its small-scale wine and liquor production facilities, as well as the family's home, which was built by the original German owners. Arrangements to visit both properties should be made in advance and together: call ☎54/504-1649.

Practicalities

Gramado can easily be reached by **bus** from Porto Alegre and Caxias do Sul, and in the summer from Torres. The **rodoviária** (☎54/286-1302) is on the main street, Avenida Borges de Medeiros, a couple of minutes' walk from the town centre. The **tourist office** (Mon–Thurs 9am–6pm and Fri–Sun 9am–8pm) at no. 1674 is extremely well organized and provides reasonable maps and comprehensive lists of local hotels and restaurants.

Most hotels offer steep discounts outside the peak summer and winter months, especially during the week, though accommodation is hard to find during the Festival de Cinema. There's an excellent **youth hostel** (☎54/295-1020) 1.5km from the centre at Avenida das Hortências 3880, towards Canela, with small dorms ($8 per person) and some double rooms (❷). The lowest-priced **hotels** are the *Planalto* across from the *rodoviária*, at Av. Borges de Medeiros 554 (☎54/286-1210; ❷), and, also in the centre, the *Dinda*, Rua Augusto Zatti 160, at the corner with Av. Borges de Medeiros (☎54/286-2810; ❷). There's no lack of more expensive places to stay: the *Casa da Montanha* at Av. Borges de Medeiros 3166 (☎54/286-2544, ⓦwww .hotelcasadamontanha.com.br; ❼) has rustic-style but extremely comfortable rooms and an indoor heated pool, while smaller, but rather more luxurious, is the *Estalagem St Hubertus*, at Rua da Carriere 974, overlooking Lago Negro (☎54/286-1273, ⓦwww.sthubertus.com; ❺), set in attractive grounds with a heated pool. A good mid-range option near the centre for families is *Pousada Sonnenhof* at Rua Nações Unidas 191 (☎54/286-7788, ⓦwww.sonnenhof .com.br; ❹), with small, well-appointed rooms and friendly service.

Gramado has some reasonably good **restaurants**. Both *Belle du Valais* at Av. das Hortênsias 1432 and *Chez Pierre* at Av. Borges de Medeiros 3022 (closed Sun), in the centre, serve tasty *fondue bourguigonne*; though very popular their house specialities, the cheese fondues, are disappointingly bland. For fairly authentic and reasonably priced northern Italian dishes, there's *Tarantino Ristorante*, also in the centre at Av. das Hortênsias 1522, by Praça Major Nicoleti. More intriguing are the game dishes at *La Caceria* (evenings only, closed Mon–Wed) in the *Hotel Casa da Montanha* (see above), which combine wild boar, venison, partridge, duck and capybara with unusual tropical fruit sauces. Rather formal and expensive, the restaurant includes some excellent and very unusual Brazilian wines on its extensive wine list.

For **getting around the backroads**, most of which are unpaved and treacherous following heavy rain, Casa da Montanha Adventures (T54/286-2544) is especially recommended. The English-speaking drivers know the region well and will take you in Land Rovers to places near Gramado and further afield, such as the Parque Nacional dos Aparados da Serra (see p.716). Prices vary according to distance and whether you can join an existing group: speak to one of the drivers at their desk at the *Hotel Casa da Montanha* (see above).

Canela

CANELA, 8km further east, down a road bordered on both sides by hydrangeas, is slightly lower, smaller and not as brashly commercialized, though it strives to be like its neighbour. Canela offers little of particular beauty within its small urban area, but it is better situated for the **Parque Estadual do Caracol** (daily 8.30am–5.30pm), 8km to the north. You can reach the park by bus – marked "Caracol Circular" (4 daily) – which leaves from Canela's *rodoviára*; get off at the restaurant-tourist complex in the park. From here, a path leads down to the foot of a waterfall, the park's main attraction, and other paths lead to different small falls at higher levels, from where there are panoramic views into the deep canyon of the Rio Caí.

Canela's **rodoviária** (T54/282-1375) is just behind the central main street, and there are regular buses here from Porto Alegre and Caxias do Sul and services at least every hour to Gramado. The **tourist office**, at Largo da Fama 227 (Mon–Sat 8am–6pm, Sun 8am–1pm; T54/282-1287), is staffed by enthusiastic students from the local tourism colleges, for which Canela has become renowned in Brazil.

There's a good **youth hostel** across the road from the *rodoviária* at Rua Ernesta Urbani 132 (T54/282-2017; $8 per person), but over winter weekends it can be difficult to find a bed. The cheapest **hotels** are *Bela Vista* at Av. Osvaldo Aranha 160 (T54/282-2136; ❷) and the very similar *Turis* at Rua Oswaldo Aranha 223 (T54/282-8436, Wwww.turishotel.tur.br; ❷), both centrally located but pretty basic, while there are a number of mid-range *pousadas* just outside the centre providing accommodation in comfortable but rustic cabins: try the *Alpes Verdes*, Rua Gilda Tanello Bolognese 1001 (T54/282-1162; ❸) and the *Vila Verde*, Rua Boaventura Garcia 292 (T54/282-4133, Wwww.hotelvilaverde.com.br; ❸), both of which are set in park-like gardens with a pool. For more luxury, the small *Quinta dos Marques*, Rua Gravataí 200 (T54/282-9813, Wwww.quintadosmarques.com.br; ❺) makes a very attractive choice.

Most visitors dine at their hotels, but if you'd rather **eat out**, your best bet is the *Coelho* at Av. Danton Corrêa 251, near the intersection of the main avenue, Osvaldo Aranha, which has an inexpensive *rodízio* of decent local-style Italian dishes. The town's **bars**, clustered along Avenida Osvaldo Aranha, tend to be livelier than those in Gramado, with students spilling into the street well into the night at weekends.

Templo Budista Chagdud Khadro Ling

Just 30km but a world away from Gramado, is the **Templo Budista Chagdud Khadro Ling** (T51/546-1563, Wwww.chagdud.org), the only Tibetan Buddhist temple complex in Latin America, attracting devotees from all over

Brazil and the United States. Situated on a hilltop outside of the largely German village of Três Coroas, the temple was founded by **Chagdud Tulku Rinpoche**, a high lama who left Tibet for Nepal following the Chinese invasion in 1959, and eventually moved to Brazil. On a clear day you can see the buildings – red in colour, adorned with yellow details and colourful symbols that sparkle like jewels – from far into the distance. Seen close-up, the remarkable site includes a huge statue of Buddha, eight large *stupas* (holy structures representing the enlightened mind), the **temple** itself with remarkable murals depicting Buddha's life, and various other buildings erected by devotees, and artists and craftsmen from Nepal. The temple is open to the public (Mon–Sat 6am–7pm and Sun 8am–7pm), but it's a good idea to phone ahead to make sure your visit is convenient. Getting to Khadro Ling is straightforward. From Porto Alegre there are several **buses** a day to Três Caroas, while from Gramado buses to Taquara stop off in Três Caroas, where you can get a **taxi** ($6) up to the temple. Apart from during retreats, it's not possible to stay at Khadro Ling, but there's a basic hotel in Três Coroas if you don't care to stay in Gramado.

Parque Nacional dos Aparados da Serra

The dominant physical feature of south central Brazil is a **highland plateau**, the result of layer upon layer of ocean sediment piling up and the consequent rock formations being lifted to form the Brazilian Shield. Around 150 million years ago, lava slowly poured onto the surface of the shield, developing into a thick layer of basalt rock. At the edge of the plateau, cracks puncture the basalt and it is around the largest of these that the **Parque Nacional dos Aparados da Serra** (Wed–Sun 9am–5pm; $2) was created.

The park lies 100km east of Canela. Approaching it from any direction, you pass through rugged cattle and sheep pasture, occasionally interrupted by the distinctive umbrella-like Paraná pine trees and solitary farm buildings. As the dirt road enters the park itself, forest patches appear, suddenly and dramatically interrupted by a canyon of breathtaking proportions, **Itaimbezinho**. Some 5800m in length, between 600m and 2000m wide and 720m deep, Itaimbezinho is a dizzying sight. The canyon and the area immediately surrounding it have two distinct climates and support very different types of vegetation. On the higher levels, with relatively little rainfall, but with fog banks moving in from the nearby Atlantic Ocean, vegetation is typical of a cloud forest, while on the canyon's floor a mass of subtropical plants flourishes. The park has abundant birdlife and is home to over 150 different species.

In the park, there's a **visitors' centre** (☏54/251-1262 or 251-1277) and a **snack bar**. From here, you can hire a guide to lead you down the steep trail (including a five-metre vertical incline that you must negotiate by rope) to the canyon floor. You'll need to be physically fit, have good hiking boots and be prepared for flash floods. Most visitors, however, follow the well-marked paths keeping to the top of Itaimbezinho, enjoying views either into the canyon (a 2hr 30min walk from the visitors' centre) or out towards the sea (a 45min walk).

Visiting the park

The Parque Nacional dos Aparados da Serra can be visited throughout the year, but spring (Oct & Nov) is the best time to see flowers. In the winter, June through August, it can get very cold, though visibility tends to be clearest. Summers are warm, but heavy rainfall sometimes makes the roads and trails impassable, and fog and low-lying clouds can completely obscure the spectacular views. Avoid April, May and September, the months with the most sustained rain. Without your own transport, or if you're not travelling as part of an organized tour, the park is difficult to reach. Although part of the park is located in Santa Catarina, access is much easier from Rio Grande do Sul. As only 1000 visitors are permitted to enter the park each day, it's advisable to phone the visitors' centre in advance to reserve a place.

To get to the park, take a bus from Porto Alegre, Gramado or Canela to **São Francisco de Paula**, 69km from the park's entrance. From São Francisco, you need to take another bus northeast to **Cambará do Sul** and ask to be let off at the entrance to the park. From here it's a further 15km to Itaimbezinho. Buses occasionally run between São Francisco or Cambará and Praia Grande (which has a couple of basic hotels, one on the main square and the other at the *rodoviária*), on the Santa Catarina side of the state line. These will drop you just 3km from Itaimbezinho. In São Francisco, you may be able to join a tour group headed for the park. Coming from Cambará, the park entrance is only 3km away and you should be able to get a taxi to take you. Visiting the park as a day-trip from Canela or Gramado is also feasible: Casa da Montanha Adventures (see p.715) escort individuals or groups for around $35 per person, which includes a delicious lunch.

An excellent way to explore the park and the wider region is on **horseback**: one-day treks cost around $45, and $400 for a seven-day trek (beginning in Torres and ending in São Francisco de Paula), including accommodation in modest local dwellings (T54/244-1901; reservations essential).

São Francisco de Paula and Cambará do Sul

The cattle towns of São Francisco and Cambará are both good places to use as a base for visiting the park. In **SÃO FRANCISCO DE PAULA**, you'll pass the **tourist office** on the way into town (daily 8am–7pm; T51/244-1602), where you may be able to get advice on getting to the park. There's a wide choice of places **to stay** in and around São Francisco, much the larger though the less attractive of the two towns. Two good places to try, both a couple of kilometers from town and well signposted are the *Pousada Pomar Cisne Branco* (T51/244-1204; **3** including dinner) and the *Hotel Cavalinho Branco* (T51/244-1263; **2**). The best place **to eat** is the *Pomar Cisne Branco*, which serves superb, inexpensive home-style meals.

In **CAMBARÁ DO SUL**, the **tourist office** is situated in the Centro Cultural (Mon–Fri 8.30–noon & 1.20–6pm, Sat & Sun 9am–noon &2–6pm; T54/244-1602), an old bright-yellow wooden building typical of the region. There are several simple but pleasant **places to stay** in the village including the *Pousada Pôr do Sol* (T54/251-1290; **2**), the *Fazenda Pindorama* (T54/251-1225; **2**) and the *Pousada Itaimbeleza* (T54/251-1365; **1**). By far the best hotel in the area, however, is the *Parador Casa da Montanha* (T54/286-2544 and 9973-9320, W www.hotelcasadamontanha.com.br; **4** full board). Although accommodation is in tents, they're secure even in the strongest of winds and have every comfort of a good hotel room. In the lodge, there's a sitting and dining area, and a terrace with views out towards a sheep-rearing *fazenda*. The food here is superb – based on local beef, mutton, squash and bean dishes, and the restaurant is open to non-guests. In Cambará itself, your eating options are limited to a couple of rustic but adequate *churrascarias*.

Caxias do Sul

Around 70km west of Gramado and 37km north of Nova Petrópolis is **CAX-IAS DO SUL**, Rio Grande do Sul's third-largest city. Italian immigrants arrived in Caxias (as the city is known) in 1875, but the only obvious indication of the city's ethnic origins is its *adegas*, now huge companies or co-operatives that produce some of the state's poorest wine. Caxias' most important wine producer is the Château Lacave but, located 9km from town, it's not worth the effort involved in getting there. A better bet is the *cantina* **tours** offered by several wine producers in the city centre that end with free tastings: Riograndense, Rua Os 18 do Forte 2346, are especially used to receiving visitors. If you're interested in the history of the region, the **Museu Casa de Pedra** (Tues–Sun 8.30am–5.30pm) is well worth a look. Housed in a late nineteenth-century stone farmhouse, it contains artefacts relating to the first Italian immigrants. The most important festival in Caxias is the **Festa Nacional da Uva**, a two-week celebration of Italian traditions and local industry – most importantly wine production. The event is held in February and March (in even-numbered years) at the Parque Exposições Centenário, on the outskirts of the city.

You'll find the **tourist office** (Mon–Fri 9am–5pm; ☎54/223-3679) at the main square, Praça Rui Barbosa, along with several inexpensive **hotels** including the *Alfred*, Rua Sinimbu 2266 (☎54/221-8655, ⓦwww.alfredhoteis .com.br; ❷), which is particularly good value. There are plenty of more expensive options, by far the best being the *Reynolds International*, Rua Dr Montaury 1441 (☎54/223-5844, ⓦwww.reynolds.com.br; ❺), a small luxury hotel.

For authentic northern Italian **food**, try *Zanottoo*, Rua Visconde de Pelotas (closed Sun evening) and *La Vindima*, Av. Júlio de Castilhos 962 (closed Sun and all Jan), both good for country-style chicken and polenta dishes, or the slightly more sophisticated *Per Mangiare*, where the menu includes game and pasta options.

Caxias is a major transport centre and **buses** run to towns throughout Rio Grande do Sul, and to states to the north, from the **rodoviária** (☎54/228-3000), seven blocks from Praça Rui Barbosa. There's also an airport (☎54/213-2566), 4km south of the city centre, with flights to Porto Alegre and São Paulo.

Flores da Cunha and around

Virtually all the towns and villages in the area to the north and west of Caixas do Sul were founded by northern Italian immigrants and, set amidst the mountainous landscape, **FLORES DA CUNHA** is considered to be the most Italian of Brazilian towns, retaining thriving Italian folk traditions. The town itself is quite unremarkable in appearance, but the **Museu Histórico** (Mon–Fri 8–11.45am & 1–6pm), in the old town hall on Rua 25 de Julho, provides a good overview of the region's history. The **tourist office** (Mon–Fri 9am–5pm) is located in the same building. There are just two **hotels**: the very plain but clean *Fiório* (☎54/292-2900, ⓦwww.hotelfiorio.com.br; ❷) on the way into town at Av. 25 de Julho 5500 (the RS-122 road), and the more comfortable *Villa Borghese Albergo* (☎54/292-2355; ❸, includes dinner), also on the outskirts of town at Rua John F. Kennedy 1031. There's one **restaurant**, *Lola's* at Rua Ernesto Alves 2107 (evenings only, closed Mon), where a delicious buffet meal with wine costs just $4. The town is a good base from which to explore the surrounding countryside and stop off at some of the *colônias* selling their homemade cheeses, salamis, liqueurs and wine. Both in town and in the region around, there are innumerable *cantinas* that welcome visitors for wine tasting.

A particularly attractive village to head for is **OTÁVIO ROCHA**, 13km southwest of town (two buses daily). The people here are almost all of Veneto origin and still maintain their pioneer forebears' dialect and customs. The village comes alive in the last two weeks of July when the **Festo do Colono** takes place, but throughout the year the hamlet is delightful. Vines are planted on just about every patch of land, extending down to the main street itself, and the smell of fermenting grapes is remarkable. If you want to stay over in Otávio Rocha, there's a good **hotel,** the *Hotel Dona Adélia* (☎54/292-1519; ❷) and a couple of restaurants serving *colono* food – huge meals at less than $4 per person. A further 7km west, **NOVA PÁDUA** makes a good place to head for: the *Albergue Belvedere Sonda*, (☎54/296-1200; reservations essential; ❹ full board) is a charming guesthouse a few kilometres from the village, with spectacular views of the Rio das Antas, and serves superb local dishes, even better than those in Otávio Rocha.

Thirty-four kilometres north of Flores da Cunha, **ANTÔNIO PRADO** was founded in 1886 by another group of northern Italian immigrants. The **Museu Municipal** in Praça Garibaldi (Tues–Fri 8.30–11.30am &1.30–5pm, Sat & Sun 11am–5pm) tells the usual story of the first pioneers, but it's Antônio Prado's wealth of **stone houses** and farm buildings that makes it particularly interesting. Until about 1940 the village and its hinterland prospered, but over the following decades the local economy stagnated and *colonos* moved as far away as the western Amazon. The town was left with dozens of disused late nineteenth- and early twentieth-century buildings, and 47 of them now have preservation orders on them – especially worth visiting are the Casa da Neni at Rua Luíza Bocchese 34, where local handicrafts, preserves and liquors are sold (9am–noon & 1.30–6pm), and the Farmácia Palombini at Av. Valdomiro Bocchese 439, whose interior remains unchanged since it opened in the 1930s. For a local map, and information on the farm buildings scattered along the *município*'s back roads, ask at the helpful **tourist office** in the Prefeitura at Praça Garibaldi 57 (Mon–Fri 8.30–11.30am & 1.30–5pm) or at the museum. Many of the best-preserved houses, built from a combination of wood and stone, are found along Linha 21 de Abril (off the RS-122 road, 6km in the direction of Flores da Cunha). The decrepit *Hotel Piemonte* (☎54/293-1280; ❷), across from Praça Garibaldi, is the only place **to stay** in Antônio Prado itself. Much nicer is the *Pousada Colonial de Rossi* (☎54/293-1771, ⓦwww.pousadaderossi.hpg.com.br; ❸ full board), 6km from town on Linha Silva Tavares, off the RS-448 road in the direction of Nova Roma.

Bento Gonçalves and around

Approach **BENTO GONÇALVES**, 40km west of Caxias, from any direction and there's no doubting that this is the heartland of Brazil's wine-producing region. On virtually every patch of land, no matter the gradient, vines are planted. Wine production entered a new era in the late 1970s as huge co-operatives developed, local *cantinas* expanded and foreign companies set up local operations. The results have been somewhat mixed. In the past, the locals relied almost exclusively on North American grape varieties and produced their own distinctive wines. Gradually, though, they were encouraged to join a co-operative or agree to sell their grapes exclusively for one company. New European and, more recently, Californian vines enabled companies to produce "finer" wines of a type until then imported. All this means that the *colonos* now rarely produce more than their own family's requirements, and high-tech stainless steel vats and rigidly monitored quality control have rapidly replaced the old oaken barrel tradition; with few exceptions, the resulting wines are, at best, mediocre.

Bento Gonçalves itself is an undistinguished-looking town whose economy, of course, totally revolves around grape and wine production. There are numerous **cantinas** in the centre of town offering free tours and tastings and a **Museu Casa do Imigrante**, at Rua Erny Hugo Dreher 127 (Tues–Fri 8–11.30am & 1.30–5.30pm, Sat 11am–5pm, Sun 9am–1pm), documenting the history of Italian immigration and life in the area. There's a **youth hostel**, the *Pousada Casa Mia* at Traversa Niterói 71 (☎54/451-1215; $7 per person), while **hotels**, of which there is no shortage, are mainly found in the streets around the very helpful **tourist office**, Rua Marechal Deodoro 70 (Mon–Fri 8–11.45am & 1–7pm, Sat 9am–5pm; ☎54/451-1088).

The surrounding area

It's worth visiting the surrounding countryside and villages, where, on the surface at least, the way of life has changed little over the years. The calendar revolves around the grape, with weeding, planting, pruning – and the maintenance of the characteristic stone walls – the main activities during the year, leading up to the harvest between January and late March. An excellent way to admire the beautiful countryside is to take the tourist **steam train** (Wed & Sat 2pm & 4pm from Bento; tickets $8 from Giordani Turismo, Rua Erny Hugo Dreher 197; ☎54/455-2788) into the vine-dominated countryside. Along its 48-kilometre route (formerly part of a line extending south to Porto Alegre), the train stops at some of the more scenic spots, of which the most spectacular is the view over the **Vale do Rio das Antas** where the river's path takes the form of a horseshoe.

Many of the villages around Bento could, from a distance at least, be mistaken for Italian ones. One of the nicest is **MONTE BELO**, from where there are fine views in all directions. With a basic, but very cheap **hotel** (❶) whose **restaurant** serves authentic *colono* food – a complete meal costs just $3 – Monte Belo is a fine base from which to wander along pathways and tracks between the vineyards. There are several buses a day to the village, but try to take one that goes along the **Linha Leopoldina**, a beautiful road along which are old stone farmhouses and other farm buildings, and a chapel, the Capela das Neves. If you are travelling by car, take the RS-470 out of Bento and turn off the road at km 68.5. You can get a map and detailed directions from the tourist office in Bento. Quite unusual in an area where wine production has become so thoroughly industrialized is the **Casa Valduga** (Ⓦwww.casavalduga .com.br), a small winery owned and run by a local family. It produces, in limited quantities, some of Brazil's finest wines. The best time to go is January through March when the grapes are harvested, but passing visitors are welcomed throughout the year for tastings. There's a restaurant (Fri–Sun noon–3pm & 9pm–midnight) serving huge quantities of excellent *colono*-style country cooking for around $10 per person. The family also maintain a *pousada* (☎54/453-1154; reservations essential; ❹); rooms are simple but they have wonderful views.

Vacaria

On the northeastern plateau, 955m above sea level, **VACARIA** is a quiet administrative and commercial centre for the surrounding cattle country. The road to Vacaria from Caxias do Sul, 100km to the south, is extremely beautiful, rising sharply from vine-clad hill slopes before reaching the near treeless *planalto* cattle country. Normally there would be absolutely nothing to detain you in town, but Vacaria comes to life when people from throughout southern Brazil and beyond come to participate in the **Rodeio Crioulo**

Internacional, one of the country's most important *rodeios*, held in the first week of February (in even-numbered years).

All the **events** that you'd expect are included, like lasso-throwing, horse-breaking and steer-riding competitions, in addition to the real purpose behind a *rodeio*, the accompanying cattle and horse shows, and song and dance events. While nattily dressed urban *gaúchos* show up in impeccably tailored *bombachas* and distinguished-looking capes, Vacaria's *rodeio* is first and foremost a popular event, attended by ordinary people of the *campanha* and cattle-ranching *serra*.

Huge **tents** are erected at the *rodeio* grounds on the outskirts of town (reached by constant buses from Vacaria's main square), in which most of the spectators and competitors stay, despite the often bitterly cold midsummer temperatures. Several simple **hotels** are on, and just off, the main square: there's usually space, even during *rodeio* week. The best equipped are the *Pampa*, Rua Júlio de Castilhos 1560 (☎54/232-1333; ❸), the *Real*, Rua Ramiro Barcelos (❷) and the *Querencia*, Rua Mal. Floriano (❷). A more fitting place to stay is the *Fazenda Capão do Índio* (☎54/231-3038; ❹ full board), 5km from town off the BR-285 in the direction of Lago Vermelho; accommodation is comfortably rustic and horse riding is available, too. You can also participate in the day-to-day work on the ranch, which is dedicated to raising horses. At the *rodeio*, **food** means meat – and only meat – and at the *rodeio* ground's restaurants you're expected to come equipped with your own sharp knife. However, in the town centre, just off the main square, there's a pizzeria where you can retreat.

The coast: the Litoral Gaúcho

The **coast** of Rio Grande do Sul is a virtually unbroken 500-kilometre-long beach, along which are dotted resorts popular with Argentines, Uruguayans and visitors from Porto Alegre and elsewhere in the state. In winter the beaches are deserted and most of the hotels closed, but between mid-November and March it's easy to believe that the state's entire population has migrated to the resorts. The attraction of this area, the **Litoral Gaúcho**, is essentially one of convenience: from Porto Alegre many of the resorts can be reached within two or three hours, making even day-trips possible. But for anyone travelling to or from points north, the beaches here can easily be ignored. Those resorts that are accessible are crowded, while – due to the influence of the powerful Rio Plate – the water is usually murky; and, even in summer, Antarctic currents often make for chilly bathing.

Torres

The northernmost point on the Litoral Gaúcho, 197km from Porto Alegre, **TORRES** is the state's one beach resort that is actually worth going out of your way for. It's considered the state's most sophisticated coastal resort, and the beaches behind which the town huddles, **Praia Grande** and **Prainha**, are packed solid on summer weekends. However, by walking across the Morro do Farol (identifiable by its lighthouse) and along the almost equally crowded Praia da Cal, you come to the **Parque Estadual da Guarita**, one of the most beautiful stretches of the southern Brazilian coast. The development of the park was supervised by the landscaper Roberto Burle Marx together with Brazil's foremost environmentalist, José Lutzenberger.

The state park is centred on a huge basalt outcrop, with 35-metre-high cliffs rising straight up from the sea, from where there are superb views up and down the coast. At several points, steps lead down from the clifftop to basalt pillars and cavern-like formations, beaten out of the cliff face over the years. Although there are areas where it's both possible, and safe, to dive from the rocks, generally the sea is inaccessible and ferocious. Continue along the clifftop, and you'll eventually reach the **Praia da Guarita**, a fairly small beach that is never as crowded as those nearer town. Just beyond a further, much smaller outcrop, there's another beach, this one stretching with hardly an interruption all the way to the border with Uruguay.

Practicalities

From the **rodoviária** (℡51/664-1787) served by buses from Porto Alegre, Florianópolis, São Paulo, Curitiba, Buenos Aires and Montevideo, walk down Avenida José Bonifácio to Avenida Barão do Rio Branco. Here, turn right for the centre and the beach (six blocks) or left (one block) for the **tourist office** (Dec–April 8am–10pm and May–Nov 8am–6pm; ℡51/626-1937). Torres has countless **hotels**, with many of the cheaper ones located on Barão do Rio Branco and the two streets running parallel to it. Even on a midsummer weekend, accommodation is surprisingly easy to track down, but try to arrive early in the day. Hotels and *pousadas* here are an undistinguished lot and you can expect to pay at least $25–50 for a double room. Worth trying are the *Vitória Praia*, Praça 15 de Novembro 16 (℡51/664-2692; ❸), the *Bauer*, Rua Ballino de Freitas 260 (℡51/664-1290; ❸) or the *Costa Dalpiaz*, Av. Bão do Rio Branco 815 (℡51/664-3224, ⓦwww.costadalpiazhotel.com.br; ❸), all of which are good value. **Youth hostel** accommodation is available in summer at Rua Júlio de Castilhos 875 (℡51/664-1865; $8 per person; closed March to mid-Dec), opposite the *rodoviária*.

All the best **restaurants** are by the river, twenty to thirty minutes' walk from the centre. Either walk along Praia Grande in the opposite direction from the lighthouse or, quicker, along Rua Sete de Setembro, a couple of streets back from the beach. Especially recommended are *Gaviota* and the *Cantinho do Pescador*, for their wide selection of seafood. In the centre, there are plenty of beachside **bars**, some serving light meals, while at Rua José Luís de Freitas 800, the *Galeto Régis* serves excellent chicken dishes (closed April–Nov).

Capão da Canoa and Tramandaí

Typical of resorts popular with day-trippers and weekend visitors are **CAPÃO DA CANOA** and **TRAMANDAÍ**, respectively 140km and 120km northeast of Porto Alegre. Unless you're spending time in Porto Alegre and want to get away briefly from the often intense summer heat, neither resort has much to recommend it. Tramandaí is the larger of the two, with more hotels, more restaurants and even more people. Both share an identical lack of character, based on wide, open beaches with little in the way of vegetation, and plenty in the way of beachside bars.

The most reasonably priced **hotels** in Tramandaí are the *Amaral Praia*, Rua Amâncio Amaral 1127 (℡51/661-2479; ❷), and the huge *Beira-Mar*, Avenida Emancipação 521 (℡51/661-1234; ❸). In the centre of Capão da Canoa try the *Maquine* at Rua Andira 320 (℡51/665-2323; ❸), or the *Kolman* at Rua Sepé 1800 (℡51/625-2022; ❸).

Parque Nacional da Lagoa do Peixe

If you are travelling south along the coast from Torres down to the Uruguayan border at Chuí, it's normally necessary to go inland via Porto Alegre. But if time's no problem, it is possible to take buses from village to village along the RS-101 road and the narrow peninsula that protects the Lagoa dos Patos from the sea. The road is unpaved and often in the most appalling state, while the landscape is barren and windswept, but the remote fishing communities along the way have consequently been protected from the ravages of tourism. The inhabitants, largely of Azorean stock but also descendants of shipwreck survivors and renegades fleeing other parts of Rio Grande do Sul, make a living by fishing, growing onions, raising chickens and sheep, and increasingly through tourism.

At the midpoint of the peninsula is the **Parque Nacional da Lagoa do Peixe**, centred on an area surrounding a long and narrow lagoon – so shallow that trucks can drive across it. The park is one of the most important **bird sanctuaries** in South America. Migrating birds stop here, attracted by the clean, brackish water rich in algae, plankton, crustacea and fish. The best time to visit is between October and April, when the lagoon shelters birds from the northern hemisphere winter, and then birds landing on their way north from the Patagonian winter. However, birdwatching opportunities are generally good year round, and even those with a passing interest in birds won't fail to be impressed by the pink flamingos. The area also provides a rich habitat for reptiles and mammals; in the winter months, sea lions share the sands with Malalhães penguins, and you might spot whales in the distance offshore, returning from their mating and feeding grounds.

There is no infrastructure for receiving visitors, so you'll need to track down someone with considerable local knowledge if you want to see anything of the park. It's best to head for **MOSTARDAS**, an attractive village dominated by simple Azorean-style buildings along its narrow streets. Basic **accommodation** is available at the *Hotel Mostardense,* Rua Bento Gonçalves 1020 (℡51/673-1368; ❶), the *Hotel Municipal,* Rua Independente 761 (℡51/673-1500; ❶) and the *Hotel Scheffer,* Rua Almirante Tamandaré (℡51/673-1277; ❶).

On Praça Prefeito Luiz Martins, the main square, is the **Casa da Cultura** (daily 8am–noon and 2–5pm), worthwhile for its display of photographs and books documenting the area; you'll also be able to pick up information on local events, such as dances, too. To find a **guide**, go to the local office of IBAMA, which administers the national parks (Mon–Fri 8am–noon and 2–5pm; ℡51/673-1464, ✉lagoadopeixe@terra.com.br), also located on the main *praça*. You might be able to latch onto a pre-arranged group; otherwise a private guide isn't likely to charge more than $30 for an early morning or late afternoon excursion to Barra da Lagoa do Peixe, where the greatest concentration of migratory birds is to be found. You'll need to count on plenty of time to enjoy the area, not only because of difficulties in gaining access to the park but because of the appalling state of the RS-101, often washed out by flash floods, and because of poor bus services between the peninsula's small settlements; before heading south of Mostardas, ask at IBAMA about the current state of the road. If you're driving, you may find it much easier to head down the peninsula on the Atlantic beach, as the sand is hard enough to take the weight of a car, although you will have to negotiate the few streams that cut across the beach and also watch out for sudden tidal surges. Also bear in mind that the climate differs widely during the year – in the winter it can be bitterly cold, while summers are warm and perfect for mosquitoes.

Pelotas

Rio Grande do Sul's second-largest city, **PELOTAS**, 270km to the south of Porto Alegre, is situated on the left bank of the Canal de São Gonçalo, which connects the Lagoa dos Patos with the Lagoa Mirim. The town was founded in 1812 as a port for the *charque* (dried meat) producers of the surrounding region; with the introduction of refrigeration in the late nineteenth century, demand for beef increased, and with it Pelotas' importance as a port and commercial centre. However, by the turn of the century, Rio Grande's port, able to take larger ships, had superseded it.

While a slowdown in investment might have been bad for the city's economy, it saved Pelotas' nineteenth-century Neoclassical centre from the developers. **Praça Coronel Pedro Osório**, the main square, is the city's heart, and most of the very elegant, stuccoed buildings with wrought-iron balconies overlooking the square date from the nineteenth century. Nearby, on Praça José Bonifácio, the **Catedral de São Francisco de Paula** is slightly unusual for these parts: while its interior has undergone alteration over the years, the exterior has not been fundamentally altered since it was built in 1832.

As a railhead, port and an important commercial centre, late nineteenth–century Pelotas was home to a considerable British community. Bearing witness to this is an Anglican church, the **Igreja Episcopal do Redentor**, a couple of blocks from the main square on Rua XV de Novembro. Built in 1883, the ivy-covered church would go unnoticed in any English town, but in Brazil it looks completely alien. In fact, though, in Rio Grande do Sul such churches have become a part of the urban landscape, with some fifty others dotted around the state.

Practicalities

The **rodoviária** (☎53/221-3311) is way out of town, with buses running into the centre every fifteen minutes. Long-distance services arrive in Pelotas, most often from Rio Grande and Porto Alegre, and less frequently from Santo Ângelo, Santa Maria, Uruguaiana and Montevideo. There's a **tourist office** (Mon–Fri 9am–6pm) at Praça Coronel Pedro Osório 6. On the same square you'll find several cheap **hotels**, of which the best are the *Rex* (❶) and the *Grande* (❷). For more comfort, try the *Curi* at Rua General Osório 719 (☎53/227-9955; ❸) or, at the top end, the *Manta* at Rua General Neto 1131 (☎53/225-2411, Ⓦwww.hoteismanta.com.br; ❺). For a city of this size and importance, the **restaurants** are generally poor but, on the main commercial street, decent (if dull) German meals are available at the *Baváriα*, Rua Sete de Setembro 306, directly opposite a Chinese restaurant, the *Shangai*. More interesting are *El Paisano*, Rua Deodoro 1093 (Tues–Sat 7pm–12.30am and Sun 11am–2pm & 7pm–midnight), an excellent Uruguayan *churrascaria* where the meat is grilled in view of the diners; and a very good Portuguese restaurant, the *Vila do Conde*, Rua Andrade Neves 1321 (closed all Mon and Sun evening), both inexpensive. Pelotas is famous for its **sweets and cakes**, and a good place to try them is *Otto Especialidades* at Rua Sete de Setembro 304, with a branch at Praça Júlio Castilhos 175, and the *Doçaria Pelotense* at the corner of Rua Sete de Setembro and 15 de Novembro.

Rio Grande and around

RIO GRANDE was founded on the entrance to the Lagoa dos Patos in 1737, at the very southern fringe of the Portuguese empire. With the growth of the *charque* and chilled beef economy, Rio Grande's port took on an increasing importance from the mid-nineteenth century. Rather more spread out than Pelotas, it does not share that city's instant charm. However, you'll find some distinguished-looking colonial and late nineteenth-century buildings in the area around Rua Floriano Peixoto and **Praça Tamandaré** (the main square), which is almost next to Largo Dr Pio and the much-renovated eighteenth-century **Catedral**. On Rua General Osório, by the corner of Rua General Neto, is the **Biblioteca Rio-grandense** (Mon–Fri 8am–noon & 2–6pm, Sat 8am–noon), dating from 1846, the oldest and still the most important library in the state. The library is especially significant for its nineteenth-century collection, which features many rare volumes. Among the city's museums, you'll want to visit the **Museu Oceanográfico** at Rua Reito Perdigão 10 (daily 9–11am & 1.30–5.30pm), perhaps the most important of its kind in Latin America and stuffed with fossils and preserved sea creatures. Also worthwhile is the **Museu Histórico da Cidade do Rio Grande** on Rua Riachuelo (Mon–Sat 9–11.30am & 2–5.30 pm), whose photographic archive and objects trace the city's history. The museum is housed in the old customs house (*alfândega*), a Neoclassical building built in 1879.

Just a stone's throw from the cathedral, the **waterfront** is always busy with ocean-going ships, fishing vessels and smaller boats. From here boats cross the mouth of the Lago dos Patos to the small village of **São José do Norte**, one of the oldest settlements in the state, where there's a simple church, **Nossa Senhora dos Navegantes**, built in 1795.

As far as **beaches** are concerned, though, you'll need to go to **Cassino**, a resort facing the Atlantic that's very popular with Uruguayans, 25km south of Rio Grande and served by buses from Praça Tamandaré. Like most of the rest of the Litoral Gaúcho, the beaches here are long, low and straight and only merit a visit if you have time between buses.

Practicalities

A few blocks from Praça Tamandaré is Rio Grande's **rodoviária** (T53/232-8444), served by buses from most cities in Rio Grande do Sul, and from cities as far north as Rio de Janeiro. Though rarely open, the **tourist office** is at Rua Riachuelo 355, in front of the Câmara de Comércio, by the waterfront.

Built in 1826, the *Paris Hotel*, on the waterfront at Rua Marechal Floriano 112 (T53/231-3866, W www.hotelvillamoura.com.br; ❷), was once the place **to stay** in Rio Grande and, after decades of neglect, much its former "Grand Hotel" feel and fabric have been restored, making it an important sight in its own right. There's an extremely pretty courtyard with a central fountain, a wood-panelled breakfast room, and while most of the bedrooms are extremely basic, some have period furnishings and offer amazing value. If the *Paris* is full, there's the *Taufik*, near the cathedral at Rua General Neto 20 (T53/231-3755; ❷), although it has no character. For **eating**, try the *Pescal*, Rua Aarechl Andrea 269 (closed Sun), which specializes in fish; the *Angola*, Rua Benjamin Constant 163 (closed Mon), for Portuguese specialities; or *Pimenta Americana* at Rua General Câmara 443 (Thurs–Sat lunch and dinner, Sun–Wed lunch only), which has an excellent all-you-can-eat buffet ($3) of hot and cold home-style Brazilian dishes.

The Uruguayan border: Chuí

Unless you're shopping for cheap Scotch whisky or visiting the casino, there's absolutely nothing in **CHUÍ** (or "Chuy" on the Uruguayan side of the frontier) to stick around for. **Buses** entering and leaving Brazil stop at an immigration office a short distance from town for passports to be stamped. The Brazilian **rodoviária** (☎53/265-1498; frequent services from Pelotas, Rio Grande and Porto Alegre), on Rua Venezuela, is just a couple of blocks from Avenida Brasil, which divides the Brazilian and Uruguayan sides of town; you can cross back and forth quite freely. Onda, one of Uruguay's main bus companies, stops on the Uruguayan side of Avenida Brasil and has frequent departures for Punta del Este and Montevideo. If you are travelling to or from western Uruguay and Treinta y Tres, you will have to walk 3km down Calle General Artigas (follow the signs to Montevideo) to the Uruguayan immigration post for an entry or exit stamp in your passport. If you need a **visa** to enter Brazil, there's a Brazilian consulate on the Uruguayan side of town at Calle Fernández 147, while in Brazil the Uruguayan consulate is at Rua Venezuela 311.

   Changing money is easy: either use a Uruguayan *casa de câmbio* or bank before travelling on into Brazil where you'll receive the equivalent of the best rates available in Brazilian cities, or wait until you cross into Chuí where there are ATMs. If you can, try to avoid **staying** in Chuí as hotels are overpriced and unpleasant; as a rule, those on the Brazilian side of the common avenue are cheaper, those on the Uruguayan side cleaner and more comfortable. **Restaurants**, even the most simple ones, are better on the Uruguayan side of the avenue – *Jesus* and *Los Leños* are both good *parillas* (*churascarrias*).

Gaúcho country: Lavras and Santa Maria

If you want to witness the everyday working life of the pampas close up, **LAVRAS DO SUL** is the place to head for. Located some 300km southwest of Porto Alegre and 100km north of Bagé, there's nothing to mark out the town from countless others in the region, dedicated to raising cattle, horses and sheep. What does make Lavras different is the local **fazenda** owners who have started taking guests, turning part of either the main house or their outhouses into *pousadas*. On arrival at a *fazenda*, you first have to show whether you can handle a horse. If you can't, you're quickly coached to develop some basic equestrian skills. Guests then join the *fazenda*'s workers in their day-to-day duties minding the livestock around the property. There are natural pools and streams for cooling off in on hot summer days, while the extremely comfortable *fazenda* buildings all have open fires for the often bitterly cold winter evenings.

   Three *fazendas* (all ➍ full board) in Lavras do Sul accept guests: *Fazenda do Sobrado* (☎51/282-1239), *Fazenda Quero-Quero* (☎51/282-1223) and *Fazenda São Crispin* (☎51/282-1207 or 9973-9886). **Reservations** are essential as the *fazendas* only have room for between six and eight guests each and will want some notice if you need collecting from the *rodoviária* in town. The *fazendas* are very similar in style and operation, but *Sobrado* is particularly attractive, the house being one of the oldest of its kind in the region, dating back to the mid-nineteenth century.

Santa Maria and around

In the centre of Rio Grande do Sul, just at the point where the *campanha* hits the escarpment leading up into the *serra*, is **SANTA MARIA**, a city of some

During the colonial era and well into the nineteenth century, Rio Grande do Sul's southern and western frontiers were ill-defined, with Portugal and Spain, and then independent Brazil, Argentina and Uruguay, maintaining garrisons to assert their claims to the region. Frontier clashes were frequent, with central government presence weak or non-existent. If anyone could maintain some measure of control over these border territories it was the **gaúchos**, the fabled horsemen of southern South America. The product of miscegenation between Spanish, Portuguese, Indians and escaped slaves, the *gaúchos* wandered the region on horseback, either individually or in small bands, making a living by hunting wild cattle for their hides. Alliances were formed in support of local *caudilhos* (chiefs), who fought for control of the territory on behalf of the flag of one or other competing power. With a reputation for being tough and fearless, the *gaúcho* was also said to be supremely callous – displaying the same indifference in slitting a human or a bullock's throat.

As the nineteenth century ended, so too did the *gaúcho*'s traditional way of life. International boundaries became accepted, and landowners were better able to exert control over their properties. Finally, as fencing was introduced and rail lines arrived, cattle turned into an industry, with the animals raised rather than hunted. Gradually *gaúchos* were made redundant, reduced to the status of mere *peões* or cattle hands.

Still, more in Rio Grande do Sul than in Argentina, some *gaúcho* traditions persist, though for a visitor to get much of a picture of the present-day way of life is difficult. In general, the cities and towns of the state's interior are fairly characterless, though travelling between towns still brings echoes of former times, especially if you get off the beaten track. Here, in the small villages, horses are not only a tool used to herd cattle, but remain an essential means of transport. While women are no differently dressed than in the rest of Brazil, men appear in much the same way as their *gaúcho* predecessors: in *bombachas* (baggy trousers), linen shirt, kerchief, poncho and felt-rimmed hat, shod in pleated boots and fancy spurs. Also associated with the interior of Rio Grande do Sul is *chimarrão* (sugarless *maté* tea), which is sipped through a *bomba* (a silver straw) from a *cuia* (a gourd). In the towns themselves, cattlemen are always to be seen, purchasing supplies or just around for a good time. But undoubtedly your best chance of getting a feel of the interior is to attend a **rodeio**, held regularly in towns and villages throughout *gaúcho* country, and most notably at Vacaria (see p.720). Branches of the state tourist office, CRTur, will have information about when and where *rodeios* are due to take place.

250,000 inhabitants. A farming, cattle, administrative and educational centre and rail junction, Santa Maria is the most important city west of Porto Alegre. And, with a pleasant, lively atmosphere (owing to the presence of three universities), it makes a good stopping-off point on the way into or out of Brazil.

Founded in 1797, it wasn't until the late nineteenth century, with the rise of the cattle economy and the arrival of the rail line, that Santa Maria became of significance. However, while there are a number of interesting buildings dating back to about 1900, nothing much remains from earlier times. On the main square in the heart of the city is the **Catedral**, Baroque in style, but built at the beginning of the twentieth century. On the same square there's another church, Anglican and – like the others in the state – built for the employees of the once important British rail line and meat-exporting interests. On Rua Daudt, a few blocks from Praça Saldanha Marinho, is another typically English building, from the same period but of otherwise uncertain origin – a curious ivy-clad house set in a beautiful garden. Many of the rail engineers at the beginning of the twentieth century were from Belgium, and they were housed in the **Vila Belga**, a row of very pretty, but dilapidated cottages built in 1903 on Rua Ernesto Beck, Rua Dr Valtier, Rua Manoel Ribas and Rua André Marques near the train station.

Practicalities

The commercial, largely pedestrianized streets run off, and parallel to, the main square on the side of town where the **ferroviária** (train station) is located (3 trains a week from Santana do Livramento, 3 from Uruguaiana and 6 from Porto Alegre). To get to the cathedral square from here, head straight along Avenida Rio Branco. Buses from all points in Rio Grande do Sul arrive at the **rodoviária** (☎55/222-4747), those from Curitiba and São Paulo use the Pluma depot, next door, while those from Montevideo run out of Planalto Turismo, beside the luxury *Itaimbé Palace Hotel*. The *rodoviária* is about fifteen minutes' walk from the city centre; cross the road and walk across the Parque Itaimbé and at the *Itaimbé Palace Hotel* turn left and walk straight on for about three blocks. There's a **tourist office** (8am–6pm) at the *rodoviária*.

Several cheap **hotels** are gathered near the *ferroviária*, but a safer inexpensive option (though a little more expensive) is the *Gloria*, Av. Rio Branco 639 (☎55/222-5656; ❷). The best place to stay in town is the *Itaimbé Palace Hotel* (☎55/222-1144; ❹), which is large, efficient, and comfortable. There are plenty of **restaurants** about, but few that are especially good. The *Vera Cruz* at Av. Nossa Senhora Medianeira 1600 and *Augusto* at Rua Floriano Peixoto 1354 both serve chicken dishes, flavoured with bacon and herbs, that are distinctive to Santa Maria.

Around Santa Maria: Vale Veneto and Mata

The immediate area around Santa Maria is now mainly given over to cattle and soya. Italians from northeastern Rio Grande do Sul have had some considerable success farming the very picturesque **Vale Veneto** (take a bus to Nova Palma), about 45 minutes from Santa Maria, but Bessarabian Jews were not so fortunate. In 1904, eighty Jewish families arrived in Santa Maria with the intention of establishing a farming colony. They were given land 15km north of the city, but it slowly became apparent that the soil would only be of use for cattle. Over a forty-year period, settlers drifted from the **Colônia Philippson** – as it was known – into Santa Maria, where there survives a small Jewish community who still maintain a synagogue (at Rua Otavio Binato 49, Santa Maria). Virtually in the middle of nowhere, on a hill surrounded by cattle pasture, is the colony's small cemetery, located within what is now the Fazenda Philippson: to get there, take any bus heading north on the BR-158 and, on the left, a few kilometres past the Oásis swimming centre (at km 311 – 14km from Santa Maria), is the *fazenda*'s clearly marked entrance (45min from town). From there, ask for directions to the cemetery.

With even just a faint interest in geology you should find a visit to **MATA** worthwhile, an hour by bus from Santa Maria. Scattered everywhere in the small town are massive petrified tree trunks. The **Museu Guido Borgomanero** (Mon–Fri 8am–6pm and Sat–Sun 9–11.30am & 1.30–5pm) has a well-catalogued collection of fossils of all kinds, and the steps leading to the local Catholic church – itself unremarkable – are made entirely of fossilized wood. If you need a **hotel** in Mata, there's the very simple *Paleon* (☎55/259-1165; ❶) by the Catholic church, and a basic **restaurant**, too.

The Jesuit missions and Iraí

For much of the seventeenth and eighteenth centuries, the **Guaraní Indians** of what is now northeastern Argentina, southeastern Paraguay and northwestern Rio Grande do Sul were only nominally within the domain of the Spanish and Portuguese empires, and instead were ruled – or protected – by the Society of Jesus, the **Jesuits** (see p.748). The first **redução** – a self-governing Indian settlement based around a Jesuit mission – was established in 1610 and, within a hundred years, thirty such places were in existence. With a total population

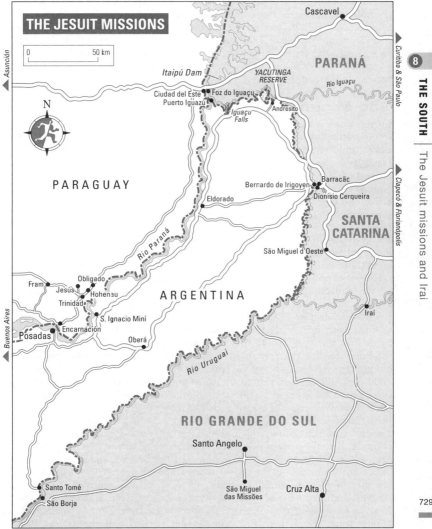

of 150,000, these mini-cities became centres of some importance, with *erva maté* and cattle the mainstay of economic activity, though spinning, weaving and metallurgical cottage industries were also pursued. As the seventeenth century progressed, Spain and Portugal grew increasingly concerned over the Jesuits' power, and Rome feared that the religious order was becoming too independent of papal authority. Finally, in 1756, Spanish and Portuguese forces attacked the missions, the Jesuits were expelled and many Indians killed. The missions themselves were dissolved, either razed to the ground or abandoned to nature, surviving only as ruins.

Brazil, Argentina and Paraguay each have one fine ruin of a Jesuit mission and, without too much difficulty, it's possible to combine a visit to all three. There are direct bus services every day between Santo Ângelo, which serves the **São Miguel** site in Brazil, and Posadas in Argentina, crossing the border at São Borja (see p.740). Posadas is a short distance from Argentina's **San Ignacio Miní** ruins and Paraguay's **Trinidad**. Alternatively, these latter two missions are an easy side-trip from the Iguaçu falls; the superb country hotel *Estancia Las Mercedes* (see p.666), roughly midway between the two areas near Eldorado, makes a convenient base.

São Miguel and around

Of the thirty former mission towns, sixteen were in present-day Argentina, seven in Paraguay and seven were situated in what is now Brazil, and almost all were completely levelled. The one exception in Brazil is **SÃO MIGUEL** (daily 8am–8pm; $1), not to be compared in extent and significance to San Ignacio Miní in neighbouring Argentina, but still of considerable visual interest, particularly for its dramatic location on a treeless fertile plain. Despite vandalism and centuries of neglect, São Miguel's ruins offer ample evidence of the sophistication of Guaraní Baroque architecture, and of *redução* life generally. Founded in 1632, to the west of the Rio Uruguai, São Miguel moved only a few years later to escape *paulista* slavers, and then a few years after that it was destroyed by a violent windstorm. After being rebuilt, its population increased rapidly and in 1687 it was relocated across the river to its present site.

The initial priority was to provide housing, so not until 1700 did work begin on the **church**, designed by the Milanese Jesuit architect Giovanni Baptista Prímoli, the ruins of which still stand. The facade is a handsome example of colonial architecture. One of the church's two towers is missing, but otherwise its stone structure is reasonably complete, the lack of a vault or dome explained by the fact that these would have been finished with wood. Other aspects of the ruins are of less interest, but the outline of the *redução*'s **walls** provides a guide to the former extent of São Miguel which, at its peak, was home to over 4000 people. The **museum** (daily 9am–6pm) has an excellent collection of stone and wood sculptures, which are beautifully displayed in Jesuit-influenced but stylistically modernist buildings designed by Lúcio Costa, the urban planner of Brasília. Every evening (6pm in winter, 8.30pm in summer; $1) there's a **sound and light show**, which, even if you don't understand the Portuguese narrative, is well worth staying for. You can actually **stay** in the quiet village here, which will give you an ideal opportunity to wander round the ruins early in the day before most of the other tourists arrive. In any case, if you're attending the sound and light show, there are no late buses returning to Santo Ângelo. Right next to the ruins, there's an excellent, new **youth hostel**, the *Pousada das Missões* (☎55/3381-1202, ⓦwww.albuergues.com.br/saomiguel; double rooms ❷ or beds in dorms $8 per person) and the *Wilson Park*

(T55/3381-2000, W www.wilsonparkhotel; ❸), a comfortable, modern hotel with a pool. There are a couple of basic **restaurants** next to the ruins, or you can eat at the *Wilson Park*.

Santo Ângelo

São Miguel is 55km from **SANTO ÂNGELO**, a town in a farming region inhabited predominantly by people of German origin. There's not much to see in the town itself, although the **Catedral**, on the main square, Praça Pinheiro Machado, is worth a look as it's a fair replica of São Miguel's church. Santo Ângelo is served by buses from throughout Rio Grande do Sul as well as from Curitiba, São Paulo and Rio. If you're planning on visiting the Jesuit ruins in Argentina and Paraguay, there's a daily **bus** to Posadas, or take a bus to the border town of São Borja and change there. The **rodoviária** is within a few blocks of Praça Pinheiro Machado; there are four buses a day to and from São Miguel, with the last going to the ruins at 5pm and returning at 7pm. A few kilometres out of town is the **airport**, with flights from Porto Alegre and São Paulo.

The best cheap **hotel** in Santo Ângelo is the *Santo Ângelo Turis* (T55/3312-4055; ❷), just off the main square at Rua Antônio Manoel 726, or for more comfort try the *Maerkil* at Av. Brasil 1000 (T55/3313-2127; ❹). The best **restaurant** in town is a *churrascaria*, the *Chico*, at Rua Antônio Manoel 1421.

San Ignacio Miní and around

Like many of the missions, **SAN IGNACIO MINÍ**, in Argentina, was initially established on another site and later relocated for safety. Consecrated in 1609 as San Ignacio-guazú across the Rio Paraná in present-day Paraguay, the mission was moved to the Rio Yabebiry in 1632 due to constant attacks by slave-hunting *bandeirantes*. This site proved unsuitable and in 1695 the mission was moved a short distance to its present location, developing into one of the largest of the *reducciónes* with, at its peak, an Indian population of over 4000. Following the Jesuits' expulsion from South America, San Ignacio Miní fell into decline, its ruins not discovered until 1897.

Of all the mission ruins, those of San Ignacio Miní (daily 7am–7pm; $1.50) are the largest in area and feature some of the most interesting museum displays. Throughout the site the buildings, trees and bushes are labelled in Spanish, so it's helpful to carry a dictionary. As you enter the site, be sure not to miss the **Centro de Interpretación Regional**, its elaborate stage-prop style displays depicting an idyllic pre-Hispanic past, the voyages of "discovery", the clash of cultures and the enslavement of the Guaraní, and finally the rise and fall of the Jesuit *reducciónes*. Among the thoroughly entertaining and thought-provoking displays is a detailed scale model of the mission prior to its abandonment.

The mission is centred around the **Plaza de Armas**, dominated by the church. Visitors can wander into the ruins of the red sandstone buildings flanking the plaza: these served as workshops, schools, cloisters and living quarters for the Indians and missionaries. Completed in 1724, and designed by the Italian Jesuit architect Giovanni Brazanelli, the huge Guaraní Baroque church was, and still is, the focal point of the mission, although only part of the facade and a few other parts of the structure remain standing. The church, like many of the other buildings, is decorated with delicate, mainly floral designs, bas-relief sculptures by Guaraní artisans. Near the exit from the ruins is a small **museum** where sculptures excavated over the years are displayed. For an excellent view across the entire mission area, climb to the top of the grandstand at the edge of the plaza. The stand itself is used for the **sound and light shows** (daily 7.30pm; $1.50): you'll obviously get more out of the show if you understand Spanish, but the music, sound effects and lighting are enough to be able to enjoy the event.

San Ignacio

San Ignacio Miní is located 60km north of Posadas, just off the main highway to Puerto Iguazú. The ruins are a few hundred metres from the centre of the sleepy little village of **SAN IGNACIO**, a pleasant place to spend a night. Especially over weekends, San Ignacio can be crowded during the day, but it empties at night. Apart from the ruins, San Ignacio is best known as the home of Uruguayan-born writer **Horacio Quiroga**, who lived here from 1910 until 1917, when his wife committed suicide, and this is where he set many of his rather gothic short stories. Quiroga's home, on Calle San Martin, has been converted into a **museum** (daily 8.30am–7.30pm) devoted to the writer's years spent in Misiones. Attached to San Ignacio's **church** is a shop with interesting **basketwork and woodcarvings** – most of the proceeds return to the Guaraní producers. In contrast, the handicrafts sold in the shops and stalls near the ruins' entrance are mainly produced in Brazil and Paraguay. Next to the church, the Jesuit and Guaraní artefacts collected by a Romanian archeologist and ethnologist in the **Museo Miguel Nadasdy** (daily 7.30am–noon & 3.30–7pm) are worth a brief look.

San Ignacio is well served by **buses**, which arrive outside the church on the main plaza every hour or so from Puerto Iguazú (4hr) and Posadas (1hr). By staying in San Ignacio you can get to the ruins early and wander around virtually alone. There are two good **accommodation** options. On the village's central plaza is the comfortable, air-conditioned *Hotel San Ignacio* (T752/470047; **2**), while near the ruins' entrance, around the corner from the *Restaurante El Jardin*, is the friendly and very clean German-run *Hospedaje Los Alemanes* (T752/470362; $7 per person). Nearby are numerous **restaurants,** catering primarily to tour groups. There's little to choose between them, except that *La Carpa Azul* has a swimming pool, wonderful on a hot summer afternoon. Argentine *pesos* are available from an **ATM** located next to the church.

Posadas

Travelling to San Ignacio Miní you're likely to pass through **POSADAS**, the capital of the Argentine province of Misiones. Apart from the pervasive red dust and a multi-ethnic population that includes descendants of German, Ukrainian, Scandinavian and other immigrants who settled in Misiones during the course of the twentieth century, the city has little of the province's frontier atmosphere. There's not much of touristic interest in Posadas but it's a useful place to stay, convenient for both the Argentine and Paraguayan ruins. Summers are intensely hot and humid, but the streets and plazas are well shaded by trees, and the ice cream is excellent, a legacy of the country's strong Italian presence.

An important commercial centre, Posadas is still small enough for you to walk to most places. Few buildings date from the city's foundation in 1870, but there are some attractive houses near the harbour in the oldest area, **La Bajada Vieja**. The city is centred on Plaza 9 de Julio, with banks (most with ATMs or currency exchange facilities) and shops concentrated on Bolívar between Azara and Junín.

The **airport**, with flights from Buenos Aires and Córdoba, is located 12km west of Posadas; minibuses ($1.50) connect the airport with the city centre via the bus terminal, or a taxi will cost $7 ($4 to the bus terminal). The **bus terminal** (☏3752/454887), on the corner of *avenidas* Mitre and Uruguay, is twelve blocks south of the city centre: most provincial centres are served, and there are regular services to and from other Argentine cities, Asunción and Rio Grande do Sul. Buses for Encarnación, across the river in Paraguay, leave from the bus terminal across the road every fifteen minutes, picking up passengers in the city centre. Midway between the bus terminal and the centre at Rioja and Colón is the well-organized **tourist office** (Mon–Fri 7am–12.30pm & 2–8pm, Sat & Sun 8am–noon & 4–8pm; ☏752/47539) which provides good maps of Posadas and local and provincial information.

Following the devaluation of the Argentine *peso*, costs of accommodation and food in Posadas are very similar to those in Brazil. **Restaurants** are concentrated on the streets extending off Plaza 9 de Julio and along Calle San Lorenzo and, as throughout Argentina, beef features prominently on menus; however, look out for *surubí*, the delicious local fish. The best restaurant in the *plaza* is *La Querencia* (closed Sun evening), which makes a point of sourcing its beef from Buenos Aires rather than using the poorer-quality local produce. The *Sociedad Española*, one block from the plaza on Calle Córdoba between Colón and Félix de Azara, offers excellent value three-course lunch specials ($3). *El Mensú*, the city's best restaurant, about six blocks north of the plaza on the corner of *calles* Coronel Reguera and Fleming, specialises in fish and pasta dishes (open dinners and weekend lunch). Reasonably priced **hotels** are easy to find. Next to the bus terminal are several basic places to stay, charging around $15 for a double room, but it's worth walking a couple of blocks in the direction of the centre to the comfortable and quiet *Residencial Córdoba*, at Santiago del Estero 2162, between Junín and Ayacucho (☏752/35451; ❷). In the centre, the least expensive place to stay is the *City Hotel* (☏752/33901; ❸), but being on Plaza 9 de Julio it's rather noisy. A couple of blocks south of the plaza at Entre Ríos 1951 is Posadas' most up-market hotel, the *Julio César* (☏3752/427930, ℮hoteljcesar@cpsarg.com; ❺), which has excellent facilities, including a pool. A few blocks further south at no. 1630 Santiago del Estero, *Le Petit* (☏752/436031; ❸), one of the city's most appealing hotels, offers spacious, air-conditioned rooms.

Brazil maintains a **consulate** at Av. Mitre 1242 with a same-day visa service, and Paraguay's consulate is at San Lorenzo between Santa Fé and Sarmiento. For **telephone calls** the Entel office is at Colón and Santa Fé, while the **post office** is at Bolívar and Ayacucho; both are within three blocks of Plaza 9 de Julio. At Colón 1574, El Pale has a very good and varied selection of regional **handicrafts**.

Trinidad and Jesús

Of the three best-preserved Jesuit mission ruins, those of **TRINIDAD** (Mon–Sat 7.30–11.30am & 1.30–5.30pm, Sun 1.30–5.30pm; $1) in Paraguay are the least visited. Founded in 1706, Trinidad was one of the last *reducciónes*, but it grew quickly and by 1728 it had a Guaraní population of over 4000. The mission was designed by the Milanese Jesuit architect Giovanni Baptista Prímoli, and the work wasn't completed until 1760, just a few years before the Jesuits' expulsion from South America. Trinidad prospered, developing *maté* plantations, cattle *estancias* and a sugar plantation and mill, and its Guaraní artisans became famous for the manufacture of organs, harps and other musical instruments, bells and statues, exported throughout the Rio Plate region and beyond. One of the most grandiose of missions, Trinidad is thought to have been the regional centre for Jesuit activity in Paraguay. Following the departure of the Jesuits, the community fell into rapid and terminal decline, the final blow coming in 1816 when Paraguay's dictator, José Gaspar Rodríguez de Francia, ordered the destruction of all Indian villages as part of his infamous scorched earth policy.

Nonetheless, Trinidad is Paraguay's best-restored Jesuit ruin and there is intense local pride in its status as a UNESCO World Heritage Monument. Occupying a hilltop position surrounded by vast areas of soya fields and cattle pasture, the site is not as extensive and the church not as large nor as complete as at San Ignacio Miní and São Miguel. Even so, much of the **church** remains in remarkable condition, including the elaborate pulpit and some of the most beautiful and intricate of **Guaraní Baroque frescoes**. Especially charming is the procession of little angels carved in sandstone that have somehow survived the centuries. Behind the ruins of the church is a small chapel: ask the guard to let you in as it contains yet more stunning wood and stone statues of angels. For an excellent view of the entire mission site and across the surrounding countryside climb the church's bell tower.

Trinidad is located 28km northeast of Paraguay's second-largest city, Encarnación. There aren't many facilities in Trinidad, which is visited by far fewer people than either San Ignacio Miní or São Miguel. By the entrance there's a restaurant that's rarely open, but at the main road at the turn-off to the ruins there are bars selling snacks and drinks. While there are no hotels, **camping** is sometimes allowed near the ruins' entrance. Most visitors stay in Posadas and cross the border for the day, or stay in Encarnación.

Ten kilometres to the north lies the Jesuit mission of **JESÚS**. Not strictly speaking ruins, Jesús (same hours and fees as Trinidad), founded in 1685 but only settled in 1763, is really an unfinished construction site, the large **church** half built when the Jesuits were ordered out of South America. What exists of the church has been restored, its beautiful arched portals resembling shamrocks, and it has an enormous half-erected guardian tower. Lacking the wealth of other missions, Jesús was not such a target of treasure seekers and remained relatively intact.

Encarnación and around

It's much cheaper to stay in **ENCARNACIÓN** than Posadas and just as convenient if visiting the missions on both sides of the river, but bear in mind that Paraguayan time is one hour behind that of Argentina. Although just one-third the size of Posadas, Encarnación is Paraguay's second-largest city. It's far from being a typical Paraguayan town, being in the centre of a region largely populated by European and Japanese immigrants and their descendants. Ukrainians and other Slavs have settled to the southwest around Fram, Germans to the northeast in the so-called *Colonias Unidas* (including Hohenau and Obligado) and Japanese to the west around La Paz and Pirapo. Unlike most other parts of the country, Spanish is heard far more than Guaraní, the national language, which is abandoned even by the migrant workers drawn from central Paraguay. For a glimpse of a more traditional Paraguay head 150km northwest to **Yuty**, a delightful village on the way to Villarica where ox-drawn carts are still more common than Toyota pick-up trucks.

There are still two parts to Encarnación (the old and the new) with the rail track being the rough dividing line. Avenida Estigarribia, the main commercial artery, extends through both parts of the city. However, the **old city**, on the slopes leading down to the river, is due to be flooded if the long-delayed Yacyretá dam is finally completed. For now, the area is one of decaying houses, public buildings and small stores selling inexpensive electronics, cameras (stock up with very cheap Fuji film) and other imports to Argentine tourists. The **post office** is near the river at Capellán Molas 377, at the intersection with Avenida Estigarribia; international postage rates are around half Brazilian rates. The **new city** on the higher ground, centred around the Plaza Artigas, is where most of the better hotels and restaurants are found and where government offices, banks and businesses are gradually being relocated.

Practicalities

US, Argentine and Brazilian **currency** are all accepted by hotels and restaurants, but Paraguayan *guaranies* are needed for bus tickets and stamps. **Changing money** is straightforward and rates are good. Banks (Mon–Fri 8.45am–12.15pm) are concentrated along Avenida Estigarribia around Plaza Artigas and are equipped with ATMs. There are also numerous *casas de câmbio* (Mon–Fri 8.30am–5pm) along Avenida Estigarribia towards the river, and at other times moneychangers offer reasonable rates at the bus terminal.

The chaotic **bus terminal** is located five blocks south of the new city centre. From Posadas, there are buses every fifteen minutes that pass by the Encarnación bus terminal before continuing to the city centre and port. The trip takes 45 minutes and **immigration procedures** on the bridge spanning the Rio Paraná are completed rapidly. If you're just crossing the border for the day you'll be waved through, but otherwise you'll have to leave the bus to have your passport stamped and then take the next bus at no extra cost. US, Australian and other citizens requiring an Argentine visa should be sure that they have valid ones.

Two types of bus services operate in Paraguay, *servicio removido* that stop to pick up or put down passengers as requested, and more expensive but much faster *servicio directo* that stop at fixed locations in towns en route and may take the form of *ejecutivo* buses that are faster, more comfortable and have toilets. There are hourly departures for Asunción and constant departures to centres in eastern Paraguay. If you're heading on **to Iguaçu Falls**, travelling via Ciudad del Este rather than Posadas is almost as fast and less expensive. The paved road passes through gently rolling terrain, once densely forested until cleared by German and German-Brazilian settlers, who produce soya and farm cattle. There are buses every two hours **to Trinidad**, or take any bus going to Jesús or to the *Colonias Unidas* and ask to be let off at the side of the main road near the ruins' entrance. There's an Argentine **consulate** in Encarnación at Dr Juan L. Mallorquín 788 on the corner with Cabañas, while the Brazilian consulate is at Memmel 452; both are less than a block from the bus terminal.

There's also a **train station**, six blocks west of Plaza Artigas, with snail-pace services for Asunción; even if you're not a train buff look out for the amazing nineteenth-century steam engines billowing out smoke as they pass through town.

Inexpensive and comfortable **hotels** are easy to find. The cheapest are near the train station (the only remotely decent one being the *Repka* at Tomás Romero Pereira 44; ❶) and directly across from the bus terminal (the best choice being the *Itapua*; ☏71/3346; ❶), but most of these are best avoided unless desperate. An excellent budget choice is the *Hotel Viena* (☏71/3486; ❷), a couple of blocks behind the bus terminal at Calle P.J. Caballero 568, near Carlos Antonio López, set in a neighbourhood of vulgar mansions (the results, it is widely believed, of rake-offs from the Yacyretá dam project). The rooms are basic but clean, the courtyard attractive and it's run by an informative German family. Near Plaza Artigas is the modern *Hotel Paraná*, at Av. Estigarribia 1414 (℡71/4480; ❸), while the *Cristal* at no. 1157 (℡71/2371; ❹) is the best hotel in town, offering excellent value and with a good restaurant.

There are numerous *heladerías* throughout the city, but the ice cream is not nearly as good as in Argentina. Instead try the refreshing national drink *terere* – *maté* served ice-cold – or Paraguayan beer, which is excellent and cheap. There are some good **parrillas** (grills): on Avenida Mariscal Estigarribia near Plaza Artigas is the excellent *Rancho Grande*, while the *Cuarajhyon*, actually on Plaza Artigas, is also reasonable. Meat, of course, dominates menus, but vegetarians can enjoy huge salads and should try *sopa paraguaya*, a national staple that is not, as its name suggests, soup but corn bread made with onion and cheese. Alternatively, the *Restaurante Chino Rubi* at Av. Mariscal Estigarribia 519, towards the river, serves large portions of acceptable, though hardly exciting, Chinese food.

The border towns

Apart from Chuí (see p.725), the most commonly used **border crossing** into Uruguay is at **Santana do Livramento**. While most buses cross into Argentina via **Uruguaiana**, you may find **São Borja** quicker if you're travelling between Jesuit mission sites or making your way north to Iguaçu Falls. Rarely do people remain in the border towns longer than it takes to go through immigration formalities, but, if you're trying to get a taste of *gaúcho* life, check to see if there's a *rodeio* about to be held somewhere around. Alternatively, use a smaller border crossing point, like **Aceguá**, near Bagé, where at least your first impressions of Uruguay or Brazil will be of cattle and ranch hands rather than duty-free shops and casinos.

Bagé and Aceguá

Of all the towns on or very near Rio Grande do Sul's border with Argentina and Uruguay, **BAGÉ** is the only one with any charm, remaining first and foremost a cattle and commercial centre, rather than a transit point. Like all towns in the *campanha*, Bagé has its own lively events, which attract people from the surrounding cattle ranches. The most important **festival**, held in January in odd-numbered years, is the **Semana Crioula Internacional**, but the *Semana de Bagé* (a folklore festival held annually from July 10 to 17), or even the *Exposição* (first half of Oct), will give you a taste of the *campanha*. For details of these and other events ask at the **tourist office** at Praça Silveira Martins (Mon–Fri 9–11.30am & 2–6pm, Sat 9am–noon). For an understanding of the region's history, a visit to the **Museu Dom Diogo de Souza**, Av. Guilayn 5759 (Tues–Fri 8.30–11.30am & 1.30–5.30pm, Sat & Sun 1.30–5.30pm), is a must. Also worth visiting is the **Museu da Gravura Brasileira** at Rua Coronel Azambuja 18 (Mon–Fri 1.30–7.30pm, Sat 1.30–6pm; closed Jan), which has a small but important collection of engravings: Rio Grande do Sul has a long tradition of this art form and some of the most important artists worked in Bagé.

Arriving from the Uruguayan border (Melo is the nearest Uruguayan town), ask to be let off at the **Polícia Federal**, a few blocks from the main square, Praça General Osório, at Rua Barão do Trunfo 1572. It's here, not at Aceguá

△ Parque Estadual de Vila Velha

(see below), that you'll need to have your passport stamped. Arriving in Bagé from elsewhere, take a "Santa Tecla" bus into the centre from the main road next to the **rodoviária** (T53/242-8122; 3 daily buses from Santa Maria and Porto Alegre, 1 each from Santo Ângelo and, via Curitiba, São Paulo). If you're leaving Brazil, have your passport stamped; failing to report to the Polícia Federal here will mean that you're likely to have difficulties entering or leaving Brazil later on.

Hotels in Bagé are plentiful, with the clean and friendly *Mini*, Avenida Sete de Setembro, near Praça General Osório (**❶**), the centre's cheapest. If you want something more refined, there's the *Hotel Fenícia* at Rua Juvêncio Lemos 45 (T53/242-8222; **❷**), while the best, largest and oldest (dating from 1850) hotel in town is the *Obinotel*, at Av. Sete de Setembro 901 (T53/242-8211; **❸**).

ACEGUÁ, 60km south and the actual frontier crossing point, is very much a back door into Brazil and Uruguay, with only a Uruguayan immigration post (remember to be stamped in or out of the country) and a few houses and stores – certainly not a place to spend a night. However, as the four buses a day in each direction between Bagé and Aceguá connect with others to and from Melo, this shouldn't be a problem – but check bus times carefully before setting out.

Changing money is best done at a *casa de câmbio* in Melo, but in Aceguá there are always plenty of men milling about offering reasonable rates for dollar bills. In Bagé, if you can't wait for the border, you can change dollars at Bradesco and many of the other banks in town are equipped with an ATM.

Santana do Livramento and around

Apart from Brazilians attracted to the casino and the duty-free shopping in Rivera, the Uruguayan border town into which **SANTANA DO LIVRAMENTO** (or simply Livramento) merges, few people stay here long. Unless you're in pursuit of *gaúchos* and intent upon taking local buses to outlying villages, the only time when Livramento is actually worth visiting in its own right is when there's a livestock exhibition, *rodeio* or cultural event on. The most important such **events** are the *Charqueada da Poesia Crioula* (last two weeks in April), the Exposição Internacional do Corriedale (March 5–12) and the *Exposição Agropecuária* (last two weeks in Sept), but check with the **tourist office** at Rua Tamandaré (Mon–Sat 7am–1pm & 3–6pm, Sun 3–8pm) to see if there are any other smaller events due, in or around the town. Livramento is also a very good place to purchase *gaúcho* **clothing and accessories**, with Correaria Gaúcha, Rua Rivadávia Correia 184, and Correaria Nova Esperança, Rua Duque de Caxias and Rua 24 de Maio, having good selections.

Otherwise, the only possible reason not to move straight on would be a visit to the surrounding *campanha*, the rolling countryside traditionally given over to raising cattle and, to a lesser extent, sheep. For a more authentic *gaúcho* experience, visit the *Fazenda Palomas* (T55/505-6417 and 9118-2640), located 20km from Livramento with the access road at km 480 of BR-158 in the direction of Porto Alegre. The 1000 hectare *fazenda* receives visitors during the daytime for horse riding or to participate in cattle round-ups and other daily activities. It's possible to stay the night in one of the four comfortable guest rooms (**❺** full board) of the late nineteenth century *fazenda* house. For another nearby excursion head to **Vila Palomas**, a village 15km from Livramento, the centre of the new and increasingly important wine industry. Of all Brazil's large **wineries**, Almadén is about the best, and their *cantina* can be visited if you give them 24 hours' notice (T55/242-5151; 9am–6pm).

Practicalities

Livramento's **rodoviária** (☎55/242-5322),at Rua Sen. Salgado Filho 335, serves most points in Rio Grande do Sul, while the **ferroviária**, in Praça Castello Branco, receives three trains a week from Santa Maria and Porto Alegre. **From Rivera**, there are several departures a day for Montevideo from the bus terminal.

If you need to stay, **hotels** are cheapest in Livramento. The *Laçador* (❶) near the park, at Rua Uruguai 1227, is good, or try the *Livramento*, opposite the *rodoviária* (☎55/242-5444; ❶). For more historical accommodation, try the *Jandaia* at Rua Uruguai 1452 (☎55/242-2288, ⓦwww.jandaiah.com.br; ❹), an old fashioned luxury hotel that has been *the* place to stay in Livramento since 1896. There's a **youth hostel** at Rua Manduca Rodrigues 615 (☎55/242-3340; $7 per person), about five blocks from the *rodoviária*, while across in Rivera there's another hostel at Uruguay 735. **Restaurants** are better in Rivera: the best is the *Dan Servanda*, Calle Carambula 1132, around the corner from the immigration office, or for excellent Uruguayan snacks and *dulces*, head for *Confeitaria City* on Avenida Sarandí.

Before **leaving** Livramento and Rivera, you'll need a Brazilian exit (or entry) passport stamp from the Polícia Federal, Rua Uruguai 1177, near the central park, and a stamp from Uruguay's Dirección Nacional de Migración, Calle Suarez 516 (three blocks from Plaza General José Artigas, Rivera's main square). If you have problems, Brazil's **consulate** in Rivera is at Calle Caballos 1159 (☎622/244-3278), and Uruguay's is in Livramento at Av. Tamandaré 2110 (☎55/242-1416). **Change money** at a *casa de câmbio* or bank in Rivera, where exchange rates are as good as you'll find in Brazil and the process much faster, or use a Brazilian ATM.

Uruguaiana

The busiest crossing point on Rio Grande do Sul's border with Argentina, **URUGUAIANA** is also one of the state's most important cattle centres. However, unless you're around while there's a livestock show or folklore festival, there's little incentive to remain here: ask about the **tourist office** (Mon–Sat 8.30am–6pm) in the Prefeitura, Praça Barão do Rio Branco. The most important annual events are the *Campeira Internacional* (a festival of regional folklore) held in the first half of March, *Semana Farroupilha* (another folklore festival) held September 13–20, and a huge livestock show, the *Expo-feira Agropecuária*, held in the first half of November. Otherwise, the **Museu Crioulo, Histórico e Artístico** (Mon–Fri 8.30am–noon & 2–5.30pm), in the cultural centre on the corner of *ruas* Santana and Duque de Caxias (by the main square), is worth a look for its interesting collection of *gaúcho*-related items.

Uruguaiana is connected to Argentina and the town of Paso de los Libres by a 1400-metre-long bridge spanning the Rio Uruguai. Frequent **local buses** connect the train and bus stations, and the centres of each city, and **immigration** formalities take place on either side of the bridge. If you have problems entering Argentina, the **consulate** in Uruguaiana is at Rua Santana 2496 (☎55/412-1925). The Brazilian consulate in Paso de los Libres is at Calle Mitre 918. You're best off **changing money** in Paso de los Libres, but failing this there are plenty of banks with ATMs in Uruguaiana. If you need **accommo-dation**, the fairly modest hotels in Uruguaiana include the *Wamosy* (☎55/412-1326; ❶) and *Mazza Tur* (☎55/412-3404; ❷), at Rua Sete de Setembro, nos 1973 and 1088 respectively. For more luxurious accommodation try the new *Elyt* at Av. Presidente Vargas 3718 (℡55/411-8800; ❸). If you're stuck in Paso de los Libres, make for the *Las Vegas* (℡3772/423490), a pleasant mid-range hotel one block from the main square, Plaza Independencia, at Sarmiento 554. **Restaurants** (for carnivores only) are better over the border in Argentina; however, in Uruguaiana, the *Casa d'Itália* at Rua Dr Maia 3112 has a varied menu to choose from.

Bus services from Uruguaiana are excellent, and you can get to or from most of the important centres, from Rio southwards. From Paso de los Libres, there are equally good services to points within Argentina, including Buenos Aires, Posadas and Puerto Iguazú. Finally, there are three **trains** a week to and from Santa Maria and Porto Alegre. There are daily **air services** from Uruguaiana to Porto Alegre and from Paso de los Libres to Buenos Aires.

São Borja

Today a fairly major border crossing point and regional trading centre, **SÃO BORJA** is best known in the rest of Brazil as the birthplace of two of the country's most controversial presidents: **Getúlio Vargas** and **João Goulart**. In São Borja, if nowhere else in Brazil, the populist Vargas remains a venerated figure, and his former home, at Av. Presidente Vargas 1772, is now open to the public as the **Museu Getúlio Vargas** (Mon–Sat 8.30am–noon & 1.30–5.30pm), containing his library and personal objects and furniture. Goulart, whose incompetent presidency led to the military's seizure of power in 1964 followed by 25 years of often ruthless rule, is someone that São Borja tries to forget.

As a **border crossing**, São Borja is most useful when travelling between the Brazilian Jesuit mission of São Miguel and those in Argentina and Paraguay. São Borja has good **bus** connections with Santo Ângelo (for São Miguel), most other important towns in Rio Grande do Sul, Curitiba, São Paulo and, across the bridge that links Brazil with Argentina, the Argentine town of Santo Tomé. From Santo Tomé there are several bus services a day to Posadas, Puerto Iguazú, Buenos Aires and other towns in Argentina.

If you need to stay over in São Borja, the cheapest **hotel** is the *Itaipu* at Rua Aparício Mariense 1167 (℡55/431-1577; ❶), while the *Executivo* at Av. Presidente Vargas 2515 (℡55/431-3741; ❷) offers slightly greater comfort. In Santo Tomé, the *Residencial Paris*, at Calle Mitre 890 on the corner of Calle Beltrán (❶), is a fall-back for budget travellers, while the best place in town is the *Hotel Santo Tomé* (℡756/20161; ❸).

Travel details

Buses

Blumenau to: Florianópolis (6 daily; 3hr); Itajaí (hourly; 2hr); Joinville (hourly; 2hr); Pomerode (hourly; 1hr).

Curitiba to: Blumenau (10 daily; 4hr); Buenos Aires (2 daily; 37hr); Florianópolis (14 daily; 5hr); Foz do Iguaçu (14 daily; 12hr); Guaraqueçaba (2 daily; 6hr); Paranaguá (hourly; 2hr); Porto Alegre (10 daily; 11hr); Prudentópolis (4 daily; 6hr); Rio (9 daily; 11hr); São Paulo (hourly; 6hr).

Florianópolis to: Blumenau (6 daily; 3hr); Buenos Aires (2 daily; 30hr); Curitiba (14 daily; 5hr); Foz do Iguaçu (2 daily; 16hr); Joinville (hourly; 3hr); Porto Alegre (10 daily; 7hr); Rio (8 daily; 19hr); Santo Amaro da Imperatriz (4 daily; 1hr); São Paulo (10 daily; 12hr).

Foz do Iguaçu to: Curitiba (14 daily; 12hr); Florianópolis (2 daily; 16hr); Itaipu (hourly; 1hr); Prudentópolis (3 daily; 7hr); Rio (4 daily; 22hr); São Paulo (7 daily; 18hr).

Joinville to: Blumenau (hourly; 2hr); Curitiba

(hourly; 2hr 30min); Florianópolis (hourly; 3hr);
Porto Alegre (2 daily; 10hr); Rio (1 daily; 15hr); São
Francisco do Sul (hourly; 1hr); São Paulo (7 daily;
9hr); Vila Dona Francesca (hourly; 45min).
Pelotas to: Porto Alegre (hourly; 3hr); Montevideo
(2 daily; 8hr); Rio Grande (hourly; 1hr)
Porto Alegre to: Buenos Aires (2 daily; 22hr);
Curitiba (10 daily; 11hr); Florianópolis (10 daily;
7hr); Livramento (4 daily; 7hr); Montevideo (3 daily;
12hr); Pelotas (hourly; 3hr); Rio (6 daily; 26hr); Rio
Grande (hourly; 1hr); São Paulo (8 daily; 18hr).

Trains

Curitiba to: Paranaguá (1–2 daily; 4hr 20min).
Porto Alegre to: Livramento (3 weekly; 14hr);
Santa Maria (daily except Sat; 7hr).

Ferries

Guaraqueçaba to: Ariri (2 weekly; 10hr);
Paranaguá (1 daily; 3hr).

Contexts

Contexts

The historical framework

Brazil's recorded history begins with the arrival of the Portuguese in 1500, although it had been discovered and settled by Indians many centuries before. The importation of millions of African slaves over the next four centuries completed the rich blend of European, Indian and African influences that formed modern Brazil and its people. Achieving independence from Portugal in 1822, Brazil's enormous wealth in land and natural resources underpinned a boom-and-bust cycle of economic development that continues to the present day. The eternal "Land of the Future" is still a prisoner of its past, as industrialization turned Brazil into the economic giant of South America, but sharpened social divisions. After a twenty-year interlude of military rule, the civilian "New Republic" has struggled, with some success, against deep-rooted economic crisis and has managed to consolidate democracy. Although social divisions remain, the current economic and political outlook is the best it has been for a generation.

Early history

Very little is known about the thousands of years that Brazil was inhabited exclusively by **Indians**. The first chroniclers who arrived with the Portuguese – Pedro Vaz da Caminha in 1500 and Gaspar Carvajal in 1540 – saw large villages, but nothing resembling the huge Aztec and Inca cities that the Spanish encountered. The fragile material traces left by Brazil's earliest inhabitants have for the most part not survived. The few exceptions – like the exquisitely worked glazed ceramic jars unearthed on Marajó island in the Amazon – come from cultures that have vanished so completely that not even a name records their passing.

The Indians fascinated the Portuguese, and many of the first Europeans to visit Brazil sent lengthy reports back home. The most vivid account was penned by a German mercenary, **Hans Staden**, who spent three nervous years among the cannibal **Tupi** after being captured in 1552. He tells how they tied his legs together, "… and I was forced to hop through the huts, at which they made merry, saying 'Here comes our food hopping towards us.'" Understandably, his memoirs were one of the first bestsellers in European history, and contained much accurate description of an Indian culture still largely untouched by the colonists. The work of Staden and the first explorers and missionaries offers a brief snapshot of Indian Brazil in the sixteenth century, a blurred photograph of a way of life soon to be horribly transformed.

It was unfortunate that the Portuguese first landed in the only part of Brazil where ritualized cannibalism was practised on a large scale; away from the Tupi areas it was rare. Nowhere was stone used for building. There was no use of metal or the wheel, and no centralized, state-like civilizations on the scale of Spanish America. There are arguments about how large the Indian population was: Carvajal described taking several days to pass through the large towns of the Omagua tribe on the Amazon in 1542 but, away from the abundant food sources on the coast and the banks of large rivers, **population** densities were much lower. The total number of Indians was probably around five million. Today there are around 300,000 in Brazil.

Conquest

The Portuguese discovery of Brazil, when **Pedro Alvares Cabral** landed in southern Bahia on April 23, 1500, was an accident, an episode in Portugal's thrust to found a seaborne empire in the East Indies during the sixteenth century. Cabral was blown off course as he steered far to the west to avoid the African doldrums on his way to Calcutta: after a cursory week exploring the coast he continued to India, where he drowned in a shipwreck a few months later. King Manuel I sent **Amerigo Vespucci** to explore further in 1501. Reserving the name of the continent for himself, he spent several months sailing along the coast, calendar in hand, baptizing places after the names of saints' days: entering Guanabara Bay on New Year's Day 1502, he called it Rio de Janeiro. The land was called Terra do Brasil, after a tropical redwood that was its first export; the scarlet dye it yielded was called *brasa*, "a glowing coal".

Portugal, preoccupied with Africa and the lucrative Far East spice trade, neglected this new addition to its empire for the first few decades. Apart from a few lumber camps and scattered stockades, the Portuguese made no attempt at settlement. Consequently, other European countries were not slow to move in, with French and English privateers using the coast as a base to raid the spice ships. Finally, in 1532, João III was provoked into action. He divided up the coastline into **sesmarias**, captaincies fifty leagues wide and extending indefinitely inland, distributing them to aristocrats and courtiers in return for undertakings to found settlements. It was hardly a roaring success: Pernambuco, where sugar took hold, and São Vicente, gateway to the Jesuit mission station of São Paulo, were the only securely held areas.

Irritated by the lack of progress, King João repossessed the captaincies in 1548 and brought Brazil under direct royal control, sending out the first governor-general, **Tomé da Sousa**, to the newly designated **capital** at Salvador in 1549. The first few governors successfully rooted out the European privateers, and – where sugar could grow – wiped out Indian resistance. By the closing decades of the century increasing numbers of Portuguese settlers were flowing in. Slaves began to be imported from the Portuguese outposts on the African coast, as **sugar plantations** sprang up around Salvador and Olinda. Brazil, no longer seen merely as a possible staging point on the way to the Far East, became an increasingly important piece of the far-flung Portuguese Empire. When Europe's taste for sugar took off in the early seventeenth century, the Northeast of Brazil quickly became very valuable real estate – and a tempting target for the expanding maritime powers of northern Europe, jealous of the Iberian monopoly in the New World.

War with the Dutch

The **Dutch**, with naval bases in the Caribbean and a powerful fleet, were the best placed to move against Brazil. A mixture of greed and pressing political motives lay behind the Dutch decision. From 1580 to 1640 Portugal was united with Spain, against whom the Dutch had fought a bitter war of independence, and they were still menaced by the Spanish presence in Flanders. Anything that distracted Spain from further designs on the fledgling United Provinces seemed like a good idea at the time. As it turned out, neither the

Spanish nor the Portuguese crowns played much of a role in the war: it was fought out between the Dutch, in the mercantile shape of the Dutch West India Company, and the Portuguese settlers already in Brazil, with Indian and *mameluco* (mixed race) backing. Although the Dutch occupied much of the Northeast for thirty years, they were finally overcome by one of South America's first guerrilla campaigns, in a war made vicious by the Catholic–Protestant divide that underlay it: few prisoners were taken and both sides massacred civilians.

In 1624 a Dutch fleet appeared off Salvador, taking the governor completely by surprise, and the city by storm. After burning down the Jesuit college and killing as many priests as they could find (like the good Calvinists they were), they were pinned down by enraged settlers for nine months and finally expelled in 1625 by a hastily assembled combined Spanish and Portuguese fleet – the only direct intervention made by either country in the conflict. When a Dutch force was once more repulsed from Salvador in 1627, they shifted their attention further north and found the going much easier: Olinda was taken in 1630, the rich sugar zones of Pernambuco were occupied, and Dutch control extended up to the mouth of the Amazon by 1641. With settlers moving in, a strong military presence and a fleet more powerful than Portugal's, Dutch control of the Northeast looked as if it would become permanent.

Maurice of Nassau was sent out as governor of the new Dutch possessions in Brazil in 1630, as the Dutch founded a new capital in Pernambuco: Mauritzstaadt, now Recife. His enlightened policies of allowing the Portuguese freedom to practise their religion, and including them in the colonial government, would probably have resulted in a Dutch Brazil had it not been for the stupidity of the Dutch West India Company. They insisted on Calvinism and heavy taxes, and when Maurice resigned in disgust and returned to Holland in 1644 the settlers rose. After five years of ambushes, plantation burnings and massacres, the Brazilians pushed the Dutch back into an enclave around Recife. The Dutch poured in reinforcements by sea, but their fate was decided by two climactic battles in 1648 and 1649 at **Guararapes**, just outside Recife, where the Dutch were routed and their military power broken. Although they held on to Recife until 1654, the dream of a Dutch empire in the Americas was over, and Portuguese control was not to be threatened again until the nineteenth century.

The bandeirantes: gold and God

The expulsion of the Dutch demonstrated the toughness of the early Brazilians, which was also well to the fore in the penetration and settling of **the interior** during the seventeenth and eighteenth centuries. Every few months, expeditions set out to explore the interior, following rumours of gold and looking for Indians to enslave. They carried an identifying banner, a *bandeira*, which gave the name **bandeirantes** to the adventurers; they became the Brazilian version of the Spanish *conquistadores*. São Paulo, thanks to its position on the Rio Tietê, one of the few natural highways that flowed east–west into the deep interior, became the main *bandeirante* centre.

The average *bandeira* would be made up of a mixed crew of people, reflecting the many – and often conflicting – motives underlying the expedition. None travelled without a priest or two (*bandeirantes* may have been cut-throats, but they were devout Catholic cut-throats), and many *bandeiras* were backed by the Jesuits and Franciscans in their drive to found missions and baptize the heathen. The majority combined exploration with plundering and could last for years, with occasional stops to plant and harvest crops, before returning to São Paulo – if they ever did: many towns on the Planalto Central or Mato Grosso have their origins in the remnants of a *bandeira*. The *bandeirantes* had to fight Indians, occasionally the Spanish, and also themselves: they were riven by tension between native-born Brazilians and Portuguese, which regularly erupted into fighting.

The journeys *bandeiras* made were often epic in scale, covering immense distances and overcoming natural obstacles as formidable as the many hostile Indian tribes they encountered, who were defeated more by diseases to which they had no resistance, than by force of arms. It was the *bandeirantes* who pushed the borders of Brazil way inland, practically to the foothills of the Andes, and also supplied the geographical knowledge that now began to fill in the blanks on the maps. They explored the Amazon, Paraná and Uruguai river systems, but the most important way they shaped the future of Brazil was in locating the Holy Grail of the New World: gold.

Gold was first found by *bandeirantes* in 1695, at the spot that is now Sabará, in Minas Gerais. As towns sprang up around further gold strikes in Minas, gold was also discovered around Cuiabá, in Mato Grosso, in 1719, adding fresh impetus to the opening-up of the interior. The 3500-kilometre journey to Cuiabá, down five separate river systems, took six months at the best of times; from São Paulo it was easier to travel to Europe. Along the way the *bandeirantes* had to fight off the Paiaguá Indians, who attacked in canoes and swam like fish, and then the Guaicuru, who had taken to the horse with the same enthusiasm the Plains Indians of North America were later to show. They annihilated entire *bandeiras*; others following observed "rotting belongings and dead bodies on the riverbanks, and hammocks slung with their owners in them, dead. Not a single person reached Cuiabá that year."

But the *paulista* hunger for riches was equal even to these appalling difficulties. By the mid-eighteenth century, the flow of gold from Brazil was keeping the Portuguese Crown afloat, temporarily halting its long slide down the league table of European powers. In Brazil, the rush of migrants to the gold areas changed the regional balance, as the new interior communities drew population away from the Northeast. The gateways to the interior, Rio de Janeiro and São Paulo, grew rapidly. The shift was recognized in 1763, when the capital was transferred from Salvador to Rio, and that filthy, disease-ridden port began its transformation into one of the great cities of the world.

The Jesuits

Apart from the *bandeirantes*, the most important agents of the colonization of the interior were the **Jesuits**. The first Jesuit missionaries arrived in Brazil in 1549 and, thanks to the influence they held over successive Portuguese kings, they acquired power in Brazil second only to that of the Crown itself. In Salvador they built the largest Jesuit college outside Rome, and set in motion a crusade to convert the Indian population. The usual method was to congregate the Indians in **missions**, where they worked under the supervision of Jesuit fathers. From 1600 onwards, dozens of missions were founded in the interior, especially in the Amazon and in the grasslands of the Southeast.

The role the Jesuits played in the conversion of the Indians was ambiguous. Mission Indians were often released by Jesuits to work for settlers, where they died like flies; and the missionaries' intrepid penetration of remote areas resulted in the spread of diseases that wiped out entire tribes. On the other hand, many Jesuits distinguished themselves in protecting Indians against the settlers, a theological as well as a secular struggle, for many Portuguese argued that the native population had no souls and could therefore be treated like animals.

The most remarkable defender of the Indians was **Antônio Vieira**, who abandoned his position as chief adviser to the king in Lisbon to become a missionary in Brazil in 1653. Basing himself in São Luís, he struggled to implement the more enlightened Indian laws that his influence over King João IV had secured, to the disgust of settlers clamouring for slaves. Vieira denied them for years, preaching a series of sermons along the way that became famous throughout Europe, as well as Brazil: "An Indian will be your slave for the few days he lives, but your soul will be enslaved for as long as God is God. All of you are in mortal sin, all of you live in a state of condemnation, and all of you are going directly to Hell!" he thundered from the pulpit in 1654, to the fury of settlers in the congregation. So high did feelings run that, in 1661, settlers forced Vieira onto a ship bound for Portugal, standing in the surf and shouting "Out! Out!"

But Vieira returned, with renewed support from the Crown, and Jesuit power in Brazil grew. It reached a peak in the remarkable theocracy of the **Guaraní missions**, where Spanish and Portuguese Jesuits founded over a dozen missions on the pampas along the Uruguayan border. Left alone for the first fifty years, they effectively became a Jesuit state, until the Treaty of Madrid in 1752 divided up the land between Spain and Portugal; the treaty ordered the missions abandoned, so that settlers could move in. The Guaraní revolted immediately and, while the Jesuit hierarchy made half-hearted efforts to get them to move, most of the priests stayed with their Guaraní flocks. Resistance was heroic but hopeless: the superior fire power of a joint Spanish–Portuguese military expedition decimated both Guaraní and Jesuits in 1756.

Jesuit involvement in the Guaraní war lent added force to the long-standing settler demands to expel them from the colony. This time, they were helped by the rise to power of the **Marquis de Pombal**, who became the power behind the Portuguese throne for much of the eighteenth century. Seeing the Jesuits as a threat to Crown control, he seized upon the Guaraní wars as an excuse to expel the Order from Brazil in 1760. The Jesuits may have been imperfect protectors, but from this time on the Indians were denied even that.

Independence

Brazil, uniquely among South American countries, achieved a peaceful transition to independence. The odds seemed against it at one point. Brazilian resentment at their exclusion from government, and at the Portuguese monopoly of foreign trade, grew steadily during the eighteenth century. It culminated, in 1789, in the **Inconfidência Mineira**, a plot hatched by twelve prominent citizens of Ouro Preto to proclaim Brazilian independence. The rebels, however, were betrayed almost before they started – their leader, **Tiradentes**, was executed and the rest exiled. Then, just as the tension seemed to be becoming dangerous, events in Europe once again took a hand in shaping Brazil's future.

In 1807, **Napoleon** invaded Portugal. With the French army poised to take Lisbon, the British navy hurriedly evacuated **King João VI** to Rio, which was declared the temporary capital of the Portuguese Empire and seat of the government-in-exile. While **Wellington** set about driving the French from Portugal, the British were able to force the opening-up of Brazil's ports to non-Portuguese shipping, and the economic growth that followed reinforced Brazil's increasing self-confidence. João was entranced by his tropical kingdom, unable to pull himself away even after Napoleon's defeat. Finally, in 1821, he was faced with a liberal revolt in Portugal that threatened to topple the monarchy, and he was unable to delay his return any longer. In April 1822 he appointed his son, **Dom Pedro**, as prince regent and governor of Brazil; when he sailed home, his last words to his son were "Get your hands on this kingdom, before some adventurer does."

Pedro, young and arrogant, grew increasingly irritated by the strident demands of the Côrtes, the Portuguese assembly, that he return home to his father and allow Brazil to be ruled from Portugal once again. On September 7, 1822, Pedro was out riding on the plain of Ypiranga, near São Paulo. Buttoning himself up after an attack of diarrhoea, he was surprised by a messenger with a bundle of letters from Lisbon. Reading the usual demands for him to return, his patience snapped, and he declared Brazil independent with the cry "Independence or death!" With overwhelming popular support for the idea, he had himself crowned **Dom Pedro I**, Emperor of Brazil, on December 1, 1822. The Portuguese, preoccupied by political crises at home and demoralized by Pedro's defection, put up little resistance. Apart from an ugly massacre of Brazilian patriots in Fortaleza, and some fighting in Bahia, the Portuguese withdrawal was peaceful and by the end of 1823 no Portuguese forces remained.

Early empire: revolt in the regions

Although independence had been easily achieved, the early decades of empire proved much more difficult. The first problem was Dom Pedro himself: headstrong and autocratic, he became increasingly estranged from his subjects, devoting more attention to scandalous romances than affairs of state. In April 1831 he abdicated, in a fit of petulance, in favour of the heir apparent, **Dom Pedro II**, and returned to Portugal. Pedro II would later prove an enlightened ruler, but as he was only five at the time there were limits to his capacity to influence events. With a power vacuum at the centre of the political system, long-standing tensions in the outlying provinces erupted into revolt.

There were common threads in all the **rebellions** in the provinces: slaves rebelling against masters, Indian and mixed-race resentment of white domination, Brazilians settling scores with Portuguese, and the poor rising against the rich. The first, and most serious, conflagration was the **Cabanagem Rebellion** in Pará, where a mass revolt of the dispossessed began in 1835. The rebels took Belém, where, in a great moment of retribution, the Indian Domingues Onça killed the governor of Pará. The uprising spread through the Amazon like wildfire and took a decade to put down. A parallel revolt, the **Balaiada**, began in Maranhão in 1838. Here the rebels took Caxias, the second city of the state, and held out for three years against the army. Similar risings in Pernambuco, Bahia and Rio Grande do Sul punctuated the 1830s and 1840s; the disruption was immense, with large areas ravaged by fighting that threatened to tear the country apart.

The crisis led to Dom Pedro II being declared emperor four years early, in 1840, when he was only fourteen. Precociously talented, he was a sensible, scholarly man, completely unlike his father. His instincts were conservative, but he regularly appointed liberal governments and was respected even by republicans. With government authority restored, the provincial rebellions had by 1850 either blown themselves out or been put down. And with **coffee** beginning to be planted on a large scale in Rio, São Paulo and Minas, and the flow of European immigrants rising from a trickle to a flood, the economy of southern Brazil began to take off in earnest.

The War of the Triple Alliance

With the rebellions in the provinces, the **army** became increasingly important in Brazilian political life. Pedro insisted they stay out of domestic politics, but his policy of diverting the generals by allowing them to control foreign policy ultimately led to the disaster of the war with Paraguay (1864–70). Although Brazil emerged victorious, it was at a dreadful cost. The **War of the Triple Alliance** is one of history's forgotten conflicts, but it was the bloodiest war in South American history, with a casualty list almost as long as that of the American Civil War: Brazil alone suffered over 100,000 casualties.

It pitted, in an unequal struggle, the landlocked republic of Paraguay, under the dictator **Francisco Lopez**, against the combined forces of Brazil, Argentina and Uruguay. Although the Paraguayans started the war, by invading Uruguay and parts of Mato Grosso in 1864, they had been sorely provoked by Brazilian meddling in Uruguay. The generals in Rio, with no more rebels to fight within Brazil, wanted to incorporate Uruguay into the empire. Paraguay saw Brazil blocking its access to the sea and invaded to pre-empt a Brazilian takeover, dragging Argentina reluctantly into the conflict through a mutual defence pact with Brazil.

The Brazilian army and navy were confident of victory as the Paraguayans were heavily outnumbered and outgunned. Yet the Paraguayans, for the first time, demonstrated the military prowess that would mark their history: united under the able leadership of Lopez, the Paraguayan army proved disciplined and fanatically brave, always defeated by numbers but terribly mauling the opposition. It turned into a war of extermination and six terrible years were only ended by the killing of Lopez in 1870, by which time the male adult population of Paraguay is said to have been reduced (by disease and starvation as well as war) to under twenty thousand, from over a million in 1864.

The end of slavery

From the seventeenth to the nineteenth century around ten million Africans were transported to Brazil as **slaves** – ten times as many as were shipped to the United States – yet the death rate in Brazil was so great that in 1860 Brazil's black population was half the size of that in the US. Slavery was always contested: slaves fled from the cities and plantations to form refugee communities called *quilombos*; the largest, **Palmares**, in the interior of the northeastern state of Alagoas, was several thousand strong and stayed independent for almost a century.

But it was not until the nineteenth century that slavery was seriously challenged. The initial impetus came from Britain, where the abolitionist movement became influential just when Portugal was most dependent on British capital and British naval protection. Abolition was regarded with horror by the large landowners in Brazil, and a combination of racism and fear of economic dislocation led to a determined rearguard action to preserve slavery. A complicated diplomatic waltz began between Britain and Brazil, as slavery laws were tinkered with *para inglês ver* – "for the English to see" – a phrase that survives in the language to this day, meaning doing something merely for show. The object was to make the British believe slavery would be abolished, while ensuring that the letter of the law kept it legal.

British abolitionists were not deceived, and from 1832 to 1854 the Royal Navy maintained a squadron off Brazil, intercepting and confiscating slave ships, and occasionally entering Brazilian ports to seize slavers and burn their ships – one of history's more positive examples of gunboat diplomacy. The slave trade was finally **abolished** in 1854 but, to the disgust of the abolitionists, slavery itself remained legal. British power had its limits and ultimately it was a passionate campaign within Brazil itself, led by the fiery lawyer **Joaquim Nabuco**, that finished slavery off. The growing liberal movement, increasingly republican and anti-monarchist, squared off against the landowners, with Dom Pedro hovering indecisively somewhere in between. Slavery became the dominant issue in Brazilian politics for twenty years. By the time full **emancipation** came, in the "Golden Law" of May 13, 1888, Brazil had achieved the shameful distinction of being the last country in the Americas to abolish slavery.

From empire to republic

The end of slavery was also the death knell of the monarchy. Since the 1870s the intelligentsia, deeply influenced by French liberalism, had turned against the emperor and agitated for a republic. By the 1880s they had been joined by the officer corps, who blamed Dom Pedro for lack of backing during the Paraguayan war. When the large landowners withdrew their support, furious that the emperor had not prevented emancipation, the **monarchy collapsed** very suddenly in 1889.

Once again, Brazil managed a bloodless transition. The push came from the army, detachments led by **Marechal Deodoro da Fonseca** meeting no resistance when they occupied Rio on November 15, 1889. They invited the royal family to remain, but Dom Pedro insisted on exile, boarding a ship to France, where he died in penury two years later in a shabby Parisian hotel. Deodoro, meanwhile, began a Brazilian tradition of ham-fisted military autocracy. Ignoring the clamour for a liberal republic, he declared himself dictator in 1891, but was forced to resign three weeks later when even the army refused to support him. His deputy, **Marechal Floriano de Peixoto**, took over, but proved even more incompetent; Rio was actually shelled in 1893 by rebellious warships, demanding Peixoto's resignation. Finally, in 1894 popular pressure led to Peixoto stepping down in favour of the first elected civilian president, **Prudente de Morais**.

Coffee with milk – and sugar

The years from 1890 to 1930 were politically undistinguished, but saw Brazil rapidly transformed economically and socially by large-scale **immigration** from Europe and Japan; they were decades of swift growth and swelling cities, which saw a very Brazilian combination of a boom-bust-boom economy and corrupt pork-barrel politics.

The boom was led by **coffee** and **rubber**, which – at opposite ends of the country – had entirely different labour forces. Millions of *nordestinos* moved into the Amazon to tap rubber, but the coffee workers swarming into São Paulo in their hundreds of thousands came chiefly from Italy. Between 1890 and 1930 over four million migrants arrived from Europe and another two hundred thousand from Japan. Most went to work on the coffee estates of southern Brazil, but enough remained to turn São Paulo into the fastest-growing city in the Americas. Urban industrialization appeared in Brazil for the first time, taking root in São Paulo to supply the voracious markets of the young cities springing up in the *paulista* interior. By 1930, São Paulo had displaced Rio as the leading industrial centre.

More improbable was the transformation of **Manaus** into the largest city of the Amazon. Rubber turned Manaus from a muddy village into a rich trading city within a couple of decades. The peak of the **rubber boom**, from the 1870s to the outbreak of World War I, financed its metamorphosis into a tropical *belle époque* outpost, complete with opera house. Rubber exports were second only to coffee, but proved much more vulnerable to competition. Seeds smuggled out of Amazônia by Victorian adventurer Henry Wickham in 1876 ended up in Ceylon and Malaya, where – by 1914 – plantation rubber pushed wild Amazon rubber out of the world markets. The region returned to an isolation it maintained until the late 1950s.

Economic growth was not accompanied by political development. Although not all the early presidents were incompetent – **Rodrigues Alves** (1902–6), for example, rebuilt Rio complete with a public health system, finally eradicating the epidemics that had stunted its growth – the majority were corrupt political bosses, relying on a network of patron–client relationships, whose main ambition seemed to be to bleed the public coffers dry. Power was concentrated in the two most populous states of São Paulo and Minas Gerais, which struck a convenient deal to alternate the presidency between them.

This way of ensuring that both sets of snouts could slurp away in the trough uninterrupted was called "**café com leite**" by its opponents: coffee from São Paulo and milk from the *mineiro* dairy herds. In fact, it was coffee with milk and sugar: the developing national habit of the sweet *cafezinho* in the burgeoning cities of the South provided a new domestic market for sugar, which ensured support from the plantation oligarchs of the Northeast. In a pattern that would repeat itself in more modern times, the economy forged ahead while politics went backwards. The saying "Brazil grows in the dark, while politicians sleep" made its first appearance around this time.

The revolution of 1930

The revolution of 1930 that brought the populist **Getúlio Vargas** to power was a critical event. Vargas dominated Brazilian politics for the next quarter-century, and the Vargas years were a time of radical change, marking a decisive break with the past. Vargas had much in common with his Argentinian contemporary, Juan Perón: both were charming, but cunning and ruthless with it, and rooted their power base in the new urban working class.

It was the **working class**, combined with disillusion in the junior ranks of the military, that swept Vargas to power. Younger officers, accustomed to seeing the armed forces as the guardian of the national conscience, were disgusted by the corruption of the military hierarchy. When the **Great Depression** hit, the government spent millions protecting coffee growers by buying crops at a guaranteed price; the coffee was then burnt, as the export market had collapsed. Workers in the cities and countryside were appalled, seeing themselves frozen out while vast sums were spent on landowners, and as the economic outlook worsened the pressure started building up from other states to end the São Paulo and Minas grip on power. This time, the transition was violent.

In 1926, **Washington Luis** was made president without an election, as the elite contrived an unopposed nomination. When Luis appeared set to do the same thing in 1930, an unstoppable **mass revolution** developed, first in Vargas's home state of Rio Grande do Sul, then in Rio, then in the Northeast. There was some resistance in São Paulo, but the worst fighting was in the Northeast, where street battles left scores dead. The shock troops of the revolution were the young army officers who led their units against the *ancien régime* in Minas and Rio, and the *gaúcho* cavalry who accompanied Vargas on his triumphant procession to Rio. Although São Paulo rose briefly against Vargas in 1932, the revolt was swiftly crushed, and Getúlio, as Brazilians affectionately knew him, embarked on the longest and most spectacular political career in modern Brazilian history.

Vargas and the Estado Novo

It was not just Vargas who took power in 1930, but a whole new generation of young, energetic administrators, who set about transforming the economy and the political system. Vargas played the nationalist card with great success, nationalizing the oil, electricity and steel industries, and setting up a health and social welfare system that earned him unwavering working-class support that continued even after his death.

Reforms this fundamental could not be carried out under the old constitutional framework. Vargas simplified things by declaring himself **dictator** in 1937 and imprisoning political opponents – most of whom were in the trade union movement, the Communist Party or the *Integralistas*, the Brazilian Fascists. He called his regime the "New State", the **Estado Novo**, and certainly its reforming energy was something new. Although he cracked down hard on dissent, Vargas was never a totalitarian dictator. He was massively popular and his great political talents enabled him to outflank most opponents.

The result was both political and economic success. The ruinous coffee subsidy was abolished, industry encouraged and agriculture diversified: by 1945 São Paulo had become the largest industrial centre in South America. With the federal government increasing its powers at the expense of state rights, regional government power was wrested out of the hands of the oligarchs for the first time.

It took **World War II** to bring Vargas down. At first Brazil stayed neutral, reaping the benefits of increased exports, but when the United States offered massive aid in return for bases and Brazilian entry into the war, Vargas joined the Allies. Outraged by German submarine attacks on Brazilian shipping, Brazil was the only country in South America to play an active part in the war. A **Brazilian Expeditionary Force**, 5000-strong, fought in Italy from 1944 until the end of the war; when they returned, the military High Command was able to exploit the renewed prestige of the army, forcing Vargas to stand down. They argued that the armed forces could hardly fight for democracy abroad and return home to a dictatorship, and, in any case, after fifteen years a leadership change was overdue. In the election that followed in 1945, Vargas grudgingly endorsed the army general **Eurico Dutra**, who duly won – but Getúlio, brooding on his ranch, was not yet finished with the presidency.

The death of Vargas

Dutra proved a colourless figure, and when Vargas ran for the presidency in 1950 he won a crushing victory, the old dictator "returning on the arm of the people", as he wrote later. But he had powerful enemies, in the armed forces and on the right, and his second stint in power was turbulent. Dutra had allowed inflation to climb, and Vargas proposed to raise the minimum wage and increase taxation of the middle classes. In the charged climate of the Cold War this was denounced by the right as veering towards communism, and vitriolic attacks on Vargas and his government were made in the press, notably by a slippery, ambitious journalist named **Carlos Lacerda**.

Vargas's supporters reacted angrily and argument turned into crisis in 1954, when shots were fired at Lacerda, missing their target but killing an air force officer guarding him. The attempt was traced to one of Vargas's bodyguards, but Vargas himself was not implicated. Even so, the press campaign rose to a crescendo, and finally, on August 25, 1954, the military High Command demanded his resignation. Vargas received the news calmly, went into his bedroom in the Palácio de Catete in Rio and shot himself through the heart.

He left an emotional suicide note to the Brazilian people: "I choose this means to be with you always . . . I gave you my life; now I offer my death. Nothing remains. Serenely I take the first step on the road to eternity, as I leave life and enter history." The initial popular reaction of stunned shock gave way to fury, as Vargas's supporters turned on the forces that had hounded him to death, burning the newspaper offices and forcing Lacerda to flee the country. Eighteen months of tension followed, as an interim government marked time until the next election.

JK and Brasília

Juscelino Kubitschek, "JK" to Brazilians, president from 1956 to 1961, proved just the man to fix Brazil's attention on the future rather than the past. He combined energy and imagination with integrity and great political skill, acquired in the hard school of the politics of Minas Gerais, one of the main nurseries of political talent in Brazil. Although the tensions in the political system were still there – constitutionalists in the armed forces had to stage a preemptive coup to allow him to take office – Kubitschek was able to serve out his full term, still the only elected civilian president to do so in modern times. And he left a permanent reminder of the most successful post-war presidency in the form of the country's new capital, Brasília, deep in the Planalto Central.

"Fifty years in five!" was his election slogan, and his economic programme lived up to its ambitious billing. His term saw a spurt in growth rates that was the platform for the "economic miracle" of the next decade; the economic boom led to wider prosperity and renewed national confidence. Kubitschek drew on both in the flight of inspired imagination that led to **the building of Brasília**.

It could so easily have been an expensive disaster, a purpose-built capital miles from anywhere, the personal brainchild of a president anxious to make his mark. But Kubitschek implanted the idea in the national imagination by portraying it as a renewed statement of faith in the interior, a symbol of national integration and a better future for all Brazilians, not just those in the South. He brought it off with great panache, bringing in the extravagantly talented **Oscar Niemeyer**, whose brief was to come up with a revolutionary city layout and the architecture to go with it. Kubitschek spent almost every weekend on the huge building site that became the city, consulted on the smallest details and had the satisfaction of handing over to his successor, **Jânio Quadros**, in the newly inaugurated capital.

1964: The road to military rule

At the time, the **military coup of 1964** was considered a temporary hiccup in Brazil's post-war democracy, but it lasted 21 years and left a very bitter taste. The first period of military rule saw the famous economic miracle (see p.757), when the economy grew at an astonishing average annual rate of ten percent for a decade, only to come to a juddering halt after 1974, when oil price rises and the increasing burden of debt repayment pushed it off the rails. But most depressing was the effective end of democracy for over a decade, and a time – from 1969 to 1974 – when terror was used against opponents by military hardliners. Brazil, where the *desaparecidos* numbered a few hundred rather than the tens of thousands butchered in Argentina and Chile, was not the worst military regime on the continent. But it is difficult to overestimate the shock even limited repression caused. It was the first time Brazilians experienced systematic brutality by a government, and even in the years of economic success the military governments were loathed right across the political spectrum.

The coup of 1964 was years in the brewing. It had two root causes: a constitutional crisis and the deepening divides in Brazilian society. In the developed South, relations between trade unions and employers went from bad to worse, as workers struggled to protect their wages against rising inflation. But it was in the Northeast that tension was greatest, as a result of the **Peasant Leagues** movement. Despite industrial modernization, the rural Northeast was still stuck in a time-warped land tenure system, moulded in the colonial period and in many ways unchanged since then. Peasants, under the charismatic leadership of **Francisco Julião** and the governor of Pernambuco, **Miguel Arraes**, began forming co-operatives and occupying estates to press their claim for agrarian reform; the estate owners cried communism and openly agitated for a military coup.

The crisis might still have been avoided by a more skilful president, but Kubitschek's immediate successors were not of his calibre. Quadros resigned after only six months, in August 1961, on the anniversary of Vargas's suicide. He apparently wanted popular reaction to sweep him back into office, but shrank from suicide and ended up shooting himself in the foot rather than the heart. The masses stayed home, and the vice-president, **João Goulart**, took over.

Goulart's accession was viewed with horror by the right. He had a reputation as a leftist firebrand, having been a minister of labour under Vargas, and his position was weakened by the fact that he had not succeeded by direct popular vote. As political infighting began to get out of control, with the country polarizing between left and right, Goulart decided to throw himself behind the trade unions and the Peasant Leagues; his nationalist rhetoric rang alarm bells in Washington, and the army began to plot his downfall, with tacit American backing.

The coup, in the tradition of Brazilian coups, was swift and bloodless. On March 31, 1964, troops from Minas Gerais moved on Rio; when the military commanders there refused to oppose them, the game was up for Goulart. After futile efforts to rally resistance in Rio Grande do Sul, he fled into exile in Uruguay, and the first in a long line of generals, **Humberto Castelo Branco**, became president.

Military rule

The military moved swiftly to dismantle democracy. Congress was dissolved, those representatives not to military taste being removed. It then reconvened with only two parties, an official government and an official opposition ("The difference," ran a joke at the time, "is that one says Yes, and the other, Yes Sir!"). All other parties were banned. The Peasant Leagues and trade unions were repressed, with many of their leaders tortured and imprisoned, and even prominent national politicians like Arrães were thrown into jail. The ferocity of the military took aback even those on the right who had agitated for a coup. Ironically, many of them were hoist with their own petard when they voiced criticism, and found themselves gagged by the same measures they had urged against the left.

The political climate worsened steadily during the 1960s. An **urban guerrilla campaign** took off in the cities – its most spectacular success was the kidnapping of the American ambassador in 1969, released unharmed in return for over a hundred political detainees – but it only served as an excuse for the hardliners to crack down even further. General **Emílio Garrastazú Médici**, leader of the hardliners, took over the presidency in 1969 and the worst period of military rule began. Torture became routine, censorship was strict and thousands were driven into exile: this dark chapter in Brazilian history lasted for five agonizing years, until Médici gave way to **Ernesto Geisel** in 1974. The scars Médici left behind him, literally and metaphorically, have still not completely healed.

The economic miracle

Despite the cold winds blowing on the political front, the Brazilian economy forged ahead from the mid-1960s to 1974, the years of the **economic miracle** – and the combination of high growth and low inflation indeed seemed miraculous to later governments. The military welcomed foreign investment, and the large pool of cheap but skilled labour was irresistible. Investment poured in, both from Brazil and abroad, and the boom was the longest and largest in Brazilian history. Cities swelled, industry grew, and by the mid-1970s Brazil was the economic giant of South America, São Paulo state alone having a GNP higher than any South American country.

The problem, though, was uneven development. Even miraculous growth rates could not provide enough jobs for the hordes migrating to the cities, and the squalid **favelas** expanded even faster than the economy. The problem was worst in the Northeast and the Amazon, where industry was less developed, and drought combined with land conflict to push the people of the interior into the cities. It was also the miracle years that saw the origins of the **debt crisis**, a millstone around the neck of the Brazilian economy in the 1980s and 1990s.

After 1974, a lot of petrodollars were sloshing around the world banking system, thanks to oil price rises. Anxious to set this new capital to work, international banks and South American military regimes fell over themselves in their eagerness to organize deals. Brazil had a good credit rating: its wealth of natural resources and jailed labour leaders saw to that. The military needed money for a series of huge development projects that were central to its trickle-down economic policy, like the **Itaipu dam**, the **Carajás** mining projects in eastern Amazônia, and a **nuclear power programme**. By the end of the 1970s the debt was at $50 billion; by 1990 it had risen to $120 billion, and the interest payments were crippling the economy.

Opening up the Amazon

The first step towards opening up the vast interior of the **Amazon** was taken by Kubitschek, who built a dirt highway linking Brasília to Belém. But things really got going in 1970, when Médici realized that the Amazon could be used as a huge safety valve, releasing the pressure for agrarian reform in the Northeast. "Land without people for people without land!" became the slogan, and an ambitious programme of highway construction began that was to transform Amazônia. The main links were the **Transamazônica**, running west to the Peruvian border, the **Cuiabá–Santarém** highway into central Amazônia, and the **Cuiabá–Porto Velho/Rio Branco** highway, opening access to western Amazônia.

For the military, the Amazon was empty space, overdue for filling, and a national resource to be developed. They set up an elaborate network of tax breaks and incentives to encourage Brazilian and multinational firms to invest in the region, who also saw it as empty space and proceeded either to speculate with land or cut down forest to graze cattle. The one group that didn't perceive the Amazon as empty space was, naturally enough, the millions of people who already lived there. The immediate result was a spiralling land conflict, as ranchers, rubber tappers, Brazil-nut harvesters, gold-miners, smallholders, Indians, multinationals and Brazilian companies all tried to press their claims. The result was – and remains today – chaos.

By the late 1980s the situation in the Amazon was becoming an international controversy, with heated claims about the uncontrolled destruction of forest in huge annual burnings, and the invasion of Indian lands. Less internationally known was the **land crisis**, although a hundred people or more were dying in land conflicts in Amazônia every year. It took the assassination in 1988 of **Chico Mendes**, leader of the rubber tappers' union and eloquent defender of the forest, to bring it home. Media attention, as usual, has shed as much heat as light, but there are grounds for hope. For all the destruction, Amazônia is very large – there is still time for more sensible development to protect what remains. (See also "Amazon Ecology and Indian Rights", p.764.)

The abertura

Growing popular resentment of the military could not be contained indefinitely, especially when the economy turned sour. By the late 1970s debt, rising inflation and unemployment were turning the economy from a success story into a joke, and the military were further embarrassed by an unsavoury chain of corruption scandals. Geisel was the first military president to plan for a return to civilian rule, in a slow relaxing of the military grip called *abertura*, the "opening-up". Yet again, Brazil managed a bloodless – albeit fiendishly complicated – transition. Slow though the process was, the return to democracy would have been delayed even longer had it not been for two events along the way: the **metalworkers' strikes** in São Paulo in 1977 and the mass **campaign for direct elections** in 1983–84.

The São Paulo strikes began in the car industry and soon spread throughout the industrial belt of São Paulo, in a movement bearing many parallels with Solidarity in Poland. Led by unions that were still illegal, and the charismatic young factory worker **Lula (Luís Inácio da Silva)**, there was a tense stand-off between army and strikers, until the military realized that having São Paulo on strike would be worse for the economy than conceding the right to free trade unions. This dramatic re-emergence of organized labour was a sign that the military could not control the situation for much longer.

Reforms in the early 1980s lifted censorship, brought the exiles home and allowed normal political life to resume. But the military came up with an ingenious attempt to determine the succession: their control of Congress allowed them to pass a resolution that the president due to take office in 1985 would be elected not by direct vote, but by an electoral college, made up of congressmen and senators, where the military party had the advantage.

The democratic opposition responded with a counter-amendment proposing a direct election. It needed a two-thirds majority in Congress to be passed, and a campaign began for **diretas-já**, "elections now". Even the opposition was surprised by the response, as the Brazilian people, thoroughly sick of the generals, took to the streets in their millions. The campaign culminated in huge rallies of over a million people in Rio and São Paulo, and opinion polls showed over ninety percent in favour; but when the vote came in March 1984 the amendment just failed. The military still nominated a third of Senate seats, and this proved decisive.

It looked like defeat; in fact it turned into victory. The moment found the man in **Tancredo Neves**, ex-minister of justice under Vargas, ex-prime minister, and a wise old *mineiro* fox respected across the political spectrum, who put himself forward as opposition candidate in the electoral college. By now it was clear what the public wanted, and Tancredo's unrivalled political skills enabled him to stitch together an alliance that included dissidents from the military's own party. In January 1985 he romped home in the electoral college, to great national rejoicing, and military rule came to an end. Tancredo proclaimed the civilian **Nova República** – the "New Republic".

The New Republic: crisis and corruption

Tragically, the New Republic was orphaned at birth. The night before his inauguration, Tancredo was rushed to hospital for an emergency operation on a bleeding stomach tumour: it proved benign, but in hospital he picked up an infection and six weeks later died of septicaemia. His funeral was the largest mass event in Brazilian history; a crowd of two million followed his coffin from the hospital where he had died in São Paulo to Guarulhos airport. The vice-president, **José Sarney**, a second-league politician from Maranhão, who had been fobbed off with a ceremonial post, suddenly found himself serving a full presidential term.

His administration was disastrous, though not all of it was his own fault: he was saddled with a ministerial team he had not chosen, and a newly powerful Congress that would have given any president a rough ride. But Sarney made matters worse by a lack of decisiveness, and wasn't helped by the sleaze that hung like a fog around his government, with **corruption** institutionalized on a massive scale. No progress was made on the economic front either. By 1990 inflation accelerated into **hyperinflation** proper, and, despite spending almost $40 billion repaying interest on the foreign debt, the principal had swollen to $120 billion. Popular disgust was so great that on every occasion Sarney found himself near a crowd of real people, he was greeted with a shower of bricks and curses. The high hopes of 1985 had evaporated: Sarney had brought the whole notion of civilian politics into disrepute, and achieved the near-impossible of making the military look good.

Collor and Franco: Marking time

Despite everything, Brazil still managed to begin the next decade on a hopeful note, with the inauguration in 1990 of **Fernando Collor de Melo**, the first properly elected president for thirty years, after a heated but peaceful campaign had managed to consolidate democracy at a difficult economic moment. In the last months of his administration, Sarney had presided over the take-off into hyperinflation, and it was clear the new president would have to come up with fast economic answers if he was to survive.

The campaign had passed the torch to a new generation of Brazilians, as the young Collor, playboy scion of one of Brazil's oldest and richest families, had squared off against **Lula**, who had come a long way since the São Paulo strikes. Now a respected – and feared – national politician, head of the Workers' Party that the strike movement had evolved into, Lula took most of the cities, but Collor's conservative rural support was enough to secure a narrow victory.

Collor's presidency began promisingly enough, as he pushed for a long-over-due opening-up of the economy and implemented the most draconian currency stabilization plan yet, the infamous **Plano Collor**, hated by the middle classes because it temporarily froze their bank accounts. The economy resisted all attempts at surgery, and inflation began to climb again. Collor became even more unstable than the economy; he was increasingly erratic in public, and rumours grew about dark goings-on behind the scenes. Thanks to fine journalism and a denunciation by Collor's own brother, apparently angry that Fernando had made a pass at his wife, it became clear that a web of **corrupt dealings** masterminded by Collor's campaign treasurer, **P. C. Farias**, had set up what was effectively a parallel government. Billions of dollars had been skimmed from the government's coffers, in a scam breathtaking even by Brazilian standards.

Impeachment proceedings were begun in Congress, but few politicians expected them to get anywhere. But then demonstrations began to take off in the big cities, led initially by students, but soon spreading to the rest of the population and numbering hundreds of thousands of angry but peaceful citizens. It rapidly became clear that if Congress did not vote impeachment through, there would be hell to pay. In September 1992 Collor was duly impeached and replaced by his vice-president, **Itamar Franco**. Farias was jailed, later to die in mysterious circumstances: he was allegedly murdered by a girlfriend who then committed suicide, but it is likely the full story of his death will never be known. His master, Collor, who may know more than most about the murder, lives in gilded self-exile in Miami, to the fury of most Brazilians. Specimen corruption charges failed, and his continued liberty is testimony to the weakness of the Brazilian legal system.

Franco, like Sarney before him, proved a buffoon left minding the shop. The real power in his government was the finance minister, **Fernando Henrique Cardoso**, who staked his claim to the succession by implementing the **Plano Real** in 1994. This finally tamed inflation and stabilised the economy, for the first time in twenty years. A grateful public duly gave him an overwhelming first-round victory in the presidential election later that year, when he trounced Lula in every state bar Brasília and the Distrito Federal.

Cardoso: stability and reform

Uniquely among modern Brazilian presidents, Cardoso, a donnish ex-academic from São Paulo universally known after his initials FHC, proved able and effective. Ironically, before he became a politician he was one of the world's most respected left-wing theorists of economic development. His political career, however, moved along a different track, as his government opened up the Brazilian economy and pushed through important political reforms.

Cardoso entered office with a clear vision of Brazil's economic and political problems, and how to cure them. On the economic front he built on the Plano Real by pushing through a privatization programme in the teeth of fierce nationalist opposition, cutting tariff barriers, opening up the economy to competition and making Brazil the dominant member of **Mercosul**, a regional trade organization that also includes Argentina, Uruguay and Paraguay, with Bolivia and Chile in the queue to join. During his first term the result was healthy growth, falling unemployment and low inflation, an achievement without precedent in modern Brazilian history. Politically, he steered a skilful middle course between dinosaurs of right and left, corrupt *caudilhos* and their patron–client politics on the one hand, and time-warped nationalists still clinging to protectionism and suspicious of the outside world on the other. In a steady if unspectacular process, a series of constitutional amendments were passed reducing the role of the state and reforming the political system.

The stabilization of the economy that Cardoso achieved through the Plano Real was not forgotten by the poor, who were the most affected by hyperinflation; Cardoso was **re-elected** in 1998, providing a much needed period of stability at the top. His second term proved more difficult, however. The Asian financial collapse of 1998 brought down much of Latin America with it, including Brazil; there was a sharp recession for a year, and GDP growth during FHC's second term ran at an anaemic annual average of just under 2 percent, barely staying ahead of population growth. But despite devaluations of the *real* foreign investment kept coming and inflation remained low, an important break with the economic patterns of the 1980s and 1990s, and a sign that at least some of Cardoso's reforms were working. Certain sectors of the economy, notably aerospace, telecommunications and agriculture, grew to become internationally competitive, and imaginative administration in health and education led to significant improvements in social indicators like life expectancy, literacy and child mortality.

Cardoso's legacy was not all positive, however. Corruption, social inequality and regional imbalances still plagued Brazil, although growing public impatience was reflected in a newly aggressive and powerful federal prosecutors system, which started to take on powerful vested interests and eventually ended the careers of a number of notoriously corrupt but very powerful national politicians. Cardoso's reliance on a broad centrist coalition limited his ability to deal with rural inequalities or really get to grips with environmental issues, and the public finances remained perennially in deficit because of a bloated public sector pensions system that is extraordinarily resistant to reform, not least because among those who benefit from it most directly are members of Congress and the judiciary. The judicial system, equally resistant to reform, is a joke, which is much more of a problem than it seems: it underlies the frightening level of violence in Brazilian society, since those using it know they will almost certainly not be brought to book, and it also encourages corruption, for the same reason.

Lula: Left turn?

Historic is an over-used word, but there is no question it is the only one to describe the **2002 election** of Lula to the presidency of Brazil, at the fourth attempt. The outcome represented the final consolidation and maturing of Brazilian democracy, as the generation that had been tear-gassed by the military and opted for armed struggle suited up and became ministers (there are four ex-guerrilla ministers in the Lula government, and his right-hand man, **José Dirceu**, had plastic surgery in Cuba and lived underground for five years). **Lula** himself is a truly historic figure whatever the fate of his government; he is the first Brazilian president not to be a member of the country's elite, and the story of his life is extraordinary. Born in desperate poverty in the Pernambuco *sertão*, like millions of Northeasterners he made the journey as a child to São Paulo on the back of a truck, and worked as a shoeshine boy before becoming a factory worker at a car plant, eventually rising to leadership of the strike movement in the early 1980s and founding the PT (Partido dos Trabalhadores, or Workers' Party), which allied the union movement to the liberal middle class and evolved into what is now the largest political party in Brazil. With FHC's retirement no other Brazilian politician has been able to match Lula's charisma, and the PT did what it had to do, learning from defeat and moderating its policies to bring it closer to the centre, where Brazilian elections are won. Lula's victory, with over 60 percent of the popular vote, was crushing.

For the first time, then, Brazil has a president who knows what life is like for the vast majority of Brazilians and is determined to attack poverty and inequality. It will not be easy satisfying popular expectations, but there are grounds for optimism. The government itself is made up of pragmatists with principles, inexperienced in government but competent. Although the general economic outlook is grim, there is plenty of scope for finding resources for social programmes by cracking down hard on corruption and focusing on reform, especially in the public sector. In their determination to concentrate spending on reducing poverty, rather than on paying pensions to those already privileged, and because of their roots in the union movement, Lula and the PT are better placed to push reform through – a situation not without irony since the PT, which consistently opposed FHC's economic reforms a few years ago, is now advancing the same measures. The early signs are good, as Lula has managed the impressive feat of pleasing both the IMF and the mass of Brazilians anxious to get poverty down and reduce inequality. If there are no external shocks, Brazil under Lula looks well set.

Brazil often – and often deservedly – gets bad press abroad, but burning rainforests and urban drug wars are only part of the Brazilian story. Now a stable and consolidated democracy, Brazil has grown and matured as its neighbours have gone backwards, limping from crisis to crisis, or worse still, sliding into economic meltdown or civil war. Brazil, along with Mexico, is where economic and political stability lies in Latin America, and whatever the short-term market blips these two countries will dominate the region's future. As the country enters the new millennium Brazilians have good reason to extend their traditional optimism to fields other than a football pitch.

Amazon ecology and Indian rights

The Amazon rainforest is not just an icon for the environmental movement, it is the largest and most biodiverse tropical forest on Earth. It is culturally diverse too; the Brazilian Amazon is home to over 300,000 Indians, some still uncontacted, speaking over 200 languages. The two issues that predominate in the environmental debate, the destruction of the rainforest and the plight of the indigenous Indian population, are in many cases inextricably linked. Brazilians tend to react with outrage at being lectured on the preservation of their environment and the protection of native peoples by North Americans and Europeans. Justifiable as Brazilian accusations of hypocrisy may be, however, they cannot hide the fact that there is a real environmental crisis in Brazil, one that has high visibility as an issue inside Brazil as well as abroad, and a real momentum for reform.

Amazon ecology

The Amazon is larger than life. It contains one fifth of the world's fresh water, sustaining the world's largest rainforest – over six million square kilometres – which in turn supports thousands upon thousands of animal and plant species, many of them still unknown. At the heart of the forest, the Amazon river is a staggering 6500km from source to mouth. But perhaps the most worrying statistic is that about 14 percent of the Brazilian Amazon has been deforested, mostly in the last 30 years, and at least as much again has been affected by selective cutting of trees and other environmental stresses, like over-hunting. With global warming promising to increase drought and hence susceptibility to fire, over the course of this century, there is real long-term danger to the integrity of this extraordinary complex of ecosystems.

Terrain

The Amazon is generally thought of as flat, steamy, equatorial forest. This is misleading – it has mountains, parts of it suffer droughts, and by no means all of it is jungle. To begin with, chunks of the Amazon are not forested at all, for the simple reason that around 25 percent of the Amazon is actually savanna, known in Brazil as **cerrado**, and concentrated in a vertical band through the central Amazon from Roraima to southern Mato Grosso, where soil and rain conditions are markedly dry. Between 5 and 10 percent of the Amazon, depending on time of year, is **várzea** (flood plain), a zone of marshes, lakes, wetlands and annually flooded forest (*igapó*) that is the most varied and among the most biodiverse of the Amazon's ecosystems, but also one of the most threatened, since for historical reasons all of the Amazon's larger cities and most of its human population are concentrated on the flood plain. The Amazon also has a long **coastline**, where mangroves alternate with sand dunes, and the largest and most ecologically complex river estuary in the world.

Amazonian rivers are equally varied. There are three main river types, classified by the nature of the area they drain. The Amazon itself is a deep brown river, the sediments scoured from the Andes giving it the colour of milky tea or coffee; other rivers of this type include the Madeira, Juruá and Purus. **Blackwater** rivers drain granite uplands with few sediments, and are stained black by chemicals released by decomposing vegetation: they are much poorer in nutrients and have much less aquatic biodiversity as a result, but have the side-benefit of being blessedly free of mosquitoes, and insects in general. Rivers of this type in the Amazon include, as the name suggests, the Rio Negro, but many other smaller rivers, like the Arapiuns near Santarém. The third type of river drains areas between these two extremes and are the most beautiful of all, with a blueish-green colour; the Tapajós is the largest river of this type.

Flora and fauna

The most distinctive attribute of the Amazon basin is the overwhelming abundance of plant and animal species. Over six thousand species of plant have been reported from one square kilometre tract of forest, and there are close to a thousand species of birds (the Amazon contains one in five of all the birds on Earth) spread about the forest. The rainforest has enormous structural diversity, with layers of vegetation from the forest floor to the canopy 30m above providing a vast number of habitats. With the rainforest being stable over longer periods of time than temperate areas (there was no Ice Age here, nor any prolonged period of drought), the fauna has also had freedom to evolve, and to adapt to often very specialized local conditions. South America has been separated from the other continents for more than 100 million years – and was separate from North America until just a few million years ago – long enough to evolve its unique flora and fauna.

Most of the **trees** found in the Amazon rainforest are tropical palms, scattered between which are the various species of larger, emergent trees. Those plants which are found growing on the forest floor are mostly tree **saplings**, **herbs** (frequently with medicinal applications) and **woody shrubs**. The best-known of all Amazon trees is the **rubber tree** (*Hevea brasiliensis*), known as *seringuera* in Brazil. Still a valuable export in Brazil today, a hundred years ago the rubber tree was the basis of an export boom that transformed the Amazon. Also familiar is the **Brazil nut tree** (*Bertholletia excelsa*), which grows to 30m and takes over ten years to reach nut-bearing maturity; once this is reached, a single specimen can produce over 450kg of nuts every year.

The big **Inga tree** (*Inga edulis*) belongs to the mimosa family, and can grow to 36m. It has colourful patchy bark, large leaves and white hair-like flowers, similar to the mimosa, but its most distinctive feature is its bean pods, sometimes over half a metre long. The pods contain sweet white pulp and large seeds that some Indian groups use to treat dysentery, others for cleaning their teeth. The **turtle-ladder vine** (*Leguminosae casalpinioideae*), known as *escada-de-jabuti* in Brazil, is an unusual-looking liana that spirals high up from the earth to blossom in the canopy of primary forests. Often these lianas are older than the trees on which they can be seen growing.

There are a vast number of different **spiky-rooted palm trees** found throughout the forest. The main trunk starts some two or three metres off the ground, with its exposed roots protected from foraging animals by spikes; in this way the trunk is kept away from flood waters and the exposed roots are able to absorb nitrogen from the atmosphere rather than the soil. One example of this type of tree is the **walking palm** (*Socratea exercisia*), the wood of which is often used for parquet flooring. Tradition has it that it developed spikes to protect itself against the now extinct giant sloth, which used to push it over. The related **stilt palm** (*Socratea exorrhiza*) also grows abundantly in the Amazon, reaching heights of up to 15m. It has a thin trunk, very thorny stilt roots that grow like a tepee above the ground, and long thin leaves that are used by some indigenous groups as a treatment for hepatitis. The most utilized part, however, is the very hard bark, which can be taken off and unwrapped in one piece for use as floor or wall slats.

Good areas for spotting **wildlife** in the Amazon are the richly diverse river banks and flood plains: here you are likely to see **caimans, macaws** and **toucans**, and you should catch sight, too, of one of a variety of **hawks**. With luck and observation you may spot a **river dolphin, capybara** or maybe even one of the **jungle cats**. In the jungle proper you're more likely to find mammals such as the **peccary** (wild pig), **tapir, tamanduá** (anteater) **tree sloth** and, very rarely, the second-largest cat in the world, the powerful **spotted jaguar**. In general though, the open spaces of the Pantanal (see p.546) are better for spotting wildlife than the Amazon, where movement through the rainforest is limited to narrow trails and rivers, and the vegetation usually makes it difficult to see more than a few yards.

The endangered forest

Advances in satellite imagery over the last twenty years have radically improved our knowledge of what is actually happening in the Amazon, how far it has gone and what the trends are over time. So far, about 14 percent of the Brazilian Amazon has been deforested. About the same amount again has suffered some fragmentation of forest cover. The amount that is deforested varies from year to year because of a number of factors, especially climate. In El Niño years, such as 1998, the Amazon is much drier than usual, fires start more easily, and deforestation is higher. In interpreting the data, what matters is not a deforestation spike in one year or another, but general trends over time. These show that deforestation climbed alarmingly in the 1970s and 1980s, but fell back in the 1990s. Furthermore, much deforested land is abandoned and re-grows over time; although it usually does not return to the level of ecological complexity it had, deforested land can re-acquire some of its biodiversity value.

In other words, all is not lost; the bulk of the Amazon is intact, and even the damaged areas need not be written off. The other thing to remember is that the frontier period of Amazonian development is largely over. The Amazon's population is stable, and rapidly urbanising; almost 70 percent of the Amazon's population lives in cities. There are no longer waves of migrants flooding to the region, or a growing rural population putting pressure on the forest. Policymakers and Amazonians themselves are realising it makes more sense to concentrate development efforts into degraded areas, where there are already roads and people living, intensifying development instead of extending it. This is unfortunate for the environmental integrity of the 20 percent or so of the Amazon in this position, but it offers the real prospect that pressure on the remaining 80 percent will diminish.

Forest clearance generally follows **road building**. When a road reached into new territories in the glory days of highway building into the Amazon in the 1970s and 1980s, it brought with it the financial backing and interests of big agricultural and industrial companies, plus an onslaught of land-seeking settlers. Historically, the great villain in the deforestation piece has been **ranching** – the latest research suggests around 80 percent of forest cleared was turned into pasture, dwarfing the deforestation caused by smallholders, commercial agriculture and logging. Forest **fires** are a major threat, generally caused by colonizing farmers and ranchers, often exacerbated by the process of selective **logging**, which opens up the forest canopy and leaves debris ripe for lighting. Alongside the logging, cattle ranching and smaller-scale farming, **hydroelectric dams** also caused serious damage to the Amazonian environment: north of Manaus, for example, the Balbina hydroelectric dam inundated an area of over 2000 square kilometres of forest, and there are plans for new dams on the Xingu river, in the central Amazon. As well as the obvious environmental impact of the flooding of this vast region, further previously unforeseen problems are now being faced. The water in the reservoir above dams is often turned acidic by the decomposing vegetation trapped underneath the surface, causing turbines to corrode.

Until the Amazon was opened up by roads, many areas were inhabited and exploited only by **Indian tribal peoples**, who had long since retreated from the main rivers. When the Spanish and Portuguese first explored the Amazon they noted that a well-established, highly organized, apparently agriculturally based Indian society thrived along the banks of the main rivers. Within two hundred years this relatively sophisticated Indian culture had vanished. Although many had died from the initial effects of new diseases (flu, smallpox, measles, etc), a large proportion had escaped into more remote areas of the forest.

The rainforest is still seen by many in Brazil as a resource to be exploited until it no longer exists, much like fossil fuels and mineral deposits. The indigenous Indians and many of the modern forest-dwellers – including rubber tappers, nut collectors and, increasingly, even peasant settlers – view the forest differently, as something which, like an ocean, can be harvested regularly if it is not overtaxed.

Chico Mendes, the Brazilian rubber tappers' union leader who was shot dead in 1988, was the best-known voice on the side of the established Amazon-dwellers: "the forest is our mother, our source of life," he argued. He was killed by hired gunmen outside his house in the state of Acre in the southwest Amazon. Acre however became the showpiece state of the Brazilian environmental movement from 1998, when a PT government led by **Jorge Viana** and dominated by old friends and colleagues of Chico Mendes implemented a radical environmental programme, including a rubber subsidy to help rubber tappers remain in the forest, and a series of innovative initiatives for marketing forest products. In fifteen years, the environmental movement in Acre has moved to the centre of Brazilian political life: Viana was triumphantly re-elected in 2002, and a close friend, **Marina da Silva**, an ex-rubber tapper from Acre who had been a colleague of Chico Mendes in the rubber tapper union movement, was sworn in as national minister of the environment in January 2003, in the incoming Lula government.

Deforestation: the regional and global consequences

In regional terms, the most serious effects of the destruction of the Amazon rainforest are twofold:

• **Local climate change**. There is now hard scientific evidence from the deforested highway corridors that removing forest reduces rainfall, creates dry seasons where there were none, and extends them where they already existed. This has obvious implications for crops, soils, flora and fauna.

• **Loss of the forest itself**. This may sound a circular argument, but the fact is that as the forest goes, so does an endless potential supply of rubber and other valuable gums, medicines, nuts, fruits, fish, game, skins and the like. Only a small proportion of the plants that exist in the Amazon have been studied, and there is a real danger of losing a genetic pool of vital importance.

Deforestation also has important global implications:

• **Global climate change**. All modelling of future climate change is controversial when you descend to specifics, but it is clear that continuing large-scale deforestation would change weather patterns in the rest of the hemisphere (ironically, given responsibilities for global warming, the agricultural areas of the US Midwest look likeliest to be affected). The destruction of the forest has two effects on the earth's atmosphere. The smoke from the vast forest clearances makes a significant direct contribution to the **greenhouse effect**; tropical deforestation as a whole accounts for around 20 percent of global carbon emissions. The exact percentage contributed by Amazonian deforestation is controversial. Few experts accept a figure of less than 5 percent of global emissions, but this is fiercely contested by the Brazilian government. Less immediately, the fewer trees there are to absorb carbon dioxide, the faster the greenhouse effect is likely to build.

• **Loss of resources**. This is a world problem almost as much as it is a regional one. A growing proportion of the chemicals or medicines found in a high-street chemist originate from rainforest products, and there can be little doubt that there are many more medical breakthroughs waiting to be discovered.

Forces driving deforestation

The blame for deforestation is often wrongly attributed. The following are some popular, but mistaken, explanations:

• **Population and land pressures**. Perhaps the most popular theory of all, certainly in Brazil, is that an unstoppable tide of humanity is swamping the forest. While there was something to this between the 1960s and the early 1990s, the rural Amazon has been losing population for a decade, and the region as a whole has a stable population with, according to the 2001 census, a small net migration to other parts of Brazil.

• **Debt**. Brazil's external debt is another popular scapegoat, but this is even less convincing. The bulk of the capital that Brazil borrowed to create the debt was invested in southern Brazil. The need to make interest payments has not been a driver of economic policy in Brazil since the debt was restructured in the early 1990s. Most of the borrowed capital that was invested in the Amazon went into the mineral sector and into building dams, neither of which were significant causes of deforestation compared to ranching and agriculture.

• **The logging industry**. Virtually no deforestation can be directly attributed to logging. The biodiversity of the Amazon means that economically useful trees are jumbled together with valueless ones. As a result clearcutting, removing forest tracts for timber, is almost unknown. Logging is more selective, resulting in the fragmentation of forest cover – degradation rather than deforestation. One often hears that logging trails open up areas into which deforesters later move, but the reverse is actually the case. Since logs have to be cut and transported from a point not too far from where they are felled, it is usually the loggers who head down the trails made by others.

• **"Big business"**. It is certainly true that most of the deforestation in the grim decades of the 1970s and 1980s was driven directly by big business, specifically the tax breaks that attracted large companies to the region, and the ignorance and arrogance that led them to think that megalomaniac development projects in the jungle would make money. But when the tax breaks were withdrawn in the early 1990s, most of the large companies left. The big companies who remain in the Amazon – mainly in mining and commercial agriculture - work in areas degraded long ago, and are not drivers of new deforestation.

A number of reasons are put forward for the continuing destruction of the rainforest. A complete answer would include the following four major factors:

• **The Brazilian economy**. Save for minerals and soya (see below), the vast bulk of what the Amazon produces is consumed within the Amazon, or goes elsewhere in Brazil. For every cubic meter of tropical hardwood that is exported, for example, nine cubic meters are consumed in Brazil, largely by the furniture and construction industry. The export of Amazonian timber is highly regulated; educated consumers in the US and EU demand proof that Amazon timber in products they buy has been sustainably produced – non-certified Amazon timber is barred from the EU, for example. There is no such demand among the vast majority of Brazilian consumers, and until there is, the domestic economy will be the single biggest driver of deforestation.

• **Soya**. While not a significant driver of deforestation at the moment, this is what keeps Brazilian environmentalists awake at night. Chunks of the central and eastern Amazon are potentially suitable for soya production. Brazil is already the world's largest soya producer, and has lower labour and land costs than the US, its main competitor. Soya has already been successfully produced on a large scale in the southern Amazon, in Mato Grosso. Once the Santarém–Cuiabá highway is asphalted, as is inevitable, a soya boom up the highway corridor is the most immediate large-scale threat the Amazon faces.

• **Government policy**. Regional development policy is one of the most unreconstructed areas of the federal government, run by old-fashioned developmentalists. Their latest contribution, Avança Brasil (Forward Brazil), a regional development plan for the Amazon published in 2000, had some good points but was woefully short on environmental safeguards, and some of the proposals, such as hydroelectric dams for the Xingú and dredging of the Tocantins to create wider channels for barge traffic, are actively harmful.

• **Amazonian states**. With a couple of exceptions, most notably Acre, Amazonian states tend to be run by old-style oligarchs, ignorant, provincial, and deeply hostile to an environmental agenda they feel is threatening to "development". As far as they can – which fortunately is not very far, given their limited resources – they tend to back policies harmful to the forest. Egregious recent examples include the partially successful attempt by the Rondônia state government to sell off chunks of the state park system between 1998 and 2002, and the dismantling of the state environment agency by the incoming state government of Mato Grosso in 2003.

Possible solutions

Deforestation happens, in the final analysis, because it makes economic sense for the person cutting the tree down. It follows that the key to preserving the forest is to make sure it makes more economic sense to keep it standing. A perfect example of the latter is the case of Belém; the largest city in the Amazon is surrounded by extensive areas of intact flood plain forest. This is because there is massive demand for *açaí*, a palm fruit central to Amazonian cuisine, and palm-heart. Both are locally consumed in large quantities, but also preserved, packed and exported to the rest of Brazil and the world. Both products come from flood-plain palm forests, and as a result, without subsidies or development projects, vast areas of flood-plain forest are preserved. Because gathering these forest products can never be mechanized, tens of thousands of livelihoods are assured, and the industry is sustainable. Overharvesting does not happen because everyone knows the level of production the ecosystem can sustain, and that they would shortly be out of a job if they went beyond it.

But this is only half the story. Gathering palm products is a living, but there is not much money in it. Or wasn't. A few years ago, DaimlerBenz was looking for a way to reassure its German shareholders of its environmental responsibility. The R&D department discovered that compressed fibres from Amazon palms could be used to stuff upholstery and also to make a material from which sunshields could be manufactured. They hooked up with the local university in Belém, which brokered a series of contracts with cooperatives in Marajó to supply and process palm fibre, creating what by local standards are scores of well-paid jobs. Everybody won: the local people, the local university (which gets a cut of each contract), the foreign corporation, the Brazilian consumer in southern Brazil driving the car, and, most of all, the environment. The Marajó villagers are now going to the university for help in reforesting deforested areas – because it makes economic sense.

So far these are isolated success stories, but they are part of a trend. Other companies looking to the Amazon to source products include Pirelli, which is producing tyres in southern Brazil with Acrean rubber; and Hermès, the French luxury goods firm, which is using *couro vegetal*, a form of latex treated to look and feel like leather, to make handbags and briefcases. A number of venture capital firms have sprung up in São Paulo, looking to finance environmentally sound but also profitable projects in the Amazon; ecotourism, organic agriculture, sustainable production of certified timber, furniture-making, fruit-pulp processing.

The principles underlying this sea-change are clear. First, long-term success usually lies in satisfying local and regional demand, not the export market. Brazilian ecotourism grew in the aftermath of 9/11, for example, because the growing number of Brazilian ecotourists compensated for the drop in international, especially American, travellers. Second, interventions are often necessary; partly the removal of subsidies that reward destruction, now largely accomplished, but also incentives to encourage more environmentally friendly land-use. A recent example is the national credit programme for family farms, PRONAF, which established a credit line for small Amazonian farmers who want to do agro-forestry, rather than straight farming, with subsidised rates of repayment. Thousands have so far taken it up. If this can be increased to tens or hundreds of thousands, it could transform the scene in the rural Amazon.

The other principles are more controversial, and are still not widely accepted by the international environmental movement, which lags way behind Brazilian environmentalism in its understanding of what needs to be done. First, it is always going to make economic sense for certain parts of the Amazon to be **dedicated to production**, not conservation. No country refuses to develop rich mineral deposits, or blocks investments in commercial agriculture with high rates of return. The choice is not whether or not to develop, but where development takes place and whether the environmental movement has any influence in channelling and controlling it. Looking at the broader picture, it makes better political and economic sense to accept the more controllable form of development – capitalism – in areas already degraded, and thus ensure the frontier fills out rather than moves on to new areas where the damage would be much greater.

Finally, it needs to be recognized that many parts of the Amazon, because of their remoteness or lack of marketable resources, are never going to be able to generate income or jobs. These areas do however provide valuable **environmental services**; their forests remove carbon from the atmosphere, reducing global warming, and keeping forests intact also protects watersheds and soil quality beyond the areas themselves. As things stand neither the Brazilian government nor the inhabitants of these areas receive any compensation for these environmental services, although perhaps in the future new markets in areas like carbon sequestration will fill some of the gap. In the meantime they should be protected, and the international community should be willing to pay most of the costs toward this, which to an extent is already happening; the Global Environment Fund is paying more than $350 million dollars over ten years from 2002 to extend and consolidate the system of federal protected areas in the Amazon. But much more needs to be done, especially for indigenous areas (see below).

The future

At the beginning of the new millennium, it is actually possible to feel optimistic about the future of the Amazon, especially when comparing the situation now to that of twenty years ago. Deforestation, while still a problem to be watched closely, is down. Crucial players, like the Brazilian president, the ministry of the environment, the World Bank and the scientific community inside and outside Brazil, are stressing environmental safeguards and the importance of reconciling conservation with development, the opposite of their positions a generation ago. Increasing areas of the Amazon are being put under strict or partial protection, and, astonishingly, 22 percent of it has been demarcated and ratified as indigenous reserves. Perhaps most encouraging, a state government – Acre – running on an explicitly environmentalist platform has been wildly successful in attracting investment and resources to a remote part of the western Amazon and was triumphantly re-elected to a second term in 2003. In Brasília, people who had been persecuted union leaders or dissident academics a decade or two ago are now running government departments or representing Brazil at international conferences. What had been a dangerous set of opinions, for which people like Chico Mendes and many others had died, was becoming, in the jargon of the bureaucrats, "mainstreamed".

It is still too early to say whether all this will be enough in the long term. Even if Brazil gets its act together, the fate of the Amazon is not only determined within Brazil. Global climate change is already having an impact in the Amazon; even without further ill-judged development, the area of dry forest vulnerable to fire will expand whatever Brazil, and Amazonians, do on their own. But it was striking, amid the chaos and shallow posturing of the third UN Conference on Environment and Development in Johannesburg in 2002, how the Brazilian organisations present stood out for their competence, sophistication and clear grasp of what needed to be done. If things come as far in the next twenty years as they have in the last twenty, and if the pressure is kept up, the satellite images may be showing recovery, instead of loss.

Indian rights

Today, there are around 330,000 Indians in Brazil, spread between more than 200 tribes speaking 180 languages or dialects. When the Portuguese first arrived in the sixteenth century, there were probably over five million indigenous inhabitants.

The **Tupi** tribe was the first Brazilian "Indian nation" to come into serious conflict with the outside world. Twelve colonies had been established in Brazil by the Portuguese king, João III, to exploit trade in wood and sugar, but slavery and death were the only things that the Tupi got out of the exchange – a pattern that was to continue for the next five hundred years in Brazil. Perhaps even more devastating than murder or slavery was the spread of white man's **disease**: dysentery and influenza hit within the first two years; smallpox and the plague followed. When the Jesuit missionaries attempted to gather the natives into "reduction" missions, epidemics killed hundreds of thousands of Indians in just a few decades.

The first century and a half of contact was funded by the need for cheap labour and new resources. Spreading steadily into the savannas of the Gê-speaking peoples, and the forests of Pará and the Amazon, the colonists established cattle ranches, plantations, lumber extraction regions and mining settlements – all of which were met by considerable native resistance. Later, the development of vulcanization in the 1870s led to an international demand for **rubber**. Prices rose rapidly and, during the boom which lasted for almost fifty years, Indians were killed, moved around and enslaved by the rubber barons.

By the second half of the twentieth century, most surviving Indian groups had taken refuge in the deep interior. The opening up of first the Centre-West region in the 1950s with the construction of Brasília, and then the Amazon from the 1960s was an unmitigated disaster for Brazil's indigenous peoples. They were dispossessed of their lands, and one of the consequences of the chaotic settlement of new frontiers was the spread of diseases, which brought many groups to the verge of extinction. The military regime regarded Indians with open racism: the Indian Code, which the military drew up in 1973 (and still technically in force today, although widely ignored), explicitly said it was a transitional set of legal regulations to be enforced until Indians were assimilated, and indistinguishable from other Brazilians. In the Amazon especially, many non-indigenous people in the areas around indigenous reserves are still openly racist, a sad legacy of their forebears who migrated there a generation ago.

Within Brazil indigenous peoples have always had defenders, notably in the Catholic church, in the universities, and even in more liberal circles in the Brazilian military and FUNAI (the federal Indian agency), where some individuals were able to make a difference. The best examples were the brothers **Claudio and Orlando Vilas-Boas**, who were able to create a reserve area in southern Mato Grosso in the 1960s, which turned out to be crucial in assuring the eventual survival of many indigenous groups of the southern Amazon. But these were isolated actions in the midst of what would best be described as accidental genocide.

The beginnings of change came in the darkest days of military repression and unrestrained road building in the late 1960s and early 1970s, when a combination of embarrassing international media coverage, foreign pressure and lobbying by the Catholic church forced the military to curb the worst excesses of development in indigenous areas, and provide emergency medical assistance –

too late in many cases. With the fall of the military regime, the situation gradually improved: the **1988 Constitution** guaranteed indigenous land rights and protection of indigenous languages and culture, and although enforcing it has been problematic, it at least provided a legal basis for enforcement, which became more and more important as a strategy during the 1990s.

The situation now is incomparably better than it was a generation ago. The presidencies of Fernando Collor and Fernando Henrique Cardoso, whatever their other shortcomings, were quite sound on indigenous issues – **Ruth Cardoso**, Fernando Henrique's wife, was an anthropology professor and very effective advocate for indigenous peoples behind the scenes – and together managed to resolve most of the outstanding issues to do with the demarcation and full legalization of indigenous areas. A remarkable 22 percent of the Brazilian Amazon is now officially indigenous land – an area more than twice the size of France. While there are still occasional invasions of indigenous lands, the combination of a free press, more responsive policing and political will at the highest levels of the Brazilian government means that invasions are much less of a problem than they once were.

Perhaps the greatest grounds for hope in the future is the strength of the **indigenous movement**. Born out of the patient organizational and educational work of the Catholic church from the 1960s, the movement rapidly outgrew its religious roots to become an important secular one, founding local associations and regional confederations, and learning from their non-indigenous colleagues in the rural union and rubber tapper movements. Prominent national leaders like **Mário Juruna**, elected federal deputy for Rio in the 1980s despite being from Mato Grosso, were important in getting the movement off the ground. Juruna died in 2002, but an able new generation of younger indigenous leaders – **Daví Yanomami, Jorge Terena, Gerson Baniwa, Escrawen Sompre** and others – have taken up the torch. An especially encouraging sign in recent years has been the central government's willingness to take important responsibilities like **education and health care** out of the hands of FUNAI – still plagued by corruption and inefficiency – and transfer them to the indigenous movement itself, with support and financing from government ministries. While this has not worked well everywhere, in many areas it has resulted not only in better education and health care for indigenous peoples, but in much greater autonomy and self-confidence, a byproduct of the training programmes which emphasized that as much teaching and health care as possible should be provided by indigenous people themselves.

Case study: the Yanomami

Straddling the hilly area of rainforest on the border between Brazil and Venezuela live the **Yanomami** tribe. One of the largest Amazon Indian groups still surviving today, there are around 10,000 living on the Brazilian side of the frontier, and around another 20,000 in Venezuela. Traditionally inhabiting circular villages of up to two hundred people, the Yanomami led a way of life that was very much in balance with the natural environment, depending on a combination of hunting, gathering and gardening.

However, in 1987, coming in the wake of local military-built airstrips and the announcement that the Yanomami were soon to be given "official" rights to their traditional land, a trickle of **gold-miners** began to invade their territory. Sufficient gold was found in the Indians' hills to bring more and more miners, or *garimpeiros*, into the Yanomami Reserve, and by 1990 there were some 45,000 *garimpeiros* in the region – far outnumbering the Yanomami. The intensified contact introduced deadly strains of disease into the tribe, with malaria epidemics especially devastating to children and old people. What made this case different from many similar episodes elsewhere in the 1980s was that it came after a presidential campaign whose winner, Fernando Collor, had made public pledges to protect Indians and the environment, which in turn attracted crowds of foreign media to cover the Yanomami story. It rapidly became a huge international embarrassment for the Brazilian government.

Demarcation of the Yanomami reserves finally happened in 1992. Nevertheless, around eleven thousand *garimpeiros* reinvaded Yanomami land in 1993, encouraged to do so by local politicians and miners' unions in the state of Roraima. Malaria, TB and other diseases tightened their grip on the tribe once again and the inevitable friction between *garimpeiros* and Indian communities exploded into **violence**. In August 1993, around ten (the full number will never be known) Yanomami of the Hashimu community were shot by gold-miners and their bodies burnt – most of the dead were women and children. This finally pushed the federal authorities to expel the miners – the deposits were already giving out – dynamiting their airstrips to ensure they stayed out. Although small crews of miners are still occasionally found, the main environmental issue for the reserve now is the rehabilitation of the areas degraded by the invasions.

The invasion emergency prompted a group of concerned Brazilians, mainly anthropologists, to found a non-governmental organization called CCPY (Comissão para a Criação do Parque Yanomami – Commission for the Creation of a Yanomami Park), which lobbied hard for Yanomami rights and set up a number of effective health and education projects in Yanomami territory. After the reserve was finally demarcated and ratified by the federal government, CCPY switched focus to lobby for effective health care and education for the Yanomami. When these were taken out of FUNAI's hands in the late 1990s, CCPY together with the Yanomami set up an independent NGO, Urihi, based in the state capital of Boa Vista, to provide health care in the Yanomami reserve but with funding from the federal ministry of health. Urihi is now the largest private sector employer in Roraima, and has set up a chain of health posts throughout the reserve as well as a very active training programme for Yanomami paramedics with training material in all the Yanomami dialects, as well as Portuguese. The results have been remarkable. In 2002, for the first time ever, there were no recorded cases of malaria in the reserve, and many Yanomami from the Venezuela side were moving across the frontier to take advantage of the better health care on the Brazilian side. Despite such advances, potential threats remain, chief among them the army, whose presence in this remote region (to guard the borders with Venezuela) has resulted in at least a dozen soldiers fathering children with Yanomami women, as well as incidences of venereal disease and social disruption.

Case study: the Makuxi

The struggle continues in Roraima. In March 1994, the **Makuxi**, Ingariko, Wapixana and Taurepang Indian groups set up roadblocks to protest at invasions of their lands by settlers, miners and road builders in a large reserve called Raposa-Serra do Sol, a stunning complex of savannas, forests, rivers and mountains that includes the Brazilian side of Mount Roraima. Although the reserve had been demarcated in the late 1980s, ratification was challenged by the state government and snarled up in the courts for years. It was a transparent

For **further information** contact:

Survival, 6 Charterhouse Buildings, London EC1M 7ET, UK ℡020/7687 8700, ℻020/7687 8701, ⊛www.survival-international.org

World Wildlife Fund in Brazil ⊛www.wwf.org.br

Also check out ⊛www.socioambiental.org and the *Brazil & Amazon Resources and Links* site at ⊛www.geocities.com/RainForest/Canopy/1316 for information and news on the Amazon, environmental issues, NGOs working in the region, maps and other more general travel and political links.

maneuver on the part of local non-indigenous interests to stall the creation of the reserve long enough for their invasions to become permanent. Although up to five hundred Indians operated the blockades, they were violently attacked. But as each barrier was bulldozed, new blockades appeared.

In 1992, Roraima's state electricity company obtained permission to study the Raposa/Serra do Sol region with a view to building a dam. This is in the traditional territory of the Makuxi Indians, of whom nearly fifteen thousand live in Brazil and some seven thousand over the border in Guyana. The proposed dam threatened to flood around forty square kilometres of Makuxi land. After years of legal battles, and much lobbying by the Makuxi and NGOs in Brazil, the dam project was finally shelved. But this did not prevent the driving of a road deep into the reserve, nor the (illegal) creation of a municipality, Uiramutã, in the heart of the reserve. An army post in Uiramutã (presumably originally placed there to deter the powerful Guyanan army from swarming southwards) could have prevented the invasions – every one of the 500 people living in the village is there illegally – but instead harasses the local indigenous villages with low-flying helicopters.

But the Makuxí are justly famous for their political skills. With support from the Catholic church, Oxfam, Rainforest Foundation, the Nature Conservancy and others, several years ago they founded a multi-ethnic indigenous association, CIR (Conselho Indígena de Roraima – the Indigenous Council of Roraima). CIR has evolved into one of the most effective regional indigenous organisations in the Amazon, and helped by other Brazilian NGOs it took the state government to court. Finally, in 2002, the Supreme Court in Brasília found in their favour, an important step in finally getting the demarcation ratified and the invaders expelled. But as of early 2003, although the omens are good with the accession of Lula to the presidency, Raposa-Serra do Sol was still the largest single piece of unfinished business for the indigenous movement in the Amazon.

C

CONTEXTS | Amazon ecology and Indian rights

Race in Brazilian society

The significance of race in Brazilian society has long been a controversial topic in Brazil. Until recently, despite the country's ethnic and racial diversity, official thinking refused to acknowledge the existence of minority groups, promoting the concept of the Brazilian "racial democracy" and denying absolutely the existence of racism or racial discrimination. If, in a country where blacks and mulattos form at least half of the population, there are few dark-skinned people at the upper levels of society – so the theory runs – this simply reflects past disadvantages, in particular poverty and lack of education.

Myth . . .

No one contributed more to the consolidation of this myth of racial brotherhood than the anthropologist **Gilberto Freyre**. In the early 1930s he advanced the view that somehow the Portuguese colonizers were immune to racial prejudice, that they intermingled freely with Indians and blacks. If **Brazilian slavery** was a not entirely benevolent patriarchy, as some people liked to believe, the mulatto offspring of the sexual contact between master and slave was the personification of this ideal. The **mulatto** was the archetypal social climber, transcending class boundaries, and was upheld as a symbol of Brazil and the integration of the nation's cultures and ethnic roots. "Every Brazilian, even the light-skinned and fair-haired one," wrote Freyre in his seminal work, *Casa Grande e Senzala*, "carries about him in his soul, when not in soul and body alike, the shadow or even birthmark, of the aborigine or negro. The influence of the African, either direct or remote, is everything that is a sincere reflection of our lives. We, almost all of us, bear the mark of that influence." The myth has endured, even in the minds of those who are also prepared to admit its flaws: "I believe in our illusion of racial harmony" said the (white) singer Caetano Velosa, in an interview in early 2000.

Accepted with, if anything, even less questioning outside Brazil than within, the concept of a racial paradise in South America was eagerly grasped. For those outside Brazil struggling against the Nazis or segregation and racial violence in the USA, it was a belief too good to pass up. "Whereas our old world is more than ever ruled by the insane attempt to breed people racially pure, like race horses or dogs", wrote the Austrian writer Stefan Zweig in exile in Brazil, "the Brazilian nation for centuries has been built upon the principle of a free and unsuppressed miscegenation, the complete equalization of black and white, brown and yellow" (*Brazil – Land of the Future*, 1942). Brazil was awarded an international stamp of approval – and its **international image** is still very much that of the happy, unprejudiced melting pot.

Anomalies were easily explained away. A romanticized image of the self-sufficient **Indian** could be incorporated into Brazilian nationalism as, deep in the forested interior and numbering only a quarter of a million, they posed no threat. Picturesque Indian names – Yara and Iraçema for girls, Tibiriça and Caramuru for boys – were given to children, their white parents seeing them as representing Brazil in its purest form. Afro-Brazilian religion, folklore and art became safe areas of interest. **Candomblé**, practised primarily in the northeastern state of Bahia and perhaps the purest of African rituals, could be seen as a quaint remnant from the past, while syncretist cults, most notably **umbanda**, combining elements of Indian, African and European religion and which have attracted mass followings in Rio, São Paulo and the South, have been taken to demonstrate the happy fusion of cultures.

. . . and reality

Many visitors to Brazil still arrive believing in the melting pot, and for that matter many leave without questioning it. It is undeniable that Brazil has remarkably little in the way of obvious **racial tension**; that there are no legal forms of racial discrimination – indeed *anti*-discrimination is enshrined in the constitution; and that on the beach the races do seem to mix freely. But it is equally undeniable that race is a key factor in determining social position. Institutional racism, born of prejudice and stereotyping, affects access to education, employment opportunities and the treatment of black people within the criminal justice system, manifested most notably in day-to-day harassment and violence from the police.

To say this in Brazil, even now, is to risk being attacked as "un-Brazilian". Nevertheless, the idea that race has had no significant effect on social mobility and that socio-economic differentials of a century ago explain current differences between races is increasingly discredited. It is true that Brazil is a rigidly stratified society within which upward mobility is difficult for anyone. But the lighter your skin, the easier it appears to be. Clear evidence has been produced that, although in general blacks and mulattos (because of the continuing cycle of poverty) have lower education levels than whites, even when they do have equal levels of education and experience whites still enjoy substantial economic benefits. The **average income** for white Brazilians is twice that for black, and while there is a growing black Brazilian middle class, it is concentrated in the arts, music and sports – black people are still hugely under-represented in the middle and upper ranks of politics, business and industry.

Perhaps the most surprising realization is that, except amongst politically developed intellectuals and progressive sectors of the Church, there seems little awareness or resentment of the link between colour and class. The black consciousness movement has made slow progress in Brazil – although grassroots community groups and national coalitions of organizations representing black people have emerged over the past decade or two – and most people continue to acquiesce before the national myth that this is the New World's fortunate land, where there's no need to organize for improved status.

Music

Brazil's talent for music is so great it amounts to a national genius. Out of a rich stew of African, European and Indian influences it has produced one of the strongest and most diverse musical cultures in the world.

Most people have heard of samba and bossa nova, or of Heitor Villa-Lobos, who introduced the rhythms of Brazilian popular music to a classical audience, but they are only the tip of a very large iceberg of genres, styles and individual talents. Music – heard in bars, on the streets, car radios, concert halls and clubs – is a constant backdrop to social life in Brazil, and Brazilians are a very musical people. Instruments help but they aren't essential: matchboxes shaken to a syncopated beat, forks tapped on glasses and hands slapped on tabletops are all that is required. And to go with the music is some of the most stunning dancing you are ever likely to see. In Brazil, no one looks twice at a couple who would clear any European and most American dance floors. You don't need to be an expert, or even understand the words, to enjoy Brazilian popular music, but you may appreciate it better – and find it easier to ask for the type of record you want – if you know a little about its history.

The roots: regional Brazilian music

The bedrock of Brazilian music is the apparently inexhaustible fund of "traditional" **popular music**. There are dozens of genres, most of them associated with a specific region of the country, which you can find in raw uncut form played on local radio stations, at popular festivals – *Carnaval* is merely the best known – impromptu recitals in squares and on street corners, and in bars and *dancetarias*, the dance halls that Brazilians flock to at the weekend. The two main centres are Rio and Salvador. There's little argument that the best Brazilian music comes from Rio, the Northeast and parts of Amazônia, with São Paulo and southern Brazil lagging a little behind. Samba, and later bossa nova, became internationally famous, but only because they both happened to get off the ground in Rio, with its high international profile and exotic image. There are, though, less famous but equally vital musical styles elsewhere in Brazil, and it's difficult to see why they remain largely unknown to audiences outside the country – especially given Western music's current obsession with the Third World.

Each local musical genre is part of a **regional identity**, of which people are very proud, and there's a distinct link between geographical rivalry and the development of Brazilian music. *Nordestinos*, in particular, all seem to know their way around the scores of Northeastern musical genres and vigorously defend their musical integrity against the influences of Rio and São Paulo, which dominate TV and national radio. A lot of people regret *carioca* and *paulista* domination of the airwaves, fearing that it's making Brazilian music homogeneous, but if anything it has the opposite effect. People react against the Southeast music by turning to their local brands – which often develop some new enriching influences, picked up along the way.

Samba

The best-known genre, samba, began in the early years of the twentieth century, in the poorer quarters of Rio, as Carnaval music, and over the decades it has developed several variations. The deafening **samba de enredo** is the set piece of Carnaval, with one or two singers declaiming a verse joined by hundreds, even thousands, of voices and drums for the chorus, as the *bloco*, the full samba school, backs up the lead singers. A *bloco* in action during Carnaval is the loudest music you're ever likely to come across, and it's all done without the aid of amplifiers: if you stand up close, the massed noise of the drums vibrates every part of your body. No recording technology yet devised comes close to conveying the sound, and recorded songs and music often seem repetitive. Still, every year the main Rio samba schools make a compilation record of the music selected for the parade, and any record with the words *Samba de Enredo* or *Escola de Samba* will contain this mass Carnaval music.

On a more intimate scale, and musically more inventive, is **samba-canção**, which is produced by one singer and a small back-up band, who play around with basic samba rhythms to produce anything from a (relatively) quiet love song to frenetic dance numbers. This style transfers more effectively in recordings than *samba de enredo*, and in Brazil its more laid-back sounds make it especially popular with the middle-aged. Reliable, high-quality records of *samba-canção* are anything by **Beth Carvalho**, acknowledged queen of the genre, **Alcione**, **Clara Nunes**, and the great **Paulinho da Viola**, who always puts at least a couple of excellent sambas on every record he makes. You can get a taste of the older samba styles that dominated Rio in the 1940s and 1950s in the records of acknowledged old-school greats like **Cartola**, **Bezerra da Silva** and **Velha Guarda de Manueira**.

Since the early 1990s, a refreshing trend in samba has been the revival of **samba-pagode**, a back-to-the-roots reaction against the increasing commercialization of samba in the 1980s. *Pagode* means a simple dance hall, and *samba de pagode* is not a different style of samba so much as a good-time samba, played by a small group, for dancing and general enjoyment in a bar or *dancetaria*. This has always flourished year-round in Rio, but since the 1970s, Carnaval and glitzy versions of *samba-canção* had increasingly become the public face of samba, dominating recording output and being heavily marketed to outsiders. Many of the musicians on whom samba depended for its continuing vitality were sidelined, reduced to making a precarious living doing live shows in the lower-income parts of Rio. Fortunately, people are now returning to *samba-pagode* in a big way, with established *sambistas* like **Agepê** and **Martinho da Vila** following their audience and switching to *pagode* on their records. A number of *pagode* groups have become major national stars, including **Zeca Pagodinho**, **Raça Negra**, **Ginga Pura** and **Banda Brasil**.

Choro

Much less known, **choro** (literally "crying") appeared in Rio around the time of World War I, and by the 1930s had evolved into one of the most intricate and enjoyable of all Brazilian forms of music. Unlike samba, which developed variations, *choro* has remained remarkably constant over the decades. It's one of the few Brazilian genres that owes anything to Spanish-speaking America, as it is clearly related to the Argentinian tango (the real River Plate versions, that is, rather than the sequined ballroom distortions that get passed off as tango outside South America). *Choro* is mainly instrumental, played by a small group: the backbone of the combo is a guitar, picked quickly and jazzily, with notes sliding all over the place, which is played off against a flute, or occasionally a clarinet or recorder, with drums and/or maracas as an optional extra. It is as quiet and intimate as samba is loud and public, and of all Brazilian popular music is probably the most delicate. You often find it being played as background music in bars and cafés; local papers advertise such places. The loveliest *choros* on record are by **Paulinho da Viola**, especially on the album *Chorando*. After years of neglect during the post-war decades *choro* is now undergoing something of a revival, and it shouldn't be too difficult to catch a *choro conjunto* in Rio or São Paulo.

Other genres

A full list of other "traditional" musical genres would have hundreds of entries and could be elaborated on indefinitely. Some of the best-known are **forró**, **maracatú**, **repentismo** and **frevo**, described at greater length in the "Northeast" chapter (starting on p.243): you'll find them all over the Northeast but especially around Recife. **Baião** is a Bahian style that bears a striking resemblance to the hard acoustic blues of the American Deep South, with hoarse vocals over a guitar singing of things like drought and migration; **axé**, a percussion musical style from Bahia that's related to samba; **carimbó** is an enjoyable, lilting rhythm and dance found all over northern Brazil but especially around Belém (a souped-up and heavily commercialized version of *carimbó* enjoyed a brief international vogue as **lambada** in the 1990s); and **bumba-meu-boi**, one of the strangest and most powerful of all styles, the haunting music of Maranhão state.

A good start, if you're interested, is one of the dozens of records by the late **Luiz Gonzaga**, also known as **Gonzagão**, which have extremely tacky covers but are musically very good. They have authentic renderings of at least two or three Northeastern genres per record. His version of a beautiful song called *Asa Branca* is one of the best loved of all Brazilian tunes, a national standard, and was played at his funeral in 1989.

The golden age: 1930–60 and the radio stars

It was the growth of radio during the 1930s that created the popular music industry in Brazil, with home-grown stars idolized by millions. The best-known was **Carmen Miranda**, spotted by a Hollywood producer singing in the famous Urca casino in Rio and whisked off to film stardom in the 1940s. Although her hats made her immortal, she deserves to be remembered more as the fine singer she was. She was one of a number of singers and groups loved by older Brazilians, like **Francisco Alves**, **Ismael Silva**, **Mário Reis**, **Ataulfo Alves**, **Trio de Ouro** and **Joel e Gaúcho**. Two great songwriters, **Ary Barroso** and **Pixinguinha**, provided the raw material.

Brazilians call these early decades *a época de ouro*, and that it really was a golden age is proved by the surviving music on record. It is slower and jazzier than modern Brazilian music, but with the same rhythms and beautiful, crooning vocals. Even in Brazil it used to be difficult to get hold of **records** of this era but after years of neglect there is now a widely available series of reissues called

Revivendo. They send catalogues abroad, if you can't make it to Brazil to buy the records: write to Revivendo Músicas Comércio de Discos Ltda, Rua Barão do Rio Branco 28/36 – 1. andar, Caixa Postal 122, Curitiba, Paraná, Brazil.

International success – the bossa nova

With this wealth of music to work with, it was only a matter of time before Brazilian music burst its national boundaries, something that duly happened in the late 1950s with the phenomenon of **bossa nova**. Several factors led to its development. The classically trained **Tom Jobim**, equally in love with Brazilian popular music and American jazz, met up with fine Bahian guitarist **João Gilberto** and his wife **Astrud Gilberto**. The growth in the Brazilian record and communications industries allowed bossa nova to sweep Brazil and come to the attention of people like Stan Getz in the United States; and, above all, there developed a massive market for a sophisticated urban sound among the newly burgeoning middle class in Rio, who found Jobim and Gilberto's slowing down and breaking up of what was still basically a samba rhythm an exciting departure. It rapidly became an international craze, and Astrud Gilberto's quavering version of one of the earliest Jobim numbers, *A Garota de Ipanema*, became the most famous of all Brazilian songs, *The Girl from Ipanema* – although the English lyric is considerably less suggestive than the Brazilian original.

Over the next few years the craze eventually peaked and fell away, though not before leaving most people with the entirely wrong impression that bossa nova is a mediocre brand of muzak well suited to lifts and airports. In North America it eventually sank under the massed strings of studio producers, but in Brazil it never lost its much more delicate touch, usually with a single guitar and a crooner holding sway. Early bossa nova still stands as one of the crowning glories of Brazilian music, and all the classics – you may not know the names of tunes like *Corcovado, Isaura, Chega de Saudade* and *Desafinado* but you'll recognize the melodies – are on the easily available double-album compilations called *A Arte de Tom Jobim* and *A Arte de João Gilberto*; Jobim's is the better of the two.

The great Brazilian guitarist **Luiz Bonfá** also made some fine bossa nova records: the ones where he accompanies Stan Getz are superb. The bossa nova records of **Stan Getz** and **Charlie Byrd** are one of the happiest examples of inter-American co-operation, and as they're easy to find in European and American shops they make a fine introduction to Brazilian music. They had the sense to surround themselves with Brazilian musicians, notably Jobim, the Gilbertos and Bonfá, and the interplay between their jazz and the equally skilful Brazilian response is often brilliant. **Live bossa nova** is rare these days, restricted to the odd bar or hotel lobby, unless you're lucky enough to catch one of the great names in concert – although Tom Jobim, sadly, died in 1995. But then bossa nova always lent itself more to recordings than live performance.

Tropicalismo

The military coup in 1964 was a crucial event in Brazil. Just as the shock waves of the cultural upheavals of the 1960s were reaching Brazilian youth, the lid went on in a big way: censorship was introduced for all song lyrics; radio and television were put under military control; and some songwriters and musicians were tortured and imprisoned for speaking and singing out – although fame was at least some insurance against being killed. The result was the opposite of what the generals had intended. A movement known as **tropicalismo** developed, calling itself cultural but in fact almost exclusively a musical movement, led by a young and extravagantly talented group of musicians. Prominent amongst them were **Caetano Veloso** and **Gilberto Gil** from Bahia and **Chico Buarque** from Rio. They used traditional popular music as a base, picking and mixing genres in a way no one had thought of doing before – stirring in a few outside influences like the Beatles and occasional electric instruments, and topping it all off with lyrics that often stood alone as poetry – and delighted in teasing the censors. Oblique images and comments were ostensibly about one thing, but everyone knew what they really meant. Chico Buarque's great song, *Tanto Mar*, for example, is apparently about the end of a party, but everyone except the censor recognized it was a salute to the Portuguese revolution, the "Revolution of the Carnations", as it's known.

It was a fine party
I had a great time
I've kept an old carnation as a memento
And even though the party's been shut down
They're bound to have forgotten a few seeds in some corner of the garden

Caetano, Gil and Chico – all of Brazil is on first-name terms with them – spent a few years in exile in the late 1960s and early 1970s, Caetano and Gil in London (both still speak fluent English with immaculate BBC accents) and Chico in Rome, before returning in triumph as the military regime wound down. They have made dozens of records between them: the best way to get to grips with their work quickly is through the compilation albums, *A Arte de. . .* , *O Talento de. . .* , or *A Personalidade de. . .* , collections of their back catalogues with all their most famous songs up to the mid-1970s. They are still the leading figures of Brazilian music, despite being in their late fifties. Gilberto Gil, after a long period in the doldrums where he experimented unsuccessfully with rock-based formats, has recently returned to form, apparently inspired by a new wave of Bahian musicians (see p.783), to whom he is a father figure. Chico Buarque's dense lyrics and hauntingly beautiful melodies are still flowing, although he produces recordings more rarely now, devoting more of his time to novel-writing and theatre. Pride of place, however, has to go to Caetano Veloso. Good though he was in the 1960s and 1970s, he is improving with age, and his records over the last fifteen years have been his best: mature, innovative, lyrical and original as ever. Highlights of his most recent work include a stunning live album *Circulado Vivo*, *Fina Estampa*, a beautiful tribute album to Spanish Latin American music, and *Livro*, an intoxicating mix of tradition and the avant-garde. His continuing originality has kept him at the leading edge of Brazilian popular music, acknowledged everywhere from the *favelas* of Rio to New York's Carnegie Hall as the greatest modern Brazilian musician.

Women singers

Brazilian music has a strong tradition of producing excellent women singers. The best of all time was undoubtedly the great **Elis Regina**, from Rio Grande do Sul, whose magnificent voice was tragically stilled in 1984, when she was at the peak of her career, by a drug overdose. She interpreted everything, and whatever Brazilian genre she touched she invariably cut the definitive version. Two of her songs in particular became classics, *Aguas de Março* and *Carinhoso*, the latter being arguably the most beautiful Brazilian song of all. Again, the *A Arte de Elis Regina* double album is the best bet, although there is also a superb record of Elis with Tom Jobim, called *Elis e Tom*. After her death the mantle fell on **Gal Costa**, a very fine singer although without the extraordinary depth of emotion Elis could project, whose version of *Aquarela do Brasil* inspired Terry Gilliam to the idea for the film "Brazil", and whose LP, named after the song, is highly recommended, along with the *A Arte de Gal Costa* compilation. And then there's **Maria Bethania**, Caetano's commercially more successful sister, who, after forty years of performing and recording, still succeeds in producing original material.

A new generation of women singers has carried the tradition forward. The most prominent amongst those who have come into their own in the 1990s has been Rio's **Marisa Monte**; the classic *Cor de Rosa e Carvão* is the best introduction to her enormous talent. Other up-and-coming women singers include **Silvia Torres**, **Belô Veloso** (a niece of Caetano), and the latest sensation, **Virginia Rodrigues**; it took a couple of albums for her remarkable voice to find the right producer, but her most recent album, *Nós*, suggests that Marisa Monte may have to look to her laurels in the years to come. A figure to emerge even more recently is **Fernanda Porto**, who also has a great voice and whose musical style is a fusion of samba and R&B.

The Bahian sound

Although Rio is the traditional capital of Brazilian music, for some years now it has been overtaken, in vitality and originality, by **Salvador**, the capital of Bahia. Bahia in general, and Salvador in particular, have always produced a disproportionate number of Brazil's leading musicians including Caetano Veloso, Maria Bethania, Gilberto Gil, Gal Costa, the Caymmi family and João Gilberto, but in recent years their status has progressed from important to dominant. The main reason is the extraordinary musical blend provided by deep African roots, Caribbean and Hispanic influences coming in through the city's port, and a local record industry that quickly realized the money-making potential of Bahian music. They didn't invent *lambada*, for example, but it was Salvador record producers who transformed it into a global hit. Tellingly, all over Brazil (except in Rio, naturally), it is now more common to hear the Salvador's *axé* Carnaval hits than samba during Carnaval.

The new Bahian sound, an exhilarating blend of Brazilian and Caribbean rhythms, is exemplified by groups like **Reflexus** and singers like **Luis Caldas**, **Margareth Menezes** and **Daniela Mercury**. Its guiding light is the percussionist and producer **Carlinhos Brown**; a great performer and songwriter in his own right, he is also the *éminence grise* behind the rise of other prominent artists like Marisa Monte with whom he joined forces, together with the experimental poet, singer and sculptor Arnaldo Antunes to create the **Tribalistas**, whose one-off CD was an amazing hit in 2002–3, described as "neo-hippy" and a blend of Brazilian sounds at their most melodic.

Contemporary singers and musicians

The number of high-quality singers and musicians in Brazilian music besides these leading figures is enormous. **Milton Nascimento** has a talent that can only be compared with the founders of *tropicalismo*, a remarkable soaring voice, a genius for composing stirring anthems and a passion for charting and celebrating the experience of blacks in Brazil. Since his emergence from Minas Gerais in the 1960s, he has become a prominent spokesperson of black Brazilians. **Fagner** and **Alceu Valença** are modern interpreters of Northeastern music, and strikingly original singers. The latter is the creator of what has been termed "*forró rock*". **Elba Ramalho** is a Northeastern woman with an excellent voice, which she too often wastes on banal rock rather than the more traditional material she excels at. **Renato Borghetti**, from Rio Grande do Sul, has done much to popularize *gaúcho*-influenced music through his skill on the accordion and his adaptations of traditional tunes. **Ney Matogrosso** has a striking falsetto voice that sounds female, but he is a man – although sometimes self-indulgent, he can be very good. **Jorge Ben** is a fine Rio singer, responsible for many modern classics of Brazilian song, including the definitive Rio verse in his *País Tropical*:

I live in a tropical country
Blessed by God with natural beauty
In February there's Carnaval
I own a guitar and drive a Beetle
I support Flamengo and have a black girlfriend called Tereza.

Vinícius de Morães and **Toquinho** are (or were in the case of Vinícius) a good singer and guitarist team, and **Dorival Caymmi** at over seventy is the doyen of Bahian musicians. Whilst all these figures have been going strongly for decades now, an artist to look out for is **Zeca Baleiro** from Maranhão who, with his *bumba-meu-boi-* and reggae-influenced style, is one of the most innovative performers to have emerged in Brazil in the 1990s.

Too many musicians these days, though, waste their time attempting to fuse Brazilian genres with rock-based formats. It's not that it can't be done – *tropicalismo* pulled it off several times in the 1960s – but the type of Brazilian rock music currently most popular in the country, appalling heavy metal and stadium rock, is completely incompatible with the subtle, versatile musical imagination of Brazilians. National radio and the dominant São Paulo radio stations pump out the worst kind of British and US FM blandness, and this has spawned a host of Brazilian imitations, almost all of them embarrassingly bad. Only a relatively few – such as **Lulu Santos** and **Charlie Brown Junior** – have succeeded in developing an enduring national following.

The other possible criticism of Brazilian music is that, while its popular roots are healthier than ever, nobody of similar stature has come up to succeed the towering figures of the 1960s and 1970s. Elis is dead, Gil, Caetano, Chico and Milton are still producing but are no longer young, and, while younger talent abounds, there's nothing at the moment that could be called genius – a lot to demand of anyone, but it's a tribute to Brazilian music that its pedigree allows us to judge it by the highest standards.

Apart from the *A Arte de. . ., O Talento de. . ., A Personalidade de. . .* and *Revivendo* series mentioned on pp.781–782, recommended recordings easily available in Brazil include the following (artists in bold, listed – as in Brazilian music stores – according to the first name of the artist):

Alceu Valença
Mágica (Barclay 1984)
Araketu
Ara Ketu (Continental 1987)
Belô Veloso
Belô Veloso (Velas 1997)
Bezerra da Silva
Se não fosse o samba (RCA Victor 1989)
Caetano Veloso
Velo (Philips 1984)
Estrangeiro (Philips 1991)
Circulado Vivo (Philips 1993)
Fina Estampa (Polygram do Brasil 1994)
Livro (Polygram do Brasil 1998)
Cartola
Cartola (Discos Marco Pereira 1990)
Chico Buarque
Ópera do Malandro (Philips 1979)
Vida (Philips 1980)
Para Todos (Philips 1994)
Uma Palavra (Ariola 1995)
Daniela Mercury
Daniela (Polygram do Brasil 1992)
Canto da Cidade (Polygram do Brasil 1993)
Dorival Caymmi
A música de Caymmi (Continental 1981)
Elis Regina and Tom Jobim
Elis e Tom (Philips 1974)
Fernanda Porto
Fernanda Porto (Trama, 2002)
Gal Costa
Aquarela do Brasil (Philips 1980)
Gilberto Gil
Parabolicamera (Philips 1991)
Gilberto Gil and Caetano Veloso
Tropicalia 2 (Philips 1994)
Jorge Ben Jor
Acústico (Universal 2002)

Maria Bethania
Ambar (EMI 1996)
Marisa Monte
M (EMI 1994)
Cor de Rosa e Carvão (EMI 1995)
Barulhinho Bom (EMI 1998)
Memórias, Crônicas e Declarações de Amor (EMI 2000)
Milton Nascimento
Clube da esquina (Polygram do Brasil 1981)
Ao vivo (Polygram do Brasil 1983)
Olodum
Egito-Madagáscar (Continental 1987)
Paulinho da Viola
Cantando (RCA Victor 1982)
Chorando (RCA Victor 1982)
Eu canto samba (RCA Victor 1989)
Bebadosamba (BMG 1996)
Reflexús
Reflexús da mãe Africa (EMI 1987)
Renato Borghetti
Renato Borghetti (RCA Victor 1987)
Silvia Torres
Silvia Torres (Melodie 1999)
Tribalistas
Tribalistas (EMI 2002)
Velha Guarda da Mangueira
E Convidados (Nikita 1999)
Vinícius de Morães
with Marilia Medalha and Toquinho
Como dizia o poeta. . . – música nova (RGE 1971)
Virginia Rodrigues
Sol Negro (Hannibal 1997)
Nós (Hannibal 1999)
Zeca Baleiro
Por onde andará Stephen Fry? (MZA, 1997)
Vô imbolá? (MZA, 1999)
Líricas (MZA, 2000)

As for Brazilian **CDs available abroad**, only the jazz/bossa nova records of Getz and his Brazilian collaborators are easily available. However, recent interest in Brazilian music has spawned a few compilation albums: notably *Brazil Classics: Volume 1* (a sort of Brazilian greatest hits) and *Volume 2* (a samba collection), both on EMI and the excellent *Forró: Music for Maids and Taxi Drivers* (Globestyle Records). One of the best international mail-order suppliers is Globestyle Records (48–50 Steele Rd, London NW10 7AS) – send an SAE for their catalogue.

C

CONTEXTS | Music

Live music and recordings

If you want to see or hear **live music**, look for suggestions in this book, buy local papers with weekend listings headed *Lazer*, which should have a list of bars with music, concerts and *dancetarias*, or ask a tourist office for advice.

Local radio is often worth listening to – you won't regret taking a transistor along and whirling the dial – and there are also local TV stations that often have **MPB** (Música Popular Brasileira) programmes; the TVE, Televisão Educativa network, funded by the Catholic Church and the Ministry of Culture, is worth checking – if you see the initials FUNARTE, it might well be a music programme.

Finally, a word about **buying recordings**. The price varies according to how well known the recording artist is. Recordings even by leading artists are less expensive than in the US or Europe, and those by more obscure artists and regional music are cheaper still. At the upper end of the scale, but dependably high quality, are the *A Arte de. . .* , *O Talento de. . .* or *A Personalidade de. . .* series, often double albums, which are basically "Greatest Hits" compilations of the best-known singers and musicians. The best place to buy any music, no matter how regional, is São Paulo, then Rio, with cities like Recife, Salvador, Belo Horizonte and Porto Alegre a long way behind. Outside Rio and São Paulo there are good music shops, but they're few and far between: look in local papers to see if there are adverts for *Loja de Disco* (record shop), with MPB or *discos nacionais* mentioned in the advert.

Books

The recent flood of books on the Amazon masks the fact that Brazil is not well covered by books in English. With some exceptions, good books on Brazil either tend to be fairly expensive or are out of print. Easily available paperbacks are given here, together with a selection of others that a good bookshop or library will have in stock or will be able to order. Apart from the novels of Jorge Amado, for example, the riches of Brazilian literature lie largely untranslated. There is still no widely available translation of Graciliano's *Barren Lives*, the best modern Brazilian novel. Where separate editions exist in the UK and US, publishers are separated by a semicolon in the listings below, with the UK company given first. University Press is abbreviated to UP, out of print to o/p.

Brazil itself has been publishing a growing number of beautifully produced coffee-table books on its architectural and artistic heritage and natural history, often with parallel English-language text. These make great souvenirs, but you'll need to snap them up as print runs tend to be small and you may not find the same book later.

The best introductions

Elizabeth Bishop *One Art* (Farrar, Straus and Giroux). One of the best American poets of the twentieth century spent much of her adult life in Brazil, living in the hills behind Petrópolis from 1951 to 1969 but travelling widely. This selection from her letters and diaries is an intimate, sharp-eyed chronicle of Brazil in those years, and much else.

Annette Haddad and Scott Doggett (eds) *Travelers' Tales: Brazil* (Travelers' Tales). A superb anthology of extracts from books and magazine articles by journalists, anthropologists, historians and other travellers to Brazil, which will make you want to search out the publications they're drawn from. Although a great read, it's a pity that more wasn't done to include the work of Brazilian authors.

D. Hess and R. DaMatta *The Brazilian Puzzle* (Columbia UP). A rare and useful collection of Brazilian perspectives on Brazilian culture; sociologists and anthropologists contribute essays on a variety of topics – race, gender, politics, the courts, sex – of variable quality, but a

Useful addresses

Anglo-Brazilian Society 32 Green St, London W1Y 3FD ☎020/7493 8493. Organizes events based on the culture and history of Brazil.

Brazilian Contemporary Arts Palingswick House, 241 King St, London W6 9LP ☎020/8741 9579, ⓦwww.brazilian.org.uk. Promotes Brazilian cultural events and festivals, and offers language classes as well.

A. Burton Garbett 35 The Green, Morden, Surrey SM4 4HJ ☎020/8540 2367. A good specialist bookseller for old and new books on Brazil.

Canning House Library 2 Belgrave Square, London SW1X 8PH ☎020/7235 2303. An excellent source of old and new books on Brazil in English.

Latin America Bureau 1 Amwell St, London EC1R 1UL ☎020/7278 2829. Publishers. A number of their titles appear in this book list.

valuable chance to see Brazil through Brazilian eyes, for a change.

Ruth Landes *The City of Women* (New Mexico UP). New edition of a classic first published in 1947: an American woman anthropologist remembers her time in Bahia studying *candomblé* and Afro-Brazilian culture. Written for the general reader, and over fifty years on still the best introduction there is to both the Northeast and racial issues in Brazil.

Claude Lévi-Strauss *Tristes Tropiques* (Picador o/p; Penguin). The great French anthropologist describes his four years spent in 1930s Brazil – the best book ever written about the country by a foreigner. There are famous descriptions of sojourns with Nambikwara and Tupi-Kawahib Indians, epic journeys and a remarkable eyewitness account of São Paulo exploding into a metropolis. Essential reading. *Saudades do Brasil: A Photographic Memoir* (Washington UP) is a beautifully produced collection that makes a wonderful companion to *Tristes Tropiques*, featuring some of the thousands of photographs Lévi-Strauss took, few of which were ever published.

Robert M. Levine and John J. Crocitti (eds) *The Brazil Reader: History, Culture, Politics* (Latin America Bureau; Duke UP). The breadth of subject matter in this thoughtful anthology is impressive, covering Brazil from colonial times to the present, using book and article extracts, original documents and historical photographs. If it wasn't for the volume's sheer weight, the book would be the perfect travel companion.

Hugh Raffles *In Amazonia: A Natural History* (Princeton UP). Superbly written mixture of history, anthropology and geography, exploring the gap between the way outsiders and Amazonians think about the region and its landscapes, and periodically very moving in its interweaving of personal memory with wider concerns.

Jan Rocha *Brazil in Focus* (Latin America Bureau; Interlink). A brief guide to Brazil's history, society and arts. Written by a journalist long resident in the country, the book is especially strong on the politics and social movements of the post-military era.

Thomas E. Skidmore *Brazil: Five Centuries of Change* (Oxford UP). Readable account of the emergence of Brazilian national identity, from the first European contact to the present day. The author, a renowned US "Brazilianist", made important contributions to the discussion of racial ideology and the analysis of twentieth-century Brazilian political development, and this book is an excellent synthesis of his work and that of other Brazilian and foreign scholars.

Travel

The Amazon

Alan Campbell *Getting to Know Waiwai: An Amazonian Ethnography* (Routledge). Superbly written and wrenching book. A Scottish anthropologist writes of two years among the Wayapí of Amapá, as they try to come to terms with Brazilian society.

Colonel P. H. Fawcett *Exploration Fawcett* (o/p). Fawcett carries his stiff upper lip in and out of some of the most disease-infested, dangerous and downright frightening parts of interior Brazil. It's a rattling good read, compiled by his son from Fawcett's diaries and letters after his disappearance. Readily available in second-hand bookshops. For more on Fawcett, see p.567.

Stephen Nugent *Big Mouth: The Amazon Speaks* (Fourth Estate o/p; Brown Trout Publications). Essential and hilarious reading, not least as an antidote to the gooey rainforest literature. Jaundiced anthropologist returns to old haunts in Belém and Santarém, debunking as he goes. There is no better guide to the complexities of modern Amazônia; convincing and depressing at the same time.

Anthony Smith *Explorers of the Amazon* (Chicago UP). A chapter devoted to each of the main explorers of the Amazon from the sixteenth to the nineteenth centuries, written for the general reader and showing that truth can be stranger than fiction; those who remember Klaus Kinski's demented portrayal of Aguirre in the film *Aguirre, Wrath of God* will be shocked to realize he actually played down the extent of the conquistador's madness.

Nigel Smith *The Amazon River Forest: A Natural History of Plants, Animals and People* (Oxford UP) An expert with the rare knack of writing clearly and interestingly for the general public tells you all you need to know about the flood plain from the year dot to the present. A great book for a long river journey, and many fine photos too.

Mato Grosso and Brasília

Richard Gott *Land Without Evil: Utopian Journeys Across the South American Watershed* (Verso). Although the subject matter is centred on eastern Bolivia, this is an important look at the swampland between the River Plate and the River Amazon, exploring the region through the adventures of missionaries and explorers and through the travels of the author himself.

Alex Shoumatoff *The Capital of Hope: Brasília and its People* (Vintage). The author talked with government officials and settlers – rich and poor – to weave a very readable account of the first 25 years of the Brazilian capital.

The South

Alexander Leonard *The Valley of the Latin Bear* (o/p). A delightful account of everyday life in an isolated German village in Santa Catarina. Although written some forty years ago, the account remains very recognizable and it's still well worth seeking out.

Guy Walmisley-Dresser *Brazilian Paradise* (o/p). Romantic reminiscences of growing up on a cattle ranch in Rio Grande do Sul in the late nineteenth century. The anecdotes are both amusing and full of insight and tell of a part of Brazil that, although distinctive in character, is all but ignored by travel writers.

History

Euclides da Cunha *Rebellion in the Backlands* (Picador; Chicago UP). Also known by its Portuguese title *Os Sertões*, this remains perhaps Brazil's greatest historical account. An epic tale of Antônio Conselheiro's short-lived holy city, the Canudos Rebellion and its brutal suppression that left some 15,000 dead (see p.278), the book is also a powerful meditation on Brazilian civilization.

R.B. Cunningham Graham *A Vanished Arcadia* (Century o/p). Cunningham Graham's passionate and rather romanticized account of the rise and fall of the Jesuit missions in South America was first published in 1901 and has become a classic on the subject.

Cyrus and James Dawsey (eds) *The Confederados: Old South Immigrants in Brazil* (Alabama UP). An extremely readable collection of essays by US and Brazilian scholars looking at different aspects of the experience of immigrants from the former Confederacy and their descendants. Contributions discuss the history of the agricultural settlements as well as the cultural (in particular religious) influence of the immigrants on the wider society and linguistic change.

Warren Dean *With Brandaxe and Firestorm* (California UP). Brilliant and very readable environmental history that tells the story of the almost complete destruction of the Mata Atlântica, the coastal rainforest of southern Brazil, from colonial times to the twentieth century.

Todd Diacon *Millennarian Vision, Capitalist Reality: Brazil's Contestado Rebellion 1912–1916* (Duke UP). An analysis of the motivation behind the men and women caught up in the Contestado Rebellion, exploring both the millennarian aspects and the response to the seizure of territory by European immigrants. The rebels attacked train stations, sawmills and immigrant colonies in Santa Catarina and Paraná but were ultimately outnumbered and outgunned. An important ground-up look at the last dramatic attempts at survival on the part of a subsistence-based economy.

Boris Fausto *A Concise History of Brazil* (Cambridge UP). The best single-volume introductory history of Brazil, written by an eminent historian from São Paulo. The author successfully demonstrates how Brazil has changed, both politically and socio-economically, despite being so often characterized by apparent historical inertia.

John Hemming *Red Gold: The Conquest of the Brazilian Indians* (Papermac; Harvard UP, o/p). The definitive history of the topic, well written and thoroughly researched. Both passionate and scholarly, it's a basic book for anyone interested in the Indian question in Brazil. A companion volume, *Amazon Frontier* (Harvard UP, US), brings the depressing story up to date.

Thomas H. Holloway *Coffee and Society in São Paulo, 1886–1934* (North Carolina UP, US, o/p). A detailed look at the labour system that evolved on the coffee plantations of São Paulo, and the experiences of two million immigrants who worked them.

Billy Jaynes Chandler *The Bandit King: Lampião of Brazil* (Texas UP, US). Compulsive reading that seems like fiction but is well-documented fact. Based on original sources and interviews with participants and witnesses, an American historian with a talent for snappy writing reconstructs the action-packed (and myth-encrusted) life of the famous social bandit, complete with fascinating photographs.

Robert M. Levine *Vale of Tears: Revisiting the Canudos Massacre in Northeastern Brazil 1893–1897* (California UP). A vivid portrait of backland life and a detailed examination of the myths behind the community, arguing that the Canudos threatened the labour supply of local landowners, causing the state government to begin its campaign against the settlement by portraying the inhabitants as degenerate fanatics. Shocking but utterly compelling reading.

Stephen Lone *The Japanese Community in Brazil, 1908–1940* (Palgrave). This is a welcome introduction to the history of Brazil's important Japanese community, drawing largely from Japanese sources. The author argues against the uniqueness of the Japanese community, suggesting that they were not particularly the subject of racism or hostility and that the hardships that were overcome were no greater – and sometimes less – than those of other immigrant groups.

Frederick C. Luebke *Germans in Brazil: A Comparative History of Cultural Conflict During World War I* (Louisiana State UP). One of the very few studies in English on Germans in Brazil. Despite the title, this social history covers the period 1818–1918, though the focus is World War I, when Brazilians of German origin began to accept that they could not remain foreigners in their own country.

Katia M. de Queiros Mattoso *To Be a Slave in Brazil, 1550–1888* (Rutgers UP, US). A history of slavery in Brazil, unusually written from the perspective of the slave. Writing for the general reader, the author divides her excellent study into three themes: the process of enslavement,

life in slavery and the escape from slavery.

Colin McEwan, Cristiana Barreto and Eduardo Neves (eds.) *Unknown Amazon: Culture in Nature in Ancient Brazil* (British Museum) Fantastically illustrated and photographed companion volume to a 2001 exhibition at the British Museum, revealing revolutionary discoveries on the scale and complexity of late prehistoric indigenous cultures in the Amazon.

Joseph A. Page *The Brazilians* (Addison-Wesley). A cultural history of Brazil in a clear if eclectic style, drawing on sources ranging from economics and political psychology to film and literature. The author is a professor of law at Georgetown University.

João José Reis *Slave Rebellion in Brazil: The Muslim Uprising of 1835 in Bahia* (Johns Hopkins UP). The last major slave rebellion in Brazil began on January 24, 1835, confronting soldiers and civilians. This is a unique portrait of urban slavery and an absorbing account of the most important urban slave rebellion in the Americas and the only one where Islam played a major role, detailing the background of the conspiracy and the brutal repression and punishment of Africans that followed.

Peter Rivière *Absent-Minded Imperialism: Britain and the Expansion of Empire in Nineteenth-Century Brazil* (Tauris). Hilarious, dryly written account of how the border between Brazil and French Guiana came to be drawn, an extraordinary and forgotten story of fanatical missionaries, mutual misunderstanding between British and Brazilian officials, and bewildered Indians stuck in the middle unaware of the diplomatic problems they were causing. A minor classic.

Eduardo Silva *Prince of the People: The Life and Times of a Brazilian Free*

Man of Colour (Verso). Was Dom Obá II d'Africa a genuine prince, or was he merely an unbalanced son of slaves with delusions? Whatever the truth, Dom Obá was revered by the poor around him, and his story also sheds light on the life of slaves and people of colour in Rio, and on popular thought during the final decades of slavery.

Stanley Stein *Vassouras: A Brazilian Coffee County, 1850–1900* (Princeton UP). Re-edition of a 1940s classic that improves with age. On the surface, a straightforward reconstruction of the rise and fall of the coffee plantation system in a town in the interior of Rio. Look closer and you see a devastating indictment of slavery, based on archive work but also, uniquely, on the memories of the last generation to have been born as slaves. Also includes a fascinating selection of photos.

Politics and society

Sue Branford and Bernardo Kucinski *Politics Transformed: Lula and the Workers' Party in Brazil* (Latin America Bureau). An impassioned and easy-to-digest look at the rise of the PT, the most powerful socialist party in the Americas, charting its development from trade union resistance to the military regime in São Paulo to the election of its leader – Lula – as president of Brazil in 2002.

Sue Branford and Jan Rocha *Cutting the Wire: The Story of the Landless Movement in Brazil* (Latin America Bureau). Written by journalists with long experience of Brazil, this book tells the story of one of the most remarkable popular movements of modern times, the MST (or Landless Workers Movement). This much-needed book discusses the historical background as well as the movement's links with wider anti-globalization struggles, deforestation and rural violence.

Gilberto Dimenstein *Brazil: War on Children* (Latin America Bureau; Monthly Review, o/p). A grim but compelling picture of life for the street children of São Paulo, but true also for most Brazilian cities. The children, living in constant fear of death squads made up of off-duty police and other vigilantes, survive as best they can as petty criminals, beggars and prostitutes, supporting one another in small gangs.

Tobias Hecht *At Home in the Street* (Cambridge UP). Excellent study of street children and those who deal with them, from death squads to social workers. Based on work in Recife, but equally applicable to any large Brazilian city.

Dan Linger *Nobody Home: Brazilian Selves Remade in Brazil* (Stanford UP). Brazil has the largest Japanese population outside Japan and many Brazilians, Japanese and not, move back and forth between the two countries doing the work the Japanese prefer to leave to others. This is a sensitive, accessible study of their lives, problems and dreams.

Maxine L. Margolis *Little Brazil: An Ethnography of Brazilian Immigrants in New York City* (Princeton UP). Since the early 1980s, there's been considerable migration from Brazil, especially to Europe and the US. The greatest concentration of expatriate Brazilians – especially educated middle classes from Minas Gerais – is in the New York City area, with most living in Long Island City and Astoria. The community's heart is Little Brazil, a one-block stretch of Manhattan's West 46th Street, and this is a thoroughly readable exploration into community life.

Roberto da Matta *Carnival, Rogues and Heroes* (Notre Dame UP, o/p). A collection of essays by one of Brazil's leading anthropologists, who also teaches in the US. They include some very stimulating – and entertaining – dissections of Carnaval.

Ruben Oliven *Tradition Matters: Modern Gaúcho Identity* (Columbia UP). This is not about the life of "cowboys" in southern Brazil, but rather an examination of the predominantly urban, middle-class social movement that prizes an idealized rural lifestyle of which it has no real experience. Oliven points up the apparent paradox in Brazil (as elsewhere) of ever-increasing cultural globalization and the strengthening of regional identity. An important study illuminating a part of Brazil largely ignored by outsiders – Brazilian as well as foreign.

Thomas Skidmore *Politics in Brazil 1930–1964; The Politics of Military Rule in Brazil 1964–85* (Oxford UP). The former is the standard work on Brazilian politics from the rise of Vargas until the 1964 military takeover. The latter continues the story to the resumption of Brazil's shaky democracy.

Gender issues

Caipora Women's Group *Women in Brazil* (Latin America Bureau). Articles, poems and interviews about life for women on farms, in fishing communities and in *favelas*. The issues repeat themselves: racism, machismo, legal rights, religious and feminist beliefs. A welcome relief from published doctoral dissertations, this is both important and highly readable, both depressing and uplifting.

Herbert Daniel and Richard Parker *Sexuality, Politics and AIDS in Brazil* (Falmer Press, US). Excellent, clearly written history of AIDS in Brazil, covering the way the epidemic has developed in relation to popular culture at one end, and government policy at the other. There are bright spots – Brazilian TV health education slots on AIDS may be the best in the world, completely frank, and often screamingly funny, but this book will help you understand how this can coexist with a scandalous lack of supervision of blood banks.

Richard Parker *Bodies, Pleasures and Passions* (Beacon Press, US). A provocative analysis of the erotic in Brazilian history and popular culture, written by an American anthropologist resident in Brazil. Tremendous subject matter and some fascinating insights into sexual behaviour, combining insider and outsider perspectives.

Daphne Patai *Brazilian Women Speak: Contemporary Life Stories* (Rutgers UP, US). Oral testimony forms the core of this very readable work that lets ordinary women from the Northeast and Rio speak for themselves to describe the struggles, constraints and hopes of their lives.

Nancy Scheper Hughes *Death Without Weeping: The Violence of Everyday Life in Brazil* (California UP). An often shocking, ultimately depressing anthropological study of *favela* women, and in particular of childbirth, motherhood and infant death. Although over-long – judicious skipping is in order – it is very accessible to the general reader, interesting, and often moving.

João Trevisan *Perverts in Paradise* (GMP, US, o/p). This is a fascinating survey of Brazilian gay life ranging from the papal inquisition to pop idols, transvestite *macumba* priests and guerrilla idols.

Race

Darién J. Davis *Afro-Brazilians: Time for Recognition* (Minority Rights Group, UK). A valuable introduction to the role of black people in Brazilian society, focusing on Afro-Brazilians in national culture and the human rights struggle. Produced for a respected British-based NGO, the report is scholarly, impassioned and essential reading for anyone wanting to understand the often contradictory nature of Brazilian racial ideology and politics.

Gilberto Freyre *The Masters and the Slaves* (California UP, US, o/p). Classic history of plantation life in the Northeast, with a wealth of detail (includes index headings like "Smutty Stories and Expressions" and "Priests, Bastards of"). Very readable, even if Freyre's somewhat simplistic theories are now out of fashion or discredited (see p.776). His *The Mansion and the Shanties* (Greenwood) deals with the early growth of urban Brazil.

George Reid Andrews *Blacks and Whites in São Paulo 1888–1988* (Wisconsin UP). Why is the notion of a racial democracy still so widely accepted while at the same time people are fully aware that for all practical purposes it's a complete myth? For large proportions of Brazilians, racism is a fact of life and this is an interesting examination of how the state has long encouraged myths of black inferiority and perpetuates racial stereotypes.

Thomas E. Skidmore *Black into White: Race and Nationality in Brazilian Thought* (Duke UP). First published in 1974, this 1993 edition has a new preface to bring the book up to date. A landmark in the intellectual history of Brazilian racial ideology, examining scientific racism and the Brazilian intellectual elite's supposed belief in assimilation and the ideal of whitening.

Frances W. Twine *Racism in a Racial Democracy* (Rutgers UP). Fascinating ethnography of racism in a small Brazilian town, by a black American sociologist interested in the differences between Brazilian and American racial politics.

The Amazon

David Cleary *Anatomy of the Amazon Gold Rush* (Macmillan o/p; Iowa UP). Clearly written introduction to an important topic, with some spectacular photographs.

Warren Dean *Brazil and the Struggle for Rubber* (Cambridge UP). Good environmental history of the rubber boom and subsequent failed attempts to set up rubber plantations in the Amazon.

Peter A. Furley (ed), *The Forest Frontier: Settlement and Change in Brazilian Roraima* (Routledge, UK). An interesting and rare look at the state of Roraima, one of Brazil's last regions to be settled by outsiders. Dry academic geography in style but a wealth of up-to-date detail on Indian life and the history of colonization, land use, environmental change and the effects of deforestation.

Susanna Hecht and Alexander Cockburn *The Fate of the Forest* (Penguin; Verso). Head and shoulders above other studies of the crisis in the Amazon. Excellently written and researched – check out the footnotes – this is as good an introduction to the problem as you will find. Very strong on Amazonian history, too – essential to understanding what's going on, but often ignored by Amazon commentators.

Gordon Macmillan *At the End of the Rainbow* (Earthscan; Columbia UP). Very interesting dissection of the issues behind the headlines about the Yanomami Indians and the invasion of their reserves by gold-miners.

Chico Mendes and Tony Gross *Fight for the Forest: Chico Mendes in His Own Words* (Latin America Bureau; Inland Book Co). Long, moving passages from a series of interviews the rubber tappers' union leader gave shortly before his assassination in 1988. Well translated and with useful notes giving background to the issues raised. Direct from the sharp end of the Amazon land crisis.

Marianne Schmink and Charles Wood *Contested Frontiers in Amazonia* (Columbia UP). The best of the more recent academic books on modern Amazônia that examines a town and region in southern Pará before, during and after the construction of the highway network. Clearly written and very interesting, especially in its description of how the Kayapo Indians adapted to a gold rush.

Candace Slater *Dance of the Dolphins* (Chicago UP). Interesting compendium of the many legends and folk tales centring on river dolphins, beautifully translated. There is a clumsy academic subtext linking the stories with environmental destruction in the Amazon, but you can skip those bits. There is no better book for giving you a feel for the popular imagination in the small towns you pass through on a river trip.

Charles Wagley *Amazon Town* (o/p). Classic anthropological study of an interior Amazon town during the 1940s that inspired generations of students. Written with incisive style and complete command of the material.

Flora and fauna

Henry Bates *The Naturalist on the River Amazon* (o/p). A Victorian botanist describes his years spent collecting in the Amazon, in an obscure but wonderful book. Bates' boyish scientific excitement illuminates every page – a fascinated, and very English, eye cast over the Amazon and its people.

Balthasar Dubs *Birds of Southwestern Brazil* (Beltrona, Switzerland). Essential reading if you're heading for the Pantanal. The main body of the book is a comprehensive annotated and illustrated list of species in the region.

Margaret Mee *In Search of the Flowers of the Amazon Forest* (Nonesuch, UK). The best of the natural history books by some way. Mee was a British botanist who dedicated her life to travelling the Amazon and painting its plant life. She died in a car crash in 1988, and this beautiful book is a fitting tribute to her. It includes descriptions of her many journeys, good photographs, and lavish reproductions of her wonderful drawings and paintings.

David L. Pearson and Les Beletsky *Brazil: Amazon and Pantanal – The Ecotravellers' Wildlife Guide* (Academic Press). The main body of this book examines the regions' ecosystems and the threats they face before moving on to chapters discussing insects, amphibians, reptiles, birds, mammals and fish. Richly illustrated and clearly written, the book will enrich any visit to the Amazon or Pantanal.

Philips Guides (Horizonte Geografico). An excellent Brazilian series of English language guides aimed at the ecotourist. So far, titles include the *Amazon, Pantanal, National Parks of Brazil, Northeast* and *South*, and all are full of practical information and photos, and especially useful for hikers, nature-lovers and beach bugs. In Brazil, good bookshops in large cities should stock them. Also check ⊛www .horizontegeografico.com.br for details on ordering them from abroad.

Helmut Sick *Birds in Brazil* (Princeton UP). An English translation of an encyclopedic Brazilian work. The illustrations are superb, but it's too hefty to travel with.

More portable guides include Hilty and Brown's *A Guide to the Birds of Colombia* (Princeton UP), and Schaunsee's *Birds of Venezuela* (Princeton UP), which both have considerable overlap for Brazil's western and northern Amazônia, while Narosky and Yzuriea's *Birds of Argentina and Uruguay: A Field Guide* (Vazques Mazzini) is valuable for southern Brazil.

Deotado Souza *All the Birds of Brazil: An Identification Guide* (DALL, Brazil). This handbook clearly describes birds that are found in Brazil, and includes location maps and fairly good colour illustrations. Although published in Brazil, don't expect to stumble across a copy there; instead purchase one from a specialist bookseller before leaving home. An essential companion for any remotely serious Brazil-bound birdwatcher.

Arts and leisure

Architecture

Lauro Cavalcanti *When Brazil Was Modern: Guide to Architecture, 1928–1960* (Princeton Architectural Press, US). This valuable guide to Brazil's unique contribution to modernist architecture discusses the work of over thirty architects, with sections on specific sites such as Brasília, Pampulha (Belo Horizonte) and the Ministry of Health and Education building in Rio. Compact, but well illustrated, the book makes a perfect travel companion for modernist junkies.

Deutsches Architektur Museum (ed) *Oscar Niemeyer: A Legend of Modernism* (Birkhäuser). This sumptuously produced book is a concise survey of Niemeyer's work from his first commissions in Rio in the early

1930s, through Pampulha and Brasília in the 1940s to 1960s, to Niterói's Museu de Arte Contemporânia of the late 1990s. Included are essays by architectural critics which, although at times overly fawning, help illuminate Niemeyer's architectural legacy.

Marta Iris Montero *Burle Marx: The Lyrical Landscape* (Thames & Hudson; California UP). A beautifully illustrated book celebrating the life and work of one of the twentieth century's foremost landscape architects, who designed many of Brazil's prominent parks, gardens and other urban spaces (the most famous of which are probably the flowing mosaics alongside Copacabana and Flamengo beaches).

Fernando Tasso Fracaso Pires *Fazenda: The Great Houses and Plantations of Brazil* (Abbeville Press). A lavish coffee-table book, richly illustrated with photographs of coffee, sugar and cattle *fazenda* houses. There's a useful historical introduc-tion discussing the importance of the *casa grande* in Brazilian society, followed by a look at individual houses, mainly in rural Rio de Janeiro and São Paulo, but also Minas Gerais, Pernambuco, Bahia and Rio Grande do Sul.

Fine art and photography

Gilberto Ferrez *Photography in Brazil 1840–1900* (New Mexico UP, US, o/p). One of the little-known facts about Brazil is that the first-ever non-portrait photograph was taken of the Paço da Cidade in Rio in 1840, by a Frenchman hot off a ship with the new-fangled Daguerrotype. This is a fascinating compendium of the pioneering work of early photographers in Brazil, including material from all over the country, although the stunning panoramas of Rio from the 1860s onward are arguably the highlight.

Daniel Levine (ed) *The Brazilian Photographs of Genevieve Naylor, 1940–1942* (Duke UP). Recently uncovered photographs by a young American photographer, mainly of Rio, Salvador and the small towns of the interior. They are a revelation: Naylor was a great photographer, interested in people and street scenes, not landscapes, and this is a unique visual record of Brazil and its people during the Vargas years.

Edward Lucie-Smith *Latin American Art of the Twentieth Century* (Thames & Hudson). It's a pity there aren't volumes on other periods in Latin American art in this excellent and easy-to-obtain series. Still, this is valuable as a look at the Brazilian scene in the context of Latin American art in general.

Edward J. Sullivan (ed) *Brazil Body & Soul* (Guggenheim Museum, US). Remarkably, there is still no thorough overview of Brazilian art history, but this lavishly illustrated catalogue to the 2001/2002 New York and Bilbao exhibition is a pretty good starting point. The catalogue offers glimpses of the art of indigenous cultures and the paintings of Frans Post and Albert Eckhout, two seventeenth-century Dutch visitors, before moving on to discuss in greater detail Baroque art and architecture, Afro-Brazilian art, and twentieth-century artistic movements including Brazil's important contributions to modernist and concrete art.

Alberto Taliani *Brazil* (Tiger Books International; Smithmark). A coffee-table book with around one hundred moody and eye-catching photos depicting Brazil as a diverse nation, including some striking juxtapositions of race, culture and wealth (or lack of it). From wildlife to beach life, and from Indians to modern architecture, the book stands as much on the thematic eye of the photographer as it does on the good-quality images themselves.

Music, dance and capoeira

Bira Almeida *Capoeira – a Brazilian Art Form* (North Atlantic Books). A *capoeira mestre* (master) explains the history and philosophy behind this African–Brazilian martial art/dance form. The book offers valuable background information for those who practise *capoeira* and for those who are merely interested.

Ruy Castro *Bossa Nova – The Story of the Brazilian Music That Seduced the World* (A Capella). A welcome translation of an excellent book by a Brazilian journalist and biographer. This is basically an oral history of *bossa nova*, packed with incidental detail on Rio nightlife and city culture of the 1950s and early 1960s. A very good read.

Alma Guillermoprieto *Samba* (Bloomsbury o/p; Vintage). The author, a trained dancer and a well-known journalist, describes a year that she spent with Rio's Mangueira samba school, introducing us to other participants who dedicate their lives to preparing for the four days of Carnaval.

Chris McGowan and Ricardo Pessanha *The Brazilian Sound: Samba, Bossa Nova and the Popular*

Music of Brazil (Temple UP). An easy-to-flick-through and well-written basic manual on modern Brazilian music and musicians. Good to carry with you if you're planning on doing some serious music buying. There's also a useful bibliography and a good discography.

Claus Schreiner *Musica Brasileira* (Marion Boyars, US). Detailed coverage of all aspects of Brazilian music from colonial times through to the present within the broader context of the country's culture and history. One for the specialist.

Caetano Veloso *Tropical Truth: A Story of Music and Revolution in Brazil* (Knopf). The maestro's account of *tropicalismo* and his early career, including exile, from the 1960s to the early 1970s. Veloso is as good a writer as you would expect, a little over-anxious to show off his learning sometimes, but this is a fascinating despatch from the culture wars of the 1960s.

Cooking

Michael Bateman *Street Café Brazil* (Conran Octopus; Contemporary Books). The title is rather deceptive, as you're unlikely to come across many of these recipes on Brazilian street stalls, but the recipes are authentic, and the lavish pictures are enough to inspire you to attempt to reproduce them at home.

Christopher Idone *Brazil: A Cook's Tour* (Pavilion; Clarkson Potter). A region-by-region look at Brazilian cooking, its origins and influences, with a few recipes thrown in as well. The colour photos of ingredients, markets and dishes are mouthwatering and the text lively and informative. It's good to see São Paulo and the Amazon being discussed separately and at length (when it comes

to cookbooks usually only Rio and Bahia get a look in), but why is the South completely ignored?

Joan and David Peterson *Eat Smart in Brazil: How to Decipher the Menu, Know the Market Foods & Embark on a Tasting Adventure* (Ginkgo Press). The title says it all: a guide for selecting food, both in shops and markets and off a menu, in Brazil. The book is divided into three main sections: a region-by-region account of food ingredients and cooking styles, with some recipes and listings of Brazilian ingredients and dishes. A must for any foodie who needs to know the difference between *pimenta malagueta*, *pimenta-do-cheiro* and *pimenta-do-reino*.

Football

Alex Bellos *Futebol: The Brazilian Way of Life* (Bloomsbury). Long overdue, accessible, literate and engaging analysis of Brazilian football, from its early history to the present day and its compulsive mixture of world-class players on the pitch and equally world-class levels of corruption. Written by a journalist with an eye for original stories such as homesick Brazilians playing in the Faroe Islands, tactics for transvestites, and much more. Essential reading.

Chris Taylor *The Beautiful Game: A Journey Through Latin American Football* (Latin America Bureau; Perennial). Pinching Pelé's catch phrase for the title, this clever paperback is a journalistic report on the football subculture in Brazil and other Latin American countries, often linked to both big business and drug trafficking.

Fiction

Jorge Amado *Gabriela, Clove and Cinnamon; Tereza Batista* (both Abacus o/p; Avon); *Dona Flor and Her Two Husbands* (Serpent's Tail; Avon); *The Violent Lands* (Collins; Avon). Amado is the proverbial rollicking good read, a fine choice for the beach or on long bus journeys. He's by far the best-known Brazilian writer abroad – there is even a French wine named after him. Purists might quibble that the local colour is laid on with a trowel, but Amado's formula of vividly tropical settings and steamy eroticism has him laughing all the way to the bank.

Mário de Andrade *Macunaíma* (Quartet Books, UK). First published in 1928, *Macunaíma* is considered one of the greatest works of Brazilian literature. In this comic tale of the adventures of a popular hero, Macunaíma, a figure from the jungle interior, Andrade presents his typical wealth of exotic images, myths and legends.

Machado de Assis *Posthumous Memoirs of Brás Cubas* (Oxford UP). The most important work by the finest novelist Brazil has yet produced. Told by one of the most remarkable characters in fiction, this is an often-hilarious tale of absurd schemes to cure the world of melancholy and half-hearted political ambitions unleashed from beyond the grave. For good translations of Machado's great short stories, *The Devil's Church and Other Stories* (Texas UP, US, o/p) and *Helena* (California UP) are worth going to some trouble to get hold of. His cool, ferociously ironic style veers between black comedy and sardonic analysis of the human condition.

Patrícia Galvão (Pagu) *Industrial Park: A Proletarian Novel* (Nebraska UP). An avant-garde novel first published in 1933. Set in the rapidly changing São Paulo factory district of Brás, this remarkable novel captures the sense of time and place, reproducing the voice of a city in the midst of rapid change.

Milton Hatoum *The Brothers* (Bloomsbury; Farrar, Straus & Giroux). Set in late nineteenth-century Manaus, this is a family saga based on Lebanese twin brothers and their relationship with their mother. Filled with local colour, this is one of the best Brazilian novels in translation to emerge in recent years.

Clarice Lispector *The Hour of the Star* (New Direction, US). The most instantly approachable translation of this work by the important Ukrainian-born writer. Her short stories are carefully constructed but, as an author to whom the existence of plot doesn't seem to matter, her books can be difficult. Other translated titles include *Family Ties* (Carcanet o/p; Texas UP) and *The Foreign Legion* (New Direction, US).

Patrícia Melo *Inferno* (Bloomsbury, UK). A thriller set in a *favela* in Rio, this is a powerful-story of an eleven year-old boy who becomes a local gang leader. Though his story's often grim, the central character is a complex figure in terms of his relationships with other gang members and his family.

Antônio Olinto *The Water House* (Carroll & Graf, US). A wonderful story about an African matriarch and her progeny over a seventy-year period, and the story of her return to West Africa from Bahia after the abolition of slavery. The family saga continues in the *King of Ketu* (R. Collings, US).

Horacio Quiroga *The Decapitated Chicken and Other Stories* (Texas UP, US). Anyone visiting the Jesuit ruins by the Argentine town of San Ignacio should read these sometimes creepy, sometimes funny, gothic horror stories set in Misiones. Also available in English is *The Exiles and Other Stories* (Texas UP, US), a more recent but not as enjoyable collection.

Graciliano Ramos *Childhood* (o/p); *São Bernardo* (o/p). Works by the Northeastern novelist who introduced social realism into modern Brazilian fiction. Neither is as good as his masterpiece *Barren Lives* (Texas UP, US), or his prison memoir, *Memórias do Cárcere* (Memories of Jail).

Darlene J. Sadlier (ed) *One Hundred Years After Tomorrow* (Indiana UP). An excellent anthology of short stories introducing the work of twenty twentieth-century Brazilian women, some famous and others less well known.

Márcio Souza *Mad Maria* (Avon, US, o/p). A comic drama set against the backdrop of the absurdity of rail construction in nineteenth-century Amazônia. Souza's excellent *The Emperor of the Amazon* (Abacus o/p; Avon o/p) is another humorous and powerful description of the decadence that characterized late nineteenth-century Amazonian society.

Antônio Torres *The Land* (Readers International). Set in a decaying town in the parched interior of the Northeast, this is a grim tale of people trapped and people trying to get away. In *Blues for a Lost Childhood* (Readers International), Torres continues with the same theme, but this time focusing on a journalist who makes it to Rio but finds life there to be a living nightmare.

João Ubaldo Ribeiro *An Invincible Memory* (Faber; HarperCollins o/p). A family saga spanning a 400-year period from the arrival of the Portuguese in Brazil to the present day, featuring anecdotes, history and myths narrated through the experiences of two Bahian families, one aristocratic, the other enslaved. The book was wildly popular when published in Brazil and is considered a national epic.

Mario Vargas Llosa *The War of the End of the World* (Faber; Penguin). Goes well with da Cunha (see p.790). The Peruvian writer produced this haunting novel, based on the events of Canudos, in the 1970s. The translation is good and the book is easy to obtain.

Language

Language

Language

Learning some Portuguese before you go to Brazil is an extremely good idea. Although many well-educated Brazilians speak English, and it's now the main second language taught in schools, this hasn't filtered through to most of the population. If you know Spanish you're halfway there: there are obvious similarities in the grammar and vocabulary, so you should be able to make yourself understood if you speak slowly, and reading won't present you with too many problems. However, Portuguese pronunciation is utterly different and much less straightforward than Spanish, so unless you take the trouble to learn a bit about it you won't have a clue what Brazilians are talking about.

Unfortunately, far too many people – especially Spanish-speakers – are put off going to Brazil precisely by the language, but in reality this should be one of your main reasons for going. Brazilian Portuguese is a colourful, sensual language full of wonderfully rude and exotic vowel sounds, swooping intonation and hilarious idiomatic expressions. You'll also find that Brazilians will greatly appreciate even your most rudimentary efforts, and every small improvement in your Portuguese will make your stay in Brazil ten times more enjoyable.

People who have learned their Portuguese **in Portugal or in Lusophone Africa** won't have any real problems with the language in Brazil, but there are some quite big differences. There are many variations in vocabulary and Brazilians take more liberties with the language, but the most notable differences are in pronunciation: Brazilian Portuguese is spoken more slowly and clearly; the neutral vowels so characteristic of European Portuguese tend to be sounded in full; in much of Brazil outside Rio the slushy "sh" sound doesn't exist; and the "de" and "te" endings of words like *cidade* and *diferente* are palatalized so they end up sounding like "sidadgee" and "djiferentchee".

The best **dictionary** currently available is the *Collins Portuguese Dictionary*. There is a pocket edition, but you might consider taking the fuller, larger version, which concentrates on the way the language is spoken today and gives plenty of specifically Brazilian vocabulary. For a **phrasebook**, look no further than *Portuguese: A Rough Guide Phrasebook*, with useful two-way glossaries and a brief and simple grammar section.

Pronunciation

The rules of **pronunciation** are complicated, but the secret is to throw yourself wholeheartedly into this explosive linguistic Jacuzzi.

Non-nasal vowels

A shouldn't present you with too many problems. It's usually somewhere between the "a" sound of "bat" and that of "father".

E has three possible pronunciations. When it occurs at the beginning or in the middle of a word, it will usually sound either a bit like the "e" in "bet"– eg *ferro* (iron) and *miséria* (poverty) – or like the "ay" in "hay"– eg *mesa* (table) and *pêlo* (hair). However, the difference can be quite subtle and it's not something you should worry about too much at the start. The third pronunciation is radically different from the other two: at the end of a word, "e" sounds like "y" in "happy", eg *fome* ("fommy", hunger) and *se* (if), which actually sounds like the Spanish "si".

I is straightforward. It's always an "**ee**" sound like the "**i**" in "police", eg *isto* (this).

O is another letter with three possible pronunciations. At the beginning or in the middle of a word, it normally sounds either the way it does in "d**o**g" – eg *loja* (shop) and *pó* (powder) – or the way it does in "g**o**"– eg *homem* (man) and *pôquer* (poker). At the end of a word "**o**" sounds like the "**oo**" in "b**oo**t", so *obrigado* (thank you) is pronounced "obri-GA-doo". And the definite article "**o**" as in *o homem* (the man) is pronounced "**oo**".

U is always pronounced like "**oo**" in "b**oo**t", eg *cruz* (cross).

There are also a variety of vowel combinations or diphthongs that sound pretty much the way you would expect them to. They are **ai** (pronounced like "**i**" in "ride"); **au** (pronounced as in "shout"); **ei** (pronounced as in "hay"); and **oi** (pronounced as in "boy"). The only one that has an unexpected pronunciation is **ou**, which sounds like "o" in "rose".

Nasal vowels

The fun really starts when you get into the **nasal vowel sounds**. Generally speaking, each "normal" vowel has its nasal equivalent. The trick in pronouncing these is to be completely uninhibited. To take one example, the word **pão** (bread). First of all, just say "pow" to yourself. Then say it again, but this time half close your mouth and shove the vowel really hard through your nose. Try it again, even more vigorously. It should sound something like "powng", but much more nasal and without really sounding the final "g".

There are two main ways in which Portuguese indicates a nasal vowel. One is through the use of the **tilde**, as in *pão*. The other is the use of the letters **m** or **n** after the vowel. As a general rule, whenever you see a vowel followed by "m" or "n" and then another consonant, the vowel will be nasal – eg *gente*. The same thing applies when the vowel is followed by "m" at the end of a word, eg *tem, bom* – in these cases, the "m" is not pronounced, it just nasalizes the vowel.

Below are some of the main nasal vowels and examples of words that use them. However, it must be emphasized that the phonetic versions of the nasal sounds we've given are only approximate.

Ã, and -am or -an followed by a consonant indicate nasal "**a**" – eg *macã* (apple), *campo* (field), *samba*.

-ão or -am at the end of a word indicate the **"owng"** sound, as explained above in *pão*. Other examples are in *estação* (station), *mão* (hand), *falam* ("FA-lowng"; they talk).

-em or -en followed by a consonant indicate a nasalized "**e**" sound – eg *tempo* (weather), *entre* (between), *gente* (people).

-em or -ens at the end of a word indicate an "**eyng**" sound – eg *tem* ("teyng"; you have or there is), *viagens* ("vee-A-zheyngs"; journeys).

-im or -in at the end of a word or followed by a consonant are simply a nasal "**ee**" sound, so *capim* (grass) sounds a bit like "ca-PEENG".

-om or -on at the end of a word or followed by a consonant indicate nasal "**o**". An obvious example is *bom* (good), which sounds pretty similar to "bon" in French.

-um or -un at the end of a word or followed by a consonant indicate nasal "**u**"– eg *um* (one).

-ãe sounds a bit like "**eyeing**" said quickly and explosively – eg *mãe* (mother).

-õe sounds like "**oing**". Most words ending in "-ão" make their plural like this, with an "s" (which is pronounced) at the end – eg *estação* (station) becomes *estações* (stations).

Consonants

Brazilian **consonants** are more straightforward than the vowels, but there are a few little oddities you'll need to learn. We've only listed the consonants where they differ from their English counterparts.

C is generally pronounced hard, as in "**cat**" (eg *campo*). However, when followed by "i" or "e", it's pronounced softly, as in "ceiling"(eg *cidade*, city). It's also pronounced softly whenever it's written with a cedilla (eg *estação*).

CH is pronounced like English "**sh**", so *chá* (tea) is said "sha".

D is generally pronounced as in English. However, in most parts of Brazil it's palatalized to sound like "**dj**"whenever it comes before an "i" or final "e". So *difícil* (difficult) is pronounced "djee-FEE-siw", and the ubiquitous preposition *de* (of) sounds like "djee".

G is generally pronounced hard as in English "**g**od" (eg *gosto*, I like). But before "e" or "i" it's pronounced like the "**s**" in English "vision" or "measure" – eg *geral* (general) and *gíria* (slang).

H is always silent (eg *hora*, hour).

J is pronounced like the "**s**" in English "vision" or "measure"– eg *jogo* (game) and *janeiro* (January).

L is usually pronounced as in English. But at the end of a word, it takes on a peculiar, almost Cockney pronunciation, becoming a bit like a "**w**". So Brasil is pronounced "bra-ZEEW". When followed by "h", it's pronounced "**ly**" as in "million"; so *ilha* (island) comes out as "EE-lya".

N is normally pronounced as in English, but when it's followed by "h" it becomes "**ny**". So *sonho* (dream) sounds like "SON-yoo".

Q always comes before "u" and is pronounced either "**k**" or, more usually, "**kw**". So *cinquenta* (fifty) is pronounced "sin-KWEN-ta", but *quero* (I want) is pronounced "KE-roo".

R is usually as in English. However, at the beginning of a word it's pronounced like an English "**h**". So "Rio" is actually pronounced "HEE-oo", and *rádio* (radio) is pronounced "HA-djee-oo".

RR is always pronounced like an English "**h**". So *ferro* is pronounced "FE-hoo".

S is normally pronounced like an English "**s**", and in São Paulo and the South this never changes. But in Rio and many places to the north, "s" sounds like English "**sh**" when it comes before a consonant and at the end of a word (*estação*, "esh-ta-SOWNG").

T is normally pronounced as in English but, like "d", it changes before "i" and final "e". So *sorte* (luck) is pronounced "SOR-chee", and the great hero of Brazilian history, Tiradentes, is pronounced "chee-ra-DEN-chees".

X is pronounced like an English "**sh**" at the beginning of a word, and elsewhere like an English "**x**" or "**z**". So *xadrez* (chess) is pronounced "sha-DREYZ", while *exército* (army) is pronounced "e-ZER-si-too".

Stress

Any word that has an accent of any kind, including a tilde, is stressed on that syllable, so *miséria* (poverty) is pronounced "mi-ZE-ree-a". If there is no accent, the following rules generally apply (the syllables to be stressed are in capitals):

• Words that end with the vowels a, e and o are stressed on the penultimate syllable. So *entre* (between) sounds like "EN-tree", and *compro* (I buy) "KOM-proo". This also applies when these vowels are followed by -m, -s or -ns: *falam* is stressed "FA-lowng".

• Words that end with the vowels i and u are stressed on the final syllable: *abacaxi* (pineapple) is pronounced "a-ba-ka-ZEE". This also applies when i and u are followed by -m, -s or -ns, so *capim* is pronounced "ka-PEENG".

• Words ending in consonants are usually stressed on the final syllable, eg *rapaz* (boy), stressed "ha-PAZ".

Some useful examples:

Rio de Janeiro HEE-oo djee zha-NEY-roo	en-TEN-djee
Belo Horizonte BE-loo o-ri-ZON-chee	**sim** (yes) SEENG (but hardly sound the final
Rio Grande do Sul HEE-oo GRAN-djee doo	"g")
Soow	**ruim** (bad) hoo-WEENG (again hardly sound
Recife he-SEE-fee	the "g")
rodoviária ho-do-vee-A-ree-a	**vinte** (twenty) VEEN-chee
onde (where) ON-djee	**correio** (post office) co-HAY-oo
não entende (he doesn't understand) now	

Brazilian Portuguese words and phrases

Basic expressions

Yes, No	sim, não	Good, Bad	bom, ruim
Please	por favor	Big, Small	grande, pequeno
Thank you	obrigado (men)/	A little, A lot	um pouco, muito
	obrigada (women)	More, Less	mais, menos
Where, When	onde, quando	Another	outro/a
What, How much	que, quanto	Today, Tomorrow	hoje, amanhã
This, That	este, esse, aquele	Yesterday	ontem
Now, Later	agora, mais tarde	But	mas (pronounced
Open, Closed	aberto/a, fechado/a	like	"mice")
Entrance, Exit	entrada, saída	And	e (pronounced like
Pull, Push	puxe, empurre		"ee" in "seek")
With, Without	com, sem	Something, Nothing	alguma coisa, nada
For	para	Sometimes	ás vezes

Greetings and responses

Hello, Goodbye	oi, tchau (like the	Excuse me	com licença
	Italian "ciao")	How are you?	como vai?
Good morning	bom dia	Fine	bem
Good afternoon/Night	boa tarde/boa	Congratulations	parabéns
	noite	Cheers	saúde
Sorry	desculpa		

Useful phrases and colloquial expressions

Do you speak English?	você fala inglês?	What's the matter?	qual é o
I don't understand	não entendo		problema?
I don't speak Portuguese	não falo	There is (is there?)	há…(?)
	português	I want, I'd like…	quero…
What's the Portuguese	como se diz	I can…	posso…
for this?	em português?	I can't…	não posso…
What did you say?	o que você	I don't know	não sei
	disse?	It's hot	está quente
My name is…	meu nome é…	It's cold	está frio
What's your name?	como se chama?	It's great	está legal
I am English/American	sou inglês/	It's boring	é chato
	americano	I'm bored, annoyed	estou chateado
Do you have…?	você tem…?	I've had it up to here	estou de saco
the time?	as horas?		cheio
Everything's fine	tudo bem	There's no way	não tem jeito
OK	tá bom	Crazy	louco/a, maluco/a
I'm hungry	estou com fome	Tired	cansado/a
I'm thirsty	estou com sede		
I feel ill	me sinto mal		
I want to see a doctor	quero ver um		
	medico		

Asking directions, getting around

Where is...?	Onde fica...?	Is this the bus to Rio?	é esse o ônibus
the bus station	a rodoviária		para Rio?
the bus stop	a parada de ônibus	Do you go to...?	você vai para...?
the nearest hotel	o hotel mais próximo	I'd like a (return)	quero uma pasagem
the toilet	o banheiro/sanitário	ticket to...	(ida e volta) para...
Left, right, straight on	esquerda, direita,	What time does it	Que horas sai
	direto	leave (arrive)?	(chega)
Go straight on	vai direto e	Far, Near	longe, perto
and turn left	dobra à esquerda	Slowly, Quickly	devagar, rápido
Where does the bus	de onde sai o ônibus		
to...leave?	para...?		

Accommodation

Do you have a room	você tem um quarto?	It's too expensive	é caro demais
with two beds/	com duas camas/	Do you have anything	tem algo mais
double bed	cama de casal	cheaper?	barato?
It's for one person/	é para uma pessoa/	Is there a hotel/	Tem um hotel/
two people	duas pessoas	campsite nearby?	camping por aqui?
It's fine, how	Está bom, quanto é?		
much is it?			

Numbers

1	um, uma	19	dezenove
2	dois, duas	20	vinte
3	três	21	vinte e um
4	quatro	30	trinta
5	cinco	40	quarenta
6	seis	50	cinquenta
7	sete	60	sesenta
8	oito	70	setenta
9	nove	80	oitenta
10	dez	90	noventa
11	onze	100	cem
12	doze	200	duzentos
13	treze	300	trezentos
14	quatorze	500	quinhentos
15	quinze	1000	mil
16	dezesseis	2000	dois mil
17	dezessete	5000	cinco mil
18	dezoito		

Days and months

Monday	segunda-feira (or segunda)	January	janeiro
Tuesday	terça-feira (or terça)	February	fevereiro
Wednesday	quarta-feira (or quarta)	March	março
Thursday	quinta-feira (or quinta)	April	abril
Friday	sexta-feira (or sexta)	May	maio
Saturday	sábado	June	junho
Sunday	domingo	July	julho

August	agosto	November	novembro
September	setembro	December	dezembro
October	outubro		

A Brazilian menu reader

Basics

açúcar	sugar	legumes/verduras	vegetables
alho e óleo	garlic and olive oil sauce	manteiga	butter
almoço	lunch	mariscos	seafood
arroz	rice	molho	sauce
azeite	olive oil	ovos	eggs
café colonial	high tea	pão	bread
café de manhã	breakfast	peixe	fish
cardápio	menu	pimenta	pepper
carne	meat	prato	plate
colher	spoon	queijo	cheese
conta/nota	bill	sal	salt
copo	glass	sobremesa	dessert
entrada	hors d'oeuvre	sopa/caldo	soup
faca	knife	sorvete	ice cream
farinha	dried manioc flour	taxa de serviço	service charge
garçom	waiter	tucupi	fermented manioc
garfo	fork		and chicory sauce
garrafa	bottle		used in Amazonian
jantar	dinner, to have dinner		cuisine

Cooking terms

assado	roasted	mal passado/	rare/well done
bem gelado	well chilled	bem passado	(meat)
churrasco	barbecue	médio	medium-grilled
cozido	boiled, steamed	milanesa	breaded
cozinhar	to cook	na chapa/na brasa	charcoal-grilled
grelhado	grilled		

Seafood (*frutos do mar*)

acarajé	fried bean cake stuffed with *vatapá* (see below)	ostra	oyster
		pescada	seafood stew, or hake
agulha	needle fish	pirarucu	Amazon river fish
atum	tuna	pitu	crayfish
camarão	prawn, shrimp	polvo	octopus
caranguejo	large crab	siri	small crab
filhote	Amazon river fish	sururu	a type of mussel
lagosta	lobster	vatapá	Bahian shrimp dish, cooked
lula	squid		with palm oil, skinned tomato
mariscos	shellfish		and coconut milk, served with
moqueca	seafood stewed in palm oil and coconut sauce		fresh coriander and hot peppers

Meat and poultry (*carne e aves*)

bife	steak	leitão	sucking pig
bife a cavalo	steak with egg and *farinha*	lingüiça	sausage
cabrito	kid	pato	duck
carne de porco	pork	peru	turkey
carneiro	lamb	peito	breast
costela	ribs	perna	leg
costeleta	chop	picadinha	stew
feijoada	black bean, pork and	salsicha	hot dog
	sausage stew	veado	venison
fígado	liver	vitela	veal
frango	chicken		

Fruit (*frutas*)

abacate	avocado	limão	lime
abacaxi	pineapple	maçã	apple
ameixa	plum, prune	mamão	papaya
caju	cashew fruit	manga	mango
carambola	star fruit	maracujá	passion fruit
cerejas	cherries	melancia	watermelon
côco	coconut	melão	melon
fruta do conde	custard apple (also *ata*)	morango	strawberry
goiaba	guava	pera	pear
graviola	cherimoya	pêssego	peach
laranja	orange	uvas	grapes

Vegetables and spices (*legumes e temperos*)

alface	lettuce	ervilhas	peas
alho	garlic	espinafre	spinach
arroz e feijão	rice and beans	macaxeira	roasted manioc
azeitonas	olives	malagueta	very hot pepper, looks like
batatas	potatoes		red or yellow cherry
canela	cinnamon	mandioca	manioc/cassava/yuca
cebola	onion	milho	corn
cenoura	carrot	palmito	palm heart
cheiro verde	fresh coriander	pepinho	cucumber
coentro	parsley	repolho	cabbage
cravo	clove	tomate	tomato
dendê	palm oil		

Drinks

água mineral	mineral water	cerveja	bottled beer
batida	fresh fruit juice with	chopp	draught beer
	cachaça	com gás/sem gás	sparkling/still
cachaça	sugar-cane rum	suco	fruit juice
café com leite	coffee with hot milk	vinho	wine
cafézinho	small black coffee	vitamina	fruit juice made with
caipirinha	rum and lime cocktail		milk

A glossary of Brazilian terms and acronyms

Agreste In the Northeast, the intermediate zone between the coast and the sertão
Aldeia Originally a mission where Indians were converted, now any isolated hamlet
Alfândega Customs
Amazônia The Amazon region
Artesanato Craft goods
Azulejo Decorative glazed tiling
Bairro Neighbourhood within town or city
Bandeirante Member of a group that marched under a bandeira (banner or flag) in early missions to open up the interior; Brazilian conquistador
Barraca Beach hut
Batucada Literally, a drumming session – music-making in general, especially impromptu
Bloco Large Carnaval group
Bosque Wood
Caatinga Scrub vegetation of the interior of the Northeast
Caboclo Backwoodsman/woman, often of mixed race
Candomblé African-Brazilian religion
Cangaceiro Outlaws from the interior of the Northeast who flourished in the early twentieth century; the most famous was Lampião
Capoeira African-Brazilian martial art/dance form
Carimbó Music and dance style from the North
Carioca Someone or something from Rio de Janeiro
Carnaval Carnival
Cerrado Scrubland
Choro Musical style, largely instrumental
Convento Convent
Correio Postal service/post office

CUT/CGT Brazilian trades union organizations
Dancetaria Nightspot where the emphasis is on dancing
Engenho Sugar mill or plantation
Estado Novo The period when Getúlio Vargas was effectively dictator, from the mid-1930s to 1945
EUA USA
Ex voto Thank-offering to saint for intercession
Favela Shantytown, slum
Fazenda Country estate, ranch house
Feira Country market
Ferroviária Train station
Forró Dance and type of music from the Northeast
Frescão Air-conditioned bus
Frevo Frenetic musical style and dance from Recife
FUNAI Government organization intended to protect the interests of Brazilian Indians; seriously underfunded and with a history of corruption
Garimpeiro Prospector or miner
Gaúcho Person or thing from Rio Grande do Sul; also southern cowboy
Gringo/a Foreigner, Westerner (not derogatory)
Ibama Government organization for preservation of the environment; runs national parks and nature reserves
Iemanjá Goddess of the sea in candomblé
Igreja Church
Largo Small square
Latifúndios Large agricultural estates
Leito Luxury express bus
Literatura de cordel Literally "string literature" – printed ballads, most common in the

Northeast but also found elsewhere, named after the string they are suspended from in country markets

Litoral Coast, coastal zone

Louro/a Fair-haired/blonde – Westerners in general

Maconha Marijuana

Macumba African-Brazilian religion, usually thought of as more authentically "African" than candomblé; most common in the North

Marginal Petty thief, outlaw

Mata Jungle, remote interior (Mata Atlântica - jungle covering the coastal parts of southern Brazil)

Mercado Market

Mineiro Person or thing from Minas Gerais

Mirante Viewing point

Mosteiro Monastery

Movimentado Lively, where the action is

MPB Música Popular Brasileira, common shorthand for Brazilian music

Nordeste Northeastern Brazil

Nordestino/a Inhabitant thereof

Nova República The New Republic – the period since the return to civilian democracy in 1985

Paulista Person or thing from São Paulo state

Paulistano Inhabitant of the city of São Paulo

Pelourinho Pillory or whipping-post, common in colonial town squares

Planalto Central Vast interior tablelands of central Brazil

Posto Highway service station, often with basic accommodation popular with truckers

Praça Square

Praia Beach

Prefeitura Town hall, and by extension city governments in general

PT Partido dos Trabalhadores or Workers' Party, the largest left-wing party in Brazil, led by Lula

Quebrado Out of order

Rodovia Highway

Rodoviária Bus station

Samba Type of music most associated with Carnaval in Rio

Selva Jungle

Senzala Slave quarters

Sertanejo Inhabitant of sertão

Sertão Arid, drought-ridden interior of the Northeast

Sesmaria Royal Portuguese land grant to early settlers

Sobrado Two-storey colonial mansion

Terreiro House where candomblé or umbanda rituals and ceremonies take place

Umbanda African-Brazilian religion especially common in urban areas of the South and Southeast

Vaqueiro Cowboy in the north

Visto Visa

Index

and small print

I

INDEX

INDEX

A Rough Guide to Rough Guides

In the summer of 1981, Mark Ellingham, a recent graduate from Bristol University, was travelling round Greece and couldn't find a guidebook that really met his needs. On the one hand there were the student guides, insistent on saving every last cent, and on the other the heavyweight cultural tomes whose authors seemed to have spent more time in a research library than lounging away the afternoon at a taverna or on the beach.

In a bid to avoid getting a job, Mark and a small group of writers set about creating their own guidebook. It was a guide to Greece that aimed to combine a journalistic approach to description with a thoroughly practical approach to travellers' needs – a guide that would incorporate culture, history and contemporary insights with a critical edge, together with up-to-date, value-for-money listings. Back in London, Mark and the team finished their Rough Guide, as they called it, and talked Routledge into publishing the book.

That first *Rough Guide to Greece*, published in 1982, was a student scheme that became a publishing phenomenon. The immediate success of the book – with numerous reprints and a Thomas Cook prize shortlisting – spawned a series that rapidly covered dozens of destinations. Rough Guides had a ready market among low-budget backpackers, but soon also acquired a much broader and older readership that relished Rough Guides' wit and inquisitiveness as much as their enthusiastic, critical approach. Everyone wants value for money, but not at any price.

Rough Guides soon began supplementing the "rougher" information about hostels and low-budget listings with the kind of detail on restaurants and quality hotels that independent-minded visitors on any budget might expect, whether on business in New York or trekking in Thailand.

These days the guides – distributed worldwide by the Penguin Group – offer recommendations from shoestring to luxury and cover more than 200 destinations around the globe, including almost every country in the Americas and Europe, more than half of Africa and most of Asia and Australasia. Our ever-growing team of authors and photographers is spread all over the world, particularly in Europe, the USA and Australia.

In 1994, we published the *Rough Guide to World Music* and *Rough Guide to Classical Music*; and a year later the *Rough Guide to the Internet*. All three books have become benchmark titles in their fields – which encouraged us to expand into other areas of publishing, mainly around popular culture. Rough Guides now publish:

- Travel guides to more than 200 worldwide destinations
- Dictionary phrasebooks to 22 major languages
- History guides ranging from Ireland to Islam
- Maps printed on rip-proof and waterproof Polyart™ paper
- Music guides running the gamut from Opera to Elvis
- Restaurant guides to London, New York and San Francisco
- Reference books on topics as diverse as the weather and Shakespeare
- Sports guides from Formula 1 to Man Utd
- Pop culture books from Lord of the Rings to Cult TV
- World Music CDs in association with World Music Network.

Visit **www.roughguides.com** to see our latest publications.

Rough Guide credits

Text editor: Yuki Takagaki
Managing Director: Kevin Fitzgerald
Series editor: Mark Ellingham
Editorial: Martin Dunford, Jonathan Buckley, Kate Berens, Ann-Marie Shaw, Helena Smith, Olivia Swift, Ruth Blackmore, Geoff Howard, Claire Saunders, Gavin Thomas, Alexander Mark Rogers, Polly Thomas, Joe Staines, Richard Lim, Duncan Clark, Peter Buckley, Lucy Ratcliffe, Clifton Wilkinson, Alison Murchie, Matthew Teller, Andrew Dickson, Fran Sandham, Sally Schafer, Matthew Milton, Karoline Densley (UK); Andrew Rosenberg, Yuki Takagaki, Richard Koss, Hunter Slaton, Chris Barsanti (US)
Design & Layout: Link Hall, Helen Prior, Julia Bovis, Katie Pringle, Rachel Holmes, Andy Turner, Dan May, Tanya Hall, John McKay, Sophie Hewat (UK); Madhulita Mohapatra,

Umesh Aggarwal, Sunil Sharma (India)
Cartography: Maxine Repath, Ed Wright, Katie Lloyd-Jones (UK); Manish Chandra, Rajesh Chhibber, Jai Prakash Mishra (India)
Cover art direction: Louise Boulton
Picture research: Sharon Martins, Mark Thomas
Online: Kelly Martinez, Anja Mutic-Blessing, Jennifer Gold, Audra Epstein, Suzanne Welles, Cree Lawson (US); Manik Chauhan, Amarjyoti Dutta, Narender Kumar (India)
Finance: Gary Singh
Marketing & Publicity: Richard Trillo, Niki Smith, David Wearn, Chloë Roberts, Demelza Dallow, Claire Southern (UK); Geoff Colquitt, David Wechsler, Megan Kennedy (US)
Administration: Julie Sanderson
RG India: Punita Singh

Publishing information

This fifth edition published November 2003 by
Rough Guides Ltd,
80 Strand, London WC2R 0RL.
345 Hudson St, 4th Floor,
New York, NY 10014, USA.
Distributed by the Penguin Group
Penguin Books Ltd,
80 Strand, London WC2R 0RL
Penguin Putnam, Inc.
375 Hudson Street, NY 10014, USA
Penguin Books Australia Ltd,
487 Maroondah Highway, PO Box 257,
Ringwood, Victoria 3134, Australia
Penguin Books Canada Ltd,
10 Alcorn Avenue, Toronto, Ontario,
Canada M4V 1E4
Penguin Books (NZ) Ltd,
182–190 Wairau Road, Auckland 10,
New Zealand
Typeset in Bembo and Helvetica to an original design by Henry Iles.

Printed in Italy by LegoPrint S.p.A
© David Cleary, Dilwyn Jenkins and Oliver Marshall 2003

856 pp includes index
A catalogue record for this book is available from the British Library

ISBN 1-84353-077-5

The publishers and authors have done their best to ensure the accuracy and currency of all the information in **The Rough Guide to Brazil;** however, they can accept no responsibility for any loss, injury, or inconvenience sustained by any traveller as a result of information or advice contained in the guide.

Help us update

We've gone to a lot of effort to ensure that the fifth edition of **The Rough Guide to Brazil** is accurate and up to date. However, things change – places get "discovered", opening hours are notoriously fickle, restaurants and rooms raise prices or lower standards. If you feel we've got it wrong or left something out, we'd like to know, and if you can remember the address, the price, the time, the phone number, so much the better.

We'll credit all contributions, and send a copy of the next edition (or any other Rough Guide if you prefer) for the best letters. Everyone who writes to us and isn't already a subscriber will receive a copy of our full-colour thrice-yearly newsletter. Please mark letters: "**Rough Guide Brazil Update**" and send to: Rough Guides, 80 Strand, London WC2R 0RL, or Rough Guides, 4th Floor, 345 Hudson St, New York, NY 10014. Or send an email to **mail@roughguides.com**

Have your questions answered and tell others about your trip at **www.roughguides.atinfopop.com**

Acknowledgements

David Cleary: Glauco Assumpção Pachalski, for diligent clubbing and barhopping in Brasília, and Marylou Carr, wife of my dreams, for everything in the Brasília chapter.

Dilwyn Jenkins would like to thank the following for their additional accounts, research and other vital support: Edilson, Cecilia and Nina; Yuki Takagaki, Richard Koss; Howard Davis; Graham Preston; Mark at Swallows and Amazons; Alex at Ecological Expeditions; and last but obviously most importantly, the family members left behind – Claire, Tess, Bethan Max and Teilo.

Oliver Marshall Thanks especially to Yuki Takagaki for her support, drive and attention to detail, and to Chris Pickard of the Brazilian Tourist Office in London for providing useful ideas and introductions. In Brazil valuable assistance was provided by many city and state tourist offices and CVBs – I'd especially like to thank Karin Luize de Carvalho of EMBRATUR. I'm grateful to Graça Salgado, Eduardo Silva and Isaura, as always, for their hospitality and local tips in Rio; to Karin Hanta for sharing lots of valuable information; and to Darién Davis, whose companionship made São Paulo and Rio more enjoyable than ever. Finally, in London, thanks to Margaret and Anneliese for their support.

The editor would like to thank Tanya Hall for tireless production work; Ed Wright, Maxine Repath and Stratigraphics for adroit mapmaking; Sharon Martins for fine picture research; Antonia Hebbert for her eagle eye; and Glenn Kaplan for pitching in.

Readers' letters

Thanks to all the readers who took the trouble to write in with their comments and suggestions (and apologies to anyone whose name we've misspelt or omitted):
Nick Bailey, Wilson Castro, Klaus R.C. Ciesielski, D. Cohn, Joe Correll, Jane Davey, Erik de Jongh, Jim Forward and Pauline McCormick, Mark Giorgi, Peter Halls, Sharon Harris, Valentina Jacome, Malcolm James, Nelson Laskowsky, Christopher Metzler, Sharon Rees, Kristin and André Santiago, Matt Schwartz, June Schwarzacher, Barrie Scott, Paul Thompson, Nigel and Edith Watt, Dave Weber, J. Weissich and Ting Hway Wong.

Photo credits

Cover Credits
main front picture Metropolitana in Brasília © Robert Harding
small front top picture Copacabana Beach © Getty
small front lower picture Macaw Robert © Harding
back top picture Nossa senhora das Dores, © Paraty Elan Fleisher
Back lower picture Jericoacoara Beach © Peter Wilson

Introduction
Buggy on beach dune © Brazil Tourist Board
Timbaleda © Marcella Haddad
Row of rum bottles © Elcio Carrico
Surf at Salvador beach © Jason P. Howe/South American Pictures
Feijoada © Jason P. Howe/South American Pictures
Carnaval, Bahia © Marcella Haddad
Boat on Amazon © Brazil Tourist Board
Church, Tiradentes © Mauricio Simonetti
Dense housing, Rio © Robert Francis/South American Pictures
Sunset, Recife © Marcella Haddad

Things Not To Miss
Daniela beach, Florianópolis, Santa Catarina © Oliver Marshall
Tijuica National Park; Atlantic rainforest © Tony Morrison/South American Pictures
Museu de Arte Contemporanea © Oliver Marshall
Last Supper by Aleijadinho © Tony Morrison/South American Pictures
Vale de Luna, Chapada dos Veadeiros © Pedro Luz Cunha/Alamy
Jabaquara Beach at Ihabela © Cristiano Burmester/Alamy
Candomble ceremony © Marcella Haddad
Fazenda do Pinhal © Francesco Venturi/CORBIS

Capoeira, Salvador © Tony Morrison/South American Pictures
Teatro Municipal, Rio © Oliver Marshall
Toco Toucan © Tony Morrison/South American Pictures
Nossa Senhora da Glória do Outeiro, Rio © Tony Morrison/South American Pictures
Rua do Amparo, Olinda © Tony Morrison/South American Pictures
Carnaval, Olinda © Tony Morrison/South American Pictures
Avenida Paulista, São Paulo © Andy Caulfield/Alamy
Iguaçu Falls © Brazil Tourist Board
Ipanema beach, Rio © Marcella Haddad
Trekking in the Chapada Diamantina © Mauricio Simonetti
Pedra Azul © Adilson Moralez
VW Beetle in Pomerode © Oliver Marshall
Odolum reggae band © Ricardo Azourty/CORBIS
Tug journey on Amazon © Tony Morrison/South American Pictures
Parati © Oliver Marshall
Mercado Municipal © Marcella Haddad
Churrascarias © Elcio Carrico
Jangada fishing boat, Iguape Beach © Tony Morrison/South American Pictures
São Miguel de Missiones © Mauricio Simonetti
Caiman, Panatal © Tony Morrison/South American Pictures
Drummers, Lapa © Marcella Haddad
Fish, Aquário Natural, Bonito © Mauricio Simonetti
Main auditorium, Manaus Opera House © Tony Morrison/South American Pictures
Igreja de Nossa Senhora Do Carmo, Ouro Preto © Jason P. Howe/South American Pictures

Teatro Nacional, Brasília © Tony Morrison/South American Pictures

Black and whites
View across Flamenco park (p.64) © Tony Morrison/South American Pictures
Ipanema beach (p.109), Rio © Marion Morrison/South American Pictures
Donkeys and herders, Ouro Preto (p.160) © Tony Morrison/South American Pictures
Diamantina, Minas (p.199) © Oliver Marshall
Buggies, Rio Grande do Norte (p.244) © Tony Morrison/South American Pictures
Cidade Alta, Salvador (p.301) © Peter M Wilson/Alamy
Carving, Igreja de São Francisco, Salvador (p.379) © Marcella Haddad
Jaguar (p.386) © Tony Morrison/South American Pictures
Exterior of Opera House (p.422) © Tony Morrison/South American Pictures
Cerrado forest (p.472) © Tony Morrison/South American Pictures
Congresso Nacional, Brasília (p.505) © Tony Morrison/South American Pictures
Corumbá, Mato Grosso do Sul (p.520) © Tony Morrison/South American Pictures
Storks, Panatal (p.551) © Mauricio Simonetti
Pinacoteca de Estado (p.572) © Elcio Carrico
Catedral Metropolitana and fountains, São Paulo (p.625) © Sue Cunningham/Alamy
Near Prudentópolis, Paraná (p.634) © Oliver Marshall
Iguaçu Falls (p.709) © Brazil Tourist Board
Parque Estadual de Vila Velha (p.737) © Gary Cook/Alamy